2009

This 12th edition published 2008
© Automobile Association Developments Limited 2008.
Automobile Association Developments Limited retains the copyright in the current edition © 2008 and in all subsequent editions, reprints and amendments to
editions. The information contained in this
directory is sourced entirely from the AA's information resources. All rights
reserved. No part of this publication may be reproduced, stored in a retrieval
system, or transmitted in any form or by any means -
electronic, photocopying, recording or otherwise - unless the written
permission of the publishers has been obtained beforehand. This book may not
be sold, resold, hired out or otherwise disposed of by way of trade in any form
of binding or cover other than that in which it is
published, without the prior consent of all relevant Publishers.

The contents of this book are believed correct at the time of printing. Nevertheless, the Publisher cannot be held responsible for any errors or omissions, or
for changes in the details given in this guide, or for the consequences of any
reliance on the information provided by the same. This does not affect your
statutory rights. Assessments of AA inspected establishments are based on the
experience of the Hotel and Restaurant Inspectors on the occasion(s) of their
visit(s) and therefore descriptions given in this guide necessarily contain an
element of subjective opinion which may not reflect or dictate a reader's own
opinion on another occasion. See pages 6-7 for a clear explanation of how,
based on our Inspectors' inspection experiences, establishments are graded. If
the meal or meals experienced by an Inspector or Inspectors during an inspection fall between award levels the restaurant concerned may be awarded the
lower of any award levels considered applicable.

Web Site addresses are included where they have been supplied and specified
by the respective establishment. Such Web Sites are not under the control of
The Automobile Association Developments Limited and as such The Automobile
Association Developments Limited has no control over them and will not accept
any responsibility or liability in respect of any and all matters whatsoever relat-
ing to such Web Sites including access, content, material and functionality. By
including the addresses of third party Web Sites the AA does not intend to solicit
business or offer any security to any person in any country, directly or indirectly.
The AA strives to ensure accuracy of the information in this guide at the time
of printing. Due to the constantly evolving nature of the subject matter the
information is subject to change. The AA will gratefully
receive any advice from our readers of any necessary updated
information. Please contact

Advertisement Sales: advertisingsales@theaa.com
Editorial Department: lifestyleguides@theaa.com

Front cover image sourced from AA photo library
Photographs in the gazetteer provided by the establishments.
Typeset/Repro: Keenes, Andover.
Printed in Italy by Printer Trento SRL, Trento
Editor: Denise Laing
Pub descriptions have been contributed by the following team of
writers: Phil Bryant, David Foster, David Halford, Julia Hynard, Denise Laing and
Jenny White.
Published by AA Publishing, a trading name of Automobile Association
Developments Limited, whose registered office is Fanum House, Basing View,
Basingstoke RG21 4EA.
Registered number 1878835.
A CIP catalogue for this book is available from the British Library.
ISBN-13: 978-0-7495-5788-1
A3681

Maps prepared by the Mapping Services Department of
The Automobile Association.
Maps © Automobile Association Developments Limited 2008.

 This product includes mapping data
licensed from Ordnance Survey® with
the permission of the Controller of Her Majesty's Stationery Office.
© Crown copyright 2008.
All rights reserved. Licence number 100021153.

Information on National Parks in England provided by
The Countryside Agency (Natural England)
Information on National Parks in Scotland provided by Scottish Natural Heritage.
Information on National Parks in Wales provided by
The Countryside Council for Wales

Contents

Using the guide　　　　　　　　　4

AA Classifications & Awards　　　6

AA Pub of the Year　　　　　　　8

Welcome to the Guide　　　　　10

Beer Festivals　　　　　　　　12

England　　14

Channel Islands　　690

Isle of Man　　691

Scotland　　692

Wales　　728

Atlas　　764

Index of Pubs　　794

Using the Guide

❶ Guide Order Pubs are listed alphabetically by name (ignoring The) under their village or town. Towns and villages are listed alphabetically within their county (a county map appears at the back of the guide). The guide has entries for England, Channel Islands, Isle of Man, Scotland and Wales in that order. Some village pubs prefer to be initially located under the nearest town, in which case the village name is included in the address and directions.

Pick of the Pubs Around 750 of the best pubs in Britain have been selected by the editor and inspectors and these are highlighted. They have longer, more detailed descriptions and a tinted background. Around 250 have a full page entry and two photographs.

❷ Map Reference The map reference number denotes the map page number in the atlas section at the back of the book and (except for London maps) the National Grid reference. The London map references help locate their position on the Central and Greater London maps.

❸ Symbols See Symbols in the panel on page 5.

❹ Address and Postcode This gives the street name and the postcode, and if necessary the name of the village is included (see 1 above). This may be up to five miles from the named location.

☎ Telephone number 📄 Fax number, email and websites: Wherever possible we have included an email address.

❺ Directions Directions are given only when they have been supplied by the proprietor.

❻ Open Indicates the hours and dates when the establishment is open and closed.

❼ Bar meals Indicates the times and days when proprietors tell us bar food can be ordered, and the average price of a main course as supplied by the proprietor. Please be aware that last orders could vary by up to 30 minutes.

---

❶ **DENHAM**   **MAP 06 TQ08** ❷

❸ **The Falcon Inn** ★★★★ INN 🍷

❹ Village Rd UB9 5BE ☎ 01895 832125

e–mail: falcon.inn@btconnect.com

❺ **dir:** *Exit M40 junct 1, follow A40/Gerrards Cross signs. Approx 200yds turn right onto Old Mill Rd. Pass church on right, enter village. Pub opposite village green.*

This traditional 16th-century inn, located opposite the green in beautiful Denham Village, is an ideal base for exploring Colne Valley Country Park. Expect excellent real ales and award-winning food. Lunch could include Spanish tortilla with mixed salad, or a home-made burger with fries; in the evening, perhaps ginger king prawns and scallops with aubergine caviar, rôsti potatoes, langoustine and herb oil, or rack of lamb with marinated courgettes, straw potatoes and red wine sauce. Lots of fish.

❻ **Open** 12-3 5-11 (Summer Sat/Sun 12-11) ❼ **Bar Meals** L served all week 12-2.30 D served all week 6.30–9.30 (Sun 12-4) ❽ **Restaurant** L served Mon-Sun 12-2.30 D served Mon-Sun 6.30-10 (Sun 12-4, 6.30-9.30)

❾ 🍺 Timothy Taylor Landlord, Bombardier, Youngs, Deuchars & Guest Ale.

❿ 🍷 11 **Facilities** Children's licence Garden **Rooms** 4 ⓫

4

8 **Restaurant** Indicates the times and days when proprietors tell us food can be ordered from the restaurant. The average cost of a 3-course à la carte meal and a 3- or 4-course fixed-price menu are shown as supplied by the proprietor. Last orders may be approximately 30 minutes before the times stated.

9 ⊕ **Brewery or Company** This is the name of the Brewery to which the pub is tied, or the Company which owns it. A free house is where the pub is independently owned and run.

◼ **The beer tankard symbol** indicates the principal beers sold by the pub. Up to five cask or hand-pulled beers are listed. Many pubs have a much greater selection, with several guest beers each week.

♀ **The wine glass symbol** followed by a number indicates the number of wines sold by the glass.

10 **Facilities** Indicates if a pub has a children's licence, a garden, allows dogs on the premises, offers parking and has a children's play area. For further information please phone the pub.

11 **Rooms** Only accommodation that has been inspected is indicated. In the case of AA accommodation only, the number of en suite bedrooms is listed. The word 'available' appearing under Rooms at the end of an entry indicates that the accommodation has been inspected by another organisation.

Notes As so many establishments take one or more of the major credit cards we only indicate if a pub does not take cards.

Key to Symbols

◉	**Rosettes** The AA's food award. Explanation on p7
★★	**Stars** Accommodation rating please see p6-7
♀	Indicates that at least six wines are available by the glass. For the exact number of wines served this way, see notes at the bottom of each entry.
NEW	Pubs appearing in the guide for the first time in 2009

AA Stars (and designators as appropriate) are shown at the beginning of an entry. The AA, in partnership with the national tourist bodies (VisitBritain, VisitScotland and the VisitWales) has introduced new Quality Standards for accommodation that is inspected. See pages 6-7 for details of AA ratings.

AA Classifications & Awards

AA Classifications & Awards

Many of the pubs in this Guide offer accommodation. Where a Star rating appears next to an entry's name in the Guide, the establishment has been inspected by the AA under common Quality Standards agreed between the AA, VisitBritain, VisitScotland and VisitWales. Where the word 'available' appears after the Room information at the end of an entry, it has been inspected by VisitBritain, VisitScotland or Visit-Wales using the same standards. These ratings are for the accommodation, and ensure that it meets the highest standards of cleanliness, with an emphasis on professionalism, proper booking procedures and prompt and efficient services. Some of the pubs in this Guide offer accommodation but do not belong to a rating scheme. In this case the accommodation is not included in their entry.

AA recognised establishments pay an annual fee that varies according to the classification and the number of bedrooms. The establishments receive an unannounced inspection from a qualified AA inspector who recommends the appropriate classification. Return visits confirm that standards are maintained; the classification is not transferable if an establishment changes hands.

The annual AA Hotel Guide and AA Bed & Breakfast Guide give further details of recognised establishments and the classification schemes. Details of AA recognised hotels, guest accommodation, restaurants and pubs are also available at www.theAA.com, along with a useful Route Planner.

AA Hotel Classification

Hotels are classified on a 5-point scale, with one star being the simplest, and five stars offering a luxurious service at the top of the range. The AA's top hotels in Britain and Ireland are identified by red stars. (★) In addition to the main **Hotel** (HL) classification which applies to some pubs in this Guide, there are other categories of hotel applicable also to pubs, as follows:

Town House Hotel (TH) - A small, individual city or town centre property, which provides a high degree of personal service and privacy

Country House Hotel (CHH) - Quietly located in a rural area

Small Hotel (SHL) - Has fewer than 20 bedrooms and is owner managed

Metro Hotel (MET) - A hotel in an urban location that does not offer an evening meal

Restaurants with Rooms (RR) - Most Restaurants with Rooms have been awarded AA Rosettes for their food, and the accommodation meets the required AA standard (see under **Guest Accommodation** for more details)

Budget Hotel (BUD) - These are usually purpose-built modern properties offering inexpensive accommodation. Often located near motorways and in town or city centres. **They are not awarded stars**

AA Guest Accommodation

Guest accommodation is also classified on a scale of one to five stars, with one being the most simple, and five being more luxurious. Yellow stars (★) indicate the very best B&Bs, Guest Houses, Farmhouses, Inns and Guest Accommodation in the 3, 4 and 5 star ratings. Stars have replaced the Diamond Classification for this type of accommodation, in accordance with Common Standards agreed between the AA and the UK tourist authorities of VisitEngland, VisitScotland and VisitWales. To differentiate them from Hotel Stars, they have been given a series of designators appropriate to the type of accommodation they offer, as follows:

Bed & Breakfast (B&B) - Accommodation provided in a private house, run by the owner and with no more than six paying guests

Guest House (GH) – Accommodation provided for more than six paying guests and run on a more commercial basis than a B&B. Usually more services, for example dinner, provided by staff as well as the owner

Farmhouse (FH) – B&B or guest house rooms provided on a working farm or smallholding

Restaurant with Rooms (RR) – Destination restaurant offering overnight accommodation. The restaurant is the main business and is open to non-residents. A high standard of food should be offered, at least five nights a week. A maximum of 12 bedrooms

Guest Accommodation (GA) – Any establishment which meets the entry requirements for the Scheme can choose this designator

Inn (INN) – Accommodation provided in a fully licensed establishment. The bar will be open to non-residents and provide food in the evenings

U A small number of pubs have this symbol because their Star classification was not confirmed at the time of going to press

A Refers to hotels rated by another organisation, eg VisitBritain

Rosette Awards

Out of the thousands of restaurants in the British Isles, the AA identifies, with its Rosette Awards, some 2000 as the best. What to expect from restaurants with AA Rosette Awards is outlined here; for a more detailed explanation of Rosette criteria please see www.theAA.com

◉ Excellent local restaurants serving food prepared with care, understanding and skill and using good quality ingredients.

◉◉ The best local restaurants, which consistently aim for and achieve higher standards and where a greater precision is apparent in the cooking. Obvious attention is paid to the selection of quality ingredients.

◉◉◉ Outstanding restaurants that demand recognition well beyond their local area.

◉◉◉◉ Amongst the very best restaurants in the British Isles, where the cooking demands national recognition.

◉◉◉◉◉ The finest restaurants in the British Isles, where the cooking stands comparison with the best in the world.

AA Pub of the Year
for England, Scotland and Wales

Selected with the help of our AA inspectors, we have chosen three very worthy winners for this prestigious award. The winners stand out for being great all-round pubs or inns, combining a good pub atmosphere, a warm welcome from friendly, efficient hosts and staff, excellent food and well-kept beers..

Pub of the year for
England

The Queens Arms, Corton Denham, Somerset
Pages 496

The ancient village of Corton Denham, just north of Sherborne on the Somerset/Dorset border is the setting for this pub. The Queens Arms is an 18th-century free house nestling in beautiful countryside. You can choose to eat in the bar or the adjoining dining room, or sit out in the garden when the weather is warm. Food and drink are taken seriously: a range of world classic bottled beers, locally brewed ales, and a selection of Somerset apple juices and ciders is enhanced by a well-chosen and reasonably priced wine and whisky list. Earthy British dishes using the freshest local and seasonal produce include light bites and sandwiches at lunch, with dishes such as poacher's risotto; and sausage and mash. In the evening, there might be confit of duck leg on bruschetta with orange and marjoram ricotta; and local venison cobbler with curly kale and baby carrots.

Pub of the year for
Scotland

The Torridon Inn, Torridon, Highlands
Page 716

The Torridon Inn stands on the shores of Loch Torridon, where it was created by converting the stable block, buttery and farm buildings of nearby Ben Demph House. The cosy bar offers a Highland welcome, and the choice of 60 malt whiskies, or the local real ale. The inn has its own restaurant where you can sample high quality, locally sourced food at any time. Hearty soups, sandwiches and bar meals are available during the day, and in the evening there's a choice of succulent starters, delicious main courses and legendary desserts. Local produce is the foundation of menus that feature venison, salmon, haggis and home-made specials. Dinner might begin with beef carpaccio with rocket and parmesan shavings; and move on to roast Scottish cod with parsley crust, creamy mash, mangetout and lemon butter sauce. Tea and coffee is served throughout the day, and there's live music some evenings.

Pub of the year for
Wales

The Bush Inn, St Hilary, Vale of Glamorgan
Page 762

The old church in this Vale of Glamorgan village has provided the backdrop for the thatched Bush Inn for more than 400 years. Bare stone walls, flag-stones, oak beams, and a huge fireplace are features of the cosy interior, with a stone spiral staircase leading to the first floor. There's a resident ghost in the shape of a highwayman who was cornered in a nearby cave and hanged on Stalling Down half a mile away. French windows lead out of the pretty dining room into the garden. Depending on which you choose, bar or restaurant menus offer choices of light bites, sandwiches and salads, chargrilled steaks, a fresh fish special of the day, and vegetarian options. Other likely choices are pan-fried rib-eye of Welsh beef; trio of mutton and mint sausages; deep-fried plaice in beer batter; and wild mushroom risotto cake. A selection of desserts appears on the blackboard menu.

Welcome to the Guide

We aim to bring you the country's best pubs, selected for their atmosphere, great food and good beer. Ours is the only major pub guide to feature colour photographs, and to highlight the 'Pick of the Pubs', revealing Britain's finest hostelries. Updated every year, this edition includes lots of old favourites, as well as plenty of new destinations for eating and drinking, and great places to stay across Britain.

Who's in the Guide?

We make our selection by seeking out pubs that are worth making a detour - 'destination' pubs - with publicans exhibiting real enthusiasm for their trade and offering a good selection of well-kept drinks and good food. We also choose neighbourhood pubs supported by locals and attractive to passing motorists or walkers. Our selected pubs make no payment for their inclusion in our guide. They are included entirely at our discretion.

Tempting Food

We are looking for menus that show a commitment to home cooking, making good use of local produce wherever possible, and offering an appetising range of freshly-prepared dishes. Pubs presenting well-executed traditional dishes like ploughman's or pies, or those offering innovative bar or restaurant food, are all in the running. In keeping with recent trends in pub food, we are keen to include those where particular emphasis is placed on imaginative modern dishes and those specialising in fresh fish. Occasionally we include pubs that serve no food, or just snacks, but are very special in other ways.

That Special Place

We look for pubs that offer something special: pubs where the time-honoured values of a convivial environment for conversation while supping or eating have not been forgotten. They may be attractive, interesting, unusual or in a good location. Some may be very much a local pub or they may draw customers from further afield, while others may be included because they are in an exceptional place. Interesting towns and villages, eccentric or historic buildings, and rare settings can all be found within this guide.

Pick of the Pubs and Full Page Entries

Some of the pubs included in the guide are particularly special, and we have highlighted these as Pick of the Pubs. For 2009 around 750 pubs have been selected by the personal knowledge of our editorial team, our AA inspectors, and suggestions from our readers. These pubs have a coloured panel and a more detailed description. From these, around 250 have chosen to enhance their entry in the 2009 Guide by purchasing two photographs as part of a full-page entry.

Smoking Regulations

A law banning smoking in public places came into force in July 2007. This covers all establishments in this guide. Some pubs provide a private area in, for example an outbuilding, for smokers. If the freedom to smoke is important to you, we recommend that you check with the pub when you book.

Tell us what you think

We welcome your feedback about the pubs included and about the guide itself.
We are also delighted to receive suggestions about good pubs you have visited and loved. A Reader Report form appears at the back of the book, so please write in or e-mail us at lifestyleguides@theAA.com to help us improve future editions. The pubs also feature on the AA website, www.theAA.com, along with our inspected restaurants, hotels and bed & breakfast accommodation.

Beer Festivals
On the Hop – a Celebration

Beer festivals, or their equivalent, are as old as the hills. The brewing of hops goes back to the beginning of human civilisation, and the combination of common crop and a fermenting process that results in alcoholic liquid has long been a cause of celebration. Beer festivals officially began in Germany with the first Munich Oktoberfest in 1810. Wherever in the world beer is brewed, today and for the last few millennia, admirers, enthusiasts, aficionados – call them what you will – have gathered together to sample and praise its unique properties. It happens throughout Europe, in Australia and New Zealand, and in America and Canada, and annual events are held in pubs all over Britain.

Beer festivals are often occasions for the whole family, when entertainment is laid on for children as well as adults. Summer is naturally a popular season for festivals, when the action can be taken outdoors. Other festivals are held in October, traditionally harvest time, but they can be at any time of the year. They can be large and well-advertised gatherings that attract a wide following for sometimes several days of unselfconscious consumption of unusual or award-winning ales; or they might be local but none the less enthusiastic get-togethers of neighbourhood or pub micro-breweries.

We list here a selection of pubs that appear in this guide, that hold usually annual beer festivals. For up-to-date information, please check directly with the pub. We would love to hear from our readers about their favourite beer festivals.
E-mail us at **lifestyleguides@theAA.com**

Bhurtpore Inn, Aston, Cheshire 01270 780917. Early June. Last year over 100 different beers, many from microbreweries.

The Burnmoor Inn, Boot, Cumbria 019467 23224. and Brook House Inn, Boot, Cumbria. 019467 23160. Joint beer festival held Thursday to Friday, 1st weekend in June. More than 70 real ales to sample, along with a barbecue, fish supper and black pudding bonanza.

Eagle & Child, Staveley, Cumbria 01539 821320. 2-4 May. Gurning, hog roast, live music, 20 beers.

The Queens Head Inn, Tirril, Cumbria 01768 863219. The Tirril Brewery's output, and other locally brewed beers, can be tasted at the annual beer and sausage festival held 12-14 September.

Wasdale Head Inn, Wasdale Head, Cumbria 019467 26229. Large numbers descend on this old drovers' inn twice a year, May & August bank hols.

The Royal Hotel, Hayfield, Derbys 01663 741721. A full entertainment programme and 50 cask ales is the reward for anyone visiting the beer festival here in the second week of October.

Greyhound, Corfe Castle, Dorset 01929 480205. The May and August BH festivals involve around 50 real ales and ciders, a hog roast, a barbecue and a seafood buffet.

The Bankes Arms Hotel, Studland, Dorset 01929 450225. 14-17 August, Morris dancing, stone carving, live music and a great selection of around 150 real ales and ciders.

The Hoop, Stock, Essex 01277 841137. The late Spring BH is at the centre of ten days of celebrations here, with 150 ales and ciders. Hog roast and barbecue.

The Boat Inn, Ashleworth, Glos 01452 700272. Visitors to the annual summer beer festival in June can choose from more than 30 different breweries

The Yew Tree, Clifford's Mesne, Gloucestershire – 01531 820719. Annual beer and cider festival in May.

Red Shoot Inn, Linwood, Hants 01425 475792. Festivals held twice a year in April and October.

The White Horse, Petersfield, Hants 01420 588387. 3-day festival June 20-22. Bouncy castle, live music, barbecues.

Cartwheel Inn, Whitsbury, Hants 01725 518362. The August festival includes Morris dancers, a spit-roasted pig, a barbecue and 25 real ales.

Swan in the Rushes, Loughborough, Leics 01509 217014. Two annual festivals in May & November. Live music, 26 beers.

Cow and Plough, Oadby, Leics 0116 272 0852. The Cow & Plough hosts beer festivals May & August BHs, and also brews its own Steamin' Billy beers.

Junction Tavern, London NW5. August BH. The pub holds beer festivals May & Aug BH, with a range of 40-plus ales served straight from the cask.

The White Horse, Fulham, London SW6 020 7736 2115. Two-day festival November with over 300 real ales and European beers.

Hill House, Happisburgh, Norfolk 01692 650004. Summer solstice beer festival each June, with the chance to sample 80 real ales, ciders and perries.

Angel Inn, Larling, Norfolk 01953 717963. August 6-8. Campsite, beers from all over the country

The White Hart, Fyfield, Oxfordshire 01865 390585. (May Day and August BH weekends festivals with at least 14 real ales, live jazz and hog roasts.

The Surrey Oaks, Newdigate, Surrey 01306 631200. Three festivals during the May & August BHs. Sample around 40 real ales and ciders.

The Owl, Little Cheverell, Wiltshire 01380 812263. Festivals have been held for around 12 years at late May BH. Bouncy castle and occasional entertainer for children, with a band or singer in the later for adults.

Smoking Dog, Malmesbury, Wiltshire 01666 825823. Last weekend in May, live music, 35 beers and ciders.

The Bridge Inn, West Lavington, Wilts 01380 813213. Charity Beer Festival August BH Sunday.

The Inn at Kippen, Kippen, Stirling 01786 871010. A small beer festival with hog roast in Aug or Sep.

England

England

BEDFORDSHIRE

BEDFORD
MAP 12 TL04

Pick of the Pubs

Knife & Cleaver Inn ★★★★ INN ◎ ♀

The Grove, Houghton Conquest MK45 3LA
☎ 01234 740387 ▤ 01234 740900
e-mail: info@knifeandcleaver.com

dir: *11m from M1 junct 12/13. 5m S of Bedford. Off A6, opp Houghton Conquest church.*

A friendly 17th-century free house, the Knife & Cleaver is located opposite the medieval church of All Saints, Bedfordshire's largest parish church. Its many historic associations include the Jacobean oak panelling in the lounge bar, which came from nearby Houghton House, formerly the home of the Conquest family, who gave their name to the village. Light meals and hand-drawn ales are served in the bar, where leather sofas and winter log fires bring welcome comfort. The seasonal menu in the conservatory restaurant is strong on fresh seafood, and also offers a varied choice of meat and vegetarian dishes. The dish of the day might be chargrilled red mullet with pesto linguine; venison and walnut casserole with herb dumplings; or chicken, bacon and apple pie. In summer, meals are also served in the cottage-style garden.

Open 12–2.30 7–11 Closed: 27–30 Dec & some BH eves
Bar Meals L served Mon-Fri 12–2.30 D served Sun-Fri 7–9.30 (Sat 12–2) Av main course £7.95 **Restaurant** L served Sun-Fri 12–2.30 D served all week 7–9.30 Av 3 course à la carte £27 ⊕ Free House ◀ Batemans XB & Village Bike-Potton Brewery. ♀ 29 **Facilities** Garden Dogs allowed Parking **Rooms** 9

The Three Tuns

57 Main Rd, Biddenham MK40 4BD ☎ 01234 354847
e-mail: thethreetuns@btinternet.com

dir: *On A428 from Bedford towards Northampton 1st right signed Biddenham. Into village, pub on right*

A traditional village pub with a public bar, lounge bar and dining room, The Three Tuns stands at the heart of beautiful Biddenham. It has recently been re-thatched and has a large garden, with decking, a patio and a play area. The old village morgue is in the back garden and the pub is haunted by a headless lady. A choice of home-made dishes includes steak, seafood platter and a daily curry, plus children's meals.

Open 11–2.30 6–11 (Sun 12–3, 7–10.30) **Bar Meals** L served all week 12–2 D served Mon-Sat 6–9 (No food Sun eve) Av main course £8.50 **Restaurant** L served all week 12–2 D served Mon-Sat 6–9 (No food Sun eve) ⊕ Greene King ◀ Greene King IPA, Abbot Ale. **Facilities** Garden Dogs allowed Parking Play Area

BLETSOE
MAP 11 TL05

Pick of the Pubs

The Falcon ♀

See Pick of the Pubs on opposite page

BOLNHURST
MAP 12 TL05

Pick of the Pubs

The Plough at Bolnhurst ♀

Kimbolton Rd MK44 2EX ☎ 01234 376274
e-mail: theplough@bolnhurst.com

dir: *On B660 N of Bedford*

This beautiful building goes back to Tudor times, as plainly testified by low beams, an intriguing layout, few windows, and open fires. In the kitchen, which you can see from the bar and the restaurant, Martin Lee and his dedicated team prepare exciting English food with a strong Italian and French influence. Sourced from farms and estates around the country, the Plough's menu is as likely to include asparagus from nearby fields as beef from distant Aberdeenshire, simply because they're the best of their kind to be had. Menus change daily to reflect market availability, but tend to offer such treats as roast sea bass with grilled root vegetables, fennel and black olive sauce; roast corn-fed Goosnargh duck breast with rösti potato, braised savoy cabbage and Armagnac sauce; or Jimmy Butler's bangers and mash with Dijon mustard and onion sauce. Follow with apple tarte Tatin and clotted cream, or European cheeses.

Open 12–3 6.30–12 (Closed Sun eve) Closed: New Year, 2wks Jan & Mon **Bar Meals** L served Tue-Sat 12–2 D served Tue-Sat 6.30–9.30 (Sun 12–2.30) Av main course £10.50 **Restaurant** L served Tue-Sat 12–2 D served Tue-Sat 6.30–9.30 (Sun 12–2.30) Av 3 course à la carte £25.30 ⊕ Free House ◀ Adnams Broadside, Nethergate Azzanewt, Batemans XB, Village Bike Potton. ♀ 12 **Facilities** Children's licence Garden Dogs allowed Parking

BROOM
MAP 12 TL14

The Cock

23 High St SG18 9NA ☎ 01767 314411 ▤ 01767 314284

dir: *Off B658 SW of Biggleswade. 1m from A1*

Unspoilt to this day with its intimate quarry-tiled rooms with latched doors and panelled walls, this 17th-century establishment is known as 'The Pub with no Bar'. Real ales are served straight from casks racked by the cellar steps. A straightforward pub grub menu includes jumbo cod, roast chicken, gammon steak, breaded lobster, and breast of Cajun chicken. There is a camping and caravan site at the rear.

Open 12–3 6–11 (Sat-Sun 12–4) **Bar Meals** L served all week 12–2.15 D served Mon-Sat 7–9 **Restaurant** L served Mon-Sat 12–2.15 D served Mon-Sat 7–9 (Sun 12–2.30) ⊕ Greene King ◀ Greene King Abbot Ale, IPA & Ruddles County. **Facilities** Garden Dogs allowed Parking Play Area

PICK OF THE PUBS

BLETSOE-BEDFORDSHIRE

The Falcon

The Falcon is set in the rolling countryside of north Bedfordshire with easy access from the A6, making it a popular destination for customers from far and wide. The 17th-century coaching inn is a great place to visit at any time of the year, with welcoming log fires in winter and a beautiful beer garden for summer dining.

Step into the relaxed ambience of the traditional country inn and you'll find an inglenook fireplace, lots of oak beams and dark wood panelling in the dining room. As you might expect at such a venerable hostelry, there's at least one resident ghost, as well as a secret tunnel leading to nearby Bletsoe Castle. To the rear of the building, a large dining terrace overlooks mature gardens leading down to the River Great Ouse. At lunchtime Falcon favourites include steak ciabatta and chicken Caesar wrap. There's also a choice of sandwiches, ploughman's and salads in a bowl, such as mozzarella, tomato and fresh basil, or poached salmon and crayfish with sweet chilli sauce. The main menu offers an extensive list of pub fare – fish

cakes, pasta, Thai curry, steak and kidney pie – plus steaks and burgers from the grill. The Friday fish menu provides some unusual options, like pangasius fillets (a delicious white fish from Vietnam) served with prawn and mustard cream sauce; or baked Nile perch supreme topped with a pesto and parmesan crust. Further interest is inspired by the daily chef's specials, with the likes of grilled lemon sole, roast leg of lamb, or baked courgettes stuffed with Mediterranean vegetables and rice.

♀
MAP 11 TL05
Rushden Rd MK44 1QN
☎ 01234 781222
🖷 01234 781222
e-mail: thefalcona6@aol.com
dir: *9m from M1 junct 13, 3m from Bedford*

Open 12–3 6–11 (Sat 12–11, Sun 12–10.30)
Bar Meals L served Mon-Sat 12–2.15 D served Mon-Sat 6–9.15 (Sun 12–8.45) Av main course £9.95
Restaurant L served Mon-Sat 12–2.15 D served Mon-Sat 6.30–9.15 (Sun 12–8.45) Av 3 course à la carte £21
⊕ Charles Wells ◖ Wells Bombardier, Wells Eagle, Red Stripe. ♀ 13
Facilities Garden Parking

England

EATON BRAY

MAP 11 SP92

The White Horse ⛾

Market Square LU6 2DG

☎ 01525 220231 📠 01525 222485

e-mail: davidsparrow@onetel.net

dir: A5 N of Dunstable onto A505, left in 1m, follow signs

For almost 20 years, David and Janet Sparrow have built their reputation on great home cooked food at this traditional 300–year-old village inn. Choose from a seasonally changing menu that might include braised lamb shank; or goat's cheese on cherry tomato and rocket salad. In addition, the daily specials menu includes a choice of fresh fish dishes. It's worth booking for the restaurant, but the same menu is also available in the bar.

Open 11.30–3 6.30–11 (Fri-Sat 6.30–11.30 Sun 12–3, 7–11) Closed: Sun eve Jan-Mar **Bar Meals** L served all week 12–2.15 D served Mon-Sat 7–9.30 (Sun 7–9) **Restaurant** L served all week 12–2.15 D served Mon-Sat 7–9.15 (Sun 7.30–9) ⊕ Punch Taverns ◀ Greene King IPA, Shepherd Neame Spitfire, Tetley's. ⛾ 8 **Facilities** Garden Parking Play Area

HARROLD

MAP 11 SP95

Pick of the Pubs

The Muntjac ★★★ INN ⛾

71 High St MK43 7BJ ☎ 01234 721500

e-mail: russell@themuntjac.co.uk

Located on the borders of three shires – Bedfordshire, Buckinghamshire and Northamptonshire – the Muntjac is a 17th-century coaching inn in a picturesque village. Head chef Gary Robbins creates a menu of contemporary dishes that reflect his desire to experiment with new ideas, flavours and presentation. He prefers to offer lighter, fish-based dishes in the summer, and the likes of casseroles in the winter. A bar menu includes pick-and-mix tapas-style snacks. On the lunch menu look for moules marinière with crusty ciabattas; chargrilled Cajun chicken with spicy potato wedges and sour cream; and toasted filled paninis. The main carte offers monkfish, bacon and pea casserole with basmati and wild rice; pan-fried pork fillet with roast apple and red cabbage coleslaw; and spiced butternut squash risotto with mascarpone. Desserts include the chef's trademark crème brûlée.

Open 12–2.30 5.30–11 (Thu 12–3) (Fri*/Sat*/Sun 12–11, *Occ close at 3) Closed: 25 Dec **Bar Meals** L served Tue-Sun 12–2.30 D served Tue-Sat 6–9 (Sun 12–5, no food Sun eve) Av main course

£7.95 **Restaurant** L served Tue-Sun 12–2.30 D served Tue-Sat 7–9 (Sun 12–3, no food Sun eve, Fri/Sat food untill 9.30) Av 3 course à la carte £25 ⊕ Free House ◀ Bill Suttons Best Bitter, John Smith's Extra Smooth, Thwaites Thoroughbred & Village Bike (Potton Brewery). ⛾ 7 **Facilities** Garden Parking **Rooms** 4

KEYSOE

MAP 12 TL06

The Chequers

Pertenhall Rd, Brook End MK44 2HR

☎ 01234 708678 📠 01234 708678

e-mail: chequers.keysoe@tesco.net

dir: On B660, 7m N of Bedford. 3m S of Kimbolton

This peaceful 15th-century country pub has been in the same safe hands for over 25 years. No games machines, pool tables or jukeboxes disturb the simple pleasures of well-kept ales and tasty home-made food. The menu offers pub stalwarts like garlic mushrooms on toast, grilled steaks, and chilli con carne, and a blackboard displays further choice plus the vegetarian options. Children's favourites include burgers, fish fingers and fresh chicken.

Open 11.30–2.30 6.30–11 Closed: Tue **Bar Meals** L served Wed-Mon 12–2 D served Wed-Sun 7–9.45 ⊕ Free House ◀ Hook Norton Best, Fuller's London Pride. **Facilities** Garden Parking Play Area **Notes** ⊛

LINSLADE

MAP 11 SP92

The Globe Inn ⛾

Globe Ln, Old Linslade LU7 2TA

☎ 01525 373338 📠 01525 850551

dir: A5 S to Dunstable, follow signs to Leighton Buzzard (A4146)

Standing on the banks of the Grand Union Canal, this friendly inn was first licensed in 1830 to serve passing canal boats. Candles and open fires set the scene for winter evenings, and there's a large garden with children's play area for warmer days. Pub favourites range from traditional fish and chips to steak and kidney pudding, whilst restaurant diners can expect mushroom ravioli; moules marinière; and slow-roast lamb shank.

Open 11–11 (Sun 11–10.30) **Bar Meals** L served Mon-Sat 12–9 D served Mon-Sat 12–9 (Sun 11–8) Av main course £8 **Restaurant** L served Mon-Fri 12–3 D served Mon-Fri 6–9 (Sat 12–9, Sun 12–8) Av 3 course à la carte £20 ⊕ Greene King ◀ Greene King Abbot Ale, Old Speckled Hen, IPA & Ruddles County Ale, Hook Norton. ⛾ 16 **Facilities** Garden Dogs allowed Parking Play Area

PICK OF THE PUBS

OLD WARDEN-BEDFORDSHIRE

Hare and Hounds

A traditional country pub on the Shuttleworth estate, near Old Warden aerodrome, home of a unique collection of aeroplanes spanning the first century of flight. As you walk towards the pub look up at the attractive carved bargeboarding under the projecting gables.

Depending on the weather, once inside you may be greeted by the warmth from the two log fires as you head either for the bar, or one of the four separate eating areas – an indication of how seriously they take their fresh, home-cooked food here. From the varied menu, starter possibilities include smoked salmon risotto with crème fraîche; baked camembert with walnut toast and cranberry sauce; and chicken liver paté. Among the reasonably priced main courses are Scottish sirloin steak with pepper butter, vine tomato and red onion, rocket and basil salad; braised wild rabbit in puff pastry with shallots, wholegrain mustard and tarragon sauce; roasted sea bass with herb salad and hand-cut chips; and gnocchi with butternut squash and pine nuts. If there's pork, it has probably come from the Shuttleworth estate. Fresh fish is delivered daily from Billingsgate Market, and many of the vegetables and herbs used in the kitchen are grown in the garden. Choices in the bar include sausage and mash, haddock and chips, and salmon with Caesar salad. For dessert there may be tarte tatin, caramelised lemon tart, and chocolate mousse, or one of an interesting selection of cheeses, including stilton from Nottinghamshire, and Gubbeens from Co Cork. Wines from around the world include some from the local Warden Abbey vineyard. On warmer days, enjoy the super views from the garden and patio area.

♀
MAP 12 TL14
SG18 9HQ
☎ 01767 627225
📠 01767 627209
dir: *From Bedford turn right off A603 (or left from A600) to Old Warden. Also accessed from Biggleswade rdbt on A1*

Open 12–3 6–11
Bar Meals L served Tue-Sun 12–2 D served Tue-Sat 6.30–9.30
Restaurant L served Tue-Sun 12–2 D served Tue-Sat 6.30–9.30
⊕ Charles Wells ◀ Wells Bomdardier Premium & Eagle IPA, Adnams. ♀ 8
Facilities Garden Parking

MILTON BRYAN — MAP 11 SP93

The Red Lion ♀

Toddington Rd, South End MK17 9HS ☎ 01525 210044
e-mail: paul@redlion-miltonbryan.co.uk
dir: *Telephone for directions*

Set in a pretty village near Woburn Abbey, this attractive brick-built pub is festooned with dazzling hanging baskets in the summer months. Comfortable, neatly maintained interior, with beams, rugs on wooden floors, and well-kept ales. Wide-ranging menu offering the likes of roast rump of lamb with potato purée, wilted spinach and ratatouille sauce; supreme of chicken stuffed with ricotta cheese, basil and Parma ham on wild rocket and roasted cherry tomato; and baked Cornish cod.

Open 11.30–3 6–11 Closed: 25–26 Dec, 1 Jan **Bar Meals** L served all week 12–2.30 D served Tue-Sat 7–9.30 ⊕ Greene King ◖ Greene King IPA, Old Speckled Hen, Abbot Ale, plus guest ales. ♀7 **Facilities** Garden Parking

NORTHILL — MAP 12 TL14

The Crown ♀

2 Ickwell Rd SG18 9AA ☎ 01767 627337 📄 01767 627279
e-mail: info@thecrown-northill.com
dir: *Telephone for directions*

A delightful 16th-century pub with chocolate box setting in an acre of garden between Northill church and the village duck pond. The grounds include a children's play area, heated patio, wooden gazebos and lighting. Inside, the unique copper-covered bar leads to an informal dining area, where the bar menu of pub favourites applies. The candlelit split-level restaurant boasts much locally-sourced produce served in home-cooked dishes such as spicy citrus scallops, Cumberland sausages, and Caribbean pork steak.

Open 11.30–3 6–11 (Fri-Sat 6–12, Summer: all day Sat-Sun) Closed: 25 Dec eve **Bar Meals** L served all week 12–3 D served Mon-Sat 6.30–9.30 Av main course £11.95 **Restaurant** L served all week 12–2.30 D served all week 6.30–9.30 ⊕ Greene King ◖ Greene King IPA, Abbot Ale, Old Speckled Hen, Olde Tripplus & guest ales. ♀8 **Facilities** Garden Dogs allowed Parking Play Area

ODELL — MAP 11 SP95

The Bell ♀

Horsefair Ln MK43 7AU ☎ 01234 720254
dir: *Telephone for directions*

A Grade II listed 16th-century thatched pub, refurbished throughout. There is a patio and aviary outside, next to a spacious garden leading down to the River Ouse. The lunch menu offers a wide choice of sandwiches, baguettes, filled jacket potatoes and light options also suitable for children. The main menu is also available at lunch or dinner, and features the likes of poached fillet of salmon with white wine sauce; home-made steak and Abbott pie, and mushroom stroganoff.

Open 11–3 6–11 (Sun 12–2.30, 7–10.30) **Bar Meals** L served all week 12–2 D served Tue-Sat 7–9 Av main course £7 **Restaurant** 12–2 6.30–9 ⊕ Greene King ◖ Greene King IPA, Abbot Ale, Ruddles County & seasonal ales. ♀6 **Facilities** Garden Parking

OLD WARDEN — MAP 12 TL14

Pick of the Pubs

Hare and Hounds ♀

See Pick of the Pubs on page 19

SHEFFORD — MAP 12 TL13

The Black Horse ♀

Ireland SG17 5QL ☎ 01462 811398 📄 01462 817238
e-mail: countrytaverns@aol.com
dir: *From S: M1 junct 12, A5120 to Flitwick. Onto A507 by Redbourne School. Follow signs for A1, Shefford (cross A6). Left onto A600 towards Bedford*

This traditional pub is set in a lovely garden surrounded by peaceful countryside. The name of the tiny hamlet is thought to be derived from the Irish navvies who built the local railway line in the 1850s. The memorable menu draws a devoted following, with imaginative meals that might include leg of lamb roasted with garlic and thyme; locally farmed pork loin with prune and apple sauce; and fillet of sea bass with warm fennel and red onion salad.

Open 11.30–3 6–11 (Sun 12–6) Closed: 25–26 Dec, 1 Jan **Bar Meals** L served Mon-Sat 12–2.30 D served Mon-Sat 6.30–10 (Sun 12–5) **Restaurant** L served Mon-Sat 12–2.30 D served Mon-Sat 6.30–10 (Sun 12–5) ◖ Greene King IPA, London Pride & Village Bike. ♀14 **Facilities** Garden Parking

SOUTHILL — MAP 12 TL14

The White Horse ♀

High St SG18 9LD ☎ 01462 813364
e-mail: jack@ravenathexton.f9.co.uk
dir: *Telephone for directions*

A village pub retaining traditional values, yet happily accommodating the needs of children and those who like sitting outside on cool days (the patio has heaters). Locally renowned for its chargrilled steaks from the Duke of Buccleuch's Scottish estate. Other main courses include Cajun chicken, chargrilled pork loin steaks, Whitby Bay scampi, and stuffed breaded plaice. Greene King beers, with London Pride up from Chiswick. Old Warden Park and its Shuttleworth Collection of old planes is nearby.

Open 11–3 6–11 (Sun 12–10.30, all day BHs) **Bar Meals** L served all week 12–2 D served all week 6–9 (Sun 12–9, Wed-Sat 6–10) ⊕ Enterprise Inns ◖ Greene King IPA, London Pride, Speckled Hen, Flowers. ♀22 **Facilities** Garden Parking Play Area

STANBRIDGE MAP 11 SP92

Pick of the Pubs

The Five Bells ♀

Station Rd, Stanbridge LU7 9JF

☎ 01525 210224 ▤ 01525 211164

dir: *Off A505 E of Leighton Buzzard*

A stylish and relaxing setting for a drink or a meal is offered by this white-painted 400-year-old village inn, which has been delightfully renovated and revived. The bar features lots of bare wood as well as comfortable armchairs and polished, rug-strewn floors. The modern decor extends to the bright, airy 75-cover dining room. There's also a spacious garden with patio and lawns. The inn offers bar meals, set menus and a carte choice for diners. The bar menu typically includes dishes such as smoked chicken, sun-dried tomato and pine nut salad; battered fish, chips and mushy peas; baked courgettes stuffed with goat's cheese and mint with a mixed salad; rib-eye steak with fries; and chicken, ham, leek and mushroom pie.

Open 12–9.30 (Sun 12–9) **Bar Meals** L served all week 12–9.30 D served all week Av main course £7.50 ∰ Fullers ◄ Greene King IPA, Timothy Taylor Landlord, London Pride. ♀ 8 **Facilities** Garden Dogs allowed Parking

SUTTON MAP 12 TL24

John O'Gaunt Inn ♀

30 High St SG19 2NE ☎ 01767 260377

dir: *Off B1040 between Biggleswade & Potton*

Situated in one of Bedfordshire's most picturesque villages, the John O'Gaunt is a traditional village inn where a guest ale features alongside the regular beers supplied in rotation from various breweries. Piped music is notable by its absence, though you may be encouraged to join in the occasional informal folk music sessions. The pub offers a large garden, and welcoming winter fires. A wide choice of good food is available most lunchtimes and evenings.

Open 12–3 7–11.30 **Bar Meals** L served Mon-Sat 12–1.30 D served Mon-Sat 7–8.30 (Sun 12.30–1.30) ◄ Rotating real ales. ♀ 8 **Facilities** Garden Dogs allowed Parking **Notes** ⊛

TILSWORTH MAP 11 SP92

The Anchor Inn ♀

1 Dunstable Rd LU7 9PU

☎ 01525 210289 ▤ 01525 211578

e-mail: tonyanchorinn@aol.com

dir: *Telephone for directions*

The only pub in a Saxon village, the Anchor dates from 1878. The restaurant is a recent addition to the side of the pub, and the whole building has been refurbished. The licensees pride themselves on their fresh food and well-kept ales. Hand-cut steaks are particularly popular (they buy the meat at Smithfield, butcher it and hang it themselves). An acre of garden includes patio seating, an adventure playground and a barbecue.

Open 12–11 **Bar Meals** L served all week 12–2.30 D served Mon-Sat 6–10 (Sun 12–7) Av main course £9 **Restaurant** L served all week 12–2.30 D served Mon-Sat 6–10 (Sun 12–7) Av 3 course à la carte £25 ∰ Greene King ◄ Greene King IPA, Abbot Ale, Wadworth 6X, guest ales. ♀ 12 **Facilities** Garden Parking Play Area

WOBURN MAP 11 SP93

The Birch at Woburn NEW ♀

20 Newport Rd MK17 9HX

☎ 01525 861414 ▤ 01525 861323

e-mail: ctaverns@aol.com

dir: *Telephone for directions*

A beautifully presented family-run establishment, The Birch is located opposite Woburn Championship Golf Course, close to Woburn Abbey and the Safari Park. It has built its reputation on the friendly service of freshly cooked food. A comprehensive menu offers a range of English and Continental dishes, and there is a griddle area where customers can make their selection from the array of fresh steaks and fish, which are then cooked to their preference by the chefs.

Open 11.30–3 6–11 Closed: Sun eve **Bar Meals** L served all week 12–5 **Restaurant** L served all week 12–2.45 D served Mon-Sat 6.30–10 ∰ Free House ◄ London Pride, Adnams, Guinness. **Facilities** Parking

BERKSHIRE

ALDERMASTON MAP 05 SU56

Hinds Head ♀

Wasing Ln RG7 4LX ☎ 0118 971 2194 ▤ 0118 971 4511

e-mail: hindshead@accommodating-inns.co.uk

dir: *M4 junct 12, A4 towards Newbury, left on A340 towards Basingstoke, 2m to village*

This 17th-century inn with its distinctive clock and bell tower still incorporates the village lock-up, which was last used in 1865. The former brew house behind the pub has been refurbished to create an additional dining area. Menu choices range from jacket potatoes and filled baguettes to whole baked sea bass; carbonara pasta; and cauliflower cheese.

Open 11.30–11 (Sun 12–10.30) **Bar Meals** L served Mon-Sat 12–2.30 D served Mon-Sat 6–9.15 (Sun 12–3, 6–8) **Restaurant** L served Mon-Sat 12–2.30 D served Mon-Sat 6–9.15 (Sun 12–3, 6–8) ∰ Fullers ◄ Fullers HSB. ♀ 12 **Facilities** Garden Parking

ALDWORTH MAP 05 SU57

Pick of the Pubs

The Bell Inn

RG8 9SE ☎ 01635 578272

dir: *Just off B4009 (Newbury-Streatley road)*

One might be surprised to discover that an establishment without a restaurant can hold its own in a world of smart dining pubs and modish gastropubs. Well, be surprised. The Bell not only survives, it positively prospers and, to be fair, it does serve some food, if only hot, crusty, generously filled rolls. And since it is one of the few truly unspoiled country pubs left, and serves cracking pints of Arkell's, West Berkshire and guest real ales, this alimentary limitation has no real disadvantage. The Bell is old, very old, beginning life in 1340 as a five-bay cruck-built manor hall. It has reputedly been in the same family for 200 years: ask Mr Macaulay, the landlord – he's been here for more than thirty of them, and has no plans to change it from the time warp it is. A 300-year-old,

Continued

21

England

ALDWORTH continued

one-handed clock still stands in the taproom, and the rack for the spit-irons and clockwork roasting jack are still over the fireplace. Taller customers may bump their heads at the glass-panelled bar hatch.

Open 11–3 6–11 (Sun, Good Fri 12–3, 7–10.30) Closed: 25 Dec & Mon (ex BH lunch) **Bar Meals** L served Tue-Sun 11–2.30 D served Tue-Sun 6–10.30 (L snacks only Wtr) ⊕ Free House ◀ Arkell's Kingsdown, 3B, West Berkshire Old Tyler & Maggs Magnificent Mild, guest ale. **Facilities** Garden Dogs allowed Parking **Notes** ☺

ASCOT
MAP 06 SU96

The Thatched Tavern ⚲

Cheapside Rd SL5 7QG ☎ 01344 620874 🗎 01344 623043
e-mail: thethatchedtaverns@4cinns.co.uk
dir: *Follow Ascot Racecourse signs. Through Ascot 1st left (Cheapside). 1.5m, pub on left*

Just a mile from the racecourse, a 17th-century building of original beams, flagstone floors and very low ceilings. In summer the sheltered garden makes a fine spot to enjoy real ales and varied choice of food. In the same safe hands for over ten years, the kitchen produces dishes like pan-fried chicken breast with cheddar mash, black pudding, Muscat and thyme sauce, seared calves' liver on bubble and squeak and steak and kidney pudding with mustard mash.

Open 12–3 5.30–11 (Fri-Sun open all day) **Bar Meals** L served all week 12–3 D served all week 7–10 (Sun 12–3, 7–9) Av main course £8 **Restaurant** L served all week 12–3 D served all week 7–10 (Sun 12–3, 7–9) Av 3 course à la carte £25 ⊕ Free House ◀ Fuller's London Pride, IPA. ⚲ 8 **Facilities** Garden Parking

ASHMORE GREEN
MAP 05 SU56

The Sun in the Wood ⚲

Stoney Ln RG18 9HF ☎ 01635 42377 🗎 01635 528392
e-mail: suninthewood@aol.com
dir: *From A34 at Robin Hood Rdbt left to Shaw, at mini-rdbt right then 7th left into Stoney Ln 1.5m, pub on left*

As the name suggests, this pub enjoys a delightful woodland setting, yet the centre of Newbury is just a stone's throw away. Expect stone floors and plenty of wood panelling within, and swings, slides, climbing frame and crazy golf outside for children. Sample a pint of Wadworth's or one of 17 wines by the glass, and enjoy home-made food such as seafood broth followed by crispy belly pork on bubble and squeak.

Open 12–2.30 6–11 Closed: Mon **Bar Meals** L served Tue-Sun 12–2 D served Tue-Sat 6–9.30 Av main course £11.50 **Restaurant** L served Tue-Sun 12–2 D served Tue-Sat 6–9.30 ⊕ Wadworth ◀ Wadworth 6X & Henrys Original IPA, Badger Tanglefoot. ⚲ 17 **Facilities** Garden Parking Play Area

BOXFORD
MAP 05 SU47

The Bell at Boxford ⚲

Lambourn Rd RG20 8DD
☎ 01488 608721 🗎 01488 658502
e-mail: paul@bellatboxford.com
dir: *A338 toward Wantage, right onto B4000, take 3rd left to Boxford*

Mock Tudor country pub at the heart of the glorious Lambourn Valley, noted for its pretty villages and sweeping Downland scenery. Cosy log fires add to the appeal in winter, and the patio is popular throughout the year with its array of flowers and outdoor heating, hog roasts, barbecues and parties.

Open 11–3 6–11 (Sat 6.30–11, Sun 7–10.30) **Bar Meals** L served Mon-Sat 12–2 D served Mon-Sat 7–10 (Sun 12–3,7–9) Av main course £6 **Restaurant** L served Mon-Sat 12–2 D served all week 7–10 (Sun 12–3) Av 3 course à la carte £24 Av 2 course fixed price £11.95 ⊕ Free House ◀ Interbrew Bass, Courage Best, Wadworth 6X, Henrys IPA. ⚲ 60 **Facilities** Garden Dogs allowed Parking **Rooms** available

See advertisement under NEWBURY

BRAY
MAP 06 SU97

Pick of the Pubs

Hinds Head Hotel ◉◉ ⚲
See Pick of the Pubs on opposite page

PICK OF THE PUBS

BRAY-BERKSHIRE

Hinds Head Hotel

With its sturdy oak panelling and beams, to its leather chairs and crackling fires, the Hinds Head has everything you'd expect from a traditional English inn. It was built in the 15th-century, though its original purpose has been lost in the mists of time. Some say it was a royal hunting lodge, or perhaps a guesthouse for the local Abbot of Cirencester.

But, whatever its origins, this much-loved tavern has been at the heart of village life in Bray for more than four centuries. Over the years the Hinds Head has hosted such illustrious events as Prince Philip's stag night in 1947, and the engagement party of Princess Margaret and Lord Snowdon in 1963. More recently, the pub has been taken over by the celebrity chef Heston Blumenthal, who also owns the famous Fat Duck, just across the street. The short, inviting menu presents an alluring sense of days gone by. Blumenthal has worked with staff at the Tudor Kitchens at Hampton Court Palace to create a range of traditional British dishes, including some lost to us for over 500 years. Starters such as dandelion salad with bacon and quails eggs; Colchester rock oysters; and tea smoked salmon with soda bread introduce main course choices that might include whole sea bream and fennel; rump steak with bone marrow sauce and triple cooked chips; shepherd's pie with grained mustard mash; or steamed mussels with garlic, lemon and parsley. For dessert, try Eccles cakes with potted stilton; lardy cake with toffee sauce and whisky ice cream; or British cheese with oatcakes and apple chutney. Meanwhile, snacks like Welsh rarebit; or steak sandwich with charred onions and watercress, make perfect partners to a pint of Greene King IPA or Marlow Rebellion.

@@ ☂
MAP 06 SU97
High St SL6 2AB
☎ 01628 626151
🖷 01628 623394
e-mail:
info@hindsheadhotel.co.uk
dir: *M4 junct 8/9 take exit to Maidenhead Central. Next rdbt take exit for Bray & Windsor. After 0.5m take B3028 to Bray*

Open 11–11 (Sun 11–10) Closed: 25–26 Dec
Bar Meals L served Mon-Sat 12–2.30 D served all week 6.30–9.30 (Sun 12–3) Av main course £15
Restaurant L served Mon-Sat 12–2.30 D served Mon-Sat 6.30–9.30 (Sun 12–4) Av 3 course à la carte £30
⊕ Free House ◀ Greene King IPA, Greene King Abbot Ale, Marlow Rebellion. ☂ 15
Facilities Parking

BURCHETT'S GREEN — MAP 05 SU88

The Crown ♀

SL6 6QZ ☎ 01628 822844
e-mail: admin@thecrownatburchettsgreen.co.uk
dir: *From M4 take A404(M), then 3rd exit*

Set amid a large rose garden overlooking the village green, this popular local has a welcoming interior with low-beamed ceilings, striking whitewashed walls and a restaurant. Head chef Michael Field uses local and organic ingredients to produce fresh, unfussy dishes including pan-fried pork chop with creamed parmesan leeks and mashed potato; traditional battered haddock and French fries; and roasted red pepper, sunblushed tomato and leek risotto.

Open 12–2.30 6.30–11 **Bar Meals** L served Tue-Sun 12–2.30 D served Tue-Sat 6.30–9.30 **Restaurant** L served Tue-Sun 12–2.30 D served Tue-Sat 6.30–9.30 ⊕ Greene King ◀ Greene King IPA, Ruddles Best. ♀ 10 **Facilities** Garden Parking

See advert on opposite page

CHADDLEWORTH — MAP 05 SU47

The Ibex ♀

Main St RG20 7ER ☎ 01488 638311 🗎 01488 639458

dir: *A338 towards Wantage, through Great Shefford then right, then 2nd left, pub on right in village*

Originally two cottages forming part of a 17th-century farm, this Grade II listed building was later used as a bakery and then an off-licence before eventually becoming a pub. In more recent years it was run by ex-jockey Colin Brown who partnered the legendary Desert Orchid for many years, and kept the cosy lounge bar with low ceilings and bench seats. Popular bar menu includes chicken and leek pie; beef and ale casserole; liver and onions; and halibut with red wine and wild mushrooms.

Open 11–11 (Sun 12–11) **Bar Meals** L served all week 12–3 D served all week 6–10 **Restaurant** L served all week 12–3 D served all week 6–10 Av 3 course à la carte £25 ⊕ Greene King ◀ Regularly changing guest ales. ♀ 7 **Facilities** Children's licence Garden Dogs allowed Parking

CHIEVELEY — MAP 05 SU47

The Crab at Chieveley ♀

North Heath, Wantage Rd RG20 8UE
☎ 01635 247550 🗎 01635 247440
e-mail: info@crabatchieveley.com
dir: *M4 junct 13. 1.5m W of Chieveley on B4494*

Break that tedious M4 journey with a pit-stop at this old thatched dining pub, one of the best seafood restaurants in England. Specialising in mouth-watering fish dishes, with fresh deliveries daily, the Fish Bar offers, for example, hot Irish oysters with chorizo as a starter, and Cornish fish curry with coconut and cardamom-scented rice as a main. In the elegant, maritime-themed restaurant, try the unfishy saltmarsh lamb confit accompanied by goats' cheese and shallot tart.

Open 11–12 (Sun 12–10.30) **Bar Meals** L served all week 12–2.30 D served all week 6–10 Av main course £14.50 **Restaurant** L served all week 12–2.30 D served all week 6–10 Av 3 course à la carte £40 Av 3 course fixed price £20 ⊕ Free House ◀ Fuller's London Pride, Boddingtons, West Berkshire, Black Sheep. ♀ 16 **Facilities** Garden Dogs allowed Parking

COOKHAM DEAN — MAP 05 SU88

Pick of the Pubs

Chequers Brasserie ♀

Dean Ln SL6 9BQ ☎ 01628 481232 🗎 01628 481237
e-mail: info@chequersbrasserie.co.uk
dir: *From A4094 in Cookham High St towards Marlow, over rail line. 1m on right*

Kenneth Grahame, who wrote *The Wind in the Willows*, spent his childhood in these parts. He'd surely have enjoyed this historic pub, tucked away between Marlow and Maidenhead in one of the prettiest villages in the Thames Valley. Striking Victorian and Edwardian villas around the green set the tone, whilst the surrounding wooded hills and dales have earned Cookham Dean a reputation as a centre for wonderful walks. Today, the Chequers offers carefully chosen wines and a good selection of real ales to go with an Anglo-French menu dedicated to the use of fresh, excellent produce. Sample the likes of seared king scallops with crayfish tail risotto; fillet of smoked haddock topped with a poached egg; whole black bream with citrus beurre blanc; and roast rack of lamb with wilted spinach and redcurrant jus.

Open 12–3.30 5.30–12 (Fri, Sat, Sun 11–12) **Restaurant** L served all week 12–2.30 D served all week 6–9.30 (Fri & Sat 12–2.20, 6–10) Av 3 course à la carte £24.95 ⊕ Free House ◀ Guinness, Greene King IPA, Rebellion Marlow Brewery. ♀ 10 **Facilities** Garden Parking

CRAZIES HILL MAP 05 SU78

Pick of the Pubs

The Horns ♀

See Pick of the Pubs on page 26

CURRIDGE MAP 05 SU47

The Bunk Inn ♀

RG18 9DS ☎ 01635 200400 📄 01635 200336

e-mail: thebunkinn@btconnect.com

dir: *M4 junct 13, A34 N towards Oxford. Take 1st slip rd then right for 1m. right at T-junct, 1st right signed Curridge*

Owned by the Liquorish family since 1991, this village free house is renowned for its cuisine and friendly atmosphere. Stay in the log fire-warmed bar in winter or, in summer, head for the attractive garden and patio. The only question is, where to dine – stylish restaurant or lovely conservatory? All food is fresh, and wherever possible, seasonal and local. An impressive carte menu, plus specials that usually include fresh Brixham fish.

Open 10–1am (Fri-Sat 10–2am, Sun 11–11) **Bar Meals** L served all week 12–2.30 D served all week 6–9.30 (Sun 6–8) **Restaurant** L served all week 12–2.30 D served all week 6–9.30 (Sun 6–8) ⊕ Free House ◗ Arkells 3B, Fuller's London Pride, plus 2 guest ales. ♀ 9 **Facilities** Garden Dogs allowed Parking Play Area

See advert on this page

THE CROWN
AT BURCHETTS GREEN

Burchetts Green • Nr Maidenhead • Berkshire • SL6 6QZ
Tel: 01628 822844 • www.thecrownatburchettsgreen.co.uk

The Crown, in the secluded village of Burchetts Green is known for its stylish restaurant. Award winning chef Michael Field produces a menu with a seductive blend of the contemporary and the traditional. The menu is English with a Mediterranean influence. Michael uses local and organic ingredients to produce fresh, unfussy dishes including pan-fried pork chop with creamed parmesan leeks and mashed potato; Roasted halibut fillet on wilted spinach and rocket with charlotte potatoes; and roasted red pepper, sunblushed tomato and leek risotto. There is also generous wine list offering new and old world wines. The Crown itself is a fine old 19th century building in a beautiful countryside and it has an attractive and-secluded rose garden.

Opening Times:
lunch & dinner Tue – Sat
also Sunday lunch
From 12 to 2.30
From 6.30 till late

THE BUNK INN

Curridge Village, Nr Hermitage, Thatcham, Berkshire RG18 9DS
Telephone (01635) 200400

Situated in a quiet village with glorious countryside surrounding, The Bunk Inn is a unique Pub with an outstanding reputation for its food, and more recently its top quality bedrooms.

Owned and run by The Liquorish Family since 1991, Michael Liquorish and his partner Ali Wright have created a most welcoming Inn, which offers something for everyone.

The À La Carte menu has a choice of seven or eight starters, main courses and puddings, and there are six special boards which change daily.

There is an excellent choice of beers and wines and the bedrooms have to be seen to be believed!

For any further information please visit our website at www.thebunkinn.co.uk

PICK OF THE PUBS

The Horns

At the end of the 19th century there were only 15 houses in Crazies Hill, the hamlet in which The Horns occupies a central position. Since then it has expanded rapidly and, incredibly, at one time supported six pubs.

This beautifully restored, 16th-century pub has three interconnecting terracotta-coloured, oak-beamed rooms full of old pine tables, with stripped wooden floors, open fires and rugby memorabilia. It started life in Tudor times as a hunting lodge, to which a barn (now the dining area) was added some 200 years ago. Today's peaceful atmosphere is untroubled by music or electronic games. The food is a traditional choice offered on a seasonal menu with popular favourites like chef's pie of the day; liver and bacon with rich onion gravy, and fish and chips with mushy peas. Other dishes include coq au vin with spring onion mash; pork tenderloin with black pudding and light Dijon mustard gravy; and salmon and haddock fishcakes with

prawn and smoked salmon sauce. Freshly-filled baguettes and home-made desserts are also available. There is an extensive and secluded garden with a children's play area and ample off-street parking. Regular jazz and comedy nights are held.

🍷
MAP 05 SU78
RG10 8LY
☎ 0118 940 1416
🖷 0118 940 4849
e-mail: reservations@
thehornspub.com
dir: *Off A321 NE of Wargrave*

Open 11–11
Bar Meals L served all week
12–3 D served all week 7–9.30
Restaurant L served all week
12–3 D served Mon-Sun 7–9.30
🍺 Brakspear 🍺 Brakspear Bitter.
Facilities Garden Dogs allowed
Parking Play Area

EAST GARSTON | MAP 05 SU37

Pick of the Pubs

The Queen's Arms Country Inn ♀

RG17 7ET ☎ 01488 648757 🖺 01488 648642
e-mail: info@queensarmscountryhotel.co.uk
dir: *M4 junct 14, 4m onto A338 to Great Shefford, then East Garston*

This 18th-century inn is pleasantly located in a small village in the Lambourn Valley, with its many racehorse training yards. It is also an excellent area for walking, being quite close to the Ridgeway. As a freehouse the Queen's Arms can offer a selection of cask-conditioned real ales, and there is also a good wine list. Bar snacks are available, and there is also a good selection of traditional country food made from fresh local ingredients. On the main menu are dishes such as goats' cheese and black pudding salad; wild boar and leek sausages; lamb cutlets; and roast peppers stuffed with brie, mushrooms and red onion served with tagliatelle. The terrace and large garden are popular in the summer, when barbecues and hog roasts take place.

Open 11–11 (Closed on 25 Dec at 2pm) **Bar Meals** L served all week 12–3 D served all week 7–10 **Restaurant** L served all week 11–3 D served all week 7–10 ⊕ Free House ◀ Fuller's London Pride, Brakspears, Guinness. ♀12 **Facilities** Garden Dogs allowed Parking

---

HARE HATCH | MAP 05 SU87

The Queen Victoria ♀

The Holt RG10 9TA ☎ 0118 940 2477 🖺 0118 940 2477
e-mail: kempjo@aol.com
dir: *On A4 between Reading & Maidenhead*

A country cottage-style pub dating back over 300 years, handily placed between Reading and Maidenhead. It offers excellent draught beers and an interesting choice of wines. The menu mainly features satisfying and traditional pub grub, but there is also a more adventurous specials board which usually includes a vegetarian option. The location of the Queen Victoria on the edge of the Chilterns means that there are some good countryside walks nearby.

Open 11–3 6–11 (Sun 12–10.30) Closed: 25–26 Dec
Bar Meals L served all week 12–2.30 D served all week 6–10 (Sun 12–9.30 Av main course £7.50 **Restaurant** L served all week 12–2.30 D served all week 6–10 Sun 12–9.30 ⊕ Brakspear ◀ Brakspear Bitter & Special. ♀11 **Facilities** Garden Parking

---

HERMITAGE | MAP 05 SU57

The White Horse of Hermitage ♀

Newbury Rd RG18 9TB ☎ 01635 200325
e-mail: thewh@btconnect.com
web: www.thewhitehorseofhermitage.co.uk
dir: *5m from Newbury on B4009. Follow signs to Chieveley, right into Priors Court Rd, turn left at mini-rdbt, pub approx 1m*

The ever-growing reputation of the WH centres on its food, best described as hearty home cooking with a Caribbean fusion twist, courtesy of the chef's flair and training. Fresh fish, speciality steaks, hand-made burgers and pies are part of a daily-changing menu that also includes fresh Shetland mussels, penne pasta with spicy Italian sausages, and four-bean chilli. Outside there is a large garden with a children's play area, plus a covered patio.

Open 12–3 5–11 (Sat all day, Sun 12–6) Closed: Mon (ex BH)
Bar Meals L served Mon-Sat 12–2.30 D served Mon-Sat 5–9 (Sun 12–6) **Restaurant** L served Mon-Sat 12–3.30 D served Mon-Sat 5–9 (Sun12–6) ⊕ Greene King ◀ Abbot Ale, Greene King IPA, Guinness. ♀9 **Facilities** Garden Dogs allowed Parking Play Area

---

HUNGERFORD | MAP 05 SU36

Pick of the Pubs

The Crown & Garter ★★★★ INN ♀
See Pick of the Pubs on page 30

The River Thames at Reading, Berkshire.

HUNGERFORD continued

Pick of the Pubs

The Swan Inn ★★★★ INN

Craven Rd, Lower Green, Inkpen RG17 9DX
☎ 01488 668326 📄 01488 668306
e-mail: enquiries@theswaninn-organics.co.uk
web: www.theswaninn-organics.co.uk
dir: *S down Hungerford High St (A338), under rail bridge, left to Hungerford Common. Right signed Inkpen (3m).*

Organic beef farmers Mary and Bernard Harris preside over this rambling 17th-century free house, which stands in fine walking country just below Combe Gibbet and Walbury Hill. In addition to ramblers, the pub is a magnet for cyclists, hang gliders, shooting parties and organic food enthusiasts. An attractive terraced garden sets the scene for al fresco summer dining, in contrast to the heavily beamed interior with its old photographic prints and open winter fires. Almost everything on the menu is prepared using their own fresh produce; meats are 100% organic and butchered on the premises, which has earned accreditation by the Soil Association and won the RSPCA Good Business Award in 2007 for the UK Independent Restaurant category. The bar menu offers traditional English favourites, while the Cygnet restaurant serves dishes like Moroccan lamb tagine, salmon teriyaki, and the full range of organic steaks; vegetarian options are also a strength.

Open 12–11 (Sun 12–10.30) Closed: 25–26 Dec **Bar Meals** L served Mon-Fri 12–2 D served all week 7–9.30 (Sat 12–2.30, Sun 12–3) Av main course £10.50 **Restaurant** L served Wed-Sat 12–2.30 D served Wed-Sat 7–9.30 (Sun lunch only 12–3) Av 3 course à la carte £27 ⊕ Free House ◀ Butts Traditional & Jester Bitter, Maggs Magnificent MIld, guest ales. **Facilities** Garden Parking Play Area **Rooms** 10

HURST   MAP 05 SU77

The Green Man ♥

Hinton Rd RG10 0BP ☎ 0118 934 2599 📄 0118 934 2939
e-mail: simon@thegreenman.uk.com
dir: *off A321, adjacent to Hurst Cricket Club*

The pub dates from 1642, when it was part of the Windsor Estate. The old black beams, low in places, are still to be seen and the building has been developed to include all the old features, while newer areas reflect a similar theme. Inside you'll find open fires, hand drawn beer and good food, from sandwiches to Sunday roasts. The garden, open to fields and woodland, includes a children's play area.

The Green Man

Open 11–3 5.30–11 (Sun 12–10.30) **Bar Meals** L served Mon-Sat 12–2.30 D served Mon-Sat 6–9.30 (Sun 12–9) **Restaurant** L served Mon-Sat 12–2.30 D served Mon-Sat 6–9.30 (Sun 12–9) ⊕ Brakspear ◀ Brakspear Bitter, Special & seasonal ales. ♥ 8 **Facilities** Children's licence Garden Parking Play Area

---

KINTBURY   MAP 05 SU36

Pick of the Pubs

The Dundas Arms

53 Station Rd RG17 9UT
☎ 01488 658263 📄 01488 658568
e-mail: info@dundasarms.co.uk
web: www.dundasarms.co.uk
dir: *M4 junct 13 take A34 to Newbury, then A4 to Hungerford, left to Kintbury. Pub 1m by canal & rail station*

Set in an area of outstanding natural beauty on the banks of the Kennet and Avon canal, this free house has been welcoming travellers since the end of the 18th century. The pub has been in the same family for many years, and proprietor David Dalzell-Piper has worked and cooked here throughout that time. Traditional beers like West Berkshire and Cornish Coaster are served in the convivial bar, whilst the simply styled restaurant is redolent of a French auberge. On warmer days, outdoor tables offer views of the narrow boats and wildlife on the canal. On the bar's blackboard menu, oxtail casserole in red wine sauce jostles with grilled halibut on saffron and fennel risotto. Meanwhile, a typical restaurant meal might start with home-potted shrimps, before moving on to grilled Kilravock pork chop with root mash and sage gravy, followed by raspberry crème brûlée.

Open 11–2.30 6–11 Closed: 25 & 31 Dec & Sun eve **Bar Meals** L served Mon-Sat 12–2 D served Tue-Sat 7–9 (Sun 12–2.30) Av main course £12 **Restaurant** D served Tue-Sat 7–9 Av 3 course à la carte £25 ⊕ Free House ◀ West Berkshire, Mr Chubbs Lunchtime Bitter, Adnams, Sharp's Cornish Coaster. **Facilities** Children's licence Parking **Rooms** available

The Crown & Garter

A family-owned, personally run 17th-century inn in a really pretty part of Berkshire. James II allegedly used to stop off here on his way to visit one of his mistresses – perhaps he wasn't in such a hurry to see her. The inn's barn was used to lay out the bodies of two lovers hanged at nearby Combe Gibbet for killing the woman's husband.

There have been four of these gruesome constructions: the original rotted away, its replacement was struck by lightning, the third lasted a hundred years or so until felled by a gale in 1949, and then there's the one you see today. The inn's ancient charm can best be seen in the bar area, where there's a huge inglenook fireplace and criss-crossing beams. You can eat here, in the restaurant, or outside in the enclosed beer garden or new patio, choosing from a variety of dishes all freshly prepared on the premises from local produce. First courses include oak-smoked salmon with horseradish cream; wild mushroom risotto with red chard salad; and oriental duck spring roll and chilli dip. Among the main courses are likely to be half a roast duck with brandy and fresh orange sauce; pan-fried lambs' liver with onions and bubble and squeak; or daily fish and seafood specials from the blackboard feature. There's also a Thai and Indonesian selection, including green, red and rendang curries. White peach soup with raspberry sherbet should slip down easily afterwards. Eight spacious en suite bedrooms have been built around a pretty cottage garden. Nearby Hungerford has some good antique shops, and Bath, Oxford and Winchester are less than an hour away. But why drive when the stunning countryside surrounding the inn is so perfect for walking, cycling, fishing or simply chilling out?

★★★★ INN 🍷
MAP 05 SU36
Inkpen Common RG17 9QR
☎ 01488 668325
e-mail: gill.hern@btopenworld.com
web: www.crownandgarter.com
dir: *From A4 to Kintbury & Inkpen. At village store left into Inkpen Rd, follow signs for Inkpen Common (2m)*

Open 12-3 5.30-11 (Sun eve 7-10.30, Closed Mon & Tue lunch)
Bar Meals L served Wed-Sat 12-2 D served Mon-Sat 6.30-9.30 (Sun 12-2.30) Av main course £10
Restaurant L served Wed-Sat 12-2 D served Mon-Sat 6.30-9.30 (Sun 12-2.30) Av 3 course à la carte £22
Free House · Mr Chubbs, Good Old Boy, Guinness, Boddingtons. 🍷 9
Facilities Garden Parking
Rooms 8

| KNOWL HILL | MAP 05 SU87 | MAIDENHEAD | MAP 06 SU88 |

Pick of the Pubs

Bird In Hand Country Inn ♀

Bath Rd RG10 9UP
☎ 01628 826622 & 822781 📠 01628 826748
e-mail: sthebirdinhand@aol.com
web: www.birdinhand.co.uk
dir: On A4, 5m W of Maidenhead, 7m E of Reading

In the same family for three generations, the inn prides itself on providing personal service in a friendly atmosphere. Parts of the building date from the 14th century, and legend has it that in the late 1700s George III wet his regal whistle here while his horse was being re-shod at the forge next door. There is a wood-panelled Oak Lounge Bar serving a range of hand-pumped ales, and an attractive restaurant overlooking the courtyard and fountain. A buffet bar is available to diners from the main bar or restaurant, while dishes from the respective menus range from steak and kidney pudding with Guinness, to roast whole stuffed quail with apricot and thyme in an oyster mushroom and grape sauce. Monthly themed evenings feature cuisines from around the world.

Open 11–3 6–11 (Sun 12–10.30) **Bar Meals** L served Mon-Sat 12–2.30 D served Mon-Sat 6.30–10 (Sun 12–9) Av main course £9.95 **Restaurant** L served Mon-Sat 12–2.30 D served Mon-Sat 7–10 (Sun 12–9) Av 3 course à la carte £18 Av fixed price £15.50 ⊕ Free House ◖ Brakspear Bitter, Hogsback TEA. ♀ 12 **Facilities** Garden Dogs allowed Parking **Rooms** available

| LECKHAMPSTEAD | MAP 05 SU47 |

Pick of the Pubs

The Stag ♀

See Pick of the Pubs on page 32

The Belgian Arms ♀

Holyport SL6 2JR ☎ 01628 634468 📠 01628 777952
e-mail: enquiries@thamessideevents.com
dir: In Holyport, 2m from Maidenhead, off Ascot road

Originally known as The Eagle, the Prussian eagle inn sign attracted unwelcome attention during the First World War. As a result, the name was changed to reflect an area where the fiercest fighting was taking place. Things are more peaceful now, and details of local walks are listed outside the pub. The attractive menu includes snacks and light lunches, as well as hot dishes like sausages, mash and onion gravy, and spicy beanburger and chips.

Open 11–3 5.30–11 (Fri-Sat 11–11, Sun 12–10.30) Closed: 25 Dec eve **Bar Meals** L served all week 12–2 D served Mon-Sun 6.30–9 ⊕ Brakspear ◖ Brakspear Best, Brakspear Special. ♀ 8 **Facilities** Garden Dogs allowed Parking

The White Hart ♀

Moneyrow Green, Holyport SL6 2ND
☎ 01628 621460 📠 01628 621460
e-mail: info@whitehartholyport.com
dir: 2m S from Maidenhead. M4 junct 8/9, follow Holyport signs then Moneyrow Green. Pub by petrol station

A busy 19th-century coaching inn offering quality home-made food, with most vegetables and herbs used – 36 varieties at the last count – freshly picked from its own organic allotment. Typical mains are caramelised breast of duck, calves' liver and bacon, venison sausages, grilled fillet of plaice, and slow-roasted tomato tart with Somerset brie. The wood-panelled lounge bar is furnished with leather chesterfields and warmed by an open fire. Poltergeists have been reported.

Open 11–12 (Fri & Sat 11am-12.30am) Closed: 1 Jan **Bar Meals** L served all week 12–2.30 D served Mon-Sat 6–9.30 Av main course £12 **Restaurant** L served all week 12–2.30 D served Mon-Sat 6–9.30 Av 3 course à la carte £25 ⊕ Greene King ◖ Guinness, IPA, Morland Original. ♀ 8 **Facilities** Garden Dogs allowed Parking Play Area

PICK OF THE PUBS

LECKHAMSTEAD-BERKSHIRE

The Stag

To look at, the privately owned, white-painted Stag could only be a pub. It lies just off the village green in a sleepy downland village and close by are the Ridgeway long-distance path and Snelsmore Common, home to nightjar, woodlark and grazing Exmoor ponies.

Needless to say, with such beautiful countryside all around, muddy wellies and wet dogs are expected – in fact, the latter are as genuinely welcome as their owners. During the winter months the wood-burning stove is always ready with its dancing flames. The bar and restaurant walls are painted in warm red, or left as bare brick, while old black and white photographs tell of village life many years ago. Surrounding farms and growers supply all produce, including venison, pheasant and fresh river trout. These fish often appear on the specials board, courtesy of a regular customer who barters them for a few glasses of Rioja, depending on their size. Aberdeen Angus beef from cattle raised next door may also feature as a special, and those lucky enough to find it there agree that

its taste and texture are sublime. Other possibilities, depending on the prevailing menu, are Cornish mussels in cream, white wine and herbs; field mushroom topped with mozzarella, olives and pesto; Thai red chicken curry and sticky lemon rice; pork fillet with sautéed chorizo and baby broad beans; beer battered fish and chips with mushy peas and homemade tartare sauce; and a daily vegetarian special. Home-made desserts include apricot bread and butter pudding with cream, and chocolate and Cointreau cheesecake. There are around 20 red and white wines, among them varieties from Australia, California and France. Compulsive workers can take advantage of a wireless internet connection, although in a pub like this it would have to be pretty urgent work.

MAP 05 SU47
Shop Ln RG20 8QG
☎ 01488 638436
e-mail: enquiries@
stagleckhampstead.co.uk
dir: *6m from Newbury on B4494*

Open 12–2.30 6–11
Bar Meals L served all week
12–2 D served all week 6–9.30 Av
main course £10
Restaurant L served all week
12–2 D served all week 6–9.30
Av 3 course à la carte £18
🍺 Brakspears, guest ales. 🍷 8
Facilities Children's licence
Garden Dogs allowed Parking

England

MARSH BENHAM   MAP 05 SU46

Pick of the Pubs

The Red House ◎ ♟

RG20 8LY ☎ 01635 582017 📄 01635 581621

e-mail: annattheredhouse@btconnect.com

dir: *5m from Hungerford, 3m from Newbury, 400yds off A4*

Very much a gastro-pub, but the spacious bar's stripped wooden floors and warmly painted walls also welcome drinkers, as does the sun-trap terrace outside. Refreshments include popular international beers alongside casks from the West Berkshire Brewery; the very respectable wine list numbers nearly 100 choices. Previously known as the Water Rat, the striking 18th-century brick-and-newly-thatched pub lies close to the banks of the River Kennet, one of Britain's prettiest chalk streams; the book-lined dining room overlooks water-meadows. Serious food as well as lighter bites meet the needs of both the ravenous and the merely peckish. Bar snacks include olives, bite-size fishcakes, and mini oriental samosas, while a three-course dinner could comprise crispy duck spring roll with plum sauce; cannon of Marsh Benham lamb with parma ham and mille-feuille of aubergine; and tiramisu with cannoli biscuit. A fixed-price menu is also served at both lunch and dinner.

Open 11.30–3 6–11 (Sun 11.30–3.30) Closed: 26 & 31 Dec–1 Jan **Bar Meals** L served Mon-Sat 11.30–2.30 D served all week 7–9.45 (Sun 7–9.30) Av main course £9.95 **Restaurant** L served Mon-Sat 12–2.30 D served Mon-Sat 7–9.30 Av 3 course à la carte £26.50 Av 3 course fixed price £17.95 ⊕ Free House ◀ Bombardier, Murphy's, London Pride. ♟9 **Facilities** Garden Parking

NEWBURY   MAP 05 SU46

See advert on this page

Pick of the Pubs

The Yew Tree Inn ◎◎ ♟

See Pick of the Pubs on page 35

The Bell at Boxford

Lambourn Rd, RG20 8DD Tel/Fax: 01488 608721/01488 658502
email: paul@bellatboxford.com   www.bellatboxford.com

The Bell is a traditional 'Inn of distinction' that is personally run by Paul and Helen Lavis, who have been your hosts for the past 22 years. Their trademark is a relaxing informal approach. 'We are serious about food and relaxed about life.'

The Good Pub's **Wine Pub of the Year**, besides offering an extensive wine list, boasts 10 modern bedrooms; shower en suite; a cosy bar with log fires and Real Ales and an à la carte restaurant providing a relaxing environment for all your needs.

The Bell's food boasts both Bar and Bistro menus. Changing daily, the blackboard menus reflect the best the Market can offer. An extensive bar menu featuring home made pies and pastas and we are known for our excellent 100% pure beef burgers.

The Bell has 10 en-suite bedrooms all with HD/TV, radio, telephone, hairdryer, trouser-press and tea & coffee making facilities. Free Wi-Fi throughout totally complimentary.

4 miles from Newbury, Hungerford and Lambourn located on the Lambourn Road in the peace and quiet of the Countryside. Ideally situated for Newbury Businesses and the Racecourse along with the beautiful Lambourn Valley.

PALEY STREET   MAP 05 SU87

Pick of the Pubs

The Royal Oak ◎◎ ♟

SL6 3JN ☎ 01628 620541

dir: *From Maidenhead take A330 towards Ascot for 2m, turn right onto B3024 signed White Waltham, 2nd pub on left*

TV and radio personality Michael Parkinson owns this inn, which is run by his son. Lovers of jazz and popular music will undoubtedly be drawn by the quality of the entertainment – Jamie Cullum, Katie Melua and James Morrison have all performed at the regular music nights – and the walls are adorned with TV and sporting memorabilia. Fullers provides the reliable ales, but the wine list is undoubtedly the star of the drinks show, which begins with over 20 champagnes to choose from; 20 wines are served by the glass. An equal lure is the accomplished and imaginative menu. Starters may include linguine with ham hock, mustard and poached egg; or hare and bacon terrine with onion marmalade. A quality line-up of main courses could offer roast halibut with potato gnocchi and wild mushrooms; or daube of Longhorn beef. Classic desserts like rhubarb trifle or steamed butterscotch pudding complete the bill.

Open 12–3 6–11 Closed: 1 Jan & Sun eve **Bar Meals** L served all week 12–2.30 D served Mon-Sat 6.30–10 **Restaurant** L served all week 12–2.30 D served Mon-Sat 6–10 ◀ Fuller's London Pride. ♟20 **Facilities** Children's licence Garden Parking

33

England

Shoulder of Mutton
Reading, Berkshire

The Only pub to be awarded in the Pride of Reading Awards 2007 and we featured on BBC 1's The One Show, providing a pie for their Mutton article. We offer a varied menu but Mutton is our speciality. Try the organic, farm reared Shoulder for £13.50. Delicious. Only 10 minutes away from Henley, see our reading listing for direction. We look forward to serving you.

Tel: 0118 947 3908

Email: shoulderofmutton@hotmail.co.uk

Website: www.readingrestaurants.co.uk

READING MAP 05 SU77

The Crown ♥

Playhatch RG4 9QN ☎ 0118 947 2872 📠 0118 946 4586
e-mail: info@thecrown.co.uk
dir: *From Reading take A4155 towards Henley-on-Thames. At 1st rdbt take 1st exit, pub 400mtrs on left*

This charming 17th-century country inn with its lovely garden and excellent restaurant nestles between the Thames and the Chilterns in an area of outstanding natural beauty. Head Chef Nana Akuffo is behind the move to buy fresh local produce wherever possible. Dinner starters may include grilled Brixham sardine fillets, or Thai beef salad; main course examples are confit of duck en croûte, and slow-roasted Cornish lamb; typical desserts are hot sticky toffee pudding, and carpaccio of fresh pineapple.

Open 10–11 **Bar Meals** L served Mon-Sat 12–2.30 D served Mon-Sat 6–9.30 (Sun 12–3 6–9) Av main course £15 **Restaurant** L served Mon-Sat 12–2.30 D served Mon-Sat 6–9.30 (Sun 12–3 6–9) Av 3 course à la carte £28 ⊕ Brakspear ◄ Brakspear Bitter, Brakspear Special, Brakspear Seasonal, Guinness. ♥ 12 **Facilities** Garden Parking **Rooms** available

The Flowing Spring ♥

Henley Rd, Playhatch RG4 9RB ☎ 0118 969 3207
e-mail: flowingspring@aol.com
dir: *3m N of Reading*

A lovely country pub overlooking the Thames flood plain at the point where the Chiltern Hills strike out north east towards Bedfordshire. The proprietor likes his establishment to be known as "a pub that serves good food, rather than a restaurant that serves lousy beer".

Representative dishes on the combined bar/restaurant menu include home-made curries, shoulder of lamb, and rib-eye steaks. It's a Fullers pub, so Chiswick, London Pride and ESB are all well kept on tap.

Open 12–11 **Bar Meals** L served Mon-Sun 12–2.30 D served Wed-Sat 6.30–9.30 Av main course £7 ⊕ Fullers ◄ London Pride, ESB, Chiswick, HSB. ♥ 7 **Facilities** Garden Dogs allowed Parking Play Area

The Shoulder of Mutton ♥

Playhatch RG4 9QU ☎ 0118 947 3908
e-mail: grnwillows@hotmail.com
dir: *From Reading follow signs to Caversham, then onto A4155 to Henley-on-Thames. At rdbt left to Binfield Heath, pub on left*

Just a stone's throw from both Reading and Henley, the Shoulder of Mutton has recently been refurbished to create a stylish, contemporary atmosphere. The conservatory was singled out for special attention, and now boasts an under floor heating system. The pub offers a varied menu; but, true to its name, mutton remains the speciality. It has featured on BBC1's The One Show, providing mutton pie for the presenters, and guests Brian Turner and Timothy Spall.

Open 12–3 6–11 (Mon 7–11, Sat 6.30–11, closed Sun eve) Closed: 26–30 Dec, 1 Jan **Bar Meals** L served all week 12–2 Av main course £10.75 **Restaurant** L served all week 12–2 D served Mon-Sat 6.30–9 Av 3 course à la carte £23 ⊕ Greene King ◄ Greene King IPA & Old Speckled Hen. ♥ 7 **Facilities** Garden Parking

See advert on this page

STANFORD DINGLEY MAP 05 SU57

The Bull Country Inn ♥

RG7 6LS ☎ 0118 974 4409 📠 0118 974 5249
e-mail: admin@thebullatstanforddingley.co.uk
dir: *A4/A340 to Pangbourne. 1st left to Bradfield. Through Bradfield, 0.3m left into Back Lane. At end left, pub 0.25m on left*

A nook-and-cranny-rich taproom bar, smoke-blackened fireplace and exposed wattle and daub make this free house a delightfully traditional setting. Family-owned, and dating from the 15th century, it remains a hub of the village while also being a destination pub. Food choices run from snacks (nachos; salads) through to main meals such as monkfish tail with Parma ham and fresh vegetables; or rack of lamb with redcurrant jus. The landlord's passion for cars is much in evidence.

Open 12–3 6–11 (Sun 7–10.30) **Bar Meals** L served all week 12–2.30 D served all week 6.30–9.30 Av main course £8.50 **Restaurant** L served all week 12.30–2.30 D served all week 6.30–9.30 (Sun 7–9.30) ⊕ Free House ◄ West Berkshire, Brakspear Bitter, West Berkshire Good Old Boy. ♥ 7 **Facilities** Garden Dogs allowed Parking

PICK OF THE PUBS

NEWBURY-BERKSHIRE

The Yew Tree Inn

This 16th-century inn belongs to the celebrated chef-turned restaurateur, Marco Pierre White.

His famed perfectionism is evident everywhere, from the immaculate styling that blends original 17th-century features with the refinement of white tablecloths and sparkling glassware, to the menu, which performs a similar trick, offering both traditional British food and time-honoured classics from the French culinary canon. Your meal might open with a parfait of foie gras; calves' tongue with celeriac remoulade; or duck rillettes, followed by lobster thermidor; Dover sole meunière; or venison with sauce grand veneur. There is a relaxed, pick-and-choose feel to the menu, which includes lighter options such as eggs Benedict, Scotch woodcock, and various soups (game consommé en croûte; bisque of lobster Newburg).

Tellingly, the desserts are described as 'puddings' and might include such familiar comforts as bread and butter pudding or rhubarb crumble. Good-value fixed-price menus are also a feature at lunchtime, early evening and on Sundays.

◉◉ ♛
MAP 05 SU46
Hollington Cross, Andover Rd,
Highclere RG20 9SE
☎ 01635 253360
🖺 01635 255035
e-mail: info@theyewtree.net
web: www.theyewtree.net
dir: *A34 toward Southampton, 2nd exit bypass Highclere, onto A343 at rdbt, through village, pub on right*

Open 10–12
Bar Meals L served all week 12–3 D served all week 6–10 (Sun 12–4, 7–9) Av main course £14.50
Restaurant L served all week 12–3 D served all week 6–10 (Sun 12–3, 7–9) Av 3 course à la carte £35
⊕ Free House ◑ London Pride, Timothy Taylor & guest ales. ♛ 8
Facilities Children's licence Garden Dogs allowed Parking

STANFORD DINGLEY continued

The Old Boot Inn ♥

RG7 6LT ☎ 0118 974 4292 ▤ 0118 974 4292

dir: *M4 junct 12, A4/A340 to Pangbourne. 1st left to Bradfield. Through Bradfield, follow Stanford Dingley signs*

Set in the glorious Pang Valley, in a village of Outstanding Natural Beauty, the original 18th-century Old Boot has been extended to include a popular conservatory. Fresh seafood choices are announced daily, and include the likes of seabass, cod, scallops, haddock and swordfish.

Open 11–3 6–11 (Sun 12–3, 7–10.30) **Bar Meals** L served Mon-Sat 12–2.15 D served all week 7–9.30 (Sun 12–2.30) **Restaurant** L served all week 12–2.15 D served all week 7–9.30 ⊕ Free House ◀ Brakspear Bitter, Interbrew Bass, West Berkshire Dr Hexters, Archers Best. ♥ 8 **Facilities** Garden Dogs allowed Parking Play Area

SWALLOWFIELD   MAP 05 SU76

Pick of the Pubs

The George & Dragon

Church Rd RG7 1TJ

☎ 0118 988 4432 ▤ 0118 988 6474

e-mail: mari.barkhuizen@btconnect.com

dir: *M4, junct 11, A33 towards Basingstoke. Left at Barge Lane to B3349 onto The Street, right onto Church Rd*

Don't judge a pub by its façade, at least not this one. It may look unassuming, but it has a smart, cosy interior with stripped low beams, terracotta-painted walls, log fires and rug-strewn floors, and it has earned quite a reputation for its food. Dining takes precedence over drinking, and booking for lunch or dinner would be prudent. Main courses include Caribbean jerk chicken with jollof rice and mojo salsa; fillet of sea bass with creamed spinach and aubergine ragoût; and wild mushroom and asparagus tagliatelle with gorgonzola cream. A typical specials board could offer a starter of smoked quail filled with winter fruits and nuts on poached apricots, followed by grilled cod with a smoked haddock, mussel and clam broth with champ mash.

Open 12–12 (Fri-Sat 12–1am, Sun 12–10.30) Closed: 25–26 Dec eve & 1 Jan eve **Bar Meals** L served Mon-Sat 12–2.30 D served Mon-Sat 7–10 (Sun 7–9) **Restaurant** L served Mon-Sat 12–2.30 D served Mon-Sat 7–10 (Sun 12–3, 7–9) Av 3 course à la carte £20.95 Av 3 course fixed price £29.95 ⊕ Free House ◀ Fuller's London Pride, Brakspears, Youngs. **Facilities** Garden Dogs allowed Parking

THATCHAM   MAP 05 SU56

The Bladebone Inn

Chapel Row, Bucklebury RG7 6PD ☎ 0118 971 2326

e-mail: jeanclaude@thebladebone.net

dir: *2m NE of Thatcham, 5m from Newbury*

Above the entrance to this historic inn hangs a bladebone, which, according to legend, originally came from a mammoth that once stalked the Kennet valley. A more probable explanation is that it was used to indicate that whale oil was sold here for use in oil-burning lamps and probably of 17th-century origin. These days the Bladebone is a stylish dining venue with a mixture of English and Mediterranean influences.

Open 12–3 6.30–11 **Bar Meals** L served Tue-Sun 12–3 D served Tue-Sat 6–10 Av main course £10 **Restaurant** L served Tue-Sun 12–3 D served Tue-Sat 6–10 Av 3 course à la carte £25 ⊕ Whitbread ◀ Fuller's London Pride, Good Old Boy. **Facilities** Garden Dogs allowed Parking

THEALE   MAP 05 SU67

Thatchers Arms ♥

North St RG7 5EX ☎ 0118 930 2070 ▤ 0118 930 2070

dir: *Telephone for directions*

Many footpaths and quiet lanes are to be found in the nearby countryside, making this warm, friendly pub something of a destination for walkers. Although in a small hamlet, the inn is also only a five-minute drive from the M4. There are good garden facilities and a separate patio area.

Open 12–2.30 6–11 **Bar Meals** L served all week 12–2.30 D served all week 6–9.30 Av main course £12.50 **Restaurant** L served all week 12–2.30 D served all week 6–9.30 Av 3 course à la carte £25 ⊕ Punch Taverns ◀ Fuller's London Pride, Brakspears, John Smiths Smooth. ♥ 8 **Facilities** Garden Dogs allowed Parking

WALTHAM ST LAWRENCE   MAP 05 SU87

The Bell ♥

The Street RG10 0JJ ☎ 0118 934 1788

e-mail: scott@thebellinn.biz

dir: *On B3024 E of Twyford (from A4 turn at Hare Hatch)*

In 1608 this 14th-century building was given to the village; it now runs as a free house with the rent going towards village charities. The Bell is renowned for its ever-changing range of real ales selected from smaller micro-breweries all over the country. It also has a growing reputation for its food – perhaps sea bass with roasted new potatoes, sunblush tomatoes, rocket and endive salad; or roast beetroot and squash salad with goat's cheese dressing.

Open 12–3 5–11 (Sat 12–11, Sun 12–10.30) **Bar Meals** L served Mon-Fri 12–2 D served Mon-Fri 7–9.30 (Sat-Sun 12–3, 7–9.30) **Restaurant** L served Mon-Fri 12–2 D served Mon-Fri 7–9.30 (Sat-Sun 12–3, 7–9.30) ⊕ Free House ◀ Waltham St Lawrence No.1 Ale plus 4 guests. ♥ 7 **Facilities** Garden Dogs allowed Parking Play Area

WARGRAVE   MAP 05 SU77

St George and Dragon ♥

High St RG10 8HY ☎ 0118 940 5021

dir: *3.5m from Henley on A321*

A friendly Thames-side pub, in one of the river's most scenic locations. Heaters on the outdoor decking make it possible to enjoy the view all year round, while inside are open kitchens, stone-fired ovens and log-burning fires. The menu offers the familiar – pizza, pasta and steaks – and the not so familiar, such as duck confit with pak choi, egg noodles, black bean and chilli sauce; and swordfish with Tuscan bean cassoulet and chorizo.

Open 12–11 **Bar Meals** L served all week 12–2 D served all week 6–9.30 (Sun 12–7) **Restaurant** L served all week 12–2.30 D served all week 6–9.30 (Sun 12–3.30, 6.30–9) ⊕ Free House ◀ Loddon Hulabaloo & Timothy Taylors Landlord. ♥ 14 **Facilities** Children's licence Garden Parking

WINKFIELD
MAP 06 SU97

Rose & Crown ♥

Woodside, Windsor Forest SL4 2DP

☎ 01344 882051 🖹 01344 885346

e-mail: info@roseandcrownascot.com

dir: *M3 junct 3 from Ascot Racecourse on A332 take 2nd exit from Heatherwood Hosp rdbt, then 2nd left*

A 200–year-old traditional pub complete with old beams and low ceilings. Hidden down a country lane, it has a peaceful garden overlooking open fields where you can see horses and llamas at pasture. A typical menu may include pan-fried fillet steak with blue cheese gratin potatoes, with seasonal vegetables and a bourguignon sauce; pavé of halibut with rosemary sauté potatoes, chargrilled asparagus and baby leeks, with horseradish cream sauce; or asparagus tortellini with basil and parmesan cheese.

Open 11–12 (9am Royal Ascot wk) **Bar Meals** L served all week 12–4 D served Tue-Sat 7–9.30 Av main course £8 **Restaurant** L served all week 12–2.30 D served Tue-Sat 7–9.30 (Sun 12–4) Av 3 course à la carte £27.50 ⊕ Greene King ◀ Morland Original, Greene King IPA & guest ale. ♥ 9 **Facilities** Garden Parking Play Area

WINTERBOURNE
MAP 05 SU47

The Winterbourne Arms ♥

RG20 8BB ☎ 01635 248200 🖹 01635 248824

e-mail: winterbournearms@tiscali.co.uk

dir: *M4 junct 13 into Chieveley Services, follow Donnington signs to Winterbourne sign. Turn right down Arlington Ln, right at T-junct, left into Winterbourne*

Formerly known as the New Inn, this large 300–year-old free house once sheltered the village shop and bakery – the remains of the bread oven survive in the restaurant. In winter the interior is candle-lit with a log fire, while the extensive gardens offer al fresco dining in summer. Local game and daily fresh fish from Brixham provide the basic ingredients for mainly British-style dishes such as pan-fried calves' liver and bacon; roasted cod; and braised ham hock.

Open 12–3 6–11 (Sun 12–10.30) **Bar Meals** L served Mon-Sat 12–2.30 D served all week 6–10 (Sun 12–4) Av main course £10 **Restaurant** L served Mon-Sat 12–2.30 D served all week 6–10 (Sun 12–4) Av 3 course à la carte £22 ⊕ Free House ◀ 6X, Ramsbury Gold, Guinness & Fuller's London Pride. ♥ 20 **Facilities** Garden Dogs allowed Parking

WORLD'S END
MAP 05 SU47

The Langley Hall Inn ♥

RG20 8SA ☎ 01635 248332 🖹 01635 248571

dir: *Exit M4 junct 13 north, take 1st slip road signed Beedon & Chieveley. Left & immediately right, inn 1.5m on left*

Friendly, family-run bar/restaurant with a reputation for freshly prepared food, real ales and a good selection of wines. Fresh fish dishes vary according to the daily catch – maybe pan-fried crevettes, grilled Dover sole, salmon fishcakes with spinach and parsley sauce, or roast cod fillet with cheese and herb crust. Other favourites are braised lamb, beef stir-fry, and Thai chicken curry. Outside there is a large patio and garden, plus a petanque court for fine weather use.

Open 11–3 5.30–11 (Closed Sun pm) Closed: 26 Dec-2 Jan **Bar Meals** L served Mon-Sat 12–3 D served Mon-Sat 6.30–9.30 (Sun 12.30–5.30) Av main course £11.75 **Restaurant** L served Mon-Sat 12–2.30 D served Mon-Sat 6.30–9.30 (Sun 12.30–3) Av 3 course à la carte £22 ⊕ Enterprise Inns ◀ West Berkshire Brewery – Good Old Boy, Mr Chubbs, Lunchtime Bitter, Deuchars IPA. ♥ 9 **Facilities** Garden Dogs allowed Parking

YATTENDON
MAP 05 SU57

Pick of the Pubs

The Royal Oak Hotel Ⓤ ◉ ♥

The Square RG18 0UG

☎ 01635 201325 🖹 01635 201926

e-mail: info@royaloakyattendon.com

dir: *M4 junct 12, A4 to Newbury, right at 2nd rdbt to Pangbourne then 1st left. From junct 13, A34 N 1st left, right at T-junct. Left then 2nd right to Yattendon*

This quintessentially English country inn dates back to the 16th century, as the timber framework will attest. The Oak – as it was formerly known – has played host to such luminaries as King Charles I and Oliver Cromwell, but today it's rarely interrupted by anything more than the clip-clop of passing horse-riders. The village bar remains popular, though the culinary emphasis is based on a brasserie-style menu and an extensive wine list, to be taken in a charmingly formal dining room. Starters like foie gras with quince purée or prawns and prunes wrapped in pancetta are the precursor to main dishes such as pan-fried red mullet in dill sauce; grilled sirloin with feta cheese; or asparagus and langoustine risotto. Round off your meal with appetising desserts like passion fruit parfait or walnut chocolate cake. Traditionally furnished bedrooms add to the appeal.

Open 11–11 **Bar Meals** L served Mon-Sat 12–2.30 **Restaurant** L served Mon-Sat 12–2.15 D served Mon-Sat 7–9.30 (Sun lunch 12–3, 7–9) Av 3 course à la carte £30 Av 3 course fixed price £15 ◀ West Berks, Good Old Boy, Mr Chubbs. ♥ 8 **Facilities** Garden Parking **Rooms** 5

BRISTOL

BRISTOL   **MAP 04 ST57**

Cornubia

142 Temple St BS1 6EN ☎ 0117 925 4415 📠 0117 929 1523
e-mail: thecornubia@hotmail.co.uk

dir: Opposite Bristol Fire Station

Characterful Georgian city centre pub built as two houses, and now owned by the Hidden Brewery company. Office workers love it, not just because of its convenience, but also for of its choice of seven changing real ales, two draught ciders and a serious collection of malts. And then there's the food – chicken and mushroom pie is an example – chalked up on a blackboard. Cornubia, by the way, is the Latinised name for Cornwall.

Open 11.30–11 (Mon-Fri 11.30–11, Sat 12–11, Sun 12–6) Closed: 25–26 Dec, 1 Jan **Bar Meals** L served all week 12–8 D served all week 11.30–9 Av main course £4.95 ◀ All Hidden Brewery ales. **Facilities** Children's licence Dogs allowed Parking

Highbury Vaults

164 St Michaels Hill, Cotham BS2 8DE ☎ 0117 973 3203
e-mail: highburyvaults@youngs.co.uk

dir: Take A38 to Cotham from inner ring dual carriageway

Once a turnpike station, this 1840s pub retains a Victorian atmosphere in its many nooks and crannies. In days when hangings took place on nearby St Michael's Hill, many victims partook of their last meal in the vaults. Today, it's a business crowd by day and students at night feasting on chilli, meat and vegetable curries, casseroles, pasta dishes, and jacket potatoes. No fried foods, no music or fruit machines and a heated garden terrace.

Open 12–12 (Sun 12–11) **Bar Meals** L served Mon-Fri 12–2 D served Mon-Fri 5.30–8.30 (Sat 12–2.30, Sun 12–3) Av main course £5.95 ⊕ Young & Co ◀ Bath Ales Gem, St Austells Tribute, Brains SA, Young's Special & Bitter. **Facilities** Garden

Robin Hood's Retreat ♀

197 Gloucester Rd BS7 8BG ☎ 0117 924 8639
e-mail: info@robinhoodsretreat.gmail.com

dir: At main rdbt at Broad Mead take Gloucester Rd exit, St Pauls. Road leads into Gloucester Rd (A38)

In the heart of Bristol this Victorian red-brick pub is popular with real ale lovers, who usually have eight to choose from. The interior has been superbly refurbished, keeping original features and adding to the richly coloured wood panelling and furniture. There's plenty of attention to detail in the food too, which is all prepared on the

premises. Favourites are slow-cooked British dishes with a French accent, and several seafood options such as devilled crab.

Open 12–11 (Sun-Wed) 12–12 (Thu-Sat) Closed: 25 Dec **Bar Meals** L served Mon-Sat 12–3 D served all week 6–9.30 (Sun 12–4) Av main course £11 **Restaurant** L served Mon-Sat 12–3 D served all week 6–9.30 (Sun 12–4, Fixed price menu Tue-Fri 6–7.30) Av 3 course à la carte £21 Av 2 course fixed price £13.50 ♀ 9 **Facilities** Garden

BUCKINGHAMSHIRE

AMERSHAM   **MAP 06 SU99**

Hit or Miss Inn ♀

Penn St Village HP7 0PX ☎ 01494 713109 📠 01494 718010
e-mail: hit@ourpubs.co.uk

dir: M25 junct 18, A404 (Amersham to High Wycombe road) to Amersham. Past crematorium on right, 2nd left into Whielden Ln (signed Winchmore Hill). 1.25m, pub on right

Michael and Mary Macken welcome you to their 18th-century cottage-style dining pub with its fires and old world beams. The Hit or Miss overlooks the cricket ground from which the pub takes its name, and there's a beautiful country garden with lawn, patio and picnic tables for warmer days. Home-cooked dishes range from well-filled sandwiches and baked potatoes to game bourguignon or grilled fresh sea bass. There are daily specials and Sunday roasts, too.

Open 11–11 (Sun 12–10.30) **Bar Meals** L served Mon-Sat 12–2.30 D served Mon-Sat 6.45–9.30 (Sun 12–8) Av main course £14 **Restaurant** L served Mon-Sat 12–2.30 D served Mon-Sat 6.45–9.30 (Sun 12–8) Av 3 course à la carte £24 ⊕ Hall & Woodhouse ◀ Badger Best, Tanglefoot, Sussex. ♀ 12 **Facilities** Children's licence Garden Dogs allowed Parking

BEACONSFIELD   **MAP 06 SU99**

Pick of the Pubs

The Royal Standard of England ♀

Brindle Ln, Forty Green HP9 1XT ☎ 01494 673382
e-mail: theoldestpub@btinternet.com

dir: A40 to Beaconsfield, right at church rdbt onto B474 towards Penn, left onto Forty Green Rd (1m)

With claims to being the oldest free house in England, this welcoming country inn has a history as long as your arm. Certainly its name dates from the Civil War when the hostelry was a Royalist headquarters. Not surprising then that the striking stained glass windows, beams, flagstone floors, and a large inglenook fireplace set the scene for many a ghost, including a 12-year-old drummer boy beheaded by the Roundheads. When it comes to food and drink, 'choice' and 'local' are the bywords; donated ingredients such as partridge make an easy transition to the specials board in exchange for a free lunch. The hearty, award-winning dishes follow traditional lines: devilled lamb's kidneys; Welsh lamb's liver and bacon; roasted pork belly. A dozen popular wines served by the glass are easily outnumbered by the variety of beers on tap, backed by some arcane and rare bottled brews to delight the cognoscenti.

Open 11–12 (Sun 12–11) **Bar Meals** L served all week 12–10 D served all week 12–10 Av main course £10 **Restaurant** L served all week 12–10 D served all week Av 3 course à la carte £19 ⊕ Free House ◀ Marston's Pedigree, Brakspear Bitter, Rebellion IPA & guest ales. ♀ 12 **Facilities** Children's licence Garden Dogs allowed Parking

PICK OF THE PUBS

BLETCHLEY-BUCKINGHAMSHIRE

The Crooked Billet

Take the evocatively named Bottledump roundabout in your stride (should it feature in your route planning) and head for this 16th-century, thatched former farmhouse in what is still a village, in spite of the Milton Keynes postcode.

While it retains much traditional charm, with original oak beams, open log fires and a large garden, the top attraction is the food and wine produced by husband-and-wife team John and Emma Gilchrist. Emma's monthly-changing menus are based on the finest ingredients, local where possible, and the suppliers – right down to the 'people of Newton Longville for growing our vegetables and herbs' – are all acknowledged in print. On offer is a range of sandwiches, wraps, burgers and goodies on toast, and a seven-course, 'whole table only' tasting menu. Falling somewhere between these two extremes are main menu starters of wild mushroom and black truffle risotto with sherry butter; soused mackerel, smoked crispy bacon, soft boiled egg and potato salad; and seared pigeon breast with chicken liver salad. Then might come fish bourride, which is 'similar to bouillabaisse but more refined'; and slow-roasted leg, chop and crispy pork belly of suckling pig, with parsnip and vanilla purée, and apple sauce. Desserts include chocolate bread and butter pudding; wheat-free ginger sponge, toffee and stem ginger and ginger ripple ice cream; and banana sundae. The cheese board has won heaps of awards, as has John Gilchrist for compiling 'best wine' lists, including his 300–bin selection here.

◎ ♀
MAP 11 SP83
2 Westbrook End, Newton Longville MK17 0DF
☎ 01908 373936
e-mail: john@thebillet.co.uk
dir: M1 junct 13, follow signs to Buckingham. 6m, signed at Buttledump rdbt to Newton Longville

Open 12–2.30 5.30–11 (Sun 12–4, 7–10.30) Closed: 25 Dec & Mon lunch
Bar Meals L served Tue-Sun 12–2 D served Mon-Thu 7–9.30
Restaurant L served Sun 12.30–3 D served Tue-Sat 7–10
⊕ Greene King ◀ Old Speckled Hen, Badger Tanglefoot, Hobgoblin, Ruddles County.
♀ 300
Facilities Garden Parking

BLEDLOW
MAP 05 SP70

The Lions of Bledlow 🍷

Church End HP27 9PE ☎ 01844 343345 📠 01844 343345

dir: *M40 junct 6, B4009 to Princes Risborough, through Chinnor into Bledlow*

This traditional free house is located at the foot of the Chilterns, just above a private railway line where steam trains run between Chinnor and Horsenden. It has a low-beamed bar and log fire, and in summer seating in the spacious garden overflows onto the village green. The menu, written on boards, might offer liver and bacon with bubble and squeak; spinach and potato cakes with chilli sauce and salad; and salmon fillet with honey mustard dressing.

Open 11.30–3 6–11 (Sun 12–3, 7–10.30) **Bar Meals** L served all week 12–2.30 D served Mon-Sat 7–9.30 (Sun 7–9) **Restaurant** L served all week 12–2.30 D served Mon-Sat 7–9.30 (Sun 7–9) ⊕ Free House ◀ Wadworth 6X, Courage Best, Marston's Pedigree, Brakspear Bitter. ♀ 10 **Facilities** Garden Dogs allowed Parking

BLETCHLEY
MAP 11 SP83

Pick of the Pubs

The Crooked Billet ⊛ 🍷

See Pick of the Pubs on page 39

BOLTER END
MAP 05 SU79

The Peacock 🍷

HP14 3LU ☎ 01494 881417

e-mail: andy.callen@thepeacockbolterend.co.uk

dir: *On B482 (Marlow to Stokenchurch road). 2m from M40 junct 5*

The oldest part of this pub dates from 1620, featuring original beams and a fireplace dating from the early 1800s. It is situated on top of the Chiltern Hills overlooking the common. At lunch alongside a bar snack selection of baguettes, ciabatta and ploughman's, the menu offers steak and chips, vegetable lasagne or cod and chips. At dinner you could expect beef Stroganoff, lamb dhansak, or halibut steak. A selection of pies is also available. Children are particularly welcome as there are two specially designated areas just for them. Quiz night every Thursday at 9pm.

Open 12–3 5.30–11 (Sat 11.30–11, Sun 12–10.30) Winter closed Sun eve and Mon. **Bar Meals** L served all week 12–2.30 D served Mon-Sat 6.30–9.30 (Sun 12–3) Av main course £11 **Restaurant** L served Mon-Sun 12–2.30 D served Mon-Sat 6.30–9.30 (Sun 12–3) Av 3 course à la carte £18.50 ⊕ Punch Taverns ◀ Brakspear Bitter, Sheppard Neame Spitfire. ♀ 8 **Facilities** Children's licence Garden Dogs allowed Parking

BOVINGDON GREEN
MAP 05 SU88

Pick of the Pubs

The Royal Oak 🍷

See Pick of the Pubs on opposite page

BRILL
MAP 11 SP61

The Pheasant Inn 🍷

Windmill St HP18 9TG ☎ 01844 237104

e-mail: rustle.ball@btconnect.com

dir: *In village centre, by windmill*

Set on the edge of Brill Common, the large garden and veranda at this 17th-century beamed inn make the most of its fine hilltop position, with stunning views over seven counties. Really a lovely spot to watch the sun set in the summer. The popular blackboard menu offers fresh salmon, plus local steaks and pheasant in season. Roald Dahl and JRR Tolkien were both frequent visitors to the pub, and the annual Brill Music Festival is on the first Saturday of July.

Open 12–11 **Bar Meals** L served Mon-Fri 12–2 D served Mon-Fri 7–9 (Sat 12–9, Sun 12–8) **Restaurant** L served Mon-Fri 12–2 D served Sun-Fri 6.30–9 (Sat 12–2.30, 7–9.30, Sun 12–2.30) ⊕ Free House ◀ Spitfire, Adnams & Tetleys. ♀ 9 **Facilities** Garden Parking

The Red Lion 🍷

27 Church St HP18 9RT ☎ 01844 238339 📠 01844 238339

e-mail: info@the-red-lion-at-brill.co.uk

web: www.the-red-lion-at-brill.co.uk

dir: *Off B4011(Thame to Bicester road)*

The Red Lion dates back to the early 17th century and was originally five separate buildings. Plenty of walking and cycling routes converge upon the village, which is overlooked by a famous windmill. Simple, traditional menus change regularly and may feature pork medallions; beer-battered cod, or lamb shank braised in red wine. In summer the secluded garden is home to fierce competitions of Aunt Sally – a local form of skittles.

Open 12–3 5.30–11 (Etr-Sep open all day) (Fri-Sat 5.30–12.30) **Bar Meals** L served Mon-Sun 12–2.30 D served Mon-Sat 6.30–9.30 (Sun lunch 12–4) Av main course £9.50 **Restaurant** L served Mon-Sun 12–2.30 D served Mon-Sat 6.30–9.30 (Sun lunch 12–4) Av 3 course à la carte £16 ⊕ Greene King ◀ Greene King IPA, Old Trip & Fireside. ♀ 7 **Facilities** Children's licence Garden Dogs allowed

PICK OF THE PUBS

BOVINGDON GREEN-BUCKINGHAMSHIRE

The Royal Oak

Just up the hill out of Marlow you'll find this delightful little whitewashed pub in the village of Bovingdon Green. It is set amid its own spacious gardens, from where you might catch a glimpse of the red kites that visit regularly.

Outside there is a sunny terrace, petanque piste and herb garden, while inside you'll find a cosy interior with a wood-burning stove, dark floorboards, rich fabrics and heritage colours. The menu offers imaginative British food making good use of fresh local produce. As part of the 'buy local where possible policy', the pub has created a European only wine list – the beers come from the Rebellion Brewery in nearby Marlow Bottom – and is making efforts to improve its green credentials in other areas, such as the recycling of waste. The menu offers a good variety of dishes from snacks to main meals. Among the 'small plate' selection you might find Oak tapas with crispy halloumi and cauliflower houmous; or beetroot-cured salmon

with hand-made pumpernickel, preserved lemons and caper berries. More robust dishes include home-made Marlow venison sausage toad-in-the-hole with port wine jus; or free-range Oxfordshire pork chop on boxty potato with sticky parsnips, onion and pork belly faggot and Calvados jus. Sunday roasts are also a popular feature, and vegetarians are not left out with options like bean cassoulet with pickled mushrooms and home-made foccacia; and roast sweet potato and Wensleydale filo parcel with pickled grapes, chicory and mizuna salad. Free WiFi is available if you're planning a working lunch or dinner.

MAP 05 SU88
Frieth Rd SL7 2JF
☎ 01628 488611
🖷 01628 478680
e-mail:
info@royaloakmarlow.co.uk
dir: *From Marlow, take A4155. In 300yds right signed Bovingdon Green. In 0.75m pub on left*

Open 11 -11 (Sun 12–10.30)
Closed: 25–26 Dec
Bar Meals L served Mon-Sat 12–2.30 D served all week 7–10 (Sun 12–4) Av main course £12.75
Restaurant L served Mon-Sat 12–2.30 D served all week 7–10 (Sun 12–4) Av 3 course à la carte £23.75
⊕ Salisbury Pubs ◀ London Pride, Brakspears, Rebellion IPA. ☙ 19
Facilities Garden Dogs allowed Parking

BUCKINGHAM
MAP 11 SP63

The Old Thatched Inn ♟
Main St, Adstock MK18 2JN
☎ 01296 712584 📄 01296 715375
e-mail: manager@theoldthatchedinn.co.uk
web: www.theoldthatchedinn.co.uk
dir: *Telephone for directions*

Listed in 1645, this lovely old thatched and beamed inn still boasts the traditional beams and inglenook fireplace. The spacious interior consists of a formal conservatory and a bar with comfy furniture and a welcoming atmosphere. Fresh fish is a speciality (try grilled turbot with tiger prawn ravioli for a typical example) and there are always two additional fish specials on a Friday. Meat options might include roast duck breast with celeriac purée, braised chicory and griottes cherry sauce.

Open 12–3 6–11 (Sat-Sun & BH 12–11) **Bar Meals** L served Mon-Fri 12–2.30 D served Mon-Fri 6–9.30 (Sat 12–9.30, Sun 12–9) **Restaurant** L served Mon-Sat 12–2.30 D served Mon-Sat 6–9.30 (Sun all day) Av 3 course à la carte £25 ⊕ Free House ◀ Hook Norton Best, Timothy Taylors, Adnams, Wadworth 6x & Old Speckled Hen. ♟ 10 **Facilities** Garden Dogs allowed Parking

The Wheatsheaf ♟
Main St, Maids Moreton MK18 1QR
☎ 01280 815433 📄 01280 814631
dir: *M1 junct 13, (or M40 junct 9, A34 to Bicester) A421 to Buckingham, then A413 to Maids Moreton*

This traditional, thatched village inn is over three hundred years old, and offers an appetising à la carte menu in the spacious conservatory overlooking the secluded beer garden. Eating options include baked cod and prawns in cream; roast aubergine stuffed with ratatouille; and home-made Thai chicken curry. Real ales and snacks can also be enjoyed in the bar, with its cosy inglenook fireplaces. Children will be delighted with the outdoor play equipment.

Open 12–3 6–11 (Sun 6–10.30, closed Mon eve) **Bar Meals** L served Mon-Sat 12–2.15 D served Tue-Sat 7–9.30 (Sun 12–2) **Restaurant** L served Mon-Sat 12–2.15 D served Tue-Sat 7–9.30 (Sun 12–2) ⊕ Free House ◀ Hook Norton, Old Speckled Hen, John Smiths, Side Pocket For A Toad & Reverend James. ♟ 10 **Facilities** Children's licence Garden Dogs allowed Parking Play Area

CHALFONT ST GILES
MAP 06 SU99

Pick of the Pubs

The Ivy House ♟
See Pick of the Pubs on opposite page

The White Hart ♟
Three Households HP8 4LP
☎ 01494 872441 📄 01494 876375
e-mail: enquiries@thewhitehartstgiles.co.uk
dir: *Off A413 (Denham/Amersham)*

Oak and brown leather furniture and a refurbished bar characterise the quiet, relaxed atmosphere of this prettily-located 100-year-old inn, giving it a welcoming, contemporary feel. The menu offers the likes of loin of pork en croute, carpet bag fillet steak, supreme of chicken, lamb shank, and calves' liver. Fish dishes include baked sea bass with vegetables and Thai fish sauce, and seared blue-fin tuna.

Open 11.30–2.30 5.30–11 (Sun, BHs All day) **Bar Meals** L served all week 12–2 D served all week 6.30–9.30 (Sun all day) **Restaurant** L served all week 12–2 D served all week 6.30–9.30 (Sun all day) Av 3 course à la carte £20 ⊕ Greene King ◀ Greene King Morland Original, Abbot Ale, Rev. James. ♟ 12 **Facilities** Garden Parking **Rooms** available

CHALFONT ST PETER
MAP 06 TQ09

Pick of the Pubs

The Greyhound Inn ♟
SL9 9RA ☎ 01753 883404 📄 01753 891627
e-mail: reception@thegreyhoundinn.net
dir: *M40 junct 1/M25 junct 16, follow signs for Gerrards Cross, then Chalfont St Peter*

The 14th-century Greyhound has a macabre place in English history. Not only are its grounds believed to be where the last man hanged for stealing sheep was executed, but a former patron was Sir George Jeffreys, known as the Hanging Judge for his harsh sentencing policy during the Monmouth Rebellion. While still a local magistrate he held court in a room above the restaurant, mention of which brings us neatly to the food here. The cooking style is essentially classic British with a modern twist, producing starters such as moules marinière, shallots, parsley, white wine and cream; chargrilled chicken Caesar salad; and avocado, orange and prawn salad with Marie Rose sauce. From a well balanced list of main courses choose from deep-fried haddock in beer batter; whole baked sea bass; pan-fried calf's liver; home-made shepherd's pie; or leg of duck confit, among many others.

Open 11–11 Closed: 1 Jan **Bar Meals** L served all week 12–3 D served all week 6–9 Av main course £10 **Restaurant** L served all week 12–3 D served all week 6–9 Av 3 course à la carte £22.50 ⊕ Enterprise Inns ◀ London Pride. ♟ 12 **Facilities** Children's licence Garden Dogs allowed Parking

The Ivy House

Set in the heart of the Chiltern Hills with views across the Misbourne Valley and the South Bucks Way, this 17th-century brick and flint free house proves popular with cask ale fans, wine lovers and diners alike. The atmosphere is cosy, warm and welcoming with open fires, comfy armchairs, old pictures, beams and brasses.

Naturally there's the odd ghost story to be told, and there is always a new beer to sample, plus more than 50 wines to choose from with some 20 available by the glass. Whisky aficionados will appreciate the good range of malts, including some rarities favored by the landlord. You can eat wherever you like, as the same menu is served in the bar, the former coach house and the restaurant. The award-winning food includes plenty of highlighted healthy options (oak-aged salmon with fresh dill, mustard, lemon and olive oil dressing), and vegetarian specials (roasted vegetable ratatouille bound in a rich Mediterranean tomato sauce, studded with melting mozzarella, served with penne pasta then finished with a sweet balsamic reduction). Seafood and fish dishes feature prominently (luxury seafood pie with a mix of fish fillets and seafood bound in a creamy sauce, laced with white wine and scented with lemon and fresh tarragon), but alternatives include steak with triple cooked chunky chips; and pan-fried pheasant breast with a West Country cider, cream and Bramley apple sauce, topped with apple crisps. The pub is also well known for its choice of home-made desserts, notably the classic bread-and-butter pudding with an extra touch of fruit and spice, served with cream, ice cream or hot custard. Following extensive refurbishment, accommodation is now provided in five en suite bedrooms with a traditional cooked breakfast to look forward to in the morning.

MAP 06 SU99
London Rd HP8 4RS
☎ 01494 872184
🖹 01494 872870
e-mail: enquiries@
theivyhouse-bucks.co.uk
dir: *On A413 2m S of Amersham & 1.5m N of Chalfont St Giles*

Open 12–3 6–11 (Sat 12–11, Sun 12–10.30)
Bar Meals L served all week 12–2.30 D served all week 6.30–9.30 (Sat 12–9.30, Sun 12–9) Av main course £13.95
Restaurant L served all week 12–2.30 D served all week 6.30–9.30 (Sat 12–10, Sun 12–9) Av 3 course à la carte £25
⊕ Free House ◼ Fuller's London Pride, Brakspear Bitter, Wadworth 6X, Hook Norton Old Hooky.
🍷 22
Facilities Garden Dogs allowed Parking Play Area
Rooms available

CHEDDINGTON   MAP 11 SP91

The Old Swan ⵏ

58 High St LU7 0RQ ☎ 01296 668226 🖹 01296 663811

e-mail: enquiries@theoldswancheddington.co.uk

dir: *From Tring towards Marsworth take B489, 0.5m. Left towards Cooks Wharf onto Cheddington, pub on left*

Formed out of three cottages in the 15th century, this delightful thatched pub is known not only for its real ales and traditional charm but also for its ghosts. A man in 18th-century dress reputedly tries to kiss ladies in the restaurant area! Food ranges from home-made lasagna or beer-battered cod through to stuffed pheasant breast or Pembrokeshire lamb hotpot. Outside there's a large garden with a children's play area.

Open 12–3 5–11 (Fri-Sun 12–11) **Bar Meals** L served Mon-Thu 12–2 D served Sun-Thu 6–9 (Fri-Sat 12–2.30, 6–9.30, Sun 12–4) Av main course £10 **Restaurant** L served Mon-Thu 12–2 D served Sun-Thu 6–9 (Fri-Sat 12–2.30, 6–9.30, Sun 12–4) Av 3 course à la carte £20 ⊕ Punch Taverns ◀ Greene King IPA, Brakspear Best, Everard's Tiger, Shepherd Neame Spitfire. ⵏ 12 **Facilities** Garden Dogs allowed Parking Play Area

CHENIES   MAP 06 TQ09

Pick of the Pubs

The Red Lion ⵏ

See Pick of the Pubs on opposite page

CHESHAM   MAP 06 SP90

The Black Horse Inn ⵏ

Chesham Vale HP5 3NS ☎ 01494 784656

dir: *A41 from Berkhamstead, A416 through Ashley Green, 0.75m before Chesham right to Vale Rd, at bottom of Mashleigh Hill, 1m, inn on left*

Set in some beautiful valley countryside, this 500–year-old pub is ideal for enjoying a cosy, traditional environment without electronic games or music. During the winter there are roaring log fires to take the chill off those who may spot one of the resident ghosts. An ever-changing menu includes an extensive range of snacks, while the main menu may feature steak and Stallion Ale pie, trout and almonds, various home-made pies, steaks and gammons, stuffed plaice, or salmon supreme.

Open 11–3 5.30–11 (Sun 12–4, 7–10.30) **Bar Meals** L served all week 12–2.30 D served Mon-Sat 6.30–9 Sun 12–3 Av main course £8.95 **Restaurant** L served all week 12–2.30 D served Mon-Sat 6.30–9 Sun 12–3 ◀ Adnams Bitter, London Pride, Speckled Hen, guest ale. ⵏ 10 **Facilities** Garden Dogs allowed Parking

The Swan ⵏ

Ley Hill HP5 1UT ☎ 01494 783075 🖹 01494 783582

e-mail: swanleyhill@btconnect.com

dir: *E of Chesham by golf course*

Once three cottages, the first built around 1520, qualifying it as one of Buckinghamshire's oldest pubs. Condemned prisoners, heading for nearby gallows, would drink 'a last and final ale' here. During the Second World War, Clark Gable, James Stewart and Glenn Miller

frequently drank here after cycling from Bovingdon airbase. Menus change several times monthly, and a blackboard features daily specials. Steamed fillet of salmon with lobster sauce is a typical dinner choice.

Open 12–3 5.30–11 (Sun 12–10.30) **Bar Meals** L served Mon-Sat 12–2.30 D served Tue-Sat 7–9.15 (Sun 12–2.30, D all wk summer) **Restaurant** L served Tue-Sat 12–2.30 D served Tue-Sat 7–9.15 (Sun 12–2.30, D all wk summer) ◀ Adnams Bitter, Fuller's London Pride, Timothy Taylor Landlord, Brakspears. ⵏ 8 **Facilities** Garden Parking

CHOLESBURY   MAP 06 SP90

Pick of the Pubs

The Full Moon ⵏ

Hawridge Common HP5 2UH ☎ 01494 758959

e-mail: annie@alberto1142.freeserve.co.uk

dir: *At Tring on A41 follow signs for Wiggington & Cholesbury. On Cholesbury Common pub by windmill*

When this 17th-century former coaching inn was first built, the local Chiltern hills were overrun with alehouses. These days, only three remain. Fortunately, the Full Moon, which graduated from The Half Moon in 1812, is something of an ideal country pub, complete with beams, flagstones, winter fires and a windmill-backed setting. Thorough menus cover a range of possibilities, from baguettes and jacket potatoes to more adventurous fare. Moroccan lamb shank; pumpkin and potato rösti; and monkfish tail wrapped in Parma ham give an indication of the range. Those looking for a Sunday lunch will find plenty of options, with chicken and porcini stroganoff; and roasted vegetable lasagne accompanying the likes of beef, turkey and lamb. In 1907, the landlord was fined for permitting drunkenness on the premises: these days the clientele is much better behaved when it comes to the eclectic selection of real ales.

Open 12–11 (Sun 12–10.30) Closed: 25 Dec **Bar Meals** L served all week 12–2 D served all week 6.30–9 (Sun 6–8) Av main course £11.10 **Restaurant** L served all week 12–2 D served all week 6.30–9 (Sun 6–8) Av 3 course à la carte £22.50 ◀ Interbrew Bass & Adnams, Fuller's London Pride, Brakspear Special, and guest ales. ⵏ 7 **Facilities** Garden Dogs allowed Parking

CUDDINGTON   MAP 05 SP71

Pick of the Pubs

The Crown ⵏ

See Pick of the Pubs on page 46

PICK OF THE PUBS

CHENIES-BUCKINGHAMSHIRE

The Red Lion

Chenies is a picturesque village in the Chess valley. It has a pretty green, an ancient parish church and a manor house that was once the home of the Dukes of Bedford. With 20 years' experience behind them, Mike and Heather Norris firmly believe the 17th-century Red Lion's popularity stems from being a pub that serves good food, not a restaurant that serves beer.

In the jukebox- and gaming machine-free bar, the noisiest thing to be heard, says Mike, are his protestations when an irritating mobile goes off, followed by its owner's often inane conversation. Get him talking about his real ales, one of which, Lion Pride, brewed by Rebellion in Marlow, is available here and here alone; other local beers come from Vale Brewery in Haddenham. There's no separate restaurant as such, although part of the bar is reserved for dining. Heather cooks everything, including fresh daily pastas; bangers with bubble and squeak; big chunks of oven-baked leg of lamb (much like Greek kleftiko); Orkneys rump steak; curries; sea bass with wholegrain mustard sauce; poached haddock with peppered red wine sauce; quorn lasagne; and sausage, apple and cheddar pie. Speaking of pies, brace yourself for the lamb version, which a visiting American serviceman once declared beat a rival pub's pies hands down. Ever since, its entry on the menu has acquired an additional adjective every time it is rewritten. Today, therefore, it reads (take a deep breath) 'The awesome, internationally acclaimed, world-renowned, aesthetically and palatably pleasing, not knowingly genetically modified, hand-crafted, well-balanced, famous, original Chenies lamb pie'. Outside, on the pub's sunny side, is a small seating area.

MAP 06 TQ09
WD3 6ED
☎ 01923 282722
🖷 01923 283797
dir: *Between Rickmansworth & Amersham on A404, follow signs for Chenies & Latimer*

Open 11–2.30 5.30–11 Sun 5.30–10.30 Closed: 25 Dec
Bar Meals L served all week 12–2 D served all week 7–10 Sun 6.30–9.30
⊕ Free House ◀ Wadworth 6X, Rebellion's, Lion's Pride, Vale Best. ♆ 10
Facilities Garden Dogs allowed Parking

PICK OF THE PUBS

CUDDINGTON-BUCKINGHAMSHIRE

The Crown

Fans of 'Midsomer Murders' may recognise Cuddington's Crown, which has been used several times as a location for the popular TV series. There's nothing sinister about the place in real life though. It's a delightful thatched and whitewashed pub at the heart of a picturesque village, and has made a name for itself as a great place to eat.

Having successfully run Annie Bailey's bar/brasserie near by for a number of years, the Berrys turned their attention to improving the Crown. Today the characterful Grade II-listed pub functions equally well as a popular local, with a choice of Fullers and Adnams brews served in the bar, augmented by an extensive wine list; several low-beamed dining areas are filled with charming prints and the glow of evening candlelight. The small patio area provides outside seating and an opportunity for al fresco dining in the summer. The eclectic menus should please all comers. Starters might include the Crown fishcake with sweet chilli jam; linguini with prawn, chilli and spring onion; avocado, smoked chicken and pine kernel salad; and roasted red pepper with shaved parmesan and croutons. On the main course menu you will find such dishes as confit duck on puy lentil stew; Thai seafood curry with coconut and lime-scented rice; honey-glazed shank of lamb; chargrilled rib-eye steak; and vegetarian alternatives such as the Mediterranean vegetable risotto with pesto. Fish dishes are a major attraction, and could include seafood pie; smoked haddock with grilled Welsh rarebit, tomato salad and chips; sea bass with crab risotto; and scallops with pancetta, salad leaves and truffle vinaigrette. The changing selection of desserts chalked up on a blackboard is guaranteed to conclude in fine style the eating-out experience here.

♀
MAP 05 SP71
Spurt St HP18 0BB
☎ 01844 292222
e-mail: david@anniebaileys.com
dir: *Off A418 between Aylesbury & Thame*

Open 12–3 6–11 (All day Sun)
Bar Meals L served Mon-Sat 12–2.30 D served Mon-Sat 6.30–10 (Sun 12–8)
Restaurant L served Mon-Sat 12–2.30 D served Mon-Sat 6.30–10 (Sun 12–8)
⊕ Fullers ◪ Fuller's London Pride, Adnams, Guinness. ♀ 9
Facilities Garden Parking

DENHAM
MAP 06 TQ08

The Falcon Inn ★★★★ INN ♀

Village Rd UB9 5BE ☎ 01895 832125
e-mail: falcon.inn@btconnect.com
dir: *M40 junct 1, follow A40/Gerrards Cross signs. Approx 200yds turn right onto Old Mill Rd. Pass church on right, enter village. Pub opposite village green*

This traditional 16th-century inn, located opposite the green in beautiful Denham Village, is an ideal base for exploring Colne Valley Country Park. Expect excellent real ales and award-winning food. Lunch could include Spanish tortilla with mixed salad, or a home-made burger with fries; in the evening, perhaps ginger king prawns and scallops with aubergine caviar, rösti potatoes, langoustine and herb oil, or rack of lamb with marinated courgettes, straw potatoes and red wine sauce. Lots of fish.

Open 12–3 5–11 (Summer Sat/Sun 12–11) **Bar Meals** L served all week 12–2.30 D served all week 6.30–9.30 (Sun 12–4) **Restaurant** L served Mon-Sun 12–2.30 D served Mon-Sun 6.30–10 (Sun 12–4, 6.30–9.30) ◧ Timothy Taylor Landlord, Bombardier, Youngs, Deuchars & guest ale. ♀ 11 **Facilities** Children's licence Garden **Rooms** 4

Pick of the Pubs

The Swan Inn ♀

See Pick of the Pubs on page 48

DORNEY
MAP 06 SU97

The Palmer Arms ♀

Village Rd SL4 6QW ☎ 01628 666612 ▤ 01628 661116
e-mail: info@thepalmerarms.com
dir: *From A4 take B3026, over M4 to Dorney*

The Palmer Arms, dating from the 15th century, is well-located in the beautiful conservation village of Dorney. Its owners are passionate about providing high standards of food and service, and like to think of their cooking as 'English with a twist'. Seasonal game dishes are always available, and fish is well represented on the menu. It is open every day of the year for lunch, afternoon tea, dinner and all-day coffee.

Open 11–11 12–11 (Mon closed 3–5, Sun 12–6) **Bar Meals** L served Mon-Sat 12–5.30 (Sun 12–4) Av main course £12 **Restaurant** L served Mon-Sat 12–2.30 D served Mon-Sat 6–9.30 (Sun 12–4) Av 3 course à la carte £22 ⊕ Greene King ◧ Greene King Abbot Ale, Old Speckled Hen, IPA, Guinness. ♀ 18 **Facilities** Garden Parking

FARNHAM COMMON
MAP 06 SU98

The Foresters ♀

The Broadway SL2 3QQ
☎ 01753 643340 ▤ 01753 647524
e-mail: barforesters@aol.com
dir: *Telephone for directions*

There's a great atmosphere at the Foresters, a pub dating back to the 1930s and built to replace a Victorian building. It's conveniently situated for discovering the delights of Burnham Beeches containing the world's largest collection of ancient beech. The quality daily menu might include fillet of brill colbert with parsley potatoes; pork loin steak with bubble and squeak and shallot and mustard sauce; and escalopes of veal with fondant potato and Irish cabbage.

Open 11–11 (Sun 12–10.30) **Bar Meals** L served Mon-Sat 12–2.30 D served Mon-Sat 6.30–10 (Sun all day) Av main course £14 **Restaurant** L served Mon-Sat 12–2.30 D served Mon-Sat 6.30–10 (Sun 12–9) Av 3 course à la carte £25 ⊕ Punch Taverns ◧ Fuller's London Pride, Draught Bass & guest ale. ♀ 10 **Facilities** Children's licence Garden Dogs allowed Parking

FARNHAM ROYAL
MAP 06 SU98

The King of Prussia ♀

Blackpond Ln SL2 3EG ☎ 01753 643006
e-mail: gm@tkop.co.uk
dir: *Telephone for directions*

This old inn has a wealth of polished wood floors and original beams running through its bar, conservatory and refurbished barn. A log fire burns in winter, and tables outside beckon on summer days. British food based on fresh seasonal fare is the overriding emphasis on the menus. You may find potted Aylesbury duck with baby leaf salad to start, followed by canon of Welsh lamb with dauphinoise potatoes, and fresh fruit meringue to finish.

Open 12–3 6–11 Closed: 1 Jan **Bar Meals** L served all week 12–2.15 D served Mon-Sat 7–9.15 (Sun 12–4.30) **Restaurant** L served all week 12–2.15 D served Mon-Sat 7–9.15 (Sun 12–4.30) Av 3 course à la carte £22.50 ⊕ Enterprise Inns ◧ Guinness, London Pride, Caffreys. ♀ 8 **Facilities** Garden Parking

PICK OF THE PUBS

The Swan Inn

The Swan is the embodiment of the traditional country inn – a double fronted Georgian property swathed in wisteria and set in the beautiful village of Denham. Though the location is wonderfully secluded, it is not too far from the bright lights by a choice of nearby motorways.

The interior is cosily welcoming with a large log fire and a collection of pictures picked up at local auctions, while outside there is a sunny terrace and gardens large enough to lose the children in. A private dining room is also available for family occasions or business meetings. Though The Swan is still very much a pub, the quality of the food is a great attraction to customers. Fresh, seasonal produce underpins a menu that re-invigorates some old favourites and makes the most of market availability with a daily changing specials board. For a starter or light meal look to the 'small plates' section of the menu, with the likes of crayfish and Cornish crab vol-au-vent with bloody Mary jelly; or white pudding sausage roll with sweet onion and port marmalade. Among the main meals you'll find plenty of variety from grilled Grimsby smoked haddock with braised leek, parsley and spring onion broth, to slow-roasted shoulder of lamb on turnip gratin with spinach purée and puy lentil jus. An interesting option is also provided for vegetarians, starting with spiced carrot and courgette fritters with pumpkin pickle and mint raita; and going on to coriander marinated halloumi burger with roast tomato, pumpkin seed pesto and sweet potato gaufrettes.

MAP 06 TQ08
Village Rd UB9 5BH
☎ 01895 832085
🖷 01895 835516
e-mail: info@swaninndenham.co.uk
dir: *From A40 take A412. In 200yds follow Denham Village sign on right. Through village, over bridge, last pub on left*

Open 11–11 (Sun 12–10.30)
Closed: 25–26 Dec
Bar Meals L served Mon-Sat 12–2.30 D served all week 7–10 (Sun 12–4) Av main course £12.75
Restaurant L served Mon-Sat 12–2.30 D served all week 7–10 (Sun 12–4) Av 3 course à la carte £23.75
⊕ Salisbury Pubs 🍺 Wadworth 6X, Courage Best, Marlow Rebellion IPA. ⛉ 19
Facilities Garden Dogs allowed Parking

England

FORD
MAP 05 SP70

Pick of the Pubs

The Dinton Hermit ★ SHL

Water Ln HP17 8XH ☎ 01296 747473 🖷 01296 748819
e-mail: dintonhermit@btconnect.com
dir: *Off A418 between Aylesbury & Thame*

A 400–year-old, listed inn deep in the Vale of Aylesbury. A sympathetic restoration and extension programme a few years ago included a 200-year-old barn constructed of packed earth known as wychert, a building method often used in this area. At lunchtime, sandwiches, the Dinton Hermit burger and a variety of main courses are served. The elegantly furnished restaurant offers starters such as marinated seared scallops with brussels sprouts, bacon and horseradish potato cake; twice-roasted duck leg with chilli mash, pak choi and hoi sin; and crispy skewered salmon with oriental spicy sauce. Among the eight main courses taken from a winter menu, might be baked John Dory with crispy pancetta, buttered spinach, ratatouille and beurre rouge; herb-stuffed corn-fed chicken supreme wrapped in Parma ham with classic jambalaya; and wild mushroom millefeuille with boursin cheese and gratinated vegetables.

Open 10–12 (Sun 12–11.30) Closed: 25–26 Dec & 1 Jan
Bar Meals L served Mon-Sat 12–2 D served all week 7–9 (Sun 12–4)
Av main course £16 **Restaurant** L served Mon-Sat 12–2
D served Mon-Sat 7–9 (Sun 12–4) Av 3 course à la carte £27 ⊕ Free
House ◀ Adnams Bitter, 6X Brakspears, London Pride, Batemans XB.
Facilities Garden Parking **Rooms** 13

FRIETH
MAP 05 SU79

The Prince Albert ♀

RG9 6PY ☎ 01494 881683
dir: *4m N of Marlow. Follow Frieth road from Marlow. Straight across at x-rds on Fingest road. Pub 200yds on left.*

Set in the Chilterns, close to Hambledon and Marlow, this traditional country pub prides itself on old world values. There are no televisions, juke boxes or games – just good conversation and a welcoming atmosphere. Warm open fires enhance the mood in winter. Expect baguettes, jacket potatoes and ploughman's lunches among the lunchtime light bites, while the evening menu typically offers jumbo battered cod, chilli con carne, lamb shank, and home-made steak and kidney pie.

Open 11–11 (Sun 12–10.30) Closed: Mon **Bar Meals** L served Mon-Sat 12.15–2.30 D served Fri-Sat 7–9.30 (Sun 12.30–3) **Restaurant** L served Mon-Sat 12.30–2.30 D served Fri-Sat 7–9.30 (Sun 12.30–3) ⊕ Brakspear ◀ Brakspear Bitter, Brakspear seasonal ales. ♀9 **Facilities** Garden Dogs allowed Parking

The Yew Tree ♀

RG9 6PJ ☎ 01494 882330 🖷 01494 883497
e-mail: enquiries@theyewtreerestaurant.com
dir: *From M40 towards Stokenchurch, through Cadmore End, Lane End right to Frieth*

Deep in the Chiltern Hills, the 16th-century, red-brick Yew Tree manages to be both traditional rustic country pub and contemporary restaurant, its unexpected pale beams contributing to the effect. Bar meals are available, although you may prefer the dining room where main courses include crispy-skinned sea bass with stir-fried vegetables and honey and soy glaze; and lamb shank, dauphinoise potatoes and garlic and thyme jus. A paddock with three llamas adjoins the substantial rear garden.

Open 12–3 6–11 (Sun 12–5) **Bar Meals** L served Tue-Sat 12–2.30 D served Tue-Sun 6–10 (Sun 12–5) **Restaurant** L served Tue-Sun 12–2.30 D served Tue-Sun 6–10 ⊕ Free House ◀ Fuller's Honeydew, Rebellion, IPA, Smuggler. ♀4 **Facilities** Garden Dogs allowed Parking Play Area

GREAT HAMPDEN
MAP 05 SP80

The Hampden Arms ♀

HP16 9RQ ☎ 01494 488255 🖷 01494 488094
e-mail: louise@thehamptonarms.fsnet.co.uk
dir: *From M40 take A4010, right before Princes Risborough. Great Hampden signed*

Whether you're celebrating a special occasion or just want a quiet pint of real ale, you'll find a warm and friendly welcome at this mock Tudor pub restaurant in the heart of the beautifully wooded Hampden Estate. The menu features such dishes as game pie set on a rich port sauce; baked halibut steak with a watercress, mussel and cream sauce; and roasted vegetables set on a rocket and parmesan salad. Lighter snacks are available, and there is a good choice of hot puddings.

Open 12–3 6–11 (Sun 7–10.30) **Bar Meals** L served all week 12–2 D served all week 6.30–9 (Fri & Sat 6.30–9.30, Sun 12–3, 7–9) Av main course £10.95 **Restaurant** L served all week 12–2 D served all week 6.30–9 (Sun 12–3, 7–9) Av 3 course à la carte £20 ⊕ Free House ◀ Adnams Bitter, Hook Norton, Tetley. ♀7 **Facilities** Garden Dogs allowed Parking

GREAT MISSENDEN
MAP 06 SP80

Pick of the Pubs

The Nags Head NEW ♀

London Rd HP16 0DG
☎ 01494 862200 🖷 01494 862945
e-mail: goodfood@nagsheadbucks.com
dir: *1m from Great Missenden on London Rd*

The Michaels family took over this much-lauded, ivy-clad, 15th-century pub in January 2008. As with their similarly award-winning Bricklayers Arms in Flaunden, they have transformed it into a foodie pub serving English traditional and French fusion cooking. They've given it a complete makeover and in the process revealed some of its hitherto hidden medieval features. In the bar, where local children's author Roald Dahl used to drink, is a big inglenook fireplace; outside is a large garden. The menus, extensively based on fresh, locally sourced organic produce, offer starters such as

Continued

Continued

49

England

GREAT MISSENDEN continued

eggs meurette; crab with home-smoked salmon; and mixed and wild mushroom feuilleté; plus mains such as best end of lamb; confit leg of Barbary duck; boned quail stuffed with mushrooms; pan-fried sea bass; and chef's vegetarian dish of the day. A broad range of desserts includes pear poached in red wine, stuffed with maple and walnut ice cream.

The Nags Head

Open 12–11.30 (Sun 12–10.30) **Restaurant** L served Mon-Sat 12–2.30 D served Mon-Sat 6.30–9.30 (Sun 12–4, 6.30–8.30) Av 3 course à la carte £28 ◀ London Pride, Timothy Taylor Landlord, Black Sheep, Old Speckled Hen. ♀ 14 **Facilities** Children's licence Garden Dogs allowed Parking **Rooms** available

Pick of the Pubs

The Polecat Inn ♀

170 Wycombe Rd, Prestwood HP16 0HJ
☎ 01494 862253 📄 01494 868393
e-mail: polecatinn@btinternet.com
dir: *On A4128 between Great Missenden & High Wycombe*

John Gamble bought the closed and dilapidated Polecat some 18 years ago, renovating and extending it to create an attractive free house, while retaining many original features. The inn dates back to the 17th century and part of its great attraction is its beautiful three-acre garden, set amidst rolling Chilterns countryside. Small low-beamed rooms radiate from the central bar, providing a great choice for sitting and relaxing over a pint or a plate of freshly cooked food. Dishes are prepared from local ingredients, including herbs from the garden. There is a lunchtime snack menu (sandwiches, warm baguettes, jacket and ploughman's) and a regular menu supplemented by a daily blackboard selection. Daily specials include roulade of chicken and pancetta with leaves and honey mustard dressing; and venison paupiettes with wild boar, juniper and apple stuffing, Calvados sauce and celeriac crisps.

Open 11.30–2.30 6–11 (Sun 12–3) Closed: 25–26 Dec, 1 Jan **Bar Meals** L served all week 12–2 D served Mon-Sat 6.30–9 ⊕ Free House ◀ Marston's Pedigree, Moorland, Old Speckled Hen, Interbrew Flowers IPA & Brakspears Bitter. ♀ 16 **Facilities** Garden Parking Play Area

Pick of the Pubs

The Rising Sun ♀
See Pick of the Pubs on opposite page

HADDENHAM   **MAP 05 SP70**

Pick of the Pubs

The Green Dragon ⓦⓦ ♀

8 Churchway HP17 8AA
☎ 01844 291403 📄 01844 299532
e-mail: pete@eatatthedragon.co.uk
dir: *From M40 A329 to Thame, then A418, 1st right after entering Haddenham*

The Green Dragon is attractively located in the old part of Haddenham, close to the village green and 12th-century church. The pub dates back to 1650 and was once a manorial court, as the last man to be executed in Buckinghamshire discovered to his cost. The garden offers two large lawned areas offering some shade and a mix of tables and chairs, some distance from the main building. Over several years pub co-owner and chef Paul Berry has built up a formidable reputation for his food, and the place gets very busy, so booking is strongly advised. The menu might start with salmon and prawn fishcakes served with herb salad and a lime and ginger dressing; or perhaps confit duck leg with a warm rhubarb and apple compote, cider and vanilla dressing. Main courses offer delights from pies and fish and chips to dishes like braised Buckinghamshire lamb shank with vegetable tagine and pak choi. Vegetarians are well catered for.

Open 12–3 6.30–11 Closed: 25 Dec & 1 Jan **Bar Meals** L served all week 12–2 D served Mon-Sat 6.30–9.15 (Sun 12–3) Av main course £12.50 **Restaurant** L served all week 12–2 D served Mon-Sat 6.30–9.15 Av 3 course à la carte £25 ⊕ Enterprise Inns ◀ IPA Deuchars Ale, Wadworth 6X & local guest ale. ♀ 10 **Facilities** Garden Parking

HAMBLEDEN   **MAP 05 SU78**

The Stag & Huntsman Inn

RG9 6RP ☎ 01491 571227 📄 01491 413810
e-mail: andy@stagandhuntsman.com
dir: *5m from Henley-on-Thames on A4155 toward Marlow, left at Mill End towards Hambleden*

Close to the glorious beech-clad Chilterns, this 400–year-old brick and flint village pub has featured in countless films and television series. Ever-changing guest ales are served in the public bar, larger lounge bar and cosy snug. Food is available in the bars as well as the dining room, from an extensive menu of home-made dishes prepared from local seasonal produce. Hambleden estate game features in season. A weekend beer festival is held in early September.

Open 11–2.30 6–11 (Sun 12–3, 7–10.30, Sat 11–3, 6–11) Closed: 25–26 Dec & 1 Jan evening **Bar Meals** L served all week 12–2 D served Mon-Sat 7–9.30 (Sun 7–9) Av main course £10 **Restaurant** L served all week 12–2 D served Mon-Sat 7–9.30 (Sun 7–9) ⊕ Free House ◀ Rebellion IPA, Wadworth 6X, guest ales. **Facilities** Garden Parking

The Rising Sun

You'll find this 250–year-old inn tucked away in the Chiltern Hills, close to the Ridgeway, down a single track, no-through-road, surrounded by beech woods and glorious scenery. It is just three miles from the Prime Minister's country retreat at Chequers and was once frequented by Harold Wilson and Ted Heath.

The original clientele were more likely to be farm labourers or bodgers who worked in the local beech woods. A network of footpaths begins just outside the front door, so it's a perfect base for country walks. An attractive new feature is the landscaped garden area with comfortable armchair seating and tables for outside wining and dining in beautiful surroundings. Rotisserie paprika-seasoned corn-fed chicken and chips is a speciality. There's some good seafood too, like hot dressed crab with cheese and grain mustard sauce, and pan-fried skate wings with scallop, lemon and capers. Otherwise look out for warm smoked chicken and bacon salad with peanut sauce; roast shoulder of lamb with a rosemary and honey sauce; charcoal grilled sirloin steak with horseradish mayonnaise; and for something lighter, roasted panini baguette with various fillings; deep-fried tiger prawns wrapped in filo pastry, served with chilli mayonnaise; deep-fried spinach and feta goujons with mixed berries in syrup; and smoked haddock and spring onion fishcake.

♟
MAP 06 SP80
Little Hampden HP16 9PS
☎ 01494 488393 & 488360
🖷 01494 488788
e-mail: sunrising@
rising-sun.demon.co.uk
web:
www.rising-sun.demon.co.uk
dir: *From A413, N of Gt Missenden, take Rignall Rd on left signed Princes Risborough 2.5m. Turn right signed 'Little Hampden only'*

Open 11.30–3 (Sun 12–3 only)
Open BH lunchtime 6.30–10
Bar Meals L served Tue-Sun
12–2 D served Tue-Sat 7–9 (Sun lunch 12–2)
Restaurant L served Tue-Sun
12–2 D served Tue-Sat 7–9 (Sun lunch 12–2) Av 3 course à la carte £22
🌐 Free House 🍺 Adnams, Spitfire, Marstons Pedigree, Brakspear Special. ♟ 10
Facilities Garden Dogs allowed Parking
Rooms available

England

HEDGERLEY — MAP 06 SU98

The White Horse ♥
SL2 3UY ☎ 01753 643225
dir: Telephone for directions

The original part of the pub is 500 years old, and over 1000 beers take their turn at the pumps during each year. At least seven real ales are always available, served by gravity. An annual beer festival is held at the end of May bank holiday. Home-made food ranges from a salad bar with pies, quiches, sandwiches and ploughman's through to curries, chilli, pasta dishes, pies and steaks.

Open 11–2.30 5–11 (Sat 11–11, Sun 12–10.30) **Bar Meals** L served all week 12–2 (Wknds 12–2.30) Av main course £6.50 ⊕ Free House ◀ Constantly changing. ♥10 **Facilities** Garden Dogs allowed Parking

KINGSWOOD — MAP 11 SP61

Crooked Billet ♥
Ham Green HP18 0QJ ☎ 01296 770239 ▤ 01296 770094
e-mail: info@crookedbillet.com
dir: On A41 between Aylesbury & Bicester

Located in peaceful Buckinghamshire countryside, this 200–year-old pub offers an extensive and tempting choice of food. Starters may include port and stilton rarebit with date and walnut bread, and tomato Cumberland sauce, or salad of queenie scallops with smoked salmon. Among the main courses can be found pasta alla Fiorentina smothered in cream cheeses and spinach; roasted sea bass fillet with shrimp velouté and parsley mash; or gratin of fine herb gnocchi with chard, turnips and carrots.

Open 11–11 **Bar Meals** L served Mon-Sat 12–2.30 D served Mon-Sat 6–9.30 (Sun 12–3.30) **Restaurant** L served Mon-Sat 12–2.30 D served Mon-Sat 6–9.30 (Sun 12–3.30) ⊕ Free House ◀ Hook Norton, Guinness, Tetley's. ♥15 **Facilities** Garden Parking Play Area

LITTLE CHALFONT — MAP 06 SU99

Pick of the Pubs

The Sugar Loaf Inn ♥
See Pick of the Pubs on opposite page

LONG CRENDON — MAP 05 SP60

Pick of the Pubs

The Angel Inn ◉ ♥
47 Bicester Rd HP18 9EE
☎ 01844 208268 ▤ 01844 202497
e-mail: angelrestaurant@aol.com
dir: A418 to Thame, B4011 to Long Crendon. Inn on B4011

Wattle-and-daub walls and inglenook fireplaces attest to the age of this former coaching inn, located in the pretty village of Long Crendon. Original materials and classic decorations have been used throughout. There is a warm bar area with leather settees, and a bright conservatory and outside patio area, which come into their own in summer. Real ales are served, along with cocktails, champagne and wine by the glass, but food is the main focus here. At lunch, choose between sandwiches with hot or cold fillings, and the more substantial fare on offer, typically English lamb with soft herb crust on vegetable ratatouille with dauphinoise potatoes and rosemary sauce; and roast fillet of halibut on vegetable fettuccine with mussel and saffron sauce. Vegetarian options, like sesame tempura vegetables with ginger noodles and wasabi, can be taken as a starter or main course.

Open 12–3 7–10 **Bar Meals** L served all week 12–3 D served Mon-Sat 7–9.30 **Restaurant** L served all week 12–2.30 D served Mon-Sat 7–9.30 ⊕ Free House ◀ Oxford Blue, IPA, Brakspear. ♥11 **Facilities** Garden Parking

MARLOW — MAP 05 SU88

The Kings Head ♥
Church Rd, Little Marlow SL7 3RZ
☎ 01628 484407 ▤ 01628 484407
dir: M40 junct 4 take A4040 S, then A4155 towards Bourne End. Pub 0.5m on right

Together with the Old Forge, this flower-adorned, 17th-century pub forms part of an attractive group of buildings a few minutes' walk from the Thames Footpath. It has an open-plan but cosy interior with original beams and open fires. In addition to sandwiches and jacket potatoes, the menu offers quite a range of more substantial meals, including salmon fillet hollandaise; mixed fish salad; lamb shank with rich minty gravy; pheasant casserole; and stir-fry duck with plum sauce.

Open 11–11 **Bar Meals** L served Mon-Sat 12–2.15 D served Mon-Sat 6.30–9.30 (Sun 12–7) **Restaurant** L served Mon-Sat 12–2.15 D served Mon-Sat 6.30–9.30 (Sun 12–7) ⊕ Enterprise Inns ◀ Fuller's London Pride, Timothy Taylor Landlord, Adnam Broadside & Deuchars IPA. ♥9 **Facilities** Garden Parking

MENTMORE — MAP 11 SP91

Pick of the Pubs

Il Maschio @ The Stag ♥
See Pick of the Pubs on page 54

PICK OF THE PUBS

LITTLE CHALFONT-BUCKINGHAMSHIRE

The Sugar Loaf Inn

The Sugar Loaf lies within the gently rolling Chiltern Hills, just a short drive from excellent walks in the Chess Valley. Built in the classic style of the late 1930's, the Sugar Loaf was originally a hotel serving the nearby Chalfont and Latimer station.

Nowadays, locals populate the comfortably furnished bar, with its oak panelled walls, wooden floors, bespoke lighting and blinds. There are open fires in winter, whilst a private rear garden and decked seating to the front and side are popular on balmy days. A range of whiskies, brandies, chilled vodkas and champagnes augments a good selection of real ales and a dozen wines served by the glass. Food service is informal, and there's an eat-anywhere policy. Simple, fresh ingredients and uncomplicated presentation characterise the menu, which offers a choice of classic European dishes with a modern twist. Lunchtime light bites and starters include mushroom and celeriac soup with garlic croutons; and roast butternut squash risotto with toasted pine nuts, as well as an appetising selection of speciality focaccia sandwiches. Main course options range from pub favourites to more adventurous dishes: try honey-roast ham with free-range eggs and chips; local Amersham sausages with spring onion mash and grain mustard jus; grilled haloumi with fresh ratatouille, spinach and polenta; grilled sea bass with roast vegetable and couscous salad; or roast cod fillet with parsnip and herb mash, mange tout and roast lemon dressing. Daily blackboard specials include lobster, oysters and game in season, and there's an all day roast on Sundays.

🍷
MAP 06 SU99
Station Rd HP7 9NP
☎ 01494 765579
e-mail:
info@thesugarloafinn.com
dir: *M25 junct 18. At 1st lights left onto A404 towards Amersham. 4m to Little Chalfont, under rail bridge, pub 500yds on right*

Open 12–3 5.30–11 Closed: 26 Dec & 1 Jan
Bar Meals L served all week 12–3 5–10
Restaurant L served Mon-Fri 12–3 D served all week 5.30–10.30 (Sun-Sat 12–4)
🍺 Adnams, Guinness, London Pride 🍷 10
Facilities Children's licence Garden Parking

PICK OF THE PUBS

MENTMORE-BUCKINGHAMSHIRE

Il Maschio @ The Stag

An imposing stone building, the Stag sits on a ridge overlooking the Vale of Aylesbury. So too does Mentmore Towers, the huge Elizabethan-style stately home built in 1855 for Baron Amschel de Rothschild.

In this idyllic setting there is a wealth of fresh resources, and head chef and co-owner Mani Rebelo has tapped into the local Chiltern farming community and suppliers for his raw materials. This way he can ensure that, whenever possible, he's using fresh, seasonal produce, humanely reared meats and fish from sustainable sources,when creating his diverse and popular dishes. The cooking is a distinctive fusion of British and Mediterranean cuisine. The lunchtime menu changes seasonally, while the evening and weekends choices are updated every 6–8 weeks. Along with the meat dishes with seasonal vegetables, there are weekly fresh fish specials and a selection of pizza, pasta's and salads. Lunch starters could include sliced San Daniele prosciutto with gallia melon; avocado with shelled prawns covered in home-made Marie Rose sauce; deep-fried breaded brie served with a cranberry dip and salad; deep fried breaded mushrooms served with a home-made garlic mayonnaise dip and salad; grilled squid and chorizo on a bed of rocket. For a main course look to smoked salmon, asparagus tips, and boiled eggs served on a bed of salad drizzled with lemon scented olive oil; free range chicken strips, smoked pancetta, parmesan shavings and anchovies on a bed of salad, croutons and home-made Caesar dressing; and warmed goat's cheese, roasted mixed peppers, grilled courgette and aubergine drizzled in home-made pesto.

MAP 11 SP91
The Green LU7 0QF
☎ 01296 668423
📠 01296 660 264
dir: *Telephone for directions*

Open 12–11
Bar Meals L served all week
12–10 D served all week 12–10
Restaurant L served all week
12–10 D served all week 12–10
⊕ Charles Wells ◀ Youngs Bitter,
Guinness, Bombardier, Eagle. ♥ 8
Facilities Children's licence
Garden Dogs allowed Parking

MOULSOE MAP 11 SP94

The Carrington Arms ♀

Cranfield Rd MK16 0HB ☎ 01908 218050 📠 01908 217850
e-mail: thecarringtonarms@4cinns.co.uk
dir: *M1 junct 14, A509 to Newport Pagnell 100yds, turn right*
signed Moulsoe & Cranfield. Pub on right

This Grade II listed building is surrounded by farm land in a
conservation area. Customers can 'create' their own menu from the
meat and seafood counter, which the chef then cooks in full view of his
expectant diners. Aberdeen beef, monkfish, tiger prawns, Colchester
oysters are all on offer, along with unusual meats like ostrich, crocodile
and kangaroo, plus vegetarian dishes and chef's specials. Friday night is
fish night and lobster is available for pre-order.

Open 12–3 5.30–11 (Sun 7–10.30) Closed: 26–27 Dec, 1 Jan
Bar Meals L served all week 12–2.30 D served all week (Sat 6–10, Sun
7–9.30) **Restaurant** L served all week 12–2.30 D served all week 6.30–10
(Sat 6–10, Sun 7–9.30) ⊕ Free House ◀ Morland Old Speckled Hen,
Greene King IPA, & guest ales. ♀ 10 **Facilities** Garden Parking

---

OVING MAP 11 SP72

The Black Boy ♀

Church Ln HP22 4HN ☎ 01296 641258 📠 01296 641271
e-mail: theblackboyoving@aol.com
dir: *4.6m N of Aylesbury*

Oliver Cromwell and his soldiers camped in the Black Boy's huge
garden after sacking nearby Bolebec Castle during the Civil War. Today,
the 16th-century pub is a rural oasis, with spectacular views over
the Vale of Aylesbury to Stowe School and beyond. Choices in the
dining room include Scottish salmon with new potatoes and seasonal
greens; local lamb shank with minted gravy and root vegetables; and a
vegetarian cheese and onion filo parcel.

Open 12–3 6–11 **Bar Meals** L served Tue-Sun 12–2 D served Tue-Sat
6.30–9 (Sun 12–3.30) **Restaurant** L served Tue-Sun 12–2 D served Tue-Sat
6.30–9 (Sun 12–3.30) Av 3 course à la carte £25 ◀ Brakspear, Rebellion,
Youngs Bitter, Batemans Bitter. ♀ 10 **Facilities** Garden Dogs allowed
Parking

RADNAGE MAP 05 SU79

The Three Horseshoes Inn ♀

Horseshoe Rd, Bennett End HP14 4EB ☎ 01494 483273

Dating from 1748, this delightful little inn is tucked away down a leafy
lane. Stone floors, original beams, a bread oven and an open fire are
among the features. The menu changes daily, and the award-winning
chef/owner uses as much local produce as possible. Outside there are
beautiful gardens.

Open 12–11 **Bar Meals** L served Mon-Sat 12–2.30 D served Mon-Sat
6–9.30 (Sun 12–4) **Restaurant** L served Mon-Sat 12–2.30 D served all
week 7–9.30 (Sun 12–4) ⊕ Free House ◀ Adnams, Brakspears, guest ales.
♀ 6 **Facilities** Garden Dogs allowed Parking

SKIRMETT MAP 05 SU79

The Frog ♀

RG9 6TG ☎ 01491 638996 📠 01491 638045
e-mail: jim.crowe@btinternet.com
dir: *Turn off A4155 at Mill End, pub in 3m*

This privately owned pub and restaurant is tucked away in the beautiful
Hambleden valley. The simple set menu offers great value for money
with options like salad of gravadlax, followed by roast loin of pork, and
sticky toffee pudding to finish. The carte offers a range of starters like
soup, garlic bread or bruschetta; followed by mains like pan-seared
salmon with curried lentils and coriander cream sauce.

Open 11.30–3 6.30–11 **Bar Meals** L served all week 12–2.30 D served all
week 6.30–9.30 **Restaurant** L served all week 12–2.30 D served all week
6.30–9.30 Av 3 course à la carte £25 Av 3 course fixed price £17.75 ⊕ Free
House ◀ Adnams Best, Hook Norton, Rebellion, Fuller's London Pride.
♀ 14 **Facilities** Garden Dogs allowed Parking

STOKE MANDEVILLE MAP 05 SP81

The Wool Pack ♀

Risborough Rd HP22 5UP
☎ 01296 615970 📠 01296 615971
dir: *4m from Aylesbury*

The gardens and landscaped decking here are ideal for a summertime
real ale. Inside there's a relaxed, informal atmosphere beneath the
thatch and low beams, and the pub's stylish interior features open
kitchens, log fires and a restaurant. The simple, up-to-the-minute menu
offers lots of comfort appeal: choose from 'Sharing Plates' with Spanish
tapas or Greek mezze; 'Fired Pizzas'; 'Pastas' such as rigatoni and
smoked haddock; or 'Rotisserie' dishes like spit chicken with lemon
and garlic confit.

Open 11–11 **Bar Meals** L served all week 12–2.30 D served all week
6–9.30 (Sun 12–7) **Restaurant** L served all week 12–2.30 D served all
week 6–9.30 (Sun 12–7) ◀ London Pride, Timothy Taylor Landlord. ♀ 10
Facilities Garden Parking

TURVILLE   MAP 05 SU79   **WEST WYCOMBE**   MAP 05 SU89

Pick of the Pubs

The Bull & Butcher ♀

RG9 6QU ☎ 01491 638283 ▤ 01491 638836
e-mail: info@thebullandbutcher.com
dir: *M40 junct 5 follow Ibstone signs. Right at T-junct. Pub 0.25m on left*

Even if you've never been to the quaint village of Turville or this delightful black-and-white-timbered 16th-century pub, you may well recognise them on sight. The village has earned itself celebrity status over the years as a popular location for numerous film and television productions: *Midsomer Murders*, *The Vicar of Dibley*, *Goodnight Mr Tom*, and *Chitty Chitty Bang Bang*. After an exhilarating walk in the glorious Chilterns, you can relax in the Well Bar or Windmill Lounge (there is a windmill on the hill above) and appreciate the original floor tiles, natural oak beams and open fires. There is also a function room ideal for leisure and corporate occasions, and a large garden and patio area. Special dishes include slow roasted saddle of Wormsley Estate venison with redcurrant sauce, dauphinoise potatoes and vegetables; and rolled lemon sole fillets, stuffed with prawns in a light lemon sauce.

Open 12–11 (Sun & BH 12–10.30) **Bar Meals** L served Mon-Fri 12–2.30 D served Mon-Fri 6.30–9.30 (Sat -Sun 12–4) **Restaurant** L served Mon-Fri 12–2.30 D served Mon-Fri 6.30–9.30 (Sat-Sun 12–4) Av 3 course à la carte £25 Av 3 course fixed price £25 ⊕ Brakspear ◀ Brakspear Bitter, Brakspear Special, Hooky Dark and Brewers selections. ♀36 **Facilities** Garden Dogs allowed Parking

Pick of the Pubs

The George and Dragon Hotel ♀

High St HP14 3AB ☎ 01494 464414 ▤ 01494 462432
e-mail: sue.raines@btconnect.com
dir: *On A40*

A traditional coaching inn with 14th-century origins inn, in a National Trust village. It was once the haunt of highwaymen stalking travellers between London and Oxford and, indeed, one unfortunate guest robbed and murdered here is rumoured still to haunt its corridors. The hotel is reached through a cobbled archway and comprises a delightful jumble of whitewashed, timber-framed buildings. The 'English-at-heart' carte menu offers an extensive selection of freshly-prepared dishes, including game from the local estate; spatchcock lemon chicken; beef Wellington with red wine and mushroom sauce; bean and wild mushroom goulash; salmon in pastry, served with crème fraîche; chargrilled steaks; and lentil and cider loaf with tomato and basil sauce. Home-made desserts include classic spotted dick, allegedly destined to become extinct according to a 2008 survey. Visitors to the area will enjoy exploring West Wycombe Caves, and the stately houses at Cliveden and Hughenden Manor.

Open 11–3 5.30–11 (Fri-Sat 11–11 Mar-Sep Sun 12–3, 6–10.30) **Bar Meals** L served Mon-Sat 12–2.30 D served Mon-Sat 6–9.30 (Sun 12–3.30, 6.30–9) Av main course £12 ⊕ Enterprise Inns ◀ Courage Best, Wells Bombardier, Timothy Taylor Landlord. ♀7 **Facilities** Children's licence Garden Dogs allowed Parking Play Area

TYLERS GREEN   MAP 06 SU99   **WHEELEREND COMMON**   MAP 05 SU89

The Old Queens Head ♀

Hammersley Ln HP10 8EY
☎ 01494 813371 ▤ 01494 816145
e-mail: info@oldqueensheadpenn.co.uk
dir: *B474 (Penn Rd) through Beaconsfield New Town towards Penn, in approx 3m left into School Rd, left again in 500yds into Hammersley Ln. Pub on corner opposite church*

In 1666, while the Great Fire was destroying countless wooden houses in London, local timber was unconcernedly being used to build this old pub. The kitchen is clearly highly versatile, producing a modern British menu offering steamed steak and parsnip suet pudding; chargrilled Oxfordshire lamb rump on celeriac and truffle gratin; and grilled pollock with herb crust and braised celery. Puddings include steamed St Clement's syrup sponge with vanilla and cinnamon custard.

Open 11–11 (Sun 12–10.30) Closed: 26 Dec **Bar Meals** L served Mon-Sat 12–2.30 D served all week 7–10 (Sun 12–4) Av main course £12.75 **Restaurant** L served Mon-Sat 12–2.30 D served all week 7–10 (Sun 12–4) Av 3 course à la carte £23.75 ◀ Morlands Original, Greene King IPA & Guinness. ♀19 **Facilities** Garden Dogs allowed Parking

The Chequers ♀

Bullocks Farm Ln HP14 3NH ☎ 01494 883070
e-mail: ray-dunse@hotmail.com
dir: *4m N of Marlow*

This picturesque 17th-century inn, with its roaring winter fires and two attractive beer gardens, is ideally located for walkers on the edge of Wheeler End Common. A solid choice of mouth-watering sandwiches and bar meals supplements the main menu, which features plenty of fresh fish and local estate game. Warm pigeon and apple salad; venison pie with red wine and juniper; and roast salmon on crushed potato tartare are typical choices.

Open 11.30–3 5.30–12 (Fri-Sun all day) **Bar Meals** L served Mon-Sat 12–2.30 D served Tue-Sat 7–9.30 (Sun 12–4) **Restaurant** L served Mon-Sat 12–2.30 D served Tue-Sat 7–9.30 (Sun 12–4) Av main course £8 ⊕ Fullers ◀ Fuller's ESB, London Pride, Jack Frost & Summer Ale, guest ale. ♀7 **Facilities** Children's licence Garden Dogs allowed Parking

WHITELEAF
MAP 05 SP80

Red Lion

Upper Icknield Way HP27 0LL
☎ 01844 344476 🖹 01844 273124
e-mail: tim_hibbert@hotmail.co.uk
dir: A4010 through Princes Risborough, turn right into The Holloway, at T-junct turn right, pub on left

Family-owned 17th-century inn in the heart of the Chilterns, surrounded by National Trust land and situated close to the Ridgeway national trail. There are plenty of good local walks with wonderful views. A cosy fire in winter and a secluded summer beer garden add to the appeal. Hearty pub fare includes prawn marie-rose, rib-eye steak, sausage and mash, vegetarian lasagne, haddock and chips, warm baguettes and jacket potatoes.

Open 12–3 5–11 (All day at wkds) **Bar Meals** L served all week 12–2 D served Mon-Sat 5–9 (Sun lunch only) Av main course £6.95 **Restaurant** L served all week 12–2 D served Mon-Sat 7–9 (Sun lunch only) Av main course fixed price £9.95 ⊕ Free House 🍺 Brakspear Bitter, Hook Norton, Guinness. **Facilities** Garden Dogs allowed Parking

---

WOOBURN COMMON
MAP 06 SU98

Pick of the Pubs

Chequers Inn 🍷

Kiln Ln HP10 0JQ ☎ 01628 529575 🖹 01628 850124
e-mail: info@chequers-inn.com
dir: M40 junct 2 through Beaconsfield towards High Wycombe. 1m left into Broad Ln. Inn 2.5m

Overlooking open Chiltern Hills countryside, this 17th-century inn makes an immediate impression with its oak posts and beams, flagstone floors and a wonderful open fireplace, blackened by a million blazing logs. An extensive lunch and dinner bar menu is offered every day, with a large selection of beers, guest ales and wines; the same menu is served in the contemporary lounge. The restaurant, attractively decorated with displays of plants, palms and memorabilia, is as ideal for a quick business lunch as for a long romantic dinner. Fresh, predominantly local ingredients are used in dishes such as red snapper, artichoke, green beans and crushed new potatoes; and saddle of rabbit stuffed with chicken mousse wrapped in bacon, with savoy cabbage and lyonnaise potatoes. Outside is a large garden area where barbecues are held in summer

---

Open All day **Bar Meals** L served Mon-Fri 12–2.30 D served Mon-Fri 6–9.30 (Open all day Sat-Sun) **Restaurant** L served all week 12–2.30 D served all week 7–9.30 ⊕ Free House 🍺 Ruddles, IPA, Abbot, guest bitter. 🍷 12 **Facilities** Children's licence Garden Parking

CAMBRIDGESHIRE

BABRAHAM
MAP 12 TL55

Pick of the Pubs

The George Inn at Babraham ◉ 🍷
See Pick of the Pubs on page 58

BARRINGTON
MAP 12 TL34

The Royal Oak 🍷

31 West Green CB22 7RZ
☎ 01223 870791 🖹 01223 870791
e-mail: info@royaloak.uk.net
dir: From Barton off M11 S of Cambridge

One of the oldest thatched pubs in England is this rambling, timbered 13th-century building overlooking what is the largest village green in England. Yet it is only six miles from Cambridge, three miles from the M11 and a mile from Shepreth Station. A wide range of fish dishes includes scallops, trout, scampi, tuna, swordfish, tiger prawns, squid and other seasonal offerings. There is also a carvery on Sunday.

Open 12–2.30 6–11 (Sun 12–10.30 high season only) **Bar Meals** L served Mon-Sat 12–2 D served Sun-Thu 6.30–9 (Sun 12–2.30, Fri-Sat 6.30–9.30) **Restaurant** D served Sun 6.30–9 ⊕ Old English Inns 🍺 IPA Potton Brewery, Adnams, Young's Bitter & Morland Original. 🍷 6 **Facilities** Garden Parking

---

BROUGHTON
MAP 12 TL27

Pick of the Pubs

The Crown 🍷

Bridge Rd PE28 3AY ☎ 01487 824428 🖹 01487 824912
e-mail: simon@thecrownbroughton.co.uk
dir: Just off A141 between Huntingdon & Warboys, by church in village centre

An idyllic, 18th-century village pub in a picturesque setting next to the church. In 1857, according to an insurance policy, it also incorporated a saddler's shop, thatched stables and piggeries. After it closed in 2000, around 40 villagers raised enough money to buy and renovate it, reopening in 2001. It is now run as a village-owned tenancy, with real ales from Greene King, Elgood's and other local breweries. Menus offer a lunchtime selection of filled ciabattas; and you'll find bangers and mash, fish and chips, and contemporary dishes like pork and apple sausages, savoy cabbage, black pudding mash and onion gravy; and Mediterranean vegetable lasagne. The main menu might come up with steamed Scottish steak and ale pudding with horseradish

Continued

PICK OF THE PUBS

The George Inn at Babraham

This family-owned 18th-century coaching inn is easily accessible from the A11 yet feels a world removed. Set in the heart of rural Cambridgeshire, it has been lovingly refurbished under the watchful eye of George Wortley, who took it over after the building was devastated by fire in 2004.

A team of craftsmen incorporated new kitchens and three restaurant areas in this now beautifully furnished and decorated village dining pub. It has become firmly established in the area, and is a popular meeting place for lunch and dinner. Chef Mark Edgeley delivers an eclectic range of food, which pairs traditional English ingredients with worldwide influences. There is no corner-cutting in the preparation: the house motto is 'a passion for detail'. For lunch you could snack on freshly baked ciabatta with fresh crayfish, wild rocket and lemon and herb mayonnaise, or enjoy heartier options such as spiced salmon fishcakes with a frisée and rocket salad and sweet chilli dipping sauce; or yellow Thai chicken and vegetable curry with wild rice, mango chutney, raita and naan bread. For more traditional tastes there might be roasted Cumberland sausage with clapshot mash and a garlic rosemary jus. An evening meal could begin with pressed ham hock terrine with honey-roasted figs and sweet grain mustard; or warm haddock, leek and gruyère tart with a wild rocket and pea shoot salad and chive cream vinaigrette, followed by whole pan-fried lemon sole with prawns, citrus butter and lemon thyme; or roast fillet of venison on caramelised parsnips with a bitter chocolate sauce. Desserts such as caramelised plum and almond tart with cinnamon ice cream cookies round it off in style.

MAP 12 TL55
High St CB2 4AG
☎ 01223 833800
e-mail: george@inter-mead.com
web: www.georgeinnbabraham.co.uk
dir: *In High St, just off A11/A505 & A1307*

Open 11.30–3 5.30–11 (Summer Sat-Sun 11.30–11)
Bar Meals L served all week 12–2.15 D served all week 6.30–9 (Food not served Sun eve in winter)
Restaurant L served all week 12–2.15 D served all week 6.30–9 (Food not served Sun eve in winter) Av 3 course à la carte £25
⊕ Free House ◀ Old Speckled Hen, Guinness, Greene King Abbot Ale. ♥ 8
Facilities Garden Parking

BROUGHTON continued

crushed potatoes and swede purée; roast cod with olive oil mash, roast fennel and caponata; or chargrilled vegetable skewer with couscous, coriander and harissa sauce.

Open 12–3 6–11 Closed: 1–11 Jan & Mon-Tue **Bar Meals** L served Wed-Sat 12–2 D served Wed-Sat 6.30–9 (Sun 12–4.30) **Restaurant** L served Wed-Sun 12–2 D served Wed-Sun 6.30–9 (Sun 12–4.30) ⊕ Free House ◼ Adnams Broadside, Elgoods Black Dog, Greene King IPA, City of Cambridge Hobson Choice. ♟ 10 **Facilities** Children's licence Garden Dogs allowed Parking

BYTHORN
MAP 12 TL07

Pick of the Pubs

The White Hart ♟

PE28 0QN ☎ 01832 710226 ◻ 01832 710226
e-mail: hartofby-thorn@btconnect.com
dir: *0.5m off A14 (Kettering-Huntingdon road)*

The White Hart, located in a peaceful village just off the A1/M1 link, is under the ownership of Jayne Masters and Justin Ackrill. The restaurant, The Hart of Bythorn (formerly known as Bennett's), has been extensively refitted. The menu is Anglo-French and changes on a monthly basis to take advantage of seasonal produce, supplemented by regular specials. Only the best quality ingredients are used by the team of chefs, and these are locally sourced wherever possible. There is a lot of history associated with the pub, beginning with John Brown who brewed his own beer on the premises in the early 19th century, where the ladies' toilets are now situated. Several people have seen a grey lady in old-fashioned dress walk in through the front wall of the pub, cross the bar and exit through the rear wall of the private dining/meeting room.

Open 12–3 6–11 (Sun 12–3, 6–10.30) Closed: Mon **Bar Meals** L served Tue-Sat 12–2 D served Tue-Sat 6–9 (Sun 12–2.30 6–8) Av main course £10 **Restaurant** L served Tue-Sat 12–2 D served Tue-Sat 6–9 (Sun 12–2.30, 6–8) Av 3 course à la carte £27.50 Av 3 course fixed price £17.95 ⊕ Free House ◼ Guinness. ♟ 6 **Facilities** Children's licence Garden Dogs allowed Parking

CAMBRIDGE
MAP 12 TL45

Pick of the Pubs

The Anchor ♟

Silver St CB3 9EL ☎ 01223 353554 ◻ 01223 327275
dir: *Telephone for directions*

Situated at the end of the medieval lane that borders Queens' College in the heart of the University city, this attractive waterside pub appeals to students and visitors alike. Hard by the bridge over the River Cam, in fine weather the riverside patio is an ideal spot for enjoying one of a range of good ales including guest beers while watching the activities on the water. The more adventurous can hire a punt for a leisurely trip to Grantchester (of Rupert Brooke and Jeffrey Archer fame), and on return sample a choice

of hearty meals from a range that includes lasagne, home-made pie, and roast beef.

Open 11–11 (Thu-Sat 11–12 Sun 12–11.30) Closed: 25 Dec **Bar Meals** L served all week 12–3 D served all week Av main course £5.50 ⊕ Greene King ◼ Greene King, IPA, Abbot Ale. ♟ 12 **Facilities** Dogs allowed

Cambridge Blue

85 Gwydir St CB1 2LG ☎ 01223 361382 ◻ 01223 505110
e-mail: c.lloyd13@ntlworld.com
dir: *In city centre*

Rowing memorabilia and pictures cover the walls of this convivial, community-spirited pub. There's an unexpectedly huge rear garden at the back, and noisy machines, including mobile phones, have no place within. Daily papers and local publications are provided, and the inn is presided over by Ajax, the resident Greek cat. Hearty regulars include Zorba pie (lamb, black olive and spinach); local sausages, mash and gravy; and Texas chilli.

Open 12–2.30 5.30–11 (Sat & Sun 12–3, Sun 6–10.30) **Bar Meals** L served all week 12–2.30 D served all week 6–9.30 (No food 25–Dec) Av main course £7 ⊕ Free House ◼ Woodforde's Wherry, Hobson's Choice, Adnams, Elgoods Black Dog Mild. **Facilities** Garden Dogs allowed Play Area

Free Press ♟

Prospect Row CB1 1DU ☎ 01223 368337
dir: *Telephone for directions*

Students, academics, locals and visitors rub shoulders in this atmospheric and picturesque back-street pub near the city centre. It has open fires and a beautiful walled garden – but no music, mobile phones or gaming machines. Punters are attracted by first-rate real ales and nourishing home-made food such as chilli with garlic bread; goat's cheese salad; filled toasted ciabattas; venison sausages; salmon filled with couscous and vegetables; and fresh pasta.

Open 12–2.30 6–11 (Sat 12–11, Sun 12–3, 7–10.30) Closed: 25–26 Dec, 1 Jan **Bar Meals** L served Mon-Fri 12–2 D served Mon-Sat 6–9 (wknds lunch 12–2.30) ⊕ Greene King ◼ Greene King IPA, Abbot Ale, Dark Mild plus guest ales. ♟ 10 **Facilities** Garden

DUXFORD
MAP 12 TL44

The John Barleycorn

3 Moorfield Rd CB2 4PP
☎ 01223 832699 ◻ 01223 832699
dir: *Turn off A505 into Duxford*

Traditional thatched and beamed English country pub situated close to Cambridge. Originally built as a coaching house in 1660, it was renamed once or twice, until 1858 when the current name was attached. The same menu is served throughout and ranges from a cheese sandwich to tournedos Rossini. Typical dishes are large leg of lamb in mint gravy, and chicken breast with garlic and herbs.

Open 11–11 (Sun 12–10.30) **Bar Meals** L served all week 12 D served all week 10 Av main course £8 ⊕ Greene King ◼ Greene King IPA, Abbot Ale, Old Speckled Hen, Ruddles Best & County. **Facilities** Garden Parking

ELSWORTH — MAP 12 TL36

The George & Dragon ♥

41 Boxworth Rd CB3 8JQ

☎ 01954 267236 📠 01954 267080

e-mail: www.georgeanddragon-elsworth.co.uk

dir: *SE of A14 between Cambridge & Huntingdon*

Set in a pretty village just outside Cambridge, this pub offers a wide range of satisfying food to locals and visitors alike. After a refurbishment there are even more fish dishes, daily specials and prime Scottish steaks on offer. Expect Mediterranean king prawns, and fresh cod, haddock or plaice from Lowestoft. For a lighter meal, ploughman's lunches and sandwiches are available. The Monday Night menus are always popular so booking is advised.

Open 11–3 6–11 (Sun 12–3, 6.30–10.30) **Bar Meals** L served Mon-Sat 12–2 D served Mon-Sat 6.30–9.30 (Sun 12–3, 6–9) Av main course £11.50 **Restaurant** L served all week 12–2 D served Mon-Sat 6.30–9.30 (Sun 12–2.30, 6–9) Av 3 course à la carte £23 ⊕ Free House ◄█ Greene King IPA, Ruddles County, Greene King Old Speckled Hen. ♥ 8 **Facilities** Garden Parking

---

ELTISLEY — MAP 12 TL25

The Leeds Arms

The Green PE19 6TG ☎ 01480 880283 📠 01480 880379

dir: *On A428 between Cambridge & St Neots*

Built towards the end of the 18th century and named after a local landowner, the Leeds Arms is a Charles Wells pub. A sample menu includes lamb shank with a mint jus, medallions of pork with Calvados sauce, chicken breast wrapped in bacon on mashed potatoes, and wild mushroom and avocado hotpot. Meat is sourced from an organic farm.

Open 11.30–2.30 6.30–11 **Bar Meals** L served all week 12–2 D served all week 6.30–9.45 Av main course £7.95 **Restaurant** L served all week 12–2 D served all week 6.30–9.45 (12–2, 7–9 on Sun) Av 3 course à la carte £15 ⊕ Charles Wells ◄█ Wells Smooth, 3 guest ales. **Facilities** Garden Dogs allowed Parking Play Area

---

ELTON — MAP 12 TL09

Pick of the Pubs

The Black Horse ♥

14 Overend PE8 6RU ☎ 01832 280240 & 280875

dir: *Off A605 (Peterborough to Northampton road)*

Antique furnishings and open log fires crank up the old world charm in this 17th-century inn, while the delightful one-acre rear garden overlooks Elton's famous church and rolling open countryside. The real ales include Everards Tiger, seasonal Nethergate brews, and Barnwell Bitter, which is brewed locally. The superb selection of food ranges from bar snacks to a full à la carte. Among the 'snacks' are sandwiches, filled baguettes jacket potatoes, a home-made pie of the day, and seasonal salads. Or you might start with portobello mushrooms topped with bacon and cheese gratin; or freshly dressed crab with brown bread and salad. Typical main courses include guinea fowl stuffed with black pudding and chorizo sausage, wrapped in Parma ham and served with a rich red wine jus; fillet of sea bass with braised pak choi, pesto and sun-blushed tomatoes; and bangers and mash.

Open 12 -11.30 **Bar Meals** L served all week 12–2 D served Mon-Sat 6–9 (Sun 12–3) Av main course £13.50 **Restaurant** L served all week 12–2 D served Mon-Sat 6–9 Av 3 course à la carte £25 ⊕ Free House ◄█ Bass, Everards Tiger, Nethergate, Barnwell Bitter. ♥ 14 **Facilities** Garden Dogs allowed Parking Play Area

The Crown Inn NEW ★★★★★ INN ♥

8 Duck St PE8 6RQ ☎ 01832 280232

e-mail: inncrown@googlemail.com

dir: *A1 junct 17, W on A605 signed Oundle/Northampton. After 3.5m turn right to Elton, 0.9m turn left signed Nassington, 0.3m on right*

In high summer The Crown, opposite the village green, is almost hidden by a beautiful chestnut tree. Chef/owner Marcus Lamb places great emphasis on the dining side, using locally sourced supplies for everything from sandwiches to Cambridge Smokery salmon and cream cheese; baked sea bass and red mullet with prawn and courgette risotto and creamy mussel sauce; venison with poached baby pear, braised red cabbage and redcurrant sauce; and beef, ale, carrot and mushroom pie.

Open 12–10.45 Closed: 1–2wks Jan Rest: 25 Dec bar only 12–2 (no food) **Bar Meals** L served Tue-Sat 12–2 D served Tue-Sat 6.30–8.45 (Sun 12–3) Av main course £10 **Restaurant** L served Tue-Sat 12–2 D served Fri & Sat 6.30–8.45 (Sun 12–3) Av 3 course à la carte £25 ⊕ Free House ◄█ Golden Crown Bitter, Greene King IPA, Deuchars IPA, Adnams & Jeffrey Hudson Bitter. ♥ 10 **Facilities** Children's licence Garden Dogs allowed Parking **Rooms** 4

ELY — MAP 12 TL58

Pick of the Pubs

The Anchor Inn ★★★★ RR ⊛ ♥

See Pick of the Pubs on opposite page

FEN DITTON — MAP 12 TL46

Pick of the Pubs

Ancient Shepherds ♥

High St CB5 8ST ☎ 01223 293280 📠 01223 293280

e-mail: ancientshepherds@hotmail.co.uk

dir: *From A14 take B1047 signed Cambridge/Airport*

Named after the ancient order of Shepherders who used to meet here, this heavily-beamed pub and restaurant was built originally as three cottages in 1540. The two bars, a lounge and a dining room all boast inglenook fireplaces. Located three miles from Cambridge in the riverside village of Fen Ditton, it provides a welcome escape for those who like to enjoy their refreshments without the addition of music, darts or pool. Among the fish dishes on the menu are fillet of sea bass on a bed of creamed leaks and home-made fishcakes. Meat eaters are equally well catered for with, among other items, half a casseroled guinea fowl in Burgundy with roast vegetables, Barnsley lamb chops, and pork loin steaks in cream and mustard sauce to choose from.

Open 12–3 6–11 (Mon, Fri-Sat 12–3, 6.30–11, Sun 12–5) Closed: 25–26 Dec **Bar Meals** L served all week 12–2 D served Tue-Sat 6.30–9 Av main course £9 **Restaurant** L served all week 12–2 D served Tue-Sat 6.30–9 Av 3 course à la carte £20 ⊕ Punch Taverns ◄█ Adnams Bitter, Greene King IPA. ♥ 8 **Facilities** Garden Dogs allowed Parking

The Anchor Inn

Sutton Gault lies on the western edge of the Isle of Ely, whose ancient cathedral stands high above the flat surrounding fens. Today this is rich agricultural country, but until the mid-17th century the fens were lawless and disease-ridden swamps, which is why, in 1630, the Earl of Bedford commissioned the Dutch engineer Cornelius Vermuyden to drain them.

Using a large contingent of Scottish prisoners of war, captured in a skirmish by Oliver Cromwell, he dug the Old and New Bedford Rivers. The Anchor was built to provide them with shelter, and it's been an inn ever since. Enter this family-run free house for a cosy atmosphere of scrubbed pine tables on gently undulating floors, evening candleglow and winter log fires. The inn continues to win wide recognition for its modern British cuisine with an emphasis on seasonal, traditional and local ingredients, notably hand-dressed Cromer crabs, Brancaster oysters and mussels, samphire, asparagus, smoked products from Bottisham and venison from the Denham Estate, together with pheasant, partridge, pigeon and wild duck in the winter. Menus may be adjusted daily to reflect a delivery of something special. The main menu is available lunchtimes and evenings and offers a typical three-course meal (taken on the riverside terrace, maybe) of grilled dates wrapped in bacon with mild grain mustard cream sauce; pork fillet with ginger cake stuffing in Parma ham with savoy cabbage and sage and onion sauce; home-made lemongrass pannacotta with sweet chilli and coconut sorbet; or unusual British farmhouse cheeses such as oven-baked Bottisham smoked camembert. Lighter lunches are available on weekdays. Plenty of wines by the glass from a long list. Some of the recently redecorated suites and rooms overlook the river.

★★★★ RR ® 🍷
MAP 12 TL58
Sutton Gault CB6 2BD
☎ 01353 778537
📠 01353 776180
e-mail: anchorinn@popmail.bta.com
dir: *From A14, B1050 to Earith, take B1381 to Sutton. Sutton Gault on left*

Open 12-3 7-11
Bar Meals L served all week 12–2 D served all week 7–9 (Sat 6.30–9.30) Av main course £13.50
Restaurant L served all week 12–2 D served all week 7–9 (Sat 6.30–9.30)
Free House · City of Cambridge Hobson's Choice, Boathouse Bitter. 🍷 12
Facilities Garden Parking
Rooms 4

FENSTANTON
MAP 12 TL36

King William IV ♟

High St PE28 9JF ☎ 01480 462467 📠 01480 468526
e-mail: mail@kingwilliampub.co.uk
dir: *Off A14 between Cambridge & Huntingdon (junct 27)*

Originally three 17th-century cottages, this rambling old inn stands next door to the clock tower in the heart of the village. Inside are low beams, a lively bar and the appropriately named Garden Room. Fresh food is cooked daily, with pork and leek sausages and King Bill vegetarian burger among the lunchtime options, while the à la carte menu offers the likes of lemon sole fillet, mignons of chicken fillet, and risotto of butternut squash.

Open 11–11 (Fri-Sat 11–1am, Sun 12–11) **Bar Meals** L served all week 12–9 D served all week 12–9 Av main course £7.50 **Restaurant** L served all week 12–2.30 D served all week 6–9 Av 3 course à la carte £26 Av 3 course fixed price £21.50 ⊕ Greene King ◖ Greene King Abbot Ale & IPA, guest ales. ♟9 **Facilities** Garden Dogs allowed Parking

FORDHAM
MAP 12 TL67

White Pheasant ♟

CB7 5LQ ☎ 01638 720414
e-mail: whitepheasant@whitepheasant.com
dir: *From Newmarket A142 to Ely, approx 5m to Fordham. Pub on left in village*

This 17th-century building stands in a fenland village between Ely and Newmarket. In recent years its considerable appeal has been subtly enhanced by improvements that preserve its period charm. Food is taken seriously here: the kitchen offers globally-influenced, traditional British dishes ranging from light bites to full à la carte meals. At the light end of the spectrum you might find the lunchtime deli plate; a salad of confit duck with orange and spring onion; or a Scottish smoked salmon croque monsieur on granary bread with vegetable crisps. A choice of 'old favourites' includes Suffolk ham with fried free range eggs and chips, while an evening meal could start with home-made local game paté with cranberry and caper relish and toasted brioche, followed by slow-roasted belly of free-range Suffolk pork with black pudding, Bramley apple, Pommery mustard mash and cider gravy. Appealing side dishes include spinach forestière and cauliflower cheese.

Open 12–3 6–11 (Sun 7–10.30) Closed: 26–29 Dec, 1 Jan **Bar Meals** L served all week 12–2.30 D served all week 7–9 **Restaurant** L served Mon-Sat 12–2.30 D served Mon-Sat 6–9.30 (Sun 12–2.30, 7–9) Av 3 course à la carte £27 ⊕ Free House ◖ Fenland Rabbit Poacher, Nethergate 3.9 & Brandon Rusty Bucket. ♟14 **Facilities** Garden Parking

FOWLMERE
MAP 12 TL44

The Chequers ♟

High St SG8 7SR ☎ 01763 208369 📠 01763 208944
e-mail: info@thechequersfowlmere.co.uk
dir: *From M11, A505, 2nd right to Fowlmere. 8m S of Cambridge, 4m E of Royston*

The pub dates from the 16th century, and was visited by Samuel Pepys in 1660, but the pub's sign – blue and red chequers – honours the British and American squadrons based nearby during World War II. These days the Chequers is known for its imaginative cooking served in the galleried restaurant, bar or attractive garden. Specials include trout and cod fishcakes with rocket salad, saffron and prawn sauce; and braised steak with bubble and squeak.

Open 12–3 6–11 Closed: 25–26 Dec eve & 1 Jan eve **Bar Meals** L served all week 12–2 D served Mon-Sat 7–9.30 (Sun 6.30–8) Av main course £13.95 **Restaurant** L served Mon-Sat 12–2 D served Mon-Sat 7–9.30 (Sun 12–3 & 6.30–8.30) Av 3 course à la carte £25 ⊕ Free House ◖ Adnams, Nethergate, Cottage, Buntingford & Archers. ♟20 **Facilities** Garden Parking

GOREFIELD
MAP 12 TF41

Woodmans Cottage

90 High Rd PE13 4NB ☎ 01945 870669 📠 01945 870669
e-mail: mdhigginson@aol.com
dir: *3m NW of Wisbech*

This friendly, family-run village pub stands in Cambridgeshire's Fenland, a mere 2m above the level of the sea nearly 10 miles away. It offers a good range of pub food, from lunchtime baguettes and jacket potatoes to bar snacks (chicken nachos with a salsa dip, beef teriyaki with mixed leaf salad), and main courses such as seared tuna steak with Lyonnaise potatoes, or steak and chips.

Open 11–2.30 7–11 Closed: 25 Dec **Bar Meals** L served Mon-Sat 12–2.30 D served Mon-Sat 6–10 (Sun 12–8) **Restaurant** L served Mon-Sat 12–2.30 D served Mon-Sat 6–10 (Sun 12–8) Av fixed price £12.50 ⊕ Free House ◖ Greene King IPA , Old Speckled Hen, Interbrew Worthington Bitter. **Facilities** Garden Dogs allowed Parking

GRANTCHESTER · MAP 12 TL45

The Rupert Brooke NEW ♟

2 Broadway CB3 9NQ ☎ 01223 840295 🖹 01223 841251
e-mail: info@therupertbrooke.com

Set in an idyllic location overlooking the meadows close to the River Cam, the Rupert Brooke is just five minutes from the centre of Cambridge. Inside, you'll find timber beams and winter log fires, with relaxing sofas and tub chairs. Watch the chefs at work in the theatre-style kitchen, creating their range of modern British dishes – winter squash and sage risotto; Grasmere Farm sausages with creamy mash; and poached smoked haddock are typical choices.

Open 11.30–3 6–11.30 (Sat-Sun, May-Aug all day) **Bar Meals** L served Mon-Sat 12–2.30 D served Mon-Fri 6–9.30 (all day summer, Sat-Sun 12–6, Sun 8 in summer) Av main course £9 **Restaurant** L served all week 12–2.30 D served Mon-Sat 6–9.30 (Sun 12–6, 8 in summer) ⊕ Enterprise Inns ◀ Harveys Sussex Best, Woodforde's Wherry, London Pride & Timothy Taylor Landlord. ♟ 12 **Facilities** Children's licence Garden Parking

---

GREAT CHISHILL · MAP 12 TL43

The Pheasant ♟

24 Heydon Rd SG8 8SR ☎ 01763 838535

dir: *Off B1039 between Royston & Saffron Walden*

Stunning views and roaring log fires characterise this traditional village free house, where Nethergates' and Greene King ales easily outsell lager. There are no gaming machines or piped music to disturb the friendly, sociable bar, and children under 14 are not allowed in. In summer, bird song holds sway in the idyllic pub garden. Freshly-made sandwiches come complete with chips and salad garnish, whilst home-made dishes like rabbit casserole, poached haddock, or wild mushroom lasagne cater for larger appetites.

Open 12–3 6–11 (Sat 12–12, Sun 12–10.30) **Bar Meals** L served all week 12–2 D served all week 6–9.30 Av main course £9 **Restaurant** L served all week 12–2 D served all week 6–9.30 ⊕ Free House ◀ Nethergates IPA & Umbel Ale, Greene King IPA. ♟ 8 **Facilities** Garden Dogs allowed Parking

---

HEMINGFORD GREY · MAP 12 TL27

The Cock Pub and Restaurant ♟

47 High St PE28 9BJ ☎ 01480 463609 🖹 01480 461747
e-mail: cock@cambscuisine.com

dir: *2m S of Huntingdon and 1m E of A14*

There's been a spring in the step of this village pub since Oliver Thain and Richard Bradley arrived a few years ago. Transforming it into an award-winning dining pub, they've retained traditional values, with well kept real ales, log fires blazing when the weather demands, and a welcome for walkers, children and dogs. In the wooden-floored restaurant fresh fish, including pan-fried halibut fillets, and chef's various home-made sausages, may prove irresistible.

Open 11.30–3 6–11 (Sun 12–4, 6.30–10.30) **Restaurant** L served all week 12–2.30 D served Mon-Thu 6.30–9 (Fri-Sat 6.30–9.30, Sun 6.30–8.30) Av 3 course à la carte £24 Av 3 course fixed price £15 ⊕ Free House ◀ Golden Jackal, Wolf Brewery, Victoria Bitter, Buntingford Highwayman IPA. ♟ 13 **Facilities** Children's licence Garden Dogs allowed Parking

---

HILDERSHAM · MAP 12 TL54

The Pear Tree ♟

CB1 6BU ☎ 01223 891680
e-mail: peartreeinn@btconnect.com

dir: *5m E of Cambridge, take A1307 to Haverhill, turn left to Hildersham*

Popular with walkers and locals alike, the Pear Tree is every inch the traditional village pub, set opposite the village green with beams and a stone floor inside and a country garden outside. It has a well-deserved reputation for its home-cooked food – perhaps deep-fried brie wedges wrapped in filo pastry with a gooseberry dip, followed by oven-baked fresh trout with fresh vegetables. Typical desserts are Bakewell tart, and bread and butter pudding.

Open 12–2 6.30–11 (Fri-Sat 12–2, 6–11, Sun 12–4, 7–10.30) **Bar Meals** L served Wed-Sat 12–2 D served Wed-Sat 6.30–9.30 (Sun 12–4, 7–9) Av main course £7 ⊕ Greene King ◀ Greene King IPA & Abbot Ale. ♟ 12 **Facilities** Garden Dogs allowed Parking

---

HILTON · MAP 12 TL26

The Prince of Wales ★★★ INN ♟

Potton Rd PE28 9NG ☎ 01480 830257

dir: *On B1040 between A14 & A428 S of St Ives*

The Prince of Wales is a traditional, 1830s-built, two-bar village inn with four comfortable bedrooms. Food options range from bar snacks to full meals, among which are grills, fish, curries brought in from a local Indian restaurant, and daily specials, such as lamb hotpot. Home-made puddings include crème brûlée and sherry trifle. The village's 400-year-old grass maze was where locals used to escape the devil.

Open 11–2.30 6–11 **Bar Meals** L served Tue-Sun 12–2 D served all week 7–9 **Restaurant** L served all week 12–2 D served Tue-Sun 7–9 ⊕ Free House ◀ Adnams, Timothy Taylor Landlord, Smoothflow, Worthingtons. ♟ 9 **Facilities** Children's licence Garden Parking **Rooms** 4

HINXTON
MAP 12 TL44

The Red Lion ♀

32 High St CB10 1QY ☎ 01799 530601 📠 01799 531201
e-mail: info@redlionhinxton.co.uk

dir: *1m from M11 junct 9.*

The Red Lion has been in Hinxton, a conservation village, since the 16th century. The bar is in the oldest part, while the spacious oak-built extension is the dining room. Pub policy is always to use fresh local produce where possible to create amply-proportioned dishes such as maize-fed chicken breast with tomato confit, purple-sprouting broccoli and sweet potato fondant; and fillet of turbot with oyster and sorrel sauce, lentil and spinach fritter and tarragon wild rice.

Open 11–3 6–11 (Sun 12–4.30, 7–10.30) **Bar Meals** L served Mon-Sat 12–2 D served Sun-Thu 6.45–9 (Sun 12–2.30, Fri-Sat 6.45–9.30) **Restaurant** L served Mon-Sat 12–2 D served Sun-Thu 6.45–9 (Sun 12–2.30, Fri-Sat 6.45–9.30) ⊕ Free House ◀ Adnams, Greene King IPA, Woodforde's Wherry, plus guest ales including Nethergates & Hobsons Choice. ♀ 12 **Facilities** Children's licence Garden Dogs allowed Parking

HOLYWELL
MAP 12 TL37

The Old Ferryboat Inn ⓐ ★★ HL ♀

Back Ln PE27 4TG ☎ 01480 463227 📠 01480 463245

dir: *A14 then right onto A1096 then A1123 right to Holywell*

Renowned as England's oldest inn, built some time in the 11th century, but with a hostelry history that goes back to the 6th. The Old Ferryboat has immaculately maintained thatch, white stone walls, and cosy interior. A pleasant atmosphere – despite the resident ghost of a lovelorn teenager – in which to enjoy hot chicken curry, roast rack of lamb, steak and ale pie, fish and chips, and Greene King ales.

Open 11.30–11 **Bar Meals** L served all week 12–2.30 D served all week 6–9.30 (Sun 12–2.30, 6–9) Av main course £8.95 ⊕ Old English Inns ◀ Greene King Abbot Ale/IPA, Old Speckled Hen, guest ales. ♀ 6 **Facilities** Garden Parking **Rooms** 7

HUNTINGDON
MAP 12 TL27

The Three Horseshoes ⓤ ♀

Moat Ln, Abbots Ripton PE28 2PA
☎ 01487 773440 📠 01487 773440
e-mail: abbotsripton@aol.com

Dating back to1654 and retaining many original features, the picturesque Three Horseshoes once had the lowest ceiling of any pub in the county. Stepping inside today, customers are greeted by three bar areas, a restaurant and a range of hand pumped Adnams real ales. Typical food includes Sunday roasts like rib of beef with Yorkshire pudding; roast loin of pork with crackling and apple sauce; and grilled tuna steak.

Open 11.30–3 6–11 Closed: Mon **Bar Meals** L served Tue-Sat 12–2 D served Tue-Sat 6.30–9.30 (Sun 12–2.30, 6.30–9) **Restaurant** L served Tue-Sat 12–2 D served Tue-Sat 6.30–9.30 (Sun 12–2.30) ◀ Adnams Bitter, Adnams Broadside, Oakhams JHB. ♀ 12 **Facilities** Garden Parking **Rooms** 5

KEYSTON
MAP 11 TL07

Pick of the Pubs

Pheasant Inn ◉ ♀

Village Loop Rd PE28 0RE
☎ 01832 710241 📠 01832 710340
e-mail: info@thepheasant-keyston.co.uk

dir: *Signed from A14, W of Huntingdon*

A charming 15th-century, thatched free house in a sleepy farming village. The traditional bar has all the oak beams, big open fires and simple wooden furniture you could wish for. Three distinct dining areas offer a choice of comfortable, intimate and relaxed places to eat and drink. In fine weather you can enjoy the garden at the rear of the pub, or sit on one of the benches at the front of the building. Expect good things of the food; owners Jay and Taffeta have worked in highly rated London restaurants. Style-wise, it is an eclectic mix, with strong influences from the south of France. Whet your appetite with a rhubarb Bellini before kicking off with fish soup with rouille, followed by braised goat with olives, carrots and coriander, pommes anna and spring greens. Three Suffolk real ales are always on offer, alongside a widely acclaimed wine list.

Open 12–3 6–11 Closed: Mon (ex BH) **Bar Meals** L served Tue-Sun 12–2.30 D served Tue-Sun 6.30–9.30 **Restaurant** L served Tue-Sun 12–2.30 D served Tue-Sun 6.30–9.30 ⊕ Huntsbridge ◀ Adnams, Village Bike Potton Brewery, Augustinian Nethergate Brewery. ♀ 16 **Facilities** Garden Parking

KIMBOLTON
MAP 12 TL16

The New Sun Inn ♀

20–22 High St PE28 0HA
☎ 01480 860052 📠 01480 869353
e-mail: newsunninn@btinternet.com

dir: *From A1 N, B645 for 7m, From A1 S B661 for 7m, From A14 B660 for 5m*

An impressive array of flowers greets visitors to this 16th-century inn near Kimbolton Castle. As well as being a real ale pub, it offers a good choice of wines by the glass. Dishes from the restaurant menu include king prawns in hot garlic and ginger oil, or whole baked Camembert to start, then venison sausages with grain mustard mash or home-made steak and kidney pudding as mains. Lighter meals, such as jacket potatoes or sandwiches are also available.

Open 11–2.30 6–11 (Sun all day) **Bar Meals** L served all week 12–2.15 D served Tue-Sat 7–9.30 **Restaurant** L served Tue-Sun 12–2 D served Tue-Sat 7–9.30 ⊕ Charles Wells ◀ Wells Bombardier & Eagle IPA, Greene King Old Speckled Hen. ♀ 12 **Facilities** Garden Dogs allowed

LITTLE WILBRAHAM
MAP 12 TL55

Hole in the Wall ◉ ♀

2 High St CB1 5JY ☎ 01223 812282

When only the gentry were allowed entry to this pub, local farm workers had to order and collect their beer through a hole in the wall. Today the pub welcomes all comers with a regular real ale and changing guests from local micro-breweries. The same honest menu applies whether customers choose to eat in the bar with open fire, the snug with coal range, or the main dining room. Try the Welsh rarebit with Fulbourn ham.

Open 11.30–3 6.30–11 (Closed Sun eve & Mon ex BH lunch)
Bar Meals L served Tue-Sun 12–2 D served Tue-Sat **Restaurant** L served Tue-Sun 12–2 D served Tue-Sat ⊕ Free House ◧ Woodforde's Wherry, Brewers Gold, Cambridge Bitter, Sparta. ♀9 **Facilities** Garden Dogs allowed Parking

MADINGLEY   MAP 12 TL36

Pick of the Pubs

The Three Horseshoes ⊛ ♀

High St CB3 8AB ☎ 01954 210221 ▤ 01954 212043
e-mail: thethreehorseshoes@huntsbridge.co.uk
dir: *M11 junct 13, 1.5m from A14*

This picturesque thatched inn enjoys a charming location; its large garden extends towards meadowland and the local cricket pitch. Inside is a small, bustling bar and a pretty conservatory restaurant. Chef-Patron Richard Stokes is a local from the fens who has eaten his way around the world, and his success can be gauged by the long queues for tables. Richard's own style is a modern take on Italian cuisine, characterised by seasonal and imaginative dishes with intense flavours. After antipasti, you could try gnocchi with salsa osso buco and gremolata, followed by chargrilled monkfish with grilled polenta, mixed leaves and anchovy-rosemary sauce; or perhaps rabbit cooked with sage, garlic and balsamic vinegar with olive oil mashed potatoes and roasted carrots and leeks. Desserts might include pannacotta or lemon tart with crème fraîche sorbet. Prior booking is advisable.

Open 11.30–3 6–11 (Sun 6–8.30) **Bar Meals** L served Mon-Fri 12–2 D served Mon-Fri 6.30–9.30 (Sat-Sun 12–2.30, Sun 6–8.30)
Restaurant L served Mon-Fri 12–2 D served Mon-Sat 6.30–9.30 (Sat-Sun 12–2.30) ◧ Adnams Bitter, Hook Norton Old Hooky, Smile's Best, Cambridge Hobsons Choice. ♀20 **Facilities** Garden Parking

MILTON   MAP 12 TL46

Waggon & Horses

39 High St CB4 6DF ☎ 01223 860313
e-mail: winningtons.waggon@ntlworld.com
dir: *A14/A10 junct. Past Tesco, through village, approx 1m set back on left*

Elgood Brewery's most southerly house, the pub is an imposing mock-Tudor building famed for its large collection of hats. Real cider is also served, from local producer Cassels. A challenging quiz is set on Wednesday nights and baltis are the speciality on Thursdays. All meals are good value and the chilli is particularly recommended. Bar billiards is popular inside, and outside there is a large child-safe garden with a slide, swings and a pétanque terrain.

Open 12–2.30 5–11 (Fri 5–12, Sat 6–11.30, Sun 7–10.30)
Bar Meals L served all week 12–2 D served all week 7–9 Av main course £5 **Restaurant** L served all week 12–2 D served all week 7–9 ◧ Elgoods Cambridge Bitter, Black Dog Mild, Golden Newt, and seasonal & guest ales.
Facilities Garden Dogs allowed Parking

NEWTON   MAP 12 TL44

The Queen's Head ♀

Fowlmere Rd CB22 7PG ☎ 01223 870436
dir: *6m S of Cambridge on B1368, 1.5m off A10 at Harston, 4m from A505*

Best described as 'quintessentially English' this 17th-century pub has been run by the same family since 1962. They continue to steadfastly ban fruit machines and piped music from the two small bars. Lunches are limited to home-made soup, Aga-baked potatoes, toast with beef dripping, and sandwiches. In the evening it's just soup and cold platters. There's no specials board since, as the landlord says, 'We have no specialist'!

Open 11.30–2.30 6–11 (Sun 12–2.30, 7–10.30) Closed: 25–26 Dec
Bar Meals L served Mon-Sat 11.30–2.15 D served Mon-Sat 7–9.30 (Sun 7–9.30) Av main course £4 ⊕ Free House ◧ Adnams Southwold, Broadside, Fisherman, Bitter & Regatta. ♀8 **Facilities** Dogs allowed Parking **Notes** ⊛

PETERBOROUGH   MAP 12 TL19

The Brewery Tap ♀

80 Westgate PE1 2AA ☎ 01733 358500 ▤ 01733 310022
e-mail: brewerytap@hotmail.com
dir: *Opposite bus station*

This is the home of multi-award-winning Oakham Ales, moved here from their home in Rutland when Peterborough's spacious old labour exchange opened its doors as the Brewery Tap in 1998. Visitors to this striking pub can see the day-to-day running of the brewery through a glass wall spanning half the length of the bar. As if the appeal of the beer range were not enough, Thai chefs beaver away producing delicious snacks, soups, salads, stir-fries and curries.

Open 12–11 (Fri-Sat 12–late) Closed: 25–26 Dec, 1 Jan
Bar Meals L served Sun-Thu 12–2.30 D served Sun-Thu 6–9.30 (Fri-Sat 12–10.30) Av main course £9 **Restaurant** L served Sun-Thu 12–2.30 D served Sun-Thu 6–9.30 (Fri-Sat 12–10.30) Av 3 course à la carte £16 Av 2 course fixed price £12.99 ⊕ Free House ◧ Oakham, Jeffery Hudson Bitter, Bishops Farewell & White Dwarf, Elgoods Black Dog & 7 guest ales. ♀7 **Facilities** Children's licence Dogs allowed

Charters Bar & East Restaurant

Upper Deck, Town Bridge PE1 1FP
☎ 01733 315700 & 315702 For Bkgs ▤ 01733 315700
e-mail: manager@charters-bar.co.uk
dir: *A1/A47 Wisbech, 2m for city centre & town bridge (River Nene). Barge moored at Town Bridge (west side).*

A 176-foot converted barge, Charters promises 'brews, blues and fine views'. It motored from Holland across the North Sea in 1991, and is moored in the heart of Peterborough on the River Nene. Twelve hand pumps dispense a continually changing repertoire of real ales, while Friday and Saturday nights welcome live music lovers to the late night blues club. The East part of the name applies to the oriental restaurant on the upper deck.

Open 12–11.30 (Fri-Sat 12–5am dependent on trade) Closed: 25–26 Dec, 1 Jan **Bar Meals** L served all week 12–3.30 Av main course £5.95 **Restaurant** L served Mon-Sat 12–2.30 D served all week 5.30–10.30 (Sun 12–3.30) Av 2 course fixed price £8.95 ⊕ Free House ◧ Oakham JHB, Oakham White Dwarf & Bishops Farewell, Elgoods Black Dog.
Facilities Children's licence Garden Dogs allowed

England

REACH
MAP 12 TL56

Dyke's End NEW ♀
CB25 0JD ☎ 01638 743816

In 1996/7 villagers saved this pub from closure and ran it as a co-operative until 2003, when it was bought by Frank Feehan, who has further refurbished and extended it. Frank's additions include the Devil's Dyke microbrewery, which produces four real ales, including a strong mild. The pub's local reputation for the quality of its food means restaurant booking is strongly advised, particularly at weekends. A fenced front garden overlooks the village green.

Open 12–3 6–11 Closed: Mon lunch **Bar Meals** L served Tue-Sun 12–2 D served Tue-Sat 7–9 Av main course £10 **Restaurant** L served Tue-Sun 12–2 D served Tue-Sat 7–9 Av 3 course à la carte £22 ⊕ Free House
🍺 Devil's Dyke microbrewery beer, Woodfordes Wherry, Adnams Bitter. ♀8
Facilities Garden Dogs allowed Parking Play Area

SPALDWICK
MAP 12 TL17

Pick of the Pubs

The George Inn ♀
High St PE28 0TD ☎ 01480 890293 🖺 01480 896847
dir: 6m W of Huntingdon on A14, junct 18 towards Spaldwick/Stow Longa

Refurbished to create a pleasing blend of traditional and modern, this fine old building retains historic features such as original beams and fireplaces. It started life as a large private residence belonging to the Dartington family, and became a coaching inn in 1679. Today it remains a serene presence beside the manor house, overlooking the village green. The bar is relaxing with its comfortable leather sofas, while the restaurant, set in a beautifully converted barn, offers a pleasing selection of traditional British and Mediterranean-influenced dishes. Typical choices include a starter of crispy duck salad with spicy chorizo, bacon lardons, croutons and plum dressing, followed by wood pigeon breasts with herb dumplings, mash, red cabbage and a chocolate red wine sauce. Finish with apple crumble tart or a delightful selection of cheeses. A good choice of wines is available by the glass, and there are plenty of well-kept real ales.

Open 12–11 (Fri-Sat 12–12) **Bar Meals** L served all week 12–2.30 D served all week 6–9.30 Av main course £11.95 **Restaurant** L served all week 12–2.30 D served all week 6–9.30 Av 3 course à la carte £25 ⊕ Punch Taverns 🍺 Adnams Broadside, Greene King IPA, Youngs Special. ♀25 **Facilities** Children's licence Garden Parking

STILTON
MAP 12 TL18

Pick of the Pubs

The Bell Inn Hotel ★★★ HL ◉ ♀
Great North Rd PE7 3RA
☎ 01733 241066 🖺 01733 245173
e-mail: reception@thebellstilton.co.uk
dir: From A1 follow signs for Stilton. Hotel on main road in village centre

The magnificent sign hanging outside the inn is a replica of the 16th-century original. Astonishingly, with its ornate wrought iron supporting bracket, it weighs two and three quarter tonnes. Samplers of the Bell's delights have included highwayman Dick Turpin, the Duke of Marlborough, Lord Byron and, more recently, Clark Gable and Joe Louis, who were stationed nearby with the USAF in World War II. But place of honour must go to stilton cheese, first served here in the early 1700s. The galleried restaurant is particularly atmospheric, offering steamed loin of monkfish; roast partridge breast; and home-made tagliatelle, while the more contemporary bistro is likely to present devilled calves' kidneys with champ potato and savoy cabbage; steamed fillet of salmon on roast pumpkin, sweet potato and kale with lemon butter sauce; and chick pea, spinach and feta cheese bake with herb oat topping and rocket salad.

Open 12–2.30 6–11 (Fri-Sat 6–12, Sat-Sun 12–3, Sun 7–11) Closed: 25 Dec **Bar Meals** L served Mon-Sat 12–2.15 D served Mon-Sat 6–9.30 (Sun 12–2.30, 7–9) Av main course £12.95 **Restaurant** L served Mon-Fri 12–2.15 D served all week 7–9.30 (Sun 12–2) Av 2 course fixed price £21.95 ⊕ Free House 🍺 Greene King Abbot Ale, Oakham JHB, Fuller's London Pride, Greene King IPA. ♀8 **Facilities** Garden Parking **Rooms** 22

STRETHAM
MAP 12 TL57

The Lazy Otter
Cambridge Rd CB6 3LU ☎ 01353 649780 🖺 01353 649314
e-mail: restaurant@lazy.otter.com
dir: Telephone for directions

Just off the A10 between Ely and Cambridge, the Lazy Otter stands overlooking the marina beside the River Great Ouse. There's been a pub on this site since the 18th century, but the old building was redeveloped in 1986; today, the large beer garden and riverside restaurant are popular summer attractions. Lunchtime brings baguettes, sandwiches and jacket potatoes, whilst main course choices include ham and eggs; baked cod au gratin; and home-made spinach lasagne.

Open 11–11 **Bar Meals** L served Mon-Sat 12–2 D served Mon-Sat 6–9 (Sun 12–7) Av main course £7.50 **Restaurant** L served Mon-Sat 12–2 D served Mon-Sat 6–9 (Sun 12–7) ◀ Greene King IPA, Morland Original, Ruddles & guest ales. **Facilities** Garden Parking Play Area

CHESHIRE

ALDFORD
MAP 15 SJ45

Pick of the Pubs

The Grosvenor Arms ♀

Chester Rd CH3 6HJ
☎ 01244 620228 📄 01244 620247
e-mail: grosvenor.arms@brunningandprice.co.uk
dir: *On B5130 S of Chester*

Sometimes described as a 'large, rather austere Victorian governess of a building', the Grosvenor was the work of a locally infamous mid-Victorian architect who, in the name of progress, destroyed many fine medieval buildings in and around Chester. It is endearing nonetheless, and viewed from the garden it's a delight of higgledy-piggledy rooflines and soft, warm Cheshire brick. The spacious, open-plan interior includes an airy conservatory and a panelled, book-filled library. On the bistro-style menu are a range of sandwiches and unusual starters such as oxtail potato cake with poached egg; and seared squid with lightly spiced couscous. Main courses range from straightforward cottage or fish pie, to rump of lamb or duck breast served with crushed dauphinoise potatoes. Desserts include the ever-popular bread and butter pudding, served here with apricot syrup. An outside terrace leads into a small but pleasing garden which, in turn, takes you out to the village green.

Open 11.30–11 (Sun 12–10.30) **Bar Meals** L served Mon-Sat 12–10 D served Mon-Sat 12–10 (Sun 12–9) ⊕ Free House ◀ Weetwood-Eastgate, Caledonian Deuchars IPA, Phoenix Arizona, Thwaites Original. ♀ 20 **Facilities** Garden Dogs allowed Parking

ASTON
MAP 15 SJ64

Pick of the Pubs

The Bhurtpore Inn ♀

See Pick of the Pubs on page 68

BARTHOMLEY
MAP 15 SJ75

The White Lion Inn

CW2 5PG ☎ 01270 882242
dir: *Telephone for directions*

Dating from 1614, this half-timbered and thatched inn with character bars is in a lovely rural setting, and has associations with the English Civil War. It offers home-cooked food like hotpot, lasagne, cottage pie, 'hot beef' baguettes, sirloin and stilton on French stick, and a selection of sandwiches.

Open 11.30–11 (Sun 12–10.30) **Bar Meals** L served all week 12–2 (Sun 12–2.30) Av main course £5 ⊕ Burtonwood ◀ Marstons Bitter, Marstons Pedigree, Mansfield Banks, plus guest. **Facilities** Garden Dogs allowed Parking

BOLLINGTON
MAP 16 SJ97

The Church House Inn ♀

Church St SK10 5PY ☎ 01625 574014 📄 01625 562026
e-mail: info@the-church-house-inn.co.uk
dir: *From A34 take A538 towards Macclesfield. Through Prestbury, then follow Bollington signs*

Exposed beams, log fires and agricultural decorations lend a homely feel to this stone-built village free house, which hit the headlines when it was bought by a group of local residents. The varied menu includes home-made soup, the inn's own sausages and pies, and other traditional British favourites. Vegetarian options feature on the daily specials board. The pub also has a small enclosed beer garden.

Open 12–3 5.30–11 (Fri-Sun all day) **Bar Meals** L served all week 12–2.30 D served all week 6.30–9.30 **Restaurant** L served all week 12–2.30 D served all week 6–9.30 Av 3 course à la carte £15 Av 3 course fixed price £7.50 ⊕ Free House ◀ Greene King IPA, Black Sheep, Interbrew Boddington's. ♀ 18 **Facilities** Parking

BROXTON
MAP 15 SJ45

The Copper Mine

Nantwich Rd CH3 9JH ☎ 01829 782293
e-mail: geoff@the-coppermine.freeserve.co.uk
dir: *At Sainsbury's rdbt take A41 (Whitchurch), left at next rdbt onto Nantwich A534, 1m, pub on right.*

A well known food venue, this pub is convenient for Cheshire Ice Cream Farm, Beeston Castle, and the Candle Factory at Cheshire Workshops. Sit in the conservatory to make the most of the beautiful

CONTINUED

PICK OF THE PUBS

ASTON-CHESHIRE

The Bhurtpore Inn

The George family has a bit of a thing about this traditional village pub. In 1849 James George leased it from the local Combermere estate, from which descendant Philip George bought it in 1895, only to sell it six years later to a Crewe brewery.

Ninety years later, in 1991, Simon and Nicky George were looking to buy their first pub and came across the boarded-up, stripped-out Bhurtpore. It ticked just about every box. Although it has been a pub since at least 1778, it was the 1826 Siege of Bhurtpore in India, where Lord Combermere had distinguished himself, that inspired its current name. With eleven real ales always available, a large selection of bottled beers and seven continental beers on tap, it is truly a free house. The award-winning food is fresh, home made and reasonably priced, both in the bar and the restaurant. Starters include spicy lamb samosas with yogurt and mint dip; potato skins with grilled cheese and bacon topping; and pork and black pudding patties with coarse grain mustard and apple sauce. In addition to typical mains such as steak, kidney and real ale pie, and breaded wholetail scampi, there is a good choice of specials, such as lamb fillet wrapped in pastry with port and cranberry sauce; fish and king prawn pie with mushrooms, egg and spring onion mash; and buffalo mozzarella with garlic bread. Finish with spiced raisin and ginger pudding with toffee sauce, or a local farmhouse ice cream. Behind the pub is a lawn with countryside views. Very much at the centre of the local community, the pub is home to an enthusiastic cricket team, a group of cyclists known as the Wobbly Wheels and, once a month, folk musicians.

🍷
MAP 15 SJ64
Wrenbury Rd CW5 8DQ
☎ 01270 780917
e-mail:
simonbhurtpore@yahoo.co.uk
dir: *Just off A530 between Nantwich & Whitchurch. Turn towards Wrenbury at x-rds in village*

Open 12–2.30 6.30–11.30 (Sun 12–11) Closed: 25–26 Dec, 1 Jan
Bar Meals L served all week 12–2 D served all week 6.45–9.30 (Sun 12–9) Av main course £9.50
Restaurant L served all week 12–2 D served all week 6.45–9.30 (Sun 12–9) Av 3 course à la carte £18.50
🌐 Free House 🍺 Salopian Golden Thread, Abbeydale Absolution, Weetwood Oasthouse Gold, Copper Dragon Golden Pippin. 🍷 10
Facilities Garden Dogs allowed Parking

BROXTON continued

views, or in summer, enjoy the patio and lawn with mature trees. Meals range from salads, sandwiches and omelettes through to main dishes such as salmon and broccoli fish cakes with a pink Caesar dressing or home-made steak burger with chips.

Open 12–3 6–11 **Bar Meals** L served Tue-Sun 12–2.30 D served Tue-Sun 6.30–9.30 Av main course £7.95 **Restaurant** L served Tue-Sun 12–2.30 D served Tue-Sun 6.30–9.30 ⊕ Free House ◀ Marstons Cream Flow, Pedigree & Banks Real Ale. **Facilities** Garden Parking Play Area

---

BUNBURY   MAP 15 SJ55

Pick of the Pubs

The Dysart Arms ♈

Bowes Gate Rd CW6 9PH
☎ 01829 260183 📠 01829 261286
e-mail: dysart.arms@brunningandprice.co.uk
dir: *Between A49 & A51, by Shropshire Union Canal*

A truly classic English village pub, built as a farmhouse in the mid-18th century, and licensed since the late 1800s. Around its central bar are several airy rooms with solid wooden tables and chairs, tiled and wooden floors, lovely open fires and a couple of large bookcases. From the terrace and immaculate garden there are views of Peckforton Castle one way, and Beeston Castle the other. Home-grown herbs are used in an appetising menu offering starters like black olive and artichoke tart, and warm goats' cheese with honey dressing. Among the main courses are steak, kidney and oyster pudding; seafood gratin; local Bunbury bangers; pan-fried duck breasts; and sweet pepper and pepper bake.

Open 11.30–11 (Sun 12–10.30) **Bar Meals** L served Mon-Sat 12 D served Mon-Sat 9.30 (Sun 12–9) ⊕ Free House ◀ Phoenix Struggling Monkey, Weetwood Eastgate, Thwaites Bitter, Roosters Yankee. ♈14 **Facilities** Garden Dogs allowed Parking

---

BURLEYDAM   MAP 15 SJ64

The Combermere Arms ♈

SY13 4AT ☎ 01948 871223 📠 01948 661371
e-mail: combermere.arms@brunningandprice.co.uk
dir: *From Whitchurch take A525 towards Nantwich, at Newcastle/Audlem/Woore sign, turn right at junct. Pub 100yds on right*

Popular with local shoots, walkers and town folk alike, this busy 17th-century inn retains great character and warmth. Three roaring fires complement the wealth of oak, pictures and old furniture. Dishes range from light bites and sandwiches to plates of grilled halibut or venison and pheasant casserole; and puddings like ginger sponge with custard. Of special note are the wine list with nearly 70 to choose from, and a cheese selection of rare and award-winning quality.

Open 12–11 **Bar Meals** L served all week 12–9.30 D served all week 12–9.30 **Restaurant** L served all week ⊕ Free House ◀ Woodlands Oak Beauty, Weetwood Cheshire Cat, Thornbridge Jaipur Monsoon, St Austells Tribute & Storm Hurricane Hubert. ♈15 **Facilities** Garden Dogs allowed Parking

---

BURWARDSLEY   MAP 15 SJ55

Pick of the Pubs

The Pheasant Inn ★★ HL ♈

See Pick of the Pubs on page 70

CHESTER   MAP 15 SJ46

Pick of the Pubs

Albion Inn

See Pick of the Pubs on page 72

Old Harkers Arms ♈

1 Russell St CH1 5AL ☎ 01244 344525 📠 01244 344812
e-mail: harkers.arms@brunningandprice.co.uk
dir: *Follow steps down from City Road onto canal path*

A buzzy meeting place with the feel of a gentlemen's club, this former Victorian warehouse on the Shropshire Union Canal is one of Chester's more unusual pubs. The bar offers over 120 malt whiskies, 24 wines by the glass, and hand pumps dispensing four regular and six guest ales. The daily-changing menu runs from light dishes such as breaded tiger prawns with pineapple salsa, through to main courses of braised lamb shoulder or Gloucester Old Spot sausages.

Open 11.30–11 (Sun 12–10.30) Closed: 25–26 Dec **Bar Meals** L served all week 12 D served all week 9.30 Av main course £10 ◀ Weetwood Cheshire Cat, Flowers Original, Wapping Bitter, Titanic Stout & Spitting Feathers. ♈24 **Facilities** Dogs allowed

---

CHOLMONDELEY   MAP 15 SJ55

Pick of the Pubs

The Cholmondeley Arms ♈

SY14 8HN ☎ 01829 720300 📠 01829 720123
e-mail: guy@cholmondeleyarms.co.uk
dir: *On A49, between Whitchurch & Tarporley*

This attractive and elegant pub was once the village school, and it remained closed until 1988 when the current owners, with the help of Lord and Lady Cholmondeley, residents of the nearby castle, embarked on its conversion. Since reopening it has won many regional, and even national, trade and newspaper awards. All food is freshly prepared, wherever possible using local produce. From its daily changing menu come hot baked prawns in sour cream and garlic; Jerusalem artichoke hummus with rosemary bruschetta; and, at lunchtimes only, devilled kidneys on toast. Usually appearing in the main courses section are braised oxtail in red wine sauce; smoked haddock fishcakes with devilled tomato sauce; leek and cheddar soufflé; hot Madras beef curry with rice and chutneys; and rack of lamb with onion and mint sauce. Going on a Sunday? Then expect roast rib-eye of beef with Yorkshire pudding and horseradish cream. Home-made puddings are a speciality.

Open 11–3 6–11 Closed: 25 Dec **Bar Meals** L served all week 12–2.30 D served all week 6.30–10 Av main course £10 **Restaurant** L served all week 12–2.30 D served all week 6.30–10 ⊕ Free House ◀ Marston's Pedigree, Adnams Bitter, Banks's, Everards Tiger Best. ♈7 **Facilities** Garden Dogs allowed Parking Play Area

PICK OF THE PUBS

BURWARDSLEY-CHESHIRE

The Pheasant Inn

This 300–year-old sandstone and half-timbered former farmhouse is set in beautiful rural surroundings, yet 15 minutes in the car will take you to the historic centre of Chester. Sitting aloft the Peckforton Hills, the views from the terrace are amongst the most magnificent in Cheshire.

During the winter, meals and drinks are served at one of the tables standing on polished wooden floorboards, or those grouped around the brick pillars warmed by open fires – one of them is reputedly the largest log fire in the county. There is also a stone-flagged conservatory and flower-filled courtyard, ideal for enjoying the well-kept ales and sophisticated cooking during the warmer summer weather. The owners aim to provide the best of food with friendly service in a relaxed environment; children are welcome during the day, but evenings are carefully preserved for adults. Sandwiches are available at lunchtime – grilled goat's cheese with red onion marmalade for example. The carte opens with nibbles like marinated Aegean and Kalamata olives, or grilled Cumberland pork and leek black pudding chipolatas with honey and mustard mayonnaise. Starters could include toasted crumpet with field mushrooms, or smoked haddock and cod fishcake. The 'Home Comforts' selection is where you'll find braised shin of beef and oxtail with creamy mash and herb dumplings; and steak, Weetwood Ale and mushroom pie with shortcrust pastry, served with chunky chips and garden peas. Puddings follow traditional lines, or select your favourite flavours from the list of Gog's Cheshire Farm ice creams made just down the road. If the thought of driving home threatens to spoil your evening, you can always opt to stay in one of the 12 en suite country-style bedrooms.

★★ HL ♛
MAP 15 SJ55
CH3 9PF
☎ 01829 770434
🖷 01829 771097
e-mail:
info@thepheasantinn.co.uk
dir: *A41 (Chester to Whitchurch), after 4m left to Burwardsley. Follow 'Cheshire Workshops' signs*

Open 11–11
Bar Meals L served Mon-Sat
12–10 D served Mon-Sat 12–10
(Sun 12–8.30)
Restaurant L served all week D
served all week
⊕ Free House ◀ Weetwood Old
Dog, Eastgate, Best, and guest
Bitter. ♛ 8
Facilities Children's licence
Garden Dogs allowed Parking
Play Area
Rooms 12

Cheshire Plain, Cheshire

Albion Inn

The Albion is Chester's last Victorian corner pub, standing in the shadow of the city's Roman wall. The home fires still burn on winter nights at this living memorial to the 1914–18 war, with its splendid cast-iron fireplace and original three-room layout, now filled with pictures, prints, artefacts and enamelled advertisements from the World War I period.

The lounge wallpaper was designed on the first day of the Great War and other objects of interest include a 1928 Steck player piano, which still performs on occasions. Trench rations are locally and regionally sourced wherever possible. Expect Penrith Cumberland sausages, Bury black puddings, McSween's haggis (traditional and vegetarian), local breads, organic free-range eggs and organic English free-range pork and chicken. The menu ranges through boiled gammon and pease pudding served with parsley sauce; McConickies corned beef hash with pickled red cabbage; and lambs' liver, bacon and onions in a rich cider gravy. The house speciality is filled Staffordshire oatcakes – the oatcakes are collected from Burslem in Staffordshire each week. Fillings include West Country brie, bacon and chutney; black pudding, bacon and cheese; and ham, leek and cheddar, among many others. Fresh vegetables and home-made desserts are also very much in evidence. Among the latter are creamy coconut pudding with caramelised oranges; and treacle tart with crème fraîche. Alternatively finish with English cheese served with fruitcake, in true northern style. A selection of club and doorstep sandwiches is also available. Please note that children are not welcome here.

MAP 15 SJ46
Park St CH1 1RN
☎ 01244 340345
e-mail: christina.mercer@
tesco.net
dir: *In city centre adjacent to Citywalls & Newgate*

Open 11–3 5–11 (Sat 11.30–3 6–11, Sun 12–2.30 7–10.30)
Closed: 25–26 Dec, 1–2 Jan
Bar Meals L served all week 12–2 D served Mon-Fri 5–8 (Sat 6–8.30, Sun eve no food) Av main course £8.50
Restaurant L served all week 12–1.45 D served Mon-Fri 5–7.45 (Sat 6–8.15, Sun eve no food)
⊕ Punch Taverns ◖ Black Sheep, Batemans, Deuchars & guest ales.
Facilities Dogs allowed
Notes ⊠

CONGLETON   MAP 16 SJ86

The Plough At Eaton ★★★★ INN ♟

Macclesfield Rd, Eaton CW12 2NH
☎ 01260 280207 📄 01260 298458
e-mail: theploughinn@hotmail.co.uk
dir: On A536 (Congleton to Macclesfield road)

Like a giant jigsaw puzzle, an ancient Welsh barn was transported here in hundreds of pieces to become a marvellously atmospheric restaurant adjoining this Elizabethan inn. From the specials menu come poached fresh salmon and prawn salad; chicken Madras with rice; and lamb Henry with mash. The carte offers lightly grilled turbot with lemon butter, and fillet steak cooked at the table. Apple crumble and custard and chocolate fudge cake are typical desserts.

Open 11–11 (Sun 12–10.30) **Bar Meals** L served all week 12–2.30 D served all week 6–9.30 (Sun 12–8) Av main course £8.95 **Restaurant** L served all week 12–2.30 D served all week 6–9.30 (Sun 12–8.30) ⊕ Free House ◀ Boddingtons, Hydes, Moore Houses, Storm Brew. ♟10 **Facilities** Garden Parking **Rooms** 17

HANDLEY   MAP 15 SJ45

The Calveley Arms ♟

Whitchurch Rd CH3 9DT
☎ 01829 770619 📄 01829 770901
e-mail: calveleyarms@btconnect.com
dir: 5m S of Chester, signed from A41. Follow signs for Handley & Aldersey Green Golf Course

First licensed in 1636, the Calveley is chock full of old timbers, jugs, pots, pictures, prints and ornaments. The food is a big attraction, with a daily changing specials menu offering starters like potted shrimps or game terrine, followed by the Calveley fish pie (halibut, salmon and prawns with a mornay sauce); or slow-cooked pheasant with mushrooms, shallots, garlic and cream. Sandwiches, baguettes and special salads are among the lighter options.

Open 12–3 6–11 (Sun 7–10.30) **Bar Meals** L served all week 12–2.15 D served all week 6–9.30 **Restaurant** L served Mon-Sat 12–2.15 D served Mon-Sat 6–9.30 (Sun 12–2.30, 7–9.30) ⊕ Enterprise Inns ◀ Castle Eden Ale, Marston's Pedigree, Black Bull & Bombardier. ♟10 **Facilities** Garden Dogs allowed Parking

HAUGHTON MOSS   MAP 15 SJ55

The Nags Head ♟

Long Ln CW6 9RN ☎ 01829 260265 📄 01829 261364
e-mail: rorykl@btinternet.com
dir: Turn off A49 S of Tarporley at Beeston/Haughton sign into Long Ln, continue for 1.75m

This typical 16th-century Cheshire black and white building, once a smithy, is every inch the traditional pub. Inside are low ceilings, crooked beams, exposed brickwork and real fires. A comprehensive set of menus offers everything from 'lite bites' served from lunchtime to early evening, to a full range of starters followed by roast poultry, grilled steaks or seafood. Children eat well on smaller portions from the menu, or choose from their own list of sausages, burgers or nuggets.

Open 12–12 (Closed 25 Dec eve only) **Bar Meals** L served all week 12–10 D served all week 12–10 Av main course £6.95 **Restaurant** L served all week 12–10 D served all week 12–10 Av 3 course à la carte £20 ⊕ Free House ◀ Flowers IPA, Bombardier & guest ales. ♟16 **Facilities** Children's licence Garden Dogs allowed Parking Play Area

HUXLEY   MAP 15 SJ56

Stuart's Table at the Farmer's Arms NEW ♟

Huxley Ln CH3 9BG ☎ 01829 781342 📄 01829 781794
e-mail: stuart@stuarttable.com

Quality British steaks are the speciality at this country pub and restaurant, which also offers a frequently changing set price menu. Start, perhaps, with tempura tiger prawns and basil mayonnaise; or caramelised onion soup with Welsh rarebit sourdough. Main courses might include roast cod with grilled Charlotte potatoes and buttered asparagus; and roast beef fillet with wild mushroom gratin and watercress purée.

Open 11–3 5–11 Closed: Mon **Bar Meals** L served Tue-Sat 12–2 (Sun 12–3) **Restaurant** L served Tue-Sat 12–2 D served Tue-Sat 6–9 (Sun, winter 12–6, summer 12–4 & 6–8.30) Av 3 course à la carte £25 Av 3 course fixed price £19.95 ◀ Black Sheep, Adnams & guest ale. ♟30 **Facilities** Garden Dogs allowed Parking Play Area

England

KNUTSFORD   MAP 15 SJ77

Pick of the Pubs

The Dog Inn ★★★★ INN ♟

Well Bank Ln, Over Peover WA16 8UP

☎ 01625 861421 📠 01625 864800

e-mail: thedog-inn@paddockinns.fsnet.co.uk

web: www.doginn-overpeover.co.uk

dir: *S from Knutsford take A50. Turn into Stocks Ln at The Whipping Stocks pub. 2m*

In the summer colourful flowerbeds, tubs and hanging baskets create quite a setting for the timbered Dog Inn, which has served ale to locals and travellers since the turn of the 19th century. In its time it has been a row of cottages, a grocer's, a shoemaker's and a farm, but now faithful regulars and visitors come for its range of cask ales from small regional breweries, large array of malt whiskies, and classic English menu prepared from ingredients sourced largely from within a six-mile radius. Starters include sticky chilli prawns; and Bury black pudding stack with bacon, while typical among the main courses are baked salmon fillet; half-roasted crispy duck; steak and ale pie; and stuffed Staffordshire oatcakes. Ever popular desserts include strawberry Pavlova, and Bramley apple pie. Stay overnight in one of the six comfortable and well-equipped en suite bedrooms and visit a nearby National Trust property.

Open 11.30–3 4.30–11 (Sun 11–11) **Bar Meals** L served Mon-Sat 12–2.30 D served Mon-Sat 6–9 (Sun 12–8.30) Av main course £10.95 **Restaurant** L served Mon-Sat 12–2.30 D served Mon-Sat 6–9 (Sun 12–8.30) ⊕ Free House ◀ Hydes Traditional Bitter, Weetwood Best, Skipton Brewery, Moorhouses. ♟ 8 **Facilities** Garden Dogs allowed Parking **Rooms** 6

LACH DENNIS   MAP 15 SJ77

The Duke of Portland ♟

Penny's Ln CW9 7SY ☎ 01606 46264

e-mail: info@dukeofportland.com

web: www.dukeofportland.com

Expect to eat well at this independent family-run pub set in the heart of the glorious Cheshire plain. The sunny, landscaped garden complements the attractively refurbished building, and the owners have a genuine commitment to local producers, many of whom have never supplied other commercial customers. Try twice-baked oak smoked salmon soufflé with lemon and vodka cream, followed by fillet of pork with russet apple, chestnut mushroom and Calvados cream.

The Duke of Portland

Open 12–11 **Bar Meals** L served Mon-Sat 12–2.30 D served Mon-Sat 5.30–9.30 (Sun 12–8) Av main course £11 **Restaurant** L served Mon-Sat 12–2.30 D served Mon-Sat 5.30–9.30 (Sun 12–8) Av 3 course à la carte £30 ◀ Thwaites Bomber, Marstons Pedigree, Banks Original, Sneck Lifter. ♟ 7 **Facilities** Children's licence Garden Parking

LITTLE NESTON   MAP 15 SJ27

The Old Harp NEW

19 Quay Side CH64 0TB

☎ 0151 336 6980 📠 0151 336 6980

e-mail: a.jones140@surfree.co.uk

dir: *From Neston town centre, at 2nd mini-rdbt, turn right onto Marshlands Rd. At bottom turn left, 200yds ahead*

Migrant Welsh coalminers named this isolated pub overlooking the Dee marshes after it had been converted from two old cottages in 1780. Although renovated over the years, it remains a simple two-roomed pub, the public bar on the left, the lounge on the right, with quarry-tiled floors and low beams. In the old days, the miners used one room, their managers the other. Bar lunches only, and a good range of real ales.

Open 12–12 **Bar Meals** L served Mon-Fri 12–2 Av main course £6 ◀ Joseph Holts, Titanic Iceberg, Timothy Taylor Landlord & guest ales. **Facilities** Children's licence Garden Dogs allowed Parking **Notes** ⊜

LOWER WHITLEY   MAP 15 SJ67

Pick of the Pubs

Chetwode Arms ♟

See Pick of the Pubs on opposite page

PICK OF THE PUBS

LOWER WHITLEY-CHESHIRE

Chetwode Arms

Adorned with window boxes and built from Cheshire brick, this 400–year-old former coaching inn is a welcoming sight in the heart of this small village. The inn's interior is as cosy and rambling as you could wish for.

There's the tap room, which welcomes walkers and their dogs; the bar room, which is tiny and has an open fire; and, leading off the bar, a warren of small, intimate dining rooms and passageways. It is said that somewhere underground, a tunnel leads from the pub to the vicarage, and then on to St Luke's church, which is believed to be the oldest brick church still standing in England. From the main dining room you can step onto a terrace overlooking the pub's own crown bowling green, one of the best kept greens in the country. There, with the wall heated gently by the sun, you can while away the hours late into the evening supping a pint of Marston's Pedigree or Jennings Cumberland. The pub's owners are English and Austrian, so expect a continental touch to the cooking.

Snacks, available until 3.30pm from Monday to Sunday, include crusty baguettes served with chips and filled with the likes of lobster tails, Marie Rose sauce and rocket, or brie, bacon and cranberry. For a more warming snack, opt for a panini filled with roasted vegetables or sirloin steak and fried onions. Starters from the main menu include black pudding and stilton rarebit on rösti; and asparagus spears wrapped in Parma ham topped with hollandaise sauce. Follow with vegetarian Thai curry; lobster and salmon ravioli in a creamy sauce with lemon and sun dried tomatoes; and osso buco. A selection of steaks cooked on volcanic stone is also available, and there are always plenty of seafood options.

MAP 15 SJ67
St Lane WA4 4EN
☎ 01925 730203
🖷 01925 730870
e-mail:
info@chetwodearms.com
dir: *On A49 2m S from M56 junct 10, 6m S of Warrington*

Open 12–11 (Winter 12–4, 5.30–11)
Bar Meals L served all week 12–3 D served all week 6–9
Restaurant L served all week 12–3 D served all week 6–9.30 (Sun 12–8)
⊕ Punch Taverns ◼ Marston's Pedigree, Banks Original, Adnams Broad, Jennings Cumberland & guest ale. ♟ 12
Facilities Garden Dogs allowed Parking Play Area

England

MACCLESFIELD   MAP 16 SJ97

The Windmill Inn ♀

Holehouse Ln, Whitely Green, Adlington SK10 5SJ

☎ 01625 574222

e-mail: thewindmill@dsl.pipex.com

dir: *Between Macclesfield & Poynton. Follow brown tourist signs on main road. Pub in 1.5m*

A beamed former farmhouse set in lovely Cheshire countryside with a landscaped garden. The pub is close to the Macclesfield Canal and fantastic walks including the Middlewood Way. Sandwiches and side orders like home-made chips are supplemented by such daily specials as beef casserole with wholegrain mustard mash and chopped parsley. Main courses include the likes of gateau of aubergines with Nantwich goats' cheese, plum tomatoes and basil.

Open 12–3 5–11 (Sat 12–11, Sun 12–10.30) **Bar Meals** L served all week 12–2.30 D served all week 6–9 (Sat 12–9.30, Sun 12–8) **Restaurant** L served all week 12–2.30 D served all week 6–9 (Sat 12–9.30, Sun 12–8) ◀ Timothy Taylor Landlord, Black Sheep, Old Speckled Hen, Tetleys & guest. **Facilities** Garden Dogs allowed Parking

MARTON   MAP 16 SJ86

Pick of the Pubs

The Davenport Arms ♀

See Pick of the Pubs on opposite page

MOULDSWORTH   MAP 15 SJ57

Pick of the Pubs

The Goshawk ♀

Station Rd CH3 8AJ ☎ 01928 740900 📄 01928 740965

dir: *A51 from Chester onto A54. Left onto B5393 towards Frodsham. Enter Mouldsworth, pub on left opposite rail station*

There is a professional yet relaxed atmosphere at The Goshawk, with its friendly staff, log fires in winter and stripped pine floors. The wide-ranging menu should have something for everyone, with light snacks such as smoked mackerel bruschetta with roast peppers; or steak burgers; meat dishes like chicken stuffed with chorizo; or steak and kidney pie; up to twelve fish dishes, including Thai baked sea bass; monkfish with mussel and clam chowder; and lobster thermidor; vegetarian choices like goats' cheese in filo pastry with Mediterranean vegetables; and several traditional desserts such as spotted dick; chocolate fudge cake; and Bakewell tart. A wide choice of wines is on offer as well as real ales like Timothy Taylors Landlord. There is a good play area for children, and the decked area to the rear overlooks one of the finest crown bowling greens in the area.

Open 12–11 Closed: 25 Dec & 1 Jan **Bar Meals** L served all week D served all week 12–9.30 (Sun 12–9) **Restaurant** L served all week D served all week 12–9.30 (Sun 12–9) ◀ Timothy Taylors Landlord, Greene King IPA, Deuchars & Speckled Hen. ♀ 14 **Facilities** Garden Parking Play Area

NANTWICH   MAP 15 SJ65

The Thatch Inn ♀

Wrexham Rd, Faddiley CW5 8JE

☎ 01270 524223 📄 01270 524674

e-mail: thethatchinn@aol.com

dir: *Follow signs for Wrexham from Nantwich, inn 4m from Nantwich*

The black-and-white Thatch Inn is believed to be the oldest as well as one of the prettiest pubs in south Cheshire. It has a three quarter acre garden, and inside you'll find oak beams, and open fires in winter. The menu is divided between options from the grill; traditional favourites (pies, roasts and casseroles); tastes from afar (nachos, lasagne, curry); and fish, summer salads, light bites and a children's menu. Speciality coffees are a feature.

Open 11–11 (Sun 12–10.30) **Bar Meals** L served all week 11–9.30 D served all week 11–9.30 (Sun 12–9.30) Av main course £7.95 **Restaurant** L served all week 12–9.30 D served all week 12–9.30 ⊕ Free House ◀ Marston Pedigree, Timothy Taylor Landlord, Weetwoods, Archers. ♀ 24 **Facilities** Garden Parking Play Area

PENKETH   MAP 15 SJ58

The Ferry Tavern ♀

Station Rd WA5 2UJ ☎ 01925 791117 📄 01925 791116

e-mail: ferrytavern@aol.com

dir: *From Widnes A562 pass Fiddlers Ferry power station & golf driving range. Turn into Tannery Lane. Right at Three Elms nursing home into Station Road*

Set on its own island between the Mersey and the St Helen's canal, this 12th-century ale house has been an inn since 1762, and welcomes walkers and cyclists from the trans-Pennine Way. Beneath the low beams in the stone-flagged bar you'll find a range of unusual guest beers and over 300 different whiskies, including 60 Irish. Lunch only is served and includes dishes such as soup, burgers and paté, plus sandwiches and jacket potatoes.

Open 12–3 5.30–11 (Fri-Sat 12–11.30, Sun 12–10.30) **Bar Meals** L served Mon-Fri 12–2 Av main course £5 ⊕ Free House ◀ Interbrew Boddingtons Bitter, Abbot Ale, Boddingtons Cask & Ruddles County. ♀ 10 **Facilities** Garden Dogs allowed Parking

PLUMLEY   MAP 15 SJ77

The Golden Pheasant Hotel ♀

Plumley Moor Rd WA16 9RX

☎ 01565 722261 📄 01565 722125

dir: *M6 junct 19, A556 signed Chester. 2m, left at Plumley/Peover signs. Through Plumley, pub in 1m opposite rail station*

In the heart of rural Cheshire, the hotel has a large restaurant, bar area, public bar, children's play area and bowling green. The menu offers substantial choice, from bar snacks such as nachos or paninis, to a more elaborate restaurant menu, including pork medallions in apricot and tarragon reduction. Real ales are pulled from the attractive handpumps installed by J.W. Lees, one of the country's few remaining independent family breweries with its own cooperage.

Open 11–11 (Sun 12–10.30) **Bar Meals** L served all week 12–2.30 D served all week 6–9.30 (Sat 12–9.30, Sun 12–8.30) Av main course £6.95 **Restaurant** L served all week 12–2.30 D served all week 6–9.30 (Sat 12–9.30, Sun 12–8.30) Av 3 course à la carte £20 Av 2 course fixed price £12.95 ⊕ J W Lees ◀ J W Lees Bitter, GB Mild & Moonraker. ♀ 10 **Facilities** Children's licence Garden Dogs allowed Parking Play Area

PICK OF THE PUBS

MARTON-CHESHIRE

The Davenport Arms

Marton's 14th-century, half-timbered church is probably the oldest of its type still in use in Europe. Opposite is this 18th-century pub, formerly a farmhouse, and nearby is the ancient Marton Oak, still producing acorns after more than a millennium.

The traditional bar has cushioned settles and leather armchairs by a log fire, while in the middle of the restaurant is a well, although purely decorative these days. Upstairs, criminals were once tried, the really bad ones ending up on a gibbet over the road. Food – and this includes chutneys, sauces and desserts – is all freshly made on the premises from locally supplied ingredients. The menu, incorporating a light lunch selection, offers fishcakes; tenderloin of pork wrapped in bacon with blue cheese and cider sauce; and breast of duck marinated with ginger, garlic and chilli, noodles and stir-fried vegetables. The lovely beer garden contains a discreet children's play area.

MAP 16 SJ86
Congleton Rd SK11 9HF
☎ 01260 224269
📄 01260 224565
e-mail: enquiries@
thedavenportarms.co.uk
web: www.thedavenportarms.
co.uk
dir: *3m from Congleton off A34*

Open 12–3 6–close (Fri-Sun all day)
Bar Meals L served Tue-Sat 12–2.30 D served Tue-Sat 6–9 (Sun 12–3, 6–8.30) Av main course £11.50
Restaurant L served Tue-Sat 12–2.30 D served Tue-Sat 6–9 (Sun 12–3, 6–8.30) Av 3 course à la carte £22.50
⊕ Free House ◀ Copper Dragon, Storm Brewing, Directors, Websters Yorkshire Bitter & Weetwood. ♟ 9
Facilities Children's licence Garden Parking Play Area

England

PLUMLEY continued

The Smoker ♟

WA16 0TY ☎ 01565 722338 📠 01565 722093
e-mail: smoker@plumley.fsword.co.uk

dir: *From M6 junct 19 take A556 W. Pub 1.75m on left*

This 400-year-old coaching inn is actually named after a white racehorse bred by the Prince Regent, although recent legislation has prompted the addition of a covered smokers' courtyard complete with heating and seating. The pub's striking wood-panelled interior of three connecting rooms provides a traditional welcoming atmosphere, with log fires, beams and copper kettles. The menu has an appealing and lengthy array of starters; main courses include Barnsley chop; deep-fried haddock; and lamb Henry.

Open 10–3 6–11 (Sun all day) **Bar Meals** L served Mon-Sat 11.30–2.30 D served Mon-Sat 6–9.15 (Sun 12–9) Av main course £8.95
Restaurant L served Mon-Sat 11.30–2.30 D served Mon-Sat 6.30–9.30 (Sun 12–9) Av 3 course à la carte £18.95 ◀ Robinson's Best, Double Hop, Robinson's Smooth. ♟ 10 **Facilities** Garden Parking Play Area

PRESTBURY   MAP 16 SJ87

Pick of the Pubs

The Legh Arms & Black Boy Restaurant ♟

SK10 4DG ☎ 01625 829130 📠 01625 827833
e-mail: legharms@hotmail.co.uk

dir: *From M6 through Knutsford to Macclesfield, turn to Prestbury at Broken Cross. Pub in village centre.*

A smart country pub with a large suntrap garden, The Legh Arms is located in one of Britain's most prosperous and charming villages. The original 15th-century inn on this site was called The Saracen's Head, to commemorate the Crusades. In 1627, when the current inn was built, the signmaker mistakenly painted a black boy's head and the image is still used today. Bonnie Prince Charlie is believed to have stayed here on his way to Derby during the ill-fated 1745 rebellion. An extensive menu in the oak-beamed restaurant ranges through pot roast pheasant, triple tomato risotto with spinach and asparagus, and grilled fillet steak. Fresh fish, delivered six days a week, is a notable feature, along with herbs from the inn's walled garden. A private dining/conference room is available.

Open 12–11 **Bar Meals** L served Mon-Sat 12–2 D served Mon-Sat 7–10 (Sun 12–10) **Restaurant** L served Mon-Sat 12–2 D served Mon-Sat 7–10 (Sun all day) Av 3 course à la carte £26 ◀ Robinson's Bitter, Hatters Mild, Guinness. ♟ 8 **Facilities** Garden Parking

SHOCKLACH   MAP 15 SJ44

Bull Inn Country Bistro

Worthenbury Rd SY14 7BL ☎ 01829 250239
e-mail: jaws@fsbdial.co.uk

This welcoming mid-19th-century pub is located in a quiet village 20 minutes from Chester. Exposed beams, many other original features, and often a cosy log fire greet visitors heading for a pint of Mansfield Cask, or a traditional pub meal. Popular are fish, chips and mushy peas, 'big and hearty' pies, curries, braised beef, pork loin with black pudding, grills, poached salmon, and vegetarian pancakes. For the kids there are burgers, pizzas and nuggets.

Open 12–3 6.30–11 (Sun 7–10.30) **Bar Meals** L served Fri-Sun 12–2.30 D served Tue-Sun 6.30–9 (Sun 7–9) Av main course £8.95
Restaurant L served Fri-Sun 12–2.30 D served Tue-Sun 6.30–9 (Sun 12–2.30, 7–9) ◀ Mansfield Cask, Pedigree, Guinness. **Facilities** Children's licence Garden Parking

SWETTENHAM   MAP 15 SJ86

Pick of the Pubs

The Swettenham Arms ♟

Swettenham Ln CW12 2LF
☎ 01477 571284 📠 01477 571284
e-mail: info@swettenhamarms.co.uk
web: www.swettenhamarms.co.uk

dir: *M6 junct 18 to Holmes Chapel, then A535 towards Jodrell Bank. 3m right (Forty Acre Lane) to Swettenham*

A riot of flowers covers the stone frontage of The Swettenham Arms, idyllically situated behind a 13th-century church. The pub itself dates back almost as far: it was once a nunnery, linked to the church by an underground passage where corpses 'rested' before burial. Expect ghost stories: indeed, in 2005, after seeing a lady apparently floating in the restaurant, a customer had to seek urgent counselling from the vicar. Following starters of home-made duck liver paté, or sautéed queen scallops, the extensive menu progresses to steamed steak and kidney pudding or cod fillet rolled with spinach, before hitting the heights of Chef's Specialities. These include roasted grey mullet filed with prawn duxelle; and beef stroganoff served with pilaff rice. Vegetarians are well catered for, and each of the specialities has a suggested wine and beer. The pub's lavender and sunflower meadow is a delight in summer.

Open 12–3 6.30–11 (all day Sun & all day all week Summer)
Bar Meals L served Mon-Sat 12–2.30 D served Mon-Sat 7–9.30 (Sun 12–9.30) **Restaurant** L served Mon-Sat 12–2.30 D served Mon-Sat 7–9.30 (Sun 12–9) ⊕ Free House ◀ Landlord, Hydes, Beartown, Pride of Pendle. ♟ 8 **Facilities** Garden Parking

TARPORLEY MAP 15 SJ56

Alvanley Arms Inn ★★★★ INN ♀

Forest Rd, Cotebrook CW6 9DS ☎ 01829 760200
e-mail: info@alvanleyarms.co.uk
dir: On A49, 1.5m N of Tarporley

There's a strong shire horse theme throughout this charming 16th-century coaching inn. Photographs, rosettes, harnesses and horseshoes decorate the walls, linking the inn to the landlords' Cotebrook Shire Horse Centre next door. Hand-pulled ales in the oak-beamed bar complement a range of freshly prepared dishes, based on ingredients from local family businesses. A typical lunchtime selection includes steak and ale pie; mushroom stroganoff with rice and crusty bead; and grilled North Sea cod.

Open 12–3 5.30–11 (Sun all day) **Bar Meals** L served all week 12–2 D served all week 6–9 (Sun 12–9) Av main course £9.95
Restaurant L served all week 12–2 D served all week 6–9 (Sun 12–9)
Av 3 course à la carte £22 ◀ Robinsons Best & guest ales. ♀ 12
Facilities Garden Parking **Rooms** 7

Pick of the Pubs

The Boot Inn ♀

Boothsdale, Willington CW6 0NH ☎ 01829 751375
dir: Off A54 Kelsall by-pass or off A51 (Chester-Nantwich), follow signs to Willington

Originally a row of red brick and sandstone cottages, this charming building became a small beer house before evolving into the inviting pub and restaurant it is today. Quarry tiled floors, old beams and open fires enhance the welcome. The kitchen uses local suppliers wherever possible. Dishes might include oak-smoked salmon with sour cream, herb dressing and salad, or spicy crab fishcakes to start, followed by baked Spanish omelette with salad and beetroot relish; Moroccan spiced chicken with couscous and minted cucumber yogurt; fisherman's pie; or natural smoked haddock with a mustard stout rarebit topping and cherry tomato chutney. For something lighter try salad platters, sandwiches, fresh baguettes and hot paninis. A booklet of circular walks is available at the pub. It includes an account of the pub's long history; among the interesting tales is the fact that a previous landlord was the father of current James Bond 007 Daniel Craig.

Open 11–12 Closed: 25 Dec **Bar Meals** L served all week 11–2.30 D served all week 6–9.30 (Sat-Sun & BHs food all day) Av main course £9.40 **Restaurant** L served all week 11–2.30 D served all week 6–9.30 ◀ Weetwood, Timothy Taylor Landlord, Bass, Tetleys. ♀ 10
Facilities Garden Dogs allowed Parking

TUSHINGHAM CUM GRINDLEY MAP 15 SJ54

Pick of the Pubs

Blue Bell Inn

SY13 4QS ☎ 01948 662172 📄 01948 662172
dir: A4, 4m N of Whitchurch, signed Bell O' the Hill

A lovely black-and-white building that oozes character with its abundance of beams, open fires and horse brasses. In what must be a unique tale from the annals of pub-haunting, it was once occupied by a duck whose spirit is reputedly sealed in a bottle buried in the bottom step of the cellar. Believe that or not, the Blue Bell remains a charming and characterful pub. Its oldest part dates to approximately 1550, and the main building was completed in 1667. It has all the features you'd expect of a timber-framed building of this date, including one of the largest working chimneys in Cheshire and a priest hole. Curios that have been discovered from within the wall structure are on show in the pub. The menu is based on traditional English fare, with specials prepared daily. Drink options include well-kept ales plus a selection of wines.

Open 12–3 6–11 (Sun 12–3, 7–11) Closed: Mon ex BH
Bar Meals L served Tue-Sun 12–2 D served Tue-Sat 6–9
Restaurant L served Tue-Sun 12–2 D served Tue-Sat 7–9 ⊕ Free House ◀ Carlins, Shropshire Gold, Oakhan JHB & guest ales.
Facilities Garden Dogs allowed Parking

WARMINGHAM MAP 15 SJ76

The Bear's Paw

School Ln CW11 3QN ☎ 01270 526317 & 526342
e-mail: enquiries@thebearspaw.co.uk
dir: M6 junct 18, A54, A533 towards Sandbach. Follow signs for village

Delightful country house hotel conveniently situated within easy reach of many Cheshire towns and some of the county's prettiest countryside. Wide-ranging menus offer an extensive selection of starters, including chicken liver paté, smoked haddock fish cake, and bacon and black pudding salad, followed by breast of chicken stuffed with spinach and brie, and red mullet on a crab mash. Beef lasagne, cod supreme and Cumberland sausage are other options.

Open 5–11 (Sat-Sun all day) Closed: 25–26 Dec & 1 Jan
Bar Meals L served Sat-Sun 12–6 D served all week 6–9 (Fri-Sat 6–9.30) Av main course £10 **Restaurant** L served Sat-Sun 12–6 D served all week 6–9 (Fri-Sat 6–9.30) Av 3 course à la carte £19 ⊕ Free House ◀ Tetley Cask, & guest ales. **Facilities** Garden Parking

England

WRENBURY

MAP 15 SJ54

The Dusty Miller ♥

CW5 8HG ☎ 01270 780537

dir: Telephone for details

A beautifully converted 16th-century mill building beside the Shropshire Union Canal. A black and white lift bridge, designed by Thomas Telford, completes the picture postcard setting. The menu, which tends to rely on ingredients from the region, offers light bites including filled rolls and a cheese platter alongside the more substantial baked hake with buttery mash and a white wine and parsley sauce, and home-made Aberdeen Angus burger with pear and apple chutney.

Open 11.30–3 6.30–11 (Fri-Sat 6.30–12) **Bar Meals** L served Tue-Sun 12–2 D served all week 6.30–9.30 (Sun 12–2.30, 7–9) Av main course £10 **Restaurant** L served Tue-Sun 12–2 D served all week 6.30–9.30 ◀ Robinson's Best Bitter, Double Hop, Old Tom, Hatters Mild & Hartleys XB. ♥ 12 **Facilities** Garden Dogs allowed Parking

WYBUNBURY

MAP 15 SJ64

The Swan ♥

Main Rd CW5 7NA ☎ 01270 841280 🖹 01270 841200
e-mail: jacqueline.harris7@btinternet.com
web: www.swaninnwybunbury.co.uk

dir: M6 junct 16 towards Chester & Nantwich. Turn left at lights in Wybunbury

The Swan, a pub since 1580, is situated in the village centre next to the church. All the food is freshly prepared on the premises and includes glazed lamb shoulder, Cumberland sausage, basil-crusted cod fillet, crispy half roast duckling, and beef, mushroom and Jennings ale pie. The menu also features hot baps, thick-cut sandwiches and salads. Sit in the garden below the church tower.

Open 12–12 (Mon 5–12) **Bar Meals** L served Tue-Sat 12–2 D served Mon-Sat 6.30–9.30 (Sun & BHs 12–8) Av main course £10.35 **Restaurant** L served Tue-Sun 12–2 D served all week 6.30–9.30 (BHs 12–8) Av 3 course à la carte £16 ◀ Unicorn, Cumbria Way & guest ales. ♥ 9 **Facilities** Children's licence Garden Dogs allowed Parking

CORNWALL & ISLES OF SCILLY

BLISLAND

MAP 02 SX17

The Blisland Inn

PL30 4JF ☎ 01208 850739

dir: 5m from Bodmin towards Launceston. 2.5 m off A30 signed Blisland. On village green

An award-winning inn in a very picturesque village on the edge of Bodmin Moor. The superb parish church was a favourite of John Betjeman who wrote about it extensively. Most of the traditional pub fare is home cooked, including a variety of puddings. Leek and mushroom bake is a perennial favourite, while lasagne, sausage and mash, and traditional farmhouse ham, egg and chips are also popular.

Open 11.30–11 (Sun 12–10.30) **Bar Meals** L served Mon-Sat 12–2.15 D served Mon-Sat 6.30–9.30 (Sun 12–2, 6.30–9) **Restaurant** L served all week 12–2.15 D served all week 6.30–9.30 (Fixed price menu Sun lunch only) ◀ Guest ales. **Facilities** Garden Dogs allowed

BODINNICK

MAP 02 SX15

Old Ferry Inn

PL23 1LX ☎ 01726 870237 🖹 01726 870116
e-mail: royce972@aol.com

dir: A38 towards Dobwalls, left onto A390. After 3m left onto B3359 then right to Bodinnick/Polruan for 5m.

This friendly, family-run free house stands just 50 yards from the scenic River Fowey, where the car ferry still makes regular crossings to Fowey

CONTINUED ON PAGE 82

Cadgwith Cove Inn

This traditional, whitewashed Cornish inn transports you right back the days when Cadgwith Cove was a smuggler's haunt. The atmospheric bars are adorned with relics that record a rich seafaring history, and it's easy to imagine that the ghosts of smugglers still gather within these cosy walls.

The inn occupies an idyllic spot on the Lizard peninsular, right on the coastal path and overlooking the cove. Appealing to both locals and tourists alike, it offers a warm welcome and authentic local colour. Ramblers with their well-behaved dogs gather here all year round, relaxing with pints of ale and listening to sea shanties sung by the Cadgwith Singers late into Friday night. On Tuesday nights the inn hosts a thriving folk club when guests are invited to join in or just sit back and enjoy the music. On any night of the week you might find yourself swapping tales with one of the fishermen whose catches feature on the popular menus. As may be expected, these are positively laden with seafood – lobster and crab of course, but also

grilled red mullet or bass, moules marinière, the special Cadgwith fish casserole, and traditional fish and chips. Meat eaters and vegetarians are also well provided for, with ingredients coming from local butchers and surrounding farms. Meals can be served in the garden in clement weather, and the large terrace with sea views is an ideal spot during the summer gig races, or for one of the regular seafood barbeques prepared by local fishermen.

MAP 02 SW71
TR12 7JX
☎ 01326 290513
🖷 01326 291018
e-mail: enquiries@
cadgwithcoveinn.com
dir: *10m from Helston on main Lizard road*

Open 12–3 7–11 (Jul-Aug & Sat-Sun open all day)
Bar Meals L served all week 12–2.00 D served all week 6.30–9.00 Av main course £8
Restaurant L served all week 12–2.00 D served all week 6–9.00 Av 3 course à la carte £15
⊕ Punch Taverns ◀ Interbrew Flowers IPA, Sharp's, Abbot Ale, guest ales.
Facilities Garden Dogs allowed Parking

81

BODINNICK continued

itself. Inside the 400–year-old building, old photographs and nautical bric-a-brac set the scene for sampling Sharp's Bitter and an extensive bar menu. Choices range from snacks to home-cooked dishes like steak and stilton pie; fresh Dover sole with prawn and lemon butter; and creamy garlic mushrooms with pasta and melted cheese.

Open 11–11 (Nov-Feb 12–10.30) Closed: 25 Dec **Bar Meals** L served all week 12–3 D served all week 6–9 (Nov-Feb 12–2, 6.30–8.30) Av main course £7.50 **Restaurant** L served Sun 12–2.30 D served all week 7–9 (Winter 7–8.30) Av 3 course à la carte £20 ⊕ Free House ◀ Sharp's Bitter, Guinness. **Facilities** Children's licence Garden Dogs allowed Parking **Rooms** available

BOLVENTOR   MAP 02 SX17

Jamaica Inn ♀

PL15 7TS ☎ 01566 86250 🖥 01566 86177
e-mail: enquiry@jamaicainn.co.uk
web: www.jamaicainn.co.uk

The setting for Daphne du Maurier's famously eponymous novel, this 18th-century inn stands high on Bodmin moor. Its Smugglers Museum houses fascinating artefacts, while the Daphne du Maurier room honours the great writer. The place is big on atmosphere, with a cobbled courtyard, beamed ceilings and roaring fires. Lunches range from hot ciabattas to grills; the evening menu served from 3pm could start with warm melted goat's cheese bruschetta, and follow with barbecued pork ribs or poached fillet of Port Isaac salmon.

Open 9 -11 **Bar Meals** L served all week 12–2.30 D served all week 2.45–9 **Restaurant** L served all week 2.30–9 D served all week 2.45–9 ⊕ Free House ◀ Doom Bar, Tribute & Jamaica Inn Ale. ♀ 8 **Facilities** Children's licence Garden Parking Play Area **Rooms** available

BOSCASTLE   MAP 02 SX09

Pick of the Pubs

The Wellington Hotel ★★ HL ◉◉ ♀

The Harbour PL35 0AQ
☎ 01840 250202 🖥 01840 250621
e-mail: info@boscastle-wellington.com
dir: In Boscastle follow signs to harbour, into Old Road. Hotel ahead

This listed 16th-century coaching inn nestles on one of England's most stunning coastlines at the end of a glorious wooded valley where the rivers Jordan and Valency meet. It retains much of its

original charm, including beamed ceilings and real log fires. The cosy atmosphere makes it easy to believe – as the locals do – that many ghostly guests and staff still linger. The traditional beamed bar provides a good selection of Cornish ales, malt whiskies and bar snacks, while the smart Waterloo restaurant is the focus of more serious dining. Food here could include monkfish pavé with pickled red cabbage, crispy angel hair and beet dressing, followed by seared fillet steak with a veal shin burger, caraway dauphinoise, onion confit, beetroot purée and marrow. Finish with excellent cheeses, or perhaps deep-fried strawberries in black pepper batter with five berry sorbet and berry salad.

Open 11–11 (Sun 10–10.30) **Bar Meals** L served Mon-Sat 12–3 D served Mon-Sat 6–10 (Sun 12–9, Summer 12–10)
Restaurant D served Fri-Wed 6.30–9 Av 3 course à la carte £28.50 ⊕ Free House ◀ St Austell HSD, St Austell Tribute, Skinners Ales-Spriggan, Wooden Hand Brewery & Cornish Blonde. ♀ 8 **Facilities** Garden Dogs allowed Parking **Rooms** 15

CADGWITH   MAP 02 SW71

Pick of the Pubs

Cadgwith Cove Inn

See Pick of the Pubs on page 81

CALLINGTON   MAP 03 SX36

The Coachmakers Arms ♀

6 Newport Square PL17 7AS
☎ 01579 382567 🖥 01579 384679
dir: Between Plymouth & Launceston on A388

Traditional stone-built pub on the A388 between Plymouth and Launceston. Clocks, plates, pictures of local scenes, old cars and antique trade advertisements contribute to the atmosphere, as do the fish tank and aviary. There's plenty of choice on the menu, from chargrilled steaks, steak and kidney pie or hot-pot, to oven-baked plaice, vegetable balti or salads. Regulars range from the local football team to the pensioners dining club. On Wednesday there's a charity quiz night, and Thursday is steak night.

Open 11–11.30 (Sun 12–10.30) **Bar Meals** L served all week 12–2 D served all week 7–9.30 Av main course £4.95 **Restaurant** L served all week 12–2 D served all week 7–9.30 Av 3 course à la carte £15 ⊕ Enterprise Inns ◀ Sharp's Doom Bar & Special, Worthing Best Bitter, Abbot Ale, Tetley. ♀ 7 **Facilities** Dogs allowed Parking

Manor House Inn NEW ♀

Rilla Mill PL17 7NT ☎ 01579 362354
dir: 5m from Callington, just off B3257

Smartly updated but still very much a traditional pub, The Manor House offers a reasonably-priced selection of home-made food. Careful attention is paid to sourcing quality local ingredients, including fresh fish. Typical choices include pie of the day; battered haddock with chips; or gruyere-filled chicken breast with dauphinoise potatoes and a garlic and tarragon sauce. Lighter options include lasagne, beefburger and chips, toasted sandwiches, and salads.

Open 11–3 5.30–11.30 (Sat-Sun & BH, all day) Closed: Mon **Bar Meals** L served Tue-Sun 12–2 D served Tue-Sun 6–9 Av main course £8 **Restaurant** L served all week 12–2 D served all week 6.30–9.30 Av 3 course à la carte £18 ⊕ Free House ◀ Sharp's Own & Special, Betty Stogs. ♀ 8 **Facilities** Children's licence Garden Parking

CONSTANTINE   MAP 02 SW72

Pick of the Pubs

Trengilly Wartha Inn ♀

See Pick of the Pubs on page 84

CRACKINGTON HAVEN   MAP 02 SX19

Coombe Barton Inn

EX23 0JG ☎ 01840 230345 📠 01840 230788
e-mail: info@coombebarton.co.uk
dir: *S from Bude on A39, turn off at Wainhouse Corner, then
down lane to beach*

The inn, parts of which are over 200 years old, was built for the
'captain' of the quarry in the days when slate was shipped out from
this small port. Expect a good choice of locally caught fish and seafood,
home-baked Cornish pasties, toasted sandwiches and home-made
chef's specials. The Sunday lunchtime carvery offers roast ribs of local
beef, leg of pork and chicken.

Open 11–11 (Fri-Sat 11–12, Sun 12–11) **Bar Meals** L served Mon-Sat
11–2.30 D served Mon-Sat 6.30–9.30 (Sun 12–2.30, 6.30–9 booking req for
Sun lunch) **Restaurant** L served all week 11–2.30 D served all week 6–10
⊕ Free House ◀ St Austell Tribute & Hick's Special Draught, Sharp's Doom
Bar, Sharp's Safe Haven, Skinners Betty Stogs. **Facilities** Dogs allowed
Parking

CUBERT   MAP 02 SW75

The Smugglers' Den Inn ♀

Trebellan TR8 5PY ☎ 01637 830209 📠 01637 830580
e-mail: paulsmuggler@aol.com
dir: *From Newquay take A3075 to Cubert x-rds, then right, then
left signed Trebellan, 0.5m*

A thatched 16th-century pub in a valley leading down to the coast.
Features include a long bar, family room, children's play area, courtyards
and huge beer garden. The no-nonsense menu may offer grilled Cornish
red mullet fillets or hot Cornish yarg bruschetta, followed by confit of
whole local partridge or Cornish beef from the grill. Regional breweries
furnish a wondrous selection of beers, culminating in over 50 candidates
for the annual real ale and pie festival over the May Day weekend.

Open 11–3 6–11 (Open all day Jul & Aug) **Bar Meals** L served all week
12–2.30 D served all week 6–9.30 Av main course £10
Restaurant L served all week 12–2.30 D served all week 6–9.30 Av 3 course
à la carte £20 ⊕ Free House ◀ Skinner's Smugglers Ale, Betty Stogs Bitter,
Sharp's Doom Bar, Trebellan Tipple. ♀ 12 **Facilities** Garden Dogs allowed
Parking Play Area

DULOE   MAP 02 SX25

Ye Olde Plough House Inn ♀

PL14 4PN ☎ 01503 262050 📠 01503 264089
e-mail: alison@ploughhouse.freeserve.co.uk
dir: *A38 to Dobwalls, take turn signed Looe*

A welcoming 18th-century free house set in the heart of the Cornish
countryside, yet only three miles from the coastal town of Looe. The
building features slate floors, wood-burning stoves, settles and old
pews, with a fenced, grassy garden outside. Lunchtime brings white or
granary baguettes, ploughman's, and hot plates such as home-cooked
ham, egg and chips; roast of the day; and beef and stilton pie. In the
evening you can cook your own steak on a preheated grillstone.

Open 12–2.30 6.30–11 (Sun 7–10.30) Closed: 25–26 Dec
Bar Meals L served all week 12–2 D served all week 6.30–9.30 (Sun
7–9.30) **Restaurant** L served all week 12–2 D served all week 6.30–9.30
(Sun 7–9.30) ⊕ Free House ◀ Sharp's Doom Bar, Butcombe Bitter,
Worthington. ♀ 9 **Facilities** Garden Dogs allowed Parking

DUNMERE   MAP 02 SX06

The Borough Arms

PL31 2RD ☎ 01208 73118
e-mail: borougharms@aol.com
dir: *From A30 take A389 to Wadebridge, pub approx 1m from
Bodmin*

Built in the 1850s for train crews taking china clay from the moors
down to the port at Padstow, but it seems much older. Walkers, cyclists
and horseriders drop in for refreshment as they follow the disused
railway line, now the 17-mile Camel Trail. The menus offer steak and
ale pie, Spanish chicken, fish and chips, tender meats from the carvery,
and snacks. Specials, mostly home made, are on the chalkboards.

Open 11–11 (Sun 12–10.30) **Bar Meals** L served all week 12–9 D served
all week 12–9 Av main course £6.95 **Restaurant** L served all week 12–9
D served all week 12–9 ◀ Sharp's Bitter, Skinner's, John Smith's Smooth.
Facilities Garden Dogs allowed Parking Play Area

FEOCK   MAP 02 SW83

The Punch Bowl & Ladle ♀

Penelewey TR3 6QY ☎ 01872 862237 📠 01872 870401
dir: *Off Truro to Falmouth road, after Shell garage at 'Playing
Place' rdbt follow signs for King Harry Ferry to right. 0.5m, pub
on right.*

This ancient and fascinating building comprises three cob-built 17th-
century farm workers' cottages and a former customhouse. Much of its
trade still comes from travellers on the King Harry Ferry, but nowadays
they are tourists. There are delightful rural views from the inn's patio,
and in warmer weather you can enjoy a drink in the walled garden.
Food includes fish pie; local mussels in Cornish cider; Malaysian
chicken; and venison steak in chocolate sauce.

Open 11.30–11 (Fri & Sat 11.30–12, Sun 12–10.30, Sun Summer 12–11)
Bar Meals L served all week 12–2.30 D served all week 6–9.15 Av main
course £8.95 **Restaurant** L served all week 12–2.30 D served all week
6–9.15 Av 3 course à la carte £26.95 ◀ IPA Tribute, HSD & Cornish Cream.
♀ 8 **Facilities** Garden Dogs allowed Parking

Trengilly Wartha Inn

This unusually named inn is situated in the hamlet of Nancenoy, in an area designated as being of outstanding natural beauty, about a mile from the village of Constantine. The name is actually Cornish and means a settlement above the trees, in this case the wooded valley of Polpenwith Creek, an offshoot of the lovely Helford River.

The six acres of gardens and meadows that surround the inn include a vine-shaded pergola just perfect for summer dining. There's a small bistro on one side of the inn, and plenty more space for eating in the informal bar area, where a conservatory extension houses the family room. Talented chefs prepare everything from scratch using the best locally produced meats, game, fish and shellfish from local waters. The bar menu offers pub favourites like beef stroganoff, steak, and wholetail scampi, as well as less traditional choices such as courgette and rosemary pancakes stuffed with Cornish feta, cashew nuts, spinach and smoked cherry tomatoes; chicken breast with chilli and cranberry butter with creamed savoy cabbage and crispy pancetta;

and warm fillet of lightly smoked, locally caught pollock with herb butter. The fixed price menu in the bistro always has a good seafood selection, but watch out, because in summer the day's boatload of fresh fish can sell out fast. Fresh home-made steak and kidney puddings are sold through the winter on Wednesday nights. Since it's a free house, there's a good selection of real ales, over 40 malt whiskies and 150 wines, with 15 available by the glass.

MAP 02 SW72
Nancenoy TR11 5RP
☎ 01326 340332
🖷 01326 340332
e-mail: reception@trengilly.co.uk
dir: *From Constantine follow signs to Nancenoy*

Open 11–3 6.30–11 (Summer 5.30–11)
Bar Meals L served all week 12–2.15 D served all week 6.30–9.30
Restaurant L served all week 12–2.15 D served all week 7.30–9.30 (No food 25 Dec)
⊕ Free House ◧ Hobsons, Three Tuns XXX, Wye Valley Butty Bach. ♀ 15
Facilities Garden Dogs allowed Parking Play Area

FOWEY   MAP 02 SX15

The Ship Inn ♀

Trafalgar Square PL23 1AZ
☎ 01726 832230 📠 01726 834931
e-mail: a1dwd@msn.com
dir: *From A30 take B3269 & A390*

One of Fowey's oldest buildings, The Ship was built in 1570 by John Rashleigh, who sailed to the Americas with the as yet unknighted Walter Raleigh. Given Fowey's riverside position, assume a good choice of fish, including Thai fishcakes; prawn risotto; and home-made crab and mussel soup. Other options include Cornish sausages, or beef and Guinness pie. St Austell ales, real fires and a long tradition of genial hospitality add the final touches.

Open 10 -1am (Winter times vary please telephone)
Bar Meals L served all week 12–2.30 D served all week 6–9
Restaurant L served all week 12–2.30 D served all week 6–9 Av 3 course à la carte £20 ⊕ St Austell Brewery ◀ St Austell Tinners Ale, Tribute & HSD.
♀ 16 **Facilities** Children's licence Dogs allowed

GOLDSITHNEY   MAP 02 SW53

The Trevelyan Arms ♀

Fore St TR20 9JU ☎ 01736 710453
e-mail: mikehitchens@hotmail.com
dir: *5m from Penzance. A394 signed to Goldsithney*

The former manor house for Lord Trevelyan, this 17th-century property stands at the centre of the picturesque village just a mile from the sea. It has also been a coaching inn and a bank/post office in its time, but these days is very much the traditional family-run Cornish pub. Food is fresh and locally sourced, offering good value for money. Typical dishes are T-bone steaks, home-made pies and curries, pasta dishes and local fish.

Bar Meals L served Sat 12–2 D served all week 6–9 (Sun 12–2.30)
Restaurant L served Sat 12–2 D served all week 6–9 (Sun 12–2.30)
⊕ Punch Taverns ◀ Morland Speckled Hen, Flowers IPA, Guinness, St Austell Tribute. ♀ 12 **Facilities** Garden Dogs allowed

GUNNISLAKE   MAP 03 SX47

The Rising Sun Inn

Calstock Rd PL18 9BX ☎ 01822 832201
dir: *From Tavistock take A390 to Gunnislake, pub through village 0.25m on left. Left at lights, 0.25m on right*

A traditional two-roomed picture postcard pub set in award winning terraced gardens overlooking the beautiful Tamar Valley. Great walks start and finish at the Rising Sun, which is understandably popular with hikers and cyclists, locals and visitors. This pub is currently not serving food.

Open 12–2.30 5–11 ⊕ Free House ◀ Spitfire, Otter, Sharp's Cornish Coaster, Skinner's Betty Stogs Bitter. **Facilities** Children's licence Garden Dogs allowed Parking **Notes** ⊗

GUNWALLOE   MAP 02 SW62

Pick of the Pubs

The Halzephron Inn ♀

TR12 7QB ☎ 01326 240406 📠 01326 241442
e-mail: halzephroninn@gunwalloe1.fsnet.co.uk
dir: *3m S of Helston on A3083, right to Gunwalloe, through village. Inn on left*

The name of this ancient inn derives from Als Yfferin, old Cornish for 'cliffs of hell', an appropriate description of its situation on this hazardous stretch of coastline. Once a haunt of smugglers, the pub stands just 300 yards from the famous South Cornwall footpath and is the only pub on the stretch between Mullion and Porthleven. Originally called the Ship, it changed its name in the late 1950s when it regained its licence after 50 'dry' years. Today it offers a warm welcome, a wide selection of ales and whiskies, and meals prepared from fresh local produce. Lunch brings a choice of platters accompanied by home-made granary or white rolls, plus specials such as lamb casserole. The evening menu shifts comfortably from the classic (pan-fried escalopes of lamb's liver) to the modern: perhaps roast cod steak on a lightly curried mussel soup, or sweet and sour pork with egg fried rice.

Open 11–2.30 6.30–11 (Summer eve 6–11) Closed: 25 Dec
Bar Meals L served all week 12–2 D served all week 7–9 (Summer 6.30–9.30) **Restaurant** L served all week 12–2 D served all week 7–9 (Summer 6.30–9.30) ⊕ Free House ◀ Sharp's Own, Doom Bar & Special, St Austell Tribute, Organic Halzephron Gold. ♀ 6
Facilities Garden Parking

England

The Gweek Inn

TR12 6TU ☎ 01326 221502 📠 01326 221502
e-mail: info@gweekinn.co.uk
dir: *2m E of Helston near Seal Sanctuary*

The lovely location of this traditional family-run village pub at the mouth of the pretty Helford River makes booking a table a wise precaution. It is known for value-for-money food, typically steak, kidney and ale pie; tagliatelle con pollo; filled jacket potatoes; and a range of salads. The chalkboard lists locally caught seafood.

Open 12–2.30 6.30–11 **Bar Meals** L served all week 12–2 D served all week 6.30–9 (7–9 in winter) Av main course £7.50 **Restaurant** L served Sun 12–2 D served all week 6.30–9 (7–9 in winter) Av 3 course à la carte £15 ⊕ Punch Taverns ◀ Old Speckled Hen, Sharp's Doom Bar, Skinners Betty Stogs, 3 guest ales. **Facilities** Garden Dogs allowed Parking Play Area

The Watermill

Lelant Downs TR27 6LQ ☎ 01736 757912
e-mail: watermill@btconnect.com
dir: *Exit A30 at junct for St Ives/A3074, turn left at 2nd mini rdbt*

Built in the 1700s to mill grain for the local estate, the watermill was converted into a pub/restaurant in the 1970s. Old mill machinery is still in place and the iron waterwheel still turns, gravity fed by the mill stream. It is a family friendly establishment, with extensive gardens and fantastic views up the valley towards Trencrom Hill. Bar meals are served, and there is a separate restaurant where steaks and fish (sea bass, sardines and mackerel perhaps) are specialities.

Open 12–11 **Bar Meals** L served all week 12–2 D served all week 6–9 **Restaurant** D served all week 6–9 ⊕ Free House ◀ Sharp's Doom Bar, Ring 'o' Bells Dreckly, Skinners Betty Stogs. **Facilities** Garden Parking Play Area

The Halfway House Inn ♀

Fore St PL10 1NA ☎ 01752 822279 📠 01752 823146
e-mail: info@halfwayinn.biz
dir: *From Torpoint Ferry or Tamar Bridge follow signs to Mount Edgcumbe*

Set among the narrow lanes and colour-washed houses of a quaint fishing village, this family-run inn has been licensed since 1850, and has a pleasant stone-walled bar with low-beamed ceilings and a large central fireplace. Locally caught seafood is a feature of the small restaurant, including crab cocktail; sautéed scallops with white wine, cream and parsley sauce; whole sea bass with toasted almonds; and baked monkfish with Mediterranean vegetables. For the lunchtime visitor there's a good selection of bar snacks.

Open 12–3 7–11 (All day in summer) **Bar Meals** L served all week 12–2 D served all week 7–9 (Winter 12–2, 7–9) Av main course £10.50 **Restaurant** L served all week 12–2 D served all week 7–9 (Sun 12–2, 7–9) Av 3 course à la carte £17 ⊕ Free House ◀ Sharp's Doom Bar & Own, Marstons Pedigree, Guinness, John Smith's Smooth. ♀ 10 **Facilities** Dogs allowed **Rooms** available

Lamorna Wink

TR19 6XH ☎ 01736 731566
dir: *4m on B3315 towards Land's End, then 0.5m to turn on left*

This oddly-named pub was one of the original Kiddleywinks, a product of the 1830 Beer Act that enabled any householder to buy a liquor licence. Popular with walkers and not far from the Merry Maidens standing stones, the Wink provides a selection of local beers and a simple menu that includes sandwiches, jacket potatoes and fresh local crab. The management have been at the Wink for over thirty years, and pride themselves on providing diners with as much local produce as possible.

Open 11–11 (Winter 11–4, 6–11) **Bar Meals** L served all week 11–3 D served all week 6–9 ⊕ Free House ◀ Sharp's Doom Bar, Skinners, Cornish Ale, Heligan Honey & Cornish Storm Lager. **Facilities** Garden Dogs allowed Parking **Notes** ☺

Pick of the Pubs

The Crown Inn ★★★ INN ♀

See Pick of the Pubs on opposite page

The Crown Inn

This ancient pub has been extensively, but sympathetically, restored. The work uncovered a huge, deep well under the porch, which is now covered by glass enabling you to peer down as you walk over it.

The pub was built in the 12th century to house the stonemasons constructing the next-door church of St Brevita, past which runs Saints' Way, the old coast-to-coast path linking Padstow and Fowey. Needless to say, with such a history, everything about this charming pub oozes tradition – its thick stone walls, granite and slate floors, low beams, open fireplaces, and large, unusual bread oven. Fowey harbour is only a few miles away, so expect the menu to offer fresh crab, scallops, mackerel and much more. Other local produce also features strongly, including meats from a butcher's in Par, fruit and veg from Bodmin and dairy products from Lostwithiel. A typical meal might begin with an appetiser of marinated olives and ciabatta bread, then a starter of locally smoked duck, Cornish charcuterie, or pan-seared scallops. Main courses include braised shoulder of local lamb with red wine and rosemary gravy; duck leg confit with roasted new potatoes and braised red cabbage; and leek and mushroom pie. Have a fresh Fowey crab sandwich at lunchtime, or a Cornish brie, bacon and watercress ciabatta; or just a proper Cornish pasty. The beers come from Sharps in Rock and Skinners of Truro, while a reasonably priced wine list offers eight wines by the glass. The pretty front garden is a lovely spot to enjoy a summer evening, perhaps with a glass of Pimms. Five bed and breakfast rooms have been added in a new annexe.

★★★ INN ♥
MAP 02 SX05
PL30 5BT
☎ 01208 872707
🖷 01208 871208
e-mail:
thecrown@wagtailinns.com
dir: *Signed off A390 via brown sign about 1.5m W of Lostwithiel*

Open 12–11
Bar Meals L served all week
12–2.30 D served all week 6–9
(Summer 12–3, 5.30–9.15) Av
main course £8.95
Restaurant L served all week
12–2.30 D served all week
6.30–9.00 (Summer 12–3,
5.30–9.15) Av 3 course à la carte
£20
⊕ Free House ◀ Sharp's Doom
Bar, Skinners Betty Stogs, Skinners
Cornish Knocker, Crown Inn
glory. ♥ 7
Facilities Garden Dogs allowed
Parking
Rooms 9

England

The Royal Oak ♥

Duke St PL22 0AG

☎ 01208 872552 & 872922 📠 01208 872922

e-mail: di_and_dave@lycos.co.uk

dir: *A30 from Exeter to Bodmin then onto Lostwithiel. Or A38 from Plymouth towards Bodmin then left onto A390 to Lostwithiel*

There is believed to be a secret tunnel connecting this 12th-century inn to Restormel Castle a short way up the River Fowey. The tunnel was some kind of escape route, perhaps for smugglers. Though there is a strong emphasis on the restaurant side of the business, The Royal Oak also has a stone-flagged public bar, cosy and welcoming with a log fire, and separate lounge bar, both serving real ales like Betty Stogs and Sharp's Doom Bar. Quality Cornish produce is used wherever possible in a menu of largely traditional fare, with dishes such as deep-fried haddock with hand-cut chips, pea purée and tartare sauce, and slow-cooked belly pork with black pudding and Bramley apple sauce. Vegetarian options are also available, like baked aubergine herb salad with wild Cornish Yarg and basil dressing.

Open 11–12 (11–11 in winter) **Bar Meals** L served all week 12–2.30 D served all week 6–9 **Restaurant** L served all week 12–2.30 D served all week 6–9 ⊕ Punch Taverns ◀ Interbrew Bass, Fuller's London Pride, Sharp's Doom Bar, Tribute. ♥ 8 **Facilities** Garden Dogs allowed Parking **Rooms** available

White Hart

Churchtown TR20 8EY ☎ 01736 740574

dir: *From A30 take B3309 at Crowlas*

Built somewhere between 1280 and 1320, the White Hart retains the peaceful atmosphere of a bygone era and offers splendid views across St Michael's Mount and Bay. Fresh fish is a feature from Thursday to Saturday, and other popular dishes are toad-in-the-hole, steak and kidney pie and home-made lasagne (including a vegetarian version). The bar offers a good choice of malts and Irish whiskies.

Open 11–2.30 6–11 **Bar Meals** L served Tue-Sun (Mon-Sun Etr-Oct) 12–2 D served Tue-Sun (Mon-Sun Etr-Oct) 7–9 Av main course £6.50 **Restaurant** L served Tue-Sun (Mon-Sun Etr-Oct) 12–2 D served Tue-Sun (Mon-Sun Etr-Oct) 7–9 ⊕ Punch Taverns ◀ Sharp's Doom Bar, Flowers IPA & Abbots. **Facilities** Garden Dogs allowed Parking **Notes** ⊛

The Heron Inn

Trenhaile Ter TR1 1SL ☎ 01872 272773 📠 01872 272773

Two miles from Truro's city centre, the pub enjoys panoramic River Fal views from its large terrace. The building may be old but its interior is light and airy, echoing the colours of the river. Local produce is used in traditional home-made dishes such as local roast ham, fried egg and chips; beef lasagne with garlic bread; and a pan-fried trio of Cornish fish. Open all day through the summer months.

Open 11–3 6–11 (Open all day Summer Jun-Sep) **Bar Meals** L served Mon-Sat 12–2 D served Mon-Sat 6.30–9 (Sun 12–2, 7–9) ⊕ St Austell Brewery ◀ HSD, Tribute, IPA, Duchy. **Facilities** Children's licence Garden Dogs allowed Parking

The New Inn ♥

TR12 6HA ☎ 01326 231323

e-mail: penny@stmartin.wanadoo.co.uk

dir: *7m from Helston*

Thatched village pub, deep in Daphne du Maurier country, dating back to Cromwellian times, although obviously Cromwell forbade his men to drink here. Attractions include the homely bars and a large, natural garden full of flowers. At lunchtime you might try a locally made pasty or moules marinière, and in the evening perhaps sea bass and chive fishcakes with tomato coulis and sautéed vegetables, or slow-roasted lamb shank with red wine and redcurrant gravy.

Open 12–3 6–11 (Sat-Sun all day in summer) **Bar Meals** L served all week 12–2.30 D served all week 6–9.30 (Sun 12–2, 7–9) **Restaurant** L served all week D served all week ⊕ Punch Taverns ◀ Flowers IPA, Sharp's Doom Bar. ♥ 10 **Facilities** Garden Dogs allowed Parking Play Area

Pick of the Pubs

Godolphin Arms ★★ SHL

TR17 0EN ☎ 01736 710202 📠 01736 710171

e-mail: enquiries@godolphinarms.co.uk

dir: *From A30 just outside Penzance follow Marazion signs. Pub 1st large building on right in Marazion, opposite St Michael's Mount*

Locations don't come much more spectacular than this: the Godolphin Arms stands atop a sea wall directly opposite St

Michael's Mount, and has superb views across the bay. It's so close that the sea splashes at the windows in the winter, and you can watch the movement of seals, dolphins, ferries, and fishing boats returning to Newlyn with their daily catch. From the traditional bar and beer terrace to the more homely restaurant and most of the stylishly-decorated bedrooms, the Mount is clearly visible. Seafood figures prominently in the restaurant: the specials blackboard lists daily choices such as lemon sole pan fried in butter and capers; moules; scallops; or seafood tagliatelle. Aside from the view, the highlight of any stay is breakfast, which includes everything from a full English breakfast to kippers on toast.

Open 8–12 (8–11 Winter) **Bar Meals** L served all week 12–2.30 D served all week 6–9 (Summer 12–3, 6–9.30) ⊕ Free House ◀ Sharp's Doom Bar & Special, St Austell Tribute, Tetley's Smooth. **Facilities** Children's licence Garden Dogs allowed Parking **Rooms** 10

MEVAGISSEY   MAP 02 SX04

The Rising Sun Inn ♥

Portmellon Cove PL26 6PL ☎ 01726 843235
e-mail: cliffnsheila@tiscali.co.uk
dir: Telephone for directions

Built partly from shipwreck timber, this listed building is superbly situated in a beautiful cove on the Southwest Coastal Path. The inn has a cosy beamed bar, snug and cellar bar serving real ale, an impressive list of speciality bottled beers, malt whiskies and wines by the glass. The kitchen offers a host of local seafood dishes – teriyaki scallops, and crispy skinned sea bass among them – plus alternatives like Cornish duck breast or stuffed aubergine.

Open 11–3 6–12 (BHs, Apr-Oct 11–12) Closed: Nov-Feb **Bar Meals** L served all week 12.30–3 (Sun 12.30–4) Av main course £6 **Restaurant** L served all week 12.30–3 D served all week 6–9 (Sun 12.30–4) Av 3 course à la carte £25 ⊕ Free House ◀ Adnams Bitter, Fuller's London Pride, Skinners, Greene King Abbot Ale & Spitfire. ♥12 **Facilities** Dogs allowed Parking **Rooms** available

The Ship Inn ★★★ INN ♥

Fore St PL26 6UQ ☎ 01726 843324 📠 01726 844368
e-mail: shipinnian@hotmail.co.uk
dir: 7m S of St Austell

The inn stands just a few yards from Mevagissey's picturesque fishing harbour, so the choice of fish and seafood dishes comes as no surprise: moules marinière, beer-battered cod, and oven-baked fillet of haddock topped with prawns and Cornish Tiskey cheese and served with a lemon and dill sauce. Other options take in baguettes, burgers, jacket potatoes, steaks, and trio of Cornish sausages served with creamy mash and rich red onion gravy.

Open 11–12 **Bar Meals** L served all week 12–3 D served all week 6–9 ⊕ St Austell Brewery ◀ St Austell Ales. ♥8 **Facilities** Dogs allowed **Rooms** 5

MITCHELL   MAP 02 SW85

Pick of the Pubs

The Plume of Feathers

TR8 5AX ☎ 01872 510387 📠 01637 839401
e-mail: enquiries@theplume.info
dir: Exit A30 to Mitchell/Newquay

Since its establishment in the 16th century, the Plume of Feathers has accommodated various historical figures – John Wesley preached Methodism from the pillared entrance, and Sir Walter Raleigh used to live locally. The present owners took over the inn some years ago and have turned it into a successful destination pub restaurant; the imaginative kitchen has an excellent reputation for its food, based on a fusion of modern European and classical British dishes, with an emphasis on fresh fish and the best Cornish ingredients. There is always a daytime specials board, which changes at 6pm to include an extensive choice of 'on the night' creations. Dinner could start with chicken liver parfait with spiced pear chutney, or salmon and cod fishcake. Mains choices include grilled Angus rib-eye steak with tomato and onion salad; and penne pasta in a wild mushroom sauce. Specials include roasted whole sea bass with crispy fennel and basil salad, and chargrilled Moroccan rack of lamb with basmati rice.

Open 9–11 **Bar Meals** L served all week 12–5 D served all week 6–10 **Restaurant** L served all week 12–5 D served all week 6–10 ⊕ Free House ◀ Doom Bar, John Smiths Smooth. **Facilities** Garden Parking Play Area

---

MORWENSTOW   MAP 02 SS21

Pick of the Pubs

The Bush Inn ♥

EX23 9SR ☎ 01288 331242 📠 01288 331630
e-mail: info@bushinn-morwenstow.co.uk
dir: Exit A39, 3m N of Kilkhampton, 2nd right into village of Shop. 1.5m to Crosstown. Inn on village green

Thirteenth-century origins make it hard to challenge The Bush's claim to be one of Britain's oldest pubs, although long before then it had been a pilgrims' chapel of rest. Understandably, 18th-century smugglers loved its isolated cliff-top hamlet location, close to a dramatic stretch of the north Cornish coast. Its unspoilt interior features stone-flagged floors, old stone fireplaces and a 'leper's squint', a tiny window through which the needy grabbed food scraps. It's very different today. Meals are freshly prepared from fresh local produce, including beef from the inn's own farm, and lamb, pork, salad and vegetables from others nearby. Local shoots provide all the game and seafood comes from home waters. In winter, warming dishes include red wine and blue cheese risotto; venison stew; and Old Cornish sausages and mash with onion gravy. In summer enjoy a plate of mussels or beer-battered pollock and chips in the large garden overlooking the valley and the Atlantic.

Open 11–12 **Bar Meals** L served all week 12–6 D served all week 6–9.30 (winter 6–9, Sun 12–3) **Restaurant** L served all week 12–3 D served all week 6–9.30 (winter 6–9) Av 3 course à la carte £22 ⊕ Free House ◀ St Austell HSD, Sharp's Doom Bar, Skinners Betty Stogs & St. Austell Tribute. ♥8 **Facilities** Children's licence Garden Dogs allowed Parking Play Area **Rooms** available

St Michael's Mount , Marazion, Cornwall

MYLOR BRIDGE — MAP 02 SW83

Pick of the Pubs

The Pandora Inn ♀

Restronguet Creek TR11 5ST
☎ 01326 372678 📠 01326 378958

dir: *From Truro/Falmouth follow A39, left at Carclew, follow signs to pub*

Rather romantically, you can reach this thatched, white-painted inn by foot, bicycle and boat. It has a breathtaking location, set right on the banks of the Restongruet Creek, with panoramic views across the water. There's seating right outside, and also at the end of the pontoon, where up to twenty boats can moor at high tide. The inn itself dates back in part to the 13th century, and its flagstone floors, low-beamed ceilings and thatched roof suggest little can have changed since. The name stems from the good ship Pandora, sent to Tahiti to capture the Bounty mutineers. Sadly, it was wrecked and the captain court-martialled. Forced into early retirement, he bought the inn. Call in for a casual lunch: perhaps smoked mackerel fillets with creamed horseradish. In the evening make a meal of grilled sea bass with spinach risotto; or home-made Cornish crab cakes in saffron dressing.

Open 10–12 (Winter 10.30–11) **Bar Meals** L served all week 12–3 D served all week 6.30–9 (Fri-Sat 6.30–9.30) Av main course £12 **Restaurant** L served all week 12–3 D served all week 7–9 (Fri-Sat 7–9.30) Av 3 course à la carte £23 Av 3 course fixed price £24 ⊞ St Austell Brewery ◀ St Austell Tinners Ale, HSD, Bass, Tribute. ♀ 12 **Facilities** Garden Dogs allowed Parking

PENZANCE — MAP 02 SW43

Dolphin Tavern

Quay St TR18 4BD ☎ 01736 364106 📠 01736 364194

A 600–year-old harbourside pub overlooking Mounts Bay and St Michael's Mount. In this building, apparently, Sir Walter Raleigh first smoked tobacco on English soil and, the following century, Judge Jeffreys held court. Haunted by not one but several ghosts. A good choice of seafish is among the options on the menu.

Open 10–12 **Bar Meals** L served all week 11–9.30 D served all week 11–9.30 Av main course £6.95 ⊞ St Austell Brewery ◀ St Austell HSD, Tinners Tribute, Cornish Cream. **Facilities** Garden Dogs allowed

The Turks Head Inn ♀

Chapel St TR18 4AF ☎ 01736 363093 📠 01736 360215
e-mail: turkshead@gibbards9476.fsworld.co.uk

dir: *Telephone for directions*

Dating from around 1233, making it Penzance's oldest pub, it was the first in the country to be given the Turks Head name. Sadly, a Spanish raiding party destroyed much of the original building in the 16th century, but an old smugglers' tunnel leading directly to the harbour and priest holes still exist. Typically available are fresh seafood choices like mussels, sea bass, John Dory, lemon sole, and tandoori monkfish, along with others such as pan-fried venison, chicken stir-fry, pork tenderloin, steaks, mixed grill and salads. A sunny flower-filled garden lies at the rear.

Open 11–11 (Mon-Sat all day, Sun 12–3, 5.30–10.30) **Bar Meals** L served Mon-Sat 11–2.30 D served Mon-Sat 6–10 (Sun 12–2.30, 6–10) **Restaurant** L served all week 11–2.30 D served all week 6–10 Av 2 course fixed price £10 ⊞ Punch Taverns ◀ Betty Stogs, 6X, Sharp's Doom Bar & guest ale. ♀ 14 **Facilities** Garden Dogs allowed

PERRANUTHNOE — MAP 02 SW52

The Victoria Inn ★★★ INN ◉

TR20 9NP ☎ 01736 710309 📠 01736 719284
e-mail: enquiries@victoriainn-penzance.co.uk

dir: *Off A394 (Penzance to Helston road), signed Perranuthnoe*

Queen Victoria stares sternly from the sign outside this pink-washed, 12th-century inn, reputedly Cornwall's oldest, and first used as a hostelry by masons building the village church. Fresh seafood is its forte, the selection changing daily according to the local catch. Among the possibilities are megrim sole stuffed with Newlyn crab and baby bay prawns, and halibut steak with avocado salsa and Moroccan orange dressing. In the garden imagine you're by the Med.

Open 12–2.30 6.30–11 Closed: 25 & 26 Dec, 1 Jan, 1st wk Jan, Sun eve & Mon off season **Bar Meals** L served all week 12–2 D served all week 6.30–9 **Restaurant** L served all week 12–2 D served all week 6.30–9 Av 3 course à la carte £22 ◀ Doom Bar, Tribute. **Facilities** Garden Dogs allowed Parking **Rooms** 2

POLKERRIS — MAP 02 SX05

The Rashleigh Inn ♀

PL24 2TL ☎ 01726 813991 📠 01726 815619
e-mail: jonspode@aol.com

dir: *Off A3082 outside Fowey*

This 300–year-old stone-built building on the beach – once a boathouse and coastguard station – became the village pub in 1915

CONTINUED

England

POLKERRIS continued

when the previous one was swept away during a storm. Panoramic views across St Austell Bay from the multi-level heated and panelled terrace. Excellent real ale selection, with two real ciders and local organic soft drinks. And superb eating: seafood such as lobster thermidor, or scallops in cream and cider; Cornish beef and lamb too; and traditional home-made desserts.

Open 11–11 (Sun 12–10.30) **Bar Meals** L served all week 12–2 D served all week 6–9 Av main course £7.95 **Restaurant** L served all week 12–2 D served all week 6–9 Av 3 course à la carte £21 ⊕ Free House ◀ Sharp's Doom Bar, Cotleigh Tawny, Blue Anchor Spingo, Timothy Taylor Landlord. ♀ 8 **Facilities** Garden Parking

POLPERRO   MAP 02 SX25

Old Mill House Inn

Mill Hill PL13 2RP ☎ 01503 272362
e-mail: oldmillhouseinn@btconnect.com
dir: *Telephone for directions*

In the heart of historic Polperro, this 16th-century inn has been extensively refurbished. Here you can sample well-kept local ales and 'scrumpy' cider beside a log fire in the bar, or sit out over lunch in the riverside garden during fine weather. Local ingredients, with an emphasis on freshly caught fish, are the foundation of dishes on the restaurant menu. Traditional roasts are served on Sundays.

Open 11–11 **Bar Meals** L served all week 12–2.30 (Sun carvery 12–3 not every wk) **Restaurant** D served Mon-Sat 7–9.30 ⊕ Free House ◀ Skinners, Erdinger Weiss ale, Skinners Mill House Ale. **Facilities** Garden Dogs allowed Parking

PORT GAVERNE   MAP 02 SX08

Pick of the Pubs

Port Gaverne Hotel ★★ HL ♀

PL29 3SQ ☎ 01208 880244 🖹 01208 880151
dir: *Signed from B3314, S of Delabole via B3267 on E of Port Isaac*

Just up the lane from a beautiful little cove, this delightful 17th-century inn is a magnet for both locals and holidaymakers. It's a meandering building with plenty of period detail, evocative of its long association with fishing and smuggling. Bread is home made, and locally supplied produce includes plenty of fresh fish. Along with a selection of ploughman's and children's favourites, the lunchtime bar menu offers a half pint of prawns with mayonnaise; seafood pie served with new potatoes and vegetables; or a

chargrilled chicken salad. At dinner you might try tomato, red onion and Cornish goats' cheese salad; pan-fried fillet of John Dory served on saffron mash with a white wine and parsley sauce; and a selection of West Country cheeses. Walkers from the Heritage Coast Path can pause for a pint of St Austell Tribute in the small beer garden, or at a table in front of the hotel.

Open 11–11 **Bar Meals** L served all week 12–2.30 D served all week 6.30–9.30 **Restaurant** D served all week 7–9.30 ⊕ Free House ◀ Sharp's Doom Bar, Bass, St Austell Tribute. ♀ 9 **Facilities** Garden Dogs allowed Parking **Rooms** 15

PORTHLEVEN   MAP 02 SW62

The Ship Inn

TR13 9JS ☎ 01326 564204 🖹 01326 564204
e-mail: cjoakden@yahoo.co.uk
dir: *From Helston follow signs to Porthleven, 2.5m. On entering village continue to harbour. Take W road by side of harbour to inn*

Dating from the 17th century, this smugglers' inn is actually built into the cliffs, and is approached by a flight of stone steps. During the winter two log fires warm the interior, while the flames of a third flicker in the separate Smithy children's room. Expect a good selection of locally caught fish and seafood, such as crab thermidor, moules marinara or the day's catch. Don't, however, expect chips, not even with a 10oz gammon steak.

Open 11.30–11 (Sun 12–10.30) **Bar Meals** L served all week 12–2 D served all week 7–9 ⊕ Free House ◀ Courage Best, Sharp's Doom Bar & Special, & guest ales. **Facilities** Garden Dogs allowed

PORTREATH   MAP 02 SW64

Basset Arms

Tregea Ter TR16 4NG ☎ 01209 842077
e-mail: bassettarms@btconnect.com
dir: *From Redruth take B3300 to Portreath. Pub on left near seafront*

Tin-mining and shipwreck paraphernalia adorn the low-beamed interior of this early 19th-century Cornish stone cottage, built as a pub to serve harbour workers. The menu makes the most of local seafood, such as mussels and fries, and home-made fish pie, but also provides a wide selection of alternatives, including half-chicken in barbecue sauce; 12oz gammon steak; curry of the day; and salads – ham, cheese, prawn and, when available, crab.

Open 11–11 (wknds & summer 11–12) **Bar Meals** L served all week 12–2 D served all week 6–9 (Summer 12–2.30, 6–9.30) Av main course £9 **Restaurant** L served all week 12–2 D served all week 6–9 (summer 12–2.30, 6–9.30) Av 3 course à la carte £16 ⊕ Free House ◀ Sharp's Doom Bar, Worthington 6X, Courage & John Smith's Smooth. **Facilities** Children's licence Garden Dogs allowed Parking Play Area

England

RUAN LANIHORNE   MAP 02 SW84

The Kings Head

TR2 5NX ☎ 01872 501263

e-mail: contact@kings-head-roseland.co.uk

dir: *3m from Tregony Bridge on A3078*

Deep in the Roseland countryside, there's a warm welcome at this rural free house. Roaring winter fires, beamed ceilings and mulled wine contrast with summer days relaxing on the terrace with a jug of Pimms. But whatever the time of year, the chef responds with seasonal menus that might include hot or cold soups, pheasant, venison and shellfish in season. Look out for the signature dish, too – slow-roasted Ruan duckling with a warm pepper sauce.

Open 12–2.30 6–11 Closed: Mon Nov-Mar **Restaurant** L served all week 12.30–2 D served all week 6.30–9 ⊕ Free House ◀ Skinners Kings Ruan, Cornish Knocker, Betty Stogs. **Facilities** Garden Dogs allowed Parking

---

ST AGNES   MAP 03 SW75

Driftwood Spars ★★★★ GA ♥

Trevaunance Cove TR5 0RT

☎ 01872 552428 🖺 01872 553701

e-mail: driftwoodspars@hotmail.com

dir: *A30 onto B3285, through St Agnes, down steep hill, left at Peterville Inn, onto road signed Trevaunance Cove*

Just off the coastal path, this family-run pub with rooms, restaurant, beer gardens and microbrewery, is housed in a 300-year-old tin miners' store, chandlery and sail loft, complete with its own smugglers' tunnel. The name comes from the huge beams that were originally spars from a shipwrecked boat. Eight hand-pulled real ales are served alongside 50 malts, 10 rums and a 40-bin wine list. Daily changing specials supplement the seasonal menu and seafood figures strongly.

Open 11-1am **Bar Meals** L served all week 12–2.30 D served all week 6.30–9.30 (All day Aug) Av main course £10 **Restaurant** L served all week 12–2.30 D served all week 6.30–9.30 (No food 25 Dec & short L 1 Jan) ⊕ Free House ◀ Carlsberg-Tetley Bitter, St Austell HSD, Cuckoo Ale, Sharp's Doom Bar & Own. ♥ 9 **Facilities** Garden Dogs allowed Parking **Rooms** 15

ST AGNES (ISLES OF SCILLY)   MAP 02 SV80

Turks Head

TR22 0PL ☎ 01720 422434

dir: *By boat or helicopter to St Mary's & boat on to St Agnes*

Named after the 16th-century Turkish pirates who arrived from the Barbary Coast, the Turks Head is Britain's most southwesterly inn. Noted for its atmosphere and superb location overlooking the island quay, this former coastguard boathouse is packed with fascinating model ships and maritime photographs. Lunchtime brings soup, salads and open rolls, while evening dishes might include blackened swordfish steak in Cajun spices, or sirloin steak with all the trimmings.

Open 10.30–11.30 Closed: Nov-Feb **Bar Meals** L served all week 12–2.30 D served all week 6–9 ⊕ Free House ◀ Skinners Betty Stogs, Sharp's Doom Bar, Ales of Scilly, Scuppered. **Facilities** Garden Dogs allowed

---

ST BREWARD   MAP 02 SX07

The Old Inn & Restaurant ♥

Churchtown, Bodmin Moor PL30 4PP

☎ 01208 850711 🖺 01208 851671

e-mail: darren@theoldinn.fsnet.co.uk

dir: *A30 to Bodmin. 16m, right just after Temple, follow signs to St Breward. B3266 (Bodmin to Camelford road) turn to St Breward, follow brown signs*

Located high up on Bodmin Moor, one of Cornwall's oldest inns is now owned and run by local man Darren Wills, the latest licensee in its 1,000–year history. The pub is well-known throughout this glorious area for its wholesome home-cooked food, frequented by many regulars who are drawn by its Moorland Grills and Sunday roasts. Sizzling platters, home-made curries and an array of fish and vegetarian options add to the menu's appeal. Check out the local Cornish wines as well.

Open 11–11 **Bar Meals** L served Mon-Fri 11–2 D served Mon-Fri 6–9 (Sat 11–9, Sun 12–2, 6–9) Av main course £8.95 **Restaurant** L served Mon-Fri 11–2 D served Mon-Fri 6–9 (Sat 11–9, Sun 12–9) Av 3 course à la carte £24.50 ⊕ Free House ◀ Sharp's Doom Bar & Special, guest ales. ♥ 20 **Facilities** Garden Dogs allowed Parking

England

ST EWE
MAP 02 SW94

The Crown Inn ☺
PL26 6EY ☎ 01726 843322 📠 01726 844720
e-mail: linda@thecrowninn737.fsnet.co.uk
dir: *From St Austell take B3273. At Tregiskey x-rds turn right. St Ewe signed on right*

Hanging baskets add plenty of brightness and colour to this delightful 16th-century inn, just a mile from the famous 'Lost gardens of Heligan', which Crown chef John Nelson co-founded and helped to restore. Well-kept St Austell ales complement an extensive menu and daily specials. Expect cod in beer batter, local steaks, rack of lamb, and liver and bacon among other favourites. Try a glass of Polmassick wine from the vineyard only half a mile away.

Open 12–3 5–11 **Bar Meals** L served all week 12–2 D served all week 6–9 **Restaurant** L served all week 12–2 D served all week 6–9 ⊞ St Austell Brewery ◀ Tribute, Hicks Special, Tinners & guest ale. ☺ 8 **Facilities** Garden Dogs allowed Parking Play Area

ST JUST (NEAR LAND'S END) MAP 02 SW33

Pick of the Pubs

Star Inn
TR19 7LL ☎ 01736 788767
dir: *Telephone for directions*

Plenty of tin mining and fishing stories are told at this traditional Cornish pub, located in the town of St Just, near Lands End. It dates back a few centuries, and was reputedly built to house workmen constructing the 15th-century church. John Wesley is believed to have been among the Star's more illustrious guests over the years, but these days the pub is most likely to be recognised for having featured in several television and film productions. A choice of local beers is served, but there is no food. Monday night is folk night, and there's live music on Thursdays and Saturdays, too, in a whole range of styles.

Open 11–11 (Sat 11–12, Sun 12–11) ⊞ St Austell Brewery ◀ St Austell HSD, Tinners Ale, Tribute, Dartmoor. **Facilities** Garden Dogs allowed **Notes** ☺

ST MAWES
MAP 02 SW83

Pick of the Pubs

The Rising Sun ☺
The Square TR2 5DJ ☎ 01326 270233 📠 01209 270198
e-mail: info@risingsunstmawes.com
dir: *From A39 take A3078 signed St Mawes, in village centre*

At the heart of Cornwall's yachting community, The Rising Sun stands by the picturesque harbour at St Mawes. The Lizard Peninsula shelters this popular yet dignified resort from the vagaries of the Atlantic, and the mild climate makes the terrace an ideal spot to relax with a drink and watch the world sail by. Innovative English cooking is offered from a flexible daily changing menu, taking account of the freshest local ingredients available. The emphasis is on wholesome food, flavour and attractive presentation so that diners enjoy every aspect of their meal. Seafood is strongly represented with crab bisque, hot smokie crumble, and grilled sea bass fillets with redcurrant dressing. Other options might be pink organic West Country duck breast with red wine sauce, and comfort food like cottage pie, beef burgers, fishcakes and chicken curry.

Open 10–11 **Bar Meals** L served all week 12–2.30 D served all week 6.30–9 (Summer all day) Av main course £10.50 **Restaurant** L served all week 12–2.30 D served all week 6.45–9 (Oct-Mar 12–2) ⊞ St Austell Brewery ◀ Hicks Special Draught, St Austell Tinners Ale, Tribute. ☺ 11 **Facilities** Garden Dogs allowed Parking

Pick of the Pubs

The Victory Inn ☺
Victory Hill TR2 5PQ
☎ 01326 270324 📠 01326 270238
e-mail: contact@victory-inn.co.uk
web: www.victory-inn.co.uk
dir: *Take A3078 to St Mawes. Pub up Victory Steps adjacent to harbour*

Close to St Mawes harbour on the Roseland Peninsula is this friendly fishermen's local, named after Nelson's flagship. Traditional yet also a modern dining pub, it serves food at lunchtime and dinner seven days a week. The warm welcome from Phil and Debbie Heslip embraces one and all, including children who are provided with paper, crayons and their own menu, while dogs are given treats. The first-floor Seaview restaurant and heated covered terrace look across the rooftops to the harbour. Not surprisingly, the freshest of local seafood is high on the list of ingredients all supplied from Cornwall; look out for sea bass fillets on smoked salmon and leek risotto; or John Dory fillets with new potatoes. Alternatively starters like chicken satay skewers marinated in ginger, or crayfish tails on mixed leaves, can be followed by slow-roasted shoulder of lamb, a mixed grill, or whole ham hock with pesto mash.

Open 11–11 Closed: Nov–Mar **Bar Meals** L served all week 12–2.30 D served all week 6.30–9.30 (Winter 6.30–9.30) **Restaurant** L served Mon–Sun 12–2.15 D served Mon–Sun 6.30–9 Av 3 course à la carte £20 ⊕ Punch Taverns ◀ Sharp's, Bass, Wadworth 6X, Adnams Broadside. ☂ 8 **Facilities** Dogs allowed

ST MAWGAN   MAP 02 SW86

Pick of the Pubs

The Falcon Inn ★★★★ INN ☂

TR8 4EP ☎ 01637 860225 🖹 01637 860884

e-mail: enquiries@thefalconinn-newquay.co.uk

dir: *From A30 (8m W of Bodmin) follow signs to Newquay/St Mawgan Airport. After 2m right into village, pub at bottom of hill*

Nestling in the sheltered Vale of Lanherne, the Falcon has a large, attractive garden with a lovely magnolia tree and walls covered with wisteria, plus a cobbled courtyard. Inside it is cosy and relaxed, with flagged stone floors and log fires in winter. The beers come from the St Austell brewery, and there are plenty of wines available by the glass with a choice of ten malt whiskies. At lunchtime, you'll find home-made soup; garlic bread made with sun-dried tomatoes and basil ciabatta; sandwiches, jacket potatoes; and bigger dishes such as seafood and broccoli mornay; tortelloni al pesto; chicken, mushroom and ale pie; and vegetable and five bean chilli. The evening menu is more substantial and may feature starters of fresh scallops; Cornish smoked salmon and shell-on prawns; antipasto misto; or roast vegetable bruschetta. Among the main courses there are always fish dishes such as red mullet, hake or trout.

Open 11–3 6–12 (Sun 12–5, 7–11) **Bar Meals** L served all week 12–2 D served all week 6–9 (Summer 12–2.30, 6–9.30) **Restaurant** L served all week 12–2 D served all week 6–9 ⊕ St Austell Brewery ◀ St Austell HSD, Tinners Ale & Tribute. ☂ 7 **Facilities** Garden Dogs allowed Parking Play Area **Rooms** 2

ST NEOT   MAP 02 SX16

The London Inn ☂

PL14 6NG ☎ 01579 320263 🖹 01579 321642

e-mail: lon.manager@ccinns.com

Dating back to the 18th century, this pub was the first coaching inn on the route from Penzance to London. The bar and dining areas have old beamed ceilings and polished flagstone floors. Seafood platter, salmon, and halibut are among the fish dishes, while other main courses include lamb shank in a spiced port sauce. Lighter fare ranges from ciabatta bread with a variety of fillings, including roast beef, chicken, bacon and cheese, to a choice of ploughman's lunches.

Open 12–3 6.30–11 **Bar Meals** L served all week 12–2 D served all week 7–9 Av main course £9.95 **Restaurant** L served all week 12–2 D served all week 7–9 Av 3 course à la carte £25 ◀ Doom Bar, Courage Best, John Smiths & guest ales. ☂ 16 **Facilities** Dogs allowed Parking

SALTASH   MAP 03 SX45

The Crooked Inn ★★★ GA

Stoketon Cottage, Trematon PL12 4RZ
☎ 01752 848177 🖹 01752 843203

e-mail: info@crooked-inn.co.uk

dir: *Telephone for directions*

Overlooking the lush Lyher Valley, a family-run inn that once housed staff from Stoketon Manor, whose ruins lie the other side of the courtyard. Traditional, home-made dishes include pie, pasta or curry of the day; battered fresh cod; breaded wholetail scampi; and 'generous, hefty, ample or copious' steaks. Boards list lunchtime, evening and vegetarian specials and there's a special Little Horrors menu. The children's playground has friendly animals, swings, slides, a trampoline and a treehouse.

Open 11–11 (Sun 11–10.30) Closed: 25 Dec **Bar Meals** L served all week 12–2.30 D served all week 6–9.30 Av main course £6.95 **Restaurant** L served all week 12–2.30 D served all week 6–9.30 ⊕ Free House ◀ Hicks Special Draught, Sharp's Own Ale, Skinner's Cornish Knocker Ale. **Facilities** Children's licence Garden Dogs allowed Parking Play Area **Rooms** 18 (15 en suite)

The Weary Friar Inn ★★★★ INN

Pillaton PL12 6QS ☎ 01579 350238 🖹 01579 350238

e-mail: info@wearyfriar.co.uk

dir: *2m W of A388 between Callington & Saltash*

This whitewashed 12th-century inn with oak-beamed ceilings, an abundance of brass, and blazing fires lies next to the Church of St

Continued

SALTASH continued

Adolphus, tucked away in a small Cornish village. A typical selection from the menu includes venison pie, spit roasted chicken, fillet steak with wild mushroom sauce, spinach and mushroom bake, and Cornish crab cakes. Salads, sandwiches, afternoon cream teas and ploughman's are also available. Curry and other themed nights are popular.

Open 11–11 (Sun 12–10.30) **Bar Meals** L served Mon-Sat 11–3 D served all week 5–9 (Sun 12–3) **Restaurant** L served all week 11–3 D served all week 5–9 ⊕ Free House ◀ St Austell Tribute, Tinners, Interbrew Bass, Fuller's London Pride. **Facilities** Garden Parking **Rooms** 12

SENNEN   MAP 02 SW32

The Old Success Inn ★★ HL

Sennen Cove TR19 7DG ☎ 01736 871232 📠 01736 871457
e-mail: oldsuccess@sennencove.fsbusiness.co.uk
dir: *Telephone for directions*

Once the haunt of smugglers and now a focal point for the Sennen Lifeboat crew, this 17th-century inn enjoys a glorious location overlooking Cape Cornwall. Its name comes from the days when fishermen gathered here to count their catch and share out their 'successes'. Fresh local seafood is to the fore, and favourites include cod in Doom Bar batter, steaks, chilli, and vegetable lasagne. Live music every Saturday night in the bar.

Open 11–11 **Bar Meals** L served all week 12–2.30 D served all week 6.15–9.30 **Restaurant** L served Sun 12–2.15 D served all week 7–9.30 Av 3 course à la carte £18.50 Av 3 course fixed price £17 ⊕ Free House ◀ Doom Bar, Skinners, Heligan Honey, Headlaunch Special. **Facilities** Garden Dogs allowed Parking **Rooms** 12

TINTAGEL   MAP 02 SX08

The Port William ★★★ INN ♀

Trebarwith Strand PL34 0HB
☎ 01840 770230 📠 01840 770936
e-mail: theportwilliam@btinternet.com
dir: *Off B3263 between Camelford & Tintagel, pub signed*

Occupying one of the best locations in Cornwall, this former harbourmaster's house lies directly on the coastal path, 50 yards from the sea. There is an entrance to a smugglers' tunnel at the rear of the ladies' toilet! Focus on the daily-changing specials board for such dishes as artichoke and roast pepper salad, warm smoked trout platter, and spinach ricotta tortelloni.

Open 11–11 (Winter 12–11, Sun 12–10.30) **Bar Meals** L served all week 12–2.30 D served all week 6.30–9.30 Av main course £8.50 **Restaurant** L served all week 12–2.30 D served all week 6–9.30 Av 3 course à la carte £15 ⊕ Free House ◀ St Austell Tinners Ale & Hicks, Interbrew Bass. ♀ 8 **Facilities** Garden Dogs allowed Parking **Rooms** 8

TORPOINT   MAP 03 SX45

Pick of the Pubs

Edgcumbe Arms ♀

Cremyll PL10 1HX ☎ 01752 822294 📠 01752 822014
e-mail: edgcumbe-arms@btconnect.com
dir: *Telephone for directions*

The inn dates from the 15th century and is located right on the Tamar estuary, next to the National Trust Park, close to the foot ferry from Plymouth. Views from the bow window seats and waterside terrace are glorious, taking in Drakes Island, the Royal William Yard and the marina. Real ales from St Austell like Cornish Cream, Tribute HS, and Tinners, and quality home-cooked food are served in a series of rooms, which are full of character with American oak panelling and stone flagged floors. A good choice of bar snacks is also offered. The inn has a first floor function room with sea views, and a courtyard garden; it also holds a civil wedding license.

Open 11–11 (Sun 12–10.30) **Bar Meals** L served all week 12–6 D served all week 6–9.30 **Restaurant** L served all week 12–6 D served all week 6–9.30 ⊕ St Austell Brewery ◀ St Austell HSD, Tribute HS, IPA, Cornish Cream. ♀ 10 **Facilities** Garden Dogs allowed Parking

TREBARWITH   MAP 02 SX08

Pick of the Pubs

The Mill House Inn

See Pick of the Pubs on opposite page

PICK OF THE PUBS

The Mill House Inn

Set in seven acres of wooded gardens on the north Cornish coast, the Mill House dates back to 1760 and was a working mill until the late 1930s. Hardly surprising, then, that it's a beautifully atmospheric stone building with log fires in the bar and residents' lounge.

Surfing beaches, the coastal path and numerous tourist attractions are dotted around the surrounding area; King Arthur's legendary castle of Tintagel is in the very next valley. Originally known as Treknow Mill, the building became a public house in 1960. 2008 saw the building of a new restaurant with the millstream diverted alongside. The slate-floored bar with its wooden tables and chapel chairs has a relaxed, family-friendly feel. Lunches, evening drinks and barbeques can be enjoyed outside on the attractive split-level terraces in fine weather. Sharps local ales and an unusual and creative wine list complement the regularly changing lunch and dinner menus, which make use of the best locally sourced ingredients. At lunchtime, traditional pub favourites such as sausages and mash or battered haddock and chips appear alongside more adventurous dishes like Tuscan bean cassoulet with dressed leaves, parmesan and ciabatta. In the restaurant, typical starters include pan-fried medallions of monkfish with local bacon and dressed leaves; and oven-baked stuffed mushrooms. You could follow with chargrilled Cornish venison steak on potato wedges with creamy wholegrain mustard sauce; or roast supreme of local chicken wrapped in Parma ham and served on couscous. Round things off with a choice of home-made traditional and contemporary desserts, or a selection from the local cheeseboard.

MAP 02 SX08
PL34 0HD
☎ 01840 770200
🖷 01840 770647
e-mail: management@
themillhouseinn.co.uk
web: www.themillhouseinn.co.uk
dir: *From Tintagel take B3263 S, right after Trewarmett to Trebarwith Strand. Pub 0.5m on right.*

Open 12–11 Closed: 25 Dec
Bar Meals L served Mon-Sat 12–2.30 (Sun 12–3)
Restaurant D served all week 6.30–9 Av 3 course à la carte £28
⊕ Free House ◀ Sharp's Doom Bar, Red Stripe, Sharp's & Wills Resolve.
Facilities Children's licence Garden Dogs allowed Parking Play Area
Rooms available

The Mill House

The Springer Spaniel

Reputedly a pub for the last 200 years, with old creeper-clad walls concealing a cosy bar with high-backed wooden settles, farmhouse-style chairs, and a wood-burning stove. The atmosphere is friendly, and there's bound to be a local willing to reveal an interesting nugget or two about the area.

This is a pub that seeks to bring the best that a traditional Cornish hostelry can offer – delectable ales, delicious food, fine wines and tip-top service. You can bring your dog, join in with the chat or read the papers, or cast an eye over the many books in the snug. Children are always welcome, and will have fun with the 'Little Jack Russell' menu which serves up chicken goujons; sausages, chips and beans; and fresh penne bolognaise. The restaurant is full of plants and flowers, with flickering candles in the evenings adding to the romantic atmosphere. In summer the small and sheltered garden is a great place to relax and enjoy the sunshine with a pint of Skinners. The fully stocked bar also includes other local brews and guest ales, all with a cask marque as well

as a wine list designed to suit the food on offer, and an eclectic range of spirits and liqueurs. Food is a big draw here, with daily-changing blackboards displaying the best of fresh and seasonal produce. Imaginative menus feature fresh fish and seafood from Cornish waters, meat and game from local farmers and estates, with organic beef and lamb from the pub owner's own farm. Seared scallops are always a wonderful summer treat, while dishes of rabbit, venison and boar represent 'wild food' at its best. Try a ciabatta filled with meltingly tender steak, or an organic beefburger and Springer chips.

♈
MAP 03 SX37
PL15 9NS
☎ 01579 370424
e-mail: enquiries@
thespringerspaniel.org.uk
web: www.thespringerspaniel.
org.uk
dir: *On A388 halfway between
Launceston & Callington*

Open 12–3 6–11 (Fri-Sat eve
6–12)
Bar Meals L served Mon-Sat
12–1.45 D served all week
6.30–8.45
Restaurant L served all week
12–1.45 D served all week
6.30–8.45
⊕ Free House ◼ Sharp's
Doom Bar, Skinners Betty Stogs,
St Austell Tribute & guest. ♈ 7
Facilities Garden Dogs allowed
Parking

TREBURLEY   MAP 03 SX37

Pick of the Pubs

The Springer Spaniel ♀

See Pick of the Pubs on opposite page

TREGADILLETT   MAP 03 SX28

Eliot Arms (Square & Compass) ♀

PL15 7EU ☎ 01566 772051

e-mail: eli.bookings@ccinns.com

dir: *From Launceston take A30 towards Bodmin. Then follow brown signs to Tregadillett*

This old coaching inn is built from Cornish stone and boasts a huge collection of clocks, Masonic regalia and horse brasses. It was believed to have been a Masonic lodge for Napoleonic prisoners, and even has its own friendly ghost! Customers can enjoy real fires in winter and lovely hanging baskets in summer. Fish features strongly, with delicacies such as moules marinière and grilled sardines. Other options include Cajun-style chicken, and home-made vegetable curry.

Open 11.30–3 6–11 (Fri-Sun all day) **Bar Meals** L served all week 12–2 D served all week 7–9 Av main course £11 **Restaurant** L served all week 12–2 D served all week 7–9 Av 3 course à la carte £20 ⊕ Free House ◀ Doom Bar, Courage Best. ♀9 **Facilities** Dogs allowed Parking

TRESCO (ISLES OF SCILLY)   MAP 02 SV81

Pick of the Pubs

The New Inn ★★ HL ⑨ ♀

New Grimsby TR24 0QQ

☎ 01720 422844 📄 01720 423200

e-mail: newinn@tresco.co.uk

dir: *By New Grimsby Quay*

Tresco is one of five inhabited islands in the Scillies, 29 miles south west of Lands End. The New Inn is the only pub remaining out of thirteen and, as you might expect, the sea has always been a big influence – even its signboard was salvaged from a wreck. The Main Bar is famous for its Cornish and Scillonian ales. On the lunchtime menu some starters, such as salmon fishcakes and grilled goat's cheese, double up as mains, while locally caught fish and seafood appear on the specials board. For evening dining, there's a choice – the quiet restaurant, the livelier Driftwood Bar, the Pavillion, or simply alfresco. The dinner menu, offering, for example, confit duck leg; pan-fried calves' liver; and even a chateaubriand for two is complemented by daily specials. On Sundays there's a traditional roast. Many of the double rooms have ocean views.

Open 11–11 (Nov, Dec, Jan 11–2.30, 6–11) **Bar Meals** L served all week 12–2 D served all week 6–9 (Limited menu Apr-Sep) **Restaurant** D served all week 7–9 Av 3 course à la carte £24.50 ⊕ Free House ◀ Skinner's Betty Stogs Bitter, Tresco Tipple, Ales of Scilly Scuppered & Firebrand, St Austell IPA. ♀12 **Facilities** Garden **Rooms** 16

TRURO   MAP 02 SW84

Old Ale House ♀

7 Quay St TR1 2HD ☎ 01872 271122 📄 01872 271817

e-mail: old.ale.house@btconnect.com

dir: *In town centre*

Olde-worlde establishment with a large selection of real ales on display, as well as more than twenty flavours of fruit wine. Lots of attractions, including live music and various quiz and games nights. Food includes 'huge hands of hot bread', oven-baked jacket potatoes, ploughman's lunches and daily specials. Vegetable stir fry, five spice chicken and sizzling beef feature among the sizzling skillets.

Open 11–11 (Sun 12–10.30) Closed: 25 Dec, 1 Jan **Bar Meals** L served all week 12–2.45 D served Mon-Fri 6.30–8.45 ⊕ Enterprise Inns ◀ Skinners Kiddlywink, Shepherd Neame Spitfire, Courage Bass, Greene King Abbot Ale. ♀9

The Wig & Pen Inn

Frances St TR1 3DP ☎ 01872 273028 📄 01872 277351

dir: *City centre near Law Courts, 10 mins from railway station*

A listed city centre pub originally known as the Star, that became the Wig & Pen when the county court moved to Truro. There is a ghost called Claire who lives in the cellar, but she is friendly! The choice of food includes such home-made dishes as steak and ale pie, curry, casseroles, steaks and vegetarian dishes, and a range of fish options such as sea bass, John Dory, mullet or monkfish.

Open 11–11 **Bar Meals** L served all week 12–2.55 D served all week 6–8.55 ⊕ St Austell Brewery ◀ St Austell, Tribute, IPA, HSD & guest ales. **Facilities** Garden Dogs allowed

TYWARDREATH   MAP 02 SX05

The Royal Inn ♀

66 Eastcliffe Rd PL24 2AJ ☎ 01726 815601 📄 01726 816415

e-mail: info@royal-inn.co.uk

dir: *A3082 Par, follow brown tourist signs for 'Newquay Branch line' or railway station. Pub opposite railway station*

Named by royal assent after a visit by King Edward VII to a local copper mine, this 19th-century inn hosted travellers and employees of the Great Western Railway. It was completely refurbished a few years ago, and today supports many Cornish micro-breweries and food producers. The open-plan bar with large log fire is a great place for, say, simple sausages and mash, while the restaurant and conservatory serves delicious local seafood such as Fowey River mussels.

Open 11.30–11 (Sun 12–10.30) **Bar Meals** L served all week 12–2 D served Mon-Sat 6.30–9 (Sun 7–9) **Restaurant** L served all week 12–2 D served Mon-Sat 6.30–9 (Sun 7–9) ⊕ Free House ◀ Sharp's Doom Bar & Special Ale, Wells Bombardier, Shepherd Neame Spitfire, Cotleigh Barn Owl. ♀11 **Facilities** Garden Dogs allowed Parking **Rooms** available

England

VERYAN
MAP 02 SW93

The New Inn ★★★★ INN ♀

TR2 5QA ☎ 01872 501362 📄 01872 501078
e-mail: jack@newinn-veryan.fsnet.co.uk

dir: From St Austell take Truro road, after 2m bear left to Tregony, through Tregony follow signs to Veryan

Based in a pair of 16th-century cottages, this unspoilt pub is found in the centre of a pretty village on the Roseland Peninsula. It has a single bar, open fires and a beamed ceiling, and the emphasis is on good ales and home cooking. Simple, satisfying dishes abound, with seafood featuring heavily: expect pan-fried bass fillet and Dover sole grilled on the bone, plus jumbo rump steak or a special like Louisiana jambalaya.

Open 12–3 6–11 (Winter 12–2.30) **Bar Meals** L served all week 12–2 D served Mon–Sat 7–9 ⊕ St Austell Brewery ◀ St Austell HSD, Dartmoor Ale & Tribute. ♀ 8 **Facilities** Children's licence Garden **Rooms** 3 (2 en suite)

WADEBRIDGE
MAP 02 SW97

The Quarryman Inn

Edmonton PL27 7JA ☎ 01208 816444
dir: Off A39 opposite Royal Cornwall Showground

Close to the famous Camel Trail, this friendly 18th-century free house has evolved from a courtyard of cottages once home to slate workers from the nearby quarry. Several bow windows, one of which features a stained-glass quarryman panel, add character to this unusual inn. Expect the likes of creamy garlic mushrooms and slow-braised leg of moorland lamb; puddings are on the blackboard. The first Tuesday night of the month features curries made to authentic recipes.

Open 12–11 (Sun 12–10.30) **Bar Meals** L served all week 12–2.30 D served all week 6–9 **Restaurant** L served all week 12–2.30 D served all week 6–9 ⊕ Free House ◀ Sharp's, Skinners, Timothy Taylor Landlord, guest ales. **Facilities** Garden Dogs allowed Parking

Swan ♀

9 Molesworth St PL27 7DD
☎ 01208 812526 📄 01208 812526
e-mail: reservations@smallandfriendly.co.uk

dir: In centre of Wadebridge on corner of Molesworth St and The Platt

A town centre hotel that is family friendly, it was originally called the Commercial Hotel, and sits alongside the Camel Trail. Typical pub food includes doorstep sandwiches and baguettes, light snacks like cheesy chips, salads, chargrill dishes, full Cornish breakfast and main courses like Tribute beer-battered cod, or curry of the day. Children's dishes include chicken nuggets made of 100% chicken breast; pizza or pork sausage.

Open 10–11 **Bar Meals** L served all week 12–3 D served all week 6–9 Av main course £6.50 ⊕ St Austell Brewery ◀ HSD, Tribute, Guinness. ♀ 13 **Facilities** Children's licence Garden Dogs allowed

WIDEMOUTH BAY
MAP 02 SS20

Bay View Inn ♀

EX23 0AW ☎ 01288 361273 📄 01288 361145
e-mail: thebayviewinn@aol.com

dir: On Marine Drive adjacent to beach in Widemouth Bay

The Bay View Inn, as its name implies, enjoys wonderful vistas of the rolling Atlantic from its Surf Bar restaurant and the large raised decking area outside. About a hundred years old, it was a guest house for many years before transformation to an inn in the 1960s. The appetising menu makes excellent use of Cornish produce in such dishes as smoked pilchard and St Marwenne cream cheese paté, and locally farmed rump steak cooked to your liking.

Open 9–1am (Sun 9–11.30) **Bar Meals** L served all week 12–2.30 D served all week 6.30–9.30 (Sun 12–3 6–9) Av main course £12.50 **Restaurant** L served all week 12–2.30 D served all week 6.30–9.30 (Sun 12–3 6–9) ⊕ Free House ◀ Skinners Spriggan Ale, Sharp's Doom Bar & Own. ♀ 17 **Facilities** Garden Dogs allowed Parking Play Area **Rooms** available

England

ZENNOR   MAP 02 SW43

Pick of the Pubs

The Gurnards Head ★★★ INN 🏵🏵 ♀

Treen TR26 3DE

☎ 01736 796928 📠 01736 795313

e-mail: gur.bookings@ccinns.com

dir: *5m from Penzance. 5m from St. Ives on B3306*

An imposing colour-washed building that dominates the coastal landscape above Gurnard's Head, this traditional Cornish pub (stone-flagged bar, open fires) is just the place to get stranded on a wind-swept winter's night. Here you can see Cornwall at its most brutal, but on warmer days there are some great walks along the coastal path or the rugged Penwith Moors, strewn with wild flowers and studded with ancient Celtic remains. The owners of the highly successful Felin Fach Griffin in Brecon have taken over the place recently, and have already stamped their upmarket brand on the place. The bar and eating areas have been refurbished, everywhere has been brightened by a few coats of paint, and the food has been given a lift as well.

Open 12–3 6–11 (Sun 7–10.30) **Bar Meals** L served all week 12–2.30 D served all week 6.30–9 Av main course £12 **Restaurant** L served all week 12–2.30 D served all week 6.30–9 Av 3 course à la carte £25 ⊕ Free House ⬛ Betty Stogs, Tribute, Cornish Knocker. ♀ 10 **Facilities** Children's licence Garden Dogs allowed Parking **Rooms** 6

The Tinners Arms ♀

TR26 3BY ☎ 01736 796927

e-mail: tinners@tinnersarms.com

dir: *Take B3306 from St Ives towards St Just. Zennor approx 5m*

The only pub in the village, this 13th-century, granite-built free house is close to the South West coastal path and is particularly popular with walkers. It has changed very little over the years, with its stone floors and low ceilings. The main bar has open fires at both ends and outside there is a large terrace with sea views. Menus make the most of fresh locally caught fish, and Tinners fish pie is a favourite.

Open 11–11 (Sun 12–10.30) (Nov-Etr wkdays 11–3 6.30–11) **Bar Meals** L served all week 12–2.30 D served Fri-Sat 6.30–9 (times vary during Summer) ⊕ Free House ⬛ Doom Bar, Zennor Mermaid, Tinners Ale. ♀ 12 **Facilities** Garden Dogs allowed Parking

AMBLESIDE   MAP 18 NY30

Pick of the Pubs

Drunken Duck Inn

★★★★★ INN 🏵🏵 ♀

See Pick of the Pubs on page 102

Wateredge Inn ★★★★ INN ♀

Waterhead Bay LA22 0EP

☎ 015394 32332 📠 015394 31878

e-mail: stay@wateredgeinn.co.uk

dir: *M6 junct 36, A591 to Ambleside, 5m from Windermere station*

The inn's name sums up its idyllic position on the banks of Lake Windermere, with Ambleside just a short stroll away. Run by the same family for over 25 years, the inn was originally developed from two 17th-century fishermen's cottages. Real ales and 14 wines by the glass can be sipped whilst appreciating the spectacular views from the heated lakeside patio. On the bar and bistro menu, choose from classic pub fare augmented by some gastro dishes.

Open 10–11 **Bar Meals** L served all week 12–4 D served all week 5–9.30 ⊕ Free House ⬛ Black Sheep, Coniston Bluebird, Colly Wobbles, Tag Lag. ♀ 13 **Facilities** Children's licence Garden Dogs allowed Parking **Rooms** 22

APPLEBY-IN-WESTMORLAND   MAP 18 NY62

The Royal Oak ♀

Bongate CA16 6UN ☎ 017683 51463 📠 017683 52300

e-mail: jan@royaloakappleby.co.uk

dir: *M6 junct 38 take B6260 to Appleby-in-Westmorland*

An inn with a long and venerable history, with parts dating back to 1100 and the rest to the 17th century. Today, a classic dog-friendly tap-room with blackened beams, an oak-panelled lounge with open fire, and a comfortable restaurant have been sympathetically modernised to serve real ales and fresh local food at reasonable prices. Settle down with a bowl of appetising olives while choosing from home-made soups, pastas, curries and blackboard specials. Excellent Sunday roasts and children's menu.

Open 8–12 **Bar Meals** L served all week 12 D served all week 12 **Restaurant** L served all week 12 D served all week 12 Av 3 course à la carte £16 ⊕ Free House ⬛ Hawkshead, Black Sheep, Timothy Taylor. ♀ 8 **Facilities** Garden Dogs allowed Parking **Rooms** available

Pick of the Pubs

Tufton Arms Hotel ♀

See Pick of the Pubs on page 104

PICK OF THE PUBS

Drunken Duck Inn

In the heart of the Lake District, this traditional whitewashed Lakeland inn has been owned by the same family for three decades. Good service, excellent food and drink, comfortable accommodation, and a friendly atmosphere are the combined holy grails of hospitality carefully observed here.

The amusing name stems from a flock of comatose ducks found by a former landlady. Thinking of her guests' stomachs, she began to pluck them for the pot, unaware that they were not dead but merely legless from drinking beer that had leaked into their feed. No such risk today – the adjoining Barngates Brewery takes good care of its award-winning real ales, which are served in the oak-floored and beamed bar, with open fire, numerous pictures, leather club chairs and beautiful Brathay Black slate bar top from the local quarry. Excellent locally sourced food is attentively served in three informal restaurant areas – two traditional, one more modern. Inventive is not a puffed up word to use for starters like twice-baked Keene's cheddar

soufflé; duck parfait, rillette of duck and brioche; and rabbit ballotine with candied red cabbage. Nor indeed for main courses such as seared loin and confit shoulder of lamb, parsnip and sweet potato purées; and butternut squash and sage risotto. Desserts too are no less resourceful: melting chocolate fondant with white chocolate and apricot trifle; and honeycomb brûlée with thyme sablé and pan-roasted plums are just two. You'd expect an excellent wine list – and there is. Each of the seventeen bedrooms comes complete with antique furniture, prints and designer fabrics.

★★★★★ INN ⊛⊛♥
MAP 18 NY30
Barngates LA22 0NG
☎ 015394 36347
🖹 015394 36781
e-mail: info@
drunkenduckinn.co.uk
dir: *From Kendal on A591
to Ambleside, then follow
Hawkshead sign. In 2.5m inn sign
on right, 1m up hill*

Open 11.30–11
Bar Meals L served all week
12–2.30 6–9
Restaurant L served all week
12–2.30 D served all week 6–9 Av
3 course à la carte £40
⊕ Free House ⬛ Barngates
Cracker Ale, Chesters Strong &
Ugly, Tag Lag, Catnap & 1 guest
ale. ♥ 20
Facilities Children's licence
Garden Parking
Rooms 17

ARMATHWAITE MAP 18 NY54

The Dukes Head Inn ★★★ INN ♥

Front St CA4 9PB ☎ 016974 72226
e-mail: info@dukeshead-hotel.co.uk
dir: *9m from Penrith, 10m from Carlisle between junc 41 & 42 off M6*

Set in the pretty red sandstone village of Armathwaite, this family-run establishment is just minutes from the M6. The River Eden runs through the village and provides wonderful walks along its banks and up into the woods beyond. Originally a farm, the pub was licensed during the construction of the Settle to Carlisle railway, and offers two comfortable bars and an airy dining room. Typical dishes are hot potted Solway shrimps, and roast duckling.

Open 11.30–12 Closed: 25 Dec **Bar Meals** L served all week 12–1.45 D served all week 6.15–9 Av main course £9.50 **Restaurant** L served all week 12–1.45 D served all week 6.15–9 Av 3 course à la carte £16 ⊕ Punch Taverns ◀ Jennings Cumberland Ale,Tetley's Bitter, Black Sheep Bitter, Guinness. ♥ 6 **Facilities** Garden Dogs allowed Parking **Rooms** 3

BAMPTON MAP 18 NY51

Mardale Inn NEW

CA10 2RQ ☎ 01931 713244
e-mail: info@mardaleinn.co.uk

A whitewashed, early 18th-century inn in one of the most rural parts of the Lake District. Menus change slightly every month, so you may not find curried winter vegetable soup in July, but pan-fried fillet of sea bass, saffron and coriander mash; roasted tenderloin of pork with black pudding and Calvados sauce; and chicken, vegetable and salsa tortillas might well feature throughout much of the year. Dogs are welcome in all public areas.

Open 11–11 **Bar Meals** L served all week D served all week **Restaurant** L served all week 11–3 D served all week 6–9 ◀ Coniston Bluebird, Timothy Taylors Landlord, Thwaites Wainwright & Hesket Newmarket Haystacks. **Facilities** Dogs allowed Parking **Rooms** available

BARBON MAP 18 SD68

The Barbon Inn ♥

LA6 2LJ ☎ 015242 76233 ▤ 051242 76574
e-mail: info@barbon-inn.co.uk
dir: *3.5m N of Kirkby Lonsdale on A683*

A 17th-century coaching inn with oak beams and open fires, the Barbon is situated in a quiet village between the lakes and dales. Pockmarks in a settle tell of a 19th-century shooting, and there's also a tale of a hanged highwayman. A good choice of wines and real ales is offered alongside dishes like Morecambe Bay potted shrimps and roast fillet of pork with Marsala sauce and apricot compote. Special diets are happily catered for.

Open 12–3 6.30–11 (Sun 6.30–10.30) Closed: 25 Dec **Bar Meals** L served all week 12–2 D served all week 6.30–9 **Restaurant** L served all week 12–2 D served all week 7–9 ⊕ Free House ◀ Theakston, Barngates Westmorland Gold, Speckled Hen, York Brewery. ♥ 20 **Facilities** Garden Dogs allowed Parking

BASSENTHWAITE MAP 18 NY23

The Pheasant ★★★ HL ⊛ ♥

See Pick of the Pubs on page 107

BEETHAM MAP 18 SD47

The Wheatsheaf at Beetham ♥

LA7 7AL ☎ 015395 62123 ▤ 015395 64840
e-mail: info@wheatsheafbeetham.com
dir: *On A6 5m N of junct 35*

This 16th-century former coaching inn, now a freehouse, stands in the village centre, close to the little River Bela. Fallow deer wander neighbouring fields, and thousands of pheasants are reared locally every year. A small bar services the dining areas, all decorated with fresh flowers and illuminated with candles in the evening. Well-behaved children may eat from their own menu in a small upstairs room before 7pm. As far as possible, seasonal menus use the freshest and finest local produce. Lunchtime light meals include hot and cold sandwiches, salads such as warm black pudding and smoked bacon, and larger plates of Cumberland sausage and mash or steak and ale pie. Sample dishes from the carte include Forest of Bowland ham hock terrine to start, Fleetwood fisherman's pie to follow, and Sandra's sticky toffee pudding to finish. The reasonably priced wine list mixes classic European with New World offerings, and a dozen are served by the glass.

Open 11.30–3 5.30–11 (Sun 12–3, 6.30–10.30) Closed: 25 Dec **Bar Meals** L served Mon-Fri 12–2 D served Mon-Fri 6–9 (Sat 12–9, Sun 12–8.30) Av main course £10 **Restaurant** L served Mon-Fri 12–2 D served Mon-Fri 6–9 (Sat 12–9, Sun 12–8.30) ⊕ Free House ♥ 12 **Facilities** Garden Parking

BLENCOGO MAP 18 NY14

The New Inn ♥

CA7 0BZ ☎ 016973 61091 ▤ 016973 61091
dir: *From Carlisle, take A596 towards Wigton, then B5302 towards Silloth. After 4m Blencogo signed on left*

This late Victorian sandstone pub has superb views of the north Cumbrian fells and Solway Plain. It is located in a farming hamlet, and the impressive menu makes good use of produce from the region – perhaps Cumbrian venison with blueberry and Drambuie sauce and wholegrain mustard mash, or lamb from Dearham, chargrilled and topped with a mustard and herb crust and served with colcannon. A selection of malt whiskies is kept.

Open 7–11 (Sun 12–3, 6.30–10.30) Closed: 1st 2wks Jan **Bar Meals** L served Sun 12–2 D served Thu-Sun 7–9 Av main course £12 **Restaurant** L served Sun 12–2 D served Thu-Sun 7–9 ⊕ Free House ◀ Yates, Carlisle State Bitter, Hesket Newmarket, Black Sheep. ♥ 10 **Facilities** Garden Parking

Tufton Arms Hotel

Appleby-in-Westmorland is a medieval market town nestled in the heart of a valley so magically unspoilt that the only possible name for it is Eden. This 16th-century family-run coaching inn is something of a local landmark, renowned for its hospitality.

It's an ideal base from which to enjoy the many countryside pursuits available locally, while less hearty types will also find much to engage them. The present owners, the Milsom family, have lovingly restored the Tufton Arms to its former Victorian splendour with rich drapes, period paintings and antique furniture. The elegant conservatory restaurant overlooks a cobbled mews courtyard; light and airy in the daytime, this room takes on an attractive glow in the evening when the curtains are closed and the lighting is low. Chef David Milsom and his kitchen team have won many accolades for their superb food: a selection of delicious dishes made from the finest and freshest local ingredients. The resulting cuisine is an appealing blend of the classical and the modern, with fresh local meat, game, fish and seafood appearing on the menu. Typical starters include chowder of smoked haddock and prawn chowder; or hot pot of wild mushroom and chorizo sausage. Move on to grilled fillets of sea bass with asparagus spears and lemon butter; pan-fried breast of pheasant with sloe gin sauce; salmon fillet with braised fennel and roast cherry vine tomatoes; or a traditional steak and kidney pie. Round off with a home-made dessert: milk chocolate cheesecake; raspberry mousse; or pannacotta with vanilla and grenadine ice cream.

🍷
MAP 18 NY62
Market Square CA16 6XA
☎ 017683 51593
📄 017683 52761
e-mail:
info@tuftonarmshotel.co.uk
dir: *In town centre*

Open 11–11 Closed: 25–26 Dec
Bar Meals L served all week
12–2 D served all week 6.30–9
Restaurant L served all week
12–2 D served all week 6.30–9
Av 3 course à la carte £27.50
Av 3 course fixed price £27.50
⊕ Free House ◖ Tufton Arms
Ale, Flower IPA, Tennants. 🍷 15
Facilities Dogs allowed Parking
Rooms available

BOOT
MAP 18 NY10

Pick of the Pubs

The Boot Inn

See Pick of the Pubs on page 108

Pick of the Pubs

Brook House Inn ★★★★ INN ♀

See Pick of the Pubs on page 109

BORROWDALE
MAP 18 NY21

The Langstrath Country Inn ♀

CA12 5XG ☎ 017687 77239

e-mail: info@thelangstrath.com

dir: *B5289 past Grange, through Rosthwaite, left to Stonethwaite. Inn on left after 1m*

Refurbishments at this family-run inn include the addition of a restaurant with spectacular views up the Langstrath valley. Dishes here could include wild boar terrine with apricot chutney; and fillet of sea bass on a warm salad of fennel with new potatoes and a lemon and caper dressing. The bar offers decent ales and an extensive wine list. Set on the coast-to-coast and Cumbrian Way walks, this is an ideal spot for hikers.

Open 12–11 Closed: Mon & Tue-Wed Nov-Mar **Bar Meals** L served Tue-Sun 12.30–2.30 D served Tue-Sun 6.30–9 Av main course £9.50 **Restaurant** D served Tue-Sat 6–9 Av 3 course à la carte £22.50 ⊕ Free House ◀ Jennings Bitter, Black Sheep, Doris 90th, Coniston Bluebird. ♀ 8 **Facilities** Garden Parking

BOUTH
MAP 18 SD38

The White Hart Inn ♀

LA12 8JB ☎ 01229 861229 📠 01229 861229

e-mail: nigelwhitehart@aol.com

dir: *1.5m from A590, 10m M6 junct 36*

Bouth today reposes quietly in the Lake District National Park, although once it housed an occasionally noisy gunpowder factory. When this closed in 1928 villagers turned to woodland industries and farm labouring instead, and some of their tools now adorn this 17th-century coaching inn. Ever-changing specials are served in the upstairs restaurant that looks out over woods, fields and fells, or the horseshoe-shaped bar, with six real ales, including Cumbrian brews, 35 malts and real cider.

Open 12–2 6–11 (Mon-Tue all day, Sat 12–11, Sun 12–10.30) **Bar Meals** L served Wed-Sun 12–2 D served Mon-Sun 6–8.45 Av main course £10.25 **Restaurant** L served Wed-Sun 12–2 D served Wed-Sun 6–8.45 ⊕ Free House ◀ Black Sheep Best, Jennings Cumberland Ale, Tetley, Yates Bitter. ♀ 7 **Facilities** Children's licence Garden Dogs allowed Parking

BOWLAND BRIDGE
MAP 18 SD48

Pick of the Pubs

Hare & Hounds Country Inn ♀

LA11 6NN ☎ 015395 68333 📠 015395 68777

dir: *M6 onto A591, left after 3m onto A590, right after 3m onto A5074, after 4m sharp left & next left after 1m*

This 17th-century coaching inn is set in the pretty little hamlet of Bowland Bridge, not far from Bowness. A traditional country pub atmosphere is fostered by the flagstone floors, exposed oak beams, ancient pews warmed by open fires, and cosy niches. The bar menu offers local Cumberland sausage with egg and chips; toasted muffin with smoked haddock; confit of duck; and king prawns in filo pastry. The seasonal main menu could offer asparagus and saffron risotto; and smoked salmon and prawn roulade as starters, followed by butternut squash, spinach and mozzarella strudel; fresh cod in batter with home-made chips; steak and ale pie; There is also a specials board with fresh fish and game always available. A safe garden with play area and swings for the children makes this pub particularly family-friendly, and there are gorgeous views all round, especially of Cartmel Fell.

Open 11–11 **Bar Meals** L served all week 12–2.30 D served all week 6–9 **Restaurant** L served all week 12–2.30 D served all week 6–9 ⊕ Free House ◀ Black Sheep, Jennings, Boddingtons, Marstons Pedigree. ♀ 10 **Facilities** Garden Parking Play Area

BRAITHWAITE
MAP 18 NY22

Coledale Inn

CA12 5TN ☎ 017687 78272 📠 017687 78272

e-mail: info@coledale-inn.co.uk

dir: *M6 junct 50, A66 towards Cockermouth for 18m. Turn to Braithwaite then towards Whinlatter Pass. Follow sign on left, over bridge to Inn*

Well away from passing traffic, this traditional pub was built as a woollen mill in the 1820s, before being converted for pencil making. It is full of attractive Victorian prints, furnishings and antiques, with a fine wine cellar. Home-made meals, such as chilli con carne, sirloin steak and fresh salmon fillet, are served in the bars and dining room. Don't expect an answer to a question about the strange-shaped tree in the garden, because no-one knows.

Open 11–11 **Bar Meals** L served all week 12–2 D served all week 6–9 **Restaurant** L served all week 12–2 D served all week 6–9 ⊕ Free House ◀ Yates, Theakstons, Jennings Best, John Smiths. **Facilities** Garden Dogs allowed Parking Play Area

The Royal Oak ★★★★ INN ♀

CA12 5SY ☎ 017687 78533 📠 017687 78533

e-mail: theroyaloak@tp-inns.co.uk

dir: *Exit M6 junct 40, A66 to Keswick, 20m. Bypass Keswick & Portinscale juncts, take next left, pub in village centre*

Set in the heart of Braithwaite village, The Royal Oak enjoys a strong following thanks to consistently high standards and friendly staff. Surrounded by high fells, this is a walkers' paradise, but the inn also serves as a focal point for locals. The interior is all oak beams and log fires and the menu follows suit with dishes ranging from a hearty 'walkers' broth' to a giant Yorkshire pudding filled with home-made lamb casserole. *CONTINUED*

BRAITHWAITE continued

Open 11–12 **Bar Meals** L served all week 12–2 D served all week 6–9 Av main course £8 **Restaurant** L served all week 12–2 D served all week 6–9 Av 3 course à la carte £16 ⊕ Marstons ◄ Jennings Lakeland Ale, Cumberland Ale, Cocker Hoop & Sneck Lifter. ♥ 8 **Facilities** Children's licence Garden Dogs allowed Parking **Rooms** 9

BRAMPTON   MAP 21 NY56

Blacksmiths Arms ★★★★ INN ♥

Talkin Village CA8 1LE ☎ 016977 3452 ▤ 016977 3396

e-mail: blacksmithsarmstalkin@yahoo.co.uk

dir: From M6 take A69 E, after 7m straightover rdbt, follow signs to Talkin Tarn then Talkin Village

The original smithy, dating from 1700, remains part of this attractive family-run village inn standing in some of northern Cumbria's most scenic countryside; the Borders, Hadrian's Wall and the Lakes are all close by. Enjoy the warm hospitality with a pint of Geltsdale from Brampton's newest microbrewery, while choosing from the menu of classic pub favourites – beef lasagne, chicken and mushroom or shepherd's pie, Cumberland sausages, fresh local trout, or Barnsley double lamb chop.

Open 12–3 6–11 **Bar Meals** L served all week 12–2 D served all week 6–9 **Restaurant** L served all week 12–2 D served all week 6–9 ⊕ Free House ◄ Copper Dragon, Yates. ♥ 20 **Facilities** Garden Parking **Rooms** 8

BROUGHTON-IN-FURNESS   MAP 18 SD28

Pick of the Pubs

Blacksmiths Arms ♥

Broughton Mills LA20 6AX ☎ 01229 716824

e-mail: blacksmithsarms@aol.com

dir: A593 from Broughton-in-Furness towards Coniston, in 1.5m left signed Broughton Mills, pub 1m on left.

The Blacksmiths Arms, set in a secluded Lakeland valley, dates back to 1577 and was originally a farmhouse called Broadstones. The interior is beautifully preserved, with the old farmhouse range, oak-panelled corridor, worn slate floors sourced from local quarries, and low beams. Gaslights in the dining room and bar still work when the electricity fails. The chef proprietor uses local suppliers who guarantee the quality produce, and serves beer from local micro-breweries. You will often find Herdwick lamb, which is reared in the Lickle Valley, on the menu, along with traditional steak pie in suet pastry made from local beef. Dishes

might include Morecambe Bay potted shrimps; Cajun chicken salad; a choice of sandwiches or baguettes or a ploughman's at lunch. The dinner menu offers main courses like oven-baked Cumberland sausage served with creamy chive mash and red onion gravy; or deep-fried cod or haddock with Cumberland beer batter, chips and mushy peas.

Blacksmiths Arms

Open 12–11 (Mon 5–11) Closed: 25 Dec **Bar Meals** L served Tue-Sun 12–2 D served all week 6–9 Av main course £9.75 **Restaurant** L served Tue-Sun 12–2 D served all week 6–9 Av 3 course à la carte £17.95 ⊕ Free House ◄ Jennings Cumberland Ale, Dent Aviator, Barngates Tag Lag, Moorhouses Pride of Pendle. ♥ 7 **Facilities** Garden Dogs allowed Parking

BUTTERMERE   MAP 18 NY11

Bridge Hotel ★★★ CHH ♥

CA13 9UZ ☎ 017687 70252 ▤ 017687 70215

e-mail: enquiries@bridge-hotel.com

web: www.bridge-hotel.com

dir: Take B5289 from Keswick

The 18th-century former coaching inn is set between Buttermere and Crummock Water in an area of outstanding natural beauty surrounded by the Buttermere fells. There are wonderful walks right from the front door. Good food and real ales are served in the character bars (Cumbrian hot pot, jewel of lamb, traditional fish and chips), and a five-course dinner in the dining room (pan-fried calves' liver and mash, chargrilled rib-eye with pomme Anna and watercress salad).

Open 9.30am–12am (All day in summer) **Bar Meals** L served all week 12–6 D served all week 6–9.30 Av main course £6.75 **Restaurant** L served Sun 12–2 D served all week 6.30–8.30 Av 5 course fixed price £29.50 ⊕ Free House ◄ Theakston's Old Peculier, Black Sheep Best, Buttermere Bitter, Boddingtons. ♥ 12 **Facilities** Children's licence Garden Parking **Rooms** 21

PICK OF THE PUBS

BASSENTHWAITE-CUMBRIA

The Pheasant

In attractive gardens and woodland near Bassenthwaite Lake, the Pheasant combines the charm of a traditional Cumbrian hostelry with the attractions of a comfortable modern hotel. First a farmhouse, then a coaching inn, this Lake District favourite dates back some 500 years and now enjoys an international reputation.

Huntsman John Peel was a regular and the Cumbrian painter Edward H Thompson (1866–1949) bartered for beer in the pub; two of his originals hang in the bar. This richly inviting area, with polished parquet flooring, panelled walls and oak settles, stocks an extensive selection of malt whiskies. The high standard of food, ranging from Cumbrian specialities to fine dining, is well known to locals and to those from further afield. Lunch and dinner are served in the attractive beamed dining room, with lighter lunches available in the lounges or bar. There are open sandwiches; stilton, walnut and apricot paté; potted local Silloth shrimps; and ploughman's platters. Typical specials include casserole of local wild venison in red wine;

pan-fried crab cakes with pickled cucumber; and baked goat's cheese tartlet. Why not treat yourself to afternoon tea with home-made scones and rum butter in one of the lounges overlooking the gardens? A private dining room is available for parties of up to 12 people, and there are 15 individually decorated bedrooms with attractive fabrics and fine antique pieces. The en suite bathrooms are particularly impressive.

★★★ HL ◎ ♀
MAP 18 NY23
CA13 9YE
☎ 017687 76234
🖷 017687 76002
e-mail: info@the-pheasant.co.uk
dir: *A66 to Cockermouth, 8m N of Keswick on left*

Open 11.30–2.30 5.30–10.30 (Sun 6–10.30) Closed: 25 Dec
Bar Meals L served all week 12–2
Restaurant L served all week 12.30–1.30 D served all week 7–9 Av 3 course fixed price £31.95
⊕ Free House ◄ Theakston Best, Interbrew Bass, Jennings Cumberland Ale. ♀ 12
Facilities Garden Dogs allowed Parking
Rooms 15

PICK OF THE PUBS

BOOT-CUMBRIA

The Boot Inn

The name is appropriate, as this award-winning traditional 16th-century free house is set in some of England's finest walking country. The Boot actually gets its name from the pretty pink granite village in which it sits, which also boasts England's oldest working watermill. A beck wends its way through the valley, crossed by a 17th-century packhorse bridge.

Scafell Pike (England's highest mountain) and Wastwater (England's deepest lake) are within rambling distance and, naturally enough, the pub attracts many cold and hungry climbers. Fortunately there's a roaring fire to warm them on cooler days, and plenty of hearty home-made Cumberland dishes to fill them up. The beamed Burnmoor Room restaurant dates back to 1578, but there's also a modern conservatory with spectacular views, and an eating area in the bar by the open fire. A fourth option is the beer garden, which has two kiddies' playing areas. Sandwiches, baguettes, jacket potatoes, and ploughman's platters (ham or cheese) on the lunch menu are supported by a grand choice of pizzas, pastas, and home-made pies

such as the Burnmoor – chicken breast with baked ham in a creamy leek sauce. Local produce is taken seriously here, with lamb, beef, eggs, cheese and sausages all coming from nearby suppliers. In the evening the range broadens with starters of Cumberland mushrooms or rollmop herrings; main courses such as lamb Henry or steaks; and traditional puds like fruit crumble or baked Alaska. Children will love the home-made burger or Bewley's sausages served with chips and beans or peas. Dogs under control are welcome. Landlords Lesley and Francis Dantinnes have left, but their successors Lesley's son Sean King and his partner Caroline Friel are determined to maintain standards.

MAP 18 NY10
CA19 1TG
☎ 019467 23224
📠 019467 23337
e-mail: enquiries@bootinn.co.uk
web: www.bootinn.co.uk
dir: *From A595 follow signs for Eskdale then Boot*

Open 11–11 Closed: 25 Dec
Bar Meals L served all week
12–4 D served all week 6–9
Restaurant D served all week
6–9
⊕ Hartleys ◀ Hartleys XB,
Old Stockport, Wards Best,
Double Hop & Unicorn.
Facilities Children's licence
Garden Dogs allowed Parking
Play Area

PICK OF THE PUBS

BOOT-CUMBRIA

Brook House Inn

Brook House Inn is run by two generations of the Thornley family. The business has grown enormously in the decade since they took over the place, attracting a wide ranging clientele, including farmers, business people and day trippers from all over the country, often arriving en masse aboard the Laàl Ratty railway.

The inn's situation in the heart of Eskdale is superb, with glorious views and fabulous walking country all around. A drying room for wet walkers is provided, and accommodation for several bikes. Between three and seven real ales are kept, according to season, 150+ malt whiskies and a great choice of wine by the glass. Home-made food is available all day, in the restaurant, bar and snug, prepared from locally supplied fresh produce. Top quality ingredients include fell-side bred lamb and local steaks, Bewley's the butcher's Cumbrian sausage, Cumberland cheeses, free range eggs and home-smoked chicken, fish, cheese and garlic, which give a unique character to some of the dishes. Home-made bread, chutney, biscuits, sauces and stocks are also a feature, showing just how seriously food is taken here. There are two lovely dining rooms, the Scafell Restaurant and The Grainstore, with its exposed beckstone granite walls, which is ideal for family parties. Daytime sandwiches and salads are served, and the evening menu is the same throughout the inn, with specials boards offering fresh fish along the lines of brill with saffron sauce; and sea bass with roasted red pepper and vine tomato salsa. From the main menu might come trio of lamb chops with Madeira and mushroom sauce; or Moroccan vegetable and bean casserole. Special desserts include rich chocolate mousse with apricot compote; and caramelised lemon tart with lime syrup.

★★★★ INN ♥
MAP 18 NY10
CA19 1TG
☎ 019467 23288
▤ 019467 23160
e-mail:
stay@brookhouseinn.co.uk
dir: *M6 junct 36, A590 follow Barrow signs. A5092, then A595. Past Broughton-in-Furness then right at lights to Ulpha. Cross river, next left signed Eskdale, & on to Boot. (NB not all routes to Boot are suitable in bad weather conditions)*
Open 11–11 (8–12 during high season) Closed: 25 Dec
Bar Meals L served all week 12–5.30 D served all week 5.30–8.30 Av main course £9.95
Restaurant L served all week 12–4.30 D served all week 6–8.30 Av 3 course à la carte £25
⊕ Free House ◀ Timothy Taylor Landlord, Hawkshead Bitter, Jennings Cumberland, Yates and guests. ♥ 10
Facilities Children's licence Garden Parking
Rooms 7

CALDBECK   MAP 18 NY34

Oddfellows Arms

CA7 8EA ☎ 016974 78227 📠 016974 78056

dir: *Telephone for directions*

This 17th-century former coaching inn is set in a scenic conservation village in the northern fells. Popular with coast-to-coast cyclists and walkers on the Cumbrian Way, the Oddfellows serves Jennings Bitter and Cumberland Ale. Lunchtime snacks include jacket potatoes, sandwiches, or hot beef in a roll, whilst specials and vegetarian blackboards supplement the regular menu. Expect bacon chops with stilton; sirloin steaks; and local trout fillets. There's a daily curry, too.

Open 11–12 **Bar Meals** L served all week 12–2 D served all week 6–8.30 Av main course £7.50 **Restaurant** L served all week 12–2 D served all week 6.30–8.30 ⊕ Marstons ◀ Jennings Bitter, Cumberland Ale. **Facilities** Garden Dogs allowed Parking

CARTMEL   MAP 18 SD37

Pick of the Pubs

The Cavendish Arms ♀

See Pick of the Pubs on opposite page

COCKERMOUTH   MAP 18 NY13

The Trout Hotel ★★★ HL ◉ ♀

Crown St CA13 0EJ ☎ 01900 823591 📠 01900 827514
e-mail: enquiries@trouthotel.co.uk

Overlooking the River Derwent, the Trout's well-appointed rooms make a good base for horse riding, cycling, fell walking, climbing and fishing trips. The patio of the Terrace Bar and Bistro, with its large heated parasols, offers al fresco dining any time of the year, while the Derwent Restaurant, dominated by a classic fireplace and ornate mirrored sideboard, offers daily changing menus featuring the best local produce, such as pheasant and pigeon breast, grilled sea bass, and mushroom risotto.

Open 11–11 **Bar Meals** L served all week 9.30–9.30 D served all week 9.30–9.30 Av main course £8.95 **Restaurant** L served Sat-Sun 12–2 D served all week 7–9.30 Av 3 course à la carte £28.50 Av 4 course fixed price £15.95 ⊕ Free House ◀ Jennings Cumberland Ale, Theakston Bitter, John Smiths, Marston's Pedigree. ♀ 24 **Facilities** Garden Parking **Rooms** 43

CONISTON   MAP 18 SD39

Pick of the Pubs

The Black Bull Inn & Hotel ♀

1 Yewdale Rd LA21 8DU
☎ 015394 41335 & 41668 📠 015394 41168
e-mail: i.s.bradley@btinternet.com

dir: *M6 junct 36, A590. 23m from Kendal via Windermere & Ambleside*

Nestling at the foot of the Old Man of Coniston mountain and adjacent to Coniston Water, this 400–year-old coaching inn has been run by the same family for nearly 30 years. Its illustrious visitors have included poets and artists, from Coleridge and Turner to Anthony Hopkins for his part in the film *Across the Lake*, a dramatisation of Donald Campbell's ill-fated water speed record attempt. Back in the 1990s behind the inn the owners' son started a micro-brewery which has gone from strength to strength; the acclaimed and award-winning real ales are not only sold behind the bar, but shipped out to 30 neighbouring hostelries. For hungry ramblers calling in at lunchtime, excellent ranges of toasted sandwiches, soups and jacket potatoes are popular. Alternatively, the restaurant menu promises hearty dishes of half a roast chicken or duck; a bowl of home-made chilli; or a salad of local Esthwaite trout fillets – perfect on a summer's day.

Open 11–11 (Sun 12–10.30) Closed: 25 Dec **Bar Meals** L served all week 12–9.30 D served all week 12–9.30 Av main course £8 **Restaurant** D served all week 6–9 (lunch available by arrangement) Av 3 course à la carte £15 ⊕ Free House ◀ Coniston Bluebird, Old Man Ale, Opium, Blacksmith & XB. ♀ 10 **Facilities** Children's licence Garden Dogs allowed Parking

Pick of the Pubs

Sun Hotel & 16th Century Inn ♀

LA21 8HQ ☎ 015394 41248 📠 015394 41219
e-mail: thesun@hotelconiston.com

dir: *From M6 junct 36, A591, beyond Kendal & Windermere, then A598 from Ambleside to Coniston. Pub signed from bridge in village.*

A 16th-century inn with a 10–room hotel attached, this was Donald Campbell's base during his final water speed record attempt. Coniston Bluebird is one of the ales behind the bar, along with guest ales like Black Cat, Black Sheep Special and Speckled Hen. The menu offers seafood paella; pan-roasted pheasant with baby spinach ragout; and Hungarian goulash with dumplings. Outside is a large quiet garden with benches, and the conservatory offers exceptional views that can be enjoyed whatever the weather.

Open 12–11 **Bar Meals** L served all week 12–2.30 D served all week 6–9 **Restaurant** L served all week 12–2.30 D served all week 6–9 ◀ Coniston Bluebird, Hawkshead, Speckled Hen & 3 guest ales. ♀ 7 **Facilities** Children's licence Garden Dogs allowed Parking Play Area **Rooms** available

PICK OF THE PUBS

CARTMEL-CUMBRIA

The Cavendish Arms

Situated within the village walls, this 450–year-old coaching inn is Cartmel's oldest hostelry. Many traces of its long history remain, from the mounting block outside the main door to the bar itself, which used to be the stables.

Oak beams, uneven floors and an open fire create a traditional, cosy atmosphere, and outside there's a tree-lined garden overlooking a stream. Lunchtime sandwiches (tuna and lemon with ground black pepper; roast topside of beef with sliced red onion); are served on locally-baked bread with a portion of chips, while hot options include home-made soup; Morecambe Bay shrimps with herb butter; and tiger prawn piri piri. An evening meal might begin with pressed game terrine with home-made apple and pistachio chutney; haddock prawn and leek fishcake; or fresh crab with a lime and ginger dressing. Move on to supreme of chicken with a goats' cheese and sun dried tomato stuffing; braised lamb shank with orange, mint and redcurrant jus; braised lamb shank, root vegetables and red wine sauce; and whole sea bass with warm Morecambe Bay shrimp vinaigrette. Desserts include sticky toffee pudding and chocolate and brandy mousse, plus a variety of Lakeland ice creams.

♀
MAP 18 SD37
LA11 6QA
☎ 015395 36240
🖺 015395 35082
e-mail:
food@thecavendisharms.co.uk
dir: *M6 junct 36, A590 signed Barrow-in-Furness. Cartmel signed. In village take 1st right*

Open 11.30–11
Bar Meals L served all week 12–2 D served all week 6–9 (Sun 12–9) Av main course £10.50
Restaurant L served all week 12–2 D served all week 6–9 (Sun 12–9) Av 3 course à la carte £18
⊕ Free House ◀ Greene King IPA, Cumberland, Bombardier, Theakstons. ♟ 8
Facilities Garden Dogs allowed Parking
Rooms available

CROOK
MAP 18 SD49

The Sun Inn ♦
LA8 8LA ☎ 01539 821351 📄 01539 821351
dir: *Off B5284*

A welcoming inn which has grown from a row of cottages built in 1711, when beer was served to travellers from a front room. The same pleasure is dispensed today by the winter fires or on the summer terrace. The bar and regular menus feature sandwiches, starters, light snacks and main courses, supplemented by a specials board: squid in tempura batter, and Cumbrian lamb shank with celeriac mash.

Open 12–2.30 6–11 (Sat 12–11, Sun 11.30–10.30) **Bar Meals** L served Mon-Fri 12–2.15 D served Mon-Fri 6–8.45 (Sat all day, Sun 12–8) **Restaurant** L served Mon-Sat 12–2.30 D served Mon-Sat 6–9 (Sun 12–8) ◀ Theakston, John Smiths's, Courage Directors, Coniston Bluebird. ♥14 **Facilities** Garden Dogs allowed Parking

---

CROSTHWAITE
MAP 18 SD49

Pick of the Pubs

The Punch Bowl Inn ★★★★★ INN
◉ ♦

See Pick of the Pubs on opposite page

ELTERWATER
MAP 18 NY30

Pick of the Pubs

The Britannia Inn
LA22 9HP ☎ 015394 37210 📄 015396 78075
e-mail: info@britinn.co.uk
dir: *Inn in village centre*

Situated in the very heart of Beatrix Potter country, The Britannia Inn was built over 400 years ago – the quintessential Lakeland inn. The Britannia really comes to life in summer when colourful hanging baskets dazzle the eye and the garden fills up with customers (and occasionally Morris dancers). In colder weather, the thick stone walls, log fires and beamed ceilings come into their own, and at any time the inn offers a big selection of real ales and a wide choice of fresh home-cooked food. Informal bar lunches might take in Cumberland sausage and mash, or home-made steak and ale pie. In the evening, start with oak-smoked salmon and prawn platter perhaps, followed by local fillets of trout, or red pesto and sweet pepper tart.

Open 9–11 (25–26 Dec 10–4) **Bar Meals** L served all week 12–2 D served all week 6.30–9.30 **Restaurant** L served all week 12–2 D served all week 6.30–9.30 (Snacks 2–5.30) Av 3 course à la carte £21 ⊕ Free House ◀ Jennings Bitter, Coniston Bluebird, Harviestoun's Bitter & Twisted, Hawkshead Bitter. **Facilities** Children's licence Garden Dogs allowed Parking **Rooms** available

---

ENNERDALE BRIDGE
MAP 18 NY01

Pick of the Pubs

The Shepherd's Arms Hotel
See Pick of the Pubs on page 114

ESKDALE GREEN
MAP 18 NY10

Pick of the Pubs

Bower House Inn ★★ HL
See Pick of the Pubs on page 115

King George IV Inn
CA19 1TS ☎ 019467 23262
e-mail: info@kinggeorge-eskdale.co.uk
dir: *From Broughton-in-Furness over Ulpha Fell towards Eskdale*

What we see today is a 17th-century coaching inn, although Roman origins are likely. It lies in one of Lakeland's finest hidden valleys, close to the narrow gauge Ravenglass & Eskdale steam railway, known affectionately as La'al Ratty. Inside are open fires, oak beams, low ceilings, flagged floors and antiques. Dishes include home-made steak and ale, curry, pan-fried liver and onions, ostrich fillet, and salmon in Martini, orange and ginger sauce. Vegetarian dishes and a children's menus, pizzas and sandwiches are also served.

Open 11–11 **Bar Meals** L served all week 12–9 D served all week 12–9 **Restaurant** L served all week 12–2 D served all week 6–9 ⊕ Free House ◀ Coniston Bluebird, Black Sheep Special, Jennings Cumberland Ales, Jennings Sneck Lifter & guest ales. **Facilities** Garden Dogs allowed Parking

---

GARRIGILL
MAP 18 NY74

The George & Dragon Inn ♦
CA9 3DS ☎ 01434 381293 📄 01434 382839
e-mail: info@garrigill-pub.co.uk
dir: *Telephone for details*

Once serving the local zinc and lead mining communities, this 17th-century coaching inn is popular with walkers who enjoy log fires that stave off that brisk North Pennine weather. Look on the menu to find local Cumberland sausage, steak and ale pie, gammon steak, battered cod or Whitby scampi. There are plenty of Yorkshire puddings, jacket potatoes or sandwiches for a lighter meal.

Open 12–11 (Tue 5–11, Fri-Sat 12–12, Sun 12–10.30) (Winter: Mon-Wed 5–11, Thu 12–2, 5–11) **Bar Meals** L served all week 12–2 D served all week 7–8.45 Av main course £6.95 **Restaurant** L served all week 12–2 D served all week 6–8.45 ⊕ Free House ◀ Black Sheep Bitter, Bombardier, guest ales. ♥9 **Facilities** Children's licence Dogs allowed

PICK OF THE PUBS

CROSTHWAITE-CUMBRIA

The Punch Bowl Inn

Not only is the Punch Bowl a bar, restaurant and hotel, it also serves as the village post office, with reception manager Linsey doubling her duties as Crosthwaite's post mistress. Set in the unspoilt Lyth Valley, the inn is going great guns.

The slate-floored bar, with its open fires, comfy sofas, original beams and low ceilings, is the perfect spot to enjoy a pint of Tag Lag, brewed with fell water by the nearby Barngates Brewery. Leather chairs, gleaming wooden floors and a beautiful pale stone fireplace make for an elegant dining room. When it comes to the food, local and seasonal are the watchwords. The menu, which is available in both bar and restaurant, lists an extraordinary range of suppliers, many of them organic. Start with baked Cumbrian cheddar cheese and spring onion soufflé with wilted spinach and parmesan cream; or naturally smoked haddock, herb risotto and poached egg. Main courses might include herb-crusted rack of lamb with a cassoulet of summer beans and rosemary; slow-cooked shin of beef with wild mushroom gratin and red wine jus; or for fish lovers, perhaps pan-seared seabass with crab and chilli mash and petit pois à la Francaise. The puddings are straightforward but alluring: poached rhubarb and pannacotta, for example, or ginger crème brûlée with toffee-grilled figs and shortbread. Each of the nine stylish bedrooms boasts flat-screen TV, Roberts Revival radios and a freestanding roll top bath.

★★★★★ INN ❀ ☂
MAP 18 SD49
LA8 8HR
☎ 015395 68237
🖹 015395 68875
e-mail:
info@the-punchbowl.co.uk
dir: *M6 junct 36, A590 towards Barrow, A5074 & follow signs for Crosthwaite. Pub by church on left*

Open 12–11
Bar Meals L served all week 12–6 D served all week 6–9.30
Restaurant L served all week 12–2.30 D served all week 6–9.15 Av 3 course à la carte £25
⊕ Free House ⬛ Tag Lag, Cat Nap, Red Bull Terrier & Erdinger.
Facilities Garden Dogs allowed Parking
Rooms 9

PICK OF THE PUBS

The Shepherd's Arms Hotel

Located on one of the most beautiful stretches of Wainwright's Coast to Coast footpath, this informal free house is a favourite with walkers. Bike hire and pony trekking can also be arranged for an enjoyable alternative day out.

Shepherd's Arms own brew heads a list of beers that includes Jennings Bitter and a regular guest ale; during colder months, welcoming open fires warm the bar, which is a venue for local musicians. A nicely varied menu is served throughout, with plenty of choice for vegetarians, as well as daily specials and à la carte options in the dining room. Dinner might begin with fresh home-made soup, or deep-fried brie with a hot redcurrant sauce, before moving on to nut and mushroom fettuccine; breaded haddock with lemon; or local sirloin steak with brandy and black pepper sauce. After finishing, perhaps, with raspberry meringue, diners can relax in the comfortable lounge.

MAP 18 NY01
CA23 3AR
☎ 01946 861249
🖹 01946 861249
e-mail:
shepherdsarms@btconnect.com
web:
www.shepherdsarmshotel.co.uk
dir: *A66 to Cockermouth (25m), A5086 to Egremont (5m) then follow sign to Ennerdale*

Open 11–2 6–11 Apr-Oct
open all day, Fri & Sat 6–12am
Bar Meals L served all week
12.15–1.45 D served all week
6.15–8.45 Av main course £7.50
Restaurant D served all week
6.30–8 Av 3 course fixed price
£17.50
⊕ Free House ◀ Jennings
Bitter, Cumberland & guests (x3).
Facilities Garden Dogs allowed
Parking

PICK OF THE PUBS

ESKDALE GREEN-CUMBRIA

Bower House Inn

This fine 17th-century stone-built former farmhouse surrounded by gardens and next to the village cricket pitch, overlooks Muncaster Fell in a scenic and unspoilt part of Cumbria.

The Bower House's traditional appeal is irresistible: the oak beamed bar, warm fires and warren of rooms welcome locals and visitors alike, and the charming candlelit restaurant is a rambling room with a traditional feel to it helped by lots of stone, log fires and horsey pictures. In here you can try some hearty, imaginative food. For dinner you could choose a starter such as Morecambe Bay potted shrimps and melba toast; smoked Herdwick lamb with minted apple chutney; or panfried calamari rings in a spicy oriental sauce, and move on to roast haunch of venison with red wine and juniper berry sauce; roast pheasant with whisky sauce; escalope of veal with ham and gruyere; chicken breast with apple and tarragon sauce; grilled duck breast on roasted fruits with red wine and plum sauce; or poached salmon with white wine and cucumber sauce. The inn has lovely rooms serving the leisure and business customer. There is a conference room and various breaks including some with a golfing them are offered during the year.

★★ HL
MAP 18 NY10
CA19 1TD
☎ 019467 23244
🖷 019467 23308
e-mail: info@bowerhouseinn.
freeserve.co.uk
web: www.bowerhouseinn.co.uk
dir: *4m off A595, 0.5m W of Eskdale Green*

Open 11–2.30 6–11
Bar Meals L served all week
12.30–2.30 D served all week
6–9 Av main course £9.95
Restaurant D served all week
7–9 Av 3 course à la carte £23 Av
4 course fixed price £20
⊕ Free House ◀ Theakston
Bitter, Jennings Bitter, Coniston
Bluebird, Hawkshead Bitter &
Dent Ales.
Facilities Garden Dogs allowed
Parking
Notes
Rooms 28

England

GOSFORTH   MAP 18 NY00

The Globe Hotel

CA20 1AL ☎ 01946 725235

e-mail: gosglobel@aol.com

dir: *On A595, 15m S of Whitehaven*

Over a pint of Jennings Bitter in this friendly, traditionally furnished village pub, contemplate a walk round the shores of nearby Wast Water, England's deepest lake. Or, better still, walk first and get back here in time for that pint to accompany home-made fellman's steak, mushroom and brown ale pie with shortcrust pastry; grilled Cumberland sausages with pickled red cabbage and rich onion gravy; or deep-fried Whitby scampi with salad, chips and peas.

Open 12 -11 **Bar Meals** L served all week 12–2 D served all week 6–9 **Restaurant** L served all week 12–2 D served all week 6–9 ⊕ Enterprise Inns ◫ Jennings Bitter, John Smiths Smooth & Cumberland Ale. **Facilities** Children's licence Garden Dogs allowed

GRASMERE   MAP 18 NY30

The Travellers Rest Inn ♥

Keswick Rd LA22 9RR ☎ 015394 35604 🖷 017687 72309

e-mail: stay@lakedistrictinns.co.uk

dir: *From M6 take A591 to Grasmere, pub 0.5m N of Grasmere*

Located on the edge of picturesque Grasmere and handy for touring and exploring the ever-beautiful Lake District, the Travellers Rest has been a pub for more than 500 years. Inside, a roaring log fire complements the welcoming atmosphere of the beamed and inglenooked bar area. An extensive menu of traditional home-cooked fare is offered, ranging from Westmorland terrine and eggs Benedict, to wild mushroom gratin and rump of Lakeland lamb.

Open 12–11 (Sun 12–10.30) **Bar Meals** L served all week 12–3 D served all week 6–9.30 (Mar-Oct, 12–9.30) **Restaurant** L served all week 12–3 D served all week 6–9.30 (Mar-Oct, 12–9.30) ⊕ Free House ◫ Jennings Bitter & Cocker Hoop, Cumberland Ale, Sneck Lifter, guest ales. ♥ 10 **Facilities** Garden Dogs allowed Parking **Rooms** available

GREAT LANGDALE   MAP 18 NY20

The New Dungeon Ghyll Hotel ★★ HL ♥

LA22 9JY ☎ 015394 37213 🖷 015394 37666

e-mail: enquiries@dungeon-ghyll.com

dir: *From M6 into Kendal then A591 into Ambleside onto A593 to B5343, hotel 6m on right*

Traditional Cumberland stone hotel dating back to medieval times, and full of character and charm. The hotel stands in its own lawned grounds in a spectacular position beneath the Langdale Pikes and Pavey Ark. Local specialities, expertly cooked, are served in the smart dining room. A sample dinner menu offers pan-fried venison in port wine, steak on haggis mash, chargrilled salmon fillet on asparagus spears, roasted vegetable risotto, whole baked rainbow trout, and crispy local lamb with mint and rosemary.

Open 11–11 (Sun 11–10.30) **Bar Meals** L served all week D served all week **Restaurant** D served all week 6.30–8.30 ⊕ Free House ◫ Thwaites Bitter, Smooth & Thoroughbred. ♥ 7 **Facilities** Garden Dogs allowed Parking **Rooms** 20

GREAT SALKELD   MAP 18 NY53

Pick of the Pubs

The Highland Drove Inn and Kyloes Restaurant ♥

See Pick of the Pubs on opposite page

HAWKSHEAD   MAP 18 SD39

Kings Arms ★★★ INN

The Square LA22 0NZ ☎ 015394 36372 🖷 015394 36006

e-mail: info@kingsarmshawkshead.co.uk

dir: *M6 junct 36, A590 to Newby Bridge, right at 1st junct past rdbt, over bridge, 8m to Hawkshead*

An inn since the 16th century, when Hawkshead was a prosperous wool town, the Kings Arms stands overlooking the square at the centre of a network of narrow streets and alleyways, unchanged over the centuries, and now a conservation area. The carved figure of a king in the bar supports the upper rooms. Eat in the bar or dining room, with options ranging from filled rustic rolls to steak and Hawkshead Ale pie.

Open 10–12 **Bar Meals** L served all week 12–2.30 D served all week 6–9.30 **Restaurant** L served all week 12–2.30 D served all week 6–9.30 ⊕ Free House ◫ Carlsberg-Tetley Bitter, Black Sheep Best, Hawkshead Gold, Hawkshead Bitter. **Facilities** Children's licence Garden Dogs allowed **Rooms** 9

PICK OF THE PUBS

GREAT SALKELD-CUMBRIA

The Highland Drove Inn and Kyloes Restaurant

A 300–year-old country inn deep in the lovely Eden Valley, on one of the old drove roads from Scotland into England. Kyloes were the original Highland cattle that were bred in the Western Isles and then driven over the short channels of water to the mainland.

Father and son team Donald and Paul Newton have turned it into the area's social hub by maintaining their well-deserved reputation for high quality food. Traditional local dishes usually feature, alongside daily specials reflecting the availability of local game and fish, and meat from herds reared and matured in Cumbria. On most days you're likely to find sea bass, brill or wild salmon sharing the menu with innovative chicken dishes, succulent steaks, and even mallard. Typical meals might be rabbit and bacon pie baked in a double crust with cider and cream; honeyed duck breast with black pudding; pan-fried plaice fillet with spiced melon and lime butter; vegetarian meze of Mediterranean appertizers; then pannacotta and stewed rhubarb. The area's many attractions include Hadrian's Wall. Despite the excellence of the food, the Highland Drove is still a pub where locals come to enjoy the wide range of cask-conditioned real ales, plenty of other beers and ciders, and a good selection of wines.

MAP 18 NY53
CA11 9NA
☎ 01768 898349
🖹 01768 898708
e-mail: highlanddroveinn@btinternet.com
dir: *Exit M6 junct 40, take A66 E'bound then A686 to Alston. After 4m, left onto B6412 for Great Salkeld & Lazonby*

Open 12–3 6–11 (Sat 12–11)
Bar Meals L served Tue-Sun 12–2 D served all week 6.30–9 (Sun 12–2, 6–8.30) Av main course £11.45
Restaurant L served Tue-Sun 12–2 D served all week 6.30–9 (Sun 6.30–8.30) Av 3 course à la carte £22.50
⊕ Free House ◖ Theakston Black Bull, John Smiths Cask, John Smiths Smooth, Theakstons Best. ♒ 14
Facilities Children's licence Garden Dogs allowed Parking

HAWKSHEAD continued

Pick of the Pubs

Queens Head Hotel ★★ HL ◉ ▼

See Pick of the Pubs on opposite page

The Sun Inn ★★★★ INN

Main St LA22 0NT

☎ 015394 36213 & 36236 📄 015394 36747

e-mail: rooms@suninn.co.uk

dir: *N on M6 junct 36, A591 to Ambleside, B5286 to Hawkshead. S on M6 junct 40, A66 to Keswick, A591 to Ambleside, B5286 to Hawkshead*

The Sun is a listed 17th-century coaching inn at the heart of the charming village where Wordsworth went to school. Inside are two resident ghosts – a giggling girl and a drunken landlord – and outside is a paved terrace with seating. Hill walkers and others will enjoy the log fires, real ales and locally-sourced food.

Open 11–12 **Bar Meals** L served Mon-Fri 12–2.30 D served Mon-Fri 6.15–9.30 (Sat-Sun all day) ⊕ Free House ◀ Jennings, Taylors Landlord, Hawkshead Bitter, Cocker Hoop, plus two guest ales. **Facilities** Garden **Rooms** 8

HESKET NEWMARKET   MAP 18 NY33

The Old Crown ▼

CA7 8JG ☎ 016974 78288

e-mail: malcolm.hawksworth@yahoo.co.uk

dir: *From M6 take B5305, left after 6m towards Hesket Newmarket*

Regulars here can sleep soundly, in the knowledge that their favourite beers will always be waiting for them. That's because the pub and its associated micro-brewery, which stands at the rear, are owned by a dedicated co-operative of local people. Real ales aside, traditional home-cooked food includes steak in Hesket Newmarket ale; breaded haddock with chips and peas; lamb and vegetarian curries; and Normandy-style chicken with bacon and mushrooms in a cream and cider sauce.

Open 12–2.30 5.30–11 (Open lunch during school holidays) Closed: Mon-Thu pm **Bar Meals** L served Fri-Sun 12–2 D served all week 6–9 Av main course £8 **Restaurant** L served Fri-Sun 12–2 D served all week 6–9 Av 3 course à la carte £17 ⊕ Free House ◀ Doris, Skiddaw, Blencathra, Helvellyn Gold. ▼ 11 **Facilities** Garden Dogs allowed

---

HEVERSHAM   MAP 18 SD48

Blue Bell Hotel

Princes Way LA7 7EE ☎ 015395 62018 📄 015395 62455

e-mail: stay@bluebellhotel.co.uk

dir: *On A6 between Kendal & Milnthorpe*

Originally a vicarage for the old village, this hotel dates back as far as 1460. Heversham is an ideal base for touring the scenic Lake District and Yorkshire Dales, but pleasant country scenery can also be viewed from the hotel's well-equipped bedrooms. The charming lounge bar, with its old beams, is the perfect place to relax with a drink or enjoy

one of the meals available on the menu, including potted shrimps, sirloin steak, Cumbrian game pie and Isle of Man crab.

Open 11–11 **Bar Meals** L served all week 12–9 D served all week 6–8.30 (Sat 12–3, 6–9) Av main course £7.95 **Restaurant** L served all week 11–9 D served all week 7–9 (Sun 11–8) Av 3 course à la carte £15 ⊕ Samuel Smith ◀ Samuel Smith Old Brewery Bitter. **Facilities** Garden Dogs allowed Parking

---

KENDAL   MAP 18 SD59

Gateway Inn ▼

Crook Rd LA8 8LX ☎ 01539 724187 📄 01539 720581

dir: *From M6 junct 36 take A590/A591, follow signs for Windermere, pub on left after 9m*

Located within the Lake District National Park, this Victorian country inn offers delightful views, attractive gardens and welcoming log fires. A good range of appetising dishes includes chicken casserole with red wine and herb dumplings, grilled fillets of sea bass with ratatouille and mussels, and roasted butternut squash filled with leeks and stilton. Traditional English favourites of liver and onions or rabbit pie are also a feature.

Open 11–11 **Bar Meals** L served all week D served all week Av main course £9 ⊕ Thwaites ◀ Thwaites Bitter, Thwaites Smooth & Cask Ales. ▼ 11 **Facilities** Garden Dogs allowed Parking Play Area

---

KESWICK   MAP 18 NY22

The Farmers

Portinscale CA12 5RN ☎ 01768 773442

dir: *Exit M6 junct 40 (Penrith) onto A66, pass Keswick B5289 junct, turn left to Portinscale*

Revitalised as one of Keswick's foremost food-led pubs, everything from stocks, soups and breads to the after-dinner mints is freshly prepared. A typical starter might be mushroom risotto with charred asparagus and parmesan crisps, followed by roast chicken thighs stuffed with haggis on bubble and squeak, or a more traditional combination like grilled lemon sole with lemon and coriander butter.

Open 12–11 **Bar Meals** L served all week 12–2 D served all week 6–9 Av main course £8.50 **Restaurant** L served all week 12–2 D served all week 6–9 Av 3 course à la carte £17.50 ◀ Jennings Bitter, Jennings Cumberland Ale, Jennings Cumberland Cream. **Facilities** Children's licence Garden

---

Pick of the Pubs

The Horse & Farrier Inn ▼

See Pick of the Pubs on page 120

PICK OF THE PUBS

HAWKSHEAD-CUMBRIA

Queens Head Hotel

This charming hotel has been part of Hawkshead since the 16th century. This is the picturesque village where William Wordsworth attended grammar school. Later, in the early 20th century, the writer and illustrator Beatrix Potter lived just up the road. Her husband was the local solicitor and his old offices, now the Beatrix Potter Gallery, are full of her illustrations.

Behind the Queen's Head's flower-bedecked exterior you'll find low oak-beamed ceilings, wood-panelled walls, an original slate floor and a welcoming fire. Among the pictures and plates on display is the curious Girt Clog, a 20-inch-long shoe made for an elephantitis sufferer in the 1820s. An extensive wine list and a selection of real ales is offered, plus a full carte menu and an ever-changing specials board. Dishes draw from the wealth of quality produce on the doorstep: trout from Esthwaite Water, pheasant from Graythwaite, traditionally cured hams and Cumberland sausage from Waberthwaite, and slow-maturing Herdwick lamb. For lunch try sandwiches, salads or light bites such as a steamed,

naturally-smoked haddock fillet with mixed leaves or chicken liver paté with orange and tequila served with toasted brioche. Heartier lunch options include a 'pot of fish' in a lemon and parsley cream sauce; or Thai curry with saffron rice. An evening meal might open with confit Barbary duck leg with a sweet plum reduction or moules marinière, followed by local pheasant with huntsman sauce; Hawkshead venison casserole; baked brill with a dill and butter sauce; or leek and blue cheese tart. The surrounding area is a haven for walkers, and Esthwaite Water is a stone's throw away. For those wishing to stay, the hotel has 12 very attractive en suite rooms.

★★ HL ◉ ♥
MAP 18 SD39
Main St LA22 0NS
☎ 015394 36271
🖷 015394 36722
e-mail: enquiries@
queensheadhotel.co.uk
dir: *M6 junct 36, A590 to Newby Bridge, 1st right, 8m to Hawkshead*

Open 11–12
Bar Meals L served Mon-Sat
12–2.30 D served all week
6.15–9.30 (Sun 12–5, 6.15–9.30)
Av main course £14.90
Restaurant L served Mon-Sat
12–2.30 D served all week
6.15–9.30 (Sun 12–5, 6.15–9.30)
Av 3 course à la carte £26
🍺 Robinsons Unicorn, Hartleys
Cumbria Way, Double Hop. ♥ 11
Facilities Children's licence
Garden
Rooms 12

The Horse & Farrier Inn

All the essential features of an inn built over 300 years ago – slate-flagged floors, beamed ceilings, open fires – may be found within the Horse & Farrier's thick, whitewashed stone walls. It stands in the picturesque hamlet of Threlkeld, at the foot of 868–metre Blencathra, with views of the even higher Skiddaw to the west and Helvellyn to the south.

Fell walkers like to make the most of this lovely setting with a beer in the garden – a case of up hill and down ale, perhaps. Hunting prints decorate the traditional-style bars, warmed in winter by crackling log fires. The inn has an excellent reputation in these parts for good food, from hearty Lakeland breakfasts to home-cooked lunches and dinners served in either the bar, or the charming period restaurant. Making full use of local, seasonal produce, the award-winning chefs beaver away in their gleaming kitchen preparing the wide range of menu choices. At lunchtime and in the evening the bar menu offers home-made curry of the day; Mediterranean vegetable lasagne and plenty more. Lunch could also be an open sandwich, a filled baguette or a salad, as well as a more substantial lamb shoulder braised in Jennings Cumberland ale; poached smoked haddock fillet; or mushroom, cherry tomato and garlic tagliatelle. At dinner, start with marinated griddled tiger prawn and water chestnut kebab; or pork, bacon and herb terrine. Then, turn your attention to poached fillet of Scottish salmon with fettucine; pan-griddled Cumberland sausage with spinach mash; or oven-baked field mushroom filled with ratatouille. Typical desserts are caramel pavlova; and lemon and lime cheesecake, both with fresh cream. The wine list ranges far and wide. All fifteen well-appointed guest rooms are en suite.

MAP 18 NY22
Threlkeld Village CA12 4SQ
☎ 017687 79688
🖷 017687 79823
e-mail:
info@horseandfarrier.com
web: www.horseandfarrier.com
dir: *M6 junct 40 follow Keswick (A66) signs, after 12m, turn right signed Threlkeld. Pub in village centre*

Open 8am-12am
Bar Meals L served Mon-Fri 12–2 D served Mon-Fri 6–9 (Sat & Sun 12–9. Jun-Oct 12–9)
Restaurant L served Mon-Fri 12–2 D served Mon-Fri 5–9 (Sat & Sun 12–9. Jun-Oct 12–9)
🌐 Jennings ◀ Jennings Bitter, Cocker Hoop, Sneck Lifter, Cumberland Ale & guest ale. 🍷 9
Facilities Children's licence Garden Dogs allowed Parking
Rooms available

Pick of the Pubs

The Kings Head ♥

Thirlspot CA12 4TN ☎ 017687 72393 📠 017687 72309
e-mail: stay@lakedistrictinns.co.uk
dir: *From M6 take A66 to Keswick then A591, pub 4m S of Keswick*

The view surrounding this 17th-century former coaching inn is truly sublime. On warm days and in summer, the garden is the best place to enjoy a meal or drink. Inside, old beams and inglenook fireplaces are traditional features of the bar, while a separate games room offers pool, snooker and darts. Popular real ales include beers from Theakstons, the Jennings brewery in nearby Cockermouth, and there is a fine selection of wines and malt whiskies. In the elegant restaurant try choosing between spicy citrus-crusted pork roast; and oven-baked sea bass, which might be preceded by filo wrapped prawns, or mushroom and thyme soup, and followed by home-made lemon and lime tartlet. On the bar menu you'll find Cumberland chargrill, beef stroganoff, wild mushroom gratin, Borrowdale trout stuffed with prawns, and Waberthwaite sausages, and there are sandwiches, cold platters and salads.

Open 12–11 (Sun 12–10.30) **Bar Meals** L served all week 12–3 D served all week 6–9.30 (Mar-Oct 12–9.30) **Restaurant** D served all week 7–8.30 ⊕ Free House ◀ Jennings Bitter, Cumberland Ale, Sneck Lifter, Cocker Hoop & guest ales. ♥ 10 **Facilities** Garden Dogs allowed Parking **Rooms** available

The Swinside Inn

Newlands Valley CA12 5UE ☎ 017687 78253
e-mail: info@theswinsideinn.com
dir: *1m from A66, signed for Newlands/Swinside*

Situated in the quiet Newlands Valley, the Swinside Inn is a listed building dating back to about 1642. From the pub there are superb views of Causey Pike and Cat Bells – among other landmarks. Nearby is the market town of Keswick, a good base for visiting the area's many attractions. Inside are two bars, traditional open fires and oak-beamed ceilings. From Easter to late October food is served all day. Extensive bar menu may offer lamb Henry, Cumberland sausage, Swinside chicken, and fresh, grilled Borrowdale trout. Friday fish night specials.

Open 11–11 **Bar Meals** L served all week 12–2 D served all week 6–8.45 Av main course £8 **Restaurant** L served all week 12–2 D served all week 6–8.45 ⊕ Scottish & Newcastle ◀ Jennings Cumberland Ale, John Smith's Smooth, Deuchars, Caledonian IPA. **Facilities** Garden Dogs allowed Parking

---

Pick of the Pubs

The Pheasant Inn ♥

Casterton LA6 2RX ☎ 01524 271230 📠 01524 274267
e-mail: info@pheasantinn.co.uk
dir: *From M6 junct 36, A65 for 7m, left onto A683 at Devils Bridge, 1m to Casterton village centre*

This whitewashed 18th-century inn is run by Annette, Ian and William Dixon. In the welcoming oak-beamed bar, with its wood-burning fireplace, you'll find a choice of real ales and wines by the glass, while meals are served in the oak-panelled restaurant, where the menu offers mostly traditional English fare. Typical main courses are roast crispy duckling with sage and onion stuffing and apple sauce; breaded scampi; tournedos Rossini with Madeira sauce; halibut steak cooked in dairy butter; seafood mixed grill; and, for vegetarians, cannelloni stuffed with finely chopped button mushrooms, asparagus spears and parsley cream sauce. There is also a daily changing selection of specials that makes the most of the markets and the seasons. In fine weather you can sit outside on the patio or lawn, which have beautiful views of the fells.

Open 12–3 6–11 (Sun 12–3, 6–10.30) **Bar Meals** L served all week 12–2 D served all week 6–9 **Restaurant** L served all week 12–2 D served all week 6–9 ⊕ Free House ◀ Theakston Best & Cool Cask, Black Sheep Best, Dent Aviator, Timothy Taylor Landlord & John Smiths. ♥ 7 **Facilities** Garden Parking

The Sun Inn ★★★★★ INN ⊛ ♥

Market St LA6 2AU ☎ 015242 71965 📠 015242 72485
e-mail: email@sun-inn.info
dir: *From M6 junct 36 take A65 for Kirkby Lonsdale. In 5m turn left signed Kirkby Lonsdale. To next T-junct, turn left. Right at bottom of hill*

Ruskin's View, famously painted by Turner, is only a few minutes' walk from this popular 17th-century pub. Rumoured to have a resident ghost, the bar is a convivial spot to enjoy a pint of such guest ales as Timothy Taylor or Coniston. Simple furniture, oak floors and open log fires to add to the atmosphere. A contemporary European-influenced menu is available in the bar, the wine library, and the intimate formal restaurant.

Open 11–11 **Bar Meals** L served all week 12–2.30 D served Sun-Thu 7–9 (Fri-Sat 6.30–9.30) **Restaurant** L served all week 12–2.30 D served Sun-Thu 7–9 (Fri-Sat 6.30–9.30) Av 3 course à la carte £25 ⊕ Free House ◀ Jennings Cumberland Ale, Timothy Taylor Landlord, guest ales. ♥ 7 **Facilities** Dogs allowed **Rooms** 11

England

KIRKBY LONSDALE continued

The Whoop Hall ★★ HL ♀

Skipton Rd LA6 2HP ☎ 015242 71284 📠 015242 72154

e-mail: info@whoophall.co.uk

dir: *From M6 take A65. Pub 1m SE of Kirkby Lonsdale*

16th-century converted coaching inn, once the kennels for local foxhounds. In an imaginatively converted barn you can relax and enjoy Yorkshire ales and a good range of dishes based on local produce. Oven baked fillet of sea bass with tagliatelle verde and tiger prawns, and stir-fried honey roast duck with vegetables and water chestnuts are among the popular favourites. The bar offers traditional hand-pulled ales and roaring log fires, while outside is a terrace and children's area.

Open 7–11 **Bar Meals** L served all week 12–6 D served all week 6–10 Av main course £7.95 **Restaurant** L served all week D served all week Av 3 course à la carte £16.20 ⊕ Free House ◄ Black Sheep, Greene King IPA, Tetley Smooth. ♀ 14 **Facilities** Children's licence Garden Dogs allowed Parking Play Area **Rooms** 24

KIRKBY STEPHEN   MAP 18 NY70

The Bay Horse ♀

Winton CA17 4HS ☎ 017683 71451

e-mail: kingotty@hotmail.com

dir: *M6 junct 38, A685 to Brough via Kirkby Stephen, 2m N*

Refurbished 16th-century coaching inn specialising in seasonally changing beers – up to 300 different types each year including Hawkeshead Bitter and Titanic Iceberg – plus Corney and Barrow wines. A simple menu is offered at lunchtime with sandwiches, light dishes and mains like home-made burgers or lasagne. The dinner menu might list half a succulent roast corn-fed chicken with rich gravy, new potatoes and fresh vegetables. The specials board changes daily.

Open 12–3 6–11 **Bar Meals** L served Tue-Sun 12-2.30 D served Tue-Sun 6–9 Av main course £8 ⊕ Free House ◄ Hawkshead Bitter plus guest ales. ♀ 14 **Facilities** Garden Dogs allowed Parking

LITTLE LANGDALE   MAP 18 NY30

Pick of the Pubs

Three Shires Inn ★★★★ INN

See Pick of the Pubs on opposite page

LOWESWATER   MAP 18 NY12

Pick of the Pubs

Kirkstile Inn ★★★★ INN ♀

See Pick of the Pubs on page 124

MELMERBY   MAP 18 NY63

The Shepherds Inn ♀

CA10 1HF ☎ 01768 881919

e-mail: theshepherdsinn@btopenworld.com

dir: *On A686 NE of Penrith*

Well-known in the North Pennines, this unpretentious sandstone pub looks across the village green towards remote moorland country, close to miles of spectacular walks. An interesting mix of well-kept real ales is constantly rotated, with regulars like Jennings Cumberland Ale, Black Sheep Best, and Courage Directors.

Open 11–3 6–11 (Sun 12–3, 7–10.30) Closed: 25 Dec **Bar Meals** L served all week 11.30–2 D served all week 6–9 Av main course £8.50 **Restaurant** L served all week 11.30–2 D served all week 6–9 ⊕ Enterprise Inns ◄ Jennings Cumberland Ale, Black Sheep Best, Courage Directors. ♀ 8 **Facilities** Children's licence Dogs allowed Parking

MUNGRISDALE   MAP 18 NY33

The Mill Inn ♀

CA11 0XR ☎ 017687 79632 📠 017687 79981

e-mail: margaret@the-millinn.co.uk

dir: *From Penrith A66 to Keswick, after 10m right to Mungrisdale, pub 2m on left*

Set in a peaceful village, this 16th-century coaching inn is handy for spectacular fell walks. Charles Dickens and John Peel once stayed here. The inn has an annual pie festival which raises money for charity with its huge selection of pies. At lunchtime, hungry walkers could tuck into local Cumberland sausages or home-made fishcakes. Evening specials always include tempting pies with fillings such as local lamb and apricot; steak with roasted onions; and spiced chicken.

Open 12–11 (Sun 12–10.30) Closed: 25–26 Dec **Bar Meals** L served week 12-2.30 D served all week 6–8.30 (High season 6–9) Av main course £6 **Restaurant** L served all week 12–2.30 D served all week 6–8.30 Av 3 course à la carte £20 ⊕ Free House ◄ Jennings Bitter & Cumberland plus guest ale. ♀ 7 **Facilities** Garden Dogs allowed Parking

NEAR SAWREY   MAP 18 SD39

Tower Bank Arms ♀

LA22 0LF ☎ 015394 36334

e-mail: enquiries@towerbankarms.com

dir: *On B5285 SW of Windermere.1.5m from Hawkshead. 2m from Windemere via ferry*

This 17th-century Lakeland inn was immortalised in Beatrix Potter's Tales of Jemima Puddleduck. The author's former home, Hilltop, now a National Trust property, is just behind the pub. Food based on local produce is served in the bar or restaurant, and children are made welcome. Typical dishes include steamed mussels with chilli, lime and lemongrass; casseroled beef cooked in Cumbrian ale, and rhubarb and ginger teacup trifle. There is also an excellent cheese slate.

Open 11–11 (Nov-Feb 11–3, 5.30–11) **Bar Meals** L served all week 12–2 D served Mon-Sat 6–9 (Sun 6–8) Av main course £11 **Restaurant** L served all week 12–2 D served Mon-Sat 6–9 (Sun 6–8) Av 3 course à la carte £20.50 ⊕ Free House ◄ Barngates Tag Lag, Hawkshead Bitter, Brodies Prime, Keswick. ♀ 7 **Facilities** Children's licence Garden Dogs allowed Parking

PICK OF THE PUBS

LITTLE LANGDALE-CUMBRIA

Three Shires Inn

The Stephenson family recently celebrated 25 years running this 19th-century inn five miles west of Ambleside in the beautiful valley of Little Langdale; third generation members now help out during school holidays and at weekends.

Named after its situation near the meeting point of three county shires – Westmorland, Cumberland and Lancashire – the inn is a perfect stop for lunch (or a beer, or afternoon tea) on many circular low level walks in the Langdale and Skelwith area. The traditional Cumbrian slate and stone building was erected in 1872, when it provided a much-needed resting place and watering hole for travellers on the journey over the high passes of Hardknott and Wrynose. The bars boasting bare beams and slate walls are warmed in winter by cosy log fires. Summertime sees locals and visitors happily ensconced at picnic tables under parasols by a lakeland stream in the landscaped garden. Refreshments include excellent

real ales from nearby and regional breweries, and a splendid selection of malt whiskies. Food sourced as locally as possible is lovingly prepared by head chef Simon Carter, whose commitment to the Three Shires for over ten years also deserves note; evening booking is advisable. Light lunches start with a range of sandwiches, baguettes and soups, or larger plates of hot food such as beef in ale pie or locally-made Cumberland sausage. A hearty evening choice could comprise a starter of smoked breast of local duckling; a main course of pork loin steak in a garlic, thyme and fennel marinade; and a traditional dessert like rich and creamy home-made rice pudding. The inn offers ten prettily furnished bedrooms with lovely views of the valley.

★★★★ INN
MAP 18 NY30
LA22 9NZ ☎ 015394 37215
🖷 015394 37127
e-mail:
enquiry@threeshiresinn.co.uk
dir: Turn off A593, 2.3m from Ambleside at 2nd junct signed for The Langdales. 1st left 0.5m. 1m up lane.

Open 11–11 (Sun-Thu 11–10.30) (Dec-Jan 12–3, 8–10.30) Closed: 25 Dec
Bar Meals L served all week 12–2 D served all week 6–8.45 (ltd evening meals Dec-Jan) Av main course £12.95
Restaurant D served all week 6–8.30 (ltd evening meals Dec-Jan) Av 3 course à la carte £25
⊕ Free House ◀ Jennings Best & Cumberland, Coniston Old Man, Hawkshead Bitter, Blacksheep Bitters.
Facilities Children's licence Garden Parking
Rooms 10

PICK OF THE PUBS

LOWESWATER-CUMBRIA

Kirkstile Inn

For some four hundred years The Kirkstile Inn, located between Loweswater and Crummock Water, has offered shelter and hospitality amidst the stunning Cumbrian fells. The inn stands in the shadow of Melbreak and makes an ideal base for walking, climbing, boating and fishing. You may prefer simply relaxing over a beer from one of the local breweries.

If you're a fan of real ale, be sure to try something from the Loweswater Brewery, which is attached to the inn: maybe Melbreak Bitter, Grasmere Dark Ale, or Kirkstile Gold at the bar, or stock up on bottles of Dark Ale and Gold to take home as a souvenir. The dining room is the oldest part of the inn, dating back to 1549, and faces south down the Buttermere Valley. Here the food matches the views in quality, with plenty of choice from lunch and dinner menus. A third menu of specials is also offered, listed on a blackboard. At lunchtime a good choice of sandwiches, filled baguettes and tortilla wraps is offered alongside pasta dishes, steak and ale pie, and Herdwick lamb sausage. Options from the main menu include smoked trout

mousse wrapped in Brougham Hall smoked salmon with cucumber pappadelle and Dijon vinaigrette to start; and a hearty main course of chicken, leek and mustard pudding, gently steamed and served with a mushroom and white wine sauce. Finish with marbled chocolate marquise, or the fruit crumble of the day, with custard, whipped cream or English Lakes ice cream. The friendly atmosphere extends through to the accommodation, comprising seven en suite rooms and a family suite. Two private lounges ensure that guests enjoy total relaxation.

★★★★ INN ♥
MAP 18 NY12
CA13 0RU
☎ 01900 85219
🖷 01900 85239
e-mail: info@kirkstile.com
dir: *From A66 Keswick take Whinlatter Pass at Braithwaite. Take B5292, at T-junct left onto B5289. 3m to Loweswater. From Cockermouth B5289 to Lorton, past Low Lorton, 3m to Loweswater. At red phone box left, 200yds*

Open 11–11 Closed: 25 Dec
Bar Meals L served all week 12–2 D served all week 6–9
Restaurant D served all week 6–9 Av 3 course à la carte £18
⊕ Free House ◼ Kirkstile Gold, Coniston Bluebird, Yates Bitter, Melbreak. ♥ 10
Facilities Children's licence Garden Dogs allowed Parking
Rooms 8

NETHER WASDALE   MAP 18 NY10

The Screes Inn

CA20 1ET ☎ 019467 26262 📠 019467 26262

e-mail: info@thescreesinnwasdale.com

dir: *To Gosforth on A595, and on for 3m, turn right signed Nether Wasdale. In village on left*

The pub is situated in the picturesque village of Nether Wasdale and makes an excellent base for walking, mountain biking or diving in this lovely area. It dates back 300 years and offers a log fire, real ales and large selection of malt whiskies. There is a good choice of sandwiches at lunchtime, and dishes include chick pea and sweet potato curry, Cumberland sausage with apple sauce, and roast leg of lamb with mint gravy.

Open 12–11 Closed: 25 Dec, 1 Jan   **Bar Meals** L served Mon-Fri 12–2.30 D served all week 6–9 (Sat -Sun 12–3)   Av main course £8.95 **Restaurant** L served Mon-Fri 12–3 D served all week 6–9 (Sat-Sun 12–3) ⊕ Free House ◀ Yates Bitter, Derwent, Whitehaven, Jennings Cumberland. **Facilities** Children's licence Garden Dogs allowed Parking

---

OUTGATE   MAP 18 SD39

Outgate Inn

LA22 0NQ ☎ 015394 36413

e-mail: outgate@outgate.wanadoo.co.uk

dir: *Exit M6 junct 36, by-passing Kendal, A591 towards Ambleside. At Clappersgate take B5285 to Hawkshead then Outgate 3m*

Once a mineral water manufacturer, and now part of Robinson's and Hartley's Brewery, whose ales are served in the bar. During the winter there's a real fire, while summer warmth should be available in the secluded beer garden. Daily specials supplement grilled local gammon with cider and peach sauce; pan-fried rump steak with beer-battered onion rings and mushrooms; and lightly grilled fillet of lemon sole. Renowned for live jazz on Fridays from March to October.

Open 11–3 6–11 (Feb-Nov 12–11, Nov-Feb Sat-Sun 11–11) **Bar Meals** L served all week 12–2.30 D served all week 6–9 **Restaurant** L served all week 12–2 D served all week 6–9 ◀ Hartleys XB, Old Stockport Bitter, Robinsons Smooth. **Facilities** Children's licence Garden Dogs allowed Parking

RAVENSTONEDALE   MAP 18 NY70

The Black Swan ★★★★ INN ☞

CA17 4NG ☎ 015396 23204

e-mail: enquiries@blackswanhotel.com

dir: *M6 junct 38 take A685 E towards Brough*

A grand, solid-looking Victorian hotel set in a peaceful village in the upper Eden valley. The sheltered garden leads across a bridge over a beck to a natural riverside glade. Local ales are served in the bar, while meals are taken in the lounge or the popular restaurant – examples include local trout fishcake; Moroccan lamb tagine with couscous; and local Cumberland sausage with colcannon mash and rich onion gravy.

Open 8–12 (Fri-Sat 8–1)   **Bar Meals** L served all week 12–2 D served all week 6–9   Av main course £10   **Restaurant** L served all week 12–2 D served all week 6–9 Av 3 course à la carte £18 ⊕ Free House ◀ Black Sheep, John Smith's, Dent, Tirril Brewery. ☞ 7 **Facilities** Garden Dogs allowed Parking **Rooms** 10

Pick of the Pubs

The Fat Lamb Country Inn ★★ HL

See Pick of the Pubs on page 127

Pick of the Pubs

King's Head ★★★ INN ☞

See Pick of the Pubs on page 128

SEDBERGH   MAP 18 SD69

The Dalesman Country Inn ☞

Main St LA10 5BN ☎ 015396 21183 📠 015396 21311

e-mail: info@thedalesman.co.uk

dir: *M6 junct 37, follow signs to Sedbergh, 1st pub in town on left*

Restored 16th-century coaching inn, noted for its dazzling floral displays and handy for a choice of glorious walks along the River Dee or up to the Howgill Fells. The menu changes every fortnight, and among the main courses are trio of chargrilled lamb chops, wild salmon fillet, home-made mushroom stroganoff, fresh swordfish nicoise, and organic chicken breast. Popular patio and garden, and a good wine selection.

Open 11–11 (Sun 12–10.30)   **Bar Meals** L served all week 12–2.30 D served all week 6–9.30 (Sat-Sun 12–9)   **Restaurant** L served all week 12–2.30 D served all week 6–9.30 (Sat-Sun 12–9) ⊕ Free House ◀ Carlsberg-Tetley, Theakston Best Bitter, Black Sheep. ☞ 9 **Facilities** Children's licence Garden Parking **Rooms** available

View over Wasdale Head from Great Gable,
Lake District National Park , Cumbria

PICK OF THE PUBS

The Fat Lamb Country Inn

There are magnificent uninterrupted views in all directions from this 17th-century former coaching inn, built solidly of local stone in open countryside midway between the Lake District and Yorkshire Dales National Parks.

As if this isn't enough, it has its own eleven-acre private nature reserve. An old Yorkshire range, with an open fire when it's needed, has survived in the small bar from the days when it was once the kitchen and main living area. If a local or a visitor doesn't hear what someone says, it won't be because of noise from the pool table, video games or juke box – there aren't any. Snacks and meals can be eaten here, or for something more elaborate there's the print- and plate-decorated restaurant. All dishes are produced on the premises from the best local ingredients available – nothing comes in ready-made, not even the bar snacks. Try cutlets of local lamb in mint jus; roast half guinea fowl with caramelised onion and apple sauce; or pan-fried tuna steak with black olive and red onion dressing. All bedrooms are centrally heated with en-suite bathrooms and tea and coffee making facilities. Outside are informal gardens and wildlife areas with a patio and picnic tables. The nature reserve calls for more comment: it arose from the interest of long-term landlord, Paul Bonsall, in bird watching and wildlife. In 1989, concerned that the land behind the pub might fall into the hands of a shooting syndicate, he bought it at auction. Over the years, with the help of the Countryside Commission and many others, he has created a splendid wildlife haven which visitors may wander round and admire those magnificent uninterrupted views.

★★ HL
MAP 18 NY70
Crossbank CA17 4LL
☎ 015396 23242
▤ 015396 23285
e-mail: fatlamb@cumbria.com
web: www.fatlamb.co.uk
dir: *On A683 between Sedbergh & Kirkby Stephen*

Open 11–2 6–11
Bar Meals L served all week 12–2 D served all week 6–9 Av main course £9
Restaurant L served all week 12–2 D served all week 6–9
⊕ Free House ◀ Black Sheep Bitter.
Facilities Children's licence Garden Dogs allowed Parking Play Area
Rooms 12

PICK OF THE PUBS

RAVENSTONEDALE-CUMBRIA

King's Head

One of the oldest buildings in Ravenstonedale, this traditional, 17th-century Cumbrian inn offers everyone a warm welcome. It stands in an unspoilt village in the upper Eden valley, an Area of Outstanding Natural Beauty between two National Parks – the Yorkshire Dales and the Lake District.

Over the years it has served as inn, courthouse, jail, cottages and temperance hotel, before becoming an inn again. In January 2005, Cumbria's worst floods in living memory devastated it – these were the floods that paralysed Carlisle. During four months' closure for extensive refurbishment, the owners took the opportunity to discreetly modernise the interior, without compromising its old-world charm. The log fire-warmed main bar and snug, for example, still feel very friendly, especially with a pint from the Black Sheep or Dent breweries, or a guest ale from another part of the country. The 50–seater Candlelight Restaurant, where one of northern England's largest collections of whisky jugs is displayed, offers extensive lunchtime and evening menus and frequently changing 'specials', all based on local produce. Begin with paté Cumberland or prawn platter, and follow with a chargrilled steak; Ravenstonedale salmon in garlic butter; turkey and ham pie; chicken korma; seafood tagliatelle; or vegetable crumble. Cumbria is red squirrel country and the proprietors support and encourage the local population. You can watch them display their acrobatic skills on aerial runs and feeding stations in the beer garden on the banks of the nearby beck. Squirrel pictures on the website were all taken here or nearby. Pool, darts, dominoes, bar skittles and shove ha'penny are available in the games room.

★★★ INN ☻
MAP 18 NY70
CA17 4NH
☎ 015396 23284
e-mail:
enquiries@kings-head.net
dir: *On A685, 7m from M6 junct 38 (Tebay)*

Open 11–3 6–11 (Fri-Sat Open all day Spring & Summer)
Bar Meals L served all week 12–2 D served all week 6–9 Av main course £10.50
Restaurant L served all week 12–2 D served all week 6–9 Av 3 course à la carte £18.50
⊕ Free House ◀ Black Sheep, Dent, Tetley's Imperial, over 100 guest ales. ☻ 6
Facilities Children's licence Garden Dogs allowed Parking
Rooms 3 (2 en suite)

TIRRIL
MAP 18 NY52

Pick of the Pubs

Queen's Head Inn ♀

CA10 2JF ☎ 01768 863219 📠 01768 863243

e-mail: bookings@queensheadinn.co.uk

dir: *A66 towards Penrith then A6 S toward Shap. In Eamont Bridge take R just after Crown Hotel. Tirril 1m on B5320.*

Dating from 1719, this privately owned, traditional free house is chock-full of beams, flagstones and memorabilia. Look in the bar for the Wordsworth Indenture, signed by the great poet himself, his brother, Christopher, and local wheelwright John Bewsher, to whom the Wordsworths sold the pub in 1836. Food includes pasta dishes, steaks, and mains such as chicken fajitas; Whitby wholetail scampi; or steamed steak and ale pudding.

Open 12–3 6–11 (Fri-Sun all day, Apr-Oct all day all wk) **Bar Meals** L served all week 12–2 D served all week 6–9.30 (Sun 6.30–8.30) Av main course £9 **Restaurant** L served all week 12–2 D served all week 6–9.30 (Sun 6.30–8.30) Av 3 course à la carte £25 ⊕ Free House ▦ Tirril Bewshers Best, Thomas Slee's Academy Ale & Charles Gough's Old Faithful, Brougham Ale & Cumbrian guest ales. ♀ 10 **Facilities** Children's licence Dogs allowed Parking

TROUTBECK
MAP 18 NY40

Pick of the Pubs

Queens Head ★★★★ INN ♀

Townhead LA23 1PW

☎ 015394 32174 📠 015394 31938

e-mail: enquiries@queensheadhotel.com

web: www.queensheadhotel.com

dir: *M6 junct 36, A590/591, W towards Windermere, right at mini-rdbt onto A592 signed Penrith/Ullswater. Pub 2m on right*

The lovely undulating valley of Troutbeck, with its maze of footpaths and felltop views, is a magnet for ramblers. True to its roots, this smart 17th-century coaching inn offers sustenance and comfortable accommodation to the weary and footsore. The bars are full of nooks and crannies, with open fires and ancient carved settles. A change of ownership has introduced Robinson's Brewery beers to the pumps, while the established focus on comfort and accomplished cooking continues. The lunch menu offers hearty but innovative fare – from baguettes stuffed with Cumbrian dry-cured bacon to pan-fried lamb's liver with sweet potato mash. The à la carte menu, available at lunch or dinner, could include starters

like home-made black pudding with roast king scallop; and main courses such as whole roast Vale of Lune red-legged partridge. Children can tuck into lamb and mint meatballs, with bramley apple Bakewell tart with Kendal ice cream to follow.

Open 11–11 (Sun 12–10.30) Closed: 25 Dec **Bar Meals** L served all week 12–5 D served all week 5–9 **Restaurant** L served all week 12–2 D served all week 6.30–9 Av 3 course à la carte £25 Av 4 course fixed price £18.50 ⊕ ▦ Robinsons Unicorn, Hartleys XB, Pride of Cumbria. ♀ 9 **Facilities** Children's licence Parking **Rooms** 16 (15 en suite)

ULVERSTON
MAP 18 SD27

The Devonshire Arms ♀

Victoria Rd LA12 0DH

☎ 01229 582537 & 480287 📠 01229 480287

This popular pub is located on the outskirts of the bustling market town of Ulverston, and is home to a wide range of cask beers and guest ales, as well as two dart teams. The menu focuses on classic pub grub, with plenty in the way of light bites: baguettes, burgers, jackets and the like, as well as some more filling mains. These range from home-made mince and onion pie to vegetable korma curry.

Open 11–2.30 5.30–11 (Autumn-Winter 6–11) **Bar Meals** L served Thu-Tue 12–2 D served Thu-Tue 6–8.30 ▦ Tetley Smooth, Jennings Cumberland & Tetley Dark Mild. ♀ 8 **Facilities** Children's licence Garden Parking

Farmers Arms ♀

Market Place LA12 7BA ☎ 01229 584469 📠 01229 582188

e-mail: roger@farmersulufreeserve.com

dir: *In town centre*

A warm welcome is extended at this lively 16th-century inn located at the centre of the attractive, historic market town. The visitor will find a comfortable and relaxing beamed front bar with an open fire in winter. Landlord Roger Chattaway takes pride in serving quality food; his Sunday lunches are famous locally, and at other times there's a varied and tempting specials menu, and lunchtime choice of hot and cold sandwiches, baguettes or ciabatta, and various salads.

Open 10–11 **Bar Meals** L served all week 11–3 D served all week 5.30–8.30 Av main course £8.95 **Restaurant** L served all week 11–3 D served all week 5.30–8.30 Av 3 course à la carte £14.95 ⊕ Free House ▦ Hawkshead Best Bitter, John Smiths. ♀ 12 **Facilities** Children's licence Garden

WASDALE HEAD
MAP 18 NY10

Wasdale Head Inn ♀

CA20 1EX ☎ 019467 26229 & 26333 📠 019467 26334

e-mail: wasdaleheadinn@msn.com

dir: *From A595 follow Wasdale signs. Inn at head of valley*

Famous mountain inn dramatically situated at the foot of England's highest mountains and beside her deepest lake. Oak-panelled walls are hung with photographs reflecting a passion for climbing. Exclusive real ales are brewed in the pub's own micro brewery and celebrated by annual beer festivals. Menus specialising in Herdwick lamb and mutton suit outdoor appetites, and there's a choice of 25 malt whiskies.

Open 11–11 (Winter 11–10) **Bar Meals** L served all week 11–9 D served all week 11–9 (Winter 12–8) Av main course £9.50 **Restaurant** D served 7–8 Av 4 course fixed price £32 ⊕ Free House ▦ Great Gable, Wasd Ale, Burnmoor, Yewbarrow. ♀ 15 **Facilities** Garden Dogs allowed Parking

Brackenrigg Inn

This white-painted roadside inn dates from the 18th century and occupies a breathtakingly beautiful position with sweeping views over Ullswater and Helvellyn. Inside there is a traditional bar with plenty of wood panelling, an open fire and a welcoming atmosphere engendered by relaxed and friendly owners Garry Smith and John Welch.

They offer a good choice of real ales, such as Coniston Bluebird, Jennings Cumberland and Copper Dragon 1816, as well as lagers and continental beers. The wine list is well-balanced and full of interest, with helpful suggestions on food and wine pairing and a very good selection by the glass. Fresh local produce is to the fore on the comprehensive menus, which include a bar and an à la carte choice. Typical choices from the bar menu include starters of smoked haddock chowder; game terrine; and French onion soup, followed perhaps by Herdwick mutton shank on a bed of mash with a white onion sauce; or local venison cobbler. From the a la carte, you could start with monkfish tail wrapped in Cumbrian air dried

ham, served with pineapple risotto cake or a caramelised red onion tart, followed by honey roasted Barbary duck breast on caramelised swede with baby vegetables and a port wine reduction; or a light garlic fish stew of locally-sourced fish and shellfish. For those who can't tear themselves away from the peace and beauty of the place, there are smart bedrooms, some housed in the newly-refurbished Stables Cottages, where a good night's sleep and a traditional Cumbrian breakfast are too tempting to ignore. Excellent wheelchair access throughout.

★★★★ INN ☛
MAP 18 NY42
CA11 0LP
☎ 017684 86206
🖷 017684 86945
e-mail: enquiries@
brackenriginn.co.uk
dir: *M6 junct 40 take A66 signed
Keswick. Then take A592 signed
Ullswater. Turn right at lake. Inn
6m from M6 & Penrith*

Open 12–11 (Nov-Mar, Mon-Fri
closed 3–5pm)
Bar Meals L served all week
12–3 D served all week 5–9 Av
main course £12
Restaurant L served all week
12–2.30 D served all week 6–9
Av 3 course à la carte £25
⊕ Free House ◀ Jennings
Cumberland, Coniston Bluebird,
Copper Dragon, Copper Dragon
1816. ☛ 12
Facilities Children's licence
Garden Dogs allowed Parking
Rooms 17

WATERMILLOCK
MAP 18 NY42

Pick of the Pubs

Brackenrigg Inn ★★★★ INN ♀
See Pick of the Pubs on opposite page

WHITEHAVEN
MAP 18 NX91

The Waterfront ♀
West Strand CA28 7LR ☎ 01946 691130 ▤ 01946 695987
e-mail: thewaterfront@aol.com
dir: *From M6 follow A66 towards Workington. Take A595 towards Whitehaven then A5094. Pub in town centre on harbourside.*

Set on Whitehaven's historic harbourside, once the third busiest port in the country. The Waterfront serves both food and drink outside in summer, where unrivalled views across the Solway can be enjoyed. There's a contemporary feel to the interior, and the friendly, knowledgeable staff are eager to make you feel at home. Modern and traditional dishes are locally sourced – the evening menu is particularly strong on chargrilled steaks with a choice of sauces.

Open 12 -11 **Bar Meals** L served all week 12–2 D served all week 6–9.30 Av main course £5.75 **Restaurant** L served all week 12–2 D served all week 6–9.30 Av 4 course à la carte £20 Av 4 course fixed price £15 ◖ Jennings Bitter, Cumberland Ale, Cocker Hoop. ♀ 16 **Facilities** Children's licence

WINDERMERE
MAP 18 SD49

The Angel Inn NEW ♀
Helm Rd LA23 3BU ☎ 015394 44080 ▤ 015394 46003
e-mail: rooms@the-angelinn.com

Occupying an unrivalled position in the centre of Bowness-on-Windermere, this former guest house is a sophisticated yet welcoming gastro-pub with a mix of modern and classic decor. Local ales vie with international beers at the bar, and good food based on local produce appears in dishes such as grilled Waberthwaite gammon steak and Cartmel Valley pheasant. Popular sunny summer garden terrace with lovely views.

Open 9–11 Closed: 25 Dec **Bar Meals** L served all week 11.30–4 D served all week 5–9 Av main course £11 **Restaurant** L served all week 11.30–4 D served all week 5–9 Av 3 course à la carte £22.50 ⊕ Free House ◖ Coniston Bluebird Bitter, Hawkshead Bitter. ♀ 12 **Facilities** Children's licence Garden Parking

Eagle & Child Inn ★★★ INN ♀
Kendal Rd, Staveley LA8 9LP ☎ 01539 821320
e-mail: info@eaglechildinn.co.uk
dir: *M6 junct 36, A590 towards Kendal then A591 towards Windermere. Staveley approx 2m*

The rivers Kent and Gowan meet at the gardens of this friendly inn, and it's surrounded by miles of excellent walking, cycling and fishing country. Several pubs in Britain share the same name, which refers to a legend of a baby found in an eagle's nest. Dishes include Fleetwood mussels in tomato, garlic and white wine sauce, local rump steak braised with onions; and roast cod loin in anchovy and parsley butter.

Open 11–11 **Bar Meals** L served all week 12–2.30 D served all week 6–9 Av main course £5 **Restaurant** L served Mon-Fri 12–2.30 D served Mon-Fri 6–9 Av 3 course à la carte £20 ◖ Black Sheep Best Bitter, Coniston, Hawkshead Bitter, Dent Ales. ♀ 10 **Facilities** Garden Dogs allowed Parking **Rooms** 5

WORKINGTON
MAP 18 NY02

The Old Ginn House
Great Clifton CA14 1TS ☎ 01900 64616 ▤ 01900 873384
e-mail: enquiries@oldginnhouse.co.uk
dir: *Just off A66, 3m from Workington & 4m from Cockermouth*

The Ginn Room was where farm horses were harnessed to a grindstone to crush crops. Today the unique rounded room is this 17th-century inn's main bar. The butter yellows, bright check curtains and terracotta tiles of the dining areas exude a warm Mediterranean glow. A menu of the usual bar food is supplemented by larger dishes such as a Ginn House steak, which is stuffed with ham and onion and topped with stilton or cheddar.

Open 11–12 Closed: 24–26 Dec, 1 Jan **Bar Meals** L served all week 12–1.45 D served all week 6–9.15 Av main course £7.50 **Restaurant** L served all week 12–1.45 D served all week 6–9.15 Av 3 course à la carte £16 ⊕ Free House ◖ Jennings Bitter, John Smiths Bitter, Murphys. **Facilities** Children's licence Garden Parking **Rooms** available

England

YANWATH MAP 18 NY52

Pick of the Pubs

The Yanwath Gate Inn ♀

CA10 2LF ☎ 01768 862386 📄 01768 899892

e-mail: enquiries@yanwathgate.com

dir: *Telephone for directions*

The Yanwath Gate Inn has been offering hospitality in the North Lakes since 1683. Today the ethos of owner Matt Edwards is to offer good quality informal dining based on produce which is usually local and organic if possible. While choosing from the regularly changing seasonal menu, enjoy a pint of Doris' 90th Birthday Ale or one of the other Cumbrian ales on offer. Fish is delivered fresh every morning so there are always half a dozen fish and seafood specials on the à la carte menu. A typical dinner choice could be smoked halibut and crème fraiche cheesecake; rolled marinated local lamb shoulder with goats' cheese mash; and brûlée of the day. A cosy reading area in the bar ensures a relaxed mood for diners who can choose to eat here by the log fire or at a table in one of the two dining rooms.

Open 11–11 **Bar Meals** L served all week 12–2.30 D served all week 6–9 Av main course £10 **Restaurant** L served all week 12–2.30 D served all week 6–9 Av 3 course à la carte £30 ⊕ Free House 🍺 Hesket Newmarket Brewery Doris's 90th Birthday Ale, Tirril, Keswick, Paulaner Hefeweizen. ♀ 12 **Facilities** Children's licence Garden Dogs allowed Parking

DERBYSHIRE

ASHBOURNE MAP 10 SK14

Barley Mow Inn

Kirk Ireton DE6 3JP ☎ 01335 370306

dir: *Telephone for directions*

On the edge of the Peak District National Park, this imposing 17th-century inn has remained largely unchanged over the years. Close to Carsington Water, ideal for sailing, fishing and bird watching. There are also good walking opportunities on nearby marked paths. Ales from the cask and traditional cider; fresh granary rolls at lunchtime and evening meals for residents only.

Open 12–2 7–11 (Sun 7–10.30) Closed: 25 & 31 Dec **Bar Meals** 12–2 (Rolls only at lunch) ⊕ Free House 🍺 Hook Norton, Burton Bridge, Whim Hartington, Archers. **Facilities** Garden Dogs allowed Parking **Notes** ⊕

Dog & Partridge Country Inn ♀

Swinscoe DE6 2HS ☎ 01335 343183 📄 01335 342742

e-mail: info@dogandpartridge.co.uk

dir: *From Ashbourne take A52 to Leek. 3m, pub on left in Swinscoe*

This country free house was extended in 1966 to accommodate the Brazilian World Cup football team, who practised in a nearby field. Nowadays the pub scores highly for its extensive menus, offering a good selection of grills, fish, poultry and vegetarian dishes. Start, perhaps, with seafood pancake, followed by pan-fried liver with apple and cranberry; or local trout with a creamy stilton sauce. To finish, there's a wide choice of sweets, ice creams and cheeses.

Open 11–11 **Bar Meals** L served all week 11–11 D served all week Av main course £9 **Restaurant** L served all week 11–11 D served all week Av 3 course à la carte £27.50 Av 3 course fixed price £21.50 ⊕ Free House 🍺 Greene King Old Speckled Hen & Ruddles County, Hartington Best, Wells Bombardier, Courage Directors. **Facilities** Garden Dogs allowed Parking Play Area **Rooms** available

BAKEWELL MAP 16 SK26

Pick of the Pubs

The Bull's Head

Church St, Ashford-in-the-Water DE45 1QB

☎ 01629 812931

e-mail: bullshead.ashford@virgin.net

dir: *Off A6, 2m N of Bakewell, 5m from Chatsworth Estate*

Formerly a coaching inn, The Bull's Head has seen the London and Manchester coaches come and go, though the village's famous well dressing is still a sight to enjoy. Everything about this cosy pub is smartly turned out, from the roses climbing round the door to the shiny brassware hanging around the bar. The interior is cosy and comfortable, with dark wooden beams, open brick fires and cosy banquettes. The menu changes very frequently, with a typical starter of Parma ham salad with stilton dressing, or chicken and pistachio terrine with raspberry vinaigrette. Main courses come as rabbit and pear sausages and celeriac mash; fennel and goats' cheese tartlet topped with Greek yoghurt; and baked cod and smoked bacon with white wine and coriander sauce. Not all the dishes are so ambitious, and simple combinations like pan-fried calves' liver with bubble and squeak, or steak and Old Stockport pie will appease the traditionalists.

Open 11–3 6–11 (Sun 12–3, 7–10.30) **Bar Meals** L served all week 12–2 D served all week 6.30–9 (Sun 7–9) Av main course £10 🍺 Old Stockport, Wards, Unicorn & Double Hop. **Facilities** Garden Parking

Pick of the Pubs

The Monsal Head Hotel 🅄 ♀

See Pick of the Pubs on opposite page

PICK OF THE PUBS

BAKEWELL-DERBYSHIRE

The Monsal Head Hotel

This distinctive balconied hotel in the heart of the Peak District National Park enjoys lovely views over Monsal Dale. With its seven en suite bedrooms, the hotel complex is ideally located for touring and walking; it's just three miles outside Bakewell, and Chatsworth House and Haddon Hall are a ten-minute drive away.

Originally built in the 19th century as the Bull's Head, it was later rebuilt as the Railway Hotel. A stone carving of a bull's head is still in place, while the hotel's real ale pub, the Stables, reflects its earlier role as the home of railway horses which collected passengers from Monsal Dale station. Today this delightful venue features original flagstone floors and seating in the former horse stalls, with horse tack on the walls and a hay rack at the back of the bar. There's a welcoming fire in winter, and a range of cask ales including Abbeydale and Thornbridge. Lagers, wheat beers and wines by the bottle or glass are also on offer. Food from a single menu covers both the bar and restaurant, and is also served in the large enclosed garden in summer.

Meat (including local lamb) and game are provided by an award-winning butcher, and fresh fish on the specials blackboard may proffer roasted whole black bream, or fillet of pollock. Light lunches feature hot or cold sandwiches, fajitas, and jacket potatoes. Cheesy garlic bread or a bowl of olives with warm ciabatta will help fill the odd corner, whilst a full three-course meal could commence with cod, pancetta and basil fishcake; continue with mushroom-filled cannelloni topped with gruyère, buffalo mozzarella and parmesan; and conclude with raspberry pavlova.

⊔ ♀
MAP 16 SK26
Monsal Head DE45 1NL
☎ 01629 640250
📠 01629 640815
e-mail:
enquiries@monsalhead.com
dir: *A6 from Bakewell towards Buxton. 1.5m to Ashford. Follow Monsal Head signs, B6465 for 1m*

Open 11.30–11 (Sun 12–10.30)
Bar Meals L served Mon-Sat 12–9.30 D served Mon-Sat (Sun 12–9) Av main course £13
Restaurant L served Mon-Sat 12–9.30 D served Mon-Sat 6–9.30 (Sun 12–9) Av 3 course à la carte £22.50
⊕ Free House ◀ Theakstons, Bradfield ales, Lloyds Monsal, Thornbridge ales & Abbeydale.
Facilities Garden Dogs allowed Parking
Rooms 7

England

BAMFORD   MAP 16 SK28

Pick of the Pubs

Yorkshire Bridge Inn ★★★★ INN �

See Pick of the Pubs on opposite page

BARLOW   MAP 16 SK37

The Tickled Trout

33 Valley Rd S18 7SL ☎ 0114 289 0893

A few miles outside Chesterfield, this quaint country pub is located at the gateway to the superb Peak District, renowned for its walking and splendid scenery. Within the pleasant, cosy atmosphere you can sample the inn's straightforward menu: among the fishy choices are fresh local trout with almond butter, beer-battered cod, and grilled monkfish with a tomato and basil sauce on a bed of couscous. The specials board offers choices for those not inclined towards seafood.

Open 12–3 6–11 (Sun 7–10.30) **Bar Meals** L served all week 12–2.30 D served all week 6.30–9 (Sun 12–3) Av main course £6.50 **Restaurant** L served all week 12–2.30 D served all week 6.30–9 ⊕ Free House ◀ Marstons Pedigree, Mansfield Smooth, Marstons Finest Creamy & guest. **Facilities** Garden Dogs allowed Parking

BASLOW   MAP 16 SK27

Rowley's ⊛⊛ ♟

Church Ln DE45 1RY ☎ 01246 583880 ▤ 01246 583818

e-mail: info@rowleysrestaurant.co.uk

dir: *A619/A623 signed Chatsworth. Baslow on edge of Chatsworth Estate*

Formerly a village pub, Rowleys combines the best of the old (drinkers are still welcome to enjoy the stone-flagged bar and open fire) with an emphasis on classy eating. Typical dishes include lobster and prawn ravioli followed by slow-braised belly pork with mashed potato, apple fondant and black pudding. Outside is a terrace with lovely church views – ideal for enjoying a pint of local cask ale.

Open 11–11 (Closed Sun eve) Closed: 1st wk Jan **Bar Meals** L served all week 12–2.30 D served Mon-Thu 5–8 Av main course £10 **Restaurant** L served all week 12–2.30 D served Mon-Fri 7–9 (Sat 7–10) ⊕ Free House ◀ Thornbridge, Black Sheep Best Bitter. ♟6 **Facilities** Parking

BIRCHOVER   MAP 16 SK26

Pick of the Pubs

The Druid Inn ♟

Main St DE4 2BL ☎ 01629 650302

dir: *From A6 between Matlock & Bakewell take B5056, signed Ashbourne. After approx 2m turn left to Birchover.*

A popular, friendly, ivy-clad dining pub in the heart of the Peak District. The Druid was built in 1607, so the old bar has plenty of character, with original tiled floor and real log fires. The same menu serves the bar/snug and two restaurants, and meals are also served on the terrace on bright sunny days. Traditional and contemporary dishes range from classic hot or cold sandwiches to a gourmet set menu. If choosing from the carte, starters may include crispy Bakewell black pudding with streaky bacon, brown sauce onions and poached free-range egg. Main courses might be Druid Inn smoked fish pie with mature cheddar cheese mash; or venison, pigeon and Guinness stew. Real ales include a Druid-badged brew from Leatherbritches in Ashbourne. Especially popular on summer weekends, this pub has many visitors who walk up to the Nine Ladies Stone Circle on Stanton Moor, or Rowtor Rocks, reached by a steep uphill path behind the inn.

Open 11–11 Closed: Sun pm Winter **Bar Meals** L served Mon-Sat 12–2.30 Sun 12–3 (D served Sun-Thu 6–9 Fri-Sat 6–9.30) **Restaurant** L served Mon-Sat 12–2.30 Sun 12–3 (D served Sun-Thu 6–9 Fri-Sat 6–9.30) (D not served in Winter) ⊕ Free House ◀ Druid Bitter & guest ale. ♟12 **Facilities** Garden Parking

The Red Lion

Main St DE4 2BN ☎ 01629 650363

e-mail: matteo@frau36.fsnet.co.uk

dir: *5.5m from Matlock, off A6 onto B5056*

Druids practised their magic amidst Rowter Rocks, a 70-yard-long pile of gritstone with fine views of the wooded hillside and valley below. The Red Lion was built in 1680 as a farmhouse and its old well, now glass-covered, still remains in the Tap Room. Expect reasonably priced home-cooked food made with local ingredients, with dishes ranging from a simple sandwich to a rustic Sardinian dish from co-owner Matteo's homeland.

Open 12–2.30 7–11 (Mon 7–9) Closed: Mon Winter **Bar Meals** L served all week 12–2.30 D served all week 7–9 **Restaurant** L served all week 12–2 D served all week 7–9 Av 3 course à la carte £15 ◀ Boddingtons, Nine ladies, Black Sheep, Ichinusa (Sardinian) & Peakstone's Rock Brewery Bitter's. **Facilities** Garden Dogs allowed Parking

BIRCH VALE   MAP 16 SK08

Pick of the Pubs

The Waltzing Weasel Inn ★★★ INN ♟

See Pick of the Pubs on page 136

PICK OF THE PUBS

BAMFORD-DERBYSHIRE

Yorkshire Bridge Inn

Dating back to at least 1826, this inn takes its name from the old packhorse bridge that crossed the River Derwent here on the border with Yorkshire. Set against a magnificent Peak District backdrop, the inn is surrounded by wonderful walking country, woodlands and a profusion of wildlife.

A short stroll away are the Ladybower and other Derwent Valley reservoirs, famed for the RAF's Dambuster training runs in 1943. The bars, plentifully beamed and with attractive chintz curtains, are cosy and welcoming in winter, although in warmer weather you might want to be in the stone-built conservatory, or outside in the courtyard or spacious beer garden. Food is prepared to order using fresh local produce and the standard menu, complemented by daily specials, lists sandwiches and filled jacket potatoes (lunchtime only), plus salads, grills and other hot dishes which are available throughout the day. Starters include nachos with melted cheese, jalapeno peppers and salsa dip; and a large Yorkshire pudding filled with creamy onion sauce and gravy. Among the main courses are pot-roasted lamb with minted gravy, vegetables and a choice of potatoes; or butternut squash and goat's cheese lasagne. The blackboard lists daily fish specials, while other regular dishes include a selection from the grill and a range of salad platters. For dessert, you could try English treacle and orange tart, or the home-made crumble of the day. The en suite bedrooms, including one with a four-poster, make a good base for touring nearby attractions like Chatsworth. The Derwent Valley reservoirs caused heated controversy when they were created in the first half of the 20th century, but have matured into beautiful attractions in their own right.

★★★★ INN ♉
MAP 16 SK28
Ashopton Rd S33 0AZ
☎ 01433 651361
🖷 01433 651361
e-mail:
info@yorkshire-bridge.co.uk
web: www.yorkshire-bridge.co.uk
dir: *A57 from M1, left onto A6013, pub 1m on right*

Open 10–11
Bar Meals L served all week
12–2 D served all week 6–9 (Sun
12–8.30) Av main course £9
Restaurant L served all week
12–2 D served all week 6–9
Av 3 course à la carte £18.25
⊕ Free House ⬤ Blacksheep,
Old Peculier, Golden Pippen,
Copper Dragon IPA. ♉ 13
Facilities Garden Dogs allowed
Parking
Rooms 14

PICK OF THE PUBS

BIRCH VALE-DERBYSHIRE

The Waltzing Weasel Inn

This intriguingly named and award-winning pub was built of local stone some 400 years ago, and is surrounded by Peak District hills. This is walking country beloved of outdoor enthusiasts, and new owners Brian Jordan and Jon Sanderson, in charge since March 2006, are ready to welcome them.

Business people are welcome too, though they are asked to turn off their mobile phones in keeping with house policy prohibiting gaming machines and music, apart from the odd live jazz session. Country antiques are a feature of the bar, while from the garden and mullion-windowed restaurant there are dramatic views of Kinder Scout. The food is produced from local produce where possible, and Fair-Trade items are also used when appropriate. Bar menu regulars include vegetarian dishes such as leek and Hartington Blue Stilton bread and butter pudding, or vegetable lasagne; and meat dishes such as rabbit with lavender, apricots and Galliano, loin of pork with pink peppercorns, and rare breed beef roast with parsnip chips

and Yorkshire pudding. There are fish dishes like pan-seared scallops wrapped in smoked bacon with a white wine, cream and brandy sauce, salmon fillet, served with mushrooms and a white wine sauce or tuna loin Mediterranean style. Be sure and try some of the Weasel's own sausages – Harvey Bangers. Menus are regularly changed so that even regular diners don't always know what to expect. Look out for occasional special events, such as the popular "lobster night".

★★★ INN ☂
MAP 16 SK08
New Mills Rd SK22 1BT
☎ 01663 743402
▤ 01663 743402
e-mail: w-weasel@zen.co.uk
dir: *W from M1 at Chesterfield*

Open 12–11 Sun 12–10.30
Bar Meals L served all week
12–9 D served all week 7–9 Av
main course £12
Restaurant L served all week
12–2 D served all week 6–9 Av 3
course fixed price £27.50
⊕ Free House ◖ Marston's Best
& Pedigree, Jennings Sneck Lifter,
Greene King IPA, Old Speckled
Hen. ☂ 10
Facilities Garden Parking
Rooms 8

BRADWELL MAP 16 SK18

The Old Bowling Green Inn 🍷

Smalldale S33 9JQ ☎ 01433 620450 📠 01433 620280
dir: *Off A6187 onto B6049 towards Bradwell*

A 16th-century coaching inn with impressive views over glorious countryside. Traditional country cooking and good value daily specials supplemented by weekly changing ales produce grilled goats' cheese with sun-dried tomatoes and caramelised onions; chicken breast in mushroom, white wine and mustard grain cream sauce; sea bass fillets on celeriac mash; and meat and potato pie. Bakewell tart and apple crumble feature among a range of tempting home-made puddings.

Open 12–11 **Bar Meals** L served all week 12–2 D served all week 6–8.30 (Sun 12–3, 6–8) Av main course £8 **Restaurant** L served all week 12–2 D served all week 6–9 (Sun 12–3, 6–8) Av 3 course à la carte £16.50 Free House Stones, Timothy Taylor, Tetleys, Kelham Gold. 🍷 8 **Facilities** Children's licence Garden Parking Play Area

BRASSINGTON MAP 16 SK25

Pick of the Pubs

Ye Olde Gate Inne

Well St DE4 4HJ ☎ 01629 540448 📠 01629 540448
e-mail: theoldgateinn@supanet.com
dir: *2m from Carsington Water off A5023 between Wirksworth & Ashbourne.*

Oak beams, black leaded ranges, an antique clock, charmingly worn tiled floors and a delightful mishmash of scrubbed pine furniture – this inn has no shortage of character. It was built in 1616 out of local stone and salvaged Armada timbers, and stands beside an old London to Manchester turnpike in the heart of Brassington, a hill village on the southern edge of the Peak District. Hand pumped Marston's Pedigree Bitter takes pride of place behind the bar, alongside guest ales such as Jennings Sneck Lifter. The menu, written daily on blackboards, features a wealth of local produce. At lunch, try fresh soups, sandwiches, filled baguettes or the house speciality, the Derbyshire fidget. The evening menu changes regularly using locally sourced seasonal produce.

Open 12–2.30 6–11 (Sat 12–3, 6–11 Sun 12–3, 7–10.30) Closed: Mon **Bar Meals** L served Tue-Sun 12–1.45 D served Tue-Sun 7–8.45 (Sun 12–2) Av main course £10.50 Marstons Pedigree, Hobgoblin & guest ales. **Facilities** Garden Dogs allowed Parking

BROUGH MAP 16 SK18

Travellers Rest ★★★ INN

Brough Ln Head S33 9HG
☎ 01433 620363 📠 01433 623338
e-mail: elliottstephen@btconnect.com
dir: *Old A625/B6147 between Sheffield & Castleton*

Between Sheffield and Castleton in the Peak District's Hope Valley. This long-established family-owned stone inn is only a few yards from a Roman encampment which exploited the local lead mines. The pub offers rooms with lovely views. Real ales include a couple of local brews, and the good value menu may feature Thai-style fishcakes followed by beef and local ale pie with chips and mushy peas. A large garden with benches is popular in summer.

Open 12–12 (Nov-Feb 12–3, 5–12) Closed: 25–26 Dec **Bar Meals** L served Mon-Sat 12–2 D served Mon-Sat 6–9 (Sun 12–6) **Restaurant** L served Mon-Sat 12–2 D served Mon-Sat 6–9 (Sun 12–6) Free House Farmers Blonde, Acorn Barnsley Bitter, Boddingtons & Worthingtons. **Facilities** Children's licence Garden Parking Play Area **Rooms** 5

CASTLETON MAP 16 SK18

The Castle 🍷

Castle St S33 8WG ☎ 01433 620578 📠 01433 622902
dir: *Exit M1 for Chesterfield, and follow Chatsworth House signs. At Chatsworth House follow Castleton signs. Pub in village centre*

The Castle in the heart of the Peak District has been a coaching inn since Charles II's reign. The four resident ghosts may go back that far too! Open fires ensure that entering on a chilly day after some brisk fell-walking is like getting into a bed that's had the electric blanket on. As for eating, you could start with black pudding and bacon salad, or salmon and broccoli fishcakes, and proceed to minted lamb cutlets or chilled Cajun salmon steak salad.

Open 12–11 (Sun 12–10.30) **Restaurant** L served all week 12–11 D served all week Vintage Inns Cask Bass, Black Sheep, Bombardier, Speckled Hen. 🍷 22 **Facilities** Garden Parking

The Peaks Inn ★★★★ INN 🍷

How Ln S33 8WJ ☎ 01433 620247 📠 01433 623590
e-mail: info@peaks-inn.co.uk
dir: *On A625 in town centre*

An attractive, stone-built village pub standing below the ruins of Peveril Castle, after which Castleton is named. The bar is warm and welcoming, with leather armchairs for weary walkers, and open log fires for their wet socks. The menu offers old favourites of steak and ale pie; bangers and mash; ham, egg and chips; beer battered cod; and a range of steaks. Rest your eyes in one of the four en suite rooms.

Open 12–12 (Fri-Sat 12–1am) **Bar Meals** L served all week 12–3 D served all week 5–9 (Summer 12–9) Av main course £6 Punch Taverns Black Sheep, Deuchars IPA, Tetley Smooth & 1 guest on rotation. 🍷 9 **Facilities** Garden Dogs allowed Parking **Rooms** 3

England

CASTLETON continued

Ye Olde Nag's Head ☻

Cross St S33 8WH

☎ 01433 620248 & 620443 📄 01433 621501

e-mail: info@yeoldenagshead.co.uk

dir: *A625 from Sheffield, W through Hope Valley, pass through Hathersage & Hope. Pub on main road*

A traditional, family-run 17th-century coaching inn with a cosy bar, and three real fires. Muddy boots are welcome, as many walkers and cyclists have been pleased to discover as they limp into the bar for a reviving pint of Timothy Taylor Landlord. County-sourced or supplied food includes all-day giant Derbyshire breakfast; steak, Guinness and mushroom pie; fish and chips; and home-made roasted vegetable strudel.

Open 9–12 **Bar Meals** L served Mon-Sat 12–6 D served Mon-Sat 6–9 (Sun Carvery 12–8) Av main course £8 **Restaurant** L served Mon-Sat 12–6 D served Mon-Sat 6–9 (Sun Carvery 12–8) ⊕ Free House ◀ Timothy Taylor Landlord, Black Sheep, Worthingtons, guest ale. ☻ 12 **Facilities** Dogs allowed Parking **Rooms** available

---

DERBY MAP 11 SK33

The Alexandra Hotel ☻

203 Siddals Rd DE1 2QE ☎ 01332 293993

dir: *Telephone for directions*

Two-roomed hotel filled with railway memorabilia. Noted for its real ale (11 hand pumps and 450 different brews on tap each year), range of malt whiskies, and friendly atmosphere. A typical menu offers chilli con carne, liver and bacon, home-baked ham with free range egg and chips, filled Yorkshire puddings, ploughman's lunches, omelettes and freshly-made filled hot and cold cobs.

Open 11–11 (Sun 12–3, 7–10.30) Closed: 25 Dec **Bar Meals** L served Tue-Sat 12–2 Av main course £3.75 ⊕ Tynemill Ltd ◀ Castle Rock, Nottingham Gold, Elsie Mo. ☻ 6 **Facilities** Garden Dogs allowed Parking **Notes** ⊜

DOE LEA MAP 16 SK46

Hardwick Inn ☻

Hardwick Park S44 5QJ ☎ 01246 850245 📄 01246 856365

e-mail: batty@hardwickinn.co.uk

web: www.hardwickinn.co.uk

dir: *M1 junct 29 take A6175. 0.5m left (signed Stainsby/Hardwick Hall). After Stainsby, 2m, left at staggered junct. Follow brown tourist signs*

Peter and Pauline Batty are the third generation of their family to run this 15th-century inn by the south gate of the National Trust's Hardwick Hall. Built from locally quarried sandstone, it retains its historic atmosphere, particularly when the open coal fires are alight in winter. On the menu are Hardwick Estate grilled Barnsley chop with a redcurrant and port sauce; grilled rainbow trout filled with crab and prawns; beef and Old Peculier sausages; and mixed grill.

Open 11.30–11 **Bar Meals** L served Mon-Sat 11.30–9.30 D served Mon-Sat 11.30–9.30 (Sun 12–9) **Restaurant** L served Tue- Sun 12–2 D served Tue-Sat 7–8.30 ⊕ Free House ◀ Theakston Old Peculier & XB, Greene King Old Speckled Hen, Black Sheep, Bombardier. ☻ 24 **Facilities** Children's licence Garden Parking Play Area

---

EYAM MAP 16 SK27

Miners Arms

Water Ln S32 5RG ☎ 01433 630853

dir: *Off B6521, 5m N of Bakewell*

This welcoming 17th-century inn and restaurant in the famous plague village of Eyam gets its name from the local lead mines of Roman times. Fish features strongly on the menu, with the likes of seafood pie, tuna steak on a bed of ratatouille, and grilled salmon fillet with a herb crust and sweet chilli sauce. Wash it all down with a pint of Theakston's Best, or Old Peculier.

Open 12–11 Closed: 26 Dec eve **Bar Meals** L served Mon-Sat 12–2 Sun 12–3 (D served Tue-Fri & Sun 6–9 Mon 6–8, Sat 7–9) **Restaurant** L served Mon-Sat 12–2 D served Mon-Sat 6–9 (Sun 12–3) ◀ Worthington's Creamflow, Theakstons Best Pedigree, John Smiths, Old Peculier. **Facilities** Garden Dogs allowed Parking

---

FENNY BENTLEY MAP 16 SK14

Pick of the Pubs

Bentley Brook Inn ★★★ INN ☻

See Pick of the Pubs on opposite page

PICK OF THE PUBS

FENNY BENTLEY-DERBYSHIRE

Bentley Brook Inn

Completely refurbished but still full of traditional charm and atmosphere, this lovely building began life as a medieval farmhouse made from wattle and daub. Its near neighbour was the manor house, whose fortifications included five square towers – you can see the only remaining one from the inn's car park.

The farmhouse was twice extended in the 1800s, and, on the second occasion, re-roofed with slate. Between the World Wars, two elderly ladies lived here in considerable style, attended to by five servants, a gardener, an under-gardener and a coachman. The house became a restaurant in 1954, and a full drinks licence was granted in the 1970s. The inn serves a selection of real ales, some brewed by the local Leatherbritches brewery. Both the bar and the restaurant, which overlooks the terrace and garden, serve everything from sandwiches to substantial home-cooked dishes. Lunch might include a home-made black pudding and bacon tartlet with a coarse grain mustard sauce followed by home-made

steak and ale pie with chips and peas. The menus are changed with the seasons and in response to the usually plentiful supply of local game. Home-made desserts include sticky toffee pudding with butterscotch sauce and ice cream; and fresh fruit pavlova with fruit coulis. Traditional English Sunday lunch is served as a three-course, three-roast carvery, and during the summer the barbecue in the garden is fired up. In the winter, snuggle up by the central open log fire and play dominoes, cards or chess – just ask at the bar.

★★★ INN ☕
MAP 16 SK14
DE6 1LF
☎ 01335 350278
🖹 01335 350422
e-mail:
all@bentleybrookinn.co.uk

Open 11–12
Bar Meals L served all week 12–3, 6–8.45 D served all week 12–8.45 (Sun 12–8)(Oct-Mar kitchen closed 3–5.30) Av main course £9
Restaurant L served all week 12 D served all week 9 (Sun 12–8) Av 3 course à la carte £20
🍺 Leatherbritches Bespoke, Leatherbritches Hairy Helmet, Goldings, Marstons Pedigree. ☕ 7
Facilities Garden Dogs allowed Parking Play Area
Rooms 11

FENNY BENTLEY continued

The Coach and Horses Inn ♀

DE6 1LB ☎ 01335 350246

e-mail: coachandhorses2@btconnect.com

dir: *On A515 (Ashbourne to Buxton road), 2.5m from Ashbourne*

A cosy refuge in any weather, this family-run, 17th-century coaching inn stands on the edge of the Peak District National Park. Besides the beautiful location, its charms include stripped wood furniture and low beams. Expect real ales and good home cooking along the lines of honey-roasted duck breast with a port and berry sauce; or whole roasted trout stuffed with pearl barley, wild mushrooms and parsley and finished with lemon butter.

Open 11–11 **Bar Meals** L served all week 12–9 D served all week 12–9 Av main course £10 **Restaurant** L served all week 12–9 D served all week 12–9 ⊕ Free House ◀ Marston's Pedigree, Timothy Taylor Landlord, Black Sheep Best, Oakham JHB. ♀ 6 **Facilities** Garden Parking

FROGGATT
MAP 16 SK27

Pick of the Pubs

The Chequers Inn ★★★★ INN ◉ ♀

Froggatt Edge S32 3ZJ

☎ 01433 630231 ▤ 01433 631072

e-mail: info@chequers-froggatt.com

dir: *On A625, 0.5m N of Calver*

An arrestingly attractive country inn, the Chequers is set below Froggatt Edge; its westward panorama of the Peak District National Park reached by a steep, wild woodland footpath from the elevated secret garden. Reminders of the building's centuries' old history include a horse-mounting block and the old stables housing logs for the crackling winter fires. The interior of wooden floors, Windsor chairs and bookcases is ideal for a contemplative beer or your choice from an innovative modern European menu (with some British favourites). The food is prepared from locally sourced produce, ranging from sandwiches and salads through to starters as varied as classic prawn cocktail, and confit duck leg with braised cabbage and roasted plums. Mains take in spiced beancake with tomato and coriander salad; seafood risotto with saffron; and pot roasted lamb shank with braised winter vegetables. Finish with chocolate brownie and Tia Maria sabayon.

Open 12–2 6–9.30 (Sat & Sun all day) Closed: 25 Dec **Bar Meals** L served Mon-Sat 12–2 D served Mon-Sat 6–9.30 (Sun 12–9) Av main course £13 ⊕ Free House ◀ Wells Bombardier Premium Bitter, Greene King IPA & Black Sheep. ♀ 9 **Facilities** Garden Parking **Rooms** 5

GREAT HUCKLOW
MAP 16 SK17

The Queen Anne Inn ★★★ INN ♀

SK17 8RF ☎ 01298 871246 ▤ 01298 873504

e-mail: angelaryan100@aol.com

dir: *A623 onto B6049, turn off at Anchor pub towards Bradwell, 2nd right to Great Hucklow*

A warm welcome awaits at this traditional country free house with its log fires, good food, and an ever-changing range of cask ales. The inn dates from 1621; a licence has been held for over 300 years, and the names of all the landlords are known. Stunning open views can be enjoyed from the sheltered south-facing garden. Specialities include lamb and pork from neighbouring farms, making Sunday lunch a particular favourite among the local cognoscenti.

Open 12–2.30 5–11 (Sat-Sun all day) Closed: Mon **Bar Meals** L served Tue-Sun 12–2 D served Tue-Sun 6.30–8.30 Av main course £9 ⊕ Free House ◀ Adnams Bitter, Shaws, Storm Brewery, Kelham Island. ♀ 10 **Facilities** Garden Parking **Rooms** 2

GRINDLEFORD
MAP 16 SK27

Pick of the Pubs

The Maynard ★★★ HL ◉◉

Main Rd S32 2HE ☎ 01433 630321 ▤ 01433 630445

e-mail: info@themaynard.co.uk

dir: *From M1 take A619 into Chesterfield, then onto Baslow. A623 to Calver, right into Grindleford*

This fine stone-built inn stands grandly in immaculately kept grounds overlooking the Derwent Valley, in the heart of the Peak District National Park. You may eat in either the Longshore Bar or in the Padley Restaurant, with its large windows facing the gardens. Choose the bar, and the menu may well offer seared breast of chicken with mushroom risotto and balsamic oil; Moroccan-spiced braised lamb with couscous; or grilled sea bass on champ with tomato and olive salsa. Opt for the restaurant and discover other possibilities, such as eggs Benedict with chive oil, or smoked haddock fishcake as starters; main courses of fillet of beef with fondant potato, wild mushrooms and caramelised red wine onion; pan-fried calf's liver with olive oil mash, onion fritters and grilled pancetta; and pan-seared red mullet with shellfish paella and lobster oil. For dessert, try sticky toffee parkin pudding with stem ginger ice cream.

Open 11–11 (Sun 12–10.30) **Bar Meals** L served all week 12–2 D served all week 6–9 Av main course £9 **Restaurant** L served Sun-Fri 12–2 D served all week 7–9.30 ⊕ Free House ◀ Abbey Dale Moonshine, Bakewell Bitter. **Facilities** Children's licence Garden Dogs allowed Parking **Rooms** 10

England

HARTSHORNE   MAP 10 SK32

The Mill Wheel ★★★★ INN ♀

Ticknall Rd DE11 7AS ☎ 01283 550335 📄 01283 552833
e-mail: info@themillwheel.co.uk
dir: *A511 from Burton-on-Trent towards Leicester. Left at island signed A514/Derby. Pub a short distance*

Amazingly this old building's huge mill wheel has not only survived for 250–odd years, but also, since restoration in 1987, still slowly turns, powered by recirculated water. The wheel is very much the focus of attention in the bar and restaurant, where freshly prepared dinner might comprise leek, spinach and coriander soup; roasted red sea bream with a tapenade; and a hot or cold dessert. En suite rooms are furnished to a high standard.

Open 12–2.30 6–11 (Sun 12–11) **Bar Meals** L served Mon-Sat 12–2.15 D served Mon-Sat 6–9.15 (Sun 12–8.30) **Restaurant** L served Mon-Sat 12–2.15 D served Mon-Sat 6–9.15 (Sun 12–7) ⊕ Free House ◀ Abbot Ale, Oakham Ale, Summer Lightning, Bass & Pedigree. ♀ 8 **Facilities** Garden Parking **Rooms** 4

HASSOP   MAP 16 SK27

Eyre Arms ♀

DE45 1NS ☎ 01629 640390
e-mail: nick@eyrearms.com
dir: *On B6001 N of Bakewell*

Formerly a farmstead and 17th-century coaching inn, this traditional free house stands in one of the most beautiful parts of rural Derbyshire. Oak settles, low ceilings and cheery log fires create a cosy atmosphere, while the secluded garden overlooks the rolling Peak District countryside with its lovely local walks. Typical dishes include local venison pie; Grand Marnier duckling; and local trout baked with butter and almonds.

Open 11.30–3 6.30–11 Closed: 25 Dec **Bar Meals** L served all week 12–2 D served all week 6.30–9 Av main course £9.50 ⊕ Free House ◀ Marston's Pedigree, Theakstons Black Bull Bitter, Black Sheep Special. ♀ 9 **Facilities** Garden Parking

HATHERSAGE   MAP 16 SK28

Millstone Inn ★★★★ INN ♀

Sheffield Rd S32 1DA ☎ 01433 650258 📄 01433 650276
e-mail: jerry@millstone.co.uk
dir: *Telephone for directions*

There are striking views over the picturesque Hope Valley from this tastefully furnished former coaching inn. Chatsworth House, Ladybower Reservoir and the Blue John Mines are among nearby attractions. An atmospheric bar, serving six traditional cask ales, adds to the appeal. The menu features hearty favourites such as fish and chips alongside the likes of Arbroath smokies with fresh tomato in a mustard and cheese sauce; or sweet potato and mushroom ragout with saffron rice.

Open 11.30 -11 **Bar Meals** L served Mon-Sat 12–9 D served Mon-Sat 12–9 (Sun 12–8) ⊕ Free House ◀ Timothy Taylor Landlord, Black Sheep, guest ales. ♀ 16 **Facilities** Garden Dogs allowed Parking **Rooms** 8

Pick of the Pubs

The Plough Inn ★★★★ INN ⊛ ♀

See Pick of the Pubs on page 142

HAYFIELD   MAP 16 SK08

The Royal Hotel ♀

Market St SK22 2EP ☎ 01663 742721 📄 01663 742997
e-mail: enquiries@theroyalhayfield.co.uk
web: www.theroyalhayfield.co.uk
dir: *Off A624*

A fine-looking, mid-18th-century building in a High Peak village. The oak-panelled Windsor Bar has log fires, and serves bar snacks and selected dishes, while the dining room offers a traditional menu from which you might select spinach and mushroom pancake, followed by rack of lamb (served pink) with rich port jus; or grilled plaice with cream and prawn sauce. Then chef's hot pudding and custard to finish. Kinder Scout looks impressive from the patio.

Open 11–1am **Bar Meals** L served Mon-Sat 12–2.15 D served Mon-Sat 6–9 (Sun 12–6) Av main course £6 **Restaurant** L served Mon-Sat 12–2.15 D served Mon-Sat 6–9 (Sun 12–6) ⊕ Free House ◀ Hydes, Howard Town, Taylors. ♀ 8 **Facilities** Children's licence Garden Parking

PICK OF THE PUBS

The Plough Inn

Set amid its own nine acres of land and surrounded by idyllic countryside on the banks of the River Derwent, this 16th-century inn is the perfect place to escape the stresses of daily life. Guests receive a warm welcome from hosts Bob and Cynthia Emery who will ensure the most comfortable of stays.

All the bedrooms are en suite; three are housed in the main building and two in September Cottage, a conversion across the courtyard from the inn. Local materials have been used throughout, leaving exposed beams and brickwork. A wide range of ales, whiskies, brandies and liqueurs, and wines from around the world, are served in the cosy bar, where a log fire burns, and meals are served in the bar or intimate restaurant. The menu, with over 40 freshly prepared dishes to choose from, is an eclectic mix of traditional and modern European cooking. Examples from the restaurant are saltimbocca of sea bass with crushed potato, French beans and tomato coulis; and saddle of rabbit wrapped in pancetta with a prune compote, sauté potatoes and rosemary velouté. Typical bar meals include the pie of the day, fish and chips, sausage and mash, and spaghetti bolognaise. The sheltered garden is a delight in summer, with tea served in the afternoons, and a pretty array of flower-filled baskets adorns the inn's external walls. Situated in the Peak District National Park, the Plough makes an ideal base from which to explore the surrounding countryside and visit nearby attractions, such as Chatsworth House, Haddon Hall, Castleton with its many caves, and the famous Blue John Mine.

★★★★ INN ⚛ ♥
MAP 16 SK28
Leadmill Bridge S32 1BA
☎ 01433 650319 & 650180
🖹 01433 651049
e-mail: sales@
theploughinn-hathersage.com
dir: *M1 junct 29, take A617W, A619, A623 and then B6001N to Hathersage*

Open 11–11 Closed: 25 Dec
Bar Meals L served Mon-Sat 11.30–2.30 D served Mon-Sat 6.30–9.30 (Sun 12–9) Av main course £12.95
Restaurant L served Mon-Sat 11.30–2.30 D served Mon-Sat 6.30–9.30 (Sun 12–9)
⊕ Free House ◖ London Pride, Old Speckled Hen, Black Sheep, Young's Bitter & Bombardier. ♥ 14
Facilities Garden Parking
Rooms 5

HOGNASTON   MAP 16 SK25

The Red Lion Inn ♥

Main St DE6 1PR ☎ 01335 370396 📠 01335 370396
e-mail: redlion@w3z.co.uk
web: www.redlionhognaston.co.uk
dir: *From Ashbourne take B5035 towards Wirksworth. Approx 5m follow Carsington Water signs. Turn right to Hognaston*

A traditional 17th-century inn on the edge of the Peak District National Park, with beautiful Carsington Water a short walk away. John Kennedy Jr and his wife once stayed here – they would have loved the beamed ceilings, open fireplaces and church pew seating. Top quality produce is prepared daily for menus serving the bar and restaurant, where Derbyshire fillet steak, Peak District bangers and mash, and fish pie are among the regulars.

Open 12–3 6–11 **Bar Meals** L served all week 12–2.45 D served all week 6.30–9 **Restaurant** L served all week 12–2.45 D served all week 6.30–9 Av 3 course à la carte £25 ⊕ Free House ◀ Marston's Pedigree, Burton Bitter & guest ales. ♥ 8 **Facilities** Garden Parking

HOLLINGTON   MAP 10 SK23

Pick of the Pubs

The Red Lion Inn ♥

Main St DE6 3AG ☎ 01335 360241 📠 01335 361209
e-mail: redlionholl@aol.com
dir: *On A52 between Ashbourne & Derby, turn off at Ednaston/Hollington sign. Pub 2m on right*

In a beautiful country setting, this spectacular 18th-century coaching inn is known for its warm and friendly atmosphere and award-winning food. Start a meal with salt and pepper cuttlefish with sweet chilli noodles; or pheasant and thyme ravioli poached in game and vegetable broth. Main courses include crispy honey-glazed Gressingham duck breast with salsify; braised osso buco of veal with root vegetables, red wine and fine herb dumplings; venison fillet medallions set on swede mash with shallot and cep marmalade; roasted loin of lamb with Puy lentil vinaigrette and ratatouille; fresh halibut fillet steak on wilted spinach with warm chive butter sauce; and chargrilled plaice with Sauvignon Blanc dressing. For dessert see if steamed bitter chocolate sponge with hot chocolate fudge sauce is available. On a fine day the gated beer garden is just the place for a pint of Adnams Broadside.

Open 12–3 6–11 **Bar Meals** L served all week 12–2 D served all week 6.30–9 (Sun 12–2.30) Av main course £7.50

Restaurant L served all week 12–2 D served all week 6.30–9 (Sun 12–2.30) Av 3 course à la carte £23 Av 2 course fixed price £9.95 ⊕ Free House ◀ Pedigree, Abbot Ale, Bass, Adnams Broadside. ♥ 8 **Facilities** Garden Dogs allowed Parking

HOPE   MAP 16 SK18

Cheshire Cheese Inn ♥

Edale Rd S33 6ZF ☎ 01433 620381 📠 01433 620411
e-mail: tcheese@gmail.com
dir: *On A6187 between Sheffield & Chapel-en-le-Frith*

Located on the old trans-Pennine salt route in the heart of the Peak District, this 16th-century inn owes its name to the tradition of accepting cheese as payment for lodgings. It has a reputation for good home-made food and hand-pulled beer served in a relaxed atmosphere with open fires. There is a choice of light bites and main meals, ranging from toasted sandwiches or jacket potatoes to a mixed grill or roasted lamb shank.

Open 12–3 6.30–11 (all day at wknds) **Bar Meals** L served all week 12–2 D served all week 6.30–9 (Sun 12–8.30) **Restaurant** L served all week 12–2 D served all week 6.30–9 (Sun 12–8.30) ⊕ Free House ◀ Slaters Toptotty, Wentworthy Pale Ale, Black Sheep Best, Hartington Bitter. ♥ 13 **Facilities** Garden Dogs allowed Parking

LITTON   MAP 16 SK17

Red Lion Inn ♥

SK17 8QU ☎ 01298 871458 📠 01298 871458
e-mail: theredlionlitton@yahoo.co.uk
dir: *Just off A623 (Chesterfield -Stockport rd), 1m E of Tideswell*

The Red Lion is a beautiful, traditional pub on the village green, very much at the heart of the local community. With its wood fires, selection of real ales and friendly atmosphere, it's a favourite with walkers and holiday-makers too. The menu offers hearty pub food at reasonable prices, such as haddock goujons to start, lambs' liver and bacon with horseradish mash to follow, and treacle sponge pudding with custard to round things off.

Open 12–11 **Bar Meals** L served Mon-Wed 12–2 D served Mon-Wed 6–8 (Thu-Sun 12–8.30) Av main course £7.95 **Restaurant** L served all week D served all week Av 3 course à la carte £16 ⊕ Free House ◀ Barnsley Bitter, Timothy Taylor, Thornbridge Hall, Kelham Island. ♥ 9 **Facilities** Garden Dogs allowed

LONGSHAW   MAP 16 SK27

Fox House ♥

Hathersage Rd S11 7TY ☎ 01433 630374 📠 01433 637102
dir: *From Sheffield follow A625 towards Castleton*

A delightfully original 17th-century coaching inn and, at 1,132 feet above sea level, one of the highest pubs in Britain. The Longshaw dog trials originated here, after an argument between farmers and shepherds as to who owned the best dog. A simple menu lists sandwiches, starters, Sunday roasts, and mains like chicken and ham pie, ground Scottish beefsteak burger, spicy prawn pasta, and lamb cutlets.

Open 11–11 (Sun 11.30–10.30) **Bar Meals** L served all week 12–5 D served all week 5–10 (Sun 12–9.30) Av main course £9 **Restaurant** L served all week 12–5 D served all week 5–10 (Sun 12–9.30) Av 3 course à la carte £18 ⊕ Vintage Inns ◀ Cask Stones, Cask Tetleys. ♥ 20 **Facilities** Garden Parking

MARSTON MONTGOMERY   MAP 10 SK13

Pick of the Pubs

The Crown Inn ★★★★ INN ◉ ♟

Riggs Ln DE6 2FF ☎ 01889 590541 ▤ 01889 591576

e-mail: info@thecrowninn-derbyshire.co.uk

dir: *From Ashbourne take A515 towards Lichfield, 5m. Turn right at Cubley x-rds, follow signs to Marston Montgomery, 1m. Pub in village centre*

Set in the idyllic hamlet of Marston Montgomery on the southern edge of the Peak District, this small inn retains plenty of traditional charm. Low ceilings, beams and leather sofas make the bar a comfortable place in which to unwind and enjoy the selection of beers and real ales, or choose from the carefully selected wine list. Outside is an elevated patio and garden area for hot summer days. The menu changes weekly, offering modern, classically-based food with a fusion twist. The daily specials board either includes a selection of fresh fish. Lunchtime brings a full à la carte menu alongside sandwiches on speciality breads and bagels. On Sundays there is a traditional roast. Typical dishes include twice-baked stilton soufflé and pickled pear salad; blade of beef and braised red cabbage; and pan-fried sea bass on black pudding and pink peppercorn mash. Seven individually designed en suite bedrooms are available.

Open 12–3 6.30–11 Closed: 25 Dec & 1 Jan **Bar Meals** L served all week 12–2.30 D served Mon-Sat 6–7.30 Av main course £8 **Restaurant** L served all week 12–2.30 D served Mon-Thu 7–9 (Fri-Sat 7–9.30) Av 3 course à la carte £23 Av 2 course fixed price £11.95 ⊕ Free House ◀ Timothy Taylor Landlord, Marstons Pedigree, Guinness. ♟ 7 **Facilities** Garden Parking **Rooms** 7

MATLOCK   MAP 16 SK35

The Red Lion ★★★★ INN

65 Matlock Green DE4 3BT ☎ 01629 584888

dir: *From Chesterfield, A632 into Matlock, on right just before junct with A615*

This friendly, family-run free house makes a good base for exploring local attractions like Chatsworth House, Carsington Water and Dovedale. Spectacular walks in the local countryside help to work up an appetite for bar lunches, steaks and a wide selection of home-cooked meals. In the winter months, open fires burn in the lounge and games room, and there's a boules area in the garden for warmer days.

Open 11–12 **Bar Meals** L served Tue-Fri 12–2 D served Tue-Sun 7–9 (Sun 12–4) **Restaurant** L served Tue-Fri 12–2 D served Tue-Sun 7–9 (Sun 12–4) ◀ Courage Directors, John Smiths & Theakstons Bitter, Peak Ales & guest ales. **Facilities** Garden Parking **Rooms** 6

MELBOURNE   MAP 11 SK32

The Melbourne Arms NEW ★★★ INN

92 Ashby Rd DE73 8ES

☎ 01332 864949 & 863990 ▤ 01332 865525

e-mail: info@melbournearms.co.uk

This restaurant on the village outskirts was tastefully converted from an 18th-century pub about 13 years ago. There are two bars, a coffee lounge and the restaurant itself, traditionally decorated – no, not red

flock wallpaper – and where an extensive menu of authentic Indian dishes is offered. With a range of English dishes and a children's menu too, there's no reason why the whole family can't find plenty to enjoy.

Open 12–11.30 (Fri-Sat 12–12) Closed: 26 Dec **Bar Meals** L served all week 12–11.30 D served all week 4–11.30 Av main course £8 **Restaurant** L served all week D served all week Av 3 course à la carte £15 ◀ Pedigree, Tetley's Smooth, Guinness. **Facilities** Garden Parking Play Area **Rooms** 7

MILLTOWN   MAP 16 SK36

The Nettle Inn ♟

S45 0ES ☎ 01246 590462

The Nettle Inn is a traditional 16th-century hostelry nestling in countryside bordering the Peak District. All the sought-after qualities of cosiness and character are here, from the flower-filled hanging baskets outside to the log fires and stone-flagged taproom floor within. Locals and visitors alike rejoice in the choice of real ales, and appreciate fully the head chef who will only serve dishes and breads, sauces, pickles and sweets if he has made them.

Open 12–3 5.30–11.30 **Bar Meals** L served all week 12–2.30 D served all week 6.30–9.30 (times vary Sat-Sun) Av main course £7.95 **Restaurant** L served all week 12–2.30 D served Sun-Fri 6.30–9.30 (Sat 6.30–10, Sun 12–4) Av 3 course à la carte £24 ⊕ Free House ◀ Bradfield Farmers Best Bitter, Bradfield Farmers Blonde, Hardy & Hansons, Olde Trip. ♟ 9 **Facilities** Children's licence Garden Dogs allowed Parking

RIPLEY   MAP 16 SK35

The Moss Cottage Hotel

Nottingham Rd DE5 3JT ☎ 01773 742555 ▤ 01773 741063

e-mail: info@mosscottagehotel.co.uk

dir: *Telephone for directions*

This red-brick free house specialises in carvery dishes, with four roast joints each day. Expect popular menu choices like prawn cocktail or mushroom dippers; ham, egg and chips; liver and onions; or battered haddock. Hot puddings include rhubarb crumble and chocolate fudge cake. Under new management.

Open 12–3 6–10 Closed: Mon-Tue lunch, Sun pm **Bar Meals** L served Wed-Sat 12–5 (Sun 12–6) Av main course £7.50 **Restaurant** L served Wed-Sun 12–2.15 D served Mon-Sat 6–9 (Sun 12–2.15, 6–6) ⊕ Free House ◀ Old Tripp, Guinness, Old Rose Scrumpy Cider & guest ale. **Facilities** Parking

ROWSLEY   MAP 16 SK26

The Grouse & Claret ★★★ INN ♟

Station Rd DE4 2EB ☎ 01629 733233 ▤ 01629 735194

dir: *On A6 between Matlock & Bakewell*

A popular venue for local anglers, this pub takes its name from a fishing fly. It is also handy for touring the Peak District or visiting the stately homes of Haddon Hall and Chatsworth House. A meal from the cosmopolitan menu might include crispy duck salad with hoi sin sauce, and chicken and seafood paella or, for the more traditionally minded, prawn cocktail followed by steak and ale pie. Food served all day.

Open 7.30–11 (Sun 7.30–10.30) **Bar Meals** L served all week 7.30–9 D served all week 7.30–9 **Restaurant** L served all week 7.30–9 D served all week 7.30–9 ⊕ ◀ Marston's Pedigree, Mansfield, Bank's Bitter. ♟ 12 **Facilities** Garden Parking Play Area **Rooms** 8

England

SHARDLOW
MAP 11 SK43

The Old Crown

Cavendish Bridge DE72 2HL ☎ 01332 792392

dir: *M1 junct 24 take A6 towards Derby. Left before river, bridge into Shardlow*

A family-friendly pub on the south side of the River Trent, where up to seven guest ales are served. It was built as a coaching inn during the 17th century, and retains its warm and atmospheric interior. Several hundred water jugs hang from the ceilings, while the walls display an abundance of brewery and railway memorabilia. Traditional food is lovingly prepared by the landlady, including sandwiches, jackets, omelettes, ham and eggs, and Cumberland sausages.

Open 11–12 (Fri-Sat 11–1, Sun 10.30–12) **Bar Meals** L served Mon-Sat 12–2 D served Mon-Thu & Sat 5–8 (Sun 12–3) ⊕ Marstons ◀ Marston's Pedigree, Jennings Cocker Hoop & 7 guest ales. **Facilities** Children's licence Garden Dogs allowed Parking Play Area

SOUTH WINGFIELD
MAP 16 SK35

The White Hart ♥

Moorwood Moor DE55 7NU

☎ 01629 534229 🖺 01629 534229

dir: *From Crich take B5035 to South Wingfield. Turn R at top of hill, pub 1 mile on L*

Classic award-winning country pub at the gateway to the Derbyshire Peak District, superbly situated for walkers and cyclists and offering wonderful views across to Wingfield Manor where Mary Queen of Scots was held captive. A good reputation for locally-sourced food and home-grown ingredients guarantees everything from bread to truffles are made in the White Hart's kitchen. Expect chicken and locally-supplied black pudding roulade, natural-smoked haddock, Bakewell pudding, and a range of Derbyshire cheeses.

Bar Meals D served Tue-Thu 6–9 Av main course £5.95 **Restaurant** D served Tue-Sat 6–9 (Sun 12–2.30) Av 3 course à la carte £26 Av 1 course fixed price £5.95 ◀ Pedigree, Guinness, Bass, guest ale. ♥ 6 **Facilities** Garden Parking

TIDESWELL
MAP 16 SK17

The George Hotel ♥

Commercial Rd SK17 8NU

☎ 01298 871382 🖺 01298 871382

e-mail: georgehoteltideswell@yahoo.co.uk

dir: *A619 to Baslow, A623 towards Chapel-en-le-Frith, 0.25m*

A 17th-entury coaching inn in a quiet village conveniently placed for exploring the National Park and visiting Buxton, Chatsworth and the

historic plague village of Eyam. Quality home-cooked food includes venison cooked in red wine sauce, roast pheasant with bacon, potatoes and mushrooms, seafood crumble, and whole rainbow trout with almonds.

Open 12–3 6–11 (Open all day Sat-Sun) **Bar Meals** L served all week 12–2 D served all week 6–9 (Sat-Sun all day Summer) Av main course £6 **Restaurant** L served all week 12–2 D served all week 6–9 (Sat-Sun all day Summer) Av 3 course à la carte £12 ⊕ Hardy & Hansons ◀ Kimberley Cool, Olde Trip Bitter, Best Bitter. ♥ 12 **Facilities** Garden Dogs allowed Parking

Three Stags' Heads

Wardlow Mires SK17 8RW ☎ 01298 872268

dir: *At junct of A623 & B6465 on Chesterfield – Stockport road.*

Grade II listed 17th-century former farmhouse, designated by English Heritage as one of over 200 heritage pubs throughout the UK. It is located in the limestone uplands of the northern Peak District, and is now combined with a pottery workshop. Well-kept real ales and hearty home-cooked food for ramblers, cyclists and locals includes chicken and spinach curry; pork, leek and stilton pie, and game in season. No children under eight.

Open 12–11 (Fri 7–11) Closed: Mon-Thu **Bar Meals** L served Sat-Sun 12.30–3 D served Fri-Sun 7.30–9.30 ⊕ Free House ◀ Abbeydale Matins, Absolution, Black Lurcher & Brimstone Bitter. **Facilities** Dogs allowed Parking **Notes** ⊗

WESSINGTON
MAP 16 SK35

The Three Horseshoes

The Green DE55 6DQ ☎ 01773 834854

e-mail: scott@3horseshoes-wessington.info

dir: *A615 towards Matlock, 3m after Alfreton, 5m before Matlock*

A century ago horses were still being traded over the bar at this late-17th-century former coaching inn and associated blacksmith's forge, to both of which activities it no doubt owes its name. For a true taste of the Peak District try Derbyshire chicken with black pudding and apple; or braised lamb shank with celeriac purée. Several local walks start or end at the pub – why not order a picnic or a hamper for refreshment?

Open 11.30–11 (Sun 12–10.30) Closed Mon in winter **Bar Meals** L served Tue-Sat, BHs 12–2 D served Tue-Thu, BHs 5.30–8.30 (Sun 12.30–4.45) **Restaurant** L served Sun in winter 12.30–3 D served Fri-Sat 7–9 (Sun 12.30–5) Av 3 course à la carte £21 ◀ Guinness, Hardys & Hansons Olde Trip, guest ale. **Facilities** Garden Dogs allowed Parking Play Area

England

DEVON

ASHBURTON

MAP 03 SX77

The Rising Sun ★★★★ INN ♀

Woodland TQ13 7JT ☎ 01364 652544 📄 01364 654202
e-mail: risingsun.hazel@btconnect.com

dir: E of Ashburton from A38 take lane signed Woodland/ Denbury. Pub on left approx 1.5m

A former drovers' inn, largely rebuilt following a fire in 1989, The Rising Sun is set in beautiful Devon countryside, convenient for Exeter, Plymouth and Torbay. Regularly changing real ales are served and an extensive wine list, including local Sharpham wine. The menu offers a good choice of fish and excellent West Country cheeses. The pub is also well known for its home-made pies (available to take home), and its monthly Pie Club evening. New Licensees 2008.

Open 11.45–3 6–12 (Sun 12–3, 7–10.30) Closed: 25 Dec
Bar Meals L served Tue-Sat 12–2.15 D served Tue-Sat 6–9.15 (Sun 12–3, 7–9.15) **Restaurant** L served Tue-Sat 12–2.15 D served Tue-Sat 6–9.15 (Sun 12–3, 7–9.15) Av 3 course à la carte £20 ⊕ Free House ◀ Princetown Jail Ale, IPA, Teignworthy Reel Ale & guest ales. ♀ 10 **Facilities** Garden Dogs allowed Parking Play Area **Rooms** 4

AVONWICK

MAP 03 SX75

The Avon Inn

TQ10 9NB ☎ 01364 73475
e-mail: rosec@beeb.net

dir: Telephone for directions

There's a distinctly Gallic flavour to this handsome whitewashed free house, just off the busy Exeter to Plymouth trunk road. In the colder months, a cheery wood-burning stove sets the scene for sea bass and salmon on spinach and crayfish rosti with lobster bisque; and galette of chestnuts, mushrooms and leeks with boursin filo parcels. Chef/ proprietor Dominique Prandi also offers more traditional English fare, including braised lamb on celeriac mash with rosemary jus.

Open 11.30–3 6–11 (Sun 12–2.30, 6–10.30) **Bar Meals** L served Mon-Sat 12–2 D served Tue-Sun 6.30–9.30 (Sun 12–3, Mon 6–11) Av main course £8 **Restaurant** L served Mon-Sat 12–2 D served Mon-Sat 6–9.30 (Sun 12–3) Av 3 course à la carte £20 ⊕ Free House ◀ Teignworthy Reel Ale, guest ale, Otter Bitter, Sharp's Doom Bar. **Facilities** Garden Parking

Pick of the Pubs

The Turtley Corn Mill ♀

TQ10 9ES ☎ 01364 646100 📄 01364 646101
e-mail: mill@avonwick.net

Milling apart, this sprawling old building has witnessed a number of activities, including chicken hatching. Its idyllic six-acre location is bordered by a river, and includes a lake with its own small island. Inside, the style is light and fresh with oak and slate floors, bookcases, old furniture and pictures galore of the chicken-hatching Trott dynasty, some of whose members still dine here. There are no fruit machines, pool tables or music, but plenty of newspapers and books to read if you wish. Daily changing menus, based extensively on local produce, offer fish stew with garlic mayonnaise; spicy chilli beef with tortilla chips, melted cheese and sour cream; coq au vin with saffron rice; and mixed bean burger

with coleslaw and fries. The cellar is well stocked with a range of local beers, including some from Summerskills in Plymouth. Plans are in hand to reintroduce corn grinding here.

Open 11.30–11 (Sun 12–10.30) Closed: 25 Dec **Bar Meals** L served Mon-Sat 12–9.30 D served Mon-Sat 12–9.30 (Sun 12–9) Av main course £10 ⊕ Free House ◀ Tamar Ale, Jail Ale, Tribute, Dartmoor IPA. ♀ 11 **Facilities** Garden Dogs allowed Parking

AXMOUTH

MAP 04 SY29

Pick of the Pubs

The Harbour Inn

Church St EX12 4AF ☎ 01297 20371
e-mail: garytubb@yahoo.com

dir: Main street opposite Church, 1m from Seaton

The River Axe meanders through its valley into Lyme Bay, but just before they meet is Axmouth harbour, which accounted for one sixth of Devon's trade during the 16th century. This cosy, oak-beamed, harbourside inn was built four centuries earlier, however. Gary and Graciela Tubb have maintained three principles – local ingredients bought from small family businesses, nothing frozen, and everything home made. A bar and bistro menu offers scampi and chips, lasagne, sausages or faggots with mash and gravy, jacket potatoes, baguettes and sandwiches. From a daily updated blackboard menu, you might want to consider pork tenderloin with prunes and bacon; swordfish steak with niçoise salad; or tagliatelle, wild mushrooms and spicy tomato sauce. The Harbour makes a great stop if you are walking the South West Coast Path between Lyme Regis and Seaton.

Open 11–3 6–11 (Summer all day, Sun 12–10.30)
Bar Meals 12–2 6.30–9 (Sun 7–9) Av main course £11
Restaurant L served all week 12–2 D served all week 6.30–9 (Sun 7–9) Av 3 course à la carte £20 ⊕ Hall & Woodhouse ◀ Badger 1st Gold, Tanglefoot, Sussex & Otter Bitter. **Facilities** Garden Dogs allowed Parking Play Area

The Ship Inn ♀

EX12 4AF ☎ 01297 21838

dir: 1m S of A3052 between Lyme & Sidmouth. Signposted to Seaton at Boshill Cross

There are long views over the Axe estuary from the beer garden of this creeper-clad family-run inn. It was built soon after the original Ship burnt down on Christmas Day 1879, and is able to trace its landlords back to 1769; the current ones have been there for over 40 years. Well kept real ales complement an extensive menu including daily blackboard specials where local fish and game feature, cooked with home-grown herbs.

Open 11–3 6–11.30 (Jan & Feb closed Sun eve) **Bar Meals** L served all week 12–2 (Summer 12–3) D served all week 6–9.30 **Restaurant** L served all week 12–2 D served all week 6–9 (Summer 12–3, 6–9.30) ⊕ Pubmaster ◀ Otter Bitter, Guinness, 6X & Stowford Press. ♀ 10 **Facilities** Garden Dogs allowed Parking Play Area

BARBROOK

MAP 03 SS74

The Beggars Roost

EX35 6LD ☎ 01598 752404

e-mail: info@beggarsroost.co.uk

dir: *A39 1m from Lynton*

Originally a manor farmhouse with attached cow barn, the buildings were converted into a hotel in the 1970s with the barn becoming the Beggars Roost. The long, low bar has tables around a warm log-burner; the restaurant on the floor above extends up into the beamed apex and is popular for parties. The pub menu offers a great range of reasonably priced favourites such as casseroles, terrines and ploughman's, while the restaurant focuses on more sophisticated fare.

Open 12–3 6–12 **Bar Meals** L served all week 12–3 D served all week 6–9 Av main course £6.95 **Restaurant** D served all week 6–9.30 Av 3 course à la carte £25 ⊕ Free House ◀ Exmoor Ale, Cotleigh Barn Owl, Exmoor Silver Stallion, Cotleigh Tawny. **Facilities** Children's licence Garden Dogs allowed Parking

BEER

MAP 04 SY28

Anchor Inn ♀

Fore St EX12 3ET ☎ 01297 20386 📄 01297 24474

e-mail: 6403@greeneking.co.uk

dir: *A3052 towards Lyme Regis. At Hangmans Stone take B3174 into Beer. Pub on seafront*

Fish from local boats feature strongly on the menu at this pretty colourwashed hotel, which overlooks the sea in the equally picture-perfect Devon village of Beer. Dine on beer-battered cod and chips; local crab with salad; smoked haddock on cheddar cheese mash with a mustard cream sauce; or chicken breast stuffed with brie, wrapped in bacon and served with a cranberry and red wine sauce.

Open 8–11 **Bar Meals** L served all week 12–3 D served all week 6–9 (Apr-Oct food all day) **Restaurant** L served all week 12–3 D served all week 6–9 (Apr-Oct Fri-Sat 6–9.30) ⊕ Greene King ◀ Otter Ale, Greene King IPA, Abbot Ale. ♀ 14 **Facilities** Children's licence Garden

BERE FERRERS

MAP 03 SX46

Olde Plough Inn

PL20 7JL ☎ 01822 840358

e-mail: oldeplough@btinternet.com

dir: *A386 from Plymouth, A390 from Tavistock*

Originally three cottages, dating from the 16th century, this inn has bags of character, with its old timbers and flagstones, which on closer inspection are revealed to be headstones. To the rear is a fine patio overlooking the River Tavey, and there are lovely walks in the Bere Valley on the doorstep. The area is ideal for birdwatchers. Dishes on offer range through fresh fish, crab, local pies, curries and stir-fries.

Open 12–3 7–11.30 **Bar Meals** L served all week 12–2 D served all week 7–9 Av main course £7 **Restaurant** L served all week 12–2 D served all week 7–9 Av 3 course à la carte £16 ⊕ Free House ◀ Sharp's Doom Bar & Own, Interbrew Flowers, guest ale. **Facilities** Garden Dogs allowed

BICKLEIGH

MAP 03 SS90

Fisherman's Cot ♀

EX16 8RW ☎ 01884 855237 📄 01884 855241

e-mail: fishermanscot.bickleigh@eldridge-pope.co.uk

dir: *Telephone for directions*

Well-appointed thatched inn by Bickleigh Bridge over the River Exe with food all day and large beer garden, just a short drive from Tiverton and Exmoor. The Waterside Bar is the place for snacks and afternoon tea, while the restaurant incorporates a carvery and à la carte menus. Sunday lunch is served, and champagne and smoked salmon breakfast is optional.

Open 11–11 **Bar Meals** L served all week 12–6 D served all week 6–9.30 **Restaurant** L served all week 12–10 D served all week ⊕ Eldridge Pope ◀ Wadworth 6X, Bass. ♀ 8 **Facilities** Garden Parking

BIGBURY-ON-SEA

MAP 03 SX64

Pilchard Inn ♀

Burgh Island TQ7 4BG ☎ 01548 810514 📄 01548 810243

e-mail: reception@burghisland.com

dir: *From A38 turn off to Modbury then follow signs to Bigbury & Burgh Island*

A small 14th-century inn located on a tiny island off the Devon coast and only accessible on foot at low tide. The adjoining art deco hotel was once a favourite haunt of the likes of Noël Coward and the Windsors, and Agatha Christie set several of her popular detective novels here. Fine real ales and ciders are part of the appeal.

Open 11.30–11 (Sun 12–10.30) **Bar Meals** L served all week 12–2.30 D served Thu-Sat 7–9 Av main course £15 ⊕ Free House ◀ Sharp's, Teignworthy, St Austell. ♀ 7 **Facilities** Children's licence Garden Dogs allowed Play Area

See advert on page 148

BRANSCOMBE

MAP 04 SY18

Pick of the Pubs

The Masons Arms ★★ HL ⊚ ♀

See Pick of the Pubs on page 149

Pilchard Inn
Bigbury-on-Sea, Devon, TQ7 4BG

The Pilchard Inn is a genuine smugglers' pub, established 1336. Owned by Burgh Island Hotel, The Pilchard serves fine wines, local draught beers and regional ciders. Food is freshly prepared by the Hotel's kitchen: bar food during the day, popular curry buffets on Fridays and evening meals on Thursdays and Saturdays. Two cosy bars, an open fire and endless sea views.

Tel: 01548 810514

BRAUNTON   MAP 03 SS43

The Williams Arms

Wrafton EX33 2DE ☎ 01271 812360 📠 01271 816595

dir: *On A361 between Barnstaple & Braunton*

Spacious thatched pub dating back to the 16th century, and adjacent to the popular Tarka Trail, named after the much-loved otter created by author Henry Williamson. The restaurant has a carvery serving fresh locally-sourced meat and various vegetable dishes. Breakfast all day.

Open 11–11 **Bar Meals** L served all week 11–9.30 D served all week 11–9.30 Av main course £7.95 **Restaurant** L served all week 12–2.30 D served all week 6.15–9.30 Av 3 course à la carte £11 ⊕ Free House ◀ Guinness, Bass, Creamflow. **Facilities** Children's licence Garden Parking Play Area

---

BRENDON   MAP 03 SS74

Rockford Inn

EX35 6PT ☎ 01598 741214 📠 01598 741265
e-mail: enquiries@therockfordinn.com

dir: *A39 through Minehead follow signs to Lynmouth. Turn left off A39 to Brendon approx 5m before Lynmouth*

A traditional 17th-century country inn on the banks of the tumbling East Lyn River. Lots of old beams and Cotleigh real ales help to characterise the bar. A plate of local beef and dumplings is accompanied by onions, carrots and potatoes stewed in rich ale gravy; sirloin steak comes with traditional vegetables; and there's a Thai vegetable dish, gaeng keow waan.

Open 12–3 6.30–10.30 Closed: Nov-Etr **Bar Meals** L served all week 11.30–2.30 D served all week 6.30–9.30 Av main course £6.95 ⊕ Free House ◀ Real ales & lagers brewed on-site. **Facilities** Children's licence Garden Dogs allowed Parking

---

BROADHEMPSTON   MAP 03 SX86

The Monks Retreat Inn

The Square TQ9 6BN ☎ 01803 812203

dir: *Exit Newton Abbot to Totnes road at Ipplepen, follow signs for Broadhempston for 3.5m*

Apparently a friendly ghost inhabits this inn – certainly it's the sort of place you'd want to linger in: the building (listed as of outstanding architectural interest) is full of fascinating features, including a panelled oak screen typical of ancient Devon houses. Sit by one of the cosy log fires and enjoy a pint of Skinner's Cornish Knocker or other decent real ales from Butcombe.

Open 12–2.30 6–11 (Sun 7–11) Closed: Mon **Bar Meals** L served Tue-Sat 12–2 D served Tue-Sat 6.30–9 (Sun 12–2.30) **Restaurant** L served Tue-Sun 12–2 D served Tue-Sun 6.30–9 ⊕ Enterprise Inns ◀ Butcombe, Guinness & Cornish Knocker. **Facilities** Children's licence Dogs allowed

---

BUCKFASTLEIGH   MAP 03 SX76

Dartbridge Inn 🅰 ★★★ INN ♥

Totnes Rd TQ11 0JR ☎ 01364 642214 📠 01364 643839
e-mail: dartbridge.buckfastleigh@oldenglishinns.co.uk

dir: *From Exeter A38, take 1st Buckfastleigh turn, then right to Totnes. Inn on left*

Standing close to the River Dart, this 19th-century building was originally a simple dwelling, then a teashop before becoming a pub. Well known for its eye-catching floral displays, inside are open fires and oak beams. The lunch/bar menu includes slow-cooked Welsh lamb, and spinach and ricotta girasole, while dinner mains are typically baked rainbow trout with pan-fried tiger prawns, gammon and other steaks, sausages and mash, and chicken Caesar salad.

Open 11–11 **Bar Meals** L served all week 12–5 D served all week 5–9.30 (Sun 11–9) Av main course £8.95 **Restaurant** L served all week 12–2 D served all week 7–9.30 ⊕ Old English Inns ◀ Scottish Courage, Abbot Ale, IPA, Otter Ale. ♥ 12 **Facilities** Parking **Rooms** 10

BUCKLAND MONACHORUM   MAP 03 SX46

Drake Manor Inn ♥

The Village PL20 7NA ☎ 01822 853892 📠 01822 853892
e-mail: drakemanor@drakemanorinn.co.uk

dir: *Off A386 near Yelverton*

Built in the 12th century for the masons constructing St. Andrews church, the Drake Manor has always been a hostelry. An extensive menu ranges from freshly baked filled baguettes, crab bisque and Glamorgan sausages to baked sea bass, lamb shank, smoked haddock risotto, and venison. In summer the gardens are full of colour, while in winter the wood-burning stoves offer a different appeal. The bar offers more than thirty malts from Aberlour to Tullibardine.

Open 11.30–2.30 6.30–11 (Sat 11.30–3, Sun 12–11 Fri-Sat 6.30–11.30) **Bar Meals** L served all week 12–2 D served Mon-Sat 7–10 (Sun 7–9.30) Av main course £5 **Restaurant** L served all week 12–2 D served Mon-Sat 7–10 (Sun 7–9.30) Av 3 course à la carte £12.50 ⊕ Punch Taverns ◀ John Smiths & Courage Best, Greene King Abbot Ale, Sharp's Doom Bar. ♥ 9 **Facilities** Garden Dogs allowed Parking

PICK OF THE PUBS

BRANSCOMBE-DEVON

The Masons Arms

Just thinking about the great age of the creeper-clad Masons Arms can stop you in your tracks. It actually dates back to 1360, when it was just a simple cider house measuring a mere 8ft x 4ft, squeezed into the middle of a row of cottages.

Today that row of cottages is an independent, family run pub and hotel offering 20 bedrooms, some set in their own peaceful gardens with views across the valley and out to sea. Once the haunt of smugglers, the Masons Arms has a bar that can hardly have changed in 200 years, with stone walls, ancient ships' beams, slate floors, and a splendid open fireplace used for spit-roasts, including Sunday lunchtimes. Five real ales are always available, including several that are locally brewed. Food is a serious business here and the restaurant maintains a standard of cooking worthy of its AA Rosette. Where possible all ingredients are grown, reared or caught locally, none perhaps more so than the lobster and crab landed on Branscombe beach, a ten-minute stroll away. There is a choice of dining experiences: in the bar, or in the waiter-serviced restaurant. The former can keep you happy with an extensive menu of sandwiches, paninis and ploughman's, starters like salad of Dartmouth kiln-roasted salmon; and Rousdon quails' eggs, asparagus and prawns, and main courses such as chicken tikka masala; lamb and baby balsamic onion casserole; and wilted spinach and brie gnocchi. In the restaurant the fixed-price, three-course dinner menu typically offers carpaccio of beef with parmesan and red onion relish; grilled fillets of sea bass; and sweet cinnamon and mascarpone risotto. In whichever part of the pub you eat, there is always a good choice of fish and seafood.

★★ HL @ ?
MAP 04 SY18
EX12 3DJ
☎ 01297 680300
🖷 01297 680500
e-mail:
reception@masonsarms.co.uk
dir: *Turn off A3052 towards Branscombe, down hill, hotel at bottom of hill*

Open 11–11 Times vary, please phone
Bar Meals L served all week 12–2 D served all week 7–9 Av main course £11
Restaurant D served all week 7–9 Av 3 course fixed price £27.50
⊕ Free House ◖ Otter Ale, Masons Ale, Tribute, Branoc & guest ales. ? 14
Facilities Children's licence Garden Dogs allowed Parking
Rooms 20

BUTTERLEIGH
MAP 03 SS90

The Butterleigh Inn 🍷

EX15 1PN ☎ 01884 855407 📠 01884 855600

e-mail: enquiries@thebutterleighinn.com

dir: *3m from M5 junct 28 turn right by Manor Hotel in Cullompton. Follow Butterleigh signs*

This 400-year-old traditional Devonshire free house is very much a friendly local. There's a mass of local memorabilia throughout the pub, and customers can choose from a selection of real ales including Butcombe Bitter, Otter and Tawny. On fine days, the garden with its huge flowering cherry tree is very popular. Booking is recommended for the restaurant, where home-made dishes and daily specials are always available.

Open 12–2.30 6–12 (Summer 12–12, Sun 12–11) (Sun 12–3 7–10.30) **Bar Meals** L served all week 12–2 D served all week 7–9 Av main course £9.95 **Restaurant** L served all week 12–2 D served all week 7–9 Av 3 course à la carte £15.95 ⊕ Free House ◀ Cotleigh Tawny Ale, Yellow Hammer & guest ale. ♀ 7 **Facilities** Children's licence Garden Dogs allowed Parking

CHAGFORD
MAP 03 SX78

Ring O'Bells 🍷

44 The Square TQ13 8AH

☎ 01647 432466 📠 01647 432466

e-mail: info@ringobellschagford.co.uk

dir: *From Exeter take A30 to Whiddon Down rdbt, 1st left onto A382 to Mortonhampstead. 3.5m to Easton Cross, right signed Chagford*

You won't find a juke box, games machines or television at this traditional West Country free house, but you can count on some lively conversation amid the open winter fires, beams and hand-carved bar. On warmer days, the sunny walled garden makes a great backdrop to a drink and a bite to eat. Three carefully kept ales are on offer together with home-cooked, locally sourced food. Dogs are very welcome.

Open 9.30–3 5–11 (Sat 10–3, 6–11, Sun 12–3, 6–10.30) **Bar Meals** L served all week 12–2 D served all week 6–9 Av main course £9.25 **Restaurant** L served all week 12–2 D served all week 6–9 ⊕ Free House ◀ Butcombe Bitter, Dartmoor Ale, Reel Ale, Tetley. ♀ 8 **Facilities** Children's licence Garden Dogs allowed

The Sandy Park Inn ★★★ INN 🍷

TQ13 8JW ☎ 01647 433267

e-mail: sandyparkinn@aol.com

dir: *From A30 exit at Whiddon Down, turn left towards Moretonhampstead. Inn 5m from Whiddon Down*

Everything about the thatched Sandy Park is just as it should be. Dogs are frequently to be found slumped in front of the fire, horse-brasses and sporting prints adorn the walls, and the beamed bar attracts locals and tourists alike, all happily setting the world to rights with the help of an eclectic wine list and good range of traditional local ales, including Otter Ale, St Austell Tribute and Sharp's Doom Bar. The candlelit restaurant is equally appealing, offering a brasserie-style menu that changes daily to make the most of local produce. Starters might include deep-fried brie with redcurrant jelly, or smoked mackerel, to be followed by venison casserole, roast cod, or spinach and mushroom pie – the perfect fare after a day spent stomping on the moors.

Open 11–11 **Bar Meals** L served Mon-Sat 12–2.30 D served Mon-Sat 6.30–9 (Sun 12–5) Av main course £9 **Restaurant** L served Mon-Sat 12–2.30 D served Mon-Sat 6.30–9 (Sun 12–5) Av 3 course à la carte £24 ⊕ Free House ◀ Otter Ale, O'Hanlons, St Austell Tribute, Exe Valley XX1. ♀ 14 **Facilities** Garden Dogs allowed Parking **Rooms** 5

Three Crowns Hotel ★★ SHL

High St TQ13 8AJ

☎ 01647 433444 & 433441 📠 01647 433117

e-mail: threecrowns@msn.com

dir: *Telephone for directions*

An impressive, 13th-century, granite-built inn with a wealth of historical associations to investigate. Take young poet and Cavalier Sydney Godolphin, for example, who was shot in the hotel doorway in 1643 and who continues to 'appear', making him the hotel's oldest resident. Period features include mullioned windows, sturdy oak beams and a massive open fireplace. Among chef's specialities are sautéed fillet of pork with mango salsa; roasted breast of duck with plum sauce; and lemon sole poached in white wine with mixed seafood sauce.

Open 8–12.30 **Bar Meals** L served all week 12–3 D served all week 6–9.30 Av main course £6 **Restaurant** L served all week 12–2.30 D served all week 6–9.30 Av 3 course à la carte £22.50 Av 3 course fixed price £19.50 ⊕ Free House ◀ Flowers Original, Boddingtons, Bass, Whitbread. **Facilities** Children's licence Dogs allowed Parking **Rooms** 17

CHARDSTOCK
MAP 04 ST30

The George Inn

EX13 7BX ☎ 01460 220241

e-mail: info@george-inn.co.uk

dir: *A358 from Taunton through Chard towards Axminster, left at Tytherleigh. Signed from A358.*

Graffiti from 1648 can be seen in the snug of this 700–year-old pub, which was once a parish house. A friendly parson named Copeland haunts the cellar, while cheerful locals who've been drinking in the George for the past 40 years preside over 'Compost Corner'. Hearty dishes include feta, spinach and mozzarella pie; pan-fried lambs' liver or beer battered cod.

Open 11–2.30 6–11 (Sat 11–3, 6–11, Sun 12–3, 7–10.30)
Bar Meals L served Mon-Sat 12–2 D served Sun-Fri 7–9 (Sat 7–9.30, Sun 12–2.30) **Restaurant** L served all week 12–2 D served all week 7–9 ⊕ Free House ◀ Branoc & guest ale. **Facilities** Garden Dogs allowed Parking

---

CHERITON BISHOP · MAP 03 SX79

Pick of the Pubs

The Old Thatch Inn ♀

EX6 6HJ ☎ 01647 24204 🖹 01647 24584
e-mail: mail@theoldthatchinn.f9.co.uk
dir: *0.5m off A30, 7m SW of Exeter*

The Old Thatch is a charming 16th-century free house located within the Dartmoor National Park, just half a mile off the main A30. It's a popular halfway house for travellers on their way to and from Cornwall, and once welcomed stagecoaches on the London to Penzance road. For a time during its long history, the inn passed into private hands and then became a tea-room, before its licence was renewed in the early 1970s. A major refurbishment during the winter of 2006, following a fire, has preserved the period appeal. Owners David and Serena London pride themselves on their high standards. All the food is prepared using fresh ingredients from the southwest, with seafood featuring strongly. Dishes change every day depending on supplies, and examples include breast of Dartmouth smoked chicken in a poppadom basket; and baked fillets of sea bream with fresh lime, tarragon and lemon grass.

Open 11.30–3 6–11 Closed: 25–26 Dec **Bar Meals** L served all week 12–2 D served all week 6.30–9 Av main course £6.75 **Restaurant** L served all week 12–2 D served all week 6.30–9 Av 3 course à la carte £25 ⊕ Free House ◀ Sharp's Doom Bar, Otter Ale, Princetown's Jail Ale, Port Stout. ♀9 **Facilities** Garden Dogs allowed Parking

---

CLAYHIDON · MAP 04 ST11

Pick of the Pubs

The Merry Harriers ♀

Forches Corner EX15 3TR
☎ 01823 421270 🖹 01823 421270
e-mail: peter.gatling@btinternet.com
dir: *A38, turn onto Ford Street (marked by brown tourist sign). At top of hill turn left, 1.5m on right*

Standing high on the Blackdown Hills, with plenty of space for a large beer garden and a five-lane skittle alley, one of the longest

in the county. Inside the characterful bar are beamed ceilings, a cosy inglenook and attractive dining areas. Peter and Angela Gatling have worked tirelessly to build the local drinks trade while expanding the food operation. More than 90 per cent of kitchen ingredients are from the surrounding hills, or further afield in the West Country. The regularly changing menus offer a wide choice, including grilled venison steak with garlic mash and whisky sauce; oven-roasted aromatic duck with a cherry sauce; and tagliatelle of wild mushrooms, rocket and parmesan. From the Firm Favourites menu come Somerset pork chop topped with apple sauce; and local steak and kidney pie. Children can select from a menu that contains kiddie curry, mad cow (steak and kidney) pie, and whizzers (organic pork and apple sausages) and chips.

Open 12–3 6.30–11 Closed: Sun pm & Mon **Bar Meals** L served Mon-Sat 12–2 D served all week 6.30–9 (Sun 12–2.30) Av main course £8.50 **Restaurant** L served Mon-Sat 12–2 D served all week 6.30–9 (Sun 12–2.30) Av 3 course à la carte £16 ⊕ Free House ◀ Otter Head, Cotleigh Harrier, Exmoor Gold, St Austell Tinners & Exe Valley Devon Pride. ♀14 **Facilities** Garden Dogs allowed Parking Play Area

---

CLEARBROOK · MAP 03 SX56

The Skylark Inn

PL20 6JD ☎ 01822 853258
e-mail: skylvic@btinternet.com
dir: *5m N of Plymouth on A386 towards Tavistock. Take 2nd right signed Clearbrook*

The beamed bar with its large fireplace and wood-burning stove characterises this attractive village inn. Although only ten minutes from Plymouth, the Skylark is set in the Dartmoor National Park and the area is ideal for cyclists and walkers. Good wholesome food is served from an extensive menu that features rainbow trout with new potatoes and salad; vegetable stew with dumplings; and a range of shortcrust pastry pies.

Open 11.30–3 6–11 (Summer Mon-Sun 11.30–11.30) **Bar Meals** L served all week 11.30–2 D served all week 6.30–9 ⊕ Unique Pub Co ◀ Interbrew Bass, Courage Best, Sharp's Special, Otter. **Facilities** Garden Dogs allowed Parking Play Area

---

CLOVELLY · MAP 03 SS32

Pick of the Pubs

Red Lion Hotel ★★ HL

The Quay EX39 5TF ☎ 01237 431237 🖹 01237 431044
e-mail: redlion@clovelly.co.uk
dir: *From Bideford rdbt, follow A39 to Bude for 10m. At Clovelly Cross rdbt turn right, follow past Clovelly Visitor Centre entrance, bear to left. Hotel at bottom of hill*

Clovelly, the famously unspoilt 'village like a waterfall', descends down broad steps to a 14th-century harbour and this charming hostelry is located right on the quay. Guests staying in the whimsically decorated bedrooms can fall asleep to the sound of waves lapping the shingle and wake to the cries of gulls squabbling for scraps. Seafood, unsurprisingly, is a priority on the modern French-influenced menu, which could offer grilled Cornish oysters with champagne sabayon, or home-made wild rabbit terrine with red onion marmalade to start, followed by

CONTINUED

CLOVELLY continued

chargrilled turbot steak; cod fillet in tempura batter with minted pea purée, or pan-seared tuna steak with grilled foie gras and shallots. Desserts are equally artful: frozen mango parfait with grapefruit confit and black peppercorn meringue sounds especially intriguing. Daytime visitors can tuck into a locally-made Cornish pasty, or a plate of cod and chips.

Open 11–1am **Bar Meals** L served all week 11–2.30 D served all week 6–8.30 Av main course £11.50 **Restaurant** L served all week 12–2.30 D served all week 7–8.30 Av 3 course fixed price £28.50 ⊕ Free House ◀ Doom Bar, Old Appledore, Guinness, Clovelly Cobbler. **Facilities** Children's licence Parking **Rooms** 11

CLYST HYDON   MAP 03 ST00

Pick of the Pubs

The Five Bells Inn ☻

EX15 2NT ☎ 01884 277288

e-mail: info@fivebellsclysthydon.co.uk

web: www.fivebellsclysthydon.co.uk

dir: *B3181 towards Cullompton, right at Hele Cross towards Clyst Hydon. 2m turn right, then sharp right at left bend at village sign.*

Originally a 16th-century thatched farmhouse, this attractive country pub in rolling east Devon countryside started serving ale about a hundred years ago, and takes its name from the five bells hanging in the village church tower. It's gone from strength to strength in recent years, thanks to its family-friendly owners and a focus on real ales, good food and cheerful hospitality. The well-maintained garden is a delight in summer, with twenty tables enjoying lovely views, and a children's play area. The interior boasts two wood fires, numerous prints and watercolours, and brass and copper artefacts. Excellent real ales are augmented by draught lagers, cider and bottled beers. When it comes to food, why not start with bacon and garlic mushroom tart, or crab cakes with sweet chilli dip. Then indulge in a West Country steak served with mushrooms, peas and chips; or a slowly cooked duck leg on a bed of colcannon with orange and spring onion.

Open 11.30–3 6.30–11 (Sun 12–3, 6.30–10.30) Closed: Mon lunch Winter **Bar Meals** L served Mon-Sat 11.30–2 D served all week 7–9 (Sun 12–2) Av main course £10 **Restaurant** L served Mon-Sat 11.30–2 D served Mon-Sat 7–9 (Sun 12–2, 6.30–10.30) Av 3 course à la carte £20 ⊕ Free House ◀ Cotleigh Tawny Ale, Otter Bitter, O'Hanlon's. ☻8 **Facilities** Garden Parking Play Area

COCKWOOD   MAP 03 SX98

Pick of the Pubs

The Anchor Inn ☻

EX6 8RA ☎ 01626 890203 📄 01626 890355

dir: *Off A379 between Dawlish & Starcross*

Overlooking a small landlocked harbour on the River Exe, this former Seamen's Mission has been a haven to sailors and smugglers for centuries. In summer customers spill out onto the veranda and harbour wall, while real fires and low beams make the interior cosy in winter. Nautical bric-a-brac abounds, with lights inside divers' helmets, ropes and pulleys, binnacles, and a wall displaying over 200 cast ship badges. A recent extension has been carefully designed to blend in with the characterful original building, making maximum use of reclaimed timbers for floors, beams, bench seating, tables and chairs. Now a further 100 customers can be comfortably seated while choosing between 30 different ways to eat mussels. If mussels don't appeal, there are scallops, oysters, crab, lobster, whole grilled plaice, Cockwood mackerel smokies with lumberjack chips. If meat is preferred, look to the range of Devon pies and sausages, or your favourite cut – it's almost certainly on the truly comprehensive menu.

Open 11–11 (Sun 12–10.30) **Bar Meals** L served Mon-Sat 12–10 D served Mon-Sat 12–10 (Sun 9–12.30) Av main course £7.95 **Restaurant** L served all week 12–2.15 D served Mon-Sat 6.30–10 (Sun 6.30–9.30) Av 3 course à la carte £14.95 ⊕ Heavitree ◀ Interbrew Bass, Timothy Taylor Landlord, Fuller's London Pride, Otter Ale. ☻10 **Facilities** Garden Dogs allowed Parking

COLEFORD   MAP 03 SS70

Pick of the Pubs

The New Inn 🅄 ☻

EX17 5BZ ☎ 01363 84242 📄 01363 85044

e-mail: enquiries@thenewinncoleford.co.uk

dir: *From Exeter take A377, 1.5m after Crediton turn left for Coleford, continue for 1.5m*

Built in the 13th century, The New Inn still serves the sleepy conservation village of Coleford with its ales. It retains original black beams and fireplaces, and the ground floor is divided into three – a restaurant partitioned by a timber and glass screen, a central bar servery, and a bar around the fireplace in the oldest section. There are six bedrooms, three in the old linney (once an open-sided barn) and three in the main building. A changing selection of locally sourced fresh fish, meat and vegetarian dishes produces starters of feta cheese and sun-dried tomato salad; and main courses including West Country faggots with wholegrain mustard mash; or roast duck breast with blackcurrant jus. During the summer, make the most of the idyllic garden, bordered by the Cole Brook, for drinking and dining alfresco. The patio also plays host to pig-roasts between late April and October.

Open 12–3 6–11 (Sun 7–10.30) Closed: 25–26 Dec **Bar Meals** L served all week 12–2 D served all week 7–10 (Sun 7–9.30) Av main course £10 **Restaurant** L served all week 12–2 D served all week 7–10 (Sun 7–9.30) Av 3 course à la carte £20 ⊕ Free House ◀ Doom Bar, Otter Ale, Exmoor Ale, Wells Bombardier & Tanglefoot. ☻8 **Facilities** Garden Parking

CORNWORTHY

MAP 03 SX85

Hunters Lodge Inn ♀

TQ9 7ES ☎ 01803 732204

e-mail: gill.rees@virgin.net

dir: Off A381, S of Totnes

Built in 1740, this country local is at the hub of village life, sponsoring a football team, charity events and a dog show (it's a dog friendly pub). There's even a Christmas party for children. Other notable features are the real log fire and resident ghost. An extensive menu offers dishes from the sea (sesame battered Brixham cod fillet), and from the land (gammon steak, Cornworthy hens' eggs) as well as a selection of pasta dishes (spaghetti carbonara).

Open 11.30–2.30 6.30–11 **Bar Meals** L served all week 12–2 D served all week 7–9 **Restaurant** L served all week 12–2 D served all week 7–9 ⊕ Free House ◖ Teignworthy Reel Ale & Springtide, guest ales. ♀ 14 **Facilities** Garden Dogs allowed Parking Play Area

---

CULMSTOCK

MAP 03 ST11

Culm Valley Inn ♀

EX15 3JJ ☎ 01884 840354 🖹 01884 841659

e-mail: culmvalleyinn@btinternet.com

dir: 2m from A38, 3m from Wellington

A former station hotel in which the owners exposed a long-hidden bar during a renovation re-creating a 'between the wars' look. The ever-changing blackboard menu displays a lengthy list of home-made dishes, mostly using locally-grown or raised ingredients, including chicken breast with a cider brandy sauce. Fish and shellfish come from South Devon or Cornwall, including shellfish platters and Portuguese fish stew. Several real ales straight from the cask.

Open 12–3 6–11 (Sat 12–11, Sun 12–10.30) Closed: 25 Dec eve **Bar Meals** L served Mon-Sat 12–2 D served Mon-Sat 7–9 (Sun 12–10.30) Av main course £12 **Restaurant** L served all week 12–2 D served Mon-Sat 7–9 Av 3 course à la carte £23 ⊕ Free House ◖ O'Hanlons Firefly, Branscombe Branoc, Warrior Golden Wolf. ♀ 50 **Facilities** Garden Dogs allowed Parking **Notes** ⊛

DALWOOD

MAP 04 ST20

Pick of the Pubs

The Tuckers Arms ♀

EX13 7EG ☎ 01404 881342 🖹 01404 881138

e-mail: davidbeck@tuckersarms.freeserve.co.uk

web: www.tuckersarms.co.uk

dir: Off A35 between Honiton & Axminster

Dating back 800 years or so, this Devon longhouse originally provided accommodation for the artisans constructing the local church across the way. Today it is a popular and hospitable village inn providing good quality sustenance for modern travellers. It enjoys a pretty setting between two ridges of the Blackdown Hills, a few yards from the Corry brook and overlooked by the ancient Viking fort of Danes Hill. Inside it is everything you would expect of a traditional, thatched inn – it has inglenook fireplaces, low beams and flagstone floors. Real ales such as Otter Bitter and Old Speckled Hen are on tap. Fish and shellfish from local fishermen

Tuckers Arms

Dalwood, Axminster, Devon EX13 7EG

This is a beautiful old English pub with a thatched roof, low beamed ceilings, flag stone floors & inglenook fireplaces. Recently under new management.

Just off the A35 to the east of Honiton, Devon. With restaurant & accommodation, the 800 year old inn, nestles beside the babbling Cory brook.

Dalwood has not been invaded by tourists – this is rural Devon hospitality at its best and quietest!

At the Tucker's Arms our à la carte menu specialises in award winning fresh fish & game, locally caught crab, mussels & sea bass is regularly featured on our menu. These are supplemented by imaginative starters, and a wide selection of local game, grill and poultry dishes. Local cheeses & clotted cream feature on the menu at all times. Double skittle alley available.

If it's a lunchtime snack you are after, a bar snacks menu with a price range to suit everyone is available Monday to Saturday 12–2pm.

Bed and Breakfast en suite rooms are available prices vary throughout seasons.

Tel: 01404 881342
Website: www.tuckersarms.co.uk
Email: reservations@tuckersarms.co.uk

(the pub is only 15 minutes from Lyme Regis) and Brixham market are shown on the daily specials board, and will generally include scallops, monkfish, lemon sole, with sea bass and seafood roast when available. Outside there is a lovely olde-English country garden and, more recently created, a covered patio with heaters.

The Tuckers Arms

Open 12–3 6.30–11 (Sun 12–10.30) **Bar Meals** L served all week 12–2 D served all week 7–8.30 (Sun 12–7.30) **Restaurant** L served all week 12–2 D served all week 7–9 Av 3 course à la carte £20.95 Av 2 course fixed price £18.95 ⊕ Free House ◖ Otter Bitter, Courage Best, Old Speckled Hen. ♀ 8 **Facilities** Garden Parking

See advert on this page

DARTMOUTH
MAP 03 SX85

Pick of the Pubs

Royal Castle Hotel ★★★ HL ♀
11 The Quay TQ6 9PS
☎ 01803 833033 📠 01803 835445
e-mail: enquiry@royalcastle.co.uk
dir: *In town centre, overlooking inner harbour*

In the 1630s two merchants built their neighbouring quayside houses in commanding positions on the Dart estuary. A century later, one had become The New Inn, and by 1782 it had been combined with its neighbour to become The Castle Inn. Further rebuilds incorporated the battlemented turrets and cornice that gave it an appearance worthy of its name. Opposite the bar is the Lydstone Range, forged in Dartmouth over 300 years ago, and on which you can still have your meat roasted during the winter. There is also a bell-board in the courtyard, with each room's bell pitched to a different note. In the upstairs Adam Room Restaurant fish and seafood dishes are always available – typically dishes will be based on red mullet, lemon sole, turbot and red snapper to name but a few. Other options might be pan-fried chicken breast on green pea and trompette mushroom risotto; rich lamb casserole, filled with fresh local vegetables.

Open 8–11.30 **Bar Meals** L served all week 11.30–10 D served all week 11.30–10 Av main course £9 **Restaurant** L served all week 12–2 D served all week 6–9.30 Av 3 course à la carte £20 ⊕ Free House ◀ Dartmoor IPA, Directors, Bass. ♀ 12 **Facilities** Dogs allowed Parking **Rooms** 25

DENBURY
MAP 03 SX86

The Union Inn ♀
Denbury Green TQ12 6DQ
☎ 01803 812595 📠 01803 814206
e-mail: unioninn@hotmail.co.uk
dir: *2m form Newton Abbot, signed Denbury*

At least 400 years old and counting. Inside are the original stone walls that once rang to the hammers of the blacksmiths and cartwrights who worked here many moons ago. Choose freshly prepared, mouth-watering starters such as moules marinière or smoked chicken in mango vinaigrette, and follow with slow-roasted shoulder of lamb with mint garlic and redcurrant jelly, or a rib-eye steak on a bed of haggis with stilton and whisky sauce.

Open 12–3 6–11 (Sat 12–11, Sun 12–10.30) **Bar Meals** L served all week 12.30–2.30 D served all week 6.30–9.30 Av main course £10 **Restaurant** L served all week 12.30–2.30 D served all week 6.30–9.30 Av 3 course à la carte £18 ⊕ Enterprise Inns ◀ Otter, 6X & London Pride. ♀ 9 **Facilities** Garden Dogs allowed Parking

DITTISHAM
MAP 03 SX85

Pick of the Pubs

The Ferry Boat ♀
Manor St TQ6 0EX ☎ 01803 722368
dir: *Telephone for directions*

Set right at the water's edge with a pontoon outside its front door, this riverside inn (the only one on the River Dart) dates back 300 years. There are tables at the front with views across the river to Greenway House and Gardens, a National Trust property that was once Agatha Christie's home. The pub has plenty of marine connections, being just a few miles upriver from the Royal Naval College in Dartmouth. The pontoon outside guarantees popularity with the boating fraternity, but the pub is also a favourite of walkers and families. In the winter months, open log fires crackle in the grates, making it a snug place to go for a pint of Hobgoblin or Adnams Broadside. Home-cooked food, made from fresh local produce, is served lunchtimes and evenings, and the bar is well-stocked with everything from ales to fine wines.

Open 11–12 (Sun 12–11) **Bar Meals** L served all week 12–2.30 D served all week 7–9 ⊕ Punch Taverns ◀ Bass, Youngs & Hobgoblin, Adnams Broadside. ♀ 9 **Facilities** Children's licence Dogs allowed

DODDISCOMBSLEIGH
MAP 03 SX88

Pick of the Pubs

The Nobody Inn ♀
See Pick of the Pubs on opposite page

DOLTON
MAP 03 SS51

Rams Head Inn ♀
South St EX19 8QS ☎ 01805 804255 📠 01805 804509
e-mail: ramsheadinn@btopenworld.com
dir: *8m from Torrington on A3124*

In a village setting, right at the centre of the county of Devon, this owner-run free house dates from the 15th century, or earlier. Original features include open fireplaces complete with bread ovens and pot stands. Traditional bar food is served alongside cask ales at lunchtime, while in the evening the restaurant menu offers something for everyone – meat, chicken and fish dishes, steaks and spicy fare – using local produce whenever possible.

Open 10–12 (Mon 5–12) **Bar Meals** L served Tue-Sun 12–2.30 D served Mon-Sat 6.30–9 (Sun 12–2.30, 7–8.30) Av main course £8 **Restaurant** L served Tue-Sun 12–2.30 D served Mon-Sat 6.30–9 (Sun 12–2.30, 7–8.30) Av 3 course à la carte £14 ⊕ Free House ◀ 4X, Flowers IPA Cask, Flowers Original, Trophy. ♀ 7 **Facilities** Garden Dogs allowed Parking **Rooms** available

PICK OF THE PUBS

DODDISCOMBSLEIGH-DEVON

The Nobody Inn

There's always quite a gathering at this charming free house. Low ceilings, blackened beams, inglenook fireplace and antique furniture all contribute to the timeless and homely atmosphere. Dating from around 1591, for many years this building served as the village's unofficial church house and meeting place, becoming a de facto inn along the way.

It was officially licensed as the New Inn in 1838; the name was changed in 1952 after the innkeeper's death, when his body was accidentally left in the mortuary whilst the funeral took place around an empty coffin. Andy and Rowena Whiteman, both trained wine-makers, took over the reins in early 2008, and quickly made an impression for great food and friendly hospitality. Their mantra of 'eat real food, drink real wine' is instrumental in their approach to change – the dining room has already been refurbished, and a new kitchen is in place. But some things are best left as they are – the bar retains its traditional ambience, and continues to intrigue customers with the breadth of refreshments on offer: unusual local ales, over 200 wines, and around 260 whiskies. The pub is also famous for the range of local cheeses on the cheeseboard, which never fails to impress; there are usually over fifteen varieties, six of which are served with water biscuits or bread in the ploughman's platter. Starters range from home-made soups and terrines to home-cured gravadlax. Main courses include fish pie, Cornish steak and chips, fresh fish of the day, and slow-cooked belly of pork. Well-behaved children and dogs are as welcome as their owners, especially when the warmer days bring out the tables and chairs in the pretty cottage garden.

♀
MAP 03 SX88
EX6 7PS
☎ 01647 252394
🖨 01647 252978
e-mail: info@nobodyinn.co.uk
dir: *3m SW of Exeter Racecourse (A38)*

Open 12–2.30 6–11 (Sun 12–3, 7–10.30) Closed: 25–26 & 31 Dec
Bar Meals L served all week 12–2 D served all week 7–10
Restaurant L served Sun 12–2 D served Tue-Sat 7.30–9
⊕ Free House ◀ Branscombe Nobody's Bitter, Sharp's Doom Bar, RCH East Street Cream, Exmoor Gold. ♀ 20
Facilities Children's licence Garden Dogs allowed Parking

England

DOLTON continued

The Union Inn

Fore St EX19 8QH ☎ 01805 804633 🖹 01805 804633

e-mail: theunioninn@dolton.wanadoo.co.uk

dir: *From A361 take B3227 to S Moulton, then Atherington. Left onto B3217 then 6m to Dolton. Pub on right*

A 17th-century free house built as a Devon longhouse. Traditionally constructed of cob, the building was converted to a hotel in the mid-19th century to serve the local cattle markets, and it remains a traditional village pub with a cosy atmosphere. There's a homely beamed bar, oak settles and sturdy wooden tables, plus good home cooking, especially Sunday roasts and traditional dishes, washed down with West Country ales.

Open 12–3 6–11 Closed: 1st 2wks Feb **Bar Meals** L served Thu-Tue 12–2 D served Thu-Tue 7–10 (Sun 12–2.30, 7–9) Av main course £6.95 **Restaurant** L served Sun 12–2.30 D served Thu-Tue 7–9 (Sun 12–2.30, 7–9) ⊕ Free House 🍺 Sharp's Doom Bar, Jollyboat Freebooter, Clearwater Cavalier, St Austell Tribute. **Facilities** Children's licence Garden Dogs allowed Parking

DREWSTEIGNTON   MAP 03 SX79

Pick of the Pubs

The Drewe Arms ⬤

The Square EX6 6QN ☎ 01647 281224

e-mail: fiona@thedrewearms.co.uk

dir: *W of Exeter on A30 for 12m. Left at Woodleigh junct follow signs for 3m to Drewsteignton*

Tucked away in a sleepy village square close to the National Trust's Castle Drogo, this quintessentially English thatched inn is an ideal place for refreshments after a country walk in the surrounding Dartmoor National Park. Built in 1646, the inn was originally known as the Druid Arms but in the 1920s the Drewe family, for whom Castle Drogo was built, persuaded the brewery to change the pub's name. Their family coat of arms is still on the sign. Traditional ales are drawn direct from the cask, housed in the original 'tap bar' and served through a hatchway into the snug. The Card Room has a log fire for cold winter days, and in summer you can relax in the attractive gardens or enjoy a game of boules. Expect half crispy roast duck, local butcher's sausages, braised lamb shank, Mediterranean chicken bake, and Thai-style red snapper, as well as sandwiches and ploughman's lunches.

Open 11–3 6–12 (Summer 11–12) **Bar Meals** L served all week 12–3 D served all week 6–9.30 Av main course £10 **Restaurant** L served all week 12–3 D served all week 6.30–9 Av 3 course à la carte £15 ⊕ Whitbread 🍺 Otter Ale, Princetowns Jail Ale. **Facilities** Garden Dogs allowed Parking

EAST ALLINGTON   MAP 03 SX74

Fortescue Arms NEW ⬤

TQ9 7RA ☎ 01548 521215

e-mail: info@fortescuearms.co.uk

A charming old country inn, the Fortescue Arms is set in the village of East Allington some four miles from Kingsbridge. Landlords, Austrian chef proprietor Werner Rott and business partner Tom Kendrick

promise real ale, fine wines, good food and a welcoming atmosphere by an open fire. Typical dishes include potted crab sealed with garlic herb butter; local lamb loin on sweet potato cake with rosemary sauce; and warm apfelstrudel with crème patissiere.

Open 12–2.30 6–11 (Sun 6–10.30) Closed: Mon lunch **Bar Meals** L served Tue-Sun 12–2.30 D served all week 6.30–9.30 **Restaurant** L served Tue-Sun 12–2.30 D served all week 7–9.30 Av 3 course à la carte £30 ⊕ Free House 🍺 Butcombe Bitter, Dartmoor IPA, Guinness & Guest ales. ⬤ 9 **Facilities** Garden Dogs allowed Parking **Rooms** available

EXETER   MAP 03 SX99

Red Lion Inn ⬤

Broadclyst EX5 3EL ☎ 01392 461271

dir: *On B3181 (Exeter to Cullompton)*

A 16th-century inn set at the heart of a delightful National Trust village, next to the church. Typical examples of the restaurant menu include monkfish medallions with bacon and tomato jus; seafood gratin; pan-fried pigeon; roast pheasant with redcurrant and red onion jus; and a range of steaks. In the bar expect ham, egg and chips; venison sausages with colcannon; and Thai curry.

Open 11–3 5.30–11 (Sun 12–3, 7–10.30) **Bar Meals** L served all week 12–2.30 D served Mon-Sat 6–9.30 (Sun 7–9) **Restaurant** L served all week 12–2.30 D served Mon-Sat 6–9.30 (Sun 7–9) ⊕ Free House 🍺 Bass, Fuller's London Pride, O'Hanlons Local Blakelys Red, Speckled Hen. ⬤ 7 **Facilities** Garden Parking

The Twisted Oak ⬤

Little John's Cross Hill EX2 9RG

☎ 01392 273666 🖹 01392 277705

e-mail: martin.bullock@virgin.net

dir: *A30 to Okehampton, follow signs for pub*

Set in a beautiful part of Ide just outside Exeter, this large pub has been turned into a quality, food-driven venue in the last few years. There is a choice of dining areas – an informal place where you can relax on the leather sofas and eat; a separate lounge bar restaurant; and a more formal conservatory area, which is adult only in the evenings. During the summer months the huge garden provides seating and a children's play area.

Open 11–3 6–11 (Sun 6–10.30) **Bar Meals** L served all week 12–2.30 D served all week 6–9.30 **Restaurant** L served all week 12–2.30 D served all week 6–9.30 🍺 O'Hanlons Firefly, Cotleighs 25, Bass, Pedigree. ⬤ 11 **Facilities** Garden Parking Play Area

EXMINSTER   MAP 03 SX98

Swans Nest ⬤

Station Rd EX6 8DZ ☎ 01392 832371

web: www.swans-nest.co.uk

dir: *From M5 junct 30 follow A379 (Dawlish Rd)*

A much extended pub in a pleasant rural location whose facilities, unusually, extend to a ballroom, dance floor and stage. The carvery is a popular option for diners, with a choice of meats served with freshly prepared vegetables, though the salad bar is a tempting alternative, with over 39 items, including quiches, pies and home-smoked chicken. A carte of home-cooked fare includes grilled lamb steak, Devon pork chop, and five-bean vegetable curry.

Swans Nest

The Church House Inn

Open 10.30–2.30 6–11 (Sun 12–2.30 7–10.30) Closed: 26 Dec
Bar Meals L served all week 12–2 D served all week 6–9.45
Restaurant L served all week 12–2 D served all week 6–9.30 ⊕ Free House
◀ Otter Bitter. ♥ 8 **Facilities** Garden Parking Play Area

Open 11–2.30 6–11 (Sat 11–3, Sun 12–3, 7–10.30) **Bar Meals** L served
all week 12–2 D served all week 6.30–9.30 Av main course £13.50
Restaurant 12–2 6.30–9.30 (closed Sun during winter) Av 3 course à la
carte £23 ⊕ Free House ◀ Skinners, Abbots, Dartmoor IPA, Church House
Bitter & guest ales. **Facilities** Dogs allowed

EXTON   MAP 03 SX98

Pick of the Pubs

The Puffing Billy ♥

Station Rd EX3 0PR ☎ 01392 877888 📠 01392 876232
e-mail: food@thepuffingbilly.com

dir: *A376 signed Exmouth, through Ebford. Follow signs for
Puffing Billy, turn right into Exton*

Named for its proximity to the Exeter-Exmouth branch line, the
16th-century Puffing Billy enjoys views of the Exe estuary. Diners
can see the serious approach to food expressed pictorially in the
original artwork on display. Enjoy mackerel rillette with marinated
aubergine, pink fir potato and tapenade salad; caramelised
scallops with truffled baby leek terrine; confit duck leg and fennel
risotto; twice-baked Cornish Blue soufflé with walnuts and French
bean salad; slow honey-roasted pork belly with creamed potato
and pine nut salad; and Crediton duckling with fondant potato,
turnip, apples and fig jus. Rhubarb crumble soufflé with ginger ice
cream is a typical dessert.

Open 12–3 6–11 Sun 12–2.30, 6–10.30 Closed: selected days
over Christmas **Bar Meals** L served Mon-Fri 12–2.15 D served
Mon-Sat 6.30–9.30 Sat 12–2, Sun 12–2.30 Av main course £8.50
Restaurant L served Mon-Fri 12–2.15 D served Mon-Sat 6.30–9.30
Sat 12–2, Sun 12–2.30 Av 3 course à la carte £29 ◀ Otter, Bass, Laffe.
♥ 12 **Facilities** Children's licence Garden Parking

HARBERTON   MAP 03 SX75

The Church House Inn

TQ9 7SF ☎ 01803 863707 📠 01803 864661
e-mail: churchhouseinnha@btconnect.com

dir: *From Totnes take A381 S. Take turn for Harberton on right,
pub by church in village centre*

Built to house masons working on the church next door (around
1100), the inn has some fascinating historic features, including a Tudor
window frame and latticed window with 13th-century glass; there's
even a resident ghost. The extensive menu is supplemented by daily
specials and a traditional roast on Sundays. There's plenty of seafood/
fish, and a family room is provided.

HAYTOR VALE   MAP 03 SX77

Pick of the Pubs

The Rock Inn ★★ HL ⚫ ♥

TQ13 9XP ☎ 01364 661305 📠 01364 661242
e-mail: inn@rock-inn.co.uk

dir: *A38 from Exeter, at Drum Bridges rdbt take A382 for
Bovey Tracey, 1st exit at 2nd rdbt (B3387), 3m left to Haytor
Vale*

Old-fashioned values are as important as ever at this cheerful
18th-century coaching inn, and the old stables recall the pub's
strategic position on the road between Widecombe-in-the-
Moor and Newton Abbot. Modern-day travellers will find nine
comfortable en suite bedrooms, all named after Grand National
winners. Open fires, antique tables and sturdy furnishings lend
a traditional feel to the rambling bars, but the cooking style is
unashamedly modern British, using excellent produce in nicely
presented dishes. Lunchtime might bring mussel and saffron
tart, whole grilled dab with sauce vierge or Devon pork sausages.
Dinner might include a main of herb-crusted bream or sea bass
with stir-fry vegetables. The children's menu offers the likes of
cottage pie and fish and chips.

Open 11–11 Closed: 25–26 Dec **Bar Meals** L served all week 12–2.30
D served all week 6.30–9.30 **Restaurant** L served all week 12–2.30
D served all week 7–9 ⊕ Free House ◀ Old Speckled Hen, St Austell
Dartmoor Best, Interbrew Bass. **Facilities** Garden Parking **Rooms** 9

HOLBETON · MAP 03 SX65

The Mildmay Colours Inn ♀

PL8 1NA ☎ 01752 830248 📠 01752 830432
e-mail: mildmay.colours@btconnect.com
dir: *S from Exeter on A38, Yealmpton/Ermington, S past Ugborough & Ermington right onto A379. After 1.5m, turn left, signed Mildmay Colours/Holbeton*

A 17th-century pub, which derives its unusual name from a famous jockey, Lord Anthony Mildmay, whose portrait and silks are hung in the pub. Home-cooked traditional food is served from extensive menus, and in summer there are gardens and terraces in which to enjoy it. New owners.

Open 11–3 6–11 (Sun 12–3, 6–10.30) **Bar Meals** L served Mon-Sat 12–2.15 D served Mon-Sat 6–9 (Sun 12–2.30) ⊕ Free House ◄ Mildmay Colours Bitter & Mildmay SP, Hellican Honey, Keel Over, Betty Stogs. ♥ 8 **Facilities** Garden Dogs allowed Parking Play Area

HOLSWORTHY · MAP 03 SS30

The Bickford Arms ★★★★ INN

Brandis Corner EX22 7XY
☎ 01409 221318 📠 01409 220085
e-mail: info@bickfordarms.com
dir: *On A3072, 4m from Holsworthy towards Hatherleigh*

This pub stood on the Holsworthy to Hatherleigh road for 300 years before it was gutted by fire in 2003. Now totally rebuilt, it retains much period charm, with beams, a welcoming bar and two fireplaces. The bar and restaurant menu offers food prepared with locally-sourced ingredients – perhaps free-range Devon duck breast with redcurrant and red wine sauce; home-made steak and ale pie; or seared salmon with lemon and dill butter.

Open 11–11 **Bar Meals** L served all week 12–2.30 D served all week 6–9.30 **Restaurant** 12–2.30 D served Thu-Sat 6–9.30 ◄ Skinners Betty Stogs, Lazy Daze & Tribute. **Facilities** Children's licence Garden Parking **Rooms** 5

HONITON · MAP 04 ST10

The Otter Inn

Weston EX14 3NZ ☎ 01404 42594
dir: *Just off A30 W of Honiton*

On the banks of the idyllic River Otter, this ancient 14th-century inn is set in over two acres of grounds and was once a cider house. Enjoy one of the traditional real ales, try your hand at scrabble, dominoes or cards, or peruse the inn's extensive book collection. A wide-ranging menu caters for all tastes and includes fresh fish, game, steak, vegetarian dishes, bar meals and Sunday lunch.

Open 10–11 (Sun 12–10.30) **Bar Meals** L served all week 12–3 D served all week 6–10 (Snacks/bar meals Sun 12–8) **Restaurant** L served all week fr 12 D served all week 6–9 ⊕ Free House ◄ Otter Ale, London Pride, guest ales. **Facilities** Children's licence Garden Dogs allowed Parking

HORNDON · MAP 03 SX58

The Elephant's Nest Inn

PL19 9NQ ☎ 01822 810273 📠 01822 810273
e-mail: info@theelephantsnest.co.uk
dir: *Off A386 N of Tavistock*

The pub got its unique name in the 1950s when a regular made a humourous remark about the then rather portly landlord. An isolated inn on the flanks of Dartmoor National Park reached via narrow lanes from Mary Tavy, the 16th-century building retains its real fires, slate floors and low beamed ceilings decorated with elephant memorabilia. Meals include lunchtime baguettes, interesting vegetarian options and a good seafood selection – smoked haddock chowder, for example.

Open 12–3 6.30–11 **Bar Meals** L served all week 12–2.15 D served all week 6.30–9 Av main course £10.95 **Restaurant** L served all week 12–2.15 D served all week 6.30–9 Av 3 course à la carte £21.65 ⊕ Free House ◄ Palmers IPA, Copper, Otter Bright, Sail Ale & guest ales. **Facilities** Garden Dogs allowed Parking

HORNS CROSS · MAP 03 SS32

Pick of the Pubs

The Hoops Inn & Country Hotel
★★★ HL ⊛ ♀

Clovelly EX39 5DL ☎ 01237 451222 📠 01237 451247
e-mail: sales@hoopsinn.co.uk
dir: *On A39 between Bideford & Clovelly*

Having made their way along tortuous footpaths to evade the revenue men, smugglers would share out their spoils in this thatched, cob-walled, 13th-century inn. Set in 16 acres of gardens and meadows on the rugged Atlantic coast, it offers charm galore. Menus are based on the freshest produce Devon can offer, including herbs, fruit and vegetables from the gardens, and a wide choice of wines by the glass from more than 220 bins. Guests may choose to eat in the bar, morning room or restaurant, where oak-panelled walls, period furniture and tables set with crisp white napkins create just the right level of formality. Seasonal menus focus on local producers and suppliers, and house specialities include terrine of Devon game with home-made piccalilli, and Exmoor venison with griottine cherry sauce.

The Hoops Inn & Country Hotel

Open 8–11 **Bar Meals** L served all week 12–9.30 D served all week 6–9.30 Av main course £12.50 **Restaurant** L served Mon-Fri 12–3 D served Mon-Fri 6–9.30 (Sat-Sun all day) Av 3 course à la carte £30 ⊕ Free House ◖ Hoops Old Ale & Best, Golden Pig. ♟ 20 **Facilities** Children's licence Garden Dogs allowed Parking **Rooms** 13

HORSEBRIDGE   MAP 03 SX47

The Royal Inn

PL19 8PJ ☎ 01822 870214
e-mail: paul@royalinn.co.uk
dir: *S of B3362 (Launceston-Tavistock road)*

The pub, with a façade enlivened by superb pointed arched windows, was once a nunnery. Standing near a bridge built over the Tamar in 1437 by Benedictine monks, it was the Packhorse Inn until Charles I pitched up one day – his seal is in the doorstep. Beef for the steaks, casseroles and stews, and the pheasant and venison on the specials board are all locally supplied. Chilli cheese tortillas are much appreciated. So is the absence of noisy machines.

Open 12–3 6.30–11 **Bar Meals** L served all week 12–2 D served all week 6.30–9 (25–26 Dec night, 1 Jan night 6.30–8) Av main course £8 **Restaurant** L served all week 12–2 D served all week 7–9 ⊕ Free House ◖ Eastreet, Bass, Skinners, Sharp's. **Facilities** Garden Dogs allowed Parking

ILFRACOMBE   MAP 03 SS54

The George & Dragon ♟

5 Fore St EX34 9ED ☎ 01271 863851
e-mail: linda.quinn5@btinternet.com
dir: *Please telephone for directions*

The oldest pub in town, The George & Dragon dates from 1360 and is reputedly haunted. The food is of the simple, no-nonsense variety – typical examples include home-cooked boozy beef; chicken curry; mixed grills; fiery chicken with sweet and sour vegetables; and home-cooked crab from the harbour when available. No fruit machines or pool table, but if you are lucky there will be a little home-produced background music.

Open 10–12 (Jul-Aug 10–1am) **Bar Meals** L served all week 12–3 D served all week 6.30–9 (Some BH food all day, Sun lunch served only in summer) Av main course £7 ⊕ Punch Taverns ◖ Brakspear, Spitfire & Betty Stogs. ♟ 7 **Facilities** Children's licence Dogs allowed **Notes** ⊜

IVYBRIDGE   MAP 03 SX65

The Anchor Inn ♟

Lutterburn St, Ugborough PL21 0NG
☎ 01752 892283 📄 01752 690534
e-mail: theanchorinn@btinternet.com
dir: *Telephone for directions*

A village inn whose origins can be traced back to the 16th century. Food is served in the bar and the à la carte restaurant, with locally farmed, organic produce being used wherever possible. Tiger prawns cooked in chilli, garlic and white wine is a likely offering among the fish dishes. Beamed ceilings, open fires and real cask ales maintain the traditional welcome, and the Anchor is ideally located for exploring the South Hams region of Devon.

Open 11.30–3 5–11 (Fri-Sat 11.30–11 Sun 12–10.30) **Bar Meals** L served all week 12–2.30 D served all week 7–10 (Sat-Sun 12–10) Av main course £7 **Restaurant** L served all week 12–2.30 D served all week 7–10 Av 3 course à la carte £22.50 ⊕ Free House ◖ Bass, Courage, Directors, local ales. ♟ 8 **Facilities** Garden Dogs allowed Parking

KINGSBRIDGE   MAP 03 SX74

The Crabshell Inn

Embankment Rd TQ7 1JZ
☎ 01548 852345 📄 01548 852262
dir: *A38 towards Plymouth, follow signs for Kingsbridge*

A traditional sailors' watering hole on the Kingsbridge estuary quayside (arrive by boat and you may moor free). As you would expect, the views from the outside tables and from the first-floor Waters Edge Restaurant are wonderful. The extensive menu and specials board range through grills, pies, pasta, jacket potatoes, salads and sandwiches, but the house speciality is fresh fish, with dishes such as monkfish provençale, and scallop and smoked bacon gratin.

Open 11–11 (Sun 12–10.30) **Bar Meals** L served all week 12–2.30 D served all week 6–9.30 (Winter 6–9) Av main course £6 **Restaurant** L served all week 12–2.30 D served all week 6–9.30 (Winter 6–9) Av 3 course à la carte £16 ⊕ Free House ◖ Bass Bitter, Crabshell Bitter, Old Speckled Hen, Worthington Cream Flow. **Facilities** Garden Dogs allowed Parking Play Area

KINGSKERSWELL   MAP 03 SX86

Barn Owl Inn ♟

Aller Mills TQ12 5AN ☎ 01803 872130 📄 01803 875279
e-mail: barnowl@eldridge-pope.co.uk
dir: *Telephone for directions*

Handy for Dartmoor and the English Riviera towns, this 16th-century former farmhouse has many charming features, including flagged floors, a black leaded range, and oak beams in a high-vaulted converted barn with a minstrel's gallery. Lunchtime snacks include toasties, wraps and baguettes, while the main menu features lots of traditional pub favourites plus an extensive tapas selection – perhaps crispy duck spring rolls, Greek lamb skewers, or chilli prawn bruschetta.

Open 11–11 (Sun 12–10.30) **Bar Meals** L served all week 12–2.30 D served all week 6–9.30 **Restaurant** 12–2.30 D served all week 6–9.30 ⊕ Eldridge Pope ◖ 6X & guest ales. ♟ 14 **Facilities** Garden Parking

England

KINGSKERSWELL continued

Pick of the Pubs

Bickley Mill Inn NEW ⚑

TQ12 5LN ☎ 01803 873201

e-mail: info@bickleymill.co.uk

dir: *From Newton Abbot on A380 towards Torquay. Right at Barn Owl Inn, follow brown tourist signs*

Originally a flour mill, dating from the 13th century, this attractive bar, restaurant and rooms is located in the wooded Stoneycombe Valley, within convenient reach of Torquay, Newton Abbot and Totnes. The mill became a free house in the early 1970s and for the next 25 years was in turn a busy pub, restaurant, bed and breakfast business and, during the 1980s, a nightclub. After a period of neglect it was bought by David and Patricia Smith, re-opening after a thorough refurbishment. The following year, the Miller's Room, a converted 18th-century barn, was opened, accommodating 30–70 people and catering for private functions. Quality produce from the southwest is used in dishes such as crispy pork belly with smashed parsnips and apples, sage and onion sauce; grilled sea bream fillets with roast vegetables and tomato sauce; and sweet potato and aubergine rogan josh.

Open 11.30–3 6.30–11 Closed: 27–28 Dec & 1 Jan **Bar Meals** L served Mon-Sat 12–2 (Sun 12–3) **Restaurant** L served Mon-Sat 12–2 D served Mon-Sat 6.30–9 (Sun 12–2.30, 6–8.30) Av 3 course à la carte £23.50 Av 2 course fixed price £11 ⊕ Free House ◖ Otter Ale, Boddingtons, Teignworthy. ♟ 8 **Facilities** Children's licence Garden Dogs allowed Parking

---

KING'S NYMPTON   MAP 03 SS61

The Grove Inn NEW ⚑

EX37 9ST ☎ 01769 580406

e-mail: info@thegroveinn.co.uk

dir: *2.5m from A377 Exeter to Barnstaple road*

A true taste of Devon is offered at this 17th-century thatched inn, set in a beautiful conservation village. Real ales, real ciders and Devon wines are on offer, by an open fire in winter. Working closely with local farmers and producers, the food is sourced as close to home as possible. Grill options, ploughman's and sandwiches all use local produce, as do dishes such as smoked trout slices with horseradish cream; and individual beef Wellington.

Open 12–3 6–11 Closed: Mon lunch ex BH **Bar Meals** L served Tue-Sat 12–2 Av main course £8 **Restaurant** L served Tue-Sun 12–2 D served Tue-Sat 6.30–9 Av 3 course à la carte £18 ⊕ Free House ◖ Exmoor Ale, Otter Ale, Bath Gem Ale, Fuller's HSB. ♟ 7 **Facilities** Children's licence Garden Dogs allowed

KINGSTON   MAP 03 SX64

The Dolphin Inn

TQ7 4QE ☎ 01548 810314 📄 01548 810314

e-mail: info@dolphininn.eclipse.co.uk

web: www.dolphin-inn.co.uk

dir: *From A379 (Plymouth to Kingsbridge road) take B3233 for Bigbury-on-Sea. Follow brown inn signs.*

Built in the 15th century to accommodate stonemasons constructing the neighbouring church, The Dolphin is just a mile from the beautiful Erme Estuary and coastal footpath. The inn retains its historic character, providing a cosy atmosphere for regular music and quiz nights. Locally produced home-cooked food ranges from fresh fish in summer to hearty winter dishes such as slow-roasted belly pork with apple sauce, cider gravy and buttered mash; or home-made steak and ale pie.

Open 11–3 6–11 (Sun 12–3, 7–10.30) Closed: Sun eve Winter **Bar Meals** L served Tue-Sun 12–2 D served Tue-Sat 6–9 (Sun 7–9) Av main course £8.95 ⊕ Punch Taverns ◖ Teignworthy Spring Tide, Four Seasons Ale, Courage Best, Sharp's Doom Bar & Otter. **Facilities** Garden Parking Play Area

---

KINGSWEAR   MAP 03 SX85

The Ship

Higher St TQ6 0AG ☎ 01803 752348

dir: *Telephone for directions*

Historic village pub overlooking the scenic River Dart towards Dartmouth and Dittisham. Located in one of South Devon's most picturesque corners, this tall, character inn is very much a village local with a friendly, welcoming atmosphere inside. Well-prepared fresh food is the hallmark of the menu. Sandwiches, baguettes and pies are available in the bar, while the restaurant menu offers crispy duck with stir-fried vegetables on egg noodles, or oven-baked cod with lemon and lime crust.

Open 12–3 6–11 (Summer all day) **Bar Meals** L served all week 12.30–2 D served all week 7–9.30 **Restaurant** L served all week 12.30–2 D served all week 7–9.30 ⊕ Heavitree ◖ Greene King IPA, Otter, Adnams, Timothy Taylor. **Facilities** Garden Dogs allowed

LEWDOWN MAP 03 SX48

Pick of the Pubs

The Harris Arms ♥

Portgate EX20 4PZ ☎ 01566 783331 📇 01566 783359

e-mail: whiteman@powernet.co.uk

dir: *From A30 take Lifton turn, halfway between Lifton & Lewdown in hamlet of Portgate*

Here is an establishment that certainly lives up to its promotional strapline: 'Eat Real Food and Drink Real Wine'. The Harris Arms is a 16th-century inn located on the old A30 close to the boundary between Devon and Cornwall, with wonderful views to Brent Tor. Honest food with substance and style is locally sourced and carefully cooked. Example starters from the specials board are Fowey River mussels steamed in cream, garlic and white wine; seared scallops with sage, lemon and capers; and marinated and grilled Cornish sardines. Main courses are no less succulent, with the likes of winter cassoulet of pheasant, chicken, rare breed pork and Merguez sausage; or pan-fried pigeon breast with griddled squash, smoked bacon and red wine sauce. Lunchtime dishes include home-made 100% beef burgers, light fish and chips, and Ploughman's with Attitude.

Open 12–3 6.30–11 Closed: Sun eve Winter & Mon
Bar Meals L served Tue–Sun 12–2 D served Tue–Sat 6.30–9 (Sun 7–9) **Restaurant** L served Tue–Sun 12–2 D served Tue–Sat 6.30–9 (Sun 7–9) ⊕ Free House ◖ Sharp's Doom Bar, Guinness Extra Cold & guest ales. ♥ 18 **Facilities** Garden Dogs allowed Parking

LIFTON MAP 03 SX38

Pick of the Pubs

The Arundell Arms ★★★ HL ⊕⊕ ♥

See Pick of the Pubs on page 162

LITTLEHEMPSTON MAP 03 SX86

Tally Ho Inn ♥

TQ9 6NF ☎ 01803 862316 📇 01803 862316

e-mail: tally.ho.inn@btconnect.com

dir: *Off A38 at Buckfastleigh. A381 between Newton Abbot & Totnes*

A traditional, family-owned 14th-century inn in a pretty village, with inglenook fireplaces and a flower-filled patio. Local suppliers are the mainstay of seasonal menus offering cod fillet with mash and parsley sauce; home-made steak and kidney pie and chips; lamb's liver and onions; fettucine with fresh pesto, topped with parmesan; and smoked salmon, watercress and poached egg on toasted granary bread. Real ales come from Devon breweries.

Open 12–3 6.30–11 Closed: 25 Dec **Bar Meals** L served Mon–Sat 12–2 (Sun 12–2.30) D served all week 7–9 Av main course £8.95 ⊕ Free House ◖ Exmoor Ale, Teignworthy Brewery Ales, Whitbread Best Bitter, guest ales. ♥ 7 **Facilities** Children's licence Garden Dogs allowed Parking

LUTON (NEAR CHUDLEIGH) MAP 03 SX97

The Elizabethan Inn ♥

Fore St TQ13 0BL ☎ 01626 775425 📇 01626 775151

e-mail: elizabethaninn@btconnect.com

dir: *Between Chudleigh & Teignmouth*

Known locally as the Lizzie, this cosy 16th-century free house boasts a pretty beer garden that makes a great destination on a fine summer's day. Local produce features strongly on the daily specials board, whilst the extensive bar menu features a choice of omelettes, risottos and warm salads. Other dishes include traditional jacket potatoes; luxury home-made fishcakes; and red Thai curry. A log fire burns in the bar on cold winter days.

Open 12–3 6–11 Closed: 25–26 Dec, 1 Jan **Bar Meals** L served all week 12–2 D served Mon–Sat 6–9.30 (Sun 7–9.30) Av main course £11 **Restaurant** L served all week 12–2 D served Mon–Sat 6–9.30 (Sun 7–9) Av 3 course à la carte £22.50 ⊕ Free House ◖ London Pride, Teignworthy Reel Ale, Otter Ale, O'Hanlon's Yellowhammer. ♥ 8 **Facilities** Garden Dogs allowed Parking

LYDFORD MAP 03 SX58

Pick of the Pubs

Dartmoor Inn ⊕⊕ ♥

EX20 4AY ☎ 01822 820221 📇 01822 820494

e-mail: info@dartmoorinn.co.uk

dir: *On A386 S of Okehampton*

Owners Karen and Philip Burgess have made their mark at this distinctive free house, which Charles Kingsley almost certainly described in his novel Westward Ho! The stylish, restrained décor extends through the cosy dining rooms and small bar, where an easy dining menu features dishes like bacon and egg salad with mustard dressing; and goats' cheese omelette with red onion. After your meal, you can even browse for beautiful accessories and home ware in the inn's own boutique.

Open 11.30–3 6.30–11 (6–11 in Summer) **Bar Meals** L served Tue–Sat 12–2.15 (Sun 12–2.15) D served Tue–Sat 6.30–9.15 Av main course £9.75 **Restaurant** L served Tue–Sat 12–2.15 (Sun 12–2.30) D served Tue–Sat 6.30–9.15 ⊕ Free House ◖ Otter Ale, Austell Hicks Special & Dartmoor Best. ♥ 6 **Facilities** Garden Dogs allowed Parking

The Arundell Arms

Run by the same family for over forty years, the Arundell Arms is one of England's premier fishing hotels. Guests have access to 20 miles of private fishing along the Tamar and its tributaries, whilst walkers and bird watchers can enjoy some of England's loveliest countryside.

Formerly known as the White Horse, this 18th-century free house was renamed in about 1815 after William Arundell took over the 'best and most respectable inn in the village'. The description is still apt. Today, the Arundell Arms exudes warmth and comfort – not only in the 'locals' bar, with its babble of conversation and simple food at lunchtime, but also in the smarter dining bar which has earned two AA rosettes for its food. You can choose to eat sandwiches (toasted fillet steak with Dijon mustard and onion rings, or Montgomery cheddar cheese with apricot chutney), or select from the starters and light snacks menu. Here you're likely to find chicken Caesar salad with garlic croutons, or butternut squash risotto for starters;

and main courses like pan-fried lambs' kidneys with smoked bacon, mushrooms and onion rings, chips and herb butter; and slowly-cooked confit of corn-fed chicken leg with a mustard mash and a peppercorn sauce. Five-course table d'hôte and à la carte menus are served in the elegant restaurant. There are 21 individually designed en suite bedrooms, and thoughtful touches are provided like home-made chocolates for after-dinner guests in the sitting room. From here you can see one of England's few remaining cockpits, now the hotel's fishing tackle room, set in the terraced garden where swifts and swallows soar overhead in the evening sunshine. Around the car park quadrangle there's a skittle alley and meeting rooms.

★★★ HL ◉◉ ♀
MAP 03 SX38
PL16 0AA
☎ 01566 784666
🖷 01566 784494
e-mail:
reservations@arundellarms.com
dir: *1m off A30 dual carriageway, 3m E of Launceston*

Open 11–11 (Fri/Sat 11–12, Sun 12–11)
Bar Meals L served all week 12–2.30 D served all week 6–10
Restaurant L served all week 12.30–2 D served all week 7.30–8
Av 3 course à la carte £40
⊕ Free House ◼ guest ales. ♀ 9
Facilities Garden Dogs allowed Parking
Rooms 21

LYMPSTONE

MAP 03 SX98

The Globe Inn ⚑

The Strand EX8 5EY ☎ 01395 263166

dir: *Telephone for directions*

Set in the estuary village of Lympstone, this traditional beamed inn has a good reputation for seafood. The separate restaurant area serves as a coffee bar during the day. Look out for bass fillets with plum sauce; monkfish kebabs; seafood platter; and seafood grill. Weekend music and quiz nights are a feature.

Open 10–3 5.30–12 **Bar Meals** L served all week 12–2 D served Mon-Sat 6.30–9.30 **Restaurant** L served all week D served Mon-Sat 7–9.30 ⊞ Heavitree ◀ London Pride, Otter, Bass. ⚑ 6 **Facilities** Dogs allowed

LYNMOUTH

MAP 03 SS74

Pick of the Pubs

Rising Sun Hotel ★★ HL ◉ ⚑

Harbourside EX35 6EG

☎ 01598 753223 📄 01598 753480

e-mail: risingsunlynmouth@easynet.co.uk

dir: *From M5 junct 25 follow Minehead signs. A39 to Lynmouth*

Overlooking Lynmouth's tiny harbour and bay is the Rising Sun, a 14th-century thatched smugglers' inn. In turn, overlooking them all, are Countisbury Cliffs, the highest in England. The building's long history is evident from the uneven oak floors, crooked ceilings and thick walls. Literary associations are plentiful: R D Blackmore wrote some of his wild Exmoor romance, *Lorna Doone*, here; the poet Shelley is believed to have honeymooned in the garden cottage, and Coleridge stayed too. Immediately behind rises Exmoor Forest and National Park, home to red deer, wild ponies and birds of prey. With sea and moor so close, game and seafood are in plentiful supply, and pheasant, venison, hare, wild boar, monkfish, crab or scallops, for example, will appear variously as starter or main course dishes. At night the oak-panelled, candlelit dining room is an example of romantic British inn-keeping at its best.

Open 11–11 (Open all day all year) **Bar Meals** L served all week 12–4 D served all week 7–9 Av main course £7 **Restaurant** L served all week 12–2 D served all week 7–9 Av 3 course à la carte £32 ⊞ Free House ◀ Exmoor Gold, Fox & Cotleigh Tawny Ale. **Facilities** Garden **Rooms** 16

LYNTON

MAP 03 SS74

The Bridge Inn

Lynbridge Hill EX35 6NR

☎ 01598 753425 📄 01598 753225

e-mail: bridgeinnlynton@hotmail.co.uk

dir: *Turn off A39 at Barbrook onto B3234. In 1m pub on right just beyond Sunny Lyn camp site*

Attractive 17th-century riverside inn overlooked by National Trust woodlands. In the cellars the remains of 12th-century salmon fishermen's cottages are still visible, and the unusually shaped windows at the front originally belonged to Charles I's hunting lodge at Coombe House, salvaged following flood damage in the 1680s. The 1952 Lynmouth Flood destroyed the Lyn Bridge and car park, but most of the pub survived intact.

Open 12–3 6–11 (Sun 7–10.30 winter) **Bar Meals** L served all week 12–2.30 D served all week 6–9.30 (Sun 7–10.30 Winter) Av main course £8.50 **Restaurant** L served all week 12–2.30 D served all week 6–9.30 ⊞ Free House ◀ St. Austell Tribute, Sharp's Doom Bar, Exmoor Fox. **Facilities** Children's licence Garden Dogs allowed Parking

MARLDON

MAP 03 SX86

The Church House Inn ⚑

Village Rd TQ3 1SL ☎ 01803 558279 📄 01803 664865

dir: *Take Torquay ring road, follow signs to Marldon & Totnes, follow brown signs to pub*

An ancient inn with a contemporary feel located between Torbay and the market town of Newton Abbott. The building dates from 1362, when it was a hostel for the builders of the adjoining village church, but it was rebuilt in 1750 incorporating beautiful Georgian windows. Typical dishes are poached monkfish on vegetable medley and prawn bisque; chargrilled Exmoor sirloin steak; and asparagus and parmesan risotto torte.

Open 11.30–2.30 5–11 (Sun 12–10.30) **Bar Meals** L served all week 12–2 D served all week 6.30–9.30 Av main course £12.50 **Restaurant** L served all week 12–2 D served all week 6.30–9.30 Av 3 course à la carte £24 ⊞ Free House ◀ Dartmoor Best, Bass, Old Speckled Hen, Greene King IPA. ⚑ 10 **Facilities** Garden Dogs allowed Parking

MEAVY   MAP 03 SX56

The Royal Oak Inn ▾

PL20 6PJ ☎ 01822 852944

e-mail: sjearp@aol.com

dir: *B3212 from Yelverton to Princetown. Right at Dousland to Meavy, past school. Pub opposite village green*

Flagstone floors, heavy beams and a welcoming open fire set the scene at this traditional 15th-century free house. Standing close to the shores of Burrator reservoir on the edge of Dartmoor, the inn is popular with cyclists and walkers. Local cask ales, ciders and fine wines accompany the locally sourced ingredients in a menu ranging from lunchtime baguettes and jackets to swordfish steaks; blackened Cajun chicken; and home-made steak and Guinness pie.

Open 11–3 6–11 (Winter, Fri-Sat 11–11, Sun 11–10.30) **Bar Meals** L served all week 12–2 D served all week 6–9 Av main course £9 **Restaurant** L served all week 12–2 D served all week 6–9 Av 3 course à la carte £18 ⊞ Free House ◀ Princetown Jail Ale, Dartmoor IPA, St Austell Tribute, Royal Oak & guest. ▾ 12 **Facilities** Dogs allowed

---

MODBURY   MAP 03 SX65

California Country Inn

California Cross PL21 0SG

☎ 01548 821449 ▤ 01548 821566

e-mail: california@bellinns.entadsl.com

web: www.californiacountryinn.co.uk

Oak beams and exposed stonework are features of this whitewashed 14th-century free house. Brass, copper and old photographs decorate the interior, and there's a landscaped garden for summer use. Menus are created from only locally supplied produce, with prime meats from the chargrill, and dishes ranging from lasagne and beer-battered cod in the bar to roast monk fish with Yealm mussels, or loin of Plympton venison in the restaurant.

Open 11–11 **Bar Meals** L served all week 12–2 D served Mon-Sat 6–9 (Sun 6–8.30) **Restaurant** D served Wed-Sat 6–9 (Sun 6–8.30) ⊞ Free House ◀ Guinness, Abbot Ale, London Pride. **Facilities** Children's licence Garden Dogs allowed Parking

---

MOLLAND   MAP 03 SS82

The London Inn

EX36 3NG ☎ 01769 550269

dir: *Telephone for directions*

Just below Exmoor lies peaceful Molland, and to find its church is to find this 15th-century inn. Historic features abound, but try and picture today's spacious dining room as the original inn, and the bar as the brewhouse. The frequently-changing menu features savoury pancakes, Welsh rarebit, mixed grill, as well as ploughman's, jackets and sandwiches.

Open 11.30–2.30 6–11 (Sun 12–3, 7–10.30) **Bar Meals** L served all week 12–2 D served all week 7–9 Av main course £8 **Restaurant** L served all week D served all week Av 3 course à la carte £19.50 ⊞ Free House ◀ Exmoor Ale, Cotleigh Tawny Bitter. **Facilities** Garden Dogs allowed Parking **Notes** ⊛

MORETONHAMPSTEAD   MAP 03 SX78

The White Hart Hotel ★★★ HL ◉ ▾

The Square TQ13 8NF ☎ 01647 441340 ▤ 01647 441341

e-mail: enquiries@Whitehartdartmoor.co.uk

web: www.whitehartdartmoor.co.uk

dir: *From A30 at Whiddon Down take A382 for Chagford & Moretonhampstead. Pub in village centre (parking in 20yds)*

This Grade II listed building was a meeting place for French officers on parole from Dartmoor's nearby prison during the Napoleonic Wars. Today the stylish hotel is renowned for its Sunday lunch with jazz, and its malt whisky selection. Bar lunches and a brasserie serve contemporary cuisine to a high standard: chargrilled aubergine and brie; pan-fried calves' liver with red onion marmalade; or roast loin of venison with butter beans.

Open 8–12 **Bar Meals** L served Mon-Sat 12.30–2.30 D served all week 6.30–9.30 (Sun 12–2.30) Av main course £8 **Restaurant** L served Sun 12–2.30 D served all week 6.30–9.30 Av 3 course à la carte £32 Av 3 course fixed price £24.95 ◀ St Austell Tribute, Otter Fursty Ferret, Doom Bar, O'Hanlons Brewing. ▾ 16 **Facilities** Children's licence Garden Dogs allowed Parking **Rooms** 29

NEWTON ABBOT   MAP 03 SX87

The Wild Goose Inn ▾

Combeinteignhead TQ12 4RA ☎ 01626 872241

dir: *From A380 at Newton Abbot rdbt take B3195 (Shaldon road), signed Milber, 2.5m into village, right at sign*

Called the Country House Inn when first licensed in 1840, the name change came about in the 1960s when nearby geese took to intimidating the pub's customers. The building has remained virtually unchanged, and outside is a peaceful walled garden overlooked by the tower of the 14th-century church next door. West Country suppliers include over a dozen breweries taking turns at the pumps, and local ingredients are served in home-made pies, catch of the day from Brixham, and grilled ribs and steaks.

Open 11–2.30 5.30–11 (Sun 12–2.30, 7–11) (Fri-Sat 5.30–12) **Bar Meals** L served all week 12–2 D served all week 7–9.30 **Restaurant** L served all week 12–2 D served all week 7–9.30 ⊞ Free House ◀ Otter Ale, Cotleigh, Sharp's Bitter, Skinner's Bitter. ▾ 16 **Facilities** Garden Parking

PICK OF THE PUBS

NOSS MAYO-DEVON

The Ship Inn

The 16th-century Ship Inn is a waterside free house that has been beautifully renovated using reclaimed materials, including English oak and local stone. Its style is simple and properly pub-like.

While appearing spacious, it also remains cosy thanks to the wooden floors, old furniture and bookcases, log fires and dozens of local pictures. The inn's tidal location is superb, making it an especially popular port of call for sailing enthusiasts who can tie their boats up right outside; walkers too throng the bar, and dogs are allowed downstairs. The daily-changing menu of home-made dishes majors on local produce, notably fish. For a light lunch the ploughman's cheeses are all sourced in Devon or Cornwall, while baguette fillings include local ham with mustard. Half a dozen bar menu choices tempt with the likes of local cod fillet in real ale batter; an eight-ounce steak burger topped with gruyère cheese; and steak

and kidney pie served with new potatoes and green vegetables. For the hearty three-course appetite, classic starters like leek and potato soup or chicken liver paté with toasted granary bread could be followed by fillet steak with wild mushroom sauce; Cajun fillet of salmon on creamed potatoes; or roast shank of Devon lamb with roasted root vegetables. Traditional puddings include apple and berry crumble with custard, or choose your favourite flavours from the list of Salcombe dairy ice creams. A good list of teas, coffees and malt whiskies complete the carte, which you can peruse at your leisure while enjoying the great views from the waterside garden and sipping a local beer such as Tamar or Dartmoor IPA.

MAP 03 SX54
PL8 1EW
☎ 01752 872387
🖷 01752 873294
e-mail: ship@nossmayo.com
web: www.nossmayo.com
dir: *5m S of Yealmpton on River Yealm estuary*

Open 11–11
Bar Meals L served Mon-Sat 12–9.30 D served Mon-Sat 12–9.30 (Sun 12–9) Av main course £10
Restaurant L served Mon-Sat 12–9.30 D served Mon-Sat 12–9.30 (Sun 12–9) Av 3 course à la carte £20
⊕ Free House ◀ Tamar, Jail Ale & Butcombe Blonde, Dartmoor IPA. ♟ 10
Facilities Garden Dogs allowed Parking

England

NEWTON ST CYRES   MAP 03 SX89

The Beer Engine ♇

EX5 5AX ☎ 01392 851282 📠 01392 851876

e-mail: info@thebeerengine.co.uk

dir: *From Exeter take A377 towards Crediton. Pub opposite rail station in village, signed from A377 towards Sweetham*

Striking whitewashed free house, once a railway hotel and these days acknowledged as one of Devon's first micro-breweries. There are daily fish deliveries from Brixham so expect sea bass, cod or haddock cooked in beer batter. Vegetarians can look forward to a good selection of choices including aubergine and tomato bake, vegetable curry and spinach lasagne. Choice of locally made bangers, starters and light meals.

Open 11–11 **Bar Meals** L served all week 12–2.15 D served Tue-Sun 6.30–9.15 (Mon 6.30–8.45) Av main course £9.50 **Restaurant** L served all week 12–2.15 D served Tue-Sun 6.30–9.15 (Mon 6.30–8.45) ⊕ Free House ◀ Engine Ales: Piston Bitter, Rail Ale, Sleeper Heavy. ♟7 **Facilities** Garden Dogs allowed Parking

NORTH BOVEY   MAP 03 SX78

Pick of the Pubs

The Ring of Bells Inn

TQ13 8RB ☎ 01647 440375 📠 01647 440746

e-mail: info@ringofbellsinn.com

dir: *1.5m from Moretonhampstead off B3212. 7m S of Whiddon Down junct on A30*

The Ring of Bells is one of Dartmoor's most historic inns, an attractive thatched property located just off the village green. It was built in the 13th century as lodgings for the stonemasons who were working on the construction of the nearby church, and remains very much at the heart of the village's social life. Visitors too are attracted by the good Devon pub food and West Country ales, and there is certainly plenty to do and see in the area, particularly walking, cycling, fishing, riding and bird watching in this beautiful moorland countryside. Hearty appetites are happily catered for with Ring of Bells classics like steak and ale pie, local bangers and mash, and lambs' liver and bacon. Alternatives range through local rabbit braised in red wine, fishcakes with sweet chilli sauce, and charred aubergine rolls stuffed with mushroom, olives and pine nuts.

Open 11–11 **Bar Meals** L served Mon-Sat 12–2.30 D served all week 6.30–9.30 (Sun 12–3) **Restaurant** L served Mon-Sat 12–2.30 D served Mon-Sat 7–9.30 (Sun 12–3, 7–9) ◀ Otter Ale, Wadworth 6x, Dartmoor Best Bitter & Butcombe Best Bitter Bass. **Facilities** Garden Dogs allowed

NOSS MAYO   MAP 03 SX54

Pick of the Pubs

The Ship Inn ♇

See Pick of the Pubs on page 165

OTTERY ST MARY   MAP 03 SY19

The Talaton Inn

Talaton EX5 2RQ ☎ 01404 822214 📠 01404 822214

dir: *Telephone for directions*

Timber-framed, well-maintained 16th-century inn, run by a brother and sister partnership. A strong seafood emphasis means that the menu may feature poached salmon hollandaise, cod and chips, seafood platter, or scampi. Blackboard specials change regularly, and may include chicken Wellington or fillet steak Rossini, for example. Good selection of real ales and malts, and a fine collection of bar games.

Open 12–3 7–11 (Summer 6–11) **Bar Meals** L served all week 12–2 D served Tue-Sat 7–9.15 **Restaurant** L served all week 12–2.15 D served Tue-Sat 7–9.15 ⊕ Free House ◀ Otter, Fuller's London Pride, O'Hanlon's, Badger Tanglefoot. **Facilities** Dogs allowed Parking

PARRACOMBE   MAP 03 SS64

Pick of the Pubs

The Fox & Goose ♇

See Pick of the Pubs on opposite page

RATTERY   MAP 03 SX76

Church House Inn ♇

TQ10 9LD ☎ 01364 642220 📠 01364 642220

e-mail: ray12@onetel.com

dir: *1m from A38 Exeter to Plymouth Rd & 0.75m from A385 Totnes to South Brent Rd*

With not that long to go until it is 1000 years old – it was built in 1028 – the pub features large open fireplaces, sturdy oak beams and a painting of a monk (don't move it, as misfortune will befall you!) in the characterful dining room, the menu offers fresh fish of all kinds, as well as venison, stilton and cranberry pie; Indonesian lamb; lots of grills; and salads, baguettes, toasted sandwiches and children's meals.

Open 11–3 6–11 (Winter 11–2.30, 6.30–10.30) **Bar Meals** L served all week 12–2 D served all week 7–9 **Restaurant** L served all week 12–2 D served all week 7–9 ⊕ Free House ◀ St Austell Dartmoor Best, Princetown Jail Ale, Skinners Betty Stogs Bitter & Otter Ale. ♟8 **Facilities** Children's licence Garden Dogs allowed Parking

PICK OF THE PUBS

PARRACOMBE-DEVON

The Fox & Goose

Originally this charming free house was no more than a couple of tiny thatched cottages serving the local farming community. The landlord enlarged the building to compete with nearby hotels after the narrow gauge Lynton and Barnstaple Railway linked Parracombe with the outside world in 1898.

Then, in 1925, the village's narrow street was sidelined by an early bypass, which may have contributed to the closure of the railway just ten years later. Through all this, the village has remained unspoilt and the pub has continued to welcome visitors and locals alike. The pub enjoys a sound reputation for its home-made food which is served in the bar, in the restaurant and outside in the paved courtyard garden overlooking the river. There's a wide selection of dishes to suit all tastes, based on produce from surrounding farms and the Devon coast. Menus keep pace with daily changes, and might include starters of the pub's own smoked mackerel and horseradish paté; or cod fish cakes, also home made, served with salad. Not surprisingly,

fish features prominently on the list of main courses: examples are local sand sole grilled with herb butter; pan-fried lemon sole fillets; and a traditional bouillabaisse, a fish stew made with a selection from the freshly landed catch. Meat lovers can choose between steaks, prime lamb loin chops, and chicken, leek and tarragon pie. Vegetarians might plump for the mushroom stroganoff or butternut squash risotto. Desserts not to be resisted are the local clotted cream ice creams, or the Foxy fondue for two – dark chocolate melted with Cointreau and orange essence, served with mixed fruits and marshmallows for dipping.

MAP 03 SS64
EX31 4PE
☎ 01598 763239
🖹 01598 763621
dir: *1m from A39 between Blackmoor Gate (2m) & Lynton (6m). Signed to Parracombe. Fox & Goose sign on approach*

Open 12–3 6–11
Bar Meals L served all week 12–2 D served Mon-Sat 6–9 (Sun 7–9) Av main course £12.95
Restaurant L served all week 12–2 D served Mon-Sat 6–9 (Sun 7–9) Av 3 course à la carte £23
⊕ Free House ◀ Cotleigh Barn Owl, Dartmoor Best, Exmoor Fox, Guinness. ♀ 10
Facilities Garden Dogs allowed Parking

ROCKBEARE MAP 03 SY09

Pick of the Pubs

Jack in the Green Inn ◉◉ ♟

See Pick of the Pubs on opposite page

SALCOMBE MAP 03 SX73

Pick of the Pubs

The Victoria Inn ♟

Fore St TQ8 8BU ☎ 01548 842604 📠 01548 844201
e-mail: info@victoriainnsalcombe.co.uk
dir: *In town centre, overlooking estuary*

From the first floor restaurant there are stunning views of the pretty harbour and the fishing boats bringing in the catch for the kitchen. Deciding which fresh fish dish to choose could be difficult: perhaps a chowder starter of handpicked Salcombe white crabmeat, prawns and other shellfish, white wine, fresh dill and Devon double cream. A main dish of slowly roasted half shoulder of new season Devon lamb encrusted with garlic and fresh herbs and served with a redcurrant and fresh mint sauce, served over a wholegrain mustard mash, could follow. Desserts include home-made apple and blackberry crumble and custard, and Devon ice creams and cheeses. New management for 2008.

Open 11–11 (may close 3–6pm during Winter) **Bar Meals** L served all week 12–2.30 D served all week 6–9 **Restaurant** D served all week 7–9 Av 3 course à la carte £18 ⊕ St Austell Brewery ◀ St Austell Tribute, Dartmoor Best, St Austell HSD, Black Prince & Tinners Tribute. ♟ 12 **Facilities** Garden Dogs allowed Play Area

SHEEPWASH MAP 03 SS40

Half Moon Inn

EX21 5NE ☎ 01409 231376 📠 01409 231673
e-mail: info@halfmoonsheepwash.co.uk
web: www.halfmoonsheepwash.co.uk
dir: *From M5 take A30 to Okehampton then A386, at Hatherleigh, left onto A3072, after 4m right for Sheepwash*

A very popular venue for anglers, this white-painted inn overlooking the village square in a remote Devon village is a Grade II listed building with fishing rights for ten miles of the River Torridge. Inside you'll find slate floors and a huge inglenook fireplace where a log fire burns in

cooler weather. Bar snacks are available at lunchtime and a set menu of traditional English fare at dinner.

Open 11.30–2.30 6–11 (Sun 12–2.30 7–10.30) Closed: 20–27 Dec **Bar Meals** L served Mon-Sat 12–1.45 D served Mon-Sat 6.30–8.30 Av main course £8 **Restaurant** L served all week D served all week 8 Av 3 course à la carte £20 ⊕ Free House ◀ Courage Best, Sharp's Own, Greene King Ruddles Best Bitter. **Facilities** Parking

SIDMOUTH MAP 03 SY18

Pick of the Pubs

Dukes NEW ★★★★ INN ♟

The Esplanade EX10 8AR
☎ 01395 513320 📠 01395 519318
e-mail: dukes@hotels-sidmouth.co.uk
dir: *M5 junct 30 onto A3052, take 1st exit to Sidmouth on right then left onto Esplanade*

Situated at the heart of Sidmouth town centre on the Esplanade, Dukes is a contemporary inn with traditional values. The interior is stylish and lively, with a relaxed continental feel in the bar. In fine weather the patio garden overlooking the sea is the perfect place to bask in the sun with a mid-morning coffee and home-baked pastry, or a pint and plate of your choice at lunchtime. Branscombe and O'Hanlons are among the real ale choices, and over a dozen wines are served by the glass. Traditional English style favourites vie with the specials board, where seafood from Brixham and Lyme Bay, and prime meats from West Country farms will be found. The head chef and his team aim to produce dishes for all tastes: potted crab, crispy duck confit and home-made banoffee pie are typical examples. If just a snack is required, sandwiches, pizzas and Devon cream teas are among the options.

Open 10–11 **Bar Meals** L served Sun-Wed 12–9 D served Sun-Wed 12–9 (Thu-Sat 12–9.30) Av main course £9.95 **Restaurant** L served Sun-Wed 12–9 D served Sun-Wed 12–9 (Thu-Sat 12–9.30) ⊕ Free House ◀ Branscombe Vale Branoc & Summa That, O'Hanlon's Firefly, Princetown Jail Ale, Otter Ale. ♟ 16 **Facilities** Garden Dogs allowed Parking Play Area **Rooms** 13

SLAPTON MAP 03 SX84

Pick of the Pubs

The Tower Inn ♟

See Pick of the Pubs on page 170

PICK OF THE PUBS

ROCKBEARE-DEVON

Jack in the Green Inn

An inn has been here for several centuries, but the name goes way back to pagan times when a 'green man' was associated with spring fertility celebrations. Now fast forward – this whitewashed pub stands just a few minutes' drive from Exeter airport.

Wood-burning stoves and leather armchairs create a cosy, welcoming interior, with several rooms geared towards meetings and celebrations. Overall the inn is best known as a dining destination because, during the many years he's been here, owner Paul Parnell has adopted a simple philosophy – to serve the best of Devon's produce in stylish surroundings, with more than a dash of good old-fashioned hospitality. The success of his culinary efforts has been recognised with two AA Rosettes. A bar snack here could be the substantial-sounding rib-eye steak with garlic Portobello mushrooms, chips and pine-nut parmesan and rocket salad; or fresh fish pie topped with cheesy potatoes and fresh vegetables. In the restaurant, a typical three-course meal might be crispy crottin Chavignol goat's cheese with Mediterranean vegetable terrine; boned and rolled skate wing with shrimps and parsley; and sticky toffee pudding. For something different, try a tasting menu of braised belly pork with spinach, apple and black pudding; Brixham fish stew; fillet of ruby red beef with braised shin faggot; mixed local cheeses; and bitter chocolate mousse with black cherry sorbet. Another possibility is a three-course 'Totally Devon' meal for £25. The wine list offers over 100 bins, selected for character and excellent value.

⊛⊛ ♀
MAP 03 SY09
London Rd EX5 2EE
☎ 01404 822240
🖷 01404 823445
e-mail:
info@jackinthegreen.uk.com
dir: *From M5 take old A30 towards Honiton, signed Rockbeare*

Open 11–2.30 6–11 (Sun 12–10.30) Closed: 25 Dec-5 Jan
Bar Meals L served Mon-Sat 11–2 D served Mon-Sat 6–9.30 (Sun 12–9.30) Av main course £14
Restaurant L served Mon-Sat 11–2 D served Mon-Sat 6–9.30 (Fixed price menu Sun 12–9.30) Av 3 course à la carte £32 Av 3 course fixed price £25
⊕ Free House ◀ Cotleigh Tawny Ale, Thomas Hardy Hardy Country, Otter Ale, Royal Oak.
♀ 12
Facilities Parking

PICK OF THE PUBS

SLAPTON-DEVON

The Tower Inn

The Tower Inn dates from the 14th century and is very much a part of the historic South Hams village of Slapton, which lies almost equidistant between Kingsbridge and Dartmouth, half a mile from the coast and Slapton Sands.

The inn owes its name to the ruined tower that overlooks the walled garden, which is all that remains of the Collegiate Chantry of St Mary. In 1347 the builders of the chantry constructed cottages for their own accommodation, so it seems likely that the inn may have been the College's guesthouse, dispensing alms and hospitality even then. The pub is approached by a narrow lane, and entered through a rustic porch. The interior comprises a fascinating series of low-ceilinged, interconnecting rooms with stone walls and fireplaces, beams, pillars and pews. These in turn are decorated with plants, a giant cartwheel, brasses, pictures and violins. An excellent range of beers, augmented by local cider and mulled wine in winter, is

being maintained by new owners. Traditional Sunday lunch with roast sirloin of beef, Yorkshire pudding and horseradish sauce is offered on a separate menu from the daily lunch and dinner selections. Lunchtime options range through sandwiches, a vegetarian pasta, local sausages, and herb crusted cod with cheese sauce. The dinner menu extends to medallions of pork tenderloin set on sautéed sugar snap peas served with pear, rosemary and lemon. Daily specials provide an additional choice of mainly fresh fish and game dishes, and a children's menu is also available. To finish, choose between pudding – maybe treacle orange tart – and a platter of West Country cheeses with Bath Olivers and oatcakes.

MAP 03 SX84
Church Rd TQ7 2PN
☎ 01548 580216
e-mail: towerinn@slapton.org
web: www.thetowerinn.com
dir: *Off A379 S of Dartmouth, turn left at Slapton Sands*

Open 12–2.30 6–11 (Sun 7–10.30) Closed: Mon lunch Winter
Bar Meals L served all week 12–2.30 D served all week 6–9 (Winter: lunch 12–2, dinner 7–9) Av main course £8
Restaurant L served all week 12–2.30 D served all week 6–9 (Winter: lunch 12–2, dinner 7–9) Av 3 course à la carte £20
⊕ Free House ◀ Butcombe Bitter, St Austell, Otter Bitter, Otter Ale & guest ales. ♥ 8
Facilities Garden Dogs allowed Parking

SOURTON
MAP 03 SX59

The Highwayman Inn

EX20 4HN ☎ 01837 861243 📄 01837 861196

e-mail: info@thehighwaymaninn.net

dir: *On A386 (Okehampton to Tavistock road). Exit A30 towards Tavistock. Pub 4m from Okehampton, 12m from Tavistock*

A fascinating old inn full of eccentric furniture, unusual architectural designs, and strange bric-a-brac. Since 1959 the vision of Welshman John 'Buster' Jones, and now run by his daughter Sally, it is made from parts of sailing ships, wood hauled from Dartmoor's bogs, and Gothic church arches. Popular with holidaymakers and international tourists, the menu consists of light snacks including pasties, platters and organic nibbles. In the garden, the kids will enjoy Mother Hubbard's Shoe, and the Pumpkin House.

Open 11–2 6–10.30 (Sun 12–2, 7–10.30) **Bar Meals** L served all week 11–1.45 D served all week ⊕ Free House ⌖ St Austell Duchy, Teignworthy. **Facilities** Garden Dogs allowed Parking Play Area

SOUTH POOL
MAP 03 SX74

The Millbrook Inn ♀

TQ7 2RW ☎ 01548 531581

e-mail: info@millbrookinnsouthpool.co.uk

dir: *Take A379 from Kingsbridge to Frogmore then E for 2m to South Pool*

This quaint 16th-century village pub is cosy and unspoilt inside, with open fires, fresh flowers, cushioned wheelback chairs, and beams adorned with old banknotes and clay pipes. Set at the head of the creek, its summer barbecues attract small boats from Salcombe and Kingsbridge. Fish is a speciality, and there's a peaceful sunny rear terrace overlooking a stream with ducks. At least two real ales always kept.

Open 12 -11 **Bar Meals** L served all week 12–2 D served all week 7–9 Av main course £7 **Restaurant** L served all week 12–2 D served all week 7–9 Av 3 course à la carte £19.50 ⊕ Free House ⌖ Bass, Sharp's Doom Bar, Otter Ale, Teignworthy Reel. ♀ 10 **Facilities** Garden Dogs allowed

SOUTH ZEAL
MAP 03 SX69

Oxenham Arms ★★ HL ♀

EX20 2JT ☎ 01837 840244 📄 01837 840791

e-mail: theoxenhamarms@aol.com

web: www.theoxenhamarms.co.uk

dir: *Just off A30 4m E of Okehampton, in village centre*

Probably built by monks in the 12th century, this inn on the edge of Dartmoor is one of the oldest in England and a scheduled Ancient

Monument. First licensed in 1477, the pub retains a historical feel with beams, flagstone floors, blazing fires and a prehistoric monolith – archaeologists believe the monks just built around it. Real ales include regular guests, while the refurbished restaurant serves simply cooked high quality produce from the owners' own farm.

Open 11–3 5–11 (Sun 12–2.30 7–10.30) **Bar Meals** L served all week 12–2.30 D served all week 6.30–9.30 (Summer all day Sat) Av main course £7 **Restaurant** L served all week 12–2.30 D served all week 6.30–9.30 Av 3 course à la carte £20 ⊕ Free House ⌖ Sharp's Doom Bar, Own, Eden & Special Ale, Archers Golden. **Facilities** Garden Dogs allowed Parking **Rooms** 8 (7 en suite)

SPREYTON
MAP 03 SX69

The Tom Cobley Tavern

EX17 5AL ☎ 01647 231314

dir: *From A30 at Whiddon Down take A3124 N. Right at Post Inn, then 1st right over bridge*

From this pub one day in 1802 a certain Thomas Cobley and his companions set forth for Widecombe Fair, recorded and remembered in the famous song. Today, this traditional village local offers a good selection of bar snacks, lighter fare and home-made main meals, including pies, salads, duck and fish dishes, as well as a good vegetarian selection. Finish off with one of the great ice creams or sorbets, including white chocolate and vodka! The garden is pretty.

Open 12–2 6–11 (Mon open Summer, BHs) **Bar Meals** L served Tue-Sat 12–2 D served Tue-Sun 7–9 **Restaurant** L served Sun 12–2 D served Wed-Sat 7–8.45 ⊕ Free House ⌖ Cotleigh Tawny Ale, Interbrew Bass, Tom Cobley Bitter, Doom Bar Tribute & real ales. **Facilities** Garden Parking

STOCKLAND
MAP 04 ST20

Pick of the Pubs

The Kings Arms Inn ♀

See Pick of the Pubs on page 172

See Pick of the Pubs on page 172

STOKE FLEMING
MAP 03 SX84

The Green Dragon Inn ♀

Church Rd TQ6 0PX ☎ 01803 770238 📄 01803 770238

e-mail: pcrowther@btconnect.com

dir: *Off A379 (Dartmouth to Kingsbridge coast road) opposite church*

A smuggler's tunnel is said to link this 12th-century inn to the beach at nearby Blackpool Sands. The pub, if not the tunnel, was built by masons labouring on the nearby church, and was first recorded as purveying ales in 1607. Lunchtime snacks include baguettes and beefburgers, while dinner brings such hearty dishes as local rare breed sausages with herb mash and onion gravy; game pie; or trawlerman's pie with vegetables.

Open 11–3 5.30–11 **Bar Meals** L served all week 12–2.30 D served all week 6.30–9 **Restaurant** L served all week 12–2.15 D served all week 6.30–8.30 (No food Sun eve in Winter) ⊕ Heavitree ⌖ Otter, Flowers IPA, Bass, 6X. ♀ 10 **Facilities** Garden Dogs allowed Parking Play Area

The Kings Arms Inn

A traditional 16th-century coaching inn tucked away in the Blackdown Hills, where real ales and good food are served in a lively atmosphere. Proprietors Shaun Barnes and John O'Leary are bringing fresh ideas and enthusiasm to this Grade II-listed thatched and whitewashed inn.

It boasts an impressive flagstoned walkway entrance, a medieval oak screen and an original bread oven, as well as an old grey-painted phone box. The atmospheric Farmers bar is a popular meeting place with locals and visitors united in their fondness of real ales such as Otter and Exmoor and a regularly changing summer guest; popular keg beers like Fosters and Kronenbourg are also available. The Cotley restaurant dining room offers a wide range of blackboard specials – the adventurous head chef is willing to try most ingredients, from pigeon breasts to ostrich fillets. But not to the detriment of traditional favourites: lunchtime filled ciabattas are served with chips and salad; soups are home made, and there's usually a curry. On the à la carte menu, expect to find gravadlax, sautéed prawns in garlic and herb butter, king prawn thermidor, and scallops in cream – fresh fish from the Devon coast is naturally a consistent feature. Other options may include venison medallions, rack of lamb and beef stroganoff. Many desserts are based on seasonal fruits which appear in cheesecakes and crumbles served with crème anglaise. The pub's skittle alley, where the village's two or three home teams practise, can be booked for other functions. This is a pub which is very much at the heart of the community; watch out for events like the Stockland Fair, when the pub comes into its own with barbecues and live music.

MAP 04 ST20
EX14 9BS
☎ 01404 881387
🖷 01404 881732
e-mail:
info@thekingsarmsinn.org.uk
dir: *Off A30 to Chard, 6m NE of Honiton*

Open 12–3 6.30–11.30 Closed: 25 Dec
Bar Meals L served Mon-Sat 12–2 D served all week 6.30–9
Restaurant L served all week 12–2 D served all week 6.30–9
⊕ Free House ◀ Otter Ale, Exmoor Ale, O'Hanlon's Yellowhammer, Firefly & Port Stout. ♀ 15
Facilities Garden Dogs allowed Parking

STOKENHAM   MAP 03 SX84

Pick of the Pubs

The Tradesman's Arms ♀

TQ7 2SZ ☎ 01548 580313 📠 01548 580313

e-mail: nick@thetradesmansarms.com

dir: *Just off A379 between Kingsbridge & Dartmouth*

The Tradesman's Arms is a fine part-thatched pub and restaurant, with beams, log-burning fires and a lovely atmosphere, tucked away on the edge of Stokenham's large, sheep-grazed village green. Over the years it has been many things including, until a few years back, a restaurant, but now it is most definitely a pub – a pub that serves excellent food, for that matter. Real ales come from the South Hams brewery in nearby Kingsbridge, and there are local ciders too, served in a cosy atmosphere of old beams and log fires. The kitchen uses fresh and, wherever possible, locally sourced ingredients extensively, as in a typical three-course meal of smoked salmon with capers and sun-blushed tomatoes, followed by fillet steak, roasted field mushrooms stuffed with paté, onion marmalade and a red wine sauce, then tarte au citron to finish. The menu is supplemented by home-made fresh fish and meat specials, and a curry of the day, all of which change regularly.

Open 11–3 6–11 (Sun 12–10.30) **Bar Meals** L served all week 12–2.30 D served Wed–Sun 6.30–9.30 **Restaurant** L served all week 12–2.30 D served Wed–Sun 6.30–9.30 ⊕ Free House ◼ Brakspear, Southams Devon Pride & Eddystone, Bass & guest ale. ♀ 18 **Facilities** Garden Dogs allowed Parking

---

STRETE   MAP 03 SX84

Pick of the Pubs

Kings Arms ◉ ♀

See Pick of the Pubs on page 174

THURLESTONE   MAP 03 SX64

The Village Inn ♀

TQ7 3NN ☎ 01548 563525 📠 01548 561069

e-mail: enquiries@thurlestone.co.uk

dir: *Take A379 from Plymouth towards Kingsbridge, at Bantham rdbt straight over onto B3197, then right into a lane signed Thurlestone, 2.5m*

Built in the 16th century as a farmhouse, this old pub prides itself on good service, well-kept ales and decent food. Like the nearby Thurlestone Hotel, it has been owned by the Grose family for over a century. Seafood is a speciality, with Salcombe crabmeat, River Exe mussels and other local fish and shellfish to choose from on the seasonal menus. Other possibilities are Cajun roasted chicken breast, sirloin and rump steaks, and beef burgers.

Open 11.30–3 6–11 (Sun 12–3, 7–10.30, Aug all day) **Bar Meals** L served all week 12–2.30 D served all week 6.30–9.30 ⊕ Free House ◼ Palmers IPA, Interbrew Bass, Sharp's Doom Bar & guest ale. ♀ 10 **Facilities** Children's licence Garden Dogs allowed Parking

---

TIPTON ST JOHN   MAP 03 SY09

Pick of the Pubs

The Golden Lion Inn NEW ♀

EX10 0AA ☎ 01404 812881

e-mail: info@goldenliontipton.co.uk

Francois (Franky) and Michelle Teissier are in their sixth year in this inviting village pub. Charmingly eclectic décor includes Art Deco prints jostling for space with Tiffany lamps and paintings by Devon artists. A combination of rustic Mediterranean and British traditional cooking produces dishes, usually titled in French, such as pork tenderloin with prunes and Armagnac sauce; breast of duck with damson sauce; and steak and kidney pudding. Blackboard specials feature fresh fish and seafood landed at nearby Sidmouth, such as sea bass stuffed with cream cheese and sage; monkfish kebabs; and lobster in garlic butter. Other specials might be haunch of venison with chocolate sauce, and braised oxtail. Vegetarians have plenty of choice, from vegetable lasagne to butter bean cassoulet. The lunch menu is simpler, with a good selection of sandwiches, ploughman's and regular pub grub. In winter the pub is closed on Sunday evenings.

Open 12–2.30 6–11 (Sat 12–3, Sun 12–3, 7–11) Closed: Sun eve Sep-Mar **Bar Meals** L served all week 12–2 D served Mon-Sat 6.30–8.30 (Sun 7–8.30) Av main course £10 **Restaurant** L served all week 12–2 D served Mon-Sat 6.30–8.30 (Sun 7–8.30) Av 3 course à la carte £25 ◼ Otter Ale, Bass & Greene King IPA. ♀ 10 **Facilities** Children's licence Garden Parking

PICK OF THE PUBS

Kings Arms

You can't go wrong with a pub whose kitchen motto is 'keep it fresh, keep it simple'. In the Kings Arms, the only pub in the village, customers are welcome to eat in the traditional terracotta-walled bar with its old photographs of the village and fish prints, or they can opt for the contemporary dining room, enlivened by specially commissioned art.

Menus are based around local and regional produce, and seafood makes up about eighty percent of it. Among the seafood dishes you might find River Yealm oysters with local chipolatas and coarse-grain mustard; grilled fillets of red mullet on warm tomato and mint vinaigrette; seared hand-dived scallops on braised Puy lentils with Pedro Xiemenes sherry dressing; Szechwan 'salt and pepper' squid with mooli and carrot salad and sweet soy sauce; Thai-style mussels with coriander, lemon grass and chili; mackerel 'escabeche' with rhubarb jelly; grilled sardines with sea salt, lemon and thyme; Spanish-style roast cod with chorizo, potatoes and peppers; grilled sea bream, pancetta, vanilla, green peppercorn and apple syrup; and

Singapore crab with black pepper, steamed pak choi and sesame oil. What's more, they also bake their own bread, brioche, oatcakes and biscuits, and make their own sausages, pickles, relishes and ice creams. At lunchtime you can opt for a light meal like Caesar salad with hot smoked salmon; or warm salad of goats' cheese with roasted baby tomato and pesto; or go for a River Yealm's oysters on ice starter, followed by mixed Devon seafood poached in a thin Thai broth.

⊚ ♀
MAP 03 SX84
Dartmouth Rd TQ6 0RW
☎ 01803 770377
🖷 01803 771008
e-mail: kingsarms_devon_fish@
hotmail.com
dir: *On A379 (Dartmouth-Kingsbridge road), 5m from Dartmouth*

Open 11.30–2.30 6.30–11 Sun 12–3 7–10.30
Bar Meals L served all week 12–2 (Sun 12–3) D served all week 6.30–9 Av main course £14
Restaurant L served all week 12–2 (Sun 12–3) D served all week 6.30–9 Av 3 course à la carte £27
🍺 Otter Ale, Adnams Bitter, Guinness. ♀ 15
Facilities Children's licence Garden Dogs allowed Parking

TOPSHAM
MAP 03 SX98

Pick of the Pubs

Bridge Inn

Bridge Hill EX3 0QQ ☎ 01392 873862

e-mail: su3264@eclipse.co.uk

dir: *A376 toward Exmouth. In 2m turn right to Topsham, 1m to Pink Pub by River Clyst*

There's been a building on this site since 1083 and a pub since 1512. Four generations of the same family have run the Bridge since great grandfather moved in during 1897, and it remains eccentrically and gloriously old fashioned. It has been described as a museum with beer, with its vernacular architecture – a mix of stone and cob – small rooms, open fires, an 18th-century malting kiln and an old malt house used for parties or overflow custom. Back in 1998 it became the only pub in England to have been officially visited by Queen Elizabeth II. This is a drinking pub with all real ales from independent breweries only, naturally cellared and served straight from the cask. There are also a few wines, including two from a local organic vineyard. Traditional bar food includes ploughman's, pasties, sandwiches and soup, all made with local ingredients. No lagers, no chips and definitely no mobile phones.

Open 12–2 6–10.30 (Sat 6–11, Sun 7–10.30) **Bar Meals** L served all week 12–2 ⊕ Free House ◀ Branscombe Vale-Branoc, Adnams Broadside, Exe Valley, O'Hanlons. **Facilities** Children's licence Garden Dogs allowed Parking **Notes** ⊛

The Lighter Inn ♀

The Quay EX3 0HZ ☎ 01392 875439 📄 01392 876013

dir: *Telephone for directions*

The imposing 17th-century customs house on Topsham Quay has been transformed into a popular waterside inn. A strong nautical atmosphere is reinforced with pictures, ship's instruments and oars beneath the pub's wooden ceilings, and the attractive quayside sitting area is popular in summer. Dishes may include whole sea bass or plaice, steaks, curries and salads, or steak, ale and mushroom pie.

Open 11–11 **Bar Meals** L served all week 12–2.30 D served all week 6.30–9 (Food all day Jul-Sep) Av main course £7.95 ⊕ Hall & Woodhouse ◀ Badger Best, Badger Tanglefoot, Sussex. ♀ 12 **Facilities** Parking

TORCROSS
MAP 03 SX84

Start Bay Inn ♀

TQ7 2TQ ☎ 01548 580553 📄 01548 581285

e-mail: clair@startbayinn.co.uk

dir: *Between Dartmouth & Kingsbridge on A379*

Formerly the Fisherman's Arms, this 14th-century inn remains popular with local fishermen working off the adjacent beach. They deliver fresh-caught fish to the kitchen, and the retired landlord still dives for scallops for his daughters to serve at the inn. Look for locally-sourced ingredients such as steaks, Devon ham, and Hannaford's beefburgers; other menu choices range from sandwiches and jacket potatoes to vegetarian options like spinach and mascarpone lasagne.

Open 11.30 -11 **Bar Meals** L served Mon-Sat 11.30–2 D served all week 6–10 (Sun 11.30–2.15, winter 6–9.30, summer 11.30–10) Av main course £7.50 ⊕ Heavitree ◀ Interbrew Flowers Original & Bass, Otter Ale. ♀ 8 **Facilities** Garden Parking

TOTNES
MAP 03 SX86

Pick of the Pubs

The Durant Arms ★★★★ INN ♀

See Pick of the Pubs on page 176

Royal Seven Stars Hotel NEW ♀

The Plains TQ9 5DD ☎ 01803 862125

e-mail: enquiry@royalsevenstars.co.uk

dir: *From A382 signed for Totnes, left at 'Darlinton' rdbt. Through lights toward town centre, continue through next rdbt and past Morrisons car park on left. 200yds on right*

A Grade II listed pub dating from 1640, set in the picturesque village of Dinton. Freshly prepared food is served in the lounge bar, snug or restaurant, and there is a good choice of wines, cask ales and lagers to go with it. A recent refurbishment has brought the pub up to date without eroding its character, and the real fires remain.

Open 9–11 (Fri-Sat 9–12) **Bar Meals** L served all week 9–9 D served all week 9–9 (Sun 11.30–9) Av main course £7.50 **Restaurant** 12–2.30 D served all week 6.30–9.30 Av 3 course à la carte £25 ◀ Speckled Hen & Courage Best. ♀ 16 **Facilities** Garden Dogs allowed Parking

Rumour ♀

30 High St TQ9 5RY ☎ 01803 864682

dir: *On main street up hill above arch on left. 5 min walk from rail station, follow signs for Totnes castle/town centre*

After a chequered history as a milk bar, restaurant and wine bar, this 17th-century building was named after a Fleetwood Mac album in the mid-1970s. Now comprehensively refurbished, including innovative heating and plumbing systems which reduce the pub's environmental footprint. Hospitable staff aim to provide the best drinking and dining experience possible. Try River Exe moules marinières, lamb shank braised in red wine, and chocolate parfait with griottine cherries.

Open 10–12 (Fri-Sat 10–12.30, Sun 6–10.30) **Bar Meals** L served Mon-Sat 12–3 D served all week 6–10 Av main course £10 **Restaurant** L served Mon-Sat 12–3 D served all week 6–10 Av 3 course à la carte £20.90 ⊕ Free House ◀ Erdinger, Abbots Ale, guest ales. ♀ 15

The Durant Arms

Locally renowned as a dining pub, the Durant Arms is situated in the picturesque village of Ashprington, just outside the Elizabethan town of Totnes in the heart of the South Hams. Proprietors Graham and Eileen Ellis are proud to uphold British values of hospitality at the award-winning 18th-century hostelry.

It was originally the counting house for the neighbouring 500–acre Sharpham Estate. For some years it was The Ashprington Inn, a smaller establishment than the Durant, which has expanded into an adjoining property. The small bar is fitted out in a traditional style, with work by local artists on display alongside horse-brasses, ferns and cheerful red velvet curtains. All dishes at the Durant are cooked to order, with a wide variety of meat, fish and fresh steamed vegetables, all sourced locally wherever possible. Local fish and seafood figure strongly in dishes such as Dartmouth smoked salmon with black pepper; or shell-on whole prawns with garlic dip, to start, and main courses of sea bass fillet on roasted vegetables with

pepper sauce; or fillets of lemon sole roulade. Alternatives might be devilled kidneys with brandy and cream; and roast half pheasant with port wine sauce. Desserts range from chocolate fondant with clotted cream to treacle sponge pudding with vanilla ice cream. Award-winning, hand-made English cheeses from nearby Sharpham's organic dairy are another speciality of the house, and wines from the Sharpham vineyard – red, white and rosé – are offered on the wine list. The little courtyard to the rear provides a cosy spot to linger over a summer meal, and eight comfortably furnished en suite bedrooms complete the package.

★★★★ INN ♥
MAP 03 SX86
Ashprington TQ9 7UP
☎ 01803 732240
dir: *Exit A38 at Totnes junct, to Dartington & Totnes, at 1st lights right for Knightsbridge on A381, in 1m left for Ashprington*

Open 11.30–2.30 6.30–11
Bar Meals L served all week 12–2.30 D served all week 7–9.15
Restaurant L served all week 12–2 D served all week 7–9.15
⊕ Free House ◖ Dartmoor Bitter, Tetley, Tribute. ♥ 8
Facilities Garden Parking
Rooms 8

TOTNES continued

Steam Packet Inn ★★★★ INN ♥

St Peter's Quay TQ9 5EW

☎ 01803 863880 📄 01803 862754

e-mail: steampacket@buccaneer.co.uk

dir: *Exit A38 towards Plymouth, 18m. A384 to Totnes 6m. Left at mini-rdbt, pass Morrisons on left, over mini-rdbt, 400yds on left*

The inn's sign depicts the Amelia, a steam packet ship that regularly called here with passengers, parcels and mail before the days of modern road and rail transport. These days the building is a welcoming riverside pub with great views, particularly from the conservatory restaurant, and plenty of waterside seating for sunny days. Typical dishes from the thoroughly modern menu include home-made crab ravioli, roast vegetable lasagne, and whole pan-roasted sea bass.

Open 11–11 (Sun 12–10.30) **Bar Meals** L served all week 12–2.30 D served Mon-Sat 6–9.30 (Sun 6–9) Av main course £13 **Restaurant** L served all week 12–2.30 D served Mon-Sat 6–9.30 (Sun 6–9) Av 3 course à la carte £25 ⊕ Buccaneer Holdings ◀ Courage Best, Butcombe, Otter Bright, Jail Ale & 1 guest ale. ♥8 **Facilities** Children's licence Garden Parking **Rooms** 4

Pick of the Pubs

The White Hart Bar ♥

Dartington Hall TQ9 6EL

☎ 01803 847111 📄 01803 847107

dir: *Totnes turn on A38 to Plymouth, approx 4m*

Surrounded by landscaped gardens, ancient deer parkland and woodland, the White Hart's location is second-to-none. Beside it is the 14th-century Dartington Hall. Inside you'll find a stylish dining venue with flagstone floors, limed oak settles, roughcast walls and a welcoming atmosphere. Enjoy the range of West Country ales, or choose from an accessible wine list that classifies bottles by taste. The innovative menu uses local and organic produce where possible to create dishes with a modern twist. You could start with roasted shallot, beetroot and goat's cheese tart with mixed leaves, or crab paté with mixed leaves and toasted brioche, followed by a Moroccan-style casserole of Devon lamb, or smoked haddock with braised spinach, poached egg and a cheddar and mustard sauce. For dessert, perhaps raspberry crème brûlée with a shortbread biscuit, or Belgian chocolate and coffee tart. Walk it off in the magnificent gardens surrounding Dartington Hall.

Open 11–11 Closed: 24–29 Dec **Bar Meals** L served all week 12–2 D served all week 6–9 **Restaurant** L served all week 12–2 D served all week 6–9 ⊕ Free House ◀ Otter Brewery Ale & Bitter. ♥8 **Facilities** Children's licence Garden Parking

---

TUCKENHAY
MAP 03 SX85

The Maltsters Arms ♥

TQ9 7EQ ☎ 01803 732350 📄 01803 732823

e-mail: pub@tuckenhay.demon.co.uk

dir: *Take A381 from Totnes towards Kingsbridge. 1m, at hill top turn left, follow signs to Tuckenhay (3m)*

Accessible only along high-banked lanes, or by boat either side of high tide, this old stone country inn on Bow Creek off the River Dart was once owned by TV chef, Keith Floyd. The daily changing menu may feature roasted woodcock with sloe gin gravy; fillets of sea bream and salmon with lemon and herb butter; and sweet potato, aubergine and spinach jalfrezi with rice. Famous for summer barbecues and occasional music events.

Open 11–11 (25 Dec 12–2 only – no food) **Bar Meals** L served all week 12–3 D served all week 7–9.30 **Restaurant** L served all week 12–3 D served all week 7–9.30 ⊕ Free House ◀ Princetown Dartmoor IPA, Young's Special, Teignworthy Maltsters Ale ♥18 **Facilities** Garden Dogs allowed Parking

---

TYTHERLEIGH
MAP 04 ST30

Tytherleigh Arms Hotel

EX13 7BE ☎ 01460 220400 & 220214 📄 01460 220814

e-mail: tytherleigharms@aol.com

dir: *Equidistant from Chard & Axminster on A358*

Beamed ceilings and huge roaring fires are notable features of this family-run, 17th-century former coaching inn. It is a food-led establishment, situated on the Devon, Somerset and Dorset borders. Fresh home-cooked dishes, using local ingredients, include lamb shank with honey and cider, steaks, and fresh seafood such as sea bass, red mullet and Lyme Bay crab thermidor. Comprehensive bar snack menu also available.

Open 11–2.30 6.30–11 **Bar Meals** L served all week 12–2.30 D served all week 6.30–9 (Sun 7–9 summer) **Restaurant** L served all week 12–2.30 D served all week 6.30–9 (Sun 7–9 summer) Av 3 course à la carte £25 ⊕ Free House ◀ Butcombe Bitter, Otter, Murphy's, Boddingtons. **Facilities** Children's licence Garden Parking **Rooms** available

---

UMBERLEIGH
MAP 03 SS62

Pick of the Pubs

The Rising Sun Inn ♥

EX37 9DU ☎ 01769 560447 📄 01769 560764

e-mail: risingsuninn@btopenworld.com

dir: *On A377 (Exeter-Barnstaple road) at junct with B3227*

Idyllically set beside the River Taw and with a very strong fly fishing tradition, the Rising Sun dates back in part to the 13th century. The traditional flagstone bar is strewn with fishing memorabilia, comfortable chairs and daily papers and magazines for a very relaxing visit. Outside is a sunny raised terrace with beautiful rural views of the valley, and the riverside walk is equally enjoyable before or after a meal. This inn is an excellent base for the touring motorist with several National Trust properties nearby. A choice of à la carte restaurant or regularly updated bar menus feature the best of West Country produce, with seasonal delights like seafood

CONTINUED

UMBERLEIGH continued

from the North Devon coast, salmon and sea trout from the Taw, game from Exmoor, and local cheeses. The daily changing specials board is often the best place to start looking. There's also a carvery every Sunday.

Open 12–3 6–11 (May-Sep all day) **Bar Meals** L served all week 12–2 D served all week 6.30–9 **Restaurant** L served all week 12–2 D served all week 6.30–9 (Sun 6.30–8.30) ⊕ Free House ◀ Cotleigh Tawny Bitter, Barn Owl, Guinness, Speckled Hen. ♀ 9 **Facilities** Children's licence Garden Dogs allowed Parking **Rooms** available

---

WIDECOMBE IN THE MOOR   MAP 03 SX77

The Old Inn ♀

TQ13 7TA ☎ 01364 621207 🖺 01364 621407
e-mail: oldinn.wid@virgin.net
dir: *Telephone for directions*

Dating from the 15th century, the Old Inn was partly ruined by fire but rebuilt around the original fireplaces. Two main bars and no fewer than five eating areas offer plenty of scope for visitors to enjoy the extensive selection of home-cooked food on offer. Sustaining main courses include home-made pies; fresh local salmon; and steaks from the grill. There are plenty of vegetarian options such as mushroom stroganoff and lasagne verde.

Open 11–11 **Bar Meals** L served all week 11.30–2.30 D served all week 6–9 (Snack menu 2.30–6, Sun all day) Av main course £7.50 **Restaurant** L served all week 11–2 D served all week 7–10 Av 3 course à la carte £11 ⊕ Free House ◀ Badger & guest ales. ♀ 12 **Facilities** Garden Dogs allowed Parking

---

WINKLEIGH   MAP 03 SS60

Pick of the Pubs

The Duke of York ♀

Iddesleigh EX19 8BG
☎ 01837 810253 🖺 01837 810253
dir: *Telephone for directions*

The atmosphere of this venerable thatched inn is blissfully unsullied by juke box, fruit machine or karaoke. Set deep in rural mid-Devon, it was originally three cottages housing craftsmen who were rebuilding the parish church; local records accurately date this work to 1387. All the timeless features of a classic country pub remain – heavy old beams, scrubbed tables, farmhouse chairs and a huge inglenook fireplace with winter fires. Popular with all, it offers decent real ales (Cotleigh Tawny, for example) and hearty home cooking, with everything freshly prepared using local produce such as meat reared on nearby farms. Examples of bar meals taken from the large blackboard menu include rainbow trout, liver and bacon, and casseroles. From the dining room menu could come Dartmouth smokehouse salmon followed by pork loin with port and tarragon sauce, then a choice of more than a dozen classic home-made desserts.

Open 11–12 **Bar Meals** L served Mon-Sat 12–10 D served Mon-Sat 12–10 (Sun 12–9.30) **Restaurant** L served all week 12–10 D served Mon-Sat 7–10 (Sun 7–9.30) ⊕ Free House ◀ Adnams Broadside, Cotleigh Tawny, guest ales. ♀ 10 **Facilities** Garden Dogs allowed

The Kings Arms ♀

Fore St EX19 8HQ ☎ 01837 83384
dir: *Village signed off B3220 (Crediton to Torrington road)*

Scrubbed pine tables and traditional wooden settles set the scene at this ancient thatched country inn in Winkleigh's central square. Wood-burning stoves keep the beamed bar and dining rooms warm in chilly weather, and traditional pub games are encouraged. Generous servings of freshly-made food include sandwiches and hot snacks, as well as roasted vegetables with goats' cheese; Lucy's fish pie; and lamb's liver with bacon. Booking is recommended at weekends.

Open 11–11 (Sun 12–10.30) **Bar Meals** L served Mon-Sat 11–9.30 D served Mon-Sat 11–9.30 (Sun 12–9) Av main course £9.95 **Restaurant** L served Mon-Sat 11–9.30 D served Mon-Sat 11–9.30 (Sun 12–9) ⊕ Enterprise Inns ◀ Butcombe Bitter, Sharp's Doom Bar & Cornish Coaster. ♀ 7 **Facilities** Children's licence Garden Dogs allowed

---

WOODBURY SALTERTON   MAP 03 SY08

Pick of the Pubs

The Digger's Rest ♀

See Pick of the Pubs on opposite page

YEALMPTON   MAP 03 SX55

Rose & Crown ❀ ♀

Market St PL8 2EB ☎ 01752 880223 🖺 01752 881058
e-mail: info@theroseandcrown.co.uk
web: www.theroseandcrown.co.uk

The Rose and Crown is a stylish spot these days, elegant without being overbearing. The food is taken seriously here, and the Pacific Rim-inspired menu includes such imaginative dishes as Falmouth bay scallops, roasted cantaloupe and coriander pesto, followed by roast breast of duck, vanilla purée and Armagnac jus. Look out for the secret garden: complete with fountain, it's a lovely spot for a romantic summer meal.

Open 12–11 **Bar Meals** L served all week 12–3 D served all week 6.30–9 **Restaurant** L served all week 12–2 D served all week 6.30–9 Av 3 course à la carte £20 Av 3 course fixed price £12.95 ◀ Doom Bar, London Pride, Courage Best. ♀ 10 **Facilities** Garden Dogs allowed Parking

PICK OF THE PUBS

WOODBURY SALTERTON-DEVON

The Digger's Rest

A picturesque country inn with thick, 500–year-old walls built of stone and cob and heavy beams under a thatched roof, the Digger's Rest was originally a Devon cider house. The interior features West Country art, antique furniture and a skittle alley. Traditionally drawn ales are served alongside home-cooked food in a relaxed, welcoming atmosphere.

The patio garden provides seating for up to 40 people and is the perfect setting for outdoor drinking and dining, especially at night when it is attractively illuminated. Simple, freshly cooked food is prepared from English and West Country produce, including fish from Brixham and Looe, Devon Ruby Red beef and Blackdown Hills pork. Meat and eggs are free range, and the kitchen is committed to supporting good husbandry and buying organic where possible. The coffee is fair trade; and the cheeses, provided by Country Cheeses of Topsham, are all unpasteurised. Start with Cornish crabcakes and tomato salsa; or coarse country paté with warm toast. A good variety of mains includes steak and ale pie; Thai green chicken curry;

Mediterranean vegetable salad; and chargrilled Cornish mackerel. From the grill come West Country steaks with a choice of sauces, or Devon Ruby Red beef burger with fries, red onion and dressed salad leaves. Desserts are not to be missed, with Digger's bread and butter pudding; individual hot treacle sponge; and rich chocolate brownie with warm chocolate sauce. Digger's nibbles are nice with a drink: houmous, tsatziki and crudités; mixed breads; and marinated Greek olives.

MAP 03 SY08
EX5 1PQ
☎ 01395 232375
📠 01395 232711
e-mail: bar@diggersrest.co.uk
dir: *2.5m from A3052. Signed from Westpoint*

Open 11–3 6–11 (All day Sat-Sun)
Bar Meals L served Mon-Sat 12–2 D served Mon-Sat 6.30–9.30 (Sun 12–2.30, 6–9) Av main course £11.95
Restaurant L served Mon-Sat 12–2 D served Mon-Sat 6.30–9.30 (Sun 12–2.30, 6–9) Av 3 course à la carte £20.95
⊕ Free House ◀ Otter Bitter, Otter Ale, Scatterbrook Devonian, Butcombe Bitter. ♀ 13
Facilities Children's licence Garden Parking

England

DORSET

ABBOTSBURY
MAP 04 SY58

Ilchester Arms ♟
9 Market St DT3 4JR ☎ 01305 871243 🖹 01305 871225

dir: *Telephone for directions*

Rambling 16th-century coaching inn set in the heart of one of Dorset's most picturesque villages. Abbotsbury is home to many crafts including woodwork and pottery. A good area for walkers, and handy for the Tropical Gardens and Swannery.

Open 11–11 (Sun 12–10.30) **Bar Meals** L served all week 12–2 D served all week 7–9 (Sun 12–2.30) Av main course £10 **Restaurant** L served all week 12–2.30 D served all week 7–9.30 (Sun 12–2.30, 7–9) Av 3 course à la carte £20 ◀ Fuller's HSB, Courage Best, Tribute, Speckled Hen. ♟ 12 **Facilities** Children's licence Garden Dogs allowed Parking

BLANDFORD FORUM
MAP 04 ST80

The Anvil Inn ★★★★ INN ♟
Salisbury Rd, Pimperne DT11 8UQ
☎ 01258 453431 🖹 01258 480182
e-mail: theanvil.inn@btconnect.com

A thatched roof, crooked beams and a cavernous fireplace are just a few of the rustic charms of this 16th-century inn located in the pretty village of Pimperne, two miles from Blandford Forum. The menu starts with ploughman's lunches, simple omelettes and salads, and runs to hearty meals including grills, fish and chips, and sausages and mash. Spicier choices include Thai vegetable curry or chicken fajitas.

Open all day **Bar Meals** L served all week D served all week ⊕ Free House ◀ Guinness, London Pride, IPA & Copper Ale. **Facilities** Children's licence Garden Dogs allowed Parking **Rooms** 12

Best Western Crown Hotel ♟
West St DT11 7AJ ☎ 01258 456626 🖹 01258 451084
e-mail: crownhotel.blandford@hall-woodhouse.co.uk
dir: *M27 W onto A31 to A350 junct, W to Blandford. 100mtrs from town bridge*

An 18th-century coaching inn which replaces an original inn destroyed by fire in 1731. Standing on the banks of the River Stour, the Crown has plenty of period atmosphere, and a separate restaurant. Begin a meal, perhaps, with cod and parsley fishcake with sweet chilli sauce, follow it with rosemary-crusted lamb cutlets with redcurrant scented gravy; or gammon steak with grilled pineapple, chips and peas. An extensive bar menu includes sandwiches and light bites.

Open 10–2.30 6–11 Closed: 25–28 Dec **Bar Meals** L served all week 12–2 D served all week 6.30–9 **Restaurant** D served Mon-Sat 7.15–9.15 (Sun 7–9) ⊕ Hall & Woodhouse ◀ Badger Tanglefoot, Best, Badger 1st Gold. ♟ 20 **Facilities** Garden Dogs allowed Parking

BOURTON
MAP 04 ST73

The White Lion Inn
High St SP8 5AT ☎ 01747 840866 🖹 01747 840191
e-mail: office@whitelionbourton.co.uk
dir: *Off A303, opposite B3092 to Gillingham*

A quintessentially English pub, built from stone in 1723 and packed with beams and flagstones, not to mention a log fire and a good choice of real ales. Food options are divided between light bites (baguettes; ham, egg and chips; Catalan style meatballs) and the Shoals restaurant menu. There's also a daily selection of fish specials. Typical starters include venison paté; meatballs; tagliatelle with seafood sauce; and mushrooms stuffed with garlic, parsley and parmesan cheese. Follow with Thai green curry; steak and kidney pie; vegetable tagine with couscous; or beef escalope with port wine sauce.

Open 12–3 5–11 **Bar Meals** L served Mon-Sat 12–2 D served all week 7–9 (Sun 12–3) Av main course £8 **Restaurant** L served Mon-Sat 12–2 D served Mon-Sat 7–9 (Sun 12–3) ⊕ ◀ Fuller's London Pride, Greene King IPA & guest ale. **Facilities** Garden Dogs allowed Parking

BRIDPORT
MAP 04 SY49

The George Hotel ♟
4 South St DT6 3NQ ☎ 01308 423187
dir: *In town centre, 1.5m from West Bay*

Handsome Georgian town house, with a Victorian-style bar and a mellow atmosphere, which bustles all day, and offers a traditional English breakfast, decent morning coffee and a good menu featuring fresh local plaice, natural smoked haddock, avacado and bacon salad, and the famous rabbit and bacon pie. Everything is home cooked using local produce.

Open 9.30–11.30 Closed: 25 Dec **Bar Meals** L served all week 12–2.30 D served Wed-Thu 6–9 ⊕ Palmers ◀ Palmers – IPA, Copper & 200, Tally Ho. **Facilities** Dogs allowed

Pick of the Pubs

Shave Cross Inn ★★★★ INN ♟
See Pick of the Pubs on opposite page

PICK OF THE PUBS

BRIDPORT-DORSET

Shave Cross Inn

No amount of guessing is likely to reveal the origins of this friendly, family-run pub's name. Back in the 13th-century, pilgrims and monks on their way to the church of St Candida and St Cross in nearby Whitchurch Canonicorum would stop here, or so the story goes, for a quick haircut.

The churchyard contains the grave of Georgi Markov, Bulgaria's 'most revered dissident', who was assassinated by a Soviet agent with a poisoned umbrella on Waterloo Bridge in 1978. Tucked away down narrow lanes, this could well be the inn that time forgot. The bar is floored with ancient blue lias flagstones from Dorset's Jurassic Coast (a World Heritage Site), and the inglenook fireplace is just right for smoking hams. Owners Roy and Mel Warburton spent a long time in Tobago, before returning in 2003 to take over and revive the pub. They brought with them their head chef, who is responsible for the authentically Caribbean touches to the menu. Examples include roast créole duck with cherry compote; jerk chicken salad with plantain,

crispy bacon and aioli; and Dorset prime fillet steak with a rum, brandy and Caribbean peppercorn sauce. Fans of traditional British food won't be disappointed though: there are plenty of other options, especially at lunchtime. These range from fresh battered haddock, and rump steak, to cheese ploughman's, and fresh crab sandwiches. Local beers come from Quay Brewery in Weymouth and Devon's Branscombe Vale. The garden has a play area for children, a thatched wishing well and a huge collection of flowers and shrubs. Ancient customs linger on in these parts. The inn houses the oldest thatched skittle alley in the country, and maintains the traditions of Morris dancing, folk singing, and ashen-faggot burning on Twelfth Night.

★★★★★ INN ☻
MAP 04 SY49
Shave Cross, Marshwood Vale
DT6 6HW
☎ 01308 868358
🖷 01308 867064
e-mail: roy.warburton@virgin.net
web:
www.theshavecrossinn.co.uk
dir: *From Bridport take B3162 2m turn left signed 'Broadoak/ Shave Cross' then Marshwood*

Open 11–3 6–11 (All day Tue-Sun in Summer, BH Mons) Closed: Mon (ex BH)
Bar Meals L served Tue-Sun 12–2.30 D served Tue-Sun 5–9.30 (Sun 12–3, 6–8 Summer)
Restaurant L served Tue-Sun 12–2.30 D served Tue-Sat 7–9.30 (Sun 6–8 Summer)
⊕ Free House ◀ Local guest ales, Branoc (Branscombe Valley), Quay Brewery Weymouth. ☻ 8
Facilities Children's licence Garden Dogs allowed Parking Play Area
Rooms 7

England

BRIDPORT continued

The West Bay ♀

Station Rd, West Bay DT6 4EW
☎ 01308 422157 🖹 01308 459717
e-mail: info@thewestbay.co.uk
dir: *From A35 (Bridport by-pass) take B3157 (2nd exit) towards West Bay. After mini-rdbt 1st left (Station Road). Pub on left*

Built in 1739, this traditional bar/restaurant lies at the foot of East Cliff, part of the impressive World Heritage Jurassic Coast. Specialities are fish and seafood – deep-fried pollock in local Palmer's ale; and crab and shellfish platter, for example – and meat dishes such as Dorset Blue Vinny rarebit on pork loin with black pudding; and spiced honey roast duck breast, sweet potato mash and pancetta jus. Desserts are served with ice cream, custard or cream.

Open 12–3 6.15–11 Closed: Sun eve **Bar Meals** L served Mon-Sat 12–2 D served Mon-Sat 6.30–9 (Sun 12–2.15) Av main course £14 **Restaurant** L served all week 12–2 D served Mon-Sat 6.30–9 Av 3 course à la carte £24 ⊕ Palmers ◀ Palmers IPA, Palmers Copper, Palmers 200, Guinness. ♀ 8 **Facilities** Children's licence Garden Parking

BUCKHORN WESTON   MAP 04 ST72

Pick of the Pubs

Stapleton Arms NEW ♀

Church Hill SP8 5HS ☎ 01963 370396
e-mail: relax@thestapletonarms.com
dir: *3.5m from Wincanton in village centre*

A stylish but unstuffy pub in a pretty village, with a spacious bar, elegant dining room, and secluded garden. Hand-pumped ales, draught farm ciders, organic fruit juices and wines from new, old and emerging wine regions accompany simple, innovative food using quality produce from small local suppliers. For a starter try French onion soup with Montgomery cheddar croutons; or black pudding wontons with winter salad and seed mustard dressing. Main courses include pan-fried Dorset red mullet with tiger prawn and coriander green curry; roasted leg of locally shot roe deer, root mash and rosemary sauce; risotto of cauliflower, Blue Vinny and charred spring onions; and a selection of tapas. Typical puddings are boozy date and walnut sponge with butterscotch sauce and crème fraîche; and white chocolate tart with white chocolate sauce. On Sundays you may carve your own roast, provided you've ordered it by the previous Thursday.

Open 11–3 6–11 (Sat-Sun 11–11) **Bar Meals** L served all week 12–3 D served Mon-Sat 6–10 (Sun 6–9.30) Av main course £10 **Restaurant** L served all week 12–3 D served Mon-Sat 6–10 (Sun 6–9.30) Av 3 course à la carte £23 ◀ Butcombe, Timothy Taylor Landlord, Hidden Brewery. ♀ 12 **Facilities** Garden Dogs allowed Parking **Rooms** available

BURTON BRADSTOCK   MAP 04 SY48

Pick of the Pubs

The Anchor Inn ♀

High St DT6 4QF ☎ 01308 897228
e-mail: info@dorset-seafood-restaurant.co.uk
dir: *2m SE of Bridport on B3157 in centre of Burton Bradstock*

A 300–year-old coaching inn, the Anchor is located just inland from a stretch of the Jurassic Coast World Heritage Site, near Chesil Beach. As you might expect from its name, the pub is full of marine memorabilia: fishing nets hang from ceilings, and old fishing tools and arty things made by the chef-proprietor from shellfish adorn the walls. Seafood is a speciality, and there is an extensive selection of main fish courses on the menu, plus 'catch of the day' specials. The bouillabaisse is a substantial version of the celebrated French dish, including a wide variety of local fish and shellfish in a creamy lobster, white wine and brandy jus, served with a hot baguette. Dorset scallops, dived for around West Bay, are seared in butter anD served in their shells with a creamy bacon and mushroom sauce, on a bed of savoury rice garnished with salad and prawns.

Open 11–11 (Sun 12–10.30) **Bar Meals** L served Mon-Sat 12–2 D served all week 6–9 **Restaurant** L served all week 12–2 D served all week 6–9 ⊕ Punch Taverns ◀ Otter Bitter, Tribute, Flowers Bitter & John Smith's. ♀ 10 **Facilities** Children's licence Parking

CATTISTOCK   MAP 04 SY59

Fox & Hounds Inn

Duck St DT2 0JH ☎ 01300 320444 🖹 01300 320444
e-mail: info@foxandhoundsinn.com
dir: *On A37, between Dorchester & Yeovil, follow signs to Cattistock*

This attractive 16th-century inn is set in the beautiful village of Cattistock. Original features include beams, open fires and huge inglenooks, one with an original bread oven. It is a fascinating building, full of curiosities, such as the hidden cupboard reached by a staircase that winds around the chimney in one of the loft areas. Traditional home-made meals include locally made faggots; mushroom stroganoff; steak and kidney pudding; fisherman's pie; and Dorset apple cake.

Open 12–2.30 7–11 **Bar Meals** L served Tue-Sun 12–2 D served all week 7–9 Av main course £8 **Restaurant** L served Tue-Sun 12–2 D served all week 7–9 ⊕ Palmers ◀ Palmers IPA, Copper Ale, Palmers 200 & Dorset Gold. **Facilities** Children's licence Garden Dogs allowed Parking

PICK OF THE PUBS

CERNE ABBAS-DORSET

The Royal Oak

Built in 1540 in the market square using the remains of a 9th-century abbey, the Royal Oak delivers all the character and atmosphere that its history suggests, thanks to a thatched roof, flagstone floors, oak beams and open fireplaces. The pretty village location enhances its charm.

Outside there's a lovely courtyard garden, and just inside the pub you'll see what is believed to be its original front door complete with its wooden lock. In 1670 a previous owner sold the pub, and with the proceeds he purchased 1800 acres of land in the United States, now the site of Capitol Hill. Fast-forward to the present day and the pub is owned by Maurice and Sandra Ridley, whose son Darran is in charge of the kitchen. Darran, a member of the Master Chefs of Great Britain, has vast international experience including stints at Buckingham Palace, the Gleneagles Hotel and on board the QE2. Dine on light bites such as a filled panini (freshly baked to order), a ploughman's or a dressed local crab salad. For a more substantial meal, you could start with River Teign oysters, grilled with garlic and parmesan or served on ice; or a warm tartlet of sun-blushed tomatoes and goats' cheese. For your main course, try venison bourguignon; lamb shank, slow cooked for seven hours in red wine, tomato, garlic and rosemary; or pie of the day (beef in ale with local blue vinney cheese is very popular). Fish dishes are also a strength, and might include simple local dressed crab salad, or monkfish cheeks with braised ox tails. Also worthy of attention are the desserts, many of which come with ice cream churned to order.

MAP 04 ST60
23 Long St DT2 7JG
☎ 01300 341797
🖹 01300 341814
e-mail:
info@theroyaloak-pub.co.uk
dir: *M5/A37, follow A37 to A352 signed Cerne Abbas, midway between Sherborne & Dorchester. Pub in centre of village*

Open 11 -11
Bar Meals L served all week 12–3 D served all week 6.30–9 Av main course £9.95
⊕ Hall & Woodhouse
🍺 Tanglefoot, Badger Best, Fursty Ferret, Stowford Press. 🍷 8
Facilities Garden Dogs allowed

CERNE ABBAS
MAP 04 ST60

Pick of the Pubs

The Royal Oak ♀

See Pick of the Pubs on page 183

CHIDEOCK
MAP 04 SY49

The Anchor Inn ♀

Seatown DT6 6JU ☎ 01297 489215

dir: *On A35 turn S in Chideock opp church & follow single track rd for 0.75m to beach*

Originally a smugglers' haunt, The Anchor has an incredible setting in a little cove surrounded by National Trust land, beneath Golden Cap. The large sun terrace and cliff-side beer garden overlooking the beach make it a premier destination for throngs of holidaymakers in the summer, while on winter weekdays it is blissfully quiet. The wide-ranging menu starts with snacks and light lunches – three types of ploughman's and a range of sandwiches might take your fancy. For something more substantial you could try freshly caught seafood – crab salad, for example.

Open 11–3 6–11 (Fri-Sun all day Summer 11–11) **Bar Meals** L served all week 12–2.30 D served all week 6–9 (Sat-Sun, Summer all day) Av main course £7.50 ⊕ Palmers ◀ Palmers 200 Premium Ale, IPA, Copper Ale. ♀ 8 **Facilities** Garden Dogs allowed Parking

CHRISTCHURCH
MAP 05 SZ19

Fishermans Haunt ♀

Salisbury Rd, Winkton BH23 7AS
☎ 01202 477283 📄 01202 478883

e-mail: fishermanshaunt@accommodating-inn.co.uk

dir: *2.5m N on B3347 (Christchurch/Ringwood road)*

Dating from 1673, this inn overlooks the River Avon and is a popular place for walkers, and anglers visiting some of the local fisheries. The area is also well endowed with golf courses. The menu offers a daily fish selection, usually including trout and whole plaice, and staples such as steak and kidney pie, battered cod, and mixed grill along with sandwiches and baked potatoes. There's a more extensive carte menu in the restaurant.

Open 10.30–3 5–11 (Sat 11–11, Sun 12–10.30) **Bar Meals** L served all week 12–2 D served all week 6–9 **Restaurant** L served Sat-Sun 12–2 D served Sat-Sun 6–9 Av 3 course à la carte £15 ⊕ Fullers ◀ Fuller's GB & HSB, London Pride & Ringwood Fortyniner. ♀ 7 **Facilities** Garden Dogs allowed Parking **Rooms** available

The Ship In Distress ◉◉

66 Stanpit BH23 3NA ☎ 01202 485123 📄 01202 483997

e-mail: enquiries@theshipindistress.com

dir: *Telephone for directions*

Once a haunt of famous Christchurch smugglers, this 300–year-old pub featured in a recent documentary film about the history of smuggling. It is located close to Mudeford Quay and has an award-winning seafood restaurant. Typical dishes are moules marinière, and baked fillet of turbot with shallots, wild mushrooms and sunblush

tomatoes. Fresh daily desserts include assiette of Belgian chocolate, and Cointreau orange mascarpone cheesecake with confit orange.

Open 11–11 Closed: 25 Dec **Bar Meals** L served all week 12–2 D served all week 7–9.30 (Sun 12–3) Av main course £10 **Restaurant** L served all week 12–2 D served all week 7–9.30 Av 3 course à la carte £30 ⊕ Punch Taverns ◀ Ringwood Best, Fortyniner, Interbrew Bass, Courage Directors. **Facilities** Garden Dogs allowed Parking

CHURCH KNOWLE
MAP 04 SY98

The New Inn ♀

BH20 5NQ ☎ 01929 480357 📄 01929 480357

dir: *From Wareham take A351 towards Swanage. At Corfe Castle turn right for Church Knowle. Pub in village centre*

A 16th-century inn of stone and thatch set in a picturesque village overlooking the Purbeck hills. Maurice and Rosemary Estop have been at this pub for over 21 years and their son Matthew is head chef. Home-made dishes feature daily-delivered fresh fish, including haddock in golden batter, roasted cod with wild mushroom and white wine sauce, fresh dressed crab, lobster, whole grilled bream or plaice, and fruits de mer. Pies, grills and sandwiches also make an appearance.

Open 11–3 6.30–11 Closed: Mon eve Jan-Feb **Bar Meals** L served all week 12–2.15 D served all week 6–9.15 **Restaurant** L served all week 12–2.15 D served all week 6–9.15 ⊕ Punch Taverns ◀ Wadworth 6X, Old Speckled Hen, Interbrew Flowers Original. ♀ 8 **Facilities** Garden Parking

CORFE CASTLE
MAP 04 SY98

The Greyhound Inn ♀

The Square BH20 5EZ ☎ 01929 480205 📄 01929 480205

e-mail: eat@greyhoundcorfe.co.uk

dir: *W from Bournemouth, take A35 to Dorchester, after 5m left onto A351, 10m to Corfe Castle*

A classic old coaching inn in the heart of the ancient village, with a large garden overlooking Corfe Castle and the Swanage Steam Railway. A lively diary of events, with music especially important, is topped by two annual beer festivals in May and August. The convivial atmosphere embraces families, groups of cyclists and walkers enjoying real ales, ciders, and delicious food – seasonally fresh and local produce embraces a wealth of winter game or summer shellfish from Swanage, Weymouth or Lulworth.

Open 11am-12.30am **Bar Meals** L served all week 12–3 D served all week 6–9 (Jul-Sep & wknds food all day) **Restaurant** L served all week 12–3 D served all week 6–9 (Jul-Sep food all day) ⊕ Enterprise Inns ◀ Fuller's London Pride, Timothy Taylor Landlord, Black Sheep, Ringwood Best. ♀ 13 **Facilities** Children's licence Garden Dogs allowed Play Area

Chesil Beach, Dorset

The COVENTRY Arms

Mill Street, Corfe Mullen BH21 3RH
Tel: 01258 857284

Situated on the main A31 between Wimborne and Bere Regis this unspoilt Pub/Restaurant is a delight for both drinkers and eaters. Real ales dispensed straight from the cask behind the bar and great, locally sourced food with a strong emphasis on fish and game cooked with skill by the team of chefs. A wonderful garden where you can

watch kingfishers going up and down the river while you sip your wine from the extensive list, makes this pub well worth a visit.

CORFE MULLEN
MAP 04 SY99

The Coventry Arms ⊛ ☗

Mill St BH21 3RH ☎ 01258 857284

dir: *On A31 (Wimborne-Dorchester road)*

Built in the 13th-century, this friendly pub was once a watermill with its own island. Beer is served direct from the cask, while an annual spring seafood festival attracts many visitors. The inn specialises in fish and game from local estates, and most of the produce is sourced from within the area. Expect such creative dishes as open ravioli of monkfish medallions and mussels; or pan-seared Sika deer's liver with smoked bacon.

Open 11–3 5.30–11 **Bar Meals** L served all week 12–2.30 D served all week 6–9.30 (Sun all day) **Restaurant** L served all week 12–2.30 D served all week 6–9.30 (Sun all day) Av 3 course à la carte £25 ⊕ Free House ◀ Fuller's HSB, Timothy Taylor Landlord. ☗ 17 **Facilities** Garden Dogs allowed Parking

See advert above

EAST CHALDON
MAP 04 SY78

The Sailors Return

DT2 8DN ☎ 01305 853847 🖹 01305 851677

dir: *1m S of A352 between Dorchester & Wool*

A splendid 18th-century thatched country pub in the village of East Chaldon (or Chaldon Herring – take your pick), tucked away in rolling downland near Lulworth Cove. Seafood includes whole local plaice, scallop and mussel Stroganoff, and wok-fried king prawns. Alternatives include half a big duck, local faggots, whole gammon hock, and vegetarian dishes. Choose from the blackboard in the beamed and flagstoned bar and eat inside or in a grassy area outside.

Open 11–11 (Sun 12–10.30) **Bar Meals** L served all week 12–2 D served all week 6–9 **Restaurant** L served all week 12–2 D served all week 6–9 (Summer 12–9) ⊕ Free House ◀ Ringwood Best, Hampshire Strongs Best Bitter, Badger Tanglefoot. **Facilities** Garden Parking Play Area

---

EAST MORDEN
MAP 04 SY99

Pick of the Pubs

The Cock & Bottle ☗

BH20 7DL ☎ 01929 459238

dir: *From A35 W of Poole turn right B3075, pub 0.5m on left*

Some 400 years ago this popular pub was a cob-walled Dorset longhouse. It acquired a brick skin around 1800, and remained thatched until 1966. The original interiors are comfortably rustic with quaint, low-beamed ceilings, attractive paintings and lots of nooks and crannies around the log fires. Additional to the lively locals' bar are a lounge bar and modern rear restaurant extension; lovely pastoral views over farmland include the pub's paddock, where vintage car and motorcycle meetings are occasionally hosted during the summer. The experienced chef serves up an appealing mix of traditional and inventive cooking, with wholesome bar and light lunch menus supporting a varied carte. Starters could include fresh dressed local crab, or crown of Charentaise melon filled with peeled prawns. To follow try whole boned wild mallard with braised red cabbage; or one of the fish dishes – pan-seared Lyme Bay scallops, or fillet of monkfish encased in peppered Parma ham.

Open 11–3 6–11 (Sun 12–3, 7–10.30) **Bar Meals** L served all week 12–2 D served Mon-Sat 6–9 (Sun 7–9) **Restaurant** L served all week 12–2 D served Mon-Sat 6–9 (Sun 7–9) Av 3 course à la carte £23.70 ⊕ Hall & Woodhouse ◀ Badger Dorset Best & Tanglefoot & Sussex. ☗ 6 **Facilities** Garden Dogs allowed Parking

England

EVERSHOT   MAP 04 ST50

Pick of the Pubs

The Acorn Inn ★★★★ INN ⊛ ♀

DT2 0JW ☎ 01935 83228 🖹 01935 83707

e-mail: stay@acorn-inn.co.uk

web: www.acorn-inn.co.uk

dir: A303 to Yeovil, Dorchester Rd, on A37 right to Evershot

A 16th-century coaching inn, this pub was immortalised as the Sow and Acorn in Thomas Hardy's *Tess of the D'Urbervilles*. It stands in an area of outstanding natural beauty, with walking, fishing, shooting and riding all nearby. Inside are two oak-panelled bars – one flagstoned, one tiled – with logs blazing in carved hamstone fireplaces. The skittle alley used to be the stables, and it's rumoured that the residents' sitting room was once used by Hanging Judge Jeffreys as a court room. Most of the food is sourced from within a 15–mile radius, and the interesting menus might typically include starters such as smoked haddock and grain mustard chowder with chive cream, and mains of fillet of cod in beer batter with home-made tartare sauce; roasted loin of Dorset lamb with braised leeks, twice-baked mushroom and cheddar soufflé and Madeira jus; and a roasted leek, red pepper and ricotta tart.

Open 11–11 **Bar Meals** L served all week 12–2 D served all week 7–9 Av main course £8.50 **Restaurant** L served all week 12–2 D served all week 7–9 Av 3 course à la carte £23.50 ⊕ Free House ◀ Draymens & guest ale. ♀ 11 **Facilities** Garden Dogs allowed Parking **Rooms** 10

FARNHAM   MAP 04 ST91

Pick of the Pubs

The Museum Inn ⊛⊛ ♀

DT11 8DE ☎ 01725 516261 🖹 01725 516988

e-mail: enquiries@museuminn.co.uk

dir: From Salisbury take A354 to Blandford Forum, 12m. Farnham signed on right. Pub in village centre

This part-thatched pub was built by General Augustus Lane Fox Pitt Rivers, the father of modern archaeology, to provide accommodation and refreshments for visitors to the nearby museum. Comprehensively refurbished, all its original features remain intact, from the stone flagged floors and inglenook fireplace to a traditional bread oven. The same attention to detail is displayed in the kitchens, where a commitment to sourcing local produce reared in traditional ways leads to an imaginative array of dishes arranged with pleasing intricacy. Try parsnip, celeriac and scrumpy apple soup, or lightly pickled Chesil Beach mackerel with crunchy vegetables garlic aioli and pink fir apple potatoes, followed by Portland fish stew with rouille croûtes and saffron potatoes; or roasted local estate venison loin with butternut squash mash, honey-glazed parsnips and sour cherry jus. For dessert, perhaps farmhouse bread and butter pudding, or citrus lemon tart with berry compote and mascarpone cream.

Open 12–3 6–10.30 Closed: 1 Jan **Bar Meals** L served Mon-Fri 12–2 D served all week 7–9.30 (Sat 12–2.30, Sun 12–3) Av main course £15 **Restaurant** L served Mon-Sat 12–2 D served all week 7–9.30 (Sun 12–3) Av 3 course à la carte £27 ⊕ Free House ◀ Ringwood Best, Hopback Summer Lightening, Timothy Taylor Landlord, Otter Gold. ♀ 14 **Facilities** Children's licence Garden Dogs allowed Parking

---

GILLINGHAM   MAP 04 ST82

The Kings Arms Inn ♀

East Stour Common SP8 5NB ☎ 01747 838325

e-mail: nrosscampbell@aol.com

dir: 4m W of Shaftesbury on A30

A family-run, 200–year-old free house, this village inn makes a great base for exploring Dorset's countryside and coast. There is a public bar with a log fire, the Mallard and Garden Room and an enclosed acre of attractive beer garden. The menus offer an extensive choice of restaurant fare and traditional pub grub. A popular choice is the Kings Arms' famous haggis, neeps and tatties with whisky gravy. A separate menu is available for children.

Open 12–3 5.30–11 (Sat-Sun 12–11) **Bar Meals** L served Mon-Fri 12–2.30 D served Mon-Fri 5.30–9.15 (Sat-Sun 12–9.15) **Restaurant** L served Mon-Fri 12–2.30 D served Mon-Fri 5.30–9.15 (Sat-Sun 12–9.15) Av 3 course à la carte £21 ⊕ Free House ◀ London Pride, Copper Ale, Tribute, Wadworth 6X. ♀ 8 **Facilities** Garden Dogs allowed Parking

GUSSAGE ALL SAINTS   MAP 04 SU01

The Drovers Inn ⚲

BH21 5ET ☎ 01258 840084

e-mail: info@thedroversinn.net

dir: *A31 Ashley Heath rdbt, right onto B3081*

Rural 16th-century pub with a fine terrace and wonderful views from the garden. Popular with walkers, its refurbished interior retains plenty of traditional appeal with flagstone floors and oak furniture. Ales include Ringwood's seasonal ales and guest beers. The menu features home-cooked pub favourites: fresh cod in home-made beer batter, curry, steak and kidney pie, and steak and chips.

Open 11.45–11 **Bar Meals** L served all week 12–2 D served all week 6–9 all day weekends Av main course £6.95 ◀ Ringwood Best, Old Thumper, Ringwood seasonal ales, Fortyniner & guest ales. ⚲ 10 **Facilities** Garden Dogs allowed Parking

---

KING'S STAG   MAP 04 ST71

The Greenman NEW ⚲

DT10 2AY ☎ 01258 817338 🖹 01258 818358

dir: *E of Sherborne on A3030*

Legend has it that King's Stag in the Blackmore Vale owes its name to Henry III's favourite white hart, hunted down and killed by a local nobleman. Built 400 years ago and full of oak beams, the pub has five separate dining areas where you can order anything from a snack to a banquet. The Sunday carvery offers a choice of five meats and eight vegetables – booking is essential.

Open 11–3 5.30–12 (Sat-Sun all day) **Bar Meals** L served all week 12–2.30 D served all week 6–9 Av main course £7 **Restaurant** L served all week 12–2.30 D served all week 6–9 ⊕ Enterprise Inns ◀ Exmoor, Spitfire, HBC, London Pride. ⚲ 9 **Facilities** Children's licence Garden Dogs allowed Parking Play Area

LODERS   MAP 04 SY49

Loders Arms

DT6 3SA ☎ 01308 422431

e-mail: janelegg@aol.com

dir: *Off A3066, 2m NE of Bridport*

Unassuming stone-built local tucked away in a pretty thatched village close to the Dorset coast. Arrive early to bag a seat in the long cosy bar or the homely dining room. A selection of mains includes scallops in Pernod and cream; fusilli with roasted vegetables, feta and pesto; wild boar sausages; and rack of lamb studded with garlic. There's a lovely garden with views of Boarsbarrow Hill, and a skittle alley that doubles as a function room.

Open 11.30–3 6–11 (Sun 11.30–11) **Bar Meals** L served all week 12.30–2 D served all week 7.15–9 **Restaurant** L served all week 12.30–2 D served all week 7.15–9 ⊕ Palmers ◀ Palmers Copper, Palmers IPA, Palmers 200. **Facilities** Garden Dogs allowed Parking

---

LOWER ANSTY   MAP 04 ST70

The Fox Inn ★★★★ INN ⚲

DT2 7PN ☎ 01258 880328 🖹 01258 881440

e-mail: foxinnansty@tiscali.co.uk

dir: *A35 from Dorchester towards Poole for 4m, exit signed Piddlehinton/Athelhampton House, left to Cheselbourne, then right. Pub in village opposite post office*

Looking more like a grand rectory than a pub, the 250–year-old Fox was built for brewer Charles Hall, later to co-found Blandford's Hall & Woodhouse brewery, whose Badger beers are, naturally enough, served in the bar. Typical main courses are pot-roasted half duck with cherry compôte and red wine jus; sautéed tiger prawn in sweet pepper and tomato sauce; and grilled fillet steak glazed with Dorset Blue Vinny cheese and herb mash.

Open 11–11 (Sun 12–10.30) **Bar Meals** L served all week 12–2 D served all week 6.30–9 **Restaurant** L served all week 12–2 D served all week 6.30–9 (Sun 12–3 Carvery) ⊕ Hall & Woodhouse ◀ Badger Tanglefoot, Badger Best, Badger Smooth & seasonal guest ale. ⚲ 11 **Facilities** Garden Parking

---

LYME REGIS   MAP 04 SY39

Pilot Boat Inn ⚲

Bridge St DT7 3QA ☎ 01297 443157

dir: *Telephone for directions*

Old smuggling and sea rescue tales are associated with this busy town centre pub, close to the sea front. However its biggest claim to fame is as the birthplace of the original Lassie, Hollywood's favourite collie. A good range of food offers sandwiches, salads and cold platters, Dorset chicken with cider sauce, local crab, real scampi and chips, and other fresh fish as available. There's also a good vegetarian choice, and a vegan three-bean casserole.

Open 11–11 Closed: 25 Dec **Bar Meals** L served all week 12–10 D served all week **Restaurant** L served all week 12–10 ⊕ Palmers ◀ Palmers Dorset Gold, IPA, 200, Bridport Bitter. ⚲ 8 **Facilities** Garden Dogs allowed

England

MARSHWOOD

MAP 04 SY39

Pick of the Pubs

The Bottle Inn ☻

DT6 5QJ ☎ 01297 678254 🖹 01297 678739

e-mail: thebottleinn@msn.com

dir: *On B3165 (Crewkerne to Lyme Regis road)*

The thatched Bottle Inn was first mentioned as an ale house back in the 17th century, and was the first pub in the area during the 18th century to serve bottled beer rather than beer from the jug – hence the name. Standing beside the B3165 on the edge of the glorious Marshwood Vale, its rustic interior has simple wooden settles, scrubbed tables and a blazing fire. Proprietor Shane Pym loves introducing new dishes onto the menu, and recent additions have included local pork tenderloin with a cream and stilton sauce; Highland chicken stuffed with smoked salmon and served with a whisky and mustard sauce; for vegetarians there is aubergine in oregano batter with caramelised onions and goat's cheese; and fish lovers will surely go for monkfish with a sun-dried tomato pesto, wrapped in Parma ham. Taking the organic food theme to its furthest reaches, the pub is home to the annual World Stinging-Nettle Eating Championships.

Open 12–3 6.30–11 **Bar Meals** L served all week 12–2 D served all week 6.30–9 Av main course £8.50 **Restaurant** L served all week D served all week ⊕ Free House ◀ Otter Ale & 3 guest ales. ☻ 7 **Facilities** Garden Parking Play Area

MILTON ABBAS

MAP 04 ST80

The Hambro Arms ☻

DT11 0BP ☎ 01258 880233

e-mail: info@hambroarms.co.uk

dir: *A354 (Dorchester to Blandford road), turn off at Royal Oak*

Traditional whitewashed 18th-century thatched pub located in a picturesque landscaped village. Enjoy an appetising bar snack or perhaps half shoulder of lamb with minted redcurrant sauce, liver and bacon, duck with orange sauce, venison sausages, or grilled sea bass, in the comfortable lounge bar or on the popular patio.

Open 11–3 6.30–11 (May-Sep 11–11) **Bar Meals** L served all week 12–2 D served all week 7–9 **Restaurant** L served all week 12–2 D served all week 7–9 ⊕ Free House ◀ Abbot Ale, Ringwood. **Facilities** Parking

MOTCOMBE

MAP 04 ST82

The Coppleridge Inn ☻

SP7 9HW ☎ 01747 851980 🖹 01747 851858

e-mail: thecoppleridgeinn@btinternet.com

dir: *Take A350 towards Warminster for 1.5m, turn left at brown tourist sign. Follow signs to inn*

An 18th-century dairy farm converted in the 1980s, the Coppleridge has been run by the Goodinge family for nearly 20 years. Flagstone floors and stripped pine add a traditional touch to the bar and restaurant. The daily-changing menu, based when possible on local produce, offers the full range of pub snacks, plus starters like venison faggot and main courses such as baked whole trout with cider. Large garden and terrace with Blackmore Vale views; secure children's playground.

The Coppleridge Inn

Open 11–3 5–11 (Sat-Sun all day) **Bar Meals** L served all week 12–2.30 D served all week 6–9 **Restaurant** L served all week 12–2.30 D served all week 6–9.30 ⊕ Free House ◀ Butcombe Bitter, Greene King IPA, Wadworth 6X, Fuller's London Pride. ☻ 10 **Facilities** Garden Dogs allowed Parking Play Area **Rooms** available

NETTLECOMBE

MAP 04 SY59

Marquis of Lorne ☻

DT6 3SY ☎ 01308 485236 🖹 01308 485666

e-mail: enquiries@marquisoflorne.com

dir: *B3066 (Bridport-Beaminster road), turn approx 1.5m N of Bridport. N of Gorecross Business Park, rdbt, through West Norton, 1m, straight over junct to Nettlecombe, inn at top of hill, 300yds on left*

A 16th-century farmhouse converted into a pub in 1871, when the Marquis himself named it to prove land ownership. Membership of the Campaign for Real Food means that much local produce is used. Daily menus offer such dishes as pigeon breast with juniper and red wine sauce, home-made curry, fresh cod fillet, and mushroom and pepper stroganoff. Desserts might be rum and chocolate truffle terrine or twice baked cheesecake. Superb gardens with beautiful views.

Open 12–3 6.30–11 (Sun all day) **Bar Meals** L served all week 12–2 D served all week 7–9.30 Av main course £10 **Restaurant** L served all week 12–2 D served all week 7–9.30 Av 3 course à la carte £20 ⊕ Palmers ◀ Palmers Copper, IPA, 200 Premium Ale. ☻ 12 **Facilities** Garden Dogs allowed Parking Play Area

NORTH WOOTTON

MAP 04 ST61

The Three Elms ☻

DT9 5JW ☎ 01935 812881 🖹 01935 812881

dir: *From Sherborne take A352 towards Dorchester then A3030. Pub 1m on right*

Real ales and locally produced ciders await you at this family-run free house overlooking scenic Blackmore Vale. Stunning views can be enjoyed from the pub garden, and the landlord prides himself on his impressive collection of about 1,600 model cars, as well as number plates from every state in America. Wide-ranging menu includes dishes like rosemary-crusted trout fillet, minted lamb shank, chicken Kiev and mixed grill. Extensive range of starters, snacks and sandwiches.

Open 11–2.30 6.30–11 (Sun 12–3, 7–10.30) Closed: 25–26 Dec **Bar Meals** L served all week 12–2 D served all week 6.30–10 (Sun 7–10) **Restaurant** L served all week 12–2 D served all week 6.30–10 ⊕ Free House ◀ Fuller's London Pride, Butcombe Bitter, Otter Ale. ☻ 10 **Facilities** Garden Dogs allowed Parking Play Area

OSMINGTON MILLS MAP 04 SY78

The Smugglers Inn ♀

DT3 6HF ☎ 01305 833125 ▤ 01305 832219

e-mail: smugglers.weymouth@hall-woodhouse.co.uk

dir: *7m E of Weymouth towards Wareham, pub signed*

Set on the cliffs at Osmington Mill with the South Coast Footpath running through the garden, the inn has beautiful views across Weymouth Bay. In the late 18th century it was the base of infamous smuggler Pierre Latour who fell in love with the publican's daughter, Arabella Carless, who was shot dead while helping him to escape during a raid. Typical dishes are chicken and bacon salad, chargrilled rump steak, and Sussex smokey (fish pie).

Open 11–11 (Sun 12–10.30) **Bar Meals** L served all week 11–6 D served all week 12–9 Av main course £7 **Restaurant** L served all week 11–6 D served all week 12–9 ⊕ Hall & Woodhouse ♀ 12 **Facilities** Children's licence Garden Dogs allowed Parking Play Area

---

PIDDLEHINTON MAP 04 SY79

The Thimble Inn

DT2 7TD ☎ 01300 348270

e-mail: thimbleinn@googlemail.com

dir: *A35 W'bound, right onto B3143, Piddlehinton in 4m*

Friendly village local with open fires, traditional pub games and good food cooked to order. The pub stands in a pretty valley on the banks of the River Piddle, and the riverside patio is popular in summer. The extensive menu ranges from sandwiches and jacket potatoes to fish choices like poached halibut on leek and white sauce; and grilled trout with almonds.

Open 12–2.30 7–11 (Sun 7–10.30) Closed: 25 Dec **Bar Meals** L served all week 12–2 D served all week 7–9 Av main course £8 **Restaurant** L served all week 12–2 D served all week 7–9 ⊕ Free House ◀ Ringwood Best, Palmer Copper Ale & Palmer IPA, Ringwood Old Thumper, Summer Lightning. **Facilities** Garden Dogs allowed Parking

---

PIDDLETRENTHIDE MAP 04 SY79

The Piddle Inn ♀

DT2 7QF ☎ 01300 348468 ▤ 01300 348102

e-mail: piddleinn@aol.com

dir: *7m N of Dorchester on B3143, in village centre*

This friendly village free house has been a pub since the 1760s, and was originally a stopover for prisoners in transit between the jails at Dorchester and Sherborne. Traditional pub games and real ales straight from the barrel accompany pub favourites like jacket potatoes; home-made chilli con carne; and Cumberland sausage and mash. The river Piddle flows past the popular beer garden.

Open 12–3 6–11 **Bar Meals** L served Tue-Sun 12–2 D served Mon-Fri 6.30–9 (Sat-Sun 12–9) **Restaurant** L served Tue-Sun 12–2 D served Mon-Sun 6.30–9 ⊕ Free House ◀ Greene King IPA, Ringwood Best, Ringwood 49er. ♀ 8 **Facilities** Children's licence Garden Dogs allowed Parking

The Poachers Inn ★★★★ INN ♀

DT2 7QX ☎ 01300 348358 ▤ 01300 348153

e-mail: info@ thepoachersinn.co.uk

dir: *6m N from Dorchester on B3143. At the Church end of Piddletrenthide*

This family-run inn beside the River Piddle continues to provide real ales, good food, fires and traditional pub games right in the heart of Thomas Hardy country. The riverside patio is especially popular in summer. There's an extensive menu, supported by daily specials that may include home-made spaghetti bolognese; seafood salad with lemon and dill; or pork and leek sausages with mustard mash. Leave room for traditional red and blackcurrant crumble!

Open 9–12 **Bar Meals** L served all week 12–9.30 D served all week 12–9.30 **Restaurant** L served all week 12–9.30 D served all week 12–9.30 Av 2 course fixed price £10 ⊕ Free House **Facilities** Garden Dogs allowed Parking **Rooms** 21

PLUSH MAP 04 ST70

The Brace of Pheasants ♀

DT2 7RQ ☎ 01300 348357 ▤ 01300 348959

e-mail: information@braceofpheasants.co.uk

dir: *A35 onto B3143, 5m to Piddletrenthide, then R to Mappowder & Plush*

Tucked away in a fold of the hills in the heart of Hardy's beloved county is this pretty 16th-century thatched village inn. With a welcoming open fire, oak beams and fresh flowers, it's an ideal place to start or end a walk. A lunch menu might offer crab, cheddar and saffron cream tarts; while for dinner pan-fried strips of chicken breast with chorizo, lime juice, cream and basmati rice could be an option.

Open 12–3 7–11 (Sun 12–3, 7–10.30) Closed: 25 Dec & Mon (ex BH) **Bar Meals** L served Tue-Sun 12.30–2.30 D served Tue-Sun 7–9.30 **Restaurant** L served Tue-Sun 12–1.30 D served Tue-Sun 7–9.30 ⊕ Free House ◀ Timothy Taylor Landlord, Ringwood Best, Dorset Brewing Co. & Palmers. ♀ 8 **Facilities** Garden Dogs allowed Parking

POOLE
MAP 04 SZ09

The Guildhall Tavern Ltd ♥

15 Market St BH15 1NB ☎ 01202 671717 🖹 01202 242346
e-mail: sewerynsevfred@aol.com

dir: *2 mins from Quay*

This former cider house is located in the Old Town, just two minutes from Poole Quay. It is owned by Severine and Frederic Grande, whose French influence is evident throughout the bi-lingual menu. Snacks and sandwiches include croque monsieur and French onion soup, while main meals range through double baked cheese soufflé; wild whole sea bass flambéed with Pernod; and hazelnut meringue with fresh raspberries.

Open 11–3.30 6.15–11 Closed: 1st 2wks Nov & Mon **Bar Meals** L served Tue-Sun 11–2.30 **Restaurant** L served Tue-Sun 12–2.30 D served Tue-Sun 6.30–9.30 Av 3 course à la carte £25 ⊕ Punch Taverns ◀ Ringwood Best. ♥ 7 **Facilities** Parking

POWERSTOCK
MAP 04 SY59

Pick of the Pubs

Three Horseshoes Inn ♥

DT6 3TF ☎ 01308 485328
e-mail: info@threehorseshoesinn.com

dir: *3m from Bridport off A3066 (Beaminster road)*

Popularly known as the Shoes, this pretty, rural Victorian inn is surrounded by some of Dorset's finest scenery. In the restaurant, fresh local produce is used wherever possible; even the herbs, for example, are picked each day from the garden. Light lunches are available, with the main carte coming into play in the evening. From these choose starters of grilled goats' cheese salad with tomato and pinenut dressing; seared scallops with orange and fennel broth; or deep-fried prawns with chilli. Main courses include Powerstock organic lamb noisettes with roasted pepper and almond dressing; braised rabbit, wild mushroom and green peppercorn sauce; pan-fried pigeon breasts with bourguignon sauce; Dorset crab mornay; and honey- and soy-roasted red snapper fillet with saffron potatoes, courgettes and mixed leaves. Desserts – all home made – include lime and ginger cheesecake, and strawberry and basil crème brûlée.

Open 11–3 6.30–11 (Sun 12–3, 6.30–10.30) **Bar Meals** L served week 12–2.30 D served all week 7–9 (Sun 12–2.30, 7–8.30) Av main course £11 **Restaurant** L served all week 12–2.30 D served all week 7–9 (Sun 7–8.30) Av 3 course à la carte £21 ⊕ Palmers ◀ Palmer's IPA, Copper Ale. ♥ 7 **Facilities** Garden Dogs allowed Parking Play Area **Rooms** available

PUNCKNOWLE
MAP 04 SY58

The Crown Inn ♥

Church St DT2 9BN ☎ 01308 897711 🖹 01308 898282

dir: *From A35, into Bridevally, through Litton Cheney. From B3157, inland at Swyre.*

There's a traditional atmosphere within the rambling, low-beamed bars at this picturesque 16th-century thatched inn, which was once the haunt of smugglers on their way from nearby Chesil Beach to visit prosperous customers in Bath. Food ranges from light snacks and sandwiches to home-made dishes like lamb chops with mint sauce; mushroom and nut pasta with French bread; and tuna steak with basil and tomato sauce.

Open 11–3 7–11 (Sun 12–3, 7–10.30 Summer 6.30–11) Closed: 25 Dec **Bar Meals** L served all week 12–2 D served all week 7–9 (Summer Mon-Fri 6.30–9) Av main course £7.60 ⊕ Palmers ◀ Palmers IPA, 200 Premium Ale, Copper, Tally Ho!. ♥ 10 **Facilities** Garden Dogs allowed Parking **Notes** ☺

SHERBORNE
MAP 04 ST61

The Digby Tap

Cooks Ln DT9 3NS ☎ 01935 813148
e-mail: peter@lefevre.fslife.co.uk

dir: *Telephone for directions*

Old-fashioned town pub with stone-flagged floors, old beams and a wide-ranging choice of real ale. A hearty menu of pub grub includes lasagne, steak and kidney pie, rump steak, gammon steak, and plaice or cod. The pub was used as a location for the 1990 TV drama *A Murder of Quality*, that starred Denholm Elliot and Glenda Jackson. Scenes from the film can be seen on the pub walls.

Open 11–2.30 5.30–11 (Sat 6–11, Sun 12–3, 7–10.30) Closed: 1 Jan **Bar Meals** L served Mon-Sat 12–1.45 ⊕ Free House ◀ Ringwood Best, Otter Ale, Sharp's Cornish Coaster & Cornish Jack, St Austell Tinners. **Facilities** Dogs allowed **Notes** ☺

Half Moon Inn ♥

Half Moon St DT9 3LN
☎ 01935 812017 🖹 01935 818130
e-mail: halfmoon@eldridge-pope.co.uk

dir: *Telephone for directions*

Standing opposite Sherborne Abbey in the heart of this charming Dorset town, the Half Moon is at the centre of local life. There's a choice of real ales, 11 wines served by the glass, and great food is served all day. Daily specials supplement the wide-ranging themed menus; typical choices include roast pork hock; chilli prawn bruschetta; Mediterranean stuffed peppers; and fisherman's crumble. Sunday roasts, desserts and children's menus are also offered.

Open 11–11 **Bar Meals** L served all week 11–6 D served all week 6–9.15 Av main course £7.95 **Restaurant** L served all week 11–3 D served all week 6–9.30 ⊕ Marstons ◀ Wadworth 6X, Otter 3.6. ♥ 11 **Facilities** Garden Parking

SHERBORNE continued

Queen's Head

High St, Milborne Port DT9 5DQ
☎ 01963 250314 📄 01963 250339
dir: *On A30*

Milborne Port has no facilities for shipping, the suffix being Old English for 'borough', a status it acquired in 1249. The building came much later, in Elizabethan times, although no mention is made of it as a hostelry until 1738. Charming and friendly bars, restaurant, beer garden and skittle alley combine to make it a popular free house in these parts.

Open 12–2.30 5.30–11 (Sun 12–10.30) **Bar Meals** L served Sat-Sun 12–1.40 D served Sat-Sun 7–9.30 (Mon-Tue 7–8.40, Wed-Fri 7–9.10) Av main course £8 **Restaurant** L served Sat-Sun 12–2 D served Sat-Sun 7–9.30 (Mon-Tue 7–8.40, Wed-Fri 7–9.10) Av 3 course à la carte £16 🌐 Enterprise Inns ◀ Butcombe Bitters, Fuller's London Pride, Hopback Summer Lightning. **Facilities** Children's licence Garden Dogs allowed Parking

Skippers Inn ☻

Horsecastles DT9 3HE ☎ 01935 812753
e-mail: chrisfrowde@tiscali.co.uk
dir: *From Yeovil A30 to Sherborne*

'You don't need a newspaper in Skippers, read the walls'. So says the proprietor about his end-of-terrace converted cider house, and Sherborne's self-styled premier fish restaurant. The crammed blackboard menu has everything from game, duck, chicken and venison to steaks, sandwiches, soup, and around 12 fresh fish dishes. On Sunday there are three roasts to choose from.

Open 11–12 (Winter 11–2.30, 6–11) Closed: 25 Dec **Bar Meals** L served Mon-Sat 11.15–2 D served Mon-Sat 6.30–9.30 (Sun 12–3, 7–10.30) **Restaurant** L served Mon-Sat 11.15–2 D served Mon-Sat 6.30–9.30 (Sun 12–2, 7–9) 🌐 Wadworth ◀ Wadworth 6X & Henrys IPA, Butcombe Bitter & guest ales. ☻8 **Facilities** Garden Parking

White Hart ☻

Bishops Caundle DT9 5ND
☎ 01963 23301 📄 01963 23301
e-mail: info@whitehartcarvery.co.uk
dir: *On A3030 between Sherborne & Sturminster Newton. 4m*

Located in the heart of the Blackmore Vale, the White Hart, dating from the 16th century was reputedly used as a courthouse by the infamous Judge Jeffries. The large enclosed family garden offers beautiful views of the wonderful Bullbarrow Hill, as well as play equipment and an

adventure trail for children. The extensive menu starts with baguettes, jacket potatoes and ploughman's, plus there are vegetarian options and a carvery, always with six choices. Jazz evenings.

Open 11.30–3 6.30–11 (Sun 12–3, 7–10.30) **Bar Meals** L served all week 12–2 D served all week 7–9 **Restaurant** L served all week 12–2 D served all week 7–9 🌐 Hall & Woodhouse ◀ Badger Gold & Hopping Hare. **Facilities** Garden Dogs allowed Parking Play Area

SHROTON OR IWERNE COURTNEY

MAP 04 ST81

Pick of the Pubs

The Cricketers ☻

DT11 8QD ☎ 01258 860421 📄 01258 861800
e-mail: cricketers@heartstoneinns.co.uk
dir: *7m S of Shaftesbury on A350, turn right after Iwerne Minster. 5m N of Blandford Forum on A360, past Stourpaine, in 2m left into Shroton. Pub in village centre*

The Cricketers nestles under Hambledon Hill, which is renowned for its Iron-Age hill-forts. A classically English pub, built at the turn of the 20th century, it is above all a welcoming local. The open plan interior comprises a main bar, sports bar and den – all light and airy rooms leading to the restaurant at the rear. This in turn overlooks a lovely garden, well stocked with trees and flowers. Inside, the cricket theme is taken up in the collection of sports memorabilia on display, and during the summer months the local cricket team really does frequent the establishment. The pub is also popular with hikers, lured from the Wessex Way, which runs conveniently through the garden. expect a menu of fresh daily choices and specials, with perhaps locally shot venison and pheasant, and fish direct from the Cornish coast.

Open 12–3 6–11 **Bar Meals** L served Mon-Sat 12–2.30 D served all week 6.30–9.30 (Sun 12–3) Av main course £12 **Restaurant** L served Mon-Sat 12–2.30 D served all week 6.30–9.30 (Sun 12–3) 🌐 Free House ◀ Tribute Cornish Ale, Ringwood Best, Butcombe. ☻10 **Facilities** Garden Parking

STOKE ABBOTT   MAP 04 ST40

The New Inn

DT8 3JW ☎ 01308 868333

dir: *1.5m from Beaminster*

A welcoming 17th-century farmhouse turned village inn, with thatched roof, log fires and a beautiful garden. It offers three real ales, and an extensive menu of light meals such as grilled black pudding with caramelised apples, and cold smoked duck breast with plum chutney, plus a good choice of baguettes, sandwiches and vegetarian dishes. Specials might include pork schnitzel with sweet chili dip, scallops wrapped in bacon, and beef and mushroom pie.

Open 12–3 7–11 (Sun 12–3 only) Closed: Mon **Bar Meals** L served Tue-Sun 12–1.30 D served Tue-Sat 7–8.30 **Restaurant** L served all week 12–1.30 D served all week 7–8.30 ⊕ Palmers ◀ Palmers IPA & 200 Premium Ale, Tally Ho, Copper IPA. **Facilities** Garden Dogs allowed Parking

STOURPAINE   MAP 04 ST80

The White Horse Inn ♥

Shaston Rd DT11 8TA ☎ 01258 453535 📠 01258 453535

dir: *From Blandford Forum on A350 towards Shaftesbury*

Typical village pub dating back to the early 18th century, sympathetically refurbished and extended. Inside, are an inglenook fireplace and two dining rooms, one opening on to the decked patio. The menu offers home-baked ham, eggs and chips; pan-fried duck breast with black cherries and brandy sauce; wholetail deep-fried scampi and chips; and mixed vegetable, pasta and blue cheese bake. Hod Hill Roman fort and the River Stour are within easy reach.

Open 12–3 6–11 (Fri-Sat 6–12) **Bar Meals** L served all week 12–2 D served Tue-Sun 6–9 **Restaurant** L served all week 12–2 D served Tue-Sun 6–9 ⊕ Hall & Woodhouse ◀ Badgers Best, Festive Pheasant, Fursty Ferret, Sussex. ♥ 8 **Facilities** Children's licence Garden Dogs allowed Parking

STRATTON   MAP 04 SY69

Saxon Arms ♥

DT2 9WG ☎ 01305 260020 📠 01305 264225

e-mail: rodsaxonlamont1@yahoo.co.uk

dir: *3m NW of Dorchester on A37, pub at back of village green between church & new village hall*

A massive thatched roof, a patio overlooking the village green, solid oak beams, flagstone floors and a log-burning stove provide a great atmosphere. Menus offer steak and ale pie, local butcher's pork and herb sausages, lasagne verde, and chicken, bacon and tarragon pie, while the specials boards may conjure up scallop and tiger prawn brochette, Portland crab, or beef in Guinness casserole. Either way, leave room for one of the many desserts.

Open 11–2.30 5.30–11 (Sat-Sun all day) **Bar Meals** L served all week 11.30–2.30 D served all week 6–9.30 **Restaurant** L served Mon-Sat 11.30–2.30 D served Mon-Sat 6–9.30 (Sun 12–9) ⊕ Free House ◀ Fuller's London Pride, Palmers IPA, Ringwood, Timothy Taylor. ♥ 15 **Facilities** Garden Dogs allowed Parking

STUDLAND   MAP 05 SZ08

The Bankes Arms Hotel

Watery Ln BH19 3AU

☎ 01929 450225 📠 01929 450307

web: www.bankesarms.com

dir: *B3369 from Poole, across on Sandbanks chain ferry, or A35 from Poole, A351 then B3351*

Close to sweeping Studland Bay, across which can be seen the prime real estate enclave of Sandbanks, is this part 15th-century, creeper-clad inn, once a smugglers' dive. It specialises in fresh fish and seafood, but also offers game casserole, lamb noisettes in mint, honey and orange sauce, and spicy pork in chilli, coriander and caper sauce. The annual beer festival held in its large garden showcases 60 real ales, music, Morris dancing and stone carving.

Open 11–11 Closed: 25 Dec **Bar Meals** L served all week 12–9.30 D served all week 12–9.30 (Winter 12.30–3, 6–9.30) **Restaurant** L served all week 12.30–3 D served all week 6–9.30 ⊕ Free House ◀ Isle of Purbeck Fossil Fuel, Studland Bay Wrecked, Solar Power & IPA. **Facilities** Children's licence Garden Dogs allowed Parking **Rooms** available

SYDLING ST NICHOLAS   MAP 04 SY69

The Greyhound Inn ★★★★ INN ♥

DT2 9PD ☎ 01300 341303 📠 01300 341303

e-mail: info@thegreyhounddorset.co.uk

dir: *Off A37 (Yeovil to Dorchester road), turn off at Cerne Abbas/ Sydling St Nicholas*

The Greyhound is a lovely 17th-century inn with a walled garden set in a picturesque village. It has a growing reputation for its food served in the cosy restaurant or the bar, where you can choose between the full menu and a light snack selection. Fresh local seafood features, including mussels with cider, leeks and cream, and fillet of sea bass in tempura batter. Otherwise chicken tagine or steak and kidney pudding.

Open 11–2.30 6–11 (Sun 12–3.30) **Bar Meals** L served Mon-Sat 12–2 D served all week 6.30–9 (Sun 12–2.30) **Restaurant** L served all week 12–2 D served all week 6.30–9 ⊕ Free House ◀ Palmer IPA, Wadworth 6X, St Austell Tinners, Old Speckled Hen & Spitfire. ♥ 12 **Facilities** Garden Parking Play Area **Rooms** 6

TARRANT MONKTON
MAP 04 ST90

The Langton Arms ★★★★ INN ⊛ ♀
DT11 8RX ☎ 01258 830225 🖹 01258 830053
e-mail: info@thelangtonarms.co.uk
dir: *A31 from Ringwood, or A357 from Shaftesbury, or A35 from Bournemouth*

An attractive 17th-century thatched inn occupying a peaceful spot in the village centre close to the church. Real ales from four pumps include a couple of oft-changing guests, while the Stables restaurant and conservatory caters comfortably for local food enthusiasts: start with marinated crispy strips of Tarrant Valley beef; and follow with slow braised Dorset lamb's liver and smoked bacon. You could finish with a good selection of regional cheeses, or lemon drizzle sponge cake with Dorset clotted cream.

Open 11.30–12 (Sun 12–10.30) **Bar Meals** L served Mon-Fri 11.30–2.30 D served Mon-Fri 6–9.30 (Sat-Sun all day) **Restaurant** L served Sun 12–2 D served Wed-Sat 7–9 ⊞ Free House ◀ Ringwood Best Bitter, Hidden Pint, Hidden Pleasure, 2 guest ales. ♀7 **Facilities** Garden Parking Play Area **Rooms** 6

TRENT
MAP 04 ST51

Pick of the Pubs

Rose & Crown Inn NEW ♀
DT9 4SL ☎ 01935 850776 🖹 01935 850776
e-mail: hkirkie@hotmail.com
dir: *Just off A30 between Sherborne & Yeovil*

An old, but newly refurbished, thatched and ivy-clad pub in a conservation village. It was actually built for the men erecting the church spire opposite in the 16th century – quite a perk, one imagines. Inside, the Trent Barrow Room, with a massive open fire, plenty of seating, old bottles and books, is somewhere to retire when the drinks have been bought. Although new to the trade, the pub's owners, Heather Kirk and Stuart Malcolm, have quickly come up with some appealing menus. Sandwiches apart, lunch could be a three-course meal starting with woodland mushroom and Blue Vinny soup; then wild boar and apple sausages with colcannon mash and merlot gravy; and lemon tart with raspberry coulis to follow. In the evening, dinner might comprise duck foie gras and pistachio terrine with plum relish; grilled lemon sole with samphire, crushed potatoes, lime and caper berry sauce; and forest fruit crumble.

Open 12–3 6–11 (Sat-Sun & BH, all day) Closed: Mon **Bar Meals** L served Tue-Fri & Sun 12–3 D served Tue-Fri 6–10 (Sat all day) Av main course £12 **Restaurant** L served Tue-Sun 12–3 D served Tue-Sun 6–10 Av 3 course à la carte £22 Av 2 course fixed price £9.95 ⊞ Wadworth ◀ 6X, Henry's IPA & Horizon. ♀8 **Facilities** Garden Dogs allowed Parking Play Area

WEST BEXINGTON
MAP 04 SY58

The Manor Hotel ★★ HL ♀
DT2 9DF ☎ 01308 897616 🖹 01308 897704
e-mail: themanorhotel@btconnect.com
dir: *On B3157, 5m E of Bridport*

Overlooking the Jurassic Coast's most famous feature, Chesil Beach, parts of this ancient manor house date from the 11th century. It offers an inviting mix of flagstones, Jacobean oak panelling, roaring fires, comfortable en suite rooms, and a cosy cellar bar serving Dorset beer and organic cider. Locally sourced dishes include grilled John Dory; Peggy's Gloucester Old Spot sausages; butternut squash risotto; and, in season, jugged hare. Muddy boots, dogs or children won't raise any eyebrows.

Open 11–11 **Bar Meals** L served all week 12–2 D served all week 6.30–9.30 **Restaurant** L served all week 12–1.30 D served all week 7–8.30 ⊞ Free House ◀ Butcombe Gold, Harbour Master. ♀7 **Facilities** Children's licence Garden Dogs allowed Parking Play Area **Rooms** 13

WEST LULWORTH
MAP 04 SY88

The Castle Inn ♀
Main Rd BH20 5RN ☎ 01929 400311 🖹 01929 400415
dir: *Follow village signs from A352 (Dorchester to Wareham road). Inn on right on B3070 through West Lulworth. Car park opposite*

In a delightful setting near Lulworth Cove, this family-run thatched village inn lies close to plenty of good walks. The friendly bars offer a traditional atmosphere in which to enjoy a pint of Ringwood Best or Gales' ales. Outside, you'll find large tiered gardens packed with plants, and in summer there's a giant outdoor chess set. The wide-ranging menu includes grills, poultry, fish and steak dishes and flambéed dishes cooked at the table.

Open 11–3 6–11 (Winter 12–2.30, 7–11) Closed: 25 Dec **Bar Meals** L served all week 11–2.30 D served all week 6–10.30 ⊞ Free House ◀ Ringwood Best, Courage, John Smiths. ♀8 **Facilities** Garden Dogs allowed Parking

WEYMOUTH   MAP 04 SY67

The Old Ship Inn ♀

7 The Ridgeway DT3 5QQ

☎ 01305 812522 📠 01305 816533

dir: *3m from Weymouth town centre, at bottom of The Ridgeway*

Copper pans, old clocks and a beamed open fire create just the right atmosphere at this historic pub, while outside the terrace offers views over Weymouth. Thomas Hardy refers to it in his novels *Under the Greenwood Tree* and *The Trumpet Major*. A good range of jacket potatoes, baguettes and salads is supplemented by traditional pub favourites, and there are fish dishes among the daily specials.

Open 12–12 (Sun 12–10.30) **Bar Meals** L served all week 12–2.30 D served all week 6–9.30 (Sun 12–4) Av main course £10.95 **Restaurant** L served Mon-Sat 12–2 D served all week 6–9.30 (Sun 12–4) Av 3 course à la carte £11.45 ⊕ Punch Taverns ◀ Greene King, Old Speckled Hen, Ringwood Best & guest ales. ♀ 7 **Facilities** Children's licence Garden Dogs allowed Parking

---

WINTERBORNE ZELSTON   MAP 04 SY89

Botany Bay Inne ♀

DT11 9ET ☎ 01929 459227

dir: *A31 between Bere Regis & Wimborne Minster*

An obvious question: how did the pub get its name? Built in the 1920s as The General Allenby, it was changed about 17 years ago in belated recognition of prisoners from Dorchester jail who were required to spend a night nearby before transportation to Australia. Since no such fate awaits anyone these days, meals to enjoy at leisure include bacon-wrapped chicken breast; steak and kidney pudding; roasted Mediterranean vegetable Wellington; and fish catch of the day. Real ales are locally brewed.

Open 11.30–3 6–11 (Mon-Sat summer 10–11) **Bar Meals** L served all week 12–2.15 D served all week 6.30–9.30 Av main course £7 **Restaurant** L served all week 12–2.15 D served all week 6.30–9.30 Av 3 course à la carte £17 ◀ Badger Best Bitter, Tanglefoot, Botany Bay Bitter, Fursty Ferret. ♀ 7 **Facilities** Children's licence Garden Dogs allowed

CO DURHAM

AYCLIFFE   MAP 19 NZ22

The County ♀

13 The Green, Aycliffe Village DL5 6LX

☎ 01325 312273 📠 01325 312273

e-mail: colettefarrell@btinternet.com

dir: *Off A167 into Aycliffe*

Quietly positioned overlooking an award-winning village green, the County can be found in Aycliffe village some four miles north of Darlington. It came into new ownership in January 2008, but the selection of good real ales remains, backed by half a dozen wines served by the glass. The bistro-type daily specials board adds variety to the menu of starters like cream of butter bean and parmesan soup with poached egg, and main courses such as plaice fillets filled with crabmeat.

Open 12–3 6–11 Closed: 25–26 Dec, 1 Jan & Sun eve **Bar Meals** L served Mon-Sat 12–2 D served Mon-Sat 6–9 (Sun 12–2.30) Av main course £11 **Restaurant** L served Mon-Sat 12–2 D served Mon-Sat 6–9 (Sun 12–2.30) Av 3 course à la carte £23 ⊕ Free House ◀ Wells Bombardier, Jennings Cumberland Ale, Castle Eden & Camerons, Theakstons Best. ♀ 7 **Facilities** Parking

---

BARNARD CASTLE   MAP 19 NZ01

Pick of the Pubs

The Morritt Arms Hotel ★★★ HL ♀

Greta Bridge DL12 9SE

☎ 01833 627232 📠 01833 627392

e-mail: relax@themorritt.co.uk

dir: *At Scotch Corner take A66 towards Penrith, after 9m turn at Greta Bridge. Hotel over bridge on left.*

Situated in rural Teesdale, The Morritt Arms has been an inn for two centuries. Here the carte offers starters of smoked haddock and potato chowder; roast pear and goats' cheese salad with a citrus reduction; seared scallops topped with a lemon crust served with a petit salad and chive oil; sweet melon and poached fruits with a port and orange syrup; and grilled black pudding with pan-fried foie gras, apricot and saffron chutney and ginger syrup. Main courses include ballantine of chicken with a wild mushroom and tarragon stuffing; cannon of lamb with a red onion crust with basil crushed potatoes and a mint and fevés jus; pan-roasted duck with parmentier potatoes and sautéed pancetta finished with honey and pepper jus; and risotto of wild mushrooms and artichokes, with deep-fried Swaledale cheese beignets. For more informal meals choose the bar, Pallatt's bistro, or the landscaped gardens.

Open 11–11 (Sun 11–10.30) **Bar Meals** L served all week 12–3 D served all week 6–9.30 (Sun 6–9) Av main course £12 **Restaurant** L served all week 12–3 D served all week 6–9.30 (Sun 7–9) Av 3 course à la carte £25 ⊕ Free House ◀ John Smith's, Timothy Taylor Landlord, Black Sheep Best, Cumberland Ale. ♀ 20 **Facilities** Garden Parking Play Area **Rooms** 27

COTHERSTONE   MAP 19 NZ01

The Fox and Hounds ♀

DL12 9PF ☎ 01833 650241 📠 01833 650518

e-mail: foxenquiries@tiscali.co.uk

dir: *4m W of Barnard Castle. From A66 onto B6277, signed*

This delightful 18th-century coaching inn in the heart of Teesdale is a perfect holiday base. Both the restaurant and the heavily beamed bar boast welcoming winter fires in original fireplaces. Fresh local ingredients are the foundation of home-made food such as a warm salad of wensleydale cheese, bacon, cranberries and apple; steak, black pudding and Black Sheep ale pie; or pan-fried crown of Holwick pheasant on bubble and squeak mash with rich gravy.

Open 12–3 6.30–11 Closed: 25–26 Dec **Bar Meals** L served all week 12–2 D served Mon-Sat 7–9 (Sun 7–8.30) **Restaurant** L served all week 12–2 D served Mon-Sat 7–9 (Sun 7–8.30) ⊕ Free House ◀ Black Sheep Best, Village Brewer Bull Bitter, Jennings Cumberland, Black Sheep Ale. ♀ 10 **Facilities** Garden Parking

DURHAM   MAP 19 NZ24

Victoria Inn

86 Hallgarth St DH1 3AS ☎ 0191 386 5269

dir: *In city centre*

Carefully nurtured by the Webster family since 1975, this unique listed inn has scarcely changed since it was built in 1899. Small rooms warmed by coal fires include the unusual off-sales booth and tiny snug, where a portrait of Queen Victoria still hangs above the upright piano. You'll find a few simple snacks to tickle the taste buds, but it's the well-kept local ales, single malts, and over 40 Irish whiskeys that are the main attraction.

Open 11.45–3 6–11 ⊕ Free House ◀ Wylam Gold Tankard, Durham Magus, Big Lamp Bitter, Jarrow Bitter. **Facilities** Dogs allowed Parking **Rooms** available

FIR TREE   MAP 19 NZ13

Duke of York Inn

DL15 8DG ☎ 01388 762848 📄 01388 767055

e-mail: suggett@firtree-crook.fsnet.co.uk

dir: *On A68 towards Scotland, 12m W of Durham*

Family owned and run for four generations, this pub offers an old world atmosphere enhanced by 'mouseman' Robert Thompson's furniture and bar fittings, and the proprietor's collection of African memorabilia and Stone Age flints. A former drovers' and coaching inn dating from 1749, it stands on the tourist route (A68) to Scotland. Typical dishes from the blackboard include home-made steak and kidney pie; fresh Amble cod in beer batter; and gammon in sherry and peaches.

Open 11–2.30 6.30–10.30 **Bar Meals** L served all week 12–2 D served all week 6.30–9 Av main course £8.95 **Restaurant** L served all week 12–2 D served all week 6.30–9 Av fixed price £20 ⊕ Free House ◀ Black Sheep, Worthington. **Facilities** Children's licence Garden Parking Play Area

HUTTON MAGNA   MAP 19 NZ11

Pick of the Pubs

The Oak Tree Inn ♥

DL11 7HH ☎ 01833 627371

dir: *6.5m along A66, W from Scotch Corner*

Expect a warm welcome at this whitewashed, part 18th-century free house run by Alastair and Claire Ross. Alastair previously spent 14 years in London working at The Savoy, Leith's and, more recently, a private members' club on the Strand. Meals in the simply furnished dining room are based around the finest local ingredients, and choices change daily depending on what is available. The three fish choices, in particular, rely on what comes in on the boats. The cooking style combines classic techniques and occasional modern flavours: you could start with crab, courgette and ginger cannelloni or warm salad of belly pork and black pudding with honey and mustard dressing. Typical mains include fillet of turbot with chive-crushed new potatoes, red pepper, tomato and black olive vinaigrette; and best end of lamb with provençale vegetables, green beans and pesto. Don't miss the list of 21 whiskies.

Open 6–11 (Sun 6–10.30) Closed: Xmas & New Year **Restaurant** D served Tue-Sun (Bookings only) Av 3 course à la carte £29.50 ⊕ Free House ◀ Wells Bombardier, Timothy Taylor Landlord & Black Sheep Best. ♥ 8 **Facilities** Dogs allowed Parking

MIDDLESTONE   MAP 19 NZ23

Ship Inn ♥

Low Rd DL14 8AB ☎ 01388 810904

dir: *On B6287 (Kirk Merrington to Coundon road)*

Beer drinkers will appreciate the string of CAMRA accolades received by this family-run pub on the village green. In the last five years regulars could have sampled well over 800 different beers. Home-cooked food is served in the bar and restaurant. The rooftop patio has spectacular views over the Tees Valley and Cleveland Hills.

Open 4–11 (Fri-Sun 12–11) **Bar Meals** L served Fri-Sun 12–2.30 D served all week 4–9 **Restaurant** L served Fri-Sun 12–2.30 D served all week 6–9 ⊕ Free House ◀ 6 guest ales. ♥ 13 **Facilities** Children's licence Dogs allowed Parking Play Area

MIDDLETON-IN-TEESDALE   MAP 18 NY92

The Teesdale Hotel ★★ HL

Market Square DL12 0QG

☎ 01833 640264 📄 01833 640651

e-mail: enquiries@teesdalehotel.com

dir: *Telephone for directions*

A tastefully modernised, family-run former coaching inn just off the Pennine Way, amid some of northern England's loveliest scenery. Noted for its striking 18th-century stone exterior and archway, while the interior is warm and friendly, with well-furnished bedrooms. All meals are home-made from local produce, with dishes typified by steak and kidney pie; gammon steak; pork chops; pan-fried Cajun salmon; chilli con carne; and vegetable goulash. Sausage and mash is a popular option for children.

Open 11–11 (Tea room open 10–4 from Etr) **Bar Meals** L served all week 12–2 D served all week 7–9 **Restaurant** L served all week 12–2.30 D served all week 7–9 ⊕ Free House ◀ Guinness, Tetley Smooth, Jennings Cumberland Ale, Jennings Red Breast. **Facilities** Dogs allowed Parking **Rooms** 14

NEWTON AYCLIFFE   MAP 19 NZ22

Blacksmiths Arms ♥

Preston le Skerne, (off Ricknall Lane) DL5 6JH

☎ 01325 314873

A former smithy dating from the 1700s, and still relatively isolated in its farmland setting. Enjoying an excellent reputation locally as a good dining pub, it offers starters of hot smoked mackerel and potato salad; cod and prawn brandade; chicken fillet goujons; and potted mushrooms. Requiring their own page on the menu are fish dishes such as grilled halibut steak with risotto, and gingered salmon. Chef's specialities include Gressingham duck breast, and pork au poivre.

Open 12–3 6–11 (Sun 6–10.30) Closed: 1 Jan & Mon **Bar Meals** L served Tue-Sat 11.30–2 D served Tue-Sat 6–9.30 (Sun 12–10.30) ⊕ Free House ◀ Ever changing selection of real ales. ♥ 10 **Facilities** Garden Parking Play Area

England

PICK OF THE PUBS

ROMALDKIRK-CO DURHAM

Rose & Crown

This substantial ivy-clad 18th-century coaching inn stands in the middle of three village greens. It overlooks ancient stocks and a water pump, not to mention the 700–year-old St Romald's Church which is also known as the Cathedral of the Dales. Step inside the award-winning inn, and you'll be met by warm smiles and the scent of fresh flowers.

Polished panelling, old beams, gleaming copper and brass artefacts, and creaking stairs add to the rustic charm. The brasserie has deep red walls decorated with large pictures of aloof French waiters. In the restaurant there's more oak panelling, crisp white tablecloths, sparkling silver and soft lights – the perfect setting for a romantic supper. Lunch in the bar from the daily changing menu could start with pan-fried haggis, neep and tattie mash and whisky cream; or a trio of smoked salmon, smoked trout and prawns with olive mayonnaise. Main courses could include grilled sea bass fillets with pea and prawn risotto; or steak, kidney and mushroom pie with Theakston's ale gravy. Desserts follow traditional lines, with the likes of hot treacle tart or toasted almond and sherry trifle. Children are well catered for with bangers, beans and chips, scrambled eggs on toast, or smoked Scotch salmon for the more sophisticated. In the evening a four-course fixed price dinner menu might offer Mr Woodall's matured Cumberland ham with fresh figs; celeriac and apple soup; pan-fried breasts of wood pigeon with parsnip tartlet; and dark chocolate torte with two sauces. A good selection of wines is served by the glass. If staying the night, twelve beautifully furnished en suite bedrooms are equipped with Bose music systems and flat-screen TVs.

★★ HL ◉◉ ♀
MAP 19 NY92
DL12 9EB
☎ 01833 650213
▤ 01833 650828
e-mail:
hotel@rose-and-crown.co.uk
dir: *6m NW from Barnard Castle on B6277*

Open 11.30–3 5.30–11 Closed: 23–27 Dec
Bar Meals L served all week 12–1.30 D served all week 6.30–9.30
Restaurant L served Sun 12–1.30 D served all week 7.30–9
⊕ Free House ◀ Theakston Best, Black Sheep Best, Emmerdale.
♀ 14
Facilities Children's licence Dogs allowed Parking
Rooms 12

England

ROMALDKIRK
MAP 19 NY92

Pick of the Pubs

Rose & Crown ★★ HL ◉◉ ♀

See Pick of the Pubs on page 197

SEDGEFIELD
MAP 19 NZ32

Dun Cow Inn ♀
43 Front St TS21 3AT ☎ 01740 620894 📠 01740 622163

dir: *At junct of A177 & A689. Inn in village centre*

An interesting array of bric-a-brac can be viewed inside this splendid old village inn, which has many flower baskets bedecking its exterior in summer. Typical offerings include Angus sirloin steaks, locally-made sausages, spring lamb cutlets, fresh Shetland mussels, and mushroom stroganoff. Pudding choices often include gooseberry crumble and chocolate fudge cake with butterscotch sauce.

Open 11–3 6.30–11 (Sun 12–11) **Bar Meals** L served Mon-Sat 12–2 D served Mon-Sat 6.30–9.30 (Sun 12–8.30) **Restaurant** L served Mon-Sat 12–2 D served Mon-Sat 7–9.30 (Sun 12–8.30) ⊕ Free House ◀ Theakston Best Bitter, John Smiths Smooth, Black Sheeps Bitter & guest ales. ♀ 8 **Facilities** Parking

TRIMDON
MAP 19 NZ33

The Bird in Hand
Salters Ln TS29 6JQ ☎ 01429 880391

dir: *Telephone for directions*

Village pub nine miles west of Hartlepool with fine views over surrounding countryside from an elevated position. There's a cosy bar and games room, stocking a good choice of cask ales and guest beers, a spacious lounge and large conservatory restaurant. Traditional Sunday lunch goes down well, as does breaded plaice and other favourites. In summer you can sit outside in the garden, which has a roofed over area for climbing plants.

Open 12–11 (Sun 12–10.30) **Bar Meals** L served Mon-Sat 12–2.30 D served Mon-Sat 5–9 Av main course £3.50 **Facilities** Garden Dogs allowed Parking

ESSEX

ARKESDEN
MAP 12 TL43

Pick of the Pubs

Axe & Compasses ♀
See Pick of the Pubs on opposite page

AYTHORPE RODING
MAP 06 TL51

Axe & Compasses NEW ♀
CM6 1PP ☎ 01279 876648

e-mail: shunt36@msn.com

Husband and wife team David and Sheila Hunt are restoring this weatherboarded, 17th-century pub, which they bought after it had stood empty for a year. Ales from small regional and craft brewers are served from barrels behind the bar. David, a skilled self-taught chef, loves to offer old favourites such as rack of lamb with spring vegetables and minted Jersey Royals, followed by treacle and pecan tart with brown bread ice cream.

Open 11–11 (Sun 12–10.30) **Bar Meals** L served Mon-Sat 12–3 D served Mon-Sat 6–10 (Sun 12–9) Av main course £12 **Restaurant** L served Mon-Sat 12–3 D served Mon-Sat 6–10 (Sun 12–9) Av 3 course à la carte £22 ⊕ Free House ◀ Brentwood Best, Nethergate Old Growler, Crouch Vale Brewers Gold, Woodfordes Wherry. ♀ 11 **Facilities** Garden Parking **Notes** ☺

BLACKMORE
MAP 06 TL60

Pick of the Pubs

The Leather Bottle ♀
The Green CM4 0RL ☎ 01277 821891

e-mail: leatherbottle@tiscali.co.uk

dir: *M25 junct 8 onto A1023, left onto A128 5m. Left onto Blackmore Rd 2m. Left towards Blackmore 2m. Right and 1st left*

According to local legend, Henry VIII used to stable his horses here when he came to visit his mistress. There has been a pub on the site for over 400 years, but the original building burned down in 1954 and was rebuilt in 1956. The present day pub is a family-run affair with James and Gwen Wallace at the helm and their daughter Sarah in charge of the restaurant. The bar is a cosy, inviting place to savour real ales, while the restaurant is smart, with modern furnishings. There's also an airy conservatory which opens onto the spacious enclosed garden. Food options include a very reasonably priced lunchtime menu, which might include seafood chowder followed by sausages and mash. Typical evening dishes are pan-fried lambs' kidneys with toasted pine nuts and balsamic syrup, followed by a pork chop with roasted root vegetables, topped with apple and date chutney.

Open 11–11 (Fri-Sat 11–12, Sun 12–11) **Bar Meals** L served Sun 12–2 **Restaurant** L served Mon-Sat 12–2 D served Mon-Sat 7–9 (Sun 12–4) Av 3 course à la carte £20 Av 2 course fixed price £9.99 ⊕ Free House ◀ Adnams Best, Adnams Broadside, Deuchars IPA, Woodfordes Wherry. ♀ 8 **Facilities** Garden

Axe & Compasses

Always just the 'Axe' in the local vernacular, this old pub stands in the centre of a pretty village through which runs Wicken Water, a gentle stream spanned by footbridges leading to picture-postcard white, cream and pink-washed thatched cottages.

The main section of the building, itself also thatched, which dates from 1650, is now the comfortable lounge containing easy chairs and settees, antique furniture and clocks, horse brasses and maybe the warming glow of an open fire. The part to the right is the public bar, built in the early 19th century as stabling, a function it performed until the 1920s. Meals in here range from sandwiches to grilled lemon sole and lambs' liver and bacon. In the cosy, softly lit restaurant area, which seats 50 on various levels, agricultural implements adorn the old beams. Here, the menu offers a good selection of starters, including pan-fried strips of duck breast with scallions and cucumber, served in a pancake with plum sauce; and lightly baked, oat-rolled fresh mackerel fillet. There's a good choice of main courses too, examples being supreme of chicken with port wine and stilton; medallions of beef fillet with rösti potato, soft green peppercorns, brandy and cream; and halibut steak with spinach, tomato, cheddar cheese, white wine and cream. Vegetarians may choose from breadcrumbed spinach and potato cake, with tomato and basil sauce; roasted vegetable vol au vent filled with cheese and mustard cream sauce; and mushroom, cream and cheese pancake. Round off with popular desserts from the trolley such as trifle of the day, or summer pudding. House wines are modestly priced. On a fine day many drinkers and diners head for the patio.

🍷
MAP 12 TL43
High St CB11 4EX
☎ 01799 550272
📠 01799 550906
dir: *From Buntingford take B1038 towards Newport. Then left for Arkesden*

Open 11.30–2.30 6–11
Bar Meals L served all week 12–2 D served all week 6.45–9.30
Restaurant L served Mon-Sat 12–2 D served Mon-Sat 6.45–9.30 (Sun 12–3, 7–10.30, Winter dinner Mon-Sat only) Av 3 course à la carte £24
Greene King Greene King IPA, Abbot Ale & Old Speckled Hen. 🍷 14
Facilities Garden Parking

BRAINTREE

MAP 07 TL72

Pick of the Pubs

The Green Dragon at Young's End ☕

Upper London Rd, Young's End CM77 8QN
☎ 01245 361030 📠 01245 362575
e-mail: info@greendragonbraintree.co.uk
dir: *At Braintree bypass take A131 S towards Chelmsford, exit at Youngs End on Great Leighs bypass*

The Green Dragon provides a comfortable venue for good drinking and dining, with winter fires creating a cosy atmosphere in the friendly bars, which are smartly decked out with lots of exposed beams and traditional furnishings. As their names suggest, the barn and hayloft restaurants provide plenty of space, maintaining the rustic theme with bare brick walls and wonderful old beams. Outside there's a large garden and heated patio area. The same blackboard and extensive printed menus are available throughout, offering light snacks and full meals ranging through fresh seafood, game in season and speciality Gloucestershire Old Spot pork dishes. One of the Old Spot recipes is slow roasted belly of pork stuffed with apricots and served with cider sauce and sage mash. Seafood specials include oysters, dressed crab, moules marinière, and halibut steak with prawns and lemon and lime butter. There is also a menu for the under 10's with planet spaghetti and toad in the hole.

Open 12–3 5.30–11 (Sun & BHs 12–11) **Bar Meals** L served Mon–Fri 12–2.30 D served Mon–Fri 6.30–9.30 (Sat-Sun 12–9) **Restaurant** L served Mon–Sat 12–2.15 D served Mon–Sat 6–9.30 (Sun 12–9) ⊕ Greene King ⬛ Greene King IPA , Abbot Ale, Ruddles County & Old Speckled Hen. ☕ 10 **Facilities** Garden Parking Play Area

BURNHAM-ON-CROUCH

MAP 07 TQ99

Ye Olde White Harte Hotel

The Quay CM0 8AS
☎ 01621 782106 📠 01621 782106
dir: *Along high street, right before clocktower, right into car park*

Directly overlooking the River Crouch, the hotel dates from the 17th century and retains many original features, including exposed beams. It also has its own private jetty. The food is mainly English-style with such dishes as roast leg of English lamb, local roast Dengie chicken and seasoning, and grilled fillet of plaice and lemon. There is also a range of bar snacks including toasted and plain sandwiches, jacket potatoes, and soup.

Open 11–11 **Bar Meals** L served all week 12–2 D served all week 7–9 Av main course £7.80 **Restaurant** L served all week 12–2 D served all week 7–9 Av 3 course à la carte £19.50 ⊕ Free House ⬛ Adnams Bitter, Crouch Vale Best. **Facilities** Dogs allowed Parking

CASTLE HEDINGHAM

MAP 13 TL73

The Bell Inn ☕

St James St CO9 3EJ ☎ 01787 460350
e-mail: bell-castle@hotmail.co.uk
dir: *On A1124 N of Halstead, right to Castle Hedingham*

An unspoilt, 15th-century former coaching inn run by the same family for something like 40 years. In the winter log fires warm the interior, while the sun usually obliges on the vine-covered patio and huge orchard garden in summer. Food from quality local suppliers is home cooked and largely traditional, although expect the Turkish chef to produce some native dishes for the specials board. Fish is hand-picked from Billingsgate or delivered fresh from Colchester.

Open 11.45–3 6–11 (Fri 11.45–12 Sat 12–11.30 Sun 12–11) Closed: 25 Dec eve **Bar Meals** L served Mon–Fri 12–2 D served Mon–Sat 7–9.30 (Sat-Sun 12–2.30, Sun 7–9) Av main course £9.50 ⊕ Grays ⬛ Maldon Gold Mighty Oak, Adnams Bitter, Mighty Oak IPA & guest ale. ☕ 8 **Facilities** Garden Dogs allowed Parking Play Area

CHAPPEL

MAP 13 TL82

The Swan Inn ☕

CO6 2DD ☎ 01787 222353 📠 01787 220012
dir: *Pub visible just off A1124 (Colchester to Halstead road), from Colchester 1st left after viaduct*

This rambling low-beamed free house stands in the shadow of a magnificent Victorian railway viaduct, and boasts a charming riverside garden with overflowing flower tubs. Fresh meat arrives daily from Smithfield, and fish from Billingsgate. Typically the seafood may include

crispy sole fillets, deep-fried monkfish or poached skate, while the grill comes into its own with prime steaks, platters of surf'n'turf, English pork chops and calves' liver and bacon. There are daily vegetarian specials, and home-made desserts too.

Open 11–3 6–11 (Sat 11–11, Sun 12–10.30) **Bar Meals** L served all week 12–2.30 D served all week 6.30–10 (Sun 12–8.30) Av main course 8.95 **Restaurant** L served all week 12–2.15 D served all week 7–10 (Sun 2–8.30) Av 3 course à la carte £15 ⊕ Free House ◀ Greene King IPA, Abbot Ale. **Facilities** Garden Dogs allowed Parking Play Area

CHELMSFORD   MAP 06 TL70

The Alma ♟

57 Arbour Ln CM1 7RG ☎ 01245 256783 ▤ 01245 256793
e-mail: the_alma@hotmail.com
web: www.thealma.biz
dir: Please telephone for directions

Named after the bloodiest battle of the Crimean war, The Alma was built in the late 19th century as an alehouse for soldiers recovering in the neighbouring hospital. The present owners have refurbished the pub to give it a contemporary edge, and the menu follows suit with a stylish mix of traditional and modern dishes – perhaps monkfish with Parma ham, a crab cake and asparagus tips; or parsnip tart with pumpkin risotto.

Open 11–11 Closed: 25 Dec pm, 26 Dec **Bar Meals** L served all week 12–2.30 D served all week 6–9.30 (Sun 12–8) **Restaurant** L served all week 12–2.30 D served all week (Sun 12–8) ⊕ Free House ◀ Greene King IPA, Spitfire, Nethergate Suffolk County, Crouch Vale Brewers Gold. ♟ 11 **Facilities** Garden Parking

CLAVERING   MAP 12 TL43

Pick of the Pubs

The Cricketers ♟
See Pick of the Pubs on page 202

COLCHESTER   MAP 13 TL92

The Rose & Crown Hotel ★★★ HL ◉◉ ♟

East St CO1 2TZ ☎ 01206 866677 ▤ 01206 866616
e-mail: info@rose-and-crown.com
dir: From M25 junct 28 take A12 N. Follow Colchester signs

Probably the oldest hotel in England's oldest town, the Rose & Crown has a bar made of cell doors from the jail that once stood on the site.

Traditional food in the oak-beamed Tudor Bar Brasserie includes fish and chips; rib-eye and sirloin steaks; lamb curry; and beef and potato pie. Or there's the refurbished East Street Grill, which offers sun-dried tomatoes, mascarpone and chicken roulade; parmesan and olive-crusted salmon; and asparagus and saffron risotto.

Open 11–2.30 6–11 (Sat-Sun all day) **Bar Meals** L served Mon-Sat 12–2 D served Mon-Sat 6–10 (Sun 12–3, 6.30–9) **Restaurant** L served all week 12–2 D served Mon-Sat 7–9.45 ⊕ Free House ◀ Tetley's Bitter, Rose & Crown Bitter, Adnams Broadside. ♟ 7 **Facilities** Parking **Rooms** 39

DEDHAM   MAP 13 TM03

Marlborough Head Hotel

Mill Ln CO7 6DH ☎ 01206 323250
e-mail: jen.permain@tiscali.co.uk
web: www.marlborough-head.co.uk
dir: E of A12, N of Colchester.

Tucked away in glorious Constable country, a 16th-century building that was once a clearing-house for local wool merchants. In 1660, after a slump in trade, it became an inn. Today it is as perfect for a pint, sofa and newspaper as it is for a good home-cooked family meal. As well as traditional favourites, such as lambs' liver and bacon, the dinner menu also includes chicken arrabbiata, seafood platter, peppered steak and roasted vegetable tagliatelle.

Open 11–11 **Bar Meals** L served all week 11–11 D served all week 11–11 (Sun 12–10.30) Av main course £7.95 **Restaurant** L served all week 11–11 D served all week 11–11 (Sun 12–10.30) ⊕ Old English Pub Co ◀ Adnams Southwold, Greene King IPA, Adnams Broadside & guest. **Facilities** Garden Parking

Pick of the Pubs

The Sun Inn ★★★★ INN ♟

High St CO7 6DF ☎ 01206 323351
e-mail: office@thesuninndedham.com
dir: From A12 follow signs to Dedham for 1.5m, pub on village high street.

Owner Piers Baker has transformed the Sun from a run-down village boozer to an inn of fine repute. With open fires, oak beams, a sun-trap terrace and walled garden, you'll find character everywhere you look. Here, a quiet pint goes hand in hand with robust food and drink; there's a decent selection of real ales and a respectable wine list, with up to sixteen wines available by the glass. Locally sourced seasonal ingredients drive the menu of modern British dishes: expect roast partridge with pear, braised lentils and baked radicchio; baked organic salmon with chickpeas, Swiss chard, chilli and mint; and molten chocolate baby cake with cream. If you can't quite tear yourself away, the Sun boasts four en-suite guest rooms with large comfy beds, crisp linen, character furniture, great showers and lazy continental breakfasts.

Open 11–11 Closed: 25-27 Dec **Bar Meals** L served Mon-Fri 12–2.30 D served Sun-Thu 6.30–9.30 (Wknds 12–3, Fri-Sat 6.30–10) Av main course £12.50 **Restaurant** L served Mon-Fri 12–2.30 D served Sun-Thu 6.30–9.30 (Wknds 12–3, Fri-Sat 6.30–10) Av 3 course à la carte £24 Av 2 course fixed price £15 ⊕ Free House ◀ Brewer's Gold Crouch Vale, Adnam's Broadside, Canary from Lowestoft, Titanic & Kaltenberg. ♟ 20 **Facilities** Children's licence Garden Dogs allowed Parking **Rooms** 5

The Cricketers

Always popular, in recent years this 16th-century inn has gained renown as the place where celebrity chef Jamie Oliver first learnt to wield a spatula. Set in the heart of a beautiful and unspoilt Essex village, the pub is still run by his parents, Trevor and Sally.

It stands near the cricket pitch, and related memorabilia decorates the brick-fronted bar and green-themed restaurant. Seasonally changing menus are offered in both areas, with fixed-price in the restaurant, and carte in the bar; the cooking reveals a distinctly Italian influence. Although fresh fish is served every day, Tuesdays are special fish days, with lobster and crab alongside whatever looks good at the market. Lunchtime bar meals feature these fruits of the sea, and sandwiches such as chargrilled free-range chicken and salad. A good range of salads also make a tasty light lunch, especially when you know they are based on produce from Jamie's organic garden; an example is the Greek salad with feta cheese, olives, sun blushed tomatoes and roasted peppers. Children's dishes are based on the same healthy ingredients (no surprise there then!), with the likes of breadcrumbed strips of organic salmon, or Braughing pork sausages; alternatively half portions from the main menu can be served. The dinner menu choices could present a dilemma: Red Poll steaks; creamed natural smoked haddock with home-made tagliatelle; lambs' liver with black pudding fritters and braised Puy lentils; Suffolk lamb; and loin of Priors Hall pork are just some of the mouth-watering main course options; desserts are all made on the premises.

MAP 12 TL43
CB11 4QT
☎ 01799 550442
🖷 01799 550882
e-mail: info@thecricketers.co.uk
dir: *From M11 junct 10, A505 E. Then A1301, B1383. At Newport take B1038*

Open 10.30–11 Closed: 25–26 Dec
Bar Meals L served all week 12–2 D served all week 7–10
Restaurant L served Sun 12–2 D served all week 6.30–9.30
Av 3 course à la carte £27.50
Av 3 course fixed price £27.50
⊕ Free House ◖ Adnams Bitter, Tetley Bitter, Greene King IPA & Adnams Broadside. ♙ 10
Facilities Garden Parking Play Area
Rooms available

EARLS COLNE   MAP 13 TL82

Pick of the Pubs

The Carved Angel ♀

Upper Holt St CO6 2PG
☎ 01787 222330 📠 01787 220013

e-mail: info@carvedangel.com

dir: *From A120 take B1024 to Coggeshall, turn right at junct with A1124, pub 300yds on right.*

Once a haven for monks and nuns escaping persecution by Henry VIII, this 15th-century village inn is now a popular gastropub with a stylish bar and restaurant. Traditional ales from Adnams and Greene King are offered alongside continental beers and a global wine list. Frequently changing menus are created from fresh seasonal ingredients, with the aim of offering a high standard of food but in a relaxed setting at reasonable prices. The kitchen turns out well-crafted dishes such as prawn tails fried in tempura with home-made tartare sauce; confit of duck with caramelised apple and a burgundy and sage reduction; and iced rhubarb parfait with a winter berries compote. The lunch special menu is particularly good value. Special events are held on a regular basis, for Mothering Sunday, Valentine's Day and so on.

Open 11.30–3 6.30–11 (Sun 6.30–10.30) Closed: 26 Dec, 1 Jan **Bar Meals** L served all week 12–2 D served all week 7–9 (Fri-Sat 7–10, Sun 12–2.30) Av main course £10 **Restaurant** L served all week 12–2 D served all week 7–9 (Fri-Sat 7–10, Sun 12–2.30) Av 3 course à la carte £19 ⊕ Free House ◀ Greene King IPA, Adnams Bitter. ♀ 14 **Facilities** Garden Parking

---

ELSENHAM   MAP 12 TL52

The Crown

The Cross, High St CM22 6DG ☎ 01279 812827

dir: *M11 junct 8 towards Takeley. Left at lights*

A pub for 200 years, with oak beams, open fireplaces and Essex pargetting at the front. The menu, which has a large selection of fresh fish, might offer baked trout with toasted almonds, steak and kidney pie, Crown mixed grill with onion rings, a choice of steaks cooked to order, or breast of duck with peppercorn sauce. There's a good choice of vegetarian choices as well, plus lighter bites and jacket potatoes.

Open 12–11 (Sun 12–10.30) **Bar Meals** L served Mon-Sat 12–9 D served Mon-Sat 6–9 (Sun lunch 12–3) Av main course £11 **Restaurant** L served Mon-Sat 12–9 D served Mon-Sat (Sun 12–4) Av 3 course à la carte £30 ◀ IPA, Broadside, Spitfire. **Facilities** Garden Dogs allowed Parking

---

FEERING   MAP 07 TL82

The Sun Inn ♀

Feering Hill CO5 9NH ☎ 01376 570442 📠 01376 570442

e-mail: andy.howard@virgin.net

dir: *On A12 between Colchester & Witham. Village 1m*

This timbered building dates from 1525, and features richly carved decorations on the bressummer and barge boards of the three gable ends. It's a lively pub, with two log fires to welcome customers in the winter months and up to 20 constantly changing real ales.

Open 12–3 5.30–11 (Sun 12–11) **Bar Meals** L served Mon-Sat 12–2.30 D served all week 6–9.30 (Sun 12–3) ⊕ Shepherd Neame ♀ 8 **Facilities** Garden Dogs allowed Parking

---

FELSTED   MAP 06 TL62

Pick of the Pubs

The Swan at Felsted ♀

See Pick of the Pubs on page 204

See Pick of the Pubs on page 204

FINGRINGHOE   MAP 07 TM02

The Whalebone ♀

Chapel Rd CO5 7BG ☎ 01206 729307 📠 01206 729307

e-mail: fburroughes1974@aol.com

dir: *Telephone for directions*

This Grade II listed 18th-century free house has panoramic views of the Roman river valley. The Whalebone has wooden floors, aubergine walls, unique artwork and sculptures, and roman blinds. The unusual name comes from bones, once fastened above the door of the pub, which came from a locally beached whale. Another unusual feature is the oak tree nearby, thought to be the largest in Essex. Legend has it that the tree grew from an acorn in the mouth of a pirate executed and buried there some centuries ago. No acorns on the menu though, just hearty home-made dishes like roasted poussin with ricotta, gorgonzola and mortadella; chargrilled sirloin steak and chips; roast belly of Suffolk pork; and roasted sea bass with vermouth braised fennel.

Open 12–3 5.30–11 (Sat-Sun all day) **Bar Meals** L served all week 12–2.30 D served Tue-Sat 7–9.30 Av main course £10.25 **Restaurant** L served all week D served Mon-Sat Av 3 course à la carte £18.75 ⊕ Free House ◀ Greene King IPA, Caledonian Deuchars IPA & 2 guest ales. ♀ 7 **Facilities** Children's licence Garden Dogs allowed Parking

---

GOSFIELD   MAP 13 TL72

The Green Man ♀

The Street CO9 1TP ☎ 01787 472746

e-mail: greenmangosfield@tesco.net

dir: *Take A131 N from Braintree then A1017 to village*

A pink-washed medley of buildings housing a smart village dining pub, where Cumberland sausage, cottage pie, haddock fillet and spinach and ricotta cannelloni feature among good value lunch and dinner possibilities. Additional choices in the evening include a full rack of ribs with honey or mustard sauce, mushrooms, onion rings and chips; rump, rib-eye and fillet steaks; and chicken supreme.

Open 11–3 6.15–11 (Sun 12–4) **Bar Meals** L served all week 12–2.30 D served Mon-Sat 6.45–9 **Restaurant** L served all week 12–2.30 D served Tue-Sat 6.45–9 ⊕ Greene King ◀ Greene King IPA, Old Speckled Hen & Abbot Ale. ♀ 6 **Facilities** Children's licence Garden Dogs allowed Parking

PICK OF THE PUBS

The Swan at Felsted

The Swan is ideally situated for exploring the pretty North Essex countryside, and only a short drive from Stansted Airport. For many years it was the village bank and was rebuilt after a disastrous fire in the early 1900s.

The imposing exterior hides within it a delightfully clean and refreshing atmosphere. Today very much a gastro-pub, the drinks range includes a guest ale, draught cider, Guinness and popular lagers as well as fine wines, successfully achieving a balance between the traditional English pub and a high quality restaurant. The pub chefs source their ingredients with an eye to keeping food miles to a minimum, and prepare their dishes to suit every palate – everything from light bites at lunchtime to more serious fare in the evening. Menus are designed to stimulate the senses while retaining a simplicity that allows the quality of the local ingredients to shine through. The lunch choice keeps in touch with their pub roots with favourite treats such as beer-battered fish and chips; Swan bacon and cheeseburger; and Wicks Manor Farm sausages. Changing seasonally, the à la carte menu offers a delightful selection of modern European dishes: crab and avocado salad; crispy pork belly dressed with home-made sweet chilli sauce; mozzarella and herb crusted fillet of cod with pommes Anna, green beans and a lemon butter sauce; aubergine gratin – these give an idea of the flavoursome cooking produced by the kitchen team. Children are welcome too; their own reasonably priced menu will not deter parents from bringing them along to enjoy a plate of bangers and mash, or fresh pasta with tomato sauce.

⌕
MAP 06 TL62
Station Rd CM6 3DG
☎ 01371 820245
🖨 01371 821393
e-mail:
info@theswanatfelsted.co.uk
dir: *Exit M11 junct 8 onto A120 signed Felsted. Pub in village centre*

Open 11–11 (Sun 12–4)
Bar Meals L served Mon-Sat 12–3 D served Mon-Sat 6–10 (Sun 12–4)
Restaurant L served Mon-Sat 12–3 D served Mon-Sat 6–10 (Sun 12–4)
⊕ Greene King ◖ IPA, Prospect, Guinness & guest ale. ☙ 9
Facilities Children's licence Garden Dogs allowed Parking

GREAT BRAXTED   MAP 07 TL81

Du Cane Arms ♟

The Village CM8 3EJ ☎ 01621 891697 📠 01621 890009

e-mail: fred@fredrodford.com

dir: *Great Braxted signed between Witham & Kelvedon on A12*

Walkers and cyclists mingle with the locals at this friendly pub, built in 1935 at the heart of a leafy village: handy for the A12 today, it is a popular spot and comes up with a variety of lively real ales and daily fresh fish. Adnams bitter boosts the beer batter for fresh cod or haddock, while the steak and kidney pie is livened up with a splash of Guinness. Thai curries, rack of lamb, and seafood curry are among the other dishes. The garden is ideal for summertime eating.

Open 11.30–3 6.30–11 **Bar Meals** L served all week 12–2 D served all week 6.30–9.30 (Winter Sun 12–4.45) **Restaurant** L served all week 12–2 D served all week 7–9.30 ⊕ Free House ◀ Adnams Bitter, Greene King IPA, John Smiths Smooth. ♟ 10 **Facilities** Garden Parking

GREAT YELDHAM   MAP 13 TL73

The White Hart ⊛ ♟

Poole St CO9 4HJ ☎ 01787 237250 📠 01787 238044

e-mail: mjwmason@yahoo.co.uk

dir: *On A1017 between Haverhill & Halstead*

Highwaymen were once locked up in a small prison under the stairs of this impressive, 500–year-old, timber-framed inn. An express lunch menu offers Adnams beer-battered cod; pork and leek sausages; and Mr Wu's chicken curry. Those with more time to spare might opt for local Auberie Estate fillet of venison; Colne Valley rack of lamb; or baked monkfish.

Open 10–12 **Bar Meals** L served Mon-Sat 12–3 D served Mon-Thu 6–9.30 Av main course £8.95 **Restaurant** L served all week 12–3 D served all week 6–9.30 Av 3 course à la carte £28 Av 3 course fixed price £19.95 ⊕ Free House ◀ Adnams Bitter, Black Sheep, Adnams Broadside. ♟ 7 **Facilities** Children's licence Garden Parking Play Area **Rooms** available

HENNY STREET   MAP 13 TL83

The Henny Swan ♟

CO10 7LS ☎ 01787 269238

e-mail: harry@hennyswan.com

dir: *From Sudbury centre take A131 to Chelmsford 1.5m, at lights turn left at Henny Street*

Set on the Essex bank of the Stour, the Henny Swan was a typical, old-fashioned rural pub now transformed into a modern dining restaurant pub. The interior is decidedly stylish, with polished wood floors, soft lighting and leather armchairs. Choice from the European-influenced, regularly changing menus is extended by at least three daily blackboard specials at both lunch and dinner. Local produce is used extensively. Start with Thai-style fishcake with sweet chilli sauce, or grilled avocado filled with stilton and crushed walnuts; and follow with chargrilled rib-eye steak with a creamy wild mushroom and bacon sauce; or seared fillet of wild salmon dusted with Cajun sauce on sweet chilli and tiger prawn linguine. Desserts might include home-made bakewell tart with strawberry compote and custard; or fresh fruit pavlova filled with lightly whipped cream.

Open 11–3 6–11 Closed: Mon (ex Apr-Oct) **Bar Meals** L served Mon-Sat 12–2.30 D served Mon-Sat 6.30–9 (Sun 12–6) **Restaurant** L served Mon-Sat 12–2.30 D served all week 6.30–9.30 (Sun 12–4) ⊕ Free House ◀ Greene King IPA, Adnams Broadside. ♟ 8 **Facilities** Garden Parking

HORNDON ON THE HILL   MAP 06 TQ68

Bell Inn & Hill House ♟

See Pick of the Pubs on page 206

INGATESTONE   MAP 06 TQ69

The Red Lion NEW ♟

Margaretting CM4 0EQ ☎ 01277 352184

e-mail: shunt36@msn.com

dir: *3m from Chelmsford town centre off A12*

The 17th-century Red Lion is what most would describe as a quintessential English pub. The bar area is decorated in warm shades of burgundy and aubergine, the restaurant in light coffee and cream. Seasonal menu highlights include steamed mussels; chicken, leek and mushroom pie; and calf's liver, smoked bacon and bubble and squeak at lunch, and deep-fried Lowestoft cod; chargrilled rib-eye steak; and butternut squash, broad bean and mushroom risotto at dinner.

Open 11–11 (Sun 12–10.30) **Bar Meals** L served all week 12–9 D served all week Av main course £12 **Restaurant** L served all week 12–3 D served all week 6–9.30 Av 3 course à la carte £22 ⊕ Greene King ◀ Greene King IPA, Abbott Ale, Old Speckled Hen, Ruddles. ♟ 11 **Facilities** Garden Parking Play Area

Bell Inn & Hill House

The Bell is a 15th-century coaching inn and Hill House, almost next door, dates from 1685. The two buildings between them provide good beer, food and accommodation in an attractive village setting only ten minutes from the Dartford Tunnel.

The inn has many original features including a courtyard balcony where luggage would once have been lifted from coach roofs; and a king post supports roof timbers over 1,000 years old. An unusual tradition takes place here every year, when the oldest villager available hangs a hot cross bun from a beam in the saloon bar; the custom dates back about 100 years, when the pub changed hands on a Good Friday. Two bars serve a selection of regularly changing real ales, amounting to around 144 different cask beers in the course of a year. The wine list is extensive and over a dozen are served by the glass; you can also purchase a bottle at the 'off-sales' price. The bar menu offers lunchtime sandwiches and light meals of pan-fried fishcakes with poached egg and hollandaise; or braised lamb's liver with mustard mash and red wine sauce. From the daily-changing restaurant menu you might start with celeriac soup with chive oil; potted local pheasant with thin oat cakes; or Cornish crab, avocado and roma tian with soda bread croutons. Main course options may include pan-fried English rib-eye steak on wild mushrooms with sauté of foie gras; roast Orsett partridge on smoked bacon mash with redcurrant jus; or confit of wild rabbit leg on spinach with rabbit pie. Stylish desserts could prove too tempting: try vanilla poached pear with blueberries and toasted almonds; or dark chocolate glazed roast pineapple and mascarpone cheesecake.

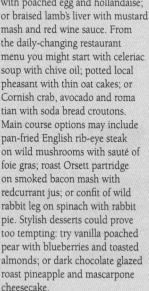

MAP 06 TQ68
High Rd SS17 8LD
☎ 01375 642463
🖷 01375 361611
e-mail: info@bell-inn.co.uk
dir: *M25 junct 30/31 signed Thurrock*

Open 11–2.30 5.30–11 (Sun 12–4, 7–10.30) Closed: 25–26 Dec
Bar Meals L served all week 12–1.45 D served Mon-Sat 6.45–9.45 (Sun food from 7) Av main course £13.95
Restaurant L served all week 12–1.45 D served Mon-Sat 6.45–9.45 (Sun food from 7) Av 3 course à la carte £27.95
⊕ Free House ◖ Greene King IPA, Interbrew Bass, Crouchvale Brewers Gold, Ruddles County.
🍷 16
Facilities Garden Dogs allowed Parking

LANGHAM

MAP 13 TM03

The Shepherd and Dog

Moor Rd CO4 5NR ☎ 01206 272711 📠 01206 273136

dir: *A12 from Colchester towards Ipswich, take 1st left signed Langham*

Situated on the Suffolk/Essex border, in Constable country, this 1928 freehouse has the classic styling of an English country pub. Widely renowned for its food, the Shepherd and Dog serves an extensive variety of meat, fish and poultry dishes, plus a vegetarian selection and a children's menu.

Open 11–3 5.30–11 (Sat 11–11, Sun 12–11) **Bar Meals** L served Mon-Fri 12–2.15 D served Mon-Fri 6–10 (Sat 11–11 Sun 12–10.30) **Restaurant** L served all week 12–2.15 D served all week 6–10 ⊕ Free House ◀ Greene King IPA, Abbot Ale & guest ales. **Facilities** Children's licence Garden Dogs allowed Parking

LITTLE BRAXTED

MAP 07 TL82

The Green Man ♀

Green Man Ln CM8 3LB ☎ 01621 891659

dir: *1.5m from A12 junct 22, follow B1389 signed to Witham. Follow signs to Little Braxted, over bridge, right into Little Braxted Lane, 1.5m, right at next T-junct, pub on right*

A traditional English pub situated in a village that frequently wins the title of Essex's 'Best Kept'. On display in the public bar are many old pictures, woodworking tools and a Dinky toy collection. The secluded garden is popular in summer, while in winter the cosy interior and open fire draw people in. Home-made dishes include lamb shank in minted red wine gravy, as well as lighter snacks and sandwiches.

Open 11.30–3.30 5–11 (Sun 12–3.30, 7–10.30) **Bar Meals** L served Mon-Sat 12–2.30 D served Mon-Sat 6–9 (Sun 12–6) **Restaurant** L served Mon-Sat 12–2.30 D served Mon-Sat 6–9 (Sun 12–6) ⊕ Greene King ◀ Greene King IPA & Mild, Morland, Old Bob, Ruddles Best. ♀ 9 **Facilities** Children's licence Garden Dogs allowed Parking

LITTLE CANFIELD

MAP 06 TL52

The Lion & Lamb ♀

CM6 1SR ☎ 01279 870257 📠 01279 870423

e-mail: info@lionandlamb.co.uk

dir: *M11 junct 8, B1256 towards Takeley & Little Canfield*

A favourite for business or leisure, this traditional country pub restaurant is handy for Stansted airport and the M11. Inside you'll find oak beams, winter log fires, and an extensive food selection. Choose sandwiches, or traditional bar food such as steak and ale pie, or go for

---

roasted scallops on saffron scented risotto followed by breast of duck with sesame pak choi, crisp noodles and oriental dressing.

Open 11–11 (Sun 12–11) **Bar Meals** L served all week 11–10 D served all week 11–10 (Sun 12–10) **Restaurant** L served all week 11–10 D served all week 11–10 (Sun 12–10) Av 3 course fixed price £25 ⊕ Greene King ◀ Old Speckled Hen, Greene King IPA, Ridleys Rumpus, Old Bob & seasonal ales. ♀ 10 **Facilities** Garden Parking Play Area

See advertisement on page 210

LITTLE DUNMOW

MAP 06 TL62

Flitch of Bacon

The Street CM6 3HT ☎ 01371 820323 📠 01371 820338

dir: *B1256 to Braintree for 10m, turn off at Little Dunmow, 0.5m pub on right*

A 15th-century country inn whose name refers to the ancient gift of half a salted pig, or 'flitch', to couples who have been married for a year and a day, and 'who have not had a cross word'.

Open 12–3 5.30–11 (Sat 6–11 Sun 12–5, 7–10.30) **Bar Meals** L served Tues-Sat 12–2 D served Mon-Sat 6.30–9 (Sun 12–3) Av main course £6.50 ⊕ Free House ◀ Fuller's London Pride, Greene King IPA. **Facilities** Garden Dogs allowed Parking

MANNINGTREE

MAP 13 TM13

Pick of the Pubs

The Mistley Thorn ◉◉ ♀

High St, Mistley CO11 1HE

☎ 01206 392821 📠 01206 390122

e-mail: info@mistleythorn.com

dir: *Exit A12 at Hadleigh, follow signs to E Berholt & Manningtree/Mistley*

This historic free house overlooks the beautiful two-mile wide Stour estuary near Colchester. Built in 1725, it stands on the site of an older pub where self-appointed Witchfinder General Matthew Hopkins condemned dozens of local women to death. Still a focal point in the village of Mistley, the pub was completely refurbished a few years ago to become a casual but upscale bistro-style restaurant, with terracotta-tiled floors and high quality furnishings. Owner Sherri Singleton, who also runs the Mistley Kitchen cookery school, serves up an accomplished menu with a strong emphasis on locally sourced and seasonal produce, organic where possible. The daily-changing menu includes plenty of fish and shellfish (Mersea Island rock oysters; seafood platter; smoked haddock

CONTINUED

MANNINGTREE continued

chowder) alongside chargrilled local rib-eye with tempura onion rings, organic leaves and hand cut fries; and home-made ricotta gnocchi with pesto and summer vegetables.

Open 12–11 **Bar Meals** L served Mon-Fri 12–2.30 D served Mon-Fri 7–10 (Sat-Sun all day) **Restaurant** L served Mon-Fri 12–2.30 D served Mon-Fri 7–9.30 (Sat-Sun all day) ⊕ Free House ◼ Greene King IPA, Adnams, St Peters. ♥ 17 **Facilities** Dogs allowed Parking

NORTH FAMBRIDGE   MAP 07 TQ89

The Ferry Boat Inn

Ferry Ln CM3 6LR ☎ 01621 740208

e-mail: sylviaferryboat@aol.com

dir: *From Chelmsford take A130 S then A132 to South Woodham Ferrers, then B1012. right to village*

A 500–year-old traditional weatherboard inn with beams, log fires and a resident ghost. It is tucked away at the end of a lovely village on the River Crouch, next to the marina, and was once a centre for smugglers. These days it is understandably popular with the sailing fraternity. In addition to the extensive menu, daily specials might include minted lamb chop, grilled sea bass, chicken korma or beef chilli.

Open 11.30–3 6.30–11 (Summer Sun all day) **Bar Meals** L served Mon-Sat 12–2 D served Mon-Sat 7–9.30 (Sun 12–2.45, 7–9) Av main course £6.95 **Restaurant** L served all week 12–1.30 D served all week 7–9 ⊕ Free House ◼ Greene King IPA, Abbot Ale, Morland. **Facilities** Garden Dogs allowed Parking

PATTISWICK   MAP 13 TL82

Pick of the Pubs

The Compasses at Pattiswick ♥

See Pick of the Pubs on opposite page

PELDON   MAP 07 TL91

The Peldon Rose NEW ♥

Colchester Rd CO5 7QJ ☎ 01206 735248 ▤ 01206 736303

e-mail: enquiries@thepeldonrose.co.uk

dir: *On B1025 Mersea Rd, just before causeway*

Locally famous as an old smugglers' inn, the Peldon Rose simply exudes character. Winter log fires burn in the bar, with its original beams and leaded windows. An airy conservatory leads out to the garden, which is ideal for summer dining. Fresh local ingredients including Mersea island fish and oysters feature on the menu; other dishes include lamb and vegetable casserole with herb dumplings; and field mushrooms with spinach, pine nut and stilton stuffing.

Open 12–2.15 6.30–9 (Fri-Sat 6.30–9.30, Sun 12–6, Summer 12–9) Closed: 25 Dec **Bar Meals** L served all week 12–2.15 D served Mon-Thu 6.30–9 (Fri-Sat 6.30–9.30, Sun 12–6, Summer 12–9) **Restaurant** L served all week 12–2.15 D served Mon-Thu 6.30–9 (Fri-Sat 6.30–9.30, Sun 12–6, Summer 12–9) ◼ Adnams Broadside, Adnams bitter, IPA, local guest bitter. ♥ 26 **Facilities** Garden Parking

RADWINTER   MAP 12 TL63

The Plough Inn

CB10 2TL ☎ 01799 599222

dir: *4m E of Saffron Walden, at junct of B2153 & B2154*

An Essex woodboard exterior, old beams, open fires and a thatched roof characterise this listed inn, once frequented by farm workers. Food is served in the 50–seat restaurant, making the Plough more a destination gastro-pub than a purely local village inn, without losing too much of the village pub feel. A typical menu includes the likes of smoked haddock parcels, lamb noisettes, partridge, duck breast, and a variety of home-made pies. Friday night is fish night.

Open 12–3 6–11 (Sun 12–4, 7–11) **Bar Meals** L served Mon-Sat 12–2 D served Mon-Sat 6.30–9 (Sun 12–3) Av main course £8.50 **Restaurant** L served all week 12–2 D served Mon-Sat 6.30–9 (Sun 12–3) ⊕ Free House ◼ Adnams Best, IPA, Woodfordes Wherry, Archers. **Facilities** Garden Dogs allowed Parking

SAFFRON WALDEN   MAP 12 TL53

Pick of the Pubs

The Cricketers' Arms ★★★★ INN ◉ ♥

Rickling Green CB11 3YG

☎ 01799 543210 ▤ 01799 543512

e-mail: reservations@cricketers.demon.co.uk

dir: *Exit B1383 at Quendon. Pub 300yds on left opposite cricket ground.*

This historic inn was built as a terrace of timber-framed cottages, and overlooks the cricket green. The cricketing connection began in the 1880s when Rickling Green became the venue for London society cricket matches, and associations with the England team and the county game continue today. The pub has been beautifully refurbished in a stripped-back, modern style, retaining traditional features such as exposed beams and stone floors, but bringing in contemporary comforts such as big leather sofas and, outside, a pretty Japanese terrace garden. One modern, all-pleasing menu serves all three dining areas. Typical starters include foie gras parfait with toasted brioche, sliced apple and red onion; home-smoked tomato and parsnip soup; and risotto of crayfish, caramelized onion, fresh herbs and parmesan. Follow with monkfish wrapped in bacon with chilli, coriander and yellow pea purée; or butternut squash risotto with tempura beetroot and parmesan shavings.

Open 12–11 **Bar Meals** L served all week 12–2.30 D served all week 7–9.30 (Sun 7–9) **Restaurant** L served all week 12–2.30 D served all week 7–9.30 (Sun 12–2.30) ⊕ Punch Taverns ◼ Greene King IPA, Jennings Cumberland & Abbot Ale. ♥ 8 **Facilities** Garden Parking **Rooms** 9

PICK OF THE PUBS

PATTISWICK-ESSEX

The Compasses at Pattiswick

Originally built as two estate workers cottages, this award-winning dining pub seems to be miles from any seriously populated area, although both Chelmsford and Colchester are only 20 minutes away.

The owners' passion for good food translates into simple, hearty rural dishes, which you can choose from a menu jam-packed with local produce, including local estate-shot game. Lunchtime offers cottage pie with roasted parsnips and carrots; beer-battered haddock, chips and minted garden peas; and vegetable and bean casserole with herb dumplings, as well as salads, croque monsieur, jacket potatoes and other snacks. For dinner, maybe crab cakes with mixed cress and sweet chilli sauce as a starter, and braised lamb shank with crushed root vegetables and redcurrant jus to follow. A fish specials board makes the most of what is available in and around the Pattiswick area. Thus you may find seared scallops on a bed of mixed leaves with plum tomato, avocado and crispy bacon; crispy squid rings and home-made aioli; poached smoked haddock with creamy mash, lightly poached egg and whole grain mustard sauce; whole grilled plaice with fine green beans, buttered new potatoes and lemon, caper butter. Wines are selected for simplicity and clarity of flavour from both New and Old World producers.

🍷
MAP 13 TL82
Compasses Rd CM77 8BG
☎ 01376 561322
📠 01376 564343
e-mail: info@
thecompassesatpattiswick.co.uk
dir: *From Braintree take A120 E towards Colchester. After Bradwell 1st left to Pattiswick*

Open 11–3 5–12 (all day Etr-Sep)
Bar Meals L served all week
12–2.45 D served Mon-Sat
6–9.30 Av main course £11.50
Restaurant L served all week
12–2.45 D served Mon-Sat 6–9.45
Av 3 course à la carte £21.50 Av 2 course fixed price £15
⊕ Free House ⌷ Wherry-Woodforde's, Adnam's, Adnam's Broadside, St Austell Tribute. 🍷 12
Facilities Garden Dogs allowed
Parking Play Area

England

SHALFORD
MAP 12 TL72

The George Inn
The Street CM7 5HH ☎ 01371 850207 📠 01371 851355
e-mail: info@thegeorgeshalford.com
dir: 5m Braintree

A hundred years ago there were five pubs in Shalford, but the George Inn, which dates back some 500 years, is the only one now. It's a traditional village pub, with oak beams and open fires, surrounded by lovely countryside. Its own George Ale is brewed at the nearby Felstar micro-brewery. The menu is written up on the blackboard daily, including steaks, chicken breast specialities and popular Oriental and Indian dishes. Fish goes down well too, particularly battered plaice, cod mornay, and salmon en croute.

Open 12–3 6.30–12 (Sat-Sun 12–12) **Bar Meals** L served Mon-Sat 12–2.30 D served all week 6.30–9 (Sun 12–3) **Restaurant** L served all week 12–2.30 D served Sun-Fri 6.30–9.30 (Sat 7–9) ⊕ Free House ◀ Greene King IPA, Fuller's London Pride, Woodfordes Wherry, George Bitter. **Facilities** Garden Parking

STANSTED AIRPORT
MAP 06 TL52

See **Little Canfield**

STOCK
MAP 06 TQ69

The Hoop ♟
21 High St CM4 9BD ☎ 01277 841137
web: www.thehoop.co.uk
dir: On B1007 between Chelmsford & Billericay

This welcoming music-free 15th-century free house on Stock's attractive village green now serves its own ale made by Brentwood Brewery, among others. In fact the annual beer festival goes from strength to strength, but the food is not to be missed either. It could be a traditional bar meal such as half a roast free-range chicken and chips, or a proper affair in the Oak Room restaurant with the likes of whole Dover sole followed by pear crumble and chocolate sauce.

Open 11–11 (Fri 11–12, Sat 11–12, Sun 12–10.30) **Bar Meals** L served Tue-Sat 11–2.30 D served Tue-Sat 6–9 (Sun 12–5) Av main course £7.50 **Restaurant** L served Tue-Sat 12–2.30 D served Tue-Sat 6–9 (Sun 12–3) Av 3 course à la carte £20 ⊕ Free House ◀ Adnams Bitter & 4 guest ales. ♟ 10 **Facilities** Garden Dogs allowed

WICKHAM BISHOPS
MAP 07 TL81

The Mitre

2 The Street CM8 3NN ☎ 01621 891378 🖹 01621 894932

dir: Off B1018 at Witham exit A12. Right at Jack & Jenny pub. Right at end of road. 1st left & follow road over bridge. 2nd pub on left

Originally the Carpenter's Arms, this friendly pub changed its name in the mid-1890s, presumably to reflect the one-time possession of the village by the Bishops of London. The pub's regular range of meat choices includes mixed grills, pies and curries, steaks, and dishes featuring duck, pork, lamb and chicken. Fish is strongly represented by dishes based on haddock, cod, trout, sea bass, swordfish, plaice, Dover sole, red mullet and sea halibut to name a few.

Open 11.30–12 **Bar Meals** L served all week 12–2.30 D served all week 6.30–9.30 (Sat-Sun all day) **Restaurant** L served all week 12–2.30 D served all week 6.30–9.30 (Sat-Sun all day) Av 2 course fixed price £5.99 ⊕ Greene King ◀ Greene King IPA, Greene King Abbot, Fireside, Ruddles & Old Bob. **Facilities** Garden Dogs allowed Parking Play Area

WOODHAM MORTIMER
MAP 07 TL80

Hurdle Makers Arms

Post Office Rd CM9 6ST ☎ 01245 225169

e-mail: hurdlemakersarms@supanet.com

dir: From Chelmsford A414 to Maldon/Danbury 4.5m through Danbury into Woodham Mortimer. Over 1st rdbt 1st left, pub on left

A Grade II listed building dating back 400 years, the Hurdle Makers Arms has been a pub since 1837. Right at the heart of village life, it has darts teams, quiz nights and regular themed food evenings. Five real ales are served, two regulars plus three weekly changing guest beers. Home-made pub food is served seven days a week, and in summer there are weekend barbecues in the large beer garden.

Open 12–3 5–11 (Sat 6.30–11, Sun 12–11) **Bar Meals** L served all week 12–2.30 D served all week 6.30–9 (Sun 12–4, 7–9) Av main course £7 **Restaurant** L served all week 12–2.30 D served all week 6.30–9 (Sun 12–4 7–9) Av 3 course à la carte £15 ◀ Abbot IPA, Mighty Oak, Adnams & guest ales. **Facilities** Garden Dogs allowed Parking Play Area

GLOUCESTERSHIRE

ALMONDSBURY
MAP 04 ST68

The Bowl ★★ HL ⊛ ☻

16 Church Rd BS32 4DT ☎ 01454 612757 🖹 01454 619910

e-mail: reception@thebowlinn.co.uk

web: www.thebowlinn.co.uk

dir: M5 junct 6 towards Thornbury. 3rd left onto Over Ln, 1st right onto Sundays Hill, next right onto Church Rd

Originally built to house monks building the village church, The Bowl became an inn in 1550. Its name derives from the shape of the valley around the nearby Severn Estuary, which can be seen from the inn. Food in the bar ranges from filled baguettes to beer battered Cornish pollock with chips, while restaurant options include fishcakes, followed by rump of lamb with potato and beetroot gratin and red wine sauce.

Open 11–3 5–11 (Sun 12–10.30) Closed: 25 Dec **Bar Meals** L served Mon-Sat 12–2.30 D served Mon-Sat 6–10 (Sun 12–8) **Restaurant** L served all week 12–2.30 D served Mon-Sat 6–9.30 Av 3 course à la carte £25 ⊕ Free House ◀ Courage Best, Smiles Best, Wickwar BOB, Moles Best. ☻ 9 **Facilities** Garden Parking **Rooms** 13

ANDOVERSFORD
MAP 10 SP01

Pick of the Pubs

The Kilkeney Inn ☻
See Pick of the Pubs on page 212

The Royal Oak Inn ☻

Old Gloucester Rd GL54 4HR ☎ 01242 820335

e-mail: royal.oak1@unicombox.co.uk

dir: 200mtrs from A40, 4m E of Cheltenham

The 17th-century Royal Oak stands on the banks of the River Coln, one of a small chain of popular food-centred pubs in the area. Originally a coaching inn, its main dining room, galleried on two levels, occupies the converted former stables. Four real ales and three varieties of draught cider are part of the allure here, and there is a good selection of coffees. New owners for 2008.

Open 11–3 5–11 **Bar Meals** L served Mon-Sat 12–2 D served all week 7–9 (Sun 12–3) **Restaurant** L served Mon-Sat 12–2 D served Mon-Sat 6–9 (Sun 12–3, 7–9) ⊕ Free House ◀ Stanway Ales, Doom Bar, Otter Ale & Broadside. ☻ 9 **Facilities** Garden Dogs allowed Parking

England

PICK OF THE PUBS

The Kilkeney Inn

Nigel and Jean White have owned the Kilkeney Inn on the main road outside Andoversford for a good few years now, having already run it for two years as managers. It's very much a desirable place to eat, but beer drinkers are obviously more than welcome and will find real ales served in good condition.

A visit to this charming country dining pub is well worth the drive out from Cheltenham, where the rolling landscapes stretch away on all sides. The best views of the Cotswolds are from the front of the pub and the mature garden at the rear with bench seating; the expanse of greenery was originally six individual plots belonging to a terrace of mid-19th century stone cottages. A patio with heaters and seating can also be used if the weather permits. Inside, a wood-burning stove warms the beamed bar whenever there's a nip in the air, and the atmosphere is welcoming and cosy whatever the weather. The lunch menu ranges from filled ciabattas, herb sausages with creamy mash, and warm chicken Caesar salad, to the

Kilkeney special: a slow-roasted shoulder of lamb with smashed root vegetables in a rich red wine and mint glaze. For dinner, try a starter of grilled goats' cheese on roasted sweet peppers. This can be followed by marinated breast of cornfed chicken with leeks and sweet potatoes; home-made beef, ale and stilton pie; or a fillet of sea bass on leek mash with a white wine sauce. Chocolate and orange cheesecake, or a basket of figs with raspberry coulis and cream, may appear among the pudding choices. It's best to book for any meal, especially the traditional Sunday lunch, the monthly fish supper, and occasional jazz lunches.

🍷
MAP 10 SP01
Kilkeney GL54 4LN
☎ 01242 820341
📠 01242 820133
dir: *On A436 1m W of Andoversford*

Open 11–3 5–11
Bar Meals L served all week 12–2.30 D served all week 6.30–9
Av main course £9
Restaurant L served all week 12–2 D served all week 6.30–9 Av 3 course à la carte £18
⊕ Free House
🍺 Bombardier, Youngs Best Bitter, St Austells Tribute. 🍷 9
Facilities Garden Parking

England

ARLINGHAM MAP 04 SO71

Pick of the Pubs

The Old Passage Inn ★★★★ RR ◉◉ ♥

Passage Rd GL2 7JR ☎ 01452 740547 📄 01452 741871
e-mail: oldpassage@ukonline.co.uk
dir: 5m from A38 adjacent M5 junct 13

The Old Passage was for centuries a ford across the river Severn, and a ferry made the regular crossing here until 1947. This delightful free house is run by Sally Pearce and her son David, with head chef Raoul Moore always in attendance. The pub has a deserved reputation as a fine dining restaurant, and is particularly renowned for its fresh fish dishes. Start, perhaps, with North Atlantic prawns and traditional mayonnaise, or devilled soft shell crabs with sweet chilli sauce. Oysters from Yealm in Devon or Fowey in Cornwall are served au nature, or amoricaine with spicy lobster sauce and gruyère cheese. Fruits de mer are also served hot or cold, with other fish dishes including roast halibut and pan-fried skate. Non-fish alternatives are limited but may include steaks or pheasant cassoulet. In summer the garden menu offers a more relaxed style of dining, with the likes of moules and chips or fish pie.

Open 12–3 7–11 (closed Sun eve) Closed: 25 Dec & Mon
Bar Meals L served Tue-Sat 12–2 D served Tue-Sat 7–9.30 (Sun 12–3) **Restaurant** L served Tue-Sun 12–2 D served Tue-Sat 7–9.30 Av 3 course à la carte £30 ⊕ Free House ◀ Wickwar. ♥ 14
Facilities Garden Dogs allowed Parking

ASHLEWORTH MAP 10 SO82

Boat Inn ♥

The Quay GL19 4HZ ☎ 01452 700272 📄 01452 700272
e-mail: elisabeth_nicholls@yahoo.co.uk
dir: Telephone for directions

This delightful free house with its tiny front parlour, flagstone floors and ancient kitchen range has been in the same family for over 300 years. The pub has a longstanding reputation for real ales, and visitors to the annual summer beer festival can choose from more than 30 different brews. A selection of traditionally filled rolls with home-made tomato chutney forms the hub of the simple but delicious food offering, available only at lunchtimes.

Open 11.30–3 6.30–11 (Winter 7–11) Closed: Mon & Wed lunch
Bar Meals L served Tue, Thu-Sun 12–2 ⊕ Free House ◀ Wye Valley, Church End, Arkells, RCH Pitchfork. ♥ 6 **Facilities** Garden Parking
Notes ◉

Pick of the Pubs

The Queens Arms ♥

The Village GL19 4HT ☎ 01452 700395
dir: From Gloucester N on A417 for 5m. At Hartpury, opposite Royal Exchange turn right at Broad St to Ashleworth. Pub 100yds past village green

Outside this 16th-century inn the front garden features two beautifully clipped, 200–year-old yew trees, while a flagstoned patio at the rear is decorated with white cast-iron garden furniture, flower tubs and hanging baskets. The interior was given a makeover by the Victorians; thankfully the original beams and iron fireplaces were untouched, now complemented by comfy armchairs and antiques. The summer floods in 2007 necessitated a change of carpet, but Tony and Gillian Burreddu have now celebrated ten happy years here. The bar stocks a good range of real ales and over a dozen wines served by the glass. The restaurant, which is really two intimate rooms, tempts with blackboards full of ideas: pub lunch plates such as liver and bacon; a specials board which includes fresh fish – halibut or sea bass, for example; starters like sherried kidneys; and main courses such as gammon with black cherries; and hand-crafted desserts like almond and amaretto tart.

Open 12–3 7–11 Closed: 25–26 Dec & 1 Jan & Sun eve (ex BHs)
Bar Meals L served all week 12–2 D served Sun-Thu 7–9 (Fri-Sat 7–10)
Av main course £10 **Restaurant** L served all week 12–2 D served Sun-Thu 7–9 (Fri-Sat 7–10) ⊕ Free House ◀ Timothy Taylor Landlord, Donnington BB, S A Brain & Company Rev James, Shepherd Neame Spitfire & Tetley Bitter. ♥ 14 **Facilities** Garden Parking

---

AWRE MAP 04 SO70

Pick of the Pubs

The Red Hart Inn at Awre ♥

See Pick of the Pubs on page 214

PICK OF THE PUBS

The Red Hart Inn at Awre

Close to the beautiful River Severn, the setting is ideal for serious hikers, or for those simply seeking a relaxing, attractive place to walk off dinner – there's even a map by the front door for inspiration! The history of this cosy, traditional free house goes back to 1483, when it was built to house the workmen who were renovating the nearby 10th-century church.

The charming interior includes all the hoped-for historic features such as flagstone floors, stone fireplaces, lots of exposed beams, and an original working well, which is now attractively illuminated – it's the kind of atmospheric place where one quick post-walk drink could turn to several, or even a meal. If you do find yourself inclined to dine, rest assured that food is taken seriously here – so much so that a list of all local growers and suppliers is provided on each table. Vegetables are organic when obtainable, and the Awre family supply the inn with beef, lamb and pork, the latter cooked with Severn cider on Sundays. Look out for Red Hart favourites like Gloucester Old Spot sausages with mash and onion gravy; and local beef steak and ale casserole with mustard mash; and from the carte, pan-roasted breast of chicken with dauphinoise potatoes, mushrooms and smoked bacon sauce; and chargrilled pork loin with glazed apples, mashed potato and Awre's Severn cider sauce. The four desserts can be enjoyed individually or taken all together on one Awesome plate: crème brûlée, chocolate torte with Bailey's pannacotta; syrup sponge pudding and custard; and apple cheesecake with crumble topping and caramel sauce.

MAP 04 SO70
GL14 1EW
☎ 01594 510220
dir: *E of A48 between Gloucester & Chepstow, access is from Blakeney or Newnham villages*

Open 12–3 6.30–11 Closed: 23 Jan–5 Feb
Bar Meals L served all week 12–2 D served all week 6–9.30 (Sun 12–2.30, 6–9) Av main course £7.95
Restaurant L served all week 12–2 D served all week 6–9.30 (Sun 12–2.30, 6–9) Av 3 course à la carte £19.95
🍺 Free House 🍺 Wye Valley Butty Bach, guest ales, Whttingtons, Archers. 🍷 11
Facilities Garden Dogs allowed Parking

BARNSLEY   MAP 05 SP00

Pick of the Pubs

The Village Pub ◉◉ ♥
GL7 5EF ☎ 01285 740421 📠 01285 740929

e-mail: reservations@thevillagepub.co.uk

dir: *On B4425 4m NE of Cirencester*

Light years away from the average local, this stone-built country pub with flagstones, oak floorboards, exposed timbers and open fireplaces has been decorated by internationally renowned interior designer Rupert Charles-Jones. The beautifully restored dining rooms with their eclectic mix of furniture, rug-strewn floors and open fires provide an atmospheric background to the busy free house, which enjoys a reputation as one of the best local eating places. The daily-changing menus are founded on quality ingredients, including locally sourced produce, traceable or organic meats, and fresh seasonal fish. Starters range from celery soup with coco beans to ham hock risotto with truffle oil, and mains from beer battered fish and chips with tartare sauce to grilled rib-eye of beef with salsify, mushrooms and lardons. Typical desserts are pear and almond tart with crème fraîche, and warm rice pudding with poached plums.

Open 11–3.30 6–11 (Fri, Sat & Sun all day) **Bar Meals** L served all week 12–2.30 D served all week 7–9.30 (Sat-Sun 12–3, Fri-Sat 7–10) Av main course £12.50 **Restaurant** L served all week 12–2.30 D served all week 7–9.30 (Sat-Sun 12–3, Fri-Sat 7–10) Av 3 course à la carte £24 ⊕ Free House ◀ Hook Norton Bitter, Wadworth 6X, Cotswold Premium. ♥ 12 **Facilities** Children's licence Garden Dogs allowed Parking

---

BERKELEY   MAP 04 ST69

The Malt House ★★★ INN ♥
Marybrook St GL13 9BA ☎ 01453 511177 📠 01453 810257

e-mail: the-malthouse@btconnect.com

dir: *M5 junct 13/14, A38 towards Bristol. Pub on main road towards Sharpness*

Within walking distance of Berkeley Castle and its deer park, this family-run free house is also handy for the Edward Jenner museum, dedicated to the life of the founding father of immunology. Inside the heavily beamed pub you'll find a varied selection of lunchtime bar food, as well as weekly home-made specials. Pub favourites like steak and ale pie rub shoulders with vegetarian stuffed peppers; and grilled halibut, butter and lime.

Open 12–11 (Mon-Tue 4–11, Sun 12–6) **Bar Meals** L served Wed-Sun 12–2 D served Mon-Sat 6–9 (Sun eve closed) **Restaurant** L served Wed-Sun 12–2 D served Mon-Sat 6–9 (Sun eve closed) ⊕ Free House ◀ Courage Directors, Old Speckled Hen & Theakstons. ♥ 6 **Facilities** Garden Parking **Rooms** 9

BIBURY   MAP 05 SP10

Catherine Wheel
Arlington GL7 5ND ☎ 01285 740250 📠 01285 740779

e-mail: catherinewheel.bibury@eldridge-pope.co.uk

dir: *Telephone for directions*

Low-beamed 15th-century pub situated in a Cotswold village described by William Morris as 'the most beautiful in England'. Inside is an original ship's timber beam, as well as various prints and photographs of Old Bibury, and blazing log fires in winter. Traditional pub food includes fresh Bibury trout, salmon and prawns, and tuna steak.

Open 11–11 (Sun 12–10.30) **Bar Meals** L served all week 12–2 D served all week 6–9.30 bar snacks 2–6 Av main course £10 **Restaurant** L served all week 12–2 D served all week 6–9 Av 3 course à la carte £20 ⊕ Eldridge Pope ◀ Wadworth 6X, Hook Norton. **Facilities** Garden Dogs allowed Parking

---

BIRDLIP   MAP 10 SO91

The Golden Heart ♥
Nettleton Bottom GL4 8LA

☎ 01242 870261 📠 01242 870599

e-mail: cathstevensgh@aol.com

dir: *On A417 Gloucester to Cirencester. 8m from Cheltenham. Pub at base of dip in Nettleton Bottom*

A centuries-old Cotswold stone inn sitting in a dip, with absolutely glorious views from its terraced gardens. The regular menu, supplemented by a daily blackboard, includes game, minted lamb steak, pork tenderloin, beef and vegetable pie, ostrich casserole, kangaroo steak and even a crocodile, zebra and rattlesnake mixed grill. For fish fans there's scampi, battered cod and chips, and pan-fried fillet of salmon. Beer-buying policy supports local breweries such as Wickwar, Archers and Goffs.

Open 11–3 5.30–11 (Summer hols all day) (Fri-Sat 11–11, Sun 12–10.30) Closed: 25 Dec **Bar Meals** L served Mon-Sat 12–3 D served Mon-Sat 6–10 (Sun 12–10) Av main course £10.25 **Restaurant** L served Mon-Sat 12–3 D served Mon-Sat 6–10 (Sun 12–10) ⊕ Free House ◀ Archers Golden, Young's Special, Wickwar, Cotswolds Way. ♥ 10 **Facilities** Garden Dogs allowed Parking

---

BISLEY   MAP 04 SO90

The Bear Inn
George St GL6 7BD ☎ 01452 770265

e-mail: kate@bearinnbisley.co.uk

dir: *E of Stroud off B4070*

The 16th-century building was originally a courthouse, and even as a pub The Bear remained a manorial court until 1838. A huge inglenook fireplace, bread oven and old priest hole are outstanding features, and the rock-hewn cellars and 58-foot well are probably Tudor. There are two distinct areas serving meals and drinks, plus a cosy family room. Food includes baguettes, burgers and Bear Essentials such as stuffed pancakes, fish and chips, and steak pie.

Open 12–3 6–11 (Sat 12–11, Sun 12–10.30) **Bar Meals** L served all week 12–2.30 D served Mon-Sat 6–9.30 (Sun lunch all afternoon) ⊕ Pubmaster ◀ Tetley, Flowers IPA, Wells Bombardier & Youngs Special. **Facilities** Garden Dogs allowed Parking

PICK OF THE PUBS

BLEDINGTON-GLOUCESTERSHIRE

The Kings Head Inn

Set back from a perfect Cotswold village green, with its brook and stone bridge, this 16th-century, honeyed-stone building was once a cider house. Much of the original structure has survived, leaving sturdy beams, low ceilings, flagstone floors, exposed stone walls, and big open fireplaces – all of which have been preserved and enhanced by more recent modernisations.

The solid oak furniture and large black kettle hanging in an inglenook are nice touches. Owners Archie and Nicola Orr-Ewing have worked hard to earn an excellent reputation for this free house – one built on well kept real ales, an extensive wine list and wonderful fresh produce in the kitchen. Ingredients are locally sourced and organic as far as possible, with beef (hung for 21 days) from the family farm and fish delivered fresh from Grimsby. In the bar, Hook Norton Best is a mainstay, alongside other real ales, including guests from local micro-breweries. Organic cider and local lagers also feature, along with over 25 malts. The wine list offers a choice of more than 40 bins, including house wines by the glass. The lunch menu includes salads

and sandwiches alongside full meals such as kiln-roasted salmon fishcake with caper and chive mayonnaise followed by local venison with Savoy cabbage, bubble and squeak and redcurrant jus. For dinner, you could try local pheasant, herb and bacon terrine with home-made chutney and crusty bread, followed by chargrilled chicken breast with sage and lemon stuffing, smashed neeps and parmentier potatoes. Puddings (all home-made on the premises) could include a chocolate caramel brownie with vanilla ice cream, or bread and butter pudding with custard. The lovely bedrooms are worth bearing in mind, with six above the pub and six more by the courtyard.

★★★★ INN ◉ ♀
MAP 10 SP22
The Green OX7 6XQ
☎ 01608 658365
🖹 01608 658902
e-mail:
kingshead@orr-ewing.com
dir: *On B4450 4m from Stow-on-the-Wold*

Open 11.30–3 6–11 (Wknds & BHs 12–11) Closed: 24–25 Dec
Bar Meals L served all week 12–2 D served Sun-Thu 7–9.00 (Fri-Sat 7–9.30)
Restaurant L served all week 12–2 D served Mon-Sat 7–9.30 (Sun & Winter ex Fri/Sat last orders 9pm) Av 3 course à la carte £25
⊕ Free House ◀ Hook Norton Bitter, Doom Bar, Vale Pale Ale, Wye Valley & Brakspear. ♀ 8
Facilities Garden Parking
Rooms 12

LEDINGTON   MAP 10 SP22

Pick of the Pubs

The Kings Head Inn ★★★★ INN ◉ ♥

See Pick of the Pubs on opposite page

OURTON-ON-THE-HILL   MAP 10 SP13

Pick of the Pubs

Horse and Groom ♥

GL56 9AQ ☎ 01386 700413 📄 01386 700413

e-mail: greenstocks@horseandgroom.info

dir: *2m W of Moreton-in-Marsh on A44*

A honey-coloured Grade II listed Georgian building with a contemporary feel combined with original period features. This is a serious dining pub, as well as a friendly place for the locals to drink. The bar offers a selection of local favourites and guest ales, whilst the blackboard menu of regularly changing dishes provides plenty of appeal for even the most regular diners. With committed local suppliers backed up by the pub's own vegetable patch, the Horse and Groom's kitchen has plenty of good raw material to work with. A typical menu might feature fennel soup with white beans; mackerel and spring onion fishcake with rosemary aioli; or pork saltimbocca with puy lentils and green peppercorn sauce. Leave room for puds like chocolate, peanut and caramel torte. In summer, the mature garden offers panoramic hilltop views.

Open 11–3 6–11 (closed Sun eve & Mon lunch) Closed: 25 Dec **Bar Meals** L served Tue-Sat 12–2 Av main course £12.50 **Restaurant** L served Tue-Sat 12–2 D served Mon-Thu 7–9 (Sun 12–2.30, Fri-Sat 7–9.30) Av 3 course à la carte £24 ⊕ Free House ◀ Hook Norton Hooky, Dorothy Goodbody-Wye Valley, Pure UBU, Tournament. ♥ 14 **Facilities** Garden Parking

CHEDWORTH   MAP 05 SP01

Hare & Hounds ★★★★ INN ◉ ♥

Foss Cross GL54 4NN ☎ 01285 720288 📄 01285 720488

e-mail: stay@hareandhoundsinn.com

web: www.hareandhoundsinn.com

dir: *On A429 (Fosse Way), 6m from Cirencester*

A 14th-century inn with various interconnecting dining areas often described as a rabbit warren. Open fires, beams and stone and polished wood floors add to the charm. It's ideally placed for touring

the Cotswolds or attending Cheltenham race meetings. There's a daily changing blackboard, along with a menu typically listing breast of Gressingham duck; baked fillet of cod; and Burmese vegetable tofu curry.

Open 11–3 6–12 **Bar Meals** L served all week 12–2.30 D served all week 7–9.45 (Sun 12–3, 7–9) Av main course £12.95 **Restaurant** L served all week 11–2.30 D served all week 6.30–9.45 (Sun 12–3, 7–9) Av 3 course à la carte £15.95 ◀ Arkells 3B & JRA 2B. ♥ 10 **Facilities** Garden Dogs allowed Parking **Rooms** 10

Pick of the Pubs

Seven Tuns ♥

Queen St GL54 4AE

☎ 01285 720242 📄 01285 720933

e-mail: theseventuns@clara.co.uk

dir: *Exit A429, turn off at junct to Chedworth. Approx half way between Northleach & Cirencester, follow signs to pub.*

Directly opposite this creeper-covered, unmistakably Cotswold inn, are a waterwheel, a spring and a raised terrace for summer dining. The pub dates back to the 17th century, and the name derives from the seven chimney pots that deck the roof. The lunch menu offers nothing too heavy – sandwiches, ploughman's, jacket potatoes and appealing Mediterranean dishes like croque monsieur, tagliatelle bolognese or minted lamb kebabs. In the evening, try chorizo, new potato and goats' cheese salad; Mexican spiced chicken supreme with avocado and tomato salsa; or home-made sage, redcurrant and beef burgers. In the beer garden there's a revolving South African barbecue and a renovated skittle alley. Live music evenings held.

Open 12–3 6–11 (July-Aug all wk, all day) (Sat 12–2am, Sun 12–10.30) **Bar Meals** L served all week 12–3 D served all week 6.30–9.30 Av main course £11 **Restaurant** L served Mon-Fri 12–2.30 D served Mon-Sat 6.30–9.30 (Sat 12–3, Sun 12–3, 6–9) ◀ Young's Bitter, Winter Warmer, Waggledance, St Georges. ♥ 12 **Facilities** Garden Dogs allowed Parking

England

England

CHIPPING CAMPDEN — MAP 10 SP13

The Bakers Arms

Broad Campden GL55 6UR ☎ 01386 840515

dir: *1m from Chipping Campden*

There is a friendly family atmosphere at this country Cotswold inn, where you can expect to find exposed stone walls, beams and an inglenook fireplace. A choice of four to five real ales is offered alongside reasonably priced meals. Choose from sandwiches, warm baguettes and filled giant Yorkshire puddings, or dishes such as mariner's pie, Thai red vegetable curry, and liver, bacon and onions with rich gravy.

Open 11.30–2.30 4.45–11 (Sun 12–10.30, Summer 11.30–11) Closed: 25 Dec **Bar Meals** L served all week 12–2 D served all week 6–9 (Apr-Oct 12–9) **Restaurant** L served all week 12–2 D served all week 6–9 ⊕ Free House ◀ Stanway Bitter, Bombardier, Donnington BB. **Facilities** Garden Dogs allowed Parking Play Area **Notes** ◉

Pick of the Pubs

Eight Bells ♀

Church St GL55 6JG
☎ 01386 840371 🖹 01386 841669
e-mail: neilhargreaves@bellinn.fsnet.co.uk
dir: *8m from Stratford-upon-Avon*

A lovely old inn, located just off the High Street of this popular Cotswold destination, the Eight Bells was built in the 14th century to house stonemasons working on the nearby church and to store the eight church bells. A cobbled entranceway leads into two atmospheric bars, which retain the original oak beams, open fireplaces and a priest's hole. In summer, the exterior is hung with flower baskets, and guests spill out into the enclosed courtyard or the beautiful terraced garden that overlooks the almshouses and church. Freshly prepared local food is offered in the bar or the modern dining room. Lunchtime sandwiches on freshly baked bread are available Monday to Saturday, and dishes range through home-made soup, bruschetta, traditional fish and chips, chicken pasanda, and roast rump of prime British beef with Yorkshires and all the trimmings. Home-made desserts take in dark chocolate torte and bread and butter pudding.

Open 12–11 Closed: 25 Dec **Bar Meals** L served all week 12–2.30 D served Mon-Thu 6.30–9 (Fri-Sun 6.30–9.30) Av main course £12.50 **Restaurant** L served all week 12–2.30 D served Mon-Thu 6.30–9 (Fri-Sun 6.30–9.30) Av 3 course à la carte £20 ⊕ Free House ◀ Hook Norton Best, Goff's Jouster, Marston Pedigree, Purity UBU & guest ales. ♀8 **Facilities** Garden Dogs allowed **Rooms** available

---

The Kings ★★★★ RR ◉

The Square GL55 6AW ☎ 01386 840256 🖹 01386 84159
e-mail: info@kingscampden.co.uk

Set in the square of a pretty Cotswold town, this smart 17th-century in has an air of relaxed elegance. There are plenty of snacks, but the full menu offers some imaginative delights: tournedos Rossini with home made chicken liver pate in a rich Madeira wine sauce; dressed crab with shell on prawns; or a gateaux of herb polenta cakes, mozzarella and plum tomatoes. Seafish comes fresh from Brixham daily. Have a look at the specials board for more choices, and take in some lovely artwork by a local painter.

Open 9–11 Closed: 25 Dec **Bar Meals** L served Mon-Fri 12–2.30 D serve all week 6.30–9.30 (Sat-Sun 12–3) **Restaurant** L served Mon-Fri 12–2.30 D served all week 6.30–9.30 (Sat-Sun 12–3) ⊕ Free House ◀ Hook Norton Best. **Facilities** Garden Dogs allowed Parking **Rooms** 14

Pick of the Pubs

Noel Arms Hotel ★★★ HL ♀

High St GL55 6AT ☎ 01386 840317 🖹 01386 841136
e-mail: reception@noelarmshotel.com
dir: *On High St, opposite Town Hall*

Charles II stayed in this 16th-century coaching inn, built like so much round here of golden Cotswold stone. It was through the carriage arch that packhorse trains used to carry bales of wool, the source of the town's prosperity, to Bristol and Southampton. Absorb the hotel's atmosphere in front of the log fire in Dover's Bar; read the papers over coffee in the conservatory; sleep in a four-poster made in 1657; and enjoy the very best food from the lush Cotswolds. The bar offers a good choice, from toasted ciabattas, sandwiches and soups, to main meals such as Thai green chicken curry with steamed rice and prawn crackers; and butter bean and roast pepper tagine with minted couscous. An evening meal might involve pan-fried sweetbreads on apple mash with vanilla vinaigrette; chargrilled tuna steak with sun-blushed tomato risotto and olive tapenade; and mango parfait with passion-fruit mousse and lime tuiles.

Open 11–11 (Sun 12–11) **Bar Meals** L served all week 12–2.30 D served all week 6–9.30 Av main course £12 **Restaurant** L served all week 12–2.30 D served all week 7–9.30 ⊕ Free House ◀ Hook Norton Best Bitter, Guinness. ♀10 **Facilities** Garden Dogs allowed Parking **Rooms** 26

The Yew Tree

The Yew Tree is situated on the slopes of the National Trust's May Hill, and were you to climb to the 971ft summit you would be able to glimpse the bluish outlines of the Welsh Mountains, Malvern Hills and the River Severn. The pretty inn was a cider house back in the 16th century and the bars are floored with quarry tiles and warmed by a crackling log fire.

Hosts Caroline and Philip are the first to admit that the inn is not the easiest place to find, but it is well worth the effort and a warm welcome is guaranteed. A good choice of real ales is offered and all the wines are imported by the inn and sold in its own wine shop. This provides a selection of over 60 wines by the bottle, with £5 added to the retail price to drink it in the pub. The seasonal menu is supported by daily blackboard specials, and there's a selection of local farmhouse cheeses. Dishes are freshly prepared, and starters could include local asparagus and mascarpone tartlet, or grilled mushrooms with spinach and bacon, topped with melted Double Gloucester. Main courses range through Awre cider bacon steaks (local air-cured bacon marinated in Severn Sider cider served with cider and cream sauce, bubble and squeak and fresh vegetables); coq au vin; or line-caught fish with roasted sweet red pepper and beurre blanc. There are some nice nibbles, too, olives, nuts, houmous with breadsticks, or a bowl of Gloucester Old Spot crackling. Special events are a regular feature with a monthly quiz and supper through the winter and occasional guest performances plus an annual beer and cider festival in May.

MAP 10 SO72
Clifford Mesne GL18 1JS
☎ 01531 820719
🖹 01531 820912
e-mail: cass@yewtreeinn.com
dir: *From Newent High Street follow signs to Clifford's Mesne. Pub at far end of village on road to Glasshouse.*

Open 12–2.30 6–11 (Sun 12–4)
Bar Meals L served Wed-Sat 12–2 D served Tue-Sat 6–9 (Sun 12–4) Av main course £10
⊕ Free House ◀ Wye Valley Butty Bach, & a selection of locally brewed ales such as Whittingtons Nine Lives. ♀ 16
Facilities Garden Dogs allowed Parking Play Area

CHIPPING CAMPDEN continued

The Volunteer Inn ♇

Lower High St GL55 6DY ☎ 01386 840688

e-mail: mark_gibbo@yahoo.co.uk

dir: *From Shipston on Stour take B4035 to Chipping Campden.*

A 300-year-old inn where, in the mid-19th-century, the able-bodied used to sign up for the militia. Ramblers can set off from here to walk the Cotswold Way. Unusually, there is a takeaway food menu, featuring home-made burger with coleslaw and fries; and spinach, ricotta and basil lasagne with a herby tomato sauce. The in-house menus, supplemented by daily specials, feature the likes of honey and ginger beef with stir-fried vegetables and crispy noodles.

Open 11–11 (Nov-Mar Mon-Fri 12–3, 5–11) **Bar Meals** L served Mon-Sat 12–2.30 (Sun 12–3) Av main course £8 **Restaurant** L served Mon-Sat 12–2.30 D served Sun-Thu 5–10 (Sun 12–3 Fri-Sat 5–10.30) Av 3 course à la carte £18 ⊕ Free House ◀ Hook Norton, Hobgoblin ♇ 12 **Facilities** Garden Dogs allowed Play Area

---

CINDERFORD　　　　　　　　**MAP 10 SO61**

The New Inn ♇

170 Ruspidge Rd, Ruspidge GL14 3AR ☎ 01594 824508

e-mail: thenewinnruspidge@fsmail.net

dir: *1.5m from Cinderford*

A traditional country pub in the heart of the Forest of Dean, The New Inn serves as a popular village local while also offering a warm welcome to visitors from further afield. A good selection of home-made pub food includes grilled steaks, an impressive choice of curries, and vegetarian dishes such as home-made spicy chilli, or butternut squash and ginger bake. Lunch is served by arrangement.

Open 5–11 (Sun & BH 12–11) **Bar Meals** L served all week 5–10 D served all week 5–10 (lunch by arrangement for 6+) Av main course £6.95 ⊕ Free House ♇ 10 **Facilities** Garden Dogs allowed Parking

---

CIRENCESTER　　　　　　　**MAP 05 SP00**

Pick of the Pubs

The Crown of Crucis ★★★ HL ♇

Ampney Crucis GL7 5RS

☎ 01285 851806 🖨 01285 851735

e-mail: reception@thecrownofcrucis.co.uk

dir: *On A417 to Lechlade, 2m E of Cirencester*

This 16th-century inn stands beside the Ampney brook in picturesque Ampney Crucis at the gateway to the Cotswolds. The

name 'Crucis' refers to the Latin cross in the nearby churchyard. The inn itself retains its historical charm while feeling comfortably up-to-date. It overlooks the village cricket green, and on summer days the evocative sound of willow on leather and the quiet stream meandering past the lawns conspire to create a perfect picture of quintessential England. Bar food is served all day, with choices ranging from snacks and salads to comforting meals such as the award-winning home-made steak and kidney pie. The restaurant menu offers starters of carpaccio of beef with roast aubergines; and chicken skewers with lime and coriander marinade, followed perhaps by breast of guinea fowl and confit leg wrapped in pancetta with a celery and cranberry sauce. Typical desserts include crème brûlée and sticky toffee pudding.

Open 10.30–11 Closed: 25 Dec **Bar Meals** L served all week 12–10 D served all week 12–10 **Restaurant** L served all week 12–2.30 D served all week 7–9.30 ⊕ Free House ◀ Doom Bar, Archers Village, John Smiths's. ♇ 10 **Facilities** Garden Dogs allowed Parking **Rooms** 25

CLIFFORD'S MESNE　　　　**MAP 10 SO72**

Pick of the Pubs

The Yew Tree ♇

See Pick of the Pubs on opposite page

COATES　　　　　　　　　　**MAP 04 SO90**

Pick of the Pubs

The Tunnel House Inn

See Pick of the Pubs on page 222

COLESBOURNE　　　　　　**MAP 10 SP01**

Pick of the Pubs

The Colesbourne Inn ♇

GL53 9NP ☎ 01242 870376

e-mail: info@thecolesbourneinn.co.uk

dir: *Midway between Cirencester & Cheltenham on A435*

A handsome 17th-century stone pub on the Colesbourne estate at the heart of the Cotswolds. Set between the historic towns of Cheltenham and Cirencester, it is ideal for exploring the villages and gentle, very English countryside of Gloucestershire. Nearby is the source of the River Thames, which can be reached on foot along delightful field and meadow paths. Dating back to 1827 and set in two acres of grounds, the Colesbourne Inn has been sympathetically restored over the years. Among the distinguishing features are a host of beams, roaring log fires, four separate dining areas, and a superb terrace and garden with stunning rural views. There is even a side entrance from the bar originally used as a chamber for smoking ham. Food is all important at the Colesbourne Inn, and fresh local produce is used wherever possible; there is an appetising range of light bites.

Open 12–3 6–11 (Sat-Sun 12–11) (Nov-Feb 12–11) **Bar Meals** L served Mon-Fri 12–1.45 D served Sun-Thu 6–8.45 (Sat-Sun 12–2.30, Fri-Sat 6–9.30) **Restaurant** L served Mon-Fri 12–1.45 D served Sun-Thu 6.30–8.45 (Sat-Sun 12–2.30, Fri-Sat 6.30–9.30) ⊕ Wadworth ◀ Wadworth 6X, Henrys IPA, Bishops Tipple/ Summersault. ♇ 20 **Facilities** Garden Dogs allowed Parking Play Area **Rooms** available

PICK OF THE PUBS

COATES-GLOUCESTERSHIRE

The Tunnel House Inn

Between the Cotswold villages of Coates and Tarlton, the Tunnel House Inn enjoys a glorious rural location down a very bumpy track by Sapperton Tunnel on the Thames and Severn Canal. It once provided accommodation for the 'navvies' building the canal, and is not far from the source of the Thames.

It was rebuilt in 1957 after a fire, and the bar has some oddities, including an upside-down table on the ceiling. In the summer or on warm spring and autumn days the garden is an ideal place for relaxing with a drink or a meal, and enjoying the views across the fields. Three log fires warm the welcoming bar in the winter months. A children's play area and spectacular walks in the surrounding countryside add to its popularity. You may dine in the restaurant area or relax in the comfortable seating in the bar. Eat lightly at lunchtime with a bacon and brie sandwich or a ploughman's, or choose from the monthly changing menu typically featuring good home-cooked dishes such as Tunnel House pie with chips and vegetables; Gloucester

Old Spot sausages with creamed mash, red onion marmalade and rich gravy; and broccoli, potato and cheese bake. Dinner, from a separate menu, could begin with pan-fried king prawns in chilli, lime and garlic butter; then lamb shank with dauphinoise potatoes, seasonal vegetables and rosemary and redcurrant gravy; with treacle tart and vanilla ice cream to follow. Children will probably opt for the usual favourites of sausage and mash; mini beefburger with cheese and bacon; fish and chips; or chicken goujons.

MAP 04 SO90
GL7 6PW
☎ 01285 770280
🖷 01285 700040
e-mail:
bookings@tunnelhouse.com
web: www.tunnelhouse.com
dir: *From Cirencester on A433 towards Tetbury, in 2m turn right towards Coates, follow brown signs to Canal Tunnel & Inn*

Open 11–3 6–11 (Open all day Fri-Sun)
Bar Meals L served Mon-Sat 12–2.15 D served all week 6.45–9.15 (Sun 12–2.30)
Restaurant L served Mon-Sat 12–2.15 D served all week 6.45–9.15 (Sun 12–2.30)
◀ Uley Old Spot, Uley Bitter, Wye Valley Bitter, Hook Norton.
Facilities Children's licence Garden Dogs allowed Parking Play Area

COLN ST ALDWYNS   MAP 05 SP10

The New Inn At Coln ♥

GL7 5AN ☎ 01285 750651 📄 01285 750657
e-mail: info@thenewinnatcoln.co.uk
web: www.new-inn.co.uk
dir: *Between Bibury (B4425) & Fairford (A417), 8m E of Cirencester*

The centre of this Cotswold village community, this pub welcomes walkers, their dogs and children too. The interior has been totally refurbished with a comfortable gastro-pub feel, so relax with a pint of Old Hooky while deciding what to eat and where; the south-facing terrace is a must in summer. Doorstep sandwiches and pan-fried lambs' kidneys are lunchtime favourites, while the dinner menu tempts with soft-boiled duck egg with pea mousse, followed by fillet of halibut with sorrel soubise.

Open 11–11 (Sun 12–10.30) **Bar Meals** L served Mon-Sat 12.30–2.30 D served all week 7–9.30 (Sun 12–3) **Restaurant** L served Mon-Sat 12.30–2.30 D served Mon-Sat 7–9.30 (Sun 12–3) Av 3 course à la carte £30 ⊕ Free House ◀ Hook Norton Best Bitter, Wadworth 6X, Donningtons BB. ♥ 12 **Facilities** Children's licence Garden Parking

COWLEY   MAP 10 SO91

Pick of the Pubs

The Green Dragon Inn ★★★★ INN ♥

See Pick of the Pubs on page 224

CRANHAM   MAP 10 SO81

The Black Horse Inn

GL4 8HP ☎ 01452 812217
dir: *A46 towards Stroud, follow signs for Cranham*

Set in a small village surrounded by woodland and commons, a mile from the Cotswold Way and Prinknash Abbey, this is a traditional inn with two open fires and two dining rooms upstairs. On the menu you'll find all sorts of pies, as well as chops, gammon, salads, casseroles and a variety of fish dishes including grilled salmon, and trout with garlic and herb butter. There's quite a bit of Morris dancing throughout the season, with the sloping garden offering lovely views across the valley.

Open 12–3 6.30–11 (Sun 8–10.30) Closed: 25 Dec **Bar Meals** L served Tue-Sun 12–2 D served Tue-Sun 6.45–9 Av main course £9 ⊕ Free House ◀ Wickwar Brand Oak, Archers, Golden Train & Village, Hancocks HB & guest ales. **Facilities** Garden Parking

DIDMARTON   MAP 04 ST88

Pick of the Pubs

The Kings Arms ★★★★ INN ♥

The Street GL9 1DT ☎ 01454 238245 📄 01454 238249
e-mail: bookings@kingsarmsdidmarton.co.uk
dir: *M4 junct 18 take A46 N signed Stroud, after 8m take A433 signed Didmarton 2m*

This attractively restored 17th-century coaching inn is locally famous for its annual Rook Night Supper, held after the cull on the sprawling Badminton Estate. The building was originally held on a 1,000-year lease from the Beaufort family at a rent of sixpence a year. Today, the Edwardian-style interior is cosy and welcoming all year round, especially when the big open fires are blazing away in winter. Both bars support local breweries, and 10 wines are available by the glass. The weekly changing seasonal menu might include smoked chicken and Moroccan salad or goats' cheese and red onion charlotte, followed by wild mushroom and red pepper tagliatelle; 10oz rib-eye steak on crushed new potato with pepper sauce; or roast haunch of Badminton venison with butter onion mash. Fish dishes might be home-smoked scallops with a pancetta and pinenut salad; monkfish with lime and banana curry, or red snapper with a sweet tomato and prawn risotto. The beautiful, large enclosed gardens incorporate a boules pitch.

Open 11–11.30 (Fri-Sat 11–11 Sun 12–10.30) **Bar Meals** L served all week 12–2.30 D served Mon-Sat 6–9 (Sun 7–9) Av main course £10 **Restaurant** L served Mon-Sat 12–2.30 D served Mon-Sat 6–9 (Sun 12–7.45) ⊕ Free House ◀ Uley Bitter, Otter, Moles Brewery, Hook Norton. ♥ 10 **Facilities** Garden Dogs allowed Parking **Rooms** 4

The Green Dragon Inn

A handsome stone-built inn dating from the 17th century and located in the Cotswold hamlet of Cockleford. The fittings and furniture are the work of the 'Mouse Man of Kilburn' (so-called for his trademark mouse) who lends his name to the popular Mouse Bar, with its stone-flagged floors, beamed ceilings and crackling log fires.

The weekly menu includes sandwiches at lunchtime, children's favourites, and a choice of starters/light meals such as smoked haddock chowder or Caesar salad. Typical fish dishes may include fillet of mackerel on ciabatta; stir-fried smoked eel with black beans and spring onions; Green Dragon fish pie; and blue swimming crab omelette. Other important features are the choice of real ales, with a monthly guest beer; the heated dining terrace; and the function room/skittle alley. Very popular at weekends.

★★★★ INN ♛
MAP 10 SO91
Cockleford GL53 9NW
☎ 01242 870271
🖷 01242 870171
dir: *Telephone for directions*

Open 11–11 (Sun 12–10.30)
Bar Meals L served all week
12–2.30 D served all week
6–10.30 (Sat 12–3, 6–10 Sun
12–3.30, 6–9) Av main course
£12.50
⊕ Free House ◀ Hook Norton,
Directors Butcombe, guest ale.
♛ 9
Facilities Children's licence
Garden Dogs allowed Parking
Rooms 9

PICK OF THE PUBS

FORD-GLOUCESTERSHIRE

The Plough Inn

Tucked away in the hamlet of Ford, this 16th-century inn is ideally situated for explorations of all that the Cotswolds have to offer. Fans of countryside activities will be particularly well served here.

The Plough regularly hosts shooting lunches, fishing is available nearby and Cheltenham racecourse is but a short drive, while the famous racing stables of Jackdaws Castle are just across the street. Inside, the inn is steeped in history and character, providing all that one associates with a traditional English pub, from flagstone floors and log fires, to sturdy pine furnishings and lively conversation. In one of its earlier incarnations, the inn served as a local courthouse, with cellars being used as cells for sheep-stealers. Under the rear lounge window are the remnants of the indoor stocks that once held miscreants – these days seating arrangements are more hospitable! Interestingly, the literal meaning of the phrase 'you're barred' becomes clear when one

sees another relic of the past – the bar that was once used to reinforce the door when court was in session. Meals made from local produce are cooked to order, and the inn is renowned for its fresh, seasonal asparagus supper. Seafood is also something of a speciality: try sea bass on a bed of wild mushroom risotto; smoked haddock with poached egg and cheese sauce; beer-battered cod; or a sumptuous lemon sole filled with crab and lobster bisque. Visitors can stay in three well-converted en suite bedrooms in what was once a stable block and hayloft.

★★★★ INN ♟
MAP 10 SP02
GL54 5RU
☎ 01386 584215
▤ 01386 584042
e-mail:
info@theploughinnatford.co.uk
dir: *4m from Stow-on-the-Wold on Tewkesbury road*

Open 11–12 (Fri-Sat 11am-1am)
Closed: 25 Dec
Bar Meals L served all week
12–2 D served all week 6.30–9
(Wknds 12–9)
Restaurant L served all week
11.30–2 D served all week 6.30–9
(Wknds 11.30–9)
◆ Donnington BB, SBA &
XXX (summer only). ♟ 7
Facilities Garden Parking Play Area
Rooms 3

PICK OF THE PUBS

FOSSEBRIDGE-GLOUCESTERSHIRE

The Inn at Fossebridge

This attractive family-run free house in the heart of the Coln Valley is ideally situated for visiting Bibury and Northleach. It's less than an hour to Stratford; Burford and Stow-on-the-Wold, sometimes called the capital of the Cotswolds, are also within easy reach. Sited within the parish of Chedworth, the first building on the site was recorded in 1634.

The inn had opened by 1759, subsequently to become known as Lord Chedworth's Arms. The name is recalled in the wonderful old bar that still exists today; it became the Inn at Fossebridge in the early 19th century. The atmospheric Bridge Bar and Restaurant is located in the oldest part of the building. Exposed beams, stone walls, flagstone floors and open fires provide the setting for the varied bar food and restaurant menus. Snacks range from sandwiches, baguettes and jacket potatoes to light meals, whilst the ever-changing specials board might feature steak and ale pie; or pan-fried sardines with chunky tomato sauce. Look to the seasonally-changing main menu for additional choices: starters of Peking duck spring rolls; deep-fried brie with marinated vegetables; and Thai fish cakes with lemon grass sauce. Main courses could find shallow-fried Billingsgate cod with chips, mushy peas and tartare sauce; chargrilled Fossebridge burger, on its own or with bacon or cheese, served with relish and mixed leaf salad. Also from the chargrill is the halibut steak, served with ratatouille, saffron potatoes and vièrge sauce. The traditional Irish stew with dumplings and colcannon mash makes a warming and hearty dish for a frosty winter's day. But leave room for a dessert: perhaps chocolate and orange sponge with dark chocolate sauce and vanilla ice cream.

★★★★ INN 🍷
MAP 05 SP01
GL54 3JS
☎ 01285 720721
🖷 01285 720793
e-mail:
info@fossebridgeinn.co.uk
web: www.fossebridgeinn.co.uk
dir: *From M4 junct 15, A419 towards Cirencester, then A429 towards Stow. Pub approx 7m on left*

Open 12–12 (Sun 12–11.30)
Bar Meals L served all week 12–3 D served Mon-Sat 6–10 (Sun 6–9.30)
Restaurant L served all week 12–3 D served Mon-Sat 6–10 (Sun 6–9.30) ⊕ Free House
🍺 Youngs, Hooky, Old Hooky & 6X. 🍷 8
Facilities Garden Dogs allowed Parking
Notes
Rooms 8

Pick of the Pubs

The Ebrington Arms NEW Ⓤ ★★★★
INN ◉ ⬥

GL55 6NH ☎ 01386 593223
e-mail: info@theebringtonarms.co.uk
dir: *Chipping Campden on B4035 towards Shipston-on-Stour. Left to Ebrington signed after 0.5m, by village green*

A hidden gem of a proper pub, just two miles from Chipping Campden in an area of outstanding natural beauty and ideally situated for access to the Cotswold Way. The inn, built in 1640, is steeped in history and retains many original features – from giant flagstone floors and beamed ceilings to log burning inglenook fireplaces that used to cook the village's bread. It's the hub of community life, with colourful locals chatting over the merits of three award-winning real ales and two ciders. As for the menu, head chef James Nixon is a great believer in low food miles and freshly harvested organic produce when available. A typical choice could be crabcakes with wilted spinach, followed by roasted rump of Cotswold lamb or a special such as fan-fried fillet of sea bream, and a pudding of chocolate pecan pie with clotted cream. Monthly music, games and quiz nights, and occasional themed food evenings are held.

Open 12–3 6–11 (Sun all day, Sat all day summer only) Closed: Mon (ex BH) **Bar Meals** L served Tue-Sun 12–2.30 D served Tue-Sat 6–9 Av main course £10 **Restaurant** L served Tue-Sun 12–2.30 D served Tue-Sat 6–9 ⊕ Free House ◖ Goffs Brewery, Jouster. ⬥ 8 **Facilities** Garden Parking **Rooms** 3

Pick of the Pubs

The Plough Inn ★★★★ INN ⬥
See Pick of the Pubs on page 225

Pick of the Pubs

The Inn at Fossebridge ★★★★ INN ⬥
See Pick of the Pubs on opposite page

Pick of the Pubs

The Crown Inn ★★★★ INN ⬥
See Pick of the Pubs on page 228

Pick of the Pubs

The White Horse ◉ ⬥
Cirencester Rd GL6 8HZ ☎ 01285 760960
e-mail: emmawhitehorse@aol.com
dir: *6m from Cirencester towards Stroud on A419*

Seagrass flooring and original artwork on the walls gives this smart dining pub a fresh, inviting feel. The White Horse has a growing reputation for modern British food, and offers a warm welcome even if all you want is a quiet drink. A large sofa and comfy chairs encourage the latter, whilst the daily-changing menu will please discerning appetites. The large seawater tank ensures a good supply of fresh seafood, with oysters, clams, mussels and lobsters available in season. Restaurant diners might select potted shrimp from the monthly changing menus, before moving on to noisettes of lamb stuffed with apricots and served with chorizo mash; Cornish lobster; or slow braised pork belly with bubble and squeak. Steamed marmalade pudding with crème anglaise is a typical dessert. A good-value fixed price menu is proving highly popular, and a lengthy, thoughtful wine list will delight oeniphiles.

Open 11–3 6–11 Closed: 24-26 Dec, 1 Jan **Bar Meals** L served Mon-Sat 12–2.30 D served Mon-Sat (Sun 12–3) Av main course £8.95 **Restaurant** L served all week 12–2.30 D served Mon-Sat 7–9.45 (Sun 12–3) Av 3 course à la carte £24 Av 2 course fixed price £15.25 ⊕ Free House ◖ Uley Bitter, Hook Norton Best, Arkells Summer Ale. ⬥ 10 **Facilities** Garden Dogs allowed Parking

England

PICK OF THE PUBS

FRAMPTON MANSELL-GLOUCESTERSHIRE

The Crown Inn

This 17th-century inn stands in the heart of the unspoilt village of Frampton Mansell and has views over the beautiful wooded Golden Valley. The interior is full of old world charm, with honey-coloured stone walls, beams, and open fireplaces where log fires are lit in winter. There is also plenty of seating in the large garden for the warmer months.

Fresh local food with lots of seasonal specials, real ales from Uley Brewery and the Wickwar Brewing Company, and a good choice of wines by the glass are served in the restaurant and three inviting bars. The menus are seasonal and freshly sourced and created. For starters you could try beetroot and Cerney Ash goat's cheese salad; or seared scallops with sliced Old Spot sausage and a chilli balsamic oil. Move on perhaps to a straightforward ploughman's with sliced Cotswold ham, brie and cheddar, pickles, parsnip crisps and red onion jam, served with crusty bread and apple; a hearty steak and Coopers Pale Ale pie with a puff pastry lid, creamy mash and vegetables; Oxford Blue cheese, leek, and field mushroom tartlet with a warm new potato and crème fraiche salad; or home-made beef burger, thickly cut chips and The Crown's home-made tomato sauce. All dishes can also be served in child-sized portions. Twelve smart bedrooms housed in an annexe make it easy to stay and enjoy the place, with plenty to do while you relax and unwind. Various events are held at the inn, including quiz nights. There are some wonderful walks and cycling routes in the surrounding countryside, and the royal residences of Highgrove and Gatcombe Park are in the neighbourhood.

★★★★ INN ☂
MAP 04 SO90
GL6 8JG
☎ 01285 760601
e-mail: enquiries@
thecrowninn-cotswolds.co.uk
dir: *A419 halfway between
Cirencester & Stroud*

Open 12–11 (Sun 12–10.30)
Bar Meals L served Mon-Sat
12–3 6–9.30 D served all week
(Sun 12–5) Av main course £11
Restaurant L served Mon-Sat
12–3 6–9.30 D served all week
(Sun 12–5)
⊕ Free House ◧ Butcombe
Bitter, Coopers Pale Ale & Laurie
Lee's Bitter. ☂ 17
Facilities Garden Parking
Rooms 12

England

GLOUCESTER
MAP 10 SO81

Queens Head ♥

Tewkesbury Rd, Longford GL2 9EJ
☎ 01452 301882 📄 01452 524368

e-mail: queenshead@aol.com

dir: *On A38 (Tewkesbury to Gloucester road) in Longford*

This 250 year-old pub/restaurant is just out of town but there's no missing it in summer when it is festooned with hanging baskets. Inside, there's a lovely old flagstone-floored locals' bar which proffers a great range of real ales, while two dining areas tempt with tasty menus. These may include beef stroganoff, or the pub's signature dish, Longford lamb – a kilo joint slowly cooked in mint gravy until it falls off the bone.

Open 11–3 5.30–11 **Bar Meals** L served all week 12–2 D served all week 6.30–9.30 **Restaurant** L served all week 12–2 D served all week 6.30–9.30 ⊕ Free House ◀ Ringwood, Landlord, Pigswill, Butty Bach. ♥ 8 **Facilities** Parking

The Lamb Inn

Open 11.30–2.30 6.30–11 **Bar Meals** L served all week 12–2 D served all week 7–9.30 (Sat-Sun 12–2.30) Av main course £8.95 **Restaurant** L served all week 12–2 D served all week 7–9.30 ⊕ Free House ◀ Hook Norton, John Smiths & guest ale. ♥ 9 **Facilities** Garden Dogs allowed Parking Play Area **Rooms** available

GREAT BARRINGTON
MAP 10 SP21

The Fox ♥

OX18 4TB ☎ 01451 844385

e-mail: info@foxinnbarrington.com

dir: *3m W on A40 from Burford, turn N signed The Barringtons, pub approx 0.5m on right*

Picturesque pub with a delightful patio and large beer garden overlooking the River Windrush – on warm days a perfect summer watering hole, and very popular with those attending Cheltenham racecourse. Built of mellow Cotswold stone and characterised by low ceilings and log fires, the inn offers a range of well-kept Donnington beers and a choice of food which might include beef in ale pie, local pigeon breasts casseroled with button mushrooms, chicken piri-piri, Thai tuna steak, and spinach, leek and chestnut pie.

Open 11–11 **Bar Meals** L served Mon-Fri 12–2.30 D served Mon-Fri 6.30–9.30 (Sat-Sun 12–9.30) Av main course £9.95 **Restaurant** L served Mon-Fri 12–2.30 D served Mon-Fri 6.30–9.30 (Sat-Sun 12–9.30) ⊕ ◀ Donnington BB, SBA. ♥ 7 **Facilities** Garden Dogs allowed Parking

GREAT RISSINGTON
MAP 10 SP11

The Lamb Inn ♥

GL54 2LP ☎ 01451 820388 📄 01451 820724

e-mail: enquiries@thelambinn.com

dir: *Between Oxford & Cheltenham off A40*

Among the attractions at this busy inn, some of which dates back 300 years, are part of a Wellington bomber which crashed in the garden in 1943, and a specially installed OS map of the area helpful for walkers. Home-cooked pub food might include pork loin steak on a mustard mash with apple and sage sauce, tagliatelle with spinach, blue cheese and pine nut cream, or chargrilled salmon, tuna and red mullet on noodles.

Open 11–12.30 **Bar Meals** L served all week 12 D served all week 9.30 Av main course £10 **Restaurant** L served all week 12 D served all week 9.30 ⊕ Free House ◀ Hollow Bottom Best Bitter, Goff's Jouster, Timothy Taylor Landlord, Fuller's London Pride. ♥ 7 **Facilities** Children's licence Garden Dogs allowed Parking

GREET
MAP 10 SP03

The Harvest Home ♥

Evesham Rd GL54 5BH ☎ 01242 602430

dir: *M5 junct 9 take A435 towards Evesham, then B4077 & B4078 towards Winchcombe, 200yds from station*

Set in the beautiful Cotswold countryside, this traditional country inn draws steam train enthusiasts aplenty, as a restored stretch of the Great Western Railway runs past the end of the garden. Built around 1903 for railway workers, the pub is handy for Cheltenham Racecourse and Sudeley Castle. Expect a good range of snacks and mains, including locally-reared beef and tempting seafood dishes.

Open 12–3 6–11 (Sun 6–10.30) **Bar Meals** L served all week 12–2 D served all week 6–9 Av main course £8 **Restaurant** L served all week 12–2 D served all week 6–9 Av 3 course à la carte £16.50 Av 2 course fixed price £5.95 ⊕ Enterprise Inns ◀ Old Speckled Hen, Goffs Jouster, Deuchars IPA. ♥ 11 **Facilities** Children's licence Garden Dogs allowed Parking

GUITING POWER
MAP 10 SP02

The Hollow Bottom ♥

GL54 5UX ☎ 01451 850392 📄 01451 850945

e-mail: hello@hollowbottom.com

dir: *Telephone for directions*

There's a horse-racing theme at this 18th-century Cotswold free house, often frequented by the Cheltenham racing fraternity. Its nooks and crannies lend themselves to an intimate drink or meal, and there's also a separate dining room, plus outside tables for fine weather. Specials include prawn cocktail on seasonal leaves with a spicy tomato sauce; grilled salmon; breast of pan-fried chicken with stilton, olive oil, tomato and spring onion; and home-made raspberry cheesecake to finish.

Open 11–12.30 **Bar Meals** L served all week 12 D served all week 9.30 Av main course £10 **Restaurant** L served all week 12 D served all week 9.30 ⊕ Free House ◀ Hollow Bottom Best Bitter, Goff's Jouster, Timothy Taylor Landlord, Fuller's London Pride. ♥ 7 **Facilities** Children's licence Garden Dogs allowed Parking

England

HINTON · MAP 04 ST77

The Bull Inn ▾

SN14 8HG ☎ 0117 9372332

e-mail: diserwhite@aol.com

dir: *From M4 junct 18, A46 to Bath 1m, turn right 1m, down hill. Pub on right*

Since it was built in the 17th century, The Bull has been an inn, a farm and a dairy. Inside it retains two inglenook fireplaces and original flagstone flooring, while outside there's a front-facing terrace and a large rear garden with a children's play area. Food served in the restaurant and bar draws on locally supplied produce and home-grown fruit and vegetables. Look out for house specialities such as truffle and chive potato pancake.

Open 12–3 6–11 (Sat 12–11, Sun 12–10.30) Closed: Mon lunch
Bar Meals L served Tue-Sat 12–2 D served Mon-Thu 6–9 (Fri-Sat 6–9.30, Sun 12–3, 7–8.30) **Restaurant** L served Tue-Sun 12–2 D served Mon-Thu 6–9 (Fri-Sat 6–9.30, Sun 7–8.30) ⊕ Wadworth ◀ Wadworth 6X & Henrys IPA, Wadworth Bishops Tipple, Wadworth Summersault plus guest ale. ▾ 12 **Facilities** Garden Dogs allowed Parking Play Area

LECHLADE ON THAMES · MAP 05 SU29

The Trout Inn ▾

St Johns Bridge GL7 3HA

☎ 01367 252313 📄 01367 252313

e-mail: chefpjw@aol.com

dir: *From A40 take A361 then A417. From M4 to Lechlade then A417 to inn*

In 1220, when workmen constructed a new bridge over the Thames, they built an almshouse to live in. In 1472 it became an inn, which it has been ever since. The bar, all flagstone floors and beams, overflows into the old boathouse. Appetising snacks, and dishes like rich lamb and vegetable hotpot; locally made faggots; and tempura-battered hake fillets are favourites. The large garden often pulsates with tractor and steam events, and jazz and folk festivals.

Open 10–3 6–11 (Summer all day) Closed: 25 Dec **Bar Meals** L served all week 12–2 D served Mon-Sat 7–10 (Sun 7–9.30) Av main course £9.50 ⊕ Unique Pub Co ◀ Courage Best, Doom Bar, Cornish Coaster, guest ales. ▾ 15 **Facilities** Garden Dogs allowed Parking Play Area

LITTLETON-ON-SEVERN · MAP 04 ST58

White Hart ▾

BS35 1NR ☎ 01454 412275

e-mail: whitehart@youngs.co.uk

dir: *M48 junct 1 towards Chepstow left on rdbt, follow for 3m, 1st left to Littleton-on-Severn*

A traditional English country pub dating back to the 1680s. It was originally a farmhouse, from which flagstone floors and other features of the old building, including two large inglenook fireplaces, survive. Food ranges from home-cooked pub classics, such as beef and ale winter stew with herb dumpling and vegetables, to modern Anglo-French dishes that usually feature among the specials. After all-day rain in the front garden, watch it set over the Severn estuary.

Open 12–3 6–11 (Sat-Sun all day) **Bar Meals** L served all week 12–2 D served all week 6.30–9.30 (Sat-Sun 12–2.30, 6–9) Av main course £8.95 ◀ Youngs Bitter, Youngs Special, Youngs Waggledance, Thatchers Heritage. ▾ 18 **Facilities** Children's licence Garden Dogs allowed Parking

LITTLE WASHBOURNE · MAP 10 SO93

The Hobnails Inn ▾

GL20 8NQ ☎ 01242 620237 📄 01242 620458

dir: *M5 junct 9, A46 towards Evesham then B4077 to Stow-on-the-Wold. Inn 1.5m on left*

Established in 1473, the Hobnails is one of the oldest inns in the county. Inside you'll find winter log fires, and you can tuck yourself into a private corner, or relax with a pint of ale on one of the leather sofas. A good range of bar snacks is supplemented by a lunchtime carvery and a fresh fish range. Outside is a lovely large garden for warmer days with views over surrounding countryside.

Open 12–2.30 6–11 (Sat-Sun 12–11 Apr-Sep) **Bar Meals** L served Mon-Sat 12–2 D served all week 6–9 (Sun 12–3) Av main course £9.95 **Restaurant** L served Mon-Sat 12–2 D served all week 6–9 (Sun 12–3) ⊕ Enterprise Inns ◀ London Pride, Flowers IPA, Hook Norton Best, Deuchars IPA. ▾ 6 **Facilities** Children's licence Garden Dogs allowed Parking

LONGHOPE · MAP 10 SO61

The Glasshouse Inn

May Hill GL17 0NN ☎ 01452 830529

dir: *Village off A40 between Gloucester & Ross-on-Wye*

The Glasshouse is unique and its popularity confirms the need for traditional pubs with no gimmicks. The inn dates back to 1450 and gets its name from Dutch glassmakers who settled locally in the 16th century. It is located in a wonderful rural setting with a country garden outside and a tranquil and dignified interior. Home-cooked dishes now include authentic Thai choices.

Open 11.30–3 6.30–11 **Bar Meals** L served Mon-Sat 12–2 D served Mon-Sat 7–9 (Sun 12–3) ⊕ Free House ◀ Butcombe, Spitfire, Black Sheep, London Pride & Greene King. **Facilities** Garden Parking

England

LOWER APPERLEY   MAP 10 SO82

The Farmers Arms ♥

Ledbury Rd GL19 4DR ☎ 01452 780307 🖹 01452 780307
e-mail: starline.estop@btconnect.com
dir: *From Tewksbury take A38 towards Gloucester/Ledbury. 2m, right at lights onto B4213 (signed Ledbury). 1.5m, pub on left*

A popular, 16th-century, timber-framed pub on the village fringe and close to the River Severn. Low beams, an open fire, regular guest ales and an extensive menu are to be found within. Home-made dishes using locally sourced produce include steak and kidney pie; honey roast ham with free range eggs and chips; and luxury fish pie.

Open 11.30–3 6–11 (Sun 12–10.30) Closed: Mon ex eve summer hols
Bar Meals L served all week 12–2.15 D served Mon-Thu 6–9 (Fri-Sat 6–9.30, Sun 12–8) Av main course £8.50 **Restaurant** L served Tue-Sun 12–2.15 D served all week 6.30–9.30 Av 3 course à la carte £17.50
⊕ Wadworth ◀ Wadworth 6X, Henry's Original IPA plus guest ales. ♥ 10
Facilities Garden Parking Play Area **Rooms** available

LOWER ODDINGTON   MAP 10 SP22

Pick of the Pubs

The Fox ♥

GL56 0UR
☎ 01451 870555 & 870669 🖹 01451 870669
e-mail: info@foxinn.net
dir: *A436 from Stow-on-the-Wold then right to Lower Oddington*

A creeper-clad 16th-century inn of Cotswold stone, The Fox is tucked away in an idyllic village setting, close to Stow-on-the-Wold, Moreton-in-Marsh and Chipping Campden. Antique furniture is set against the polished flagstone floor, beams and log fires in the bar, and the Red Room, dedicated to dining, has a fine collection of drawings, water colours and oil paintings. In summer, the enclosed garden with its covered, heated terrace comes into its own. The menu is supported by daily changing blackboards, and food is prepared from fresh, local produce. Home-cured gravadlax is a speciality starter, followed perhaps by slow-cooked lamb shank in red wine with rosemary and cranberries. Ecclefechan tart with whisky syrup and cream provides a satisfying conclusion.

Open 12–3 6.30–11 (Apr-Oct 12–11) Closed: 25 Dec
Bar Meals L served all week 12–2.30 D served Mon-Sat 6.30–10 (Sun 6.30–9.30) **Restaurant** L served all week 12–2.30 D served Mon-Sat 6.30–10 (Sun 6.30–9.30) ⊕ Free House ◀ Hook Norton Best, Abbot Ale, Ruddles County, Wickwar's Old Bob. ♥ 12 **Facilities** Garden Parking

LYDNEY   MAP 04 SO60

The George Inn ♥

St Briavels GL15 6TA ☎ 01594 530228 🖹 01594 530260
e-mail: george_inn@tiscali.co.uk
dir: *Telephone for directions*

In a quiet village high above the Wye Valley and close to the Forest of Dean, this pretty white-washed pub overlooks a moody 12th-century castle ruin. The interior includes an 8th-century Celtic coffin lid set into one of the walls. The pub is famous for braised shoulder of lamb and Moroccan lamb, along with popular dishes such as traditional steak and kidney, and beef and Guinness pies.

Open 11–2.30 6.30–11 **Bar Meals** L served all week 11–2.30 D served all week 6.30–9.30 **Restaurant** L served all week 11–2.30 D served all week 6.30–9.30 ⊕ Free House ◀ RCH Pitchfork, Freeminers, London Pride, Archers. ♥ 10 **Facilities** Garden Parking

MARSHFIELD
MAP 04 ST77

The Catherine Wheel

39 High St SN14 8LR ☎ 01225 892220
e-mail: bookings@thecatherinewheel.co.uk
dir: *Between Bath, Bristol & Chippenham on A420. 5m from M4 junct 18*

Simple, stylish decor complements the clean lines of this 16th-century inn, with its exposed brickwork and large open fireplaces. Menus are also simple and well presented, with favourites at lunchtime including jacket potatoes and ploughman's. In the evening look forward to smoked mackerel and crab fishcakes, followed by one of the specials such as venison and pheasant stew. A small but sunny patio is a lovely spot for a summertime pint brewed by nearby Cotswold and Bath-based breweries.

Open 12–3 6–11 (Sun 12–10.30) **Bar Meals** L served all week 12–2 D served all week 7–9 (Sun 12–3) **Restaurant** L served all week 12–2 D served all week 7–9 (Sun 12–3) ⊕ Free House ◖ Courage Best, Abbey Ales Bellringer & guest ale. **Facilities** Garden Dogs allowed Parking

The Lord Nelson Inn ★★★ INN ♥

1 & 2 High St SN14 8LP ☎ 01225 891820 & 891981
e-mail: thelordnelsoninn.@btinternet.com
dir: *On A420 between Bristol & Chippenham*

Located in a village on the outskirts of Bath, this 17th-century coaching inn is family run and has a good reputation for its home-made food and quality cask ales. There are log fires in winter and a patio for summer use. Dishes range from home-made burger with hand cut chips, to collops of monkfish with saffron and red pepper dressing, and timbale of white and wild rice.

Open 12–2.30 5–11 (Sun all day) **Bar Meals** L served all week 12–2.30 D served all week 6.30–9 (Sun 12–3) Av main course £7.50 **Restaurant** L served all week 12–2 D served all week 6.30–9 (Sun 12–3, 6–8) Av 3 course à la carte £19.95 ⊕ Enterprise Inns ◖ Courage Best, Bath Gem & 6X. ♥ 12 **Facilities** Children's licence Garden Dogs allowed Play Area **Rooms** 3

MEYSEY HAMPTON
MAP 05 SP10

The Masons Arms ♥

28 High St GL7 5JT ☎ 01285 850164 ▤ 01285 850164
dir: *6m E of Cirencester off A417, beside village green.*

With its origins as far back as 1725, this charming village free house is an ideal haven for travellers, and the bar remains a convivial focus of village life. A varied menu of home-made dishes, light bites and vegetarian options is served in the bar and the re-styled restaurant; daily specials might include Italian-style chicken; minted lamb chops; or fresh pan-fried swordfish. There's a carvery on Sundays.

Open 11.30–3.00 6–11.30 (Sun 12–11.30) **Bar Meals** L served all week 12–3 D served all week 6.30–9.30 (Fri-Sat 6–9.30) Av main course £8.50 **Restaurant** L served all week 12–2.30 D served all week 7–9.30 (Fri-Sat 6.30–9.30) Av 3 course à la carte £16 ⊕ Free House ◖ Hook Norton Best, guest ales. ♥ 14 **Facilities** Children's licence Garden Dogs allowed Parking Play Area

MINCHINHAMPTON
MAP 04 SO80

The Old Lodge NEW ★★★★ INN ♥

Minchinhampton Common GL6 9AQ
☎ 01453 832047 ▤ 01453 834053
e-mail: old-lodge@food-club.com
dir: *Telephone for details*

A 400–year-old Cotswold inn, high on Minchinhampton Common, where cattle range free and from where you can see Wales. The stylish restaurant, adorned with paintings and sculptures, has floor-to-ceiling windows that look directly onto the common. Typically on the menu are roast monkfish tail with curried parsnip purée and mussel broth; braised shank of lamb with dauphinoise potato, french beans and paprika sauce; and porcini mushroom risotto with shaved parmesan.

Open 11–11 Closed: 25 & 31 Dec **Bar Meals** L served Mon-Fri 11–3 D served Mon-Fri 6–10 (Sat-Sun all day) Av main course £3.95 **Restaurant** L served Mon-Fri 12–3 D served Mon-Fri 6–10 (Sat-Sun all day) Av 3 course à la carte £24.95 ◖ Abbot Ale, Stroud Budding, IPA, Otter Bitter & Ruddles County. ♥ 10 **Facilities** Garden Dogs allowed **Rooms** 6

Pick of the Pubs

The Weighbridge Inn ♥

See Pick of the Pubs on opposite page

NAILSWORTH
MAP 04 ST89

Pick of the Pubs

The Britannia ♥

See Pick of the Pubs on page 234

PICK OF THE PUBS

MINCHINHAMPTON-GLOUCESTERSHIRE

The Weighbridge Inn

The Weighbridge is situated in a lovely part of the South Cotswolds, which is becoming ever more popular with holidaymakers and walkers. The 17th-century free house stands on the original London to Bristol packhorse trail, now a footpath and bridleway, ideal for exploring this Area of Outstanding Natural Beauty on foot.

At one time the innkeeper also looked after the weighbridge, which served the local woollen mills; these included the long defunct Longfords Mill, memorabilia from which is displayed around the inn. Behind the scenes there has been careful renovation, but original features of the bars and upstairs restaurant, with massive roof beams reaching almost to the floor, remain untouched. The drinking areas are just as cosy while, outside, the patios and arbours offer good views of the Cotswolds. The proprietors feel that in an ever changing world some things should remain the same. The customers agree and find comfort in the familiar surroundings, to which some have been accustomed for over 60 years. The inn prides itself on the quality of its food, all cooked from scratch. The famous '2 in 1' pies have been made here for 30 years, comprising the filling of your choice (such as pork, bacon and celery; or chicken, ham and leek) topped with home-made cauliflower cheese and a pastry lid. Also popular are the Sunday roasts and the daily specials that supplement the regular menu, which itself changes every five weeks. The future for the inn is really more of the same: great food, great service and great company.

♀
MAP 04 SO80
GL6 9AL
☎ 01453 832520
🖷 01453 835903
e-mail: enquiries@2in1pub.co.uk
dir: *Between Nailsworth & Avening on B4014*

Open 12–11 (Sun 12–10.30)
Closed: 25 Dec & 10 days Jan
Bar Meals L served all week
12–9.30 D served all week
12–9.30 Av main course £9
Restaurant L served all week
12–9.30 D served all week
12–9.30 Av 3 course à la carte £20
⊕ Free House ◀ Wadworth 6X,
Uley Old Spot & Laurie Lee. ♀ 16
Facilities Garden Dogs allowed
Parking

233

PICK OF THE PUBS

The Britannia

An impressive 17th-century former manor house occupying a delightful position on the south side of Nailsworth's Cossack Square. The interior is bright and uncluttered with low ceilings and cosy fires, an open-plan design and a blue slate floor.

Outside you'll find a pretty garden with plenty of tables, chairs and umbrellas for making the most of warm, sunny days. Whether inside or out, a pint of well-kept Otter Bitter, Wickwar Bob or Bath Gem is sure to go down well. The brasserie-style menu is an interesting blend of modern British and continental food, with ingredients bought from local suppliers and from Smithfield Market. You can go lightly with just a starter from the new tapas menu, or a small main (Thai fishcakes; steak ciabattas; or crispy duck salad); sample a pasta dish such as linguini with pesto; or tackle a hearty main dish like lamb shank with braised vegetables; fish and chips with mushy peas; or salmon with braised fennel. Puddings are a popular event at the Britannia,

with plenty of favourites that might include fruit crumble and custard; or sticky rice pudding; and for calorie addicts, chocolate brownie or cookies with ice cream and chocolate sauce. The owners import their own wines, so the list is well worth browsing through.

MAP 04 ST89
Cossack Square GL6 0DG
☎ 01453 832501
e-mail: pheasantpluckers2003@
yahoo.co.uk
dir: *From A46 S'bound right at town centre rdbt. 1st left. Pub directly ahead*

Open 11–11 (Fri-Sat 11–12)
Closed: 25 Dec
Bar Meals L served Mon-Fri
11–2.45 D served Mon-Fri
5.30–10 (Sat-Sun all day)
Restaurant L served Mon-Fri
11–2.45 D served Mon-Fri 5.30–10
(Sat-Sun all day)
♟ 10
Facilities Garden Dogs allowed
Parking

England

NAILSWORTH continued

Pick of the Pubs

Egypt Mill ★★ HL 🍷
GL6 0AE ☎ 01453 833449 📠 01453 839919
e-mail: reception@egyptmill.com
dir: *M4 junct 18, A46 N to Stoud. M5 junct 13, A46 to Nailsworth*

Situated in the charming Cotswold town of Nailsworth, this converted corn mill contains many features of great character, including the original millstones and lifting equipment. The ground floor bar and bistro enjoy a picturesque setting, and its views over the pretty water gardens complete the scene. There is a choice of eating in the bistro or restaurant, and in both there is a good selection of wines by the glass. For those who like to savour an aperitif before dining, try the large Egypt Mill Lounge. Tempting starters might offer ham hock and pea risotto; smoked salmon and avocado parcels; and salmon and lobster sausages. Main courses include the likes of saddle of lamb Greek style; calves' liver and bacon; breast of duck with apple and blackberry risotto; and Brixham fish and potato pie.

Open 7–11 **Bar Meals** L served all week 12–2 D served all week 6.30–9 (Sun 12–9) **Restaurant** L served all week 12–2 D served all week 7–9 (Sun 12–9) 🍺 Free House 🍺 Boddingtons, Archers Best, Cats Whiskers, Wickwar Cotswold Way. 🍷 10 **Facilities** Garden Parking **Rooms** 28

Pick of the Pubs

Tipputs Inn 🍷
See Pick of the Pubs on page 236

NAUNTON   MAP 10 SP12

The Black Horse
GL54 3AD ☎ 01451 850565
dir: *Telephone for directions*

Renowned for its home-cooked food and Donnington real ales, this friendly inn enjoys a typical Cotswold village setting beloved of ramblers and locals alike. The Black Horse provides a traditional English menu featuring liver and bacon, cottage pie, and broccoli and cheese bake.

Open 11.30–3 6–11 **Bar Meals** L served all week 12–2 D served all week 6.30–9.30 **Restaurant** L served all week 12–2 D served all week 6.30–9.30 🍺 🍺 Donnington BB, SBA. **Facilities** Garden Dogs allowed Parking

NETHER WESTCOTE   MAP 10 SP22

Pick of the Pubs

The Westcote Inn 🍷
See Pick of the Pubs on page 238

NEWLAND   MAP 04 SO50

Pick of the Pubs

The Ostrich Inn
GL16 8NP ☎ 01594 833260 📠 01594 833260
e-mail: kathryn@theostrichinn.com
dir: *Follow Monmouth signs from Chepstow (A466), Newland signed from Redbrook*

A 13th-century inn situated in a pretty village on the western edge of the Forest of Dean and adjoining the Wye Valley, both areas of outstanding natural beauty. To this day it still retains many of its ancient features, including a priest hole. With wooden beams and a welcoming log fire in the large lounge bar throughout the winter, visitors can enjoy a relaxed and friendly setting for a wide selection of cask-conditioned beers and good food. Diners are served in the small, intimate restaurant, the larger lounge bar, the garden and the patio. In the bar expect simpler dishes, such as salmon spinach fishcakes; steak and ale pie; and penne pasta. The monthly changing menu in the restaurant offers more sophistication in the form of slow-roasted spiced belly pork with pak choi; and supreme of Nile perch from Lake Victoria with black tiger prawns and chive cream sauce. No one will frown at your muddy boots.

Open 12–3 6.30–11.30 (Sat 6–11.30) **Bar Meals** L served all week 12–2.30 D served all week 6.30–9.30 (Sat 6–9.30) Av main course £8.50 **Restaurant** L served all week 12–2.30 D served all week 6.30–9.30 (Sat 6–9.30) Av 3 course à la carte £23.50 🍺 Free House 🍺 Timothy Taylor Landlord, Butty Bach, Pigs Ear, Old Hooky. **Facilities** Garden Dogs allowed

Tipputs Inn

This 17th-century pub-restaurant has been decked out in impeccable style, so that mellow Cotswold stone and stripped floorboards blend nicely with modern, clean-lined furniture and a touch of grandeur in the form of a giant candelabra. Located in the heart of the Cotswolds, the Tipputs Inn is owned by Nick Beardsley and Christophe Coquoin.

They started out as chefs together more than 12 years ago, but admit to spending less time in the kitchen these days now that they have to create menus for this and their other Gloucestershire food pubs. Much of their time is spent on selecting and importing some of their menu ingredients and wines direct from France. The menus cater for most requirements: starters are served all day, and might include such exotic choices as sautéed Spanish chorizo with mushrooms and peppers tossed in spinach leaves; pigeon breast with beetroot and hazelnut salad and a port and honey dressing; and rabbit and pork terrine wrapped in Parma ham. The list of lighter meals takes in Gloucester Old Spot sausage and mash with shallot gravy; fettuccine pasta with cashew nuts and parmesan shavings; haddock in beer batter with home-made chips; and rib-eye steak sandwich on ciabatta with caramelised onions and chips. Larger mains are served for four hours at lunchtime and in the evenings: look out for whole roasted mackerel with shallots, cherry tomsatoes, garlic and thyme; steak and kidney pie; farmed rabbit with a bean and vegetable casserole; pork tenderloin medallions pan fried with apples and cider on a celeriac and potato mash; wild mushroom risotto served with a mixed leaf salad; and onion and mushroom tart topped with gruyere.

MAP 04 ST89
Bath Rd GL6 0QE
☎ 01453 832466
🖹 01453 832010
e-mail: pheasantpluckers2003@yahoo.co.uk
dir: *A46, 0.5m S of Nailsworth*

Open 11–11 Closed: 25 Dec
Bar Meals L served all week 11–10 D served all week 11–10 Av main course £11
Restaurant L served all week 11–10 D served all week 11–10 Av 3 course à la carte £23
⊕ Free House ◀ Greene King IPA, Abbot Ale & Stroud Brewery. ₹ 12
Facilities Garden Dogs allowed Parking

NORTH CERNEY
MAP 05 SP00

Bathurst Arms ♥

GL7 7BZ ☎ 01285 831281

e-mail: james@bathurstarms.com

dir: 5m N of Cirencester on A435

Antique settles, flagstone floors, stone fireplaces, beams and panelled walls characterise this former coaching inn, in a pretty village setting. The garden, including a boules pitch, stretches down to the River Churn. A special wine room offers over 100 wines with a good choice by the glass. Fresh fish, and produce from ethically minded farmers feature in dishes such as roasted loin of Gloucester Old Spot pork, luxury fish pie, and winter vegetable hot pot.

Open 12–3 6–11 (Sun 12–3 7–10.30) **Bar Meals** L served all week 12–2 D served Mon-Sat 6–9 (Sun 7–9) Av main course £11 **Restaurant** L served Mon-Sat 12–2 D served Mon-Thu 6–9 (Fri-Sat 6–9.30, Sun 12–2.30, 7–9) ⊕ Free House ◀ Hook Norton, Cotswold Way, rotating guest ales. ♥ 10 **Facilities** Garden Dogs allowed Parking **Rooms** available

NORTHLEACH
MAP 10 SP11

Pick of the Pubs

The Puesdown Inn ★★★★ INN ◉◉ ♥

Compton Abdale GL54 4DN

☎ 01451 860262 🗎 01451 861262

e-mail: inn4food@btopenworld.com

dir: On A40 between Oxford & Cheltenham, 3m W of Northleach

A former coaching inn whose name means 'windy ridge' in ancient English. Standing as it does 800ft up, there's a grand view from the garden, not that the guest 'marooned in the worst blizzard of the century' here in February 1947 would have known. Much longer ago a poacher died on the doorstep, an arrow in his back, about whom the owners tell spooky tales. Interior colours are warm and rich, and there are lots of cosy sofas and log fires, clearly provided only for Habibe, a tabby cat who moves for no-one. The restaurant has earned two AA Rosettes for food such as supreme of corn-fed chicken with pancetta, lentils and fondant potato; lamb cutlets with a herb crust, rösti and rosemary jus; and roast pollack with crispy squid and squid ink risotto. The inn supports Prince Charles's Mutton Renaissance Campaign, so look for the proof on the menu.

Open 11–3 6–11 (Fri-Sat 11–11) **Bar Meals** L served all week 12–3 D served Mon-Sat 6–10.30 **Restaurant** L served all week 12–3 D served Mon-Sat 6.30–10.30 (Sun 6.30 – 9.30) Av 3 course à la carte £28 ⊕ Free House ◀ Hook Norton Best Bitter, Hooky Dark, Old Hooky, Haymaker. ♥ 15 **Facilities** Garden Dogs allowed Parking **Rooms** 3

OAKRIDGE
MAP 04 SO90

The Butcher's Arms

GL6 7NZ ☎ 01285 760371 🗎 01285 760602

dir: From Stroud A419, left for Eastcombe and Bisley signs. Just before Bisley right to Oakridge, brown signs for pub

Traditional Cotswold country pub with stone walls, beams and log fires in the renowned Golden Valley. Once a slaughterhouse and butchers shop. A full and varied restaurant menu offers steak, fish and chicken dishes, while the bar menu ranges from ploughman's lunches to home-cooked daily specials.

Open 11–3 6–11 Closed: 25–26 Dec, 1 Jan **Bar Meals** L served Tue-Sun 12–2 D served Tue-Sat 6.30–9.30 **Restaurant** L served Sun 12–3 D served Tue-Sat 7–9 ⊕ Free House ◀ Greene King Abbot Ale, Wickwar Bob, Archers Best, Buttcombe Bitter. **Facilities** Garden Dogs allowed Parking

OLDBURY-ON-SEVERN
MAP 04 ST69

The Anchor Inn ♥

Church Rd BS35 1QA ☎ 01454 413331

dir: From N A38 towards Bristol, 1.5m then right, village signed. From S A38 through Thornbury

Parts of this Cotswold stone pub, formerly a mill, date from 1540. The large garden by a stream has plenty of seats for summer dining, and a popular boules piste. Bar snacks include filled ciabattas, crayfish mayonnaise, and home-baked ham with eggs. Crispy roast belly of pork, Oldbury sausages and mash, jalfrezi chicken curry, Devon crab and scallop gratin and smoked haddock and salmon pie feature on the main menu.

Open 11.30–2.30 6.30–11 (Sat 11.30–11, Sun 12–10.30, Summer 6–11) **Bar Meals** L served Mon-Sat 11.30–2.30 D served Mon-Thu 6.30–9 (Sun 12–3, 6–9, Fri-Sat 6.30–9.30, Summer 6–9.30) **Restaurant** L served Mon-Sat 11.30–2.30 D served Mon-Sat 6.30–9 (Sun 12–3, 6–9) ⊕ Free House ◀ Interbrew Bass, Theakston Old Peculier, Butcombe Best & Otter Bitter. ♥ 12 **Facilities** Garden Parking

The Westcote Inn

The Westcote Inn, a 300-year-old malthouse, has been lovingly restored with many previously hidden period details now revealed. In such a traditional British pub you'd expect to be served 'Great British Food' (to quote the menu) and you will be, although European influences are apparent. Everything is freshly produced and makes abundant use of organic ingredients.

There's a comprehensive lunch and supper menu served throughout the pub that might begin with salt beef and green bean salad; Welsh rabbit; potted Morecambe Bay shrimps and home-made soda bread; or smoked mackerel salad with endive and Jersey Royals. Main courses could include Gloucestershire Old Spot sausages with mash and onion gravy; Westcote beef burger with Devon Oak cheddar cheese and chips; or fillet of sea bass with wild seashore vegetables and cockles. Desserts list rich dark chocolate tart, and trinity burnt cream with blueberries, among others. For a light lunch look out for a choice of ploughman's (cheddar, brie or ham); various sandwiches (medium rare beef and horseradish, Severn and Wye smoked salmon, or roast chicken and sage); or perhaps an all-day breakfast. And vegetarians have their own menu: double baked stilton potato soufflé; Welsh onion cake with fried duck's egg; or Little Wallop goat's cheese, beetroot and wild herbs. Every bottle on the sensibly priced wine list can be served by the glass, whatever its price. Two acres of gardens include a spectacular patio overlooking what must be one of the best views in the Cotswolds. In the summer, hog roasts and barbecues are popular features.

🍷
MAP 10 SP22
OX7 6SD
☎ 01993 830888 & 07976 971672
🖨 01993 831657
e-mail: info@westcoteinn.co.uk
web: www.westcoteinn.co.uk
dir: *20m from Oxford on A40 towards Cheltenham. At Burford rdbt follow signs A424 towards Stow-on-the-Wold*

Open 11–11
Bar Meals L served all week
12–2.30 D served all week
7–9.30 Av main course £12.95
Restaurant L served all week
12–2.30 D served all week 7–9.30
Av 3 course à la carte £27
⊕ Free House ◪ Hookie,
Landlord, London Pride
& Guinness. 🍷 30
Facilities Garden Dogs allowed
Parking Play Area
Rooms available

PAINSWICK · MAP 04 SO80

Pick of the Pubs

The Falcon Inn ♀

New St GL6 6UN ☎ 01452 814222 📄 01452 813377

e-mail: bleninns@clara.net

dir: *On A46 in centre of Painswick*

Boasting the world's oldest known bowling green in its grounds, the Falcon dates from 1554 and stands at the heart of a conservation village. For three centuries it was a courthouse, but today its friendly service extends to a drying room for walkers' gear. A sampling of dishes from the menu includes whole trout and almonds; gammon and egg; sirloin steak; chilli crust beef fillet; duck leg confit on a bed of sherry and puy lentils with Madeira sauce; penne pasta arrabiatta; stuffed pork loin with apricot and pistachios; steamed seabass fillet with scallop mousseline; and minted lamb chop with fennel, asparagus and Jerusalem artichoke garnish.

Open 11–11 (Sun 12–10.30) **Bar Meals** L served all week 12–2.30 D served all week 7–9.30 Av main course £22 **Restaurant** L served all week 12–2.30 D served all week 7–9.30 ⊕ Free House ◀ Greene King IPA, Otters Ale, Wye Valley. ♀ 10 **Facilities** Children's licence Garden Dogs allowed Parking

PAXFORD · MAP 10 SP13

Pick of the Pubs

The Churchill Arms ◉ ♀

GL55 6XH ☎ 01386 594000 📄 01386 594005

e-mail: info@thechurchillarms.com

dir: *2m E of Chipping Campden, 4m N of Moreton-in-Marsh*

Husband and wife team Sonya Kidney and Leo Brooke-Little took over this delightful Cotswold village inn in 1997. Popular with outdoor types, it offers local beers, a wide choice of wines, and quality modern pub food from local suppliers. The frequently changing menu reflects the inclusion of new ideas. Try goujons of plaice with beetroot relish; breast of pheasant, port and green peppercorns; and triple chocolate torte with raspberry parfait.

Open 11–3 6–11 **Bar Meals** L served all week 12–2 D served all week 7–9 Av main course £12 **Restaurant** L served all week 12–2 D served all week 7–9 ⊕ Free House ◀ Hook Norton Bitter, Arkells, Moonlight. ♀ 10 **Facilities** Garden

POULTON · MAP 05 SP00

Pick of the Pubs

The Falcon Inn ♀

London Rd GL7 5HN ☎ 01285 850844

e-mail: info@thefalconpoulton.co.uk

dir: *From Cirencester E on A417 towards Fairford*

At the heart of the Cotswold village of Poulton, the Falcon has been transformed from a straightforward village local into a stylish and sophisticated gastro pub which has become popular with

drinkers and diners from far and wide. For beer drinkers this is a real ale paradise, with up to half a dozen breweries represented behind the colourful handles; the choice continues with many wines available by the glass. Diners too have decisions to make. Especially good value is the fixed-price two-course lunch menu, which offers choices of three starters and three main courses: home-made mushroom soup with truffle cream, for example, could be followed by leg of duck confit with braised red cabbage and potato dauphinoise. A dessert can be added if desired, and probably will be when the menu offers the likes of warm home-made chocolate fudge cake with chocolate sauce and clotted cream.

Open 11–3 7–11 (Sun 12–3, 7–10.30. Summer 5–11)
Bar Meals L served Mon-Sat 12–2 **Restaurant** L served all week 12–2 D served Mon-Sat 7–9 (Summer 12–2.30, 5–9.30) Av 3 course à la carte £22 ⊕ Free House ◀ Hook Norton – Wickwar Bob ♀ 9 **Facilities** Dogs allowed Parking

SAPPERTON · MAP 04 SO90

Pick of the Pubs

The Bell at Sapperton ♀

GL7 6LE ☎ 01285 760298 📄 01285 760761

e-mail: thebell@sapperton66.freeserve.co.uk

dir: *From A419 halfway between Cirencester & Stroud follow signs for Sapperton. Pub in village centre near church*

The Bell is on the edge of the Cirencester Park, at the heart of the Cotswolds, an area popular with walkers, cyclists and horse riders. Those popping in for a light meal can enjoy something from the snack menu, perhaps washed down with a pint of locally brewed real ale. Ingredients used in the kitchen are all carefully sourced from local suppliers, and bread is made on the premises using Shipton Mill flour. Dairy products come from a local farm, and locally sourced meats might include rare breed Belted Galloway beef from the local National Trust Estate of Ebworth. Wild mushrooms, game, fruit and vegetables are also generally from the local area. Try a chalkboard special like braised Old Spot pig cheeks with parsnip mash, ginger and lime sauce; or take a good look at the dinner menu, with choices like pure bred Hereford rib-eye steak with a garnish of roast tomato, mushrooms and fries.

Open 11–2.30 6.30–11 (Sun times vary) Closed: 25 & 31 Dec, 3–10 Jan **Bar Meals** L served all week 12–2 D served all week 7–9.30 (Sun 7–9) Av main course £14.50 **Restaurant** L served all week 12–2 D served all week 7–9.30 (Sun 7–9) Av 3 course à la carte £30 ⊕ Free House ◀ Uley Old Spot, Bath Ales, Butcombe Best, Cotswold Way. ♀ 16 **Facilities** Garden Dogs allowed Parking

SHEEPSCOMBE   MAP 04 SO81

Pick of the Pubs

The Butchers Arms ♥

GL6 7RH ☎ 01452 812113 🖹 01452 814358

e-mail: mark@butchers-arms.co.uk

dir: *1.5m S of A46 (Cheltenham to Stroud Rd), N of Painswick*

Set on the sunny side of Sheepscombe valley, this award-winning pub has a garden terrace with lovely views of beech-wooded slopes on all sides. Deer hunted by Henry VIII in his royal park used to hang in the bar – hence the pub's name. The area attracts many walkers, riders and tourists, all made welcome by hosts Mark and Sharon and their young team. A delightful range of hand-pulled real ales is offered in the bar, all served in fine condition. The menus include dishes made from produce raised in fields within sight of the pub. Light meals and salads are augmented by traditional favourites such as home-made cottage pie, creamy seafood tagliatelle, beer-battered fish and chips, and grilled steaks. The 'Young Person's Menu' keeps children happy, or an adult-sized main course can be divided in two. An ever-changing specials board above the fireplace completes the choice.

Open 11.30–2.30 6.30–11.30 (Sat-Sun all day Summer)
Bar Meals L served Mon-Sat 12–2.30 D served Mon-Sat 7–9.30 (Sun 12–9) Av main course £9.75 **Restaurant** L served Mon-Sat 12–2.30 D served Mon-Sat 7–9.30 (Sun 12–9) Av 3 course à la carte £21 ⊕ Free House ◀ Otter Ale, Hook Norton Bitter, guest ales. ♥ 10 **Facilities** Children's licence Garden Dogs allowed Parking

SOMERFORD KEYNES   MAP 04 SU0

Pick of the Pubs

The Bakers Arms ♥

GL7 6DN ☎ 01285 861298 🖹 01453 832010

dir: *Leave A419 signed Cotswold Water Park. Cross B4696 for 1m, follow signs for Keynes Park and Somerford Keynes*

A beautiful chocolate box pub built from Cotswold stone, with low-beamed ceilings and inglenook fireplaces. Dating from the 15th century, the building was formerly the village bakery and stands in mature gardens ideal for al fresco dining. Discreet children's play areas and heated terraces add to its broad appeal. Somerford Keynes is in the Cotswold Water Park, and the man-made beach of Keynes Park is within easy walking distance, while the nearby Thames Path and Cotswold Way make the pub popular with walkers.

Open 11–11 (Fri-Sat 11–12) **Bar Meals** L served all week 12–2.45 D served all week 6–9.30 (Sun all day) Av main course £8.50 **Restaurant** L served all week 12–2.45 D served all week 6–9.30 (Sun all day) Av 1 course fixed price £5 ⊕ Enterprise Inns ◀ Courage Best, 6X, Hook Norton, London Pride. ♥ 8 **Facilities** Children's licence Garden Dogs allowed Parking Play Area

SOUTHROP   MAP 05 SP1

Pick of the Pubs

The Swan at Southrop ◉◉ ♥

See Pick of the Pubs on opposite page

STONEHOUSE   MAP 04 SO8

The George Inn

Peter St, Frocester GL10 3TQ

☎ 01453 822302 🖹 01453 791612

dir: *M5 junct 13, onto A419 at 1st rdbt 3rd exit signed Eastington left at next rdbt signed Frocester. Approx 2m on right in village*

An award-winning 18th-century coaching inn, unspoiled by juke box or fruit machine. Instead, crackling log fires and a sunny courtyard garden give the place all-year-round appeal. The Cotswold Way and a network of leafy paths and lanes are on the doorstep. Expect a warm welcome, a selection of real ales including three local brews, and good home-cooked food from nearby suppliers. Tuck in to half a roast chicken, or Frocester Fayre faggots with mash, peas and gravy.

Open 11.30–2.30 5–11 (Fri-Sun 11.30–11) **Bar Meals** L served all week 12–2 D served Mon-Sat 6.30–9.30 (Sun carvery 12.30–3) Av main course £9 **Restaurant** L served all week 12–2 D served Mon-Sat 6.30–9.30 (Sun carvery 12.30–3) ◀ Deuchars IPA, Blacksheep & 3 guest ales. **Facilities** Garden Parking

PICK OF THE PUBS

SOUTHROP-GLOUCESTERSHIRE

The Swan at Southrop

The Swan is a creeper clad, early 17th-century Cotswold inn with a classic location on the village green at Southrop. This is an area of Gloucestershire, close to the borders of Oxfordshire and Wiltshire, which is renowned for gentle strolls and picturesque country rambles.

The inn has recently changed hands and is now run by Graham Williams with Bob Parkinson as chef, both of them formerly of bibendum in London. Their aim is to provide food of excellent quality at village inn prices. The Swan's interior, comprising a bar, snug and restaurant, is surprisingly light and airy for such a historic building, but cosy too in winter with the log fire. Another attractive feature is the skittle alley, where larger parties can be catered for. Accommodation in four bedrooms is also planned for the future. In addition to the carte there is a good-value, short, fixed-price lunch menu of two or three courses, including a vegetarian option (linguine with broccoli, red onion, pine nuts and parmesan). From the carte you might choose confit tuna salad with borlotti beans, chorizo and poached egg to start, or Thai duck salad with sour fruits, chilli, mint and coriander. Mains range through escargots de Bourgogne; grilled entrecote steak with Béarnaise sauce, pomme frites and green salad; and fillet of halibut with watercress salad, baby artichokes, courgette relish and aïoli. Meals finish with the likes of chocolate fondant with vanilla ice cream, or a selection of cheeses with leaves and fig chutney.

☺☺♥
MAP 05 SP10
GL7 3NU
☎ 01367 850205
🗎 01367 850555
dir: *Off A361 between Lechlade & Burford*

Open 11.30–3.30 6.30–11
Bar Meals L served all week
12–2 D served all week 7–9
Restaurant L served all week
12–2.30 D served all week 7–10
(Closed Sun pm in winter) Av 3
course à la carte £28
⊕ Free House ◀ Hook Norton,
Wadworth 6X, Timothy Taylor
Landlord, Marstons. ♥ 10
Facilities Dogs allowed

STOW-ON-THE-WOLD MAP 10 SP12

Pick of the Pubs

The Eagle and Child ★★★ HL ◉◉ ♥

See Pick of the Pubs on opposite page

The Unicorn ★★★ SHL ◉ ♥

Sheep St GL54 1HQ ☎ 01451 830257 ▤ 01451 831090
e-mail: reception@birchhotels.co.uk

Attractive hotel of honey-coloured limestone, hand-cut roof tiles and abundantly flowering window boxes, set in the heart of Stow-on-the-Wold. The interior is stylishly presented with Jacobean pieces, antique artefacts and open log fires. Light meals are served in the bar (sandwiches and salads, plus beef and Guinness stew, and beer-battered fish and chips), and a dinner menu of modern British dishes is available in the elegant Georgian setting of the restaurant.

Open 12 -11 (Winter 12–3, 7–11) **Bar Meals** L served all week 12–2 D served all week 7–9 Av main course £9.95 **Restaurant** L served all week 12–2 D served all week 7–9 Av 3 course à la carte £20 ♥ 6 **Facilities** Garden Dogs allowed Parking **Rooms** 20

STROUD MAP 04 SO80

Pick of the Pubs

Bear of Rodborough Hotel ★★★ HL ♥

See Pick of the Pubs on page 244

The Ram Inn

South Woodchester GL5 5EL
☎ 01453 873329 ▤ 01453 873329
e-mail: jewantsum@aol.com

dir: *A46 from Stroud to Nailsworth, right after 2m into South Woodchester (follow brown tourist signs)*

From the terrace of the 17th-century Cotswold stone Ram there are splendid views over five valleys, although proximity to the huge fireplace may prove more appealing in winter, with plenty of outdoor seating in summer. Rib-eye steak, at least two fish dishes, home-made lasagne and Sunday roasts can be expected, washed down by regularly changing real ales such as Uley Old Spot, Wickwar BOB and Archer's Golden. The Stroud Morris Men regularly perform.

Open 11–11 (Sun 12–10.30) **Bar Meals** L served all week 12–2.30 D served Mon-Sat 6–9.30 (Sun 6–8.30) Av main course £7 **Restaurant** L served all week 12–2.30 D served Mon-Sat 6–9.30 (Sun 6–8.30) ⊕ Free House ◀ Uley Old Spot, Otter Ale, Stroud Budding, Stroud Tom Long & Butcombe Bitter. **Facilities** Garden Dogs allowed Parking

Pick of the Pubs

Rose & Crown Inn ♥

The Cross, Nympsfield GL10 3TU
☎ 01453 860240 ▤ 01453 861564
e-mail: gadros@aol.com
dir: *M5 junct 13 off B4066, SW of Stroud*

An imposing, 400–year-old coaching inn of honey-coloured local stone in the heart of the village close to the Cotswold Way and therefore a popular stop for walkers and cyclists. It could well be the highest pub in the Cotswolds, but whether it is or not is irrelevant as the views over the Severn are stunning anyway. Inside, the inn's character is preserved with natural stone, wood panelling, a lovely open fire and some local real ales. In the galleried restaurant, main courses include faggots cooked in onion gravy, enchiladas, and salmon en croûte. Just as satisfying might be Eastern Promise, a baked baguette filled with roast duck, spring onion, cucumber and hoi sin sauce. The kids will enjoy the playground area, which has a swing, slides and a climbing bridge.

Open 12 -11 **Bar Meals** L served all week 12–9.30 D served all week 6–9.30 **Restaurant** L served all week 12–9.30 D served all week 6–9.30 ⊕ Free House ◀ Uley, Pigs Ear & Otter. ♥ 7 **Facilities** Children's licence Garden Dogs allowed Parking Play Area

The Woolpack Inn

Slad Rd, Slad GL6 7QA
☎ 01452 813429 ▤ 01452 813429
dir: *2m from Stroud, 8m from Gloucester*

Situated in the Slad Valley close to the Cotswold Way, an area immortalised by Laurie Lee in his book *Cider with Rosie*, this is a friendly local that offers good real ales and is popular with walkers and dog owners.

Open 12–3 5–11 (Sat-Sun all day) **Bar Meals** L served all week 12–2.30 D served all week 6–9.30 Av main course £7.95 **Restaurant** L served all week 12–2.30 D served Mon-Sat 6–9.30 ⊕ Free House ◀ Uley Pig's Ear, Old Spot, Laurie Lee. **Facilities** Garden Dogs allowed Parking

PICK OF THE PUBS

STOW-ON-THE-WOLD-GLOUCESTERSHIRE

The Eagle and Child

Certified by the Guinness Book of Records as the oldest inn in England, The Eagle and Child is part of the Royalist Hotel. The site is said to date back to 947 AD and was once a hospice to shelter lepers. Historic finds include a 10th-century Saxon shoe, a leper hole, witches' marks in the rooms, a bear pit, thousand-year-old timbers and an ancient frieze.

The names of inn and hotel alike recall Stow on the Wold's place in history as the site in 1646 of the final battle of the English Civil War. Intriguingly, the name Digbeth Street is thought to be a derivative of 'duck bath'. Bucolic as it sounds, it actually refers to the somewhat grim sight of ducks swimming in the blood of fallen Royalist casualties as it flowed copiously over the cobblestones. The inn and hotel have recently been taken over by local hoteliers Mark and Janine Vance, who have set about creating a luxurious package. In the cheerful pub, sample ham hock, curly kale pressé and apple purée; and smoked chicken with mascarpone risotto. Mains might include steak, kidney and thyme suet pudding with roast parsnips;

smoked haddock, mussel and clam chowder; and slow braised lamb shank with ratatouille and garlic mash. Diners at the award-winning restaurant might start with stilton pannacotta and carpaccio of beef, followed by such assured dishes as Cornish mackerel, pomme gratin and oxtail tortellini, or braised osso buco, ox cheeks and wild mushroom. The hotel has 14 bedrooms, each a textbook example of how to blend the contemporary and tradition for maximum stylish impact.

★★★ HL ◉◉ ❢
MAP 10 SP12
GL54 1HY
☎ 01451 830670
🖷 01451 870048
e-mail:
stay@theroyalisthotel.com
dir: *From Moreton-in-Marsh train station take A429 Fosseway to Stow-on-the-Wold. At 2nd lights turn left onto Sheep St. (A436). Establishment 100yds on left*

Open 11–11
Bar Meals L served all week
12–2.30 D served all week 6–9.30
Restaurant L served all week
12–2.30 D served all week 7–9.30
Av 3 course à la carte £20
⊕ Free House ◀ Hook
Norton, London Pride,
Goffs & Donnington. ❢ 8
Facilities Garden Dogs allowed
Parking
Rooms 14

PICK OF THE PUBS

Bear of Rodborough Hotel

Built in the 17th century, this former alehouse stands 600 ft above sea level, surrounded by 300 acres of National Trust land. Its name comes from the bear-baiting that used to take place nearby. The hotel is worth seeking out for all sorts of reasons: comfortable accommodation, open log fires, stone walls and solid wooden floors.

An interesting beam over the front doors reads "Through this wide opening gate none come too early, none return too late", reputedly carved by louche sculptor and typographer, Eric Gill. Spot the running bear design incorporated into the ceiling beams in the elegant Box Tree restaurant and Tower Room. Additional character is occasionally provided in the form, if that's the right word, of a resident ghost whose unknown identity is often discussed late at night in the Grizzly Bar (best pronounced the hillbilly way), as likely as not over pints of Gloucestershire brews from Uley and Wickwar. The restaurant offers a contemporary British menu, so one might start with baby toad-in-the-hole with red wine jus and redcurrant jelly; or poached salmon and citrus salad; continue with Bibury trout; faggots with buttered mash; or wild mushroom risotto; and finish with a dessert from the daily specials. Sandwiches include Single Gloucester cheese with Uley's Old Spot ale and apple chutney. There are two wine lists, one containing a short, modestly priced selection, the other running to the full 60 bins. Outside is a croquet lawn created in the 1920s by a former resident called Edmunds, a partner in a well-known firm of proud Stroud nurserymen.

★★★ HL ☻
MAP 04 SO80
Rodborough Common GL5 5DE
☎ 01453 878522
📄 01453 872523
e-mail:
info@bearofrodborough.co.uk
web: www.cotswold-inns-hotels.
co.uk/bear
dir: *From M5 junct 13 follow signs for Stonehouse then Rodborough*

Open 10.30–11
Bar Meals L served Mon-Sat
12–2.30 D served Mon-Sat
6.30–10 (Sun 12–2, 6.30–9.30)
Restaurant D served Mon-Sat
7–9.30 (Sun 7–9)
⊕ Free House ◀ Uley Bitter,
Bob from Wickwar Brewery,
Stroud, Wadworth. ☻ 6
Facilities Garden Dogs allowed
Parking Play Area
Rooms 46

England

Pick of the Pubs

Gumstool Inn ♀

Calcot Manor GL8 8YJ
☎ 01666 890391 ▤ 01666 890394
e-mail: reception@calcotmanor.co.uk
dir: *3m W of Tetbury*

The cheerful and cosy Gumstool is part of Calcot Manor Hotel, set in 220 acres of Cotswold countryside. The hotel is a successful conversion of a 14th-century stone farmhouse built by Cistercian monks, set around a flower-filled courtyard. Monthly menus offer a good choice, with typical starters of Arbroath smokies gratin (only traditionally smoked haddock from within five miles of Arbroath may use the town's name); chicken liver salad with avocado, crispy bacon and garlic croûtes; and plum tomato and caramelised red onion tart with tallegio cheese and rocket. Among the mains might be Cornish fish stew in a rich shellfish broth; roasted wild duck with spiced pear and redcurrant port wine sauce; and slow-braised lamb hotpot. Desserts include bread and butter pudding with clotted cream; baked toffee apple and nut cheesecake; and home-made sorbets and ice creams. As a free house, Gumstool stocks a good selection of real ales.

Open 11.30–2.30 5.30–11 (Sat 11.30–11, Sun 12–10.30)
Bar Meals L served all week 12–2 D served Mon-Sat 5.30–9.30 (Sun 5.30–9) Av main course £8 **Restaurant** L served all week 12–2 D served Mon-Sat 7–9.30 (Sun 7–9) Av 3 course à la carte £35 ⊕ Free House ◀ Atlantics Sharp's IPA, Matthews Bob Wool, Wickwar Cotswold Way & Butcomb Blonde. ♀ 12 **Facilities** Garden Parking Play Area

Pick of the Pubs

The Priory Inn ★★★ SHL ♀

London Rd GL8 8JJ
☎ 01666 502251 ▤ 01666 503534
e-mail: info@theprioryinn.co.uk
dir: *M4 junct 17, A429 towards Cirencester. Left onto B4014 to Tetbury. Over mini-rdbt onto Long Street, pub 100yds around corner on right*

A thriving gastro-pub, hotel and coffee bar at the centre of Tetbury life. The aim is to provide excellent value modern rustic cuisine with a minimum of food miles. Monthly newsletters keep customers informed of the local suppliers who have provided their supper. Children are especially welcome, with a specialised menu of home-made dishes and junior cocktails, plus the opportunity to decorate a personalised wood-fired pizza. Adults are equally coddled with a lunch menu that might include a sandwich of pickled cherry tomato and Godsell's Three Virgins cheese; or fresh sardines, tomato and oregano on toasted home-made bread. The evening meal could begin with devilled lambs' kidneys, and continue with melted Cotswold blue brie over mushrooms with a jerusalem artichoke gratin. Try a scoop of Westonbirt ice cream with the warm chocolate fondant for dessert. Live music every Sunday evening.

Open 11–11 **Restaurant** L served Mon-Fri 12–3 D served Mon-Fri 6–10 (Sat-Sun 12–10) Av 3 course à la carte £25 ⊕ Free House ◀ Uley Bitter, Cotswold Premium Lager, Archers Ale, Stowford Press Cider. ♀ 10 **Facilities** Children's licence Garden Parking Play Area **Rooms** 14

The Trouble House ◉◉ ♀

Cirencester Rd GL8 8SG ☎ 01666 502206
e-mail: info@thetroublehouse.co.uk
dir: *On A433 between Tetbury & Cirencester*

An old Cotswold inn whose troubled past includes landlords who committed suicide, farmworkers who destroyed new-fangled agricultural machinery, and ghosts. Or is it named after the nearby flood-prone area known as The Troubles? No one knows. Inside are wooden floors, black beams, open fires, pastel-coloured walls and subtle lighting. Freshly prepared rustic cooking includes roasted squid stuffed with sun-dried tomatoes, mozzarella and chilli lentils; and double-cooked rib-eye of pork with mushy peas and mustard sauce.

Open 11.30–3 6.30–11 (Sun 12–3) (Oct-May Tue-Sat 7–11) Closed: 25 Dec-5 Jan Sun eve & Mon **Bar Meals** L served Tue-Sun 12–2 D served Tue-Sat 7–9.30 Av main course £15 **Restaurant** L served Tue-Sun 12–2 D served Tue-Sat 7–9.30 Av 3 course à la carte £30 ⊕ Wadworth ◀ Wadworth 6X & Henrys IPA. ♀ 12 **Facilities** Garden Dogs allowed Parking

TEWKESBURY   MAP 10 SO83

The Fleet Inn ♥

Twyning GL20 6FL ☎ 01684 274310
e-mail: enquiries@fleet-inn.co.uk
dir: *M5 junct 8, M50 junct, 3m from Tewkesbury A38*

The gardens of this idyllic 15th-century pub run right down to the banks of the River Avon. The traditional bars and themed areas provide a wide range of dishes. Produce is locally sourced, and might include steak and kidney parcels; pheasant breast on colcannon mash; or half shoulder of lamb in mint and rosemary gravy. There's a boules court to keep the teenagers happy, and a pets' corner for the little ones.

Open 11–11   **Bar Meals** L served Mon-Sat 12–2.30 D served all week 6–9 Av main course £9   **Restaurant** L served all week 12–2.30 D served all week 6–9 Av 3 course à la carte £18 ⊕ Enterprise Inns ◖ Bombardier, Banks, Cat's Whiskers. ♥ 10   **Facilities** Children's licence Garden Parking Play Area

TODENHAM   MAP 10 SP23

Pick of the Pubs

The Farriers Arms ♥

Main St GL56 9PF ☎ 01608 650901 🖩 01608 650403
e-mail: info@farriersarms.com
dir: *Right to Todenham at N end of Moreton-in-Marsh. 2.5m from Shipston-on-Stour*

A traditional Cotswold pub built as a church house in 1650, later becoming an ironworks, before acquiring a beer licence in 1840. It has all the features you'd associate with a country local: polished flagstone floors, exposed stone walls, wooden beams and a large inglenook fireplace. Outside, a suntrap patio garden offers views of the church. The bar and restaurant menu changes daily to offer a good range of freshly prepared dishes using local produce.

Starters range from home-made chicken liver parfait to duo of Todenham sausages with grain mustard sauce, while typical main courses include braised steak and Hook Norton ale pie with puff pastry; cod in beer batter with chips and mushy peas; and roast vegetables and goat's cheese cannelloni. In the Aunt Sally season maybe have a game yourself, or just watch 'the professionals' as they compete against other local league players.

Open 12–3   6.30–11 (Sun 7–10.30)   **Bar Meals** L served Mon-Sat 12–2 D served Sun-Thu 7–9 (Fri-Sat 7–9.30, Sun 12–2.30) Av main course £12   **Restaurant** L served Mon-Sat 12–2 D served Sun-Thu 7–9 (Fri-Sat 7–9.30, Sun 12–2.30) ⊕ Free House ◖ Hook Norton Best, Archers Golden, Wye Valley Butty Bach, Timothy Taylor Landlord. ♥ 11   **Facilities** Garden Dogs allowed Parking

TORMARTON   MAP 04 ST77

Best Western Compass Inn ★★ HL ♥

GL9 1JB ☎ 01454 218242 🖩 01454 218741
e-mail: info@compass-inn.co.uk
dir: *From M4 junct 18 take A46 N towards Stroud. After 200mtrs 1st right towards Tormarton, continue for 300mtrs*

A charming 18th-century inn, set in six acres of grounds in the heart of the Gloucestershire countryside, right on the Cotswold Way. Its extensive facilities include an orangery, 26 bedrooms and space for functions. Light bites and more fulsome meals can be taken in the bar, while the restaurant offers the likes of chicken liver paté with brioche, followed by roasted pork fillet with sage mash, caramelised apple and grain mustard sauce.

Open 7–11 Closed: 25–26 Dec   **Bar Meals** L served all week 11–7 D served all week 7–10   Av main course £9   **Restaurant** L served all week 7–10 D served all week 7–10 Av 3 course à la carte £20 ⊕ Free House ◖ Interbrew Bass, Butcombe Gold & Butcombe. ♥ 9   **Facilities** Garden Dogs allowed Parking   **Rooms** 26

UPPER ODDINGTON   MAP 10 SP22

Pick of the Pubs

The Horse and Groom Inn ♥

GL56 0XH ☎ 01451 830584
e-mail: info@horseandgroom.uk.com
dir: *1.5m S of Stow-on-the-Wold, just off the A436*

In a Cotswold conservation village just a mile and a half from Stow-on-the-Wold, this immaculate 16th-century stone inn welcomes with beams, flagstone and English oak floors, and open log fires in winter. In warmer weather the terrace is perfect for

CONTINUED ON PAGE 248

The Old Fleece

Delightful coaching inn dating back to the 18th century and built of Cotswold stone with a traditional stone roof. The interior benefited from a complete refurbishment and makeover in the last couple of years. Among the features that help to create just the right atmosphere and ambience are wooden floors, wood panelling and exposed stone.

The pub's surroundings are equally inviting, with miles of stunning countryside and footpaths to explore. From the Old Fleece, you can walk to Rodborough, Minchinhampton and Selsley Commons, or go one step further and connect eventually with the scenic Cotswold Way long-distance trail. Owners Nick and Christophe are passionate about their pub, and are well-known in the Stroud valley for fine fresh food, sharp service and customer comforts. Predominantly French chefs prepare quality, freshly produced dishes seven days a week and ingredients are sourced locally or directly – London for meat and Bristol and Birmingham for vegetables and fish. Start perhaps with warm Greek salad with cherry tomato, focaccia bread and sweet thyme dressing; or steak and caramelised onion on toast. The main course is an event to linger over: try chicken breast with boudin noir, wrapped in bacon with an apple and cream sauce; venison fillet with rich chocolate and balsamic sauce; braised lamb shank served with rosemary jus and roasted garlic mash; or for fish lovers, salmon and tarragon fishcakes with a ginger and chilli mayonnaise; marinated chilli tuna; and fish pie. To round off you could choose banana waffle with a creamy caramel sauce; balsamic parfait with a raspberry coulis; or apple and honey tart with mascarpone cheese. Well kept Greene King Abbot Ale and Otter Ale go down well on their own.

MAP 04 SO80
Bath Rd, Rooksmoor GL5 5NB
☎ 01453 872582
e-mail: pheasantpluckers2003@
yahoo.co.uk
dir: *2m S of Stroud on A46*

Open 11–11 Closed: 25 Dec
Bar Meals L served Mon-Fri
11–2.45 D served Mon-Fri 5.30–10
(Sat-Sun all day) Av main course
£12.95
Restaurant L served Mon-Fri
11–2.45 D served Mon-Fri 5.30–10
(Sat-Sun all day) Av 3 course à la
carte £23
 Bass, Greene King
Abbot Ale, Otter Bitter. 12
Facilities Garden Dogs allowed
Parking

England

UPPER ODDINGTON continued

dining outside, where tables overlook dry stone walls and pretty stone-built cottages. There's a great selection of cask ales from local breweries; the most recent addition – the Cotswold Brewing Company – is just three miles away in Foscot. If wine is preferred, at least 25 are served by the glass. The best of regional food is the head chef's quest. Daily blackboard specials feature four starters and four main courses, two of which are fish. Expect the likes of fresh fig, Parma ham and melon salad with a balsamic reduction; pan-fried chicken livers with olive jus; and seared sea bream fillets with ratatouille sauce. Desserts such as prune and sherry tart maintain the high standard.

Open 12–3 5.30–11 (Sun 5.30–10.30) **Bar Meals** L served all week 12–2 D served Mon-Sat 6.30–9.30 (Sun 7–9) **Restaurant** L served all week 12–2 D served Mon-Sat 6.30–9.30 (Sun 7–9) ⊕ Free House ◀ Wye Valley Butty Bach, Wye Valley Best, Hereford Pale Ale, Wickwar Bob Cotswold Premium Lager. ♀ 25 **Facilities** Children's licence Garden Parking Play Area

WINCHCOMBE — MAP 10 SP02

The White Hart Inn and Restaurant ♀

High St GL54 5LJ ☎ 01242 602359 📄 01242 602703
e-mail: enquiries@the-white-hart-inn.com
dir: *In centre of Winchcombe on B4632*

A traditional 16th-century coaching inn with a Swedish twist, the White Hart has been refurbished to offer a beamed bar and Swedish-style restaurant. Enjoy snacks (antipasti, olives), a pizza or a Swedish hotdog at the bar – followed by an Italian ice-cream dessert. Dinner in the restaurant could be Scandinavian seafood platter; or pan-fried cod with red caviar mashed potato.

Open 8am-12 Closed: 25 Dec **Bar Meals** L served all week 11–10 D served all week 6–10 **Restaurant** L served all week 11–10 D served all week 6–10 Av 3 course à la carte £25 Av 3 course fixed price £16.95 ◀ Archers Golden, Uley Old Spot, Whittingtons Cats Whiskers, Greene King IPA. ♀ 8 **Facilities** Children's licence Garden Dogs allowed Parking **Rooms** available

WITHINGTON — MAP 10 SP01

The Mill Inn

GL54 4BE ☎ 01242 890204 📄 01242 890195
dir: *3m from A40 between Cheltenham & Oxford*

Until 1914 the innkeeper also had to find time to grind corn in this 450-year-old inn on the banks of the River Coln. Inside are stone-flagged floors, oak panelling and log fires, while outside is a peaceful lawned garden with 40 tables. Lunch or dinner is selected from a wide selection of light meals and more substantial main courses, including blackened Cajun chicken, steak and ale pie, Barnsley chop, and quorn and vegetable chilli.

Open 11.30-3 6–11 (Summer all day) (Sat-Sun 11.30–12) **Bar Meals** L served Mon-Fri 12–2 (Sat-Sun 12–2.30) D served all week 6–9 ⊕ Samuel Smith ◀ Samuel Smith Old Brewery Bitter, Samuel Smith Sovereign, Alpine Lager, Pure Brew Lager. **Facilities** Garden Dogs allowed Parking

WOODCHESTER — MAP 04 SO80

Pick of the Pubs

The Old Fleece ♀

See Pick of the Pubs on page 247

GREATER LONDON

CARSHALTON — MAP 06 TQ26

Greyhound Hotel ♀

2 High St SM5 3PE ☎ 020 8647 1511 📄 020 8647 4687
e-mail: greyhound@youngs.co.uk
dir: *5 min from Carshalton station on foot, 20 min train journey from Victoria Station*

Standing directly opposite the ponds in Carshalton Park, this distinctive former coaching inn has a welcoming fire in the bar in winter months. Records dating back to 1706 show that the white-painted building was formerly a centre for cock-fighters and race-goers. Today's visitors will find an interesting range of filled ciabattas and snacks, together with more substantial options like home-made steak and kidney pudding; and hake fillet in Young's beer batter, hand cut chips and mushy peas.

Open 11–12 (Sun 12–11.30) **Bar Meals** L served all week 12–3 D served all week 6.30–10 (Sun 12–9) Av main course £10 **Restaurant** D served all week 6.30–10 (Sun 12–9) ⊕ Young & Co ◀ Youngs Special, Winter Warmer, PA & Waggle Dance. ♀ 17 **Facilities** Parking

TWICKENHAM

See **London Plan 2 C2**

The White Swan ♀

Riverside TW1 3DN ☎ 020 8892 2166
e-mail: whiteswan@massivepub.com

Sitting right by the Thames since 1690, with an outside balcony and garden on the river's edge (tides permitting), while inside there's old wood and, as you might expect in this neck of the woods, walls covered with rugby memorabilia. Food is revered too, with a 'help yourself' buffet laid out in the summer, and at weekends a wonderful barbecue cooked on the patio. Winter brings out Sunday roasts and solidly traditional fare.

Open 11–11 (Sun 12–10.30) **Bar Meals** L served all week 12–2.30 D served Tue-Sat 6–9.30 (Sun 12–5) Av main course £7.25 ◀ IPA, Bombardier, Twickenham Ale, Deuchars. ♀ 10 **Facilities** Garden Dogs allowed

GREATER MANCHESTER

ALTRINCHAM

MAP 15 SJ78

Pick of the Pubs

The Victoria NEW ♥

Stamford St WA14 1EX ☎ 0161 613 1855

e-mail: the.victoria@yahoo.co.uk

After two years of closure, the fully refurbished Victoria reopened in mid-2006. It's a small, one-roomed pub, with the bar to one side, and what the owners call 'the restaurant' the other. As well as the main menu, which is changed every eight weeks, there's a lunch menu of sandwiches, salads and other quick-to-prepare dishes. Starters might well include sarsaparilla-glazed pork ribs; smoked duck pikelet; and kipper and poached egg salad. Among the main courses are possibilities such as steamed pink veal pudding; shoulder of mutton hotpot; oven-roasted monkfish; and goat's cheese and butternut squash ravioli, while typical puddings are brandy-soaked spotted dick; and white chocolate and gingernut cheesecake. The search is on for products no longer widely seen on menus, and by the time this guide appears the menu may also be offering tripe, smoked eel and pressed tongue, if, say the owners, they can find a meat press.

Open 12–11 (Sun 12–6) Closed: 26 Dec & 1–2 Jan
Bar Meals L served Mon-Sat 12–3 D served Mon-Sat 5.30–9.30 (Sun 12–4) Av main course £15 **Restaurant** L served Mon-Sat 12–3 D served Mon-Sat 5.30–9.30 (Sun 12–4) Av 3 course à la carte £25 ● Old Speckled Hen, Jennings Cumberland, Flowers IPA. ♥ 9

CHEADLE HULME

MAP 16 SJ88

The Church Inn ♥

Ravenoak Rd SK8 7EG
☎ 0161 485 1897 📠 0161 485 1698
e-mail: church_inn@yahoo.co.uk
dir: 3m from Stockport

A family-run and family-friendly pub, this is Cheadle Hulme's oldest hostelry. With welcoming log fires in winter and a furnished front patio for warmer days, the pub is open all day every day for drinks, and food is served in both bar and restaurant. The appeal of the menu and specials board is broadly cosmopolitan, with starters such as calamari strips or chicken satay; and main courses like steak au poivre or ham hock with bubble and squeak.

Open 11–11 (Sun 12–10.30) **Bar Meals** L served Mon-Sat 11.30–2.30 D served Mon-Sat 5.30–9.30 (Sun 12–7.30) Av main course £9.50
Restaurant L served Mon-Sat 11.30–2.30 D served Mon-Sat 5.30–9.30 (Sun 12–7.30) Av 3 course à la carte £20 Av 3 course fixed price £11.95 ● Robinsons Best Bitter, Hatters Mild, Robinsons Old Stockport plus 2 guest ales. ♥ 18 **Facilities** Garden Parking

DENSHAW

MAP 16 SD91

The Rams Head Inn ♥

OL3 5UN ☎ 01457 874802 📠 01457 820978

e-mail: ramsheaddenshaw@aol.com

dir: From M62 junct 22, 2m towards Oldham

From its position 1212 feet above sea level, this 400-year-old country inn offers panoramic views over Saddleworth. Log fires and collections of memorabilia are features of the interior, where blackboard menus list everything available and food is cooked to order. Seafood figures strongly, with dishes such as crayfish tails with ginger crème fraîche, and monkfish wrapped in Parma ham. Another attraction is 1212 at The Rams Head, a farm shop, deli, bakery, tearooms and pattisserie.

Open 12–2.30 6–11 (Sun 12–10.30) Closed: 25 Dec & Mon (ex BH)
Bar Meals L served Tue-Sat 12–2.30 (BH Mon 12–3) D served Tue-Sat 6–10 (Sun 12–8.30) **Restaurant** L served Tue-Sat 12–2.30 D served Tue-Sat 6–10 (BH Mon 12–3, Sun 12–8.30) ⊕ Free House ● Carlsberg-Tetley Bitter, Timothy Taylor Landlord, Black Sheep Bitter. ♥ 8 **Facilities** Parking

DIDSBURY

MAP 16 SJ89

Pick of the Pubs

The Metropolitan ♥

See Pick of the Pubs on page 250

LITTLEBOROUGH

MAP 16 SD91

The White House ♥

Blackstone Edge, Halifax Rd OL15 0LG
☎ 01706 378456
dir: On A58, 8m from Rochdale, 9m from Halifax

A coaching house built in 1671, standing 1,300 feet above sea level on the Pennine Way, with panoramic views of the moors and Hollingworth Lake far below. Not surprising, then, that it attracts walkers and cyclists who rest up and sup on Theakstons and regular guest ales. A simple menu of pub grub ranges from sandwiches and starters like garlic and herb mushrooms, to grills, curries, chillis and traditional plates of home-made steak and kidney pie.

Open 12–3 6–11 Closed: 25 Dec **Bar Meals** L served Mon-Sat 12–2 D served Mon-Sat 6.30–9 (Sun 12–9) ⊕ Free House ● Timothy Taylor Landlord, Theakstons Bitter, Exmoor Gold, Blacksheep. **Facilities** Parking

PICK OF THE PUBS

DIDSBURY-GREATER MANCHESTER

The Metropolitan

Built as a hotel by the old Midland Railway for passengers on its route into Manchester, the 'Met' still punches above its weight architecturally, but then that's how Victorian railway companies liked to gain a competitive edge over their rivals. Look in particular at the decorative floor tiling, the ornate windows, the impressive roof timbering, and the delicate plasterwork.

Sadly, during the latter part of the 20th century the building became very run down, until in 1997 it was given a sympathetic renovation, reopening as a gastropub, now one of several eating and drinking places in this buzzy southern city suburb. Its huge, airy interior is well filled with antique tables and chairs, which suit the mainly young, cosmopolitan clientele. Indeed, the Met does get very busy at peak times, but the addition of an outside bar with attractive furniture and patio heaters helps to spread the load. The lunchtime menu will almost certainly offer grilled Cumberland sausage on a ragout of smoked bacon, tomato, baby onions and herb potatoes; and the 'famous' 100 per cent prime beef burger with hand-cut chunky chips.

In the evening look for oven-baked whole sea bream stuffed with spring onion, ginger, red pepper and basil, and passion fruit and chilli coulis; pan-fried English fillet steak with horseradish and Meaux mustard mash, parmentier carrots and tarragon jus; and baked coconut and sweet chilli risotto cakes with coriander, beansprout and spring onion salad. There are also pies big enough for two – braised steak, mushroom and stout; and smoked haddock with salmon and prawn. Ploughman's can be assembled from a wide choice of cheeses, and sandwiches are all garnished with salad and coleslaw.

🍷
2 Lapwing Ln M20 2WS
☎ 0161 374 9559
📠 0161 282 6544
e-mail:
info@the-metropolitan.co.uk
dir: *M60 junct 5, A5103 turn right onto Barlow Moor Rd, then left onto Burton Rd. Pub at the x-rds. Right onto Lapwing Lane for car park.*

Open 11.30–11 (Fri-Sat 11.30–12am) Closed: 25 Dec
Bar Meals L served all week 12–6 D served all week 6–7 (Sun 12–6) Av main course £9
Restaurant L served all week 12–6 D served all week 6–9.30 (Fri-Sat 12–10, Sun 12–9) Av 3 course à la carte £20
🍺 Timothy Taylor Landlord, Deuchars IPA, Hoegarden, Staropramen & Guinness. 🍷 8
Facilities Garden Parking

MANCHESTER   MAP 16 SJ89

Dukes 92

14 Castle St, Castlefield M3 4LZ
☎ 0161 839 8646 📠 0161 832 3595
e-mail: info@dukes92.com
dir: *In Castleford town centre (off Deansgate)*

Beautifully-restored 19th-century stable building with a vast patio beside the 92nd lock of the Duke of Bridgewater canal, opened in 1762. The interior is full of surprises, with minimalist décor downstairs and an upper gallery displaying local artistic talent. A new grill restaurant supplements a lunchtime bar menu and evening pizza choices, as well as the renowned cheese and paté counter with its huge range of British and continental cheeses, salad selection, and choice of platters for sharing.

Open 11.30–11 (Fri-Sat 11.30–1am, Sun 12–10.30) Closed: 25–26 Dec, 1 Jan **Bar Meals** L served Mon-Thu 12–2.30 (Fri-Sun 12–5.30, pizza available 12–10) **Restaurant** L served Mon-Thu 12–4.30 D served all week 5.30–10 (Fri-Sat 12–10.30, Sun 12–9.30) ⊕ Free House ◀ Interbrew Boddingtons Bitter, Boddingtons. **Facilities** Garden Parking

Marble Arch

73 Rochdale Rd M4 4HY
☎ 0161 832 5914 📠 0161 819 2694
dir: *Located in city centre, northern quarter of Manchester*

A listed building with a strikingly original interior, the Marble Arch is a fine example of Manchester's Victorian heritage. It's also home to the award-winning organic Marble Brewery, with six regular and eight seasonal house beers. Snacks and more substantial meals are served in the bar – the pies are deservedly popular. Sample the likes of steak and Marble ale pie; black pudding and potato salad; and pot-roast chicken in Marble ginger beer.

Open 11.30–11 (Thu-Fri 11.30–12, Sat-Sun 12–12) Closed: 25–26 Dec **Bar Meals** L served all week 12–7 D served all week 12–7 (Sun 12–6) Av main course £7.50 ⊕ Free House ◀ GSB, Marble Best, Ginger Marble, Lagonda.

The Queen's Arms

6 Honey St, Cheetham M8 8RG ☎ 0161 835 3899
dir: *Telephone for directions*

The Queen's is part of a loose grouping of real ale pubs in Manchester's Northern Quarter. The original tiled frontage shows that it was once allied to the long-vanished Empress Brewery. Its clientele spans the socio-economic spectrum from 'suits' to bikers to pensioners, all seemingly happy with the heavy rock on the jukebox. Food is available, but it's the brewed, distilled and fermented products that attract, including an impressive 'menu' of bottled lagers, fruit beers, vodkas and wines.

Open 12–11 (Sun 12–10.30, 25 Dec 12–3, 7.30–10.30) **Bar Meals** L served all week 12–8 D served all week Av main course £3.50 ◀ Timothy Taylors Landlord, Phoenix Bantam, guest ales. **Facilities** Children's licence Garden Dogs allowed Play Area **Notes** ⊜

MELLOR   MAP 16 SJ98

The Moorfield Arms ★★★ INN ⌾

Shiloh Rd SK6 5NE ☎ 0161 427 1580 📠 0161 427 1582
e-mail: info@moorfieldarms.co.uk
dir: *From Marple station down Brabyns Brow to lights. Right into Town St. 3m, left into Shiloh Rd. 0.5m, pub on left*

This pub enjoys picturesque views of Kinder and the surrounding Pennine hills from its secluded position on the edge of the moors. The building dates from 1640 and retains plenty of old world charm and atmosphere, including a log fire. Its accommodation makes it an ideal base for outdoor activities. The menu includes hot sandwiches, lunchtime snacks, an extensive selection from the grill, and signature dishes such as steak and ale pie or lamb Henry.

Open 12–3 6.30–11.30 **Bar Meals** L served Mon-Sat 12–2 D served Mon-Sat 6.30–10 (Sun 12–9) **Restaurant** L served Mon-Sat 12–2 D served Mon-Sat 6.30–10 (Sun 12–9) ⊕ Free House ◀ Pedigree Bitter, Guinness, Marsden & guest ales. ⌾ 16 **Facilities** Garden Parking **Rooms** 4

The Oddfellows Arms ⌾

73 Moor End Rd SK6 5PT ☎ 0161 449 7826
e-mail: amollimited@hotmail.co.uk
dir: *Telephone for details*

A friendly welcome can be expected in this c1650 building, which has had a liquor licence since 1805. It changed its name from 'The Angel Inn' in 1860 to accommodate the Oddfellows Society, a forerunner of the Trades Unions. Seafood options include lobster and tiger prawn linguini, and Basque seabass with crispy rocket salad.

Open 12–3 5.30–11 (Sun 12–7) Closed: 25–26 Dec, 31 Dec-1 Jan **Bar Meals** L served Tue-Sun 12–2 D served Tue-Sat 6.30–9.30 Av main course £12 **Restaurant** L served Sun 12–4 D served Tue-Sat 7–9.30 ⊕ Free House ◀ Adnams Southwold, Marston's Pedigree, Bitter, Fennicks Arizona & guest. ⌾ 8 **Facilities** Garden Dogs allowed Parking

OLDHAM   MAP 16 SD90

The Roebuck Inn ⌾

Strinesdale OL4 3RB ☎ 0161 624 7819 📠 0161 624 7819
e-mail: sehowarth1@hotmail.com
dir: *From Oldham Humps Bridge take Huddersfield Rd, right at 2nd lights onto Ripponden Rd, after 1m right at lights onto Turfpit Ln, follow for 1m*

Historic inn located on the edge of Saddleworth Moor in the rugged Pennines, 1,000 feet above sea level. Part of the pub was once used as a Sunday school, while the upstairs lounge served as a morgue. This may explain the presence of the ghost of a girl who drowned in the local reservoir. The menu offers an extensive choice from vegetarian dishes and steaks to fish dishes; from the fish board perhaps smoked haddock with poached egg and hollandaise sauce.

Open 12–2.30 5–12 (Fri-Sun all day) Closed: Mon lunch **Bar Meals** L served all week 12–2.15 D served all week 5–9.30 (Fri 12–9.15, Sun 12–8.15) Av main course £6.80 **Restaurant** L served all week 12–2.15 D served all week 5–9.30 (Fri 12–9.15, Sun 12–8.15) Av 3 course à la carte £18 Av 3 course fixed price £10.80 ⊕ Free House ◀ Tetleys, guest ale. ⌾ 8 **Facilities** Garden Dogs allowed Parking Play Area

England

England

Pick of the Pubs

The White Hart Inn ◎◎ ♟

Stockport Rd, Lydgate OL4 4JJ

☎ 01457 872566 📄 01457 875190

e-mail: bookings@thewhitehart.co.uk

dir: *From Manchester A62 to Oldham. Right onto bypass, A669 through Lees. In 500yds past Grotton brow of hill turn right onto A6050*

There are two major elements to this attractive 18th-century coaching inn's appeal: an award-winning restaurant, and the fact that the characters Compo, Clegg and Cyril from *Last of the Summer Wine* were based on former regulars here. Over the years the inn has served as a brewery, kennels, prison, school and weaver's cottage, before returning at last to its original purpose as a hostelry. Several different eating areas include the brasserie, a contemporary restaurant, the intimate library, and the new Oak Room. Beer comes from local breweries and there's an extensive wine list. The food itself has been totally revamped; the emphasis now is on well executed pub food, with plenty of choice (including six options for children) and some classic local dishes. In the restaurant expect the likes of carpaccio of beetroot with Cheshire goat's cheese fritters; grilled line-caught Anglesey sea bass fillet; and rum baba with cherries and clotted cream.

Open 12–12 (Sun 12–11) **Bar Meals** L served Mon-Sat 12–2.30 D served Mon-Sat 6–9.30 (Sun 1–7.30) **Restaurant** L served Sun 1–3.30 D served Tue-Sat 6.30–9.30 ⊕ Free House ◀ Timothy Taylor Landlord, J W Lees Bitter, Carlsberg-Tetley Bitter, Copper Dragon & Golden Best. ♟ 16 **Facilities** Garden Parking

---

STALYBRIDGE   MAP 16 SJ99

The Royal Oak NEW

364 Huddersfield Rd, Millbrook SK15 3EP

☎ 0161 338 7118

A family-run pub, once a coroner's evidence room, and later owned by the late Jackie Blanchflower of Man United, who took it on in 1967, two weeks before the breathalyser was introduced. The head chef (also the owner) trained in Italy, has a flair for sauces and steaks, and sources all meats from a butcher who frequently dines here with his family – what better endorsement can there be? The wine list is short but well chosen.

Open 5.30–11 (Sat 4–11, Sun 12–10.30, Summer Fri 12–3) Closed: Mon & Tue **Bar Meals** L served Summer Fri 12–2 D served Wed-Fri 5.30–9 (Sat 4–9, Sun 12–7) Av main course £8.95 **Restaurant** D served Wed-Fri 5.30–9 (Sat 4–9, Sun 12–7) Av 3 course à la carte £21 Av 3 course fixed price £13.50 ⊕ Free House ◀ Boddingtons, John Smiths. **Facilities** Garden Dogs allowed Parking

Stalybridge Station Buffet Bar

The Railway Station, Rassbottom St SK15 1RF

☎ 0161 303 0007

dir: *Telephone for directions*

Unique Victorian railway station refreshment rooms dating from 1885 and including original bar fittings, open fire and a conservatory. Decorated throughout with railway memorabilia, much donated by the regulars. There's always a good choice of real ales, and the bar hosts regular beer festivals and folk nights. Expect the pub's famous black pudding and black peas, pasta bake, pies, liver and onions, and sausage and mash on the bar menu.

Open 11–11 **Bar Meals** L served all week 11–8 ⊕ Free House ◀ Boddingtons, Bass & Flowers IPA. **Facilities** Garden Dogs allowed Parking **Notes** ◎

STOCKPORT   MAP 16 SJ89

The Arden Arms ♟

23 Millgate SK1 2LX ☎ 0161 480 2185

e-mail: steve@ardenarms.com

dir: *M60 junct 27 to town centre. Across mini-rdbt, at lights turn left. Pub on right of next rdbt behind Asda*

An award-winning gem of a pub is this early 19th-century coaching inn on the edge of Stockport's historic market place. Its last major 'modernisation' was in 1908, so the interior alone makes a visit worthwhile. Bear in mind that dinner is not served, although high quality lunches include pan-fried mackerel; seared rump steak; goat's cheese fritter; and roasted red pepper with wild mushroom stroganoff stuffing. Drinking and eating in the courtyard is pleasant in summer.

Open 12–12 **Bar Meals** L served all week 12.30–2.30 (Sat-Sun 12.30–4) Av main course £7.50 ◀ Robinsons: Unicorn Bitter, Hatters Mild, Robin Bitter,Double Hop & seasonal ales. ♟ 7 **Facilities** Garden Dogs allowed **Notes** ◎

The Nursery Inn ♟

Green Ln, Heaton Norris SK4 2NA

☎ 0161 432 2044 📄 0161 442 1857

e-mail: nursery@hydes37.eclipse.co.uk

dir: *Green Ln off Heaton Moor Rd. Pass rugby club on Green Ln, at end on right. Little cobbled road, pub 100yds on right*

Originally the main headquarters of Stockport County Football Club, with players changing in what is now the pub's interior, and the pitch at the rear. The Nursery dates back to 1939, with the wood panelling in the lounge/dining room reflecting the period. Food is available at lunchtime only – jacket potatoes, sandwiches and baguettes in the bar, and smoked haddock and tuna steak in the restaurant.

Open 11.30–11 (Fri 11.30–11.30, Sat 11.30–12 Sun 12–11.30) **Bar Meals** L served Mon-Sat 12–2.30 (Sun 12–4) **Restaurant** L served Mon-Sat 12–2.30 (Sun 2 sittings: 12.30 & 2.30) ◀ Hydes Bitter, Hydes Jekylls Gold, Hydes Seasonal Ales, Harp Irish. ♟ 7 **Facilities** Garden Dogs allowed Parking **Notes** ◎

England

WIGAN   MAP 15 SD50

Bird I'th Hand

Gathurst Rd, Orell WN5 0LH ☎ 01942 212006

dir: *Telephone for directions*

Handy for Aintree races, this lively pub may well have once been the home of Dr Beecham of 'powders' fame. Home-made food, freshly prepared from market produce, characterises the imaginatively designed menu which offers the likes of stuffed chicken breast, beef stroganoff, Great Grimsby fish pie, Bird special farmhouse stew, liver and onions, and Brixham plaice. Extensive range of starters.

Open 12–11 (Fri-Sat 12pm-3am) **Bar Meals** L served all week 12–9 D served all week 12–9 **Restaurant** L served Mon-Sat 12–9 D served Mon-Sat 12–9 (Sun 12–8) ◀ John Smiths, Directors Bitter, Foster Chesnut Mild, guest ale. **Facilities** Garden Dogs allowed Parking Play Area

HAMPSHIRE

ANDOVER   MAP 05 SU34

Wyke Down Country Pub & Restaurant ♞

Wyke Down, Picket Piece SP11 6LX
☎ 01264 352 048 🖹 01264 324661
e-mail: info@wykedown.co.uk

dir: *3m from Andover town centre/A303. Follow signs for Wyke Down Caravan Park.*

The pub has been in its time a family farm and a base for Irish navvies building a railway cutting on the Waterloo line outside Andover. The restaurant, which opened over a decade ago, stands on the site of the old farm buildings. A good selection of dishes includes home-made burgers prepared from 100% beef steak, steaks, slow roast lamb shank, mushroom stroganoff, and fresh fish from the blackboard specials.

Open 12–3 6–11 (Sun 6–10.30) Closed: 25 Dec-2 Jan **Bar Meals** L served all week 12–2 D served all week 6–9 (Fri-Sat 6–9.30, Sun 6.30–8.30) **Restaurant** L served Sun-Fri 12–2 D served all week 6–9 (Fri-Sat 6–9.30, Sun 6.30–8.30) ⊕ Free House ◀ Guinness. ♞6 **Facilities** Children's licence Garden Parking Play Area

AXFORD   MAP 05 SU64

The Crown at Axford ♞

RG25 2DZ ☎ 01256 389492
e-mail: crownaxford@yahoo.co.uk

dir: *From Basingstoke take A339 towards Alton. Under M3 bridge, turn next right onto B3046 towards New Alresford. Axford in approx 5m*

The Crown is a small country inn set at the northern edge of the pretty Candover Valley. Here you can enjoy your choice from a selection of real ales and wines, with some bread and olives to keep you going, and order dishes like pork, beer and watercress sausages. The food is all home cooked from local produce wherever possible, including fish, game, and veggie dishes from the board. Organic specials are a feature.

Open 12–3 6–11 (Sat 11–11 Sun 12–10.30) **Bar Meals** L served Mon-Sat 12–2.30 D served Mon-Sat 6.30–9.30 (Sun 12–8) Av main course £10 **Restaurant** L served Mon-Sat 12–2.30 D served Mon-Thu 6.30–9 (Fri-Sat 6.30–9.30, Sun 12–8) ⊕ Free House ◀ London Pride, Youngs Bitter, Triple FFF. ♞7 **Facilities** Children's licence Garden Dogs allowed Parking

BASINGSTOKE   MAP 05 SU65

Hoddington Arms ♞

Upton Grey RG25 2RL
☎ 01256 862371 🖹 01256 862371
e-mail: monca777@aol.com

dir: *Telephone for directions*

The McCutcheon family and their dog Foxo run this charming 250–year-old village pub, popularly known as the Hodd, where a log fire burns, cask ales are served and fresh-cooked food is displayed on a blackboard. Choose a delicious home-made pie; oven-roasted salmon on a bed of strawberries; Slovak pork goulash; chargrilled vegetables with rich tomato provençale and rice; or a special, such as beef Madras. The enclosed garden features an adventure playground.

Open 12–3 6–11 (Sun 7–10.30) **Bar Meals** L served all week 12–2 D served Mon-Sat 6–9 **Restaurant** L served all week 12–2 D served Mon-Sat 6–9 Av 3 course à la carte £20 ⊕ Greene King ◀ Greene King IPA, Old Speckled Hen, Ruddles Best. ♞7 **Facilities** Garden Dogs allowed Parking Play Area

BAUGHURST   MAP 05 SU56

Pick of the Pubs

The Wellington Arms ◎◎ ♀

Baughurst Rd RG26 5LP ☎ 0118 982 0110

e-mail: info@thewellingtonarms.com

web: www.thewellingtonarms.com

dir: *Exit M4 junct 12 follow signs to Newbury along A4. At rdbt take left turn to Aldermaston. At rdbt at top of hill take 2nd exit, at T-junct turn left, pub 1m on left.*

A pretty whitewashed building with a large lawned garden surrounded by fields and woodland, an ideal setting for 35 free-range rare breed chickens, whose eggs are used in the kitchen and sold on the bar. There are beehives too, and herbs are grown just outside the kitchen door. Impressive menus show attention to detail, bread is baked by a craft baker, three fish deliveries arrive weekly direct from Brixham, all beef comes from Orkney, and Henwood Farm in Ashford Hill delivers fresh organic vegetables and salads daily. A simple lunch menu from Wednesday to Friday offers choices at a fixed price: potted pork rillettes with dill pickles could be followed by twice-baked goat's cheese soufflé on sautéed spinach, and completed with steamed chocolate and hazelnut sponge. At other times the blackboard may offer Cornish mussels steamed in olde English cider to start, and a main course of Orkney Island beef, shallot and red wine.

Open 12–2.30 6.30–9.30 Closed: Sun eve, Mon & Tue am
Restaurant L served Wed-Sun 12–2.30 D served Tue-Sat 6.30–9.30 Av 3 course à la carte £28 Av 3 course fixed price £15 ⊕ Punch Taverns
◀ Wadworth 6X. ♀ 12 **Facilities** Garden Parking

BEAUWORTH   MAP 05 SU52

The Milburys ♀

SO24 0PB ☎ 01962 771248 📄 01962 7771910

e-mail: info@themilburys.co.uk

dir: *A272 towards Petersfield, after 6m turn right for Beauworth*

A rustic hill-top pub dating from the 17th century and named after the Bronze Age barrow nearby. It is noted for its massive, 250-year-old treadmill that used to draw water from the 300ft well in the bar, and for the far-reaching views across Hampshire that can be savoured from the lofty garden. The African Oasis restaurant has a distinctly South African flavour.

Open 11–3 6–11 (Sun 6–10.30) **Bar Meals** L served all week 12–2 D served all week 6.30–9.30 Av main course £9 **Restaurant** L served all week 12–2 D served all week 6.30–9.30 Av 3 course à la carte £10 ⊕ Free House ◀ Theakstons Old Peculier, Triple FFF Altons Pride, Deuchars, guest ale. ♀ 8 **Facilities** Garden Dogs allowed Parking

BENTLEY   MAP 05 SU74

The Bull Inn ♀

GU10 5JH ☎ 01420 22156 📄 01420 520772

dir: *2m from Farnham on A31 towards Winchester*

15th-century beamed coaching inn in a Hampshire village made famous by a reality TV show called *The Village*. Inside are open log fires, two separate bars and a restaurant. Extensive selection of pub food complemented by braised shank of lamb with sweet potato mash and rosemary sauce; pan-fried fillet of salmon with a lemon and chive butter; and roasted hock of ham with swede and potato purée.

Open 11–11 **Bar Meals** L served Mon-Sat 12–2.30 D served Mon-Sat 6.30–9.30 (Sun 12–8.30) **Restaurant** L served Mon-Sat 12–2.30 D served Mon-Sat 6.30–9.30 (Sun 12–8.30) ⊕ Free House ◀ Courage Best, Ringwood Best, Young's Bitter, Fuller's London Pride. ♀ 8 **Facilities** Garden Dogs allowed Parking

BENTWORTH   MAP 05 SU64

The Star Inn

GU34 5RB ☎ 01420 561224

e-mail: matt@star-inn.com

dir: *Just off A339 signed from Lasham x-rds.*

Handy for the Woodland Trust's property at Home Farm, The Star occupies a charming spot in prime Hampshire countryside. It's an attractive pub, with eye-catching floral displays in summer and a safe, secluded garden. Foodwise, you can choose from good value favourites such as sandwiches, baked potatoes and omelettes; or larger meals like home-made steak and kidney pie; Mexican style enchiladas; or a wide variety of fish dishes.

Open 12–3 5–11 (Fri, Sat, Sun all day) **Bar Meals** L served all week 12–2 D served all week 6.30–9 Av main course £10 **Restaurant** L served all week 12–2 D served all week 6.30–9 (Sun 7–9) ⊕ Free House ◀ Fuller's London Pride, Ringwood Best, Doom Bar, ESB. **Facilities** Garden Parking

Pick of the Pubs

The Sun Inn ♀

See Pick of the Pubs on opposite page

PICK OF THE PUBS

BENTWORTH-HAMPSHIRE

The Sun Inn

This delightful flower-decked pub is either the first building you pass as you enter Bentworth from the Basingstoke-Alton road, or the last one out, depending on which way you are travelling, and it always seems to come as a surprise. Originally two cottages, it now has three interconnecting rooms, each with its own log fire and brick and wood floors.

The bar is the middle room, right in front of the door. Pews, settles, scrubbed pine tables with lit candles in the evening add to the homely atmosphere. Food is hearty and traditional, with beef Stroganoff; minted lamb; a range of meat and vegetarian curries; liver and bacon; cheesy haddock bake; filled Yorkshire puddings; braised steak in red wine and mushroom sauce; and Mediterranean lamb. Game in season includes venison, cooked in Guinness with pickled walnuts, and pheasant. Everything, from the soup to the dessert, is home made. A thriving free house, it offers several hand-pumped real ales, including Timothy Taylor Landlord, Ringwood's Best and Old Thumper, both from Hampshire breweries, Fuller's London Pride,

and Stonehenge Pigswill. There is much to see and do in the area: Gilbert White's House and the Oates Museum in Selborne are not far away, and neither are Jane Austen's House at Chawton, nor the Watercress Line at Alresford. Also within easy reach is Basing House in Old Basing, on the outskirts of Basingstoke, where important Civil War sieges and bombardments brought about the ruin of the house, though parts of it are being restored.

MAP 05 SU64
Sun Hill GU34 5JT
☎ 01420 562338
dir: *Telephone for directions*

Open 12–3 6–11 (Sun 12–10.30)
Bar Meals L served all week
12–2 D served all week 7–9.30
⊕ Free House ◖ Cheriton
Pots Ale, Ringwood Best & Old
Thumper, Brakspear Bitter, Fuller's
London Pride.
Facilities Garden Dogs allowed
Parking

BOLDRE
MAP 05 SZ39

The Hobler Inn ♥

Southampton Rd, Battramsley SO41 8PT ☎ 01590 623944
e-mail: hedi@alcatraz.co.uk
dir: *2m from Brockenhurst, towards Lymington on main road*

On the main road between Brockenhurst and Lymington, with a large grassed area and trestle tables ideal for families visiting the New Forest. It's more London wine bar than local, but still serves a well-kept pint of Ringwood. Hot lunchtime snacks like Welsh rarebit or Boston baked beans on toast are good value. Mains include a variation on the classic shepherd's pie but with added Nepalese spices.

Open 11–11 **Bar Meals** L served all week 12–6 D served all week 6–9.30 Av main course £6 **Restaurant** L served all week 12–6 D served all week 6–9.30 Av 3 course à la carte £18 Av 2 course fixed price £9.95 ◀ Ringwood, Ringwood Best, Timothy Taylor. ♥ 10 **Facilities** Garden Parking

Pick of the Pubs

The Red Lion ♥

Rope Hill SO41 8NE ☎ 01590 673177 📄 01590 674036
dir: *1m from Lymington off A337. From M27 junct 1 through Lyndhurst & Brockenhurst towards Lymington, follow signs for Boldre*

The Red Lion has a mention in the Domesday Book, although today's inn dates from the 15th century, when it was created from a stable and two cottages. It remains the quintessential New Forest pub. Inside you'll find a rambling series of beamed rooms packed with rural memorabilia. Head chef Richard West delights in creating traditional, home-made dishes based around the bounty of excellent produce that is available locally. Venison from Forest herds and fish from local catches are commonly on the menu. Begin with caramelized onion and goats' cheese tart, or classic prawn cocktail, before sampling such popular dishes as wild rabbit slow braised with white wine and fresh thyme and served on buttered mash; twice-roasted belly pork on roasted winter vegetables with home-made gooseberry sauce; or fish pie. Booking is recommended, as are Angela's jam roly-poly and whiskey bread and butter pudding among other desserts.

Open 11–3 5.30–11 (Sun 12–3.30 6–10.30) **Bar Meals** L served Mon-Sat 12–2.30 D served Mon-Sat 6–9.30 (Sun 12–3.30, 6–9) **Restaurant** L served Mon-Sat 12–2.30 D served Mon-Sat 6–9.30 (Sun 12–3.30, 6–9) ⊕ Free House ◀ Ringwood Best, Ringwood Fortyniner, Marstons Pedigree, Guinness & guest ales. ♥ 18 **Facilities** Garden Dogs allowed Parking

See advertisement under LYMINGTON

BRAMDEAN
MAP 05 SU62

The Fox Inn ♥

SO24 0LP ☎ 01962 771363
e-mail: thefoxinn@callnetuk.com
dir: *A272 between Winchester & Petersfield*

The crest fixed to the exterior of this 400–year-old pub commemorates the day when the Prince of Wales (later king George IV) stopped by for refreshments. Situated in the beautiful Meon Valley surrounded by copper beech trees, The Fox serves locally sourced food including a good blackboard selection of fresh fish dishes – perhaps supreme of halibut with lime and chilli butter. Other typical choices include pork fillet with stilton and brandy sauce.

Open 11–3 6–11 (Winter 6.30–11) **Bar Meals** L served all week 12–2 D served all week 7–9 ⊕ Greene King ◀ Ruddles County & IPA Smooth. ♥ 7 **Facilities** Garden Parking

BROOK
MAP 05 SU21

Pick of the Pubs

The Bell Inn ★★★ HL ⊚⊚ ♥

SO43 7HE ☎ 023 8081 2214 📄 023 8081 3958
e-mail: bell@bramshaw.co.uk
web: www.bellinnbramshaw.co.uk
dir: *From M27 junct 1 (Cadnam) take B3078 signed Brook, 0.5m on right*

Since it was established in 1782 the Bell has been owned continuously by the same family. Features of the handsome building include white-painted window shutters, an imposing inglenook fireplace and beamed bedrooms. Bar food ranges from hot and cold snacks (omelettes, sandwiches, burgers) to daily specials featuring fresh fish and local game in season. A daily menu offers a wider choice.

Open 11–11 **Bar Meals** L served all week 12–9.30 D served all week Av main course £11 **Restaurant** 12–3 D served all week 7.30–9.30 ⊕ Free House ◀ Ringwood Best, Guinness & guest ale. ♥ 10 **Facilities** Garden Parking Play Area **Rooms** 25

BUCKLERS HARD MAP 05 SU40

The Master Builders House Hotel ★★★

HL 🏵🏵 ♟

SO42 7XB ☎ 01590 616253 📠 01590 616297
e-mail: res@themasterbuilders.co.uk
dir: *From M27 junct 2 follow signs to Beaulieu. Left onto B3056. Left to Bucklers Hard. Hotel 2m on left*

Once home to master shipbuilder Henry Adams, this idyllic 18th-century inn is situated on the banks of the River Beaulieu, in the historic ship-building village of Bucklers Hard. Ducks, boats and river walks are all on the doorstep. Bar food includes braised lamb shank set on creamed potato with red wine and rosemary jus; and fisherman's pie with crusty bread and salad, served alongside a choice of real ales and decent wines.

Open 11–11 (Nov-Mar Sun-Thu 11–6) **Bar Meals** L served all week 12–2.30 D served all week 7–9 **Restaurant** L served all week 12–3 D served all week 7–10 ⊕ Free House 🍺 Greene King IPA, Abbots, Old Hooky. ♟14 **Facilities** Garden Parking **Rooms** 25

BURLEY MAP 05 SU20

The Burley Inn ♟

BH24 4AB ☎ 01425 403448
e-mail: info@theburleyinn.co.uk
dir: *4m from Ringwood*

Before it became a pub, this spacious Edwardian building was where the local doctor practised, the waiting room now being the bar and dining areas. The menu offers a broad choice, including pie of the day; beef bourguignonne; salmon in white wine and chive sauce; and lasagne and vegetable tagine. The inn stands in the heart of the New Forest, so take care when driving as ponies, donkeys and cattle freely roam the local roads.

Open 9–11 (Sun 9–10.30) **Bar Meals** L served all week 12–6 D served all week 12–9.30 **Restaurant** L served all week 11–6 D served all week 11–9.30 ⊕ Free House 🍺 Ringwood Best, Ringwood Old Thumper. ♟11 **Facilities** Garden Dogs allowed Parking

CADNAM MAP 05 SU31

Sir John Barleycorn ♟

Old Romsey Rd SO40 2NP
☎ 01202 746162 📠 01202 743080
e-mail: hedi@alcatraz.co.uk
dir: *From Southampton M27 junct 1 into Cadnam*

Reputedly the oldest inn in the New Forest, this friendly establishment is formed from three 12th-century cottages, one of which was once home to the charcoal burner who discovered the body of King William Rufus. A thorough menu covers all the options from quick snacks and sandwiches to toad-in-the-hole; chicken, leek and bacon pie; and Thai chicken curry. The name derives from a folksong celebrating the transformation of barley to beer.

Open 11–11 **Bar Meals** L served all week 12–7 D served all week 6–9.30 Av main course £6 **Restaurant** L served all week 12–7 D served all week 6–9.30 Av 3 course à la carte £17 Av 2 course fixed price £9.95 🍺 Ringwood, Ringwood Best, London Pride. ♟10 **Facilities** Garden Parking

CHALTON MAP 05 SU71

Pick of the Pubs

The Red Lion ♟

PO8 0BG ☎ 023 9259 2246 📠 023 9259 6915
e-mail: redlionchalton@fullers.co.uk
dir: *Just off A3 between Horndean & Petersfield. Follow signs for Chalton*

Originally established in 1147 as a workshop and residence for the craftsmen working on St Michael's church across the road, the Red Lion is believed to be Hampshire's oldest pub. By 1460 it had become a hostel for church dignitaries, and it was later extended to accommodate coachmen on their regular journey from London to Portsmouth. Its licence was granted in 1503, and by the 1700s it was extended again. Built of wood, white daub and thatch, this ancient building blends effortlessly into the hills and trees of the South Downs. There are spectacular views from the large garden and modern dining room. The popular snack menu includes ciabatta rolls and traditional ploughman's, as well as the likes of home-made meatballs, and filled jacket potatoes. The blackboard menu changes daily: look out for Southdown pork fillet with Cumberland sauce; or smoked haddock fillet with cheese and chive sauce.

Open 11.30–11 (Sun 11.45–10.30) **Bar Meals** L served Mon-Thu 12–9 D served Mon-Thu 12–9 (Fri-Sat 12–9.30, Sun 12–8) Av main course £8.95 **Restaurant** L served Mon-Thu 12–9 D served Mon-Thu 12–9 (Fri-Sat 12–9.30, Sun 12–8) Av 3 course à la carte £18.20 🍺 Fuller's GB, HSB, Butser, London Pride. ♟20 **Facilities** Garden Dogs allowed Parking

England

CHARTER ALLEY   MAP 05 SU55

The White Hart Inn ♀

White Hart Ln RG26 5QA
☎ 01256 850048 🖹 01256 850524
e-mail: enquiries@whitehartcharteralley.com
web: www.whitehartcharteralley.com
dir: *From M3 junct 6 take A339 towards Newbury. Turn right to
Ramsdell. Right at church, then 1st left into White Hart Lane*

On the outskirts of the village overlooking open farmland and
woods, this pub draws everyone from cyclists and walkers to real ale
enthusiasts. Dating from 1818, it originally refreshed local woodsmen
and coach drivers visiting the farrier next door. Today's more
sophisticated menu is likely to include corn-fed chicken stuffed with
wild mushrooms, a grilled sirloin steak, or chef's curry of the day. Look
to the blackboard for specials and fish dishes.

Open 12–2.30 7–11 (Sun 12–3, 7–10.30) Closed: 25–26 Dec, 1 Jan
Bar Meals L served all week 12–2 D served Tue–Sat 7–9 Av main course
£7.50 **Restaurant** L served all week 12–2 D served Tue–Sat 7–9 Av 3 course
à la carte £20 ⊕ Free House ⬛ West Berkshire Mild, Palmers IPA, Triple
FFF Alton Pride. ♀ 7 **Facilities** Garden Dogs allowed Parking

CHAWTON   MAP 05 SU73

The Greyfriar

Winchester Rd GU34 1SB ☎ 01420 83841 🖹 01420 83841
e-mail: info@thegreyfriar.co.uk
dir: *Just off A31 near Alton. Access to Chawton via A31/A32 junct.
Follow Jane Austen's House signs*

A terrace of 16th-century cottages opposite Jane Austen's house,
which was divided into a 'beer shop' and grocery in the 1860s. Proper
pub status followed with a license granted to the Chawton Arms;
for reasons unknown it became the Greyfriar in 1894. Today it's a
family-run and friendly place to enjoy Fullers beers and quality food
from a varied and imaginative menu. Expect the likes of sautéed fresh
asparagus, Scottish scallops grilled in the shell, and main courses that
include fresh lamb reared in the village.

Open 12–11 (Sun 12–10.30) **Bar Meals** L served Mon–Sat 12–2
D served Mon–Sat 7–9.30 (Sun 12–3, 6–8.30) Av main course £12
Restaurant L served Mon–Sat 12–2 D served Mon–Sat 7–9.30 (Sun 12–3,
6–8.30) ⬛ Fuller's London Pride, ESB & seasonal ales. **Facilities** Garden
Dogs allowed Parking Play Area

CHERITON   MAP 05 SU52

Pick of the Pubs

The Flower Pots Inn

SO24 0QQ ☎ 01962 771318 🖹 01962 771318
dir: *A272 toward Petersfield, left onto B3046, pub 0.75m on
right*

This friendly red brick village pub was built as a farmhouse in
the 1840s by the head gardener of nearby Avington Park. There
are two bars: the rustic, pine-furnished public bar and the cosy
saloon with its comfy sofa, both with welcoming open fires in
winter. A large, safe garden allows young ones to let off steam.
Simple home-made food is the order of the day: expect toasted
sandwiches, jacket potatoes and tasty hotpots – perhaps beef
bourguignon, spicy mixed bean, or lamb and apricot – served with
a choice of crusty bread, basmati rice, garlic bread or jacket potato.
There are also ploughman's (with cheese, ham or beef), and giant
baps filled with a choice of beef, pork steak and onions, bacon
and mushroom, cheese, or coronation chicken. Be sure to try the
award-winning beers like Pots Ale or Goodens Gold, brewed in
the micro-brewery across the car park.

Open 12–2.30 6–11 (Sun 12–3, 7–10.30) **Bar Meals** L served all
week 12–2 D served Mon–Sat 7–9 (Wed eve curry only, no dinner BHs)
Av main course £7 ⊕ Free House ⬛ Flower Pots Bitter & Goodens
Gold. **Facilities** Garden Dogs allowed Parking **Notes** ◉

CHILWORTH   MAP 05 SU41

Chilworth Arms NEW ♀

Chilworth Rd SO16 7JZ ☎ 023 8076 6247
dir: *3m N of Southampton on A27 Romsey road*

Formerly known as the Clump Inn, this gastropub is warmed by log
fires and furnished with leather sofas. There's a great mix of freshly
prepared dishes, from simple pizzas to well-aged steaks, fresh fish
and traditional pub classics, many with a hint of Italian about them.
Regularly changing real ales vie for popularity with continental beers,
fine wines and fresh juices. Eat in the spacious dining area, or out on
the covered patio.

Open 11–11 **Bar Meals** L served Mon–Sat 12–9.30 D served Mon–Sat
12–9.30 (Sun 12–8.30) Av main course £10 **Restaurant** L served Mon–Sat
12–2.30 D served Mon–Sat 6–10 (Sun 12–8.30) Av 3 course à la carte £20
⊕ Free House ⬛ Timothy Taylor Landlord. ♀ 15 **Facilities** Children's
licence Garden Parking

CRAWLEY   MAP 05 SU43

The Fox and Hounds ♀

SO21 2PR ☎ 01962 776006 🖹 01962 776006
e-mail: liamlewisairey@aol.com
dir: *A34 onto A272 then 1st right into Crawley*

Just north west of Winchester, at the heart of a peaceful Hampshire
village, this mock Tudor inn enjoys a burgeoning reputation for
simple well-cooked food. Restored to former glories, it features
beamed rooms warmed by log fires that create a welcoming, lived-in
atmosphere. Typical menu choices include Old English sausages on
bubble and squeak, steak and ale pie, salmon fillet with hollandaise
sauce, dressed crab salad, and pork fillet with black pudding.

Open 12–3 6–11 (Sun 12–4, Sat-Sun 6–12) **Bar Meals** L served all week 12–2 D served all week 6–9 Av main course £8.95 **Restaurant** L served all week 12–2 D served all week 7–9 ∰ Free House ◀ Wadworth 6X, Ringwood Best, Fuller's London Pride & HSB. ♀36 **Facilities** Children's licence Garden Parking Play Area

---

CRONDALL   **MAP 05 SU74**

Pick of the Pubs

The Hampshire Arms ♀

Pankridge St GU10 5QU
☎ 01252 850418 📄 01252 850418
e-mail: dining@thehampshirearms.co.uk
dir: *From M3 junct 5 take A287 S towards Farnham. Follow signs to Crondall on right*

The Hampshire Arms bar is light and elegant, as are the two main dining areas and intimate alcoves. Throughout the public rooms open fires, exposed beams and candlelight combine to create a delightfully welcoming atmosphere. The building dates from the 18th century and began as two cottages, but over the years it has also been a courthouse, a post office and a bakery. Outside there is a large landscaped garden with a patio area. For a leisurely lunch you could try chef's special chicken liver parfait with red onion marmalade, freshly made brioche and sultanas soaked in jasmine tea, as a starter. Smoked salmon and haddock fishcakes with buttered spinach and French butter sauce are an established favourite, as is the classic dessert, French lemon tart, served with chocolate chip shortbread. The mid-week fixed-price menu offers value for money with seared scallops with apple and ginger purée and soft herb salad; and roast rump of lamb with three mustards, wilted greens and lamb reduction.

Open 11–3 6–11.30 (Sat all day, Sun12–10.30) **Bar Meals** L served Tue-Sun 12–2.30 D served Tue-Sat Av main course £8 **Restaurant** L served Tue-Sun 12–2.30 D served Tue-Sat 6.30–9.30 Av 3 course à la carte £31.50 ∰ Greene King ◀ Greene King IPA, Abbot Ale, Ruddles County,. ♀10 **Facilities** Garden Parking

---

DAMERHAM   **MAP 05 SU11**

The Compasses Inn ♀

SP6 3HQ ☎ 01725 518231 📄 01725 518880
e-mail: info@compassesinn.net
web: www.compassesinn.net
dir: *From Fordingbridge (A338) follow signs for Sandleheath/ Damerham. Signed from B3078*

The Compasses is a perfect example of the traditional family-run country free house. Set next to the village green, it is an ideal spot for a tranquil summer pint or a winter warmer round the welcoming open fires. The ales are augmented by over 100 malt whiskies and a good selection of wines. Freshly prepared food is served in the bar, dining room or garden: it ranges from a simple home-baked bread ploughman's to pan-fried sea bass with prawns.

The Compasses Inn

Open 11–3 6–11 (Sat all day, Sun 12–4, 7–10.30) **Bar Meals** L served all week 12–2.30 D served all week 7–9.30 (Sun 7–9) **Restaurant** L served all week 12–2.30 D served all week 7–9.30 (Sun 7–9) Av 3 course à la carte £20 ∰ Free House ◀ Ringwood Best, Hop Back Summer Lightning, Courage Best, Palmers IPA. ♀8 **Facilities** Children's licence Garden Dogs allowed Parking

---

DOWNTON   **MAP 05 SZ29**

The Royal Oak ♀

Christchurch Rd SO41 0LA ☎ 01590 642297
e-mail: royaloak@alcatraz.co.uk
dir: *On A337 between Lymington & Christchurch*

Two miles south of the New Forest and just one mile from the beach at Lymington, this renovated pub is renowned for its food. Snack on a traditional ploughman's platter or daytime sandwiches such as warm chicken, chorizo and rocket or brie and bacon. Main meals include salmon fish cakes with tomato and chilli jam; sirloin steak with peppercorn sauce; and gourmet burgers.

Open 11–11 (Sun 11.30–11) Closed: 25 Dec **Bar Meals** L served all week 12–6 D served all week 6–9.30 **Restaurant** L served all week 12–6 D served all week 6–9.30 ∰ Enterprise Inns ◀ Ringwood Best Bitter, Fuller's London Pride & HSB. ♀15 **Facilities** Garden Parking

---

DUMMER   **MAP 05 SU54**

The Queen Inn ♀

Down St RG25 2AD ☎ 01256 397367 📄 01256 397601
e-mail: richardmoore49@btinternet.com
dir: *M3 junct 7, follow Dummer signs*

You can dine by candlelight from the restaurant menu at this 16th-century village pub with low beams and huge open log fire. Alternatively you'll find lunchtime savouries like Welsh or Scottish rarebits alongside the sandwiches and jackets. A bar menu offers everything from starters and healthy options to flame grills, house favourites, and specials like chargrilled half chicken peri peri and beef bourguignon. Beers include guest ales, and the wine list is commendably unpretentious.

Open 11–3 6–11 (Sun 12–3, 7–10.30) **Bar Meals** L served all week 12–2 D served Mon-Sat 6–9.30 (Sun 7–9) **Restaurant** L served all week 12–2 D served all week 6–9.30 ∰ Enterprise Inns ◀ Courage Best & John Smiths, Fuller's London Pride, Old Speckled Hen & guest ales. ♀10 **Facilities** Garden Parking

England

EAST END

MAP 05 SZ39

The East End Arms

Main Rd SO41 5SY ☎ 01590 626223 📠 01590 626223
e-mail: joanna@eastendarms.co.uk
dir: *From Lymington towards Beaulieu (past Isle of Wight ferry), 3m to East End*

Close to Beaulieu and historic Buckler's Hard, this New Forest inn combines the authenticity of a proper local with a growing reputation as a gastropub. Ringwood ales are drawn straight from the wood in The Foresters Bar, where stone floors and open fires create a homely, traditional feel. The atmospheric lounge bar, with its sofas and winter fires, is a comfortable setting for a meal from the daily-changing, brasserie-style menu. Locally sourced fish/ seafood make a strong showing in dishes such as grilled sardine fillets with chive butter, followed by grilled sea bass fillet with spring onion and coriander risotto. An alternative might be goat's cheese cheesecake with red onion jam, followed by grilled rib-eye steak with herb butter and chips. The pub is well worth the drive down country lanes or a short diversion from the nearby Solent Way long distance footpath.

Open 11.30–3 6–11 (Sat 11.30–11, Sun 12–9) **Bar Meals** L served all week 12–2.30 **Restaurant** L served Tue-Sun 12–2.30 D served Tue-Sat 7–9.30 (Mon baguettes only) ⊕ Free House ◀ Ringwood Best, Archers & Fortyniner. **Facilities** Garden Dogs allowed Parking

EAST MEON

MAP 05 SU62

Ye Olde George Inn 🍷

Church St GU32 1NH ☎ 01730 823481 📠 01730 823759
e-mail: yeoldgeorge@aol.com
dir: *S of A272 (Winchester/Petersfield). 1.5m from Petersfield turn left opposite church*

This 15th-century inn is located in a lovely old village on the River Meon, close to a magnificent Norman church. Its open fires, heavy beams and rustic artefacts create an ideal setting for a good choice of real ales and freshly prepared food in the bar or restaurant. Fish features strongly with dishes of baked sea bass with samphire and balsamic olive dressing, or poached halibut with mussel sauce.

Open 12–3 6–11 (Sat 11–3) **Bar Meals** L served all week 12–2 D served all week 7–9 Av main course £9.50 **Restaurant** L served all week 12–2 D served all week 7–9 Av 3 course à la carte £16.95 ⊕ Hall & Woodhouse ◀ Badger Best, Tanglefoot & King & Barnes Sussex. 🍷 8 **Facilities** Garden Dogs allowed Parking

EASTON

MAP 05 SU53

The Chestnut Horse 🍷

SO21 1EG ☎ 01962 779257 📠 01962 779037
dir: *From M3 junct 9 take A33 towards Basingstoke, then B3047. Take 2nd right, then 1st left*

This 16th-century dining pub has gained a well-earned local reputation for the quality of its food. Old tankards and teapots hang from the low-beamed ceilings in the two bar areas, where a large open fire is the central focus through the winter months. The romantic candlelit restaurants are equally inviting: plates adorn the light, panelled Green Room, and there's a wood-burning stove in the darker low-beamed Red Room. Fans of good food on a shoestring will want to seek out the excellent value set price menu that might open with Thai fishcakes, and go on to lamb navarin with pomme purée. From the carte, you might start with a tian of fresh Dorset crab with crayfish tails or pan-seared loin and rillette of rabbit with horseradish cream and hazelnut oil, then continue with marinated ostrich fillet with tomato and marjoram polenta, or a prime Scotch sirloin with peppercorn sauce. Dessert choices include plum tart Tatin with butterscotch sauce. There's also a traditional roast on Sunday.

Open 11–3 5.30–11 (Sat all day Winter Sun 11–6) **Bar Meals** L served all week 12–2.30 D served all week 6–9.30 (Sun 12–4 winter, 12–8 summer) Av main course £12.95 **Restaurant** L served all week 12–2.30 D served all week 6–9.30 (Sun 12–4 winter, 12–8 summer) Av 3 course à la carte £25 Av 2 course fixed price £10 ⊕ Hall & Woodhouse ◀ Chestnut Horse Special, Badger First Gold, Tanglefoot. 🍷 9 **Facilities** Garden Dogs allowed Parking

The Cricketers Inn 🍷

SO21 1EJ ☎ 01962 779353 📠 01962 779010
e-mail: cricketersinn@btconnect.com
dir: *M3 junct 9, A33 towards Basingstoke, right at Kingsworthy onto B3047. In 0.75m turn right. Pub signposted*

Standing on a corner in the heart of a popular village, this 1904 pub is a real local, with a single L-shaped bar and cricketing memorabilia on the walls. Look out for crusty doorstep sandwiches and open toasties, in addition to filled Yorkshires and specials of ribs, sweet and sour chicken and cottage pie. New landlord for 2008.

Open 12–3 6–11 (Fri-Sat 6–11.30) **Bar Meals** L served all week 12–2 D served Mon-Sat 7–9 Av main course £8 ⊕ Marstons ◀ Ringwood, guest ales. 🍷 8 **Facilities** Children's licence Garden Dogs allowed Parking

EAST TYTHERLEY   MAP 05 SU22

Pick of the Pubs

The Star Inn Tytherley ★★★★ INN

@ @ ☂

SO51 0LW ☎ 01794 340225

e-mail: info@starinn.co.uk

dir: *5m N of Romsey off A3057, left for Dunbridge on B3084. Left for Awbridge & Kents Oak. Through Lockerley then 1m*

Set in the smallest village in the Test Valley, the 16th-century Star Inn stands overlooking the village cricket green. You'll find seasonal Ringwood beers and other guest ales behind the bar, plus an extensive international wine list, carefully compiled to offer a selection of good 'quaffing' wines as well as fine bottles for a special occasion. Dine where you like, in the bar, at dark-wood tables in the main dining room, or outside on the patio in summer, where you can also play chess on a king-sized board. Lunchtime brings a variety of platters (cheese, fish or pork pie), sandwiches (perhaps crayfish and chorizo, or brie, parma ham and tomato), and a good value two course choice (Winchester cheese soufflé, and pheasant roly poly), plus a carte. Choose from the evening supper menu (parsnip and cheddar bread and butter pudding, or venison casserole), while the dinner carte serves up pork tenderloin, or grilled gilthead bream fillets.

Open 11–3 6–11 Closed: Sun eve & Mon (ex BH)
Bar Meals L served Tue-Sat 12–2 D served Tue-Fri 7–9 (Sun 12–2.30)
Restaurant L served Tue-Sat 12–2 D served Tue-Sun 7–9 (Sun 12–2.30) ⊕ Free House ◖ Ringwood Best, Seasonal Ringwood ales, Hidden Quest & guest ales. ☂ 9 **Facilities** Children's licence Garden Dogs allowed Parking Play Area **Rooms** 3

EMSWORTH   MAP 05 SU70

The Sussex Brewery ☂

36 Main Rd PO10 8AU ☎ 01243 371533 ▤ 01243 379684

dir: *On A259 (coast road), between Havant & Chichester*

A fresh 'carpet' of sawdust is laid daily in the bars of this traditional 17th-century pub that boasts wooden floors, large open fires and a typically warm welcome. Fully 15 sausage recipes are on offer containing all kind of fillings, from traditional to exotic. Daily specials might include fresh local fish, steaks, or rack of lamb.

Open 11–11 **Bar Meals** L served all week 12–2.30 D served all week 7–9.30 Av main course £8 **Restaurant** L served all week 12–2.30 D served all week 7–9.30 ⊕ Young & Co ◖ Youngs Special, Youngs Ordinary, Waggle Dance, Bombardier Tribute. ☂ 9 **Facilities** Garden Dogs allowed Parking

EVERSLEY   MAP 05 SU76

The Golden Pot ☂

Reading Rd RG27 0NB ☎ 0118 973 2104 ▤ 0118 973 4042
e-mail: jcalder@goldenpot.co.uk
web: www.golden-pot.co.uk

dir: *Between Reading & Camberley on B3272 approx 0.25m from Eversley cricket ground*

Dating back to the 1700s, this welcoming pub has a warming fire connecting the bar and restaurant, and both offer wide-ranging menus: look out for baguettes at lunchtime, and bar dishes like escalope of venison with crème fraîche borscht. The restaurant menu offers the likes of seared king scallops followed by chicken and mozzarella roulade. Monday evenings offer Swiss rösti night with live music.

Open 11.30–3 5.30–11 Closed: 25–26 Dec, 1 Jan **Bar Meals** L served Mon-Sat 12–2.15 D served Mon-Sat 6–9.15 (Sun 12–2)
Restaurant L served Sun-Fri 12–2 D served Mon-Sat 7–9 ⊕ Greene King ◖ Greene King Ruddles Best, Abbot Ale, Greene King IPA. ☂ 8 **Facilities** Garden Dogs allowed Parking

FORDINGBRIDGE   MAP 05 SU11

The Augustus John ☂

116 Station Rd SP6 1DG ☎ 01425 652098
e-mail: enquiries@augustusjohn.com

dir: *12m S of Salisbury on A338 towards Ringwood*

A change of hands has introduced all embracing plans for a transformation of this pub, named after the renowned British portrait painter who lived in the village. Since John was not universally liked, the name caused local controversy; some villagers preferred the previous Railway Hotel, or even the Load of Hay. Plans include improvements to the kitchen and seating areas, a wider choice of lunchtime snacks, and more dishes based on locally-sourced produce.

Open 11.30–3.30 5–12 (Fri-Sun all day) (Mon-Sun all day from Easter)
Bar Meals L served Mon-Sat 12–2.30 D served Mon-Sat 6.30–9.30 (Sun 7–9) **Restaurant** L served all week 11.30–2.30 D served all week 6.30–9.30 ⊕ Marstons ◖ Ringwood Best, Pedigree. ☂ 8 **Facilities** Garden Dogs allowed Parking

England

FRITHAM
MAP 05 SU21

The Royal Oak 🍷

SO43 7HJ ☎ 023 8081 2606 📄 023 8081 4066

e-mail: royaloakfritham@btopenworld.com

dir: *M27 junct 1, B3078 signed Fordingbridge. 2m, then left at x-rds signed Ocknell & Fritham. Then follow signs to Fritham*

A small traditional thatched pub dating from the 15th century, deep in the New Forest. Walkers, cyclists and horse-riders delight in the large garden overlooking the forest and the pub's own farm. Unaltered for 100 years and with no jukebox or fruit machine, the three small bars focus on serving good real ales and simple plates of local food: quiches, sausages, pork pies and sausage rolls are all home made using the farm's pigs; chicken breasts are cured and smoked in apple wood, also by the pub.

Open 11–3 6–11 (Summer Sat 11–11, Sun 12–10.30) **Bar Meals** L served Mon-Fri 12–2.30 (Sat-Sun 12–3) Av main course £6.50 ⊕ Free House ◀ Ringwood Best & Fortyniner, Hop Back Summer Lightning, Palmers Dorset Gold, Bowman Ales Swift One. ♗ 12 **Facilities** Garden Dogs allowed **Notes** ☺

GOSPORT
MAP 05 SZ69

The Seahorse NEW 🍷

Broadsands Dr PO12 2TJ ☎ 023 9251 2910

e-mail: simonl29@aol.com

dir: *A32 onto Military Rd, 2nd exit rdbt onto Gomer Ln, 0.5m on left*

Much more than just a local pub, the newly refurbished Seahorse now includes Leonard's restaurant, as well as a large bar with terrace. This is a family-run business, where head chef Simon Leonard uses locally sourced ingredients to create a wide range of traditional and speciality dishes. Typical choices include boiled ham, duck egg and hand-cut chips; mutton suet pudding; and chargrilled steak with wild mushrooms.

Open 11–12 (Sun 12–10.30) Rest: 25 Dec 1 Jan **Bar Meals** L served Mon-Sat 12–2.30 D served Mon-Thu & Sun 6–8.45 (Fri & Sat 6–9.45, Sun 12–4) Av main course £8 **Restaurant** L served Mon-Sat 12–2.30 D served Tue-Thu & Sun 6–8.45 (Fri & Sat 6–9.45, Sun 12–4) Av 3 course à la carte £17 ⊕ Enterprise Inns ◀ London Pride, Worthington. ♗ 8 **Facilities** Garden Parking

HAMBLEDON
MAP 05 SU61

The Vine at Hambledon 🍷

West St PO7 4RW ☎ 02392 632419

e-mail: landlord@vinepub.com

dir: *Just off B2150 between Droxford (A32) and Waterlooville (A3)*

A cosy little pub with a welcoming atmosphere, tucked away in the main street of the pretty village of Hambledon. Over the past few years Tom and Vicki Faulkner have made an impression with their modern menus built around traditional British cooking. Look out for starters like scallops wrapped in Parma ham with a truffle scented green bean salad, and mains such as pan-fried fillet of turbot with braised butterbean and chorizo ragout.

Open 11.30–3 6–11 (Sun 12–4, 7–10.30) **Bar Meals** L served all week 12–2 D served Mon-Sat 7–9 (Sun 12–4) Av main course £10 **Restaurant** L served all week 12–2 D served Mon-Sat 7–9 Av 3 course à la carte £19 ◀ Ringwood Best, Jennings Cockerhoop, Ringwood 49er, "Vine" House Bitter. ♗ 11 **Facilities** Children's licence Garden Dogs allowed

HAMBLE-LE-RICE
MAP 05 SU40

Pick of the Pubs

The Bugle 🍷

See Pick of the Pubs on opposite page

HANNINGTON
MAP 05 SU55

Pick of the Pubs

The Vine at Hannington NEW 🍷

See Pick of the Pubs on page 264

HARTLEY WINTNEY
MAP 05 SU75

The Phoenix Inn 🍷

London Rd, Phoenix Green RG27 8RT

☎ 01252 842484 📄 01252 845508

dir: *On A30 between Hook & Hartley Wintney. 3m from M3, 7m from M4*

In 2007 Kristian and Georgina Minter took a long lease on the Phoenix, and have worked ceaselessly to revive the pub's motoring heritage – it was the unofficial HQ of the Vintage Sports Car Club in the 1930s. The former 17th-century coaching inn now welcomes increasing numbers of classic car and motorbike owners. Sip a pint of guest ale while choosing perhaps from Kristian's delicious carte, tempura whitebait with garlic aioli, and braised lamb shank or pot-roasted pheasant.

Open 12–11 **Bar Meals** L served Mon-Sat 12–2.30 D served all week 7–9.30 (Sun 12–3.30) **Restaurant** L served Mon-Sat 12–2.30 D served Tue-Sat 7–9.30 (Sun 12–3.30) Av 3 course fixed price £13.95 ⊕ Punch Taverns ◀ Courage Best, Adnams Bitter, guest ales. ♗ 12 **Facilities** Children's licence Garden Dogs allowed Parking

HAVANT
MAP 05 SU70

The Royal Oak 🍷

19 Langstone High St, Langstone PO9 1RY

☎ 023 9248 3125 📄 023 9247 6838

dir: *Telephone for directions*

Occupying an outstanding position overlooking Langstone Harbour, this historic 16th-century pub is noted for its rustic, unspoilt interior. Flagstone floors, exposed beams and winter fires contrast with the waterfront benches and secluded rear garden for alfresco summer drinking. Light lunches such as rich tomato soup or chicken Caesar salad support a dinner menu that includes slow-cooked Welsh lamb; baked salmon fillet; and British ham hock glazed with honey mustard.

Open 11–11 **Bar Meals** L served all week 12–6 D served all week 6–9 Av main course £6.95 **Restaurant** L served all week 12–6 D served all week 6–9 Av 3 course à la carte £13.95 ◀ Interbrew Flowers, Greene King IPA, Ruddles County, Speckled Hen. ♗ 16 **Facilities** Garden Dogs allowed

PICK OF THE PUBS

HAMBLE-LE-RICE-HAMPSHIRE

The Bugle

This historic Grade II listed waterside pub has been restored to its former glory, much to the appreciation of local drinkers. It sparked a successful rescue campaign by villagers when housing developers threatened to demolish the site, and was subsequently bought by local independent operators.

Under their ownership it was lovingly refurbished in close consultation with English Heritage, using traditional methods and materials. Features include exposed beams and brickwork, an oak bar and a wood burning stove, plus a heated terrace with lovely views over the River Hamble. Rotating ales brewed in the region make an ideal partner for one of the appetising bar bites: locally made chipolatas and hot English mustard perhaps, or half a pint of shell-on prawns with marie rose sauce. Sandwiches are also served until 2.30pm – the Bugle classic club sandwich, for example, or minute steak and caramelised onion. Diners might like to try a starter of warm smoked mackerel salad, or a parfait of foie gras and chicken livers served with onion relish and toast. Main courses and pub classics include penne with wild mushrooms, shaved parmesan and truffle oil; pan-fried salmon with crushed potatoes and watercress; roasted chicken breast, colcannon potatoes, green beans and a red wine sauce; and sausages and mash with fine beans and onion gravy. These are augmented by the chalkboards displaying daily specials. The range of desserts is short but pleasing: chocolate tart with vanilla ice cream, chef's crumble of the day, or baked vanilla cheesecake with rum and raisin syrup. The wine list is also concise but offers good scope nonetheless, with several bottles priced under the £20 mark and ten served by the glass.

MAP 05 SU40
High St SO31 4HA
☎ 023 8045 3000
🖹 023 8045 3051
e-mail:
manager@buglehamble.co.uk
dir: *M27 junct 8, follow signs to Hamble. In village centre turn right at mini-rdbt into one-way cobbled street, pub at end*

Open 11–11 (Fri-Sat 11–12, Sun 12–10.30)
Bar Meals L served Mon-Thu 12–2.30 D served Mon-Thu 6–9.30 (Fri 12–3, 6–10, Sat 12–10, Sun 12–9)
Restaurant L served Mon-Thu 12–2.30 D served Mon-Thu 6–9.30 (Fri 12–3, 6–10, Sat 12–10, Sun 12–9) Av 3 course à la carte £19.95
🍺 Rotating locally brewed ales, Courage Best. ☗ 8

The Vine at Hannington

A traditional village pub high up on the beautiful Hampshire Downs. It was originally the Wellington Arms, since the land once belonged to the eponymous Duke, then became the Shepherd's Crook and Shears, until 1960 when it was renamed after the local Vine and Craven Hunt.

The Vine at Hannington is a delightful country pub where visitors can be assured of a warm welcome, friendly service and delicious home-made pub food. A menu of home-cooked country pub food at affordable prices changes with the seasons and always includes daily specials. Many of the herbs, salad leaves and vegetables used are grown in the pub garden. Typical dishes are mozzarella cheese and roasted vegetable crumble; Manydown Farm's locally reared Aberdeen Angus steak with cherry tomatoes, onions and mushrooms; pan-fried chicken breast in mushroom sauce; and grilled fish of the day. From the specials board come roast pheasant wrapped in bacon with port and redcurrant gravy; Moroccan lamb tagine; and grilled skate wing with black butter and capers. The wine list should satisfy most tastes. The Vine at Hannington has a large garden for summer, and a cosy woodburner to relax by in winter. It is on the Wayfarers Walk, and there are many other stunning countryside walks and cycle routes nearby.

NEW ♚
MAP 05 SU55
RG26 5TX
☎ 01635 298525
🖷 01635 298027
e-mail: info@
thevineathannington.co.uk
web:
www.thevineathannington.co.uk
dir: *Hannington signed from A339 between Basingstoke & Newbury*

Open 12–3 6–11 Sat–Sun all day (Closed Sun eve in Winter)
Bar Meals L served all week 12–2 D served all week 6–9 Av main course £9
Restaurant L served all week 12–2 D served all week 6–9 Av 3 course à la carte £18
◖ Black Sheep, Bombardier.
♟ 10
Facilities Children's licence Garden Dogs allowed Parking Play Area

HOOK
MAP 05 SU75

Crooked Billet ♀

London Rd RG27 9EH ☎ 01256 762118 ▤ 01256 761011
e-mail: richardbarwise@aol.com
web: www.thecrookedbillethook.co.uk
dir: From M3 take Hook ring road. At 3rd rdbt turn right onto A30 towards London, pub on left 0.5m by river

The present pub dates back to 1935, though there has been a hostelry on this site since the 1600s. Food to suit all appetites includes half shoulder of lamb in mint gravy; Billet toad in the hole with mash and onion gravy; home-made steak and kidney pie; fresh cod fillets in beer batter; and a range of ploughman's with hot French bread.

Open 11.30–3 6–11.30 (Fri 6–12, Sat-Sun 11.30–12) **Bar Meals** L served Mon-Sat 12–2.30 D served Sun-Thu 7–9.30 (Fri & Sat 7–10, Sun 12–3 Av main course £8 **Restaurant** L served all week 12–2.30 D served Sun-Thu 7–9.30 (Fri-Sat 7–10) ⊕ Free House ◀ Courage Best, Director John Smith's, Hogs Back TEA, Timothy Taylor Landord. ♀ 8 **Facilities** Garden Dogs allowed Parking Play Area

HORSEBRIDGE
MAP 05 SU33

John O'Gaunt Inn ♀

SO20 6PU ☎ 01794 388394
e-mail: johnogaunt@aol.com
dir: A3057 (Stockbridge to Romsey road). Horsebridge 4m from Stockbridge, turn right at brown information board.

Walkers from the nearby Test Way, fishermen from the River Test and the winter shooting fraternity all frequent this small country inn, six miles north of Romsey. It provides a great atmosphere for well-kept ales and generously priced food. The menu showcases fresh local produce, with dishes such as homemade steak and kidney pudding, liver and bacon, followed by a good selection of puddings. A traditional roast at Sunday lunchtime too.

Open 11–3 6–11 (Sat-Sun all day) Closed: 4–5 Jan **Bar Meals** L served all week 12–2.45 D served Tue-Sat 6–9.30 Av main course £7 **Restaurant** L served Tue-Sun 12–2.45 D served Tue-Sat 6–9.45 ⊕ Free House ◀ Ringwood Best Bitter, Ringwood Fortyniner, Palmers IPA & Thatchers. ♀ 8 **Facilities** Children's licence Garden Dogs allowed Parking

IBSLEY
MAP 05 SU10

Old Beams Inn ♀

Salisbury Rd BH24 3PP ☎ 01425 473387 ▤ 01202 743080
e-mail: hedi@alcatraz.co.uk
dir: On A338 between Ringwood & Salisbury

Old Beams is a beautiful old thatched and timber framed village inn located at the heart of the New Forest with views of countryside and ponies. It has a beer garden with a decked area and patio, and a cosy old world interior revitalised by a recent refurbishment. Pub food favourites based on local and New Forest produce dominate the menu, and on Friday night (fish night) there's a large selection.

Open 11–12 **Bar Meals** L served all week 12–6 D served all week 6–9.30 Av main course £9.50 **Restaurant** L served all week 12–6 D served all week 6–9.30 Av 3 course à la carte £19 Av 2 course fixed price £11.95 ◀ IPA, Speckled Hen. ♀ 10 **Facilities** Garden Parking

ITCHEN ABBAS
MAP 05 SU53

The Trout ♀

Main Rd SO21 1BQ ☎ 01962 779537 ▤ 01962 791046
e-mail: thetroutinn@aol.com
dir: M3 junct 9, A34, right onto A33, follow signs to Itchen Abbas, pub 2m on left

A 19th-century coaching inn located in the Itchen Valley close to the river itself. Originally called The Plough, it is said to have been the location that inspired Charles Kingsley to write *The Water Babies*. Freshly cooked, locally sourced produce is served in the bar and restaurant: trout, of course, perhaps pan fried, home-made fishcakes, and a lunchtime selection that includes baguettes, wraps, foccacias and salads.

Open 12–3 6–11 (Sat-Sun Mar-Oct all day) Closed: 26 Dec & 1 Jan **Bar Meals** L served all week 12–2.15 D served all week 6.30–9 (Sun 12–5) Av main course £11 **Restaurant** L served all week 12–2.15 D served Mon-Sat 6.30–9 Av 3 course à la carte £21 ⊕ Greene King ◀ Greene King IPA, Morland Speckled Hen. ♀ 9 **Facilities** Children's licence Garden Dogs allowed Parking Play Area

LINWOOD
MAP 05 SU10

Pick of the Pubs

The High Corner Inn NEW ♀

BH24 3QY ☎ 01425 473973
e-mail: highcorner@wadworth.co.uk
dir: From A338 Ringwood to Salisbury road, follow brown tourist signs into forest. Pass Red Shoot Inn, after 1m turn down gravel track at Green High Corner Inn

High Corner is set amid seven beautiful acres of woodland, abundant with wildlife, in the heart of the New Forest, about a mile from the village of Linwood and four miles from the town of Ringwood. The inn dates from the 1700s and both bars are oak beamed and have open fireplaces. Outside there are views across the patio and gardens to the forest itself. A complete range of home-cooked meals and bar snacks is served; daily specials are shown on chalkboards and a carvery is available on Sunday.

CONTINUED

England

LINWOOD continued

Typical dishes are home-made game terrine; hunter's chicken; beer battered cod; and High Corner hot pot. Children are made welcome and they will delight in the adventure playground. The inn is also dog-friendly.

Open 11–11 (Closed Mon-Fri 3–6 winter) **Bar Meals** L served Mon-Fri 12–2.30 D served Mon-Fri 6–9.30 (Sat & Sun 12–9.30) Av main course £8.95 ⊕ Wadworth ◀ Wadworth 6X, Horizon, IPA, Red Shoot Forest Gold & Toms Tipple. ♀ 14 **Facilities** Garden Dogs allowed Parking Play Area **Rooms** available

LITTLETON   MAP 05 SU43

Pick of the Pubs

The Running Horse ★★★★ INN
☺☺ ♀

88 Main Rd SO22 6QS
☎ 01962 880218 ▤ 01962 886596
e-mail: runninghorseinn@btconnect.com
dir: *3m from Winchester, signed from Stockbridge Rd*

Situated on the outskirts of Winchester, this pretty rural gastro-pub offers a unique blend of atmosphere, food and luxurious accommodation. The modern décor features leather tub chairs around a roaring winter fire, just the place to enjoy the well kept locally brewed real ales. But the focus here is undoubtedly on good eating, and the chefs source seasonal produce of impeccable freshness. Choose between dining alfresco on the front or rear terrace, casually in the bar, or more formally in the stylish restaurant. Dinner might begin with tomato and grilled cheese mille feuilles, or oriental crab and salmon fishcakes. Main courses include sea bass fillets with lyonnaise potatoes; slow-cooked steak and ale pie; and pan-fried lamb's liver with wilted spinach and mashed potatoes. Vegetarians are well served, too; tempura mozzarella with rocket and sun-blushed tomato is a typical choice.

Open 11–3 5.30–11 Closed: 25 Dec **Bar Meals** L served all week 12–2 D served all week 6.30–9.30 **Restaurant** L served all week 12–2 D served all week 6.30–9.30 ◀ Ringwood Best, Palmers. ♀ 15 **Facilities** Garden Dogs allowed Parking **Rooms** 9

LONGPARISH   MAP 05 SU44

Pick of the Pubs

The Plough Inn ♀
See Pick of the Pubs on opposite page

LOWER WIELD   MAP 05 SU64

Pick of the Pubs

The Yew Tree ♀
SO24 9RX ☎ 01256 389224 ▤ 01256 389224
dir: *Take A339 from Basingstoke towards Alton. Turn right for Lower Wield*

This charming free house first served ale in 1845, but is a mere babe compared with the nearby 650-year-old yew that gave it its name. In winter a crackling log fire burns in the bar, but as the days lengthen attention turns to the adjacent cricket ground. In fact, this pub's association with England's favourite summer sport has been immortalised in Elizabeth Gibson's book *Cricket and Ale*. The resident Cheriton Pots ale is backed up by a selection of guest beers from up to 15 local breweries, as well as a bi-annually changing wine list. The Yew Tree's local reputation is for good fun and good food, and the hearty Mediterranean-influenced menu won't disappoint. Goat's cheese bruschetta with home-made pesto, could be followed by oven-roasted chicken breast wrapped in Parma ham with oven-roasted vegetables and peppercorn sauce. Finish with rhubarb, apple and ginger crumble, or pecan pie with clotted cream.

Open 12–3 6–11 (Sun all day Summer) Closed: 1st 2wks Jan & Mon **Bar Meals** L served Tue-Sun 12–2 D served Tue-Sat 6.30–9 (Sun 6.30–8.30) ⊕ Free House ◀ Cheriton Pots, Hidden Pint, Tripple fff Moondance, Hogsback Tea & Itchen Valley Hampshire Rose. ♀ 13 **Facilities** Garden Dogs allowed Parking

LYMINGTON   MAP 05 SZ39

The Kings Arms ♀
St Thomas St SO41 9NB ☎ 01590 672594
dir: *Approaching Lymington from N on A337, left onto St Thomas St. Pub 50yds on right*

King Charles I is reputed to have patronised this historic coaching inn, which these days enjoys an enviable reputation for its cask ales, housed on 150-year-old stillages. Local Ringwood ales as well as national brews are served. It is a real community pub, with a dartboard and Sky TV, and the open brick fireplaces are used in winter.

Open 11–11 (Sun 12–10.30) **Bar Meals** L served all week 12–2.30 D served all week 6.30–9 Av main course £8 **Restaurant** L served all week 12–2.30 D served all week 6–8.30 ⊕ Whitbread ◀ Weekly rotating guest ales. **Facilities** Garden **Notes** ⊜

The Plough Inn

The River Test runs close by this charming old Hampshire inn, which dates from 1721. The Plough lies just a mile from the main A303, making it an ideal meeting place for both family and business get-togethers.

Walkers following the Test Way along one of southern England's finest chalk streams will literally stumble across it, as the footpath cuts right through the inn's car-park! Owners Paul and Sarah Bingham have carried out extensive renovation to create a warm and comfortable atmosphere; expect flagstone and oak floors complemented by leather chairs, subtle soft furnishings and open log fires. Their short, simple menu provides a good balance between traditional and more inventive dishes. Starters range from simple garlic bread, or sweetcorn soup with chicken dumplings, to sautéed frog's legs with garlic Provençale and toasted pine nuts. Main course dishes are no less appetising: chicken and chorizo cassoulet

with tomato, tarragon and borlotti beans; roasted saddle of venison with celeriac and apple; game pie; and pan-fried monkfish medallions with cumin roasted carrots and black pudding are typical choices. Leave space for delicious desserts like vanilla rice pudding with rhubarb and ginger; and apple and frangipane tart with cinnamon ice cream. There's also a selection of lunchtime baguettes; raisin bread or hot open toasted sandwiches; and ploughman's, served with home-made real ale chutney and piccalilli. Look out, too for the set-price Ramblers' lunch. In addition to a good value 32–bin wine list, a limited edition selection from Paul and Sarah's private cellar is also on offer.

MAP 05 SU44
SP11 6PB
☎ 01264 720358
e-mail: eat@theploughinn.info
dir: *From M3 junct 8 take A303 towards Andover. In approx 6m take B3048 towards Longparish*

Open 11–2.30 6–11 Closed: 25 Dec & Sun eve
Bar Meals L served all week 12–2.30 D served Mon-Sat 6.30–9 Av main course £5
Restaurant L served all week 12–2 D served Mon-Sat 6.30–9
⊕ Enterprise Inns ◀ Ringwood, Fuller's London Pride, Wadworth 6x, HSB. ⚑ 10
Facilities Children's licence Garden Dogs allowed Parking

Red Lion Boldre

Rope Hill, Boldre, Lymington Hants SO41 8NE

Tel: 01590 673177

c.15th Century

'Simply Traditional'

This quintessential New Forest pub offers a genuine welcome for meals or drinks. Log fires, beamed ceilings, woodland garden. A real old-fashioned forest pub atmosphere with traditonal menu items, using local produce.

LYMINGTON continued

Mayflower Inn ♟

Kings Saltern Rd SO41 3QD

☎ 01590 672160 ▤ 01590 679180

e-mail: info@themayflower.uk.com

dir: A337 towards New Milton, left at rdbt by White Hart, left to Rookes Ln, right at mini-rdbt, pub 0.75m

A favourite with yachtsmen and dog walkers, this solidly built mock-Tudor inn overlooks the Lymington River, with glorious views to the Isle of Wight. There's a magnificent garden with a purpose-built play area for children and an on-going summer barbecue in fine weather. Light bites and big bowl salads are backed up with heartier choices like traditional lamb and rosemary hotpot, pan-fried liver and bacon, and beer battered fish of the day.

Open 11–12 (Sun 12–10.30) **Bar Meals** L served all week 12–9.30 D served all week 6.30–9.30 Av main course £8.50 **Restaurant** L served all week 12–9.30 D served all week 6.30–9.30 ⊕ Enterprise Inns ◀ Ringwood Best, Fuller's London Pride, 6X, Goddards Fuggle Dee Dum. ♟8 **Facilities** Garden Dogs allowed Parking Play Area

---

LYNDHURST

MAP 05 SU3●

New Forest Inn ♟

Emery Down SO43 7DY ☎ 023 8028 4690

dir: M21 junct 1 follow signs for A35/Lyndhurst. In Lyndhurst follow signs for Christchurch, turn right at Swan Inn towards Emery Down

Delightfully situated in the scenic New Forest, this rambling inn lies on land claimed from the crown by use of squatters' rights in the early 18th century. Ale was once sold from a caravan which now forms the front lounge porchway. Lovely summer garden and welcoming bars with open fires and an extensive menu.

Open 11–11 (Winter Mon-Fri 11.30–3 Sat-Sun 11–11) **Bar Meals** L served Mon-Sat 12–2.30 D served all week 6–9.30 (Sun 12–3.30) **Restaurant** L served all week 11–2.30 D served all week 6–9.30 ⊕ Enterprise Inns ◀ Ringwood Best, Fuller's London Pride, Abbot Ale, Old Hooky. ♟8 **Facilities** Children's licence Garden Dogs allowed Parking

The Oak Inn ♟

Pinkney Ln, Bank SO43 7FE

☎ 023 8028 2350 ▤ 023 8028 4601

e-mail: oakinn@fullers.co.uk

dir: From Lyndhurst signed A35 to Christchurch. After Christchurch follow A35 1m, turn left at Bank sign

Ponies, pigs and deer graze outside this former ciderhouse. Behind the bay windows are a traditional woodburner, antique pine and an extensive collection of bric-a-brac. There is also a large beer garden for those fine summer days. A wide selection of fresh seafood, including Selsey crab gratin, and seared tuna steak, features among an interesting choice of dishes, including the local wild boar sausages and daily pies.

Open 11.30–3 6–11.30 (Sun 12–10.30) **Bar Meals** L served all week 12–2.30 D served Mon-Sat 6–9.30 (Sun 6–9) ⊕ Fullers ◀ Ringwood Best, Hop Back Summer Lightening, London Pride, Fuller's HSB. ♟9 **Facilities** Garden Dogs allowed Parking

The Trusty Servant

Minstead SO43 7FY ☎ 023 8081 2137

e-mail: enquiries@trustyservant.co.uk

dir: Telephone for directions

Popular New Forest pub overlooking the village green and retaining many Victorian features. The famous sign is taken from a 16th-century Winchester scholar's painting portraying the qualities of an ideal college servant. The menu prides itself on its real food, good value and generous portions. You might sample snacks, home-made pies, steaks

...om the grill, venison or tenderloin of pork. There's also a good choice
f vegetarian dishes, such as sizzling Thai vegetable stir-fry.

Open 11–11 (Sun 12–10.30) **Bar Meals** L served all week 12–9 D served
ll week 7–10 **Restaurant** L served all week 12–2.30 D served all week
–10 ⊕ Enterprise Inns ◀ Ringwood Best, Fuller's London Pride,
Wadworth 6X, Timothy Taylor Landlord. **Facilities** Garden Dogs allowed
arking

MAPLEDURWELL
MAP 05 SU65

The Gamekeepers ?

Tunworth Rd RG25 2LU

☎ 01256 322038 🗎 01256 322038

e-mail: costellophil@hotmail.co.uk

dir: M3 junct 6, take A30 towards Hook. Turn right after The
Hatch pub. The Gamekeepers signed.

A very rural location for this 19th-century pub, which has a large
secluded garden and, unusually, a well inside the building. Settle
back in a leather settee with a pint, and enjoy the cosy atmosphere
of low wooden beams and flagstone floors. An extensive menu
includes an impressive range of seafood: loin of cod wrapped in
Serrano ham, crispy pan-fried sea bass fillets, red snapper, salmon
and monkfish.

Open 12–3 5–1 **Bar Meals** L served Mon-Sat 12–3 D served Mon-Sat
5.30–9.30 (Sun 12–4, 6–9.30) Av main course £10 **Restaurant** L served
Mon-Sat 12–2.30 D served Mon-Sat 5.30–9.30 (Sun 12–4, 6–9.30) Av
3 course à la carte £25 ⊕ Hall & Woodhouse ◀ Badgers First Gold,
Tanglefoot, Sussex Best, Fursty Ferret. ? 12 **Facilities** Children's licence
Garden Dogs allowed Parking

MICHELDEVER
MAP 05 SU53

Half Moon & Spread Eagle ?

Winchester Rd SO21 3DG

☎ 01962 774339 🗎 01962 774339

e-mail: debbiethickett@hotmail.co.uk

dir: From Winchester take A33 towards Basingstoke. In 5m turn
left after small car garage. Pub 0.5m on right

Old drovers' inn located in the heart of a pretty thatched and timbered
Hampshire village, overlooking the cricket green. The pub, comprising
three neatly furnished interconnecting rooms, has a real local feel, and
a few years back reverted to its old name having been the Dever Arms
for eight years. An extensive menu ranges through Sunday roasts,
Moon burgers, honeyed salmon supreme with lime courgettes, fresh
battered cod, and half shoulder of minted lamb.

Open 12–3 6–11 **Bar Meals** L served all week 12–2 D served Sun-Thu
6–9 (Fri-Sat 6–9.30) Av main course £8.50 **Restaurant** L served all week
12–2 D served Sun-Thu 6–9 (Fri-Sat 6–9.30) ⊕ Greene King ◀ Greene
King IPA, Abbot Ale, guest ales. ? 9 **Facilities** Garden Dogs allowed
Parking Play Area

MONXTON
MAP 05 SU34

Pick of the Pubs

The Black Swan ?

High St SP11 8AW ☎ 01264 710260 🗎 01264 710961

dir: Exit A303, at rdbt follow signs for Monxton, pub on main
road.

Thatch and clay tiles characterise the roofs of Monxton's houses
and cottages, some built in the 16th century. The Black Swan on
the Portway (the Roman road that linked Old Sarum, just north
of Salisbury, and Winchester) dates from 1662, possibly earlier.
For a long time it was known as Ye Swan; who blackened its
name and why is not known, but the change occurred in the
19th century, by which time it was a popular refreshment stop.
Travellers heading for one or other of the two cathedral cities
would have their horses fed and watered in the stable block, now
the restaurant. This has been extended to accommodate up to 65
diners enjoying the pub's classic English and modern cuisine. Up
to ten daily specials feature local game such as braised pheasant;
and fish dishes: scallops with creamed leeks and crispy bacon; or
John Dory fillet on steamed rice with a spicy tomato salsa. Quiz
night on Sundays.

Open 12–11 **Bar Meals** L served all week 12–2.30 D served
Mon-Thu 6–9.30 (Fri-Sat 6–10, Sun 7–9.30) Av main course
£10 **Restaurant** L served all week 12–2.30 D served Mon-Thu
6–9.30 (Fri-Sun 6–10) Av 3 course à la carte £21 ⊕ Enterprise
Inns ◀ Timothy Taylor Landlords, Ringwood Best Bitter, Summer
Lightning, London Pride. ? 9 **Facilities** Children's licence Garden
Dogs allowed Parking

THE FOX

North Waltham,
Hampshire RG25 2BE

Tel: 01256 397288
email: info@thefox.org

Converted from three flint cottages, built in the early 1600s, this traditional village pub has a warm and welcoming atmosphere, with exposed beams and open wood fires. It is set in large award winning gardens, which are a riot of colour in the summer, with splendid views over the Hampshire countryside.

The cosy Village Bar stocks an excellent range of well kept real ales and offers a traditional 'Bar Snack' menu.

The Restaurant menus feature only the freshest local produce, game and daily delivered fresh fish, all wonderfully cooked and beautifully presented. The menu changes monthly to reflect the seasons. Starters include Seared King Scallops and Stilton & Mushroom Filo Tart. Main courses list the likes of Hampshire Venison, with glazed shallots, wild mushrooms, savoy, creamed swede and sauté potatoes and a Port glaze, and Sea Bass, steamed with Ginger and Coriander. The puddings, all made daily, including Chocolate Clafoutis, Crème Brulée and Fresh Pineapple 'Alaska' are worth a visit alone.

The food is complemented by an extensive wine list with at least 10 wines available by the glass.

Each month the FOX holds special evenings including a monthly Wine Tasting Dinner, and a 'Traditional' Jazz Supper. Check the Events page on the web at www.thefox.org.

The FOX is situated at the South edge of North Waltham village, close to J7 on the M3, just off the A30 and A303. Open 11–11; Food Served 12–2.30 and 6.30–9.30.

MORTIMER WEST END

MAP 05 SU66

The Red Lion NEW ♥

Church Rd RG7 2HU ☎ 0118 970 0169 📠 0118 970 1729

Original oak beams and an inglenook fireplace are the mark of this traditional pub, which dates back to 1650. Quality food and a range of real ales are served, with dishes to suit all tastes. Where possible produce is locally sourced, including free-range chicken and eggs, and English beef hung for 21 days. Home-made pies are a speciality – seafood, venison, wild boar, and steak with house ale – and there's a daily changing specials board.

Open 11–11 (Sun 12–10.30) **Bar Meals** L served Mon-Fri 12–2 D served Mon-Fri 12–9 (Sat 12–9.30, Sun 12–7) Av main course £7.95 **Restaurant** L served Mon-Fri 12–2 D served Mon-Fri 7–9 (Sat 12–9.30, Sun 12–7) ⊕ Hall & Woodhouse ◀ Tanglefoot, Badger First Gold, Guinness. ♥ 10 **Facilities** Garden Dogs allowed Parking Play Area

---

NEW ALRESFORD

MAP 05 SU53

Pick of the Pubs

The Globe on the Lake

See Pick of the Pubs on opposite page

NORTH WALTHAM

MAP 05 SU54

Pick of the Pubs

The Fox ♥

RG25 2BE ☎ 01256 397288

e-mail: info@thefox.org

dir: *From M3 junct 7 take A30 towards Winchester. Village signed on right. Take 2nd signed road*

A peaceful village pub down a quiet country lane enjoying splendid views across fields and farmland – an ideal stop off the M3 just south of Basingstoke. Built as three farm cottages in 1624, the Fox can offer families three large level gardens, one of which is a dedicated children's play area, and superb flower borders and hanging baskets in summer. The husband and wife team of Rob and Izzy MacKenzie split their responsibilities between bar and kitchen. Amidst over a thousand miniatures on show Rob ensures that the beers are kept in top condition, while Izzy produces mouthwatering traditional dishes using seasonal produce; she prepares everything by hand from the mayonnaise upwards. A dedicated bar menu proffers the likes of ham, double egg and chips; and cottage pie. The monthly-changing restaurant choice may include smoked salmon tagliatelli; crispy duck cakes; and pan-fried breast of pheasant with confit leg.

Open 11–12 (Sun 11–10.30) **Bar Meals** L served all week 12–2.30 D served Mon-Sat 6–9.30 (Sun 6–9) Av main course £6.95 **Restaurant** L served all week 12.30–2.30 D served Mon-Sat 6.30–9.30 (Sun 6.30–9) Av 3 course à la carte £21.95 ⊕ Punch Taverns ◀ Ringwood Best Bitter, Adnams Broadside, Tribute & guest ale. ♥ 11 **Facilities** Children's licence Garden Dogs allowed Parking Play Area

See advert on this page

OLD BASING

MAP 05 SU65

The Millstone ♥

Bartons Ln RG24 8AE ☎ 01256 331153

e-mail: millstone@wadworth.co.uk

dir: *From M3 junct 6 follow brown signs to Basing House*

Basingstoke's techno-doorstep is only a DVD's flip away, which makes this attractive old building's rural location, beside the River Loddon, all the more delightfully surprising. Nearby are the extensive ruins of Old Basing House, one of Britain's most famous Civil War sites. Typical main dishes might include battered or grilled cod; creamy vegetable korma; and spinach, mushroom and brie filo parcel. Snacks include baguettes, boccattas and ciabattas, jacket potatoes and ploughman's.

Open 11.30–11 (Sun 12–10.30) **Bar Meals** L served all week 12–2.30 D served all week 6–9.30 (Sat-Sun 12–9.30) ⊕ Wadworth ◀ Wadworth 6X, Wadworth JCB, Henrys Smooth & Henrys IPA. ♥ 9 **Facilities** Garden Dogs allowed Parking

PICK OF THE PUBS

NEW ALRESFORD-HAMPSHIRE

The Globe on the Lake

n an outstanding setting on the banks of a reed-fringed lake and wildfowl sanctuary, The Globe s a convivial hostelry facing a prime Hampshire waterscape. The lake was created by Bishop de Lucy in the 12th century as a fish pond, and the great weir remains to this day an outstanding piece of medieval engineering.

An inn on the site since then was probably all but destroyed during Alresford's great fire of 1689. The Globe was rebuilt as a coaching inn, sitting at the bottom of the town's superb Georgian main street. Waterfowl frequent the garden, sunbathing between the picnic benches or by the children's playhouse. Inside the bar, a log fire blazes on cooler days, while a smart dining room and unusual garden room share the stunning outlook over the water. In summer freshly prepared food can be enjoyed in the garden and on the heated rear terrace. The daily changing blackboard features several fish dishes, like tiger prawns cooked with fresh lime and chilli; or fresh fillet of hake in beer batter with home-made tartare sauce

and chips. Other specialities may include Meon Valley pork and leek sausages; Alresford watercress flan with a hint of English mustard; oven-roasted partridge; or sautéed lambs' liver with crispy bacon. At least ten puddings, all at the same price, range from the typically English (bread and butter pudding, custard) to the exotic (citrus meringue crush with kumquat citrus sauce). A mailing list keeps regulars informed of special events, when the chef's team will prepare a menu to suit – such as the Hampshire Food Festival, a musical quiz, or Burns' Night. Real ales, of course, plenty of house wines including one from a Hampshire vineyard, and local apple juice all supplement the perfect views.

MAP 05 SU53
The Soke, Broad St SO24 9DB
☎ 01962 732294
🖹 01962 732221
e-mail: duveen-conway@
supanet.com
dir: *Telephone for directions*

Open 11–3 6–11 (Summer Sat-Sun all day) Closed: 25–26 Dec
Bar Meals L served all week
12–2 D served all week 6.30–9
(wknds 12–2.30) Av main course
£9.50
Restaurant L served all week
12–2 D served all week 6.30–9
(wknds 12–2.30) Av 3 course à la carte £20
⊕ Unique Pub Co
◀ Wadworth 6X, Ringwood, Henley Brakspear Bitter, Fuller's London Pride.
Facilities Garden Play Area

OVINGTON   **MAP 05 SU53**

The Bush ☺

See Pick of the Pubs on opposite page

OWSLEBURY   **MAP 05 SU52**

The Ship Inn ☺

Whites Hill SO21 1LT ☎ 01962 777358 📠 01962 777458
dir: *M3 junct 11 take B3335. Follow Owslebury signs*

Situated on a windswept chalk ridge on the edge of a pretty village, the Ship dates back more than 300 years. A quaint old bar with low beams and ship's timbers add to the appeal. From the pub there are striking views towards the Solent and the South Downs. Daily menus might include grilled herbed lamb cutlets, fillet of hake, pot roast guinea fowl, and lobster and mixed seafood tagliatelle. Good choice of lunchtime meals and snacks.

Open 11–3 6–11 (Fri-Sun & Jul-Aug 11–11) **Bar Meals** L served Mon-Thu 12–2 D served Mon-Thu 6.30–9.30 (Fri-Sun 12–11) **Restaurant** L served Mon-Sat 12–2 D served Mon-Sat 6.30–9.30 (Sun 12–8.30) ⊕ Greene King ◀ Greene King IPA, IPA, Speckled Hen, Abbots & Ruddles Best. ☺ 15 **Facilities** Garden Dogs allowed Parking Play Area

PETERSFIELD   **MAP 05 SU7**

The Good Intent ★★★★ INN ☺

40–46 College St GU31 4AF
☎ 01730 263838 📠 01730 302239
e-mail: pstuart@goodintent.freeserve.co.uk
dir: *Telephone for directions*

Candlelit tables, open fires and well-kept ales characterise this 16th-century pub, and in summer, flower tubs and hanging baskets festoon the front patio. Regular gourmet evenings are held and there is live music on Sunday evenings. Sausages are a speciality (up to 12 varieties) alongside a daily pie and the likes of seafood chowder and Thai fish curry. As members of the Campaign For Real Food they have well-established links with the local junior school.

Open 11–3 5.30–11 **Bar Meals** L served all week 12–2.30 D served all week 6–9.30 **Restaurant** L served all week 12–2 D served all week 6–9.30 ⊕ Fullers ◀ Fuller's HSB, GB & Butser. **Facilities** Garden Dogs allowed Parking **Rooms** 3 (2 en suite)

The Trooper Inn

Alton Rd, Froxfield GU32 1BD
☎ 01730 827293 📠 01730 827103
e-mail: info@trooperinn.com
dir: *From A3 take A272 Winchester exit towards Petersfield (NB do not take A272 to Petersfield). 1st exit at mini-rdbt for Steep. 3m, pub on right*

There's a relaxed atmosphere throughout the pine-furnished interior of this isolated free house, which stands high on the downs west of Petersfield. The building has had a chequered history since its first bricks were laid at the start of the 17th century, and it's said that it was used as a recruiting centre at the outset of the First World War. More recently, the 'pub at the top of the hill' faced closure in the mid-1990s before it was rescued and given a new lease of life by the present owners. Winter log fires now warm the bar, and the charming restaurant features wooden settles and a vaulted ceiling. Here, the locally-sourced menu ranges from fresh fig, feta and Parma ham salad to wild boar steak with Calvados sauce. Other options include poached fresh mussels, home-made vegetable lasagne, and fisherman's pie.

Open 12–3 6–12 Closed: 25–26 Dec & 1 Jan & Sun eve **Bar Meals** L served Mon-Sat 12–2 D served Mon-Thu 6.30–9 (Sun 12–2.30, Fri-Sat 6.30–9.30) **Restaurant** L served Mon-Sat 12–2 D served Mon-Thu 6.30–9 (Sun 12–2.30, Fri-Sat 6–9.30) ⊕ Free House ◀ Ringwood Best, Ballards, local guest ales. **Facilities** Garden Parking

The Bush

Once a refreshment stop on the Pilgrim's Way linking Winchester and Canterbury, The Bush is as delightful as it is hard to find.

Tucked away just off a meandering lane, and overhung by trees, the rose-covered building is a vision of a bygone age. A gentle riverside stroll along the Itchen flowing past the pretty garden will set you up for a leisurely drink or lingering meal. While the outside is white painted and light, the interior is dark and atmospheric; there's a central wooden bar, high backed seats and pews, stuffed animals on the wall and a real fire. The regularly-changing menu makes good use of local produce. Choices range from bar snacks such as sandwiches and ploughman's lunches through to satisfying gastro-pub meals such as organic smoked trout mousse with warm toast, followed by slow-roasted belly pork on braised Savoy cabbage with organic cider jus.

Finish with Eton mess or rhubarb crumble. You will probably find a wine to suit your palate, with around 12 served by the glass. Real ales keep their end up too, with various Wadsworth ales (it's a Wadsworth house), including Summersault and JCB. Film crews love this spot.

🍷
MAP 05 SU53
SO24 0RE
☎ 01962 732764
📠 01962 735130
e-mail:
thebushinn@wadworth.co.uk
dir: *A31 from Winchester, E to Alton & Farnham, approx 6m turn left off dual carriageway to Ovington. 0.5m to pub*

Open 11–3 6–11 (Sun 12–3, 7–10.30) Closed: 25 Dec
Bar Meals L served all week 12–2.30 D served all week 6.30–9.30 (Sun 7–8.30)
🍺 Wadworth 🍺 Wadworth 6X, IPA & Farmers Glory, JCB, Summersault. 🍷 12
Facilities Garden Dogs allowed Parking

England

PETERSFIELD continued

The White Horse Inn ♀

Priors Dean GU32 1DA ☎ 01420 588387 📠 01420 588387

e-mail: info@stuartinns.com

dir: *A3/A272 to Winchester/Petersfield. In Petersfield left to Steep, 5m then right at small x-rds to East Tisted, take 2nd drive on right*

Also known as the 'Pub With No Name' as it has no sign, this splendid 17th-century farmhouse was originally used as a forge for passing coaches. The blacksmith sold beer to the travellers while their horses were attended to. Restaurant dishes include carrot and cashew nut roast, and Gressingham duck breast with fondant potato and spiced grape chutney. Special fresh fish dishes are available on Fridays and Saturdays.

Open 11–2.30 6–11 (Sat 12–11, Sun 12–10.30) **Bar Meals** L served all week 12–2.30 D served Mon-Sat 7–9.30 **Restaurant** L served all week 12–2.30 D served Mon-Sat 7–9.30 ⊕ Fullers ◀ No Name Best, No Name Strong, Fuller's London Pride & HSB, Bass. ♀ 7 **Facilities** Garden Dogs allowed Parking

PILLEY   MAP 05 SZ39

The Fleur de Lys ♀

Pilley St SO41 5QG ☎ 01590 672158

e-mail: hrh7@btinternet.com

dir: *From Lymington A337 to Brockenhurst. Cross Ampress Park rdbt, right to Boldre. At end of Boldre Ln turn right. Pub 0.5m*

Dating from 1014, parts of the building pre-date the forest which surrounds it; as the Fleur de Lys, it has been serving ales since 1498. Today this traditional thatched inn exudes centuries of character, warmed by an open fire and two wood burning stoves; outside is a large landscaped garden with wooden tables and chairs. The emphasis here is on fine dining, with a concise menu which may feature pan-fried rabbit loin; marinated saddle of New Forest venison; and chocolate and marshmallow soufflé.

Open 11.30–3 6–11 (Sun 12–3, 7–10.30) **Bar Meals** L served Mon-Sat 12–2.30 D served all week 6.30–9.30 **Restaurant** L served all week 12–2.30 D served Mon-Sat 6.30–9.30 ⊕ Enterprise Inns ◀ Ringwood Best & guest ales. ♀ 10 **Facilities** Garden Dogs allowed Parking

PORTSMOUTH & SOUTHSEA   MAP 05 SZ6•

The Wine Vaults ♀

43–47 Albert Rd, Southsea PO5 2SF

☎ 023 9286 4712 📠 023 9286 5544

e-mail: winevaults@freeuk.com

dir: *Telephone for directions*

Originally several Victorian shops, now converted into a Victorian-style alehouse with wooden floors, panelled walls, and seating from old churches and schools. Partly due to the absence of a jukebox or fruit machine, the atmosphere is relaxed, and there is a good range of real ales and good-value food. A typical menu includes beef stroganoff, Tuscan vegetable bean stew, grilled gammon steak, salads, sandwiches and Mexican specialities.

Open 12–11 (Fri-Sat 12–12 Sun 12–10.30) **Bar Meals** L served all week 12–9.30 D served all week 12–9.30 **Restaurant** L served all week 12–9.30 D served all week 12–9.30 ⊕ Free House ◀ Fuller's London Pride, Discovery, guest ales. ♀ 20 **Facilities** Children's licence Garden Dogs allowed

ROCKBOURNE   MAP 05 SU1•

Pick of the Pubs

The Rose & Thistle ♀

SP6 3NL ☎ 01725 518236

e-mail: enquiries@roseandthistle.co.uk

web: www.roseandthistle.co.uk

dir: *Follow Rockbourne signs from A354 (Salisbury to Blandford Forum road), or from A338 at Fordingbridge follow signs to Rockbourne.*

This is a picture postcard pub if ever there was one, with a stunning rose arch, flowers around the door and a delightful village setting. The low-beamed bar and dining area are furnished with country house fabrics, polished oak tables and chairs, cushioned settles and carved benches, and homely touches include floral arrangements and a scatter of magazines. Open fires make this a cosy retreat in cold weather, whilst the summer sun encourages visitors to sit in the neat cottage garden. Lunchtime favourites are listed as pork and London Pride sausages with wholegrain mustard mash, or a vegetarian wild mushroom stroganoff, supplemented by fish dishes and blackboard specials. In the evening, venison steak with cider and fruit chutney; pork fillet with a confit of apricots; and duck breast with stir-fried vegetables and noodles could be among ever-changing specials.

Open 11–3 6–11 (Sun Oct-Apr close at 8) **Bar Meals** L served all week 12–2.30 D served all week 6.30–9.30 (Sun seasonal variation) Av main course £10 **Restaurant** L served all week 12–2.30 D served all week 6.30–9.30 (Sun seasonal variation) ⊕ Free House ◀ Fuller's London Pride, Adnams Broadside, Palmers Copper Ale. ♀ 18 **Facilities** Children's licence Garden Parking

---

ROCKFORD   **MAP 05 SU10**

The Alice Lisle ♀

Rockford Green BH24 3NA
☎ 01425 474700 📄 01425 483332

Well-known New Forest pub with landscaped gardens overlooking lake, popular with walkers and visitors to the region. It was named after the widow of one of Cromwell's supporters who gave shelter to two fugitives from the Battle of Sedgemoor. Choose from a varied menu which might include salmon and crab cakes, honey minted lamb shoulder, liver and bacon, and Mexican enchilada. There's a good range of starters and children's dishes.

Open 11–3 5.30–11 (Sun all day) **Bar Meals** L served all week 12–2 D served all week 6–9 (Sun 12–8) Av main course £7.95 **Restaurant** L served all week 12–2 D served all week 6–9 (Sun 12–8) ⊕ Fullers ◀ HSB, Ringwood, Winter Brew, 49er. ♀ 7 **Facilities** Children's licence Garden Dogs allowed Parking Play Area

---

ROMSEY   **MAP 05 SU32**

Pick of the Pubs

The Dukes Head ♀

Greatbridge Rd SO51 0HB ☎ 01794 514450
dir: *Telephone for directions*

A long, whitewashed, 400–year-old pub a little way out of Romsey, and little more than a hefty cast from the Test, England's leading trout river. There are large gardens at the front and rear, while inside are the main bar, the snug and four other rooms, all themed. Andy Cottingham and Suzie Russell have made their mark by shifting the balance of the menu more firmly towards fish and seafood. This means you can reliably expect dishes featuring turbot, halibut, oysters, mussels and scallops, and much more, but if you don't want fish there'll almost certainly be a succulent fillet steak, duck breast or local game, such as venison. Food is largely locally sourced, seasonally influenced as far as possible, and freshly prepared. Andy is an acknowledged wine expert and is proud of his well-balanced wine list. Go on a Sunday for wonderful live jazz, most likely outside in the summer, and on a Tuesday night for blues and folk.

Open 11–11 **Bar Meals** L served Mon-Sat 12–3 D served all week 7–10 Av main course £8 **Restaurant** L served all week 12–3 D served all week 7–10 Av 3 course à la carte £28 Av 2 course fixed price £12.50 ⊕ Free House ◀ Fuller's London Pride, Ringwood Best Bitter, 49ers, Summer Lightning. ♀ 8 **Facilities** Garden Dogs allowed Parking

The Three Tuns ♀

58 Middlebridge St SO51 8HL ☎ 01794 512639

dir: *On Romsey bypass, 0.5m from main entrance of Broadlands Estate*

Around 400 years old, centrally placed in this old market town, with its fine abbey, and a short walk from the front gates of Broadlands, country seat of Earl Mountbatten. Quality local ingredients form the basis of all meals, though the new landlords have taken the emphasis off 'gastropub', and are now offering decent, normal pub food. Game comes from the Broadlands estate.

Open 12 -11 (Mon 5–11) Closed: Mon lunch **Bar Meals** L served Tue-Sun 12–9 D served Mon-Sat 6.30–10.30 Av main course £12 **Restaurant** L served Tue-Sun 12–3 D served Mon-Sat 6.30–9.30 ◀ Ringwood Best, Fuller's HSB, London Pride. ♀ 8 **Facilities** Garden Dogs allowed Parking

---

ROWLAND'S CASTLE   **MAP 05 SU71**

The Castle Inn ♀

1 Finchdean Rd PO9 6DA
☎ 023 9241 2494 📄 023 9241 2494
e-mail: rogerburrell@btconnect.com

dir: *N of Havant take B2149 to Rowland's Castle. Pass green, under rail bridge, pub 1st on left opposite Stansted Park*

A Victorian building directly opposite Stansted Park, part of the Forest of Bere. Richard the Lionheart supposedly hunted here, and the house and grounds are open to the public for part of the year. Traditional atmosphere is boosted by wooden floors and fires in both bars. Menu options include pies, lasagne, curry, steaks, local sausages, and chilli.

Open 10.30–12 (Fri-Sat 10.30–1am) **Bar Meals** L served Mon-Sat 12–6 D served all week 6–9 (Sun 12–3, Winter Tue-Sat 6–9) Av main course £7.25 **Restaurant** L served Mon-Sat 12–6 D served all week 6–9 (Sun 12–3, Winter Tue-Sat 6–9) Av 3 course à la carte £19.50 ⊕ Fullers ◀ Fuller's Butser, HSB, London Pride & guest ales. ♀ 8 **Facilities** Children's licence Garden Dogs allowed Parking

The Fountain Inn

34 The Green PO9 6AB
☎ 023 9241 2291 📄 023 9241 2291
e-mail: fountaininn@amserve.com

dir: *Telephone for directions*

Set by the village green in pretty Rowlands Castle, The Fountain is a lovingly refurbished Georgian inn complete with resident ghost. Food is served in Sienna's bistro, where dishes include hand rolled, stone baked pizzas, pasta dishes, and specials like flame-grilled chicken and Serrano ham salad, and crusted fillet steak with a roasted vegetable chutney.

Bar Meals 12–3 D served Tue-Sat 5–8 Av main course £9 **Restaurant** L served Fri-Sun 12–3 D served Tue-Sat 6.30–10 (Sun 12–4) Av 3 course à la carte £15 Av 3 course fixed price £19.95 ⊕ Free House ◀ Ruddles IPA, Abbot, Ruddles Cask. **Facilities** Garden Dogs allowed Parking Play Area

ST MARY BOURNE   MAP 05 SU45

The Bourne Valley Inn ▼

SP11 6BT ☎ 01264 738361 🖹 01264 738126
e-mail: bournevalleyinn@btinternet.com
dir: *Telephone for directions*

Located in the charming Bourne valley, this popular traditional inn is the ideal setting for conferences, exhibitions, weddings and other notable occasions. The riverside garden abounds with wildlife, and children can happily let off steam in the special play area. Typical menu includes deep fried brie or a cocktail of prawns, followed by rack of lamb with a redcurrant and port sauce, salmon and prawn tagliatelle, steak and mushroom pie, crispy haddock and chips and warm duck salad.

Open 11–11 (Sun 12–10.30) **Bar Meals** L served all week 12–2 D served all week 7–9 **Restaurant** L served all week 12–2 D served all week 7–9 ⊕ Free House ◀ guest ales. ▼ 8 **Facilities** Children's licence Garden Dogs allowed Parking Play Area

SELBORNE   MAP 05 SU73

The Selborne Arms ▼

High St GU34 3JR ☎ 01420 511247 🖹 01420 511754
e-mail: info@selbornearms.co.uk
web: www.selbornearms.co.uk
dir: *From A3 follow B3006, pub on left in village centre*

Real fires and a warm welcome make this traditional pub a safe bet for a leisurely drink; but try, if you can, to fit in a meal. Chef and co-owner Nick Carter showcases the best local food and drink – perhaps home-made pâté of Bowtell's pork with aromatic spices and Mr Whitehead's cider served with home-made apple and cider bread; or pan-fried saddle of Blackmoor venison on spiced braised red cabbage with a quince game sauce.

Open 11–3 6–11 (Fri 5.30–11, Sat-Sun all day) **Bar Meals** L served all week 12–2 D served Mon-Sat 7–9 (Sun 7–8.30) **Restaurant** L served all week 12–2 D served Mon-Sat 7–9 (Sun 7–8.30) ◀ Courage Best, Ringwood 49er, Suthwyk Bloomfields, local guest ales. ▼ 10 **Facilities** Garden Dogs allowed Parking Play Area

SILCHESTER   MAP 05 SU6●

Calleva Arms NEW ▼

Little London Rd, The Common RG7 2PH
☎ 0118 970 0305
dir: *A340 from Basingstoke, signed Silchester*

Standing opposite the village green, the pub is popular with walkers, cyclists, and visitors to the nearby Roman town of Calleva Atrebatum. A pleasant, airy conservatory has been added to the original 18th-century building, and the large garden offers al fresco dining in fine weather. Separate lunchtime and evening menus offer freshly prepared dishes ranging from warm granary baguettes to slow-cooked gammon hock with parsley sauce. Watch the blackboard for daily specials, too.

Open 11–3 5.30–11 (Sat 11–11.30, Sun 12–11) **Bar Meals** L served all week 12–2 D served all week 6.30–9 Av main course £7.50 ◀ London Pride, HSB, Guinness. ▼ 8 **Facilities** Garden Dogs allowed Parking

SOUTHAMPTON   MAP 05 SU4●

The White Star Tavern & Dining Rooms ▼

28 Oxford St SO14 3DJ
☎ 023 8082 1990 🖹 023 8090 4982
e-mail: reservations@whitestartavern.co.uk
dir: *Exit M3 junct 13. Take A33 to Southampton, towards Ocean Village & Marina.*

This former seafarers' hotel has been stylishly renovated to create an attractive venue incorporating a good blend of old and new. The all-day menu includes light bites like chicken liver and foie gras parfait; pub classics such as beer-battered haddock and chips; main dishes of pan-fried brisket of beef; and desserts such as roasted pear and almond tart. On sunny days you can take a pavement table and watch the world go by on Southampton's restaurant row.

Open 7–11 (Sat-Sun 9–12am) Closed: 25–26 Dec, 1 Jan **Bar Meals** L served Mon-Thu 12–2.30 D served Mon-Thu 6.30–9.30 (Fri-Sat 12–3, 6.30–10, Sun 12–9) Av main course £11 **Restaurant** L served Mon-Thu 12–2.30 D served Mon-Thu 6.30–9.30 (Fri-Sat 6.30–10, Sun 12–9) Av 3 course à la carte £24.95 ⊕ Enterprise Inns ◀ London Pride. ▼ 8

SOUTHSEA   MAP 05 SZ69

See **Portsmouth & Southsea**

PICK OF THE PUBS

SPARSHOLT-HAMPSHIRE

The Plough Inn

The Plough seems to have started life about 200 years ago as a coach house for Sparsholt Manor on the other side of the road, becoming an alehouse just 50 years later. It stands in beautiful countryside, close enough to Winchester to draw many of its well-heeled citizens out for a meal or just a drink – perhaps after a walk in nearby Farley Mount Country Park.

From the outside, you can see that it has been much extended but, once inside, the main bar and dining areas blend together very harmoniously, helped by judicious use of farmhouse-style pine tables, a mix of wooden and upholstered seats, collections of agricultural implements, stone jars, wooden wine box end-panels and dried hops. The dining tables to the left of the entrance have a view across open fields to wooded downland, and it's at this end you'll find a blackboard menu offering lighter dishes exemplified by seafood pasta and basil cream sauce with garlic bread; pork and chive sausages with parsley mash and red wine gravy; and beef, ale and mushroom pie. The menu board at the right-hand end of the bar offers meals of a slightly more serious nature – maybe game casserole with herb dumplings; lamb shank with braised red cabbage and rosemary jus; seabass fillets with lemon mash and buttered leeks; and tomato, olive and courgette tart with a roasted pepper coulis. Lunchtime regulars know that 'doorstep' is the most apt description for the tasty sandwiches, perhaps crab and mayonnaise, or beef and horseradish. Puddings include plum and almond tart, melon, mango and ginger parfait, and pecan pie with clotted cream. Wadworth of Devizes supplies the real ales and there's a good wine selection. Booking is definitely advised for any meal. There's a good-sized car park and a delightful garden.

MAP 05 SU43
Main Rd SO21 2NW
☎ 01962 776353
🖷 01962 776400
dir: *From Winchester take B3049 (A272) W, left to Sparsholt, Inn 1m*

Open 11–3 6–11 (Sun 12–3, 6–10.30) Closed: 25 Dec
Bar Meals L served all week 12–2 D served all week 6–9
Restaurant L served all week 12–2 D served all week 6–9
⊕ Wadworth ◗ Wadworth Henry's IPA, 6X, Old Timer & JCB. ♟ 14
Facilities Garden Dogs allowed Parking Play Area

SPARSHOLT
MAP 05 SU43

Pick of the Pubs

The Plough Inn ♀

See Pick of the Pubs on page 277

STEEP
MAP 05 SU72

Pick of the Pubs

Harrow Inn ♀

GU32 2DA ☎ 01730 262685

dir: Off A3 to A272, left through Sheet, take road opposite church (School Lane) then over A3 by-pass bridge

The Harrow has been in the same family since 1929 and is now run by third generation sisters Claire and Nisa McCutcheon. They keep things just as their parents liked them, in traditional style, attracting visitors from all over the world. The tile-hung, 500–year-old building is tucked away down a sleepy lane, and comprises two tiny bars, one Tudor, one Victorian. There is no till, the toilets are across the road, and beer barrels are kept behind the bar, with the beer dispensed via brass taps. Quiz nights have raised thousands of pounds for charities over the years, when teams of farmers, WI members, cricketers and regulars fill the pub to bursting. Funds are also raised by local Tony Clear, who grows flowers in the pub field and sells them at the public bar door. Good old-fashioned country food is served, including house favourite ham and pea soup.

Open 12–2.30 6–11 Closed: Sun eve Oct-Apr **Bar Meals** L served all week 12–2 D served all week 7–9 Av main course £8 ⊕ Free House ◀ Ringwood Best, Oakleaf Bitter, Hop Back GFB, Bowman Ales & Suthwyk Bloomfields Bitter. **Facilities** Garden Dogs allowed Parking **Notes** ⊜

STOCKBRIDGE
MAP 05 SU33

Mayfly ♀

Testcombe SO20 6AZ
☎ 01264 860283 🖨 01264 861304
web: www.themayfly.co.uk

dir: Between A303 & A30, on A3057

The Mayfly has one of the prettiest locations in Hampshire, on an island between the River Test and another smaller river to the rear. Access from the car park is via a small bridge. The current licensees have been here more than 20 years, and they offer an all day buffet-style selection of hot and cold meats, quiches and pies, along with hot and cold daily specials. The pub is ideal for walkers and cyclists on the nearby Test Way.

Open 10–11 **Bar Meals** L served all week 11–9 D served all week Av main course £9.50 ◀ Wadworth 6X, Ringwood 49er, Abbot Ale, Hobgoblin. ♀ 2◀ **Facilities** Children's licence Garden Dogs allowed Parking

The Peat Spade ◉ ♀

Longstock SO20 6DR ☎ 01264 810612
e-mail: info@peatspadeinn.co.uk

dir: Telephone for directions

The Test, probably the country's finest trout river, flows within yards of this gabled Victorian pub. Peat, rather poor quality admittedly, was indeed once dug in these parts. A satisfying meal might be smoked eel, bacon salad and horseradish; corned beef hash, duck egg and HP sauce (that's what the menu says); or pear and frangipane tart with clotted cream. Good use of local organic produce. Stockbridge, fly-fishing capital, is down the road.

Open 11.30–3 6.30–11 Closed: 25–26 Dec **Bar Meals** L served Mon-Sat 12–2.30 D served Mon-Sat 7–9.30 (Sun 12–3, 7–9) **Restaurant** L served all week 12–2 D served all week 7–9.30 ⊕ Free House ◀ Ringwood Best, Ringwood 49er & guest ales. ♀ 10 **Facilities** Children's licence Garden Dogs allowed Parking

STRATFIELD TURGIS
MAP 05 SU65

The Wellington Arms ★★★ HL ♀

RG27 0AS ☎ 01256 882214 🖨 01256 882934
e-mail: wellington.arms@virgin.net

dir: On A33 between Basingstoke & Reading

Looking at this Grade II listed hotel today, it is hard to believe it was originally a farmhouse. The Wellington Arms is an ideal base for visiting the nearby Stratfield Saye estate, formerly the home of the Duke of Wellington. Well-kept real ales complement a good selection of eating options, including liver and bacon served with bubble and squeak; steak and kidney pudding; fanned avocado, cherry, tomato and bacon salad; and smoked salmon and prawn platter.

Open 11–11 (Sun 12–10.30) **Bar Meals** L served all week 12–10 D served all week 12–10 (Sun 12–9.30) **Restaurant** L served Sun-Fri 12–2 D served Mon-Sat 6.30–9.30 Av 3 course à la carte £24 ⊕ Hall & Woodhouse ◀ Badger Best Bitter & Tanglefoot. ♀ 12 **Facilities** Garden Dogs allowed Parking **Rooms** 28

TANGLEY
MAP 05 SU35

The Fox Inn ♀

SP11 0RU ☎ 01264 730276 🖨 01264 730478
e-mail: info@foxinntangley.co.uk

dir: A343, 4m from Andover

The 300–year-old brick and flint cottage that has been the Fox since 1830 stands on a small crossroads, miles, it seems, from anywhere. The blackboard menu offers reliably good lunchtime snacks and imaginative evening dishes. Enjoy a pint of Archers Village or Stonehenge Pigswill in the tiny, friendly bar, and a perhaps moules marinière or sea bass fillets in the unpretentious restaurant.

Open 12–11 (Sun 12–10.30) Closed: 25 Dec, 1 Jan **Bar Meals** L served all week 12–2.30 D served all week 6.30–10 Av main course £9 **Restaurant** L served Mon-Sat 12–2.30 D served Mon-Sat 6.30–10 (Sun 12–8) Av 3 course à la carte £20 ⊕ Free House ◀ London Pride, Adnams. ♀ 12 **Facilities** Garden Dogs allowed Parking

Meon Valley, Hampshire

The Jolly Farmer Country Inn

The Jolly Farmer Inn at Warsash offers a superb menu every lunchtime and evening. Among the many choices are succulent steaks, locally caught seafood dishes and our daily specials board.

To complement the food we have a selection of Traditional Real Ales and an excellent Wine List.

Outside, there is a large Beer Garden, Patio Area and ample parking. For children we have a purpose built play area.

Fleet End Road, Warsash, Hampshire SO31 9JH
Tel: 01489 572500   Fax: 01489 885847
Email: mail@thejollyfarmer.uk.com
Website: www.thejollyfarmer.uk.com

TICHBORNE   MAP 05 SU53

Pick of the Pubs

The Tichborne Arms ♀

SO24 0NA ☎ 01962 733760 🗎 01962 733760
e-mail: n.burt@btinternet.com
dir: *Off A31 towards Alresford, after 200yds right at Tichborne sign*

A heavily thatched free house in the heart of the Itchen Valley, dating from 1423 but destroyed by fire and rebuilt three times; the present red-brick building was erected in 1939. An interesting history is attached to this idyllic rural hamlet, which was dramatised in the feature film *The Tichborne Claimant*. The pub displays much memorabilia connected with the film's subject, Tom Castro's impersonation and unsuccessful claim to the title and estates of Tichborne. Real ales straight from the cask are served in the comfortable atmospheric bars, and all food is home made. Traditional choices range from steak, ale and stilton pie; crab salad; pheasant casserole; chicken, tarragon and mushroom pie; and fish pie to toasted sandwiches and filled jacket potatoes. Expect hearty old-fashioned puddings. A large, well-stocked garden is ideal for summer eating and drinking, with a beer festival the first weekend in June.

Open 11.30–2.30 6–11 **Bar Meals** L served all week 11.30–2 D served all week 6.30–9.30 ⊕ Free House ◀ Hopback Brewery, Palmers, Bowman, Flowerpots. ♀ 8 **Facilities** Garden Dogs allowed Parking

---

UPPER FROYLE   MAP 05 SU74

The Hen & Chicken Inn ♀

GU34 4JH ☎ 01420 22115 🗎 01420 23021
e-mail: bookings@henandchicken.co.uk
dir: *2m from Alton, on A31 next to petrol station*

Highwayman Dick Turpin is said to have hidden upstairs in this 18th-century coaching inn. Today it retains a traditional atmosphere thanks to large open fires, wood panelling and beams – but the post boxes above the inglenook remain empty. Food ranges from snacks to meals such as home-made linguine niçoise with a poached quail egg, followed by pan-fried calves' liver with bubble and squeak and red wine sauce; and then spotted dick with custard.

Open 11.45–3 5.30–11 (Fri-Sat 11–11 Sun 12–10.30) **Bar Meals** L served Mon-Sat 12–2.30 D served Mon-Sat 6–9 (Sun 12–9) **Restaurant** L served Mon-Sat 12–2.30 D served Mon-Sat 6–9 (Sun 12–9) ⊕ Hall & Woodhouse ◀ Badger Best, Tanglefoot, King & Barnes Sussex Ale. ♀ 8 **Facilities** Garden Dogs allowed Parking Play Area

---

WARSASH   MAP 05 SU40

The Jolly Farmer Country Inn ♀

29 Fleet End Rd SO31 9JH
☎ 01489 572500 🗎 01489 885847
e-mail: mail@thejollyfarmeruk.com
dir: *Exit M27 junct 9 towards A27 Fareham, right onto Warsash Rd. Follow for 2m, left onto Fleet End Rd*

Multi-coloured classic cars are lined up outside this friendly pub close to the Hamble River, and boasting its own golf society and cricket team. The bars are furnished in a rustic style with farming equipment on the walls and ceilings. There's also a patio and a purpose-built children's play area. Grills, including 8oz gammon steaks, and house specialities such as shank of lamb, chicken stroganoff, and fresh fillet of plaice characterise the menu.

Open 11–11 **Bar Meals** L served Mon-Sat 12–2.30 D served Mon-Sat 6–10 (Sun all day) Av main course £9.95 **Restaurant** L served all week 12–2.30 D served all week 6–10 ⊕ Whitbread ◀ Fuller's London Pride & HSB, Interbrew Flowers IPA. **Facilities** Garden Dogs allowed Parking Play Area

See advert on this page

PICK OF THE PUBS

WHITWAY-HAMPSHIRE

Carnarvon Arms

The Carnarvon Arms was built in the mid-1800s as a coaching inn to serve travellers visiting nearby Highclere Castle. The castle is the Carnarvon family seat and home of the present Lord and Lady Carnarvon, whose most famous ancestor was perhaps the 5th Earl who opened Tutankhamun's tomb in 1923.

Fresh from an extensive refurbishment, the pub is now a stylish country inn with a warm and friendly bar, decorated in fresh natural colours and furnished with rich leather upholstery. The bar menu tempts with a kettle-cooked ham and mozzarella sandwich, or a plate of Mr Parson's local sausages with mash and shallot sauce. In the dining room, with its stunning vaulted ceiling, the Egyptian-inspired wall coverings pay homage to those remarkable excavations in the Valley of the Kings. Modern British food based on fresh seasonal ingredients at sensible prices is the objective of executive chef Rob Clayton, served in a relaxed and informal atmosphere. The full carte ranges from starters of potted duck liver with girolle paté with a fig and

orange compote; to main courses such as pot-roast pork collar with spices and ginger, chive potatoes and red wine sauce; and oven-roasted skate wing with Pommery mustard mash, romanesco and pomegranate dressing. Puddings in the best tradition include tarts and crumbles, in addition to modern-day favourites such as a trio of chocolate desserts – mousse, brûlée and fondant. An excellent cheeseboard with named varieties is served with pressed fruits. Children are served 'proper food for small people', such as grilled fish with cheese pasta followed by warm toffee pudding with toffee sauce; vegetarian and set-price lunch menus are also available.

MAP 05 SU45
Winchester Rd RG20 9LE
☎ 01635 278222 🖷 01635 278444
e-mail: info@carnarvonarms.com
web: www.carnarvonarms.com
dir: *M4 junct 13 onto A34 S to Winchester. Exit A34 at Tothill Services and follow signs to Highclere Castle, Pub on right hand side*

Open all day
Bar Meals L served Mon-Fri 12–2.30 (Sat 12–6.30)
Restaurant L served Mon-Sat 12–2.30 D served Sun-Thu 6.30–9 (Sun 12–3, Fri & Sat 6.30–9.30) Av 3 course à la carte £25 Av 2 course fixed price £9.95
🍺 guest ales. 🍷 15
Facilities Garden Dogs allowed Parking
Rooms available

England

WELL MAP 05 SU74

The Chequers Inn 🍷

RG29 1TL ☎ 01256 862605 📄 01256 861116

e-mail: roybwells@aol.com

dir: *From Odiham High St turn right into Long Ln, follow for 3m, left at T-junct, pub 0.25m on top of hill*

Set deep in the heart of the Hampshire countryside, in the village of Well near Odiham, this 15th-century pub is full of charm and old world character, with a rustic, low-beamed bar, log fires, scrubbed tables and vine-covered front terrace. The menu offers good pub food such as steak and Tanglefoot pie, fishcakes, slow whole roast pheasant; and the chef's ultimate beefburger, served with home-made chips, new potatoes or creamy mash.

Open 12–3 6–11 (Sat 12–11, Sun 12–10.30) **Bar Meals** L served Mon-Fri 12–2.30 D served Mon-Fri 6.30–9.30 (Sat 12–9.30, Sun 12–8) **Restaurant** L served Mon-Fri 12–2 D served Mon-Fri 6.30–9 (Sat 12–9.30, Sun 12–8) Hall & Woodhouse Fursty Ferret, Badger First Gold, Tanglefoot, Pickled Partridge & Hopping Hare. 🍷 8 **Facilities** Garden Dogs allowed Parking

WHERWELL MAP 05 SU34

The White Lion 🍷

Fullerton Rd SP11 7JF ☎ 01264 860317 📄 01264 860317

dir: *M3 junct 8, A303, then B3048 to Wherwell; or A3057 (S of Andover), B3420 to Wherwell*

The White Lion is a well-known, historic pub in the heart of the Test Valley. Parts of it date back to before the Civil War, during which one of Cromwell's cannon balls smashed the front door, while another shot down the chimney and is still on display today. Pub favourites include ploughman's lunch, crispy battered haddock, the pie of the day and a daily curry. Salad platters feature smoked Hampshire trout or local ham.

Open 11–2.30 6–11 (Sun 7–10.30, Mon-Wed 6–10.30) Closed: 25 Dec **Bar Meals** L served Mon-Sat 12–2 D served Mon-Sat 7–9 (Sun 7–8.30) **Restaurant** L served Mon-Sat 12–2 D served Mon-Sat 7–9 (Sun 7–8.30) Punch Taverns Ringwood Best Bitter, Tetley Smooth Flow, Bass Bitter. 🍷 12 **Facilities** Garden Dogs allowed Parking

WHITCHURCH MAP 05 SU44

Watership Down Inn 🍷

Freefolk Priors RG28 7NJ ☎ 01256 892254

e-mail: mark@watershipdowninn.co.uk

dir: *On B3400 between Basingstoke & Andover*

Enjoy an exhilarating walk on Watership Down before relaxing with a pint of well-kept local ale at this homely 19th-century inn named after Richard Adams' classic tale of rabbit life. The menu choices range from sandwiches, jacket potatoes, salads and ploughman's through to liver and bacon casserole, sausage and mash, mushroom stroganoff, Somerset chicken, and braised lamb shank in a red wine gravy. Just don't expect any rabbit dishes!

Open 11.30–3.30 6–11 **Bar Meals** L served all week 12–2.30 D served all week 6–9.30 (Sun 7–8.30) Free House Oakleaf Bitter, Butts Barbus Barbus, Triple FFF Pressed Rat & Warthog, Hogs Back TEA. 🍷 8 **Facilities** Garden Parking Play Area

WHITSBURY MAP 05 SU11

The Cartwheel Inn 🍷

Whitsbury Rd SP6 3PZ ☎ 01725 518362

dir: *From Ringwood take A338 to Salisbury. In 8m exit at Fordingbridge North & Whitsbury. 4th right (Alexandria Rd), continue to end, right. Inn in 3m*

Handy for exploring the New Forest, visiting Breamore House and discovering the remote Mizmaze on the nearby downs, this extended, turn-of-the-century one-time wheelwright's and shop has been a pub since the 1920s. Well-known for being Grand National winner Desert Orchid's local; the horse re-opened the Cartwheel after its 2004 renovation with a pint of Ringwood Best.

Open 11.30–3 5.30–11 (Sat all day, Sun 12–10.30) **Bar Meals** L served all week 12–2 D served all week 6–9 (Sun 12–2.30) **Restaurant** L served all week D served all week (Sun 12–2.30, 6–9) Av 3 course à la carte £19 Ringwood 49er, Old Thumper, Ringwood Best, Ringwood Seasonal. 🍷 20 **Facilities** Garden Dogs allowed Parking Play Area

WHITWAY MAP 05 SU45

Pick of the Pubs

Carnarvon Arms 🍷

See Pick of the Pubs on page 281

WICKHAM MAP 05 SU51

Greens Restaurant & Pub 🍷

The Square PO17 5JQ ☎ 01329 833197

e-mail: DuckworthGreens@aol.com

dir: *2m from M27, on corner of historic Wickham Square*

The enduring popularity of Greens, on a corner of Wickham's picturesque square, is entirely down to the standards set by Frank and Carol Duckworth, who have run it for 24 years. Drinkers will find award-winning real ales from nearby Droxford, while front-of-house staff trained in guest care ensure a warm and welcoming reception for diners. Modern European cooking may offer warm salad of pigeon breast; roast cumin-scented rump of English lamb; and chocolate truffle parfait.

Open 11–3 6–11 Closed: Sun eve & Mon **Bar Meals** L served Tue-Sat 12–2 D served Tue-Sat 6.30–9.30 (Sun 12–4) **Restaurant** L served Tue-Sat 12–2 D served Tue-Sat 6.30–9.30 (Sun 12–4) Free House Hopback Summer Lightning, Youngs Special, Guinness, Timothy Taylor & local ales. 🍷 10 **Facilities** Garden Parking

PICK OF THE PUBS

WINCHESTER-HAMPSHIRE

The Wykeham Arms

When you open the curved, glazed doors into this pub's main bar you enter not just a local but an institution. Its two bars are nearly always full of people talking, laughing and warming themselves by the open fires. Photographs, paintings and ephemera fill most vertical surfaces.

The 'Wyk' is located in Winchester's ancient back streets close to the cathedral. Old Winchester College desks are placed inkwell to inkwell (Willie Whitelaw carved 'Manners Makyth Man', the motto of Winchester College, on one), and a good choice of wines is kept, with up to 20 by the glass. Both bars lead to intimate dining areas, where you can choose a sandwich if you are in a hurry – perhaps honey baked gammon and mustard mayonnaise, or avocado and camembert cheese with lemon and dill mayonnaise. The daily menu might offer a light dish of creamy wild mushroom, red onion, spinach and goat's cheese linguini with rocket; grilled pork and leek sausages with mashed potatoes and spicy tomato relish; or smoked chicken and mango salad

with a honey and lemon dressing. For something more substantial, consider a starter of crayfish ravioli served with a mango and fennel salad and prawn and brandy sauce; or salad of pan-seared breast of pigeon with grilled black pudding and pesto dressing. Move on to baked breast of free range chicken stuffed with smoked Applewood and baby spinach, with saffron risotto; chargrilled fillet of beef with grain mustard mash, caramelised shallots, steamed sugarsnaps and a Madeira jus; or chargrilled loin of yellow fin Tuna with Mediterranean couscous, fine leaves and pesto dressing. There is a small walled garden outside.

MAP 05 SU42
75 Kingsgate St SO23 9PE
☎ 01962 853834
🖷 01962 854411
e-mail: wykehamarms@
accommodating-inns.co.uk
dir: *Near Winchester College & Winchester Cathedral*

Open 11–11 Closed: 25 Dec
Bar Meals L served all week
12–2.30 D served Mon-Sat
6.30–8.45 (Sun 12–1.30) Av main
course £14.50
Restaurant L served all week
12–2.30 D served Mon-Sat
6.30–8.45 (Sun 12–2) Av 3 course
à la carte £25
◀ Butser Bitter, HSB, London
Pride, Chiswick. ♟ 18
Facilities Garden Dogs allowed
Parking
Rooms available

WINCHESTER MAP 05 SU42

The Westgate Inn ★★★ INN ⬤

2 Romsey Rd SO23 8TP
☎ 01962 820222 📄 01962 820222
e-mail: wghguy@yahoo.co.uk
dir: Pub on corner Romsey Rd & Upper High St

This establishment stands at the top end of Winchester's main shopping street, opposite the medieval West Gate and historic Great Hall. The popular bar serves home-cooked meals, and also houses The Gourmet Rajah, an innovative Indian restaurant. Expect a mix of English, Indian and Bangladeshi; chicken anjali in lemongrass and lime sauce perhaps, or bhindi gosht (steamed lamb cooked with okra); and fish dishes such as salmon ka sula.

Open 11–11 **Bar Meals** L served all week 12–2.30 D served all week 6.30–10 Av main course £8.50 **Restaurant** L served all week 12–2.30 D served all week 6.30–10 Av 3 course à la carte £15 ⊕ Marstons 🍺 Jennings Cumberland, Banks Original, Marstons Burton Bitter. ⬤ 7 **Facilities** Dogs allowed **Rooms** 6

Pick of the Pubs

The Wykeham Arms ⬤

See Pick of the Pubs on page 283

HEREFORDSHIRE

ASTON CREWS MAP 10 SO62

Pick of the Pubs

The Penny Farthing Inn

HR9 7LW ☎ 01989 750366 📄 01989 750922
dir: 5m E of Ross-on-Wye

A whitewashed 17th-century blacksmith's shop and coaching inn high above the River Wye valley. From its large, sloping garden you can take in views of the Malvern Hills, the Black Hills and the Forest of Dean. Inside are lots of nooks and crannies with oak beams, antiques, saddlery and cheerful log fires. At least two real ales and local cider are guaranteed to be on tap, and the wine list focuses on lesser known wineries to bring quality at a reasonable price. The same objective applies to the menu, which capitalises on the wealth of local vegetable and fruit growers' produce, and some of the best meat in the country. The lunchtime bar menu ranges from sandwiches, baguettes and jacket potatoes, to the pub's pie of the week, and chef's home-made curry. Main courses in the restaurant may feature braised local lamb shank with colcannon mash, or chargrilled Herefordshire beef steaks with all the trimmings.

Open 12–3 6–11 (Fri-Sun all day May-Sept) Closed: Sun eve, Mon lunch Winter **Bar Meals** L served Mon-Sat 12–2 D served all week 6–9 (Sun 12–4) Av main course £8.95 **Restaurant** L served Mon-Sat 12–2 D served all week 6–9 (Sun 12–4) Av 3 course à la carte £19 🍺 John Smiths, Abbot Ale, Wadworth 6X. **Facilities** Garden Dogs allowed Parking

AYMESTREY MAP 09 SO46

Pick of the Pubs

The Riverside Inn ⬤

See Pick of the Pubs on opposite page

BODENHAM MAP 10 SO55

England's Gate Inn ⬤

HR1 3HU ☎ 01568 797286 📄 01568 797768
dir: Hereford A49, turn onto A417 at Bosey Dinmore hill, 2.5m on right

A pretty black and white coaching inn dating from around 1540, with atmospheric beamed bars and blazing log fires in winter. A picturesque garden attracts a good summer following, and so does the food. The menu features such dishes as pan-fried lamb steak with apricot and onion marmalade, roasted breast of duck with parsnip mash and spinach, and wild rice cakes with peppers on a chilli and tomato salsa.

Open 11–11 (Sun 12–10.30) **Bar Meals** L served all week 12–2.30 D served all week 6–9.30 Av main course £8.95 **Restaurant** L served all week 12–2.30 D served all week 6–9.30 Av 3 course à la carte £16.95 ⊕ Free House 🍺 Wye Valley Bitter, Butty Bach, Shropshire Lad, guest ales. ⬤ 7 **Facilities** Garden Dogs allowed Parking

Railway Inn

Dinmore HR1 3JP ☎ 01568 797053
dir: 7m from Hereford on A49 (Hereford-Leominster road). Turn right at sign on Dinmore Hill.

This 17th-century inn was originally built for railway construction workers and enjoys a picturesque setting by the river, with wonderful views of the Herefordshire countryside from the large gardens. Light snacks are served at lunchtime, but in the evenings full meals are available: perhaps spicy Cornish crab cake with noodle salad and a sweet chilli sauce followed by pan-fried duck breast with braised red cabbage and a red wine and grape reduction.

Open 11.30–2.30 6.30–11 Closed: Mon, Tue lunch, Sun eve Winter **Bar Meals** L served Wed-Sat 12–2 **Restaurant** L served Wed-Sat 12–2 D served Tue-Sat 7–9 (Sun 12–2.30) ⊕ Enterprise Inns 🍺 Butty Bach, Wye Valley Bitter & John Smith's. **Facilities** Children's licence Garden Parking

PICK OF THE PUBS

The Riverside Inn

Alongside the lovely River Lugg, overlooking a fine old stone bridge, this delightful black-and-white inn is set amongst the peaceful woodland and meadows of the Welsh Marches. Anglers certainly appreciate the mile of private fly fishing for brown trout and grayling.

It's great for walkers too, situated as it is about halfway along the Mortimer Way and close to several circular routes in the vicinity. Walking packages are offered by the inn, with transportation to and from start/finish points included in the room price. The interior, with its wood panelling, low beams and log fires, engenders a relaxed atmosphere reflecting 300 years of hospitality. Owner Richard Gresko has a very focused approach to food, and locally grown and reared produce is used as much as possible in his kitchen. Visitors are welcome to take a stroll round the pub's extensive vegetable, herb and fruit gardens. Real ales and ciders are locally sourced, and the menu mainly consists of English-style cuisine. Popular dishes include home-made smooth chicken liver paté with Riverside chutney; home-made steak and kidney pudding; roasted haunch of local venison on sweet and sour red cabbage; seared lambs' liver and bacon; tenderloin of local pork with a cheese and mushroom crust on a bed of pea purée with a Dijon sauce; and supreme of chicken wrapped in smoked bacon, stuffed with apricot and pistachio anD served with a creamy apricot sauce. As befits a Herefordshire location, locally bred fillet and sirloin of beef always feature, but so too do vegetarian dishes such as mint and pea fritters with roasted peppers, and aubergine with fresh tomato and basil sauce. Gluten and dairy-free dishes can also be prepared for allergy sufferers if booked ahead.

MAP 09 SO46
HR6 9ST
☎ 01568 708440
📠 01568 709058
e-mail:
theriverside@btconnect.com
web: www.theriversideinn.org
dir: *On A4110 18m N of Hereford*

Open 11–3 6–11 Open All day in summer
Bar Meals L served all week 12.30–2.15 D served all week 7–9.15 (Sun 6.30–8.30) Av main course £8.95
Restaurant L served all week 12–2.15 D served all week 7–9.15 (Sun 6.30–8.30) Av 3 course à la carte £23.95
⊕ Free House ◀ Wye Valley Seasonal. ♟ 7
Facilities Garden Dogs allowed Parking

CANON PYON   MAP 09 SO44

The Nags Head Inn

HR4 8NY ☎ 01432 830252

dir: Telephone for directions

More than four hundred years old, with flagstone floors, open fires and exposed beams to prove it. A comprehensive menu might entice you into starting with slices of smoked salmon drizzled with brandy, lemon and cracked pepper, then to follow with medallions of lamb in a sticky Cumberland sauce, breast of Gressingham duck in a rich morello cherry sauce, or butterflied sea bass on sauteed strips of carrot and chopped coriander. Vegetarian options include stuffed peppers and tagliatelle. Curry nights and Sunday carvery. The large garden features a children's adventure playground.

Open 11–2.30 6–11 **Bar Meals** L served Tue–Sun 12–2.30 D served all week 6.30–9.30 (Sun 12–9) Av main course £5.95 **Restaurant** L served Tue–Sun 12–2.30 D served all week 6.30–9.30 (Sun 12–9) Av 2 course fixed price £8.95 ⊕ Free House ◖ Fuller's London Pride, Boddingtons, Flowers, Nags Ale. **Facilities** Garden Parking Play Area

---

CRASWALL   MAP 09 SO23

The Bulls Head

HR2 0PN ☎ 01981 510616

e-mail: info@tehbullsheadpub.com

dir: From A465 turn at Pandy. Village in 11m

Although not easy to find, you'll be pleased you persisted when you reach this 400–year-old drovers' inn below 640–metre Black Hill. If you like your pubs unchanged, then enjoy its flagstone floors, wood-burning fires, serving hatch, and bare-topped tables in the charming dining areas. New owners are beefing up the home-made pies, pasties and huffers at lunchtime, while dinner might be braised John Dory; confit shoulder of Marches lamb; or chargrilled Herefordshire steak.

Open 11–3 7–11 (Sat 11–11, Sun 11–6) Closed: Winter (check with pub) **Bar Meals** L served all week 12–2.50 D served Mon-Sat 7–9 Av main course £10 **Restaurant** L served all week 12–2.50 D served Mon-Sat 7–9 Av 3 course à la carte £22 ⊕ Free House ◖ Butty Bach, Organic Bitter, Old Bull Spinny Dog. **Facilities** Garden Dogs allowed

---

DORSTONE   MAP 09 SO34

Pick of the Pubs

The Pandy Inn

HR3 6AN ☎ 01981 550273 📄 01981 550277

e-mail: magdalena@pandyinn.wanadoo.co.uk

dir: Off B4348 W of Hereford

Richard de Brito was one of the four Norman knights who killed Thomas à Becket in Canterbury Cathedral in 1170. After 15 years in the Holy Land he returned to England to build a chapel at Dorstone as an act of atonement. He is believed to have built The Pandy to house the workers, later adapting it to become an inn, which is now one of the oldest in the county. Later, during the Civil War in the 17th century, Oliver Cromwell is known to have taken refuge here. The ancient hostelry is located opposite the village green and part of it retains its original flagstone floors and beams. The large garden, which offers 19 tables and a children's playground, has views of Dorstone Hill. Food is freshly prepared daily and the seasonal menu includes Pandy pies and home-made puddings. Farmhouse ciders are served alongside local cask ales.

Open 12–3 6–11 Closed: Mon (Oct-Jan) **Bar Meals** L served all week 12–3 D served all week 6–9.30 **Restaurant** L served all week 12–3 D served all week 6–11 ⊕ Free House ◖ Wye Valley Bitter & Butty Bach. **Facilities** Children's licence Garden Dogs allowed Parking Play Area

---

FOWNHOPE   MAP 10 SO53

The Green Man Inn ⛟

HR1 4PE ☎ 01432 860243 📄 01432 860920

e-mail: greenman.hereford@thespiritgroup.com

dir: From M50 take A449 then B4224 to Fownhope

This white-painted 15th-century coaching inn has a host of beams inside and out. Set in an attractive garden close to the River Wye, it's an ideal base for walking, touring and salmon fishing. The extensive menu has something for everyone, with a range of chunky sandwiches, jacket potatoes, burgers and ciabatta melts. Then there are hand-made pies, gourmet grills, and main course favourites like sausages and mash. All this, and sticky puddings too! New owners.

Open 11–11 (Sun 12–10.30) **Bar Meals** L served Mon-Sat 12–6 D served Mon-Sat 12–10 (Sun 12–9.30) Av main course £9 **Restaurant** L served Mon-Sat 12–6 D served Mon-Sat 12–10 (Sun 12–9.30) ◖ John Smith's Smooth, Bombardier. ⛟ 8 **Facilities** Children's licence Garden Parking

HAMPTON BISHOP   MAP 10 SO53

The Bunch of Carrots ♀

HR1 4JR ☎ 01432 870237 📄 01432 870237

e-mail: bunchofcarrotts@buccaneer.co.uk

web: www.bunch-of-carrots.co.uk

dir: From Hereford take A4103, A438, then B4224

The name has nothing to do with crunchy orange vegetables – it comes from a rock formation in the River Wye, which runs alongside this friendly pub. Inside, expect real fires, old beams and flagstones. There is an extensive menu plus a daily specials board, a carvery, salad buffet, and simple bar snacks – Thai fishcakes, perhaps. Real ale aficionados should certainly sample the local organic beer.

Open 11–3 6–11 (Sat 11–11, Sun 12–10.30) **Bar Meals** L served all week 12–9 D served all week Av main course £10 **Restaurant** L served all week 12–2.30 D served all week 6–10 (Sun 12–9) ⊕ Free House 🍺 Directors, Butcombe, Organic Bitter & Local ale. ♀ 11 **Facilities** Garden Dogs allowed Parking Play Area

See advert on this page

HEREFORD   MAP 10 SO53

The Crown & Anchor ♀

Cotts l n, Lugwardine HR1 4AB

☎ 01432 851303 📄 01432 851637

e-mail: c_a@oz.co.uk

dir: 2m from Hereford on A438. Left into Lugwardine down Cotts Lane

Old Herefordshire-style black-and-white pub with quarry tile floors and a large log fire, just up from the bridge over the River Lugg. Among the many interesting specials you might find fillets of Torbay sole with mussels and white wine; mushrooms in filo pastry with wild mushroom and marsala sauce; seafood tagliolini; supreme of chicken stuffed with wild mushrooms and chestnuts with cranberry and white wine sauce; or Brother Geoffrey's pork sausages with juniper and red wine sauce and mash. A long lunchtime sandwich list is available.

Open 12–11 Closed: 25 Dec **Bar Meals** L served all week 12–2 D served all week 7–10 Av main course £9 ⊕ Enterprise Inns 🍺 Worthington Bitter, Timothy Taylor Landlord, Marstons Pedigree, Butcombe Ale. ♀ 8 **Facilities** Garden Dogs allowed Parking

---

England

KIMBOLTON   MAP 10 SO56

Pick of the Pubs

Stockton Cross Inn

HR6 0HD ☎ 01568 612509

e-mail: info@stocktoncrossinn.co.uk

dir: *On A4112, off A49 between Leominster & Ludlow*

A drovers' inn dating from the 17th century, the Stockton Cross Inn stands beside a crossroads where alleged witches, rounded up from the surrounding villages such as Ludlow, were hanged. This grisly past is at odds with the peace and beauty of the setting, which includes a pretty country garden with umbrellas and trees for shade. The building itself is regularly photographed by tourists and featured on calendars and chocolate boxes. Owners Mike Bentley and Samantha Rosenberg, along with head chef Will Hayward, have introduced a popular traditional Sunday roast, as well as establishing a good reputation with their appealing menu of pub favourites (gammon steak with egg, plum tomato, field mushroom and home-made chips) and contemporary dishes such as sweet potato lasagne with potato coulis, vegetables and new potatoes. All meals are prepared on the premises using organic produce wherever possible.

Open 12–3 7–11 (6.30–11 Summer) **Bar Meals** L served all week 12–2.15 D served Tue-Sat 7–9 (Sun 12–2.30) **Restaurant** L served all week 12–2.15 D served Tue-Sat 7–9 ⊕ Free House ⬛ Wye Valley Butty Bach, Teme Valley This, Hobson's Town Crier, Flowers Best Bitter. **Facilities** Garden Dogs allowed Parking

---

KINGTON   MAP 09 SO25

Pick of the Pubs

The Stagg Inn and Restaurant ◉◉ ♥

Titley HR5 3RL ☎ 01544 230221 📠 01544 231390

e-mail: reservations@thestagg.co.uk

dir: *Between Kington & Presteigne on B4355*

The pub is sited at the meeting point of two drovers' tracks, and wool would have been weighed here (the pub was previously called the Balance). The extra 'g' in the pub's current name is a mystery, but its popularity is not – it's a bustling place surrounded by great countryside, with authentic décor of local stone and furniture from the area's antique markets. Chef patron Steve Reynolds makes great use of locally sourced ingredients, starting with herbs, vegetables and soft fruit from the garden. The cheese trolley numbers around 20 regional varieties, so it might be wise to order a pint from the sumptuous range of real ales on

offer before trying to choose the components for a three-cheese ploughman's. Alternative bar snacks are cod goujons or veal sausages with mash, while typical main course options may include fillet of Herefordshire beef, or Madgetts Farm duck breast.

Open 12–3 6.30–11 Closed: Sun eve & Mon **Bar Meals** L served Tue-Sat 12–2 D served Tue-Thu 6.30–10 Av main course £9 **Restaurant** L served Tue-Sat 12–2 D served Tue-Sat 6.30–10 Av 3 course à la carte £27 ⊕ Free House ⬛ Hobsons-Town Crier, Old Henry & Best Bitter, Black Sheep, Brains Rev James. ♥ 10 **Facilities** Garden Dogs allowed Parking

---

LEDBURY   MAP 10 SO7:

The Farmers Arms ♥

Horse Rd, Wellington Heath HR8 1LS ☎ 01531 632010

dir: *Through Ledbury, pass rail station, right into Wellington Heath, 1st right for pub*

Handy for the breathtaking high ground of the Malvern Hills and the seductive charms of Ross and the Wye Valley, this refurbished country inn retains lots of character and charm. In addition to the changes inside there is an outdoor decked seating area with a large heated canopy perfect for alfresco eating. The bar menu includes lots of pub favourites – ploughman's, local sausages of the week, fish and chips, steak and ale pudding plus a choice of grills.

Open 12–3 6–11 **Bar Meals** L served all week 12–3 D served all week 6–10 **Restaurant** L served all week 12–3 D served all week 6–10 ⊕ Enterprise Inns ⬛ guest ales. ♥ 8 **Facilities** Children's licence Garden Dogs allowed Parking Play Area

---

Pick of the Pubs

The Feathers Hotel ★★★ HL ◉ ♥

High St HR8 1DS ☎ 01531 635266 📠 01531 638955

e-mail: mary@feathers-ledbury.co.uk

dir: *S from Worcester A449, E from Hereford A438, N from Gloucester A417*

The higgledy-piggledy black and white exterior of the Feathers Hotel is a familiar landmark on Ledbury's main street. This fine old coaching inn dates back to 1564, and a few minutes' drive brings you to some of the loveliest countryside in the Welsh Borders. Once inside the panelled oak interior, enjoy the house speciality of a Bloody Mary in front of a roaring fire, before perusing a menu that makes the most of the region's fine produce. Start with sautéed pigeon breast, smoked bacon and lambs lettuce; or ham hock, parsley and boiled egg terrine with home-made piccalilli; followed by grilled John Dory fillet with garlic mash, mussel beignets and caviar beurre blanc. Carnivores can tuck into the likes of roast rump of local lamb with potato galette, or fillet of Herefordshire beef, with celeriac purée, creamed savoy cabbage and bacon.

Open 11–11 (Sun 12–10.30) **Bar Meals** L served all week 12–2 **Restaurant** L served all week 12–2 D served all week 7–9.30 Av 3 course à la carte £25 ⊕ Free House ⬛ Fuller's London Pride, Greene King Old Speckled Hen, Timothy Taylor Landlord. ♥ 18 **Facilities** Garden Parking **Rooms** 20

The Talbot ♥

14 New St HR8 2DX ☎ 01531 632963 🖺 01531 633796
e-mail: talbot.ledbury@wadworth.co.uk
dir: *Follow Ledbury signs, turn into Bye St, 2nd left into Woodley Rd, over bridge to junct, left into New St. Pub on right*

It's easy to step back in time with a visit to this late 16th-century black-and-white coaching inn. Dating from 1596, the oak-panelled dining room (appropriately called Panels), with fine carved overmantle, still displays musket-shot holes after a skirmish between Roundheads and Cavaliers. Choose from a good selection of local ales, and menus with starters of whitebait or duck and orange paté, and main dishes of local faggots and onion gravy, or pan-fried lambs' liver.

Open 11.30–3 5–11 (Fri-Sat 5–12) **Bar Meals** L served Mon-Sat 12–2.15 D served Mon-Sat 6.30–9.15 (Sun 12–2.30) Av main course £5.50
Restaurant L served Mon-Sat 12–2.15 D served all week 6.15–9.15 (Sun 1.30–2.30) Av 3 course à la carte £19.95 ⊕ Wadworth ◀ Wadworth 6X & Henrys Original IPA, Wye Valley Butty Bach, Wadworth guest ales & Henry's Smooth. ♥ 15 **Facilities** Parking **Rooms** available

The Trumpet Inn

Trumpet HR8 2RA ☎ 01531 670277
dir: *4m from Ledbury, at junct of A438 & A417*

This traditional black and white free house dates back to the late 14th century. The former coaching inn and post house takes its name from the days when mail coaches blew their horns on approaching the crossroads. The cosy bars feature a wealth of exposed beams, with open fireplaces and a separate dining area. Light sandwich lunches and salad platters complement main dishes like salmon fishcakes; kleftiko; or vegetable stroganoff.

Open 12–11 (Sun 12–10.30) **Bar Meals** L served all week 12–3 D served all week 6–9 (Sun 6–8.30) **Restaurant** L served all week 12–3 D served all week 6–9 (Sun 6–8.30) ⊕ Free House ◀ Wadworth 6X, Henrys IPA, Old Father Time. **Facilities** Garden Dogs allowed Parking

---

LEOMINSTER   MAP 10 SO45

The Grape Vaults ♥

Broad St HR4 8BS ☎ 01568 611404
e-mail: jusaxon@tiscali.co.uk
dir: *Telephone for directions*

An unspoilt pub with a small, homely bar complete with real fire – in fact it's so authentic that it's Grade II-listed, even down to the fixed seating. Real ale is a popular feature, and includes microbrewery products. The good food includes turkey and ham pie, bubble and squeak with bacon and egg, steak and ale pie, and various fresh fish dishes using cod, plaice, salmon and whitebait. No music, gaming machines, or alcopops!

Open 11–11 **Bar Meals** L served all week 12–2 D served Mon-Sat 5.30–9 Av main course £6.50 ⊕ Punch Taverns ◀ Banks Bitter, Pedigree, Original guest ales. ♥ 6 **Notes** ⊛

The Royal Oak Hotel

South St HR6 8JA ☎ 01568 612610 🖺 01568 612710
e-mail: reservations@theroyaloakhotel.net
dir: *Town centre, near A44/A49 junct*

Coaching inn dating from around 1733, with log fires, antiques and a minstrels' gallery in the original ballroom. The pub was once part of a now blocked-off tunnel system that linked the Leominster Priory with other buildings in the town. Good choice of wines by the glass and major ales, and a hearty menu offering traditional British food with a modern twist.

Open 10–3 6–11 (Sat 10–11, Sun 12–10.30) **Bar Meals** L served all week 12–2.30 D served all week 7–9 **Restaurant** L served Sun 12–2 D served all week 7–9.30 ⊕ Free House ◀ Shepherd Neame Spitfire, Wye Valley Butty Bach. **Facilities** Garden Dogs allowed Parking

---

LITTLE COWARNE   MAP 10 SO65

The Three Horseshoes Inn ♥

HR7 4RQ ☎ 01885 400276 🖺 01885 400276
e-mail: janetwhittall@threehorseshoes.co.uk
dir: *Off A456 (Hereford/Bromyard). At Stokes Cross follow Little Cowarne/Pencombe signs*

They no longer shoe horses at the blacksmith next door, but this old ale house's long drinking pedigree – 200 years and counting – looks secure. The hop-bedecked bar serves real ales and cider from nearby orchards, while meals made extensively from fresh local ingredients can be enjoyed in the restaurant or garden room. Prawn and haddock smokies to start, fillet of pork with crispy belly to follow, and a home-made ice cream are typical choices.

Open 11–3 6.30–11 Closed: 25–26 Dec, 1 Jan & Sun eve Winter
Bar Meals L served Mon-Sat 12–2 D served Mon-Sat 6.30–9.30 (Sun 12–3, 7–9) **Restaurant** L served all week 12–2 D served all week 6.30–9.30 Av 3 course à la carte £20 ⊕ Free House ◀ Marston's Pedigree, Greene King Old Speckled Hen, Wye Valley Bitter, John Smiths's. ♥ 12
Facilities Garden Parking **Rooms** available

MADLEY   MAP 09 SO43

The Comet Inn ♥

Stoney St HR2 9NJ ☎ 01981 250600
e-mail: stevewilson@thecometinn.co.uk
dir: *6m from Hereford on B4352*

Located on a prominent corner position and set in two and a half acres, this black and white 19th-century inn was originally three cottages, and retains many original features and a roaring open fire. A simple, hearty menu includes steak and ale pie, shank of lamb, grilled gammon, chicken curry, cod in crispy batter, mushroom stroganoff, and a variety of steaks, baguettes, and jacket potatoes.

Open 12–3 6–11 (Open all day Fri-Sun & BHs) **Bar Meals** L served all week 12–3 D served Mon-Sun 6–9 (Sat all day, Sun 12–4) Av main course £5 **Restaurant** L served all week 12–2 D served Mon-Sat 7–9.30 Av 3 course à la carte £15 ⊕ Free House ◀ Hook Norton Best Bitter, Wye Valley Bitter, Tetley Smooth Flow, Carlsberg Tetley. ♥ 22 **Facilities** Garden Dogs allowed Parking Play Area

England

MICHAELCHURCH ESCLEY   MAP 09 SO33

The Bridge Inn ☙

HR2 0JW ☎ 01981 510646 🖹 01981 510646

e-mail: nickmaddy@aol.com

dir: From Hereford take A465 towards Abergavenny, then B4348 towards Peterchurch. Left at Vowchurch & on to village

By Escley Brook, at the foot of the Black Mountains and close to Offa's Dyke, there are 14th-century parts to this oak-beamed family pub: the dining room overlooks the garden, abundant with rose and begonias, and the river – an ideal area for walkers and nature lovers. On rainy days guests may prefer the games room. Speciality dishes include steak and kidney with crispy dumplings.

Open 12–11 **Bar Meals** L served all week 12–6 D served all week 6–9 **Restaurant** L served all week 12–3 D served all week 6–9.30 ⊕ Free House ◀ Wye Valley ales, John Smiths, Bridge Bitter. ☙20 **Facilities** Garden Dogs allowed Parking Play Area

MUCH MARCLE   MAP 10 SO63

The Slip Tavern ☙

Watery Ln HR8 2NG

☎ 01531 660246 🖹 01531 660700

e-mail: thesliptavern@aol.com

dir: Follow signs off A449 at Much Marcle junction

Curiously named after a 1575 landslip which buried the local church, this country pub is delightfully surrounded by cider apple orchards. An attractive conservatory overlooks the award-winning garden, where summer dining is popular, and there's also a cosy bar. It's next to Westons Cider Mill, and cider is a favourite in the bar.

Open 11.30–2.30 6–11 (Sun 12–3, 7–10.30) **Bar Meals** L served Tue-Sun 12–2.30 D served Tue-Sat 6.30–9 Av main course £7 **Restaurant** L served Tue-Sun 11.30–2 D served Tue Sat 6.30–9.30 Av 3 course à la carte £18 ⊕ Free House ◀ John Smiths, Tetleys Smooth Flow, guest ales. ☙8 **Facilities** Garden Parking Play Area

ORLETON   MAP 09 SO46

The Boot Inn

SY8 4HN ☎ 01568 780228 🖹 01568 780228

e-mail: thebootorleton@hotmail.com

dir: Follow A49 S from Ludlow (approx 7m) to B4362 (Woofferton), 1.5m off B4362 turn left. Inn in village centre

A black and white timbered inn, The Boot dates from the 16th century, and in winter a blazing fire in the inglenook warms the bar. A range

of snacks and a regular menu, including a generous mixed grill, roast duck and a salad selection, are supplemented by specials such as pork chop with apple and cider sauce, vegetable lasagne, and fish pie with a cheesy mash topping.

Open 12–3 6–11 **Bar Meals** L served Tue-Sun 12–2 D served all week 7– Av main course £11 **Restaurant** L served Tue-Sun D served all week 7–9 Av 3 course à la carte £18 ⊕ Free House ◀ Hobsons Best, Local Real Ales, Woods, Wye Valley. **Facilities** Children's licence Garden Dogs allowed Parking Play Area

PEMBRIDGE   MAP 09 SO35

New Inn

Market Square HR6 9DZ

☎ 01544 388427 🖹 01544 388427

dir: From M5 junct 7 take A44 W through Leominster towards Llandrindod Wells

Worn flagstone floors and open fires characterise this unspoilt black and white timbered free house. Formerly a courthouse and jail, the building dates from the early 14th century. In summer, customers spill out into the pub's outdoor seating area in the Old Market Square. It attracts locals and summer tourists alike with dishes of lamb and vegetable hotpot; cream cheese and spinach lasagne; and trout fillets in lemon butter.

Open 11–2.30 6–11 **Bar Meals** L served Mon-Sat 12–2 D served Mon-Sat 7–9.30 (Sun 12–3, 7–10.30) **Restaurant** 12–2 7–9.30 ⊕ Free House ◀ Fuller's London Pride, Three Tuns from Bishops Castle, Black Sheep Best, Timothy Taylor. **Facilities** Garden Parking

PETERSTOW   MAP 10 SO52

The Red Lion Inn

HR9 6LH ☎ 01989 730202

dir: On A49, 2m from Ross-on-Wye

A traditional country pub with oak beams and log fires on the A49 between Ross-on-Wye and Hereford. Choice is what the Red Lion is all about – from the real ales to the extensive menu of pub favourites served in both bar and restaurant. Thai fishcakes and marie rose prawns are typical starters, with representative mains being bangers and mash and chargrilled steaks. Many dishes can be served as light bites suitable for children or the smaller appetite.

Open 12–3 5.30–11.30 (Sat all day, Sun 12–5) **Bar Meals** L served Mon-Sat 12–2.30 D served all week 6–9 (Sun 12–3) Av main course £12 **Restaurant** L served Mon-Sat 12–2.30 D served all week 6–9 (Sun 12–3) ⊕ Enterprise Inns ◀ Otto Bitter, Timothy Taylor Landlord, Malvern Hills Black Pear, Dorothy Goodbody's Golden Ale. **Facilities** Children's licence Garden Parking Play Area

PICK OF THE PUBS

SELLACK-HEREFORDSHIRE

The Lough Pool Inn at Sellack

Pronounced 'luff pool', this typical Herefordshire black and white half-timbered pub takes its name from the old English or Gaelic for an enclosed piece of land with water. It is indeed idyllically situated in an area of outstanding natural beauty, nestling beside the eponymous pool.

Based on a 16th-century cottage which was once the home of the village blacksmith and butcher, it has all the character to be expected in such a venerable building – flagstone floors, duck-or-grouse beams, warming log fires, and at the rear, a restaurant with solid rustic tables and chairs. David and Jan Birch are passionate about the superb produce on their doorstep, a passion shared by head chef Lee Jones who combines the produce with his culinary skill to produce award-winning dishes. The menus are seasonal, changing when tempting local specialities become available, such as asparagus, strawberries, soft fruits from neighbouring farms, and estate game. Herbs are grown in the garden, and vegetables and salad crops, organic when possible, are specially grown by a supplier in How Caple. Vegetarians and 'Little Foodies' have their own menus, and a daily specials boards adds some interesting options such as pan-fried lambs' kidneys on toast, or whole roasted baby haddock. Fresh fish such as this is caught in British waters and delivered daily; salmon, often from the Orkneys, is wild when permitted. For refreshment, real ales, some made with hops from the nearby Wye Valley, are backed by local ciders, perry and varieties of pure apple juice from the county's orchards; expertly chosen wines from specialist local merchants complete the drinks range. Outside, the peaceful garden leads to lovely walks on the new Herefordshire Trail to the River Wye.

☺☺🍸
MAP 10 SO52
HR9 6LX
☎ 01989 730236 📠 01981 570322
e-mail: David@loughpool.co.uk
dir: *4m NW from Ross-on-Wye, 2m off A49 Hereford Rd. Follow signs for Sellack*

Open 11.30–3 6.30–11 (Sun 12–3, 6.30–10.30) Closed: 25 Dec & Mon & Sun eve in Winter, Jan-Feb & Nov
Bar Meals L served all week 12–3 D served all week 7–9.15
Restaurant L served all week 12–3 D served all week 7–9.15 (Fixed menu Sun L only) Av 3 course à la carte £24 Av 2 course fixed price £15.75
🍺 Free House 🍺 Wye Valley, John Smiths, Butcombe Bitter, Old Speckled Hen. 🍷 10
Facilities Garden Dogs allowed Parking

| ROSS-ON-WYE | MAP 10 SO52 |

The Moody Cow ♥

Upton Bishop HR9 7TT ☎ 01989 780470

dir: *Accessed from M50 junct 3 or junct 4. Upton Bishop on B4221*

An old stone-built inn with a patio area offering plenty of shaded seating in summer, and a rustic bar with exposed stone walls and farmhouse seating. Here, local Wye Valley bitter figures among the real ales, alongside a good selection of wines by the glass. Beyond the bar are two further rooms, and there's a restaurant in a converted barn. Just one menu is served throughout.

Open 12–2.30 6.30–11 (Sun 12–3) Closed: Mon **Bar Meals** L served Tue-Sun 12–2 D served Tue-Sat 7–9 **Restaurant** L served Tue-Sun 12–2 D served Tue-Sat 7–9 ⊕ Free House ◀ Wye Valley Best, Butcombe Bitter,. ♥ 7 **Facilities** Garden Dogs allowed Parking

| SELLACK | MAP 10 SO52 |

Pick of the Pubs

The Lough Pool Inn at Sellack ◉◉ ♥

See Pick of the Pubs on page 291

| SHOBDON | MAP 09 SO46 |

The Bateman Arms ★★★★ INN

HR6 9LX ☎ 01568 708374

e-mail: martin.batemanarms@hotmail.co.uk

dir: *On B4362 off A4110 NW of Leominster*

An 18th-century, three-storey building of striking appearance, with old cobbled paving lining its street frontage. There's character inside too, where you can sit in the bar beneath ancient oak beams on 300–year-old wooden settles and enjoy a baguette, sandwich or jacket potato. Seasonal choices in the restaurant include Tex-Mex chilli topped with cheese on rice; chicken curry; deep-fried cod in beer batter; and roasted courgettes filled with pea risotto. Bedrooms are furnished in traditional style.

Open 12–3 7–11 **Bar Meals** L served all week 12–2 D served all week 7–9 **Restaurant** L served all week 12–2 D served all week 7–11 ⊕ Free House ◀ Wye Valley, Stowford Press & Guinness. **Facilities** Garden Parking **Rooms** 9

| SYMONDS YAT (EAST) | MAP 10 SO51 |

Pick of the Pubs

The Saracens Head Inn ★★★★ INN ♥

See Pick of the Pubs on opposite page

| TILLINGTON | MAP 09 SO44 |

The Bell

HR4 8LE ☎ 01432 760395 🖹 01432 760580

e-mail: beltill@aol.com

dir: *NE Hereford, on road to Weobley via Burghill*

Run by the same family since 1988, The Bell offers something for everybody, with quiet gardens, a formal dining area and a traditional public bar complete with oak parquet flooring, an open fire and a dart board. The varied menus cover all dining requirements, from bar snacks to more elaborate meals: smoked salmon terrine, followed by roast Madgett's Farm duck breast, or venison, wild boar and pheasant casserole, perhaps.

Open 11–3 6–11 (Sat-Sun 11–11) **Bar Meals** L served Mon-Sat 12–2.15 D served Mon-Sat 6–9.15 (Sun 12–2.30) **Restaurant** L served all week 12–2.15 D served Mon-Sat 6–9.15 Av 3 course à la carte £25 ◀ London Pride, Hereford Bitter, other local ales. **Facilities** Garden Dogs allowed Parking Play Area

| ULLINGSWICK | MAP 10 SO54 |

Pick of the Pubs

Three Crowns Inn ◉ ♥

HR1 3JQ ☎ 01432 820279 🖹 08700 515338

e-mail: info@threecrownsinn.com

dir: *From Burley Gate rdbt take A465 toward Bromyard, after 2m left to Ullingswick, left after 0.5m, pub 0.5m on right*

An unspoilt country pub in deepest rural Herefordshire, where food sources are so local that their distance away is measured in fields rather than miles. A hand-written sign offering to buy surplus fruit and veg gives locals a gentle reminder, as they sup their favourite real ale at the bar. Parterres in the garden grow varieties of produce that are not easy, or even possible, to buy commercially. Among them is a pea whose provenance can be traced back to a phial found by Lord Carnarvon in Tutankhamun's tomb. The daily-changing menus are refreshingly brief and uncomplicated; half a dozen options within each course are all priced the same – so eating to a budget is easily accomplished. A typical selection could be fish soup with rouille and croutons, followed by poached knuckle of Shropshire veal, or fish such as grilled Cornish gurnard. Puddings include chocolate truffle torte.

Open 12–2.30 7–11 Closed: 25 Dec, 1 Jan & Mon **Bar Meals** L served all week 12–2.30 D served all week 7–9.30 **Restaurant** L served all week 12–2 D served all week 7–9.30 Av 3 course à la carte £26 Av 3 course fixed price £14.45 ⊕ Free House ◀ Hobsons Best, Wye Valley Butty Bach & Dorothy Goodbody's, guest ales. ♥ 9 **Facilities** Garden Parking

PICK OF THE PUBS

The Saracens Head Inn

Once a cider mill, the Saracens Head lies on the east bank of the River Wye where it flows into a steep wooded gorge. This is the yat, the local name for a gate or pass, while Robert Symonds was a Sheriff of Herefordshire in the 17th century.

The inn's own ferry across the river to Symonds Yat West is hand operated, just as it has been for the past 200 years. You can eat in the lounge, dining room, flag-floored bar, or on one of the two sunny riverside terraces. Regularly changing menus and daily specials boards offer both traditional – egg Florentine with toasted brioche, for example – and modern, such as open ravioli of Cornish crab, spring onion and sweet ginger foam. Main courses might be straightforward, like chargrilled English rib-eye steak with hand-cut chips, field mushrooms and vine tomatoes; or something traditional but differentiated in some way, such as braised shank of Welsh lamb with parsnip purée and roasted cocotte potatoes; or roasted fillet of monkfish wrapped in pancetta, with wild mushrooms, roasted new potatoes and poached baby leeks. Then there might be the wholly modern dish, such as warm tart of smoked garlic and aubergine, with mixed leaf salad. The inn is situated in an area of outstanding natural beauty on the edge of the Royal Forest of Dean, so a stay in one of the nine en suite bedrooms is a must for exploring the unspoiled local countryside. Activities available nearby include walking, cycling, mountain biking, canoeing, kayaking, climbing, abseiling, potholing and, free to residents, fishing.

★★★★ INN ♛
MAP 10 SO51
Ross-on-Wye HR9 6JL
☎ 01600 890435
🖷 01600 890034
e-mail: contact@
saracensheadinn.co.uk
web: www.saracensheadinn.co.uk
dir: *From Ross-on-Wye take A40 to Monmouth. In 4m take Symonds Yat East turn. 1st right before bridge. Right in 0.5m. Right in 1m*

Open 11–11
Bar Meals L served all week 12–2.30 D served all week 6.30–9
Restaurant L served all week 12–2.30 D served all week 6.30–9
⊕ Free House ◀ Theakstons Old Peculier, Old Speckled Hen, Wye Valley Hereford Pale Ale, Wye Valley Butty Bach & Buttcombe Bitter. ♛ 7
Facilities Garden Parking
Rooms 9

WALFORD
MAP 10 SO52

The Mill Race NEW
HR9 5QS ☎ 01989 562891
e-mail: enquiries@millrace.info
dir: From Ross-on-Wye on Walford road, 3m on right after village hall

Following total renovation in 2005, there's a great mix of old and new here, with exposed original stone balanced by red, grey and green rendered walls. Real fires in winter; in summer, patio doors open into the external dining area with views over fields to Goodrich Castle. Watch the kitchen at work preparing simple, well-cooked food including confit of duck; beef and Wye Valley ale pie; marinated mackerel fillets; and mixed bean goulash.

Open 11–3 5–11 (Sat 11–11, Sun 12–10.30) Bar Meals L served Mon-Fri 12–2 D served Mon-Sat 6–9.30 (Sat 12–2.30, Sun 12–2.30, 6–9) Av main course £11 Restaurant L served Mon-Fri 12–2 D served Mon-Thu 6.30–9 (Fri 6.30–9.30, Sat 12–2.30 & 6.30–9.30, Sun 12–2.30) Av 3 course à la carte £22.50 ⊕ Free House ◀ Wye Valley Bitter, Guest Ales, Guinness. ♥ 8 Facilities Garden Parking

WALTERSTONE
MAP 09 SO32

Carpenters Arms
HR2 0DX ☎ 01873 890353
dir: Off A465 between Hereford & Abergavenny at Pandy

There's plenty of character in this 300–year-old free house located on the edge of the Black Mountains where the owner, Mrs Watkins, was born. Here you'll find beams, antique settles and a leaded range with open fires that burn all winter. Popular food options include beef and Guinness pie; beef lasagne; and thick lamb cutlets. Ask about the vegetarian selection, and large choice of home-made desserts.

Open 12–3 7–11 Bar Meals L served all week 12–3 D served all week 7–9.30 Restaurant L served all week 12–3 D served all week 7–9.30 ⊕ Free House ◀ Wadworth 6X, Breconshire Golden Valley & Rambler's Ruin. Facilities Garden Parking Play Area Notes ⊗

WELLINGTON
MAP 10 SO44

The Wellington
HR4 8AT ☎ 01432 830367
e-mail: thewellington@hotmail.com
dir: Off A49 into village centre. Pub 0.25m on left

Owners Ross and Philippa Williams left London to create one of Herefordshire's finest gastropubs. They're doing well, with Ross quickly becoming an award-winning champion of food prepared from local, seasonal produce. Start with smoked pheasant breast with potato scone and whisky and pink peppercorn sauce; followed by pedigree Hereford sirloin with field mushrooms, thyme and horseradish butter; and then clotted cream rice pudding with winter fruit compote. Sunday lunch could be roast haunch of venison.

Open 12–3 6–11 (Sun 7–10.30 excl Winter) Closed: Mon lunch & Sun eve Winter Bar Meals L served Tue-Sun 12–2 D served Mon-Sat 7–9 Av main course £8 Restaurant L served Tue-Sun 12–2 D served Tue-Sun 7–9 Av 3 course à la carte £25 ⊕ Free House ◀ Hobsons, Wye Valley Butty Bach, Timothy Taylor Landlord & guest Real Ales. ♥ 8 Facilities Garden Dogs allowed Parking Play Area

WEOBLEY
MAP 09 SO45

Pick of the Pubs

The Salutation Inn ◉
Market Pitch HR4 8SJ
☎ 01544 318443 ▤ 01544 318405
e-mail: salutationinn@btinternet.com
dir: A44, then A4112, 8m from Leominster

A black and white timber-framed pub dating back more than 500 years and situated in a corner of the country renowned for its hops, cattle and apple orchards. The inn, sympathetically converted from an old ale house and adjoining cottage, is the perfect base for exploring the lovely Welsh Marches and enjoying a host of leisure activities, including fishing, horse riding, golf, walking, and clay shooting. The book capital of Hay-on-Wye and the cathedral city of Hereford are close by. The inn's restaurant offers a range of award-winning dishes created with the use of locally sourced ingredients. Chef's specials are also served in the traditional lounge bar with its welcoming atmosphere and cosy inglenook fireplace. Starters include confit of duck and pan-seared Cornish scallops, while main courses range from roast rump of Welsh lamb, and oven-baked fillet of salmon, to whole roast breast of chicken, and medley of sea bass and oysters.

Open 11–11 (Sun 12–10.30) Bar Meals L served all week 12–2.30 D served all week 6.30–9.30 (Sun 6.30–8) Av main course £10 Restaurant L served all week 12–2.30 D served Mon-Sat 7–9 Av 3 course à la carte £25 ⊕ Free House ◀ Hook Norton Best, Coors Worthington's Creamflow, Wye Valley Butty Bach, Flowers Best Bitter. Facilities Children's licence Garden Parking

WHITNEY-ON-WYE
MAP 09 SO24

Pick of the Pubs

Rhydspence Inn ★★★★ INN
HR3 6EU ☎ 01497 831262 ▤ 01497 831751
e-mail: info@rhydspence-inn.co.uk
dir: N side of A438 1m W of Whitney-on-Wye

Once a manor house, the Rhydspence Inn was also a favourite watering hole for Welsh and Irish drovers taking cattle, sheep and geese to market in London. These days the pub is rather more elegant, with a cosy bar and spacious dining room giving way to stunning views over the Wye Valley. The pub also has literary connections, appearing in On The Black Hill by Bruce Chatwin, and apparently acting as a site of inspiration for Shakespeare while penning *Much Ado About Nothing*. Food options range from simple bar snacks such as steak and kidney pie or beef lasagna to more elaborate dining: perhaps honey-fried scallops with a lime, soy and ginger dressing, followed by roast monkfish on sweet pepper compote. The friendly ghost of a former landlady is said to frequent the inn, though only when young children are staying.

Open 11–2.30 7–11 **Bar Meals** L served Mon-Sat 11–1.45 D served all week 7–8.45 (Sun 12–2) Av main course £10 **Restaurant** L served Mon-Sat 11–1.45 D served all week 7–8.45 (Sun 12–2) Av 3 course à la carte £27 ⊕ Free House ◖ Robinsons Best & Interbrew Bass. **Facilities** Garden Parking **Rooms** 7

WOOLHOPE
MAP 10 SO63

The Crown Inn ♥

HR1 4QP ☎ 01432 860468 ▤ 01432 860770

e-mail: menu@crowninnwoolhope.co.uk

dir: *B4224 to Mordiford, left after Moon Inn. Pub in village centre*

Matt and Annalisa Slocombe, who have the Scrumpy House Restaurant and Bar in Much Marcle, have now purchased the freehold of this pub. It is a mainly 18th-century inn, dating back to about 1520 (as indicated by a mounting block at the front of the original building), located in a conservation area close to Hereford, Ross-on-Wye and Ledbury. One hundred percent home-cooked, old fashioned pub food is now served, along with well kept ales and ciders.

Open 12–3 6.30–11 (Sun 6.30–10.30, Mon-Fri Winter 7–11) **Bar Meals** L served all week 12–2 D served all week 6.30–9.30 (Winter 7–9.30) Av main course £8.50 **Restaurant** L served all week 12–2 D served all week 6.30–9.30 (Winter 7–9.30) ⊕ Free House ◖ Wye Valley Best, Black Sheep, guest ales. ♥ 6 **Facilities** Garden Parking

---

HERTFORDSHIRE

ALDBURY
MAP 06 SP91

The Greyhound Inn ♥

19 Stocks Rd HP23 5RT

☎ 01442 851228 ▤ 01442 851495

e-mail: greyhound@aldbury.wanadoo.co.uk

dir: *Telephone for directions*

This quintessentially English country pub looks out over the village duck pond and ancient stocks. Nestled beneath the Chiltern Hills and close to the National Trust's renowned Ashridge Estate, the Greyhound is also ideal for walks. Log fires warm the bar in winter, whilst summer brings the option of an alfresco lunch. Hearty, traditional dishes could include free-range pork sausages with onion gravy; chilled salmon salad; or butternut squash, sage and pine nut risotto.

Open 11–11 Closed: 25 Dec **Bar Meals** L served Mon-Sat 12–2.30 D served Mon-Sat 6.30–9.30 (Sun 12–4) **Restaurant** L served Mon-Sat 12–2.30 D served Mon-Sat 6.30–9.30 (Sun 12–4) ⊕ Hall & Woodhouse ◖ Badger Best, Tanglefoot, King & Barnes Sussex. ♥ 10 **Facilities** Garden Dogs allowed Parking

---

Pick of the Pubs

The Valiant Trooper ♥

Trooper Rd HP23 5RW

☎ 01442 851203 ▤ 01442 851071

dir: *A41 at Tring junct, follow rail station signs 0.5m, at village green turn right, 200yds on left*

Family-run free house in a pretty village whose ancient stocks and duckpond often feature in films. The deeds date back to 1752, when it was The Royal Oak; it became The Trooper Alehouse in 1803, allegedly because the Duke of Wellington once discussed tactics here with his troops. In the 1880s a landlord would remove his wooden leg and bang it on the counter – maybe his way of calling 'Time!' The old stable block, which has also served as scout hut and local bikers' club, is now a comfortable 40–seater restaurant offering daily blackboard specials such as duck breast with oriental stir-fry; pork loin steak with sage sauce; sausage and mash with onion gravy; and grilled mackerel stuffed with tomato and onion. Hikers and cyclists descend from the surrounding Chiltern Hills for a pint of Tring Brewery's Jack O'Legs, or regularly changing guest beers. Dogs are welcome too.

Open 11.30–11 (Sun 12–10.30) **Bar Meals** L served Tue-Sat 12–2 D served Tue-Sat 6.30–9.15 (Sun 12–2.30) Av main course £9 **Restaurant** L served Tue-Sat 12–2 D served Tue-Sun 6.30–9.15 (Sun 12–2.30) Av 3 course à la carte £20 ⊕ Free House ◖ Fuller's London Pride, Oakham J.H.B, Tring Jack O'Legs & 2 guest ales. ♥ 8 **Facilities** Garden Dogs allowed Parking Play Area

---

ARDELEY
MAP 12 TL32

The Jolly Waggoner

SG2 7AH ☎ 01438 861350

dir: *Telephone for directions*

Cream-washed 500–year-old pub with exposed beams, roaring fires, antique furniture and a popular cottage garden. The inn also benefits from a lovely village setting and a variety of local walks. All the food is home made from fresh ingredients, ranging from appetising sandwiches to à la carte dining. Fish is something of a speciality, like dressed crab salad, swordfish or sea bass. Alternatively, try loin of lamb, calves' liver or steak and kidney pie.

Open 12–3 6–11 **Bar Meals** L served all week 12–2 D served all week 6.30–9 (Sun 12–3) Av main course £12 **Restaurant** L served all week 12.30–2 D served all week 6.30–9 ⊕ Greene King ◖ Greene King IPA & Abbot Ale. **Facilities** Garden Parking

England

ASHWELL
MAP 12 TL23

The Three Tuns 🍷

High St SG7 5NL ☎ 01462 742107 📄 01462 743662
e-mail: claire@tuns.co.uk
dir: *Telephone for directions*

The building, dating from 1806, replaces an earlier one first recorded as a public house in 1700. Original features survive in the two bars and large dining room, probably once a smokehouse, judging by the rows of old hanging hooks. The daily menu might offer crayfish tails in marie rose sauce; oriental sweet and sour pork with basmati rice; grilled swordfish with black olive, garlic, tomato and pepper tapenade; and home-made apple and blackberry crumble.

Open 11–11.30 (Fri-Sat 11–12, Sun 12–10.30) **Bar Meals** L served all week 12–2.30 D served all week 6.30–9.30 **Restaurant** L served all week 12–2.30 D served all week 6.30–9.30 ⊕ Greene King ◀ Greene King IPA, guest, Abbot. 🍷 12 **Facilities** Garden Dogs allowed Parking Play Area

BARLEY
MAP 12 TL43

The Fox & Hounds

High St SG8 8HU ☎ 01763 848459 📄 01763 849274
e-mail: jamesburn1972@aol.com
dir: *A505 onto B1368 at Flint Cross, pub 4m*

Set in a pretty village, this former 17th-century hunting lodge is notable for its pub sign which extends across the lane. It has real fires, a warm welcome and an attractive garden. The owners have certainly made their mark with their home-cooked food, offering a menu with a good range of dependable choices, including sirloin steak with chips and onion rings; barbecued ribs; chilli and lasagne.

Open 12–11 (Sun 12–10.30 Winter Mon-Fri 12–3, Sat-Sun all day) **Bar Meals** L served all week 12–10 D served all week 12–10 (Sun 12–9) Av main course £8 **Restaurant** L served 12–10 D served 12–10 Av 3 course à la carte £13.95 ⊕ Punch Taverns ◀ IPA, 6X, Adnams Best, Old Speckled Hen & guest ales. **Facilities** Garden Dogs allowed Parking Play Area

BUNTINGFORD
MAP 12 TL32

The Sword Inn Hand ★★★★ INN 🍷

Westmill SG9 9LQ ☎ 01763 271356
e-mail: welcome@theswordinnhand.co.uk
dir: *Off A10 1.5m S of Buntingford*

Midway between London and Cambridge, and welcoming travellers since the 14th century – you can't miss the oak beams, flag floor and open fireplace. It styles itself a 'real English', family-run pub offering a large selection of snacks, specials, beers and wines. Fresh produce is delivered daily to create stilton-crusted chicken breast with creamy leek sauce; duck Wellington with wild mushroom sauce; and fillet of roasted monkfish with pea and mint risotto.

Open 12–3 5–11 (Fri-Sun all day) **Bar Meals** L served all week 12–2.30 D served all week 6.30–9.30 (Sun winter 12–5 summer 12–7) **Restaurant** L served Mon-Sat 12–2.30 D served all week 7–9.30 (Sun 12–5) ⊕ Free House ◀ Greene King IPA, Young's Bitter, Shephard Neame Spitfire & guest ales. 🍷 8 **Facilities** Garden Dogs allowed Parking Play Area **Rooms** 4

COTTERED
MAP 12 TL32

The Bull at Cottered 🍷

Cottered SG9 9QP ☎ 01763 281243
e-mail: cordell39@btinternet.com
dir: *On A507 in Cottered between Buntingford & Baldock*

A traditional village local in a picturesque setting, with low-beamed ceilings, antique furniture, cosy fires and pub games; the well-tended garden offers an alternative dining venue in summer. The menu presents a comprehensive carte of all home-made brasserie-style food, which could kick off with mixed olives; garlic bread topped with Serrano ham and mozzarella; or fresh Devon crab. Steaks, pastas, an excellent range of salads and the day's fish dish are all freshly prepared.

Open 12–2.30 6.30–11 (Sun 12–11) **Bar Meals** L served Mon-Sat 12–2 D served all week 6.30–9.30 (Sun 12–3) **Restaurant** L served Mon-Sat 12–2 D served all week 6.30–9.30 (Sun 12–3) ⊕ Greene King ◀ Greene King IPA & Abbot Ale. 🍷 7 **Facilities** Garden Parking

FLAUNDEN
MAP 06 TL00

Pick of the Pubs

The Bricklayers Arms 🍷

See Pick of the Pubs on opposite page

HEMEL HEMPSTEAD
MAP 06 TL00

Pick of the Pubs

Alford Arms 🍷

See Pick of the Pubs on page 298

HEXTON
MAP 12 TL13

The Raven 🍷

SG5 3JB ☎ 01582 881209 📄 01582 881610
e-mail: jack@ravenathexton.f9.co.uk
dir: *5m W of Hitchin. 5m N of Luton, just outside Barton-le-Clay*

This neat 1920s pub is named after Ravensburgh Castle in the neighbouring hills. It has comfortable bars and a large garden with a terrace and play area. Snacks include ploughman's and salad platters, plus tortilla wraps, filled baguettes and jacket potatoes. The main menu offers lots of steak options, and dishes like smoky American chicken, whole rack of barbecue ribs, Thai red vegetable curry and an all-day breakfast.

Open 11–3 6–11 (Sat 11–11 Sun 12–10.30) **Bar Meals** L served all week 12–2 D served all week 6–10 (Sat-Sun 12–9) Av main course £9.50 **Restaurant** L served all week 12–2 D served all week 6–10 (Sat-Sun 12–9) ⊕ Enterprise Inns ◀ Greene King Old Speckled Hen, Fuller's London Pride, Greene King IPA. 🍷 24 **Facilities** Garden Parking Play Area

PICK OF THE PUBS

FLAUNDEN-HERTFORDSHIRE

The Bricklayers Arms

In 1722, this award-winning pub in Hogpits Bottom was nothing more than a pair of brick and flint cottages. One was a butcher's, the other a blacksmith's forge, with a village shop added later. These days it's an award-winning, nationally recognised restaurant. Its secret is a happy marriage between traditional English and French fusion cooking.

Tucked away in deepest rural Hertfordshire, it's a favourite with locals, walkers and all those who seek a sunny and secluded garden to linger in during the summer months. The ivy-covered exterior gives way to an immaculate interior, complete with low beams, exposed brickwork, candlelight and open fires. The French influence comes from Michelin-trained head chef Claude Paillet, and the four chefs he has in turn trained. As far as possible he uses fresh organic produce from local producers and suppliers to create seasonal core menus, and two-starter, two-main course daily specials. A good way to begin might be brochette of tiger prawns with vegetable stir-fry and light curry cream; or a selection of home-smoked fish with lemon coriander butter and tomato chutney. Then to continue with sea bass pan-fried in olive oil with creamy Chardonnay, red pepper, shallot and basil sauce; or ale-marinated steak and kidney pie served with chive mash. But be sure to save space for dessert, as the Bricklayers is held in high esteem for its pudding menu. See if hot apple and cinnamon tart; or chocolate layered mousse trio with panacotta ice cream are being served when you visit . More than 120 wines appear on a worldwide list. During the summer you can take lunch in the terraced garden.

MAP 06 TL00
Hogpits Bottom HP3 0PH
☎ 01442 833322
📠 01442 834841
e-mail: goodfood@
bricklayersarms.com
web: www.bricklayersarms.com
dir: *M25 junct 18 onto A404
(Amersham road). Right at
Chenies for Flaunden*

Open 12–11.30
Bar Meals L served Mon-Sat
12–2.30 D served Mon-Sat
6.30–9.30 (Sun 12–4, 6.30–8.30)
Av main course £14
Restaurant L served Mon-Sat
12–2.30 D served Mon-Sat
6.30–9.30 (Sun 12–4, 6.30–9)
⊕ Free House ◗ Old Speckled
Hen, Greene King IPA, London
Pride, Timothy Taylor. ♀ 12
Facilities Garden Dogs allowed
Parking

PICK OF THE PUBS

HEMEL HEMPSTEAD-HERTFORDSHIRE

Alford Arms

An attractive Victorian pub, the Alford Arms is set in the hamlet of Frithsden surrounded by National Trust woodland. The pretty garden overlooks the village green, and historic Ashridge Forest is close by – the perfect place to walk off your meal.

Cross the threshold and you'll immediately pick up on the warm and lively atmosphere, derived in part from the buzz of conversation and the background jazz music. The rich colours and eclectic mixture of furniture and pictures in the dining room and bar also make an impression. Staff are renowned for their good humour and trouble is taken to ensure an enjoyable experience for customers; and if you can't make it back to the office free WiFi is available. The seasonal menu balances innovative dishes with more traditional fare, and everything is prepared from fresh local produce whenever possible. There's a great choice of light dishes or 'small plates', from rustic breads with roast garlic and olive oil, to king prawn and spring onion bread and butter pudding with goat's cream and beetroot dressing; or oak smoked bacon on bubble and squeak with hollandaise sauce and poached egg. Main meals with a similarly imaginative approach include sea bass kiev on confit vine tomatoes with cauliflower and watercress purée; and crispy Oxfordshire pork belly and onion roly poly with sticky roast parsnips. Puddings have an interesting tweak too, such as baked fig clafoutis with aged balsamic and Amaretto custard; or treacle tart with lemon grass crème fraîche. The British cheese plate is a tempting alternative to finish, with Alford oatcakes, sticky malt loaf and fig jam.

MAP 06 TL00
Frithsden HP1 3DD
☎ 01442 864480
🖶 01422 876893
e-mail:
info@alfordarmsfrithsden.co.uk
dir: *From Hemel Hempstead on A4146 take 2nd left at Water End. In 1m left at T-junct, right after 0.75m. Pub 100yds on right*

Open 11 -11 (Sun 12–10.30)
Closed: 25–26 Dec
Bar Meals L served Mon-Sat
12–2.30 D served all week 7–10
(Sun 12–4) Av main course
£12.75
Restaurant L served Mon-Sat
12–2.30 D served all week 7–10
(Sun 12–4) Av 3 course à la carte
£23.75
⊕ 🍺 Marstons Pedigree, Brakspear, Flowers Original, Rebellion IPA. 🍷 19
Facilities Garden Dogs allowed
Parking

HINXWORTH   MAP 12 TL24

Three Horseshoes

High St SG7 5HQ ☎ 01462 742280

dir: *E of A1 between Biggleswade & Baldock*

Thatched 18th-century country pub with a dining extension into the garden. Parts of the building date back 500 years, and the walls are adorned with pictures and photos of the village's history. Samples from a typical menu include chicken of the wood, lamb cutlets with champ, rainbow trout with almonds, sea bass provençale, steak and Guinness pie, bacon and cheese pasta bake, and roasted Tuscan red peppers.

Open 12–3 6–11 (Sat-Sun all day) Closed: Mon lunch
Bar Meals L served Tue-Fri 12–2 D served Tue-Thu 6–8.30 (Fri-Sat 6–9, Sat-Sun 12–2.30) **Restaurant** L served Tue-Fri 12–2 D served Tue-Thu 6–8.30 (Fri-Sat 6–9, Sat-Sun 12–2.30) ⊕ Greene King ◄ Greene King IPA, Abbot Ale, guest ales. **Facilities** Garden Parking

HITCHIN   MAP 12 TL12

The Greyhound ★★★ INN ♥

London Rd, St Ippolyts SG4 7NL ☎ 01462 440989

e-mail: greyhound@freenet.co.uk

dir: *1.5m south of Hitchin on B656*

The Greyhound was rescued from dereliction by the present owner who previously worked for the London Fire Brigade. It is now a popular, family-run hostelry surrounded by pleasant countryside yet handy for the M1 and Luton Airport. The food is unpretentious, generous and competitively priced, with only steaks and sea food main courses breaking the ten-pound barrier. Enjoy starters of deep-fried calamari or crayfish cocktail, and carry on with liver and bacon casserole, or peppered pork.

Open 7–2.30 5–12 **Bar Meals** L served all week 12–2 D served all week 5–9 **Restaurant** L served Mon-Sat 12–2 D served Mon-Sat 5–9 (Sun 12–8) ⊕ Free House ◄ Adnams, guest. ♥ 8 **Facilities** Parking **Rooms** 5

HUNSDON   MAP 06 TL41

Pick of the Pubs

The Fox and Hounds ♥

2 High St SG12 8NH

☎ 01279 843999 🖹 01279 841092

e-mail: info@foxandhounds-hunsdon.co.uk

web: www.foxandhounds-hunsdon.co.uk

dir: *From A414 between Ware & Harlow take B180 in Stanstead Abbotts N to Hunsdon*

Nestled in a sleepy village in the heart of the Hertfordshire countryside, this pub has a warm, welcoming atmosphere and a large pretty garden. The bar is stocked with a fine array of locally brewed real ales, and meals can be taken in the bar, the lounge and the large, homely dining room. Expect serious, inspired cooking that combines classics with modern touches. Lunch could begin with mussels, cider, leeks and cream; or sautéed squid, chorizo and butter beans, followed by roast skate wing, lentils and salsa verde; or perhaps calves' liver persillade and duck fat potato cake. For dinner, perhaps celeriac, chestnut and pancetta soup; or sliced breast of mallard with watercress salad, followed by whole roast partridge and braised lentils; or fillet of black bream, mussels and saffron. Clementine and Campari jelly is an elegant way to round matters off.

Open 12–4 6–11 Closed: Last wk Jan & 1st wk Feb, Sun & Mon eve **Bar Meals** L served Tue-Sat 12–3 D served Tue-Sat 6–10.30 (Sun 12–4) Av main course £13 **Restaurant** L served Sun 12–3 D served Thu-Sat 7–10 Av 3 course à la carte £35 Av 2 course fixed price £13 ⊕ Free House ◄ Adnams Bitter, Adnams Broadside & Guinness. ♥ 10 **Facilities** Children's licence Garden Dogs allowed Parking Play Area

Cliveden, Taplow, Buckinghamshire

LITTLE HADHAM MAP 06 TL42

The Nags Head ♈

The Ford SG11 2AX ☎ 01279 771555 ▤ 01279 771555
e-mail: paul.arkell@virgin.net
dir: M11 junct 8 take A120 towards Puckeridge & A10. Left at
lights in Little Hadham. Pub 1m on right

Formerly a coaching inn, this 16th-century pub has also been a
brewery, a bakery and Home Guard arsenal in its time. The 1960s
group Fairport Convention once performed in concert opposite and
the pub ran dry! Open brickwork and an old bakery oven are among
the features. An extensive menu offers everything from braised lamb
joint and roast spiced duck breast to pasta carbonara and vegetarian
mixed grill. Plenty of starters and more than 20 fish courses.

Open 11.30–3 6–11 (Sun 12–3.30 7–10.30) **Bar Meals** L served all week
12–2 D served Mon-Thu 6–9 (Fri-Sat 6–9.30, Sun 7–9) Av main course £8
Restaurant L served all week 12–2 D served Mon-Thu 6–9 (Fri-Sat 6–9.30,
Sun 7–9) Av 3 course à la carte £17.95 ⊕ Greene King ◄ Greene King
Abbot Ale, IPA, Old Speckled Hen & Ruddles County Ale, Marstons Pedigree.
♈ 6 **Facilities** Garden

OLD KNEBWORTH MAP 06 TL22

The Lytton Arms ♈

Park Ln SG3 6QB ☎ 01438 812312 ▤ 01438 817298
e-mail: thelyttonarms@btinternet.com
dir: From A1(M) take A602. At Knebworth turn right at rail
station. Follow Codicote signs. Pub 1.5m on right

The pub was designed around 1877 by Lord Lytton's brother-in-law,
who happened to be the architect Sir Edwin Lutyens. It replaced the
previous inn, now a residence next door. Also next door, in a much
grander way, is the Lytton estate, the family home for centuries. On the
simple but wide-ranging menu are Mrs O'Keefe's flavoured sausages;
chicken or vegetable balti; honeyroast ham; chargrilled lamb's liver and
bacon; and fisherman's pie.

Open 11–11 (Sun 12–10.30) **Bar Meals** L served Mon-Sun 12–2.30
D served Mon-Sat 6.30–9.30 (Sun 12–5) Av main course £8
Restaurant L served Mon-Sun 12–2.30 D served Mon-Sat 6.30–9.30 (Sun
12–5) Av 3 course à la carte £17.50 ⊕ Free House ◄ Fuller's London Pride,
Adnams Best Bitter, Broadside, Wherry. ♈ 30 **Facilities** Children's licence
Garden Dogs allowed Parking

POTTERS CROUCH MAP 06 TL10

The Hollybush ♈

AL2 3NN ☎ 01727 851792 ▤ 01727 851792
e-mail: info@thehollybushpub.co.uk
dir: Ragged Hall Ln off A405 or Bedmond Ln off A4147

The Hollybush is a picturesque country pub with a quaint, white-
painted exterior, attractively furnished interior and a large enclosed
garden. An antique dresser, a large fireplace and various prints
and paintings help to create a delightfully welcoming atmosphere.
Traditional pub fare is offered: ploughman's, burgers, jacket potatoes,
salads, platters and toasted sandwiches. The pub is close to St Albans
with its Roman ruins and good local walks.

Open 12–2.30 6–11 (Sun 7–10.30) **Bar Meals** L served all week 12–2
D served Wed-Sat 6–9 Av main course £9 ⊕ Fullers ◄ Fuller's Chiswick
Bitter, Fuller's London Pride, ESB & seasonal ales. ♈ 7 **Facilities** Garden
Parking

RICKMANSWORTH MAP 06 TQ09

The Rose and Crown ♈

Harefield Rd WD3 1PP ☎ 01923 897680
e-mail: roseandcrown@morethanjustapub.com
dir: M25 junct 17/18, follow Northwood signs. Past Tesco, pub
1.5m on right

This 17th-century former farmhouse hosts events ranging from wine
tastings to a monthly farmers' market. Inside the wisteria-clad building
you'll find low-beamed ceilings and real fires, whilst the large garden
looks out across the lovely Colne Valley. There's a strong emphasis on
varied home-cooked food, supplied locally wherever possible. Baked
lemon pollock fillet with fennel and parsnip mash; chicken pot roast;
and juniper, venison and pigeon pie are typical dishes.

Open 12–11 (Sun 12–10.30) **Bar Meals** L served all week 12–6 D served
all week 6–10 (Sun 12–9.30) Av main course £10 **Restaurant** L served all
week 12–6 D served all week 6–10 (Sun 12–9.30) Av 3 course fixed price
£14.50 ◄ London Pride & Deuchars IPA. ♈ 11 **Facilities** Garden Dogs
allowed Parking Play Area

ROYSTON MAP 12 TL34

Pick of the Pubs

The Cabinet Free House and Restaurant ◉ ♈

See Pick of the Pubs on page 302

ST ALBANS MAP 06 TL10

Rose & Crown ♈

10 St Michael St AL3 4SG
☎ 01727 851903 ▤ 01727 761775
e-mail: ruth.courtney@ntlworld.com
dir: Telephone for details

Traditional 16th-century pub situated in a beautiful part of St Michael's
'village', opposite the entrance to Verulanium Park and the Roman
Museum. It has a classic beamed bar with a huge inglenook, and a
summer patio filled with flowers. The pub offers a distinctive range of
American deli-style sandwiches, which are served with potato salad,
kettle crisps and pickled cucumber. The "Cotton Club", for example,
has a roast beef, ham, Swiss cheese, mayo, tomato, onion, lettuce and
horseradish mustard filling.

Open 11.30–3 5.30–11 (Open all day Sat-Sun) **Bar Meals** L served all
week 12–2 D served Mon-Sat 6–9.30 (Sat-Sun 12.30–2.30) Av main course
£8 **Restaurant** L served Mon-Sat 12–2 6–9.30 (Sat-Sun 12–2.30) ⊕ Punch
Taverns ◄ Adnams Bitter, Tetley Bitter, Fuller's London Pride, Courage
Directors. ♈ 20 **Facilities** Children's licence Garden Dogs allowed Parking

PICK OF THE PUBS

ROYSTON-HERTFORDSHIRE

The Cabinet Free House and Restaura

The Cabinet, meaning small room or meeting place, is a 16th-century country inn and restauran located in the little village of Reed just off the A10 London to Cambridge road, within easy striking distance of the capital. It's situated on a chalk ridge at almost the highest point in Hertfordshire, with the Roman highway Ermine Street passing just to the west.

There has been a settlement here for many centuries – the community is mentioned in the Domesday Book of 1086. Now in the capable hands of Tracey Hale and Angus Martin, the refurbished inn has a cosy and comfortable interior with low beamed ceilings and an open fire. The lovely surroundings lend themselves to special occasions, particularly weddings, and the premises are licensed for civil ceremonies. The menu is an eclectic mix, based on personal taste and sound cooking techniques rather than a particular type of cuisine. Prices in whole pounds give the menu an attractive and uncluttered look, as well as helping the budget conscious. Food is prepared from the best local produce, but draws inspiration from around the world

to offer an interesting variety of dishes including traditional favourites. The restaurant and snug lunchtime offerings range from soup of the day or cured salmon and scrambled eggs, to steak and ale suet pudding or loin of pork with braised cabbage and horseradish mash. Comfort desserts include rice pudding with home-made jam, and Eton mess. Evening suppers are equally appealing while moving up a gear or two in complexity: a typical choice could start with warm scallops with sweet chilli sauce and crème fraîche; continue with pan-seared sea bass with pickled tomatoes, bok choy and lime; and round off with baked lemon tart.

◎ ♀
MAP 12 TL34
High St, Reed SG8 8AH
☎ 01763 848366
e-mail:
thecabinet@btconnect.com
dir: *2m S of Royston, just off A10*

Open 12–3 5.30–12 Open all day
Sat-Sun Closed: 1 Jan
Bar Meals L served Tue-Sun
12–3 D served Tue-Sat 5–9 Av
main course £13
Restaurant L served Tue-Sun
12–3 D served Tue-Sat 5–9 Av 3
course à la carte £26 Av 3 course
fixed price £18
◀ Woodfordes Wherry, Adnams,
Old Speckled Hen, Nelson's
Revenge. ♀ 8
Facilities Garden Dogs allowed
Parking

England

STANDON   MAP 06 TL32

The Kick & Dicky ♀

G11 1NL ☎ 01920 821424

e-mail: kickanddicky@btinternet.com

This family-run free house stands in a sleepy hamlet amid rolling countryside, just half a mile from the A120 and 15 minutes from Stanstead. Food includes a set price menu, tapas every Wednesday night, a changing carte (casserole of veal shank on couscous; pan-fried mackerel on bok choy) and light lunch choices such as roasted pepper and olive salad with grilled haloumi or sausages, mash and gravy.

Open 12–2.30 6–11 Closed: 1st wk Jan **Bar Meals** L served Tue-Sun 12–2 D served Tue-Sat 7–9.30 (Sun 1–2) Av main course £8.50 **Restaurant** L served Tue-Sat 12–2 D served Tue-Sat 7–9.30 Av 3 course à la carte £26 ⊕ Free House ◀ Greene King IPA, Ruddles County, Adnams & Adnams Broadside. ♀7 **Facilities** Garden Parking

---

STAPLEFORD   MAP 06 TL31

Papillon Woodhall Arms ★ ★ ★ INN ♀

7 High Rd SG14 3NW ☎ 01992 535123 📠 01992 582772

e-mail: papillonwoodhall@aol.com

dir: On the A119, between the A602 and Hertford

Two other Papillon restaurants in Hertfordshire preceded the 1998 redevelopment of the Woodhall Arms; the result is this pink-washed, twin-gabled building behind a neat white picket fence. The bar serves well kept real ales in a welcoming atmosphere, and an eclectic mix of snacks or pub lunches. Papillon is known for its mix of English and continental styles in dishes based on fresh produce, including a large selection of fish. Accommodation in ten en suite bedrooms.

Open 11–2.30 6.30–11 **Bar Meals** L served all week 12–2.30 D served Sun-Fri 6.30–10 **Restaurant** L served all week 12–2 D served all week 6.30–10 (Sun 12–2.30, 6.30–9.30) Av 3 course à la carte £20 Av 2 course fixed price £11.95 ⊕ Free House ◀ Greene King IPA, Archers, Cottage, Nethergate. ♀10 **Facilities** Garden Dogs allowed Parking **Rooms** 10

TEWIN   MAP 06 TL21

The Plume of Feathers ♀

Upper Green Rd AL6 0LX

☎ 01438 717265 📠 01438 712596

dir: E from A1(M) junct 6 towards WGC, follow B1000 towards Hertford. Tewin signed on left

Built in 1596, this historic inn, firstly an Elizabethan hunting lodge and later the haunt of highwaymen, boasts several ghosts including a 'lady in grey'. Interesting menus change daily, and include a tapas bar from noon till close. Other options available are Moroccan spiced baby shark with king prawns and couscous, honey-roast duck with sweet potato wontons, or slow-roasted belly pork with bacon and cabbage. Be sure to book in advance.

Open 11–11 **Bar Meals** L served all week 12–2.30 D served Mon-Sat 6–9.30 (Summer all day) Av main course £10 **Restaurant** L served all week D served Mon-Sat (Sun 12–4) Av 3 course à la carte £20 ⊕ Greene King ◀ IPA, Abbot Ales. ♀30 **Facilities** Garden Dogs allowed Parking

---

WALKERN   MAP 12 TL22

The White Lion ♀

31 The High St SG2 7PA ☎ 01438 861251

dir: B1037 from Stevenage

In rolling chalk downland, Walkern manages to keep a respectable distance from nearby Stevenage, Britain's first 'new town'. The bar in this 16th-century pub has oak beams, an inglenook, leather sofas, newspapers and a computer for those who still need to surf the net over a pint of Greene King or cup of hot chocolate. The informal restaurant offers a traditional pub menu, with ham, egg and chips, fillet of beef stroganoff, and succulent steaks.

Open 12-2.30 4.30-11.30 (Fri 12–2, 4.30–12, Sat 12–12, Sun 12–10.30) **Bar Meals** L served all week 12–2.30 D served Tue-Sat 6–9.30 (Sun 12–5) Av main course £8 **Restaurant** L served all week 12–2.30 D served Tue-Sat 6–9.30 (Sun 12–5) Av 3 course à la carte £21 ⊕ Greene King ◀ Greene King IPA & Abbot Ales, Guinness. ♀8 **Facilities** Children's licence Garden Dogs allowed Parking Play Area

---

WESTON   MAP 12 TL23

The Rising Sun ♀

21 Halls Green SG4 7DR

☎ 01462 790487 📠 01462 790846

e-mail: therisingsun@hotmail.co.uk

dir: A1(M) junct 9 take A6141 towards Baldock. Turn right towards Graveley. In 100yds take 1st left.

Set in picturesque Hertfordshire countryside, the Rising Sun offers a regularly changing menu. Starters include stilton mushrooms, and salmon fishcakes with dill sauce. Main courses include chargrilled steaks, salmon with dill and mustard sauce, or smoked fish crumble. A huge choice of sweets, and blackboard specials change daily. The owners say that their pub may be hard to find on your first visit, but that it's well worth the trouble.

Open 11–2.30 6–11 (Sat-Sun all day Apr-Sep) **Bar Meals** L served all week 12–1.45 D served all week 6–8.45 (Sun 12–7.45) **Restaurant** L served all week 12–1.45 D served all week 6–8.45 (Sun 12–7.45) ⊕ McMullens ◀ McMullen Original AK Ale, Macs Country Best. **Facilities** Garden Dogs allowed Parking Play Area

PICK OF THE PUBS

WILLIAN-HERTFORDSHIRE

The Fox

Around 250 years old, the Fox is opposite the village pond and next to the parish church. Its previous names were several: it was the Orange Tree until 1867, then the Dinsdale Arms (after the family who owned the village), then the Willian Arms.

In 2004 businessman Cliff Nye took it over, his second venture in the hospitality trade after a very successful start in north Norfolk. The building was immaculately restyled with flair and creativity, the bar modern but laid back with local artists' work on display, and a glazed atrium ceiling on the restaurant extension. Outside are a Spanish-style courtyard and two beer gardens, a good indication that this gastro-pub is also a welcoming watering hole; the range of beers includes real ales and a weekly guest, supported by over a dozen wines served by the glass. Young and friendly staff serve food from the daily-changing menu, which includes fish and shellfish introduced by the Norfolk connection: Cyril's hand-picked Brancaster mussels in a marinière sauce; pan-fried grey mullet on a butternut squash; and herb-crusted fillet of plaice with sautéed new potatoes and courgettes. Chef's specials are always worth a look: spiced fish and crab cakes are served with mixed leaves and saffron mayonnaise; and a chargrilled T-bone steak is accompanied by hand-cut chips. A typical dinner menu offers starters like Letzer's smoked salmon with cucumber ribbons, capers and fresh black pepper; main courses such as roast crown of partridge wrapped in bacon served with a savoury bread and butter pudding and sweet sultana sauce; and desserts of caramelised pear pain perdu, with maple syrup drizzle and mascarpone.

@ ♥
MAP 12 TL23
Baldock Ln SG6 2AE
☎ 01462 480233
🖷 01462 676966
e-mail:
restaurant@foxatwillian.co.uk
web: www.foxatwillian.co.uk
dir: *A1(M) junct 9 towards Letchworth, 1st left to Willian, 0.5m on left*

Open 12–11 (Fri-Sat 12–12, Sun 12–10.30)
Bar Meals L served Mon-Sat 12–2 Av main course £12.50
Restaurant L served Mon-Sat 12–2 D served Mon-Sat 6.45–9.15 (Sun 12–2.45)
⊕ Free House ◀ Adnam Bitter & Broadside, Woodfordes Wherry, Fuller's London Pride, Timothy Taylor Landlord. ♥ 14
Facilities Children's licence Garden Dogs allowed Parking

WILLIAN

MAP 12 TL23

Pick of the Pubs

The Fox ◎ ♀

See Pick of the Pubs on opposite page

KENT

BIDDENDEN

MAP 07 TQ83

Pick of the Pubs

The Three Chimneys ♀

Biddenden Rd TN27 8LW ☎ 01580 291472

dir: *From A262 midway between Biddenden & Sissinghurst, follow Frittenden signs. (Pub seen from main road). Pub immediatley on left in hamlet of Three Chimneys*

The name of this 15th-century pub/restaurant is supposedly derived from trois chemins, which is what French prisoners during the Seven Years War (1756–63) called a nearby three-way road junction. Beyond this point was out of bounds, but a friendly sentry would light the candelabra in the window by the pub door to indicate that no English officials were inside. The prisoners could then safely slip in for a swift pint. The pub retains its original small-room layout, with low beams, wood-panelling, flagstone floors, old settles and warming fires. Food is freshly cooked to order from a menu featuring starters of marinated anchovy salad; sautéed chicken livers, mushrooms and bacon on toast; and garlic and herb bruschetta with roasted aubergine and peppers; and main courses such as roast fillet of cod with Icelandic prawns; duck leg confit with creamed potato, braised Puy lentils, chorizo and bacon; and grilled fillet steak.

Open 11.30–3 5.30–11 (Sun 12–3, 7–10.30) Closed: 25 Dec **Bar Meals** L served all week 12–1.50 D served Mon-Sat 6–9.45 (Sun 6.30–9) Av main course £15.95 **Restaurant** L served Mon-Sat 12–1.50 D served Mon-Sat 6.30–9.45 (Sun 12–2.30, 7–9) ⊕ Free House ◀ Adnams, Harveys Old & special. ♀ 10 **Facilities** Garden Dogs allowed Parking

BODSHAM GREEN

MAP 07 TR14

Pick of the Pubs

Froggies At The Timber Batts NEW

School Ln TN25 5JQ
☎ 01233 750237 📠 01233 750176
e-mail: joel@thetimberbatts.co.uk

dir: *4m E of Wye*

A venerable building dating to the 15th century, and a pub since 1747 after housing hop-growers who brewed for their own consumption. Named after a nearby wood yard, Froggies was added when French chef JoÎl Gross took it over in 2002. No surprise then that the wine list and dishes based on locally sourced produce are classically French. Seared scallops with lardons, and pan-fried duck foie gras with apricots are typical starters. Main courses encompass game from local shoots: roasted partridge with olives; pheasant poached in cider; and pan-fried venison saddle. A seafood platter can be provided with 48 hours notice. Desserts may include classic crème brûlée, and crêpes

Suzette. Or you could just enjoy a real ale in one of the beamed bars where log fires crackle in winter. A monthly evening of magic, a charity weekend in June, a firework display on Bastille Day, and countryside views from the garden are all added bonuses.

Open 12–3 6.30–12 (Sat-Sun all day summer) Closed: 25–26 Dec **Bar Meals** L served Mon-Sat 12–2.30 D served all week 7–9.30 (Sun 12.30–3) Av main course £15 **Restaurant** L served Mon-Sat 12–2.30 D served all week 7–9.30 (Sun 12.30–3) Av 3 course à la carte £30 ⊕ Free House ◀ Adnams, London Pride, Woodfordes Wherry. **Facilities** Garden Dogs allowed Parking

BOSSINGHAM

MAP 07 TR14

The Hop Pocket

The Street CT4 6DY ☎ 01227 709866 📠 01227 709866
e-mail: forgan50@aol.com

dir: *Telephone for directions*

Birds of prey and an animal corner for children are among the more unusual attractions at this family pub in the heart of Kent. Canterbury is only five miles away and the county's delightfully scenic coast and countryside are within easy reach. All meals are cooked to order, using fresh produce. Expect fish pie, supreme of chicken, spicy salmon, Cajun beef, chilli nachos and fish platter. Extensive range of sandwiches and omelettes.

Open 11–3 6.30–11 **Bar Meals** L served Tue-Sun 12–2.30 D served all week 7–9.15 (Sun 12–3, 6.30–9) **Restaurant** L served Tue-Sun 12–2 D served all week 7–9.15 ◀ London Pride, Shepherd Neame Admiral, Master Brew, Adnams. **Facilities** Garden Dogs allowed Parking

BRABOURNE

MAP 07 TR14

The Five Bells ♀

The Street TN25 5LP ☎ 01303 813334 📠 01303 814667
e-mail: fivebells@aol.com

dir: *5m E of Ashford*

A 16th-century free house pub surrounded by rolling hills and orchards and the perfect pit stop for walkers and cyclists. Originally a poor house, the old stocks are located across the road, while inside are whitewashed walls and a huge inglenook fireplace. An extensive menu and a range of popular daily specials include traditional steak and kidney pie; liver and bacon with sage and onion gravy; and fillet of salmon with creamed leeks and smoked salmon mash.

Open 11.30–3 6.30–11 **Bar Meals** L served all week 12–2 D served all week 6.30–9.30 Av main course £8 **Restaurant** L served all week 12–2 D served all week 6.30–9.30 (Sun 12–2.30) ⊕ Free House ◀ Shepherd Neame Master Brew, London Pride, Greene King IPA, Adnams. ♀ 12 **Facilities** Garden Dogs allowed Parking Play Area

PICK OF THE PUBS

BROOKLAND-KENT

The Royal Oak

The history of this marshland pub is well documented, right back to when it was built as a house in 1570. A succession of parish clerks and sextons lived here until 1736 when Jacob Ferriss took over on the death of his father. Young Ferriss, however, was obviously a bit of an entrepreneur and, with his rector's consent, added the role of ale-keeper to his job description.

His drinks licence recognised this non-secular calling by forbidding him to 'suffer ale to be tippled during divine service'. The job-sharing soon died out and it has been a pub ever since. The bar serves classic pub fare, along the lines of home-cooked honey-roast ham; steak and kidney pudding; and triple-decker toasted sandwiches. In the restaurant, regularly changing dishes draw on local, seasonal produce; available all-year round though are traditional roast beef (cooked rare) and, in weekly rotation, loin of pork, leg of Romney lamb or crown of turkey. Typical starters include smoked fish salad, deep-fried squid and grilled goats' cheese, with further main course possibilities of pheasant breasts stuffed with mushroom duxelle wrapped in bacon; mixed seafood herb pancake; trio of handmade sausages; and Mediterranean vegetables with spicy couscous. Among the puddings might be crumble of the day, toffee crème brûlée, or honeycomb crunch ice cream. A well-kept and tranquil garden borders the churchyard of St Augustine, one of only four in England with a separate bell tower. Romney Marsh has several more remarkable medieval churches.

MAP 07 TQ92
High St TN29 9QR
☎ 01797 344215
e-mail: dzrj@btinternet.com
dir: *A259, 5m E of Rye. In village by church*

Open 12–3 6–11 Closed: Sun eve
Bar Meals L served Mon-Sat
12–2.30 D served Mon-Sat
6.30–9.30
Restaurant L served all week
12–2.30 D served Mon-Sat
6.30–9.30
⊕ Enterprise Inns ◀ Harvey's
Best Bitter, Adnams Best Bitter.
♥ 8
Facilities Garden Dogs allowed
Parking
Rooms available

BROOKLAND

MAP 07 TQ92

Pick of the Pubs

The Royal Oak ♥

See Pick of the Pubs on opposite page

Pick of the Pubs

Woolpack Inn

See Pick of the Pubs on page 308

BURHAM

MAP 06 TQ76

The Golden Eagle

80 Church St ME1 3SD ☎ 01634 668975
e-mail: kathymay@btconnect.com
web: www.thegoldeneagle.org
dir: *S from M2 junct 3 or N from M20 junct 6 on A229, signs to Burham*

This popular free house has every appearance of a traditional English inn, set on the North Downs with fine views of the Medway Valley. What sets it apart is its 20-year history of serving oriental food. The chef's specialities are spare ribs, mee goreng, king prawn sambal, wortip crispy chicken, and sweet and sour crispy pork. Banana split and chocolate fudge cake are among the more occidental puddings. Vegetarians are well catered for.

Open 11.30–3 6.30–11 Closed: 25–26 Dec **Bar Meals** L served Mon-Sat 12–2 D served Mon-Sat 7–10 (Sun 12–2.30, 7–9.30) Av main course £7.95 **Restaurant** L served Mon-Sat 12–2 D served Mon-Sat 7–10 (Sun 12–2.30, 7–9.30) Av 3 course fixed price £14 ⊕ Free House ⬤ Wadworth 6X, Boddingtons. **Facilities** Parking

CANTERBURY

MAP 07 TR15

The Chapter Arms ♥

New Town St, Chartham Hatch CT4 7LT ☎ 01227 738340
e-mail: david.durell@vmicombox.co.uk
dir: *3m from Canterbury. Off A28 in Chartham Hatch or A2 at Upper Harbledown*

A charming and picturesque free house, now in new hands, in over an acre of gardens overlooking apple orchards. It was once three cottages owned by Canterbury Cathedral's Dean and Chapter – hence the name. Any day's menu might offer Kentish lamb stew; chicken Kiev; pan-fried Scottish steak; or grilled halibut and king prawns. On Sundays, there's beef suet pudding, and steak and kidney pie. Live Sixties music and jazz evenings are popular.

Open 11–3 6.30–11 (Summer Sat-Sun & BH all day) Closed: 25 Dec eve **Bar Meals** L served Mon-Sat 12–2 D served all week 6.30–9 (Sun 12–4) **Restaurant** L served all week 12–2 D served Mon-Sat 7–9 (Closed Sun eve) ⊕ Free House ⬤ Shepherd Neame Master Brew, guest ales. ♥ 10 **Facilities** Garden Dogs allowed Parking Play Area

Pick of the Pubs

The Dove Inn ◉ ♥

Plum Pudding Ln, Dargate ME13 9HB
☎ 01227 751360 🗎 01227 751360
e-mail: pipmacgrew@hotmail.com
dir: *5m NW of Canterbury, A299 Thanet Way, turn off at Lychgate service station*

Between Faversham and Whitstable, tucked away in a sleepy hamlet and surrounded by orchards and farmland. The Dove is a splendid Victorian country pub with a reputation for well-kept Shepherd Neame ales and good food based on locally sourced ingredients. The interior is simple and relaxed, with stripped wooden floors and scrubbed tables. Outside is a large formal garden where, appropriately, a dovecote and doves present an agreeably scenic backdrop when sampling a quiet pint. The menu is refreshingly brief with half a dozen choices at each stage, but succeeds in offering something for everyone: seared scallops with crispy smoked bacon and vanilla and parsnip purée is an irresistible starter; this could be followed by chump of lamb with braised pearl barley and black cabbage. Choose from desserts such as orange tart with vanilla mascarpone, or caramelised apple with toasted brioche and Calvados crème fraîche.

Open 11–3 6–11 (Fri 12–11) Closed: Mon **Bar Meals** L served Tue-Sat 12–2.30 D served Tue-Sat 7–9.30 (Sun 12–4) Av main course £16 **Restaurant** L served Tue-Sat 12–2.30 D served Tue-Sat 7–9.30 (Sun 12–4) Av 3 course à la carte £30 ⊕ Shepherd Neame ⬤ Shepherd Neame Master Brew & Spitfire. ♥ 8 **Facilities** Children's licence Garden Dogs allowed Parking

PICK OF THE PUBS

BROOKLAND-KENT

Woolpack Inn

Surrounded by the dykes and reed beds of Romney Marsh, this remote 15th-century inn is an ideal place to finish a walk, perhaps with a glass of real ale and a hearty meal.

The Woolpack Inn is a lovely old whitewashed building dating back more that 600 years. It is believed there was once a secret tunnel through which smugglers could escape from pursuing Excise men. It is ideally situated for those exploring this unique and beautiful part of Kent with many walks in the area to study nature, go fishing or just to stop, think and let the world go by. The place oozes charm and character with an old spinning wheel, which was used to divide up the smugglers' contraband, still mounted from the ceiling. Open beams, some of which came from local shipwrecks, and an inglenook fireplace, with a roaring log fire in winter, add to the atmosphere. Outside there are two beer gardens with lawns, shrubs,

hanging baskets, picnic benches and a barbecue area – perfect for families. The wholesome home-made food is prepared by cooks, not celebrity chefs. The portions are of a sensible size, offering excellent value. Sandwiches and jacket potatoes are always available, while main meals include half a pheasant with shallots, apples and apricots in a white wine and cream sauce; a wealth of steak options; spaghetti bolognese; and moules marinière with a crusty baguette. There is also a wide choice of vegetarian dishes such as lasagne or stilton and vegetable bake. For dessert, why not smuggle in another treat with the likes of bread and butter pudding or hot chocolate fudge cake?

MAP 07 TQ92
Beacon Ln TN29 9TJ
☎ 01797 344321
web:
www.thewoolpackbrookland.co.uk
dir: *1.5m past Brookland towards Rye on A259*

Open 11–3 6–11 (Sat 11–11, Sun 12–10.30)
Bar Meals L served Mon-Fri 12–2.30 D served Mon-Fri 6–9 (Sat-Sun 12–9)
⊕ Shepherd Neame
◀ Shepherd Neame Spitfire Premium Ale & Master Brew Bitter.
Facilities Garden Dogs allowed Parking Play Area

CANTERBURY continued

Pick of the Pubs

The Granville ♟

St End, Lower Hardres CT4 7AL

☎ 01227 700402 📄 01227 700925

dir: *On B2068, 2m from Canterbury towards Hythe*

Named after the Tudor warship, the Granville is a handsome solid building firmly anchored in the ancient village of Lower Hardres, just a five-minute drive from Canterbury city centre. With ample parking, a patio and large beer garden at the rear where summer barbecues take place, this Shepherd Neame pub is an ideal family venue, and dogs too are made welcome. Nevertheless this is not a place for pub grub. The short but lively menu is designed for sophisticated tastebuds, offering for starters the likes of rock oysters with shallot vinegar, smoked local wigeon (a small wild duck) with mustard fruits, and antipasti. Main courses always comprise three meat and three fish dishes: slow-roast Waterham Farm chicken with truffle cream sauce, and Dungeness brill fillet braised in Macvin and morels are two examples. There is no children's menu as such, but portions from the main menu can be served where appropriate.

Open 12–3 5.30–11 (Sun 12–10.30) Closed: 25–26 Dec
Bar Meals L served Tue-Sun 12–2.30 Av main course £13.95
Restaurant L served Tue-Sat 12–2 D served Tue-Sat 7–9 (Sun 12–2.30) Av 3 course à la carte £27 ⊕ Shepherd Neame ◀ Masterbrew and 1 seasonal ale. ♟ 6 **Facilities** Garden Dogs allowed Parking

The Old Coach House ♟

A2 Barnham Downs CT4 6SA

☎ 01227 831218 📄 01227 831932

e-mail: fairestltd@aol.com

dir: *7m S of Canterbury on A2. Turn at Jet petrol station.*

A former stop on the original London to Dover coaching route, and listed in the 1740 timetable, this inn stands some 300 metres from the Roman Way. Noteworthy gardens with home-grown herbs and vegetables, weekend spit-roasts, and unabashed continental cuisine mark it as an auberge in the finest Gallic tradition. Food options include seafood, venison and other game in season, plus perhaps rib of beef with rosemary, and grilled lobster with brandy sauce.

Open 4–11 **Bar Meals** D served all week 6.30–9 Av main course £7.50
Restaurant D served all week 6.30–9 Av 3 course à la carte £24 Av 2 course fixed price £18.50 ⊕ Free House ◀ Interbrew Whitbread Best Bitter. ♟ 5 **Facilities** Garden Parking

Pick of the Pubs

The Red Lion ♟

High St, Stodmarsh CT3 4BA

☎ 01227 721339 📄 01227 721339

e-mail: tiptop-redlion@hotmail.com

dir: *From Canterbury take A257 towards Sandwich, left into Stodmarsh*

Known to locals as The Old Junk Shop because of its impressively cluttered interior, the Red Lion was built in 1475 and until relatively recently was surrounded by hop fields. Fresh flowers adorn the tables, along with bric-a-brac that ranges from an antique sewing machine to the stuffed head of a water buffalo. Lunches are served daily, with Sunday roasts alternating weekly between beef, pork and lamb. Among the fish dishes might be baked sea bass with fresh tarragon and lime; pan-fried scallops and baby leeks; or Bantry Bay mussels with roasted peppers and free-range chicken chunks. Dishes tend to be seasonal and locally sourced: Stodmarsh lamb perhaps, or casseroled rabbit. Desserts are equally hearty, along the lines of a pineapple and Malibu crumble. Or you could simply enjoy a pint of Old Speckled Hen by the fire.

Open 10.30–11.30 **Bar Meals** L served Mon-Sat 12–2.15 D served all week 7–9.15 (Sun L 2 sittings, 12 & 2) **Restaurant** L served Mon-Sat 12–9.15 D served all week 7–9.15 (Sun 12–2.30) Av 3 course à la carte £22 ⊕ Free House ◀ Greene King IPA, Ruddles County, Speckled Hen. ♟ 7 **Facilities** Children's licence Garden Dogs allowed Parking Play Area

Pick of the Pubs

The White Horse Inn ⊛ ♟

53 High St, Bridge CT4 5LA

☎ 01227 832814 📄 01227 832814

dir: *3m S of Canterbury, just off A2*

This medieval and Tudor building was originally a staging post close to a ford on the main Dover to Canterbury road, and still provides a stirling service to modern travellers. An enormous log fire burning in the beamed bar during the winter months provides a guaranteed warm welcome, whilst the extensive garden is popular for al fresco dining on warmer days. Fullers and Shepherd Neame are amongst the real ales served in the bar, with up to ten wines available by the glass. You'll find a strong emphasis on food, with seasonal dishes created from the best local ingredients. Choose between the relaxed blackboard bar menu, and more formal dining in the restaurant.

Open 11–3 6–11 (Sun 12–5) Closed: 25 Dec, 1 Jan
Bar Meals L served Tue-Sun 12–2 D served Tue-Sat 6.30–9
Restaurant L served Tue-Sun 12–2 D served Tue-Sat 7–9 ◀ Shepherd Neame Masterbrew, Greene King Abbot Ale, Fuller's London Pride, Greene King IPA. ♟ 10 **Facilities** Garden Parking

England

CHARING   MAP 07 TQ94

The Bowl Inn ♟

Egg Hill Rd TN27 0HG ☎ 01233 712256 📄 01233 714705
e-mail: info@bowl-inn.co.uk

dir: *M20 junct 8/9, take A20 to Charing then take A252 towards Canterbury. Left at top of Charing Hill down Bowl Road, 1.25m*

Built as a farmhouse in 1512, the Bowl stands on top of the North Downs, high above Charing. The small but varied menu of mostly traditional country pub snacks includes Kent-cured ham, English cheddar ploughman's, and hot bacon and sausage sandwiches. Relax in front of the huge old inglenook fireplace and play pool on an unusual rotating hexagonal table, dominoes or shut-the-box. Even in summer, if necessary, the south-facing sun terrace is covered and heated.

Open 4–11.30 (Fri-Sun 12–11.30) **Bar Meals** L served Fri-Sun 12–9.30 D served all week 12–9.30 ⊕ Free House ◀ Fuller's London Pride, Adnams Southwold, Harveys Sussex Best, Whitstable IPA. ♟ 8 **Facilities** Garden Dogs allowed Parking

---

CHIDDINGSTONE   MAP 06 TQ54

Pick of the Pubs

Castle Inn ♟

See Pick of the Pubs on opposite page

CHILHAM   MAP 07 TR05

The White Horse ♟

The Square CT4 8BY ☎ 01227 730355

dir: *Take A28 from Canterbury then A252, 1m turn left*

One of the most photographed pubs in Britain, The White Horse stands next to St Mary's church facing onto the 15th-century village square, where the May Fair is an annual event. The pub offers a traditional atmosphere and modern cooking from a monthly-changing menu based on fresh local produce. Dishes include fillet steak poached in red wine, and cod and smoked haddock fishcakes served with a sweet chilli sauce.

Open 11–11 breakfast 8.30–10 (Sun 12–10.30, Jan-Feb 12–3, 7–11) **Bar Meals** L served all week 12–3 D served Tue-Sat 5.30–9 ⊕ Free House ◀ Flowers Original, Fuller's London Pride, Greene King Abbot Ale, Adnams Best. **Facilities** Garden

---

CHILLENDEN   MAP 07 TR25

Pick of the Pubs

Griffins Head ♟

See Pick of the Pubs on page 312

DARTFORD   MAP 06 TQ57

The Rising Sun Inn ★★★ INN ♟

Fawkham Green, Fawkham DA3 8NL
☎ 01474 872291 📄 01474 872779

dir: *0.5m from Brands Hatch Racing Circuit & 5m from Dartford*

A pub since 1702, The Rising Sun stands on the green in a picturesque village not far from Brands Hatch. Inside you will find an inglenook log fire and a cosy restaurant. Starters include crispy soy duck; stilton and bacon field mushrooms; and tempura tiger prawns. Follow with pork loin with honey and herb crust; Portuguese chicken piri-piri; or sea bass fillets with mango and garlic beurre. There is also an extensive range of steaks.

Open 11.30–11 **Bar Meals** L served all week 12–9.30 D served Mon-Sat 6.30–9.30 (Sun 12–9) **Restaurant** L served Mon-Sat 12–2.15 D served Mon-Sat 6.30–9.30 (Sun 12–9) ⊕ Free House ◀ Courage Best, Courage Directors, London Pride, Timothy Taylor Lanlords. ♟ 7 **Facilities** Garden Parking **Rooms** 5

DEAL   MAP 07 TR35

The King's Head

9 Beach St CT14 7AH ☎ 01304 368194 📄 01304 364182
e-mail: booking@kingsheaddeal.co.uk

dir: *A249 from Dover to Deal, on seafront*

Traditional 18th-century seaside pub, overlooking the seafront and situated in one of the south-east's most picturesque coastal towns. Deal's famous Timeball Tower is a few yards away and the pub is within easy reach of Canterbury, Walmer Castle and the Channel Tunnel. Bar meals include steaks, sandwiches and seafood, and there is a daily-changing specials board.

Open 10–11 (Sun 12–10.30) **Bar Meals** L served all week 11–2.30 D served all week 6–9 (Jun-Sep 11–9) Av main course £5.95 ⊕ Free House ◀ Shepherd Neame Master Brew, Spitfire, Fuller's London Pride. **Facilities** Garden Dogs allowed Play Area **Rooms** available

Castle Inn

Glance at the mellow exterior of the Castle Inn, and it's easy to see why this charming old building has starred in films as diverse as Elizabeth R, Room with a View, The Life of Hogarth and The Wicked Lady. The interior is equally photogenic, with its heavy beams, nooks and crannies, period furniture and curios.

Outside, you'll find the vine-hung courtyard and Garden Bar, whilst across a bridge lies the lawn with its beautifully tended flowerbeds. The Castle Inn is first mentioned in 1420, when it was known as Waterslip House; Thomas Weller bought the building in 1712, and began selling ale in about 1730. Today, you can sample Larkins Traditional and Larkins Porter, brewed just up the road at Larkins Farm. The wine list runs to well over 100 bins, while whisky lovers can, preferably over time, work their way through 30 malts from Aberlour to Tomintoul. The bar menu offers soup with ciabatta bread; beef or smoked salmon open sandwiches; and a range of hot dishes that includes pie and mash; chilli con carne with rice; and a

daily vegetarian pasta. The more sophisticated restaurant menu starts with smoked Lock Fyne salmon; deep fried brie with mixed leaves and cranberry sauce; and melon and Parma ham. Main course options include poached lemon sole with prawn and white wine sauce; duck breast with dauphinoise potatoes and plum relish; and wild mushroom, baby spinach and Madeira risotto with freshly shaved parmesan. Round things off with crepes Suzette; panacotta with Bailey's; or home-made apple strudel with clotted cream.

MAP 06 TQ54
TN8 7AH
☎ 01892 870247
🖷 01892 871420
e-mail: info@castleinn.co.uk
dir: *1.5m S of B2027 between Tonbridge & Edenbridge*

Open 11–11
Bar Meals L served Mon-Sat 11–6 D served all week 7–9.30 (Sun 12–6 & 7–9.30)
Restaurant L served Thu-Mon 12–2 D served Wed-Mon 7–9.30
⊕ Free House ◖ Larkins Traditional, Harveys Sussex, Young's Ordinary, Larkins Porter.
♀ 10
Facilities Children's licence Garden Dogs allowed

Griffins Head

A Kentish Wealden hall house, dating from 1286 when Edward I was on the throne. It was once occupied by the monks of All Saints Church who farmed the surrounding land until 1539, when Henry VIII's dissolution of the monasteries brought their occupation to an end. After that it reverted to being a farm again, and remained so until the mid-18th-century.

It was given a full licence to sell alcohol to coincide with the arrival of coaches on the main Canterbury to Deal road. Inside is evidence of its long history, with inglenook fireplaces and beamed bars among many original features. Fine Kentish ales and home-made food have helped this old inn to make its mark with visitors as well as locals, among them Kent's cricketing fraternity. The menu is typically English, and specialises in game from local estates in season, and locally caught fish where possible. Typical dishes include lamb stew, braised steak, onions and mash, mussels marinière, and prawn chowder. Warm salads are another house speciality, and these might range from steak and roasted vegetable to a lightweight summer meal like sautéed prawn, squid, or scallops in garlic butter, all with salad. Other traditional pub dishes include lasagna, cottage pie, and ham, egg and chips. Desserts are also well worth trying, and these might vary from apple crumble or fruit pie on cooler days to chocolate chiller thriller; chocolate nemesis; raspberry almond torte; or home-made ice creams like passionfruit, ginger, or raspberry and strawberry. Outside is a very pretty garden where drinkers and diners can linger at their leisure. A vintage car club meets here on the first Sunday of every month.

♀
MAP 07 TR25
CT3 1PS
☎ 01304 840325
🖹 01304 841290
dir: *A2 from Canterbury towards Dover, then B2046. Village on right*

Open 10.30–11
Bar Meals L served all week 12–2 D served Mon-Sat 7–9.30
Restaurant L served Sun-Fri 12–2 D served Mon-Sat 7–9.30
⊕ Shepherd Neame
🍺 Shepherd Neame. ♀ 10
Facilities Garden Parking

DOVER
MAP 07 TR34

The Clyffe Hotel ♀

High St, St Margaret's at Cliffe CT15 6AT

☎ 01304 852400 📠 01304 851880

e-mail: stay@theclyffehotel.com

dir: *3m NE of Dover*

Quaint Kentish clapperboard building dating back to the late 16th century. In its time it has been a shoemaker's and an academy for young gentlemen. Just a stone's throw from the Saxon Shore Way and the renowned White Cliffs of Dover. The main bar and neatly furnished lounge lead out into the delightful walled rose garden. Seared fillet of tuna and lightly steamed halibut are among the seafood specialities; other options include pan-fried chicken breast and penne pasta.

Open 11–12 (Sat-Sun 11-1am) **Bar Meals** L served all week 12–2.30 D served Mon-Sat 6–9.30. Av main course £9 **Restaurant** L served all week 12–2.30 D served Mon-Sat 6–9.30 Av 3 course à la carte £22 ⊕ Free House ⬛ Interbrew Bass, Boddingtons, Fuller's London Pride. ♀30 **Facilities** Children's licence Garden Dogs allowed Parking Play Area

FAVERSHAM
MAP 07 TR06

Shipwrights Arms ♀

Hollowshore ME13 7TU ☎ 01795 590088

dir: *A2 through Ospringe then right at rdbt. Right at T-junct then left opposite Davington School, follow signs*

Step back in time to this remote pub on the Swale marshes, first licensed in 1738, and once a favourite with sailors and fishermen waiting to dock in Faversham. The pub still draws its water from a well. Examine the maritime artefacts in the many nooks and crannies, while downing a gravity-fed, Kent-brewed cask ale. Home-cooked food includes locally caught fish in season, and English pies and puddings during the winter.

Open 12–3 6–11 (Sun 6–10.30) Closed: Mon (Oct-Mar) **Bar Meals** L served Tue-Sat 12–2.30 D served Tue-Sat 7–9 Av main course £8.25 **Restaurant** L served Tue-Sun 12–2.30 D served Tue-Sat 12–2.30 ⊕ Free House ⬛ Local ales. **Facilities** Garden Dogs allowed Parking

FOLKESTONE
MAP 07 TR23

The Lighthouse Inn ♀

Old Dover Rd, Capel le Ferne CT18 7HT

☎ 01303 223300 📠 01303 842270

dir: *Telephone for directions*

Perched on the edge of Dover's famous White Cliffs, with sweeping Channel views, the Lighthouse began as an ale house in 1840, later

becoming, successively, a billiard hall, convalescent home, psychiatric hospital and country club, while more recently still Channel Tunnel builders headquartered here. Most food is home made, from traditional bar meals like chilli con carne, to items on the carte and specials board, both of which offer a good choice of fish dishes.

Open 11–11 (Sun 11-10.30) **Bar Meals** L served all week 12–2.30 D served all week 6–9 (Sun 12–8.30) **Restaurant** L served all week 12–2.30 D served all week 6–9 (Sun 12–8) Av 3 course à la carte £20 Av 3 course fixed price £9.95 ⊕ Oxford Hotels ⬛ Abbot Ale, IPA & guest ales. ♀8 **Facilities** Children's licence Garden Parking Play Area

FORDCOMBE
MAP 06 TQ54

Chafford Arms ♀

TN3 0SA ☎ 01892 740267 📠 01892 740703

e-mail: bazzer@chafford-arms.fsnet.co.uk

dir: *On B2188 (off A264) between Tunbridge Wells & East Grinstead*

A lovely, mid-19th-century tile-hung village pub. Demand never flags for starters of smoked Weald trout with horseradish, and deep-fried mushrooms with garlic dip, nor indeed does it for main courses such as steaks, chicken Kiev, and signature dishes like hot and cold seafood platter for two, grilled lemon sole, prawn provençale, and courgette and aubergine cannelloni.

Open 11.45–11 (Sat all day) **Bar Meals** L served all week 12.30–2.15 D served Tue-Sat 7.15–9.15 Av main course £6.95 **Restaurant** L served all week 12.30–2.15 D served Tue-Sat 7.15–9.15 ⊕ Enterprise Inns ⬛ Larkins Bitter, Wadworth 6X. ♀9 **Facilities** Garden Dogs allowed Parking

GOODNESTONE
MAP 07 TR25

The Fitzwalter Arms NEW ♀

The Street CT3 1PJ ☎ 01304 840303

dir: *Signed from B2046 & A2*

The 'Fitz', hostelry to the Fitzwalter Estate, has been a pub since 1702. Quintessentially English, it is a place of conviviality and conversation. Jane Austen was a frequent visitor to nearby Goodnestone Park after her brother, Edward, married into the family. On the menu, roast loin of pork with sticky rib, crackling and apple sauce; pan-fried black bream fillet with squid and gremolata; and leek and Lincolnshire poacher gratin with pommery mustard sauce.

Open 12–3 6–11 (Fri-Sun all day) **Bar Meals** L served Wed-Sat & Mon 12–2 (Sun 12–2.30) **Restaurant** L served Wed-Sat & Mon 12–2 D served Wed- Sat & Mon 7–9 (Sun 12–2.30) Av 3 course à la carte £23 ⊕ Shepherd Neame ⬛ Masterbrew, Spitfire. ♀12 **Facilities** Garden

England

GOUDHURST   MAP 06 TQ73

Green Cross Inn

TN17 1HA ☎ 01580 211200 📠 01580 212905

dir: *A21 from Tonbridge towards Hastings turn left onto A262 towards Ashford. 2m, Goudhurst on right*

Food orientated pub in an unspoiled corner of Kent, originally built to serve the Paddock Wood-Goudhurst railway line, which closed in 1968. The dining-room is prettily decorated with fresh flowers, and the whole pub has been upgraded. Main courses in the bar range from home-made steak, kidney and mushroom pie with shortcrust pastry, to calves' liver and bacon Lyonnaise. Restaurant fish dishes might include fillet of turbot with spinach and a creamy cheese sauce.

Open 11–3 6–11 (Closed Sun eve winter) **Bar Meals** L served all week 12–2.30 D served Mon-Sat 7–9.45 Av main course £10 **Restaurant** L served all week 12–2.30 D served Mon-Sat 7–9.45 Av 3 course à la carte £22.50 ⊕ Free House ◀ Harveys Sussex Best Bitter, Guinness. **Facilities** Garden Parking

Pick of the Pubs

The Star & Eagle ★★★★ INN 🍷

High St TN17 1AL ☎ 01580 211512 📠 01580 212444

e-mail: starandeagle@btconnect.com

dir: *Just off A21 towards Hastings. Take A262 into Goudhurst. Pub at top of hill next to church*

A commanding position at 400 feet above sea level gives the 14th-century Star & Eagle outstanding views of the orchards and hop fields that helped earn Kent the accolade 'Garden of England'. The vaulted stonework suggests that this rambling, big-beamed building may once have been a monastery, and the tunnel from the cellars probably surfaces underneath the neighbouring parish church. These days, it's a place to unwind and enjoy fine traditional and continental food, prepared under the guidance of Spanish chef/proprietor Enrique Martinez. A typical meal might be field mushrooms stuffed with bacon and stilton; smoked salmon pasta with creamy dill sauce; and warm Belgian chocolate pudding. From his restaurant menu, possibilities include soup de poisson laced with brandy and fresh cream and Scottish rope mussels with chilli. Follow with pot-roast shoulder of lamb baked Spanish style; or sautéed calves' livers; and to finish, crepe Suzette with orange and chocolate ice cream.

Open 11–11 **Bar Meals** L served all week 12–2.30 D served Mon-Sat 7–9.30 (Sun 7–9) Av main course £12 **Restaurant** L served all week 12–2.30 D served Mon-Sat 7–9.30 (Sun 7–9) Av 3 course à la carte £30 Av 3 course fixed price £22 ⊕ Free House ◀ Adnams Bitter, Harvey's & Grasshopper. 🍷24 **Facilities** Garden Parking **Rooms** 8

GRAVESEND   MAP 06 TQ67

The Cock Inn

Henley St, Luddesdowne DA13 0XB

☎ 01474 814208 📠 01474 812850

e-mail: andrew.r.turner@btinternet.com

dir: *Telephone for directions*

Seven handpumps deliver a wonderful array of well-kept real beers at this traditional English alehouse in the beautiful Luddesdowne Valley. Woodburning stoves in the two bars with exposed beams set the warm ambience, with not a fruit machine, jukebox or television in sight. Orders for excellent home-made food (pies, scampi, rib of beef) are taken at the bar; there is no dedicated restaurant, so table reservations cannot be made. No children under 18.

Open 12–11 (Sun 12–10.30) **Bar Meals** L served all week 12–3 D served Mon-Sat 6–9 Av main course £7.50 ⊕ Free House ◀ Adnams Southwold, Adnams Broadside Shepherd Neame Masterbrew, Goacher's Real Mild Ale & Woodfordes Wherry. **Facilities** Garden Dogs allowed Parking

HARRIETSHAM   MAP 07 TQ85

The Pepper Box Inn 🍷

ME17 1LP ☎ 01622 842558 📠 01622 844218

e-mail: pbox@nascr.net

dir: *From A20 in Harrietsham take Fairbourne Heath turn. 2m to x-rds, straight over, 200yds, pub on left*

A delightful 15th-century country pub enjoys far-reaching views over the Weald of Kent from its terrace, high up on the Greensand Ridge. The pub takes its name from an early type of pistol, a replica of which hangs behind the bar. Typical dishes might include pot-roasted lamb shanks, local seasonal game, sea bass and Thai-style monkfish.

Open 11–3 6.30–11 **Bar Meals** L served all week 12–2.15 D served Tue-Sat 7–9.45 (Sun 12–3) Av main course £10.50 **Restaurant** L served Tue-Sat 12–2 D served Tue-Sat 7–9.45 ⊕ Shepherd Neame ◀ Shepherd Neame Master Brew, Spitfire, seasonal ales. 🍷6 **Facilities** Garden Dogs allowed Parking

HAWKHURST
MAP 07 TQ73

Pick of the Pubs

The Great House ♥

Gills Green TN18 5EJ

☎ 01580 753119 📄 01622 851881

e-mail: enquiries@thegreathouse.net

dir: *Just off A229 between Cranbrook & Hawkhurst*

The Great House is a wonderfully atmospheric 16th-century free house with a warm and comfortable ambience. There are three dining areas to choose from, and the Orangery which opens onto a Mediterranean-style terrace overlooking a pretty garden. From the bar menu who can choose bangers and mash, liver and bacon, or or one of various ploughman's. Alongside the deli board selection (cheese, fish, antipasti, charcuterie), there are starters of pan-seared scallops, say, or traditional Mediterranean fish soup, which may be followed by braised lamb shank with seasonal root vegetables; fish pie; pr slow-roast pork belly with a rich claret sauce. Imaginative desserts might take in warm chocolate and nuts brownies with chocolate sauce, or lavender crème brûlée. Part of the pub has been transformed into a deli/farmers' market.

Open 11–11 (Sun 11–10.30) **Bar Meals** L served all week 12–9.30 D served all week 12–9.30 Av main course £8.50 **Restaurant** L served all week 12–9.30 D served all week 12–9.30 Av 3 course à la carte £23 Av 2 course fixed price £11.95 ⊕ Free House ◀ Harveys, Guinness, Youngs & St Miguel. ♥ 13 **Facilities** Children's licence Garden Parking

The Queens Inn

Rye Rd TN18 4EY ☎ 01580 753577 📄 01580 754241

e-mail: info@thequeensinn.co.uk

dir: *In Hawkhurst, just off A21*

16th-century coaching inn with a wisteria-covered façade and an imposing entrance portico. Have a drink in the cosy reception area, the smart Wine Bar, the more cosmopolitan Piano Bar, the front garden, or heated courtyard. Seasonal menus offer snacks and salads, traditional English dishes, such as Guinness pie, and the more international pan-fried barramundi (Australia's favourite fish); mushroom, pinenut and coriander burrito; cannon of lamb en croûte; and tagliatelle carbonara.

Open 8.30–12 **Bar Meals** L served Mon-Sat 12–10 D served Mon-Sat 12–10 (Sun 12–8.30) **Restaurant** L served Sun 12–10 D served Fri-Sat 12–10 (Sun 12.30–8.30) Av 3 course à la carte £15 ⊕ Enterprise Inns ◀ Harveys Ale. **Facilities** Children's licence Garden Parking

HEVER
MAP 06 TQ44

The Wheatsheaf

Hever Rd, Bough Beech TN8 7NU ☎ 01732 700254

dir: *M25 & A21 take exit for Hever Castle & follow signs. 1m past Castle on right*

Originally built as a hunting lodge for Henry V, this splendid creeper-clad inn has some stunning original features. Timbered ceilings and massive stone fireplaces set off various curios, such as the mounted jaw of a man-eating shark, and a collection of musical instruments. There's a light lunch menu Monday to Friday (pie and mash; ploughman's), and a daily specials such as moules marinière followed

by oven-roasted guinea fowl breast with caramelised orange and ginger stuffing.

The Wheatsheaf

Open 11–11.30 **Bar Meals** L served all week 12–10 D served all week 12–10 **Restaurant** L served all week 12–10 D served all week 12–10 ⊕ Free House ◀ Harveys Sussex Bitter, Shepherd Neame, Greene King Old Speckled Hen, Grasshopper. **Facilities** Garden Dogs allowed Parking

HODSOLL STREET
MAP 06 TQ66

The Green Man

TN15 7LE ☎ 01732 823575

e-mail: the.greenman@btopenworld.com

dir: *On North Downs between Brands Hatch & Gravesend on A227*

Set in the picturesque village of Hodsoll Street on the North Downs, this family-run 300–year-old pub is loved for its decent food and real ales. Food is prepared to order using fresh local produce, and includes a wide variety of fish (especially on Wednesday, which is fish night). Curry takes centre stage on Thursday nights, while Tuesday night is steak night. Live music features every second Thursday of each month.

Open 11–2.30 6–11 (Fri-Sat 11–11, Sun 12–10.30) **Bar Meals** L served all week 12–2 D served Mon-Sat 6.30–9.30 (Sun 6.30–9) Av main course £10 **Restaurant** L served all week 12–2 D served Mon-Sat 6.30–9.30 (Sun 6.30–9) Av 2 course fixed price £10 ⊕ Enterprise Inns ◀ Fuller's London Pride, Harveys, Old Speckled Hen & guest ale. **Facilities** Children's licence Garden Dogs allowed Parking Play Area

IDEN GREEN
MAP 06 TQ73

The Peacock ♥

Goudhurst Rd TN17 2PB ☎ 01580 211233

dir: *A21 from Tunbridge Wells to Hastings, onto A262, pub 1.5m past Goudhurst*

Grade II listed building dating from the 14th century with low beams, an inglenook fireplace, old oak doors, real ales on tap, and a wide range of traditional pub food. A large enclosed garden with fruit trees and picnic tables on one side of the building is popular in summer, and there's also a patio.

Open 12–11 (Sun 12–10.30) **Bar Meals** L served all week 12–2.45 D served Mon-Sat 6–8.45 (Sun 12–3) Av main course £6.95 **Restaurant** L served all week D served all week ⊕ Shepherd Neame ◀ Shepherd Neame Master Brew, Spitfire and seasonal ales. ♥ 12 **Facilities** Garden Dogs allowed Parking

England

IGHTHAM
MAP 06 TQ55

Pick of the Pubs

The Harrow Inn 🍷

Common Rd TN15 9EB ☎ 01732 885912

dir: *1.5m from Borough Green on A25 to Sevenoaks, signed Ightham Common, turn left into Common Road, 0.25m on left.*

Within easy reach of both M20 and M26 motorways, yet tucked away down country lanes close to the National Trust's Knole Park and Ightham Mote, this Virginia creeper-hung stone inn dates back to the 17th century and beyond. The bar area comprises two rooms with a great brick fireplace, open to both sides and piled high with blazing logs; meanwhile the restaurant boasts a vine-clad conservatory that opens to a terrace that's ideal for summer dining. Menus vary with the seasons, and seafood is a particular speciality: fish aficionados can enjoy dishes such as crab and ginger spring roll; swordfish with Cajun spice and salsa; or pan-fried fillets of sea bass with lobster cream and spinach. Other main courses have included Bishop's Finger (one of Shepherd Neame's fine beers) baked sausage with gammon, fennel, red onions and garlic; and tagliatelle with a wild mushroom, fresh herb, lemongrass and chilli ragoût. Look out for the grass floor!

Open 12–3 6–11 (Sun eve & Mon) Closed: 26 Dec, 1 Jan
Bar Meals L served Tue-Sun 12–2 D served Tue-Sat 6–9
Restaurant L served Tue-Sun 12–2 D served Tue-Sat 6–9 Av 3 course à la carte £25 ⊕ Free House ◀ Greene King Abbot Ale, IPA. 🍷 8
Facilities Garden Parking

IVY HATCH
MAP 06 TQ55

Pick of the Pubs

The Plough at Ivy Hatch

High Cross Rd TN15 0NL ☎ 01732 810100

e-mail: enquiries@theploughpub.net

dir: *From M20 junct 2 take A20 then A227 through Ightham towards Tonbridge. Ivy Hatch 4.5m from Sevenoaks & 5m from Tonbridge*

When owner Michelle Booth took over the Plough in 2005, her aim was to showcase local produce and to reinstate the inn as 'an integral part of the local community'. Three years on, this cosy county pub is going from strength to strength. Set deep in Kent countryside, and just a quarter of a mile from the National Trust's 14th-century Ightham Mote, it's the perfect spot for a lingering lunch or supper. Food is sourced from nearby wherever possible, while wine, beer and bottled water alike derive from Kent. This eco-friendly attentiveness extends to the rubbish, which is all recycled. A typical menu might offer Kentish mussels in cider and cream, followed by roast local pheasant; casserole of wild rabbit; or slow roast pork belly with caramelised Hassleback apples and sage gravy. There's a terrace and garden ideal for al fresco dining.

Open 12–3 6.30–11 (summer 10–3, 5.30–11) **Bar Meals** L served all week 12–2.30 D served all week 6–9.30 (Sun 12–8) Av main course £8.95 **Restaurant** L served all week 12–2.30 D served all week 7–9.30 (Sun 12–8, summer brunch 10–12 all week) Av 3 course à la carte £23 Av 3 course fixed price £15 ⊕ Free House ◀ Harveys, Westerham & Larkins, Goachers. **Facilities** Garden Parking

LAMBERHURST
MAP 06 TQ63

The Swan at the Vineyard 🍷

The Down TN3 8EU ☎ 01892 890170
web: www.theswan.org
dir: *Telephone for directions*

Outside the Swan, which dates from the 1700s, is a beautiful floral display; inside there are open fireplaces and leather couches, and as many as three ghosts. There are two dining areas, one traditional, the other a 'cellar restaurant', with high-back leather chairs and an art gallery. A comprehensive menu features coq au vin; coconut and galangal Thai risotto with tiger prawns; and spinach and chanterelle lasagne. Try one of the award-winning English wines.

Open 12–11 **Bar Meals** L served Mon-Sat 12–2.15 D served all week 6–9.15 (Sun 12–3.30) Av main course £8.95 **Restaurant** L served Mon-Sat 12–2.15 D served all week 6–9.15 (Sun 12–3.30) Av 3 course à la carte £25 ◀ Harveys Best, Adnams Broadside, Bombardier, Adnams Regatta. 🍷 11
Facilities Garden Dogs allowed Parking Play Area

LEIGH
MAP 06 TQ54

The Greyhound Charcott 🍷

Charcott TN11 8LG ☎ 01892 870275
e-mail: GHatcharcott@aol.com
dir: *From Tonbridge take B245 N towards Hildenborough. Left onto Leigh road, right onto Stocks Green road. Through Leigh, right then left at T-junct, right into Charcott (Camp Hill)*

This cosy pub has been welcoming locals and visitors for around 120 years. Tony French, who took over four years ago, has maintained the traditional atmosphere in which music, pool table and fruit machine have no place. Winter brings log fires, while in summer you can enjoy the garden. Meals could include wild boar terrine with apple chutney, followed by local saddle of venison with roasted root vegetables and mashed potatoes. Well-kept real ales.

Open 12–3 5.30–12 (Sat-Sun 12–12) **Bar Meals** L served Mon-Sat 12–2 D served Mon-Sat 6.30–9.30 (Sun 12–6) Av main course £8.95 **Restaurant** L served Mon-Sat 12–2 D served Mon-Sat 6.30–9.30 (Sun 12–6) ⊕ Enterprise Inns ◀ Harvey, Black Sheep & Timothy Taylors Landlord. ☕ 8 **Facilities** Children's licence Garden Dogs allowed Parking

---

LINTON   MAP 07 TQ75

The Bull Inn ☕

Linton Hill ME17 4AW ☎ 01622 743612
e-mail: dominic@lintonbull.co.uk
dir: *S of Maidstone on A229 (Hastings road)*

A traditional 17th-century coaching inn in the heart of the Weald with stunning views from the glorious garden, and a large inglenook fireplace and wealth of beams inside. A tasty bar menu includes lasagna, spinach and ricotta tortellini, cod and chips, and bubble and squeak, as well as sandwiches, baguettes, and ploughman's. From the restaurant menu comes pan-fried venison steak wrapped in pancetta, served on sautéed oyster mushrooms.

Open 11–11 **Bar Meals** L served all week 12–3 D served Mon-Sun 7–10 (Sun 12–7) Av main course £8 **Restaurant** L served all week 12–3 D served all week 7–10 Av 3 course à la carte £8 ⊕ Shepherd Neame ◀ Shepherd Neame Master Brew & Spitfire, seasonal ale. ☕ 7 **Facilities** Garden Dogs allowed Parking

---

LITTLEBOURNE   MAP 07 TR25

King William IV

4 High St CT3 1UN
☎ 01227 721244 🖶 01227 721244
e-mail: sam@bowwindow.co.uk
dir: *From A2 follow signs to Howletts Zoo. After zoo & at end of road, pub straight ahead*

Located just outside the city of Canterbury, the King William IV overlooks the village green and is well placed for Sandwich and Herne Bay. With open log fires and exposed oak beams, this friendly inn is a good place for visitors and locals.

Open 11–11 (Sun 12–10.30) **Bar Meals** L served all week 12–2.30 D served Tue-Sat 6–9 Av main course £10 **Restaurant** L served all week 12–2.30 D served all week 6–9 ⊕ Free House ◀ John Smith's, Sussex Harveys. **Facilities** Parking

---

MAIDSTONE   MAP 07 TQ75

The Black Horse Inn ★ ★ ★ ★ INN ☕

Pilgrims Way, Thurnham ME14 3LD
☎ 01622 737185 🖶 01622 739170
e-mail: info@wellieboot.net
dir: *M20 junct 7, A249, right into Detling. Opposite Cock Horse Pub turn onto Pilgrims Way*

Tucked beneath the steep face of the North Downs on the Pilgrims Way, this homely and welcoming free house has an open log fire in winter. The building is thought to have been a forge before its conversion to an inn during the middle years of the 18th century. The bar and restaurant menus range from traditional favourites like steak and ale pudding to sea trout on saffron rice with roasted red onions.

Open 11–11 **Bar Meals** L served all week 12–6 D served all week 6–10 **Restaurant** L served all week 12–6 D served all week 6–10 ⊕ Free House ◀ Kents Best, London Pride, Greene King IPA, Black Sheep & Late Red. ☕ 30 **Facilities** Garden Dogs allowed Parking **Rooms** 16

MARKBEECH   MAP 06 TQ44

The Kentish Horse

Cow Ln TN8 5NT ☎ 01342 850493
dir: *3m from Edenbridge & 7m from Tunbridge Wells*

Surrounded by Kent countryside, this pub is popular with ramblers, cyclists and families. The inn dates from 1340 and is said to have a smuggling history; it also boasts a curious street-bridging Kentish sign. The menu is cooked simply from fresh ingredients, and can be served anywhere in the pub or garden. Under new management.

Open 12–11 (Sun 12–10.30) **Bar Meals** L served Mon-Sat 12–2.30 D served Mon-Sat 7–9.30 (Sun 12–3.30) **Restaurant** L served Mon-Sat 12–2.30 D served all week 7–9.30 (Sun 12–3.30) ◀ Harvey's Larkins, plus guest ales. **Facilities** Garden Dogs allowed Parking Play Area

---

NEWNHAM   MAP 07 TQ95

The George Inn ☕

44 The Street ME9 0LL ☎ 01795 890237 🖶 01795 890726
dir: *4m from Faversham*

The George is an attractive country inn with a large beer garden. Despite the passing of the centuries, the inn retains much of its historic character with beams, polished wooden floors, inglenook fireplaces and candlelit tables. Food is served in the bar and 50–seater restaurant. Bar snacks range from sandwiches to sausage and mash, while main meals could include pan-fried fillet of red snapper with crushed potatoes, baby fennel, fresh scampi and rosemary butter; or peppered duck breast with celeriac mash and cherry and port sauce. Regular events include live jazz, quizzes and murder mystery evenings.

Open 11–3 6.30–11 (Sun 12–4, 7–11) **Bar Meals** L served all week 12–2.15 D served all week 7–9.15 Av main course £12 **Restaurant** L served all week 12–2.15 D served all week 7–9.15 Av 3 course à la carte £25 ⊕ Shepherd Neame ◀ Shepherd Neame Master Brew, Spitfire, Bishops Finger, Kent Best & seasonal ale. ☕ 8 **Facilities** Garden Parking

England

PENSHURST

MAP 06 TQ54

Pick of the Pubs

The Bottle House Inn ♀

See Pick of the Pubs on opposite page

The Leicester Arms

High St TN11 8BT ☎ 01892 870551

dir: *From Tunbridge Wells take A26 towards Tonbridge. Left onto B21765 towards Penshurst*

Once part of the Penshurst Place estate, this picturesque establishment is named after Viscount De L'Isle, Earl of Leicester and grandson of the former owner. The dining room is worth a visit for its food and for its views over the weald and the river Medway. Dishes range from traditional bar bites to Ardennes paté with tomato and mozzarella salad and red pesto, followed by Hungarian goulash or game pie.

Open 11–11.30 **Bar Meals** L served all week 12–9.30 D served all week 12–9.30 **Restaurant** L served all week 12–9.30 D served all week 12–9.30 ⊕ Enterprise Inns ◀ Old Speckled Hen, Shepherd Neame, Master Brew, Fuller's London Pride. **Facilities** Garden Dogs allowed Parking

Pick of the Pubs

The Spotted Dog ♀

Smarts Hill TN11 8EE
☎ 01892 870253 📠 01892 870107
e-mail: info@spotteddogpub.co.uk
dir: *Off B2188 between Penshurst & Fordcombe*

When the trees are bare this 15th-century, typically Kentish weatherboarded pub enjoys fine views over the Weald from the rear terrace. In summer the trees are thick with foliage, but it's still a lovely spot for a drink or meal. The rambling interior cuts the mustard too, with beams, four open fireplaces, tiled and oak floors, and those little nooks and crannies that just seem to crop up in old pubs. Deciding where and what to eat is simple, as the single menu offers both traditional favourites and more sophisticated fare, and applies throughout the pub at lunchtimes and evenings. There are staples like ham, eggs and chips, and fish and chips, although some qualification might be necessary: the ham is honey-baked, the eggs free-range, and the fish is beer-battered cod. Otherwise there are starters like home-made chicken liver parfait with plum chutney, and mains of Kentish sausages with wholegrain mustard mash and red onion jus.

Open 11–3 6–11 (Seasonal times vary, ring for details)
Bar Meals L served all week 12–2.30 D served all week 6–9.30 (Sun 12–6) Av main course £8.95 **Restaurant** L served all week 12–2.30 D served all week 6–9.30 (Sun 12–6) ⊕ Free House ◀ Harveys Best, Larkins Traditional, guest ale. ♀ 9 **Facilities** Garden Dogs allowed Parking

PLUCKLEY

MAP 07 TQ94

Pick of the Pubs

The Dering Arms ♀

See Pick of the Pubs on page 320

The Mundy Bois ♀

Mundy Bois TN27 0ST
☎ 01233 840048 📠 01233 840193
e-mail: helen@mundybois.com
dir: *From A20 at Charing exit towards Pluckley. Right into Pinnock at bottom of Pluckley Hill. Next right into Mundy Bois Rd. 1m left*

An ale house since 1780 and formerly named the Rose and Crown, this creeper-clad pub is on the outskirts of Pluckley, considered to be the most haunted place in England. A blackboard menu features frequently changing dishes created from local produce where possible, and a nearby farm specializing in rare breeds. A patio dining area allows al fresco eating, and the garden has an adventure playground.

Open 11.30–3 6–11 (Sat 11.30–11) **Bar Meals** L served Mon-Sat 12–2 D served all week 6.30–9.30 (Sun 12–4) Av main course £7.95
Restaurant L served Wed -Sat 12–2.30 D served Wed-Thu 6.30–9 (Fri-Sat 6.30–9.30, Sun 12–4) Av 3 course à la carte £20 ⊕ Free House ◀ Master Brew, Youngs. ♀ 10 **Facilities** Garden Dogs allowed Parking Play Area

The Bottle House Inn

A well-regarded dining pub, the Bottle House was built as a farmhouse in 1492, and later divided into two properties. Thomas Scraggs, 'a common beer seller of Speldhurst', leased one of them in 1806 and obtained a license to sell ales and ciders.

It was registered as an alehouse at each subsequent change of hands, at a time when hop-growing was the major local industry. During the 19th century it also housed a shop, a farrier and a cobbler, and there was a skittle alley at the back. The pub was said to be the originator of the ploughman's lunch, made with bread from the old bakery next door and cheese donated by Canadian soldiers billeted near by. The building was completely refurbished in 1938 and granted a full licence; it was reputedly named after all the old bottles discovered during these works. Today, low beams and a copper-topped counter give the bar a warm, welcoming atmosphere. Choose from the range of Harveys hand-pumped beers and eight wines by the glass

before settling at a bench seat on the pergola-covered patio or in the garden. The menu has something for everyone, starting with several varieties of garlic bread. A dozen different starters encompass battered curried squid balls, and deep-fried sesame-coated brie. Main course choices are even more extensive, ranging from Indian spiced chicken kebab, to fillet of beef Wellington, to pheasant breast stuffed with wild boar paté. Fish dishes are well represented, with up to ten options including swordfish, skate, scampi, salmon and cod. Desserts include the ever-popular banoffee pie, fruits of the forest roulade, and sticky toffee pudding. A children's menu features favourite savouries served with baked beans and chips, with ice cream to follow.

MAP 06 TQ54
Coldharbour Rd TN11 8ET
☎ 01892 870306
🖷 01892 871094
e-mail: info@
thebottlehouseinnpenshurst.co.uk
web: www.
thebottlehouseinnpenshurst.co.uk
dir: *From Tunbridge Wells take A264 W, then B2188 N. After Fordcombe left towards Edenbridge & Hever. Pub 500yds after staggered x-rds*

Open 11–11 (Sun 11–10.30)
Closed: 25 Dec
Bar Meals L served Mon-Sat
12–10 D served Mon-Sat 12–10
(Sun 11.30–9)
Restaurant L served Mon-Sat
12–10 D served Mon-Sat 12–10
(Sun 11.30–9)
⊕ Free House ◼ Larkins Ale,
Harveys Sussex Best Bitter. ♛ 8
Facilities Children's licence
Garden Dogs allowed Parking

The Dering Arms

The elegant, well-appointed Dering Arms was built in the 1840s as a hunting lodge to serve the Dering Estate, which at that time was one of the largest estates in the area. The impressive building with its curved Dutch gables and uniquely arched windows was built as a smaller replica of the main manor house.

Inside you'll find two traditional bars, simply furnished and complete with roaring fires in winter. There's also an intimate restaurant, as well as a family room with a grand piano where customers are encouraged to try their hand. Chef/patron James Buss has managed this distinctive inn with passion and flair since 1984. "I run the kitchen personally", he explains, "in order to maintain the high standards I feel are essential." Everything is made on the premises, right down to the breakfast marmalade – the kitchen also makes good use of fresh vegetables from the family farm, and herbs from the pub garden. The extensive menus reflect James' own love of fresh fish and seafood. Starters could include pan-fried soft herring roes with crispy smoked bacon; grilled sardines with rosemary butter; or half a pint of prawns with home-made mayonnaise. Main course options feature blackboard specials like venison steak with potato and celeriac purée; casseroled guinea fowl with sherry and tarragon sauce; and black bream fillet with marsh samphire and beurre blanc. Desserts range from oranges in caramel with Grand Marnier, to chocolate fudge cake with warm walnut sauce. Black tie gourmet evenings are held throughout the winter, giving diners a chance to sample a seven-course meal of unusual and intriguing dishes. Of interest are the Classic Car meetings held every 2nd Sunday of the month from midday.

MAP 07 TQ94
Station Rd TN27 0RR
☎ 01233 840371
🖷 01233 840498
e-mail: jim@deringarms.com
dir: *M20 junct 8, A20 to Ashford. Right onto B2077 at Charing to Pluckley*

Open 11–3 6–11 Closed: 26–29 Dec
Bar Meals L served Tue-Sun 12–2 D served Tue-Sat 7–9.30
Restaurant L served Tue-Sun 12–2 D served Tue-Sat 7–9.30 Av 3 course à la carte £30
Free House Goacher's Dering Ale, Maidstone Dark, Gold Star, Old Ale. 7
Facilities Garden Dogs allowed Parking

ST MARGARET'S AT CLIFFE   MAP 07 TR34

Pick of the Pubs

The Coastguard

St Margaret's Bay CT15 6DY ☎ 01304 853176

e-mail: thecoastguard@talk21.com

dir: *2m off A258 between Dover & Deal, follow St Margarets at Cliffe signs. Through village towards sea*

St Margaret's Bay is one of the most delightful spots on the Kentish coast, with breathtaking white cliffs and beach walks, not to mention The Coastguard's famed food and hospitality. The pub stands only a stone's throw from the water's edge and has spectacular views out to sea. Its menu includes award-winning fish dishes such as roast skate wing with samphire and cockles or fresh fish pie. The cooking is imaginative and makes excellent use of local produce – perhaps sirloin beef steak from a local farm, seared on sea salt with garlic butter and served with double-fried chips and the pub's 'garden of Kent' fresh salad. Other typical dishes include hot devilled crab; sea bass roasted on pebbles with a seaweed dressing; and chargrilled aubergine with a basil, pine nut and parmesan crust served with roast ratatouille and Kentish new potatoes. Excellent wines, whiskies, bottled beers and real ales.

Open 11–11 **Bar Meals** L served all week 12.30–2.45 D served all week 6.30–8.45 Av main course £12 **Restaurant** L served all week 12.30–2.45 D served all week 6.30–8.45 ⊕ Free House ◀ Gadds of Ramsgate, Hop Daemon, Adnams, Caledonian. **Facilities** Garden Dogs allowed Parking Play Area

---

SANDWICH   MAP 07 TR35

George & Dragon Inn ♥

Fisher St CT13 9EJ ☎ 01304 613106 🖹 01304 621137

dir: *Between Dover & Canterbury*

An attractive, heavily beamed period pub/restaurant with plenty of character and close to the renowned Royal St Georges golf course, a favourite of James Bond creator Ian Fleming. A varied menu includes a good range of starters, followed by whole Dover sole, braised guinea fowl, smoked tuna steak, and lamb and potato vindaloo. Pizzas are prepared on the premises and cooked in a wood-burning oven, and there is a popular carvery on Sunday.

Open 11–3 6–11 (Sun 7–10.30) Closed: 25–26 Dec **Bar Meals** L served all week 12–2.15 D served Mon-Sat 6–9.15 (Sun 7–9.15) **Restaurant** L served all week 12–2.15 D served Mon-Sat 6–9.15 (Sun 7–9.15) ⊕ Enterprise Inns ◀ Shepherd Neame Master Brew, Youngs Special, Harveys Sussex Best, Adnams Broadside. ♥ 7 **Facilities** Garden Dogs allowed

---

SELLING   MAP 07 TR05

The Rose and Crown

Perry Wood ME13 9RY ☎ 01227 752214

e-mail: perrywoodrose@btinternet.co.uk

dir: *From A28 right at Badgers Hill, left at end. 1st left signed Perry Wood. Pub at top*

Set amidst 150 peaceful acres of woodland, this 16th-century pub's beamed interior is decorated with hop garlands, corn dollies, horse brasses and brass cask taps. The perfumed summer garden includes a children's play area and bat and trap pitch. Expect a choice of four real ales including a guest, and a menu high in comfort factor. The ploughman's is served with huffkin, a bread made with eggs, milk and ground paragon wheat – a little like brioche but less sweet. Game menu in season.

Open 11–3 6.30–11 (Sun 12–4, 7–10.30) Closed: 25–26 Dec eve, 1 Jan eve **Bar Meals** L served Mon-Sat 12–2 D served Tue-Sat 7–9.30 (Sun 12–2.30, 7–9) Av main course £8.95 **Restaurant** L served all week 12–2 D served Tue-Sat 7–9.30 ⊕ Free House ◀ Adnams Southwold, Harveys Sussex Best Bitter, Goacher's Real Mild Ale. **Facilities** Garden Dogs allowed Parking Play Area

---

SEVENOAKS   MAP 06 TQ55

The White Hart Inn ♥

Tonbridge Rd TN13 1SG ☎ 01732 452022

e-mail: sportingheros@btclick.com

A 16th-century inn close to Knole House, one of Kent's most famous and historic homes, noted for its glorious deer park. The pub's attractive garden, spacious terrace and traditional period interior draw customers from all corners of the county. The menu offers everything from shank of lamb with garlic mash, and breast of chicken in artichoke sauce, to steak and kidney pudding, and beer-battered cod. Bloomer sandwiches, ploughman's and baguettes make good snacks.

Open 11–3.30 6–12 **Bar Meals** L served all week 12–2.30 D served Mon-Sat 6–9.30 (Sun 12–4.30) Av main course £8.50 **Restaurant** L served all week 12–2.30 D served Mon-Sat 6–9 (Sun 12–4.30) Av 3 course à la carte £21 ◀ Harveys Sussex, Shepherd Neame Spitfire, Adnams Best, guest ales. ♥ 8 **Facilities** Children's licence Garden Parking Play Area

---

SMARDEN   MAP 07 TQ84

The Bell ♥

Bell Ln TN27 8PW ☎ 01233 770283

dir: *Telephone for directions*

Built in the year 1536, the Bell was originally a farm building on a large estate. It was used as a blacksmiths forge right up until 1907, but it had also been an alehouse since 1630. A typical menu includes seared king scallops with spinach and a crab sauce, chargrilled chicken breast with mozzarella, basil and wild mushroom sauce, gammon steak with beetroot mash and parsley sauce, and tournedos of monkfish rossini.

Open 12–3 5.30–11 (Fri-Sat 12–11 Sun 12–10.30) **Bar Meals** L served all week 12–2.30 D served all week 6.30–9.30 (Fri-Sat 6.30–10) Av main course £11 **Restaurant** L served all week 12–2.30 D served all week 6.30–9.30 (Fri-Sat 6.30–10) ⊕ Free House ◀ Shepherd Neame Master Brew Spitfire, Interbrew Flowers IPA, Fuller's London Pride, seasonal ales. ♥ 15 **Facilities** Garden Dogs allowed Parking

England

SMARDEN continued

Pick of the Pubs

The Chequers Inn ♥

The Street TN27 8QA
☎ 01233 770217 📄 01233 770623
e-mail: reception@thechequerssmarden.com
dir: Through Leeds village, left to Sutton Valence/Headcorn then left for Smarden. Pub in village centre

A ghost is said to haunt the bedrooms of the Chequers – an atmospheric 14th-century inn with a clapboard façade in the centre of one of Kent's prettiest villages. The inn has its own beautiful landscaped garden with large duck pond and attractive south-facing courtyard. Real ales such as Speckled Hen are served in the low beamed bars. Here the food ranges from club sandwiches and jacket potatoes to smoked ham, eggs and chips, and lambs' liver with bacon. For an à la carte meal two separate restaurants offer a choice of ambience: the Red Restaurant has an opulent and romantic setting, while the Gold Restaurant is less formal in style and suitable for the whole family; both serve the same menus. Typical starters are smoked duck salad, or lambs' kidney croûte, while main courses may include apple roasted pork loin steak, Barbary duck breast, and saddle of rabbit.

Open 11–11 (Sun 12–10.30) **Bar Meals** L served all week 12–2.30 D served all week 6–9.30 (Sun 12–3, 6–8.30) Av main course £9.95 **Restaurant** L served all week 12–2.30 D served all week 6.30–9.30 (Sun 12–3, 6–8.30) Av 3 course à la carte £22.50 Av 2 course fixed price £9.95 ⊕ Free House ◀ Harveys, IPA, Abbot, Speckled Hen. ♥ 9 **Facilities** Garden Dogs allowed Parking

---

SPELDHURST   MAP 06 TQ54

Pick of the Pubs

George & Dragon ♥

Speldhurst Hill TN3 0NN
☎ 01892 863125 📄 01892 863216
e-mail: julian@speldhurst.com
dir: Telephone for directions

Built around 1500, the George and Dragon is a venerable timber-clad village hostelry. Some say its origins are earlier, when Speldhurst would have seen archers departing for the Battle of Agincourt. At the beginning of the 17th century the curative powers of the village's iron-rich waters were discovered, which put nearby Tunbridge Wells on the map. Today's customers enjoy a modern gastro-pub, where refreshments include a range of local organic fruit juices. The menu offers half a dozen eclectic choices at each stage: you could start with local smoked eel on toast, and follow with Ashdown Forest wild mushroom risotto; or lunch lightly on a plate of Kentish hop pork sausages. The fish selection is exceptional, with sea bass, sea bream, brill, turbot, skate, lobster, mussels and razor clams all making regular appearances. Food can be served in the two gardens – one a modern layout with bay trees and herbs, the other a Mediterranean garden with 200-year-old olive tree.

Open 11–11 **Bar Meals** L served all week 12–3 D served Mon-Sat 7–10.30 **Restaurant** L served all week 12–2.30 D served Mon-Sat 6–10 ⊕ Free House ◀ Harveys Best, Sussex Pale, Larkins & Porter. ♥ 10 **Facilities** Children's licence Garden Dogs allowed Parking

---

TENTERDEN   MAP 07 TQ8.

White Lion Inn ♥

57 High St TN30 6BD ☎ 01580 765077 📄 01580 764157
e-mail: whitelion.tenterden@marstonstaverns.co.uk
dir: On A28 (Ashford to Hastings road)

A 16th-century coaching inn on a tree-lined street of this old Cinque Port, with many original features retained. The area is known for its cricket connections, and the first recorded county match between Kent and London was played here in 1719. The menu offers plenty of choice from calves' liver and bacon, shoulder of lamb, and Cumberland cottage pie to tuna pasta bake and various ploughman's.

Open 7–11 (Fri-Sat 7–12) **Bar Meals** L served all week D served all week (Sun 12–8.30) Av main course £8 **Restaurant** L served all week D served all week (Sun 12–8.30) Av 3 course à la carte £17 ◀ Greene King IPA, Adnams Broadside, Banks, Marstons Pedigree. ♥ 10 **Facilities** Garden Dogs allowed Parking

---

TONBRIDGE

See **Penshurst**

TUNBRIDGE WELLS (ROYAL) MAP 06 TQ5.

Pick of the Pubs

The Beacon ★★★★ INN ♥

See Pick of the Pubs on opposite page

The Crown Inn ♥

The Green, Groombridge TN3 9QH ☎ 01892 864742
e-mail: crowngroombridge@aol.com
dir: Take A264 W of Tunbridge Wells, then B2110 S

Dating back to 1585, this charming free house was a favourite haunt for Keira Knightley and the cast of *Pride and Prejudice* during filming at Groombridge Place in 2005. Low beams and an inglenook fireplace are the setting for the lunchtime bar menu, which features toasted ciabattas, jackets and hot pub favourites. Evening diners might choose grilled cod with prawn and parsley butter; chicken and home-made ratatouille; or sun-blushed tomato pasta with peppers and roquette.

Open 11–3 6–11 (Summer Fri-Sun all day) **Bar Meals** L served all week 12–3 D served Mon-Sat 7–9 (Sun 12–4) **Restaurant** L served all week 12–3 D served Mon-Sat 7–9 (Sun 12–4) ⊕ Free House ◀ Harveys IPA, Greene King IPA & Abbot Ale, Larkins. ♥ 8 **Facilities** Garden Dogs allowed Parking Play Area

PICK OF THE PUBS

The Beacon

Set high on a sandstone outcrop with one of the best views in southeast England, The Beacon began life in 1895 as the country home of Sir Walter Harris, a lieutenant of the City of London. He commissioned only the finest craftsmen, so the property has a host of impressive architectural features, including some fine stained glass windows, patterned ceilings and an oak-panelled bar.

After Harris's death the house passed through various hands, including those of a Mayor of Tunbridge Wells, until the Second World War when it became a hostel for Jewish refugee girls. Located along the wooded, attractively-named Tea Garden Lane, The Beacon has 17 acres of grounds to explore, with lakes, woodland walks and a chalybeate spring. First used in 1708, this predates by 40 years its more famous counterpart in The Pantiles at Tunbridge Wells. You can enjoy a drink on the terrace in summer or by the log fire in the bar on cooler days. Draught beers and a good selection of wines are offered, with plenty of choice by the glass. Food is served in the newly-refurbished restaurant or one of three private dining rooms. A

separate spacious function room is also available, with its own bar. The menus take full seasonal advantage of county-grown produce to which, as a member of Kentish Fare, the kitchen is strongly committed. You could start with truffle boudin blanc with a wild mushroom soup, or marbled terrine with home-grown grape chutney, followed by herb-baked half mallard with a game and wild mushroom pastry parcel and caramelized endive, or haddock fillet battered in Harvey's ale with hand-cut chips and mushy peas. Home-made desserts include hazelnut pannacotta and sticky toffee pudding with butterscotch sauce. Three bedrooms are available (two doubles and a single): the Georgian Room, the Colonial Room and the Contemporary Room.

★★★★ INN ♟
MAP 06 TQ53
Tea Garden Ln, Rusthall TN3 9JH
☎ 01892 524252
🖹 01892 534288
e-mail: beaconhotel@
btopenworld.com
web: www.the-beacon.co.uk
dir: *From Tunbridge Wells take A264 towards East Grinstead. Pub 1m on left*

Open 11–11 (Sun 12–10.30)
Bar Meals L served all week
12–2.30 D served all week
6.30–9.30
Restaurant L served Mon-Sat
12–2.30 D served Mon-Thu
6–9.30 (Fri-Sat 6.30–10, Sun 12–5,
6.30–9.30)
⊕ Free House ◀ Harveys Best,
Timothy Taylor Landlord, Larkins
Traditional. ♟ 12
Facilities Children's licence
Garden Parking Play Area
Rooms 3

England

Pick of the Pubs

The Hare on Langton Green ♀

Langton Rd, Langton Green TN3 0JA
☎ 01892 862419 📄 01892 861275
e-mail: hare@brunningandprice.co.uk
dir: *From Tunbridge Wells follow A264 towards East Grinstead. Village on A264*

There has been an inn on this site since the 16th century, though the previous version was partially destroyed in a fire in 1900. What remained was too dilapidated to restore, and the present Victorian-Tudor model was built a year later. In a spooky twist, a woman holding a child is said to haunt the main staircase and cellar, though what era she dates back to nobody can say. On the comfortably comprehensive daily-changing menu starters and main dishes might include rabbit rillettes; teriyaki chicken skewers; and baked figs with rocket and air-dried ham, to be followed by classic cassoulet; ham hock with mustard and cider sauce' or smoked haddock and mussel casserole topped with a poached egg. Light bites and sandwiches are also available. In addition to Greene King IPA and Abbot ales, there's an impressive range of malt whiskies and wines by the glass.

Open 12–11 (Fri-Sat 12–12, Sun 12–10.30) **Bar Meals** L served Mon-Thu 12–9.30 D served Mon-Thu 12–9.30 (Fri-Sat 12–10, Sun 12–9) **Restaurant** L served Mon-Thu 12–9.30 D served Mon-Thu (Fri -Sat 12–10, Sun 12–9) ⊕ Greene King ◀ Greene King IPA & Abbot Ale. ♀ 16 **Facilities** Garden Dogs allowed Parking

WESTERHAM   MAP 06 TQ45

The Fox & Hounds ♀

Toys Hill TN16 1QG ☎ 01732 750328
e-mail: hickmott1@hotmail.com
web: www.foxhoundstoyshill.co.uk
dir: *Telephone for directions*

High up on Kent's Greensand Ridge, this late-18th-century ale house adjoins a large National Trust estate incorporating an old water tower now protected as a home for hibernating bats. The pub has been revamped to include a traditionally styled restaurant, where home-prepared starters include anchovy and balsamic onion tart, and deep-fried brie with cranberry sauce, while among the mains are skate wing with capers, lamb shank with garlic mash, and daily specials.

Open 11.30–3 6–11 (Sat-Sun all day) Closed: 25 Dec **Bar Meals** L served all week 12–2 D served Tue-Sat 6–9 (Sat 12–2.30, Sun 12–3) **Restaurant** L served all week 12–2 D served Tue-Sat 6–9 Sun 12–3 ⊕ Greene King ◀ Greene King IPA, Abbot Ale, Ruddles County. ♀ 9 **Facilities** Garden Dogs allowed Parking

Pick of the Pubs

The Farmhouse ♀

97 The High St ME19 6NA
☎ 01732 843257 📄 01622 851881
e-mail: enquiries@thefarmhouse.biz
dir: *M20 junct 4, S on A228. Right to West Malling. Pub in village centre*

A modern gastro-pub, The Farmhouse occupies a handsome Elizabethan property at the heart of the village of West Malling. It has a relaxing atmosphere with a stylish bar and two dining areas, while outside is a spacious walled garden with an area of decking. Alongside the deli board selection (cheese, fish, antipasti, charcuterie), there are stone-baked pizzas, toasted paninis and salads (chicken Caesar, ocean, wood pigeon and roquefort). Starters range from home-made soup with crusty bread, to the chef's signature dish of fresh scallops. Main courses follow through with seared fillet of sea bass with sweet potato mash, leek fondue and saffron rice; or traditionally reared Kentish Limousin beef with black pepper, blue cheese or garlic butter sauce. Bar food is available all day. The 15th-century barn at the rear of the pub has been transformed into a deli/farmers' market.

Open 11–11 (Sun 11–10.30) **Bar Meals** L served all week 12–9.30 D served all week 12–9.30 Av main course £9 **Restaurant** L served all week 12–9.30 D served all week 12–9.30 Av 3 course à la carte £23 Av 2 course fixed price £11.95 ⊕ Free House ◀ Harveys, Guinness, Leffe, Youngs & St Miguel. ♀ 13 **Facilities** Children's licence Garden Parking

Pick of the Pubs

The Sportsman ◉◉ ♀

Faversham Rd CT5 4BP
☎ 01227 273370 📄 01227 262314
dir: *3.5m W of Whitstable*

Reached via a winding lane across open marshland from Whitstable, and tucked beneath the sea wall, the Sportsman may seem an unlikely place to find such good food. The rustic yet comfortable interior, with its wooden floors, stripped pine furniture and interesting collection of prints has a warm and welcoming feel. The full range of Shepherd Neame ales is served, including seasonal brews, and there is an excellent wine list. Remember that food is not served on Sunday evenings or Mondays, or you could be disappointed. The daily menu is based on local produce, with fish dishes steamed wild sea bass with a mussel pistou, or seared Thornback ray with cockles, sherry vinegar and brown butter. Starters also feature lots of seafood, typically rock oysters and hot chorizo. Amongst the mains is braised shoulder of Monkshill Farm lamb and mint sauce.

Open 12–3 6–11 Closed: 25 Dec **Bar Meals** L served Tue-Sat 12–2 D served Tue-Sat 7–9 (Sun 12–3) **Restaurant** L served Tue-Sat 12–2 D served Tue-Sat 7–9 (Sun 12–3) ⊕ Shepherd Neame ◀ Shepherd Neame Late Red, Spitfire, Masterbrew, Porter. ♀ 8 **Facilities** Garden Dogs allowed Parking

England

VYE

MAP 07 TR04

he New Flying Horse ♥

pper Bridge St TN25 5AN

☎ 01233 812297 📄 01233 813487

-mail: newflyhorse@shepherd-neame.co.uk

ir: *Telephone for directions*

his 17th-century posting house retains much of its original character
ter being refurbished. Winter log fires warm the bar and dining
ea, where you'll find a good selection of meals. In warmer weather,
ustomers can wine and dine in the prize-winning garden, which was
eatured at the 2005 Chelsea Flower Show. Expect a wide range of
easonal specials, classic dishes and vegetarian options, produced from
ne finest local ingredients.

pen 11–11 Closed: Mon-Fri eve Oct-May **Bar Meals** L served all week
2–2 D served all week 6–9 Av main course £9.95 **Restaurant** L served all
eek 12–2.30 D served all week 6–9 ⊕ Shepherd Neame ◀ Masterbrew
pitfire, Plus guests. ♥ 8 **Facilities** Garden Dogs allowed Play Area
ooms available

LANCASHIRE

BASHALL EAVES

MAP 18 SD64

Pick of the Pubs

The Red Pump Inn ♥

Clitheroe Rd BB7 3DA

☎ 01254 826227 📄 01254 826750

e-mail: info@theredpumpinn.co.uk

web: www.theredpumpinn.co.uk

dir: *3m from Clitheroe, NW, follow 'Whitewell, Trough of
Bowland & Bashall Eaves' signs.*

'Three miles from Clitheroe, a million miles from hectic' is the
promise of this friendly old inn. The pub was built in 1756 and
restored by owners Jon and Martina Myerscough. Drinking
and eating areas divide into a bar, a snug with real fire, a large
dining room and a rather special coach house café and deli.
Local, regional and national cask-conditioned ales make this a
true beer-lover's paradise; wines old and new suit every pocket
and taste, with more than ten served by the glass. The menu
makes impressive use of local produce, including hare, pheasant,
venison, and partridge. Extra-matured local beef comes into its
own on weekly steak nights, and Fridays see a celebration of fish
and seafood in dishes such as potted crayfish tails; calamari with

aïoli; and fresh hake, sea bass and snapper feature regularly. Bread
and preserves are home made, herbs come from the garden,
and a vegetable plot is underway that will eventually make the
restaurant self-sufficient.

Open 12–2.30 6–11 (Sun 12–9.30, BHs 12–5) Closed: Mon (Winter)
Bar Meals L served Mon-Sat 12–2 D served Mon-Sat 6–9 (Sun 12–7,
Spring & Autumn 12–8) **Restaurant** L served Mon-Sat 12–2 D served
Mon-Sat 6–9 (Sun 12–7, Spring & Autumn 12–8)) ⊕ Free House
◀ Timothy Taylor Landlord, Black Sheep, Moorhouses, Grindleton
Brewhouse. ♥ 10 **Facilities** Garden Parking **Rooms** available

BILSBORROW

MAP 18 SD53

Owd Nell's Tavern ♥

Guy's Thatched Hamlet, Canal Side PR3 0RS

☎ 01995 640010 📄 01995 640141

e-mail: info@guysthatchedhamlet.com

dir: *M6 junct 32 N on A6. In approx 5m follow brown tourist signs
to Guy's Thatched Hamlet*

The Wilkinson family has owned and run Guy's Thatched Hamlet
beside the Lancaster Canal for nearly 30 years, of which this country-
style tavern forms a part. Flagstone floors, fireplaces and low ceilings
create an authentic ambience. Excellent real ales are supplemented by
a lovingly assembled collection of wheat beers, fruit beers and pilsners.
All-day fare is typified by Carol's home-made steak and kidney suet
pudding, 'whale-sized' beer-battered cod and chips, and apple tart.

Open 9–3am Closed: 25 Dec **Bar Meals** L served all week 11–9 D served
all week 11–9 **Restaurant** L served Mon-Fri 12–2.30 D served Mon-Fri
5.30–10.30 (Sat 12–1am, Sun 12–10.30) ⊕ Free House ◀ Boddingtons
Bitter, Jennings Bitter, Copper Dragon, Black Sheep. ♥ 40 **Facilities** Garden
Dogs allowed Parking Play Area

See advert on page 326

**Drink
Eat
Sleep
Play
Shop
Dance**

Open All Day Everyday
Family Owned & Run Thatched Hamlet
Free from the Brewer – wide range of Independent Brewers Ales
An ever-changing selection with "The Landlords Choice"
Cask Marque 2007 & "Ask if it's Cask" Supporters
Big Screen TV, Conference Facilities
Canalside Patios & Duck Watching, Tavern Deck Patio Area
Cricket Ground, Floodlit Crown Green Bowling Green & Thatched Pavilions
Guy's Lodge – From £52.00, Spa Rooms Available.
Guy's Thatched Hamlet, Canalside, Bilsborrow, Nr Garstang, PR3 0RS
Tel: (01995) 640010
www.guysthatchedhamlet.com

BLACKBURN   MAP 18 SD62

Pick of the Pubs

Clog and Billycock NEW ♞

Billinge End Rd, Pleasington BB2 6QB ☎ 01254
e-mail: enquiries@clogandbillycock.com
dir: *M6 junct 29 onto M65 junct 3, follow signs for Pleasington*

Named after the attire of an early landlord (a billycock is black felt hat, a predecessor of the bowler), this brand new venture opened its doors in August 2008. It's in the quaint village of Pleasington on the quiet edges of Blackburn's western suburbs, where the River Darwen flows out of town. The building has undergone an expensive renovation, but the result is a warm and relaxing pub in which to enjoy Thwaites ales, draught ciders, fine wines and superb food. Sharrock's Lancashire cheese on toast with

local cured streaky bacon makes an excellent light lunch. The ploughman's is a microcosm of the pub's real food objectives: Blackstick's Blue, Sandham's Creamy Lancashire, honey roast ham, Forager's collared pork, pickled free-range egg, celeriac and walnut salad, home-made pickles, piccalilli and organic bread. Hot options may include battered deep-fried haddock with marrowfat peas and real chips in dripping; Simpson's Dairy rice pudding could complete a meal to remember. Children are welcomed with fun educational sheets and competitions.

Open 12–11 (Sun 12–10.30) Closed: 25 Dec **Bar Meals** L served Mon-Sat 12–2 D served Mon-Fri 6–9 (Sat 5.30–9, Sun 12–8.30) Av main course £9.50 **Restaurant** L served Mon-Sat 12–2 D served Mon-Fri 6–9 (Sat 5.30–9, Sun 12–8.30) ◀ Thwaites Bomber, Wainwright & Original. ♟8 **Facilities** Garden Dogs allowed Parking

Pick of the Pubs

The Millstone at Mellor ★★ HL ◉◉ ♞

See Pick of the Pubs on opposite page

BLACKO   MAP 18 SD8

Moorcock Inn

Gisburn Rd BB9 6NG
☎ 01282 614186 ▤ 01282 614186
e-mail: boo@patterson1047.freeserve.co.uk
dir: *M65 junct 13, take A682 to Blacko*

Family-run country inn with traditional log fires and good views towards the Pendle Way, ideally placed for non-motorway travel to the Lakes and the Yorkshire Dales. Home-cooked meals are a speciality, with a wide choice including salads and sandwiches, and vegetarian and children's meals. Tasty starters like cheesy mushrooms, and garlic prawns are followed by lasagne, various steak choices, pork in orange and cider, and trout grilled with lemon and herb butter.

Open 12–3 6–10 (Sat all day, Sun 12–8) Closed: Mon eve
Bar Meals L served Mon-Sat 12–2 D served Tue-Sat 6–9.30 (Sun 12–7.30) Av main course £7.95 **Restaurant** L served Mon-Sat 12–2.30 D served Tue-Sat 6–9 (Sun 12–7) ⊕ Thwaites ◀ Thwaites Best Bitter, Smooth. **Facilities** Garden Parking

BURROW   MAP 18 SD67

Pick of the Pubs

The Highwayman NEW ♞

See Pick of the Pubs on page 328

CARNFORTH MAP 18 SD47

Old Station Inn

Station Ln, Burton LA6 1HR
☎ 01524 781225 📠 01524 782662
e-mail: willparks@hotmail.co.uk
dir: From M6 take A6 signed Milnthorpe (Kendal), 3m before
Milnthorpe turn right signed Burton/Holme

Built in 1860 to serve the nearby mainline railway, this Victorian free
house was formerly the Station Hotel. Seafood is a speciality, and a
single menu is served in the bar and restaurant. Choices include grilled
mackerel with garlic butter; and seared marlin with saffron rice and
chargrilled peppers.

Open 12–11 Bar Meals L served all week 12–9 D served all week 12–9
(Sun 12–8) Av main course £10 Restaurant L served all week 12–9 D
served all week 12–9 (Sun 12–8) Av 3 course à la carte £20 Av 2 course
fixed price £11.95 ⊕ Free House ◀ Jennings, Lancaster Brewery & 4 guest
ales. Facilities Garden Dogs allowed Parking Play Area

CATFORTH MAP 18 SD43

The Running Pump 🍷

Catforth Rd PR4 0HH ☎ 01772 690265
e-mail: the.runningpump@unicom.co.uk
dir: M6 junct 32 onto A6 at Broughton B5269

Built as cottages for agricultural workers, the pub takes its name from
one of the many natural springs in the area. There is a long, beamed
bar and adjacent snug, both with log fires, where snacks are served,
while in the restaurant a modern menu is offered. Specials include
grilled fillet of sea bass on curried new potatoes and dressed leaf salad;
and warm chocolate cookie with home-made vanilla ice cream.

Open 11–12 Bar Meals L served Tue-Sat 12–2.30 D served Tue-Sat 6–9.30
(Sun 12–9) Restaurant L served Tue-Sat 12–2 D served Tue-Sat 6–9.30
(Sun 12–8.30) ◀ Robinsons, Unicorn Best Bitter, Old Tom (at Christmas) &
other seasonal ales. Facilities Parking

CHIPPING MAP 18 SD64

Dog & Partridge

Hesketh Ln PR3 2TH ☎ 01995 61201 📠 01995 61446
dir: M6 junct 31A, follow Longridge signs. At Longridge left at 1st
rdbt, straight on at next 3 rdbts. At Alston Arms turn right. 3m,
pub on right

Dating back to 1515, this pleasantly modernised rural pub in the Ribble
Valley enjoys delightful views of the surrounding fells. The barn has
been transformed into a welcoming dining area, where home-made
food on the comprehensive bar snack menu is backed by a specials
board offering the likes of hot potted shrimps with toast; tiger prawns
in filo with sweet and sour dip; roast baby leg of lamb; and pan-fried
cod with potato cake.

Open 11.45–3 6.45–11 (Sun 11.45–10.30) Closed: Mon
Bar Meals L served Tue-Sat 12–1.45 Restaurant L served Tue-Sat
12–1.30 D served Tue-Sat 7–9 (Sun 12–3, 3.30–8.30) Av 3 course à la carte
£22 Av 4 course fixed price £16.50 ⊕ Free House ◀ Carlsberg-Tetley.
Facilities Parking

CLITHEROE MAP 18 SD74

Pick of the Pubs

The Assheton Arms 🍷

See Pick of the Pubs on page 330

The Shireburn Arms ★★★ HL 🍷

Whalley Rd, Hurst Green BB7 9QJ
☎ 01254 826518 📠 01254 826208
e-mail: sales@shireburnarmshotel.com
web: www.shireburnarmshotel.com
dir: Telephone for directions

A privately run, 17th-century inn with super views, in the heart of the
Ribble Valley. Lord of the Rings author J R R Tolkien used to drink
here when visiting his son at Stonyhurst College nearby. The menu
ranges from sandwiches and salads to steak and kidney pudding; roast
sirloin of beef with Yorkshire pudding; vegetable lasagne; and poached
salmon supreme. A conservatory links the restaurant with the patio
and gardens.

Open 11–11 Bar Meals L served Mon-Sat 12–2 D served Mon-Sat
5.30–9.30 (Sun 12–9) Restaurant L served Mon-Sat 12–2 D served
Mon-Sat 6–9 (Sun 12–8) Av 3 course à la carte £20 Av 2 course fixed price
£9.95 ⊕ Free House ◀ Theakstons Best Bitter, Mild & guest ales. 🍷 10
Facilities Garden Dogs allowed Parking Play Area Rooms 22

The Assheton Arms

This stone-built country pub is well placed for a moorland walk up Pendle Hill, which looms over the village, and might be more familiar to viewers of the BBC serial Born and Bred as The Signalman's Arms, set in the 1950s.

The pub is named after Lord Clitheroe's family (they own the whole village), and the Assheton coat of arms on the sign above the inn's door includes a man holding a scythe incorrectly. The story behind this is that during the English Civil War the Asshetons supported Cromwell and one day a party of the kings' men was passing by. A prominent member of the family, not wishing to be discovered, leapt over a wall into a field where he picked up a scythe, meaning to pass himself off as a farm worker. His ruse worked, despite the fact that having never used a scythe before he was holding it the wrong way. Since that narrow escape the image of the scythe has been incorporated into the family emblem. Present-day visitors will find the single bar and

sectioned rooms furnished with solid oak tables, wingback settees, the original stone fireplace, and a large blackboard listing the range of daily specials. Seafood is offered from the blackboard according to availability, and you can expect beer battered haddock and chips, and lemon sole with parsley butter. An interesting selection of small dishes includes Mrs Whelan's Burnley black pudding with piccalilli and mustard; and Leagrams organic Lancashire cheese platter with crusty bread and apple cider chutney. Main courses take in a choice of vegetarian dishes (broccoli bake; vegetarian chilli; cauliflower and mushroom provençale), as well as traditional Lancashire hot pot; venison casserole, and a range of steaks.

MAP 18 SD74
Downham BB7 4BJ
☎ 01200 441227
🖷 01200 440581
e-mail: asshetonarms@aol.com
dir: *From A59 to Chatburn, then follow Downham signs*

Open 12–3 7–11 (Sat-Sun open all day)
Bar Meals L served Mon-Sat 12–2 D served Mon-Sat 7–10 (Sun 12–9) Av main course £10.50
🍴 Free House 🍺 Lancaster Bomber, Thwaits bitter, Daniels Smooth. 🍷 22
Facilities Dogs allowed Parking

FENCE | MAP 18 SD83

Fence Gate Inn ♀

Wheatley Lane Rd BB12 9EE
☎ 01282 618101 📄 01282 615432
e-mail: info@fencegate.co.uk
dir: *From M65 junct 13 towards Clayton-le-Moors, 1.5m, pub set back on right opposite T-junct for Burnley*

An extensive property, the Fence Gate Inn was originally a collection point for cotton delivered by barge and distributed to surrounding cottages to be spun into cloth. Food is served both in the bar and the Topiary Brasserie. Highlights are a selection of sausages starring Lancashire's champion leek and black pudding with a hint of sage. There is a good choice of pasta, and dishes like medallions of organic Salmesbury pork fillet.

Open 12–12 (Sat 12–1) **Bar Meals** L served all week 12–2.30 D served Mon-Fri 6.30–9.30 (Sat 6.30–8, Sun 6–8.30) **Restaurant** L served all week 12–2.30 D served all week 6.30–9.30 ⊕ Free House ◀ Theakston, Directors, Deuchers, Moorhouse & Bowland. ♀ 16 **Facilities** Garden Parking

Ye Old Sparrow Hawk Inn ♀

Wheatley Lane Rd BB12 9QG
☎ 01282 603034 📄 01282 603035
e-mail: mail@yeoldsparrowhawk.co.uk
dir: *M65 junct 13, A6068, at rdbt take 1st exit 0.25m. Turn right onto Carr Hall Rd, at top turn left 0.25m, pub on right*

Sipping a pint outside the half-timbered Sparrowhawk on a summer's evening is one of life's great pleasures. The pub stands at the gateway to Pendle Forest, famous for its witches, but here, you'll find friendly service and stylish surroundings. The classically trained chefs work with locally sourced fresh ingredients to create menus that include fish pie with seasonal greens and bacon lardons; sausages with bubble and squeak; and chargrilled tuna with roasted Mediterranean vegetables.

Open 12–11 **Bar Meals** L served Mon-Fri 12–2.30 D served Mon-Fri 5–9.30 (Sat 12–9.30, Sun 12–8) **Restaurant** L served Mon-Fri 12–2.30 D served Mon-Fri 5–9 (Sat 12–9.30, Sun 12–8) ◀ Thwaites Cask, Draught Bass, Moorhouse Blonde Witch, Black Sheep Best. ♀ 13 **Facilities** Garden Dogs allowed Parking

FORTON | MAP 18 SD45

Pick of the Pubs

The Bay Horse Inn ♀

LA2 0HR ☎ 01524 791204 📄 01524 791204
e-mail: bayhorseinfo@aol.com
dir: *1m S from M6 junct 33*

The quirky history of this inn recounts how it gave its name in the 19th century to the local railway station and surrounding area, even though no settlement actually existed. And how it was not this inn, but another one which had been called the Rising Sun. Suffice to say that today the pub is beautifully situated and traditional in style, with a warm welcome, real cask beers and a good selection of malt whiskies. It also specialises in simple, fresh and imaginative dishes from an award-winning chef who is wholly self-taught. Craig Wilkinson exercises his culinary skills on the very best of local ingredients, elevating standard pub fare to unashamedly gastro levels. How else could a lunch menu offer warm potted Morecambe Bay shrimps with herb butter, followed perhaps by shank of Cumbrian lamb with creamy blue cheese potatoes, thyme and ale gravy.

Open 12–3 6.30–11 (Sun 12–11) Closed: Mon **Bar Meals** L served Tue-Sat 12–1.45 D served Tue-Sat 7–9.15 (Sun 12–3) Av main course £15.95 **Restaurant** L served Tue-Sat 12–1.45 D served Tue-Sat 7–9.15 (Sun 12–3) Av 3 course à la carte £19.95 Av 3 course fixed price £14.50 ◀ Thwaites Lancaster Bomber, Moorhouses Pendle Witch, Masham Brewery & Black Sheep. ♀ 11 **Facilities** Garden Parking

GOOSNARGH | MAP 18 SD53

The Bushell's Arms ♀

Church Ln PR3 2BH ☎ 01772 865235 📄 01772 865235
dir: *Take A6 N to Garstang, right onto Whittingham Lane, after 3m left into Church Lane. Pub on right of village green*

Dr Bushell was a philanthropic Georgian who built not just a hospital for his villagers but this pub too, opposite the village green and church; it seems that patients were entitled to a daily pint. It has transmogrified to a Spanish bar and restaurant, with a menu devoted entirely to reasonably-priced tapas. According to your hunger, choose from a simple dish of olives to plates of fajitas or seafood paella.

Open 12–2 6–11 (Fri-Sat 6–1am, Sun 6–10.30) **Bar Meals** L served all week 12–2 **Restaurant** L served all week 12–2 D served all week 6–9.45 ⊕ Enterprise Inns ◀ Black Sheep, Tetleys Extra Cold. ♀ 12 **Facilities** Children's licence Garden Parking

HASLINGDEN   MAP 15 SD72

Farmers Glory

Roundhill Rd BB4 5TU ☎ 01706 215748 📄 01706 215748

dir: *On A667, 8m from Blackburn, Burnley & Bury, 1.5m from M66*

Stone-built 300–year-old pub situated high above Haslingden on the edge of the Pennines. Formerly a coaching inn on the ancient route to Whalley Abbey, it now offers locals and modern A667 travellers a wide-ranging traditional pub menu of steaks, roasts, seafood, pizzas, pasta, curries and sandwiches. Entertainment every Wednesday and Friday, and a large beer garden with ornamental fishpond.

Open 12–3 6.30–12.30 **Bar Meals** L served all week 12–2.30 D served all week 6.30–9.30 Av main course £7 **Restaurant** L served all week 12–2.30 D served all week 6.30–9.30 Av 3 course à la carte £12.95 ⊕ Punch Taverns ◀ Tetley Bitter, Lees Speckled Hen, Jennings. **Facilities** Garden Parking

---

HESKIN GREEN   MAP 15 SD51

Farmers Arms ♒

85 Wood Ln PR7 5NP ☎ 01257 451276 📄 01257 453958

e-mail: andy@farmersarms.co.uk

dir: *On B5250 between M6 & Eccleston*

Long, creeper-covered country inn with two cosy bars decorated with old pictures and farming memorabilia. Once known as the Pleasant Retreat, this is a family-run pub proud to offer a warm welcome and a traditional theme. Typical dishes include steak pie, fresh salmon with prawns and mushroom, rack of lamb, and chicken curry.

Open 12–11 (Sun 12–10.30) **Bar Meals** L served all week 12–9.30 D served all week Av main course £6 **Restaurant** L served all week 12–9.30 D served all week ⊕ Enterprise Inns ◀ Timothy Taylor Landlord, Pedigree, Black Sheep, Tetley. ♒ 7 **Facilities** Garden Dogs allowed Parking Play Area

---

HEST BANK   MAP 18 SD46

Hest Bank Hotel ♒

2 Hest Bank Ln LA2 6DN
☎ 01524 824339 📄 01524 824948
e-mail: hestbankhotel@hotmail.com

dir: *From Lancaster take A6 N, after 2m left to Hest Bank*

Comedian Eric Morecambe used to drink at this canalside former coaching inn, first licensed in 1554. Awash with history and 'many happy ghosts', it now offers cask ales and a wide selection of meals all day, with local suppliers playing an important role in maintaining food quality. The good-value menu may range from a large pot of Bantry Bay mussels to the pub's own lamb hotpot made to a traditional recipe.

Open 11.30–11 (Sun 11.30–10.30) **Bar Meals** L served all week 12–9 D served all week No food 25 Dec **Restaurant** L served all week 12–9 D served all week Av 3 course à la carte £12 Av 2 course fixed price £6.95 ⊕ Punch Taverns ◀ Interbrew Boddingtons, Timothy Taylor Landlord, Deuchars IPA, Blacksheep Bitter & guest ales. ♒ 7 **Facilities** Garden Parking

---

LANCASTER   MAP 18 SD4◀

The Stork Inn

Conder Green LA2 0AN ☎ 01524 751234 📄 01524 75266◀

e-mail: the.stork@virgin.net

dir: *M6 junct 33 take A6 north. Left at Galgate & next left to Conder Green*

White-painted coaching inn spread along the banks of the Conder Estuary, with a colourful 300–year-history that includes several name changes. The quaint sea port of Glasson Dock is a short walk along the Lancashire Coastal Way, and the Lake District is easily accessible. Seasonal specialities join home-cooked food like steak pie, locally-smoked haddock, salmon fillet with bonne femme sauce, and Cumberland sausage with onion gravy and mashed potatoes.

Open 11–11 (Sun 12–10.30) **Bar Meals** L served all week 12–3 D served all week 6–9 Av main course £6.95 **Restaurant** L served all week 12–2.30◀ D served all week 6–9 ⊕ Free House ◀ Boddingtons, Pedigree, Black Sheep, guest ales. **Facilities** Garden Dogs allowed Parking Play Area

---

The Sun Hotel and Bar ♒

LA1 1ET ☎ 01524 66006 📄 01524 66397

e-mail: info@thesunhotelandbar.co.uk

dir: *6m from junct 33 of M6*

The original inn was built in the 1600s where the medieval Stoop Hall once stood. Now Lancaster's oldest licensed premises, the Sun's popular bar serves both hand-pulled ales brewed in the city alongside world beers; if a glass of wine is your preferred tipple, you will have to choose between two dozen options. Attractive menus start with luxury breakfasts, encompass reasonably priced lunches, and the cheese, cold meat and paté boards are especially noteworthy.

Open 10–1am **Bar Meals** L served all week 12–3 D served Sun-Thu 4–9 (Fri-Sat 4–7) Av main course £6 ◀ Thwaites Lancaster Bomber, Leifmans Frambozen, Lancaster Duchy, Lancaster Blonde. ♒ 24 **Facilities** Children's licence Garden **Rooms** available

Pick of the Pubs

The Waterwitch ♥

The Tow Path, Aldcliffe Rd LA1 1SU
☎ 01524 63828 📄 01524 34535
e-mail: thewaterwitch@mitchellsinns.co.uk
dir: 6m from junct 33 of M6

The Waterwitch takes its name from three longboats that worked the adjacent Lancaster canal in the late 18th century. It occupies an old stables, tastefully converted to retain original features such as stone walls and interior slab floors. In just a few years the pub has acquired celebrity status and a clutch of awards, yet it still remains a genuine pub with the broad appeal of a wine bar and restaurant. It is noted for its ever-changing selection of fine cask-conditioned real ales, impressive wine list and guest cheeses. The talented team of chefs work with locally-sourced produce including fish that arrives daily from Fleetwood harbour. Traditional, classical and international influences combine on menus that might include king prawns with a Thai stir fry; Cumberland sausages on herb mash with red wine jus; or lamb steak with rosemary, mint and mustard on couscous.

Open 10–12 **Bar Meals** L served all week 12–3 D served all week 5–9 (Sun 12–5 6–9) Av main course £12.95 **Restaurant** L served all week 12–3 D served all week 5–9.30 (Sun 12–5, 6–9) Av 3 course à la carte £25 ◀ Thwaites Lancaster Bomber, Warsteiner, Moorhouse Ales, Lancaster Brewery Bitters. ♥ 27 **Facilities** Garden

Ye Olde John O'Gaunt ♥

53 Market St LA1 1JG
☎ 01524 65357 📄 01524 65357
dir: M6 junct 33 A6 towards Lancaster. Right at 7th set of lights. Pub on right of Market St in 50yds

Quaint, small and very old, this building was originally built for Lancaster's chief constable in 1725 but has been a pub since 1850. If you love live music, real ale or whisky this place is probably hard to beat, with its seven live music sessions a week, excellent selection of ales and up to 100 malts. Home-made food could include cullen skink; chilli con carne; and tuna pasta.

Open 11–11 (Fri-Sat 11–11.30) **Bar Meals** L served Mon-Sat 11.30–2.30 ⊞ Punch Taverns ◀ Boddingtons, Greene King Abbot, Timothy Taylor Landlord, Deuchars. ♥ 15 **Facilities** Children's licence Garden Dogs allowed **Notes** ⊜

ORMSKIRK   MAP 15 SD40

Eureka NEW ♥

78 Halsall Ln L39 3AX ☎ 01695 570819
e-mail: siloutaylor@eurekaormskirk.co.uk
dir: 0.5m from town centre, at junct of County Rd & Southport Rd, turn left onto Halsall Ln

Although in a quiet housing estate (finding it is a clue to the name) this community pub attracts customers from a much wider area. In addition to a constantly changing specials board, the standard menu offers hot filled crispy baguettes; 'original' meals in a basket; baked jacket potatoes; 'mighty and meaty' mixed grill; and fresh haddock and chips. In August there's a beer festival with up to sixteen real ales on offer.

Open 12–12 **Bar Meals** L served Tue-Sat 12–2.30 D served Wed-Sat 5–7.30 (Sun 12–7) Av main course £6 **Restaurant** L served Tue-Sun D served Wed-Sun ⊞ Free House ◀ London Pride, Timothy Taylors Landlord, Black Sheep, Tetley Cask. ♥ 8 **Facilities** Children's licence Garden Dogs allowed Parking Play Area

PARBOLD   MAP 15 SD41

Pick of the Pubs

The Eagle & Child ♥

Maltkiln Ln, Bispham Green L40 3SG
☎ 01257 462297 📄 01257 464718
dir: 3m from M6 junct 27. Over Parbold Hill, follow signs for Bispham Green on right

Many years ago, legend has it, the local landowner Lord Derby and his wife were childless, but he fathered a child following an illicit liaison with a girl from the village. The child was placed in an eagle's nest so that when the lord and his wife were out walking they happened to hear the child cry. The lady insisted that the little boy was a gift from God, so they took him home and reared him as their son. Hence the pub's name (known locally as the Bird and Bastard). The pub maintains its traditional atmosphere and offers five regularly changing guest ales and a beer festival every May. All the food is made on the premises with ingredients from local suppliers. A good choice of dishes includes grilled sea bass with crabmeat and oriental vegetables; medallions of beef fillet with pepper sauce, and a vegetarian five-bean chilli and rice.

Open 12–3 5.30–11 (Sun 12–10.30) **Bar Meals** L served Mon-Sat 12–2 D served Mon-Thu 6–8.30 (Fri-Sat 6–9, Sun 12–8.30) Av main course £10 **Restaurant** L served Mon-Sat 12–2 D served Mon-Thu 6–8.30 (Fri-Sat 6–9, Sun 12–8.30) ⊞ Free House ◀ Moorhouse Black Cat Mild, Thwaites Bitter, 5 guest ales. ♥ 6 **Facilities** Garden Dogs allowed Parking

PRESTON — MAP 18 SD52

Pick of the Pubs

Cartford Country Inn & Hotel

Little Eccleston PR3 0YP ☎ 01995 670166
e-mail: info@thecartfordinn.co.uk
web: www.thecartfordinn.co.uk
dir: *10m from Blackpool M55 junct 3, off A586*

A former farmhouse, possibly 400 years old and a hostelry for probably 200 of them. Today the pleasantly rambling, three-storey inn stands sentinel by the toll bridge over the tidal River Wyre, a few miles from its meeting with the Irish Sea. Now run by Julie and Patrick Beaumé, the inn was completely refurbished in 2007 and offers a pleasant mix of traditional and gastro elements; a timeless log fire still burns in the winter grate, while polished wood floors and chunky dining furniture are decidedly up-to-date. Some of the ales are produced by the pub's own Hart Brewery at the back. Imaginative food starts with a choice of nibbles, continues with wood platters of antipasti or seafood, and culminates in the full menu experience: Lytham large prawns, followed by the chef's signature dish of oxtail and beef in real ale suet pudding, and finishing with chocolate fondant with mascarpone cream. There's a beer garden with river views, and live music some Friday nights.

Open 11–11 Closed: 25 Dec **Bar Meals** L served Tue-Sat 12–2 D served Mon-Thu 5.30–9 (Fri-Sat 5.30–10, Sun 12–8.30) Av main course £10 **Restaurant** L served Tue-Sat 12–2 D served Mon-Thu 5.30–9 (Fri-Sat 5.30–10, Sun 12–8.30) Av 3 course à la carte £20 ⊕ Free House ◀ Hart ales, Fuller's London Pride, Moorhouse, guest ales. **Facilities** Parking **Rooms** available

RAWTENSTALL — MAP 15 SD8

The Boars Head

69 Church St, Newchurch BB4 9EH ☎ 01706 214687
dir: *From Rawtenstall right at lights onto Newchurch Rd, past market 1.5m. Pub on right set back behind green*

Dating from 1674 and located on one of the oldest streets in Newchurch, The Boar's Head has been refurbished in a style befitting its venerable age. Expect open fires, real ales and magnificent views of the Rossendale valley from the beer garden. In summer you could use the pub's own bowling green – balls are kept behind the bar. Food-wise, don't miss the chunky home-made chips. Other treats might include Lancashire hotpot or home-made lamb curry.

Open 4–12 (Fri-Sun 12–1am) **Bar Meals** L served Fri-Sun 12–2 D served all week 4–8 Av main course £6 ⊕ Punch Taverns ◀ Black Sheep Best Bitter, Old Speckled Hen, White Ale, Tetleys Mild. **Facilities** Children's licence Garden Parking

RIBCHESTER — MAP 18 SD63

The White Bull ♀

Church St PR3 3XP ☎ 01254 878303
dir: *M6 junct 31, A59 towards Clitheroe. B6245 towards longridge. Pub 100mtrs from Roman Museum in town centre*

Ancient Roman columns welcome patrons to this Grade II listed pub in the centre of Ribchester, with its beer garden overlooking the former Roman bathhouse. Despite its 18th-century origins as a courthouse, you'll find a warm and friendly atmosphere in which to sample the local hand-pumped beers. Lunchtime sandwiches, and specials like haggis, and neeps and tatties, support a main menu that might include pheasant and bacon pie; Lancashire hot pot; or crisp salmon fillet.

Open 12–12 (Mon 5–12) **Bar Meals** L served Mon-Sat 12–2.30 D served Mon-Sat 6–9.30 (Sun 12–8) Av main course £10 **Restaurant** L served Mon-Sat 12–2.30 D served Mon-Sat 6–9.30 (Sun 12–8) Av 3 course à la carte £22 ⊕ Enterprise Inns ◀ John Smiths, Copper Dragon Bitter, Bowland Brewery Bitter, Moorhouses. ♀8 **Facilities** Garden Parking

SAWLEY — MAP 18 SD74

The Spread Eagle ♀

BB7 4NH ☎ 01200 441202 🖹 01200 441973
dir: *Just off A159 between Clitheroe & Skipton, 4m N of Clitheroe*

This whitewashed pub stands on the banks of the River Ribble, affording lovely views from every table. There is a 17th-century bar with oak beams and a log fire, where a great choice of real ale, malt whiskies and wines by the glass is offered. Dishes served in the modern dining room might include smoked chicken salad; and seared fillet of sea bass with pumpkin velouté. Themed evenings (Turkish, Portuguese, Burns', Valentine's) are held regularly.

Open 12–2 6–9 Closed: 1st wk Jan & Sun eve, Mon **Bar Meals** L served Tue-Sat 12–2 **Restaurant** L served Tue-Sun 12–2 D served Tue-Sat 6–8.45 ⊕ Free House ◀ Sawley's Drunken Duck, Black Sheep, Hoegarrden. ♀16 **Facilities** Garden Parking

Forest of Bowland at Slaidburn, Lancashire

SLAIDBURN

MAP 18 SD75

Hark to Bounty Inn ♥

Townend BB7 3EP ☎ 01200 446246 📠 01200 446361
e-mail: manager@hark-to-bounty.co.uk
web: www.harktobounty.co.uk
dir: From M6 junct 31 take A59 to Clitheroe then B6478, through Waddington, Newton, onto Slaidburn

A family-run 13th-century inn known as The Dog until 1875 when Bounty, the local squire's favourite hound, disturbed a post-hunt drinking session with its loud baying. The squire's vocal response obviously made a lasting impact. View the ancient courtroom, last used in 1937. The current family of landlords have been here some 25 years, and the kitchen offers the likes of black pudding with brandy and stilton; local organic pork with mustard and brown sugar; Bowland lamb shoulder with root vegetable and redcurrant gravy; or smoked mackerel kedgeree.

Open 11–11 **Bar Meals** L served Mon-Sat 12–2 D served Mon-Sat 6–9 (Sun 12–8) **Restaurant** L served Tue-Sat 12–2 D served Tue-Sat 6–9 (Sun all day) ⊕ Scottish Courage ◀ Theakston Old Peculier, Theakstons Bitter, Archers Best, Moorhouses. ♥ 8 **Facilities** Children's licence Garden Dogs allowed Parking

TUNSTALL

MAP 18 SD67

Pick of the Pubs

The Lunesdale Arms

LA6 2QN ☎ 015242 74203 📠 015242 74229
e-mail: info@thelunesdale.co.uk
dir: M6 junct 36. A65 Kirkby Lonsdale. A638 Lancaster. Pub 2m on right

Presided over by an ever-popular landlady, this bright and cheery pub in a small village in the beautiful Lune Valley has established quite a reputation for its food, wines, and fine regional beers. Everything is freshly prepared, with meat supplied mainly by local farms, most of the salad leaves and vegetables grown organically, and all the bread baked in the pub's kitchens. Light meals at lunchtime might include chicken Florentine; lamb's liver with bacon and mash; or just a bowl of parsnip, lime and ginger soup. At dinnertime there could be slow-roasted shoulder of lamb on Vermont baked beans; fillets of plaice with salmon, sun-blushed tomato and langoustine sauce; or sirloin steak with béarnaise sauce. Puddings include rhubarb fool with a Grasmere gingerbread biscuit; chocolate brownie and ice cream; or mango and passion fruit parfait.

Open 11–3.30 6–1 Closed: 25–26 Dec & Mon (ex BH) **Bar Meals** L served Tue-Fri 12–2 D served Tue-Sun 6–9 (Sat-Sun 12–2.30) **Restaurant** L served Tue-Fri 12–2 D served Tue-Sun 6–9 (Sat-Sun 12–2.30) ⊕ Free House ◀ Black Sheep, Dent Aviator, Guinness. **Facilities** Garden Dogs allowed Parking

WHALLEY

MAP 18 SD7.

Pick of the Pubs

Freemasons Arms ♥

8 Vicarage Fold, Wiswell BB7 9DF ☎ 01254 822218
e-mail: freemasons@wiswell.co.uk
dir: From A59, onto A671, Wiswell is 1st left

During its two hundred years or more of existence monks from nearby Whalley Abbey have lived here, and freemasons used to meet in secret here, hence the name. It has a spacious bar area, a rather refined dining room upstairs and an enthusiastic proprietor, Ian Martin, who insists on carefully sourced, seasonal food – probably the principal reason for its good local reputation. Starters or lighter dishes can include risotto cake with spiced tomato sauce and gorgonzola cream; large prawns with pancetta and tomato and vodka dressing; chicken ravioli with wild mushroom sauce; and seared king scallops with roast beetroot. Main courses include chargrilled Bowland pork chop; slow roast shoulder of lamb; and Goosnargh duck confit with sautéed artichokes. There's always a good choice of fish, perhaps grilled salmon with creamed leeks and parsley sauce; brochette of monkfish and king scallops with potato purée; sea bass with sautéed pak choi and red wine and ginger sauce; or sole goujons with lemon, garlic and parsley mayonnaise.

Open 12–3 6–11 Closed: 25–26 Dec, 1–2 Jan & Mon & Tue **Bar Meals** L served Wed-Sat 12–2 D served Wed-Sat 6–9.30 (Sun 12–8) **Restaurant** L served Wed-Sat 12–2 D served Wed-Sat 6–9.30 (Sun 12–8) ⊕ Free House ◀ Bowland Brewery Hen Harrier, Black Sheep Bitter, Moorhouse Pride of Pendle, Guinness. ♥ 15

Pick of the Pubs

The Three Fishes ◉ ♥

See Pick of the Pubs on opposite page

WHALLEY-LANCASHIRE

The Three Fishes

The Three Fishes is a Ribble Valley Inn, exemplifying the Ribble Valley philosophy, which is 'to harvest the finest ingredients from the pick of the local artisan suppliers, create a menu inspired by tradition but influenced by contemporary twists, add the finest local ales, and present everything superbly in a pub full of atmosphere, character and charm'.

A public house throughout its 400 years of existence, The Three Fishes is supposedly named after the 'three fishes pendant' in the coat of arms of John Paslew, last abbot of nearby Whalley Abbey. Look above the entrance to see them carved in stone. They are said to represent the three rivers – Hodder, Calder and Ribble – that meet within the parish. The 21st-century interior very much respects the past and retains its most attractive features, including the big open fires. The strength of the menu of regional and British classics comes from using Lancashire and the northwest's finest produce, supplied by local food heroes whose contributions are honoured around the walls and in a map plotting their locations on the back of the menu.

A selection of nibbles immediately sparks interest, including cauliflower fritters accompanied by curried mayonnaise; and elmwood platters – ploughman's, house cured meats, or local seafood – which are great as a starter or for sharing. Local flavour abounds in main courses such as Lancashire hotpot of heather-reared Bowland lamb with pickled red cabbage; and a Fleetwood fish and seawater prawn pie, with a mashed potato topping sprinkled with Mrs Kirkham's Lancashire cheese. Salads, lunchtime sandwiches and light meals are also available, while children have their own menu of proper food in smaller portions.

MAP 18 SD73
Mitton Rd, Mitton BB7 9PQ
☎ 01254 826888
🖷 01254 826026
e-mail:
enquiries@thethreefishes.com
web: www.thethreefishes.com
dir: *M6 junct 31, A59 to Clitheroe. Follow signs for Whalley, take B6246 for 2m*

Open 12–11 Closed: 25 Dec
Bar Meals L served Mon-Sat 12–2 D served Sun-Fri 6–9 (Sat 5.30–9, Sun 12–8.30) Av main course £9.95
⊕ Free House ◀ Thwaites Traditional, Thwaites Bomber, Bowland Brewey Hen Harrier. ♟ 8
Facilities Children's licence Garden Dogs allowed Parking

England

WHITEWELL MAP 18 SD64

Pick of the Pubs

The Inn At Whitewell ★★★★★ INN

Forest of Bowland BB7 3AT
☎ 01200 448222 01200 448298
e-mail: reception@innatwhitewell.com
dir: *From B6243 follow Whitewell signs*

Whitewell lies in the heart of the Forest of Bowland surrounded by magnificent fell country. This ancient inn, parts of which date from the 13th century, stands on the east bank of the River Hodder. Approximately seven miles of water can be fished by guests, and the two acres of riverside grounds incorporate an extensive herb garden that supplies the kitchen. The somewhat eccentric interior is packed with a random collection of bric-a-brac and furnishings. Bar lunch dishes could include Whitewell fishcakes or chicken liver paté à la Ballymaloe; more hearty plates may encompass Cumberland bangers and champ, or grilled Norfolk kipper. Bar suppers follow similar lines, or you can choose à la carte starters such as seared king scallops, and follow with chargrilled fillet of beef with home-made chipped potatoes; or breast of lamb slow-cooked with tomatoes and garlic. Children and dogs welcome.

Open 11–3 6–11 **Bar Meals** L served all week 12–2 D served all week 7.30–9.30 Av main course £9.50 **Restaurant** D served all week 7.30–9.30 Av 3 course à la carte £26.50 Free House Marston's Pedigree, Bowland Bitter, Copper Dragon, Boddingtons Bitter. 20 **Facilities** Garden Dogs allowed Parking **Rooms** 23

YEALAND CONYERS MAP 18 SD57

The New Inn

40 Yealand Rd LA5 9SJ ☎ 01524 732938
e-mail: charlottepinder@hotmail.com
dir: *M6 junct 35, follow signs for Kendal (A6) approx 3m, past Holmere Hall, next junct on left, up hill turn left at T-junct. Pub on left*

A beamed bar and large stone fireplace are among the attractive features of this 17th-century inn, set in the picturesque village of Yealand Conyers. Cask conditioned ales are offered alongside mulled wine in winter and home-made lemonade in summer, plus an extensive range of malt whiskies. Food, served in the bar, restaurant or beer garden, ranges from warm baguettes and jacket potatoes to Cumberland sausage; beef in beer; stuffed peppers; and fresh salmon.

Open 11.30–11 (Sun 12–10.30) **Bar Meals** L served Mon-Sat 11.30–9.30 D served Mon-Sat 11.30–9.30 (Sun 12–9.30) **Restaurant** L served Mon-Sat 11.30–9.30 D served Mon-Sat 11.30–9.30 (Sun 12–9.30) Hartleys XB, Robinson's Seasonal Bitter, Old Tom. **Facilities** Garden Dogs allowed Parking

LEICESTERSHIRE

BELTON MAP 11 SK42

Pick of the Pubs

The Queen's Head ★★★★ RR

See Pick of the Pubs on opposite page

BIRSTALL MAP 11 SK50

Pick of the Pubs

The Mulberry Tree

White Horse Ln LE4 4EF
☎ 0116 267 1038 0116 267 1039
e-mail: will@mulberrypubco.com
dir: *M1 junct 21A, A46 towards Newark 5.5m. Exit A46 at Loughborough*

Set by Watermead Country Park in the heart of old Birstall, the Mulberry Tree offers peaceful waterside dining and a heated courtyard in addition to its bar and restaurant. The building, originally called the White Horse, dates from the 18th century when it was used for coal storage by the barges that plied the Grand Union canal. Today it's a sought-after gastro-pub whose executive head chef, Walter Blakemore, counts Claridges and Le Caprice among his previous kitchens. Expect well-sourced food of a high order, with starters such as black pudding and crispy bacon salad; and spiced crab cake on green onion risotto. The main courses, each with a helpful wine recommendation, follow classic lines varying from pan-fried beef fillet (hung for 21 days) to pot roasted free range chicken; fish may include grilled swordfish or roast scallops. Desserts are all home made and irresistible, like warm Bakewell tart with raspberry ripple ice cream.

Open 12–3 5.30–11.30 (Sat-Sun 12–11) **Bar Meals** L served all week 12–2.30 D served Mon-Sat 6–9.30 **Restaurant** L served all week 12–2.30 D served all week 6–9.30 Av 3 course à la carte £22 10 **Facilities** Garden Parking

PICK OF THE PUBS

BELTON-LEICESTERSHIRE

The Queen's Head

Henry and Ali Weldon purchased the Queen's Head six years' ago and over a period of six months transformed the traditional village ale house into a modern gastro-pub with six individually designed en suite bedrooms.

The place has all round appeal, whether you want to relax with a pint of real ale and a newspaper from the comfort of a leather sofa in the bar, or enjoy the culinary creations of chef Mark Billings in the bistro or restaurant. During the summer months you can also take a drink in the garden or dine outside on the terrace. The bar menu ranges through ciabatta sandwiches, salads and old favourites like fish and chips. The set menu, which changes frequently, and the seasonal carte offer a great variety of dishes prepared from the best of fresh and, wherever possible, local produce. You might try smooth chicken liver parfait with tomato chutney and toasted brioche; then sea bream with basil mash, sautéed squid, chorizo and courgettes. Finish in style with dark chocolate terrine with raspberries and pistachio tuille; or Colston Bassett stilton with celery, grapes, crackers and a glass of Taylor's LBV Port. The pub is just a five-minute hop in the car from Nottingham East Midlands Airport, the M1, or Donington Park Motor Racing Circuit, and throughout the year it runs a range of events including cookery demonstrations and wine tasting evenings. The cookery demonstrations take place in the kitchen; several seasonal dishes are produced, showing skills that are often thought too difficult to try at home. Guests then have the opportunity to relax with a glass of wine and enjoy the dishes they have seen being prepared.

★★★★ RR ⊛⊛ ♥
MAP 11 SK42
2 Long St LE12 9TP
☎ 01530 222359
🖷 01530 224860
e-mail: enquiries@
thequeenshead.org
web: www.thequeenshead.org
dir: *On B5324 between Coalville & Loughborough*

Open 11–3 6–11 (Fri 7–10, Sat-Sun all day) Closed: 25–26 Dec
Bar Meals L served Mon-Sat 12–2.30 D served Mon-Fri 7–9.30 (Sun 12–4) Av main course £15
Restaurant L served Mon-Sat 12–2.30 D served Mon-Sat 7–9.30 (Sun 12–4) Av 3 course à la carte £30 Av 3 course fixed price £17
⊕ Free House ◀ Worthington, Beaver, Pedigree & Queens Special ♥ 14
Facilities Garden Dogs allowed Parking
Rooms 6

The Three Horseshoes Inn
Breedon on the Hill, Derby, DE73 8AN

Situated in North West Leicestershire near to the Derbyshire border, The Three Horseshoes Inn sits in the centre of the enchanting village of Breedon-on-the-Hill, an ideal centre point for a day out or weekend visit to the area. Located opposite the old village 'Lock-up'- an ancient stone built structure with Breedons magnificent church standing high above on the limestone rock, it can be seen for miles around! Whether you are looking for a light lunch, business dinner, or intimate dining for two The Three Horseshoes Inn is an excellent eaterie and veritable delight waiting to be discovered.

Lunch: 12am – 2.00pm
Dinner: 5.30pm – 9.15pm
Tel: 01332 695129
Website: www.thehorseshoes.com

Open 11.30–2.30 5.30–11 (Sun 12–3.30) Closed: 25–26, 31 Dec-1 Jan & Sun eve **Bar Meals** L served Mon-Sat 12–2 D served Mon-Sat 5.30–9.15 (Sun 12–3) Av main course £7 **Restaurant** L served Mon-Sat 12–2 D served Mon-Sat 5.30–9.15 (Sun 12–3) Av 3 course à la carte £30 ⊕ Free House ◀ Marstons Pedigree, Speckled Hen, Theakstons, Directors Bitter. **Facilities** Garden Parking

See advert on this page

BRUNTINGTHORPE   MAP 11 SP68

Joiners Arms ♥

Church Walk LE17 5QH ☎ 0116 247 8258
e-mail: stephen@thejoinersarms.co.uk
dir: *4m from Lutterworth*

More restaurant than village pub, with restored natural oak beams, tiled floor, pleasant décor, and lots of brassware and candles. Menus change constantly, although old favourites staying put include medallions of Scottish beef with dauphinoise potatoes and diane sauce; calves' liver, smoked bacon, mash and red wine jus; and grilled halibut with sautéed potatoes and petit pois, with specials boards offering additional choices. Maybe caramelised rice pudding or raspberry soufflé afterwards.

Open 12–1.45 6.30–11 Closed: Mon **Bar Meals** L served Tue-Sun 12–1.45 D served Tue-Sat 6.30–9.30 **Restaurant** L served Tue-Sun 12–1.45 D served Tue-Sat ⊕ Free House ◀ Greene King IPA, John Smiths, Guinness. ♥ 8 **Facilities** Parking

---

BREEDON ON THE HILL   MAP 11 SK42

The Three Horseshoes

Main St DE73 8AN ☎ 01332 695129
e-mail: Ian@thehorseshoes.com
web: www.thehorseshoes.com
dir: *5m from M1 junct 23a. Pub in centre of village*

Originally a farrier's – the stables can still be seen in the courtyard – the Three Horseshoes is around 250 years old and Grade II listed. Opposite the pub is an original round house lockup, for the detention of felons. A hearty menu is served amid the warm wood, old beams and welcoming pub atmosphere. Typical dishes are grilled asparagus with balsamic vinegar, main courses of lamb shank with mustard mash, and home-made puddings like treacle oat tart.

EAST LANGTON   MAP 11 SP79

Pick of the Pubs

The Bell Inn ♥

Main St LE16 7TW ☎ 01858 545278 📠 01858 545748
dir: *From Market Harborough on A6 N towards Leicester, 3rd right at rdbt 2m, follow The Langtons signs on B6047, 1.5m. Take 1st right signed East Langton*

A creeper-clad, 16th-century listed building tucked away in a quiet village with good country walks all around. The cosy inn has a pretty walled garden, low beams and an open log fire. Peter Faye and Joy Jesson are enthusiastic owners, proud to offer local meats, vegetables and cheeses as well as locally brewed ales. The Langton micro-brewery operates from outbuildings, and produces two regular brews as well as seasonal ales. The wine list is carefully chosen too, and there is always a selection of bin ends and special wines too. There's a wide range of food on menus in both the

Long Bar and Green Room, from starters and light bites to more hearty fare. Starters include the likes of marinated wild wood pigeon breast on a beetroot and thyme purée, with a saffron beurre blanc. Main courses might offer choices like loin of lamb encased in a green herb and mixed peppercorn crust, on a purée of celeriac, parsnip and sweet basil leaves, complemented by a Puy lentil and Pancetta sauce.

Open 12–2.30 7–11 Closed: 25 Dec **Bar Meals** L served all week 12–2 D served Mon-Sat 7–9.30 (Sun 12–2.30) Av main course £10 **Restaurant** L served all week 12–2 D served Mon-Sat 7–9.30 Av 3 course à la carte £25 ⊕ Free House ◀ Greene King IPA & Abbot Ale, Langton Bowler Ale & Caudle Bitter. ♀7 **Facilities** Children's licence Garden Parking

---

FLECKNEY

MAP 11 SP69

The Old Crown ♀

High St LE8 8AJ ☎ 0116 240 2223

e-mail: old-crown-inn@fleckney7.freeserve.co.uk

dir: *Telephone for directions*

Close to the Grand Union Canal and Saddington Tunnel, a traditional village pub that is especially welcoming to hiking groups and families. Noted for good real ales and generous opening times (evening meals from 5pm) offering a wide choice of popular food. The garden has lovely views of fields and the canal, as well as a pétanque court.

Open 11–11 (Sun 12–10.30) **Bar Meals** L served all week 12–2 D served Tue-Sat 5–9 Av main course £8 **Restaurant** L served all week 12–2 D served Tue-Sat 8–9 ⊕ Everards Brewery ◀ Everards Tiger & Beacon, Courage Directors, Adnams Bitter, Greene King Abbot Ale. **Facilities** Garden Dogs allowed Parking Play Area **Notes** ☺

GRIMSTON

MAP 11 SK62

The Black Horse

3 Main St LE14 3BZ ☎ 01664 812358

e-mail: wymeswold@supanet.com

dir: *Telephone for directions*

A traditional 16th-century coaching inn displaying much cricketing memorabilia in a quiet village with views over the Vale of Belvoir. Plenty of opportunities for country walks, or perhaps a game of pétanque on the pub's floodlit pitch. Good home-cooked meals with daily specials, including lots of game and fish. Look out for the squirrel hotpot! Fish choices and specials include monkfish, lemon sole, whole grilled plaice, and Arctic char.

Open 12–3 6–11 (Sun 12–7) **Bar Meals** L served Mon-Sat 12–2 D served Mon-Sat 6–9 (Sun 12–3) Av main course £8.95 **Restaurant** L served Mon-Sat 12–2 D served Mon-Sat 6–9 (Sun 12–3) ⊕ Free House ◀ Adnams, Marstons Pedigree, Archers, Belvoir Mild & guest ales. **Facilities** Children's licence Garden Dogs allowed

---

HALLATON

MAP 11 SP79

Pick of the Pubs

The Bewicke Arms ♀

1 Eastgate LE16 8UB

☎ 01858 555217 📠 01858 555598

dir: *S of A47 between Leicester & junct of A47/A6003*

On Easter Monday 1770, a local chatelaine was saved from being gored by a raging bull when a hare ran across the bull's path. In gratitude, she arranged for two hare pies and a generous supply of ale to be made available to the parish poor each succeeding Easter Monday. The Bewicke Arms is now famous for this annual hare pie event – with scrambling and bottle kicking thrown in for good measure. For the rest of the year, the 400-year-old thatched inn serves Grainstore Triple B amongst other real ales, and robust meals such as chilli con carne with real steak, and local gammon with home-made chips. The climbing frame and gardens are child friendly, as are the fish fingers offered on the junior menu. There is a tea shop and gift shop attached. New landlord for 2008.

Open 12–3 5–11 (Sun all day, Winter 7–11) Closed: Etr Mon **Bar Meals** L served all week 12–2 D served Mon-Sat 7–9.30 (Food on Sun May-Oct) **Restaurant** L served all week 12–2 D served Mon-Sat 7–9.30 ⊕ Free House ◀ Grain Store Brewery, Greene King IPA, Grainstore Triple B, guest ales. ♀18 **Facilities** Garden Parking Play Area

---

HATHERN

MAP 11 SK52

The Anchor Inn ♀

Loughborough Rd LE12 5JB ☎ 01509 842309

e-mail: daytondevil@hotmail.com

dir: *M1 junct 24, A6 towards Leicester. Pub 4.5m on left*

The Anchor was once a coaching inn, with stables accessed through an archway off what is now the A6. Alongside a good range of real ales are snacks galore, a lengthy restaurant menu and plenty of vegetarian options. Rosemary and garlic coated brie wedges could be followed with Cajun chicken; fillet steak sizzler, or beef madras. Unquestionably family-friendly, there's a fenced-off children's play area in the garden.

Open 12–11.30 **Bar Meals** L served Mon-Sat 12–3 D served Mon-Sat 5–10 (Sun 12–9) **Restaurant** L served all week 12–9.30 D served all week 12–9.30 ⊕ Everards Brewery ◀ Everards Tiger, Original, Pitch Black, Abbot Ale. ♀20 **Facilities** Children's licence Garden Parking Play Area

KNOSSINGTON   MAP 11 SK80

The Fox & Hounds NEW ♀

6 Somerby Rd LE15 8LY ☎ 01664 454676

dir: *4m from Oakham in Knossington*

High quality food and helpful, friendly service are the hallmarks of this 500–year-old pub. Set in the village of Knossington close to Rutland Water, the building retains lots of traditional features, and the large rear garden and sitting area are ideal for al fresco summer dining. A typical lunch menu might include grilled lamb rump with ratatouille and tapenade; vegetable tart with stilton; or salmon with roasted aubergine, red pepper and coriander salsa.

Open 12–3 5.30–11 (Sat 12–12, Sun 12–10.30) **Bar Meals** L served Tue-Sat 12–3 D served all week 7–9 Av main course £12 **Restaurant** L served Tue-Sun 12–3 D served Tue-Sat 7–9.30 (Sun–Mon 7–9) Av 3 course à la carte £23 ⊕ Free House ◀ Pedigree, Bombardier & Guinness. ♀ 8 **Facilities** Garden Dogs allowed Parking Play Area

---

LONG CLAWSON   MAP 11 SK72

The Crown & Plough ★★★★ INN ♀

East End LE14 4NG ☎ 01664 822322 📠 01664 822322

e-mail: crownandplough@btconnect.com

dir: *Located in centre of village, 3m from A606 Melton to Nott rd*

Following an extensive programme of refurbishment, the pub retains the atmosphere of a village local but with a contemporary flavour. It has a good reputation for the quality of its food served from one menu throughout the bar, snug, restaurant and landscaped garden. There's a good choice of fish (pan-fried sea bass with home-made tagliatelle, mussels and clams), and the likes of whole roast partridge with gratin potatoes and Savoy cabbage.

Open 12–2 5–11 (Tue-Thu 12–2, 5–11, Fri-Sun 12–12) **Bar Meals** L served Tue-Sat 12–2 D served Tue-Sat 6.30–9.30 (Sun 12–8) Av main course £8 **Restaurant** L served Tue-Sun 12–8 D served Tue-Sat 6.30–9.30 ◀ Shepherd Neame, Spitfire, Lancaster Bomber, Marstons Pedigree. **Facilities** Garden Parking **Rooms** 5

LOUGHBOROUGH   MAP 11 SK51

The Swan in the Rushes ♀

21 The Rushes LE11 5BE ☎ 01509 217014 📠 01509 217014

e-mail: swanintherushes@castlerockbrewery.co.uk

dir: *On A6 (Derby road). Pub in front of Sainsbury's*

A 1930s tile-fronted real ale pub, it was acquired by the Castle Rock chain in 1986, making it the oldest in the group. A major extension in 2007 added a new kitchen and first-floor drinking terrace, extended the function room and bar so it now seats 80, and enlarged the family/dining area. It always offers ten ales, including six guests, and hosts two annual beer festivals, acoustic open-mic nights, folk club, and skittle alley. Expect traditional pub grub.

Open 11–11 (Fri–Sat 11–12) (Sun 12–11) **Bar Meals** L served Mon-Sat 12–3 D served Mon-Sat 6–9 Av main course £5.95 ⊕ Tynemill Ltd ◀ Castle Rock Harvest Pale, Adnams Bitter, Hop Back Summer Lightning & 6 guests. ♀ 11 **Facilities** Dogs allowed Parking

---

MOUNTSORREL   MAP 11 SK51

The Swan Inn ★★★★ INN

10 Loughborough Rd LE12 7AT

☎ 0116 230 2340 📠 0116 237 6115

e-mail: swan@jvf.co.uk

dir: *On A6 between Leicester & Loughborough*

A listed freehouse, originally two cottages built in 1688 of brick and Mountsorrel granite on the banks of the River Soar. Exposed beams, flagstone floors and roaring log fires in winter characterise the interior, while outside is a secluded riverside garden. Cask-conditioned beers and fine wines accompany lime-cured gravadlax with ginger and buckwheat blinis; locally farmed Charolais steaks; and home-made jam sponge or tiramisu. Light lunches and snacks include pasta with a choice of sauces.

Open 12–2.30 5.30–11 (Sat 12–11 Sun 12–3, 7–10.30) **Bar Meals** L served all week 12–2 D served Mon-Sat 6.30–9.30 Av main course £10 **Restaurant** L served all week 12–2 D served Mon-Sat 6.30–9.30 Av 3 course à la carte £19 ⊕ Free House ◀ Black Sheep Bitter, Theakstons XB, Old Peculier, Ruddles County. **Facilities** Garden Dogs allowed Parking **Rooms** 1

MOWSLEY   MAP 11 SP68

Pick of the Pubs

The Staff of Life ♀

See Pick of the Pubs on opposite page

NETHER BROUGHTON   MAP 11 SK62

The Red House NEW ♀

23 Main St LE14 3HB ☎ 01664 822429 📠 01664 823805

e-mail: jim@mulberrypubco.com

Contemporary design has been introduced to this traditional village pub to great effect. The lounge bar opens into an airy restaurant, and a conservatory area overlooks the outdoor bar, terrace and courtyard grill. Immaculate gardens include a small play area and a permanent marquee for weddings, parties and corporate functions. Dishes range from locally sourced pork pie, or sausages of the week in the bar, to diver-caught scallops, or braised lamb shank in the restaurant.

Open 7.30–11.30 (Sun 7.30–10.30) **Bar Meals** L served Mon-Sat 12–2.30 D served all week 6–9 Av main course £7 **Restaurant** L served Mon-Sat 12–2.30 D served Mon-Sat 6–10 (Sun 12–4) Av 3 course à la carte £25 ◀ Guinness, Red House Special. ♀ 18 **Facilities** Garden Parking Play Area

PICK OF THE PUBS

MOWSLEY-LEICESTERSHIRE

The Staff of Life

That this well-proportioned building looks like a private Edwardian home will come as no surprise – for that is what it was before the village pub relocated here. Set back from the road, there is a small patio area to the front and additional outside seating in the garden at the rear.

Inside traditional features include high-backed settles and flagstone floors in the bar where, if you look up, you'll see not only a fine wood-panelled ceiling but also the wine cellar. Wines served by the glass number nearly 20 at the last count; and there are usually four real ales to choose from. Overlooking the patio garden is the dining area where carefully prepared and presented dishes mix British and international influences. Daily-changing lunchtime blackboard menus from Tuesday to Saturday present a selection of good old-fashioned pub classics: sandwiches and ploughman's of course, but also plates of Joseph Morris faggots on mash with rich gravy; Aberdeen Angus cottage pie with black bomber cheddar topping;

and lemonade-battered fresh fish, hand-cut chips and home-made tartar sauce. The more extensive evening carte makes the most of seasonal produce in starters such as home-made soups; and seared king scallops on tarragon-scented black pudding. Main dishes may include smoked haddock and prawn chowder; roast chicken breast stuffed with chargrilled red peppers on thyme courgettes; and roasted butternut squash with pine nut risotto. Try a dessert milk and praline chocolate fondant with hot chocolate sauce, made by Linda O'Neill, once a member of Ireland's Panel of Chefs. Traditional Sunday lunches, featuring roasts mainly sourced from local farms, are great family affairs and good value too.

MAP 11 SP68
Main St LE17 6NT
☎ 0116 240 2359
dir: *Exit M1 junct 20, A5199 to Market Harborough. Left in Husbands Bosworth onto old A50 (Leicester). Pub 3m turn right*

Open 12–3 6–11 (Sun 12–close)
Bar Meals L served Tue-Sat 12–2.30 D served Mon-Sat 6.30–9.15 (Sun 12–3.30) Av main course £8.50
Restaurant L served Tue-Sun 12–2.30 D served Mon-Sat 6.30–9.15 Av 3 course à la carte £23
⊕ Free House ◀ Marstons, Banks Original. ♟ 19
Facilities Garden Parking

NEWTOWN LINFORD   MAP 11 SK50

Pick of the Pubs

The Bradgate ☺

37 Main St LE6 0AE

☎ 01530 242239 📄 01530 249391

e-mail: lynne@mulberrypubco.com

dir: M1 junct 22, A50 towards Leicester 1.5m. At 1st rdbt
left towards Newton Linford 1.5m, at end of road turn right
0.25m. Pub on right

Long a favourite with locals and walkers, both as a watering
hole and for fine dining. A recent makeover has left the pub
with a modern, natural look, partly owing to the extensive use
of light wood bar, flooring and furniture, and off-white walls.
The food is very much in keeping, meeting the demand for style
and innovation on the plate. Start with spiced crab cake, green
onion risotto and sweet chilli oil; follow with braised pork with
fondant potato and summer cabbage and light apple and white
wine sauce; or roast scallops with pak choi and sweet potato;
and finish with warm pear galette and almond and Armagnac ice
cream. The pub is family friendly with a children's menu and a
large play area. Dogs on a lead are welcome in the beer garden.

Open 11.30–3 5.30–11 (Sat 11.30–11, Sun 12–10.30)
Bar Meals L served all week 12–2.30 D served Mon-Thu 6–9 (Fri-Sat
6–9.30) **Restaurant** D served Mon-Sat 6–9 (Sun 6–9.30) 🍺 Tiger,
Sunchase, Original & guest ales. ☺ 10 **Facilities** Garden Parking Play
Area

OADBY   MAP 11 SK60

Pick of the Pubs

Cow and Plough ☺

Gartree Rd, Stoughton Farm LE2 2FB

☎ 0116 272 0852 📄 0116 272 0852

e-mail: enquiries@steaminbilly.co.uk

dir: 3m Leicester Station A6 to Oadby. Turn off to BUPA
Hospital, pub 0.5m beyond

Formerly a Victorian dairy farm, this much-loved free house dates
back to 1989, when licensee Barry Lount approached the owners
of Stoughton Grange Farm, who were then in the process of
opening the farm to the public. The farm park attraction has since
closed, but the Cow and Plough continues to prosper,

hosting functions and events such as beer festivals in the former
farm buildings. The pub also brews its own award-winning
Steamin' Billy beers, named after the owners' Jack Russell terrier.
The interior is decorated with historic inn signs and brewing
memorabilia, providing a fascinating setting in which to enjoy
food from the regularly-changing menus. Typical choices include
warm chicken, chorizo and spinach salad with pan juices followed
by prawn, mussel and fennel linguini with salad. Heartier options
include 21 day hung sirloin steak with black pudding, potatoes and
peppercorn sauce; and a dessert of bramley apple pie.

Open 12–3 5–11 (Sat-Sun 12–11) **Bar Meals** L served Tue-Sat 12–3
D served Tue-Sat 6.30–9.30 (Sun 12–5) **Restaurant** L served Tue-Sat
12–3 D served Tue-Sat 6.30–9.30 (Sun 12–5) Av 3 course à la carte
£16.95 Av 2 course fixed price £13.95 ⊕ Free House 🍺 Steamin Billy
Bitter, Steamin Billy Mild, Skydiver, London Pride & Abbeydale. ☺ 8
Facilities Garden Dogs allowed Parking

OLD DALBY   MAP 11 SK62

Pick of the Pubs

The Crown Inn

Debdale Hill LE14 3LF ☎ 01664 823134

e-mail: jack100harrison@aol.com

web: www.crownolddalby.co.uk

dir: A46 turn for Willoughby/Broughton. Right into
Nottingham Ln, left to Old Dalby

A classic creeper-covered, old-style pub dating from 1509, set in
extensive gardens and orchards, with small rooms, all with open
fires. The owners place a strong emphasis on fresh seasonal
produce: if the food doesn't come from Leicestershire, and
admittedly the fish doesn't because it is landed in Brixham, the
county's suppliers are otherwise wholeheartedly supported.
There's a good choice of real ales to help wash down a meal, or to
enjoy without food: Wells Bombardier, Hook Norton, and Harvest
Pale are among the selection.

Open 12–3 6–11 (Winter 12–2.30, 6.30–11) **Bar Meals** L served
Tue-Sun 12–2 D served Mon-Sat 7–9.30 Av main course £12.50
Restaurant L served Tue-Sun 12–2 D served Tue-Sat 7–9.30 Av 3
course à la carte £20 ⊕ Free House 🍺 Wells Bombardier, Hook
Norton, Courage Directors, Castle Rock Hemlock. **Facilities** Garden
Dogs allowed Parking

REDMILE   MAP 11 SK73

Peacock Inn Ⓤ ♥

Church Corner, Main St NG13 0GA
☎ 01949 842554 📠 01949 843746
e-mail: reservations@thepeacockinnredmile.co.uk
dir: *From A1 take A52 towards Nottingham. Turn left, follow signs for Redmile & Belvoir Castle. In Redmile at x-rds turn right. Pub at end of village*

Set beside the Grantham Canal in the Vale of Belvoir, this 16th-century stone-built pub is only two miles from the picturesque castle. The inn has a local reputation for good quality food and real ales, and offers a relaxed setting for wining and dining. The menus are based on local seasonal produce; try smoked haddock with creamed spinach tagliatelle, or lamb Wellington with dauphinoise potatoes, followed by an eminently tempting raspberry and white chocolate cheesecake.

Open 12–9 (Fri–Sat 12–2.30 6–9.30, Sun 12–4 6–9) **Bar Meals** L served Mon-Sat 12–2.30 D served Sun-Thu 6–9 (Fri–Sat 6–9.30, Sun 12–4) Av main course £9.95 **Restaurant** L served Sun 12–4 D served Sun-Thu 6–9 (Fri-Sat 6–9.30) Av 3 course à la carte £19.95 Av 2 course fixed price £12.95 ⊕ Charles Wells ◀ Youngs Bitter, Bombardier. ♥ 8 **Facilities** Children's licence Garden Dogs allowed Parking

SADDINGTON   MAP 11 SP69

The Queens Head

Main St LE8 0QH ☎ 0116 240 2536
dir: *Between A50 & A6 S of Leicester, NW of Market Harborough*

A traditional prize-winning English pub with terrific views from the restaurant and garden over the Saddington Reservoir. The inn specialises in real ale and good food, with four specials boards to supplement the evening menu. Foil-cooked cod fillet, roast Banbury duck, lamb shank with garlic mash, steak and ale pie, monkfish medallions with Parma ham, and pan-fried tuna steak with sweet pepper and oyster sauce guarantee something for everyone.

Open 12–3 5.30–11 **Bar Meals** L served all week 12–2 D served Mon-Sat 6.30–9.30 (Sun 12.30–3) Av main course £6.50 **Restaurant** L served all week 12–2 D served Mon-Sat 6.30–9.30 Av 3 course à la carte £20 ⊕ Everards Brewery ◀ Everards Tiger Best & Beacon Bitter + guests. **Facilities** Garden Parking

SILEBY   MAP 11 SK61

The White Swan

Swan St LE12 7NW ☎ 01509 814832 📠 01509 815995
dir: *Telephone for directions*

Behind the unassuming exterior of this 1930s building you'll find a free house of some character, with a book-lined restaurant and a homely bar with an open fire. A wide selection of home-made rolls, baguettes and snacks is on offer; menus change twice weekly, and there are blackboard specials, too. Typical main course choices include baked pheasant with chestnut and cranberry stuffing; plaice with prawns in garlic butter; and roast lamb with garlic and rosemary.

Open 12–2.30 7–11 Closed: 1–7 Jan, Sun eve & Mon, May-Sep Sun lunch **Bar Meals** L served Tue-Sun 12–1.30 D served Tue-Sat 7–9.30 **Restaurant** D served Tue-Sat 7–9.30 ⊕ Free House ◀ Marston's Pedigree, Carlsberg-Tetley Ansells, Banks, Fuller's London Pride. **Facilities** Garden Parking

SOMERBY   MAP 11 SK71

Stilton Cheese Inn ♥

High St LE14 2QB ☎ 01664 454394
dir: *From A606 between Melton Mowbray & Oakham follow signs to Pickwell & Somerby. Enter village, 1st right to centre, pub on left*

This attractive 17th-century inn enjoys a good reputation for its food, beer, wine and malt whiskies. Built from mellow local sandstone, it stands in the centre of the village of Somerby surrounded by beautiful countryside. An interesting range of food from the regularly-changing specials board includes fresh salmon and spinach wrapped in pastry; wild mushroom risotto with garlic bread; and rack of lamb in mint and redcurrant glaze.

Open 12–3 6–11 **Bar Meals** L served all week 12–2 D served Mon-Sat 6–9 (Sun 7–9) Av main course £7.50 **Restaurant** L served all week 12–2 D served Mon-Sat 6–9 (Sun 7–9) Av 3 course à la carte £15.25 ⊕ Free House ◀ Grainstore Ten Fifty, Brewster's Hophead, Belvoir Star, Tetley's Cask. ♥ 10 **Facilities** Garden Parking

England

STATHERN MAP 11 SK73

Pick of the Pubs

Red Lion Inn ◉ ♀

Red Lion St LE14 4HS
☎ 01949 860868 📄 01949 861579
e-mail: info@theredlioninn.co.uk

dir: *From A1 (Grantham), A607 towards Melton, turn right in Waltham, right at next x-rds then left to Stathern*

Set in the heart of the picturesque Vale of Belvoir, this is an inn for all seasons: you can enjoy home-made lemonade on the terrace in the summer, or warm yourself with mulled wine and chestnuts roasted on the open fires in winter. The interior includes a stone-floored bar and a comfortable lounge with plenty of magazines and newspapers. There is also an informal dining area and an elegant dining room. Traditional pub values underpin everything from the service to the food, which ranges from pub classics to innovative country cooking. Whatever you choose, expect an exuberant romp through the finest local produce: perhaps hare terrine with quince compote followed by braised lamb shoulder with rosemary gratin and ratatouille, and apple and pear crumble for dessert. With a couple of day's notice you can take home breads, meats and sauces supplied by the Red Lion's sister pub, The Olive Branch at Clipsham in Rutland.

Open 12–3 6–11 (Sat 12–11, Sun 12–6.30) Closed: 1 Jan & Mon **Bar Meals** L served Tue-Sat 12–2 D served Tue-Sat 7–9.30 (Sun 12–3) **Restaurant** L served Tue-Sat 12–2 D served Tue-Sat 7–9.30 (Sun 12–3) Av 3 course fixed price £16 🍴 Grainstore Olive Oil, Brewster's VPA, Exmoor Gold & London Pride. ♀8 **Facilities** Garden Dogs allowed Parking Play Area

---

THORPE LANGTON MAP 11 SP79

The Bakers Arms ♀

Main St LE16 7TS ☎ 01858 545201 📄 01858 545924

dir: *Take A6 S from Leicester then left signed 'The Langtons', at rail bridge continue to x-rds. Straight on to Thorpe Langton. Pub on left*

A thatched pub set in a pretty village, with plenty of period charm and an enthusiastic following. The modern pub food is one of the key attractions, though this remains an informal pub rather than a serious dining pub or restaurant. An intimate atmosphere is created with low beams, rug-strewn quarry-tiled floors, large pine tables, and open fires. The area is popular with walkers, riders and mountain bikers.

Open 12–3 6.30–11 Closed: Mon **Bar Meals** L served Sun D served Tue-Sat 6.30–9.30 **Restaurant** L served Sat-Sun 12–2.15 D served Tue-Sat 6.30–9.30 Av 3 course à la carte £25 🌐 Free House 🍴 Langton Brewery & Bakers Dozen Bitter. ♀9 **Facilities** Garden Parking

---

WOODHOUSE EAVES MAP 11 SK51

The Wheatsheaf Inn ★★★ INN ♀

Brand Hill LE12 8SS ☎ 01509 890320 📄 01509 890571
e-mail: richard@wheatsheafinn.net

dir: *M1 junct 22, follow Quorn signs*

Around the turn of the 19th century, when local quarrymen wanted somewhere to drink, they built themselves the Wheatsheaf. It's what locals call a Dim's Inn, a succession of pubs run by three generations of the Dimblebee family. Bistro-style menus include chargrilled prime steaks and vegetarian options like butternut squash and cashew nut roast. Fresh fish is a feature of the daily chalkboard – maybe monkfish and scallops pan-fried in garlic butter with sweet chilli sauce.

Open 12–2.30 6–11 (Sat–Sun all day in summer) **Bar Meals** L served Mon-Fri 12–2 D served Mon-Sat 7–9.30 (Sat-Sun 12–2.30) **Restaurant** L served Mon-Sat 12–2 D served Mon-Sat 7–9.30 (Sun 12–2.30, Sat–Sun all day summer) 🌐 Free House 🍴 Greene King Abbot Ale, Draught Burton Ale, Timothy Taylor Landlord, Adnams Broadside. ♀14 **Facilities** Garden Dogs allowed Parking **Rooms** 2

LINCOLNSHIRE

ALLINGTON MAP 11 SK84

The Welby Arms ★★★★ INN ♀

The Green NG32 2EA ☎ 01400 281361 📄 01400 281361

dir: *From Grantham take either A1 N, or A52 W. Allington 1.5m*

With views across the village green, its frontage covered with greenery, this pub matches popular expectations of how a pub should look. Guest ales are on offer while Timothy Taylor's Landlord, one of the fixtures, goes into the steak and mushroom pie. Other popular choices include casseroled lamb with a herb scone; poached chicken breast in tarragon; chargrilled steaks; Welby fish pie; and cheese and spinach pancakes. There's also a tempting array of home-made sweets.

Open 12–2.30 6–11 (Sun 12–4, 6–10.30) **Bar Meals** L served Mon-Sat 12–2 Av main course £4.95 **Restaurant** L served Mon-Sat 12–2 D served all week 6.30–9 🌐 Free House 🍴 John Smith's, Interbrew Bass, Timothy Taylor Landlord, Greene King Abbot. ♀10 **Facilities** Garden Parking **Rooms** 3

ASWARBY

MAP 12 TF03

The Tally Ho Inn ♀

NG34 8SA ☎ 01529 455205 🖷 01529 455773

e-mail: enquire@tally-ho-aswarby.co.uk

dir: *3m S of Sleaford on A15 towards Bourne/Peterborough*

Built from sturdy old pillars and beams and exposed stonework, this handsome inn is located on the Aswarby Estate and has strong connections with major hunts and other field sports. The old English garden, complete with fruit trees, overlooks estate parkland and grazing sheep. Favourite dishes at lunch and dinner include suet pudding with braised beef and mushrooms, and lamb and stilton casserole. Baguettes and toasted sandwiches are also served at lunchtime.

Open 11–11 (Sun 11–10.30) **Bar Meals** L served all week 12–2 D served all week 6–9.30 (Sun 7–9) Av main course £12 **Restaurant** L served Mon-Sun 12–2 D served Mon-Sun 6–9.30 (Sun 7–9) Av 3 course à la carte £21 ⊕ Free House ◀ Tiger, Batermans XB & XXXB. ♀ 7 **Facilities** Garden Dogs allowed Parking

BARNOLDBY LE BECK

MAP 17 TA20

The Ship Inn ♀

Main Rd DN37 0BG ☎ 01472 822308 🖷 01472 823706

e-mail: silgy386@aol.com

dir: *M180 junct 5, A18 past Humberside Airport. At Laceby Junction rdbt (A18 & A46) straight over follow Skegness/Boston signs. Approx 2m turn left signed Waltham & Barnoldby le Beck*

Fresh seafood is the star at this 18th-century inn, whose own fishing boats bring in a daily haul of cod, turbot, plaice, skate and brill. The bar is filled with maritime bric-a-brac, while outside is a beautiful garden. Besides the line-caught fish options, typical dishes include oven-roasted lamb noisettes on rosemary rösti with a vegetable medley and a garlic and redcurrant jus; and gammon steak with egg, onions, grilled tomato and chips.

Open 12–3 6–11 **Bar Meals** L served Mon-Sat 12–2 D served all week 7–9.30 (Sun 12–2.30) **Restaurant** L served all week 12–2 D served all week 7–9.30 ⊕ Punch Taverns ◀ Black Sheep Best, Tetley's Smooth, Boddingtons & Spitfire. ♀ 7 **Facilities** Garden Parking

BELCHFORD

MAP 17 TF27

The Blue Bell Inn

1 Main Rd LN9 6LQ ☎ 01507 533602

dir: *Off A153 between Horncastle & Louth*

This welcoming pub in the heart of the Wolds is run by husband and wife team Darren and Shona, with Darren as chef. Expect cask ales and comfortable armchairs plus freshly cooked food written up on daily blackboards. Dishes range from ham and home-made piccalilli ciabatta roll, served with coleslaw, salad garnish and crisps, to whole roast partridge stuffed with pork and apple and served on a truffle mash with smoked bacon and shallot sauce.

Open 11.30–2.30 6.30–11 Closed: 2nd & 3rd wk Jan, Sun eve & Mon **Bar Meals** L served Tue-Sat 11.30–2 D served Tue-Sat 6.30–9 **Restaurant** L served Tue-Sun 11.30–2 D served Tue-Sat 6.30–9 ⊕ Free House ◀ Black Sheep, Timothy Taylor Landlord & guest. **Facilities** Garden Parking

BOURNE

MAP 12 TF02

The Wishing Well Inn ♀

Main St, Dyke PE10 0AF ☎ 01778 422970 🖷 01778 394508

dir: *Take A15 towards Sleaford. Inn in next village*

This Lincolnshire village free house started life in 1879 as a one-room pub called the Crown. Several extensions have since been sympathetically executed with recycled stone and timbers; the well that gives the pub its name, previously in the garden, is now a feature of the smaller dining room. Loyal customers return again and again to enjoy a comprehensive menu of traditional favourites in the warm and welcoming atmosphere. Outside, an attractive beer garden backs onto the children's play area.

Open 9–11 (Winter 9–3, 5–11) **Bar Meals** L served all week 12–9 D served all week 12–9 Av main course £8.95 **Restaurant** L served all week 12–2 D served all week 5.30–9 (Summer all day) Av 2 course fixed price £11.50 ⊕ Free House ◀ Greene King Abbot Ale, Spitfire, 3 guest ales. ♀ 7 **Facilities** Children's licence Garden Parking Play Area

See advert on this page

England

BRIGG
MAP 17 TA00

The Jolly Miller ♀

Brigg Rd, Wrawby DN20 8RH ☎ 01652 655658
e-mail: dandmigib@aol.com

dir: *1.5m E of Brigg on A18, on left*

Popular country inn a few miles south of the Humber Estuary. The pleasant bar and dining area are traditional in style, and there's a large beer garden. The menu offers a good range of food: tuck into a chip butty; vegetable burger bap; home-made curry; or steak with onion rings. Puddings include hot chocolate fudge cake and banana split. Play area and children's menu. Coach parties accepted with advanced booking.

Open 12 -12 (Tue 3–11, Fri–Sat 12–1) **Bar Meals** L served all week 12–7.30 D served all week 12–7.30 (Sun 12–3) Av main course £6
Restaurant L served all week 12–7.30 D served all week 5–7.30 (Sun 12–3) ⊕ Enterprise Inns ◀ Guinness, John Smith Extra Smooth & 2 guest ales.
Facilities Children's licence Garden Parking Play Area

COLEBY
MAP 17 SK96

The Bell Inn ♀

3 Far Ln LN5 0AH ☎ 01522 810240 📄 01522 811800

dir: *8m S of Lincoln on A607. In village turn right at church*

One of the three original buildings that became today's rural Bell Inn actually was a pub, built in 1759. The dining area is also divisible by three – a brasserie, a restaurant, and a terrace room. Main courses may include braised shoulder of lamb on Greek-style potatoes; steamed steak and mushroom pudding; and smoked tofu and sweet potato strudel. A separate fish and seafood menu may offer grilled haddock on a sweet potato, goat's cheese and aubergine gâteau.

Open 11.30–3 5.30–11 (Sun 11.30–10.30) Closed: 1–14 Jan
Bar Meals L served Mon-Sat 12–2.30 D served Mon-Sat 5.30–9 (Sun 12–8)
Restaurant L served Mon-Sat 12–2.30 D served Mon-Sat 5.30–9.30 (Sun 12–3, 5.30–8.30) ⊕ Pubmaster ◀ Carlsberg-Tetley Bitter, Batemans XB, Wadworths 6X, Jennings. ♀8 **Facilities** Garden Dogs allowed Parking

CONINGSBY
MAP 17 TF25

The Lea Gate Inn ♀

Leagate Rd LN4 4RS ☎ 01526 342370 📄 01526 345468
e-mail: theleagateinn@hotmail.com
dir: *Off B1192 just outside Coningsby*

The oldest licensed premises in the county, dating from 1542, this was the last of the Fen Guide Houses that provided shelter before the treacherous marshes were drained. The oak-beamed pub has a priest's

hole and a very old inglenook fireplace among its features. The same family have been running the pub for over 25 years. Both the bar and restaurant serve food and offer seasonal menus with lots of local produce (including game in season) and a good vegetarian choice.

Open 11.30–2.30 6.30–11 (Sun 12–2.30, 6.30–10.30) **Bar Meals** L served all week 12–2 D served all week 6.30–9.30 Av main course £8.95
Restaurant D served all week 6.30–9.15 Av 3 course à la carte £20 ⊕ Free House ◀ Theakstons XB, Bombardier. ♀7 **Facilities** Garden Parking Play Area **Rooms** available

DONINGTON ON BAIN
MAP 17 TF28

The Black Horse Inn ★★★ INN ♀

Main Rd LN11 9TJ ☎ 01507 343640 📄 01507 343640
e-mail: mike@blackhorse-donington.co.uk

dir: *Telephone for directions*

Ideal for walkers, this old-fashioned country pub is set in a small village in the heart of the Lincolnshire Wolds on the Viking Way. A large grassed area surrounded by trees is ideal for enjoying a drink or dining alfresco on sunny days. Dining options include the non-smoking dining room, the Blue Room, and the Viking Snug.

Open 12–3 6–11 **Bar Meals** L served all week 12–2 D served all week 7–9 (Sat-Sun 7–9.30) **Restaurant** L served all week 12–2 D served all week 7–9 (Sat-Sun 7–9.30) ⊕ Free House ◀ John Smiths, Greene King, Theakstons.
Facilities Garden Dogs allowed Parking **Rooms** 8

EWERBY
MAP 12 TF14

The Finch Hatton Arms

43 Main St NG34 9PH ☎ 01529 460363 📄 01529 461703
dir: *From A17 to Kirkby-la-Thorne, then 2m NE. 2m E of A153 between Sleaford & Anwick*

Originally known as the Angel Inn, this 19th-century pub was given the family name of Lord Winchelsea, who bought it in 1875. After a chequered history and a short period of closure, it reopened in the 1980s and these days offers pub, restaurant and hotel facilities. It offers an extensive and varied menu to suit all tastes and budgets, but with its traditional ale and regular customers it retains a 'local' atmosphere.

Open 11.30–2.30 6.30–11 Closed: 25–26 Dec **Bar Meals** L served all week 11.30–2 D served all week 6.30–10 (Sun 6.30–9.30) Av main course £10 **Restaurant** L served all week 11.30–2 D served all week 6.30–10 (Sun 6.30–9.30) Av 3 course à la carte £18 ⊕ Free House ◀ Everards Tiger Best, Dixons Major, guest ale. **Facilities** Children's licence Garden Parking

FREISTON
MAP 12 TF34

Kings Head

Church Rd PE22 0NT ☎ 01205 760368
dir: *From Boston towards Skegness on A52 follow signs for RSPB Reserve Freiston Shore*

Originally two tied cottages, this pub dates from the 15th century and retains its old world charm. According to the season, you'll be delighted by the award-winning flower displays outside or the large coal fire inside. The landlady, Ann, has been here 26 years and makes all the food, using only local produce, while partner Bill provides a warm welcome in the bar. Hearty dishes, such as steak or rabbit pie, are served with fresh vegetables.

Open 11–11 (Sun 12–3 7.30–10.30) **Bar Meals** L served Mon-Tue 12–2 D served Fri-Sat 7–9 (Sun 12–3) **Restaurant** L served Mon-Sat 12–2 D served Fri-Sat 7–9 (Sun 12–3) ⊕ Batemans ◀ Batemans XB & Dark Mild, Worthington Cream Flow & John Smiths, Guinness. **Facilities** Parking **Notes** ⊛

FROGNALL   MAP 12 TF11

The Goat ☻

155 Spalding Rd PE6 8SA ☎ 01778 347629

e-mail: graysdebstokes@btconnect.com

dir: A1 to Peterborough, A15 to Market Deeping, old A16 to Spalding, pub about 1.5m from junct of A15 & A16

Families are welcome at this cosy, friendly country free house, which has an open fire, large beer garden and plenty to amuse the children. Main courses include beef stroganoff; pork in sweet and sour sauce; leek and mushroom pie; warm bacon and stilton salad; and home-made prawn curry. Beer is taken seriously, with five different guest ales each week and regular beer festivals throughout the year.

Open 11.30–3 6–11 (Sun 12–10.30) Closed: 25 Dec **Bar Meals** L served all week 12–2 D served all week 6.30–9.30 (Sun 12–9) Av main course £8 **Restaurant** L served all week 12–2 D served all week 6.30–9.30 (Sun 12–9) Av 3 course à la carte £16 ⊕ Free House ◀ guest ales: e.g. Elgood, Batemans, Abbeydale, Nethergate. ☙ 16 **Facilities** Garden Parking Play Area

---

GEDNEY DYKE   MAP 12 TF42

The Chequers ☻

PE12 0AJ ☎ 01406 362666 🖨 01406 362666

dir: From King's Lynn take A17, 1st rdbt after Long Sutton take B1359

In a pretty village close to the Wash, this 18th-century country inn has a good selection of food. Local quails eggs with bacon; or bang bang chicken, and fish specials like marinaded loin of tuna with tomato salsa; or baked sea bass with lobster fish cake are popular. Lincolnshire pork and leek sausages; and wild mushroom gateau crîpe with parmesan shavings are non-fish options. Well-chosen ales, patio garden and outdoor eating in summer.

Open 12–2 7–11 (Fri-Sat 7–12, Sun 12–2 7–10.30) Closed: 26 Dec **Bar Meals** L served Tue-Sun 12–2 D served Tue-Sun 7–9 (Sun 12–2.30) **Restaurant** L served Tue-Sun 12–2 D served Tue-Sun 7–9 (Sun 12–2.30, 7–9) ⊕ Free House ◀ Adnams Best, Greene King Abbot Ale, Speckled Hen, IPA. ☙ 10 **Facilities** Garden Parking

---

GRANTHAM   MAP 11 SK93

The Beehive Inn

10/11 Castlegate NG31 6SE ☎ 01476 404554

dir: A52 to town centre, L at Finkin St, pub at end

Grantham's oldest inn (1550) is notable for having England's only living pub sign – a working beehive high up in a lime tree. Otherwise, this simple town hostelry offers a good pint of Newby Wyke and good-value, yet basic bar food. Kids will enjoy the bouncy castle that appears during the summer.

Open 12–11 (Fri-Sat 12–12) **Bar Meals** L served all week 12–2 Av main course £4 ⊕ Free House ◀ Newby Wyke Real Ales, Everards. **Facilities** Garden

---

HECKINGTON   MAP 12 TF14

The Nags Head ☻

34 High St NG34 9QZ ☎ 01529 460218

dir: 5m E of Sleaford on A17

Overlooking a village green boasting the only eight-sailed windmill in the country. This listed, white-painted coaching inn, built in 1645, was reputedly visited by highwayman Dick Turpin after stealing some horses. He was later captured in York. On the menu: home-made pies, including chicken and stilton, beef and ale, and homity; salmon, scampi, mussels, haddock and sea bass. Patio garden with lots of tables and play area.

Open 11 -12.30 **Bar Meals** L served all week 12–2 D served all week 7–9 ⊕ Punch Taverns ☙ 15 **Facilities** Garden Parking

---

HOUGH-ON-THE-HILL   MAP 11 SK94

The Brownlow Arms ★★★★★ INN ⊛

High Rd NG32 2AZ ☎ 01400 250234 🖨 01400 251993

e-mail: armsinn@yahoo.co.uk

web: www.thebrownlowarms.com

dir: Take A607 (Grantham to Sleaford road). Hough-on-the-Hill signed from Barkston

Named after its former owner, Lord Brownlow, this 17th-century stone inn looks like a well-tended country house. A menu of modern classic dishes includes baked cheese soufflé with ham, leeks and cream to start, perhaps, then slow-cooked shoulder of lamb, crushed winter roots, Rioja and red wine jus; followed by caramelised lemon tart with blackcurrant sorbet. A landscaped terrace looks out over tree-lined fields. Take advantage of one of the four en suite double bedrooms.

Open 6.30–11 (Sun 12–3) Closed: 25–27 Dec, 1–20 Jan, 1wk Sep & Mon **Restaurant** L served Sun 12–2 D served Tue-Sat 6.30–9.30 ⊕ Free House ◀ Timothy Taylor Landlord, Marstons, Pedigree. **Facilities** Garden Parking **Rooms** 4

LINCOLN

MAP 17 SK97

Pyewipe Inn

Fossebank, Saxilby Rd LN1 2BG

☎ 01522 528708 🖩 01522 525009

e-mail: enquiries@pyewipeinn.co.uk

dir: *From Lincoln on A57 past Lincoln/A46 Bypass, pub signed in 0.5m*

First licensed in 1778, the Pyewipe (local dialect for lapwing) stands in four acres alongside the Roman-built Fossedyke Navigation. From the grounds there's a great view of nearby Lincoln Cathedral. All food is bought locally and prepared by five qualified chefs. With up to eight menu boards to choose from, expect beef, mushroom and Guinness pie; fillet of lamb with onion mash and roasted garlic; thyme chicken on saffron risotto, and much more.

Open 11–11 (Sun 12–10.30) **Bar Meals** L served all week 12–9.30 D served all week Sun 12–9 Av main course £9 **Restaurant** L served all week 12–9.30 D served all week 12–9 Av 3 course à la carte £19 ⊕ Free House ◾ Timothy Taylor Landlord, Greene King Abbot Ale, Interbrew Bass, Bombardier. **Facilities** Garden Dogs allowed Parking

The Victoria

6 Union Rd LN1 3BJ ☎ 01522 536048

dir: *From city outskirts follow signs for Cathedral Quarter. Pub 2 mins' walk from all major up-hill car parks*

Situated right next to the Westgate entrance of the Castle and within a stone's throw of Lincoln Cathedral, a long-standing drinkers' pub with a range of real ales, including six changing guest beers, as well as two beer festivals a year. It also offers splendid meals made from exclusively home-prepared food including hot baguettes and filled bacon rolls, Saturday breakfast and Sunday lunches. House specials include sausage and mash, various pies, chilli con carne and home-made lasagne.

Open 11–11 (Fri–Sat 11–11.30, Sun 12–11) **Bar Meals** L served all week 12–2.30 (Sat 11–2.30, Sun 12–2) **Restaurant** L served Sun 12–2 ⊕ Tynemill Ltd ◾ Timothy Taylor Landlord, Batemans XB, Castle Rock Harvest Pale, guest ales. **Facilities** Garden

---

Pick of the Pubs

Wig & Mitre ♥

32 Steep Hill LN2 1LU

☎ 01522 535190 🖩 01522 532402

e-mail: email@wigandmitre.com

dir: *At top of Steep Hill, adjacent to cathedral & Lincoln Castle car parks*

In the historic heart of Lincoln, the Wig & Mitre is a mix of the 14th and 16th centuries, as well as a bit of new build. But it all works and this music-free pub provides food in perpetual motion from 8am to around midnight every day, all year round. The comprehensive breakfast menu – to include champagne if you want – runs until noon, while sandwiches and light meals, such as minute steak au poivre, are available until 6pm. A meal from the main menu could include Iranian Sevruga caviar with blinis and crème fraîche; followed by pan-fried pork cutlet, honey-roast parsnip, and apple and mustard compote; or perhaps roasted fillet of halibut with wild mushrooms, baby onions and lentils; and

finally a special pudding from the blackboard. The board also lists specials such as Lincolnshire Poacher sausages with champ mash. Real ales support an extensive wine list.

Open 8am-12pm **Bar Meals** L served all week 8am-10pm D served all week 8am-10pm Av main course £13.95 **Restaurant** L served all week 8am-10pm D served all week 8am-10pm Av 3 course à la carte £19.95 ⊕ Free House ◾ Black Sheep Special, Batemans XB. ♥ 34 **Facilities** Dogs allowed

---

LOUTH

MAP 17 TF38

Masons Arms

Cornmarket LN11 9PY ☎ 01507 609525 🖩 0870 7066450

e-mail: info@themasons.co.uk

dir: *In town centre*

This Grade II listed building, located in the heart of Georgian Louth, dates back to 1725. In the days when it was known as the Bricklayers Arms, the local Masonic lodge met here. The CAMRA award-winning Market Bar is for beer lovers, while the 'upstairs' restaurant offers an à la carte menu where you might find honey roast ham, fried egg and home-made chips; steak and kidney pie; and cauliflower cheese.

Open 10–11 (Fri-Sat 10–12, Sun 12–11) **Bar Meals** L served Mon-Sat 12–2.30 D served Mon-Sat 6–8.30 (Sun 12–3) Av main course £6.95 **Restaurant** L served Sun 12–3 ⊕ Free House ◾ Abbeydale Moonshine, Marston's Pedigree, Batemans XB Bitter, XXXB & 2 guest ales. **Facilities** Children's licence **Rooms** available

---

NEWTON

MAP 12 TF03

The Red Lion

NG34 0EE ☎ 01529 497256

e-mail: theredlion@netbreeze.co.uk

dir: *10m E of Grantham on A52*

Dating from the 17th century, the Red Lion is particularly popular with walkers and cyclists, perhaps because the flat Lincolnshire countryside makes for easy exercise. Low beams, exposed stone walls and an open fire in the bar help to create a very atmospheric interior. Popular dishes include haddock in beer batter, lemon sole with parsley butter sauce, breadcrumbed scampi, and home-made steak and ale pie. The carvery serves cold buffets on weekdays, hot ones on Friday and Saturday evenings, and Sunday lunchtime.

Open 12–3 6–11 (Sun 12–4, 7–10.30) **Bar Meals** L served all week 12–2 D served Mon-Sun 7–9 (Thu-Sat 6–9) **Restaurant** L served Sun 12–2 D served Mon-Sat 7–9 (Thu-Sat 6–9) ⊕ Free House ◾ Batemans, Everards & guest ales. **Facilities** Garden Dogs allowed Parking

PARTNEY   MAP 17 TF46

Red Lion Inn

PE23 4PG ☎ 01790 752271 📠 01790 753360

e-mail: enquiries@redlioninnpartney.co.uk

dir: On A16 from Boston, or A158 from Horncastle

This peaceful village inn at the foot of the Lincolnshire Wolds offers a warm welcome. It also has a reputation for good home-cooked food using local produce, so walkers and cyclists take refreshment here between visits to the nearby nature reserves and sandy beaches. The comprehensive menu includes many favourites: starters such as prawn cocktail, and deep-fried mushrooms; main courses of lamb or pork chops, chicken curry, and beef casserole; and specials too, like half a honey-roast chicken.

Open 12–3 7–11 (Sun 12–2.30, 7–10.30) Closed: Mon **Bar Meals** L served Tue-Sun 12–2 D served Tue-Sat 7–9.30 (Sun 7–9) Av main course £8 **Restaurant** L served Tue-Sun 12–2 D served Tue-Sat 7–9.30 (Sun 7–9) ⊕ Free House ◀ Black Sheep, Guinness, Tetleys & guest ales. **Facilities** Garden Parking **Rooms** available

---

RAITHBY   MAP 17 TF36

Red Lion Inn

PE23 4DS ☎ 01790 753727

dir: A158 from Horncastle, right at Sausthorpe, left to Raithby

Traditional beamed black-and-white village pub, parts of which date back 300 years. Log fires provide a warm welcome in winter. A varied menu of home-made dishes includes seabass with lime stir fry vegetables, roast guinea fowl with tomato, garlic and bacon, and medallions of beef with peppercorn sauce.

Open 12–3 7–11 **Bar Meals** L served Tue-Sun 12–2 D served Tue-Sat 7–9 **Restaurant** L served Tue-Sun 12–2 D served Tue-Sat 7–9 ⊕ Free House ◀ Raithby, Greene King IPA, Tetley Smooth. **Facilities** Children's licence Garden Dogs allowed Parking

---

SKEGNESS   MAP 17 TF56

Best Western Vine Hotel ★★★ HL ♛

Vine Rd, Seacroft PE25 3DB

☎ 01754 763018 & 610611 📠 01754 769845

e-mail: info@thevinehotel.com

dir: In Seacroft area of Skegness. S of town centre

Substantially unchanged since 1770, the Vine is the second oldest building in Skegness. Set amid two acres of gardens, the ivy-covered hotel was bought by the brewer Harry Bateman in 1927. This charming hostelry offers comfortable accommodation and a fine selection of Bateman's own ales. The bar menu ranges from soup or a simple sandwich to bistro-style salads and substantial mixed grills; there's a traditional Sunday carvery, too.

Open 11–11 (Sun 12–10.30) **Bar Meals** L served all week 12–2.15 D served all week 6–9.15 (Sat-Sun all day) Av main course £7 **Restaurant** L served all week 12.30–2 D served all week 6.30–9.15 (Sun 12–2.30) Av 3 course à la carte £20 ⊕ Free House ◀ Batemans XB & XXXB, Valiant & Blacksheep. ♛ 8 **Facilities** Children's licence Garden Dogs allowed Parking **Rooms** 24

SOUTH WITHAM   MAP 11 SK91

Blue Cow Inn & Brewery

High St NG33 5QB

☎ 01572 768432 📠 01572 768432

e-mail: enquiries@bluecowinn.co.uk

dir: Between Stamford & Grantham on A1

Just in Lincolnshire, with the Rutland border a few hundred yards away, this once-derelict, 13th-century inn stands close to the source of the River Witham. Part-timbered outside, the interior has a wealth of beamed ceilings and walls, stone floors and open log fires when the easterly winds whip across the Fens from Siberia. Simon Crathorn brews his own beers. The inn has a patio beer garden for warm evenings.

Open 12–11 **Bar Meals** L served all week 12–2.30 D served all week 6–9.30 **Restaurant** L served all week 12–2.30 D served all week 6–9.30 Av 3 course à la carte £15 ⊕ Free House **Facilities** Garden Dogs allowed Parking **Rooms** available

---

STAMFORD   MAP 11 TF00

The Bull & Swan Inn ♛

24a High St, St Martin's PE9 2LJ

☎ 01780 763558 📠 01780 763558

e-mail: bullandswan@btconnect.com

dir: A1 for B1081 towards Stamford. Pub on right in outskirts of town

A 17th-century coaching inn retaining many original features, close to historic Burghley House. There are two log fires in winter and a large patio garden for summer use. Live music is provided indoors every Sunday in winter and in the garden every Friday in summer. The menu ranges from sandwiches to steaks or moules marinière, while daily specials offer roasted smoked duck breast or medallions of pork.

Open 11.30–11 (Mon 5–11, Sun 12–11) **Bar Meals** L served Tues-Sun 12–2 D served Mon-Sat 6.30–9 (Sat Lunch 12–5) Av main course £10 **Restaurant** L served Tue-Sun 12–2 D served Mon-Sat 6.30–9 Av 3 course à la carte £16 ◀ Jennings Cumberland, Greene King Abbot Ale, Adnams Bitter, guest ales. ♛ 12 **Facilities** Garden Dogs allowed Parking

STAMFORD continued

The George of Stamford ★★★ HL

71 St Martins PE9 2LB

☎ 01780 750750 ▤ 01780 750701

e-mail: reservations@georgehotelofstamford.com

dir: *From Peterborough take A1 N. Onto B1081 for Stamford, down hill to lights. Hotel on left*

Forty coaches a day – 20 heading for London, 20 for York – once stopped at this 16th-century inn to change horses, which explains the doors marked with the names of the two cities. It is a magnificent building, full of fascinating rooms, and widely known for its famous gallows inn sign across the road that welcomed travellers, while warning highwaymen to keep going. Today's visitors will appreciate the welcoming log fires, oak-panelled restaurants, medieval crypt, walled Monastery Garden and cobbled courtyard. Various menus are available: in the bistro-style restaurant the food ranges from pastas to fish and chips; in the York Bar find sandwiches to goulash. Specific dishes include Brittany seafood platter; chick pea and vegetable tagine with coriander couscous; fillet of English beef with cottage pie; and wild mushroom risotto. The hotel has 47 individually designed, well equipped bedrooms.

Open 11–11 (Sun 12–11) **Bar Meals** L served Mon-Sat 11.30–2.30 (Sun 12–2.30) Av main course £7.25 **Restaurant** L served all week 12.30–2.30 D served all week 7.30–10.30 Av 3 course à la carte £35.30 Av 2 course fixed price £19.45 ⊕ Free House ◀ Adnams Broadside, Fuller's London Pride, Greene King Ruddles Bitter. ♀ 14 **Facilities** Garden Dogs allowed Parking **Rooms** 47

SURFLEET SEAS END MAP 12 TF22

The Ship Inn

154 Reservoir Rd PE11 4DH

☎ 01775 680547 ▤ 01775 680541

e-mail: info@shipinnsurfleet.com

dir: *Off A16 (Spalding to Boston). Follow tourist signs towards Surfleet reservoir then The Ship Inn signs*

A fenland pub by the lock gates controlling the Rivers Glen and Welland, and Vernatti's Drain. Dating from only 2003, it occupies the footprint of an earlier hostelry, which the drainage-fixated Vernatti built in 1642. The bar is panelled in hand-crafted oak, while upstairs is the restaurant overlooking the marshes. Locally sourced food includes Whitby scampi; home-made pies; roast rib of Lincolnshire beef; and pan-fried salmon in the restaurant.

Open 11.30–3 6–11 (Fri-Sat 6–12) **Bar Meals** L served Tue-Sun 12–2 D served Tue-Sat 6.30–9 Av main course £9 **Restaurant** L served Sun 12–2 D served Fri-Sat 7–9 Av 3 course à la carte £21 ⊕ Free House ◀ Cottage Brewery selection, Tom Woods Bitter, Hydes Smooth & local micro breweries. **Facilities** Parking

---

WOODHALL SPA MAP 17 TF16

Village Limits Country Pub, Restaurant & Motel ♀

Stixwould Rd LN10 6UJ

☎ 01526 353312 ▤ 01526 352203

e-mail: info@villagelimits.co.uk

dir: *At rdbt on main street follow Petwood Hotel signs. Motel 500yds past Petwood Hotel*

The pub and restaurant are situated in the original part of the building, so expect bare beams and old world charm. Typical meals include chargrilled chicken breast with a creamy mushroom and pepper sauce, and steaks with various sauces. There's a good choice of real ales to wash it all down. Under new management for 2008.

Open 12–2.30 6.30–11 Closed: Mon & Sun eve **Bar Meals** L served Tue-Sun 12–2 D served Tue-Sat 6.30–9 Av main course £10 **Restaurant** L served Tue-Sun 12–2 D served Tue-Sat 6.30–9 Av 3 course à la carte £18.50 ⊕ Free House ◀ Bateman XB, Black Sheep Best, Barnsley Bitter, Tetley's Smooth Flow. ♀ 8 **Facilities** Garden Parking **Rooms** available

---

WOOLSTHORPE MAP 11 SK83

The Chequers Inn ★★★★ INN ◉ ♀

See Pick of the Pubs on opposite page

PICK OF THE PUBS

WOOLSTHORPE-LINCOLNSHIRE

The Chequers Inn

Just a stone's throw from Belvoir Castle, the Chequers Inn mixes modern style with traditional features including five real fires. There are further delights outside – the pub has a cricket pitch and castle views from the mature garden.

For refreshment, the fully-stocked bar meets every whim and taste: an extensive range of beers embraces real ales and continental lagers; the wine list includes over twenty served by the glass, including champagne; and fifty single malts hide some lesser known drams among the usual favourites. You can sit down to eat here too if you like, with two tables available for reservation. Alternatively try the Bakehouse Restaurant, which contains the oven from the pub's previous incarnation as the village bakery, built in 1646. The more intimate Red Room is ideal for a private party. The strong emphasis on home cooking and quality ingredients brings locally sourced produce to the table, including steaks and sausages. Bar snacks include a ploughman's of Colston Basset stilton, Lincolnshire Poacher and carved ham; a red pepper, feta cheese and rocket sandwich with frites and salad; and a home-made burger with mature cheddar and hand-cut chips. An excellent value two- or three-course fixed price lunch menu could offer mussels marinières, followed by a fillet of salmon with sautéed potatoes, and apple crumble with clotted cream to finish. Alternatively the à la carte choice could tempt with crisp lamb sweetbreads with warm shallot and red wine vinegar dressing; medallions of monkfish, roast garlic mash, braised carrots and tarragon butter sauce; and sticky toffee pudding with butterscotch sauce.

★★★★ INN ◉ ♉
MAP 11 SK83
Main St NG32 1LU
☎ 01476 870701
e-mail: justinnabar@yahoo.co.uk
dir: *Approx 7m from Grantham. 3m from A607. Follow heritage signs to Belvoir Castle*

Open 12–3 5.30–11
Bar Meals L served Mon-Sat 12–2.30 D served Mon-Sat 6–9.30 (Sun 12–4, 6–8.30)
Av main course £13.50
Restaurant L served Mon-Sat 12–2.30 D served Mon-Sat 6–9.30 (Sun 12–4, 6–8.30) Av 3 course à la carte £25 Av 3 course fixed price £16.50
⊕ Free House ◀ Olde Trip & Brewster's Marquis. ♉ 25
Facilities Children's licence Garden Dogs allowed Parking
Rooms 4

England

LONDON

E1

Town of Ramsgate ♀   Plan 2 F4

62 Wapping High St E1W 2NP ☎ 020 7481 8000

dir: *0.3m from Wapping tube station & Tower of London*

A 500-year-old pub close to The City, decorated with bric-a-brac and old prints. Judge Jeffries was caught here while trying to flee the country and escape the kind of justice he dealt out. Press gangs used to work the area, imprisoning men overnight in the cellar. The owners continue to offer real ale and value for money bar food, which can be enjoyed on the decked terrace overlooking the river Thames.

Open 12–12 **Bar Meals** L served all week 12–9 D served all week 12–9 ⊕ Free House ◀ Adnams, Youngs, Fuller's London Pride. ♀ 7 **Facilities** Garden Dogs allowed

E9

Pick of the Pubs

The Empress of India ♀   Plan 2 F4

130 Lauriston Rd, Victoria Park E9 7LH

☎ 020 8533 5123 📄 020 8533 4483

e-mail: info@theempressofindia.com

dir: *From Mile End Station turn right onto Grove Rd which will lead onto Lauriston Rd*

Queen Victoria became Empress of India in 1877, a few years before this archetypal East End public house was built. It later became a nightclub, a print works and, most recently, a floristry training school until Ed and Tom Martin added it to their London pub portfolio. The beautifully styled interior includes a carpet that must be unique since it has the pub's name woven into it. The bar serves classic cocktails, draught beers and fine wines from around the globe. Modern British food served from the open kitchen includes rotisseried rare breed beef, whole leg of Norfolk lamb, suckling pig, roe deer, duck and organic free range chicken. Other suggestions are a pint of prawns with mayonnaise; toad in the hole with onion gravy and mash; and baked halibut with braised iceberg lettuce and smoked mussel velouté. Puddings include raspberry and frangipane tart – how Hackney's changed!

Open 9 –11 Closed: 25–26 Dec **Restaurant** L served Mon-Sat 12–3 D served Mon-Sat 6–10 (Sun 12–4, 6.30–9.30) ◀ Greenwich Meantime Helles Lager, Greenwich Meantime Indian Pale Ale, Paulaner Weiss ale. ♀ 30 **Facilities** Children's licence

E14

Pick of the Pubs

The Grapes ♀   Plan 2 G4

76 Narrow St, Limehouse E14 8BP

☎ 020 7987 4396 📄 020 7987 3137

dir: *Telephone for details*

Charles Dickens once propped the bar up here, and so taken was he by its charms that the pub appears, thinly disguised, as The Six Jolly Fellowship Porters in his novel *Our Mutual Friend.* While the novelist might still recognise the interior, the surroundings have changed dramatically with the development of Canary Wharf and the Docklands Light Railway. However, the tradition of old-fashioned values is maintained by the provision of the best cask conditioned ales in the atmospheric bar downstairs, while in the tiny upstairs restaurant only the freshest fish is served. This is a fish lover's paradise with a menu that includes sea bass, monkfish, Dover sole and bream, all available with a range of different sauces. Meat eaters and vegetarians should not, however, be deterred from experiencing this evocative slice of old Limehouse; traditional roasts are served on Sundays, and sandwiches and salads are always available.

Open 12–3 5.30–11 (Fri-Sat 12–11, Sun 12–10.30) Closed: 25–26 Dec, 1 Jan **Bar Meals** L served Mon-Fri 12–2 D served Mon-Sat 7–9 (Sat brunch 12–2.30, Sun 12–3.30) Av main course £7.50 **Restaurant** L served Mon-Fri 12–2.15 D served Mon-Sat 7.30–9.15 (Sun roast only 12–3.30) Av 3 course à la carte £28 ⊕ Punch Taverns ◀ Adnams, Marstons Pedigree, Tetley's Bitter, Timothy Taylor Landlord. ♀ 6 **Facilities** Dogs allowed

Pick of the Pubs

The Gun ◉ ♀   Plan 2 G4

27 Coldharbour, Docklands E14 9NS

☎ 020 7515 5222 📄 020 7515 4407

e-mail: info@thegundocklands.com

dir: *From South Quay DLR, east along Marsh Wall to mini rdbt. Turn left, over bridge then 1st right.*

Destroyed by fire several years ago, this grade two listed 18th-century pub re-opened in 2004 following painstaking restoration works carried out in close consultation with English Heritage. It stands on the banks of the Thames directly across the water from the Millennium Dome and a stone's throw from Canary Wharf. The surrounding area was once home to the dockside iron foundries which produced guns for the Royal Navy fleets. The Gun itself used to shelter smugglers. There is still a spy hole on the secret circular staircase that was once used to look out for the 'revenue men'. Today the modern pub menu is a major attraction, with choices ranging from bar food (pint o' prawns with aioli; Irish rock oysters; beef shin burger with fat chips) to evening meals such as ham hock and confit foie gras terrine, followed by braised daube of beef with Alsace bacon and truffle mash.

Open 11–12 (Sat 11.30–12, Sun 11.30–10.30) Closed: 26 Dec **Bar Meals** L served Mon-Fri 12–3.45 D served Mon-Sat 6–10.30 (Sat 11–4, Sun 11–4, 6–9.30) Av main course £15 **Restaurant** L served Mon-Fri 12–3 D served Mon-Sat 6–10.30 (Sat 11–4, Sun 11–4, 6–9.30) Av 3 course à la carte £26 ◀ Guinness. ♀ 22 **Facilities** Children's licence Garden

EC1

Pick of the Pubs

The Bleeding Heart Tavern ⊕ ♀
Plan 1 E4

19 Greville St EC1N 8SQ

☎ 020 7242 8238 🗎 020 7831 1402

e-mail: bookings@bleedingheart.co.uk

dir: *Close to Farringdon tube station, at corner of Grenville St & Bleeding Heart Yard*

Standing just off London's famous Leather Lane, the first record of this old tavern dates from 1746, when Holborn had a boozer for every five houses. It traded until 1946, was a grill for 52 years, and reopened as The Tavern Bar in 1998. Today the Tavern offers traditional real ales and a light lunchtime menu if you're pressed for time. Downstairs, the warm and comforting dining room features an open rotisserie and grill serving free-range organic British meat, game and poultry alongside an extensive wine list. Typical menu choices might start with split pea and ham soup or potted shrimps, as a prelude to omelette Arnold Bennett; south Devon beef burger with coleslaw and fries; or smoked haddock with poached egg, bubble and squeak. Desserts include walnut Bakewell tart with clotted cream, and the Tavern is also open for a choice of continental or full English breakfasts.

Open 7am-11pm Closed: BHs, 10 days at Xmas, Sat & Sun **Bar Meals** L served Mon-Fri 11 D served Mon-Fri 6–10.30 (Breakfast available 7am-10.30am) **Restaurant** L served Mon-Fri 12–3 D served Mon-Fri 6–10.30 Av 3 course à la carte £19.95 ⊕ Free House ◀ Adnams Southwold Bitter, Broadside & Fisherman. ♀ 17

Pick of the Pubs

The Eagle ♀
Plan 1 E4

159 Farringdon Rd EC1R 3AL ☎ 020 7837 1353

dir: *Angel/Farringdon tube station. Pub at north end of Farringdon Rd*

The Eagle, which opened in 1990, was a front-runner of a new breed of stylish eating and drinking establishments that we now know as gastro pubs. Farringdon Road was more downbeat in those days but Clerkenwell is quite a trendy district now. The Eagle is still going strong, despite considerable competition, and remains one of the neighbourhood's top establishments. The airy interior includes a wooden-floored bar and dining area, a random assortment of furniture, and an open-to-view kitchen that produces a creative, modern, daily-changing menu drawing on the worlds' cuisine.

Typical of the range are escalivada, a Spanish-style roast vegetable salad with sherry vinegar and parsley; osso buco alla Milanese with saffron risotto; and Romney Marsh lamb chops with grilled artichokes and olives. A tapas selection is also available. Draught and bottled beers, and an international wine list are all well chosen.

Open 12–11 Closed: Sun eve & some BHs **Bar Meals** L served Mon-Fri 12.30–3 D served Mon-Sat 6.30–10.30 (Sat-Sun 12.30–3.30) Av main course £9.50 ⊕ Free House ◀ Wells Eagle IPA & Bombardier. ♀ 14 **Facilities** Dogs allowed

Pick of the Pubs

The Jerusalem Tavern
Plan 1 F4

55 Britton St, Clerkenwell EC1M 5NA

☎ 020 7490 4281 🗎 020 7250 3780

e-mail: beers@stpetersbrewery.co.uk

dir: *100mtrs NE of Farringdon tube station; 300mtrs N of Smithfield*

Named after the Priory of St John of Jerusalem, this historic tavern has been in four different locations since it was established in the 14th century. The current building dates from 1720, when a merchant lived here, although the frontage dates from about 1810, by which time it was the premises of one of Clerkenwell's many watch and clockmaker's workshops. A fascinating and wonderfully vibrant corner of London that has only recently been 'rediscovered', centuries after Samuel Johnson, David Garrick and the young Handel used to drink in this tavern. Its dark, dimly-lit Dickensian bar, with bare boards, rustic wooden tables, old tiles, candles, open fires and cosy corners, is the perfect film set – and that is what is has been on many occasions. The Jerusalem Tavern, a classic pub in every sense of the description, is open every weekday and offers the full range of bottled beers from St Peter's Brewery (which owns it), as well as a familiar range of pub fare, including game pie, risotto, sausage and mash and various roasts.

Open 11–11 Closed: 25 Dec-1 Jan, Sat & Sun **Bar Meals** L served Mon-Fri 12–3 D served Tue-Thu 5–9.30 Av main course £8 ⊕ St Peters Brewery ◀ St Peters (complete range).

Pick of the Pubs

The Peasant ♀
Plan 1 D3

240 St John St EC1V 4PH

☎ 020 7336 7726 🗎 020 7490 1089

e-mail: eat@thepeasant.co.uk

dir: *Exit Angel & Farringdon Rd tube station. Pub on corner of St John St & Percival St*

In the heart of Clerkenwell, this award-winning gastro-pub dating from 1860 retains many original Victorian features and is now Grade II listed. Customers delight in the lovingly restored mahogany horseshoe bar with its original inlaid mosaic floor, and a fabulous conservatory. The upstairs restaurant has had similar treatment and is beautifully lit by period chandeliers. An extensive range of pumped and bottled beers is supplemented by organic cider, rums, malt whiskeys and a good wine list. Light bites are served in the bar: mussels steamed in bacon, chilli and Leffe draught; fillet of haddock, Welsh rarebit crust, bubble and squeak;

Continued

England

EC1 continued

and sardine Caesar salad are three examples. The restaurant menu offers accomplished cooking in starters like sautéed lambs' kidneys with cassava gnocchi and walnut pesto; and main courses such as grass-fed Argentinian grilled rib-eye steak with roast shallots, red peppers and steamed curly kale.

Open 12–11 Closed: 24 Dec–2 Jan **Bar Meals** L served all week 12–11 D served all week 6–11 (Sun all day) Av main course £9 **Restaurant** L served all week 12–3.30 D served Mon–Sat 6–11 Av 3 course à la carte £35 ⊕ Free House ◖ Bombardier, Dekonick Belgian Ale, Crouch Ale, Brewers Gold. ☙12 **Facilities** Garden Dogs allowed

The Well ☙   Plan 1 F5

180 Saint John St, Clerkenwell EC1V 4JY
☎ 020 7251 9363 ▤ 020 7404 2250
e-mail: drink@downthewell.co.uk
dir: *Farringdon tube station left to junction, left onto St John, pub on corner on right*

A gastropub in trendy Clerkenwell offering a regularly changing, modern European lunch and dinner menu, an extensive wine selection, and lots of draught and bottled beers. The lower ground features a leather-panelled aquarium bar with exotic tropical fish in huge tanks. Start with twice-baked goat's cheese soufflé, or snails with Pernod and garlic butter; then Huntsman sausages with mashed potato and red onion jam; or pan-fried halibut with cep purée and port jus.

Open 11–12 (Fri-Sat 11–1am, Sun 11–11) **Bar Meals** L served Mon–Fri 12–3 D served Mon–Sat 6–10.30 (Sat–Sun 10.30–1 Brunch, 12–4 Lunch, Sun 6–10) Av main course £12 **Restaurant** L served Mon–Fri 12–3 D served Mon–Sat 6–10.30 (Sat -Sun 10.30–1 Brunch, 12–4 Lunch, Sun 6–10) ◖ San Miguel, Paulaner, Red Stripe, Kronenbourg. **Facilities** Children's licence

Ye Olde Mitre ☙   Plan 1 E4

1 Ely Court, Ely Place, By 8 Hatton Garden EC1N 6SJ
☎ 020 7405 4751web:
www.pub-explorer.com
dir: *From Chancery Lane tube station exit 3 walk downhill to Holborn Circus, left into Hatton Garden. Pub in alley between 8 & 9 Hatton Garden*

A famous old establishment, hidden up an alleyway off Hatton Garden, Ye Olde Mitre dates from 1546. Queen Elizabeth once danced around the cherry tree in the corner of the bar. These days there's also a lounge and an outside beer barrel area. Three permanent real ales are served and a minimum of two changing guest ales weekly. The snack menu offers toasted sandwiches, pork pies, scotch eggs, sausages, pickled eggs and gherkins.

Open 11–11 (2nd wknd Aug 12–5) Closed: 25 Dec, 1 Jan, BH, Sat & Sun (ex 2nd wknd Aug) **Bar Meals** L served Mon–Fri 11.30–9.30 ⊕ Punch Taverns ◖ Adnams Bitter, Adnams Broadside, Deuchars IPA, Roosters. ☙9 **Facilities** Garden

EC2

Old Dr Butler's Head   Plan 1 F4

Mason's Av, Coleman St, Moorgate EC2V 5BT
☎ 020 7606 3504 ▤ 020 7600 0417
e-mail: olddrbutlershead@shepherdneame.co.uk
dir: *Telephone for directions*

This City pub is the only surviving tavern displaying the sign of Dr Butler, purveyor of 'medicinal ale'. It was rebuilt after the Great Fire, although the frontage is probably Victorian. Pub lunches and Shepherd Neame real ales are served in the Dickensian gas-lit bar, while upstairs, the Chop House restaurant offers a traditional English menu featuring steak and kidney pudding, and chargrilled lamb cutlets. The City is largely empty at weekends, so the pub closes.

Open 11–11 Closed: Sat & Sun **Bar Meals** L served Mon–Fri 12–3 **Restaurant** L served Mon–Fri ⊕ Shepherd Neame ◖ Shepherd Neame Spitfire, Bishops Finger Master Brew, Shepherd Neame Best.

EC4

The Black Friar   Plan 1 F3

174 Queen Victoria St EC4V 4EG ☎ 020 7236 5474
dir: *Telephone for directions*

Located on the site of Blackfriar's monastery, where Henry VIII dissolved his marriage to Catherine of Aragon and separated from the Catholic church. The pub has made several TV appearances because of its wonderful Art Noveau interior. It is close to Blackfriars Bridge and gets very busy with after-work drinkers. A traditional-style menu includes steak and ale pie, sausage and mash, and sandwiches.

Open 11.30–11 (Sat 11.30–11, Sun 12–9.30) **Bar Meals** L served all week 12–9 D served all week 12–9 ◖ Fuller's London Pride, Adnams, Timothy Taylor, Speckled Hen. **Facilities** Garden

The Old Bank of England ☙   Plan 1 E4

194 Fleet St EC4A 2LT ☎ 020 7430 2255 ▤ 020 7242 3092
e-mail: oldbankofengland@fullers.co.uk
dir: *Pub by Courts of Justice*

This magnificent building previously housed the Law Courts' branch of the Bank of England. Set between the site of Sweeney Todd's barbershop and his mistress' pie shop, it stands above the original bank vaults and the tunnels in which Todd butchered his unfortunate victims. Aptly, bar meals include an extensive range of pies, but other treats include soup, sandwiches, burgers, sharing platters, and hearty meals such as bangers and mash.

Open 11–11 Closed: BHs **Bar Meals** L served Mon–Fri 12–9 D served Mon–Fri 12–9 (Fri Dinner until 8) Av main course £8.50 ⊕ Fullers ◖ London Pride, ESB, Chiswick, Discovery & seasonal. ☙8 **Facilities** Garden

Pick of the Pubs

The White Swan ⊛ ♟   Plan 1 E4

108 Fetter Ln, Holborn EC4A 1ES

☎ 020 7242 9696 📄 020 7404 2250

e-mail: info@thewhiteswanlondon.com

dir: *Nearest tube: Chancery Lane. From station towards St Paul's Cathedral. At HSBC bank left into Fetter Lane. Pub on right*

In 2003, serial London pub owners Tom and Ed Martin gutted the old Mucky Duck and created this handsome, traditional city watering hole. Upstairs is a mezzanine area and a beautifully restored dining room with mirrored ceiling and linen-clad tables. Of course, this being the hedge-funding City, eating can be a rushed business. No problem, the weekday Express Menu delivers two courses in one hour – in at twelve, out at one. An example might be split pea and ham hock soup; followed by potato and aubergine cannelloni, creamed leeks and grilled courgettes. In the more sedate dining room try steak tartare, quail's egg and sauce vièrge; followed by pan-fried haddock, butterbean and bacon cassoulet and truffle mash. Fish comes fresh from Billingsgate market each morning, including the pint of prawns that appears on the pub menu, alongside grilled rib-eye steak; and pure pork sausages, with mash and red onion jam.

Open 11–11 (Wed-Thu 11–12, Fri 11–1) Closed: Sat, Sun & BH **Bar Meals** L served Mon-Fri 12–3 D served Mon-Fri 6–10 Av main course £11 **Restaurant** L served Mon-Fri 12–3 D served Mon-Fri 6–10 Av 3 course à la carte £29 Av 2 course fixed price £24 ◀ London Pride, Red Stripe, Greene King IPA, Guinness. ♟ 10

N1

Pick of the Pubs

The Barnsbury ♟   Plan 2 F4

209–211 Liverpool Rd, Islington N1 1LX

☎ 020 7607 5519 📄 020 7607 3256

e-mail: info@thebarnsbury.co.uk

The Barnsbury, in the heart of Islington, is a welcome addition to the London scene as a gastropub that gets both the prices and food right. The recent addition of a walled garden has added a secluded and sought-after summer oasis for al fresco dining. The food is cooked from daily supplies of fresh produce which have been bought direct from the market, resulting in interesting menus with a slight nod to international cuisine. Starters include leek and smoked haddock chowder; Welsh rarebit crouton with scallops and tiger prawns, and Thai fragrant salad; and chargrilled halloumi, aubergine, parsley and harissa oil. Mains include choices like roast chicken breast with pappardelle and wild mushroom sauce; chargrilled ribeye steak with béarnaise sauce, chips and salad; and goat's cheese and ricotta ravioli, artichokes and sun dried tomatoes. Desserts range through lemon mousse brûlée; French apple tart with butterscotch sauce and Calvados crème fraîche; and chocolate mousse with oranges in Grand Marnier.

Open 12–11 Closed: 24–26 Dec, 1 Jan **Bar Meals** L served all week 12–3 D served all week 6.30–10 (Sun 6.30–9.30) **Restaurant** L served all week 12–3 D served all week 6.30–10 (Sun 6.30–9.30) ⊕ Free House ◀ Timothy Taylor Landlord, Fuller's London Pride, guest ale. ♟ 12 **Facilities** Garden

The Compton Arms ♟   Plan 2 F4

4 Compton Av, Off Canonbury Rd N1 2XD

☎ 020 7359 6883

e-mail: thecomptonarms@ukonline.co.uk

dir: *Telephone for directions*

George Orwell was once a customer at this peaceful pub on Islington's back streets. The late 17th-century building has a rural feel, and is frequented by a mix of locals, actors and musicians. One local described it as "an island in a sea of gastro-pubs". Expect real ales from the hand pump, and good value steaks, mixed grills, big breakfasts and Sunday roasts. The bar is busy when Arsenal are at home.

Open 12–11 (Sat Arsenal match days 11–11) Closed: 25 Dec afternoon **Bar Meals** L served Mon-Fri 12–2.30 D served all week 6–8.30 (Sat-Sun 11–4) Av main course £6 ⊕ Greene King ◀ Greene King IPA, Abbot Ale, Morlands, plus guest ale. ♟ 8 **Facilities** Garden Dogs allowed

The Crown ♟   Plan 2 F4

116 Cloudsley Rd, Islington N1 0EB ☎ 020 7837 7107

e-mail: crown.islington@fullers.co.uk

dir: *From tube station take Liverpool Rd, 6th left into Cloudesley Sq. Pub on opposite side of Square*

This Grade II listed Georgian building in the Barnsbury village conservation area of Islington boasts one of only two remaining barrel bars in London. It specialises in high quality gastro food, and has an unusual range of branded rums. The daily changing menu typically features starters to share like spare ribs or assorted platters with Turkish flatbreads, and mains such as lamb burgers, a variety of sausages, fishcakes, and steak and ale pie. Vegetarians are well catered for.

Open 12–11 (Sun 12–10.30) Closed: 25 Dec **Bar Meals** L served Mon-Fri 12–3 D served Mon-Fri 6–10 (Sun12–9.30, Sat 12–5, 6–10.30) Av main course £9.50 ⊕ Fullers ◀ Fuller's London Pride, Organic Honeydew & ESB. ♟ 12 **Facilities** Garden Dogs allowed

Pick of the Pubs

The Drapers Arms ⊛ ♟   Plan 2 F4

44 Barnsbury St N1 1ER

☎ 020 7619 0348 📄 020 7619 0413

e-mail: info@thedrapersarms.co.uk

dir: *Turn right from Highbury & Islington station, 10mins along Upper Street. Barnsbury St on right opposite Shell service station*

Smart Islington gastro-pub offering one menu throughout, though it is preferable to book the upstairs dining room which attracts a good crowd – celebrities from television, politics and the arts among others. If a more contemplative pint is sought, retire to the secluded and peaceful garden. The downstairs open plan bar is illuminated by large picture windows, its unfussy interior furnished with a mix of squashy sofas and solid wooden tables. Beers major on popular European lagers and pilsners augmented by Fullers' brews, with around twenty wines served by the glass. A wide choice of food includes a range of appetising starters, from parma ham and potato pancakes, to chorizo and baby squid with frisée salad. For a main course try three meat ragu with garlic parsley

CONTINUED

England

N1 continued

and spaghetti, or the catch of the day with ratte potatoes. To finish, savour the delights of passion fruit Pavlova, or apple and berry crumble with clotted cream.

Open 12–11 (Sun 12–10.30) Closed: 24–27 Dec, 1–2 Jan **Bar Meals** L served all week 12–3 D served Mon-Sat 7–10 (Sun 6.30–9.30) Av main course £14 **Restaurant** L served Sun 12–3 D served Mon-Sat 7–10.30 Av 3 course à la carte £26 ⊕ Free House ◀ Old Speckled Hen, Courage, San Miguel, Paulaner. ♥ 18 **Facilities** Garden Dogs allowed

Pick of the Pubs

The Duke of Cambridge ♥   Plan 2 F4

30 St Peter's St N1 8JT

☎ 020 7359 3066 📄 020 7359 1877

e-mail: duke@dukeorganic.co.uk

dir: *Telephone for directions*

A pioneer in sustainable eating out, the Duke of Cambridge was the first UK pub certified by the Soil Association. Founder Geetie Singh has combined her passion for food and ethical business to create a leader in green dining. The company recycles and reuses wherever possible, and even the electricity is wind and solar sourced. The Marine Conservation Society has given its stamp of approval to the Duke's fish purchasing policy – and, with 100% organic wines and a daily-changing menu, you can feel really virtuous about tucking into a few courses with a glass of your favourite tipple. Try a delicious starter like apple, radish and snow pea salad, followed perhaps by slow-braised ham hock with spring greens, creamed potatoes and Dijonnaise sauce. Sweet cherry pie, and honeyed figs with Jersey ice cream are among the desserts.

Open 12–11 (Sun 12–10.30) Closed: 25–26 Dec **Bar Meals** L served Mon-Fri 12.30–3 D served Mon-Sat 6.30–10.30 (Sat-Sun 12.30–3.30, Sun 6.30–10) Av main course £13.50 **Restaurant** L served Mon-Fri 12.30–3 D served Mon-Sat 6.30–10.30 (Sat-Sun 12.30–3.30, Sun 7–10) ⊕ Free House ◀ Eco Warrior, St Peter's Best Bitter, East Kent Golding. ♥ 12 **Facilities** Children's licence Dogs allowed

The House ⊛ ♥   Plan 2 F4

63–69 Canonbury Rd N1 2DG

☎ 020 7704 7410 📄 020 7704 9388

e-mail: info@inthehouse.biz

dir: *Telephone for directions*

This successful gastro-pub has featured in a celebrity cookbook and garnered plenty of praise since it opened its doors a few years ago. Expect a thoroughly modern menu delivering devilled kidneys and ceps on toasted brioche with smoked bacon; chargrilled rib of Buccleuch beef with a mustard and shallot crust, gratin dauphinoise, green beans and jus gras; traditional favourites like shepherd's pie, and smoked haddock with bubble and squeak.

Open 12–11 Closed: 24 Dec, 1 Jan & Mon lunch (ex BH) **Bar Meals** L served Tue-Fri 12–2.30 D served Mon-Sat 5.30–10.30 (Sat-Sun 12–3.30, Sun 6.30–9.30) Av main course £15 **Restaurant** L served Tue-Fri 12–2.30 D served Mon-Sat 5.30–10.30 (Sat-Sun 12.30–3.30, Sun 6.30–9.30) Av 3 course fixed price £17.50 ◀ Adnams, Guinness. ♥ 8 **Facilities** Garden Dogs allowed

The Northgate ♥   Plan 2 F4

113 Southgate Rd, Islington N1 3JS

☎ 020 7359 7392 📄 020 7359 7393

dir: *Nearest tube stations: Old Street & Angel. (7 mins from bus 21/76/141 from Old Street & 5 mins on bus 38/73 from Angel)*

This popular pub was transformed from a run-down community local into a friendly modern establishment serving excellent food. There's a regular guest beer, two real ales, and a good mix of draught lagers and imported bottled beers. The menu changes daily, and might include smoked haddock fishcake, slow-roast tomatoes with lemon butter; roast confit duck leg, mustard mash and Savoy cabbage; and roast aubergine, goats' cheese and onion tart with mixed leaves.

Open 12–11 (Sat 12–12, Sun 12–10.30, Mon 5–11) Closed: 24–26 Dec, 1 Jan **Bar Meals** L served all week 12–10.30 D served all week 6.30–9.30 Av main course £12 **Restaurant** L served Sat-Sun 12–10.30 D served all week 6.30–9.30 Av 3 course à la carte £20 ◀ IPA, Fuller's London Pride & guest ales. ♥ 18 **Facilities** Garden Dogs allowed

N6

Pick of the Pubs

The Flask ♥   Plan 2 E5

Highgate West Hill N6 6BU ☎ 020 8348 7346

e-mail: info@theflaskhighgate.co.uk

dir: *Telephone for directions*

A 17th-century former school in one of London's loveliest villages. Dick Turpin hid from his pursuers in the cellars, and TS Elliot and Sir John Betjeman enjoyed a glass or two here. The interior is listed and includes the original bar with sash windows which lift at opening time. Enjoy a glass of good real ale, a speciality bottled beer (choice of 15), or a hot toddy while you peruse the menu, which changes twice a day. Choices range through sandwiches and platters to char-grills and home-made puddings.

Open 12–11 **Bar Meals** L served all week 12–3 D served all week 6–10 (Sun 12–9.30) Av main course £8 ◀ Adnams, Timothy Taylor Landlord, Caledonian IPA, Harveys Sussex. ♥ 12 **Facilities** Garden Dogs allowed

N19

The Landseer ♥   Plan 2 E5

37 Landseer Rd N19 4JU ☎ 020 7263 4658

e-mail: info@thelandseer.wanadoo.co.uk

dir: *Nearest tube stations: Archway & Tufnell Park*

Sunday roasts are a speciality at this unpretentious gastro pub. Well-kept beers like Marston's Pedigree, Courage Director's and Green King IPA are supported by a range of wines served by the glass. This is an ideal spot to relax with the weekend papers, or while away an evening with one of the pub's extensive library of board games. Weekend lunches and daily evening meals are served from separate bar and restaurant menus.

Open 5–11 (Sat-Sun 12–12) Closed: 25 Dec **Bar Meals** L served Sat-Sun 12–5 D served all week 6–10 (Sun 6–9.30) Av main course £9 **Restaurant** L served Sat-Sun 12–5 D served all week 6–10 (Sun 12.30–5, 6–9.30) ⊕ Free House ◀ Marston's Pedigree, Courage Directors, Greene King IPA. ♥ 11 **Facilities** Children's licence Garden Dogs allowed

NW1

The Chapel

Plan 1 B4

48 Chapel St NW1 5DP

☎ 020 7402 9220 📄 020 7723 2337

e-mail: thechapel@btconnect.com

dir: By A40 Marylebone Rd & Old Marylebone Rd junct. Off Edgware Rd by tube station

There's an informal atmosphere at this bright and airy Marylebone gastro-pub with stripped floors and pine furniture. The open-plan building derives its name from nothing more than its Chapel Street location, but it enjoys one of the largest gardens in central London with seating for over 60 customers. Fresh produce is delivered daily, and served in starters like broccoli and watercress soup, and mains such as pan-roasted chicken breast with sautéed ratte potatoes.

Open 12–11 (Sun 12–10.30) Closed: 25–26 Dec, 1 Jan, Etr **Bar Meals** L served Mon-Sat 12–2.30 D served all week 7–10 (Sun 12.30–3) Av main course £13 **Restaurant** L served Mon-Sat 12–2.30 D served all week 7–10 (Sun 12.30–3) 🍴 Punch Taverns 🍺 Greene King IPA & Adnams. **Facilities** Garden Dogs allowed

---

Pick of the Pubs

The Engineer ♀

Plan 2 E4

65 Gloucester Av, Primrose Hill NW1 8JH

☎ 020 7722 0950 📄 020 7483 0592

e-mail: info@the-engineer.com

dir: Telephone for directions

Situated in a very residential part of Primrose Hill close to Camden Market, this unassuming corner street pub is worth seeking out. Built by Isambard Kingdom Brunel in 1841, it attracts a discerning dining crowd for imaginative and well-prepared food and a friendly, laid-back atmosphere. Inside it is fashionably rustic, with a spacious bar area, sturdy wooden tables with candles, simple decor and changing art exhibitions in the restaurant area. A walled, paved and heated garden to the rear is extremely popular in fine weather. The fortnightly-changing menu features an eclectic mix of inspired home-made dishes and uses organic or free-range meats. Typical examples could be miso-marinated cod with wasabi mash and soy sherry sauce; or chicken breast stuffed with pumpkin, ricotta and sage with warm pasta and asparagus. Side dishes include Baker fries or rocket and parmesan salad, while desserts include apple and blackberry chimichanga.

Open 9am-11pm **Bar Meals** L served Mon-Fri 12–3 D served all week 7–11 (Sat-Sun 12.30–4) **Restaurant** L served Mon-Fri 12–3 D served all week 7–11 (Sat-Sun 12.30–4) 🍺 Erdinger, Bombardier, Hook Norton. ♀10 **Facilities** Children's licence Garden Dogs allowed

The Globe ♀

Plan 1 B4

43–47 Marylebone Rd NW1 5JY

☎ 020 7935 6368 📄 020 7224 0154

e-mail: globe.1018@thespiritgroup.com

dir: At corner of Marylebone Rd & Baker St, opposite Baker St tube station

The Globe Tavern is contemporaneous with the adjoining Nash terraces and the Marylebone Road itself. The first omnibus service from Holborn stopped here, and the Metropolitan Railway runs beneath the road outside. Built in 1735, the pub retains much of its period character, and the owners proudly serve traditional English fare. A good choice of real ales is offered alongside dishes such as posh bacon and eggs; city deli salad; and 8oz Aberdeen Angus burger.

Open 10–11 (Fri-Sat 10–11.30, Sun 12–10.30) Closed: 25 Dec, 1 Jan **Bar Meals** Fri-Sat 10–11.30 L served Mon-Sat 11–9.30 D served Mon-Sat 11–9.30 (Sun 12–9) Av main course £6.99 **Restaurant** L served Mon-Sat 12–9.30 D served Mon-Sat 12–9.30 (Sun 12–9) 🍴 Punch Taverns 🍺 Scottish Courage Best, Bombardier, Youngs, IPA. ♀17

Pick of the Pubs

The Lansdowne ♀

Plan 2 E4

90 Gloucester Av, Primrose Hill NW1 8HX

☎ 020 7483 0409 📄 020 7586 1723

e-mail: thelansdownepub@thelansdownepub.co.uk

dir: From Chalk Farm underground station cross Adelaide Road, turn left up bridge approach. Follow Gloucester Ave for 500yds. Pub on corner

In 1992, Amanda Pritchett started The Lansdowne as one of the earliest dining pubs in Primrose Hill. Stripping the pub of its fruit machines, TVs and jukebox, she brought in solid wood furniture and back-to-basics décor; today, it blends a light, spacious bar and outdoor seating area with a slightly more formal upper dining room. All that apart, however, its success depends on the quality of its cooking. All food is freshly prepared on the premises, using organic or free-range ingredients wherever possible, and portions are invariably generous. The seasonal menu offers spiced red lentil soup with Greek yoghurt; home-cured bresaola with rocket, capers and parmesan; pan-fried sardines on toast with watercress; confit pork belly with prunes, potatoes and lardons; poached sea trout with crushed herb potatoes; polenta with roast pumpkin, buffalo mozzarella and walnut; hot chocolate fondant with double cream; and peaches poached in saffron with yoghurt and nuts.

Open 12–11 (Sat-Sun 9.30–11) Closed: 26 Dec **Bar Meals** L served all week 12–3 D served all week 7–10 (Sun 12.30–3.30, 7–9.30, Pizza 12.30–6, 7–10), Av main course £14 **Restaurant** L served Sat-Sun 1–3 D served Tue-Sun 7–10 Av 3 course à la carte £28 🍺 Bass 🍺 Staropramen. ♀6 **Facilities** Dogs allowed

NW1 continued

The Queens ♥ — Plan 2 E4

49 Regents Park Rd, Primrose Hill NW1 8XD

☎ 020 7586 0408 📠 020 7586 5677

e-mail: thequeens@geronimo-inns.wanadoo.co.uk

dir: *Nearest tube – Chalk Farm*

In one of London's most affluent and personality-studded areas, this Victorian pub looks up at 206ft-high Primrose Hill. Main courses may include seared calves' liver with bacon and sage mash, roast vegetable Yorkshire pudding, smoked chicken with mango and mange-tout peas, and whole roasted plaice with prawns and pancetta. On Sundays there's a selection of roasts, as well as fish, pasta and salad. Beers include Youngs and guests.

Open 11–11 (Fri-Sat 11–12, Sun 12–10.30) **Bar Meals** L served all week 12–3 D served all week 7–10 (Sat 12–5, Fri-Sat 7–10.30) Av main course £9.50 **Restaurant** L served all week 12–3 D served all week 7–10 (Sun 7–9) ⊕ ♥ 12 **Facilities** Dogs allowed

NW3

The Holly Bush ♥ — Plan 2 E5

Holly Mount, Hampstead NW3 6SG

☎ 020 7435 2892 📠 020 7431 2292

e-mail: info@hollybushpub.com

dir: *Nearest tube: Hampstead. Exit tube station onto Holly Hill, 1st right*

The Holly Bush was once the home of English portraitist George Romney and became a pub after his death in 1802. The building has been investigated by 'ghost busters', but more tangible 21st-century media celebrities are easier to spot. Depending on your appetite, the menu offers snacks and starters; smaller plates (a pint of prawns; Adnams rarebit); bigger plates (organic 21–day hung rump steak, pan-roast chicken) and a choice of sausages and pies, including vegetarian versions.

Open 12–11 **Bar Meals** L served Mon-Fri 12.30–4 D served Mon-Fri 4–10 (Sat 12–10, Sun 12–9) Av main course £9 **Restaurant** L served Tue-Fri D served Tue-Fri 6.30–10 (Sat 12–10, Sun 12–9) Av 3 course à la carte £20 ◀ Harveys Sussex Best, Adnams Bitter & Broadside, London Pride. ♥ 10 **Facilities** Children's licence Dogs allowed

Spaniards Inn ♥ — Plan 2 E5

Spaniards Rd, Hampstead NW3 7JJ

☎ 020 8731 6571 📠 020 8731 6572

dir: *Telephone for directions*

Believed to be the birthplace of highwayman Dick Turpin, this former tollhouse is a famous landmark beside Hampstead Heath. Named after two brothers who fought a fatal duel in 1721, it was mentioned by Bram Stoker in *Dracula*, and is still much frequented by celebrities. Traditional British fare is on offer, such as fish and chips, sausage and mash, and steamed steak and kidney pudding. In summer the stone flagged courtyard provides a shady retreat.

Open 11–11 (Sat-Sun 10–11, Summer Fri-Sat 11–12) **Bar Meals** L served all week 11–10 D served all week 11–10 (Sat-Sun 10–10) Av main course £7.50 **Restaurant** L served all week 12–10 D served all week (Sat-Sun 10–10) Av 3 course à la carte £15 ◀ Fuller's London Pride, Adnams Best, Marstons Old Empire, Oakhams JHB & guest ales. ♥ 16 **Facilities** Garden Dogs allowed Parking

Ye Olde White Bear ♥ — Plan 2 E5

Well Rd, Hampstead NW3 1LJ

☎ 020 7435 3758

dir: *Telephone for directions*

A Victorian family-run pub with a Hampstead village feel and a clientele that spans dustmen to Hollywood stars; there has been a pub here since 1704. Look out for the theatrical memorabilia, and there's a patio at the rear, but the real reason to come is the beer: a rolling selection of regional ales, with the list of 20 beers changing every ten weeks, adds up to about 100 different brews in a year.

Open 11–11 (Thu-Sat 11–11.30) **Bar Meals** L served all week 12–9 D served all week 12–9 **Restaurant** L served all week 12–9 D served all week 12–9 Av 3 course à la carte £17 ◀ A rolling selection of 6 ales from all over the UK. ♥ 12 **Facilities** Garden

NW5

Dartmouth Arms ♥ — Plan 2 E5

35 York Rise NW5 1SP ☎ 020 7485 3267

e-mail: info@darmoutharms.co.uk

dir: *5 min walk from Hampstead Heath*

Comedy nights, regular quizzes and themed food nights (perhaps steak or mussels) are popular fixtures at this pub close to Hampstead Heath. Food choices include a brunch menu, 'posh' sandwiches, a selection from the grill and platters themed by country (Spanish, Greek, English). Alongside the specials board, there are always hearty meals like bangers and mash or burgers. English ciders are a speciality.

Open 11–11 (Sat 10–11, Sun 10–10.30) **Bar Meals** L served Mon-Fri 11–3 D served Mon-Fri 6–10 (Sat-Sun 10–10) Av main course £7.95 **Restaurant** L served Mon-Fri 11–3 D served Mon-Fri 6–10 (Sat & Sun 10–10) ⊕ Punch Taverns ◀ Adnams, Archers & London Pride. ♥ 7 **Facilities** Dogs allowed

---

Pick of the Pubs

The Junction Tavern ♥ — Plan 2 E5

101 Fortess Rd NW5 1AG

☎ 020 7485 9400 📠 020 7485 9401

dir: *Between Kentish Town and Tufnell Park tube stations.*

This friendly local, halfway between Kentish Town and Tufnell Park underground stations, is handy for Camden and the green spaces of Parliament Hill and Hampstead Heath. The pub specialises in real ales, with over a dozen usually on offer at any one time, from country-wide breweries based anywhere between Kent (Shepherd Neame) and Edinburgh (Deuchar's). Regular beer festivals celebrate the amber liquid, when enthusiasts in the conservatory or large heated garden choose from a range of up to 30 beers hooked to a cooling system and served straight from the cask. The daily-changing seasonal menus offer an interesting choice at lunch and dinner, plus a good-value set Sunday lunch with two options per course. There's pan-fried chicken livers, black pudding and baby onions on toast to start, with slow-roast pork belly with spring onion mash and red cabbage to follow. Finish with lemon tart and Chantilly cream.

Open 12–11 (Sun 12–10.30) Closed: 24–26 Dec, 1 Jan
Bar Meals L served Mon-Sat 12–3 D served Mon-Sat 6.30–10.30 (Sun 12–4, 6.30–9.30) Av main course £13 **Restaurant** L served Mon-Sat 12–3 D served Mon-Sat 6.30–10.30 (Sun 12–4, 6.30–9.30) Av 3 course à la carte £24 ⊕ Enterprise Inns ◀ Caledonian Deuchars IPA, guest ales & 4 real ale pumps. ♀ 12 **Facilities** Garden Dogs allowed

The Lord Palmerston ♀   Plan 2 E5

33 Dartmouthhill Park NW5 1HU ☎ 020 7485 1578
e-mail: lordpalmerston@geronimo-inns.co.uk

dir: *From Tuffnel Park Station turn right and continue straight up Dartmouth Park Hill. Pub on right, corner of Chetwynd Rd*

Stylishly revamped London pub in the Dartmouth Park conservation area. It has two open fires in winter and fully opening windows in summer, plus a large front terrace and rear garden for dining. Food is taken seriously, with dishes ranging from vegetarian cassoulet to guinea fowl breast with bubble and squeak and roasted shallot tarragon sauce. Four real ales and five continental lagers are always on tap.

Open 12–11 (Sun 12–10.30) **Bar Meals** L served all week 12–3 D served all week 7–10 (Sun 12–9) Av main course £12 **Restaurant** L served all week 12–3 D served all week 7–10 (Sun 12–9) Av 3 course à la carte £20 ◀ Adnams Best, Sharp's Eden Ale. ♀ 25 **Facilities** Children's licence Garden Dogs allowed

Pick of the Pubs

The Vine   Plan 2 E5

86 Highgate Rd NW5 1PB
☎ 020 7209 0038 🖺 020 7209 9001
e-mail: info@thevinelondon.co.uk
dir: *Telephone for directions*

What looks like an Edwardian London pub on the outside has a very contemporary feel on the inside, with its copper bar, wooden floors, huge mirrors and funky art. Comfy leather sofas and an open fire make for a relaxed atmosphere. The Vine is billed as a bar, restaurant and garden, and the latter is a great asset – fully covered for year round use and popular for wedding receptions. Two dramatically decorated rooms are also available upstairs for private meetings or dinner parties. Lunchtime dishes range from bruschetta, and free-range burgers to linguine dressed with fresh blue swimmer crab. In the evening you might choose between chargrilled tuna with pak choi and roasted sesame oil, oven baked whole sea bass with cherry tomatoes and mussels, pasta with wild boar ragu and truffle oil, or home-made beefburgers.

Open 12–11 Closed: 26 Dec **Bar Meals** L served all week 12.30–3 D served all week 6.30–10.30 **Restaurant** L served all week 12–3.30 D served all week 6–10.30 ⊕ Punch Taverns ◀ Fuller's London Pride, IPA, Spitfire & guest ales. **Facilities** Garden Parking

NW6

The Salusbury Pub and Dining Room ♀   Plan 2 D4

50–52 Salusbury Rd NW6 6NN ☎ 020 7328 3286
e-mail: thesalusbury@aol.com
dir: *100mtrs left from Queens Park tube & train station*

Gastropub with a lively and vibrant atmosphere, offering a London restaurant-style menu without the associated prices. The award-winning wine list boasts more than a hundred wines including mature offerings from the cellar. The owners are appreciated by a strong local following for continuity of quality and service. Example dishes are roast sea bream with Roman artichokes, leg of duck confit with lentils and cotechino, and Angus rib-eye steak.

Open 12–11 Closed: 25–26 Dec & 1 Jan **Bar Meals** L served Tue-Sun 12.30–3.30 D served all week 7–10.15 (Sun 7–10) Av main course £12 **Restaurant** L served Tue-Sun 12.30–3.30 D served all week 7–10.15 (Sun 7–10) Av 3 course à la carte £25 ◀ Broadside, Bitburger, Guinness, Staropramen & Aspall Cider. ♀ 13 **Facilities** Dogs allowed

NW8

Pick of the Pubs

The Salt House ♀   Plan 2 D4

63 Abbey Rd, St John's Wood NW8 0AE
☎ 020 7328 6626 🖺 020 7604 4084
e-mail: salthousemail@majol.co.uk
dir: *Turn right outside St Johns Wood tube. Left onto Marlborough Place, right onto Abbey Rd, pub on left*

Describing itself as a mere scuttle from the Beatles' famous Abbey Road zebra crossing, this 18th-century inn promises a two-fold commitment to good food: to source excellent ingredients and to home cook them. With the exception of the odd bottle of ketchup, everything, including bread, buns and pasta, is made on site. Meanwhile, meats are Rare Breed Survival Trust accredited and fish has been caught by Andy in Looe. Espeto of chicken livers, chorizo, smoked bacon with lemon and parsley farofa; or aromatic crispy duck with hoi sin sauce could be followed by glazed crispy pork with black pudding mash; Catalan-style chargrilled fillet of wild halibut; or rack of Elwy Valley lamb with dauphinoise potatoes. A function room is available for larger parties, while heaters allow for al fresco dining even on inclement days.

Open 10–12 **Bar Meals** 10–5 5–10 Av main course £8 **Restaurant** 12–5 6–10.30 Av 3 course à la carte £30 ◀ Abbot Ale, Guinness. ♀ 14 **Facilities** Children's licence Dogs allowed

England

NW10

The Greyhound ♀ Plan 2 D4

64–66 Chamberlayne Rd NW10 3JJ

☎ 020 8969 8080 📄 020 8969 8081

e-mail: thegreyhound@breadandhoney.net

dir: *Corner of Chamberlayne Rd & Mortimer Rd*

This pub was created from a derelict building, much to the delight of the locals, who have been flocking in ever since. Customers range from a smattering of supermodels to young families and older couples, all clearly enjoying the friendly atmosphere. There's an eclectic wine list, and a menu each for the bar and dining room. Expect dishes such as pumpkin risotto, breaded calamari, roast duck breast with sweet potato puree and wild sea trout and baby leeks.

Open 12–12 (Mon 5–11) Closed: 25–26 Dec, 1 Jan **Bar Meals** L served Fri-Sat 12.30–3 D served Mon-Sat 6.30–10.30 (Sun 12.30–7) Av main course £10.50 **Restaurant** L served Sat 12.30–3 D served Mon-Sat 6.30–10.30 (Sun 12.30–7) Av 3 course à la carte £20 Av 2 course fixed price £12.50 🍺 Free House 🍺 Guinness, guest ales. ♀ 14 **Facilities** Garden Dogs allowed

William IV Bar & Restaurant ♀ Plan 2 D4

786 Harrow Rd NW10 5JX

☎ 020 8969 5944 📄 020 8964 9218

dir: *Telephone for directions*

The William IV enjoys a strong local following of people drawn to the revitalized interior including a music-orientated bar (Virgin Records around the corner), and modern European food. A very flexible array of dishes typically includes chargrilled sirloin steak with chips and beetroot pesto; baked plaice with green beans; and pea, broad bean and mint tart. Plenty of fish.

Open 12–11 (Fri-Sat 12–1, Sun 12–10.30) Closed: 25 Dec, 1 Jan **Bar Meals** L served all week 12–3 D served all week 6–10.30 (Sun 12–4.30) Av main course £10 **Restaurant** L served all week 12–3 D served all week 6–10.30 Av 3 course à la carte £18 🍺 Free House 🍺 Fuller's London Pride. ♀ 7 **Facilities** Garden

SE1

The Anchor ♀ Plan 1 F3

Bankside, 34 Park St SE1 9EF

☎ 020 7407 1577 & 7407 3003 📄 020 7407 7023

e-mail: anchor.0977@thespirit.group.com

dir: *Telephone for directions*

In the shadow of the Globe Theatre, this historic pub lies on one of London's most famous tourist trails. Samuel Pepys supposedly watched the Great Fire of London from here in 1666, and Dr Johnson was a regular, with Oliver Goldsmith, David Garrick and Sir Joshua Reynolds. The river views are excellent, and inside are black beams, old faded plasterwork, and a maze of tiny rooms. A varied menu includes fish and chips, pan-fried halibut with olives, and cod in crispy bacon served on wilted spinach.

Open 11–11 (Thu-Sat 11–12) Closed: 25 Dec **Bar Meals** L served all week 12–8 D served all week **Restaurant** L served all week 12–2.30 D served all week 5–10 🍺 Courage Directors, Greene King IPA, Adnams Broadside, Bombardier & guest ales. ♀ 14 **Facilities** Garden

The Anchor & Hope ◉◉ ♀ Plan 1 E2

36 The Cut SE1 8LP

☎ 020 7928 9898 📄 020 7928 4595

e-mail: anchorandhope@btconnect.com

dir: *Nearest tube: Southwark & Waterloo*

Despite picking up many accolades for its cooking, the Anchor and Hope remains a down-to-earth and friendly place; children, parents, and dogs with owners are all welcome. In fine weather, pavement seating allows you to watch the world go by as you enjoy a pint, or one of many wines sold by the glass. The wine list is notable for its straightforward approach to prices, which are mainly listed in whole pounds. Many half bottles can be bought for half the cost of full ones – something appreciated by the pub's faithful diners. The short menu, too, is refreshingly unembroidered. Starters might include oak smoked Irish salmon or duck hearts on toast, followed by hearty main courses such as potato and Ardrahan cheese pie; duck, fennel and olives; and grilled lemon sole. Rhubarb and custard pot, and lemon meringue pie are among the list of trusted desserts.

Open 11–11 (Closed Sun eve, Mon 5–11) Closed: Last 2 wks Aug, BH, Xmas, New Year **Bar Meals** L served Tue-Sat 12–2.30 D served Mon-Sat 6–10.30 (Sun from 2) Av main course £13 **Restaurant** L served Tue-Sat 12–2.30 D served Mon-Sat 6–10.30 (Sun from 2) 🍺 Bombardier, Youngs Ordinary, IPA, Erdinger. ♀ 18 **Facilities** Garden Dogs allowed

The Bridge House Bar & Dining Rooms ♀ Plan 1 G2

218 Tower Bridge Rd SE1 2UP

☎ 020 7407 5818 📄 020 7407 5828

e-mail: the-bridgehouse@tiscali.co.uk

dir: *5 min walk from London Bridge/Tower Hill tube stations*

The nearest bar to Tower Bridge, The Bridge House has great views of the river and city and is handy for London Dungeons, Borough Market, Tate Modern, London Eye, Globe Theatre and Southwark Cathedral. It comprises a bar, dining room and new café, plus facilities for private functions. Typical dishes are chargrilled steak, beer battered haddock, and calves' liver with black pudding, smoked bacon, parsley mash and red wine gravy.

Open 11.30–11 (Thu-Sat 11.30–12) Closed: 25–26 Dec **Bar Meals** L served all week 11.30–10.30 D served all week Av main course £8.50 **Restaurant** L served all week 11.30–2.30 D served all week 5.30–10.30 Av 3 course à la carte £19.95 🍺 Adnams 🍺 Adnams Best Bitter, Adnams Broadside, Adnams Explorer & guest ale. ♀ 32

England

Pick of the Pubs

The Fire Station ◉ ☻   Plan 1 D2

150 Waterloo Rd SE1 8SB

☎ 020 7620 2226 📄 020 7633 9161

e-mail: firestation.waterloo@pathfinderpubs.co.uk

dir: *Turn right at exit 2 of Waterloo Station*

Oak beams, black leaded ranges, an antique clock, charmingly worn tiled floors and a delightful mishmash of scrubbed pine furniture – this inn has no shortage of character. It was built in 1616 out of local stone and salvaged Armada timbers, and stands beside an old London to Manchester turnpike in the heart of Brassington, a hill village on the southern edge of the Peak District. Hand pumped Marston's Pedigree Bitter takes pride of place behind the bar, alongside guest ales such as Jennings Sneck Lifter. The menu, written daily on blackboards, features a wealth of local produce. At lunch, try fresh soups, sandwiches, filled baguettes or the house speciality, the Derbyshire fidget. The evening menu changes regularly using locally sourced seasonal produce.

Open 11–11 (Mon-Tue 11–12, Wed-Thu 11–1) Closed: 25–26 Dec, 1 Jan **Bar Meals** L served all week 12–5.30 D served all week 5.30–10.30 Av main course £6.95 **Restaurant** L served all week 12–2.45 D served all week 5–11 (Sat 12–11, Sun 12–9.30) Av 3 course à la carte £14.50 ◀ Adnams Best Bitter, Fuller's London Pride, Young's Bitters, Shepherd Neame Spitfire. ☻ 8

Pick of the Pubs

The Garrison ☻   Plan 1 G2

See Pick of the Pubs on page 364

The George Inn   Plan 1 G3

77 Borough High St SE1 1NH

☎ 020 7407 2056 📄 020 7403 6956

e-mail: 7781@greeneking.co.uk

dir: *From London Bridge tube station, take Borough High St exit, left. Pub 200yds on left*

The only remaining galleried inn in London and now administered by the National Trust. This striking black and white building may have numbered one William Shakespeare among its clientele, and Dickens mentioned it in *Little Dorrit* – his original life assurance policy is displayed along with 18th-century rat traps. The honestly-priced pub grub includes hot and cold sandwiches, salads, and Wiltshire ham, duck egg and chips; and salmon and broccoli fishcakes.

Open 11–11 (Sun 12–10.30) Closed: 25–26 Dec **Bar Meals** L served all week 12–5 D served Mon-Sat 6–9 (Sun 5–10) **Restaurant** D served Mon-Sat 5–10 ⬡ Greene King ◀ Greene King Abbot Ale, George Inn Ale, IPA & Old Speckled Hen. **Facilities** Garden

The Market Porter ☻   Plan 1 F3

9 Stoney St, Borough Market, London Bridge SE1 9AA

☎ 020 7407 2495 📄 020 7403 7697

dir: *Close to London Bridge Station*

Traditional tavern serving a market community that has been flourishing for about 1,000 years. Excellent choice of real ales. Worth noting is an internal leaded bay window unique in London. The atmosphere is friendly, if rather rough and ready, and the pub has been used as a location in *Lock, Stock and Two Smoking Barrels, Only Fools and Horses*, and *Entrapment*. Menu includes bangers and mash, roasted lamb shank, beetroot and lemon marinated salmon, and a hearty plate of fish and chips. Early morning opening.

Open 6am-8.30am 11–11 (Sat 12–11 Sun 12–10.30) **Bar Meals** L served all week 12–3 **Restaurant** L served all week 12–3 D served all week 6–9 ⬡ Free House ◀ Harveys Best, wide selection of international ales. ☻ 10

The Old Thameside ☻   Plan 1 F3

Pickford's Wharf, Clink St SE1 9DG

☎ 020 7403 4243 📄 020 7407 2063

dir: *Telephone for directions*

Just two minutes' walk from Tate Modern, the Millennium Bridge and Shakespeare's Globe, this former spice warehouse is also close to the site of England's first prison, the Clink. The pub features a large outdoor seating area that overhangs the River Thames, and the friendly staff are always happy to point bewildered tourists in the right direction! Traditional pub fare includes fish and chips, sausage and mash, curries and vegetarian pies.

Open 12–11 (Fri-Sat 11–12) Closed: 25 Dec **Bar Meals** L served all week 12–10 Av main course £6.95 **Restaurant** L served all week D served all week ◀ Fuller's London Pride, Adnams Bitter, Landlords Ale. ☻ 10 **Facilities** Children's licence Garden

SE5

The Sun and Doves ☻   Plan 2 F3

61–63 Coldharbour Ln, Camberwell SE5 9NS

☎ 020 7733 1525

e-mail: mail@sunanddoves.co.uk

dir: *Located on the corner of Caldecot Rd and Coldharbour Ln*

This attractive Camberwell venue is recognized for good food, drink and art – the pub showcases local artists, many of whom are well known. For a London pub it has a decent sized garden, planted in Mediterranean style, and a paved patio offers fixed seating for the summer months. The menu is stylishly simple, with snacks like the pub's own club sandwich; Welsh rarebit; or merguez with rocket. The honestly priced lunch and dinner menu offers quiche of the day, a plate of Serrano ham and salami, cottage pie; hand-made sausages; eggs Benedict; and chargrilled rib-eye steak.

Open 12–11 Closed: 25–26 Dec **Bar Meals** L served Mon-Sat 12 D served Mon-Sat 10 (Sun 12–9) **Restaurant** L served all week 12 D served all week 10 ◀ Old Speckled Hen & Ruddles. ☻ 9 **Facilities** Garden Dogs allowed

The Garrison

This artfully restyled London pub looks ordinary enough from the outside. But the interior sports a delightful hotch potch of decorative themes, from French brasserie chic to the type of limed-and-whitewashed look you might expect in a trendy seaside café.

Antique odds and ends, including mismatched chairs and tables, add to the quirky charm. In the four years since it opened the pub has established a solid following, resulting in a villagey, community vibe. A day of inspired eating begins with the most complete breakfast menu, amongst which you will find an omelette du jour; smoked haddock, poached egg, potato pancake and hollandaise; French toast with banana, bacon and maple syrup; and cinnamon porridge. For lunch, try starters such as smoked chicken, fennel, celeriac and new potatoes à la greque with watercress; Suffolk rabbit ballotine, with spring pea and mint salad; or seared and spiced blue fin tuna, fennel and tomato. To follow, half a dozen main course options

embrace Orkney calves' liver, corn dumplings, smoked bacon and marjoram, with a devilled sauce; beef and Guinness pie with mashed Desirée potatoes, swede and Brussels sprouts; and the Garrison's own kedgeree. Side dishes include chips; green beans; and baby gem, carrot, radish and boiled egg salad. Traditional desserts such as sticky toffee pudding and dark chocolate brownie are served with ice cream. Many of the same choices are available in the evening, while bar snacks include olives; chilli rice crackers; salt and pepper squid with house chilli jam; and prawn toast. The wine list is compact but fairly comprehensive, with a dozen served by the glass; other drink choices range from St Peter's Organic ale to Cidre Breton.

Plan 1 G2
99–101 Bermondsey St SE1 3XB
☎ 020 7407 3347
📄 020 7407 1084
e-mail: info@thegarrison.co.uk
dir: *From London Bridge tube station, E towards Tower Bridge 200mtrs, right onto Bermondsey St. Pub in 100mtrs*

Open 8–11 (Sat 9–11, Sun 9–10.30)
Bar Meals L served Mon-Fri 12.30–3.30; D served Mon-Fri 6.30–10 (Sat 12.30–4 6.30–10 Sun 6–9.30)
Restaurant L served Mon-Sat 12–3.30 D served Mon-Sat 6.30–10 (Sun 12.30–4, 6–9.30) Av 3 course à la carte £35
⊕ Free House 🍺 St Peters Organic Ale, Paulaner, Celis White. 🍷 12

England

SE10

The Cutty Sark Tavern ♥   Plan 2 G3

4–6 Ballast Quay, Greenwich SE10 9PD

☎ 020 8858 3146

dir: *Nearest tube: Greenwich. From Cutty Sark ship follow river towards Millennium Dome (10 min walk)*

Originally the Union Tavern, this 1695 waterside pub was renamed when the world famous tea-clipper was dry-docked upriver in 1954. Inside, low beams, creaking floorboards, dark panelling and from the large bow window in the upstairs bar, commanding views of the Thames, Canary Wharf and the Millennium Dome. Well-kept beers, wines by the glass and a wide selection of malts are all available, along with bangers and mash, seafood, vegetarian specials and Sunday roasts. Busy at weekends, especially on fine days.

Open 11–11 (Sun 12–10.30) **Bar Meals** L served all week 12 D served all week 9 (Sun 12–5) Av main course £9 ⊕ Free House ◖ Fuller's London Pride, St Austells Tribute, Adnams Broadside, Addlestones Cider. ♥ 8
Facilities Children's licence Garden

Pick of the Pubs

Greenwich Union Pub   Plan 2 G3

56 Royal Hill SE10 8RT

☎ 020 8692 6258 ▤ 020 8305 8625

e-mail: andy@meantimebrewing.com

dir: *From Greenwich DLR & main station exit by main ticket hall, turn left, 2nd right into Royal Hill. Pub 100yds on right*

Comfortable leather sofas and flagstone floors help to keep the original character of this refurbished pub intact. Interesting beers (including chocolate and raspberry!), lagers and even freshly-squeezed orange juice, along with a beer garden make this a popular spot. Try a foccacia sandwich; pearl barley risotto with courgette and radicchio; or chicken with spicy broccoli and sweet shallots; or, if it's fish you're after, grilled fillet of sea bass with seasonal vegetable ratatouille, or sauté of fresh mussels in white wine, cream and chives. The Meantime Brewery Co, which brews the beers on offer, was the only UK brewery to win awards at the 2004 Beer World Cup.

Open 12–11 (Sat 11–11, Sun 11.30–10.30) **Bar Meals** L served Mon-Sun 12.30–10 D served Mon-Sun (Sat-Sun 10–9) Av main course £8 ⊕ Free House ◖ Kolsch, Pilsener, Wheat ale, Raspberry ale & Chocolate ale. **Facilities** Children's licence Garden Dogs allowed

Pick of the Pubs

North Pole Bar & Restaurant ♥   Plan 2 G3

See Pick of the Pubs on page 366

SE16

The Mayflower ♥   Plan 2 F3

117 Rotherhithe St, Rotherhithe SE16 4NF

☎ 020 7237 4088 ▤ 020 7064 4710

dir: *Exit A2 at Surrey Keys rdbt onto Brunel Rd, 3rd left onto Swan Rd, left at T-junct, pub 200mtrs on right*

From the patio here you can see the renovated jetty from which the eponymous 'Mayflower' embarked on her historic voyage to the New World. Billed as 'London's riverside link with the birth of America' the pub has a collection of memorabilia, as well as an unusual licence to sell both British and American postage stamps. Pub fare includes stuffed pork loin; Cajun chicken supreme; and fresh pasta with smoked bacon, spinach and mushrooms, plus plenty of fish and seafood.

Open 11–3 5.15–11 (Sun 12–10.30, May-Oct 11–11) **Bar Meals** L served Mon-Fri 12–2.30 D served Mon-Fri 6.30–9.30 (Sat-Sun 12–9)
Restaurant L served Mon-Fri 12–2.30 D served Mon-Fri 6.30–9.30 (Sun 12–9) ⊕ Greene King ◖ Greene King Abbot Ale, IPA, Old Speckled Hen. ♥ 30 **Facilities** Garden Dogs allowed

SE21

The Crown & Greyhound ♥   Plan 2 F2

73 Dulwich Village SE21 7BJ

☎ 020 8299 4976 ▤ 020 8693 8959

dir: *Telephone for directions*

With a tradition of service and hospitality reaching back to the 18th century, the Crown and Greyhound counts Charles Dickens and John Ruskin amongst its celebrated patrons. Modern day customers will find three bars and a restaurant in the heart of peaceful Dulwich Village. The weekly-changing menu might feature bean cassoulet with couscous; or an 8oz Angus burger with cheddar cheese and potato wedges. There are daily salads, pasta and fish dishes, too.

Open 11–11 (Sun 12–10.30) **Bar Meals** L served all week 12–10 D served all week Sun 12–9 Av main course £7 **Restaurant** L served all week 12–10 D served all week Sun 12–9 ◖ Fuller's London Pride & guest ales. ♥ 15 **Facilities** Garden Dogs allowed

North Pole Bar & Restaurant

Guests like to begin their evening here with a signature cocktail in the bar, then climb the spiral staircase to the stylish Piano Restaurant, where the resident pianist tinkles away on the ivories Thursday to Saturday evenings.

Having reached this point, look up and you'll see goldfish swimming around in the chandeliers, but don't worry, they're for real and nothing to do with any cocktail consumed earlier. In the basement is the South Pole club, where you can dance until 2am Wednesdays to Saturdays. To complete the picture there's also a terrace, which makes an ideal spot for a glass of Pimms on a summer evening. An extensive bar menu is available all day, every day from 12 until 10.30pm, with choices ranging from sandwiches, baguettes, wraps and salads to grills. The cooking style in the Piano Restaurant is modern European, with starters typified by sautéed scallops, chorizo, coriander and tomato salsa; duck ravioli stuffed with shiitake

mushrooms, ginger, and sesame and cherry sauce; and lamb patty, with smashed chick peas, red cabbage, spiced yoghurt and lemon oil. Any one of these could be followed by ballottine of cornfed chicken with savoy cabbage, pancetta, fondant potato and cep cream; pan-fried halibut on artichoke purée, buttered asparagus and light basil velouté; or wild mushroom tart with creamed leeks, mixed leaves and truffle oil. For dessert, perhaps strawberry cheesecake, or white and dark chocolate brownie. Sundays bring roast dinners in the bar and the restaurant and live jazz, funk and Latin music downstairs. Lager lovers might like to know that the beers here are Artois, Carling, Hoegaarden and Staropramen.

Plan 2 G3
131 Greenwich High Rd,
Greenwich SE10 8JA
☎ 020 8853 3020
🖷 020 8853 3501
e-mail: natalie@
northpolegreenwich.com
web:
www.northpolegreenwich.com
dir: *From Greenwich rail station turn right, pass Novotel. Pub on right (2 min walk)*

Open 12–12 (Thu 12–1am, Fri-Sat 12–2am)
Bar Meals L served all week 12–10.30 D served all week 12–8
Restaurant L served Sun 12–4 D served all week 6.50–10 Av 3 course à la carte £25 Av 3 course fixed price £19.95
⊕ Free House ◖ Guinness. ♟20
Facilities Children's licence

England

SE22

Franklins 🍴🍷 Plan 2 F2

157 Lordship Ln, Dulwich SE22 8HX ☎ 020 8299 9598
e-mail: info@franklinsrestaurant.com

dir: *0.5m S from East Dulwich station along Dog Kennel Hill & Lordship Lane*

Franklins is as much pub as it is bar/restaurant, and there are real ales and lagers on tap here, including Whitstable Bay and Guinness among them. The restaurant interior is stripped-back, modern and stylish with bare floors, exposed brick walls and smartly clothed tables, while the bar is more traditional. The appreciative clientele enjoy the no-frills short menu, which opens with the likes of sweetbread terrine, steamed mussels, and wet garlic soup. Main courses continue in the same unfussy vein, with choices such as mutton faggots and pease pudding, Old Spot belly with fennel and black pudding, and Glamorgan sausages, spinach and tomato. Bar snacks include Welsh rarebit, and there are comforting desserts like rhubarb and custard, and bread and butter pudding. From Monday to Friday the excellent value set lunch menus allow the option of two or three courses.

Open 12–12 Closed: 25–26 & 31 Dec, 1 Jan **Bar Meals** L served all week 12–6 D served all week 6–10.30 Av main course £14 **Restaurant** L served all week 12–6 D served all week 6–10.30 Av 3 course à la carte £25 Av 2 course fixed price £15 ⊕ Free House 🍺 Whitstable Bay Organic Ale, Guinness. ♀ 11 **Facilities** Dogs allowed

SE23

The Dartmouth Arms 🍷 Plan 2 F2

7 Dartmouth Rd, Forest Hill SE23 3HN
☎ 020 8488 3117 🖺 020 7771 7230
e-mail: info@thedartmoutharms.com

dir: *800mtrs from Horniman Museum on South Circular Rd (E)*

The long-vanished Croydon Canal once ran behind this transformed old pub, and you can still see the towpath railings at the bottom of the car park. Smart bars serve snacks, traditional real ales, Continental lagers, cocktails, coffees and teas, while the restaurant offers Barnsley chop with sweetbreads, carrot, savoy cabbage and rosemary jus; and pan-fried sea bass with herb mash and pea cream.

Open 12–12 (Fri-Sat 12–1, Sun 12–11) Closed: 25–26 Dec, 1 Jan **Bar Meals** L served Mon-Sat 12–3.30 D served Mon-Sat 6.30–10.30 (Sun 12–9) Av main course £12.95 **Restaurant** L served Mon-Sat 12–3.30 D served Mon-Sat 6.30–10.30 (Sun 12–9, cost fixed price menu varies) Av 3 course à la carte £24 Av 3 course fixed price £18.50 ⊕ Enterprise Inns 🍺 Old Speckled Hen, London Pride & Brakspears. ♀ 10 **Facilities** Garden Parking

SW1

The Albert 🍷 Plan 1 D2

52 Victoria St SW1H 0NP
☎ 020 7222 5577 & 7222 7606 🖺 020 7222 1044
e-mail: thealbert.westminster@thespiritgroup.com

dir: *Nearest tube – St James Park*

Built in 1854, this Grade II Victorian pub is named after Queen Victoria's husband, Prince Albert. The main staircase is decorated with portraits of British Prime Ministers, from Salisbury to Blair, and the pub is often frequented by MPs. To make sure they don't miss a vote, there's even a division bell in the restaurant. The pub was the only building in the area to survive the Blitz of WWII, with even its old cut-glass windows remaining intact. The traditional menu includes a carvery, buffet, a selection of light dishes and other classic fare.

Open 11–11 (Sun 12–10.30) Closed: 25 Dec, 1 Jan **Bar Meals** L served all week 11–10 D served all week **Restaurant** L served all week 12–9.30 D served all week 5.30–9.30 🍺 Bombardier, Courage Directors & Best, London Pride, John Smiths. ♀ 14

The Buckingham Arms 🍷 Plan 1 D2

62 Petty France SW1H 9EU ☎ 020 7222 3386
e-mail: buckinghamarms@youngs.co.uk

dir: *Nearest tube: St James's Park*

Known as the Black Horse until 1903, this elegant, busy Young's pub is situated close to Buckingham Palace. Popular with tourists, business people and real ale fans alike, it offers a good range of simple pub food, including the 'mighty' Buckingham burger, nachos with chilli, chicken ciabatta and old favourites like ham, egg and chips in its long bar with etched mirrors.

Open 11–11 (Sat 11–5.30, Sun 12–5.30) **Bar Meals** L served all week 11 D served Mon-Fri 9 (Sun 12–4) ⊕ Young & Co 🍺 Youngs Bitter, Special & Winter Warmer & Bombardier. ♀ 11 **Facilities** Dogs allowed

The Clarence 🍷 Plan 1 D3

55 Whitehall SW1A 2HP
☎ 020 7930 4808 🖺 020 7321 0859

dir: *Between Big Ben & Trafalgar Sq*

This apparently haunted pub, situated five minutes' walk from Big Ben, the Houses of Parliament, Trafalgar Square and Buckingham Palace, has leaded windows and ancient ceiling beams from a Thames pier. Typical of the menu choice are sausage and mash; pesto penne pasta with brie or chicken; and pie of the day. Daily specials are available. The pub has a friendly atmosphere and is handy for the bus and tube.

Open 10–12am (Sun-Tue 10–11) Closed: 25 Dec **Bar Meals** L served all week all day D served all week Av main course £5 **Restaurant** L served all week D served all week Av 3 course à la carte £15 🍺 Scottish & Newcastle 🍺 Bombardier, Fuller's London Pride, Youngs, Adnams Broadside & guest ale. ♀ 17

SW1 continued

The Grenadier ♟ Plan 1 B2

18 Wilton Row, Belgravia SW1X 7NR ☎ 020 7235 3074

dir: *From Hyde Park Corner along Knightsbridge, left into Old Barracks Yd, pub on corner*

Regularly used for films and television series, the ivy-clad Grenadier stands in a cobbled mews behind Hyde Park Corner, largely undiscovered by tourists. Famous patrons have included King George IV and Madonna! Outside is the remaining stone of the Duke's mounting block. Expect traditional favourites on the blackboard, and keep an eye out for the ghost of an officer accidentally flogged to death for cheating at cards.

Open 11–11 (Sun 11–10.30) **Bar Meals** L served all week 12–2.30 D served all week 6–9.30 **Restaurant** L served all week 12–3 D served all week 6–9 **●** Fuller's London Pride, Wells Bombardier, Timothy Taylor Landord, Shepherd Neame Spitfire. **♟** 10 **Facilities** Dogs allowed

Pick of the Pubs

Nags Head Plan 1 B2

53 Kinnerton St SW1X 8ED ☎ 020 7235 1135

dir: *Telephone for directions*

Is this London's smallest pub? The award-winning Nag's Head is certainly compact and bijou, with a frontage like a Dickens shop and an unspoilt interior. Located in a quiet mews near Harrods, its front and back bars, connected by a narrow stairway, boast wooden floors, panelled walls, and low ceilings. It was built in the early 19th-century to cater for the footmen and stable hands who looked after the horses in these Belgravia mews. The full Adnams range is served, along with a good value menu: daily specials, a help yourself salad bar, and traditional favourites such as real ale sausages, mash and beans; steak and mushroom pie; and chilli con carne are all on offer. Typical salads include brie of stilton salad and smoked salmon salad. There are also ploughman's lunches and sandwiches.

Open 11–11 (Sun 12–10.30) **Bar Meals** L served all week 11–9.30 D served all week **⊕** Free House **●** Adnams Best, Broadside, Fisherman & Regatta. **Notes** ⊛

The Orange Brewery ♟ Plan 1 C1

37–39 Pimlico Rd SW1W 8NE ☎ 020 7730 5984

dir: *Nearest tube – Sloane Square or Victoria*

The name comes from local associations with Nell Gwynne, a 17th-century purveyor of oranges and a favourite of Charles II. The building dates from 1790, and fronts onto an appealing square. Beers are brewed in the cellar, including SW1, SW2 and Pimlico Porter, and regulars will find a different guest beer every month. Expect traditional pub food; steak, Guinness and suet pudding, chicken curry, or scampi and chips are favourites.

Open 11–11 (Sun 12–10.30, bar food all day) **Bar Meals** 12–5 3–8.30 (Sat-Sun 12–4, 5–8.30) Av main course £6 **⊕** Scottish & Newcastle **●** Greene King IPA, Old Speckled Hen, Bombardier, London Pride. **♟** 18 **Facilities** Dogs allowed

The Wilton Arms ♟ Plan 1 B2

71 Kinnerton St SW1X 8ED

☎ 020 7235 4854 📄 020 7235 4895

e-mail: wilton@shepherd-neame.co.uk

This early 19th-century hostelry is named after the 1st Earl of Wilton, but known locally as The Village Pub. In summer it is distinguished by its flower-filled baskets and window boxes. High settles and bookcases create individual seating areas in the air-conditioned interior, and a conservatory covers the old garden. Shepherd Neame ales accompany traditional pub fare: salt beef doorstep with horseradish and mustard dressing; fish and chips; and garlic battered chicken goujons.

Open 11–11 **Bar Meals** L served Mon-Sat 12–3.45 D served Mon-Sat 5.30–9.30 Av main course £6.95 **⊕** Shepherd Neame **●** Spitfire, Holsten, Orangeboom, Bishops Finger. **♟** 7

SW3

The Admiral Codrington ♟ Plan 1 B2

17 Mossop St SW3 2LY

☎ 020 7581 0005 📄 020 7589 2452

e-mail: admiral.codrington@333holdingsltd.com

dir: *Telephone for directions*

The local nickname for this smart and friendly gastro-pub is, inevitably, The Cod. Although this old Chelsea boozer was given a complete makeover that resulted in a stylish new look when it re-opened, it still retains a relaxed and homely feel. The modern British menu runs to vodka-cured salmon; Wag Yu beef sausages; roast breast of Norfolk chicken; and porcini risotto. Virtually all the well-chosen wines are available by the glass.

Open 11.30–12 (Sun 12–10.30) **Bar Meals** L served Mon-Sat 12–2.30 (Sun 12–4) **Restaurant** L served Mon-Sat 12–2.30 D served all week 6.30–11 (Sun 12–4) Av 3 course à la carte £25 **●** Guinness, Black Sheep, Spitfire. **♟** 20 **Facilities** Garden

Pick of the Pubs

The Builders Arms ♦   Plan 1 B1

13 Britten St SW3 3TY ☎ 020 7349 9040

e-mail: buildersarms@geronimo-inns.co.uk

dir: *From Sloane Square tube station down Kings Rd. At Habitat turn right onto Chelsea Manor St, at end turn right onto Britten St, pub on right*

Just off Chelsea's famous Kings Road, a three-storey Georgian back-street pub built by the same crew that constructed St Luke's church over the way. Inside, leather sofas dot the spacious informal bar area, where a brief, daily changing menu offers a good choice of modern English food with a twist, but if further ideas are needed, consult the specials board. Starters on the main menu might include mackerel and dill fishcake with spicy tomato ketchup; mussels and clams with Magners Irish cider, red onion and cream sauce; and sautéed chicken livers with smoked Black Forest bacon and broad beans. Typical main courses are baked codling fillet with parmentier potatoes and mustard lentils; pan-fried sea bass with caramelised shallot and gremolata; and courgette, sun-blushed tomato and feta risotto. There are more than 30 bins, with French producers just about taking the lead. When the sun shines the outdoor terrace is highly popular.

Open 11–11 (Thu-Sat 11–12) Closed: 25-26 Dec **Bar Meals** L served Mon-Fri 12-2.30 D served all week 7–10 (Sat-Sun 12–4) **Restaurant** L served Mon-Fri 12-2.30 D served all week 7–10 (Sat-Sun 12–4) ◄ Adnams, London Pride, Deuchars IPA. ♦ 16 **Facilities** Dogs allowed

Pick of the Pubs

The Coopers of Flood Street ♦   Plan 1 B1

87 Flood St, Chelsea SW3 5TB

☎ 020 7376 3120 📄 020 7352 9187

e-mail: Coopersarms@youngs.co.uk

dir: *From Sloane Square tube station, straight onto Kings Road. Approx 1m W, opposite Waitrose, left. Pub half way down Flood St*

A quiet backstreet Chelsea pub close to the Kings Road and the river. Celebrities and the notorious rub shoulders with the aristocracy and the local road sweeper in the bright, vibrant atmosphere, while the stuffed brown bear, Canadian moose and boar bring a character of their own to the bar. Food is served here and in the quiet upstairs dining room, with a focus on meat from the pub's own organic farm. The fresh, adventurous menu also offers traditional favourites that change daily: seared king scallops and chorizo; grilled chicken, bacon, avocado and sunblushed tomato salad might precede chargrilled harissa lamb steak with Moroccan vegetable couscous; bangers and mash with onion gravy; and ricotta and spinach tortellini. Good staff-customer repartee makes for an entertaining atmosphere.

Open 11–11 (Sun 12-10.30) **Bar Meals** L served all week 12-9.30 D served all week ⊕ Young & Co ◄ Youngs Special, Youngs Bitter, Wells Bombardier, Guinness. ♦ 15 **Facilities** Garden Dogs allowed

The Cross Keys   Plan 2 E3

1 Lawrence St, Chelsea SW3 5NB

☎ 020 7349 9111 📄 020 7349 9333

e-mail: xkeys.nicole@hotmail.co.uk

dir: *From Sloane Square walk down Kings Rd, left onto Old Church St, then left onto Justice Walk, then right*

A fine Chelsea pub close to the Thames and dating from 1765 that's been a famous bolthole for the rich and famous since the 1960s. The stylish interior includes the bar and conservatory restaurant, plus the Gallery and the Room at the Top – ideal for private parties. A set menu might offer porcini mushroom risotto, and smoked haddock and leek fishcake, while the carte goes for steamed mussels and clams mariniere, and grilled swordfish steak with fennel and orange salad.

Open 12–12 (Sun 12–11) Closed: 23-29 Dec, 1–4 Jan & BH **Bar Meals** L served all week 12–3 D served Mon-Fri 6–8 Av main course £15 **Restaurant** L served all week 12–3 D served all week 6–11 (Sat 12–4, 7–11 Sun 12–4, 7-10.30) ⊕ Scottish & Newcastle ◄ Directors, Best, Guinness.

The Phene Arms ♦   Plan 1 B1

Phene St, Chelsea SW3 5NY

☎ 020 7352 3294 📄 020 7352 7026

e-mail: info@thephenearms.com

dir: *200yds from Kings Rd*

Built in 1851 and named after a doctor who introduced tree planting to London's streets, the pub was once George Best's local. It has a bar, a restaurant area, and a roof terrace, great for basking in the summer. Christian and Kerstin Sandefeldt offer a northern French/Scandinavian menu, thus Swedish meatballs with lingonberries appear alongside roasted halibut with white haricot beans. Fondue and raclette are served on Sundays and Mondays.

Open 11–12 (Sun 12-10.30) **Bar Meals** L served all week 12–4 D served all week 4–10 (Sun 4–9) Av main course £8 **Restaurant** L served only for large pre-booked groups 12–7 D served all week 7–10 (Sun 4–9) Av 3 course à la carte £23 ⊕ Free House ◄ Adnams Bitter Broadside, Fuller's London Pride. ♦ 12 **Facilities** Garden Dogs allowed

The Pig's Ear NEW ♦   Plan 2 E3

35 Old Church St SW3 5BS

☎ 020 7352 2908 📄 020 7352 9321

e-mail: thepigsear@hotmail.co.uk

An award-winning gastropub off the King's Road, specialising in traditional beers and continental cuisine, with food sourced from top quality suppliers. The lunch menu offers spinach and potato gnocchi with wild mushrooms, parmesan and truffle oil; and Angus rib-eye steak with french fries, leaf salad and red wine and shallot butter. In the Blue Room, red gurnard fillets with cockles, samphire and salsa verde; and Gressingham duck magret with colcannon, swiss chard and greengage jam.

Open 12–11 (Sun 12-10.30) **Bar Meals** L served Mon-Fri 12–3 D served Mon-Sat 7–10 (Sat 12-3.30, Sun 12-3.30, 7–9.30) Av main course £15 **Restaurant** L served Sat & Sun 12–4 D served Mon-Sat 7–10 Av 3 course à la carte £35 ◄ Pigs Ear, Deuchars IPA, Guinness. ♦ 10

SW4

Pick of the Pubs

The Belle Vue ♀   Plan 2 E3

1 Clapham Common Southside SW4 7AA
☎ 020 7498 9473 📠 020 7627 0716
e-mail: sean@sabretoothgroup.com
dir: *Telephone for directions*

An independently owned freehouse overlooking the 220 acres of Clapham Common, one of South London's largest green spaces. Free internet access makes it a great place to catch up on work or leisure pursuits, with a coffee, hot snack or some tapas-style nibbles close at hand. A daily changing bistro-style lunch and dinner menu specialises in fish and shellfish, such as pan-fried giant tiger prawns in Thai spices; grilled marlin steak with pepper sauce; dressed Cornish crab salad; and chef's special fish pie. Other possibilities are braised leg of rabbit; steak and kidney pie; Thai green chicken curry; and Mediterranean vegetarian lasagne. Sunday lunch is very popular, and in addition to all the regular roasts are fish and vegetarian dishes. The wine list features over 25 wines and champagnes by the glass, and Harvey's Sussex Bitter is the house real ale.

Open 11–11 (Sun & Thu 11–12, Fri-Sat 11am-1am) Closed: 25–26 Dec **Bar Meals** L served all week 12.30–3.30 D served all week 6.30–10 Sat-Sun all day Av main course £6.50 ⊕ Free House ◖ Harveys Sussex Bitter, Courage Directors Bitter. ♀ 35

The Coach & Horses ♀   Plan 2 E3

173 Clapham Park Rd SW4 7EX
☎ 020 7622 3815 📠 020 7622 3832
e-mail: info@barbeerian-inns.com
dir: *5 mins walk from Clapham High Street & Clapham Common tube station*

Despite its urban location, this attractive coaching inn feels like a country pub. It draws a wide clientele, from locals to trendy young professionals. As the owner says: "Fine wines and Guinness sold in equal amounts." Good roast dinners make it particularly busy on Sundays, whilst Saturday is barbeque day. Samples from a specials board include chicken kebabs, marinated in lemon and fresh herbs with wild rice, warm pitta and coriander chutney; chunky vegetable stew with herb dumplings and crusty bread; and hearty fish pie with a puff pastry lid.

Open 12 -11 (Sun 12–10.30) **Bar Meals** L served all week 12.30–2.30 D served all week 6–9.30 Sat 12.30–3, 6–9; Sun 12.30–5, 7–9 Av main course £10 ◖ London Pride, Adnams. ♀ 8 **Facilities** Children's licence Garden Dogs allowed

The Royal Oak ♀   Plan 2 E3

8–10 Clapham High St SW4 7UT ☎ 020 7720 5678
e-mail: savagecorp@mac.com
dir: *Telephone for directions*

Home to pubs, bars and restaurants galore, these days Clapham High Street has a real neighbourhood feel about it. This traditional London boozer doesn't look much from outside, but its funky gastropub interior admirably compensates. A typical menu

offers rib of beef with horseradish; mushroom and tarragon sausage toad-in-the-hole; and fresh fish, including oysters, and potted salmon. Seaside-brewed Adnams real ales are very much at ease in this urban environment.

Open 12 -11 (Sun 12–10.30) **Bar Meals** L served all week 12–6 D served all week 6–10.30 Av main course £8.50 ⊕ Enterprise Inns ◖ Adnams Broadside, Adnams Bitter Guinness. ♀ 8 **Facilities** Children's licence Dogs allowed

The Windmill on the Common ♀   Plan 2 E2

Clapham Common South Side SW4 9DE
☎ 020 8673 4578 📠 020 8675 1486
e-mail: windmillhotel@youngs.co.uk
dir: *5m from London, just off South Circular 205 at junct with A24 at Clapham*

The original part of this unusually-named pub was known as Holly Lodge and at one time was the property of the founder of Youngs Brewery. The Windmill offers a varied menu with something for all tastes and appetites – sandwiches, wraps, grills, salads and steaks. Vegetarian dishes include dishes such as home-made butternut squash ravioli and wild mushroom risotto.

Open 11–12 (Sun 12–11) **Bar Meals** L served Mon-Fri 12–3 D served Mon-Fri 6–10.30 (Sat 12–10, Sun 12–9) **Restaurant** L served Mon-Fri 12–3 D served Mon-Fri 6–10.30 (Sat 12–10, Sun 12–9) ⊕ Young & Co ◖ Youngs SPA & PA, Wells Bombardier. ♀ 17 **Facilities** Children's licence Garden Parking **Rooms** available

SW6

Pick of the Pubs

The Atlas ♀   Plan 2 D3

16 Seagrave Rd, Fulham SW6 1RX
☎ 020 7385 9129 📠 020 7386 9113
e-mail: theatlas@btconnect.com
dir: *2 mins walk from West Brompton tube station*

Located in a fashionable part of London where a great many pubs have been reinvented to become trendy diners or restaurants, here is a traditional local that remains true to its cause. The spacious bar area – split into eating and drinking sections – attracts what in rural enclaves would be quaintly referred to as outsiders, but to be a local here you can even come from Chelsea, Hampstead or Hammersmith. Dinner menus might feature starters such as roast butternut squash risotto with sage, sweet peppers and parmesan, followed by a variety of tempting mains that may include grilled rib-eye steak with celeriac and parsnip mash and oregano, tomato and chilli jam; pan-roasted salmon fillet with baked fennel and leeks with cream and olives and salsa fresca; and roast duck leg with figs, dates, cinnamon, bay and white wine mashed potato with wholegrain mustard and salsa verde. One of only a handful of London pubs to have a walled garden.

Open 12–11 (Sun 12–10.30) Closed: 24 Dec-1 Jan **Bar Meals** L served Mon-Sat 12.30–3 D served Mon-Sat 7–10.30 (Sun 12.30–4, 7–10) Av main course £12 ⊕ Free House ◖ Fuller's London Pride, Adnams Broadside, London Pride, Caledonian IPA. ♀ 13 **Facilities** Garden

The Imperial ♥
Plan 1 B1

577 Kings Rd SW6 2EH
☎ 020 7736 8549 📠 020 7731 3874
dir: *Telephone for directions*

Mid 19th-century food pub in one of London's most famous and fashionable streets, with a paved terrace at the back. Vibrant and spacious inside, with wooden floors, striking features, and a lively and varied clientele. A selection of pizzas, sandwiches, salads, and burgers feature on the popular menu. Look out for the wild boar sausage with bubble and squeak.

Open 12–11 Closed: BHs **Bar Meals** L served Mon-Sat 12–2.30 D served Mon-Fri 7–9.30 Av main course £6 ◀ T.E.A, London pride. ♥7 **Facilities** Garden

The Salisbury Tavern ♥
Plan 2 D3

21 Sherbrooke Rd SW6 7HX
☎ 020 7381 4005 📠 020 7381 1002
e-mail: thesalisbury@333holdingsltd.com
dir: *Telephone for directions*

Since this sister pub to Chelsea's famous Admiral Codrington opened in 2003, it has quickly established itself as one of Fulham's most popular bar-restaurants. Its elegantly simple, triangular bar and dining area, fitted out with high-backed banquettes as well as individual chairs, is given a lofty sense of space by a huge skylight. Modern European menus offer a great selection of snacks, full all-day English breakfast, and home-made dishes.

Open 12–11 Closed: 24–26 Dec **Bar Meals** L served all week 12–4 D served all week 6–11 Av main course £10 **Restaurant** L served all week 12–2.30 D served Mon-Sat 6.30–11 (Sun 6.30–10) Av 3 course à la carte £21.50 ◀ Wells Bombardier, Greene King IPA, Fuller's London Pride. ♥16 **Facilities** Children's licence Dogs allowed

Pick of the Pubs

The White Horse ♥
Plan 1 A1

1–3 Parson's Green, Fulham SW6 4UL
☎ 020 7736 2115 📠 020 7610 6091
e-mail: whitehorsesw6@btconnect.com
dir: *140mtrs from Parson's Green tube*

This coaching inn has stood on this site since at least 1688, and has advanced impressively since then, with its polished mahogany bar and wall panels, open fires and contemporary art on the walls. A large modern kitchen is behind the imaginative, good value meals served in the bar and Coach House restaurant. For lunch, you might try basil-infused seared tuna with Greek salad, or pork sausages with mash, summer cabbage and beer onion gravy. In the evening there might be seared turbot with summer vegetable and black-eye bean broth, or chowder of gurnard, conga eel and smoked bacon. Every dish from the starters through to the desserts comes with a recommended beer or wine, and the choice of both is considerable. In fact the 2-day beer festival held annually in November with over 300 beers waiting to be sampled is a magnet for lovers of real ale and European beers.

Open 11–12 (Fri-Sat 11–1) **Bar Meals** L served all week 12–10.30 D served all week 12–10.30 Av main course £8.25 **Restaurant** L served all week 12–10.30 D served all week 12–10.30 Av 3 course à la carte £20 ◀ Adnams Broadside, Fuller's ESB, Harveys Sussex Best Bitter, Oakham JHB. ♥20 **Facilities** Garden Dogs allowed

SW7

The Anglesea Arms ♥
Plan 1 A1

15 Selwood Ter, South Kensington SW7 3QG
☎ 020 7373 7960
e-mail: enquiries@angleseaarms.com
dir: *Telephone for directions*

The interior has barely changed since 1827, though the dining area has been tastefully updated with panelled walls and leather-clad chairs; a heated and covered terrace is ideal for smokers. Lunch and dinner menus place an emphasis on quality ingredients, fresh preparation and cosmopolitan flavours. Expect the likes of parma ham, pistachio nuts, caramelised onion and feta salad; spaghetti carbonara; or pappardelle, duck, prosciutto and tomato ragu with aged pecorino. Sunday lunches are popular, booking advisable.

Open 11–11 (Sun 12–10.30) Closed: 25–26 Dec **Bar Meals** L served Mon-Fri 12–3 D served Mon-Fri 6.30–10 (Sat 12–5 & 6–10, Sun 12–5 & 6–9.30) Av main course £11 **Restaurant** L served Mon-Fri 12–3 D served Mon-Fri 6.30–10 (Sat 12–5 & 6–10, Sun 12–5 & 6–9.30) Av 3 course à la carte £19 ⊕ Free House ◀ Fuller's London Pride, Adnams Bitter, Broadside, Brakspear. ♥21 **Facilities** Garden Dogs allowed

Pick of the Pubs

Swag and Tails ◉ ♥
Plan 1 B2

See Pick of the Pubs on page 372

SW8

The Masons Arms ♥
Plan 2 E3

169 Battersea Park Rd SW8 4BT
☎ 020 7622 2007 📠 020 7622 4662
e-mail: themasonsarms@ukonline.co.uk
dir: *Opposite Battersea Park BR Station*

More a neighbourhood local with tempting food than a gastro-pub, the worn wooden floors and tables support refreshingly delightful staff and honest, modern cuisine. Here you'll find a warm and welcoming atmosphere, equally suited to a quiet romantic dinner, partying with friends, or a family outing. Open fires in winter and a summer dining terrace. Daily changing menus feature escobar fillet with paw paw and cucumber salad, pan-fried blackened tuna, and spinach and duck spring roll.

Open 12–11 (Sun 12.30–10.30) **Bar Meals** 12–3 6–10 (Sat 12–5, Sun 12.30–4) Av main course £19 **Restaurant** 12–3 6–10 (Sat 12–5, Sun 12.30–4) Av 3 course à la carte £19 ⊕ Free House ◀ Star of Promise, London Pride. ♥12 **Facilities** Garden Dogs allowed

PICK OF THE PUBS

Swag and Tails

A neighbourhood institution set in a quiet backstreet off Knightsbridge, this flower bedecked Victorian pub is just three or four minutes' walk from Harrods, Harvey Nichols, the V&A and Hyde Park. Long established owners have built up a successful and welcoming pub-restaurant business with a discerning local trade.

The clientele is predominantly up-market – this is an extremely wealthy area – comprising residents and local business people, as well as ladies lunching or taking a break from shopping. Stripped wooden floors, original wood panelling, large windows and mirrors create a light and airy feel, rather different from the typically sombre pub of this era. The atmosphere is relaxed and informal, made cosy in winter by a roaring fire, and staff are friendly, knowledgeable and well trained. Food is a priority, with an ever-changing menu to keep the regulars coming back several times a week. Seasonal changes are reflected in the choice of dishes and variety of quality fresh produce used. Cooking encompasses traditional British fare as well as Thai, Mediterranean and other international options. Typical of the range are appetisers like houmous with hot pitta bread; smoked haddock terrine with tomato and red onion salad; and roasted romero pepper, buffalo mozzarella and peach salad. Main course examples are devilled chicken livers with pousse and shallots on a granary croûte; quesadillas with guacamole, sour cream and salsa; and roast pork fillet with sun-dried tomato mash, buttered spinach and balsamic jus. The choice of desserts is short but sweet: date sponge pudding with caramel sauce and vanilla ice cream; or almond and white chocolate chip brownie with warm chocolate sauce are typical of the half-dozen on offer.

☺ ▾
Plan 1 B2
10/11 Fairholt St, Knightsbridge
SW7 1EG
☎ 020 7584 6926
🖷 020 7581 9935
e-mail:
theswag@swagandtails.com
dir: *3–4 mins walk form Harrods. Off Brompton Rd turn onto Montpelier St, 1st left onto Cheval Place, 2nd right onto Montpelier Walk, take 1st left .*

Open 11–11 Closed: BHs, Xmas & New Year, Sat & Sun
Bar Meals L served Mon-Fri 12–3 D served Mon-Fri 6–10
Restaurant L served Mon-Fri 12–3 D served Mon-Fri 6–10 Av 3 course à la carte £27
⊕ Free House ◪ Adnams Bitter, Wells Bombardier Premium Bitter. ▾ 13
Facilities Dogs allowed

England

The Chelsea Ram ☻ Plan 2 E3

32 Burnaby St SW10 0PL ☎ 020 7351 4008

e-mail: bookings@chelsearam.co.uk

dir: *Telephone for directions*

A popular neighbourhood gastro-pub, The Chelsea Ram is located close to Chelsea Harbour and Lots Road, a little off the beaten track. There is a distinct emphasis on fresh produce in the monthly-changing menu, which includes fish and meat from Smithfield Market. Start with a selection of bread, marinated olives and balsamic vinegar, or enjoy a mezze selection or crispy fried calamari to share. Among the main courses, a modern approach to some old favourites includes battered haddock with minted pea purée and hand cut chips, or pork and leek sausages with creamy mash and caramelised red onion gravy. Alternatives are the Ram burger with Apple Wood cheddar, or hand-made sun-dried tomato and mascarpone ravioli with rocket and toasted pine nuts. Finish with a nostalgic knickerbocker glory topped with hot fudge sauce or a selection of English cheeses, oat biscuits and home-made chutney.

Open 11–11 (Sun 12–10.30) **Bar Meals** L served Mon-Sat 12–3 D served Mon-Sat 6.30–10 (Sun 12–3.30, 7–9.30) Av main course £10 **Restaurant** L served all week 12–3 D served all week 6.30–10 (Sun 12–3.30, 7–9.30) Av 3 course à la carte £20 ⊕ Young & Co ◀ Youngs Bitter, Bombardier, Guinness. ☻ 16 **Facilities** Children's licence Dogs allowed

The Hollywood Arms ☻ Plan 1 A1

45 Hollywood Rd SW10 9HX

☎ 020 7349 7840 📄 020 7349 7841

e-mail: hollywoodarms@youngs.co.uk

dir: *1min from Chelsea & Westminster Hospital, 200mtrs down Hollywood Rd on the right hand side if you are travelling from Fulham rd.*

This listed building is one of Chelsea's hidden treasures. The interior has been elegantly refurbished, augmenting its original charm with rich natural woods, pastel shades and modern fabrics. The large upstairs lounge has elegant mouldings around the ceiling and large open fires at each end, with the bar centred on its length; four huge picture windows make the ambience light and airy. The ground floor pub and restaurant retains much of its traditional atmosphere. Here the chefs lovingly create menus from scratch using high quality ingredients; some, such as cheeses and cured meats, have won national or international recognition. Small plates will produce Rannoch Smokery smoked goose breast, or salt and pepper squid, while main courses offer the home-made half-pound beefburger and chips, Welsh lamb cutlets, or Muffs of Bromborough Old English herb sausages. Award-winning Burtree House Farm puddings are among the desserts.

Open 11–11.30 (Thu-Sat 11–12, Sun 12–10) **Bar Meals** 12–4 D served all week 6–9 (12–10.30) Av main course £9.95 **Restaurant** L served Mon-Sun 11–3 D served all week 6–10 (Sun 12–10.30) Av 3 course à la carte £10 ⊕ Young & Co ◀ Guinness. ☻ 12 **Facilities** Children's licence Dogs allowed

Lots Road Pub and Plan 2 E3
Dining Room ☻

114 Lots Rd, Chelsea SW10 0RJ ☎ 020 7352 6645

e-mail: lotsroad@thespiritgroup.com

dir: *5–10 mins walk from Fulham Broadway Station*

Situated in the heart of Chelsea's bustle, this is the kind of establishment the term gastro-pub was coined for – a smart, comfortable, well-designed space which segues smoothly between jaunty bar area and the more secluded and grown-up restaurant. Slate grey and cream walls and wooden tables create a light, pared-down feel, and attentive staff are set on making you feel comfortable. There's an excellent wine list, and cocktails both quirky and classic. The menu changes daily, and offers plenty of imaginative, modern dishes. Start with the likes of warm smoked chicken, chorizo and chick pea salad; or a spicy fish cake with tartare sauce; after that, perhaps Toulouse sausages with creamy mash and onion gravy; or a whole Scottish trout with spinach and parsley risotto. Puddings are delightfully rich – think sticky toffee pudding – and the more restrained will enjoy cheeses served with Bath Olivers.

Open 11–11 (Fri-Sat 11–12) **Bar Meals** L served all week 12–10.30 D served all week 12–10.30 (Sun 12–10) Av main course £9 **Restaurant** L served all week 12–3 D served all week 12–10.30 (Sun 12–10) Av 3 course à la carte £20 ◀ Wadworth 6X, London Pride, Adnams, Guinness. ☻ 33 **Facilities** Children's licence Dogs allowed

The Sporting Page ☻ Plan 1 A1

6 Camera Place SW10 0BH

☎ 020 7349 0455 📄 020 7352 8162

e-mail: sportingpage@frontpagepubs.com

dir: *Nearest tube – Sloane Square or South Kensington*

A small whitewashed pub happily tucked away between the King's and Fulham Roads. Its rather smart interior of varnished pine and rosewood and sporting murals undoubtedly appeals to people unwinding here after a day's work. Its popular modern British menu includes traditional comfort food such as bangers and mash, smoked haddock and salmon fishcakes, and spaghetti carbonara. Despite its side street location there's seating for 60 outside.

Open 11–11 Closed: 25–26 Dec **Bar Meals** L served all week 12–2.30 D served Mon-Fri 7–10 Av main course £8 ⊕ Front Page Pubs Ltd ◀ Wells Bombardier & Fuller's London Pride. ☻ 12 **Facilities** Garden Dogs allowed

England

SW11

The Castle ♀ Plan 2 E3

115 Battersea High St SW11 3HS
☎ 020 7228 8181 📠 020 7924 5887
e-mail: thecastle@tiscali.co.uk
dir: Approx 10min walk from Clapham Junction

Built in the mid-1960s to replace an older coaching inn, this ivy-covered pub tucked away in 'Battersea Village', has rugs and rustic furnishings on bare boards inside, and an outside enclosed patio garden. A typical menu offers fresh salmon and dill fishcakes; Cajun chicken sandwich; organic lamb steak; and fresh swordfish steak with avocado salsa.

Open 12–11 Closed: 25–26 Dec **Bar Meals** L served all week 12–3 D served all week 7–9.45 (Sun 12.30–4.30, 6–9.30) Av main course £8.50 🍺 Young & Co 🍺 Youngs Bitter & Special, Goddard's Winter Warmer. ♀ 14 **Facilities** Garden Dogs allowed Parking

---

Pick of the Pubs

The Fox & Hounds ♀ Plan 2 E3

66 Latchmere Rd, Battersea SW11 2JU
☎ 020 7924 5483 📠 020 7738 2678
e-mail: foxandhoundsbattersea@btopenworld.com
dir: From Clapham Junction exit onto High St turn left, through lights into Lavender Hill. After post office, left at lights. Pub 200yds on left

London still has hundreds of Victorian corner pubs, like the Queen Vic in *EastEnders*, and the Fox & Hounds is one of these. The style is simple, retaining the relaxed feel of a true neighbourhood local, with bare wooden floors, an assortment of furniture, a walled garden, extensive patio planting and a covered and heated seating area. The food, however, has changed immeasurably since the late 19th century. Fresh ingredients are delivered daily from the London markets, and the Mediterranean-style menu changes accordingly. You might start with an antipasti platter to share, or chicken breast salad with coucous. Pasta, available in starter or main course portions, includes conchiglie with green beans, butternut squash, cream and parmesan, while going up the scale are dishes such as pan-roasted lamb steak with cumin and coriander, served with melted onion and almond rice.

Open 12–3 5–11 (Fri-Sat 12–11, Sun 12–10.30, Mon 5–11) Closed: Etr wknd & 24 Dec-1 Jan & Mon lunch **Bar Meals** L served Fri-Sat 12.30–3 D served all week 7–10.30 (Sun 12.30–4) Av main course £12.50 🍺 Free House 🍺 Deuchars IPA, Harveys Sussex Best Bitter, Fuller's London Pride. ♀ 14 **Facilities** Garden Dogs allowed

SW13

The Bull's Head ♀ Plan 2 D3

373 Lonsdale Rd, Barnes SW13 9PY
☎ 020 8876 5241 📠 020 8876 1546
e-mail: jazz@thebullshead.com
dir: Telephone for directions

Facing the Thames and established in 1684, the Bull's Head has become a major venue for mainstream modern jazz and blues. Nightly concerts draw music lovers from far and wide, helped in no small measure by some fine cask-conditioned ales, over 200 wines, and more than 80 malt whiskies. Traditional home-cooked meals are served in the bar, with dishes ranging from haddock and crab to a variety of roasts and pies. Popular home-made puddings. An important and intrinsic feature of the pub is the Thai menu, available throughout the pub in the evening.

Open 11–11.30 Closed: 25 Dec **Bar Meals** L served all week 12–3 D served all week 6–11 Av main course £5.90 **Restaurant** D served all week 6–11 🍺 Young & Co 🍺 Young's Special, Bitter, Winter Warmer, St Georges. ♀ 32 **Facilities** Garden Dogs allowed

---

Pick of the Pubs

The Idle Hour ♀ Plan 2 D3

62 Railway Side, Barnes SW13 0PQ ☎ 020 8878 5555
e-mail: theidlehour@aol.com
dir: Railway Side off White Hart Ln from rail crossing. No 62 just past school

As the name suggests, this small organic gastro pub is just the spot for whiling away an afternoon. The location – hidden away from the main drag – makes it a favourite with shy celebrities. The enclosed garden is stylishly designed, as is the interior with its roaring fire. The emphasis on organic produce extends from food to all the wines as well as many of the soft drinks. Sundays see all-day opening for an organic roast, or spit-roast pig in summer. The weekday menu changes regularly and features some traditional choices alongside more adventurous dishes. Typical starters include goats' cheese with roasted beetroot, or tomato and white bean soup. Main courses might include tuna Niçoise; home-made steak and Guinness pie; and pea and mint risotto with parmesan cheese. The dessert menu takes in such delight as rhubarb crumble, bread and butter pudding, and chocolate brownies.

Open 5–1am (Sun all day for organic roasts Sat 12–1) **Bar Meals** L served Sat-Sun 1–9 D served all week 7–10 (Sun 1–9) **Restaurant** L served Sun D served all week Av 3 course à la carte £17.50 🍺 Free House 🍺 Heineken, Red Stripe, Hoegaarden, Leffe & Adnams. ♀ 12 **Facilities** Children's licence Garden

PICK OF THE PUBS

SW15-LONDON

The Spencer Arms

The Spencer Arms was transformed a few years ago from an attractive and cosy Victorian tavern overlooking Putney Common's leafy woods and dog-walking trails into an equally attractive and cosy gastropub.

In the process owner Jamie Sherriff has created a large sunlit bar area and dining room, and a relaxed fireside area with leather banquettes, all tricked out in pastels and dark wood. Parents with children to park quietly while they enjoy a drink should do so near the bookshelves and games chest. Chef Tom Bath offers two daily changing lunch and dinner menus which incorporate the best ingredients sourced from – and how unusual is this? – not necessarily local suppliers. For example, meats come from a highly regarded butchers in Coventry, fish is landed by day-boats and trawlers into Falmouth, Plymouth and Lowestoft, RSPCA-accredited salmon is reared in Sutherland, Kentish farms produce the cheeses, and fruit and vegetables

are delivered daily from London's New Covent Garden market. Bar snacks include a wide selection of freshly prepared British-style tapas such as potted shrimps, mini-shepherd's pie and salt-cod fritters, as well as comforting classics like Welsh rarebit, and steamed cockles with shallot vinegar. The main menus feature Loch Duart salmon with crayfish; corn-fed poussin with stuffing balls; venison chop with creamed cabbage; and the somewhat unexpected duck burger with goats' cheese and home-made beetroot pickle. But we're back in 'old favourite' territory with desserts like bread and butter pudding, stewed plums with soft meringue, and home-made apple crumble. Children have their own menu.

⊕ ♀
Plan 2 D3
237 Lower Richmond Rd, Putney
SW15 1HJ
☎ 020 8788 0640
🖷 020 8788 2216
e-mail:
info@thespencerarms.co.uk
dir: *Corner of Putney Common & Lower Richmond Rd, opposite Old Putney Hospital*

Open 10–12 Closed: 25 Dec, 1 Jan
Bar Meals L served all week 12–7 D served all week 12–7 Av main course £12
Restaurant L served Mon-Fri 12.30–2.30 D served Mon-Sat 6.30–10 (Sat-Sun 12–4, Sun 6.30–9.30) Av 3 course à la carte £22.50 Av 2 course fixed price £18.50
⊕ Free House ◖ Guinness, London Pride. ♀ 18
Facilities Garden Dogs allowed

SW15

Pick of the Pubs

The Spencer Arms ♀   Plan 2 D3

See Pick of the Pubs on page 375

SW18

Pick of the Pubs

The Alma Tavern ♀   Plan 2 E3

499 Old York Rd, Wandsworth SW18 1TF

☎ 020 8870 2537

e-mail: alma@youngs.co.uk

dir: *Opposite Wandsworth town rail station*

A delicately restored late-Victorian corner pub retaining much of its original decoration, from its shiny green external tiling and second floor dome to the solid mahogany staircase, carved fireplace and delicately painted mirrors. Sensitive alterations have simplified the layout to a civilised, one-roomed bar, with bare wood floors and unique handmade furniture providing a relaxed setting. Here you can sit with a frothing cappuccino, a pint of Young's or Wells, or a bowl of marinated olives with bread and oils. At the back of the pub is a spacious restaurant opening on to the colourful courtyard, where an all-day menu offers dishes such as seared chicken livers on crostini; pan-fried sardines; grilled salmon with warm couscous salad; and Moroccan vegetable tagine. Desserts include rhubarb crumble and custard; and honey-poached pear with caramel sauce and vanilla ice cream.

Open 11–12 (Sun 12–11) **Bar Meals** L served Mon-Sat 12–10.30 D served Mon-Sat 12–10.30 **Restaurant** L served Mon-Sat 12–4 D served Mon-Sat 6–10.30 (Sun 12–9.30) ⊕ Young & Co ◑ Youngs Bitter, Youngs Special, Youngs Winter Warmer, Youngs guest/seasonal ales. ♀ 17 **Facilities** Garden Dogs allowed Parking

Pick of the Pubs

The Cat's Back ♀   Plan 2 D3

86–88 Point Pleasant, Putney SW18 1NN

☎ 020 8877 0818 & 8874 2937

e-mail: info@thecatsback.com

dir: *2 min walk from Wandsworth Park, by river*

Built in 1865 for lightermen on the Thames and Wandle, this vestige of a once working riverside stands defiant, as new

apartments advance from all sides. Its unique name is simply explained: when a regular's lost moggy turned up again after a month, they were the owner's words as he entered the bar. The character of this wonderfully idiosyncratic London boozer is evident, from the old globe-topped petrol pump out among the tables and chairs on the pavement, to the collection of dodgy Victorian photographs and other paraphernalia inside. Food is served all day in the first-floor dining room, where the chef uses his overseas experience to inspire home-cooked duck breast with berry jus; jumbo shrimps in coconut milk with rice; red tuna with black and white sesame, mash and teriyaki; and medallions of polenta with ratatouille and fried onion. Live music can break out at any time.

Open 11–12.30 (Fri-Sat 11am-2am) Closed: 24–31 Dec **Bar Meals** L served all week 12–10.30 D served all week 12–10.30 **Restaurant** L served Sun D served Mon-Sat 6.30–10.30 (Sun 1–4) Av 3 course à la carte £25 Av 4 course fixed price £29 ⊕ Free House ◑ guest ales. **Facilities** Dogs allowed

Pick of the Pubs

The Earl Spencer ♀   Plan 2 D2

260–262 Merton Rd, Southfields SW18 5JL

☎ 020 8870 9244 📠 020 8877 2828

e-mail: theearlspencer@hotmail.com

dir: *Exit Southfields tube station, down Replingham Rd, left at junct with Merton Rd, to junct with Kimber Rd*

Located just five minutes from Southfields tube, this airy Edwardian pub has been renovated in true gastro-pub style. Traditional log fires and polished wood furnishings have been retained, and a good selection of wines and beers complements the high standard of cooking. The emphasis is on home-cooked food from a daily changing menu using only fresh, seasonal ingredients. Bread is baked daily, and fish is home-smoked. From the eclectic modern British menu starters might include creamy parsnip soup with parsnip crisps; chicken liver paté with toast and spiced crab apples; or beer-battered scallops with pea and mint purée. Typical main course choices include slow roast pork belly with mash and red cabbage; pan-fried trout with purple sprouting broccoli and new potatoes; and a vegetarian mezze with couscous salad and flatbread. For the true gourmet there are also special gastronomic evenings in the function room.

Open 11–11 (Sun 12–10.30) Closed: 25 Dec **Bar Meals** L served Mon-Sat 12.30–2.30 D served Mon-Sat 7–10 (Sun 12–3, 7–9.30) **Restaurant** L served Mon-Sat 12.30–2.30 D served Mon-Sat 7–10 (Sun 12.30–3, 7–9.30) Av 3 course à la carte £23 ◑ Guinness, Hook Norton, London Pride. ♀ 12 **Facilities** Garden

The Freemasons ♀   Plan 2 E3

2 Northside, Wandsworth Common SW18 2SS
☎ 020 7326 8580 📠 020 7223 6186
e-mail: info@freemasonspub.com

The aim of this stylish, popular pub is to get back to basics: to provide excellent, affordable food while maintaining all the ambiance of the friendly local. The space has been considered well, and with details like a round, black walnut bar, an open kitchen, modern art on the walls and plenty of sofas to settle into. Both food and drink are taken seriously, and there's are daily changing menus.

Open 12–11 (Sun 12–10.30, Fri-Sat 11–12) Closed: 25–26 Dec, 1 Jan **Bar Meals** L served Mon-Sat 12–3 D served Mon-Sat 6.30–10 (Sun 12.30–5, 6.30–9.30) Av main course £11 **Restaurant** L served Mon-Sat 12–3 D served Mon-Sat 6.30–10 (Sun 12.30–5, 6.30–9.30) Av 3 course à la carte £20 ⊕ Free House ◀ Timothy Taylor, Tiger Ale, Guinness. ♀ 20 **Facilities** Garden Dogs allowed

The Old Sergeant ♀   Plan 2 D2

104 Garrett Ln, Wandsworth SW18 4DJ
☎ 020 8874 4099 📠 020 8874 4099

Traditional, friendly and oozing with character, The Old Sergeant enjoys a good reputation for its beers, but also offers some decent malt whiskies. It's a great place to enjoy home-cooked food too: the menu could include salmon fish cakes with a sweet chili sauce, duck and orange sausages with coriander mash and gravy, or Thai fishcakes. One of the first pubs bought by Young's in the 1830s.

Open 12–11 (Sun 12–10.30) **Bar Meals** L served all week 12–2.30 D served all week 6–9.30 (Sun 12–9) Av main course £7.50 **Restaurant** L served Mon-Fri D served Mon-Fri (Thu-Sat 7–9.30 only) Av 3 course à la carte £20 ⊕ Young & Co ◀ Youngs Ordinary, Youngs Special. ♀ 12 **Facilities** Garden Dogs allowed

The Ship Inn ♀   Plan 2 E3

Jew's Row SW18 1TB
☎ 020 8870 9667 📠 020 8874 9055
e-mail: drinks@theship.co.uk
dir: *Wandsworth Town BR station nearby. On S side of Wandsworth Bridge*

Situated next to Wandsworth Bridge on the Thames, the Ship exudes a lively, bustling atmosphere. The saloon bar and extended conservatory area lead out to a large beer garden, and in the summer months an outside bar is open for business. There is a popular restaurant, and all-day food is chosen from a single menu, with the emphasis on free-range produce from the landlord's organic farm. Expect the likes of lamb cutlets, chargrilled marlin fillet, shepherds pie, and peppers stuffed with hazelnuts and goat's cheese.

Open 11–11 (Sun 11–10.30) **Bar Meals** L served all week 12–10 D served all week 7–10.30 (Sun 7–10) Av main course £9 **Restaurant** L served all week 12–10.30 D served all week (Sun 12–10) Av 3 course à la carte £18 ⊕ Young & Co ◀ Youngs: PA, SPA, Waggle Dance, Winter Warmer. ♀ 15 **Facilities** Garden Dogs allowed

SW19

The Brewery Tap ♀   Plan 2 D2

68–69 High St, Wimbledon SW19 5EE
☎ 020 8947 9331
e-mail: thebrewerytap@hotmail.com

A small, cosy one room pub, big on sports like football, rugby and cricket. It is also the closest pub to the Wimbledon tennis championships. Breakfast is served till 12.30pm, and snacks take in wooden platters, sandwiches and salad bowls. More substantial lunches are hot salt beef, and bangers and mash (with veggie sausage alternative). The only evening food is tapas on Wednesday. Special events are held for Burns' Night, Bastille Day etc.

Open 12–11 (Fri-Sat 12–12 Sun 11–10.30, 25 Dec 12–2) **Bar Meals** L served Mon-Sat 12–2.30 (Sun 12–4) ⊕ Enterprise Inns ◀ Fuller's London Pride, Adnams, guest ales. ♀ 13 **Facilities** Dogs allowed

W1

The Argyll Arms ♀   Plan 1 C4

18 Argyll St, Oxford Circus W1F 7TP ☎ 020 7734 6117
dir: *Nearest tube – Oxford Circus*

A tavern has stood on this site since 1740, but the present building is mid-Victorian and is notable for its stunning floral displays. There's a popular range of sandwiches and the hot food menu might offer vegetarian moussaka, beef and Guinness pie, chicken and leek pie, haddock and lasagne.

Open 11–11 (Sun 12–10.30) Closed: 25 Dec **Bar Meals** L served all week 11–10 D served all week (Sun 11–9) Av main course £6.95 **Restaurant** L served all week (Sun 12–9) ◀ Bass, Fuller's London Pride, Greene King IPA & guest ales. ♀ 15

French House ♀   Plan 1 D4

49 Dean St, Soho W1D 5BG
☎ 020 7437 2477 📠 020 7287 9109
e-mail: fhrestaurant@aol.com
dir: *Telephone for directions*

Historic pub used by the Free French during World War II, and Soho bohemians since the 1950s when the likes of Dylan Thomas, Francis Bacon and Brendan Behan were regulars. The bar is small – they do not serve pints – and the music is the conversation. There is a small restaurant on the first floor where the menu changes regularly, including dishes like braised lamb shank, fillet steak, and black bream fillet with citrus cannellini stew.

Open 12–12 (Sun-Mon 12–11) **Bar Meals** L served Mon-Sat 12–3 **Restaurant** L served Mon-Sat 12–3 D served Mon-Sat 5.30–11 Av 3 course à la carte £25.30 ⊕ Free House ◀ Budvar, Kronenbourg, Leffe, Guinness & Becks. ♀ 22

W1 continued

Red Lion ♀   Plan 1 C3

No 1 Waverton St, Mayfair W1J 5QN

☎ 020 7499 1307 📄 020 7409 7752

e-mail: gregpeck@globalnet.co.uk

dir: *Nearest tube – Green Park*

Built in 1752, The Red Lion is one of Mayfair's most historic pubs. Originally used mainly by 18th-century builders, the clientele is now more likely to be the rich and famous of Mayfair, yet the friendly welcome remains. The pub was used as a location in the 2001 Brad Pitt and Robert Redford movie, *Spy Game*. The bar menu has a traditional pub feel, offering the likes of steak and stilton pie, Cumberland sausage, chicken masala, rack of pork ribs, and steak sandwich. Piano music on Saturday nights.

Open 11.30–11.20 Closed: 25–26 Dec, 1 Jan, Sat & Sun am **Bar Meals** L served Mon-Sat 12–3 D served all week 6–9.30 Av main course £7.10 **Restaurant** L served Mon-Sat 12–2.30 D served all week 6–9.30 Av 3 course à la carte £25 ⊕ Punch Taverns ◀ Greene King IPA, London Pride, Bombardier, Youngs Ordinary. ♀ 10

W2

The Cow ♀   Plan 2 D4

89 Westbourne Park Rd W2 5QH

☎ 020 7221 5400 📄 020 7727 8687

e-mail: thecow@btconnect.com

dir: *Telephone for directions*

A gastro-pub popular with the Notting Hill glitterati, The Cow has a bustling downstairs bar and a tranquil first floor dining room. 'Eat heartily and give the house a good name' is the sound philosophy of the Cow, which specialises in oysters and Guinness. Try Cow pie or seafood platter in the bar, or go upstairs for sautéed squid with chorizo, peppers and chickpeas; or Welsh Black rump with bubble and squeak.

Open 12–11 Closed: 25 Dec **Bar Meals** L served all week 12–4 D served all week 6–10.30 **Restaurant** L served Sat-Sun 12–4 D served all week 6–11 ⊕ Free House ◀ London Pride, Guinness. ♀ 10

The Prince Bonaparte ♀   Plan 2 D4

80 Chepstow Rd W2 5BE

☎ 020 7313 9491 📄 020 7792 0911

dir: *Telephone for directions*

A first-generation gastro pub where Johnny Vaughan filmed the Strongbow ad. Renowned for its bloody Marys, good music and quick, friendly service, the pub proves popular with young professionals and has DJ nights on Fridays and Saturdays. The building is Victorian, with an airy and open plan interior. Typical meals include sausages and mash, tomato and mozzarella bruschetta, sea bass with spinach, and spicy chicken gnocchi.

Open 12–11 (Sun 12–10.30) **Bar Meals** L served all week 12.30–10 D served all week 12.30–10 (Fri-Sat 12–9) Av main course £8.50 **Restaurant** L served all week 12.30–3 D served all week 6.30–10 (Sun 6.30–9) Av 3 course à la carte £20 ⊕ Bass ◀ Fuller's London Pride, Staropramen, Greene King IPA, guest. ♀ 13 **Facilities** Dogs allowed

The Westbourne ♀   Plan 2 D4

101 Westbourne Park Villas W2 5ED

☎ 020 7221 1332 📄 020 7243 8081

dir: *On corner of Westbourne Park Rd & Westbourne Park Villas*

Classic Notting Hill pub/restaurant favoured by bohemian clientele, including a sprinkling of celebrities. Sunny terrace is very popular in summer. Tempting, twice-daily-changing menu is listed on a board behind the bar and might include baked filo roll with butternut squash, ricotta, sage and nutmeg ; pot roasted pheasant with bacon, shallots, oyster mushrooms, garlic mash and winter greens; or fillet of seabass baked with lentils, chicory, thyme, white wine and Vermouth.

Open 12–11 (Mon 5–11 Sun 12–10.30) Closed: 24 Dec-2 Jan **Bar Meals** L served Tue-Sun 12.30–3 D served all week 7–10 (Sat-Sun 7–9.30) Av main course £12 **Restaurant** L served Tue-Sun 12.30–3 D served all week 7–10 (Sat-Sun 7–9.30) Av 3 course à la carte £22 Av 2 course fixed price £10.50 ⊕ Free House ◀ Leffe, Warsteiner, Hoegaarden, Old Speckled Hen. ♀ 9 **Facilities** Garden Dogs allowed

W4   MAP 06 TQ27

Pick of the Pubs

The Devonshire House ⊛ ♀   Plan 2 C3

126 Devonshire Rd, Chiswick W4 2JJ

☎ 020 8987 2626 📄 020 8995 0152

e-mail: info@thedevonshire.co.uk

dir: *150yds off Chiswick High Rd. 100yds from Hogarth rdbt & A4*

A laid back and unpretentious gastro-pub located in a leafy district of Chiswick, the Devonshire House was formerly known as the Manor Tavern. Its transformation into an attractive, light and airy bar and restaurant happened a few years back. It serves an interesting mix of modern British and Mediterranean dishes, and changes daily depending on the fresh produce currently available. You can whet your appetite with some marinated olives, French farmhouse bread or oriental spiced crackers and nuts before launching in to the menu proper. A typical three courses might comprise salad of smoked eel and new potatoes with horseradish cream; roast saddle of new season lamb, farci, pea purée and caramelised pearl onions; and roast winter plums on toasted brioche and mascarpone ice cream. Children are made to feel welcome with a secure garden to play in, plus books, crayons and games to keep them entertained.

Open 12–11 Closed: 25–26 Dec **Bar Meals** L served Tue-Sun 12–3 D served Tue-Sun 7–11 **Restaurant** L served Tue-Sun 12–3 D served Tue-Sun 7–11 ⊕ Unique Pub Co ◀ London Pride, Guinness. ♀ 15 **Facilities** Children's licence Garden Dogs allowed

The Pilot ♀   Plan 2 C3

56 Wellesley Rd W4 4BZ

☎ 020 8994 0828 📄 020 8994 2785

e-mail: the.pilotpub@ukonline.co.uk

dir: *Telephone for directions*

A large garden makes this Chiswick pub a real winner, especially in summer, while indoors the atmosphere is always friendly and welcoming. An exciting menu includes pan-seared bison with sweet potato, spring onion hash and red wine jus; steamed barracuda on asmine rice cooked in Asian crab broth with pak choi; and stuffed baby squid with wild rice and chorizo.

Open 12–11 (Sun 12–10.30) Closed: 25 Dec **Bar Meals** L served Mon-Sun 12–3.30 D served Mon-Sun 4.30–10 Sat 12–10, Sun 12–9.30 Av main course £9.50 **Restaurant** L served all week 12–3.30 D served all week 5.30–10 Av 3 course à la carte £18.50 ◀ Staropramen, London Pride. ☻ 10 **Facilities** Garden

Pick of the Pubs

The Swan ☻   Plan 2 C3

1 Evershed Walk, 119 Acton Ln W4 5HH
☎ 020 8994 8262 🖺 020 8994 9160
e-mail: theswanpub@btconnect.com
dir: *Pub on right at end of Evershed Walk*

A friendly gastro-pub, The Swan is much appreciated by locals for its international range of beers and cosmopolitan atmosphere. A pub for all seasons, it has a welcoming wood panelled interior and a large lawned garden and patio area for outdoor refreshments. Good food is at the heart of the operation, and you can sit and eat wherever you like. The menu of modern, mostly Mediterranean cooking has a particular Italian influence. Spiced red lentil and carrot soup with star anise and allspice; and linguine alla Genovese (with potatoes, green beans and pesto) will bring in the vegetarians. Other options might be roast sea bream with Lisbon potatoes and chive aïoli; or gnochetti Sardi with wild boar sausages, tomatoes and oregano. Finish with Donald's chocolate and almond cake with cream; or apple and date crumble served with vanilla ice cream.

Open 5–11 (Sat-Sun 12–11) Closed: 23 Dec-2 Jan, Etr **Restaurant** L served Sat-Sun 12.30–3 D served Mon-Sat 7–10.30 (Sun 7–10) Av 3 course à la carte £24 ⊕ Free House ◀ London Pride, Deuchars IPA & Guinness. ☻ 14 **Facilities** Garden Dogs allowed

W5

The Red Lion ☻   Plan 2 C3

13 St Mary's Rd, Ealing W5 5RA
☎ 020 8567 2541 🖺 020 8840 1294
e-mail: red.lionealing@bt.click.com
dir: *Telephone for directions*

The pub opposite the old Ealing Studios, the Red Lion is affectionately known as the 'Stage Six' (the studios have five), and has a unique collection of film stills celebrating the Ealing comedies of the 50s. Sympathetic refurbishment has broadened the pub's appeal, and the location by Ealing Green has a leafy, almost rural feel, plus there's an award-winning walled garden. Pub food ranges through oysters, burgers, bangers and mash, and fillet steak.

Open 11–11 (Thu-Sat 11–12) **Bar Meals** L served all week 12–4 D served Mon-Sat 7–9.30 ⊕ Fullers ◀ Fuller's London Pride, Chiswick, ESB. ☻ 10 **Facilities** Garden Dogs allowed

The Wheatsheaf ☻   Plan 2 C4

41 Haven Ln, Ealing W5 2HZ ☎ 020 8997 5240
dir: *1m from A40 junct with North Circular*

Just a few minutes from Ealing Broadway, this large Victorian pub has a rustic appearance inside. Ideal place to enjoy a big screen sporting event or a drink among wooden floors, panelled walls, beams from an old barn, and real fires in winter. Traditional pub grub includes cottage pie; beer battered cod and chips; steak, ale and mushroom pie; pork and leek sausage and mash; and vegetable lasagne.

Open 12–11 (Sat 11–11, Sun 12–10.30) **Bar Meals** L served all week 12–3 D served Mon-Sat 6–9 (Sat 12–8, Sun 12–5) Av main course £6.25 ⊕ Fullers ◀ Fuller's London Pride, ESB & Chiswick, seasonal ales. ☻ 10 **Facilities** Garden Dogs allowed

W6

Pick of the Pubs

Anglesea Arms ◉ ☻   Plan 2 D3

35 Wingate Rd W6 0UR
☎ 020 8749 1291 🖺 020 8749 1254
e-mail: anglesea.events@gmail.com
dir: *Telephone for details*

Real fires and a relaxed atmosphere are all part of the attraction at this traditional corner pub. Behind the Georgian façade the decor is basic but welcoming, and the place positively hums with people eagerly seeking out the highly reputable food. A range of simple, robust dishes might include starters like pigeon, duck and foie gras terrine, Anglesea charcuterie platter, or butternut squash and goats' curd risotto. Among main courses could be slow-cooked belly of pork, wild sea bass, lentils, wild mushrooms and red wine, pot-roast stuffed saddle of lamb, and toasted sea bass with saffron potatoes. Puddings are also exemplary: expect poached pear, brandy snap and pear sorbet, chocolate, pecan and hazelnut 'brownie' cake with vanilla ice cream, or perhaps buttermilk pudding with pineapple and almond biscotti. A savoury alternative might be Cornish yarm with chutney and water biscuits.

Open 11–11 (Sun 12–10.30) Closed: 24–31 Dec **Bar Meals** L served Mon-Sat 12.30–2.45 D served Mon-Sat 7–10.30 (Sun 12.30–3.30, 7–10) Av main course £13.50 **Restaurant** L served Mon-Sat 12.30–2.45 D served Mon-Sat 7–10.45 (Sun 12.30–3.30, 7–10) Av 3 course à la carte £26 ⊕ Free House ◀ Greene King, Old Speckled Hen, Fuller's London Pride, Timothy Taylor Landlord. ☻ 20

England

W6 continued

The Dartmouth Castle NEW ♀   Plan 2 D3

26 Glenthorne Rd, Hammersmith W6 0LS

☎ 020 8748 3614 📠 020 8748 3619

e-mail: dartmouth.castle@btconnect.com

George and Richard Manners took over the Dartmouth Castle in Hammersmith a couple of years ago. While their aim is to keep the place very much a pub – somewhere to relax over a pint or two – the food is proving an even greater attraction. The monthly changing Mediterranean menu ranges from imaginative sandwiches (grilled chicken and pancetta with avocado and tomato) to dishes such as Tuscan lamb shank with olives, glazed carrots and polenta croutons; or saltimbocca of monkfish, with Parma ham, sage and sautéed potatoes. Vegetarian aren't forgotten either, with linguine alla Genovese, or wild mushroom risotto, both available as a starter or main course. Typical desserts are tiramisù, or chocolate and almond cake with cream. The range of beers includes two real ales on tap at any one time, and there's a 34-bottle wine list with 13 available by the glass. Facilities extend to a beer garden and function room.

Open 12–11 (Sun 12–10.30) Closed: Etr & 23 Dec–2 Jan
Bar Meals L served Mon-Sat 12–3 D served Mon-Sat 6–10 (Sun 12–9.30) Av main course £12 ◀ London Pride & Guest ales. ♀ 14
Facilities Garden Dogs allowed

The Stonemasons Arms ♀   Plan 2 D3

54 Cambridge Grove W6 0LA

☎ 020 8748 1397 📠 020 8846 9636

e-mail: stonemasonsarms@fullers.co.uk

dir: *Hammersmith tube. Walk down King St, 2nd right up Cambridge Grove, pub at end*

This welcoming West London gastro-pub must boast some of the most unusual sausages in the capital, including kangaroo and crocodile. They're just one of the innovations on a punchy menu inspired by traditional British and continental dishes. If kangaroo doesn't appeal, try smoked eel, chorizo and rocket salad; marinated tuna; and a bowl of home-made damson ice cream. Look out also for the Kriek beer jelly, a perfect accompaniment to chicken liver paté.

Open 11–11 (Sun 12–10.30) **Bar Meals** L served Mon-Fri 12–3 D served Mon-Fri 6–10 (Sat-Sun all day) **Restaurant** L served Mon-Fri 12–3 D served all week 6–10 (Sat 12–10, Sun 12–9.30) ⊕ Fullers ◀ London Pride, Organic Honeydew, Kirin. ♀ 16

W8

The Churchill Arms ♀   Plan 2 D3

119 Kensington Church St W8 7LN ☎ 020 7727 4242

dir: *Off A40 (Westway). Nearest tube-Notting Hill Gate*

Thai food is the speciality at this traditional 200–year-old pub with strong emphasis on exotic chicken, beef, prawn and pork dishes. Try Kaeng Panang curry with coconut milk and lime leaves, or Pad Priew Wan stir-fry with sweet and sour tomato sauce. Oriental feasts notwithstanding, the Churchill Arms has many traditional British aspects including oak beams, log fires and an annual celebration of Winston Churchill's birthday.

Open 11–11 (Thu-Sat 11–12) **Bar Meals** L served all week 12–10 D served Mon-Sat Av main course £5.85 **Restaurant** L served all week 12–10 D served Mon-Sat Av 3 course à la carte £10 Av 1 course fixed price £5.85 ⊕ Fullers ◀ Fuller's London Pride, ESB & Chiswick Bitter. ♀ 25
Facilities Garden Dogs allowed

Mall Tavern ♀   Plan 2 D4

71–73 Palace Gardens Ter, Notting Hill, Kensington W8 4RU ☎ 020 7727 3805 📠 020 7792 9620

e-mail: info@malltavern.co.uk

dir: *E along Bayswater Rd, 2nd turn on right*

This 100–year-old pub in the heart of Notting Hill was taken over in 2006 by two young chefs, so the focus on food is not unexpected. An extensive daily specials board includes starters (six rock oysters), main courses (corn-fed chicken breast) and desserts (passionfruit cheesecake). The set price lunch menu is served seven days per week, while a new range of 'lite bites' caters for the less than famished. Drinks include continental beers and 20 wines served by the glass.

Open 12–11.30 Closed: 25–26 Dec **Bar Meals** L served all week 12–11.30 D served all week 12–11.30 **Restaurant** L served Mon-Fri 12–3 D served all week 7–11 (Sat 11–4, Sun 12–4) Av 3 course fixed price £15.50 ⊕ Enterprise Inns ◀ Becks Vier, Staropramen, Leffe Blond, Tiger & Peroni. ♀ 20
Facilities Garden Dogs allowed

The Scarsdale ♀   Plan 2 D3

23A Edwardes Square, Kensington W8 6HE

☎ 020 7937 1811 📠 020 7938 2984

dir: *Exit Kensington High Street Station, turn left & continue for 10 mins along High St. Edwards Sq is next left after Odeon Cinema.*

A 19th-century, free-standing local with a stone forecourt enclosed by railings, just off Kensington High Street. The Frenchman who developed the site was supposedly one of Bonaparte's secret agents. There's so much about this place, not least its intriguing mix of customers, that ensures you don't forget which part of London you are in. The food is modern European and highly praised, but the stupendous Bloody Marys are the real talking point.

Open 12–11 (Sun 12–10.30) Closed: 25–26 Dec **Bar Meals** L served Mon-Sat 12–10 D served Mon-Sat 12–10 (Sun 12–9) **Restaurant** L served Mon-Sat 12–2.30 D served Mon-Sat 6–10 (Sun 12–3, 6–9) ⊕ Punch Taverns ▩ London Pride, Old Speckled Hen, Youngs, Greene King IPA. ♚ 20 **Facilities** Garden Dogs allowed

The Windsor Castle ♚   Plan 2 D4

114 Campden Hill Rd W8 7AR ☎ 0207 243 9551

dir: From Notting Hill Gate, take south exit towards Holland Park, left opposite pharmacy

Established in 1845, this pub takes its name from the royal castle, which could once be seen from the upper-floor windows. Unchanged for years, it boasts oak panelling and open fires, and is reputedly haunted by the ghost of Thomas Paine, author of *The Rights of Man*. A good variety of food is served in the bar, from speciality sausages and mash, to salads, sandwiches, snacks like half-a-dozen oysters, and lamb with roasted vegetables.

Open 12–11 (Sun 12–10.30) **Bar Meals** L served all week 12–3.30 D served all week 5–10 (Sat 12–10, Sun 12–9) ▩ Staropramen, Timothy Taylor Landlord, Fuller's London Pride, Adnams Broadside. ♚ 10 **Facilities** Garden Dogs allowed

---

W9

The Waterway ♚   Plan 2 D4

54 Formosa St W9 2JU

☎ 020 7266 3557 ▤ 020 7266 3547

e-mail: olly&tridge@theebury.co.uk

Trendy Maida Vale restaurant and bar in a canalside setting with a large decking area where popular barbecues are held. The bar is also a great place to relax with its comfy sofas and open fires, and there is an interesting choice of drinks, including cocktails and champagne by the glass. The restaurant menu offers a choice of modern European food.

Open 12–11 **Bar Meals** L served all week 12 D served all week 10.30 (Sun 12–10) Av main course £14 **Restaurant** L served Mon-Sat 12–3.30 D served Mon-Sat 6.30–10.30 (Sun 12–4, 6.30–10) Av 3 course à la carte £30 ▩ Guinness, Hoegaarden. ♚ 10 **Facilities** Garden Dogs allowed

---

W10

Pick of the Pubs

The Fat Badger NEW   Plan 2 D4

310 Portobello Rd W10 5TA ☎ 020 8969 4500

e-mail: rupert@thefatbadger.com

Notting Hill's Portobello Road is famous for its antique shops and Saturday street market. Right at its heart is this former drinking pub, which once had a reputation for loud music, but is now reborn as the place to relax with good beers and hearty, mainly British, food. The wood-floored bar has plenty of tables and chairs to choose from and offers snacks such as Falmouth Bay oysters. The main menu gives a wide choice, including Irish stew; smoked eel with beetroot, apple and watercress; crubeens (salted pig's trotters) with red onion marmalade; and parmesan pancake with wild mushrooms and rocket. On Sunday lunchtimes the place is

always busy with locals enjoying, perhaps, seared scallops with peas, bacon and mint; roast Herefordshire beef and Yorkshire pudding; or pickled beetroot salad, soft-boiled egg and mustard cream. Desserts include blood orange granita; sticky toffee pudding; and St Emilion au chocolat.

Open 12–11 (Sat 11-12, Sun 12–10.30) Closed: 25–26 Dec **Bar Meals** L served Mon-Fri 12–3 D served Mon-Fri 6.30–10 (Sat 11–5, 6.30–10.30, Sun 12–5, 6.30–9) **Restaurant** L served Mon-Fri 12–3 D served Mon-Fri 6.30–10 (Sat 11–5, 6.30–10.30, Sun 12–5, 6.30–9) Av 3 course à la carte £30 Av 3 course fixed price £12.50 ▩ Guinness. **Facilities** Children's licence Dogs allowed

Golborne Grove ♚   Plan 2 D4

36 Golborne Rd W10 5PR

☎ 020 8960 6260 ▤ 020 8960 6961

e-mail: golborne@groverestaurants.co.uk

dir: From Ladbroke Grove tube, up Ladbroke Grove, right into Golborne Rd

A popular dining destination, this award-winning gastro-pub is located at the north end of Notting Hill, with a ground floor bar area and function room upstairs. Local architectural photos, 1920's Venetian mirrors and squashy 1960's sofas contribute to the appealing interior. The drinks range encompasses beers, cocktails and a reasonable wine list. Fish features strongly in dishes like pan-fried red snapper fillet with roast vegetables and pine kernels, cous cous and Greek salad.

Open 12–11 (Sat 12–12, Sun 12–11.30) **Bar Meals** L served all week 12.30–3.45 D served all week 6.30–10.15 **Restaurant** L served all week 12.30–3.45 D served all week 6.30–10.15 Av 3 course à la carte £20 Av 3 course fixed price £15 ⊕ Enterprise Inns ▩ Fuller's London Pride, Guinness. ♚ 10 **Facilities** Garden Dogs allowed

The North Pole ♚   Plan 2 D4

13–15 North Pole Rd W10 6QH

☎ 020 8964 9384 ▤ 020 8960 3774

e-mail: northpole@massivepub.com

dir: Right from White City tube station, past BBC Worldwide, turn right at 2nd lights, 200yds on right. 10 mins walk

A trendy modern gastro-pub with large windows and bright décor, formerly owned by Jade Jagger, and just five minutes' walk from BBC Worldwide. Expect leather sofas, armchairs, daily papers, a good range of wines by the glass, cocktails and a lively atmosphere in the bar. Separate bar and restaurant menus continue to show real interest, with simply described modern fusion dishes. Fish dishes feature haddock, prawns, whitebait, oysters and mussels.

Open 12–11 **Bar Meals** L served all week 12–3 D served all week 6–9.30 (Fri & Sun 12–4) Av main course £10 **Restaurant** L served all week 12–3 D served all week 6–9.30 (Fri & Sun 12–4, 6–9.30) ⊕ Free House ▩ Fosters, Kronenbourg, San Miguel, Guinness. ♚ 14 **Facilities** Children's licence Dogs allowed

W11

Portobello Gold U ♀   Plan 2 D4

95–97 Portobello Rd W11 2QB ☎ 020 7460 4900

e-mail: reservations@portobellogold.com

dir: *From Notting Hill Gate Tube Station, follow signs to Portobello Market.*

This quirkily stylish Notting Hill pub cum brasserie was born in the mid-1980s, and has been in the same ownership ever since. A catastrophic fire in 2004 necessitated complete refurbishment, but the appeal is as powerful as ever, with programmes of live (but not too loud) music and artworks to accompany an eclectic range of beers and funky international menus. Food is served in the bar or in the lush tropical conservatory; booking essential.

Open 10-12 Closed: 25 Dec-1 Jan **Bar Meals** L served Mon-Sat 11–5 D served Mon-Sat 5–11 (Sun 12–9) **Restaurant** L served Mon-Sat 12–11 D served Mon-Sat 7–11 (Sun 1–8) Av 3 course à la carte £23 ⊕ Enterprise Inns ◀ Staropramen, Guinness, London Pride, Hoegaarden & Harveys Sussex Ales. ♀ 14 **Facilities** Dogs allowed **Rooms** 8

W14

The Cumberland Arms ♀   Plan 2 D3

29 North End Rd, Hammersmith W14 8SZ

☎ 020 7371 6806 🖹 020 7371 6848

e-mail: thecumberlandarmspub@btconnect.com

dir: *From Kensington Olympia, exit station & turn left, at Hammersmith Rd turn right, at T-jet (North End Rd) turn left, continue for 100yds & pub is on left.*

Close to Olympia, the Cumberland is one of the most popular gastro-pubs in this part of London. Its rich blue-painted façade with gold lettering is a welcoming sight, and mellow furniture and stripped floorboards characterise the interior; pavement benches and tables help alleviate the pressure inside. Friendly staff, an affordable wine list and well-kept ales are the draw for those seeking after-work refreshment. It's also a great place for tasty plates of unpretentious Mediterranean food, with a daily-changing selection of Italian, Spanish and North African dishes. Lunchtime sandwiches may include mozzarella with slow-roasted tomatoes and pesto, or grilled Italian sausage with tomato and chilli jam. Mixed antipasti could include marinated feta and chickpea salad, poached mackerel fillet on crostini with salsa verde, and pan-roasted pork ribs. Main courses are typified by rabbit and porcini risotto with parmesan; spaghetti with beef meatballs, tomato and oregano; and grilled red tuna with couscous salad and salsa fresca.

Open 12–11 Closed: 23 Dec-2 Jan **Bar Meals** L served Mon-Sat 12.30–3 D served Mon-Sat 7–10.30 (Sun 12.30–4, 7–10) Av main course £11.50 ◀ London Pride, Deuchars Caledonian. ♀ 12 **Facilities** Garden

The Havelock Tavern ♀   Plan 2 D4

57 Masbro Rd, Brook Green W14 0LS

☎ 020 7603 5374 🖹 020 7602 1163

dir: *Nearest tubes: Shepherd's Bush & Olympia*

The Havelock is still run very much as a boozer despite being a gastropub – but with the good food. It is popular with lunchtime customers who want a quick one-course meal before returning to work. In the evenings it offers more substantial food with a reasonably priced, ever-rolling two/three course menu.

Open 11–11 (Sun 12–10.30) Closed: 5 days at Xmas & Etr Sun **Bar Meals** L served Mon-Sat 12.30–2.30 D served Mon-Sat 7–10 (Sun 12–3, 7–9.30) ⊕ Free House ◀ Flowers Original Cask, Marston's Pedigree, Fullers London Pride. ♀ 11 **Facilities** Garden

WC1

The Bountiful Cow NEW ♀   Plan 1 E4

51 Eagle St, Holborn WC1R 4AP ☎ 020 7404 0200

e-mail: manager@roxybeaujolais.com

web: www.thebountifulcow.co.uk

dir: *230mtrs NE from Holborn Tube Station, via Procter St. Walk through 2 arches into Eagle St. Pub between High Holborn & Red Square*

Roxy Beaujolais, also proprietor of the ancient Seven Stars behind the Law Courts, found this second pub a few streets away and decided to specialise in serving the finest steaks and exceptionally large burgers at 'unbeatable prices'. Her architect husband's design achieves the right balance between funky bistro and stylish saloon, aided by dozens of pictures and posters glorifying beef. Five cuts of beef feature on the menu: onglet (for sandwiches), rib-eye, sirloin, fillet and T-bone, all aged many weeks for tenderness and flavour, and all available with melted goat's cheese, Béarnaise or green peppercorn sauce. Non-beef options include starters of duck rillettes, lemony Greek salad and smoked salmon, and mains of grilled chorizo and tomato; dill-cured herring and potato salad; and Welsh rarebit with Guinness. Adnams, Harveys and Timothy Taylor supply the real ales. Free jazz on Saturday nights usually features the outstanding Shura Greenberg Trio.

Open 11–11 Closed: Sun & BHs **Bar Meals** L served Mon-Sat 12–3 D served Mon-Sat 5–10.30 Av main course £11.40 **Restaurant** L served Mon-Sat 12–3 D served Mon-Sat 5–10.30 Av 3 course à la carte £22.80 ◀ Adnams Best, Adnams Broadside, Harveys Best, Dark Star.

Pick of the Pubs

The Lamb ♟   Plan 1 E4

94 Lamb's Conduit St WC1N 3LZ ☎ 020 7405 0713

e-mail: lambwc1@youngs.co.uk

dir: *Russell Square, turn right, 1st right, 1st left, 1st right*

This building was first recorded in 1729, was 'heavily improved' between 1836–1876, and frequented by Charles Dickens when he lived nearby in Doughty Street (now housing the Dickens Museum). This really is a gem of a place, with its distinctive green-tiled façade, very rare glass snob screens, dark polished wood, and original sepia photographs of music hall stars who performed at the nearby Holborn Empire. The absence of television, piped music and fruit machines allows conversation to flow, although there is a working polyphon. Home-cooked bar food includes a vegetarian corner (vegetable curry, or burger), a fish choice including traditional fish and chips; and steaks from the griddle, plus pies and baked dishes from the stove. Favourites are steak and ale pie (called the Celebration 1729 pie); sausage and mash; liver and bacon; and fried egg and chips. For something lighter, try a ploughman's or a vegetable samosa with mango chutney.

Open 11–12 (Sun 12–4, 7–10.30) **Bar Meals** L served all week 12–3 D served Mon-Thu & Sat 6–9 Av main course £7 ⊕ Young & Co ◗ Youngs (full range). ♟ 11 **Facilities** Garden

---

WC2

The Lamb and Flag ♟   Plan 1 D3

33 Rose St, Covent Garden WC2E 9EB

☎ 020 7497 9504 🗎 020 7379 7655

dir: *Leicester Square, Cranbourne St exit, turn left into Garrick St, 2nd left*

Licensed during the reign of Elizabeth 1, the Lamb and Flag exudes a strong atmosphere, with low ceilings and high-backed settles both striking features of the bar. In 1679 the poet Dryden was almost killed in a nearby alley. These days office workers and Covent Garden tourists throng the surrounding streets. Typical examples of the varied menu include mince beef and onion pie with mash, cauliflower cheese, and toad in the hole.

Open 11–11 (Fri-Sat 11–11.30, Sun 12–10.30) Closed: 25–26 Dec, 1 Jan **Bar Meals** L served Mon-Fri 11–3 (Sat 11–5, Sun 12–5) ◗ Courage Best & Directors, Young's PA & Special, Wells Bombardier, Greene King IPA. ♟ 10

Pick of the Pubs

The Seven Stars   Plan 1 E4

53 Carey St WC2A 2JB ☎ 020 7242 8521

e-mail: manager@roxybeaujolais.com

dir: *From Temple N via The Strand & Bell Yard to Carey St. From Holborn SE via Lincoln's Inn Fields & Searle St to Carey St*

This pub survived the Great Fire of 1666, eventually to become a favourite with judges, barristers and litigants taking breathers from duty in the Royal Courts of Justice over the road. Pit musicians from West End shows also beat a path here. A precious example of a London pub that has escaped being tarted up, it is a good bet for food thanks to the efforts of chef, cookbook writer and broadcaster Roxy Beaujolais, who owns the pub with Nathan Silver. Look out for her inspiringly-named 'elegant fish pie' or her 'Afghan beef and ginger pie'. Other treats could include Roxy's 'marvellous meat loaf' with salad, or a large bowl of steaming Shetland mussels. Even if you don't need the loo, pretend you do for the fun of navigating the ridiculously narrow Elizabethan stairs. Ms Beaujolais and Mr Silver also own The Bountiful Cow off High Holborn.

Open 11–11 (Sat 12–11, Sun 12–10.30) Closed: 25–26 Dec, 1 Jan, Good Fri, Etr Sun **Bar Meals** L served Mon-Fri 12–5 D served Mon-Fri 5–9.30 (Sat 12–11, Sun 12–10.30) Av main course £9.50 ⊕ Free House ◗ Adnams Best, Broadside, Hophead, Harveys & Dark Star Best.

MERSEYSIDE

BARNSTON
MAP 15 SJ28

Fox and Hounds ☺

Barnston Rd CH61 1BW
☎ 0151 648 7685 📄 0151 648 0872
e-mail: ralphleech@hotmail.com
dir: *M53 junct 4 take A5137 to Heswell. Right to Barnston on B5138. Pub on A551*

The pub, located in a conservation area, was built in 1911 on the site of an alehouse and barn. Its Edwardian character has been preserved in the pitch pine woodwork and leaded windows. Incredible collections of 1920s/1930s memorabilia include ashtrays, horse brasses, police helmets and empty whisky cases. Six real ales and 12 wines by the glass are served alongside a range of bar snacks such as toasted ciabatas and jacket potatoes. Daily specials may include beef pie, lamb shank, fish of the day and lasagne.

Open 11–11 (Sun 12–10.30) **Bar Meals** L served Mon-Sat 12–2 (Sun 12–2.30) Av main course £7.50 **Restaurant** L served Mon-Sat 12–2 (Sun 12–2.30) ⊕ Free House 🍺 Websters Yorkshire Bitter, Theakston, Best & Old Peculier & guest ales. ☺ 12 **Facilities** Garden Dogs allowed Parking

LIVERPOOL
MAP 15 SJ39

Everyman Bistro ☺

9–11 Hope St L1 9BH ☎ 0151 708 9545 📄 0151 703 0290
e-mail: bistro@everyman.co.uk
dir: *In front of Metropolitan Cathedral. Bistro in basement of Everyman Theatre*

A favourite haunt of Liverpool's media, academic and theatrical fraternity – Bill Nighy and Julie Walters started out in the theatre above. But you don't need to write erudite leader columns, wear a mortar board, or worry about saying 'Macbeth' out loud to enjoy dishes from the twice-daily changing menus, such as Aberdeen Angus beef with mushrooms and rice; Greek lamb with organic beans and marinated feta; or roast salmon fillet with gazpacho mayonnaise and salad.

Open 12–12 (Fri 12-2am, Sat 11-2am) Closed: Sun & BHs
Bar Meals L served Mon-Thu 12–12 D served Mon-Thu 12–12 (Fri 12-2am, Sat 11-2am) Av main course £7.95 **Restaurant** L served Mon-Sat 12–5 D served Mon-Sat 5–12 Av 3 course à la carte £13.95 ⊕ Free House 🍺 Cains Bitter, Black Sheep, Derwent Pale Ale, Copper Dragon. ☺ 8

SOUTHPORT
MAP 15 SD31

The Berkeley Arms

19 Queens Rd PR9 9HN ☎ 01704 500811
e-mail: enquiries@berkeley-arms.com

Part of the Berkeley Arms Hotel, just off Southport's famous Lord Street. There are never fewer than eight real ales on sale at any one time here, which gives the pub a shrine-like status among beer drinkers. The pub does not serve food.

Open 12–11 🍺 Adnams Southwold, Banks Bitter, Hawkshead Bitter, Landlord. **Facilities** Garden Dogs allowed Parking

NORFOLK

BAWBURGH
MAP 13 TG10

Pick of the Pubs

Kings Head ☺

See Pick of the Pubs on opposite page

BINHAM
MAP 13 TF93

Chequers Inn

Front St NR21 0AL ☎ 01328 830297
e-mail: steve@binhamchequers.co.uk
dir: *On B1388 between Wells-next-the-Sea & Walsingham*

The Chequers is now home to the Front Street Brewery, but even though they brew their own beer they still have regular Norfolk/East Anglian guest ales. The pub has been owned by a village charity since the early 1600s and was originally a trade hall. Many stones from the nearby priory were used in its construction. The daily changing menu offers dishes such as Norfolk duck paté, fresh lobster thermidor, and plum crumble.

Open 11.30–2.30 6–11 (Sun 12–2.30, 7–10.30) (Opens late Fri-Sat night)
Bar Meals L served all week 12–2 D served Mon-Sat 6–9 (Sun 7–9) Av main course £9.25 **Restaurant** L served all week D served all week ⊕ Free House 🍺 Binham Cheer 3.9%, Callums Ale 4.3%, Unity Strong 5%, Seasonal specials & micro brewery on site. **Facilities** Children's licence Garden Parking

BLAKENEY
MAP 13 TG04

The Kings Arms ☺

Westgate St NR25 7NQ ☎ 01263 740341 📄 01263 740391
e-mail: kingsarmsnorfolk@btconnect.com
dir: *From Holt or Fakenham take A148, then B1156 for 6m to Blakeney*

This Grade II listed free house is located on the beautiful north Norfolk coast, close to the famous salt marshes, and is run by Marjorie and Howard Davies, who settled here after long and successful showbiz careers. The Kings Arms is an ideal centre for walking, or perhaps a ferry trip to the nearby seal colony and world-famous bird sanctuaries. Locally-caught fish and seasonal seafood feature on the menu, together with local game, home-made pies and pastas.

Open 11–11 **Bar Meals** L served Mon-Sat 12–9.30 D served Mon-Sat 12–9.30 (Sun 12–9) Av main course £6.50 ⊕ Free House 🍺 Greene King Old Speckled Hen, Woodforde's Wherry Best Bitter, Marston's Pedigree, Adnams Best Bitter. ☺ 12 **Facilities** Garden Dogs allowed Parking Play Area

Kings Head

A genuine village pub with heavy timbers and bulging walls, The Kings Head has stood beside the restful river Yare since the 17th century. Set opposite the village green, it is big on traditional charm in the form of wooden floors, log fires, comfy leather seating and pine dining furniture.

Whatever the weather, this is an ideal place to relax after an exhausting shopping spree in nearby Norwich. The place to be on long summer evenings is the south-facing patio or the secluded, landscaped garden. Seasonal menus offer a wide choice of modern British, European and Oriental dishes, all using the best quality local produce, including herbs and vegetables from the pub garden and flour from nearby Letheringsett Mill. Lunch can be anything from the quick and easy, such as a filled roll or ciabatta, to heartier options such as roast breast of pheasant with sweet potato purée, wild mushroom polenta cake, truffled peas and crispy bacon; mille-feuille of Mediterranean vegetables with pesto, slow-cooked tomatoes, goat's cheese, rocket and parmesan; or baked gypsy eggs with chorizo, tomatoes, peas, spinach and smoked paprika. An evening meal could begin with smoked mackerel paté, pickled cucumber, lemon and hot toast; seared breast of wood pigeon with bacon lardoons, black pudding and pine nut salad; or Japanese-style slow-cooked sea bass with soy, chilli, ginger and pak choi. Follow with roast belly of pork with sage mash, black pudding apple relish, green beans and red wine jus; fish stew; or pan-roasted cod with squid ink risotto, tiger prawns, pak choi and oyster sauce. Eton mess or sticky toffee pudding are typical desserts. The famed Sunday roast lunch menu offers a choice of four local meats, all sourced from within 15 miles of the pub.

MAP 13 TG10
Harts Ln NR9 3LS
☎ 01603 744977
🖷 01603 744990
e-mail: anton@
kingshead-bawburgh.co.uk
dir: *From A47 W of Norwich take B1108 W*

Open 11.30–11 (Sun 12–10.30)
Closed: 25–27 Dec eve, 1 Jan eve
Bar Meals L served all week
12–2 D served Mon-Sat 5.30–9
(Sun 6.30–9) Av main course
£9.50
Restaurant L served all week
12–2 D served all week 6.30–9 Av
3 course à la carte £27.50
⊞ Free House ◀ Adnams,
Woodforde's Wherry, Greene King
IPA, Courage Directors. ♟ 18
Facilities Children's licence
Garden Parking

PICK OF THE PUBS

BLAKENEY-NORFOLK

White Horse Hotel

A short, steep stroll from Blakeney quayside stands the 17th-century White Horse, formerly a coaching inn. The same team has run it for many years. Blakeney itself is a gem, with narrow streets of flint-built fishermen's cottages winding down to a small tidal harbour.

The creeks and estuary beyond are surrounded by vast sea lavender marshes, and the mud flats are home to samphire and mussels, while skylarks, redshanks and oyster-catchers fill the skies. The shingle ridge of Blakeney Point dominates the horizon: a thousand acres of marram grass dunes and wide open spaces. A twice-yearly changing menu is based loosely around the shellfish seasons, thus you can expect simply cooked mussels through the winter and crab in spring and summer. As you might expect, all the shellfish and much of the fish comes from along this very stretch of coast, while local estates provide game, fruit and even asparagus. You may eat in the bustling bar, the light, airy conservatory, or the more formal Stables dining room. Apart from fish, the restaurant menu offers wild boar casserole with sweet and sour red cabbage; and grilled mustard breast of guinea fowl on curly kale. A blackboard of daily specials, again with the accent on fish, adds further choice. Begin with warmed salad of pigeon breast, bacon, pine kernels and a sharp raspberry dressing; then roast loin of English lamb, herb-crushed potatoes, redcurrant sauce; or grilled fillet of sea bass with crayfish butter, rocket salad and new potatoes. Desserts are limited to chocolate, strawberry or vanilla ice cream, and a selection of cheeses. A 50-bin wine list, a dozen of which are available by the glass, and four well-kept real ales complete the picture.

MAP 13 TG04
4 High St NR25 7AL
☎ 01263 740574
🖹 01263 741303
e-mail: enquiries@
blakeneywhitehorse.co.uk
dir: *From A148 (Cromer to King's
Lynn road) onto A149 signed to
Blakeney*

Open 11–11
Bar Meals L served all week
12–2.15 D served all week 6–9 Av
main course £10
Restaurant D served all week
7–9 Av 3 course à la carte £25
⊕ Free House ◀ Adnams Bitter,
Woodfordes Wherry, Adnams
Broadside, Yetmans. ♀ 12
Facilities Garden Parking

LAKENEY continued

Pick of the Pubs

White Horse Hotel ♀

See Pick of the Pubs on opposite page

LICKLING MAP 13 TG12

Pick of the Pubs

The Buckinghamshire Arms ♀

Blickling Rd NR11 6NF ☎ 01263 732133
e-mail: bucksarms@tiscali.co.uk
dir: *From Cromer (A140) take exit at Aylsham onto B1354, follow signs to Blickling Hall.*

'The Bucks', a late 17th-century coaching inn by the gates of Blickling Hall (NT), is Norfolk's most beautiful inn, say its owners. Anne Boleyn's ghost is said to wander in the adjacent courtyard and charming garden. The lounge bar and restaurant, with their solid furniture and wood-burning stoves, are appealing too. Meals can be taken in either, with menus offering fresh local food served in both traditional and modern ways, with starters such as brie wedge in beer batter; baked crab; and Waldorf salad. Sample main courses, alL served with salad or vegetables, new potatoes or chips, include venison with port and blackberries; grilled whole lemon sole; home-made lasagne; sautéed lambs' kidneys with Marsala; and salmon and prawn tagliatelle. The Victorian cellar houses real ales from Norfolk, Suffolk and Kent.

Open 11.30–3 6–11 (Sun 12–3, 7–10.30) Closed: 25 Dec
Bar Meals L served all week 12–2.30 D served Tue-Sat 7–9 Av main course £9.95 **Restaurant** L served all week 12–2 D served Tue-Sat 7–9 Av 3 course à la carte £25 ⊕ Free House ◀ Adnams, Woodforde's, Fuller's. ♀ 10 **Facilities** Garden Parking

---

BRANCASTER STAITHE MAP 13 TF74

Pick of the Pubs

The White Horse ★★★ HL ◉◉ ♀

PE31 8BY ☎ 01485 210262 ▤ 01485 210930
e-mail: reception@whitehorsebrancaster.co.uk
dir: *A149 (coast road), midway between Hunstanton & Wells-next-the-Sea*

Situated on the north Norfolk coast, with panoramic views across tidal creeks, marshes and seemingly endless sandy beaches. Scrubbed pine tables and high-backed settles help to create a bright, welcoming atmosphere at this popular gastropub, from whose conservatory restaurant and adjoining sun deck you can see over Brancaster Marsh to Scolt Head Island. The pub, extensively refurbished in 2007, has a reputation for making good use of fresh local produce on its daily-changing menus, especially shellfish (seasonal) grown in beds at the bottom of the garden. Also highly regarded are pan-fried Norfolk steak; local goat's cheese and caramelised onions en croûte; and slow-roasted rump of English lamb. Baguettes come with an extensive variety of fillings, while the bar menu includes smoked salmon and poached

egg Benedict; and corned beef hash with fried egg on toasted muffin. Fifteen tastefully furnished en suite bedrooms look out over the ever ebbing and flowing tide.

Open 11–11 (Sun 12–10.30) **Bar Meals** L served all week 11–9 D served all week 11–9 Av main course £7.25 **Restaurant** L served all week 12–2 D served all week 6.30–9 ⊕ Free House ◀ Adnams Best Bitter, Fuller's London Pride, Woodforde's Wherry & guest. ♀ 17 **Facilities** Garden Dogs allowed Parking **Rooms** 15

BURNHAM MARKET MAP 13 TF84

Pick of the Pubs

The Hoste Arms ★★★ HL ◉◉◉ ♀

The Green PE31 8HD
☎ 01328 738777 ▤ 01328 730103
e-mail: reception@hostearms.co.uk
dir: *Signed off B1155, 5m W of Wells-next-the-Sea*

Over the centuries this building has been a courthouse, a livestock market, and even a Victorian brothel. Built as a manor house in 1550, it has been an inn since 1720 but fell into decline during the last century. Paul Whittome rescued it in 1989 and turned it into a beautifully presented hotel with striking interior design courtesy of his wife Jeanne. The inn now has 36 stylish bedrooms and several restaurant areas. Recent additions include an orangery and a cellar, which houses over 200 fine wines in a temperature-controlled environment. The brasserie-style menu includes plenty of local specialities; perhaps hot-smoked Holkham venison with portabella mushroom and black pudding on toasted brioche, followed by fillet of Norfolk pork with turnip and potato hash, cabbage, pumpkin and caraway seed purée. Brancaster oysters are served six ways, from natural to hot with tomato chutney and emmental. Additional light lunch options include sandwiches.

Open 11–11 **Bar Meals** L served all week 12–2 D served all week 6–9 Av main course £13 **Restaurant** L served all week 12–2 D served Sun-Thu 6–9 (Fri 7–9.30) ⊕ Free House ◀ Woodforde's Wherry Best, Greene King Abbot Ale, Adnams Best Bitter, Adnams Broadside & Nelson's Revenge. ♀ 11 **Facilities** Garden Dogs allowed Parking **Rooms** 35

Blickling Hall and gardens, Norfolk

BURNHAM THORPE **MAP 13 TF84**

Pick of the Pubs

The Lord Nelson ⚲

See Pick of the Pubs on page 391

CLEY NEXT THE SEA **MAP 13 TG04**

Pick of the Pubs

The George Hotel ⚲

High St NR25 7RN ☎ 01263 740652 📠 01263 741275
e-mail: thegeorge@cleynextthesea.com
dir: *On A149 through Cley next the Sea, approx 4m from Holt*

Located near the sea and marshes, The George is stands on historic Cley's winding High Street. The beer garden backs onto the marshes, from where you can see Cley's famous mill, while the lovely oak-floored bar provides a year-round welcome. You can snack in the lounge bar or dine in the light, Painting-filled restaurant. At lunchtime the menu runs from sandwiches (hot chicken, avocado, crispy bacon and red pesto mayonnaise; or brie, smoked ham and fresh mango) to starters and light meals such as warm pan-fried chicken liver, duck liver and rocket salad with balsamic dressing; or hearty main courses – perhaps home-made steak, kidney and suet pudding. Dinner brings starters of roast parsnip and honey soup laced with cream, followed by braised pork belly with spiced red cabbage, wilted spinach and honey glaze. Seafood is a real strength.

Open 11–11 (Sun & BHs 11–10.30) **Bar Meals** L served all week 12–2 D served all week 6.30–9 (Sun 12–2.30) Av main course £10.95 **Restaurant** L served all week 12–2 D served all week 6.30–9 (Sun 12–2.30) Av 3 course à la carte £20 🍴 Free House 🍺 Greene King IPA, Abbot Ale, Yetmans ales & Leffe. ⚲ 8 **Facilities** Garden Dogs allowed Parking

COLTISHALL **MAP 13 TG21**

Kings Head ⚲

26 Wroxham Rd NR12 7EA
☎ 01603 737426 📠 01603 736542
dir: *A47 (Norwich ring road) onto B1150 to North Walsham at Coltishall. Right at petrol station, follow to right past church. Pub on right by car park*

This 17th-century free house stands on the banks of the River Bure, right in the heart of the Norfolk Broads. Hire cruisers are available at nearby Wroxham, and fishing boats can be hired at the pub. If you prefer to stay on dry land you'll find a warm welcome at the bar, with a range of real ales that includes Adnams Bitter, Directors and Marston's Pedigree. There's an inviting menu, too, served in both the bar and the restaurant.

Open 11–3 6–11 (Sun all day) Closed: 26 Dec **Bar Meals** L served all week 12–2 D served all week 7–9 Av main course £12.50 **Restaurant** L served all week 12–2 D served all week 7–9 Av 3 course à la carte £25 🍴 Free House 🍺 Adnams Bitter, Directors, Marston's Pedigree. ⚲ 10 **Facilities** Parking

DEREHAM **MAP 13 TF91**

Yaxham Mill ★★★★ INN ⚲

Norwich Rd, Yaxham NR19 1RP
☎ 01362 851182 📠 01362 691482
e-mail: yaxhammill@hotmail.co.uk
dir: *From Norwich take A47 towards Swaffham. At East Dereham take B1135. Yaxham 2m*

A converted windmill in the middle of open Norfolk countryside and dating back to 1810. The miller's house and chapel were transformed into a restaurant and bar. Menus cater for all tastes, with grilled lemon sole, minted lamb steak, sweet and sour chicken, and chilli con carne among other dishes. Home-made pies, including steak and kidney and cottage, are something of a speciality.

Open 12–3 6–11 (Sun 6–10.30) **Bar Meals** L served Mon-Sat 12–2 D served all week 6.30–9 (Sun 12–8) Av main course £8.95 **Restaurant** L served all week 12–2 D served all week 6.30–9 Av 3 course à la carte £17.50 🍴 Free House 🍺 Bombardier, Youngs & 2 guest ales. ⚲ 8 **Facilities** Garden Parking **Rooms** 12

EAST RUSTON **MAP 13 TG32**

The Butchers Arms ⚲

Oak Ln NR12 9JG ☎ 01692 650237
dir: *Off School Road opposite East Ruston allotment*

A quintessential village pub, originally three cottages built in the early 1800s. You won't find a jukebox, TV or pool table, but outside is 'Mavis', a 1954 Comma fire engine. Landlady Julie Gollop takes pride in creating a welcoming atmosphere, serving a good choice of real ales, and preparing a menu of traditional home-cooked favourites: mushrooms with garlic dip; and deep-fried whitebait; and grilled steaks.

CONTINUED

EAST RUSTON continued

Open 12–3 6.30–11 (Summer 6–11) **Bar Meals** L served all week
12–2 D served all week 7–8.30 (Summer 7–9) Av main course £10
Restaurant L served all week 12–2 D served all week 7–8.30 (Summer
6.30–9) Av 3 course à la carte £18.20 ∰ Free House ◀ Adnams,
Woodfordes, Old Speckled Hen, Greene King IPA. ♥ 7 **Facilities** Children's
licence Garden Dogs allowed Parking **Notes** ◉

EATON   MAP 13 TG20

The Red Lion ♥

50 Eaton St NR4 7LD ☎ 01603 454787 📄 01603 456939
e-mail: redlioneaton@hotmail.co.uk
dir: Off A11, 2m S of Norwich city centre

This heavily-beamed 17th-century coaching inn has bags of character,
thanks to its Dutch gables, panelled walls and inglenook fireplaces.
The covered terrace enables customers to enjoy one of the real ales or
sample the extensive wine list outside during the summer months. The
extensive lunch menu offers everything from toasted paninis to wing
of Lowestoft skate with prawns and capers; or roast Aylesbury duckling
with sausage stuffing.

Open 11–3 6–11 (Sun 12–3, 7–10.30) **Bar Meals** L served Mon-Sat
12–6 D served Mon-Sat 7–9 (Sun 12–8.30) **Restaurant** L served all week
12–2.15 D served all week 7–9 ∰ Enterprise Inns ◀ Old Speckled Hen,
Courage Directors, Greene King IPA, Adnams Bitter. ♥ 10 **Facilities** Garden
Parking

ERPINGHAM   MAP 13 TG13

Pick of the Pubs

The Saracen's Head

NR11 7LX ☎ 01263 768909 📄 01263 768993
e-mail: saracenshead@wolterton.freeserve.co.uk
dir: A140, 2.5m N of Aylsham, left through Erpingham, pass
Spread Eagle on left. Through Calthorpe follow priority of rd
to Aldborough, bear left (straight on) to pub

Standing as it does in the middle of nowhere, the Saracen's Head
is an ideal escape from the rat-race. This former coach house was
built in 1806 and modelled on a Tuscan farmhouse. There's no
piped music, no fruit machines, and no ordinary pub food – just
daily-changing menus reflecting owner Robert Dawson-Smith's
enduring passion for cooking up some of Norfolk's most delicious
wild and tame treats. According to seasonal availability, these may
include wok-sizzled sirloin strips with anchovy, or pot-roast leg of
lamb with red and white beans. A good array of seafood could
feature baked Cromer crab, or grilled bass with white wine. The
delightful walled garden features the Shed, a small workshop run
by Robert's daughter; this is the place to seek out that essential
piece of retro furniture or modern artwork.

Open 12–3 6–11.30 (Sun 12–3, 7–10.30) Closed: 25 Dec
Bar Meals L served all week 12.30–2 D served all week 7.30–9 Av
main course £12.25 **Restaurant** L served all week 12.30–2 D served
all week 7.30–9 Av 3 course à la carte £24 Av 2 course fixed price
£8 ∰ Free House ◀ Adnams Best Bitter, Woodforde's Wherry.
Facilities Garden Parking

FAKENHAM   MAP 13 TF9

The Wensum Lodge Hotel

Bridge St NR21 9AY ☎ 01328 862100 📄 01328 863365
e-mail: enquiries@wensumlodge.fsnet.co.uk
dir: In town centre

Wensum Lodge is a converted mill dating from around 1700, idyllically
located by the River Wensum, for which the hotel has fishing rights.
Home-cooked food is prepared from locally supplied ingredients, with
baguettes, jacket potatoes and an all-day breakfast on the light bite
menu. The carte might have baby peeled prawns on dressed leaves
with chilli dip; and Wensum burger topped with bacon, cheese, salad
and relish in a toasted bun served with fries.

Open 11–11 **Bar Meals** L served all week 11.30–3 D served all week
6.30–9.30 (Sun 12–3, 6.30–9) **Restaurant** L served all week 11.30–3
D served all week 6.30–9.30 (Sun 12–3, 6.30–9) ∰ Free House ◀ Greene
King Abbot Ale & IPA, Old Mill Bitter. **Facilities** Garden Parking

The White Horse Inn ★★★★ INN

Fakenham Rd, East Barsham NR21 0LH
☎ 01328 820645 📄 01328 820645
e-mail: subalpine19@whsmith.net.co.uk
dir: 1.5m N of Fakenham on minor road to Little Walsingham

Ideally located for birdwatching, walking, cycling, fishing, golf and
sandy beaches, this refurbished 17th-century inn offers en suite rooms
and a characterful bar with log-burning inglenook. Good range of
beers and malt whiskies. Fresh ingredients are assured in daily specials
with fish especially well represented. Typical choices include chicken
breast stuffed with stilton, peppered mackerel fillets, sweet and sour
pork, and venison steak. There is also a grill menu. Birdwatching tours
can be arranged.

Open 11.30–3 6.30–11 **Bar Meals** L served all week 12–2 D served all
week 7–9.30 Av main course £9.95 **Restaurant** L served all week 12–2
D served all week 7–9.30 ◀ Adnams Best, Adnams Broadside, Tetley, Wells
Eagle IPA. **Facilities** Garden Parking **Rooms** 3

GREAT RYBURGH   MAP 13 TF92

The Boar Inn

NR21 0DX ☎ 01328 829212 📄 01328 829421
dir: Off A1067 4m S of Fakenham

The village, deep in rural Norfolk, has one of the county's unusual
round-towered Saxon churches. Opposite is the 300–year-old Boar,
dispensing a good variety of food, including beef Madras with rice,
sweet and sour chicken with noodles, plaice fillet with prawns in
mornay sauce, scallops, lemon sole, and prime Norfolk steaks.
Specials include skate wing with garlic and herb butter, and wild
boar steak with cranberry and red wine jus. Bar/alfresco snacks and
children's meals.

Open 12–2.30 5.30–12 (1 May-30 Sep all day) **Bar Meals** L served all
week 12–2 D served all week 7–9 **Restaurant** L served all week 12–2
D served all week 7–9 Av 3 course à la carte £15 ∰ Free House ◀ Courage
Best & guest ale. **Facilities** Garden Parking

PICK OF THE PUBS

BURNHAM THORPE-NORFOLK

The Lord Nelson

Horatio Nelson was born in Burnham Thorpe in 1758. The pub, originally called the Plough, was already over 100 years old; in 1798 its name was changed to honour his victory over the French at the Nile. Visitors today can soak up an atmosphere that has changed little since; you can even sit on Nelson's high-backed settle.

There's no bar – drinks are served from the taproom, with real ales straight from the cask. When Nelson was without a ship, he spent many hours in the pub composing letters of protest to the Admiralty. On the declaration of war against France in 1793, he celebrated being given a command by treating the whole village to a meal upstairs. After his death at Trafalgar in 1805, his body was immersed in a barrel of rum to preserve it for the long journey home. Sailors started taking nips of this questionable marinade in an effort to acquire his gifts. They called it 'Nelson's Blood'; now a secret blend of 100 proof Navy rum and spices is made and sold here, despatched around the world, and used locally to make Nelson's Blood Bitter. The team running the

place is headed by Simon Alper and Peter De Groeve who took over two years ago, Simon with long experience on the drinks side, and Peter importing a wealth of European food influences from his native Belgium. His aim is to provide a different eating experience based on traditional produce, in dishes such as duck with a Norfolk lavender sauce; Holkham Venison with tiger prawns in garlic sauce, and asparagus Flamande; and rabbit pie. Desserts may include white chocolate delight with Lady Nelson sauce. Families are welcomed, and children will enjoy the huge garden. Dirty wellies and soggy doggies straight from the beach are no problem in 'Nelson's local'.

MAP 13 TF84
Walsingham Rd PE31 8HL
☎ 01328 738241
🖨 01328 738241
e-mail:
simon@nelsonslocal.co.uk
dir: *B1355 (Burnham Market to Fakenham road), pub 9m from Fakenham & 1.75m from Burnham Market. Pub near church opposite playing fields*

Open 12–3 6–11 (Sun 12–10.30, Summer hols 12–11) Closed: Mon (ex school hols)
Bar Meals L served Mon-Fri 12–2 D served Mon-Sat 6–7.30 (Sat-Sun 12–2.30) Av main course £7.95
Restaurant L served Mon-Fri 12–2 D served Mon-Thu 7–9 (Sat-Sun 12–2.30, Fri-Sat 7–9.30) Av 3 course à la carte £24 Av 3 course fixed price £19.95
🍺 Greene King 🍺 Greene King Abbot Ale & IPA, Woodforde's Wherry, Nelson's Blood Bitter.
🍷 13
Facilities Garden Dogs allowed Parking Play Area

HAPPISBURGH

MAP 13 TG33

The Hill House ♥

NR12 0PW ☎ 01692 650004 📠 01692 650004

dir: *5m from Stalham, 8m from North Walsham*

Expect to be corrected if you pronounce Happisburgh the way it's spelt – it's Haze-borough. Once the favourite haunt of the creator of Sherlock Holmes, Sir Arthur Conan Doyle, this 16th-century coaching inn offers good value bar food, a wide selection of fish and seafood, steaks and other meat dishes, as well as a vegetarian selection. Look out for the Summer Solstice beer festival for the chance to sample over 80 real ales and ciders.

Open 12–3 7–11.30 (Thu-Sun & Summer all day) **Bar Meals** L served all week 12–2.30 D served Mon-Sat 7–9.30 (Sun 7–9) Av main course £10 **Restaurant** L served all week 12–2.30 D served Mon-Sat 7–9.30 (Sun 7–9) Av 3 course à la carte £17.50 ⊕ Free House ◀ Shepherd Neame Spitfire, Buffy's, Woodforde's Wherry, Adnams Bitter. ♥ 10 **Facilities** Children's licence Garden Dogs allowed Parking Play Area

HEVINGHAM

MAP 13 TG12

Marsham Arms Freehouse ♥

Holt Rd NR10 5NP ☎ 01603 754268

e-mail: nigelbradley@marshamarms.co.uk

web: www.marshamarms.co.uk

dir: *On B1149 N of Norwich airport, 2m through Horsford towards Holt*

Built as a roadside hostel for poor farm labourers by Victorian philanthropist and landowner Robert Marsham. Some original features remain, including the large open fireplace, and there's a spacious garden with paved patio and a dedicated family room. A goodly range of fresh fish dishes includes cod, haddock, sea bass, herrings and crab. Specialities such as minted lamb casserole and the local butcher's sausages are backed by a daily blackboard. Desserts like chocolate brownies are home made.

Open 11–11 **Bar Meals** L served Mon-Sat 11.30–2.30 D served Mon-Sat 6–9.30 (Sun 12–2.30, 6.30–9) **Restaurant** L served all week 12–2.30 D served Mon-Sat 6–9.30 (Sun 6.30–9) ⊕ Free House ◀ Adnams Best, Woodforde's Wherry Best Bitter, Mauldens, Worthington. **Facilities** Garden Parking Play Area **Rooms** available

HEYDON

MAP 13 TG1:

Earle Arms ♥

The Street NR11 6AD ☎ 01263 587376

e-mail: haitchy@aol.com

dir: *Signed between Cawston & Corpusty on B1149 (Holt to Norwich road)*

Heydon is one of only thirteen privately owned villages in the country and is often used as a film location. It dates from the 16th century, and inside are log fires, attractive wallpapers, prints and a collection of bric-a-brac. One of the two rooms offers service through a hatch, and there are tables outside in the pretty back garden. Locally reared meat goes into dishes like braised lamb shank or fillet of beef marchand de vin. Fish choices include plaice goujons, crayfish omelette, and sea bass fillet with lemon butter.

Open 12–3 6–11 Closed: Mon **Bar Meals** L served Tue-Sun 12–2 D served Tue-Sun 7–8.30 **Restaurant** L served Tue-Sun 12–2 D served Tue-Sun 7–8.30 ⊕ Free House ◀ Adnams, Woodforde's Wherry. **Facilities** Garden Parking

HOLKHAM

MAP 13 TF8·

Pick of the Pubs

Victoria at Holkham ★★ SHL 🏵🏵 ♥

Park Rd NR23 1RG ☎ 01328 711008 📠 01328 711009

e-mail: victoria@holkham.co.uk

dir: *On A149, 3m W of Wells-next-the-sea*

The Victoria stands at the gates of landlord Tom Coke's Palladian ancestral home, Holkham Hall, just minutes from the golden sands of Holkham Beach. Its opulent, colonial-style interior is full of furniture and accessories from Rajahstan and other exotic places. Outside is a courtyard where summer barbecues are popular. Tom Coke would argue that the Victoria's main attraction is what he calls 'some of the most consistently good food in North Norfolk'. Key words here are fresh, local and seasonal, whether it be shellfish, fish or samphire from the north Norfolk coast, beef from farms on the Holkham estate, organic chickens from a tenant farmer, venison from the herd of fallow deer or, in the winter, wild game from family shoots. An eclectic, yet sensibly priced, wine list proves popular, and there are always several real ales on tap.

Open 12–12 **Bar Meals** L served out of season only D served all week **Restaurant** L served all week 12–2.30 D served all week 7–9 ◀ Adnams Best, Woodforde's Wherry, guest ale. ♥ 12 **Facilities** Children's licence Garden Dogs allowed Parking Play Area **Rooms** 10

HORSEY
MAP 13 TG42

Nelson Head ♥

The Street NR29 4AD ☎ 01493 393378

dir: *On B1159 (coast road) between West Somerton & Sea Palling*

Located on a National Trust estate, which embraces nearby Horsey Mere, this 17th-century inn will, to many, epitomise the perfect country pub. It enjoys the tranquility of a particularly unspoilt part of the Norfolk coast – indeed, glorious beaches are only half an hour's walk away – and the sheltered gardens look out towards the dunes and water meadows. Fresh cod, plaice and home-made fish and prawn pie are usually available. Local beers are Woodforde's Wherry and Nelson's Revenge.

Open 11–3 6–11 (Winter hrs vary Etr-Oct all day) **Bar Meals** L served all week 12–3 D served all week 6–8.30 Av main course £7.50 **Restaurant** L served all week 12–2 D served all week 6–8.30 Av 3 course à la carte £12 ⊕ Free House ◀ Woodforde's Wherry & Nelson's Revenge. ♥ 7 **Facilities** Garden Dogs allowed Parking Play Area

HORSTEAD
MAP 13 TG21

Recruiting Sergeant ♥

Norwich Rd NR12 7EE ☎ 01603 737077 📠 01603 736905

dir: *On B1150 between Norwich & North Walsham*

The name of this inviting country pub comes from the tradition of recruiting servicemen by giving them the King or Queen's shilling in a pint of beer. It offers good food, ales and wines in homely surroundings with a patio and lawned garden for alfresco dining. The menu is ever changing, with inventive dishes such as fresh oysters with a tabasco, lime and red onion dressing, duck breast on an apple and potato rosti and chicken breast stuffed with mozzarella and chorizo. There is also a vast daily specials menu, including fish and vegetarian dishes.

Open 11–11 **Bar Meals** L served all week 12–2 D served all week 6.30–9 (Fri-Sat 6.30–9.30, Sun 12–9) Av main course £15 **Restaurant** L served all week 12–2 D served all week 6.30–9 (Sun 12–9) Av 3 course à la carte £20 ⊕ Free House ◀ Adnams, Woodeforde's, Greene King Abbot Ale, Scottish Courage. ♥ 13 **Facilities** Garden Dogs allowed Parking

HUNSTANTON
MAP 12 TF64

The King William IV NEW

Heacham Rd, Sedgeford PE36 5LU

☎ 01485 571765 📠 01485 571743

e-mail: info@thekingwilliamsedgeford.co.uk

dir: *On B1454*

The King William first became an ale house in 1836, and while much has changed in the intervening years, the traditional character of the inn, with its log fires and beautiful rural surrounding, remains to be cherished. House specialities include Brancaster mussels, local sea bass and popular steak and ale pies. A daily curry is also offered, and afternoon tea is served in the bar and garden.

Open 11–11 (Mon 6–11, Sun 12–10.30) Closed: Mon lunch (ex BH) **Bar Meals** L served Tue-Sat 12–2 D served Mon-Sat 6.30–9 (Sun 12–9 summer, 12–8 winter) Av main course £11 **Restaurant** L served Tue-Sat 12–2 D served Mon-Sat 6.30–9 (Sun 12–9 summer, 12–8 winter) Av 3 course à la carte £18 ⊕ Free House ◀ Woodfordes's Wherry, Adnams Bitter, Guinness & guest ale. **Facilities** Garden Dogs allowed Parking **Rooms** available

ITTERINGHAM
MAP 13 TG13

Pick of the Pubs

Walpole Arms ♥

See Pick of the Pubs on page 394

KING'S LYNN
MAP 12 TF62

The Stuart House Hotel, Bar & Restaurant ★★ HL

35 Goodwins Rd PE30 5QX

☎ 01553 772169 📠 01553 774788

e-mail: reception@stuarthousehotel.co.uk

dir: *Follow signs to town centre, pass under Southgate Arch, immediate right, in 100yds, turn right*

A short walk from the historic town centre, the Stuart House is set in its own delightful grounds, with a patio and beer garden. Cask conditioned ales and home-cooked dishes are served in the bar, and there is a separate restaurant offering a carte menu and daily specials. A programme of events includes regular live music, murder mystery dinners and an annual beer festival.

Open 6–11 **Bar Meals** D served all week 7–9.15 (Lunch available for pre-booked parties of 12 or more) **Restaurant** D served all week 7–9.15 (Lunch available for pre-booked parties of 12 or more) Av 3 course à la carte £25 ⊕ Free House ◀ Adnams, Woodforde's, Greene King, Oakham JHB. **Facilities** Children's licence Garden Parking Play Area **Rooms** 18

England

PICK OF THE PUBS

ITTERINGHAM-NORFOLK

Walpole Arms

Long-term Norfolk residents Richard Bryan and Keith Reeves, together with their respective families, combined their talents in 2001 when they took over this traditional village pub in the beautiful north Norfolk countryside.

Richard's lifetime passion for food has been partly channelled into broadcasting, notably as producer of BBC TV's *Masterchef*, while Keith is a highly respected wine merchant, supplying customers throughout East Anglia. With the addition of chef Andy Parle, a veteran of Michelin-starred restaurants in Norwich and London, the team seem to have every base covered, and the success of this award-winning venture proves that they have indeed got the recipe right. The Walpole arms has been a pub since 1836, although the oak-beamed bar suggests something older. In fact, Robert Horace Walpole, a direct descendant of Britain's first prime minister, once owned it. Today it is both a real pub and a dining destination. Andy and his team use the best seasonal and

local produce to create thoroughly modern and inspired pub food. Both restaurant and bar offer a daily changing three-course carte; on Saturdays a special brunch menu is served, and on Sundays there's a delicious roast. Typical starters include Moroccan style broad bean, feta and pomegranate salad; and ballotine of turkey, bacon and chestnut with cranberry relish. Follow with slow roast belly pork with saffron and chick pea stew and black kale; or Morston mussels with salsa rosso and crusty bread. Wash it down with wine from Keith's comprehensive wine list, and finish with desserts such as drop scones with quince compote, pistachio ice cream and crème fraîche. Outside are large grassy areas with tables and a vine-covered patio.

MAP 13 TG13
NR11 7AR
☎ 01263 587258
🖹 01263 587074
e-mail: goodfood@thewalpolearms.co.uk
web: www.thewalpolearms.co.uk
dir: *From Aylsham towards Blickling. After Blickling Hall take 1st right to Itteringham*

Open 12-3 6-11 (Sun 7-10.30)
Closed: 25 Dec
Bar Meals L served all week 12-2 D served Mon-Sat 7-9.30 (Sun 12.30-2.30) Av main course £12
Restaurant L served Sat-Sun 12-2 D served Mon-Sat 7-9.30 (Sun 12.30-2.30) Av 3 course à la carte £22.50
🍺 Adnams Broadside & Bitter, Woodforde's Wherry Best Bitter & Walpole. 🍷 12
Facilities Garden Dogs allowed Parking Play Area

England

LARLING   MAP 13 TL98

Pick of the Pubs

Angel Inn ♀

NR16 2QU ☎ 01953 717963 📄 01953 718561

dir: *5m from Attleborough, 8m from Thetford. 1m from station.*

This 17th-century former coaching inn on the Norwich to Thetford road has been run by three subsequent generations of the same family. The heavily-beamed public bar has a homely, local feel, while the characterful lounge bar has wheel-back chairs, an oak settle, oak-panelled walls, a wood-burning stove and a huge collection of water jugs. The cooking is underpinned by local ingredients wherever possible: home-made daily specials might be cod cooked in a crispy Adnams bitter batter, or home-made steak and kidney pie. A selection of spicier options includes Thai green chicken curry and prawn Madras, while snacks range from home-made beef burgers through to Welsh rarebit or a simple omelette with your choice of fillings. The pub stands within the Brecks of Norfolk, close to Snetterton racing circuit and on the edge of Thetford Forest.

Open 10–11 **Bar Meals** L served Sun-Thu 12–9.30 D served Sun-Thu 12–9.30 (Fri-Sat 12–10) Av main course £8.95 **Restaurant** L served Sun-Thu 12–9.30 D served Sun-Thu 12–9.30 (Fri & Sat 12–10) Av 3 course à la carte £18 ⊕ Free House ◑ Adnams Bitter, Wolf Bitter, Caledonian Deuchars IPA, Timothy Taylor Landlord & Mauldons. ♀ 10 **Facilities** Garden Parking Play Area **Rooms** available

LITTLE FRANSHAM   MAP 13 TF91

The Canary and Linnet

Main Rd NR19 2JW ☎ 01362 687027

dir: *On A47 between Dereham & Swaffham*

A pretty, former blacksmith's cottage fulfilling the key requirements of a traditional English country pub – low ceilings, exposed beams and an inglenook fireplace. Its sign once showed footballers in Norwich City (Canaries) and Kings Lynn (Linnets) strips, but now features two birds in a cage. Food offered throughout the bar, conservatory restaurant and garden includes steak and ale pie, medallions of pork in stilton sauce, and seared Cajun spiced swordfish steak with lime and coriander dressing.

Open 12–3 6–11 (Sun 12–3, 7–10) **Bar Meals** L served all week 12–2 D served all week 6–9 **Restaurant** L served all week 12–2 D served all week 6–9.30 ⊕ Free House ◑ Greene King IPA, Tindall's Best, Adnams Bitter, Wolf. **Facilities** Garden Dogs allowed Parking

LITTLE WALSINGHAM   MAP 13 TF93

The Black Lion Hotel ♀

Friday Market Place NR22 6DB

☎ 01328 820235 📄 01328 821407

e-mail: lionwalsingham@btconnect.com

dir: *From King's Lynn take A148 & B1105, or from Norwich take A1067 & B1105.*

A former coaching inn, dating in part from 1310, built to accommodate Edward III and Queen Philippa of Hainault when they visited the shrine at Walsingham (the hotel takes its name from her coat of arms). The friendly bar has a welcoming fire in winter, and in the restaurant the seasonal menu might offer scrumpy pork hock; rainbow trout Cleopatra; and spinach, cherry tomato and mozzarella herb pudding.

Open 12–3 6–1 (Sat 11-1am) **Bar Meals** L served all week 12–2.30 D served all week 7–9 Av main course £8 **Restaurant** L served all week 12–2.30 D served all week 7–9 Av 3 course à la carte £16 ⊕ Enterprise Inns ◑ Woodforde's Wherry, Blacksheep Special, John Smiths Smooth & Woodforde's Nelson's Revenge. ♀ 9 **Facilities** Garden Dogs allowed

MARSHAM   MAP 13 TG12

The Plough Inn ♀

Norwich Rd NR10 5PS ☎ 01263 735000 📄 01263 735407

e-mail: enq@ploughinnmarsham.co.uk

dir: *on A140, 10m N of Norwich*

A warm welcome is assured at this 18th-century countryside inn, ideally located for the North Norfolk coast and the Broads. The pumps serve both real ales and lagers, while menus based on local and seasonal produce include traditional favourites such as pork sausages and mash; steak and ale pie; and home-made beefburgers. A specials board proffers fresh fish; gluten- and wheat-free meals are also a speciality.

Open 12–3 6–11 (Tue 5–11, Sun 6–10.30) **Bar Meals** L served all week 12–2.30 D served Mon-Sat 6.30–9 (Sun 6.30–8.30) Av main course £9.95 **Restaurant** L served all week 12–2.30 D served Mon-Sat 6.30–9 (Sun 6.30–8.30) Av 3 course à la carte £20 ⊕ Free House ◑ IPA, Adnams, John Smiths. ♀ 9 **Facilities** Garden Parking **Rooms** available

PICK OF THE PUBS

NORWICH-NORFOLK

The Mad Moose Arms

A traditional neighbourhood pub with a decidedly stylish ground floor bar, all vibrant red walls, exposed brickwork and gleaming wood.

Here the menu offers light meals, salads, sandwiches and daily specials such as crayfish, beetroot and candied lemon salad; chestnut, mushroom, saffron and baby spinach risotto; and pan-fried salmon, fine beans, crushed new potatoes, tomato and shallot dressing. Upstairs is the elegant 1up restaurant with chandeliers, sea-green drapes and a feature wall depicting a fairytale forest. Confident and ambitious cooking is typified by starters of buckwheat blinis with warm smoked fish, pickled red cabbage and horseradish crème fraîche; and confit of wild Norfolk rabbit, with quince and lemon aioli. To follow, slow-cooked Suffolk pork with creamed kale, pancetta, braised puy lentils, butternut squash and pease pudding; and seared sea bream with fondant potato, wilted romaine lettuce, pickled cucumber, crisp Parma ham and mustard jus.

@@ 🍷
MAP 13 TG20
2 Warwick St NR2 3LB
☎ 01603 627687
📄 01508 494946
e-mail:
madmoose@animalinns.co.uk
web: www.themadmoose.co.uk

Open 12–12 (Fri-Sat 12–12.30)
Closed: 25 Dec
Bar Meals L served all week
12–2 D served all week 6–10 Av
main course £7.50
Restaurant L served Sun 12–2
D served Mon-Sat 7–10 Av 3
course à la carte £27.50 Av 2
course fixed price £15
🌐 Free House 🍺 Adnams
Broadside & Greene King IPA. 🍷 9
Facilities Garden

MUNDFORD
MAP 13 TL89

Crown Hotel
Crown Rd IP26 5HQ ☎ 01842 878233 🖹 01842 878982
dir: *A11 to Barton Mills junct, then A1065 to Brandon & onto Mundford*

Built in 1652, the Crown has been many things – a famous hunting lodge; the local magistrates' court; even a doctors' waiting room. Its most unusual feature, in these pancake-flat parts, is that it is set into a hill! Traditional food is served in the bar, and a more elaborate menu is available in the restaurant; perhaps tian of Brixham crab followed by lamb rump with flageolet purée, fondant potato, garlic confit and mint jus.

Open 11–2am **Bar Meals** L served all week 12–3 D served all week 7–10 **Restaurant** L served all week 12–3 D served all week 7–10 ⊕ Free House ◀ Courage Directors, Marston Pedigree, Archers, Greene King IPA & guest ales. **Facilities** Garden Dogs allowed Parking

NORWICH
MAP 13 TG20

Adam & Eve ♀
Bishopsgate NR3 1RZ ☎ 01603 667423 🖹 01603 667438
e-mail: theadamandeve@hotmail.com
dir: *Telephone for directions*

First recorded as an alehouse in 1249, the Adam & Eve is Norwich's oldest pub – it was frequented by workmen constructing the nearby cathedral. Choose from a good selection of ales and wines before taking a bench seat beneath award-winning flower-filled baskets in summer. The menu of favourite bar foods ranges from crispy coated garlic mushrooms, to chicken and ham pie, to large Yorkshire pudding filled with beef or sausages; daily specials are on the chalk board.

Open 11–11 (Sun 12–10.30) Closed: 25–26 Dec, 1 Jan **Bar Meals** L served Mon-Sat 12–7 (Sun 12–2.30) ⊕ Enterprise Inns ◀ Adnams Bitter, Theakston Old Peculier, Greene King IPA, Wells Bombardier. ♀ 10 **Facilities** Parking

Pick of the Pubs

The Mad Moose Arms ◉◉ ♀
See Pick of the Pubs on opposite page

Ribs of Beef ♀
24 Wensum St NR3 1HY ☎ 01603 619517 🖹 01603 625446
e-mail: roger@cawdron.co.uk
dir: *From Tombland (in front of cathedral) turn left at Maids Head Hotel. Pub on right on bridge (200yds)*

Welcoming riverside pub incorporating remnants of the original 14th-century building destroyed in the Great Fire in 1507. Once used by the Norfolk wherry skippers, it is still popular among boat owners cruising the Broads. The menu offers a wide range of sandwiches, burgers and jacket potatoes, as well as Scottish salmon and dill fish cakes, Adnams' braised brisket of beef, vegetarian lasagne, and a choice of omelettes.

Open 11–11 (Fri-Sat 11-12) **Bar Meals** L served Mon-Fri 12-2.30 D served by arrangement (Sat-Sun 12–5) Av main course £6.95 ⊕ Free House ◀ Woodforde's Wherry, Adnams Bitter, Adnams Broadside, Marston's Pedigree & Elgoods Mild. ♀ 8

REEPHAM
MAP 13 TG12

The Old Brewery House Hotel Ⓤ
Market Place NR10 4JJ ☎ 01603 870881 🖹 01603 870969
dir: *Off A1067 (Norwich to Fakenham road), B1145 signed Aylsham*

A grand staircase, highly polished floors and wooden panelling characterise this fine hotel, originally built as a private residence in 1729. It became a hotel in the 1970s, retaining many of its Georgian features. Alongside the real ales and fine wines, there's a bar menu of freshly produced dishes.

Open 11–11 (Sun 12–10.30) **Bar Meals** L served all week 12–2 D served all week 6.30–9.15 (Sun 12–2.15, 7–9) **Restaurant** L served all week 12–2 D served all week 6.30–9.30 Av 3 course à la carte £20 ⊕ Free House ◀ IPA, Greene King Abbot Ale & Old Speckled Hen. **Facilities** Garden Dogs allowed Parking **Rooms** 23

RINGSTEAD
MAP 12 TF74

Pick of the Pubs

The Gin Trap Inn ★★★★ INN ◉ ♀
See Pick of the Pubs on page 398

SALTHOUSE
MAP 13 TG04

The Dun Cow
Coast Rd NR25 7XG ☎ 01263 740467
dir: *On A149 coast road, 3m E of Blakeney, 6m W of Sheringham*

Overlooking some of the country's finest freshwater marshes, the front garden of this attractive pub is inevitably popular with birdwatchers and walkers. The bar area was formerly a blacksmith's forge, and many original 17th-century beams have been retained. Children are welcome, but there's also a walled rear garden reserved for adults. The menu includes snacks, pub staples like burgers and jacket potatoes, and main courses like gammon steak, pasta and meatballs, plaice and chips, and lasagne.

Open 11–11 (Sun 12–10.30) **Bar Meals** L served all week 12–8.45 D served all week 12–8.45 Av main course £7 ⊕ Pubmaster ◀ Greene King IPA & Abbot Ale, Adnams Broadside. **Facilities** Garden Dogs allowed Parking

PICK OF THE PUBS

RINGSTEAD-NORFOLK

The Gin Trap Inn

The Gin Trap was built in 1667 and is situated on the famous Peddars Way, the last two miles of which run from the old world pub down to the sea. The sprawling, white-painted building stands in the attractive village of Ringstead, just a few miles inland from the North Norfolk coast and Hunstanton.

From the early 70s until a re-fit just a few years ago, the pub was packed with old gin traps and farm implements (hence the name). A few gin traps are still displayed for customers' interest, over the front door and incorporated into light fittings in the oak beamed-bar area. The pub has a relaxed and friendly atmosphere with a blazing log burner going throughout the winter and a pretty garden to sit out in during the summer. Walkers pop in for drinks and a meal to fortify them on their way, and dogs are very welcome. Landlords Steve Knowles and Cindy Cook have their own two great danes, who are regularly seen in the pub. Food is taken very seriously, and the snacks board includes local mussels in season and a selection of hand cut sandwiches including some based on speciality breads, such as ciabatta and focaccia. The menu is available throughout the bar, the cosy dining room and the 40–seater conservatory dining area. Typical dishes are six Thornham oysters on ice with shallot and red wine vinegar dressing; and confit Courtyard Farm organic saddleback pork belly with creamed leeks and wholegrain mustard velouté. Desserts range from rich chocolate and orange marquise with pistachio crème anglaise, to sticky toffee pudding with butterscotch sauce.

★★★★ INN ⊛ ⚲
MAP 12 TF74
High St PE36 5JU
☎ 01485 525264
e-mail:
thegintrap@hotmail.co.uk
dir: *A149 from King's Lynn towards Hunstanton. In 15m turn right at Heacham for Ringstead*

Open 11.30–2.30 6–11 (Open all day Summer)
Bar Meals L served Mon-Fri 12–2 D served Sun-Thu 6–9 (Sat-Sun 12–2.30, Fri-Sat 6–9.30) Av main course £11
Restaurant L served Mon-Fri 12–2 D served Sun-Thu 6–9 (Sat-Sun 12–2.30, Fri-Sat 6–9.30) Av 3 course à la carte £24
⊕ Free House ◀ Adnams Best, Woodforde's Wherry, plus guest ales. ⚲ 8
Facilities Garden Dogs allowed Parking
Rooms 3

NETTISHAM   MAP 12 TF63

Pick of the Pubs

The Rose & Crown ★★ HL 🏵 ♈

Old Church Rd PE31 7LX
☎ 01485 541382 📄 01485 543172
e-mail: info@roseandcrownsnettisham.co.uk
dir: *10m N from King's Lynn on A149 signed Hunstanton. Inn in village centre between market square & church*

With its rose-covered façade, the 14th-century Rose & Crown is everything you'd expect from a North Norfolk village inn – twisting passages and hidden corners, low ceilings and old beams, uneven pamment floors and log fires, excellent beers and a relaxed, informal atmosphere. The pretty walled garden was once the village bowling green. Each of the three convivial bars has its own character (and characters!). The menu partners traditional pub favourites with more exotic dishes, all prepared to a high standard and using, where possible, locally supplied produce. Beef, for example, comes from cattle that grazed the nearby salt marshes; fishermen still in their waders deliver Brancaster mussels and Thornham oysters; and strawberries and asparagus grow all around. A regularly changing menu offers, for example, braised oxtail; king prawn Thai curry; pan-roasted lamb rump; and sweet potato ravioli. Sixteen stylish bedrooms offer outstanding bed and breakfast accommodation.

Open 11–11 (Sun 12–10.30) **Bar Meals** L served Mon-Fri 12–2 D served Sun-Thu 6.30–9 (Sat-Sun 12–2.30, Fri-Sat 6.30–9.30) **Restaurant** L served Mon-Fri 12–2 D served Sun-Thu 6.30–9 (Sat-Sun 12–2.30, Fri-Sat 6.30–9.30) ⊕ Free House 🍺 Adnams Bitter & Broadside, Interbrew Bass, Fuller's London Pride, Greene King IPA. ♈20 **Facilities** Garden Dogs allowed Parking Play Area **Rooms** 16

STOKE HOLY CROSS   MAP 13 TG20

Pick of the Pubs

The Wildebeest Arms 🏵🏵 ♈

See Pick of the Pubs on page 400

STOW BARDOLPH   MAP 12 TF60

Pick of the Pubs

The Hare Arms ♈

PE34 3HT ☎ 01366 382229 📄 01366 385522
e-mail: trishmc@harearms222.wanadoo.co.uk
dir: *From King's Lynn take A10 to Downham Market. After 9m village signed on left*

Trish and David McManus have been licensees at this attractive ivy-clad pub for 32 years. The pub was built during the Napoleonic wars and takes its name from the surrounding estate, ancestral home of the Hare family since 1553. The Hare has preserved its appeal and become deservedly popular. The L-shaped bar and adjoining conservatory are packed with decades-worth of fascinating bygones; the cat warms itself by the fire and peacocks wander around outside. An extensive menu of regular pub food is supplemented by daily specials, including the award-winning steak and peppercorn pie, and fish dishes like whole sea bream with lemon and lime butter. The silver service restaurant offers an à la carte menu Monday to Saturday evening with a range of steaks, vegetarian options and dishes such as slow-cooked lamb shank; Gressingham duck in caramelised orange sauce, and monk fish medallions with red pepper risotto.

Open 11–2.30 6–11 (Sun 12–10.30) Closed: 25–26 Dec **Bar Meals** L served Mon-Sat 12–2 D served Mon-Sat 7–10 (Sun 12–10) Av main course £9 **Restaurant** L served Sun 12–10 D served Mon-Sat 7–9.30 Av 3 course à la carte £30 ⊕ Greene King 🍺 Greene King, Abbot Ale, IPA & Old Speckled Hen & guest ale. ♈7 **Facilities** Garden Parking

SWANTON MORLEY   MAP 13 TG01

Darbys Freehouse

1&2 Elsing Rd NR20 4NY
☎ 01362 637647 📄 01362 637928
e-mail: louisedarby@hotmail.co.uk
dir: *From A47 (Norwich to King's Lynn) take B1147 to Dereham*

Built in the 1700s as a large country house, then divided into cottages in the late 19th century. In 1987, after the village's last traditional pub closed, it was converted into the pub you see today, while retaining its old beams and inglenooks. Traditional pub food includes steak and mushroom pudding, braised lamb shank, chargrilled pork loin, scampi, beer-battered haddock, steaks, curries and a vegetarian selection. Children have their own menu and a play area.

Open 11.30–3 6–11 (Sat 11.30–11, Sun 12–10.30) **Bar Meals** L served Mon-Fri 12–2.15 D served Mon-Fri 6.30–9.45 (Sat 12–9.45, Sun 12–8.45) **Restaurant** L served all week 12–2.15 D served all week 6.30–9.45 ⊕ Free House 🍺 Woodforde's Wherry, Badger Tanglefoot, Adnams Broadside, Adnams Best. **Facilities** Garden Dogs allowed Parking Play Area

PICK OF THE PUBS

STOKE HOLY CROSS-NORFOLK

The Wildebeest Arms

There is a colourful history behind the unique name of this village pub. It used to be called the Red Lion, but was re-named in honour, if that's the right phrase, of a former landlord known to his regulars as 'the wild man' or 'beasty'.

A sophisticated calm now imbues the large open-plan, oak-beamed bar and dining area, furnished with bare wooden tables, and decorated with yellow rag-wash. What strikes the first-time visitor, however, is the collection of African tribal art, which seems to reference the pub's name, with its masks, primitive instruments, large carved hippos and a giraffe. According to the locals, most people come for the food, and indeed the pub is popular with a discerning Norwich clientele. The Wildebeest also has a wine list which gives helpful tasting notes, and 14 are served by the glass. A good-value, fixed-price lunch menu du jour of two or three courses offers three choices at each course: how about starting with roast butternut squash and split lentil soup, with chives; continuing with pan-fried fillet of salmon with herb crushed new potatoes, purple sprouting broccoli and fennel duxelle; and finishing with apple and cinnamon crumble with whisky ice cream. A dinner menu du jour along similar lines features more complex cooking reflected in a slightly higher fixed price. Alternatively you can choose from the dinner carte which has a good selection of British dishes with French undertones, in starters like pan-fried pigeon breast with braised lentils, crisp Alsace bacon and celeriac; in main courses such as rosemary roasted loin of local lamb with a Dijon crust; and in desserts like classic crème brûlée with passion fruit sorbet and tuile biscuit.

❀❀ ♥
MAP 13 TG20
82–86 Norwich Rd NR14 8QJ
☎ 01508 492497
📄 01508 494946
e-mail:
wildebeest@animalinns.co.uk
web: www.thewildebeest.co.uk
dir: *From A47, take A140 turn left to Dunston. At T-junct turn left, Wildebeest Arms on right*

Open 12–3 6–11 (Sun 12–3, 7–10.30) Closed: 25–26 Dec
Restaurant L served Mon-Sat 12–2 D served all week 7–10 (Sun 12.30–2.30) Av 3 course à la carte £27.50
⊕ Free House ◪ Adnams. ♥ 14
Facilities Garden Parking

THOMPSON   MAP 13 TL99

Pick of the Pubs

Chequers Inn ☻

See Pick of the Pubs on page 402

THORNHAM   MAP 12 TF74

Pick of the Pubs

Lifeboat Inn ☻

Ship Ln PE36 6LT ☎ 01485 512236 📠 01485 512323
e-mail: reception@lifeboatinn.co.uk
dir: *A149 to Hunstanton, follow coast road to Thornham, pub 1st left*

The Lifeboat is a 16th-century inn overlooking Thornham Harbour and the salt marshes. Despite being extended, its original character has been retained. Inside, the warm glow of paraffin lamps enhances the welcoming atmosphere, while the adjoining conservatory is renowned for its ancient vine and adjacent walled patio garden. The best available fish and game feature on the frequently changing menus, in the form of Brancaster mussels – always a popular starter – steamed in Chardonnay with lemon grass, ginger and double cream. For a satisfying main course try local partridge casserole with Guinness and mushrooms, bacon, herbs and creamy horseradish mash. Numerous attractions lie within easy reach of the inn, including Thornham beach, Blakeney, Cley, Sandringham and Nelson's birthplace at Burnham Thorpe.

Open 11–11 **Bar Meals** L served all week 11 D served all week 11 Av main course £10 **Restaurant** D served all week 6.30–9.30 Av 3 course à la carte £27.50 ⊕ Free House ◀ Adnams, Woodforde's Wherry, Greene King IPA, guest ales. ☻ 10 **Facilities** Garden Dogs allowed Parking Play Area

Pick of the Pubs

The Orange Tree ★★★★ RR

◉◉ ☻

High St PE36 6LY
☎ 01485 512213 📠 01485 512424
e-mail: email@theorangetreethornham.co.uk

This refurbished country pub stands by the ancient Peddar's Way, opposite the church in one of North Norfolk's lovely coastal villages. Two large beer gardens and a children's play area add to the Orange Tree's family appeal; roast Sunday lunch is also popular, served from midday through to 6pm. The bar and restaurant are very stylish, but the building still has that special feel of a traditional rural pub. Lunchtime snacks start with a range of ciabattas, ploughman's, jacket potatoes and salads, and light lunches include baked oyster rarebit grilled with cheese, Guinness, Parma ham and Worcester sauce. Naturally the menu incorporates the best local seafood, which appears on the specials board as pan-fried hake with parsley mash, mussel and crayfish beurre blanc; and seared fillet of sea bass with gremolata potatoes and celeriac purée. Meats supplied by the butcher in Dersingham go into plates of Cumberland sausages served with champ mash and red onion; and traditional lasagne.

Open 11–11 (Sun 12–10.30) **Bar Meals** L served Mon-Sat 12–2 D served Mon-Sat 6–9 (Sun 12–5.30, Summer Sun all day) **Restaurant** L served all week 12–2 D served Mon-Sat 6–9 ⊕ Punch Taverns ◀ Greene King IPA, Adnams Bitter & Guinness. ☻ 10 **Facilities** Garden Dogs allowed Parking Play Area **Rooms** 6

PICK OF THE PUBS

Chequers Inn

The 16th-century Chequers, with its unusual low-slung thatched roof, is hidden among the trees on the edge of Thompson village. Like its namesakes elsewhere, it takes its title from the use of a chequered cloth to make calculations, often of wages, at least halfway intelligible to medieval agricultural workers.

Manor courts, dealing with rents, lettings of land, and small crimes, were held here in the 18th century; later it became a doctor's surgery. Original features inside include exposed beams and timbers, while old farming memorabilia hangs from the walls. Food may be chosen from the bar menu, carte or daily specials board. Carte starters include devilled whitebait; deep-fried breaded mushrooms with garlic mayonnaise; and chef's own chicken liver paté. There's plenty of main course choice, such as pan-fried beef medallions with shallots, leeks, garlic and double cream; lamb cutlets with redcurrant, rosemary and garlic sauce; breast of chicken with wild mushrooms and tarragon sauce; baked sea bass with thyme, sun-blushed tomatoes and lime; and a good choice of fish, including baked sea bream with thyme, sun-blushed tomato and garlic. Nut roast, cheesy pancake and vegetable lasagne should satisfy vegetarian tastes. Among the specials look out for steak and kidney pudding; smoked duck breast with crisp leaf salad and orange and hazelnut dressing; and seafood linguine with garlic, wine and cream sauce. Finally, for dessert, there may well be home-made apple pie, treacle sponge and spotted dick. A climbing frame and swings in the garden will appeal to younger visitors, and the views extend over open land and woods. Nearby is the eight-mile Great Eastern Pingo Trail that navigates a succession of glacially formed swampy depressions in the ground.

MAP 13 TL99
Griston Rd IP24 1PX
☎ 01953 483360
🖷 01953 488092
e-mail: richard@
chequers_inn.wanadoo.co.uk
dir: *Between Watton & Thetford off A1075*

Open 11.30–2.30 6.30–11 (Sun 12–3, 6.30–10.30)
Bar Meals L served all week 12–2 D served all week 6.30–9.30
Av main course £8.50
Restaurant L served all week 12–2 D served all week 6.30–9.30
Av 3 course à la carte £25
⊕ Free House ◀ Fuller's London Pride, Adnams Best, Wolf Best, Greene King IPA. ♟ 7
Facilities Garden Dogs allowed Parking Play Area
Rooms available

THORPE MARKET MAP 13 TG23

Green Farm Restaurant & Hotel

North Walsham Rd NR11 8TH
☎ 01263 833602 🗎 01263 833163
e-mail: enquiries@greenfarmhotel.co.uk
web: www.greenfarmhotel.co.uk
dir: *On A149*

This 16th-century flint-faced former farmhouse overlooks the village green and features a pubby bar as well as a restaurant with an interesting menu. Typical dishes may include grilled marinated breast of duck served on a herbal ratatouille with a sage and balsamic jus, roasted pork cutlet with a sweet pepper crust and spicy garlic and okra sauce, or seabass on roasted fennel and lemon cream sauce.

Open 10–11 **Bar Meals** L served all week 12–2 D served all week 6.30–8.30 (Fri-Sat 6.30–9) Av main course £9.50 **Restaurant** L served all week 12–2 D served all week 6.30–8.30 (Fri-Sat 6.30–9) Av 3 course à la carte £30 Av 5 course fixed price £26 ⊕ Free House ◀ Greene King IPA, Wolf Best Bitter. **Facilities** Garden Dogs allowed Parking

TITCHWELL MAP 13 TF74

Pick of the Pubs

Titchwell Manor Hotel ★★★ HL ⊛⊛

PE31 8BB ☎ 01485 210221 🗎 01485 210104
e-mail: margaret@titchwellmanor.com
dir: *A149 between Brancaster & Thornham*

In the same hands for nearly twenty years, this Victorian manor house has been tastefully updated with a light modern décor. The emphasis here is very much on food. Smart public rooms include a lounge, informal bar, and a delightful conservatory restaurant. From its pretty walled garden the sea views are glorious, and

its proximity lends a major influence to the menus. Uncluttered menus are priced simply in whole pounds, the cooking is skilled and interesting, and the presentation is studied. Lunch options include sandwiches, starters such as Brancaster oysters, and light cooked meals of pan-fried lemon sole with new potatoes, or deep-fried haddock with minted mushy peas. For dinner you might find bream or halibut, with roast rack of lamb or seared Holkham venison if meat is preferred. Families are particularly welcome, and there is a colourful children's menu for under 12s, with lots of choice.

Open 11–11 **Bar Meals** L served all week 12–2 D served all week 6.30–9.30 **Restaurant** L served all week 12–2 D served all week 6.30–9.30 ⊕ Free House ◀ Greene King IPA. **Facilities** Garden Dogs allowed Parking **Rooms** 16

WARHAM ALL SAINTS MAP 13 TF94

Pick of the Pubs

Three Horseshoes

NR23 1NL ☎ 01328 710547
dir: *From Wells A149 to Cromer, then right onto B1105 to Warham*

A gaslit main bar, stone floors, scrubbed wooden tables and a grandfather clock ticking in the corner – this charming gem first opened its doors in 1725. Real ales are served directly from the cask through a hole in the bar wall, and the largely original interior includes a curious green and red dial in the ceiling – a rare example of Norfolk twister, an ancient pub game. Vintage posters, clay pipes, photographs and memorabilia adorn the walls, while down a step are old one-arm bandits. The pub is well known for its home cooking, with local game and shellfish; steak, kidney and Wherry bitter pie; Norfolk chicken and leek suet pudding; and woodman's pie (mushrooms and nuts in red wine sauce). Please don't ask for chips, though. Home-made puddings are listed over the fire in the main bar.

Open 12–2.30 6–11 (Sun 6–10.30) **Bar Meals** L served all week 12–1.45 D served all week 6–8.30 ⊕ Free House ◀ Greene King IPA, Woodforde's Wherry. **Facilities** Garden Dogs allowed Parking **Notes** ⊛

WELLS-NEXT-THE-SEA MAP 13 TF94

Carpenter's Arms NEW ♛

High St, Wighton NR23 1PF ☎ 01328 820752

Gareth and Rebecca Williams took over the pub in April 2007 after six months' closure, and Gareth's cooking is proving very popular. The menu offers fresh, locally sourced classic British food (Adnams beer battered haddock with hand cut chips and mushy peas; home-made steak and kidney pudding; pan-fried calves' liver and bacon with mustard mash). The pub is family and pet friendly with quirky décor and a wood fire inside and large beer garden outside.

Open 12–2.30 6–11 Closed: Mon lunch **Bar Meals** L served Tue-Sun 12–2.30 D served Tue-Sun 6.30–9 Av main course £8 **Restaurant** L served Tue-Sun 12–2.30 D served Tue-Sun 6.30–9.30 Av 3 course à la carte £18 ⊕ Free House ◀ Adnams, Woodfordes Wherry, Norfolk Honey Ale. ♛ 7 **Facilities** Children's licence Garden Dogs allowed Parking

PICK OF THE PUBS

WELLS-NEXT-THE-SEA-NORFOLK

The Crown

A former coaching inn, The Crown overlooks the tree-lined green known as The Buttlands. Striking contemporary décor and furnishings work well with the old-world charm of the 17th-century building.

Food is served in the bar with its old beams and open fire, or the sunny coloured restaurant or vibrant orangery, while on fine days you can sit outside on the sun deck. In style, the cooking brings together modern British and Pacific Rim flavours, along with traditional options for the more conservative of diners. One thing is certain though – you can be sure of ambitious and freshly prepared food made from the best ingredients. The bar menu is divided into three sections, from 'savoury little things' to sandwiches and more hearty options. Goat's cheese and rosemary brûlée with toast and tomato pickle, or smoked ham, butterbean and almond terrine on toasted brioche with onion marmalade might suit smaller appetites; hungrier folk will be satisfied by a more substantial confit of duck leg with chargrilled aubergine; paella with monkfish crab claws, squid, clams and chorizo, or baked fillet of cod with saffron mash and celeriac remoulade. The regularly changing restaurant menu might take in flash-fried squid, bacon and black pudding, or terrine of lamb shank and sweetbreads with sauerkraut, followed by Thai marinated duck breast with seared scallops and chilli jam, or feta, parmesan and basil risotto with roasted cherry tomatoes. Round off with such sophisticated sweet things as olive oil chocolate mousse or Mumma Coughbroughs apple and walnut pudding with clotted cream.

⊚ ♟
MAP 13 TF94
The Buttlands NR23 1EX
☎ 01328 710209
🖹 01328 711432
e-mail: reception@
thecrownhotelwells.co.uk
dir: *10m from Fakenham on B1105*

Open 11 -11
Bar Meals L served all week
12–2.30 D served all week
6.30–9.30
Restaurant D served all week
7–9
⊕ Free House ◖ Adnams Bitter,
Woodforde's Wherry, guest
ale. ♟ 14
Facilities Children's licence
Garden Dogs allowed Parking
Rooms available

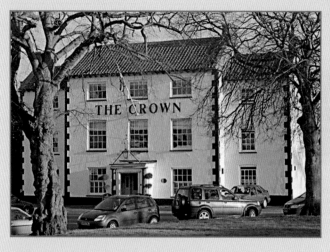

PICK OF THE PUBS

Wiveton Bell

This pretty, 17th-century inn overlooks the village green just a mile from Blakeney on Norfolk's beautiful north coast. Inside, subdued lighting and candles enhance the setting created by an inglenook fireplace, cushioned settles, carver chairs, scrubbed wooden tables and oil paintings.

Customers are just as likely to be walkers with muddy boots (and muddy dogs) as members of the area's business community. The restaurant, awarded an AA Rosette following a refurbishment in 2007, is strong on local produce such as mussels, crabs, oysters and lobsters, and game from the Holkham Hall Estate. Signature dishes include pan-fried pigeon breasts with spiced red cabbage, chorizo and thyme jus; slow-roast Norfolk pork belly, with pomme purée and creamy apple and cider sauce; braised oxtail with venison faggots and Guinness jus; and fisherman's pie. Among the blackboard specials are pan-fried local sea bass with ratatouille, fondant potatoes and fennel and black olive tapenade; and butternut squash with spiced couscous, red pepper coulis and parmesan, rocket and spinach salad. If you want something lighter at lunchtime, there'll be chicken and bacon bruschetta, omelette Arnold Bennett, or a fine steak sandwich. Some of the Norfolk beers come from neighbouring brewery Yetmans, whose owner regards the Bell as his brewery taproom. In summer the sheltered gardens come into their own for drinking and dining, not least because of their lovely views of the village church and over open countryside. The gardens even have their own bar, which is accessed through the cellar, itself a curiosity. Nice touches are the wind-up torches and umbrellas left in the bus shelter on the green for customers to use on the way to and from their cars.

❀ ♥
MAP 13 TG04
Blakeney Rd NR25 7TL
☎ 01263 740101
e-mail:
enquiries@wivetonbell.co.uk
web: www.wivetonbell.com
dir: *1m from Blakeney. Wiverton Rd off A149*

Open 12–3 5.30–11 (Sun eve closed Oct-Etr)
Bar Meals L served all week 12–3 D served all week 6–9.30 (Sun eve closed Oct-Etr) Av main course £9.95
Restaurant L served all week 12–3 D served all week 6–9.30
⊕ Free House ◂▮ Woodforde's Nelson's Revenge, Wherry. ♥ 18
Facilities Garden Dogs allowed Parking

WELLS-NEXT-THE-SEA continued

Pick of the Pubs

The Crown ✿ ⚑

See Pick of the Pubs on page 404

WEST BECKHAM   MAP 13 TG13

The Wheatsheaf ⚑

Manor Farm, Church Rd NR25 6NX ☎ 01263 822110
e-mail: danielclarejoe@tiscali.co.uk
dir: *2m inland from Sheringham on A148, turn opposite Sheringham Park.*

Former manor house converted to a pub over 20 years ago that retains many original features. Sample one of the real ales from Woodfordes Brewery and relax in the large garden. The extensive menu caters for all appetites, large or small, and may feature saddle of lamb stuffed with spinach and stilton with a brandy gravy, pork and oregano meatballs in a tomato sauce on tagliatelle with garlic bread, or chick pea, pepper and pineapple curry served with home-made chapattis.

Open 11.30–3 6.30–11 (Sun 12–3, 7–10, Winter 12–3, 6.30–11)
Bar Meals L served all week 12–2 D served Mon-Sat 6.30–9
Restaurant L served all week 12–2 D served Mon-Sat 6.30–9 ⊕ Free House ◀ Woodforde's Wherry Best Bitter, Nelson's Revenge, Norfolk Nog, Greene King IPA & guest ales. ⚑ 7 **Facilities** Garden Dogs allowed Parking Play Area

---

WINTERTON-ON-SEA   MAP 13 TG41

Fishermans Return ⚑

The Lane NR29 4BN ☎ 01493 393305 📄 01493 393951
e-mail: fishermans_return@btopenworld.com
dir: *8m N of Great Yarmouth on B1159*

Long beaches and National Trust land are within walking distance of this 300-year-old brick and flint pub – ideal for a spot of bird or seal watching. Under the same ownership for over 30 years, the Fisherman's Return has a popular menu that, aptly, includes good fish and seafood options from the blackboard (moules marinière; whole grilled plaice) plus snacks and jacket potatoes.

Open 11–2.30 6–11 (Sat 11–11, Sun 12–10.30) **Bar Meals** L served all week 12–2 D served all week 6.30–9 Av main course £9.25 ⊕ Free House ◀ Woodforde's Wherry & Norfolk Nog, Adnams Best Bitter & Broadside and Greene King IPA & guest ales. ⚑ 10 **Facilities** Garden Dogs allowed Parking Play Area

---

WIVETON   MAP 13 TG04

Pick of the Pubs

Wiveton Bell ✿ ⚑

See Pick of the Pubs on page 405

WOODBASTWICK   MAP 13 TG31

The Fur & Feather Inn ⚑

Slad Ln NR13 6HQ ☎ 01603 720003 📄 01603 722266
dir: *From A1151 (Norwich to Wroxham road), follow brown signs for Woodforde's Brewery. Pub next to Brewery*

This idyllic country pub is ideal for real ale lovers: Woodforde's Brewery is next door, and of course the ales are offered here, straight from the cask. The pub was originally two farm cottages, and now boasts three cosy bar areas and a smart restaurant where you can enjoy steak and ale pie, home baked ham, and goats' cheese, pepper and tomato lasagne, for example, followed by pannacotta and Norfolk honey or a baked vanilla cheesecake maybe.

Open 11.30–3 6–11 (Summer Mon-Sat 11.30–11, Sun 12–10.30)
Bar Meals L served all week 12–2 D served all week 6–9 (Sun 12–2.30) Av main course £10 **Restaurant** L served Mon-Sat 12–2 D served all week 6–9 (Sun 12–2.30) ⊕ Woodforde's ◀ Woodforde's Wherry, Sundew, Norfolk Nog, Nelsons Revenge. ⚑ 10 **Facilities** Garden Parking

---

NORTHAMPTONSHIRE

ASHBY ST LEDGERS   MAP 11 SP56

The Olde Coach House Inn

CV23 8UN ☎ 01788 890349 📄 01788 891922
e-mail: oldcoachhouse@traditionalfreehouses.com
dir: *M1 junct 18 follow A361/Daventry signs. Village on left*

A late 19th-century farmhouse and outbuildings, skilfully converted into a pub with dining areas and meeting rooms, set in a village that dates way back to the Domesday Book of 1086. The village was home to Robert Catesby, one of the Gunpowder plotters. Beer is taken seriously here, with up to eight regularly changing real ales and legendary beer festivals. The pub also serves fresh, high quality food in comfortable surroundings, and holds summer barbecues.

Open 12–11 (Sun 12–10.30) **Bar Meals** L served all week 12–8.30 D served all week 12–8.30 Av main course £7 **Restaurant** L served all week D served all week Av 3 course à la carte £20 ⊕ Free House ◀ Everards Original, Everards Tiger, Marstons Pedigree, guest ale. **Facilities** Garden Parking Play Area

---

ASHTON   MAP 11 SP74

The Old Crown ⚑

1 Stoke Rd NN7 2JN ☎ 01604 862268
dir: *M1 junct 15. 1m from A508 from Roade*

Attractive 17th-century inn with traditional beamed interior and walls decorated with many prints and mirrors. Outside there are two attractively-planted gardens for alfresco dining. Snacks such as soups, sandwiches and salads are available, along with main courses like seared fennel-crusted tuna on Mediterranean couscous; charred aubergine and coconut curry; five-herb roasted chicken breast with potato and celeriac mash; and steamed steak, mushroom, bacon, stilton and herb suet pudding.

Open 12–3 6–11 (Sat-Sun all day) **Bar Meals** L served Mon-Sat 12–2.30 D served Tue-Sun 6.30–9.30 (Sun 12–4) Av main course £7.95 **Restaurant** L served Mon-Sun 12–2.30 D served Mon-Sat 6.30–9 (Sun 12–3) ◀ Wells, Bombardier, Red Stripe, guest ale. ⚑ 7 **Facilities** Garden Parking

PICK OF THE PUBS

BULWICK-NORTHAMPTONSHIRE

The Queen's Head

This charming old building is thought to have been a pub since the 17th century, although parts of it date back to 1400. The name comes from the Portuguese wife of Charles II, Katherine of Braganza, who was well known for her very elaborate hair-dos.

Overlooking the village church, it is every inch the quintessential English pub, with exposed beams, four open fireplaces, wooden beams and flagstone floors in a warren of small rooms. Relax by the fire or on the patio with a pint of Spitfire or a local Rockingham Ale, and some hearty pub food. Many ingredients are sourced from the surrounding area, and the pub is well known for its use of local game like teal, woodcock, partridge and pheasant. Lunch brings sandwiches, interesting snacks (chorizo sausages; toasted seeds) and full meals such as duck and chicken liver terrine with quince jelly followed by Cornish crab, tomato, fennel and saffron risotto with basil. Many of the dishes incorporate Italian influences and ingredients.

The evening menu opens with the likes of Jerusalem artichoke soup with crisp pancetta and white truffle oil; or buffalo mozzarella with a salad of fresh figs, rocket, parmesan and spiced fig vinegar. Follow with roast saddle of rabbit with a pine nut, parsley, garlic and sage stuffing and a morel mushroom sauce; or poached potato gnocchi with spinach and leeks in a goats' cheese and sage sauce with white truffle oil. Typical desserts include almond and apricot tart with Devonshire cream; and warm lemon and almond polenta cake. The menu is backed by a comprehensive wine list, while ale lovers will find guest ales sourced from microbreweries alongside the regular selection at the bar.

MAP 11 SP99
Main St NN17 3DY
☎ 01780 450272
e-mail: queenshead-bulwick@
tiscali.co.uk
dir: *Just off A43, between Corby & Stamford*

Open 12–3 6–11 (Sun 7–10.30)
Closed: Mon
Bar Meals L served Tue-Sat
12–2.30 D served Tue-Sat 6–9.30
(Sun 12–3)
Restaurant L served Tue-Sat
12–2.30 D served Tue-Sat 6–9.30
(Sun 12–3) Av 3 course fixed
price £15
⊕ Free House ◀ Shepherd
Neame, Spitfire & guest ales,
Rockingham Ales & Newby
Wyke. ♀ 9
Facilities Garden Dogs allowed
Parking

England

BADBY
MAP 11 SP55

The Windmill Inn

Main St NN11 3AN ☎ 01327 702363 📄 01327 311521
e-mail: info@windmillinn-badby.com
dir: *M1 junct 16 take A45 to Daventry then A361 S. Village in 2m*

A traditional thatched pub dating back to the 17th century, with beamed and flagstone bars and a friendly, relaxed atmosphere. Theme nights are very popular, including a Winter Sportsmen's dinner, though the cask-conditioned ales and home-cooked food are a draw at any time. Close by are Blenheim Palace and Warwick Castle and nearby is the only thatched youth hostel in England and Wales.

Open 11.30–3 5.30–12 (Sat-Sun 11.30–12) **Bar Meals** L served Mon-Sat 12–2 D served Mon-Sat 7–9.30 (Sun 12–2.30, 7–9) **Restaurant** L served Mon-Sat 12–2 D served Mon-Sat 7–9.30 (Sun 12–2.30, 7–9) ⊕ Free House ◀ Bass , Flowers OB, Boddingtons, Timothy Taylor Landlord. **Facilities** Garden Dogs allowed Parking

BULWICK
MAP 11 SP99

Pick of the Pubs

The Queen's Head 🍷

See Pick of the Pubs on page 407

CHACOMBE
MAP 11 SP44

Pick of the Pubs

George and Dragon

Silver St OX17 2JR ☎ 01295 711500 📄 01295 710516
e-mail: thegeorgeanddragon@msn.com
dir: *From M40 junct 11 take Daventry road. Chacombe 1st right*

An attractive, honey-stoned, 16th-century pub tucked away beside the church in a pretty village protected by Conservation Area status. There's a welcoming feel to the three comfortable bars, where the traditional atmosphere is upheld by an abundance of low beams, simple wooden chairs and settles, log fires (which really are lit), and warm terracotta decor. The blackboards list an interesting selection of food, from sandwiches and baked butternut squash or jacket potatoes (filled with flaked tuna and lemon mayonnaise, prawns with a lime dressing), to favourites and specials: you'll find fish pie at lunchtime, along with fish and chips; pork and apple burgers; root vegetable bake; smoked duck salad; and warm bacon and green leaf salad. In the evening the menu lists starters like goats' cheese and caramelized pears; with such main dishes as smoked salmon and avocado salad; steak and Everard Tiger beer pie; and wild mushroom risotto.

Open 12–11 (Sun 12–10.30) **Bar Meals** L served all week 12–2.30 D served Mon-Sat 6.30–9.30 (Sun 12–3) Av main course £10 **Restaurant** L served all week 12–2.30 D served Mon-Sat 6–9.30 (Sun 12–3) ⊕ Free House ◀ Everards Tiger, Everards Beacon & guest ales. **Facilities** Garden Dogs allowed Parking

CLIPSTON
MAP 11 SP78

The Bulls Head 🍷

Harborough Rd LE16 9RT ☎ 01858 525268
dir: *On B4036 S of Market Harborough*

American airmen once pushed coins between the beams as a good luck charm before bombing raids, and the trend continues with foreign paper money pinned all over the inn. In addition to its good choice of real ales, the pub has an amazing collection of over 500 whiskies. The menu includes shark steaks, whole sea bass, hot toddy duck, and steak pie.

Open 11.30–3 5.30–11 (Sat-Sun all day in summer) **Bar Meals** L served all week 12–2.30 D served all week 6.30–9 **Restaurant** L served all week 12–2.30 D served all week 6.30–9 ⊕ Free House ◀ Tiger, Beacon, guest & seasonal ales. 🍷 14 **Facilities** Children's licence Garden Dogs allowed Parking

COLLYWESTON
MAP 11 SK90

Pick of the Pubs

The Collyweston Slater ★★★★ INN
⊛ 🍷

See Pick of the Pubs on opposite page

CRICK
MAP 11 SP57

The Red Lion Inn

52 Main Rd NN6 7TX ☎ 01788 822342 📄 01788 822342
e-mail: ptm180@tiscali.co.uk
dir: *From M1 junct 18, 0.75m E on A428, follows signs for Crick from new rdbt*

A thatched, stone-built coaching inn dating from the 17th century, with beams and open fires. The Marks family, landlords here for over 25 years, give their regulars and visitors exactly what they want – a friendly atmosphere, real ales and traditional food. The daily home-made steak pie is a lunchtime favourite, while fillet and sirloin steaks are a speciality in the evening. Fish eaters will find trout, stuffed lemon sole, salmon and seafood platter.

Open 11–2.30 6.15–11 (Sun 12–3, 7–10.30) **Bar Meals** L served all week 12–2 D served Mon-Sat 6.30–9 Av main course £6.50 ⊕ Wellington Pub Co ◀ Websters, Wells Bombardier, Greene King Old Speckled Hen & guest ale. **Facilities** Garden Dogs allowed Parking

PICK OF THE PUBS

COLLYWESTON-NORTHAMPTONSHIRE

The Collyweston Slater

Collyweston slates have been used as a roofing material since Roman times. Although Jurassic limestone rather than true slate, it can be split along natural cleavage lines in the same way.

Since its 2006 refit this popular village gastropub has been well reviewed. It has a light, modern interior, which still allows the original oak timbering and slate to conjure up visions of former times. In the AA-Rosette restaurant, the short, frequently-changing menus make the most of seasonal produce, and are backed by an extensive and well-put together wine list and a good range of real ales: look out for ales by Everard's of Leicester, including Slater Ale which is brewed specially for the pub although the brewery name is coincidental. Typical starters are cream of leek and potato soup; chicken liver parfait and red onion jam; and steamed mussels with ginger and spring onion cream. Six mains are usually offered, among

them perhaps tenderloin of pork, smoked bacon, braised leeks and roast potatoes; fillet of salmon, wilted spinach, sauté potatoes and bois boudrin; and broccoli and stilton tart, toasted almonds, spinach and red onion salad. Ice creams and sorbets apart, desserts include sticky toffee pudding, and vanilla pannacotta with roasted pineapple and pink peppercorns. The wines are widely sourced, from Argentina to the USA, by way of France, Hungary, Italy and South Africa, and there's a selection of five champagnes. Overnight guests have a choice of four rooms and one luxury suite with a double Jacuzzi. Although a main road passes the pub, guests have observed that the double-glazing does its job well.

★★★★ INN ◉ ♥
MAP 11 SK90
87–89 Main Rd PE9 3PQ
☎ 01780 444288
e-mail:
info@collywestonslater.co.uk
dir: *4m SW of Stamford, A43 2m off A1 junct*

Open 10.30–3 5–11 (Sat 10.30–11, Sun 12–4) Closed: 25 Dec, 2 Jan
Bar Meals L served Mon-Sat 12–2 D served all week 6–9.30 (Sun 12–2.30) Av main course £10
Restaurant L served Mon-Sat 12–2 D served all week 6–9 (Sun 12–2.30) Av 3 course à la carte £24 Av 3 course fixed price £16
◪ Slaters Ale, Tiger, Bitter, Original Bitter. ♥ 8
Facilities Garden Parking
Rooms 5

England

FARTHINGSTONE
MAP 11 SP65

Pick of the Pubs

The Kings Arms

Main St NN12 8EZ ☎ 01327 361604 📄 01327 361604
e-mail: paul@kingsarms.fsbusiness.co.uk
dir: *M1 junct 16, A45 towards Daventry. At Weedon take A5 towards Towcester. Right signed Farthingstone*

Tucked away in perfect walking country near Canons Ashby (a National Trust property), this 18th-century Grade II listed inn is every inch the traditional country pub – albeit it a highly distinctive one, with gargoyles peering from the stonework. On fine days many visitors come to see the beautiful garden bursting with flowers, vegetables and herbs; in less hospitable weather the cosy interior can be relied upon for real fires and a warm welcome. The pub has a retail business specialising in Cornish fish, and this passion for excellent ingredients is reflected on the short menu where dishes might include game casserole; spicy sausage and bean casserole; Italian chicken with salad; a meat platter of smoked duck, salami, ham and black pudding; a Loch Fyne fish platter or a British cheese platter. Naturally the commitment to sourcing regional specialities extends to the excellent real ales.

Open 12–2.30 7–11 (Fri 6.30–11, Sat-Sun 12–3.30)
Bar Meals L served Sat-Sun 12–2 (Some Fri eve specials 7.30–10) Av main course £8.25 ⊕ Free House ◀ Gt. Oakley, Thwaites Original, Adnams, Brakspear Bitter. **Facilities** Garden Dogs allowed Parking
Notes ⊛

FOTHERINGHAY
MAP 12 TL09

Pick of the Pubs

The Falcon Inn ⊛ ♥

PE8 5HZ ☎ 01832 226254 📄 01832 226046
e-mail: info@thefalcon-inn.co.uk
dir: *N of A605 between Peterborough & Oundle*

King Richard III was born in Fotheringhay in 1452; 115 hundred years later the population balance was restored when Mary Queen of Scots was beheaded here. The attractive 18th-century, stone-built Falcon, in gardens redesigned by award-winning landscape architect, Bunny Guinness, overlooks the outstanding church, which looks truly magical at night when floodlit. It's a real local, with a tap bar regularly used by the real ale-fuelled village darts team. The menus, in both the bar and charming conservatory restaurant, rely extensively on locally sourced ingredients, offering pan-fried venison with parsnip mash; roast fillet of salmon with cannellini beans; and fricassée of mushrooms, leeks, and tagliatelle. Affogato (vanilla ice cream with espresso) is definitely worth trying for dessert, or stick with Bakewell tart, or some local cheeses. The wine list is well chosen, from a Chilean sauvignon blanc at £11.95 to a chart-topping Champagne at £150.

Open 12–3 6–11 (Sat 6–12, Sun 12–3, 7–10.30) **Bar Meals** L served Mon-Sat 12–2.15 D served Mon-Sat 6.15–9.15 (Sun 12–3, 6.15–8.30) Av main course £8 **Restaurant** L served Mon-Sat 12–2.15 D served Mon-Sat 6.15–9.15 (Sun 12–3, 6.15–8.30) Av 3 course à la carte £25 ⊕ Free House ◀ Greene King IPA, Barnwell Bitter, Fools Nook & guest ales.
♥ 15 **Facilities** Garden Parking

GRAFTON REGIS
MAP 11 SP74

The White Hart ♥

Northampton Rd NN12 7SR ☎ 01908 542123
e-mail: alan@pubgraftonregis.co.uk
dir: *M1 junct 15 on A508 between Northampton & Milton Keynes*

In 1464, Edward IV married Elizabeth Woodville in this historic village, where the stone-built thatched White Hart was first licensed in 1750. The restaurant menu might list salmon fillet with prawn sauce, or mature Welsh fillet steak topped with home-made chicken liver paté. From the lounge menu, you can choose from the likes of mustard and sugar-baked ham; steak, stilton and mushroom pie; or home-made lasagne. Round off with raspberry charlotte or banoffee pie.

Open 12–2.30 6–11 (Sun 7–10.30) Closed: Mon **Bar Meals** L served Tue-Sun 12–2 D served Tue-Sat 6–9.30 (Sun 7–9) **Restaurant** L served Tue-Sun 12–1.30 D served Tue-Sat 6.30–9 ⊕ Free House ◀ Greene King, Abbot Ale & IPA. ♥ 14 **Facilities** Garden Parking

---

GREAT OXENDON
MAP 11 SP78

Pick of the Pubs

The George Inn ♥

LE16 8NA ☎ 01858 465205 📄 01858 465205
e-mail: info@thegeorgegreatoxendon.co.uk
dir: *Telephone for directions*

Parts of this country dining pub are up to 600 years old, and the building reputedly accommodated soldiers after the battle of Naseby. Original beams, a lovely log fire and old photographs lend stacks of charm. Today the George has a county-wide reputation for excellent food and service, but customers are still welcome to call in for a pint or a glass of wine from the extensive list. Three dining areas comprise the cosy restaurant, a conservatory overlooking award-winning gardens, and a patio. Owner David Dudley and his son Philip offer lunchtime choices ranging from a simple bowl of marinated olives to substantial meals like rib-eye steak; or local sausages and mash with onion gravy. The impressive dinner menu includes Barbary duck with red cabbage and plum sauce; pan-fried sea bass with crushed potatoes and olive tapenade; and tempura vegetables with sweet chilli dip.

Open 11.30–3 5.30–11 Closed: 25 Dec Sun & BH eves
Bar Meals L served all week 12–2 D served Mon-Sat 6–10
Restaurant L served all week 12–2 D served Mon-Sat 6–10 ⊕ Free House ◀ Batemans guest ale, Adnams Bitter, Youngs Special, Timothy Taylor Landlord. ♥ 12 **Facilities** Garden Parking

HARRINGTON   MAP 11 SP78

Pick of the Pubs

The Tollemache Arms ☕

49 High St NN6 9NU ☎ 01536 710469

e-mail: markandjo@tollemacheharrington.com

dir: *6m from Kettering, off A14 junct 3. Follow signs for Harrington*

A popular retreat from the nearby towns of Northampton, Kettering and Market Harborough, this thatched and whitewashed pub stands in the lovely Northamptonshire village of Harrington. There are open fires in the winter months and panoramic views from the large garden. Food and drink are served all day, every day, from midday. Light bites include sandwiches, ploughman's and omelettes, while main menu dishes combine modern, classic and traditional influences. Start with rich coarse local paté served

with winter fruit chutney and toasted brioche, or black pearl scallops wrapped in oak smoked salmon, gently roasted, with vine tomatoes and a mango, sage and lime dressing. Mains range from a half pound sausage knot set on mustard crushed new potatoes with onion gravy and fresh vegetables; and pan-seared butter-flied sea bass on a cucumber and mint salsa served with new potatoes. Skittles knockout evenings and quizzes are regular events.

Open 12–11 (Sun 12–10.30) **Bar Meals** L served all week 12–9.30 D served all week 12–9.30 Av main course £11.95 **Restaurant** L served all week 12–6 D served all week 6–9.30 Av 3 course à la carte £20 ⓦ Charles Wells ◀ Bombardier, Eagle IPA, Draught Red Stripe & 2 guest ales. ☕ 17 **Facilities** Garden Parking

See advert on this page

KETTERING   MAP 11 SP87

The Overstone Arms ☕

Stringers Hill, Pytchley NN14 1EU

☎ 01536 790215 📠 01536 791098

dir: *1m from Kettering, 5m from Wellingborough*

The 18th-century coaching inn is at the heart of the village and has been home to the Pytchley Hunt, which over the years has attracted many royal visitors. Years ago guests would travel up from London, staying here or at Althorp Hall, mainly for the hunting. Despite its rural location, the pub is just a mile from the busy A14. Home-made pies, grilled trout, steaks, lasagne and curry are typical dishes.

Open 12–2.30 6.30–11 **Bar Meals** L served all week 12–2 D served all week 7–9.30 **Restaurant** L served all week 12–2 D served all week 7–9.30 ⓦ Unique Pub Co ◀ Greene King, Marston's Pedigree, Interbrew Bass, Adnams Bitter. ☕ 8 **Facilities** Garden Parking

England

LOWICK

MAP 11 SP98

The Snooty Fox ♀

NN14 3BH ☎ 01832 733434

e-mail: the.snooty.fox@btinternet.com

dir: *Off A14, 5m E of Kettering on A6116. Straight over at 1st rdbt, left into Lowick*

Exquisite carved beams are among the more unusual features at this 16th-century building which has been a pub since 1700. Originally the manor house, it is supposedly haunted by a horse and its rider killed at the Battle of Naseby. The kitchen specialises in grill and rotisserie cooking, so check out the rack of Cornish lamb, Gloucester Old Spot pork belly, sirloin steaks, and others. Fresh Cornish fish is also a feature, as is a good wine list.

Open 12–12 Closed: 25 Dec **Bar Meals** L served all week 12–2.30 D served all week 6–9.30 **Restaurant** L served all week 12–2 D served all week 6.30–9.30 Av 2 course fixed price £12 ⊕ Free House ◀ Jennings Cumberland, Greene King IPA, Fuller's London Pride, Morland Old Speckled Hen & Morland Original. ♀ 7 **Facilities** Garden Parking

---

NORTHAMPTON

MAP 11 SP76

The Fox & Hounds ♀

Main St, Great Brington NN7 4JA

☎ 01604 770651 ▤ 01604 770164

e-mail: althorpcoachinn@aol.com

web: www.althorp-coaching-inn.co.uk

dir: *From A428 pass main gates of Althorp House, left before rail bridge. Great Brington 1m*

Flagstone floors, beams and open fires, not to mention a beautiful walled garden, are some of the charms of this 16th-century coaching inn, which stands on the Althorp Estate, ancestral home of the Spencer family. Equally praiseworthy are the numerous guest ales and reputation for quality food. Jacket potatoes and ciabatta sandwiches feature on the snack menu; other meals include chicken stuffed with haloumi cheese; tom yam tiger prawns, and grilled Scottish salmon.

Open 11–11 (Sun 12–10.30) **Bar Meals** L served all week 12–2.30 D served all week 6.30–9.30 (Sun 6.30–8.30) Av main course £7.95 **Restaurant** L served all week 12–2.30 D served all week 6.30–9.30 (Sun 6.30–8.30) Av 3 course à la carte £21.95 ⊕ Free House ◀ Greene King IPA, Speckled Hen, Fuller's London Pride, Abbot Ale. ♀ 8 **Facilities** Garden Dogs allowed Parking

OUNDLE

MAP 11 TL08

The Montagu Arms ♀

Barnwell PE8 5PH ☎ 01832 273726 ▤ 01832 275555

e-mail: ianmsimmons@aol.com

dir: *Off A605 opposite Oundle slip road*

One of Northamptonshire's oldest inns, the Montagu Arms was originally three cottages dating from 1601, housing the workmen building the nearby manor house. The inn has a large garden, well equipped for children's play, and overlooks the brook and village green of the royal village of Barnwell. An extensive menu serving the bar and restaurant ranges through snacks and sharing platters, and dishes such as Rutland sausages and mash, stuffed chicken, and crispy fish pie.

Open 12–3 6–11 (Sat-Sun all day) **Bar Meals** L served all week 12–2.30 D served all week 7–10 Av main course £8 **Restaurant** L served all week 12–2.30 D served all week 7–10 Av 3 course à la carte £15 ⊕ Free House ◀ Digfield Ales, Adnams Broadside, Hop Back Summer Lightning, Fuller's London Pride. ♀ 14 **Facilities** Garden Parking Play Area

---

SIBBERTOFT

MAP 11 SP68

Pick of the Pubs

The Red Lion ♀

See Pick of the Pubs on opposite page

PICK OF THE PUBS

SIBBERTOFT-NORTHAMPTONSHIRE

The Red Lion

This friendly 300–year-old pub offers an appealing blend of contemporary and classic decor, with oak beams, leather upholstery and a smartly turned out dining room. The quiet garden is a favourite with local walkers and cyclists, and in fine weather lunch can be taken on the patio or lawns. Children are also made welcome, and enjoy the outdoor play area.

Food and wine are taken seriously here, reflected in awards for both the drinks list and the kitchen in recent years. In the bar reliable real ales from Adnams and Timothy Taylor are served alongside premium imports from Germany and Czechoslovakia. Wine is the special passion of owner Andrew Banks, and he offers over 200 bins which include 20 served by the glass; all wines on the list are available for purchase at a take-home price. The concise monthly changing menu is based on locally sourced ingredients, producing starters such as honeyed goat's cheese with sweet red onions; and duck and port terrine with orange and apricot chutney. Main courses may offer beef and onion cobbler with stilton scone; or pheasant with herb polenta and Adnams sauce. Lest the breadth of wine choice should bemuse or confuse, thoughtful drinking suggestions are sometimes printed on the menu to complement the dishes: a Sartori Marani perhaps, with seared salmon and sautéed new potatoes; or a Californian Pinot Noir with a local rib-eye steak with crisp salad and chunky chips. Desserts are equally mouthwatering, ranging from vanilla pannacotta with sticky berries to cherry tart with crème fraîche. A function room across the courtyard is popular for out-of-office meetings, perhaps because broadband has yet to reach Sibbertoft. Regular themed evenings include a weekly curry night and monthly wine dinners, an excellent introduction to the impressive list.

♇
MAP 11 SP68
43 Welland Rise LE16 9UD
☎ 01858 880011
e-mail: andrew@
redlionwinepub.co.uk
dir: *From Market Harborough take A4304, straight through Lubenham, then left through Marston Trussell up to Sibbertoft*

Open 12–2 6–11 (Sun 12–5)
Bar Meals L served Wed-Sat
12–2 D served Mon-Sat 6.30–9.45
(Sun 12–3) Av main course £4.50
Restaurant L served Wed-Sat
12–2 D served all week 6.30–9.45
(Sun 12–3) Av 3 course à la carte
£19 Av 2 course fixed price £7.50
⊕ Free House ◖ Adnams,
Boddingtons, Timothy Taylor.
♇ 20
Facilities Garden Parking Play
Area

STOKE BRUERNE

MAP 11 SP74

The Boat Inn

NN12 7SB ☎ 01604 862428 📄 01604 864314
e-mail: info@boatinn.co.uk
web: www.boatinn.co.uk
dir: *In village centre, just off A508 or A5*

Just across the lock from a popular canal museum, this waterside free house has been run by the same family since 1877. Beneath its thatched roof you'll find cosy bars, open fires and flagstone floors, as well as a traditional skittle alley. Home-made soups, burgers and baguettes support more substantial meals such as chef's paté with toasted bloomer followed by Gressingham duck breast with apricot and bacon stuffing.

Open 9–11 Closed: Mon-Thu 3–6 in winter **Bar Meals** L served all week 9.30–9 D served all week **Restaurant** L served Tue-Sun 12–2 D served Mon-Sat 7–9 (Sun 6.30–8.30) ⊕ Free House ◀ Banks Bitter, Marstons Pedigree, Adnams Southwold, Frog Island Best. **Facilities** Children's licence Garden Dogs allowed Parking

WADENHOE

MAP 11 TL08

Pick of the Pubs

The King's Head ⚑

Church St PE8 5ST ☎ 01832 720024
e-mail: info@kingsheadwadenhoe.co.uk
dir: *From A605, 3m from Wadenhoe rdbt. 2m from Oundle.*

The stone-built, partially thatched 16th-century inn lies at the end of a quiet country lane. What better to do on a warm afternoon than sit in its extensive gardens, with pint or spritzer in hand, and watch passing rivercraft on the slow-flowing Nene. The warm and welcoming interior has quarry-tiled and bare-boarded floors, heavy oak-beamed ceilings, pine furniture and open log fires. Vegetables and herbs come from the inn's own garden, and other local sources provide most of the remaining produce. Dishes include hearty home-made classics such as butcher's sausages, mash and onion gravy; beer-battered haddock, hand-cut chips and garden peas; and chicken, bacon and goats' cheese salad. Seafood and game in season are offered daily, while typical year-round dishes include tomato tarte Tatin; braised lamb shank; and pork chop. Nearly 20 wines are available by the glass. Challenge the locals to a game of Northamptonshire skittles – if you dare.

Open 11–3 5.30–11 (Sun 12–4) Closed: Sun eve in Winter **Bar Meals** L served all week 12–2.15 D served Mon-Sat 7–9.15 (Sun 12–3.30) Av main course £10 **Restaurant** L served all week 12–2.15 D served Mon-Sat 6.30–9.15 (Sun 12–3.30) ⊕ Free House ◀ 1 Kings Head Bitter, Barnwell Bitter, JHB, Tribute. ⚑ 18 **Facilities** Garden Dogs allowed Parking

WESTON

MAP 11 SP54

Pick of the Pubs

The Crown ⚑

See Pick of the Pubs on opposite page

WOLLASTON

MAP 11 SP96

Pick of the Pubs

The Wollaston Inn NEW ⚑

87 London Rd NN29 7QS ☎ 01933 663161
e-mail: info@wollaston-inn.co.uk
dir: *From Wellingborough, onto A507 towards Wollaston. After 2m, over rdbt, then immediately left, Inn at top of hill*

The late John Peel was once the resident Sunday night DJ here. Back in those days it was the Nags Head, but Chris Spencer took over in 2003, reinvented it as a restaurant within a pub and gave it a new name. His loving restoration of the 350–year-old building's historical features provides the backdrop to Italian leather sofas and casual tables and chairs. A commitment to please both formal and casual diners is reflected in reasonably priced set lunch menus (available until 7pm), and an evening carte of seasonal dishes. These offer daily changing selections such as venison haunch steak; Thai red chicken curry; Mediterranean vegetable and buffalo mozzarella stack; and lots of fresh fish and seafood, such as lobster and monkfish thermidor; baked mackerel, sunblush tomato and courgette risotto; and organic sustainable cod, braised oxtail and caramelised apple. Service is attentive wherever you eat – bar, restaurant, patio or garden.

Open 11–11 (Sun 11–10.30) **Bar Meals** L served all week 11–7 D served all week 5–10 Av main course £8.50 **Restaurant** L served all week 11–7 D served all week 5–10 Av 3 course à la carte £27 ◀ Burton Bitter, Black Sheep & Guinness. **Facilities** Children's licence Garden Parking

WOODNEWTON

MAP 11 TL09

The White Swan

22 Main St PE8 5EB ☎ 01780 470381
dir: *5m off A605/A47*

Welcoming village local comprising a simple, single oblong room, one end focusing on the bar and wood-burning stove, the other set up as a dining area. The regularly changing blackboard menu may offer home-made soup; parsnip and pancetta spaghetti; pan-fried pork fillet medallions; lemon grass plaice with coriander salsa and coconut rice. Finish with a traditional home-made sweet, like fruit crumble or sticky toffee pudding.

Open 12–2.30 6–11 (Sun 12–3.30) **Bar Meals** L served Wed-Sun 12–1.30 D served Tue-Sat 6.30–8.30 (Sun 12–2.30) **Restaurant** L served Wed-Sun 12–1.30 D served Tue-Sat 6.30–8.30 Sun 12–2.30 ⊕ Free House ◀ Adnams, London Pride, Bass, Batemans. **Facilities** Garden Parking

PICK OF THE PUBS

The Crown

Llama trekking and Lord Lucan are two of the unusual associations with this attractive 16th-century inn. The former is available in the village, while the latter was allegedly spotted having a pint in the pub the night after his children's nanny was famously murdered. However the inn's history stretches back much further than that.

It's been serving ales since the reign of Elizabeth I, with the first recorded owner being All Souls College, Oxford. A cross-country route dating back to 1593 provides the first documented evidence of the Crown. The present owner, Robert Grover, acquired the freehold for the inn in 2003, having long believed in its potential as a dining destination. His policy has always been to serve food prepared from fresh ingredients, complemented by a 45-bin wine list. The result? After a significant upswing in trade, the pub has gained a central role in the community; the traditional roast on Sunday has proved a particular hit with the locals. Lunchtime bites include a range of paninis and omelettes. A typical evening menu might start with deep-fried brie and Parma ham in filo pastry; chicken samosa with onion bhaji, poppadom, mango chutney and minted raita; or smoked trout paté with lemon and dill vinaigrette on toasted ciabatta. Follow these with main courses such as vegetarian penne pasta with parmesan and rocket; curried salmon and haddock fishcakes, lemon mayonnaise, mixed leaves and chips; or beef casserole with roasted parsnips and buttered mash. Nearby attractions include Sulgrave Manor, the ancestral home of George Washington, and Silverstone racing circuit.

MAP 11 SP54
Helmdon Rd NN12 8PX
☎ 01295 760310
🖷 01295 760310
e-mail:
thecrown-weston@tiscali.co.uk
dir: *Accessed from A43 or B4525*

Open 12–3 6–12 (Sun 6–11.30)
Closed: 25 Dec, Mon-Tue lunch
Bar Meals L served Wed-Sun
12–2.30 D served Mon-Sat 6–9.30
🌐 Free House 🍺 Greene King
IPA , Hook Norton Best, Black
Sheep, Landlord. 🍷 7
Facilities Garden Dogs allowed
Parking

NORTHUMBERLAND

ALLENHEADS

MAP 18 NY84

The Allenheads Inn

NE47 9HJ ☎ 01434 685200 🖹 01434 685200

e-mail: philann@phomer.fsbusiness.co.uk

dir: *From Hexham take B6305, then B6295 to Allenheads*

An 18th-century free house with a lively atmosphere, the Allenheads Inn is situated in the fabulous countryside of the North Pennines, perfect for walking and exploring the nearby market towns and enjoying the many local attractions. Relax in the popular Antiques Bar, or the unusually-named Forces Room, and enjoy pies, chilli, curry, burgers, or one of the pub's seasonal specials.

Open 12–11 **Bar Meals** L served all week 12–2 D served all week 7–9 Av main course £7.50 **Restaurant** L served all week 12–2 D served all week 7–9 ⊕ Free House ◀ Greene King Abbot Ale, Timothy Taylor Landlord, Black Sheep Bitter and guest ales. **Facilities** Garden Dogs allowed Parking

ALNWICK

MAP 21 NU11

Masons Arms

Stamford, Nr Rennington NE66 3RX ☎ 01665 577275

e-mail: bookings@masonsarms.net

dir: *NE of Alnwick on B1340, 0.5m past Rennington*

A tastefully modernised 200–year-old coaching inn, known by the local community as Stamford Cott. It is a useful staging post for visitors to Hadrian's Wall, Lindisfarne and the large number of nearby golf courses. The substantial home-cooked food is available in the bar and the restaurant, and is made using the best of local produce. Typical examples include lemon sole with prawns and parsley sauce; Northumbrian game casserole; and curry.

Open 12–2 6.30–11 (Sun 7–10.30) **Bar Meals** L served all week 12–2 D served all week 6–9 (Winter 6.30–8.30) **Restaurant** L served all week 12–2 D served all week 6–9 (Winter 6.30–8.30) Av 3 course à la carte £16 ⊕ Free House ◀ John Smiths's, Theakston Best, Secret Kingdom, Gladiator. **Facilities** Children's licence Garden Dogs allowed Parking **Rooms** available

BELFORD

MAP 21 NU13

Blue Bell Hotel ★★★ HL

Market Place NE70 7NE ☎ 01668 213543 🖹 01668 213787

e-mail: bluebell@globalnet.co.uk

dir: *Off A1, 15m N of Alnwick , 25m S of Berwick-upon-Tweed*

Richard Burton and Elizabeth Taylor are among a host of illustrious movie stars and television celebrities who have stayed at this 17th-century coaching inn on the A1 London to Edinburgh route. Choices from the restaurant menu may include chicken liver pate with oatcakes as a starter, followed by grilled sirloin steak on roast asparagus with a stilton crust; and gingered rhubarb crumble with English custard to round off.

Open 11–2.30 6.30–11 **Bar Meals** L served all week 11–2 D served all week 6.30–9 **Restaurant** L served all week 12–2 D served all week 7–9 ⊕ Free House ◀ Interbrew Boddingtons Bitter, Northumbrian Smoothe, Calders, Tetleys Smooth. **Facilities** Garden Parking **Rooms** 17

BERWICK-UPON-TWEED

MAP 21 NT95

The Rob Roy ⬧

Dock Rd, Tweedmouth TD15 2BE

☎ 01289 306428 🖹 01289 306428

e-mail: therobroy@hotmail.com

dir: *Exit A1 2m S of Berwick at A1167 signed Scremerston, right at rdbt signed Spittal, 1m to Albion pub on left*

Ideally situated for exploring the coasts and castles of Northumberland and Berwickshire, the Rob Roy was built as a Tweed-side cottage 150 years ago. Today it's a privately-run hostelry with salmon fishing paraphernalia decorating the bar. Fresh fish is a speciality and the seafood platter for two, with eight different varieties of fish and shellfish, is popular with locals and tourists alike. Alternatives on the bar menu could be deep-fried squid, or pork medallions sautéed in masala.

Open 12–2.30 7–11 Closed: 25 Dec **Bar Meals** L served Tue-Sun 12–2 D served Tue-Sat 6.30–8.45 Av main course £8.50 **Restaurant** L served Tue-Sun 12–1.45 D served Tue-Sat 6.30–8.45 ⊕ Free House ◀ Rob Roy Bitter. ⬧ 8

England

PICK OF THE PUBS

EGLINGHAM-NORTHUMBERLAND

Tankerville Arms

The Tankerville Arms nestles in idyllic countryside about seven miles from Alnwick. Inside it is warm and welcoming, with traditional features that enhance its character.

A variety of tables and chairs and loads of bric-a-brac, along with a warm welcome, make it easy to feel at home here, and the pub attracts everyone from grandparents with children to families and young people – all are equally well catered for. The secret weapon here is chef Bryan Hornsey who has put his unique stamp on the food. Fresh local produce is given careful but innovative handling by a kitchen working at the peak of its talents, and the results appear on the same menu throughout the pub. Look out for starters like Eyemouth dressed crab with caper and lemon dressing, or home-made Glendale pork and apricot terrine with fresh fig jam. Main courses include pollock with a confit of cherry tomatoes and tarragon dressing; or braised brisket of Glendale beef, roasted shallots and smoked bacon gravy with horseradish mash. For dessert look no further than old favourite spotted dick with fresh egg custard, and the more sophisticated iced mint parfait with lavender marinated fruits. A great range of beers can be enjoyed on their own or with a meal, like Black Sheep Best, or Mordue Workie Ticket.

MAP 21 NU11
NE66 2TX
☎ 01665 578444
🖷 01665 578444
dir: *B6346 from Alnwick*

Open 11–11
Bar Meals L served all week
12–9.30 D served all week 6–9.30
Av main course £8.95
Restaurant L served all week
12–9.30 D served all week 6–9.30
Av 3 course à la carte £19.50
🍺 Free House 🍺 Black Sheep
Best, Mordue Workie Ticket,
Hadrian and Border Tyneside
Blond
Facilities Garden Parking Play
Area

417

PICK OF THE PUBS

FALSTONE-NORTHUMBERLAND

The Pheasant Inn

This sprawling stone-walled building in the north Tyne Valley dates back to 1624. It was originally a large farmstead, but for over 250 years one room was always used as a locals' bar. Its permanent change of use came about in 1974, and 1975 saw the conversion of some of the farm buildings into bedrooms.

In 1985 it was taken over by the Kershaws, who have continually improved and upgraded it. However they have succeeded in keeping the rustic atmosphere intact – around the walls old photos record local people engaged in long-abandoned trades and professions. Robin and Irene's cooking is fresh, generous and tasty, producing wholesome traditionally English fare. Meals may be taken al fresco in the pretty grassed courtyard with a stream running through, or in the oak-beamed restaurant with its cottagey furnishings and warm terracotta walls. The bar menu changes daily according to season, but classic dishes like steak and kidney pie, home-made soups, lasagne, ploughman's and sandwiches are always available. Restaurant menu

starters could embrace grilled fresh asparagus with a balsamic dressing; sweet marinated herrings; and creamy garlic mushrooms in puff pastry. Sample main courses from the blackboard might be slow-roasted Northumbrian lamb; cider baked gammon; home-made game pie; and fish from North Shields quay. Sandra's sticky toffee pudding is always an irresistible way to finish. Nearby is Kielder Water, the largest artificial lake in Europe and a magnet for walkers, cyclists and sailors. There's also Hadrian's Wall, some of England's least spoilt countryside and coastline, and sights such as Alnwick Castle and gardens. Guests tempted to stay can book one of eight en suite bedrooms, with views over the stunning landscape.

★★★★ INN
MAP 21 NY78
Stannersburn NE48 1DD
☎ 01434 240382
🖹 01434 240382
e-mail: enquiries@
thepheasantinn.com
dir: *A69, B6079, B6320, follow signs for Kielder Water*

Open 11–3 6–11 (Opening times vary, ring for details) Closed: 25–26 Dec & Mon-Tue (Nov-Mar)
Bar Meals L served all week 12–2.30 D served all week 7–9 Av main course £11.95
Restaurant L served Mon-Fri 12–2.30 D served all week 7–9 (Sun 12–2)
⊕ Free House ◀ Theakston Best, Marstons Pedigree, Timothy Taylor Landlord, Wylam Gold.
Facilities Garden Dogs allowed Parking Play Area
Rooms 8

418

BLANCHLAND   MAP 18 NY95

The Lord Crewe Arms

DH8 9SP ☎ 01434 675251 🖹 01434 675337

e-mail: lord@crewearms.freeserve.co.uk

dir: 10m S of Hexham via B6306

Once the abbot's house of Blanchland Abbey, this is one of England's oldest inns. Antique furniture, blazing log fires and flagstone floors make for an atmospheric setting. Wide-ranging, good-value bar and restaurant menus with specials offer filled rolls, salads, savoury bean hot pot, and game pie. Watch out, there are lots of ghosts!

Open 11–11 **Bar Meals** L served all week 12–2 D served all week 7–9.15 **Restaurant** D served all week 7–9.15 ⊕ Free House ◖ Black Sheep, John Smiths, Guinness. **Facilities** Garden Dogs allowed Parking **Rooms** available

CARTERWAY HEADS   MAP 19 NZ05

Pick of the Pubs

The Manor House Inn ♀

DH8 9LX ☎ 01207 255268

dir: A69 W from Newcastle, left onto A68 then S for 8m. Inn on right.

A small family-run free house enjoying spectacular views across open moorland and the Derwent Reservoir from its lonely position high on the A68. Built circa 1760, the inn has been completely refurbished and looks better than ever. The cosy stone-walled bar, with its log fires, low-beamed ceiling and massive timber support, offers a good range of well-kept real ales and around 70 malt whiskies. The bar and lounge are ideal for a snack, while the restaurant is divided into two dining areas, the larger of which welcomes families with children. Typical dishes include soups and pastas of the day, salads and wraps, and hearty main courses of braised lamb shank with roasted root vegetables; or pan-fried calves' liver with bubble and squeak. Home-made puddings are a feature, as is the choice of up to 16 local cheeses, and many of these products can be purchased in the recently-opened farm shop and deli.

Open 11–11 **Bar Meals** L served Mon-Sat 12–9.30 D served Mon-Sat (Sun 12–9) **Restaurant** L served all week 12–2.30 D served Mon-Sat 7–9.30 (Sun 7–9) ⊕ Free House ◖ Theakstons Best, Mordue Workie Ticket, Greene King Ruddles County, Courage Directors & Wells Bombardier. ♀ 12 **Facilities** Children's licence Garden Dogs allowed Parking **Rooms** available

CHATTON   MAP 21 NU02

The Percy Arms Hotel ♀

Main Rd NE66 5PS ☎ 01668 215244 🖹 01668 215277

dir: From Alnwick take A1 N, then B6348 to Chatton

Traditional 19th-century forming coaching inn, situated in the heart of rural Northumberland. Expect a warm, traditional pub welcome, as well as a selection of fine beers, wines and tempting food. Bar menu includes Aberdeen Angus steaks, deep-fried haddock, steak and kidney pie and a wide selection of fish and seafood dishes. Bar games include snooker, pool and darts, but those who wish to can still enjoy a quiet pint in comfort.

Open 11–11 (Sun 12–10.30) **Bar Meals** L served all week 12–2 D served all week 6.30–9 **Restaurant** L served all week 12–1.30 D served all week 6.30–8.30 ⊕ Jennings ◖ Jennings Cumberland Cream, guest ales. ♀ 7 **Facilities** Children's licence Garden Parking **Rooms** available

CORBRIDGE   MAP 21 NY96

The Angel of Corbridge ♀

Main St NE45 5LA ☎ 01434 632119 🖹 01434 633496

e-mail: info@theangelofcorbridge.co.uk

dir: 0.5m off A69, signed Corbridge

Stylish 17th-century coaching inn overlooking the River Tyne. Relax with the daily papers in the wood-panelled lounge or attractive bars, or enjoy a home-made dish or two from the extensive menu choice. Options include pan-fried chicken breast with spicy cous cous, salmon and lemon fish cakes and risotto of asparagus and leek.

Open 10–11 (Sun 11–10.30) **Bar Meals** L served Mon-Thu 12–7 D served Mon-Thu 6–7 (Fri-Sat 12–6) Av main course £10 **Restaurant** L served all week 12–3 (Sun 12–4) D served Mon-Sat 6–9 Av 3 course à la carte £25 ⊕ Free House ◖ Timothy Taylor Landlord & local ales. ♀ 10 **Facilities** Children's licence Garden Parking

CRASTER
MAP 21 NU21

Cottage Inn 🍷

Dunstan Village NE66 2UD
☎ 01665 576658 📠 01665 576788
e-mail: enquiries@cottageinnhotel.co.uk
dir: NW of Howick to Embleton road

Set in six acres of woodland, in an area of outstanding natural beauty, this 18th-century inn lies in a hamlet close to the coast. Nearby is Dunstanburgh Castle, one of Northumberland's great historic landmarks. Inside is a beamed bar, together with a restaurant, conservatory and patio. One menu serves all and includes the ever-popular Craster kippers, steak and game pie, venison sausages, and vegetable risotto. Local ingredients are used wherever possible.

Open 11–12 **Bar Meals** L served all week 12–2.30 D served all week 6–9.30 Av main course £8.50 **Restaurant** L served all week 12–2.30 D served all week 6–9.30 Av 3 course à la carte £19 ⊕ Free House ◀ Mordue, Tetley's, Farne Island, Black Sheep & Landlord. 🍷 7 **Facilities** Garden Parking Play Area

Jolly Fisherman Inn

Haven Hill NE66 3TR ☎ 01665 576461
e-mail: muriel@silk8234.fsnet.co.uk
dir: Exit A1 at Denwick, follow Dunstanburgh Castle signs

The first landlord, in 1847, was a fisherman – presumably a jovial fellow. The pub stands right by the water in this tiny fishing village world-renowned for its kippers. The menu is not extensive, but it makes full use of the sea's bounty with home-made kipper paté; crabmeat soup with whisky and cream; and oak-smoked or fresh salmon sandwiches. For something different, try Geordie stottie cake pizza. Nearby Dunstanburgh Castle is worth a visit.

Open 11–3 6.30–11 (Jun-Aug all day) **Bar Meals** L served Mon-Sat 11–2.30 (Sun 12–2.30) ⊕ Punch Taverns ◀ Black Sheep, John Smith's, Speckled Hen. **Facilities** Garden Dogs allowed Parking **Notes** ⊜

EGLINGHAM
MAP 21 NU11

Pick of the Pubs

Tankerville Arms
See Pick of the Pubs on page 417

ETAL
MAP 21 NT9

Black Bull 🍷

TD12 4TL ☎ 01890 820200 📠 07092 367 733
e-mail: blackbulletal@aol.com
dir: 10m N of Wooler right off A697, left at junct for 1m then left into Etal

The Black Bull stands by the ruins of Etal Castle, not far from the River Till, with the grand walking country of the Cheviots on the doorstep. The only thatched pub in Northumberland, it serves traditional pub food such as mince and dumpling with potatoes and vegetables; or home-made steak and ale pie. Lighter options include soup, sandwiches, and toasted teacakes.

Open 11–3.30 5.30–11 (summer all day) Closed: Mon in winter **Bar Meals** L served all week 12–2 D served all week 6–9 (in summer all day) **Restaurant** L served all week 11.30–2.30 D served all week 6–9.30 (in summer all day) ⊕ Pubmaster ◀ Jennings, Deuchers & John Smith Smooth. **Facilities** Children's licence Garden Parking

FALSTONE
MAP 21 NY7

The Blackcock Inn ★★★ INN

NE48 1AA ☎ 01434 240200 📠 01434 240200
e-mail: thebcinn@yahoo.co.uk
dir: Exit A1 junct 43 to Hexham and follow A6079 to Bellingham, brown signs to Kielder & Falstone

Nestled close to Kielder Water, the Blackcock is an ideal base for walking, boating and fishing; it is also handy for the Rievers cycle route. Stone walls, log fires and original beams reflect the 18th-century origins of this traditional family-run free house. The food draws on excellent local produce, with options ranging from light lunchtime snacks through to full evening meals in the intimate Chatto's restaurant. On Sundays, expect a traditional roast and freshly cooked puddings.

Open 12–2 7–11 (Sat-Sun 12–3, Sun 7–10.30) Closed: Tue low season **Bar Meals** L served Wed-Sun 12–2 D served all week 7–8.30 **Restaurant** L served Wed-Sun 12–2 D served all week 7–8.30 ⊕ Free House ◀ John Smiths, Worthington & guest ale. **Facilities** Children's licence Garden Dogs allowed Parking Play Area **Rooms** 6 (4 en suite)

Pick of the Pubs

The Pheasant Inn ★★★★ INN
See Pick of the Pubs on page 418

PICK OF THE PUBS

HEDLEY ON THE HILL-NORTHUMBERLAND

The Feathers Inn

From its hilltop position, this small stone-built free house overlooks the splendid adventure country of the Cheviots. The three-roomed pub is well patronised by the local community, but visitors too are frequently charmed by its friendly and relaxed atmosphere. Families are welcome, and a small side room can be booked in advance if required.

Old oak beams, coal fires, rustic settles, and stone walls decorated with local photographs of rural life make an ideal setting for the appreciation of the bar's four cask ales; there's also a good selection of traditional pub games like shove ha'penny and bar skittles. But the chances are that most people will be here for a plate or two of food. Award-winning chef Rhian Cradock puts on a spectacular menu that changes every day to use the freshest of local ingredients. He goes to great lengths to publicise the provenance, food miles and animal husbandry behind his food. Regional dishes from the North East sit alongside great British classics, some enhanced with a sprinkling of Rhian's favourite Mediterranean flavours from Spain,

Italy and North Africa. Home-made black pudding, wild salmon from the south Tyne, game from local shoots, rare-breed local cattle and Longhorn beef all feature. You'll find old fashioned stews, pies and suet puddings alongside delicious offal preparations and simply grilled fish. Rhian also believes in simply plated but immaculately prepared desserts. A memorable three-course meal could comprise truffled wild mushroom, celeriac and chestnut soup; river trout fillet with crayfish, watercress, crushed heritage potatoes and a chive velouté; and pink rhubarb and preserved ginger parfait with shortbread biscuits. The Northumbrian cheeseboard is another source of pride – it never fails to impress.

MAP 19 NZ05
NE43 7SW
☎ 01661 843607
🖷 01661 843607
e-mail:
marina@thefeathersinn.com
web: www.feathersinn.com
dir: *Telephone for directions*

Open 12–3 6–11 (Sun 12–3, 7–10.30) Closed: 25 Dec
Bar Meals L served Sat-Sun 12–2.30 D served Tue-Sun 7–9
⊕ Free House ◖ Mordue Workie Ticket, Big Lamp Bitter, Fuller's London Pride, Northumberland County.
Facilities Children's licence Parking

GREAT WHITTINGTON MAP 21 NZ07

Pick of the Pubs

Queens Head Inn ♥

NE19 2HP ☎ 01434 672267 📠 01434 672267

dir: *Turn off A69 towards Jedburgh, then N on A68. At rdbt take 3rd exit onto B6318, 1st left signed Great Whittington*

At the heart of Hadrian's Wall country this old pub/restaurant, once a coaching inn, radiates a welcoming atmosphere in comfortable surroundings of beamed rooms, oak settles and open fires. In addition to real ales there are eleven wines by the glass. Menus combine the best of local and European ingredients, without losing touch with the classics. Expect starters like tempura of black pudding with a beetroot and red onion relish and crisp salad. Follow that with a main course such as pork tenderloin on an orange and onion marmalade with black pudding fritters and cider and sage jus. Traditional desserts include old favourites like sticky toffee pudding, bread and butter pudding, and baked vanilla cheesecake.

Open 12–3 5.30–1am (Fri-Sat 12–12, Sun 12–10.30) **Bar Meals** L served Mon-Thu 12–2.30 D served Mon-Thu 6–9 (Fri-Sun 12–9.30) Av main course £12 **Restaurant** L served Mon-Thu 12–2.30 D served Mon-Thu 6–9 (Fri-Sat 12–9.30, Sun 12–9) Av 3 course à la carte £29.50 ⊕ Free House ◀ Farne Island, Auld Hemp & Nels Best. ♥ 11 **Facilities** Garden Parking

---

HALTWHISTLE MAP 21 NY76

Milecastle Inn

Military Rd, Cawfields NE49 9NN ☎ 01434 321372
e-mail: clarehind@aol.com
web: www.milecastle-inn.co.uk
dir: *From A69 into Haltwhistle. Pub approx 2m at junct with B6318*

From the garden of this stone-built rural inn there are good views of Hadrian's Wall. Inside are open fires and, of course, a resident

ghost. Daily specials supplement separate bar and restaurant menus, which offer numerous home-made pies and grills; pheasant in garlic and Madeira; chicken tikka masala; seafood medley; and stilton and vegetable crumble.

Open 12–9 (Nov-Mar 12–3, 6–11) **Bar Meals** L served all week 12–3 D served all week 6–9 (summer all day) **Restaurant** L served all week 12–3 D served all week 6–9 (All day Apr-Nov) ⊕ Free House ◀ Big Lamp, Prince Bishop, Carlsberg-Tetley, Castle Eden. **Facilities** Garden Parking

---

HAYDON BRIDGE MAP 21 NY86

The General Havelock Inn ♥

Ratcliffe Rd NE47 6ER ☎ 01434 684376 📠 01434 684283
e-mail: generalhavelock@aol.com
dir: *On A69, 7m west of Hexham*

General Havelock was a hero of the Indian mutiny, although the inn now bearing his name was built from traditional Northumbrian stone in 1766. You can gaze down to the River Tyne from both the restaurant, housed in a converted barn, and the tranquil south-facing terrace. Locally-sourced ingredients combine in modern yet traditional dishes like terrine of local game with Cumberland sauce; and chicken escalope with a herb crust. Home-made desserts include egg custard tart with nutmeg ice cream.

Open 12–2.30 7–11 Closed: Mon **Bar Meals** L served Tue-Sun 12–2 D served Tue-Sat 7–9 (Sun 12–2, 8–11) **Restaurant** L served Tue-Sun 12–2 D served Tue-Sat 7–9 (Sun 12–2, 8–11) ⊕ Free House ◀ Hesket Newmarket, Wylam Magic, Helvellyn Gold, Matfen Brewery – Neil's Best. ♥ 9 **Facilities** Children's licence Garden Dogs allowed

---

HEDLEY ON THE HILL MAP 19 NZ05

Pick of the Pubs

The Feathers Inn

See Pick of the Pubs on page 421

Hadrian's Wall at Rapishaw Gap, Northumberland

HEXHAM
MAP 21 NY96

Pick of the Pubs

Battlesteads Hotel & Restaurant

Wark NE48 3LS ☎ 01434 230209 📠 01434 230039
e-mail: info@battlesteads.com
dir: *10m N of Hexham on B6320 (Kielder road)*

Built as a farmhouse in 1747, this family-run hotel is close
to Hadrian's Wall and Kielder Forest. There's a cosy fire in
the bar, where four cask ales and bottle-conditioned beers
from neighbourhood micro-breweries are served. A major
refurbishment in 2007 saw the building transformed into a
stylish country inn with an 80-seat restaurant; the light and
airy conservatory leads to a secret walled beer garden. Meals,
snacks and sandwiches are served throughout the day. Freshly
cooked dishes make good use of seasonal game, local lamb,
and Cumbrian beef, while fish comes from the quay at North
Shields. Among the lunchtime options are the Northumbrian
smoked platter comprising cheese, fish and meats from the Bywell
Smokery; and pan-fried locally caught trout. At dinner a smattering
of international choices for the more cosmopolitan palate may
include Moroccan lamb cooked with mint, chillis, coriander and
cumin, and served with fruit couscous.

Open 11–11 Closed: Winter Mon-Fri between 3–6 **Bar Meals** L served
all week 12–3 D served all week 6.30–9.30 **Restaurant** L served all
week 12–3 D served all week 6.30–9.30 ⊕ Free House ◀ Wylam
Gold Tankard, Black Sheep Special, Durham White Velvet, Durham
Magus. **Facilities** Children's licence Garden Dogs allowed Parking
Rooms available

Pick of the Pubs

Dipton Mill Inn ⍟

Dipton Mill Rd NE46 1YA ☎ 01434 606577
e-mail: ghb@hexhamshire.co.uk
dir: *2m S of Hexham on HGV route to Blanchland, B6306,
Dipton Mill Rd*

The millstream runs right through the gardens of this
quintessentially English country pub, once part of a farm. The
rugged local countryside around Hadrian's Wall is something of a
walker's dream, and there is an assortment of other Roman sites
in the area to explore. Alternatively, you could play golf nearby
or enjoy an afternoon at Hexham races just down the road.
The Dipton Mill is the home of the Hexhamshire Brewery ales,
including Devil's Water and Old Humbug. Food is served evenings

and lunchtimes with all dishes being freshly prepared and using
local produce where possible. Perhaps sample haddock baked
with tomato and basil; steak and kidney pie; dressed crab salad; or
chicken in a sherry sauce. To follow, try syrup sponge and custard
– perfect after a day of bracing Northumberland winds.

Open 12–2.30 6–11 (Sun 12–3) Closed: 25 Dec **Bar Meals** L served
all week 12–2 D served Mon-Sat 6.30–8.30 Av main course £7.50
⊕ Free House ◀ Hexhamshire Shire Bitter, Old Humbug, Devil's
Water, Devil's Elbow & Whapweasel. ⍟ 17 **Facilities** Children's licence
Garden **Notes** ⊛

Miners Arms Inn

Main St, Acomb NE46 4PW ☎ 01434 603909
dir: *17m W of Newcastle on A69, 2m W of Hexham.*

Close to Hadrian's Wall in peaceful surroundings, this welcoming
village pub with open hearth fire dates from 1746. Pride is taken in
the range and quality of the ales and in the good home-cooked food,
but note that weekday opening time is 5pm and no food is served on
Monday evenings. Sunday lunches are especially popular, when North
Acomb beef or lamb roasts are accompanied by home-made Yorkshire
puddings, roast potatoes and a selection of vegetables. Pleasant beer
garden, families welcome.

Open 5–11 (Etr, Sum, Xmas Hols 12–11) **Bar Meals** L served Sat-Sun
12–2.30 D served Tue-Sat 6–8.30 **Restaurant** L served Sat-Sun & Holidays
12–2.30 D served Tue-Sat 6–8.30 ⊕ Free House ◀ Black Sheep Bitter,
Yates, Durham White Velvet, Boddingtons. **Facilities** Children's licence
Garden Dogs allowed **Notes** ⊛

Rat Inn NEW ⍟

NE46 4LN ☎ 01434 602814
e-mail: info@theratinn.co.uk
dir: *2m from Hexham, Bridge End (A69) rdbt, take 4th exit signed
Oakwood. Inn 500yds on right*

Set in the picturesque hamlet of Anick, The Rat has spectacular views
across Hexham and the Tyne Valley. A classic country pub with a
stunning summer garden and log fires in winter, it offers a classy
selection of traditional food cooked to order using local ingredients.
Examples include pigeon and black pudding salad followed by herb-
crusted rack of lamb with courgettes provençale and dauphinoise
potatoes. Excellent real ales.

Open 12–3 6–11 (Sat-Sun 12–11) **Bar Meals** L served Tue-Sat 12–2
D served Tue-Sat 6–9 (Sun 12–3) Av main course £10 **Restaurant** L served
Tue-Sat 12–2 D served Tue-Sat 6–9 (Sun 12–3) Av 3 course à la carte
£20 ⊕ Free House ◀ John Smiths, Guinness, Bass & Deuchars. ⍟ 8
Facilities Children's licence Garden Parking

LONGFRAMLINGTON
MAP 21 NU10

Pick of the Pubs

The Anglers Arms

See Pick of the Pubs on opposite page

PICK OF THE PUBS

The Anglers Arms

Deep in rural Northumberland, this former coaching inn dates from the 1760s, since when it has commanded the picturesque Weldon Bridge over the River Coquet. The interior reveals an abundance of bric-a-brac, antiques and fishing memorabilia, as well as attractive hand-painted wall tiles.

A carefully tended half-acre of garden contains a children's play park and plenty of general space to eat and drink. Bar meals, such as Whitby wholetail scampi, Northumbrian sausage casserole, and oriental sizzling platter are popular, but for more style and a different set of options you may dine in the main restaurant or even in the somewhat unusual surroundings of a converted railway carriage. In both you'll find starters such as scallop and bacon salad; black pudding with mashed potato, poached egg and cheese sauce; and smoked chicken and wild mushroom tartlet. Main courses include pork tenderloin wrapped in Parma ham with bubble and squeak and cognac sauce; cod and crab fishcakes with asparagus and tenderstem broccoli; roast halibut with king prawns and Greenland mussels in white wine sauce; and warm tomato and feta quiche with red onion chutney. Turn to the blackboard for daily changing desserts and selections of Continental and English cheeses, including one with nettles and herbs made locally at Otterburn. Sandwiches include baked ham, and brie and beef tomato, while duck and orange is a possibility from the list of salads. The Anglers is a good base for walking in the Cheviot Hills and visiting Northumberland's famous castles.

MAP 21 NU10
Weldon Bridge NE65 8AX
☎ 01665 570271 & 570655
📠 01665 570041
e-mail: johnyoung@
anglersarms.fsnet.co.uk
dir: *From N, 9m S of Alnwick
right Weldon Bridge sign. From S,
A1 to by-pass Morpeth, left onto
A697 for Wooler & Coldstream.
7m, left to Weldon Bridge*

Open 11–11 (Sun 12–11)
Bar Meals L served Mon-Sat
12–9.30 D served Mon-Sat
12–9.30 (Sun 12–9)
Restaurant L served all week
12–2 D served all week 7–9
⊕ Free House ◀ Worthington,
Boddingtons & 3 guest ales.
Facilities Children's licence
Garden Dogs allowed Parking
Play Area

PICK OF THE PUBS

NEWTON-ON-THE-MOOR-NORTHUMBERLAND

The Cook and Barker Inn

From its elevated position in the picturesque village of Newton-on-the-Moor, this traditional inn commands outstanding views of the Cheviot Hills and the Northumbrian coast. Not long ago the inn's owner purchased a 400–acre farm, which is in the process of converting to organic methodologies.

The aim is to furnish food from the farm directly to customers' plates in the Cook and Barker's restaurant. Not surprisingly, dedication such as this produces accomplished dishes of notable quality on the bar and lounge daily menu, where starters may include crab and prawn risotto with spinach and parmesan; goats' cheese tart with beetroot; and chargrilled sardines with hoi sin sauce. Main dishes vary from savoury minced beef and dumplings to grilled gammon steak with free-range egg and roasted tomato. Seafood alternatives could comprise grilled lobster and prawn salad with buttered new potatoes; seared tuna loin with pepper, fresh lime and niçoise salad; or hot and cold seafood platter. The à la carte is sub-divided to help meet the demands of different appetites and varying tastes of the inn's patrons. Appetisers, for example, range from slow-cooked crispy belly pork with seared West Coast scallops and a sweet sesame and chilli dressing; to oak-smoked salmon parcel filled with prawns, crab and bacon. 'Forest and fields' is where to find the likes of prime Northumbrian T-bone steaks, or pan-fried pheasant with creamed cabbage, bacon and a wild mushroom jus. And the fish selection 'Fresh from the sea' continues with the likes of pan-fried lemon sole with baby capers; and roast fillet of sea bass with grilled Mediterranean vegetables, pesto and balsamic dressing.

★★★★ INN ☻
MAP 21 NU10
NE65 9JY
☎ 01665 575234
🖷 01665 575887
dir: *0.5m from A1 S of Alnwick*

Open 11–3 6–11
Bar Meals L served all week
12–6 D served all week 6–9 Av
main course £8
Restaurant L served all week
12–2 D served all week 7–9 Av 3
course à la carte £25 Av 3 course
fixed price £25
⊕ Free House ◀ Timothy Taylor
Landlord, Theakstons Best Bitter,
Fuller's London Pride, Batemans
XXXB. ☻ 12
Facilities Garden Parking
Rooms 19

PICK OF THE PUBS

SEAHOUSES-NORTHUMBERLAND

The Olde Ship Hotel

Set above the tiny bustling harbour, the Olde Ship is a fully residential hotel with a long established reputation for good food and drink in comfortable, relaxing and old fashioned surroundings.

The former farmhouse dates from 1745 and has been in the present owner's family for over 90 years. As a farmhouse it owes its unusual location to the grain export business of earlier times, but since 1812 it has proved to be the perfect place for a pub. On the right sort of day you can enjoy a pint of Black Sheep in the garden while watching the local fishing boats bob up and down below. The interior is nautically themed and the main saloon bar is full of character, packed with memorabilia and lit by stained glass windows and the welcoming glow of the open fire. Next to this is the low, beamed Cabin Bar, with wooden floor made of pine ships' decking. The hotel's corridors and boat gallery also display treasure troves of antique nautical artefacts

and seafaring mementos, such as diving helmets, oars, fish baskets, branding irons, lamps and the nameplate from the 'Forfarshire' of Grace Darling fame. Popular bar foods include locally caught seafood, freshly made sandwiches and home-made crab or vegetable soup. Main courses take in bosun's fish stew, gamekeeper's casserole and vegetable lasagne, followed by golden sponge; chocolate pear crumble; and apricot brioche tart with mascarpone cheese and apricots. Bedrooms are neat and well appointed, and some have views over to the bird and seal sanctuary on the Farne Islands. Boats will take you there from the nearby pier.

★★ SHL ♟
MAP 21 NU23
9 Main St NE68 7RD
☎ 01665 720200
🖷 01665 721383
e-mail:
theoldeship@seahouses.co.uk
dir: *Lower end of main street above harbour*

Open 11–11 (Sun 12–11)
Bar Meals L served all week
12–2 D served all week 7–8.30
Restaurant L served Sun 12–2
D served all week 7–8.15 (end
Nov-end Jan no dinner)
⊕ Free House ◀ Black Sheep,
Theakstons, Best Scotch, Ruddles.
♟ 10
Facilities Children's licence
Garden Parking
Rooms 18

LONGHORSLEY MAP 21 NZ19

Linden Tree ★★★★ HL 🏵🏵

Linden Hall NE65 8XF ☎ 01670 500033 📄 01670 500001

e-mail: lindenhall@macdonald-hotels.co.uk

dir: *Off A1 on A697, 1m N of Longhorsley*

This popular pub was originally two large cattle byres. It takes its name from the linden trees near Linden Hall, the impressive Georgian mansion (now hotel) in whose grounds it stands. The brasserie-style menu might include a ham and pease pudding sandwich; a traditional Caesar salad; home-made Craster kipper paté with brown bread, butter and lemon; spaghetti carbonara; and (from its Taste of Northumberland selection) home-made steak and suet pudding.

Open 8–11 (Sun 12–10.30) **Bar Meals** L served Mon-Sat 8am-9.30 D served Mon-Sat (Sun 8–9) Av main course £10 **Restaurant** L served Mon-Sat 12–2 D served Mon-Sat 6.45–9.30pm (Sun 12–4, 6–9) ⊕ Free House ◀ Worthington 1744, Greene King IPA **Facilities** Children's licence Garden Parking Play Area **Rooms** 50

LOW NEWTON BY THE SEA MAP 21 NU22

The Ship Inn

The Square NE66 3EL ☎ 01665 576262

e-mail: forsythchristine@hotmail.com

dir: *NE from A1 at Alnwick towards Seahouses*

The beach is only a stroll away from this pretty inn, which overlooks the green. Low Newton was purpose-built as a fishing village in the 18th century and remains wonderfully unspoilt. Bustling in summer and a peaceful retreat in winter, The Ship offers plenty of fresh, locally caught fish and free-range meats. Try kipper paté, followed by Borders' sirloin steak with onion marmalade, with local unpasteurised cheese to finish. The pub now has its own microbrewery.

Open 11–4 6.30–11 (School holidays all day) **Bar Meals** L served Tue-Sat 12–2.30 7–8 Av main course £10 ⊕ Free House ◀ Original Northumberland, Farm Island Local Brewery, guest ales. **Facilities** Garden Dogs allowed **Notes** 😊

NETHERTON MAP 21 NT90

The Star Inn

NE65 7HD ☎ 01669 630238

dir: *7m from Rothbury*

Owned by the same family since 1917, this pub has also been in every edition of the CAMRA real ale guide. No food is served, but cask ales in the peak of condition are the speciality.

Open 7.30–10.30 (Fri 7.30–11) Closed: Mon & Thu ⊕ Free House ◀ Castle Eden Ale. **Facilities** Parking **Notes** 😊

NEWTON-ON-THE-MOOR MAP 21 NU10

Pick of the Pubs

The Cook and Barker Inn ★★★★ INN ♥

See Pick of the Pubs on page 426

ROWFOOT MAP 21 NY6

The Wallace Arms

NE49 0JF ☎ 01434 321872 📄 01434 321872

e-mail: www.thewallacearms@btconnect.com

dir: *Telephone for directions*

The pub was rebuilt in 1850 as the Railway Hotel at Featherstone Park station, when the now long-closed Haltwhistle-Alston line (today's South Tyne Trail) was engineered. It changed to the Wallace Arms in 1885. Sample menu includes modestly-priced haddock fillet in beer batter, salmon fillet in lemon and tarragon sauce, steak and ale pie, grilled sirloin steak, and smoked haddock and prawn pasta. There are light snacks, burgers and sandwiches, if you prefer.

Open 11–3 4–12 (Opening times vary, ring for details) **Bar Meals** L served all week 12–2.30 D served all week 6–9 **Restaurant** L served all week 12–2.30 D served all week 6–9 ⊕ Free Hous ◀ Hook Norton Old Hooky, Young's Special, Greene King IPA, Greene King Abbot Ale. **Facilities** Garden Parking **Rooms** available

SEAHOUSES MAP 21 NU2

Pick of the Pubs

The Olde Ship Hotel ★★ SHL ♥

See Pick of the Pubs on page 427

WARDEN MAP 21 NY9

The Boatside Inn ♥

NE46 4SQ ☎ 01434 602233

e-mail: sales@theboatsideinn.com

web: www.theboatsideinn.com

dir: *Off A69 W of Hexham, follow signs to Warden Newborough & Fourstones*

Attractive stone-built inn situated where the North and South Tyne rivers meet, beneath Warden Hill Iron Age fort. The name refers to the rowing boat that ferried people across the river before the bridge was built. It is a popular destination for walkers, promising real ale and good food cooked from local produce. Dishes include seafood stew, battered haddock, and slow roast lamb shoulder. There is also a garden with a lawn area and barbecue.

Open 11–11 **Bar Meals** L served Mon-Sat 12–2 D served Mon-Sat 6.30–9 (Sun 12–9) **Restaurant** L served all week 12–2 D served all week 6.30–9 (Sun 12–9) ⊕ Free House ◀ Black Sheep, John Smiths, Mordue & Wylan ♥ 15 **Facilities** Children's licence Garden Dogs allowed Parking

PICK OF THE PUBS

WHALTON-NORTHUMBERLAND

Beresford Arms

*he landlords at this ivy-covered coaching inn have worked hard to maintain the feel of a
roper' country pub, while at the same time ensuring it conveys a modern feel.*

lies in the picturesque village
f Wharton, popular with cyclists
nd walkers enjoying the delights
f nearby Kielder Forest and
Jorthumberland National Park.
et opposite the village hall, it also
rovides a welcome focus for village
fe. Start a meal with home-made
oup, or prawn and avocado salad
vith Marie Rose sauce; follow with
rilled Wallington Hall rib-eye steak
vith tomato, mushrooms, onion
ngs and chips; or one of Stevie's
Vonders, such as grilled fillet of
ea bass on spiced couscous with
n oriental sauce; and finish with
 crumble, or something that's
ound to involve fresh berries,
hipped cream or chocolate sauce.
Doorstop' sandwiches are served
 lunchtime. 'Elves, leprechauns
nd kids under 4ft 9ins' can opt

for chicken or crispy fish goujons,
beefburger or sausages.

MAP 21 NZ18
NE61 3UZ
☎ 01670 775225
🖷 01670 775351
e-mail: beresford.arms@
btconnect.com
dir: *5m from Morpeth town
centre on B6524*

Open 11–3 5.30–11 (May-Sep
all day)
Bar Meals L served all week
12–2 D served Mon-Sat 6–9 (Sun
12–5) Av main course £11
Restaurant L served Sun 12–3
D served Fri-Sat 6–9 Av 3 course à
la carte £25
⊕ Enterprise Inns ◀ Black
Sheep, Timothy Taylor Landlord,
John Smiths.
Facilities Garden Parking

WARENFORD   MAP 21 NU12

Pick of the Pubs

The White Swan ♀

NE70 7HY ☎ 01668 213453 📠 01668 213453

dir: *100yds E of A1, 10m N of Alnwick*

This 200–year-old coaching inn stands near the original toll
bridge over the Waren Burn. Formerly on the Great North Road,
the building is now just a stone's throw from the A1. Inside,
you'll find thick stone walls and an open fire for colder days;
in summer, there's a small sheltered seating area, with further
seats in the adjacent field. The Dukes of Northumberland once
owned the pub, and its windows and plasterwork still bear the
family crests. Visitors and locals alike enjoy the atmosphere and
award-winning Northumbrian dishes: try Seahouses kippers with
creamy horseradish sauce; venison pudding with lemon suet
crust and fresh vegetables; or roast pork hock with wine and
herbs. Vegetarians are well catered for, with interesting dishes
like beetroot and potato gratin; artichoke and leek pancakes; and
celeriac pan Haggarty with fresh tomato sauce.

Open 12–2 7–11 (Sun 7–10) **Bar Meals** L served Sun 12–2 D served
Tue-Sun 7–9 Av main course £8.50 **Restaurant** L served Sun 12–1.30
7–9.30 (Sun 12–4) Av 3 course à la carte £16.50 ⊕ Free House
🍺 John Smith's. ♀ 8 **Facilities** Garden Parking

WHALTON   MAP 21 NZ18

Pick of the Pubs

Beresford Arms

See Pick of the Pubs on page 429

NOTTINGHAMSHIRE

BEESTON   MAP 11 SK53

Victoria Hotel ♀

Dovecote Ln NG9 1JG ☎ 0115 925 4049 📠 0115 922 3537
e-mail: hopco.victoriabeeston@virgin.net

dir: *M1 junct 25, A52 E. right at Nurseryman PH, right opp
Rockaway Hotel into Barton St 1st left*

The Victoria dates from 1899 when it was built next to Beeston Railway
Station, and the large, heated patio garden is still handy for a touch of
train-spotting. It offers an excellent range of traditional ales, continental
beers and lagers, farm ciders, a good choice of wines by the glass and
single malt whiskies. Dishes on the menu you may find Lincolnshire
sausages, and smoked chicken and bacon pasta. Half the menu is
meat-free or vegan.

Open 11–11 (Sun 12–11) Closed: 26 Dec **Bar Meals** L served Mon-Sat
12–8.45 D served Mon-Sat (Sun 12–7.45) **Restaurant** L served Mon-Sat
D served Mon-Sat 12–8.45 (Sun 12–7.45) ⊕ Free House 🍺 Batemans XB,
Castle Rock Harvest Pale, Castle Rock Hemlock, Everards Tiger & 6 guest
ales. ♀ 30 **Facilities** Garden Dogs allowed Parking

BINGHAM   MAP 11 SK7

The Chesterfield ♀

Church St NG13 8AL ☎ 01949 837342
e-mail: eat@thechesterfield.co.uk

dir: *6m E of Nottingham, Bingham off A52 & A46 junct. Pub just
off market square*

One of the earliest buildings in the centre of this small market town,
the Chesterfield has recently been refurbished in contemporary style.
The pub now features a stylish bar and gastro-style restaurant, as well
as a private dining room and garden. Lunchtime brings snacks and
sandwiches, plus a traditional Sunday roast. Typical restaurant choices
include rack of lamb with apricots and cheese; seared fresh salmon
salad; and grilled haloumi with cous cous and curry sauce.

Open 12–11 (Sat-Sun 12–12) **Bar Meals** L served Mon-Sat 12–2.30
D served all week 5–10 **Restaurant** L served all week 12–2.30 D served
all week 5–10 Av 3 course à la carte £20 Av 2 course fixed price £12
🍺 Timothy Taylor Landlord, Marston Pedigree, Wells Bombardier, Shepher
Neame Spitfire & Fuller's London Pride. ♀ 12 **Facilities** Garden Parking

BLIDWORTH   MAP 16 SK5

Fox & Hounds ♀

Blidworth Bottoms NG21 0NW ☎ 01623 792383
e-mail: info@foxandhounds-pub.com

dir: *Right off B6020 between Ravenshead & Blidworth*

A traditional country pub, extensively refurbished a few years ago
to create attractive surroundings in which to eat and drink. It was
probably built as a farmhouse in the 19th century, when Blidworth
Bottoms was a thriving community, with shops and a post office. A
reputation for good pub food comes from dishes such as steak and a
pie; Mediterranean chicken; blackened salmon in Cajun spices; home
made vegetarian cottage pie; and hot chilli con carne.

Open 11.30–12 **Bar Meals** L served all week D served all week Av main
course £7.95 **Restaurant** L served all week D served all week ⊕ Greene
King 🍺 H&H Cask Bitter, Olde Speckled Hen, Olde Trip H&H. ♀ 9
Facilities Children's licence Garden Dogs allowed Parking Play Area

England

CAUNTON   MAP 17 SK76

Pick of the Pubs

Caunton Beck ♀

NG23 6AB ☎ 01636 636793 🖨 01636 636828

e-mail: email@cauntonbeck.com

dir: *6m NW of Newark on A616*

No ordinary free house, this reassuringly civilised village pub-restaurant opens daily for breakfast and carries on serving food until around midnight, just like its sister, the Wig & Mitre in Lincoln. It is built around a beautifully restored 16th-century cottage with herb gardens and a colourful rose arbour. Real ales complement a worthy international wine list, including a wide choice by the glass. The main menu, served throughout, offers dishes such as carved breast of Gressingham duck with glazed fig tartlet and an orange reduction; and pan-fried red mullet with wilted bok choi and egg noodles, plus suggestions for accompanying wines. In addition to breakfast and snack menus, blackboard specials include pan-seared calves' liver with red onion and sage marmalade and crisp parma ham; and roast fillet of Scottish salmon with celeriac and caper rémoulade. Lemongrass and lime iced parfait, and warm treacle tart with toffee anglaise are popular desserts.

Open 8–12 **Bar Meals** L served all week 8–10 D served all week 8–10 Av main course £13.95 **Restaurant** L served all week 8–10 D served all week 8–10 Av 3 course à la carte £26.25 Av 3 course fixed price £13.95 ⊕ Free House ◀ Batemans Valiant, Marstons Pedigree, Tom Woods Best Bitter. ♀ 34 **Facilities** Garden Dogs allowed Parking

CAYTHORPE   MAP 11 SK64

Black Horse Inn

NG14 7ED ☎ 0115 966 3520

dir: *12m from Nottingham off road to Southwell (A612)*

Three generations of the same family have run this small, beamed country pub where old-fashioned hospitality is guaranteed. It has its own small brewery, producing Caythorpe Dover Beck bitter, a coal fire in the bar, and delicious home-cooked food prepared from seasonal ingredients. Fresh fish is a speciality; other choices might include Chinese dim sum; king prawns in garlic and cream sauce; fillet steak; and omelettes with various fillings. Good local walks.

Open 12–3 5.30–11 (Sat 6–11, Sun 8–10.30) Closed: Mon lunch (ex BHs) **Bar Meals** L served Tue-Sat 12–1.45 D served Tue-Thu 7–8.30 Av main course £8.50 **Restaurant** L served Tue-Sat 12–1.45 D served Tue-Thu 7–8.30 Av 3 course à la carte £25 ⊕ Free House ◀ Greene King Abbot Ale, Black Sheep, Dover Beck Bitter,. **Facilities** Garden Dogs allowed Parking **Notes** ⊜

COLSTON BASSETT   MAP 11 SK73

Pick of the Pubs

The Martins Arms Inn ♀

School Ln NG12 3FD ☎ 01949 81361 🖨 01949 81039

dir: *Off A46 between Leicester & Newark*

This award-winning 18th-century inn stands right at the heart of the village, next to a market cross that dates back to 1257. The listed building has a real country house feel to it, with period furnishings, traditional hunting prints and winter fires in the Jacobean fireplace. An impressive range of real ales, including Black Sheep Best and Timothy Taylor Landlord, is served. Regional ingredients are a feature of dishes like braised lamb shank with parsnip mash; beer-battered fish and chips; honey roast cannon of pork with braised cabbage and black pudding fritter; and game pie with roasted new potatoes. From the specials menu come pan-fried pheasant breast with wild mushrooms and a red wine sauce, and there are scrumptious desserts like banana and toffee bread and butter pudding with banana compote. For a quick snack try ciabatta sandwiches filled with roasted vegetables and four cheese perhaps, or sausage and red onion marmalade.

Open 12–3 6–11 (Sun 7–10.30) Closed: 25 Dec eve **Bar Meals** L served all week 12–2 D served Mon-Sat 6–10 Av main course £12.50 **Restaurant** L served all week 12–2 D served Mon-Sat 6–9 Av 3 course à la carte £25 ⊕ Free House ◀ Marston's Pedigree, Interbrew Bass, Greene King Abbot Ale, Timothy Taylor Landlord. ♀ 7 **Facilities** Garden Dogs allowed Parking

ELKESLEY   MAP 17 SK67

Robin Hood Inn ♀

High St DN22 8AJ ☎ 01777 838259

e-mail: a1robinhood@aol.com

dir: *5m SE of Worksop off A1 towards Newark-on-Trent*

Parts of this unassuming village inn date back to the 14th century. Ceilings and floors are deep red, while the green walls are adorned with pictures of food. The comprehensive choice is served in both the bar and restaurant, and includes a fixed price menu, carte and daily specials board. Devilled kidneys with baked mushrooms followed by roast breast of corn-fed chicken with spinach and sweet peppers will satisfy the heartiest of appetites.

Open 11.30–3 6–11 Closed: Sun eve & Mon lunch **Bar Meals** L served Tue-Sun 12–2 D served Mon-Sat 6–9 **Restaurant** L served Tue-Sun 12–2 D served Mon-Sat 6.30–9 Av 3 course à la carte £20 Av 2 course fixed price £11.50 ⊕ Enterprise Inns ◀ John Smiths Extra Smooth & guest ale. ♀ 8 **Facilities** Garden Parking Play Area

HALAM
MAP 17 SK65

The Waggon and Horses ♀

The Turnpike, Mansfield Rd NG22 8AE

☎ 01636 813109 🖹 01636 816228

e-mail: info@thewaggonathalam.co.uk

dir: *from A614 at White Post Farm rdbt follow signs to Farnsfield. In Halam, pub on right*

Set in the heart of a small village, The Waggon and Horses is a hub for local activities. Its home-cooked food also draws visitors from further afield. The ever-changing blackboard menus might include starters of warm scallop and bacon salad or ham hock terrine with date and apple chutney, followed by slow-cooked lamb with carrot and swede mash; or pan-fried pheasant with leeks and bacon. Special dietary requirements can be accommodated.

Open 11.30–3 5.30–11 (Sun 11.30–4) Closed: 25–26 Dec
Bar Meals L served all week 12–2.15 D served Mon-Sat 6–9.15
Restaurant L served all week 12–2.15 D served Mon-Sat 6–9.15
◀ Thwaites Bomber, Thwaites Original, Warsteiner, Thwaites Smooth. ♀ 8
Facilities Garden Parking

HARBY
MAP 17 SK87

Bottle & Glass NEW ♀

High St NG23 7EB ☎ 01522 703438 🖹 01522 703436

e-mail: email@bottleandglassharby.com

dir: *S of A57 (Lincoln to Markham Moor road)*

This tastefully modernised hotel is conveniently located between the town centre and the seafront, and has lively bars that transform Thursday to Sunday nights with their carnival atmosphere. Public areas are smartly presented and include the stylish Bazil Brasserie.

Open 9am-11 **Bar Meals** L served all week 9am-10 D served all week 9am-10 Av main course £12.95 **Restaurant** L served all week 9am-10 D served all week 9am-10 Av 3 course à la carte £23.50 Av 3 course fixed price £13.95 ⊕ Free House ◀ Youngs Bitter, Farmers Blonde & Black Sheep. ♀ 34 **Facilities** Garden Dogs allowed Parking

KIMBERLEY
MAP 11 SK44

The Nelson & Railway Inn

12 Station Rd NG16 2NR

☎ 0115 938 2177 🖹 0115 938 2179

dir: *1m N of M1 junct 26*

The landlord of more than 30 years gives this 17th-century pub its distinctive personality. Next door is the Hardy & Hanson brewery that supplies many of the beers, but the two nearby railway stations that once made it a railway inn are now sadly derelict. A hearty menu of pub favourites includes soup, ploughman's, and hot rolls, as well as grills and hot dishes like home-made steak and kidney pie; gammon steak; and mushroom stroganoff.

Open 11–12 (Sun 12–11) **Bar Meals** L served Mon-Fri 12–2.30 D served Mon-Fri 5.30–9 (Sat 12–9, Sun 12–6) **Restaurant** L served Mon-Fri 12–2.30 D served Mon-Fri 5.30–9 (Sat 12–9, Sun 12–6) ⊕ Hardy & Hansons ◀ Hardys, Hansons Best Bitter, Cool & Dark, Olde Trip. **Facilities** Children's licence Garden Dogs allowed Parking **Rooms** available

LAXTON
MAP 17 SK76

The Dovecote Inn ♀

Moorhouse Rd NG22 0SX ☎ 01777 871586

e-mail: dovecote-inn@btconnect.com

dir: *Exit A1 at Tuxford through Egmanton to Laxton*

Like most of the village of Laxton, this family-run, 18th-century pub is Crown Estate property belonging to the Royal Family. Outside is a delightful beer garden with views of the church. The interior includes a bar and three cosy wining and dining rooms. Here the seasonal, home-cooked dishes could include game pie or 21–day matured steak followed by Auntie Mary's ever-popular desserts, which she has been producing for the Dovecote for over 14 years.

Open 11.30–3 6.30–11.30 (Fri-Sat 6–11.30) **Bar Meals** L served Mon-Sat 12–2 D served Mon-Sat 6.30–9 (Sun 12.30–6.30) Av main course £10 **Restaurant** L served Mon-Sat 12–2 D served Mon-Sat 6.30–9 (Sun 12.30–6.30) ⊕ Free House ◀ Mansfield Smooth, Banks Smooth, Marston's Pedigree, Bombardier & Black Sheep. ♀ 10 **Facilities** Garden Dogs allowed Parking

MORTON
MAP 17 SK75

Pick of the Pubs

The Full Moon Inn ♀

See Pick of the Pubs on opposite page

NOTTINGHAM
MAP 11 SK53

Cock & Hoop ♀

25 High Pavement NG1 1HE

☎ 0115 852 3231 🖹 0115 852 3236

e-mail: drink@cockandhoop.co.uk

web: www.cockandhoop.co.uk

dir: *Follow tourist signs for 'Galleries of Justice'. Pub opposite.*

Tasteful antiques, a real fire, a cellar bar and some striking bespoke artwork characterize this traditional Victorian alehouse. It stands opposite the Galleries of Justice, where Lord Byron is said to have watched hangings from his lodgings above the pub.

Open 12–1am Closed: 25–26 Dec **Bar Meals** L served all week 12–10 D served all week Av main course £15 ⊕ Free House ◀ Deuchars IPA, Cock & Hoop, London Pride, Timothy Taylors Landlord. ♀ 7
Facilities Children's licence Dogs allowed

PICK OF THE PUBS

MORTON-NOTTINGHAMSHIRE

The Full Moon Inn

Tucked away in the remote hamlet of Morton, on the outskirts of the minster town of Southwell, The Full Moon is five minutes' walk from the River Trent. This makes it a popular destination for cyclists and ramblers, especially in summer when the pub garden comes into its own.

It's a traditional country inn boasting hundreds of years of history – old photographs show previous landlords, and one of the original pub signs is still in place; two log fires in the bar emphasize the warm and welcoming atmosphere. After being taken over by William and Rebecca White in 2007, today's choice of real ales bears witness to the fact that Will takes the Full Moon's freehouse status very seriously. With handles bearing the names of Black Sheep, Bombardier and Woodforde's Wherry (to name only three), this is a true beer drinker's haven. Wines too are interesting and fairly priced, with eight served by the glass. Rebecca is in charge of the kitchen, where the emphasis is on farm fresh food sourced locally when possible; facts sheets on Rebecca's

suppliers are in preparation. Traditional English dishes may include shepherd's pie with cauliflower cheese and fresh mint sauce, and bangers and mash. From the specials board expect aromatic duck pancakes; wild venison with beetroot and squeak; and slow-roasted shoulder of lamb. Fish is a strength too, but you'll need to look to the specials board. The reason is simple: Will and Rebecca rely on their fishmonger to choose their fish for them, to ensure they receive the best the market has to offer; they don't put it on the specials board until it's been delivered. There's plenty here to keep children occupied too, and dogs are also welcome. There is a designated indoor play area, an outdoor castle and a sand pit.

� MAP 17 SK75
Main St NG25 0UT
☎ 01636 830251
🖷 01636 830554
e-mail: info@
thefullmoonmorton.co.uk
dir: *Newark A617 to Mansfield. Past Kelham, turn left to Rolleston & follow signs to Morton*

Open 10–3 6–11 (Sun 12–3)
Bar Meals L served Mon-Sat 12–2.30 D served Mon-Sat 6–9.30 (Sun 12–3, 6–9) Av main course £12
Restaurant L served Mon-Sat 12–2.30 D served Mon-Sat 6–9.30 (Sun 12–3, 6–9) Av 3 course à la carte £25 Av 3 course fixed price £15
⊕ Free House ◀ Ruddles Best, Bombardier, Dover Beck, guest ales. � 8
Facilities Children's licence Garden Dogs allowed Parking Play Area

England

NOTTINGHAM continued

Fellows Morton & Clayton

54 Canal St NG1 7EH ☎ 0115 950 6795 📄 0115 953 9838

e-mail: info@fellowsmortonandclayton.co.uk

dir: *Telephone for directions*

Surrounded by the impressive Castle Wharf complex, with a cobbled courtyard overlooking the Nottingham canal, 'Fellows' was converted from a former warehouse in 1979. The pub, which has been under the same tenancy since 1990, is a regular Nottingham in Bloom award winner. The varied menu includes chargrilled chicken and bacon salad; spicy bean burger on toasted ciabatta; and Spanish haddock with smoked salmon and seafood. Sandwiches and lighter lunches too.

Open 11–11 (Fri-Sat 11–12) **Bar Meals** L served Mon-Sat 11–9 D served Mon-Sat 11–9 (Sun 12–6) **Restaurant** L served Mon-Sat 11.30–2.30 (Sun 12–6) ⊞ Enterprise Inns ◀ Timothy Taylor Landlord, Fuller's London Pride, Nottingham EPA, Deuchars IPA. **Facilities** Garden Parking

Ye Olde Trip to Jerusalem ♀

1 Brewhouse Yard, Castle Rd NG1 6AD

☎ 0115 947 3171 📄 0115 950 1185

e-mail: 4925@greeneking.co.uk

dir: *In town centre*

Said to be Britain's oldest inn, the Trip is surely one of the most unusual. Parts of the building penetrate deep into the sandstone of Castle Rock, and customers are warned to look out for uneven steps, floors and low doorways. It also would be wise to avoid cleaning the Cursed Galleon. The menu caters for most tastes, ranging from burgers, wraps and jacket potatoes to main course dishes like stilton and vegetable crumble; smoked haddock fish pot; and hickory barbecue chicken.

Open 10.30–12 (Sun-Thu 10.30–11) **Bar Meals** L served Mon-Fri 12–8 (Sat-Sun 12–6) ⊞ Greene King ◀ Ye Olde Trip Ale, guest ales, Greene King IPA, Abbot Ale. ♀ 11 **Facilities** Children's licence Garden

RUDDINGTON   MAP 11 SK53

Three Crowns ♀

23 Easthorpe St NG11 6LB ☎ 0115 921 3226

e-mail: simon@nottinghamthai.co.uk

dir: *A60 towards Loughborough. Right at 1st lights into Ruddington Village, right & right again, pub 500yds on left*

A modern pub with an authentic Thai restaurant next door, where traditionally attired waitresses from the Land of Smiles glide between the tables. Lunchtime pub snacks include baguettes, omelettes, burgers, traditional pies and Thai stir-fries. The restaurant serves pork, chicken, beef, duck, fish and seafood curries of various strengths, and other Thai dishes, as well as steaks. Traditional roasts and other non-Thai meals are served on Sundays.

Open 12–3 5–11 (Sat-Sun all day) **Bar Meals** L served Tue-Sat 12–2 D served Tue-Sat 6.30–10 Av main course £13 **Restaurant** D served Tue-Sat 6.30–10 Av 3 course à la carte £25 Av 3 course fixed price £20 ⊞ Free House ◀ Adnams, Nottingham Brewery, Timothy Taylor Landlord, Cottage Brewery. ♀ 18 **Facilities** Dogs allowed

THURGARTON   MAP 17 SK64

The Red Lion ♀

Southwell Rd NG14 7GP ☎ 01636 830351

dir: *On A612 between Nottingham & Southwell*

This 16th-century inn was once a monks' alehouse. Pub food can be enjoyed in the bar, restaurant or garden. Main courses include beef and Guinness casserole, chicken breast in garlic and mushroom sauce, or a variety of steaks. For a lighter option, try a salad with roast ham or poached salmon and prawn; or the cheese platter with local blue stilton. Look out for the 1936 newspaper cutting reporting the murder of a previous landlady by her niece!

Open 11.30–2.30 6.30–11 (Sat-Sun & BHs all day) **Bar Meals** L served Mon-Fri 12–2 D served Mon-Thu 6.30–9 (Fri 6.30–9.30, Sat-Sun 12–9.30) Av main course £7.95 **Restaurant** L served Mon-Fri 12–2 D served Mon-Thu 6.30–9 (Fri 6.30–9.30, Sat-Sun 12–9.30) Av 3 course à la carte £14 ⊞ Free House ◀ Greene King Abbot Ale, Jennings Cumberland, Carlsberg-Tetley, Black Sheep & Mansfield Cask. ♀ 7 **Facilities** Garden Parking

TUXFORD   MAP 17 SK77

The Mussel & Crab ♀

NG22 0PJ ☎ 01777 870491 📄 01777 872302

e-mail: musselandcrab1@hotmail.com

dir: *From Ollerton/Tuxford junct of A1& A57. N on B1164 to Sibthorpe Hill. Pub 800yds on right*

Fish and seafood dominate the menu at this quirky pub with a fabulous curved zinc bar and a multitude of eating areas. You can play liar dice, admire the fish in the gents' toilets, and sit on large carved wooden hands in the bar. Up to 22 blackboards offer constantly changing dishes featuring snapper, sole, sea bass, crab, lobster, locally shot wild pigeon breast, and cheese soufflé and much more.

Open 11–2.30 6–11 **Bar Meals** L served Mon-Sat 11.30–2.30 D served Mon-Sat 6–10 (Sun 11.30–2.45, 6–9) **Restaurant** L served Mon-Sat 12–2.30 D served Mon-Sat 6–10 (Sun 12–2.45, 6–9) Av 3 course à la carte £25 ⊞ Free House ◀ Tetley Smooth, Tetley Cask, Guinness. ♀ 16 **Facilities** Garden Dogs allowed Parking

England

OXFORDSHIRE

ABINGDON · · · · · · · · · · · · MAP 05 SU49

The Merry Miller ♥

Cothill OX13 6JW ☎ 01865 390390 ▤ 01865 390040

e-mail: rob@merrymiller.co.uk

dir: *1m from Marcham interchange on A34*

Any inventory of the Merry Miller must include its wealth of risqué prints. Despite the beams, flagstones and stripped pine tables, the interior of this 17th-century former granary is more redolent of Tuscany – which at least ensures that the pasta dishes feel at home! But lunch could just as easily be a club sandwich or seafood salad bowl, whilst evening diners might choose roasted Gressingham duck; or tomato, goat's cheese and Puy lentil tartlettes.

Open 12–2.45am (Fri-Sat 12–11 Sun 12–10.30) **Bar Meals** L served all week 12–2.45 D served all week 6.30–9.45 (Sun all day) **Restaurant** L served all week 12–2.45 D served all week 6.30–9.45 Av 3 course à la carte £20 ⊕ Greene King ◀ Greene King IPA & Old Speckled Hen. ♥ 15 **Facilities** Garden Dogs allowed Parking

ADDERBURY · · · · · · · · · · · · MAP 11 SP43

Red Lion ▲ ★★ HL ♥

The Green OX17 3LU ☎ 01295 810269 ▤ 01295 811906

dir: *Off M40 3 m from Banbury*

A fine stone-built coaching inn on the Banbury to Oxford road, overlooking the village green. Established in 1669, the Red Lion was once known as the King's Arms, and had a tunnel in the cellar used by Royalists in hiding during the Civil War. Enter the rambling, beamed interior to find daily newspapers, real ales, good wines and a varied menu, with plenty of fish choices like home-made Thai salmon fish cakes, chargrilled tuna steaks, and salmon steak parcels.

Open 11–11 (Fri-Sat 11–11.30) **Bar Meals** L served all week 12–3 D served all week 7–9.30 (Sat-Sun & BHs 12–9.30) **Restaurant** L served all week 12–3 D served all week 7–9.30 (Sun 12–9.30) ⊕ Greene King ◀ Greene King IPA, Abbot Ale, Old Speckled Hen. ♥ 11 **Facilities** Garden Parking **Rooms** 12

ARDINGTON · · · · · · · · · · · · MAP 05 SU48

Pick of the Pubs

The Boar's Head ★★★★ INN ⊛⊛ ♥

See Pick of the Pubs on page 436

BAMPTON · · · · · · · · · · · · MAP 05 SP30

The Romany

Bridge St OX18 2HA ☎ 01993 850237 ▤ 01993 852133

e-mail: romany@barbox.net

dir: *Telephone for details*

A shop until 20 years ago, The Romany is housed in an 18th-century building of Cotswold stone with a beamed bar, log fires and intimate dining room. The choice of food ranges from bar snacks and bar meals to a full à la carte restaurant menu, with home-made specials like hotpot, Somerset pork, or steak and ale pie. There is a good range of vegetarian choices. Regional singers provide live entertainment a couple of times a month.

Open 11–11 **Bar Meals** L served all week 12–2 D served all week 6.30–9 Av main course £6 **Restaurant** L served all week 12–2 D served all week 6.30–9 ⊕ Free House ◀ Archers Village, plus guests. **Facilities** Garden Dogs allowed Parking Play Area

BANBURY · · · · · · · · · · · · MAP 11 SP44

The George Inn

Lower St, Barford St Michael OX15 0RH ☎ 01869 338226

dir: *Telephone for directions*

Handy for both Banbury and Oxford, this 300–year-old thatched village pub features old beams, exposed stone walls and open fireplaces. It stands in a large garden, with a patio and orchard, overlooking open countryside. Live music is an established tradition, and the pub hosts a variety of rock, folk and solo artists. There's a good choice of real ales, and options from the single menu include baguettes, baked potatoes, pasta, pies, and fish and chips.

Open 12–3 7–11 (Sun 12–4) **Bar Meals** D served 7–9 ⊕ Free House ◀ Timothy Taylor Landlord, IPA, Copper Ale, Greene King. **Facilities** Garden Dogs allowed Parking **Notes** ⊛

The Wykham Arms ♥

Temple Mill Rd, Sibford Gower OX15 5RX

☎ 01295 788808

e-mail: info@wykhamarms.co.uk

web: www.wykhamarms.co.uk

dir: *Between Banbury & Shipston-on-Stour off B4035. 20m S of Stratford-upon-Avon*

A centuries-old thatched inn built of mellow stone with lovely countryside views, where drinkers and diners congregate in intimate beamed rooms. The bar menu is typified by fresh mussels with shallots and garlic; and spaghetti carbonara. Restaurant main courses may include Shiraz-poached blade of Lighthorne lamb with savoy cabbage and dauphinoise potato; confit Barbary duck leg with bubble and squeak and creamed spinach; and pan-fried skate wing with herb risotto, sautéed spring onion and olives.

Open 11–3 6–11.30 Closed: Mon **Bar Meals** L served Tue-Sat 12–2.30 D served Tue-Sat 6.30–9.45 (Sun 12–3.30) **Restaurant** L served Tue-Sat 12–2.30 D served Tue-Sat 7–9.45 (Sun 12–3) Av 3 course à la carte £25 ⊕ Free House ◀ Hook Norton Best, Guinness, St Austell Tribute, Adnams Broadside. ♥ 17 **Facilities** Children's licence Garden Dogs allowed Parking

435

PICK OF THE PUBS

The Boar's Head

In the 19th century Lord Wantage laid out the now-famous Lockinge Estate, within which lies the lovely downland village of Ardington. He would be delighted that it remains very much as he left it.

The Boar's Head has been serving the still-flourishing local community for the past 150 years, and today is a happy combination of village pub, first-class restaurant and superb accommodation. Candles, fresh flowers and blazing log fires create just the right romantic atmosphere, with scrubbed pine tables giving a rustic touch. Everything, from bread to ice cream, and from pasta to pastries, is made on the premises. The menu, which changes regularly, is varied and well known for its fish – the chef's speciality – which comes up daily from Cornwall. A typical meal could consist of mackerel and black pudding salad with walnut vinaigrette; or grilled ceps with truffle carpaccio, followed by fillet of Lockinge venison with wild mushrooms and fondant potato; breast of Gressingham duck with roasted beetroots and cabbage; or tranche of Newlyn cod with braised lettuce, peas and bacon. Assiette of chocolates with raspberry ripple or hot Grand Marnier soufflé with iced chocolate cream would make a satisfying finale. Should you feel inclined to take advantage of one of three well-appointed guest suites, you could explore the region further since Ardington is an ideal base for walking or cycling, and footpaths wind down through nearby villages or run up to the ancient Ridgeway a few miles away. Golfers will be delighted by several excellent courses nearby, while fly-fishers can try their luck in the village's well-stocked trout lakes.

★★★★ INN ⊛⊛ ♥
MAP 05 SU48
Church St OX12 8QA
☎ 01235 833254
🖹 01235 833254
e-mail: info@
boarsheadardington.co.uk
dir: *Off A417 E of Wantage, next to village church*

Open 12–3 6.30–11
Bar Meals L served all week
12–2.30 D served all week 7–10
Restaurant L served all week
12–2.15 D served all week 7–10
⊕ Free House ⊠ Hook
Norton Old Hooky, West
Berkshire Brewery Dr. Hexter's,
Warsteiner, Butts Brewery. ♥ 8
Facilities Garden Parking
Rooms 3

436

BANBURY continued

Ye Olde Reindeer Inn

47 Parsons St OX16 5NA
☎ 01295 264031 📄 01295 264018
e-mail: tonypuddifoot@aol.com
dir: 1m from M40 junct 11, in town centre just off market square

The oldest pub in Banbury, the Reindeer dates back to 1570. During the Civil War, Oliver Cromwell met his men here in the magnificent Globe Room, which still has its original panelling. A great range of cask ales is kept and a large selection of malt whiskies. Mulled wines are another house speciality. Pick of the menu is the very popular bubble and squeak and Yorkshire pudding filled with sausage, onion and gravy.

Open 11–11 (Sun 12-3.30) **Bar Meals** L served Mon-Sat 11–2.30 D served Mon -Sat (Sun 12–3) **Restaurant** L served Mon-Sat 12–2 D served Mon-Sat 12–2 (Sun 12–3) ⊕ Hook Norton ◀ Hook Norton, Best , Hook Norton Haymaker, Old. **Facilities** Garden Parking

---

BARNARD GATE   MAP 05 SP41

Pick of the Pubs

The Boot Inn ♈

OX29 6XE ☎ 01865 881231
e-mail: info@theboot-inn.com
dir: Off A40 between Witney & Eynsham

The Boot is a popular place renowned for its collection of footwear given by celebrities such as the Bee Gees, George Best and Jeremy Irons. Exposed beams, stone-flagged floors and a roaring log fire in winter set the scene at the inn, which is surrounded by beautiful countryside on the edge of the Cotswolds, near the ancient village of Eynsham and just a few miles west of Oxford. There is a pleasant garden for summer use, a welcoming bar and secluded dining areas. Beers from well-known and reliable brewers are on tap, and the wine list would satisfy the most cosmopolitan of oenophiles. The lunch menu offers salads, sandwiches and a selection from the chargrill – burgers, chops and steaks. Dinner options are along the lines of duck breast with kumquat brochette; twice roasted lamb shank; and roast vegetable parcels stuffed with mozzarella.

Open 11–3 6–11 (Sun and summer all day) Closed: 26 Dec **Bar Meals** L served Mon-Sat 12–2.30 D served all week 7–10 (Sun 12–3) Av main course £9.95 **Restaurant** L served all week 12–2.30 D served Mon-Sat 7–10 (Sun 7–9) ⊕ Free House ◀ Hook Norton Best, Adnams Best, Fuller's London Pride, Youngs Best. ♈ 7 **Facilities** Garden Parking

---

BECKLEY   MAP 05 SP51

Pick of the Pubs

The Abingdon Arms ♈

High St OX3 9UU ☎ 01865 351311
e-mail: chequers89@hotmail.com
dir: M40 junct 8, follow signs at Headington rdbt for Beckley

Expect a warm welcome at this cosy, traditional pub set in a pretty village to the north of Oxford. It has been smartly updated, and good food is also helping to put it on the map, backed by excellent beers from Brakspear's. A range of sandwiches and bar snacks is available at lunchtime, while a full meal could include marinated crab with chilli, coriander and rocket, followed by chargrilled medallions of lamb with spinach mash and mustard cream sauce. The atmosphere in the pub is always friendly, and there are roaring log fires in winter. In the summer you can sit on the patio and enjoy the spectacular views of Otmoor. Some years ago this area was popular with the writer Evelyn Waugh, and today it is just round the corner from an RSPB bird reserve. There are opportunities for many pleasant walks in the area.

Open 12–3 6–11 (Sat-Sun all day) **Bar Meals** L served all week 12–2.30 D served Mon-Sat 7–9.30 (Sun 12–3, Summer 6.30–8.30) Av main course £10 **Restaurant** L served all week 12–2.30 D served Mon-Sat 7–9.30 (Sun 12–3, 6.30–8.30) Av 3 course à la carte £20 ⊕ Brakspear ◀ Brakspears Bitter, Brakspear Special & Brakspear guest. ♈ 8 **Facilities** Garden Parking

---

BLACK BOURTON   MAP 05 SP20

Pick of the Pubs

The Vines ♈

See Pick of the Pubs on page 438

BLOXHAM   MAP 11 SP43

The Elephant & Castle

OX15 4LZ ☎ 0845 873 7358
e-mail: bloxhomelephant1@btconnect.com
dir: Just off A361, in village centre

The arch of this 15th-century Cotswold-stone coaching inn still straddles the former Banbury to Chipping Norton turnpike. Locals play darts or shove-ha'penny in the big wood-floored bar, whilst the two-roomed lounge boasts a bar-billiards table and a large inglenook fireplace. The reasonably priced menu offers a range of sandwiches and crusty filled baguettes, plus pub favourites like roast chicken breast with stuffing, crispy battered cod, and seafood platter.

Open 10–3 5–11 (Sat-Sun all day) **Bar Meals** L served Mon-Sat 12–2 **Restaurant** L served Mon-Sat 12–2 ⊕ Hook Norton ◀ Hook Norton Best Bitter, Hook Norton seasonal ales, guest ales. **Facilities** Garden Parking Play Area

PICK OF THE PUBS

BLACK BOURTON-OXFORDSHIRE

The Vines

Long acclaimed for its fine dining in elegant surroundings, this stone-built Cotswold hotel is set in the beautiful village of Black Bourton, surrounded by its own delightful gardens. John Clegg of the BBC's Real Rooms team famously designed and decorated The Vines restaurant and bar.

The effect is stunning – very different from the more predictable styles favoured for a building of this character. Here you can enjoy lunch or dinner from the carte or special daily menus of modern British dishes with an international twist. Particularly popular are the likes of slow-cooked shin of beef in Hook Norton ale, and duck and Cointreau paté with blueberry dressing, all created from fresh local produce. The good-value Light Bights menu is ideal for lunch or supper, and there's also a traditional Sunday lunch, plus a special children's selection. To complement the food, the cellar offers a choice of over 36 Old and New World wines. The spacious lounge area with its leather sofas is a comfortable place to relax with a drink or light snack while enjoying a chat or a game of chess, particularly by a cosy log fire on a cold evening. On sunny days you can eat outside on the patio and play a nostalgic game of Aunt Sally. The Vines provides a superb setting for a wedding reception, anniversary or other special event, and owners Ahdy and Karen Gerges pride themselves on their professional planning expertise. The hotel is ideally placed for anyone on business in Oxford, Swindon, Witney or Brize Norton and makes an ideal base for exploring the Cotswolds. Burford is less than four miles away.

🍷
MAP 05 SP20
Burford Rd OX18 2PF
☎ 01993 843559
🖷 01993 840080
e-mail: info@vineshotel.com
web:
www.vinesblackbourton.co.uk
dir: *From A40 Witney, take A4095 to Faringdon, then 1st right after Bampton to Black Bourton*

Open 12–3 6–11 (Sun 7–11)
Closed: Mon lunch
Bar Meals L served Tue-Sun 12–2 D served Mon-Sun 6.30–9.30 (Sun 7–9.30) Av main course £13.80
Restaurant L served Tue-Sun 12–2 D served Tue-Sun 6.30–9.30
🌐 Free House 🍺 Old Hookey, Tetley Smooth. 🍷 7
Facilities Children's licence Garden Parking

BRIGHTWELL BALDWIN　　MAP 05 SU69

Pick of the Pubs

The Lord Nelson Inn ♀

See Pick of the Pubs on page 440

BROADWELL　　MAP 05 SP20

Chilli Pepper ♀

GL7 3QS ☎ 01367 860385
e-mail: info@chilli-pepper.net
dir: *A361 from Lechlade to Burford, after 2m right to Kencot Broadwell, right after 200mtrs. Right at x-rds*

Attractive 16th-century Cotswold stone inn overlooking the manor and parish church. It used to be known as The Five Bells Broadwell, but the change of name has brought a hot new look. The bars are full of character with beams and flagstones, and there are lots of places to eat. The menu takes in starters like Caesar salad with chargrilled chicken, and then pan-fried fillet of venison with a cream wild berry and brandy sauce.

Open 12–2.30 6–12 (please phone for summer opening) Closed: 25–26 Dec **Bar Meals** L served Tue-Sun 12–2.30 D served Tu-Sat 6–10 Av main course £9 **Restaurant** L served Tue-Sun 12–2.30 D served Tue-Sat 6–9.30 Av 3 course à la carte £25 ⊕ Free House ◀ Greene King IPA. ♀ 12 **Facilities** Garden Dogs allowed Parking

BROUGHTON　　MAP 11 SP43

Saye and Sele Arms ♀

Main Rd OX15 5ED
☎ 01295 263348 📄 01295 272012
e-mail: mail@sayeandselearms.co.uk
dir: *3m from Banbury Cross*

A pretty stone-built 16th-century pub just five minutes' walk from Broughton Castle, home to Lord and Lady Saye and Sele. Licensed for 300 years, today's good selection of real ales includes three regularly changing guests. It's also known for its food, and chef/proprietor Danny McGeehan's 'real' pies are always on the menu. They include lamb and apricot; beefsteak, kidney and ale; chicken, bacon, mushroom and tarragon; and minced beef, cheddar and stilton. His bread and butter pudding is not to be missed either.

Saye and Sele Arms

Open 11.30–2.30 7–11 (Sun 12–5) Closed: 25 Dec Sun eve **Bar Meals** L served Mon-Sat 12–2 D served Mon-Sat 7–9.30 (Sun 12–3) **Restaurant** L served Mon-Sat 12–2 D served Mon-Sat 7–9.30 (Sun 12–3) ⊕ Free House ◀ Wadworth 6X, Adnams Southwold, 2 guest ales. ♀ 8 **Facilities** Garden Dogs allowed Parking

BURCOT　　MAP 05 SU59

The Chequers ♀

OX14 3DP ☎ 01865 407771 📄 01865 407771
e-mail: enquiries@thechequers-burcot.co.uk
dir: *On A415 (Dorchester to Abingdon road)*

A timber framed, thatched country pub, The Chequers was once a staging post for barges on the Thames. It dates back 400 years, but the beam over the large inglenook fireplace is even older. There is a snack and light meal menu available at lunchtime, while diners might try crab claw fishcakes on lime salad with chilli dip; Gloucester Old Spot grilled chops; or Hooky beer-battered haddock with chunky chips, peas and tartare sauce.

Open 12–11 **Bar Meals** L served Mon-Sat 12–2.30 D served Mon-Sat 6–9.30 (Sun 12–3) **Restaurant** L served Mon-Sat 12–2.30 D served Mon-Sat 6–9.30 (Sun 12–3) Av 3 course à la carte £22 ⊕ Free House ◀ Hook Norton Bitter, Ridgway. ♀ 21 **Facilities** Garden Parking

PICK OF THE PUBS

The Lord Nelson Inn

In Nelson's day this 17th-century pub was known as the Admiral Nelson, but when, in 1797, our naval hero was elevated to the peerage, its name was elevated too. For more than a century after that, passing travellers and villagers slaked their thirst here.

In 1905, following complaints from the church and the local squire about over-indulgent estate workers, the inn was closed and it became a shop, a post office and then a private house. In 1971 a couple driving past liked the look of it, bought it, renewed its licence and restored it to its former glory, decorating the interior in traditional style, in keeping with its age. These days, it's always full of fresh flowers and lit candles. During the summer the pretty, weeping willow-draped garden, and the rear terrace, are popular places to eat and drink. All the food is freshly cooked, using local produce where possible. The lunch menu may offer stir-fry beef with hoi sin, plum sauce and noodles; or fillet of sea bass with sweet chilli dressing; while at

dinner there may be local partridge with bacon and mixed vegetables; fresh oven-roasted poussin with lardons and Italian herbs; lamb cutlets with fresh rosemary; fillet of cod with a herb crust; and ratatouille feuilleté with tomato confit and basil. Typical weekly specials include fillet steak; fresh grilled John Dory with capers; and noisettes of English lamb with fresh rosemary. Real ales served in the beamed bar are supplied by Black Sheep, Brakspear, John Smiths, and West Berkshire Brewery, and the comprehensive wine list includes 20 by the glass. In the early 1990s the RSPB chose the nearby Chiltern escarpment to reintroduce the red kite – you'll be unlucky not to see at least one.

MAP 05 SU69
OX49 5NP
☎ 01491 612497
dir: *Off B4009 between Watlington & Benson*

Open 11–3 6–11 (Sun 7–11)
Bar Meals L served all week 12–2.30 D served all week 6–10.30 (Sun 7–10)
Restaurant L served all week 12–2.30 D served all week 6–10.30 (Sun 7–10) Av 3 course à la carte £25 Av 2 course fixed price £11.95
⊕ Free House ◖ West Berkshire Brewery, Brakspear, John Smiths & Black Sheep. ♚ 20
Facilities Garden Parking

BURFORD
MAP 05 SP21

Pick of the Pubs

The Inn for All Seasons ★★ HL ♟

See Pick of the Pubs on page 443

Pick of the Pubs

The Lamb Inn ★★★ SHL ◎◎ ♟

See Pick of the Pubs on page 444

CHADLINGTON
MAP 10 SP32

The Tite Inn ♟

Mill End OX7 3NY ☎ 01608 676475 📄 0870 7059308

e-mail: willis@titeinn.com

dir: *3m S of Chipping Norton*

Sixteenth-century Cotswold-stone free house where, in 1642, Royalist troops sank a few stiffeners before the Battle of Edgehill nearby. The lunch menu features Thai coconut chicken curry with basmati rice; lambs' kidneys braised in red wine; and bobotie, a South African sweet and spicy meatloaf. At dinner try deep-fried goujons of plaice with tartare sauce; baked gammon with Dijon cream sauce; or vegetarian Brazil nut roast with fresh tomato sauce.

Open 12–2.30 6.30–11 (Sun 12–3, 7–10.30) Closed: 25–26 Dec
Bar Meals L served Tue-Sun 12–2 D served Tue-Sun 7–9 (Sun 12–2.30)
Av main course £9.95 **Restaurant** L served Tue-Sun 12–2 D served
Tue-Sat 6.30–9 (Sun 12–2.30) Av 3 course à la carte £19 ⊕ Free House
◀ Ramsbury, Sharp's, Cotswold Premium Lager & 4 guest ales. ♟ 8
Facilities Garden Dogs allowed Parking

CHALGROVE
MAP 05 SU69

Pick of the Pubs

The Red Lion Inn

The High St OX44 7SS ☎ 01865 890625

e-mail: annie@redlionchalgrove.co.uk

dir: *B480 from Oxford Ring road, through Stadhampton, left then right at mini-rdbt, at Chalgrove Airfield right into village*

Rather unusually, the cruck-framed, 15th-century Red Lion is one of only two pubs in the country owned by its local parish church. How appropriate, then, that the new owners are Suzanne and

Raymond Sexton who, incidentally, was Jamie Oliver's dad's chef for 10 years. From the front garden there is a view of the memorial to Col John Hampden, a key political figure fatally wounded in a nearby Civil War skirmish. From a 'menu that tries to please everyone' come starters of grilled field mushrooms with poached egg and hollandaise; and spiced lamb patties with caraway and cucumber dressing. Main dishes include pork fillet wrapped in Parma ham with Dijon mustard and tarragon sauce; salted king scallops with chorizo risotto; and the more prosaic cod in batter. Sandwiches and side orders are available at lunchtime, and children have their own special menu.

Open 11.30–3 6–11.30 (Summer, Sat-Sun all day)
Bar Meals L served all week 12–3 Av main course £11.50
Restaurant L served Mon-Sat 12–2 D served Mon-Sat 6–9 (Sun 12–3) Av 3 course à la carte £22 Av fixed price £14 ⊕ Free House
◀ Fuller's London Pride, Adnams Best, Timothy Taylors Landlord.
Facilities Garden Dogs allowed Play Area

CHARLBURY
MAP 11 SP31

Pick of the Pubs

The Bull Inn ♟

See Pick of the Pubs on page 447

CHECKENDON
MAP 05 SU68

The Highwayman ♟

Exlade St RG8 0UA ☎ 01491 682020 📄 01491 682229

e-mail: thehighwayman@skyeinns670.fsnet.co.uk

dir: *On A4074 (Reading to Wallingford road)*

An early 17th-century listed inn which has undergone a major refurbishment programme. The emphasis in the character bar is on wooden floors and open fireplaces. The famous Maharajah's Well nearby is surrounded by numerous walks in the glorious Chiltern beechwoods. Seared salmon fillet, pan-fried calves' liver, and honey mustard and lemon chicken escalope are typical examples from the inviting menu.

Open 12–3 6–11 (Sat-Sun & BH all day) **Bar Meals** L served all week 12–3 D served all week 7–9.30 **Restaurant** L served all week 12–2.30 D served all week 7–9.30 ⊕ Free House ◀ Fuller's London Pride, Loddon Ferryman's Gold, Butlers Brewers & guest ale. **Facilities** Garden Dogs allowed Parking Play Area

CHINNOR **MAP 05 SP70**

Pick of the Pubs

The Sir Charles Napier ◎◉ ♀

Spriggs Alley OX39 4BX

☎ 01494 483011 🖹 01494 485311

dir: *M40 junct 6 to Chinnor. Turn right at rdbt, up hill to Spriggs Alley*

Once an old beer house, probably much frequented by bodgers, the itinerant wood-turners who worked in these Chiltern beech woods. Today, it is a true destination pub with huge log fires, comfortable sofas and an eclectic jumble of old furnishings, in which lunchtime customers may well still be lingering at dusk. Inside and out are works in stone, marble and wood by local sculptor Michael Cooper, while regulars are inclined to drift in with fungi, berries, pheasants and pigeons for the pot. In summer lunch is served on the vine- and wisteria-shaded terrace that overlooks extensive lawns and herb gardens. Try guinea fowl wrapped in pancetta with globe artichoke, ratatouille and basil jus; or roast mallard with smoked bacon, ceps, lentils and red wine sauce. Pan-fried gurnard with crayfish beurre blanc is a blackboard special. An extensive wine list includes bottles from unusual places, such as Oregon, Canada and Lebanon.

Open 12–3.30 6.30–12 Closed: 25–26 Dec, Sun eve & Mon **Bar Meals** L served Tue-Fri 12–2.30 D served Tue-Thu 7–9.30 Av main course £11.50 **Restaurant** L served Tue-Sat 12–2.30 D served Tue-Sat 7–10 (Sun 12–3.30) Av 3 course à la carte £32 Av 2 course fixed price £16.50 ⊕ Free House ⬛ Wadworth 6X, Wadwoth IPA. ♀ 15 **Facilities** Garden Parking

CHIPPING NORTON **MAP 10 SP3**

The Chequers ♀

Goddards Ln OX7 5NP

☎ 01608 644717 🖹 01608 646237

e-mail: enquiries@chequers-pub.co.uk

dir: *In town centre, next to theatre*

Log fires, low ceilings and soft lighting make for a cosy atmosphere in the bar of this popular 16th-century inn. By contrast, the courtyard restaurant is wonderfully bright and airy. Well-kept real ale, good wines and decent coffee are served along with freshly prepared contemporary dishes. Look for starters like wild mushroom risotto; and mains including baked cod in Parma ham with sun-dried tomato and pine nut cous cous; and chicken stir-fry with cashew nuts.

Open 11–11 (Sun 12–10.30) Closed: 25 Dec **Bar Meals** L served all week 12–2.30 D served Mon-Sat 6–9.30 (Sun 12–5) Av main course £9.50 **Restaurant** L served all week 12–2.30 D served Mon-Sat 6–9 (Sun 12–5) Av 3 course à la carte £17.50 ⊕ Fullers ⬛ Fuller's Chiswick Bitter, London Pride & ESB, Organic Honeydew. ♀ 18

CHISLEHAMPTON **MAP 05 SU5**

Pick of the Pubs

Coach & Horses Inn ★★★ INN ♀

Watlington Rd OX44 7UX

☎ 01865 890255 🖹 01865 891995

e-mail: enquiries@coachhorsesinn.co.uk

dir: *On B480 (Watlington Road), 5m from Oxford*

A young girl killed during the Civil War is believed to haunt this delightful 16th-century inn. Set in peaceful countryside on the old Roman road Icknield Street, the inn, as the name attests, once provided hospitality for the stage coaches travelling from Birmingham to London. Among the features inside are roaring log fires, quaint beams and an old bread oven. Start with warm duck and home-cured bacon salad, before tucking into the likes of open steak and kidney pie, or pan-fried chicken with cider and mustard sauce. Vegetarians might like roasted butternut squash risotto; spinach, tomato and mushroom lasagne; or peppers stuffed with rice, sun-dried tomatoes, basil and coriander. The daily specials fish board could include mixed seafood grill; fresh fillet of sea bass; and red snapper. Grills, poultry and game are also perennial favourites.

Open 11.30–11 **Bar Meals** L served all week 12–2 D served Mon-Sat 7–10 **Restaurant** L served all week 12–2 D served Mon-Sat 7–10 ⊕ Free House ⬛ Hook Norton Best, London Pride, Old Hooky. ♀ 8 **Facilities** Garden Parking **Rooms** 9

PICK OF THE PUBS

BURFORD-OXFORDSHIRE

The Inn for All Seasons

In its lifetime this 16th-century coaching inn has been a garage, a filling station and two quarry cottages whose occupants quarried the stone for St Paul's Cathedral. Within its solid Cotswold stone walls is a treasure-trove of ancient oak beams, inglenooks and contemporary furniture.

There are several guest ales, among them always a Wychwood from nearby Witney, and a large selection of wines by the glass. The Sharp family has owned the Inn since 1986; Matthew Sharp, the chef, has worked with the Roux Brothers and Anton Mosimann. Connections with the right people in Brixham guarantee a wonderful supply of fish for specials such as grilled fillet of yellow fin tuna on a classic salad nicoise with an anchovy dressing and parmesan shavings; flash-fried squid with lime and baby spinach leaf salad; and grilled troncon of turbot with tarragon potatoes and a béarnaise sauce. If you prefer land over sea, look to the main menu for starters such as River Dart salmon confit with a cucumber and avocado salsa; stilton and toasted walnut salad with a herb dressing; and chicken, chorizo and mushroom terrine wrapped in Parma ham. Main courses might be sautéed wild mushrooms and penne pasta tossed in parmesan and fresh herb butter; and roast chump of lamb on a minted pea puree, with Madeira sauce. Desserts might include warm pineapple and Satsuma served with vanilla ice cream. For those seeking a lunchtime snack, there are grilled paninis, and mouthwatering snacks such as bubble and squeak with bacon and fried egg, or steamed Oxfordshire suet pudding with tangy sauce alongside the main a la carte menu. There is a good selection of wines by the glass.

★★ HL ♥
MAP 05 SP21
The Barringtons OX18 4TN
☎ 01451 844324
📄 01451 844375
e-mail:
sharp@innforallseasons.com
web: www.innforallseasons.com
dir: *3m W of Burford on A40*

Open 11–2.30 6–11 (Sun 12–3, 7–10.30)
Bar Meals L served Mon-Sat 11.30–2.30 D served Mon-Sat 6.30–9.30 (Sun 12–2.30, 7–9) Av main course £13.50
Restaurant L served Mon-Sat 11.30–2.30 D served Mon-Sat 6.30–9.30 (Sun 12–2.30, 7–9)
⊕ Free House ◀ Wadworth 6X, Interbrew Bass, Wychwood, Badger. ♥ 15
Facilities Children's licence Garden Dogs allowed Parking Play Area
Rooms 10

PICK OF THE PUBS

BURFORD-OXFORDSHIRE

The Lamb Inn

A traditional English inn with stone flagged floors, real ale and log fires set at the heart of the Cotswolds. Originally built in 1420 as weavers' cottages, this charming old inn is in complete harmony with its surroundings. The honey-coloured stone building lies just off the centre of Burford, with easy access to the shops.

In summer you can visit the walled cottage garden, admire the herbaceous borders and perhaps take lunch on the sheltered courtyard terrace. The welcoming bar draws in staying guests and locals alike, exchanging news and views while enjoying a glass of real ale or wine. Lunching or dining in these surroundings is a relaxing option, with the bar and fireside menu offering nibbles (olives, garlic bread, tapenade); traditional sandwiches served with kettle chips and green salad; and starters like salmon rillettes; classic chicken Caesar salad with char-grilled chicken and anchovies; and scallops, black pudding and mash. Light meals may include eggs Benedict with smoked salmon; and roasted tiger prawns with warm garlic potato salad. A spacious restaurant with mullioned windows overlooks the lovely garden and courtyard, while the cheerful interior combines original features with modern fabrics, enhanced by flowers, candles and light jazz. There's nothing old-world about the menus, which present a delicious blend of English and international cooking. Local suppliers provide most of the ingredients, and menus change regularly. Always included is a fish board, and main menu dishes such as lamb and date tagine with spicy bulgar wheat; game pie with chips and pickled onions; Cumberland sausage and lamb kidney casserole; goat's cheese and red onion tart; and on Sundays, traditional roasts.

★★★ SHL ◎◎ ♥
MAP 05 SP21
Sheep St OX18 4LR
☎ 01993 823155
🖻 01993 822228
e-mail:
info@lambinn-burford.co.uk
web: www.cotswold-inns-hotels.
co.uk/lamb
dir: *M40 junct 8, follow A40 &
Burford signs, 1st turn down hill
into Sheep St*

Open 11–11
Bar Meals L served all week
12–2.30 D served all week
6.30–9.30 Av main course £9.50
Restaurant L served all week
12–2.30 D served all week 7–9.30
Av 3 course fixed price £32.50
⊕ Free House ◄ Hook Norton
Best, Brakspear. ♥ 9
Facilities Garden Dogs allowed
Rooms 17

CHRISTMAS COMMON MAP 05 SU79

Pick of the Pubs

The Fox and Hounds ▾

OX49 5HL ☎ 01491 612599

e-mail: kiran.daniels@btconnect.com

dir: M40 junct 5, 2.5m to Christmas Common (on road towards Henley)

Renovations in recent years have transformed this charming 500–year-old inn into a stylish dining pub with an immaculate interior, a large restaurant complete with open-plan kitchen, and four cosy bar areas. Changing special and an imaginative menu that places a clear emphasis on quality ingredients, local where possible, produces lunchtime sandwiches (perhaps Welsh rarebit; or Scottish smoked salmon with cucumber and cream cheese; and excellent value hot dishes. Typical choices include roast red onion, oven-dried tomato, butternut, rocket and three cheese tart; and "lunch for a fiver" deals such as Angus beef and celeriac hash with a fried free-range egg and walnut mustard. From the evening menu come starters of chicken liver parfait with red onion marmalade and toast; and mains like roast local partridge with colcannon and rosemary gravy; or Aberdeen Angus rib-eye steak with sautéed potatoes, roast vine tomatoes, Spanish onion and parsley butter.

Open 12–3 5.30–11 Closed: 25 Dec, 31 Dec eve **Bar Meals** L served all week 12–2.30 D served all week 7–9.30 **Restaurant** L served all week 12–2.30 D served all week 7–9.30 Av 3 course à la carte £25 Av 1 course fixed price £5 ⊕ Brakspear ◀ Brakspear Bitter, Special & seasonal ales. ▾14 **Facilities** Garden Dogs allowed Parking

CHURCH ENSTONE MAP 11 SP32

Pick of the Pubs

The Crown Inn ▾

Mill Ln OX7 4NN ☎ 01608 677262

dir: Off A44, 15m N of Oxford

Award-winning chef Tony Warburton runs this stone-built 17th-century free house on the eastern edge of the Cotswolds with his wife Caroline. During the summer season you can while away the long evenings eating or drinking in the quiet and secluded rear garden, which is sheltered from the wind but enjoys the best of the late sunshine. Inside you'll find a traditional rustic bar with an open fire; a spacious, slate floored conservatory; and a richly decorated beamed dining room. All meals are prepared on the premises using fresh produce, including pork, beef and game from the local farms and estates. Starters may include cream of leek and potato soup; or pan-fried wood pigeon with red cabbage and crispy bacon. Main course choices range from steak and Hooky pie to poached smoked haddock with cauliflower fritter and cheesy mash. A home-made pudding such as cheesecake with blackcurrants will round things off nicely.

Open 12–3 6–11 (Sun 12–4) Closed: 26 Dec, 1 Jan & Mon **Bar Meals** L served Tue-Sun 12–2 D served Tue-Sat 7–9 Av main course £10 **Restaurant** L served Tue-Sun 12–2 D served Tue-Sat 7–9 Av 3 course à la carte £19.45 ⊕ Free House ◀ Hook Norton Best Bitter, Timothy Taylor Landlord & Hobgoblin. ▾8 **Facilities** Garden Dogs allowed Parking

CLIFTON MAP 11 SP43

Duke of Cumberland's Head

OX15 0PE ☎ 01869 338534 📄 01869 338643

e-mail: info@dukeatclifton.com

dir: A4260 from Banbury, then B4031 from Deddington. (7m from Banbury)

Built in 1645, this thatched and beamed stone pub was named to honour the Duke whose forces fought for his uncle, Charles I, at the nearby Battle of Edge Hill; important strategic decisions were supposedly made around the pub's inglenook fireplace. Today it offers a choice of real ales, two dining rooms, and a wonderful garden in summer. The menu may start with avocado and prawns, continue with beef braised in beer, and finish with tiramisu.

Open 12–2.30 6.30–11 (Closed Mon Lunch) Closed: 25 Dec **Bar Meals** L served Tue-Sun 12–2 D served Mon-Sat 6–9 Av main course £11 **Restaurant** L served Wed-Sun 12–2 D served Wed-Sat 7–9.30 Av 3 course à la carte £21.50 Av 3 course fixed price £20 ◀ Hook Norton, Adnams, Deuchars & Black Sheep. **Facilities** Garden Dogs allowed Parking

CRAY'S POND MAP 05 SU68

Pick of the Pubs

The White Lion ▾

See Pick of the Pubs on page 448

England

England

CUMNOR   MAP 05 SP40

Pick of the Pubs

Bear & Ragged Staff ♀

28 Appleton Rd OX2 9QH

☎ 01865 862329 🖹 01865 865947

dir: *A420 from Oxford, right to Cumnor on B4017*

A 700–year-old pub allegedly haunted by the mistress of the Earl of Warwick. With a tad more certainty it is believed that Oliver Cromwell's brother Richard chiselled out the royal crest above one of the two massive, original fireplaces, which with the wooden beams and floors, help to create a powerfully historic atmosphere. The pub caters for a wide cross-section of locals, as well as being popular with visitors from further afield, many drawn by the extensive menu. Starters include roasted garlic king prawn skewers; timbale of salmon, crab and prawns; and crispy duck spring rolls with vermicelli noodles. Mains to consider are roasted vegetable tagliatelle; chargrilled tuna steak with chorizo and sweet chilli sauce; medallions of oriental pork with fresh ginger, spring onions and egg noodles; home-made steak and kidney pudding; fillet of Appleton beef (hung for four weeks); and the locally renowned Cape bobotie.

Open 12–11 (Sun 12–10.30) **Bar Meals** L served all week 12–2.30 D served all week 6–9.30 **Restaurant** L served all week 12–3 D served all week 6–9 ⊕ Morrells ◀ IPA, Old Speckled Hen, Abbot Ale, Old Hooky. **Facilities** Garden Parking Play Area

The Vine Inn ♀

11 Abingdon Rd OX2 9QN

☎ 01865 862567 🖹 01865 862567

dir: *A420 from Oxford, right onto B4017*

An old village pub whose name, when you see the frontage, needs no explanation. In 1560, the suspicious death of an Earl's wife in Cumnor Place first had people asking 'Did she fall, or was she pushed?'. A typical menu here could include lamb shank with a red wine and mint sauce, pan-fried fillet steak with brandy and mushroom sauce, and the day's fresh fish. There's also a good range of snacks. Children love the huge garden.

Open 11–3 6–11 (Sun 12–10.30) **Bar Meals** L served all week 12–2.15 D served all week 6–9.15 (Sat 12–3, Sun 12–6) **Restaurant** L served all week 12–2.15 D served all week 6.30–9.15 (Sat 12–3 Sun 12–6) ⊕ Punch Taverns ◀ Adnams Bitter, Tetely Bitter, Hook Norton, guest ales. ♀7 **Facilities** Children's licence Garden Dogs allowed Parking Play Area

CUXHAM   MAP 05 SU69

The Half Moon ♀

OX49 5NF ☎ 01491 614151

e-mail: info@thehalf-moon.com

dir: *M40 junct 6 follow Watlington signs. Right at T-junct, 2nd right to Cuxham. Across rdbt, Pub in 1m on right, just past Cuxham sign*

Owner Eilidh Ferguson grows the vegetables and salad leaves that end up on the dining plates at this 16th-century thatched pub. Her partner and chef Andrew Hill smokes the salmon and prepares the game from surrounding farms. Typically, you could expect dishes such as duck

hearts on toast; fried Harlesford Farm organic mutton with bubble and squeak; roast chicken with Caesar salad; grilled dab with caper butter; and vegetable meze. Large beer garden.

The Half Moon

Open 12–2.30 5.30–11 (Closed Sun eve Winter) **Bar Meals** L served Mon-Sat 12–2 D served all week 6–9 (Sun 12–3) Av main course £12.50 **Restaurant** L served Mon-Sat 12–2 D served all week 6–9 (Sun 12–3) Av 3 course à la carte £24.50 ⊕ Brakspear ◀ Brakspear Ordinary, 4 seasonal ales. ♀8 **Facilities** Garden Dogs allowed Parking

DEDDINGTON   MAP 11 SP43

Pick of the Pubs

Deddington Arms ★★★ HL ◉ ♀

Horsefair OX15 0SH ☎ 01869 338364 🖹 01869 337010

e-mail: deddarms@oxfordshire-hotels.co.uk

dir: *M40 junct 11 to Banbury. Follow signs for hospital, then towards Adderbury & Deddington, on A4260.*

This historic old coaching inn has been welcoming travellers since the 16th century. It overlooks the picturesque market square in Deddington, one of the gateways to the Cotswolds, and offers innovative, freshly prepared food served in friendly surroundings. Good quality ales and an international wine list add to the experience. Settle in the oak beamed bar with its flagstone floors and cosy fireplace for a bar snack, or move to the elegant restaurant where a meal might begin with pan-fried pigeon breast with apple fritters and Irish cider jus, followed by roasted rump of lamb with basil mash, puy lentils and paysanne vegetables. A tempting dessert menu might offer espresso ice cream parfait with bitter chocolate sorbet, and there's also an enticing selection of traditional cheeses. Accommodation includes 27 en suite bedrooms with cottage suites and four-poster luxury.

Open 11–12 (Fri-Sat 11–1am) **Bar Meals** L served all week 12–2 D served all week 6.30–9 Av main course £9.50 **Restaurant** L served all week 12–2 D served all week 6.30–10 (Sun 7–9) Av 3 course à la carte £27.50 ⊕ Free House ◀ Tetleys Bitter, Greene King IPA, Deuchars & guest ale. ♀8 **Facilities** Parking **Rooms** 27

PICK OF THE PUBS

CHARLBURY-OXFORDSHIRE

The Bull Inn

This fine 16th-century coaching inn with a smart stone exterior presides over the main street of Charlbury (named Sheep Street – which gives an indication of the agricultural preoccupations that once held sway in these parts), a beautifully preserved Cotswold town surrounded by lovely countryside.

Despite the proximity to the great outdoors, the inn is also close to Woodstock and only 15 minutes from Oxford by train to Charlbury Station. The interior is full of period character, with exposed beams and inglenook fireplaces, where log fires burn in cooler weather. There's a traditional bar with wooden floors and a tastefully furnished lounge and dining room. Outside, the vine-covered terrace is a delightful spot to sit and enjoy a drink or a meal in summer weather. Food is served in both the bar and restaurant, with options ranging from lunchtime sandwiches and light snacks in the bar, to a full à la carte menu in the restaurant. Diners might like to start with Malay chicken satay, served with spicy peanut sauce, or perhaps black pudding, crispy

bacon and poached egg on a bed of leaves. Main courses range from such classic English fare as beef and Hook Norton ale pie with a puff pastry lid, to a fresh line-caught Devon crab on a bed of mixed leaves with buttered new potatoes and lemon mayonnaise; or from pan-fried calve's liver with smoked streaky bacon on a bed of mashed potatoes, to skewered monkfish, salmon, chicken and smoked bacon, on a timbale of rice with a chilli and coconut drizzle.

MAP 11 SP31
Sheep St OX7 3RR
☎ 01608 810689
e-mail: info@bullinn-charlbury.com
web: www.bullinn-charlbury.com
dir: *Off A44 (Chipping Norton to Oxford road) turn at Enstone onto B4022. Pub on left at x-rds in village. Or M40 junct 8, A40, A44 follow Woodstock/Blenheim Palace signs. Through Woodstock take B4437 to Charlbury*

Open 11.30–2.30 6–11
Bar Meals L served Tue-Fri 12–2 D served Tue-Sat 7–9 (Sat-Sun 12–2.30) Av main course £10.50
Restaurant L served Tue-Fri 12–2 D served Tue-Sat 7–9 (Sat-Sun 12–2.30) Av 3 course à la carte £25
⊕ Free House ◀ Hook Norton Bitter & a range of guest ales. ♀ 8
Facilities Garden Parking

PICK OF THE PUBS

CRAY'S POND-OXFORDSHIRE

The White Lion

Up in the Chilterns, in the hamlet of Crays Pond, stands the popular 250–year-old White Lion. A nearby field is the home of the annual Woodcote Rally, the third largest steam, vintage and veteran transport fair in England. As you might expect, while it's on, the pub acts as the organisers' unofficial headquarters.

Photographs taken at rallies during the last 40 or so years line the deep terracotta walls. Also worth a browse is the collection of fascinating old menus from famous restaurants around the world. The beamed ceilings are low, so be prepared to stoop. For several reasons, the food is of a high standard: partly through working closely with local producers, partly because each dish is prepared to order, and partly because the menu is changed daily. New French managers for 2007, Magali Magnein and Loïc Genestier, have brought a gastropub atmosphere and thoroughly French menus with them. From a daily choice of around eight starters and main courses, supplemented by some specials, you might find crab salad

with asparagus and coriander and tomato mayonnaise; scallops with creamy lemon and coriander sauce; pork and prune terrine; half lobster casserole with baby vegetables and saffron jus; and fillet steak with wild mushrooms and red wine sauce. Desserts are likely to include warm gooey chocolate with coffee ice cream, and crème brûlée. A selection of farmhouse cheeses is kept in peak condition. There is always a good choice of Devon fish and seafood on the menu, and everything is home made. The view from outside extends across the Thames Valley.

🍷
MAP 05 SU68
Goring Rd, Goring Heath
RG8 7SH
☎ 01491 680471
📠 01491 684254
e-mail: reservations@
thewhitelioncrayspond.com
dir: *From M4 junct 11 follow signs to Pangbourne, through toll bridge to Whitchurch. N for 3m into Crays Pond*

Open 10–3 6–11 Closed: 25–26 Dec, 1 Jan
Bar Meals L served Tue-Sun 12–1.30 D served Tue-Sat 6–9.30 Av main course £13.95
Restaurant L served Tue-Sun 12–2 D served Tue-Sat 6.30–9 Av 3 course à la carte £22.50 Av 3 course fixed price £28.40
🍺 Greene King 🍺 IPA, Abbot Ale, Guinness. 🍷 11
Facilities Garden Dogs allowed Parking Play Area

DEDDINGTON continued

The Unicorn ♀

Market Place OX15 0SE ☎ 01869 338838 🖹 01869 338592
e-mail: welcome@unicorninn.net
web: www.unicorninn.net
dir: 6m S of Banbury on A4260

Populated by friendly locals and smiling staff, visitors feel welcome too in this 17th-century coaching inn overlooking the market square. Exposed beams and an open fire characterise the bar; for warmer days the tranquillity of the secret walled garden is preserved by parents keeping children and dogs under control. Unpretentious food cooked by chefs Jude and Simon includes warm mixed salads, steak and gammon grills, open sandwiches, and perhaps cheese and mushroom omelette. Fresh fish deliveries six days per week make seafood a particular strength.

Open 12–11 (Fri-Sat 12–12) **Bar Meals** L served Mon-Sat 12–2.30 6.30–9 (Sun 12–3, No dinner Sun winter) Av main course £9 **Restaurant** L served Mon-Sat 12–2.30 D served all week 6–9.30 (Sun 12–3. No dinner Sun winter) Av 3 course à la carte £18 ◀ Hook Norton, Fuller's London Pride. ♀ 8 **Facilities** Garden

---

DORCHESTER (ON THAMES) MAP 05 SU59

Fleur De Lys Ⓤ ♀

9 High St OX10 7HH ☎ 01865 340502 🖹 01865 340502
e-mail: mail@fleurdorchester.co.uk

Dating from around 1525, this lovely old pub is located on the High Street of the picturesque village. It has retained much of its original character with a pretty garden and cosy bar and dining room. Traditional British fare is served, including steak, stilton and port wine pie; and crab and ginger fishcakes, all made in-house. Vegetarians are well catered for, too, with dishes such as baked aubergines stuffed with ratatouille, or steamed vegetarian pudding.

Open 11–11 (Sun 12–10.30) Closed: (Winter 3–6) **Bar Meals** L served Mon-Sat 12–2.30 D served Mon-Sat 7–9.30 (Sun 12–3.30, 6.30–9.30) Av main course £8.95 **Restaurant** L served Mon-Sat 12–2.30 D served Mon-Sat 7–9.30 (Sun 12–3.30, 6.30–9.30) Av 3 course à la carte £17.90 Av 2 course fixed price £10 ⊕ Free House ◀ Brakspear, Hooky, Guinness. ♀ 8 **Facilities** Garden Dogs allowed Parking **Rooms** 5

Pick of the Pubs

The George ★★★ HL

25 High St OX10 7HH
☎ 01865 340404 🖹 01865 341620
e-mail: thegeorgehotel@fsmail.net

dir: From M40 junct 7, A329 S to A4074 at Shillingford. Follow Dorchester signs. From M4 junct 13, A34 to Abingdon then A415 E to Dorchester

DH Lawrence was a frequent visitor to this 15th-century coaching inn, believed to be one of the oldest public houses in Britain. The George stands at the centre of the picturesque village of Dorchester. Inside, oak beams and inglenook fireplaces help to create a welcoming atmosphere, while outside there is an attractive garden. The Potboys bar is a traditional taproom – just the spot to enjoy a pint of Brakspear while tucking into steak and Guinness pie; vegetable curry or goats' cheese and pesto roasted peppers. The Carriages restaurant, with its secret garden, serves a full menu with, for example, chicken and wild mushroom terrine or spiced sausage, black pudding and poached egg salad as starters. Main courses might be sea bass and mushroom risotto; pan-seared tun steak or tian of roast vegetables with rocket pesto.

Open 11–11 (Sun 12–10.30) Closed: 25 Dec & 1 Jan **Bar Meals** L served all week 12–2.30 D served Mon-Sat 6.30–9.30 (Sun 6.30–10) **Restaurant** L served all week 12–2.30 D served Sun-Thu 6.30–9.30 (Fri & Sat 6.30–10) Av 3 course à la carte £25 ◀ Brakspear & Wadworth 6X. **Facilities** Garden Parking **Rooms** 17

DORCHESTER (ON THAMES) continued

Pick of the Pubs

The White Hart ★★★ HL 🏵 ♀

High St OX10 7HN

☎ 01865 340074 📠 01865 341082

e-mail: whitehart@oxfordshire-hotels.co.uk

dir: *A4074 (Oxford to Reading), 5m from M40 junct 7/ A329 to Wallingford*

The White Hart is located eight miles south of Oxford right at the centre of the High Street in the historic village of Dorchester-on-Thames. The inn has been providing hospitality to travellers for around 400 years, and the bars attract locals, residents and diners alike. Log fires and candlelight create an intimate atmosphere for the enjoyment of innovative dishes prepared from fresh ingredients. A good-value fixed-price lunch is available Monday to Saturday, with a choice of three starters, mains and desserts; perhaps Caesar salad, seared salmon on pomme purée and pepper coulis, and raspberry meringue tart with berry compote. The carte menu doubles your choice and includes imaginative dishes such as home-made gravadlax with dill, sweet potato salad and lemon oil, followed by glazed suckling pig with rosemary and apricots, dauphnoise potato and port sauce.

Open 11–11 **Bar Meals** L served all week 12–2.30 D served all week 6.30–9.30 **Restaurant** L served all week 12–2.30 D served all week 6.30–9.30 🍺 Free House 🍴 Greene King, Marstons Pedigree,. St Austell Tribute, Deuchars Caledonian IPA. ♀ 12 **Facilities** Parking **Rooms** 28

EAST HENDRED   **MAP 05 SU48**

The Wheatsheaf ♀

Chapel Square OX12 8JN

☎ 01235 833229 📠 01235 821521

e-mail: info@thewheatsheaf.org.uk

dir: *2m from A34 Milton interchange*

Formerly used as a courthouse, this 16th-century pub stands in a pretty village close to the Ridgeway path. Spit-roasts and barbecues are popular summer features of the attractive front garden, which overlooks the village. Bar meals include baguettes; a venison burger with hand cut chips; and classic Greek salad with French bread. The restaurant menu might offer twice-baked cheddar, stilton and spinach soufflé, followed by noisette of lamb with mint and blackcurrant jus and dauphinoise potatoes.

Open 11.30–3 6–11 **Bar Meals** L served all week 12–2 D served all week 6.30–9 **Restaurant** L served Mon-Sat 12–2 D served all week 6.30–9.30 (Sun 12–2.30) Av 3 course à la carte £20 🍺 Greene King 🍴 IPA, 2 guest ales. ♀ 8 **Facilities** Garden Dogs allowed Parking

FARINGDON   **MAP 05 SU29**

Pick of the Pubs

The Lamb at Buckland ♀

Lamb Ln, Buckland SN7 8QN

☎ 01367 870484 📠 01367 870675

e-mail: enquiries@thelambatbuckland.co.uk

dir: *Just off A420 3m E of Faringdon*

The 18th-century Lamb displays a fair few appropriately ovine artefacts. It has a village location on the fringe of the Cotswolds in the Vale of the White Horse and is renowned for its excellent food. A reliable menu, supplemented by daily specials, offers the likes of veal kidneys sautéed with shallots, smoked bacon, fresh herbs and mushrooms; and breast of Gressingham duck, roasted pink and served with apple and Calvados sauce. Items from the specials board might include brace of roast teal with sage and onion stuffing, or medallions of Scotch beef fillet with wild mushroom sauce. Friday night is fish night – a piscatorial extravaganza – with dishes like cullen skink, home-smoked sprats, monkfish and prawn ragout, and seared fillet of wild sea bass served with shrimp and saffron risotto.

Open 10.30–3 5.30–11 Closed: 24 Dec-7 Jan, Sun eve & Mon am **Bar Meals** L served Tue-Sun 12–2 D served Tue-Sat 6.30–9.30 **Restaurant** L served Tue-Sun 12–2 D served Tue-Sat 6.30–9.30 (Sun 12–3) 🍺 Free House 🍴 Hook Norton, Adnams Broadside, Arkells 3Bs. ♀ 12 **Facilities** Garden Parking

Pick of the Pubs

The Trout at Tadpole Bridge ♀

Buckland Marsh SN7 8RF ☎ 01367 870382

e-mail: info@trout-inn.co.uk

dir: *Halfway between Oxford & Swindon on A420 take road signed Bampton, pub approx 2m*

In July 2007 this 17th-century pub was flooded, along with all the other inns along this stretch of the River Thames. Thanks to the Hurculean efforts of staff and regulars the bar was re-opened within six days, but the restaurant and rooms took much longer to repair. Ironically the pub had only recently been refurbished when the flood struck, but following its second, unexpected refurbishment the Trout is better than ever. A new chef has introduced more slow-cooked and braised dishes – his beef and mushroom steamed pudding is a particular hit – and dishes are still based on locally sourced ingredients. Daily specials include braised lamb faggots with grainy mustard mash and cumin

Savoy cabbage; or turbot poached in Merlot with braised onions and salsify. The wine list continues to expand and the selection of local ales is a big attraction to the walkers and boaters who frequent the inn.

Open 11.30–3 6–11 Closed: 25 Dec-1 Jan **Bar Meals** L served all week 12–2 D served Mon-Sat 7–9 **Restaurant** L served all week 12–2 D served Mon-Sat 7–9 ⊕ Free House ◀ Ramsbury Bitter, Youngs PA Bitter, Butts Barbus, West Berkshire Brewery Mr Chubbs Lunchtime Bitter. ♀ 10 **Facilities** Garden Dogs allowed Parking

---

FIFIELD   MAP 10 SP21

Merrymouth Inn ♀

Stow Rd OX7 6HR ☎ 01993 831652 ▤ 01993 830840
e-mail: tim@merrymouthinn.fsnet.co.uk
dir: *On A424 between Burford & Stow-on-the-Wold*

A beautifully restored Cotswold inn dating back to the 13th century. At that time it was owned by the monks of nearby Bruern Abbey, to which hitherto undiscovered underground passages are said to lead. A blackboard of fresh fish, vegetarian and other daily specials includes such dishes as a warm salad of scallops and bacon and gilt head sea bream with fennel and tomato. Home-made puddings include raspberry marshmallow meringue.

Open 12–2.30 6–10.30 **Bar Meals** L served all week 12–2 D served all week 6.30–9 (Sun 7–8.30) Av main course £10 **Restaurant** L served all week 12–2 D served all week 6.30–9 (Sun 7–9) Av 3 course à la carte £21 ⊕ Free House ◀ Hook Norton Best Bitter, Adnams Broadside. ♀ 7 **Facilities** Garden Dogs allowed Parking

---

FILKINS   MAP 05 SP20

The Five Alls ♀

GL7 3JQ ☎ 01367 860306
e-mail: info@thefivealls.co.uk
dir: *A40 exit Burford, Filkins 4m, A361 to Lechlade*

Dating from the 1700s, this Cotswold stone pub has a peaceful village setting in a popular walking area. The interior is all bare wood floors, terracotta walls and rustic furniture, with the odd leather sofa thrown in for good measure. Home-made fare ranges from the all-day bar menu with plates of deep-fried five-spice baby squid, and steak and Brakspear Ale pie; to the carte offering lunch of crab salad niçoise, or a dinner dish of jugged hare with spring greens.

Open 11–3 5.30–11 (Sat-Sun all day) **Bar Meals** L served Mon-Sat 12–2.30 D served all week 6.30–9 (Sun 12–4) Av main course £12 **Restaurant** L served Mon-Sat 12–2.30 D served all week 6.30–9 (Sun 12–4) Av 3 course à la carte £28 ⊕ Brakspear ◀ Brakspear Bitter, Brakspear Special & Brakspear/Wychwood seasonal ales. ♀ 8 **Facilities** Garden Dogs allowed Parking

---

FRINGFORD   MAP 11 SP62

The Butchers Arms

OX27 8EB ☎ 01869 277363
e-mail: butcherarms@aol.com
dir: *4m from Bicester on A4421 towards Buckingham*

Flora Thompson mentioned this traditional village pub in her 1939 novel *Lark Rise to Candleford* about life on the Northamptonshire/ Oxfordshire border. A good selection of fresh fish and other seafood, including mussels, crab and king prawns, is offered, as well as liver,

bacon and onions, peppered fillet steak, half a roast duck, and steak and kidney pie. Pumps display Adnams Broadside labels. From the patio watch the cricket during the summer.

The Butchers Arms

Open 12–11.30 **Bar Meals** L served Mon-Sat 12–9.30 D served Mon-Sat 12–9.30 (Sun 3 sittings 12, 2, 3.30) Av main course £9.95 **Restaurant** L served Mon-Sat 12–9.30 D served Mon-Sat 12–9.30 (Sun 12–4) ⊕ Punch Taverns ◀ Adnams Broadside, Hooky Bitter & Old Speckled Hen. **Facilities** Dogs allowed Parking

---

FYFIELD   MAP 05 SU49

Pick of the Pubs

The White Hart ♀

See Pick of the Pubs on page 452

GORING   MAP 05 SU68

Miller of Mansfield ♀

High St RG8 9AW ☎ 01491 872829 ▤ 01491 873100
e-mail: reservations@millerofmansfield.com
dir: *From Pangbourne take A329 to Streatley. Right on B4009, 0.5m to Goring*

This beautiful old building has been completely renovated. There is a full bar menu and a restaurant open for breakfast, lunch and dinner 365 days a year. Modern European menus might offer roast loin of venison or grilled fillet of sea bass in the restaurant, and fish and chips or steak sandwich in the bar. There is a marble paved area in the garden with plants and statues under a canopy with gas heating.

Open 8–11 **Bar Meals** L served all week 11–10 D served all week 11–10 (Sun 12–4, 6.30–9.30) Av main course £11.95 **Restaurant** L served all week 12–3 D served all week 6–10 Av 3 course à la carte £22 ⊕ Free House ◀ Good Old Boy, Rebellion IPA, Organic Jester. ♀ 15 **Facilities** Garden Dogs allowed Parking

PICK OF THE PUBS

FYFIELD-OXFORDSHIRE

The White Hart

It might not give much away from the outside, but the interior of this former chantry house is breathtaking. It was built in 1442 to house two priests and five almsmen (poor men) whose sole duty was to pray for the soul of the lord of the manor, the chapel's founder.

Among the many original features is a tunnel – probably an escape route for priests during the Dissolution of the Monasteries – that runs from the corner of the bar to the manor house. In the cosy low-ceilinged bar, centre stage is taken by a large inglenook fireplace. In stark contrast is the main restaurant, a grand hall of a place with soaring eaves and beams, huge stone-flanked window surrounds and flagstone floors, overlooked by a minstrels' gallery. Mark and Kay Chandler are passionate 'foodies' and work closely with nearby farms and suppliers; they even exchange food and wine for locals' home-grown produce, and menus change daily. Each dish is prepared to order and everything is made on the premises, including bread

and pasta from locally milled flour. Apart from starters that might include braised hare suet pudding with garlic velouté, or home-cured salmon gravadlax with marinated cucumber salad, there are antipasti, mezze and fish sharing-boards for two. Typical main courses are wild sea bass fillet with pumpkin and parmesan tartlet, toasted hazelnuts and warm broccoli salad; and slow-roasted belly of Kelmscott pork with celeriac and cider jus. Save room for the deliciously tempting pudding menu, especially the hot chocolate fondant with pistachio ice cream. The extensive and varied wine list includes wine from the local vineyard. Two annual beer festivals are held (on May Day and August bank holiday) with at least 12 real ales, and hog roasts.

MAP 05 SU49
Main Rd OX13 5LW
☎ 01865 390585
e-mail:
info@whitehart-fyfield.com
web: www.whitehart-fyfield.com
dir: *6m S of Oxford just off A420 (Oxford to Swindon road)*

Open 12–3 5.30–11 (Sat 12–11, Sun 12–10.30) Closed: Mon
Bar Meals L served Tue-Sat 12–2.30 D served Tue-Sat 6.30–9.30 (Sun 12–4) Av main course £15
Restaurant L served Tue-Sat 12–2.30 D served Tue-Sat 6.30–9.30 (Sun 12–4) Av 3 course à la carte £26 Av 2 course fixed price £15
⊕ Free House ◀ Ale, Hooky Bitter, Village Idiot, Black Beauty & guest ales. ♈ 14
Facilities Garden Parking Play Area

GREAT TEW   MAP 11 SP42   HENLEY-ON-THAMES   MAP 05 SU78

Pick of the Pubs

The Falkland Arms ♚

OX7 4DB ☎ 01608 683653 🖹 01608 683656

e-mail: falklandarms@wadworth.co.uk

dir: *Off A361, 1.25m, signed Great Tew*

This 500-year-old inn takes its name from Lucius Carey, 2nd Viscount Falkland, who inherited the manor of Great Tew in 1629. Nestling at the end of a charming row of Cotswold stone cottages, the Falkland Arms is a classic: flagstone floors, high-backed settles and an inglenook fireplace characterise the intimate bar, where a huge collection of beer and cider mugs hangs from the ceiling. Home-made specials such as beef and ale pie or salmon and broccoli fishcakes supplement the basic lunchtime menu, served in the bar or the pub garden. In the evening, booking is essential for dinner in the small dining room. Expect parsnip soup or grilled goats' cheese salad, followed by chicken breast with bacon and mushrooms in shallot sauce; salmon and prawns with lemon and dill sauce; or mushroom and herb stroganoff.

Open 11.30–2.30 6–11 (Sat 11.30–3, Sun 12–3, 7–10.30 Summer all day Sat-Sun) **Bar Meals** L served all week 12–2 **Restaurant** L served all week 12–2 D served Mon-Sat 7–8 ⬢ Wadworth ⬛ Wadworth 6X & Henry's IPA & guest ales. ♟ 12 **Facilities** Garden Dogs allowed

---

HAILEY   MAP 11 SP31

Bird in Hand ♚

Whiteoak Green OX29 9XP ☎ 01993 868321 🖹 01993 868702

e-mail: welcome@birdinhandinn.co.uk

web: www.birdinhandinn.co.uk

dir: *From Witney N onto B4022 through Hailey to Whiteoak Green for 5m. At Charlbury S onto B4022 for 5m*

Set in the Oxfordshire countryside just outside the village of Hailey, this classic Cotswold stone inn is Grade-II listed and dates from the 16th century. The beamed interior has huge inglenook fireplaces, with log fires in winter. Food ranges from traditional rarebit on toast topped with a poached egg, to marinated Cotswold game casserole; or home-made faggots with onion gravy and mashed potato.

Open 11–11 **Bar Meals** L served all week 12–3 D served Sun-Thu 6–9 (Fri-Sat 6–10) Av main course £9 **Restaurant** L served Mon-Sat 12–2.30 D served Mon-Thu 6–9 (Fri-Sat 6–10, Sun 12–6) ⬢ Buccaneer Holdings ⬛ Old Hooky, Butcombe & Directors. ♟ 14 **Facilities** Garden Parking

See advert on page 454

The Baskerville Arms

Station Road, Lower Shiplake, Henley-on-Thames, RG9 3NY

Tel: 0118 940 3332

Email: enquiries@thebaskerville.com

The only pub situated in the picturesque village of Shiplake, just a few yards from the Thames and a stones throw from Henley-on-Thames.

Always at least 3/4 cask conditioned beers on tap. 5-excellent rooms and an award winning restaurant highly commended for its food (runner up in 'The-Best Rural pub with Accommodation' award from Tourism South East), and last but not least a superb garden with summer barbecues.

Pick of the Pubs

The Cherry Tree Inn ★★★★ INN ⬢ ♚

Stoke Row RG9 5QA

☎ 01491 680430 🖹 01491 682168

e-mail: info@thecherrytreeinn.com

dir: *B481 towards Reading & Sonning Common 2m, follow Stoke Row sign*

There's a confident blend of ancient and modern inside this 400-year-old listed building. Originally three flint cottages, the Cherry Tree has been comprehensively re-fitted, mixing the original flagstone floors, beamed ceilings and fireplaces with contemporary décor, strong colours and comfortable modern

CONTINUED

HENLEY-ON-THAMES continued

furnishings. The contemporary theme continues throughout the pub, which offers Brakspear real ales, fine malt whiskies and over 40 different wines, including 12 served by the glass. Service is informal, with a variety of classic European dishes prepared from fresh local ingredients. Lunchtime choices include grilled focaccia with goats' cheese, peppers and pesto; as well as more substantial dishes like belly of pork with black pudding and creamy mash. à la carte options range from chargrilled rib-eye steak, to grilled squid and chorizo salad. Outside, the large south-facing garden is perfect for alfresco summer dining.

Open 12–11 (Sun 12–10.30) Closed: 25–26 Dec **Bar Meals** L served all week 12–4 D served all week 7–10 **Restaurant** L served Mon-Sat 12–3 D served Mon-Sat 12–10 (Sun 12–4, 7–10) Av 3 course à la carte £25 ⊕ Brakspear. ◀ Brakspear Bitter, Brakspear Organic, Douvel, Orval. ♀ 12 **Facilities** Garden Parking

PICK OF THE PUBS

HENLEY-ON-THAMES-OXFORDSHIRE

The Five Horseshoes

The Five Horseshoes is located in an area of outstanding natural beauty, with stunning views across the Chilterns and numerous walks available from the door. The building dates from the 17th-century and prides itself on its traditional atmosphere with old pub games, log fires, heavy beams and brass features.

The grounds incorporate two large beer gardens, from where the views stretch to a distance of 30 miles. Summer weekend barbeques and bank holiday Monday hog roasts are held in one of the gardens; while the other is available for private hire with a marquee for special occasions. Inside there is a large conservatory restaurant and two snug bar areas serving real ales and a choice of wines and champagnes by the glass. Food focuses on the freshest produce, locally sourced where possible. The bar menu offers Henley breads with dipping oil and Five Horseshoes' classics such as pork pie; beer battered fish and chunky chips; burgers; and Charolais sirloin steak. Seasonal fare from the monthly changing Room With a View menu might

include ham hock and guinea fowl terrine with sweetcorn purée and mead vinaigrette; today's line-caught fish; or roast haunch of wild Berkshire venison with potato rösti, grelots and peppercorn sauce. An intriguing dessert entitled tea, toast and jam comprises Earl Grey brûlée, pain perdue and rhubarb compote. Gourmet picnic hampers are now available to order in advance – perfect for the nearby Henley Regatta. Hikers and mountain bikers are welcome, but are asked to leave muddy boots at the door. Dogs are permitted in the gardens and bar. Afternoon teas are served during summer at weekends.

MAP 05 SU78
Maidensgrove RG9 6EX
☎ 01491 641282
📠 01491 641086
e-mail: admin@
thefivehorseshoes.co.uk
web:
www.thefivehorseshoes.co.uk
dir: *From Henley-on-Thames take A4130, in 1m take B480 to right, signed Stonor. In Stonor left, through woods, over common, pub on left. (5m from Henley)*

Open 12–3.30 6–11 (Sat 12–11, Sun 12–6) Closed: Sun eve
Bar Meals L served Mon-Fri 12–2.30 D served all week 6.30–9.30 (Sat 12–3, Sun 12–4) Av main course £9
Restaurant L served Mon-Fri 12–2.30 D served all week 6.30–9.30 (Sat 12–3, Sun 12–4) Av 3 course à la carte £25
🍺 Brakspear 🛢 Brakspear Ordinary, Special & Seasonal.
🍷 11
Facilities Garden Dogs allowed Parking

PICK OF THE PUBS

HENLEY-ON-THAMES-OXFORDSHIRE

WhiteHartNettlebed

Both Royalist and parliamentary soldiers made a habit of lodging in local taverns where possible during the English Civil War, and this 15th-century inn was one such billeting house for troops loyal to the king.

During the 17th and 18th-century, the area was plagued by highwaymen, including the notorious Isaac Darkin, who was eventually caught, tried and hung at Oxford Gaol. These days, the beautifully restored hotel is favoured by a stylish crowd who appreciate the chic bar, restaurant and bistro, not to mention the welcoming atmosphere. Dining styles vary from doorstop Brakspear ham and whole grain mustard sandwiches in the bar, to an inviting à la carte restaurant menu. You could begin with rolled braised pigs' trotters with warm potato salad; or seared scallops with lobster sausages; and move on to local wood pigeon and foie gras with fondant potatoes and Sauternes juice; or provençal polenta tian, glazed goats' cheese and roast garlic. Keep an eye out for blackboard specials: the catch of the day could be gilthead bream with mussel ragout and Pernod jus; or sea bass fillet with crushed new potatoes. A lengthy wine list includes some extravagant options, or you could visit for afternoon tea and the delights of home-made muffins, scones and an excellent array of teas. Weddings, meetings and parties can be hosted, with the option of using the elegant red and orange rooms. Twelve luxurious en-suite bedrooms are named and decorated after different flavours: sample Blackcurrant, Caramel or Pistachio, each of which has an accompanying recipe.

★★★ HL ◉◉ ♀
MAP 05 SU78
High St, Nettlebed RG9 5DD
☎ 01491 641245
🖷 01491 649018
e-mail:
info@whitehartnettlebed.com
dir: *On A4130 between Henley-on-Thames & Wallingford*

Open 7am-11
Bar Meals L served all week
12–2.30 D served all week 6–10
(Sun 12–3)
Restaurant L served all week
12–2.30 D served all week 6–9.30
(Sun 12–3)
🍺 Brakspear, Guinness. ♀ 12
Facilities Garden Parking Play
Area
Rooms 12

HENLEY-ON-THAMES continued

Pick of the Pubs

WhiteHartNettlebed ★★★ HL ◉◉ ♥

See Pick of the Pubs on opposite page

HOOK NORTON   MAP 11 SP33

Pick of the Pubs

The Gate Hangs High ★★★★ INN

Whichford Rd OX15 5DF

☎ 01608 737387 🖷 01608 737870

e-mail: gatehangshigh@aol.com

dir: *Off A361 SW of Banbury*

This rural pub is set amid beautiful countryside near the mystical Rollright Stones and Hook Norton, where the cask-conditioned, dry-hopped ales served here are brewed. It is on the old drovers' road from Wales to Banbury and a tollgate that once stood outside was said to hang high enough for small creatures to pass under, although owners of larger beasts had to pay. In the low-beamed bar, polished horse brasses reflect the glow from the candles, pretty wall lights and roaring log fire. A £10 set menu is offered October, November, January, February and March, from Monday to Friday – a typical example being bacon and mushroom salad, battered cod and chips, and bread pudding and custard. Otherwise popular options include lunchtime sandwiches served with chips and salad and dishes such as steak and Hooky ale pie; and swordfish steak with horseradish cream. The pub also has a cocktail menu.

Open 12–3 6–11 (Fri-Sat all day, Sun 12–4, 7–10.30) Closed: 25 Dec eve **Bar Meals** L served all week 12–2.30 D served all week 6–10 **Restaurant** L served Mon-Fri 12–2.30 D served Mon-Fri 6–10 (Sat 12–11, Sun 12–10.30) ⊕ Hook Norton ◀ Hook Norton – Best, Old Hooky, Haymaker & Generation. **Facilities** Garden Dogs allowed Parking **Rooms** 4

Sun Inn ♥

High St OX15 5NH ☎ 01608 737570 🖷 01608 737535

e-mail: joyce@the-sun-inn.com

dir: *5m from Chipping Norton, 8m from Banbury, just off A361*

A traditional Cotswold stone inn with oak beams, flagstone floors and an inglenook fireplace. Select from the full range of Hook Norton ales while deliberating over the comprehensive food options. Sandwiches include a four-ounce marinated rump steak with fried onions; bar snacks tempt with the likes of creamy chicken, bacon and mushroom crêpe; and main meal choices like slow-roasted pork knuckle provençale are augmented by a daily changing fish board. Take-away service also available.

Open 11.30–3 6–11.30 **Bar Meals** L served all week 12–2 D served all week 7–9.30 Av main course £7.50 **Restaurant** L served all week 12–2 D served all week 7–9.30 Av 3 course à la carte £21 ⊕ Hook Norton ◀ Hook Norton Best Bitter, Old Double Stout, Hooky Dark, 303 & Twelve Days. ♥ 8 **Facilities** Garden Parking

KELMSCOTT   MAP 05 SU29

The Plough Inn

GL7 3HG ☎ 01367 253543 🖷 01367 252514

e-mail: plough@kelmscottgl7.fsnet.co.uk

dir: *From M4 onto A419 then A361 to Lechlade & A416 to Faringdon, pick up signs to Kelmscott*

The Plough dates from 1631 and is set in the beautiful village of Kelmscott a short walk from Kelmscott Manor, once home to William Morris. The inn is on the Thames Path midway between Radcot and Lechlade, so is a haven for walkers and boaters. Cotswold stone walls and flagstone floors set the scene for real ales and an extensive menu. Dishes include tempura of seafood with sweet chilli sauce, and pot roasted whole partridge.

Open 11–12 (Fri-Sat 11–2am) **Bar Meals** L served all week 12–2.30 D served Mon-Sat 7–9 Av main course £14 **Restaurant** L served all week 12–2.30 D served all week 7–9 (Restaurant closed to non-residents Sun eve) ⊕ Free House ◀ Hook Norton, Timothy Taylor, Wychwood. **Facilities** Garden Dogs allowed Parking

LEWKNOR   MAP 05 SU79

The Leathern Bottel ♥

1 High St OX49 5TW ☎ 01844 351482

dir: *0.5m from M40 junct 6 north or south*

Run by the same family for more than 25 years, this 16th-century coaching inn is set in the foothills of the Chilterns. Walkers with dogs, families with children, parties for meals or punters for a quick pint are all made equally welcome. In winter there's a wood-burning stove, a good drop of Brakspears ale, nourishing specials and a quiz on Sunday. Summer is the time for outdoor eating, the children's play area, Pimm's and Morris dancers.

Open 11–3 6–11 Closed: 25–26 Dec **Bar Meals** L served all week 12–2 D served Sun-Thu 7–9.30 (Fri-Sat 7–10) ⊕ Brakspear ◀ Brakspear Ordinary, Special. ♥ 12 **Facilities** Garden Dogs allowed Parking Play Area

The Radcliffe Camera, Oxford

LOWER SHIPLAKE   MAP 05 SU77

The Baskerville Arms ★★★★ INN ♥

Station Rd RG9 3NY ☎ 0118 940 3332 ▤ 0118 940 7235
e-mail: enquiries@thebaskerville.com
dir: Just off A4155, 1.5m from Henley

This welcoming pub stands on the popular Thames Path just a few minutes from historic Henley-on-Thames. Brick-built on the outside, modern-rustic inside, it boasts an attractive garden where summer barbecues are a common fixture. Light meals are served in the bar, while the restaurant offers the likes of seared sea bass with shellfish bisque and saffron risotto; and chargrilled rib-eye steak with home-made chips. Booking is essential during Henley Regatta (early July).

Open 11.30–2.30 6–11 (Sun 11.30–2.30, 5.30–11) **Bar Meals** L served Mon-Sat 12–2 D served Mon-Sat 7–9.30 (Sun 12–2.30)
Restaurant L served all week 12–2 D served Mon-Sat 7–9.30 Av 3 course à la carte £22 Av 2 course fixed price £11.50 ◀ London Pride, Loddon Hoppit, Bass, Timothy Taylor. ♥ 8 **Facilities** Garden Dogs allowed Parking Play Area **Rooms** 5

See advertisement under HENLEY-ON-THAMES

LOWER WOLVERCOTE   MAP 05 SP40

Pick of the Pubs

The Trout Inn ♥

See Pick of the Pubs on page 460

MARSTON   MAP 05 SP50

Victoria Arms ♥

Mill Ln OX3 0PZ ☎ 01865 241382
e-mail: kyffinda@yahoo.co.uk
dir: From A40 follow signs to Old Marston, sharp right into Mill Lane, pub in lane 500yds on left

Friendly country pub situated on the banks of the River Cherwell, occupying the site of the old Marston Ferry that connected the north and south of the city. The old ferryman's bell is still behind the bar. Popular destinations for punters, and fans of TV sleuth Inspector Morse, as the last episode used this as a location. Typical menu includes lamb cobbler, steak and Guinness pie, spicy pasta bake, battered haddock, and ham off the bone.

Open 11.30–11 Closed: Oct-Apr afternoons **Bar Meals** L served 12–2.30 D served Mon-Sat 6–9 (Sun 12–6) ● Wadworth ◀ Henrys IPA, Wadworth 6X, JCB, guest ales. ♥ 15 **Facilities** Garden Dogs allowed Parking

MIDDLETON STONEY   MAP 11 SP52

Best Western Jersey Arms Hotel ★★ HL ♥

OX25 4AD ☎ 01869 343234 ▤ 01869 343565
e-mail: jerseyarms@bestwestern.co.uk
dir: 3m from junct 9/10 of M4. 3m from A34 on B430

This charming family-run free house was built as an ale house in the 13th century, on what used to be the estate of Lord Jersey. The cosy bar offers a good range of popular bar food with the extensive menu supplemented by daily blackboard specials. In the beamed and panelled Livingston's restaurant with its Mediterranean terracotta décor, the cosmopolitan brasserie-style menu features dishes like salad Niçoise; spinach and cream cheese pancakes; and duck confit with cherry and cinnamon sauce.

Open 12–11 **Bar Meals** L served all week 12–2.15 D served Mon-Sat 6.30–9.30 (Sun 6.30–9) Av main course £10.95 **Restaurant** L served all week 12–2.15 D served all week 6.30–9.30 Av 3 course à la carte £23 ⊕ Free House ◀ Interbrew Flower. **Facilities** Garden Parking **Rooms** 20

MILTON   MAP 11 SP43

Pick of the Pubs

The Black Boy Inn ♥

See Pick of the Pubs on page 462

MURCOTT   MAP 11 SP51

The Nut Tree Inn ◉◉ ♥

Main St OX5 2RE ☎ 01865 331253
dir: M40 junct 9, A34 towards Oxford. Left onto B4027 signed Islip. At Red Lion turn left. Right signed Murcett, Fencott & Charlton-on-Otmoor. Pub on right in village

Once three 15th-century cottages, this rustic, thatched inn in nearly four acres overlooks the village pond. Stripped oak beams, wood-burning stoves and unusual carvings characterise the interior. Menus offer olive oil-poached fillet of wild Scottish halibut; roast breast of free-range chicken; and filled baguettes. The pub's Gloucester Old Spot/Tamworth-cross sows gradually make their way on to the menu, but if Chloe, the biggest, produces a runt it'll be spared to become the pub dog substitute.

Open 12–11 (Sun in winter 12–6) **Bar Meals** L served Mon-Sat 12–9 D served Mon-Sat 12–9 (Sun 12–9) Av main course £7.50
Restaurant L served Mon-Sat 12–2.30 D served Mon-Sat 7–9 (Sun 12–3) Av 3 course à la carte £30 Av 2 course fixed price £15 ⊕ Free House ◀ Hook Norton, Wadworths 6X, Oxfordshire Ales, Pigswill. ♥ 10 **Facilities** Garden Dogs allowed Parking

PICK OF THE PUBS

LOWER WOLVERCOTE-OXFORDSHIRE

The Trout Inn

An old riverside inn on the banks of the Isis, as the Thames is known here. It was built around 1133 as a hospice to serve Godstow Nunnery, the ruins of which are on the opposite bank. Following the Dissolution of the Monasteries, some of the abbey's stones were removed and used to rebuild the former hospice as a hostelry.

With stone walls, slate roof, leaded windows, great oak beams, flagged floors and ancient fireplaces (always lit in winter), it is arguably Oxford's most atmospheric inn. Matthew Arnold and Lewis Carroll certainly knew it, as did Colin Dexter's fictional Inspector Morse. A single menu sets out to meet all tastes. Start with a prawn cocktail, Irish mussels, or maybe breaded flat mushrooms. Then deliberate between a chargrilled steak, or hake fillet in coriander and coconut crumb; breaded wholetail scampi with dressed mixed salad and seasoned chips, or minted lamb burger with onion; beef, mushroom and ale pie. Listed as pub classics are lemon and cracked pepper glazed chicken; and chargrilled calves' liver and bacon. Freshly cut sandwiches (Gloucestershire ham and Wexford Cheddar; and salt beef with gherkins and English mustard, for example) are served with seasoned chips. A short but perfectly adequate wine list offers examples from Australasia, South America, South Africa, Italy and Spain. Mulled wine is served in winter; Pimm's in summer. A ghost, well known locally as The White Lady, visits the Trout regularly. She is Rosamund, the much-loved mistress of Henry II, who 'embowered' her here. Her feet are never seen, as the floor level is now higher than that of the old hospice. She also knocks bottles off tables and stands behind people in the bar (but never buys her round!).

🍷
MAP 05 SP40
195 Godstow Rd OX2 8PN
☎ 01865 302071
🖨 01865 302072
dir: *From A40 at Wolvercote rdbt (N of Oxford) follow signs for Wolvercote, through village to pub*

Open 11–11
Bar Meals L served all week
D served all week
🍺 Vintage Inns ◀ Bass, Adnams.
🍷 20
Facilities Garden Parking

OXFORD MAP 05 SP50

The Anchor ♥

2 Hayfield Rd, Walton Manor OX2 6TT
☎ 01865 510282 ▤ 01865 510275
e-mail: charlotte@theanchoroxford.com

dir: A34 (Oxford ring road N), exit Peartree rdbt, 1.5m then right at Polstead Rd, follow road to bottom, pub on right

Following its major refurbishment, the Art Deco-styled Anchor is particularly popular with North Oxford's well-heeled locals, very much back on the map in fact for its well-kept ales, carefully chosen wines and good quality seasonal British food. Lunchtime specials include roast monkfish with courgettes, peas, bacon and spinach, while the main menu offers belly pork with black pudding and greens; and smoked haddock fishcakes with ginger lime mayo. Bar snacks and sandwiches are also available.

Open 11–11 (Sun 12–10.30) Closed: Xmas **Bar Meals** L served Mon-Sat 12–2.30 D served Mon-Sat 6–9.30 (Sun 12–3, 7–9) Av main course £11 **Restaurant** L served Mon-Sat 12–2.30 D served Mon-Sat 6–9.30 (Sun 12–3, 7–9) Av 3 course à la carte £22 ⊕ Wadworth ◀ Wadworth 6X, Henrys IPA, Bishops Tipple. ♥ 11 **Facilities** Parking

Turf Tavern ♥

4 Bath Place, off Holywell St OX1 3SU
☎ 01865 243235 ▤ 01865 243838
e-mail: turftavern.oxford@laurelpubco.com

dir: Telephone for directions

Situated in the heart of Oxford, approached through hidden alleyways and winding passages, this famous pub lies in the shadow of the city wall and the colleges. It is especially popular in the summer when customers can relax in the sheltered courtyards. Eleven real ales are served daily, from a choice of around 500 over a year, along with some typical pub fare. The pub has been featured in TV's *Inspector Morse*, and was frequented by JRR Tolkien.

Open 11–11 (Sun 12–10.30) **Bar Meals** L served all week 12–7.30 D served all week ⊕ Greene King ◀ Traditional ales, changing daily. ♥ 6 **Facilities** Garden Dogs allowed

PISHILL MAP 05 SU78

Pick of the Pubs
The Crown Inn ♥
See Pick of the Pubs on page 465

RAMSDEN MAP 11 SP31

Pick of the Pubs
The Royal Oak ♥
See Pick of the Pubs on page 466

ROKE MAP 05 SU69

Home Sweet Home ♥

OX10 6JD ☎ 01491 838249 ▤ 01491 835760

dir: Just off the B4009 from Benson to Watlington, signed on B4009

Long ago converted from adjoining cottages by a local brewer, this pretty 15th-century inn stands in a tiny hamlet surrounded by lovely countryside. Oak beams and the large inglenook fireplace dominate a friendly bar with an old-fashioned feel. Starters might include spicy nachos topped with cheese for two to share; while main courses run to Cornish crab fishcakes with home-made tartare sauce; or calves' liver and bacon with an onion gravy. Extensive Sunday menu.

Open 11–2.30 6–11 (Sun 12–3) Closed: 25–26 Dec **Bar Meals** L served all week 12–2 D served Mon-Sat 6–9 **Restaurant** L served Mon-Sun 12–2 D served Mon-Sat 7–9 ⊕ Free House ◀ Black Sheep, Loddon Brewery ales- Hoppit & Branoc. ♥ 10 **Facilities** Garden Dogs allowed Parking

SHENINGTON MAP 11 SP34

The Bell ♥

OX15 6NQ ☎ 01295 670274
e-mail: the_bellshenington@hotmail.com

dir: M40 junct 11 take A422 towards Stratford. Through Wroxton. Shenington signed on left

Overlooking a picturesque village green surrounded by mellow stone houses, this attractive and comfortable 300–year-old pub is conveniently located for exploring much of the nearby Oxfordshire countryside as well as the Cotswolds. The pub offers home-cooked food prepared in-house, and the blackboard menu changes frequently. Specialities include lamb and mint casserole; chicken wrapped in bacon with stilton sauce; and duck with port and black cherries. Expect treacle tart or fruit pavlova to follow.

Open 12–2.30 7–11 **Bar Meals** L served Tue-Sun 12–2 D served all week 7–11 Av main course £8.95 **Restaurant** L served Tue-Sun 12–2 D served all week 7–10 ⊕ Free House ◀ Hook Norton, Flowers. ♥ 8 **Facilities** Garden Dogs allowed

SHIPTON-UNDER-WYCHWOOD MAP 10 SP21

Pick of the Pubs
The Shaven Crown Hotel ♥
See Pick of the Pubs on page 468

PICK OF THE PUBS

MILTON-OXFORDSHIRE

The Black Boy Inn

Now in new hands, this perfect 16th-century coaching inn was completely refurbished in 2007. Yet somehow the stylish interior and solid pine furniture are entirely in keeping with such an old building. Located in the picturesque village of Milton, the pub's name is thought to be associated with the dark-skinned Charles II; other popular theories naturally include a reference to the slave trade.

The long room has a real wood stove at one end and a comfortable dining room at the other; in between is the bar, from which extends a conservatory-style dining room overlooking a gravelled courtyard. Outside is a patio and a lovely half-acre garden with plenty of seating and space for the children to run around. A rotating list of guest ales and a selection of wines by the glass ensure that drinkers can enjoy the relaxed and informal atmosphere of this quintessentially English free house, while modern British food based on fresh seasonal ingredients at sensible prices is the objective of executive chef Rob Clayton. Plenty of pub classics including the likes of beer-battered cod and home-made chips with crushed peas; and chicken, leek and tarragon pie with mash and curly kale. Choose from starters such as cream of leek and potato soup with hot-smoked trout; and lightly cooked Scottish salmon with baby leaf salad. Main courses could include pan-roasted scallops with sautéed Jerusalem artichokes, pancetta and wild mushrooms; double-cooked shoulder of lamb with braised red cabbage and gratin potatoes; and marinated guinea fowl breast with olive potato cake and baby spinach leaves in honey vinaigrette. Excellent desserts, vegetarian options and a wide range of fresh salads and tasty sandwiches complete the choice.

MAP 11 SP43
OX15 4HH
☎ 01295 722111
e-mail: info@blackboyinn.com
web: www.blackboyinn.com
dir: *From Banbury take A4260 to Adderbury. After Adderbury turn right signed Bloxham. Onto Milton Road to Milton. Pub on right*

Open 12–11 (Sun 12–10.30)
Bar Meals L served Mon-Sat 12–2.30
Restaurant L served Mon-Sat 12–2.30 D served Mon-Thu 6.30–9 (Sun 12–3, Fri-Sat 6.30–9.30) Av 3 course à la carte £20
🍺 Rotating guest ales. ♟ 8
Facilities Garden Dogs allowed Parking Play Area

SOUTH MORETON   MAP 05 SU58

The Crown Inn ♚

High St OX11 9AG ☎ 01235 812262

e-mail: dallas.family@ntlworld.com

dir: *From Didcot take A4130 towards Wallingford. Village on right*

Friendly village pub located midway between Wallingford and Didcot. It prides itself on its home-prepared food, and has real ale on tap. Families are welcome and customers come from far and wide. During the summer the garden is very popular. Dishes include steaks, shoulder of lamb, fresh battered haddock, and salmon fillet hollandaise.

Open 11–3 5.30–11 (Sat 12–12, Sun 12–10.30) Closed: 1 Jan **Bar Meals** L served Mon-Sat 12–2.30 D served Mon-Sat 7–10 (Sun 12–8) Av main course £9.50 **Restaurant** L served Mon-Sat 12–2.30 D served Mon-Sat 6.30–10 (Sun 12–8) Av 3 course à la carte £20 ⊕ Wadworth ◀ Wadworth 6X & Henrys IPA, guest ales. ♛ 12 **Facilities** Garden Dogs allowed Parking

SOUTH STOKE   MAP 03 SU58

The Perch and Pike ♚

RG8 0JS ☎ 01491 872415 📠 01491 871001

e-mail: info@perchandpike.co.uk

dir: *On Ridgeway Hiking Trail, 1.5m N of Goring, 4m S of Wallingford*

The Perch and Pike, just two minutes' walk from the River Thames, was the village's foremost beer house back in the 17th century. There is plenty of atmosphere in the original pub and in the adjoining barn conversion, which houses the 42-seater restaurant. Food ranges from a selection of sandwiches to the likes of smoked haddock and salmon fish cakes, and venison with celeriac mash and Madeira jus.

Open 12–3 6–11 (Fri-Sat 11–1), Sun 12–10.30) **Bar Meals** L served Mon-Sat 12–2.30 D served Mon-Sat 7–9.30 Av main course £10 **Restaurant** L served Sun 12–2.30 D served Mon-Sat 7–9.30 Av 3 course à la carte £21 ⊕ Brakspear ◀ Brakspear ales. ♛ 7 **Facilities** Children's Licence Garden Dogs allowed Parking

STADHAMPTON   MAP 05 SU69

Pick of the Pubs

The Crazy Bear ★ ★ ★ ★ ★ GA ◉◉ ♚

Bear Ln OX44 7UR ☎ 01865 890714 📠 01865 400481

e-mail: enquiries@crazybear-oxford.co.uk

dir: *M40 junct 7 turn left onto A329, 4m, left after petrol station, 2nd left again into Bear Lane*

From the outside it looks like a traditional 16th-century pub, but The Crazy Bear's interior is utterly distinctive, combining contemporary and art deco influences. The bar is quite traditional, except that it serves champagne and oysters as well as more conventional bar snacks. There are two award-winning restaurants, one serving Thai food, and the other modern British, as well as some stylish bedrooms and a wonderful garden with a waterfall and statues. The extensive food choices should please everyone: 'all day' breakfasts are served from 7am to 10am and from noon

until 10pm, and include such tantalising offerings as duck eggs Benedict or farm-smoked haddock kedgeree. Lunch options include sandwiches and a good value set menu during the week. The main menu, available all day, might feature sautéed foie gras with chives and aged balsamic, followed by fillet of venison with fondant potato, braised red cabbage and juniper sauce.

Open 11–11 **Bar Meals** L served all week 12–10 D served all week 12–10 Av main course £15 **Restaurant** L served all week 12–6 D served all week 6–10 (Sun 12–10) Av 3 course à la carte £35 Av 3 course fixed price £19.50 ⊕ Free House ◀ Old Speckled Hen, Greene King IPA, Ruddles County. ♛ 15 **Facilities** Garden Parking **Rooms** 17

STANTON ST JOHN   MAP 05 SP50

Star Inn ♚

Middle Rd OX33 1EX

☎ 01865 351277 📠 01865 351006

e-mail: murwin@aol.com

dir: *B4027 take Stanton exit, then 3rd left into Middle Rd, pub 200yds on left*

Although the Star is only a short drive from the centre of Oxford, this popular pub still retains a definite 'village' feel. The oldest part dates from the early 17th century, and in the past, the building has been used as a butcher's shop and an abattoir. The garden is peaceful and secluded. A varied menu features shoulder of lamb in redcurrant and rosemary, spinach and mushroom strudel, or roast vegetable and goats' cheese tart.

Open 11–2.30 6.30–11 **Bar Meals** L served all week 12–2 D served Mon-Sat 6.30–9.30 (Sun 12–2, 7–9.30) Av main course £8.50 ⊕ Wadworth ◀ Wadworth 6X, Henrys IPA & JCB. ♛ 7 **Facilities** Garden Dogs allowed Parking Play Area

The Talkhouse ♚

Wheatley Rd OX33 1EX

☎ 01865 351648 📠 01865 351085

e-mail: talkhouse@fullers.co.uk

dir: *Village signed from Oxford ring road*

First recorded as a pub in 1783, the Talkhouse comprises three bar and dining areas, all with a Gothic look and a welcoming atmosphere. A recently refurbished thatched property, it offers a good range of cask ales. Various bar meals (shepherd's pie, sausage and mash) are supplemented by a carte and various omelettes.

Open 12–11 **Bar Meals** L served all week 12–3 D served all week 6–9 Av main course £12 **Restaurant** L served all week 12–3 D served all week 6–9.30 Av 3 course à la carte £20 Av 2 course fixed price £15.50 ⊕ Fullers ◀ London Pride, ESB, Discovery & Guinness. ♛ 6 **Facilities** Garden Dogs allowed Parking

STOKE ROW   MAP 05 SU68

Pick of the Pubs

Crooked Billet ♥

See Pick of the Pubs on page 469

SWALCLIFFE   MAP 11 SP33

Stag's Head ♥

OX15 5EJ ☎ 01295 780232 📄 01295 788977

dir: *6m W of Banbury on B4035*

This friendly, 600 year-old thatched village inn enjoys picture postcard looks and a pretty village setting. It seems that Shakespeare used to drink here, until he was barred! Blending a traditional pub feel with a family-friendly environment, the Stag also offers a beautiful terraced garden and play area. Freshly prepared dishes include goat's cheese tart with chips or salad; moules marinière with chorizo and crusty bread; and Oxfordshire liver and bacon with red wine and onion gravy. Look out for the landlord's own paintings of local scenes.

Open 12–2.30 6–11 Closed: Sun eve **Bar Meals** L served Tue-Sat 12–2 D served Tue-Sat 6.30–9.30 (Sun 12–3) Av main course £7.95 **Restaurant** L served Tue-Sun 12–2 D served Tue-Sat 6.30–9.30 (Sun 12–3) ⊕ Free House ◀ Adnams Bitter, Deuchars IPA, Wye Valley IPA, Badgers Gold. ♥8 **Facilities** Garden Dogs allowed Play Area

---

SWERFORD   MAP 11 SP33

Pick of the Pubs

The Mason's Arms ⊛ ♥

Banbury Rd OX7 4AP

☎ 01608 683212 📄 01608 683105

e-mail: themasonschef@hotmail.com

dir: *Between Banbury & Chipping Norton on A361*

Originally a Masonic Lodge, this award-winning 300 year-old pub was rundown and empty until proprietors Bill and Charmaine Leadbeater took over in 2003. After refurbishing the inn, re-laying the lawns and flowerbeds, and adding a new dining room, it now has an informal ambience and an unrivalled dining experience. With menus like 'Bill's food' and 'Bill's specials', there's no room for doubt about who runs the kitchen. Bill puts a modern, personal twist on old-fashioned cuts of meat such as lamb shanks, belly of pork and ox tongue. Lunchtime brings light bites and hot dishes, as well as daily specials. Main menu choices might start with deep-fried whitebait, sour cream and cayenne pepper, followed by braised chicken and potatoes with saffron and white wine; courgette and mushroom clafoutis; or seared red gurnard with Caesar salad and new potatoes. Iced blackberry parfait or steamed syrup and lemon sponge are typical desserts.

Open 10–3 6–11 (Jul-Aug all day) Closed: 25–26 Dec & Sun eve **Bar Meals** L served Mon-Sat 12–2.15 D served Mon-Sun 7–9.15 (Sun lunch 12–3) Av main course £8.10 **Restaurant** L served all week 12–2.15 D served all week 7–9.15 Av 3 course à la carte £25 Av 3 course fixed price £19.95 ⊕ Free House ◀ Hook Norton Best & Brakspear Special. ♥7 **Facilities** Children's licence Garden Parking

---

SYDENHAM   MAP 05 SP7(

Pick of the Pubs

The Crown Inn

Sydenham Rd OX39 4NB ☎ 01844 351634

e-mail: haydn.hughes3@btinternet.com

dir: *M49 junct 6 take B4009 towards Chinnor. Left at Kingston Blount. Or off B4445 (Thame to Chinnor road), 4m from Thame*

This pretty 17th-century inn lies in a picturesque village opposite its 900–year-old church. Refurbished to incorporate both traditional and modern styles, old photographs hang harmoniously on the walls alongside contemporary paintings. Croque monsieur and filled baguettes and jacket potatoes appear on the lunchtime snacks menu, while the regular carte offers a selection of British, French and Mediterranean-style food, with fish featuring regularly: perhaps monkfish with Parma ham, escalope of salmon, or fillets of sea bass. A Thai menu broadens the geographical purview even further.

Open 12–2.30 6–11 (Oct-Mar 6–10 Mon-Tue May-Sep 12–5 Sun) **Bar Meals** L served Sun-Fri 12–2 D served Mon-Thu 6.30–9 (Fri/Sat Dinner 7–9.30) ◀ Greene King IPA, Ruddles County & Guinness. **Facilities** Garden Parking

---

TADMARTON   MAP 11 SP3:

The Lampet Arms ★★★ GA

Main St OX15 5TB

☎ 01295 780070 📄 01295 788066

dir: *Take B4035 from Banbury to Tadmarton, 5m*

Victorian-style free house offering well-kept ales and hearty home cooking. The pub is named after Captain Lampet, the local landowner who built it and mistakenly believed he could persuade the council to have the local railway line directed through the village, thereby increasing trade. Typical menu choices include steaks; chicken Kiev; steak and ale pie; chilli con carne; and a selection of sandwiches and baguettes.

Open 12–12 (Sun 12–11.30) **Bar Meals** L served all week 12–3 D served all week 7–9 Av main course £7.50 **Restaurant** L served all week 12–3 D served all week 7–9 ⊕ Free House ◀ Hook Norton, Theakstons, Guinness, John Smiths. **Facilities** Children's licence Garden Dogs allowed Parking **Rooms** 4

PICK OF THE PUBS

PISHILL-OXFORDSHIRE

The Crown Inn

A pretty, 15th-century brick and flint coaching inn, but with 11th-century origins as an alehouse. It's important to get the village name straight. The wags who separate the two syllables of Pishill are probably right, since old maps do show a second 's'.

Quite simply, in days gone by waggon drivers would stop at the inn for a swift half after the stiff climb from Henley-on-Thames, while their waiting horses would relieve themselves (an explanation even Great Aunt Maude can handle). Eight or nine centuries ago there was a thriving monastic community here; later, when Henry VIII was persecuting Catholics, many priests were smuggled up the hill from the big house at nearby Stonor and hidden in the Crown's priest's hole (reputably the largest in the country). One such priest, Father Dominique, met a sticky end whilst hiding out at The Crown and his ghost still haunts the pub on the anniversary of his death, although nobody is quite sure when that is. Fast forward to the 1960s when it became a favourite music venue for fans of George Harrison, Ringo Starr, Dusty Springfield and other live performers in the old barn. Nowadays the barn is available for weddings and other functions. Under the supervision of new owner Lucas Wood, menus are changed daily, and there is a selection of daily specials. Start with prawn, avocado and smoked salmon cocktail, and move on to braised lamb shank on a vegetable and potato rosti with redcurrant sauce. Mouthwatering puddings include banana pancakes with maple syrup and vanilla ice cream. On a fine day sit in the extensive gardens overlooking the valley.

MAP 05 SU78
RG9 6HH
☎ 01491 638364
🖶 01491 638364
e-mail: lhdwood@hotmail.com
dir: *On B480 off A4130, NW of Henley-on-Thames*

Open 11.30–2.30 6–11 (Sun 12–3, 7–10.30) Closed: 25–26 Dec
Bar Meals L served all week 12–2.30 D served all week 7–9.30 (Sun 12–3, 7–9) Av main course £6
Restaurant L served all week 12–2.30 D served all week 7–9.30 (Sun 12–3, 7–9) Av 3 course à la carte £22
⊕ Free House ◀ Brakspears, West Berkshire Brewery. ♟ 8
Facilities Garden Parking

The Royal Oak

This 17th-century former coaching inn is set opposite the church in the pretty Cotswold village of Ramsden. Once upon a time a stopping point for the London to Hereford stagecoach, these days the inn is more popular with walkers eager to explore the lovely surrounding countryside.

Whether walking or not, however, the inn makes a fine place to stop for refreshment, and its old beams, warm fires and stone walls provide a very cosy welcome. It is a free house with beers sourced from local breweries, such as Hook Norton Old Hookey and Bitter, Adnam's Broadside and Young's Special. The wine list has over 200 wines, specialising in those from Bordeaux and Languedoc, many of them available by the glass. The bar menu regularly features a pie of the week, and there are also favourites such as real Italian meatballs; home-made beef burgers; and wild mushroom pasta with shitake and porcini. Every Thursday evening there is a special offer of steak with wine and dessert. The main menu features such treats as, for starters, moules marinière with Hebridean mussels; chicken liver parfait with cognac and raisins; or baked avocado, cheese and prawn gratin. Main courses include roast half shoulder of new season Westwell lamb with rosemary and garlic jus; smoked haddock cooked with whisky, cream and cheese; confit of duck leg with quince sauce and puy lentils; and pan-fried calves' liver with wild mushroom sauce. Several fish dishes are always on offer, such as seared yellow fin tuna; roast fillet of Atlantic cod with tapenade crust; and salmon with whisky and horseradish.

🍷
MAP 11 SP31
High St OX7 3AU
☎ 01993 868213
🖷 01993 868864
dir: *From Witney take B4022 towards Charlbury, then right before Hailey, through Poffley End*

Open 11.30–3 6.30–11 Closed: 25 Dec
Bar Meals L served all week 12–2 D served all week 7–10
Restaurant L served all week 12–2 D served all week 7–10
Free House Hook Norton Old Hooky, Best, Adnams Broadside, Youngs Special. 🍷 30
Facilities Garden Dogs allowed Parking

TETSWORTH · MAP 05 SP60

The Old Red Lion

40 High St OX9 7AS

☎ 01844 281274 📄 01844 281863

e-mail: fitz@the-red-lion-tetsworth.co.uk

dir: *Oxford Service area, turn right onto A40. At T-junct turn left then right onto A40 signed Stokenchurch, via Milton Common to Tetsworth*

This pink-washed pub is right on the village green, which conveniently has a large enclosed children's play area. Nemards restaurant comprises one eating areas behind the bar, the other in the quieter Library. In addition to dishes such as pan-fried potato gnocchi with tomato sauce, peas and mozzarella, the menu shows Afro-Caribbean influences with, for example, pan-fried barracuda on a bed of callaloo with coconut and ginger sauce. Check for live jazz and blues nights.

Open 11.30–3 6.30–11 (Sat 11.30–3, Sun 12–8) **Bar Meals** L served Mon-Sat 12–2.30 Av main course £10.50 **Restaurant** L served all week 12–2.30 D served Tue-Sat 6.30–9.30 (Mon 6.30–9) ⊕ Free House **Facilities** Garden Dogs allowed Parking

THAME · MAP 05 SP70

The Swan Hotel ♀

9 Upper Hight St OX9 3ER

☎ 01844 261211 📄 01844 261954

dir: *M40 junct 7, A329 to Thame. Hotel in town centre*

Dating from the 16th century, this former coaching inn overlooks the market square at Thame. The Tudor-painted ceiling is a feature of the upstairs restaurant, where you can enjoy freshly cooked Thai food. Downstairs in the cosy bar you'll find an open fire, bar snacks and a good selection of beers such as Hook Norton, Brakspears and Shepherd Neame.

Open 11–11 (Thurs 11–12, Fri-Sat 11am-1am, Sun 12–11) **Bar Meals** L served all week 12–3 D served Mon-Sat 6–10.30 (Sun 12–4/5) Av main course £9 **Restaurant** L served all week 12–3 D served Mon-Sat 6–10.30 (Sun 12–5) Av 3 course à la carte £20 Av 2 course fixed price £18 ⊕ Free House ◀ Hook Norton, London Pride, Brakspears, Shepherd Neame Spitfire & Otter. ♀10 **Facilities** Dogs allowed Parking

TOOT BALDON · MAP 05 SP50

Pick of the Pubs

The Mole Inn ♀

OX44 9NG ☎ 01865 340001 📄 01865 343011

e-mail: info@themoleinn.com

dir: *5m SE from Oxford city centre off B480*

This stone-built, Grade II listed pub has been the subject of an extensive renovation programme in recent years. The top-notch makeover has earned it a glowing and well-deserved reputation, due in no small measure to the efforts of award-winning chef/host Gary Witchalls. Inside, a great deal of care and attention has been lavished on this classic old local, and now customers can relax in black leather sofas amid stripped beams and solid white walls.

The dining areas are equally striking with their intimate lighting and terracotta floors. Gary's inspired menu draws plenty of foodies from nearby Oxford and further afield, tempted by dishes such as loin of Old Spot pork with Toulouse Savoy cabbage and mustard mash; sea scallops, crayfish and crab risotto; or squab pigeon with bubble and squeak, celeriac fondant and smoked bacon velouté.

Open 12–11 Closed: 25 Dec, 1 Jan **Bar Meals** L served Mon-Sat 12–2.30 D served Mon-Sat 7–9.30 (Sun 12–10) **Restaurant** L served Mon-Sat 12–2.30 D served Mon-Sat 7–9.30 (Sun 12–4, 6–9) ⊕ Free House ◀ Hook Norton, London Pride, Spitfire, Guinness. ♀11 **Facilities** Garden Parking

WANTAGE · MAP 05 SU38

The Hare ♀

Reading Rd, West Hendred OX12 8RH

☎ 01235 833249 📄 01235 833268

dir: *At West Hendred on A417 between Wantage (3m W) & Didcot (5m E)*

A late 19th-century inn mid-way between Wantage and Didcot, modernised in the 1930s by local brewers, Morland, and featuring a colonial-style verandah and colonnade. Inside it retains the more original wooden floors, beams and open fire.

Open 12–3 6–12 (Fri-Sun 11.30–11) **Bar Meals** L served all week 12–2 D served 7–9 Av main course £7 **Restaurant** L served all week 12–2 D served 7–9 Av 3 course à la carte £16 ⊕ Greene King ◀ Greene King Abbot Ale, IPA, Morland Original. ♀8 **Facilities** Garden Dogs allowed Parking

WHEATLEY · MAP 05 SP50

Bat & Ball Inn ♀

28 High St OX44 9HJ

☎ 01865 874379 📄 01865 873363

e-mail: bb@traditionalvillageinns.co.uk

dir: *Through Wheatley towards Garsington, take left turn, signed Cuddesdon*

Do not be surprised to discover that the bar of this former coaching inn is packed to the gunnels with cricketing memorabilia. The owners claim that their collection puts to shame even that of Lords cricket ground! The comprehensive menu, supplemented by daily specials, is likely to feature steaks, fresh-baked pie of the day, herb-battered fresh cod, and maybe chargrilled Toulouse sausages. Lighter meals include lasagne, lamb Peshwari, and warm spinach and pancetta salad.

Open 11–11 **Bar Meals** L served all week 12–2.45 D served all week 6.30–9.45 (Sun 12–9.30) **Restaurant** L served all week 12–2.30 D served all week 6.30–9.30 (Sun 12–9.30) ⊕ Free House ◀ Marston's Pedigree, House LBW Bitter, Guinness. ♀10 **Facilities** Garden Dogs allowed Parking

PICK OF THE PUBS

The Shaven Crown Hotel

Believed to be one of the ten oldest inns in England, The Shaven Crown is steeped in history, having been built as a hospice to the neighbouring Bruern Monastery. Built of honey-coloured Cotswold stone around a medieval courtyard, parts of it, including the gateway, are up to 700 years old.

Following the Dissolution of the Monasteries, Queen Elizabeth I used it as a hunting lodge before giving it to the village in 1580, when it became the Crown Inn. It was not until 1930 that a brewery with a touch of humour changed the name to reflect the tonsorial hairstyles adopted by monks. The leader of the British Union of Fascists, Oswald Mosley, was held under house arrest here during World War II. Not surprisingly none of the rooms are named after him, whereas the small and cosy drinking area with a log fire is, as you might expect, called the Monks Bar (and it serves Oxfordshire real ales). Bar food includes salads and pastas, steak and kidney pie, sausage and mash, and chicken curry. The carte offers starters of deep-fried brie with raspberry coulis; and roast carrot and parsnip salad with walnut dressing. Popular main courses are pheasant casserole with winter vegetables; venison steak with wild mushroom and chive sauce; fresh fish is delivered daily; and, for vegetarians, goats' cheese tart with red pepper coulis. Pre-dinner drinks can be taken in the impressive Great Hall, and in the intimate candlelit dining room. Outside, apart from the enclosed courtyard, is a tree-dotted lawned area.

MAP 10 SP21
High St OX7 6BA
☎ 01993 830330
📠 01993 832136
e-mail:
relax@theshavencrown.co.uk
dir: *On A361, halfway between Burford & Chipping Norton opposite village green & church*

Open 12–2.30 5–11 (Sat-Sun all day)
Bar Meals L served all week 12–2 D served all week 6–9.30 (Sat-Sun all day) Av main course £9.50
Restaurant L served Sat & Sun 12–2 D served all week 7–9 Av 3 course à la carte £20
⊕ Free House ◧ Hook Norton Best, Old Hooky & Archers Wychwood, Hobgoblin, Arkells.
🍷 10
Facilities Garden Dogs allowed Parking

PICK OF THE PUBS

STOKE ROW-OXFORDSHIRE

Crooked Billet

It seems a shame to spoil the secret, but this charmingly rustic pub, tucked away down a single track lane in deepest Oxfordshire, is a popular hideaway for the well-heeled and the well-known. It dates back to 1642 and was once the haunt of highwayman Dick Turpin; forced to hide here from local law enforcers, he whiled away the hours by courting the landlord's pretty daughter, Bess.

Many of its finest features are unchanged, including the low beams, tiled floors and open fires that are so integral to its character. Famous customers, several of whom were introduced to the pub by the late George Harrison, have included Kate Winslet, who famously held her first wedding reception here; Eastenders cast members; and Jeremy Paxman. Menus are the work of award-winning chef/proprietor Paul Clerehugh. Local produce and organic fare are the mainstays of his kitchen, to the extent that he will even exchange a lunch or dinner for the locals' excess veg. Begin perhaps with seared partridge breasts with creamed cabbage, lardons, chestnuts and juniper jus; or crispy duck salad, frisée, spring onions, cucumber and chilli dressing. To follow, there's a good range of fish mains, including seared tuna with soba noodles and bok choy; lemon sole, hollandaise sauce and sugarsnaps; halibut with prawns and mussels, sautée potatoes and baby spinach; and whole prepared lobster with lemon butter and chipped potatoes. Alternatives might include roast rack of the pub's own lamb, dauphinoise potatoes and baby summer vegetables; or pan-fried English calves' liver with bacon crisps, carrot and parsnip rösti. Notwithstanding the occasional famous face, the pub hosts music nights, free wine tastings and other events, and contributes some of its profit to the daily meals it provides for a local primary school.

MAP 05 SU68
RG9 5PU
☎ 01491 681048
📠 01491 682231
dir: *From Henley to Oxford on A4130. Left at Nettlebed for Stoke Row*

Open 12–10
Bar Meals L served all week 12–2.30 D served all week 7–10
Restaurant L served all week 12–2.30 D served all week 7–10 (Sun all day) Av 3 course à la carte £13.50
🍺 Brakspear 🍺 Brakspear Bitter.
♟ 12
Facilities Garden Parking

PICK OF THE PUBS

White Hart

Tucked away in the quiet village of Wytham, close to the A34, is this smart gastropub, concealed within a traditional Cotswold stone inn. If it looks familiar, it may be because it has featured in some of the Inspector Morse television programmes. It serves real ale, but is predominantly a place to eat, and boasts an extensive wine list.

There are a number of rooms inside, all with warming fires, as well as a splendid conservatory. When it is warm enough to sit outside, the Mediterranean-style terrace is a charming and comfortable place to relax. The proprietor sources eggs, chicken, pork and bacon from a local farm less than a mile away, and all the meat is either free range or organic. The well presented menu is supplemented by the specials boards with fresh fish and game dishes always featured in season. Among the many starters are carpaccio of beef with wild rocket; asparagus spears wrapped in pancetta with lemon hollandaise; smoked haddock fishcakes; or a selection of all of them to share as an antipasti plate. Main courses include pork fillet with white bean,

tomato and spinach broth with crispy Parma ham; mussels, clams and prawn linguini with coriander and chilli oil; chicken breast wrapped in pancetta with sun-dried tomato tagliatelle; pink duck breast with potato fondant and parsnip purée; local sausages with cannellini bean and belly pork stew; or one of the dishes from the specials board. For those who are still hungry, there are some tasty desserts, such as raspberry panacotta with lemon and vanilla syrup; or pears poached in red wine with mascarpone cheese.

💡
MAP 05 SP40
OX2 8QA
☎ 01865 244372
🖹 01865 248595
e-mail: whitehartwytham@
btconnect.com
dir: *Just off A34 NW of Oxford*

Open 12–10
Bar Meals L served Mon-Sat
12–3 D served Mon-Sat 6.30–10
(Sun 12–9) Av main course
£14.50
Restaurant L served Mon-Sat
12–3 D served Mon-Sat 6.30–10
(Sun 12–9) Av 3 course à la carte
£25 Av 2 course fixed price £10
🍺 Hook Norton & Landlord.
💡 15
Facilities Garden Parking

WITNEY MAP 05 SP31

The Bell Inn

Standlake Rd, Ducklington OX29 7UP

☎ 01993 702514 📠 01993 706822

e-mail: danny@dpatching4.wanadoo.co.uk

dir: *1m S of Witney in Ducklington, off A415 (Abingdon road)*

Nearly 700 years have passed since the men building the adjacent church also erected their own living accommodation. Their hostel eventually became the Bell, and much extended over the years, it even embraces William Shepheard's former brewery, which closed in 1886. Today it is a popular, traditional village local, with many original features – and a collection of some 500 bells. Home-made pies, stews and burgers are a speciality, and there's a pig roast on Boxing Day.

Open 12–3 5–11 (Fri-Sun 12–11) Closed: 25–26 Dec & 1 Jan **Bar Meals** L served all week 12–2 D served Mon-Sat 6–9 Av main course £10 **Restaurant** L served all week 12–2 D served Mon-Sat 6–9 Av 3 course à la carte £19 ⊕ Greene King ◀ Greene King, IPA & Old Speckled Hen, Morland Original, Guinness. **Facilities** Garden Parking Play Area

The Three Horseshoes

78 Corner St OX28 6BS ☎ 01993 703086

dir: *From Oxford on A40 towards Cheltenham take 2nd turn to Witney. At rdbt take 5th exiti to Witney. Over flyover, through lights. At next rdbt take 5th exit into Corn St. Pub on left*

Built of Cotswold stone, this historic Grade II-listed pub is situated in Witney's original main street. Inside, the stone walls add to the charm of the part wooden, part flagged floors and low ceilings; two large log fires blaze in winter. Traditional pub lunches serve home-made cottage pie or chilli con carne, while evening menus may proffer cured calves' tongue or slow-roast belly pork. Visit on the last Friday of the month (excluding December) for a complete fish menu.

Open 12–3 6.30–11 (Sun 12–4.30) **Bar Meals** L served all week 12–2 D served Mon-Thu 6.30–9 (Sun 12–3) Av main course £9.50 **Restaurant** L served all week 12–2 D served Mon-Sat 6.30–9 (Sun 12–3) Av 3 course à la carte £25 ◀ Harveys Sussex Ale, Marstons Pedigree, Greene King Abbot, Guinness. **Facilities** Garden

WOOLSTONE MAP 05 SU28

The White Horse ★★★ INN

SN7 7QL ☎ 01367 820726 📠 01367 820566

e-mail: whitehorse@btconnect.com

dir: *Off A420 at Watchfield onto B4508 towards Longcot signed for Woolstone*

Unusual windows add to the appeal of this black-and-white-timbered, thatched, Elizabethan village pub. Upholstered stools line the traditional bar, where a fireplace conceals two priest holes, visible to those who don't mind getting their knees dirty. Lunchtime bar snacks include fajitas, burgers and fish and chips. An extensive menu of freshly prepared English and international dishes in the oak-beamed restaurant includes steak and ale pie, curries, steaks, fish pie and mushroom stroganoff.

Open 11.30–3 5.30–11 (Sat in summer 11.30–11) **Bar Meals** L served Mon-Sat D served Mon-Sat Av main course £10 **Restaurant** L served all week 12–2.30 D served Mon-Sat 6–9 Av 3 course à la carte £22 ◀ Arkells, Guinness, Stowford & Press Cider. **Facilities** Garden Dogs allowed Parking

WYTHAM MAP 05 SP40

Pick of the Pubs

White Hart ♀

See Pick of the Pubs on opposite page

RUTLAND

BARROWDEN MAP 11 SK90

Pick of the Pubs

Exeter Arms ♀

LE15 8EQ ☎ 01572 747247 📠 01572 747247

e-mail: info@exeterarms.com

dir: *From A47 turn at landmark windmill, village 0.75m S. (6m E of Uppingham & 17m W of Peterborough)*

Barrowden is an attractive stone village in the Welland Valley, not far from Rutland Water. In the centre, overlooking the village green and duck pond, is the Exeter Arms and its half-acre garden for lazy summer days. It is a 17th-century building that in the past has been a smithy, dairy and postal collection point. Now it is a welcoming pub serving home-made beers and good pub grub. The ales are brewed in the barn next door and rejoice in names such as Beech, Bevin, Hopgear, Owngear and Attitude Two. A typical menu features the likes of soup of the day; or prosciutto, brie and tomato wrap with redcurrant and port dressing. Popular main courses are grilled sea bass fillets; fish pie; or steak and ale pie made with the pub's Barrowden beer. Desserts such as treacle tart and custard or chocolate brownies with chocolate sauce and ice cream ensure a happy ending.

Open 12–2.30 6–11 (Sun & BHs 7–10.30) **Bar Meals** L served Tue-Sat 12–2 Av main course £9.95 **Restaurant** L served Tue-Sun 12–2 D served Tue-Sat 6.30–9 ◀ Beech, Bevin, Owngear, Hopgear. ♀ 10 **Facilities** Garden Dogs allowed Parking

Normanton church, Empingham, Rutland

CLIPSHAM MAP 11 SK91

Pick of the Pubs

The Olive Branch ★★★★ INN

Main St LE15 7SH ☎ 01780 410355 01780 410000
e-mail: info@theolivebranchpub.com
dir: *2m off A1 at B664 junct, N of Stamford*

A 19th-century pub saved from closing over ten years ago by three local young men. Today it is a highly successful business that has expanded to include a second pub, the Red Lion Inn at Stathern. The Olive Branch has an attractive front garden and terrace, and a beautifully refurbished interior with shelves of books and an eclectic mix of antique and pine furniture. Chestnuts roast on the open fires in winter, and home-made lemonade and barbecues are summer fixtures. In the bar excellent local ales, including the specially brewed Olive Oil, sit alongside continental beers such as Leffe. Regional suppliers are crucial to the food operation, which combines traditional, classic and modern influences: a shallot tatin and stilton and smoked duck breast salad, for example, could be followed by casseroled venison from Clipsham Woods. Produce available to buy includes complete dinner party menus based on the kitchen's recipes.

Open 12-3.30 6-11 (Sun 12-10.30, Sat 12-11 summer) Closed: 26 Dec-1 Jan **Bar Meals** L served Mon-Sat 12-2 D served Mon-Sat 7-9.30 (Sun 12-3, 7-9) **Restaurant** L served Mon-Sat 12-2 D served Mon-Sat 7-9.30 (Sun 12-3, 7-9) Av 3 course à la carte £30 Av 3 course fixed price £18.50 Grainstore 1050 & Olive Oil, Fenland, Brewster's, VPA. 10 **Facilities** Garden Dogs allowed Parking **Rooms** 6

COTTESMORE MAP 11 SK91

The Sun Inn

25 Main St LE15 7DH ☎ 01572 812321
e-mail: cheviotinns@hotmail.co.uk
dir: *3m from Oakham on B668*

Dating back to 1610, this whitewashed thatched pub boasts oak beams and a cosy fire in the bar. A well-priced menu supplemented by specials is on offer: chicken, leek and ham pie, steaks and grills, and plenty of fish choices like whole sea bass, swordfish steak and red snapper fillet are served. Lunchtime snacks include baguettes; ham, eggs and chips; and ploughman's. Apparently the ghost of a young girl is sometimes seen behind the bar.

Open 11.30-2.30 5-11 (Fri 11-3, Sat 11.30-11.30 & Sun 12-11) **Bar Meals** L served Mon-Sat 12-2.15 D served Mon-Thu 6-9 (Fri-Sat 5.30-9.30, Sun 12-8.30) **Restaurant** L served Mon-Sat 12-2.15 D served Mon-Thu 6-9 (Fri-Sat 5.30-9.30, Sun 12-8.30) Everards Brewery Adnams Bitter, Everards Tiger, Guinness, 2 guest ales. 9 **Facilities** Garden Dogs allowed Parking

EMPINGHAM MAP 11 SK90

The White Horse Inn ★★★ INN

Main St LE15 8PS ☎ 01780 460221 01780 460521
e-mail: info@whitehorserutland.co.uk
dir: *From A1 take A606 signed Oakham & Rutland Water. From Oakham take A606 to Stamford*

Just a short stroll from Rutland Water, this former 17th-century courthouse has lost none of its period charm. After pedalling around the popular 23-mile lakeside track, the warm welcome, open fire, beamed bar and comfortable restaurant are a recipe for total relaxation. Specials like duck breast, sauté potatoes and redcurrant jus, or red mullet with chilli and prawn dressing should fill the energy gap, too!

Open 8-11 Closed: 25 Dec **Bar Meals** L served Mon-Sat 12-2.15 D served Mon-Sat 7-9.30 (Sun 12-9) Av main course £9 **Restaurant** L served Mon-Sat 12-2.15 D served Mon-Sat 7-9.30 (Sun 12-9) Av 3 course à la carte £18.50 Enterprise Inns John Smith's, Grainstore Triple B, Ruddles Best, Abbot Ale. 9 **Facilities** Garden Dogs allowed Parking

EXTON MAP 11 SK91

Pick of the Pubs

Fox & Hounds

See Pick of the Pubs on page 474

GLASTON MAP 11 SK80

The Old Pheasant

Main Rd LE15 9BP ☎ 01572 822326 01572 823316
e-mail: info@theoldpheasant.co.uk
dir: *On A47 between Leicester & Peterborough. Just outside Uppingham.*

The stuffed head of a wild boar presides over the bar of this picture-perfect inn, which also features a smart stone-walled restaurant complete with evocative relics of farming history. Menus are constructed around quality produce, locally sourced where possible. Seasonal game from shoots is regularly featured, alongside trout from nearby rivers. Try home-cured gravadlax, honey glazed duck breast, and chocolate marquise, or an excellent range of cheeses.

Open 8-11 Closed: 2-7 Jan **Bar Meals** L served all week 12-2 D served Mon-Sat 6.30-9 Av main course £12 **Restaurant** L served all week 12-2 D served Mon-Sat 6.30-9 Av 3 course à la carte £23 Free House Pheasant Ale, Timothy Taylor Landlord, Fuller's London Pride, Everards Original & Greene King Abbot Ale. 8 **Facilities** Children's licence Garden Parking

PICK OF THE PUBS

EXTON-RUTLAND

Fox & Hounds

This imposing 17th-century building stands opposite the green in the centre of Exton, a charming village with its many stone and thatched cottages. Barnsdale Gardens and the amenities of Rutland Water are not far away. At the rear of the pub is a large walled garden, which makes a perfect setting for an al fresco meal or a marquee reception.

The pub has a reputation for good food and hospitality, and is an ideal stopping-off point for those making the most of the many good walks in the surrounding area. Its menu is the work of Italian chef/proprietor Valter Floris and his team, and combines the best of traditional English and Italian cuisine. There is an impressive list of over 25 authentic, thin-crust pizzas (for evenings only), which are certainly not on the small side. The 'casual lunch' lunch menu features panini, salads, traditional sandwiches and filled ciabattas, while the main menu opens with the likes of Scottish salmon with red onions, capers and cream cheese; asparagus and gruyere tart on a bed of salad drizzled with extra virgin olive oil; and paté with chutney. Main

dishes are pan-fried lambs' liver and bacon with onion gravy and creamy mashed potato; or perhaps linguini with jumbo prawns and Scottish smoked salmon in a garlic cream sauce. There is also a regularly changing menu of desserts such as sticky ginger sponge with ginger wine sauce, or baked cheesecake. This is a very popular inn, especially when village events, such as the spring bank holiday street market, are taking place.

MAP 11 SK91
19, The Green LE15 8AP
☎ 01572 812403
🖷 01572 812403
e-mail: sandra@
foxandhoundsrutland.co.uk
dir: *Take A606 from Oakham towards Stamford, at Barnsdale turn left, after 1.5m turn right towards Exton. Pub in village centre*

Open 11–3 6–11
Bar Meals L served all week
12–2 D served Mon-Sat 6.30–9
Av main course £10
Restaurant L served all week
12–2 D served all week 6.30–9 Av
3 course à la carte £20
⊕ Free House ◀ Greene King
IPA, Grainstore Real Ales, John
Smiths Smooth, Timothy Taylor.
♟ 8
Facilities Garden Dogs allowed
Parking Play Area

LYDDINGTON

MAP 11 SP89

Old White Hart ☻

51 Main St LE15 9LR ☎ 01572 821703 ▤ 01572 821965

e-mail: mail@oldwhitehart.co.uk

dir: *From A6003 between Uppingham & Corby take B672*

Set amongst the sandstone cottages of rural Lyddington, this honey-coloured stone free house close to Rutland Water has retained its original beamed ceilings, stone walls and open fires, and is surrounded by well-stocked gardens. Greene King and Timothy Taylor are amongst the beers on offer, along with interesting, freshly prepared food. The menu includes English mustard toad in the hole, and there are fish and vegetarian choices plus daily specials.

Open 12–3 6.30–11 Closed: 25 Dec **Bar Meals** L served Mon-Sat 12–2 D served Mon-Sat 6.30–9 (Sun 12–2.30) Av main course £12 **Restaurant** L served Mon-Sat 12–2 D served Mon-Sat 6.30–9 (Sun 12–2.30) Av 3 course à la carte £23 ⊕ Free House ◀ Greene King IPA & Abbot Ale, Timothy Taylor Landlord, Fuller's London Pride, Timothy Taylor Golden Best. ☻ 8 **Facilities** Garden Parking Play Area

---

OAKHAM

MAP 11 SK80

Barnsdale Lodge Hotel ★★★ HL ◉ ☻

The Avenue, Rutland Water, North Shore LE15 8AH

☎ 01572 724678 ▤ 01572 724961

e-mail: enquiries@barnsdalelodge.co.uk

web: www.barnsdalelodge.co.uk

dir: *A1 onto A606. Hotel 5m on right, 2m E of Oakham*

A former farmhouse, Barnsdale Lodge has been in the proprietor's family since 1760 as part of the adjoining Exton Estate. It stands overlooking Rutland Water in the heart of this picturesque little county. There's a cosy bar with comfortable chairs and a courtyard with outdoor seating. The bistro-style menu draws on local produce and offers dishes such as lobster bisque and individual Wellington of lamb fillet. There is also an attractive summer lunch menu.

Open 7–11 **Bar Meals** L served all week 12.15–2.15 D served all week 7–9.30 **Restaurant** L served all week 12–2.15 D served all week 7–9.30 Av 3 course à la carte £25 ⊕ Free House ◀ Rutland Grainstore, Courage Directors, John Smith's, Guinness. ☻ 10 **Facilities** Garden Dogs allowed Parking Play Area **Rooms** 44

The Blue Ball ☻

6 Cedar St, Braunston-in-Rutland LE15 8QS ☎ 01572 722135

e-mail: blueball@rutlandpubco.net

dir: *From A1 take A606 to Oakham. Village SW of Oakham. Pub next to church.*

A 17th-century thatched inn with open log fires and a cosy bar area, reputedly Rutland's oldest pub. There are five dining areas under low-beamed ceilings, where typical dishes include pork fillet served with a brandy, cream and peppercorn sauce with caramelised apples; chicken breast with a mushroom and tarragon sauce; and spinach and ricotta tortellini in a tomato sauce with shavings of gran padano cheese.

Open 12–3 6–11 (Sat-Sun all day) **Bar Meals** L served all week 12–2 D served Mon-Sat 6.30–9 (Sat-Sun 12–3) Av main course £10.95 **Restaurant** L served all week 12–2 D served Mon-Sat 6.30–9 (Sat-Sun 12–3) Av 3 course à la carte £22 ⊕ Free House ◀ Old Speckled Hen, Greene King IPA & Guinness. ☻ 13 **Facilities** Children's licence Garden Dogs allowed Parking

The Grainstore Brewery

Station Approach LE15 6RE

☎ 01572 770065 ▤ 01572 770068

e-mail: grainstorebry@aol.com

web: www.grainstorebrewery.com

dir: *Next to Oakham rail station*

Founded in 1995, Davis's Brewing Company is housed in the three-storey Victorian grain store next to Oakham railway station. Finest quality ingredients and hops are used to make the beers that can be sampled in the pub's Tap Room. Filled baguettes and stilton and pork pie ploughman's are of secondary importance, but very tasty all the same. Go for the brewery tours and blind tastings; or attend the annual beer festival during the August Bank Holiday.

Open 11–11 (Fri-Sat 11–12) **Bar Meals** L served all week 11–2.30 ⊕ Free House ◀ Rutlands Panther, Triple B, Ten Fifty, Steaming Billy Bitter. **Facilities** Garden Dogs allowed Parking

---

Pick of the Pubs

The Old Plough ☻

2 Church St, Braunston LE15 8QT

☎ 01572 722714 ▤ 01572 770382

e-mail: info@oldploughrutland.com

dir: *From A1 to Stansford, A606 to Oakham, at 1st mini-rdbt right onto High St, to rail crossing. Left then 2nd left signed Braunston. In Braunston 1st building on left.*

This very popular country pub dates back to 1783. Braunston itself is one of Rutland's finest villages, and the pub enjoys a picturesque location just a short distance from Rutland Water. An old red brick coaching inn that has kept its traditional identity despite being tastefully modernised, The Old Plough's interior includes a traditional tiled floor, a real fire and mellow yellow walls in the bar; and a bright, airy conservatory dining room with a black and white tiled floor and modern pine furniture. The large, landscaped beer garden has a very popular floodlit pétanque pitch. Expect lots of speciality evenings and various weekend entertainments, plus an enthusiasm for good food which extends to candle-lit dinners in the picturesque conservatory, as well as light lunches on the terrace. The menu typically delivers favourites such as liver, bacon and onions, Cajun chicken, and beer-battered cod fillet.

Open 11–11 (Fri-Sat 11–12) **Bar Meals** L served all week 12–2.30 D served all week 6–9.30 (Sun 12–9) Av main course £9.95 **Restaurant** L served all week 12–2.30 D served all week 6–9.30 (Sun 12–9) Av 3 course à la carte £19 ⊕ Free House ◀ Boddingtons, Bass Cask, Greene King IPA, Grainstore. ☻ 9 **Facilities** Garden Dogs allowed Parking Play Area

PICK OF THE PUBS

WING-RUTLAND

Kings Arms

The Kings Arms, dating from 1649, is situated in the quaint village of Wing, near Rutland Water. It is run by David and Gisa Goss, and son James, who has been head chef since the family arrived in 2004.

James trained in Switzerland, Denmark and Germany and by December 2006 had earned an AA Rosette for his excellent food, which uses only fresh and, as far as practicable, local ingredients. All sauces, speciality breads, chutneys, dips, ice creams and sorbets are made in-house. The weekly changing menus offer an extensive choice of dishes, featuring starters of scallops with steamed green beans and creamy bacon and shallot vinaigrette; and deep-fried haloumi with tomato salad, capers, pesto and mixed leaves. Main dishes include Aberdeen Angus beef from Speyside served in a variety of ways; herb, lemon and ricotta roast poussin with charred Mediterranean vegetables and warm cherry tomato and chorizo compote; fresh oysters and mussels from Norfolk; and wild mushroom stroganoff with jasmine rice and steamed vegetables. The pub now has its own smoke house, and depending on season can offer smoked Rutland trout, pike, veal sweetbreads, whole smoked hams, pancetta, parma-style ham and venison haunch bresaola. Beer drinkers will want to know that Grainstore Cooking Spitfire and Timothy Taylor Landlord are available in the bar, while an extensive wine list offers over 20 wines by the glass. Eight en suite letting rooms are available, set away from the pub with their own private entrance. Guests with light boats and motorised campers are welcome to use the large off-road car park.

★★★★ INN ◉ ♥
MAP 11 SK80
Top St LE15 8SE
☎ 01572 737634
🖺 01572 737255
e-mail:
info@thekingsarms-wing.co.uk
dir: *1m off B6003 between Uppingham & Oakham*

Open 12–3 6.30–11 Closed: Sun eve & Mon Winter, Sun eve & Mon lunch Summer
Bar Meals L served Tue-Sun 12–2 D served Tue-Sat 6.30–9 (Sun 6.30–8) Av main course £10
Restaurant L served Tue-Sun 12–2 D served Tue-Sat 6.30–9 (Sun 6.30–8) Av 3 course à la carte £24 Av 2 course fixed price £10
◉ Free House ◀ Timothy Taylor Landlord, Shepherd Neame Spitfire, Grainstore Cooking & Rutland Panther. ♥ 20
Facilities Garden Parking
Rooms 8

England

SOUTH LUFFENHAM
MAP 11 SK90

The Coach House Inn

3 Stamford Rd LE15 8NT

☎ 01780 720166 ▤ 01780 720866

e-mail: thecoachhouse123@aol.com

dir: *On A6121, off A47 between Morcroft & Stamford*

Horses were once stabled here while weary travellers enjoyed a drink in what is now a private house next door. Now elegantly refurbished, it offers a comfortable 40–seater dining room and a cosy bar. A short, appealing menu in the Ostler's Restaurant might feature goats' cheese, poached pear and walnut tart, followed by fillet of beef with chicken liver paté and rösti potatoes.

Open 12–2.30 5–11 Closed: 25 Dec, 1 Jan, Sun eve & Mon morning **Bar Meals** L served Tue-Sun 12–2 D served Mon-Sat 6.30–9 Av main course £8 **Restaurant** L served Tue-Sun 12–2 D served Mon-Sat 6.30–9 Av 3 course à la carte £20 ⊕ Free House ◀ IPA, Adnams, Timothy Taylor Landlord & Guinness. **Facilities** Dogs allowed Parking **Rooms** available

STRETTON
MAP 11 SK91

Pick of the Pubs

The Jackson Stops Inn ♀

Rookery Rd LE15 7RA ☎ 01780 410237

For those keen on tracking down uniquely named pubs, this is a winner. You can guarantee nowhere else will have acquired its name by virtue of an estate agent sign that once hung outside for so long that locals dispensed with the original moniker of The White Horse Inn! The thatched stone inn actually dates from the 17th century, and has plenty of appealing features: log fires, scrubbed wood tables and no fewer than four dining rooms, as well as a 90–bin wine list. The new owners offer a frequently changing menu with starters like crayfish and avocado basket; and Thai fish cakes with sweet chilli sauce; followed by slow roasted lamb shanks with mint mash and red wine gravy; steak and mushroom pudding; and locally sourced sausages with mash.

Open 12–3 6–11 Closed: Sun eve & Mon **Bar Meals** L served Tue-Sat 12–2 D served Tue-Sat 6.30–9.30 (Sun 12–3, limited L menu Tue) **Restaurant** L served Tue-Sat 12–2 D served Tue-Sat 6.30–10 (Sun 12–3, limited L menu Tue) Av 3 course à la carte £20 ⊕ Free House ◀ Oakham Ales JHB, Aldershaws Old Boy, Adnams Broadside, Timothy Taylor Landlord. ♀ 7 **Facilities** Garden Dogs allowed Parking

Ram Jam Inn ★★★ INN

The Great North Rd LE15 7QX

☎ 01780 410776 ▤ 01780 410361

dir: *On A1 N'bound carriageway past B668, through service station into car park*

The inn is thought to have got its current name some time during the 18th century when the pub sign advertised 'Fine Ram Jam', though few people, if indeed anyone, are sure what that might have been. These days, the informal café-bar and bistro exude warmth. The patio overlooks the orchard and paddock, and in fine summer weather is set for alfresco dining from the comprehensive all-day menu.

Open 7–11 Closed: 25 Dec **Bar Meals** L served all week 12–8 D served all week 12–8 **Restaurant** L served all week 12–8 D served all week 12–8 ⊕ Free House ◀ John Smith's Cask and Smooth, Marstons Pedigree, Greene King IPA. **Facilities** Garden Parking Play Area **Rooms** 7

WING
MAP 11 SK80

Pick of the Pubs

Kings Arms ★★★★ INN ⊛ ♀

See Pick of the Pubs on opposite page

SHROPSHIRE

BISHOP'S CASTLE
MAP 15 SO38

Boars Head ♀

Church St SY9 5AE ☎ 01588 638521 ▤ 01588 630126

e-mail: sales@boarsheadhotel.co.uk

dir: *In town centre*

One of Bishop's Castle's earliest surviving buildings, this former coaching inn was granted its first full licence in 1642. According to legend, it escaped being destroyed by fire during the Civil War because many of the Royalists were drinking here at the time. The integrity of the pub remains intact, with exposed beams, log fires and a chimney containing a priest hole. An appetising menu offers the likes of Spanish paella and chicken in cream and sherry sauce.

Open 11.30–11 (Sun 12–10.30) **Bar Meals** L served all week 12–3 D served all week 6.30–9 (Sun 12–9.30) Av main course £8 **Restaurant** L served all week 12–3 D served all week 6.30–9 Av 3 course à la carte £20 ⊕ Free House ◀ Courage Best & Courage Directors & regular guests. ♀ 8 **Facilities** Children's licence Parking

BISHOP'S CASTLE continued

The Three Tuns Inn 🍷

Salop St SY9 5BW ☎ 01588 638797

e-mail: timce@talk21.com

dir: *From Ludlow take A49 through Craven Arms, then left onto A489 to Lydham, then A488 to Bishop's Castle*

A traditional timber-framed town centre inn established in 1625, and a brewery since 1642; tours can be arranged. The full range of Three Tuns ales can be enjoyed more or less in peace – without piped music or fruit machines, just occasional live jazz or summer Morris dancing. Well-priced menus may offer Greek salad or Clunbury Hall organic smokehouse salmon, which could be followed by 28-day-hung sirloin steak, or chargrilled supreme of chicken; desserts are on the blackboard.

Open 12–11 (Sun 12–10.30) **Bar Meals** L served all week 12–3 D served Mon-Sat 7–9 Av main course £9 **Restaurant** L served all week 12–3 D served Mon-Sat 7–9 Av 3 course à la carte £16 Free House Tuns XXX, Steamer, Scrooge, Clerics Cure (all by Three Tuns). 🍷 10 **Facilities** Garden Dogs allowed

BRIDGNORTH MAP 10 SO79

Halfway House Inn ★★★ INN 🍷

Cleobury Rd, Eardington WV16 5LS

☎ 01746 762670 📠 01746 768063

e-mail: info@halfwayhouseinn.co.uk

dir: *M5 junct 6, A449 towards Kidderminster. Follow ring road to right. At next rdbt take A442 N towards Bridgnorth. 12m, take A458 towards Shrewsbury. Follow brown tourist signs to pub*

In 1823 Princess Victoria and her entourage rested at this 16th-century coaching inn, then the Red Lion. On enquiring where they were, she was told "Half way there, ma'am". The pub is renowned for the quality and quantity of its locally sourced home-cooked food, three local real ales, forty malts, and around a hundred wines. Dishes range from a simple ploughman's to a 16oz Shropshire rump steak. The inn and adjoining holiday cottages can sleep fifty.

Open 5–12 (Sat-Sun all day) Closed: Sun eve ex BHs **Bar Meals** L served Sat-Sun 12.30–2.30 D served Mon-Sat 5.30–8.30 **Restaurant** L served Sat-Sun 12.30–2.30 D served Mon-Sat 5.30–8.30 Av 3 course fixed price £22.50 Free House Holden's Golden Glow, Wood's Shropshire Lad, Hobson's Town Crier, Draught Guinness & Weston's Export Cider. 🍷 10 **Facilities** Garden Parking Play Area **Rooms** 10

Pheasant Inn

Linley Brook WV16 4TA ☎ 01746 762260

e-mail: pheasant-inn@tiscali.co.uk

dir: *From Bridgnorth take B4373. Pub 400yds up lane signed from B4373. 2.5m from Broseley*

Run by a husband and wife team for nearly 25 years, this is a perfect, traditional country pub. There are no games machines or piped music. Open fires and wood burners heat its two rooms, where locals play bar billiards, dominoes and card games. Food includes excellent gammon and beefsteaks, from a prize-winning local butcher; home-made curry, lasagna and chilli; and plaice with chips and peas. Local walks include one leading down to the River Severn.

Open 12–2.30 6.30–11 (Sat-Sun 12–3, Sun 6.30–10.30, summer 6–11) **Bar Meals** L served all week 12–2 D served all week 6.30–9 Free House Hobson Bitter, Hobson Town Crier, Wye Valley HPA, Salopian Shropshire Gold. **Facilities** Garden Parking **Notes**

BURLTON MAP 15 SJ42

Pick of the Pubs

The Burlton Inn 🍷

SY4 5TB ☎ 01939 270284 📠 01939 270204

e-mail: robertlesterrce@yahoo.co.uk

dir: *10m N of Shrewsbury on A528 towards Ellesmere*

This pretty old building has been transformed into a classy, contemporary interpretation of an 18th-century inn, with a fresh looking dining area, a soft furnished space for relaxation, and a traditional bar – the perfect place for a pint of Robinson Unicorn or Oldham Best among other real ales. A good choice of food is offered, including a list of starters doubling as light meals – maybe venison terrine or Thai style mussels. Among the main courses is a choice of steaks; pan-fried glazed belly pork with flavours of soy, coriander, celery, leek and onion, served with parsnip mash and fresh vegetables; and grilled sea bass fillets on pea, goats' cheese and pancetta risotto. Don't miss the home-made desserts. Outside there is a lovely patio area, carefully planted to provide a blaze of colour in summer.

Open 11–3 6–11 (Sun 12–4, 7–10.30) Closed: 25 Dec, 1 Jan **Bar Meals** L served all week 12–2 D served Mon-Sat 6.30–9.45 (Sun 7–9.30) **Restaurant** L served all week 12–2 D served Mon-Sat 6.30–9.45 (Sun 7–9.30) Robinsons Unicorn, Double Hop, Old Stockport, Smooth. 🍷 12 **Facilities** Garden Parking

BURWARTON   MAP 10 SO68

Pick of the Pubs

The Boyne Arms NEW ♉

Bridgnorth Rd WV16 6QH ☎ 01746 787214
e-mail: theboynearms@btconnect.com
dir: *On B4364, between Ludlow and Bridgnorth*

A Grade II listed Georgian former coaching inn in the village of
Burwarton, surrounded by idyllic Shropshire countryside. Part of
the Boyne estate, the pub has belonged to Lord Boyne's family
for generations. Its striking roadside position draws travellers and
locals alike; a beautiful mature walled garden at the rear includes
a children's playground, making it perfect for families. Four real
ales plus a real cider are always on the hand pumps. The stable
bar with wood burning stove and solid beams doubles hosts
games and functions, while the tap room is the locals' favourite.
The refurbished dining room, with crisp white napery and
attentive friendly service, is the setting for chef Jamie Yardley's
well-presented dishes which combine fresh regional produce with
classic French flavours. Seared scallops with boudin noir could be
followed by pan-roasted breast of Goosnargh duck and puy lentils,
with a simple lemon tart and crème fraîche to finish.

Open 11–3.30 6–11.30 (Sat-Sun all day) **Bar Meals** L served
Mon-Sat 12–2.30 D served Tue-Sat 7–9.15 Av main course £14.50
Restaurant L served all week 12–2.30 D served Tue-Sat 7–9.15 Av 3
course à la carte £23 Av 2 course fixed price £11.95 ◗ Timothy Taylor
Landlord, Shropshire Lad, Bridgnorth Bitter, Town Crier & Queen Bee.
♉ 8 **Facilities** Garden Parking Play Area

CHURCH STRETTON   MAP 15 SO49

The Royal Oak

Cardington SY6 7JZ ☎ 01694 771266
dir: *Telephone for details*

Reputedly the oldest pub in Shropshire, dating from 1462, this Grade
II listed pub is all atmosphere and character. Nestling in the out-of-
the-way village of Cardington, the pub, with its low beams, massive
walls and striking inglenook, is a great place to seek out on cold winter
days. In the summer it is equally delightful with its peaceful garden and
patio. Packed lunches are available on request and there's a walkers'
guide to the area.

Open 12–3 7–12 (Fri 6-1am, Sat 7-1am, Sun 7-12am) **Bar Meals** L served
Tue-Sun 12–2 D served Tue-Sat 7–9 Av main course £7.50
Restaurant L served Tue-Sun 12–2 D served Tue-Sat 7.30–9 ⊕ Free House
◗ Hobsons Best Bitter, Duck, Hopsons, Three Tuns XXX. **Facilities** Garden
Parking Play Area

CLEOBURY MORTIMER   MAP 10 SO67

Pick of the Pubs

The Crown Inn ★★★★ INN ♉

See Pick of the Pubs on page 480

CLUN   MAP 09 SO38

The Sun Inn ♉

10 High St SY7 8JB ☎ 01588 640559
e-mail: info@thesunatclun.co.uk
web: www.thesunatclun.co.uk
dir: *On A498 N of Knighton. Or from A49 at Craven Arms take
B4368 W to Clun*

A 15th-century inn of cruck frame construction set in a pretty
Shropshire village. There are two bars, the stone-flagged snug and
carpeted lounge furnished with settles and featuring a piece of 17th-
century wallpaper. The new landlords are continuing to serve freshly
prepared food, which in fine weather can also be enjoyed outside on
the patio area.

Open 12–3 6–11.30 (Fri-Sat 12–12, Sun 12–11) **Bar Meals** L served all
week 12–2.15 D served Mon-Sat 6–8.45 **Restaurant** L served all week
12–2.15 D served all week 6–8.45 ◗ Jennings Cockerhoop, Camerons
Creamy Bitter, Banks Original & guest ales. **Facilities** Garden Dogs allowed
Parking

COCKSHUTT   MAP 15 SJ42

The Leaking Tap ♉

Shrewsbury Rd SY12 0JQ
☎ 01939 270636 📠 01939 270746
e-mail: nicklaw@btconnect.com

This friendly pub in the centre of Cockshutt village features beamed
bars and log fires, and serves a selection of guest ales and food cooked
from local produce. Lunchtime or evening menus are available,
including a vegetarian selection, might include oven-baked salmon
with roasted fennel; almond crusted fish cakes; and baked cod with
herbs and stilton.

Open 12–3 6–11 **Bar Meals** L served all week 12–2 D served Mon-Sat
6–9.30 Av main course £9.50 **Restaurant** L served all week 12–2 D served
Mon-Sat 6–9.30 Av 3 course à la carte £17 ◗ Banks Bitter, Banks Original,
guest ales. ♉ 12 **Facilities** Parking

PICK OF THE PUBS

CLEOBURY MORTIMER-SHROPSHIRE

The Crown Inn

A quick glance at this 16th-century, one-time coaching inn suggests that it is constructed from Virginia creeper, so densely does its foliage cover every square inch of the façade, except the windows. It is surrounded by tumbling streams, lush farmland and wooded valleys.

The Crown was once estate owned and its informal Rent Room bar was where local tenants paid whatever they owed. In the full service Poacher's Restaurant you can dine beneath exposed beams warmed, if necessary, by fires blazing in the large inglenooks. Fresh local produce lies behind the seasonal menus featuring not just traditional dishes, but also more adventurous house specialities. The daily blackboards offer a dizzying choice, with starters such as trio of breadcrumbed deep-fried local cheeses with Burgundy and redcurrant sauce; fresh crab and mussel chowder; and broccoli and goat's cheese pancakes with parmesan crust. The Crown is particularly well known for its fish dishes, nailing its colours to the mast in a big way with a particularly

generous selection, including whole roast silver bream with charred corn, avocado and coriander salsa; medallions of monkfish on dauphinoise potatoes with chervil cream; and sautéed king scallops on courgette spaghetti with cucumber and chilli oil. But fish is not the whole story, of course, and the boards continue with roast breast of Barbary duck with orange and Armagnac glaze; traditional faggots with mushy peas, onion gravy and golden chips; pork tenderloin with mushrooms, cream and white wine; and breast of chicken filled with banana, wrapped in bacon and melted smoked cheese on a light mustard sauce. Bedrooms are individually furnished and all offer en suite facilities. There's a duck pond in the surrounding immaculately kept gardens.

★★★★ INN ♥
MAP 10 SO67
Hopton Wafers DY14 0NB
☎ 01299 270372
🖺 01299 271127
dir: *On A4117 8m E of Ludlow, 2m W of Cleobury Mortimer*

Open 12–3 6–12
Bar Meals L served all week
12–2.30 D served all week 6–9.30
Sun 12–3 7–9 Av main course
£9.50
Restaurant L served all week
12–2.30 D served all week 7–9.30
Av 3 course à la carte £25.50 Av 2
course fixed price £13.95
⊕ Free House ◀ Timothy Taylor
Landlord, Hobsons Best + guest
ales. ♥ 10
Facilities Garden Parking Play
Area
Rooms 18

CRAVEN ARMS
MAP 09 SO48

The Sun Inn ♥

Corfton SY7 9DF ☎ 01584 861239

e-mail: normanspride@aol.com

dir: On B4368 7m N of Ludlow

The Sun really is a family affair. Landlady Teresa Pearce uses local produce in a delicious array of traditional dishes, while husband Norman brews the Corvedale ales on site, using local borehole water. First licensed in 1613, this historical pub in beautiful Corvedale is popular with walkers, who can be found tucking into the likes of faggots and mushy peas; lamb hotpot; or vegetarian casserole and dumplings. Keep an eye out for regular small beer festivals.

Open 12–2.30 6–12 (Fri-Sat 6–1am) **Bar Meals** L served Mon-Sat 12–2.30 D served Mon-Sat 6–9 (Sun 12–2.45, 7–9) **Restaurant** L served Mon-Sat 12–2 D served Mon-Sat 6–9 (Sun 12–2.45, 7–9) ⊕ Free House ◀ Corvedale Normans Pride, Secret Hop, Dark & Delicious, Julie's Ale. ♥ 14 **Facilities** Children's licence Garden Dogs allowed Parking Play Area

CRESSAGE
MAP 10 SJ50

The Riverside Inn ♥

Cound SY5 6AF ☎ 01952 510900 🖷 01952 510926

dir: On A458 7m from Shrewsbury, 1m from Cressage

In three acres of garden alongside the River Severn, this extensively refurbished coaching inn offers river view dining both outdoors and in its modern conservatory. The same menu is served throughout, with its traditional and exotic pub dishes: perhaps Peking duck pancakes with hoisin sauce, or 'Pee-kai' chicken breasts with satay sauce, and spinach, sorrel and mozzarella parcels.

Open 12–3 6–11 (Sat-Sun all day summer) **Bar Meals** L served all week 12–2.30 D served all week 6.30–9.30 **Restaurant** L served all week 12–2.30 D served all week 7–9.30 ⊕ Free House ◀ Shropshire Gold, Worthington, 4 guest ales. ♥ 8 **Facilities** Garden Dogs allowed Parking

HODNET
MAP 15 SJ62

The Bear at Hodnet

TF9 3NH ☎ 01630 685214 🖷 01630 685787

e-mail: reception@bearathodnet.co.uk

dir: At junct of A53 & A442 turn right at rdbt. Inn in village centre

Allison and Ben Christie took over the Bear in May 2007. Steeped in history, the original beams, small cellars, and a secret passage all contribute to the inn's atmospheric attributes. Tasty English staples on the menu use traditionally fed rare breed meats from the family farm – Dexter beef, Gloucester Old Spot pork and Southdown lamb to name but three. The inn was always a centre of entertainment, and medieval banquets in the baronial hall are still renowned in the locality.

Open 10.30am-1am Closed: Sun eve **Bar Meals** L served all week 12–2.30 D served Mon-Sat 6–9.30 (Sun 12–2.30 roast only) Av main course £9.95 **Restaurant** L served all week 12–2.30 D served Mon-Sat 6–9.30 ⊕ Free House ◀ Theakston, Worthers, guest ales. **Facilities** Garden Parking

IRONBRIDGE
MAP 10 SJ60

The Malthouse ♥

The Wharfage TF8 7NH

☎ 01952 433712 🖷 01952 433298

e-mail: enquiries@themalthouseironbridge.com

dir: Telephone for directions

An inn since the 1800s, the Malthouse is located in the village of Ironbridge, now a designated UNESCO World Heritage Site famous for its natural beauty and award-winning museums. Party menus are available for both the popular jazz bar and the restaurant, while the main menu ranges from lasagne or faggots to monkfish and pancetta baked and served with sweet chorizo, mussel and tomato cassoulet.

Open 11–11 (Sun 12–3, 6–10.30) **Bar Meals** L served all week 12–2.30 D served all week 6–9.30 **Restaurant** L served all week 12–2 D served all week 6.30–9.45 ⊕ Punch Taverns ◀ Directors, Greene King IPA & Badger. ♥ 10 **Facilities** Children's licence Garden Parking

LLANFAIR WATERDINE
MAP 09 SO27

Pick of the Pubs

The Waterdine ★★★★★ RR ◉◉ ♥

LD7 1TU ☎ 01547 528214

e-mail: info@waterdine.com

dir: 4.5m W of Knighton off B4355, turn right opposite Lloyney Inn, 2m into village, last on left opp church

This beautiful old inn stands on the border between England and Wales, which is marked by the River Teme as it runs through the bottom of the garden. The Waterdine has a long history of supplying scrumpy to sheep drovers and farmers, and proudly continues its tradition as a peaceful haven for weary travellers. There are two dining rooms, the Garden Room looking out over the lovely Teme, and the Taproom, tucked away in the oldest part of the building with heavy beams and a stone floor. Chef owner Ken Adams has a highly productive garden, and his menus are based on home-grown and locally supplied organic produce, so dishes are appropriately seasonal. Typical examples are Cornish crab fishcake with beurre blanc; roast poussin with wild mushrooms and white wine sauce; and rack of Kerry lamb with lamb and kidney brochette.

Open 12–3 7–11 Closed: 1wk winter, 1wk spring, Sun eve **Bar Meals** L served Tue-Sun (bookings only) 12–1.45 **Restaurant** L served Tue-Sun 12–1.45 D served Tue-Sat 7–9 ⊕ Free House ◀ Wood Shropshire Legends, Parish Bitter & Shropshire Lad. ♥ 8 **Facilities** Garden Parking **Rooms** 3

LUDLOW   MAP 10 SO57

The Church Inn ★★★★ INN ♥

Buttercross SY8 1AW ☎ 01584 872174 📄 01584 877146
web: www.thechurchinn.com
dir: In town centre

The inn stands on one of the oldest sites in Ludlow, dating back some seven centuries, and through the ages has been occupied by a blacksmith, saddler, druggist and barber-surgeon. These days it enjoys a good reputation for decent beer and traditional pub food – cod in beer batter, locally made faggots, and three cheese pasta and broccoli bake. There are nine en suite bedrooms with televisions and tea-making facilities.

Open 11–11 **Bar Meals** L served Mon-Fri 12–2.30 D served all week 6.30–9 (Sat 12–3.30, Sun 12–3) **Restaurant** L served Mon-Fri 12–2.30 D served all week 6.30–9 (Sat 12–3.30, Sun 12–3) ⊕ Free House ◀ Hobsons Town Crier, Old Hooky, Weetwood, Wye Valley Bitter. ♥ 14 **Facilities** Dogs allowed **Rooms** 8

The Clive Bar & Restaurant with Rooms

★★★★★ RR ◉◉ ♥

Bromfield SY8 2JR
☎ 01584 856565 & 856665 📄 01584 856661
e-mail: info@theclive.co.uk
web: www.theclive.co.uk
dir: 2m N of Ludlow on A49, between Hereford & Shrewsbury

This classy bar and eatery stands on the Earl of Plymouth's Estate, once home to Robert Clive, who laid the foundations of British rule in India. Built as a farmhouse in the 18th century, the building became a pub in the 1900s. These days it houses a bar serving traditional ales and light snacks, and a stylish restaurant where meals might include Shropshire ham hock and parsley terrine followed by roast monkfish with vegetable pilaf.

Open 11–11 (Sun 11–10) Closed: 25–26 Dec **Bar Meals** L served Mon-Sat 12–3 D served Mon-Sat 6.30–9.30 (Sat-Sun 12–10) Av main course £11 **Restaurant** L served Mon-Sat 12–3 D served Mon-Sat 6.30–9.30 (Sat-Sun 12–10) Av 3 course à la carte £25 ⊕ Free House ◀ Hobsons Best Bitter, Interbrew Worthington Cream Flow, Caffreys. ♥ 10 **Facilities** Garden Parking **Rooms** 15

The Roebuck Inn ★★★★ INN ◉◉

Brimfield SY8 4NE ☎ 01584 711230 📄 01584 711654
dir: Just off A49 between Ludlow & Leominster

This country inn dating back to the 15th century offers cosy bars with inglenooks and wood panelling, a bright, airy dining room and comfortable bedrooms. Imaginative food includes lemon spiced gravadlax; pan-seared scallops; goats' cheese fritters; or smoked chicken ravioli to start, and main courses ranging from roast rack of lamb or chicken breast to glazed chilli and ginger salmon or steamed fillets of sole.

Open 11.30–3.30 6.30–11 **Bar Meals** L served all week 12–2.30 D served all week 7–9 (Sun 12–3.30) **Restaurant** L served all week 12–2.30 D served all week 7–9.30 (Sun 12–3.30) ⊕ Free House ◀ Bank's Bitter, Camerons Strongarm, Marstons Pedigree plus guests. **Facilities** Garden Dogs allowed Parking **Rooms** 3

Pick of the Pubs

Unicorn Inn ♥

Corve St SY8 1DU ☎ 01584 873555 📄 01584 876268
dir: A49 to Ludlow

Dating from the early 17th century, this low, attractive timber-framed building backs on to the once flood-prone River Corve. During the great flood of 1885 a photograph was taken of men sitting drinking around a table in the bar while water lapped the doorway. Apparently it wasn't unusual for empty beer barrels to float out of the cellar and down the river. Log fires in winter and the sunny riverside terrace in summer prove very appealing. Both bar and restaurant menus are served at lunch and dinner 364 days per year. The candlelit restaurant dining room offers good British and European dishes with fillet of beef, mixed peppers and onion souvlaki; roulade of chicken and apricots with cambozola cheese sauce; and lamb Shrewsbury. In the bar you could try duck Koresh with chelo – an Iranian dish served with basmati rice – or the more prosaic battered cod, salad and chips.

Open 12–3 6–11 (Sun 12–3.30, 6.30–10.30) Closed: 25 Dec **Bar Meals** L served all week 12–2.15 D served all week 6–9.15 (Sun 6.30–9.15) Av main course £7 **Restaurant** L served all week 12–2.15 D served all week 6–9.15 Av 3 course à la carte £22.50 ⊕ Free House ◀ Timothy Taylor Landlord, Fuller's London Pride, Thwaites Original, guest ales. ♥ 8 **Facilities** Garden Dogs allowed Parking

MADELEY

MAP 10 SJ60

All Nations Inn NEW

20 Coalport Rd TF7 5DP ☎ 01952 585747 ▤ 01952 585747

dir: *On Coalport Rd, overlooking Blists Hill Museum*

Only three families have owned this friendly, largely unspoilt pub since it opened as a brewhouse in 1831. And a brewhouse it has remained. There's no jukebox, pool or fruit machine, although Six Nations rugby matches are shown on a TV perched on barrels. No restaurant either, but quality rolls and pork pies are available all day. From the outside eating area you can see Blists Hill Victorian Town open air museum.

Open 12–12 **Bar Meals** L served all week Av main course £3.50 ⊕ Free House ◀ Dabley Ale, Dabley Gold, Coalport Dodger Mild & guest ales. **Facilities** Children's licence Garden Dogs allowed Parking **Notes** ☺

The New Inn

Blists Hill Victorian Town, Legges Way TF7 5DU
☎ 01952 601018 ▤ 01785 252247

e-mail: sales@jenkinsonscaterers.co.uk

dir: *Between Telford & Broseley*

Here's something different – a Victorian pub that was moved brick by brick from the Black Country and re-erected at the Ironbridge Gorge Open Air Museum. The building remains basically as it was in 1890, and customers can buy traditionally brewed beer at five-pence farthing per pint – roughly £2.10 in today's terms – using pre-decimal currency bought from the bank. The mainly traditional menu includes home-made soup, steak and kidney pudding, and ham and leek pie.

Open 11–4 Closed: 24–25 Dec, 1 Jan **Bar Meals** L served all week 12–3 Av main course £7.50 **Restaurant** L served all week 12–3 ◀ Banks Bitter, Banks Original, Pedigree. **Facilities** Garden Parking Play Area

MARTON

MAP 15 SJ20

The Sun Inn ♀

SY21 8JP ☎ 01938 561211

e-mail: suninnmarton@googlemail.com

dir: *On B4386 Shrewsbury to Montgomery road, in centre of Marton opposite village shop.12m from Shrewsbury, 9m from Welshpool.*

This classic stone free house dates back to 1760 and is surrounded by glorious Shropshire countryside. Both bar and restaurant have been attractively refurbished, with the contemporary restaurant offering a modern English and Mediterranean menu and an impressive selection of fresh fish dishes. A typical meal might include a starter of asparagus and quail's egg salad with parmesan cracknels followed by breast of suckling with pomegranate, molasses and sherry, served with okra.

Open 12–2 7–11 Closed: Mon **Bar Meals** L served Wed-Sun 12–2 D served Tue-Sat 7–9.30 Av main course £7.95 **Restaurant** L served Wed-Sun 12–2 D served Tue-Sat 7–9.30 Av 3 course à la carte £18.95 Av 2 course fixed price £12.95 ⊕ Free House ◀ Hobsons Best Bitter, Worthington Creamflow & guest ales. ♀ 12 **Facilities** Garden Parking

MUCH WENLOCK

MAP 10 SO69

The Feathers Inn NEW ♀

Brockton TF13 6JR ☎ 01746 785202 ▤ 01746 712717

e-mail: feathersatbrockton@googlemail.com

dir: *From Much Wenlock follow signs to Ludlow on B4378 for 3m*

A 16th-century pub full of wonderful nooks and crannies, a vast inglenook, big mirrors, stone busts and local art on display, all of which help to create a friendly, relaxed atmosphere. Menus are based on the freshest, largely locally sourced ingredients, with a regularly updated specials board, listing, for example, cornfed chicken breast, asparagus and white wine; and Scottish salmon fillet, pea purée and mint hollandaise. Wines are sourced from all over the world.

Open 12–2 6.30–9.30 Closed: 1–4 Jan Mon **Bar Meals** L served Tue-Sun 12–2 D served Tue-Sat 6.30–9.30 (Sun 6.30–9) **Restaurant** L served Tue-Sun 12–2 D served Tue-Sat 6.30–9.30 (Sun 6.30–9) Av 3 course à la carte £25 Av 3 course fixed price £14.95 ⊕ Free House ◀ Hobsons Ale, Guinness, Boddingtons, Worfield Brewery Ales. **Facilities** Children's licence Garden Parking

The George & Dragon ♀

2 High St TF13 6AA ☎ 01952 727312

e-mail: angelagray111@hotmail.com

dir: *On A458 halfway between Shrewsbury & Bridgnorth*

Hundreds of water jugs hanging from the ceiling are among the astonishing collection of brewery memorabilia in this historic Grade II listed pub. Sited next to the market square, Guildhall and ruined priory, the inn's welcomes everyone, from locals to walkers and their dogs. Good food cooked to order ranges from black pudding with caramelised red cabbage, to baked ham with parsley sauce, or rack of Shropshire lamb. Leave room for the day's crumble or old English sherry trifle.

Open 12–11 (Opens later busy nights & Fri) **Bar Meals** L served all week 12–2.30 D served Mon-Tue, Thu-Sat 6–9 **Restaurant** L served all week 12–2.30 D served Mon-Tue, Thu-Sat 6.30–9 ◀ Greene King Abbot Ale, IPA, Hobsons Town Crier, Timothy Taylor Landlord. ♀ 8 **Facilities** Dogs allowed

Longville Arms

Longville in the Dale TF13 6DT
☎ 01694 771206 ▤ 01694 771742

dir: *From Shrewsbury take A49 to Church Stretton, then B4371 to Longville*

Prettily situated in a scenic corner of Shropshire, ideally placed for walking and touring, this welcoming country inn has been carefully restored. Solid elm or cast-iron-framed tables, oak panelling and wood-burning stoves are among the features that help to generate a warm, friendly ambience. Favourite main courses on the bar menu and specials board include steak and ale pie, chicken wrapped in bacon and stuffed with paté, mixed fish platter, and a range of steaks.

Open 12–3 6.30–11 **Bar Meals** L served all week 12–2.15 D served all week 6.30–9.15 **Restaurant** L served Sun 12–2.15 D served Fri-Sat 7–9.15 ⊕ Free House ◀ Local guest ales. **Facilities** Garden Dogs allowed Parking Play Area

England

MUCH WENLOCK continued

The Talbot Inn ♀

High St TF13 6AA ☎ 01952 727077 🖹 01952 728436

e-mail: the_talbot_inn@hotmail.com

dir: *M54 junct 4, follow Ironbridge Gorge Museum signs, then Much Wenlock signs. Much Wenlock on A458, 11m from Shrewsbury, 9m from Bridgnorth*

Dating from 1360, the Talbot was once a hostel for travellers and a centre for alms giving. The delightful courtyard was used in the 1949 Powell and Pressburger film Gone to Earth. Daily specials highlighted on the varied menu may include steak and kidney pie, baked seabass, Shropshire pie and cod mornay.

Open 11–3 6–11 (Sun 12–3, 7–10.30 Summer, Sat-Sun 11–11) Closed: 25 Dec **Bar Meals** L served all week 12–2.30 D served all week 7–9.30 **Restaurant** L served all week 12–2.30 D served all week 7–9.30 ⊕ Free House ◀ Bass. ♀7 **Facilities** Garden Parking

---

Pick of the Pubs

Wenlock Edge Inn

Hilltop, Wenlock Edge TF13 6DJ

☎ 01746 785678 🖹 01746 785285

e-mail: info@wenlockedgeinn.co.uk

dir: *4.5m from Much Wenlock on B4371*

This inn perches at one of the highest points of Wenlock Edge's dramatic wooded ledge. Originally a row of 17th-century quarrymen's cottages, the cosy interior contains a small country-style dining room and several bars, one with a wood-burning stove. Outside, a furnished patio takes full advantage of the views stretching across Apedale to Caer Caradoc and the Long Mynd. Start your meal with Bantry Bay mussels; home-made chicken liver paté; or oak smoked salmon, followed by a hearty main course like home-made steak and ale pie or roast vegetable and blue stilton wellington. Puddings include warm chocolate brioche pudding with rich chocolate sauce; and the pub favourite sticky toffee pudding with home-made toffee sauce. The lunchtime menu offers freshly baked baguette sandwiches as well as a range of hot dishes.

Open 12–3 7–11 **Bar Meals** L served Wed-Sat 12–2 D served Wed-Sat 7–9 (Sun 12–3) Av main course £8.50 **Restaurant** L served Wed-Sat 12–2 D served Wed-Sat 7–9 (Sun 12–3) ⊕ Free House ◀ Hobsons Best & Town Crier, Salopian Shropshire Gold, Three Tuns Brewery Edge Ale exclusive to Wenlock Edge Inn. **Facilities** Garden Dogs allowed Parking

---

MUNSLOW   MAP 10 SO58

Pick of the Pubs

The Crown Country
Inn ★★★★ INN ⊛⊛ ♀

See Pick of the Pubs on opposite page

NORTON   MAP 10 SJ70

Pick of the Pubs

The Hundred House Hotel ★★ HL ⊛⊛ ♀

See Pick of the Pubs on page 486

PAVE LANE   MAP 10 SJ7

The Fox NEW ♀

TF10 9LQ ☎ 01952 815940 🖹 01952 815941

e-mail: fox@brunningandprice.co.uk

dir: *1m S of Newport, just off A41*

A big Edwardian-style pub, with a mix of private corners and sunny spacious rooms, all wrapped around a busy central bar. The largest, vaulted room leads on to a large south-facing terrace with views over wooded hills. On the menu are faggots with wholegrain mustard mash mushy peas and onion gravy; grilled mackerel fillets with chorizo, butterbean and potato cassoulet; and spinach and ricotta raviolini in white wine sauce with toasted pine-nuts.

Open 12–11 (Sun 12–10.30) Closed: 26 Dec **Bar Meals** L served all week 12–10 D served all week 12–10 (Sun 12–9.30) **Restaurant** L served all week 12–10 D served all week 12–10 (Sun 12–9.30) ◀ Timothy Taylor Landlord, Woods Shropshire Lad, Twaites Original, Titanic Mild. **Facilities** Garden Parking

---

PICKLESCOTT   MAP 15 SO4

Bottle & Glass Inn

SY6 6NR ☎ 01694 751345

e-mail: masonsarmsinn@aol.om

dir: *Turn off A49 at Dorrington between Shrewsbury & Church Stretton*

The hamlet of Pickelscott lies in the northern foothills of the Long Mynd, or Mountain. The landlord of this 16th-century pub, who has been here for 30–odd years, occasionally hears the ghost of a wooden-legged predecessor tap-tapping around, somehow upsetting the pub's electrics. A typical starter is Roquefort-stuffed pear with green mayonnaise: homity pie; game and red wine casserole; and haddock with cheese sauce on spinach are among the main courses.

Open 12–3 6–12 Closed: Sun eve & Mon **Bar Meals** L served Tue-Sun 12–2 D served Tue-Sat 7–9 Av main course £12.50 **Restaurant** L served Tue-Sun 12–2 D served Tue-Sat 7–9 Av 3 course à la carte £20 ⊕ Free House ◀ Hobsons, Three Tuns XXX, Wye Valley Butty Bach. **Facilities** Dogs allowed Parking

PICK OF THE PUBS

The Crown Country Inn

The Crown has a lovely setting, below the rolling hills of Wenlock Edge in the Vale of the River Corve. A three-storey, Grade-II listed Tudor building, it retains many original features, like the sturdy oak beams, flagstone floors and prominent inglenook fireplace in the main bar.

It doesn't take much to imagine how it must have felt to be on trial here when the inn was once Hundred House, where courts dished out punishment to local miscreants. Perhaps the black-clothed Charlotte sometimes seen in the pub was one of them. Owners Richard and Jane Arnold have a strong commitment to good food. In fact, Richard is not only head chef but has also been a Master Chef of Great Britain for more than a decade. Meals are served in the main bar, the Bay dining area, and the Corvedale Restaurant. Top quality local produce is acquired from trusted sources and is featured strongly in light dishes such as saute of button mushrooms in creamy Shropshire Blue cheese, with apricot and walnut crust; and freshly prepared naturally smoked haddock kedgeree with poached eggs and truffle oil. Taken from the evening menu are the day's fresh fish with a fricassée of red Camargue rice and crayfish tails; and crispy slow-cooked belly of Muckleton Gloucester Old Spot pork with rösti potato, onion marmalade, chorizo and chive cream sauce. An impressive cheeseboard lists a dozen English and Welsh cheeses in order of strength, but for something sweet there's parfait of honeycomb, banana and rum with compote of fruit and shortbread. The restaurant is also available for private parties. Three large bedrooms are located in a converted Georgian stable block.

★★★★ INN ◉◉ ♟
MAP 10 SO58
SY7 9ET
☎ 01584 841205
e-mail:
info@crowncountryinn.co.uk
dir: *On B4368 between Craven Arms & Much Wenlock*

Open 12–2 6.30–11 Closed: 25 Dec, Sun eve & Mon
Bar Meals L served Tue-Sun 12–2 D served Tue-Sat 6.30–9
Restaurant L served Tue-Sun 12–2 D served Tue-Sat 6.30–9 Av 3 course à la carte £25
⊕ Free House ◀ Holden's Black Country Bitter, Black Country Mild, Holden's Golden Glow, Holden's Special Bitter & Three Tuns Brewery 3X. ♟ 7
Facilities Children's licence Garden Parking Play Area
Rooms 3

PICK OF THE PUBS

NORTON-SHROPSHIRE

The Hundred House Hotel

This fine, creeper-clad building has been lovingly run by the Phillips family for the past 21 years. The main part is Georgian, but the half-timbered, thatched barn in the courtyard is 14th century and was used as a courthouse in medieval times.

Downstairs there's a complex warren of lavishly decorated bars and dining rooms with exposed brickwork, beamed ceilings, quarry-tiled floors and oak panelling and, everywhere you look, aromatic bunches of drying herbs and flowers. Mellow brick, stained glass, Jacobean panelling, open log fires and cast-iron cooking pots from Ironbridge create, to quote a guest, "A haven of kindness, comfort and service". The quirky charm extends to the bedrooms (free WI-fi access) and to the beautiful herb and flower gardens. Food is in the modern English/Continental style, with seasonality a particular virtue. Stocks, pies and pasta are all home made. In the bar/brasserie, among many other dishes, you can order pan-fried potato cakes; Greek salad;

and a mezze of houmous, tomato, fennel and smoked aubergine salads. From the à la carte you might try tea-smoked duck breast with sesame, orange and ginger dressing followed by roast Apley partridge stuffed with mushroom and cotechino. Don't miss the specials menu though, or you'll go without such treats as venison terrine with fig, pear and hazelnut salad; chicken gumbo, or monkfish, salmon and scallop casserole with lobster and tarragon bisque. A long and lovely dessert menu offers raspberry and meringue ice cream terrine; tiramisu; and crème brûlée.

★★ HL ◉◉ ♀
MAP 10 SJ70
Bridgnorth Rd TF11 9EE
☎ 01952 730353
🖷 01952 730355
e-mail: reservations@
hundredhouse.co.uk
dir: *On A442, 6m N of
Bridgnorth, 5m S of Telford centre*

Open 11–2.30 6–11 (Sun
11–10.30) Closed: 25–26 Dec eve
Bar Meals L served Mon-Sat
12–2.15 D served Mon-Sun 6–9
(Sun 7–9) Av main course £8.95
Restaurant L served all week
12–2.15 D served Mon-Sat 6–9 Av
3 course fixed price £19.95
⊕ Free House ◀ Heritage Bitter,
Highgate Saddlers Bitter, Highgate
Dark Mild, Everards Tiger. ♀ 16
Facilities Garden Parking
Rooms 10

SHIFNAL   MAP 10 SJ70

Odfellows Wine Bar ♀

Market Place TF11 9AU ☎ 01952 461517 📠 01952 463855

e-mail: reservations@odley.co.uk

web: www.odleyinns.co.uk

dir: M54 junct 4, 3rd exit at rdbt, at next rdbt take 3rd exit, past petrol station, round bend under rail bridge. Bar on left

quirky, popular wine bar owned by Odley Inns, which explains the 'd' spelling. Drinks include regional real ales and ciders, as well as organic herbal teas. The carefully prepared food, served in an elevated dining area and attractive conservatory, is ethically sourced from local suppliers. Menus offer chargrilled free-range chicken breast with sautéed chorizo; slow-cooked Much Wenlock lamb stuffed with apricots; and grilled seabass fillets with tomato, olive and pinenut salsa. Live music every Sunday.

Open 12 -12 Closed: 25–26 Dec, 1 Jan **Bar Meals** L served Mon-Sat 12–2.30 D served Mon-Sat 6–9.30 (Sun 12–9) Av main course £7 **Restaurant** L served Mon-Sat 12–2.30 D served Mon-Sat 6–9.30 (Sun 12–9) Av 3 course à la carte £20 ⊕ Free House ◖ Salopian, Wye Valley, Holdens, Ludlow Gold & Three Tuns. ♀ 12 **Facilities** Parking **Rooms** available

---

SHREWSBURY   MAP 15 SJ41

The Armoury ♀

Victoria Quay, Victoria Av SY1 1HH

☎ 01743 340525 📠 01743 340526

e-mail: armoury@brunningandprice.co.uk

dir: Telephone for directions

The original armoury building, abandoned in 1882, was 'moved' here from the Armoury Gardens in 1922. In 1995 it was renovated, opened as a pub and renamed The Armoury. With its riverside location and large warehouse windows, it makes an impressive pub. Recent alterations have seen the place opened out into a combined restaurant and bar area, and the same menu is served throughout. Real ales include Shropshire Lad and Three Tuns Steamer.

Open 12–11 (Sun 12–10.30) Closed: 25–26 Dec **Bar Meals** L served Mon-Sat 12–9.30 D served Mon-Sat 6–9.30 (Sun 12–9) ◖ Roosters APA, Salopian Shropshire Gold, Deuchars IPA, Woods Shropshire Lad. ♀ 16

The Mytton & Mermaid Hotel ★★★ HL

◉◉ ♀

Atcham SY5 6QG ☎ 01743 761220 📠 01743 761292

e-mail: admin@myttonandmermaid.co.uk

dir: From M54 junct 7 signed Shrewsbury, at 2nd rdbt take 1st left signed Ironbridge/Atcham & follow for 1.5m, hotel on right after bridge

This tastefully decorated, Grade II listed country house hotel on the banks of the Severn effortlessly recalls the atmosphere of its original coaching inn days. Mad Jack Mytton was a profligate local squire, while the mermaid was the crest of former owner Clough Williams-Ellis's Portmeirion Hotel in North Wales. In the candlelit restaurant the seasonal, locally sourced menu might suggest Wenlock Edge pork, leek and bacon sausages; smoked haddock fillet; or fresh steamed mussels.

Open 11-12 Closed: 25 Dec **Bar Meals** L served Mon-Sat 12–2.30 D served all week 6.30–10 (Sun 12–3) Av main course £14.95 **Restaurant** L served Mon-Sat 12–2.30 D served all week 7–10 (Sun 12–3) Av 3 course à la carte £32.50 Av 3 course fixed price £29.50 ⊕ Free House ◖ Shropshire Lad, Shropshire Gold, Hobsons Best. ♀ 12 **Facilities** Garden Parking **Rooms** 20

The Plume of Feathers

Harley SY5 6LP ☎ 01952 727360 📠 01952 728542

e-mail: feathersatharley@aol.com

dir: Telephone for directions

Nestling under Wenlock Edge, this 17th-century inn has stunning views across the valley. Look for the Charles I oak bedhead, full size cider press and inglenook fireplace. Food reflects the seasons, with a changing fish menu; bar meals such as Shropshire baked ham with egg and chips; and restaurant dishes such as lamb en croûte stuffed with wild mushroom and leek gratin, with oxtail gravy; or pan-fried duck breast with black cherry sauce. A refurbishment is planned for 2009.

Open 12–3 5–11 (Sat 12–11.30, Sun 12–10.30) **Bar Meals** L served all week 12–2 D served all week 6.30–9 (Sun 12–9) **Restaurant** L served all week 12–2 D served all week 6.30–9 (Sun 12–9) ⊕ Free House ◖ Worthingtons, Guinness, Directors, & guest ales. **Facilities** Children's licence Garden Parking Play Area

STOTTESDON — MAP 10 SO68

Fighting Cocks

1 High St DY14 8TZ ☎ 01746 718270 📄 01746 718270
e-mail: sandrafc-5@hotmail.com
dir: *11m from Bridgnorth off B4376*

This unassuming 17th-century coaching inn once reputedly brewed an ale containing chicken – it was called the Cock Inn until the 1980s. Traditional values are maintained in an annual apple celebration when locals bring fruit to be crushed in the press, taking the juice home to make cider. On a more progressive note the pub also serves as a contact point for computer users, and live music is performed every Saturday. Food, home made with locally-sourced produce, combines European with occasional Asian flavours.

Open 6–12 (Fri 5–12, Sat-Sun 12–12) **Bar Meals** L served Sat-Sun 12–2.30 D served Tue-Sat 7–9 **Restaurant** L served Sat-Sun 12–2.30 D served Tue-Sat 7–9 ⊕ Free House 🍺 Hobsons Best, Hobsons Town Crier, Hobsons Mild, Wye Valley HPA & Wye Valley Bitter. **Facilities** Garden Dogs allowed Parking

UPPER AFFCOT — MAP 09 SO48

The Travellers Rest Inn ♥

SY6 6RL ☎ 01694 781275 📄 01694 781555
e-mail: reception@travellersrestinn.co.uk
dir: *on A49, 5m S of Church Stretton*

Locals and passing trade enjoy the friendly atmosphere, great range of real ales and good pub grub at this traditional south Shropshire inn on the A49 between Church Stretton and Craven Arms. Food to suit the appetite and the pocket is served all day until 9pm. Expect to see starters of smoked mackerel or prawn cocktail, traditional mains like steak or chilli con carne, and spotted Dick or treacle sponge.

Open 11–11 **Bar Meals** L served all week 11.30–8.30 D served all week 11.30–8.30 (Sun 12–8.30) 🍺 Wood Shropshire Lad, Hobsons Best Bitter, Bass, Guinness. ♥ 14 **Facilities** Children's licence Garden Dogs allowed Parking

WENTNOR — MAP 15 SO39

The Crown Inn

SY9 5EE ☎ 01588 650613 📄 01588 650436
e-mail: crowninn@wentnor.com
dir: *From Shrewsbury A49 to Church Stretton, follow signs over Long Mynd to Asterton, right to Wentnor*

Outdoor enthusiasts of all persuasions will appreciate the location of this 17th-century coaching inn below the Long Mynd. Its homely atmosphere which owes much to log fires, beams and horse brasses, makes eating and drinking here a pleasure. Meals are served in the bar or separate restaurant. Typical daily changing, traditional home-made dishes include pork tenderloin filled with marinated fruits; pan-fried breast of duck with a burnt orange sauce; and grilled sea bass with couscous.

Open 12–3 6–11 (Sat 12–11, Sun 12–10.30 Summer Sat-Sun all day) Closed 25 Dec **Bar Meals** L served all week 12–2 D served all week 6–9 Sat-Sun 12–9 Av main course £6 **Restaurant** L served all week 12–2 D served all week 6–9 Sat-Sun 12–9 ⊕ Free House 🍺 Hobsons, Old Speckled Hen, Three Tuns, Wye Valley. **Facilities** Garden Parking Play Area

WESTON HEATH — MAP 10 SJ71

Pick of the Pubs

The Countess's Arms ♥

TF11 8RY ☎ 01952 691123 📄 01952 691660
e-mail: countesssarms@countessarms.co.uk
dir: *1.5m from Weston Park. Turn off A5 onto A41 towards Newport*

Described as a large contemporary eatery in a refurbished traditional pub, the interior of the Countess's Arms spectacularly belies its outside appearance, as all the internal walls and floors have been removed and an extension has been added. The internal structure now comprises a spacious gallery bar from where customers can look down on the blue glass mosaic-tiled bar below. The establishment is owned by restaurateur and food critic the Earl of Bradford, whose family seat is just down the road. Bar snacks include chilli nachos, seafood dim sum, sausage with bubble and squeak, and Countess burger with hand-cut chips. Full meals, served in the Gallery Bar or Garden Room Restaurant, offer imaginative combinations like roast pork fillet, haggis and field mushroom 'Wellington' with roasted vegetables, or chargrilled teriyaki halloumi with sesame noodle salad and sweet chilli dressing. The place is particularly popular for its jazz night on Fridays.

Open 12–11 (Sun 12–10.30) **Bar Meals** L served all week 12–6
D served all week 6–9.30 (Sun 12–8.30) **Restaurant** L served
all week 12–6 D served all week 6–9.30 (Sun 12–8.30) ⊕ Free
House ◖ Woods, Shropshire Lad, Salopian, Shropshire Gold. ♀ 10
Facilities Garden Parking

WHITCHURCH   MAP 15 SJ54

Willeymoor Lock Tavern ♀

arporley Rd SY13 4HF ☎ 01948 663274

ir: 2m N of Whitchurch on A49 (Warrington/Tarporley)

former lock keeper's cottage idyllically situated beside the Llangollen
anal. Low-beamed rooms are hung with a novel teapot collection;
here are open log fires and a range of real ales. Deep-fried fish and a
hoice of grills rub shoulders with traditional steak pie, chicken curry
nd vegetable chilli. Other options include salad platters, children's
hoices and gold rush pie for dessert.

pen 12–3 6–11 (Sun 12–2.30, 7–10.30) Closed: 25 Dec & 1 Jan
ar Meals L served all week 12–2 D served all week 6–9 (Winter Sun 7–9)
estaurant L served all week 12–2 D served all week 6–9 ⊕ Free House
Abbeydale, Moonshine, Weetwood, Oakham JHB. ♀ 8 **Facilities** Garden
arking Play Area **Notes** ⊛

WOORE   MAP 15 SJ74

Swan at Woore ♀

Nantwich Rd CW3 9SA ☎ 01630 647220

ir: A51 (Stone to Nantwich road). 10m from Nantwich

efurbished 19th-century dining inn by the A51 near Stapley Water
ardens. Four separate eating areas lead off from a central servery.
aily specials boards supplement the menu, which might include
ispy confit of duck, slow roast knuckle of lamb, roasted salmon
vegetable linguine, or red onion and garlic tarte Tatin. There's a
parate fish menu, offering grilled red mullet fillets, perhaps, or seared
na on roasted sweet peppers.

pen 12–12 **Bar Meals** L served Mon-Sat 12–6 D served Mon-Sat 6–9
at 6–9.30) Av main course £8 ⊕ Inn Partnership ◖ Wells Bomdardier,
ddingtons. ♀ 6 **Facilities** Garden Dogs allowed Parking

APPLEY   MAP 03 ST02

The Globe Inn

TA21 0HJ ☎ 01823 672327

e-mail: globeinnappley@btconnect.com

dir: From M5 junct 26 take A38 towards Exeter. Village signed
in 5m

The Globe is known for its large collection of Corgi and Dinky cars,
Titanic memorabilia, old advertising posters and enamel signs. The inn
dates back 500 years and is hidden in maze of lanes on the Somerset-
Devon border. Food from baguettes to main courses includes plenty
for vegetarians, like spicy three-bean and vegetable pie, alongside pan-
fried pollack fillet with tapenade; and mushroom stuffed free-range
chicken breast with white wine and sage butter sauce.

Open 11–3 6.30–12 Closed: Mon (ex BH) **Bar Meals** L served Tue-Sun
12–2 D served Tue-Sun 7–9.30 **Restaurant** D served Tue-Sun 7–9.30
⊕ Free House ◖ Palmers Copper Ale, Palmers 200, Exmoor Ales, Appleys
Ale. **Facilities** Garden Parking Play Area

ASHCOTT   MAP 04 ST43

The Ashcott Inn ♀

50 Bath Rd TA7 9QQ
☎ 01458 210282 ▤ 01458 210282

dir: M5 junct 23 follow signs for A39 to Glastonbury

Dating back to the 16th century, this former coaching inn has an
attractive bar with beams and stripped stone walls, as well as quaint
old seats and an assortment of oak and elm tables. Outside is a
popular terrace and a delightful walled garden. A straightforward
menu offers 'Home Favourites' such as Cumberland sausages, pasta
carbonara, Spanish omelette and steak baguette, while poultry and
seafood choices include chicken provençal, tuna steak with salad, or
chicken tikka masala. Vegetarians may enjoy mushroom stroganoff with
gherkins and capers, or stilton and walnut salad.

Open 11–11 **Bar Meals** L served all week D served all week Av main
course £7 **Restaurant** L served all week 12–9.30 D served all week
(Sun 12–8.30) Av 3 course à la carte £17 ⊕ Heavitree ◖ Otter. ♀ 12
Facilities Garden Dogs allowed Parking Play Area

England

ASHCOTT continued

Ring O'Bells ♀

High St TA7 9PZ ☎ 01458 210232
e-mail: info@ringobells.com
dir: *M5 junct 23 follow A39 & Glastonbury signs. In Ashcott turn left, at post office follow church & village hall signs*

A free house run by the same family for over 20 years. Parts of the building date from 1750, so the traditional village pub interior has beams, split-level bars, an old fireplace and a collection of bells and horse brasses. Local ales and ciders are a speciality, while all food is made on the premises. Look to the good value specials board for cheesy cauliflower soup followed by fresh ling fillet, with treacle pudding to finish. Attractive patio and gardens.

Open 12–3 7–11 (Sun 7–10.30) Closed: 25 Dec **Bar Meals** L served all week 12–2 D served all week 7–10 Av main course £8
Restaurant L served all week 12–2 D served all week 7–10 Av 3 course à la carte £16 ⊕ Free House ◀ guest ales, Somerset cider. ♀ 8
Facilities Garden Parking Play Area

ASHILL   MAP 04 ST31

Square & Compass

Windmill Hill TA19 9NX ☎ 01823 480467
e-mail: squareandcompass@tiscali.co.uk
dir: *Turn off A358 at Stewley Cross service station (Windmill Hill) 1m along Wood Road, behind service station*

There's a warm, friendly atmosphere at this traditional free house, beautifully located overlooking the Blackdown Hills in the heart of rural Somerset. Lovely gardens make the most of the views, and the refurbished bar area features hand-made settles and tables. There is a good choice of home-cooked food, including beef casserole with cheesy dumplings; tasty shortcrust game pie; and duck breast with port and orange sauce. The barn next door was built by the owners from reclaimed materials for use as a music venue.

Open 12–2.30 6.30–late (Sun 7–late) Closed: 25 Dec & Tue-Thu lunch
Bar Meals L served all week 12–2 D served all week 7–9.30 ⊕ Free House
◀ Exmoor Ale & Gold Moor Withy Cutter, Wadworth 6X, Branscombe Bitter,
WHB. **Facilities** Garden Dogs allowed Parking

AXBRIDGE   MAP 04 ST45

Lamb Inn

The Square BS26 2AP ☎ 01934 732253 📠 01934 733821
dir: *10m from Wells & Weston Super Mare on A370*

Parts of this rambling 15th-century free house were once the guildhall, but it was licensed in 1830 when the new town hall was built. Standing across the medieval square from King John's hunting lodge, the pub's comfortable bars have log fires; there's also a skittle alley and large terraced garden. Snacks and pub favourites support contemporary home-made dishes such as pan-fried salmon in cheese and chive coating; and Mediterranean roasted vegetable pancakes in stilton sauce.

Open 11.30–11 (Mon-Wed 11.30–3, 6–11) **Bar Meals** L served all week 12–2.30 D served Mon-Sat 6.30–9.30 Av main course £8.50 ⊕
◀ Butcombe, Butcombe Gold & guest ales. **Facilities** Garden Dogs allowed

---

BABCARY   MAP 04 ST52

Red Lion NEW ♀

TA11 7ED ☎ 01458 223230 📠 01458 224510
e-mail: redlionbabcary@btinternet.com

Totally refurbished by the owners in 2002, the Red Lion is a beautiful, stone-built free house. Rich, colour-washed walls, heavy beams and simple wooden furniture set the tone in the friendly bar, whilst French doors lead out into the garden from the restaurant. Granary sandwiches, ciabattas and hot pub favourites are served in the bar. In the restaurant, expect grilled lamb chops and olive mash; stuffed aubergine with couscous; and daily fishy specials.

Open 12–3 6–12 **Bar Meals** L served all week 12–3 D served Mon-Sat 7–9.30 (Sun 7–9) Av main course £7.50 **Restaurant** L served all week 12–2.30 D served Mon-Sat 12–9.30 Av 3 course à la carte £21.50 ⊕ Free House ◀ Teignworthy Reel Ale, O'Hanlons, Otter, Bath Ales. ♀ 12
Facilities Garden Dogs allowed Parking Play Area

BATH   MAP 04 ST76

Pick of the Pubs

The Hop Pole

7 Albion Buildings, Upper Bristol Rd BA1 3AR
☎ 01225 446327 📠 01225 471876
e-mail: hoppole@bathales.co.uk
dir: *20 min walk from City of Bath on A4 towards Bristol. Pub located opposite Victoria Park*

Opposite the Royal Victoria Gardens and just off the canal path, this is a great spot for quaffing summer ales. One of just six pubs belonging to Bath Ales, a fresh young micro brewery, The Hop Pole has a stripped-down, stylish interior and a garden to the rear complete with patio heaters and pétanque pitch. The atmospheric old skittle alley has been transformed into a restaurant, where the home-cooked food ranges from imaginative bar snacks and sandwiches (Cornish crab mayonnaise, for example, or home-made houmous) through to full meals. You could start with chicken liver parfait or carpaccio of beef, before moving on to honey roast breast of Barbary duck, or medallions of monkfish with chargrilled Mediterranean vegetables, sun-dried tomatoes and pesto. For dessert, perhaps bread and butter pudding with clotted cream, or cheeses with Bath Oliver biscuits.

Open 12–11 (Fri-Sat 12–12) **Bar Meals** L served all week 12–2 D served Mon-Sat 7–9 (Sun 12–2.30) Av main course £8.95
Restaurant L served Sun 12–2.30 D served Mon-Sat 7–9 ◀ Bath Ales: Gem, Spa, Barnstormer, Festivity & Wild Hare. **Facilities** Garden

Pick of the Pubs

King William ♀

36 Thomas St BA1 5NN ☎ 01225 428096
e-mail: info@kingwilliampub.com
dir: *At junct of Thomas St & A4 (London Rd), on left leaving Bath towards London. 15 mins walk from Bath Spa main line station*

Since buying this 19th-century city tavern five years ago, Charlie and Amanda Digney have transformed the run-down old boozer into a stylish and sophisticated gastro-pub. Now the friendly and unpretentious free house offers the best of everything: four real ales from local brewers, organic cider, and over 20 wines served by the glass. Standing on a corner site just off the London Road, the King William boasts a cosy snug in the cellar and a chic upstairs restaurant to showcase the couple's passion for good food. Meat and poultry are free range or organic, and seafood is delivered daily from the Cornish coastline. Lunchtime guests might choose a plate of cider-steamed mussels, or braised oxtail with ox heart and horseradish mash. A typical dinner could comprise pig cheek with braised lentils; pink gurnard with squid, garlic and lemon; and apple fritters with golden syrup and clove ice cream.
Open 12–3 5–12 (Closed lunch Mon-Thu Jun-Aug Sat-Sun 12–12) Closed: 25–26 Dec **Bar Meals** L served all week 12–2.30 D served Mon-Sat 6.30–10 **Restaurant** L served Sun (or prior booking) 12–3 D served Wed-Sat 6.30–10 (Private bookings) Av 3 course à la carte £26 Av 2 course fixed price £24.50 ⊕ Free House ◀ Copper Ale, Peroni, Danish Dynamite, Staropramen & Amarillo. ♀ 21 **Facilities** Dogs allowed

The Old Green Tree ♀

2 Green St BA1 2JZ ☎ 01225 448259
dir: *In town centre*

Loved for its faded splendour, this 18th-century, three-roomed, oak-panelled pub has a dim and atmospheric interior and a front room decorated with World War II Spitfires. Food ranges from pub basics like soup and bangers and mash ('probably the best sausages in Bath') through to smoked duck and poached apple salad; or mussels in white wine and cream sauce. Great for real ales, German lager, malt whiskies and real coffee.
Open 11–11 (Sun 12–10.30) Closed: 25 Dec **Bar Meals** L served all week 12–3 Av main course £8.50 ⊕ Free House ◀ Spire Ale, Brand Oak Bitter, Pitchfork, Mr Perrretts Stout & Summer Lightning. ♀ 12 **Notes** ⊛

Pack Horse Inn ♀

Hods Hill, South Stoke BA2 7DU
☎ 01225 832060 🖷 01225 830075
e-mail: info@packhorseinn.com
dir: *2.5m from Bath city centre, take A367 (A37). Take B3110 towards Frome. Take South Stoke turn on right*

This country inn maintains a tradition of hospitality that dates back to the 15th century. It was built by monks to provide shelter for pilgrims and travellers, and still has the original bar and inglenook fireplace. Outside an extensive garden overlooks the surrounding countryside. All the meals are home made, from sandwiches and snacks to main courses of spinach, pea and forest mushroom risotto; Normandy chicken, or pepper smoked mackerel fillet with horseradish sauce.
Open 11.30–2.30 6–11 (Sat 11–11, Sun 12–10) **Bar Meals** L served all week 12–2 D served Tue-Sun 6–9 Av main course £8 ◀ Butcombe Bitter, 6X, London Pride & Real Ciders. ♀ 6 **Facilities** Children's licence Garden Dogs allowed

The Raven ♀

7 Queen St BA1 1HE ☎ 01225 425045
e-mail: enquiries@theravenofbath.co.uk
dir: *Between Queen Sq & Milsom St*

Real ale lovers flock to this traditional, family-owned free house, set in two Georgian townhouses on a quiet cobbled street in the centre of Bath. Two hundred ales have been served in the past year alone, including the exclusively brewed Raven and Raven's Gold. And what better accompaniment for your pint than a home-made pie with mash and gravy? Or you could try chicken of Aragon, lamb, or mushroom and asparagus.
Open 11.30–11.30 (Fri-Sat 11.30–12) Closed: 25–26 Dec **Bar Meals** L served all week 12–2.30 D served Mon-Sat 6–8.30 (Sat all day, Sun 12.30–4) Av main course £7.25 ⊕ Free House ◀ Raven & Raven's Gold. ♀ 7

The Star Inn

23 Vineyards BA1 5NA ☎ 01225 425072
e-mail: landlord@star-inn-bath.co.uk
dir: *On A4, 300mtrs from centre of Bath*

Often described as a rare and unspoilt pub of outstanding historic interest, and listed on the National Inventory of Heritage Pubs, this impressive building stands amid Bath's glorious Georgian architecture, and was first licensed in 1760. Famous for its pints of Bass served from the jug and including many original features such as 19th-century Gaskell and Chambers bar fittings and a lift to transport barrels from the cellar. Large selection of rolls at lunchtime.
Open 12–2.30 5.30–12 (Sat-Sun 12–12) ⊕ Punch Taverns ◀ Bellringer, Bass, Bath Star, Staropramen & Doom Bar. **Facilities** Dogs allowed

England

BECKINGTON
MAP 04 ST85

Woolpack Inn △ ★★ SHL ♦

BA11 6SP ☎ 01373 831244 📠 01373 831223
e-mail: 6534@grenneking.co.uk
dir: *Just off A36 near junction with A361*

Standing on a corner in the middle of the village, this charming, stone-built coaching inn dates back to the 1500s. Inside there's an attractive, flagstoned bar and outside at the back, a delightful terraced garden. The lunch menu offers soup and sandwich platters, and larger dishes such as home-made sausages and mash; fresh herb and tomato omelette; steak and ale pie; and beer-battered cod and chips. Some of these are also listed on the evening bar menu.

Open 11–11 (Sun 12–10.30) **Bar Meals** L served all week 12–2.30 D served all week 6.30–9.30 (Sun 11–3, 6.30–9) **Restaurant** L served all week 12–2.30 D served all week 6.30–9.30 (Sun 12–3) Av 3 course à la carte £22 ⊕ Old English Inns ◀ Greene King IPA, Abbot Ale, guest ale. ♦ 8 **Facilities** Garden Dogs allowed Parking **Rooms** 11

BICKNOLLER
MAP 03 ST13

The Bicknoller Inn

32 Church Ln TA4 4EL ☎ 01984 656234
e-mail: info@bicknollerinn.co.uk

A 16th-century thatched country inn set around a courtyard with a large garden under the Quantock Hills. Inside you'll find traditional inglenook fireplaces, flagstone floors and oak beams, as well as a theatre-style kitchen and restaurant. Meals range from sandwiches and pub favourites like hake in beer batter (priced for an 'adequate' or 'generous' portion), to the full three courses with maybe smoked salmon; chicken supreme cooked in red wine, and warm treacle tart.

Open 12–3.30 6–12 (Summer 11.30–11) **Bar Meals** L served all week 12–3 D served all week 6–9.30 Av main course £7.50 **Restaurant** L served all week 12–3 D served all week 6–9.30 Av 3 course à la carte £25 ◀ Palmers Copper, Palmers IPA, guest ales. **Facilities** Garden Dogs allowed Parking Play Area

BLAGDON
MAP 04 ST5⁵

The New Inn ♦

Church St BS40 7SB ☎ 01761 462475 📠 01761 463523
e-mail: newinn.blagdon@tiscali.co.uk
dir: *From Bristol take A38 S then A368 towards Bath, through Blagdon left onto Church Ln, past church on right*

A lovely old country pub in the village of Blagdon at the foot of the Mendips, the New Inn offers open fires, traditional home-cooked food, and magnificent views across fields to Blagdon Lake. The menu is locally sourced, and ranges through snacks, salads and main meals such as brewer's beef (the meat marinated in Wadworth bitter); deep-fried breaded plaice, with chips, jacket or baby potatoes; and vegetable risotto served with a side salad.

Open 11–3 6–11 **Bar Meals** L served all week 12–2 D served all week 7– Av main course £8 **Restaurant** L served all week 12–2 D served all week 7–9 ⊕ Wadworth ◀ Wadworth 6X, Henry's IPA, J.C.B & Guinness. ♦ 16 **Facilities** Garden Dogs allowed Parking

BLUE ANCHOR
MAP 03 ST0⁴

The Smugglers ♦

TA24 6JS ☎ 01984 640385 📠 01984 641697
e-mail: simonandsuzie@aol.com
dir: *Off A3191, midway between Minehead & Watchet*

'Fresh food, cooked well' is the simple philosophy at this friendly 300–year-old inn, standing just yards from Blue Anchor's sandy bay. The Cellar Bar menu features a range of sandwiches, baguettes, filled baked potatoes, pizzas, pastas, grills, salads and speciality sausages, as well as plenty of fish and seafood. Honey-roast ham, chicken tikka korma, and minted lamb cutlets are listed among the 'comfort food' selection. In fine weather diners eat in the large walled garden.

Open 12–11 (Nov-Etr 12–3, 7–11, wknds 12–3, 6–11) **Bar Meals** L served all week 12–10 D served all week 12–10 **Restaurant** 12–3 D served Thu-Sun 7–10 ⊕ Free House ◀ Smuggled Otter, Otter Ale. ♦ 6 **Facilities** Children's licence Garden Dogs allowed Parking Play Area

BRADFORD-ON-TONE   MAP 04 ST12

White Horse Inn ♀

Regent St TA4 1HF ☎ 01823 461239

e-mail: donnamccann31@btinternet.com

web: www.whitehorseinnbradford.co.uk

dir: *N of A38 between Taunton & Wellington*

Dating back over 300 years, this stone-built inn stands opposite the church in the heart of a delightful thatched village. It has a bar area, restaurant, garden and patio, and serves real ales brewed in the southwest and home-cooked food prepared from locally sourced ingredients – try half shoulder of lamb with orange, cranberry and port jus; or vegetarian stuffed peppers. Pig roasts and barbecues are catered for, and there's a boules pitch in the garden.

Open 11.30–3 5.30–12 (Winter 6–12) Closed: Jan-Feb, Oct-Nov Sun-Mon eve **Bar Meals** L served all week 12–2 D served all week 6.30–9 **Restaurant** L served all week 12–2 D served all week 6.30–9 ⊕ Enterprise Inns ◀ Cotleigh Tawney, John Smith's, Whitbread Best, Sharp's Doom Bar. ♀ 7 **Facilities** Garden Dogs allowed Parking

BUTLEIGH   MAP 04 ST53

The Rose & Portcullis ♀

Sub Rd BA6 8TQ ☎ 01458 850287 🖹 01458 850120

dir: *Telephone for directions*

This stone built 16th-century free house takes its name from the coat of arms granted to the local lord of the manor. Thatched bars and an inglenook fireplace are prominent features of the cosy interior; there's also a skittle alley, garden, and children's play area. Grills and pub favourites like ham, egg and chips rub shoulders on the menu with more adventurous fare: oriental duck with ginger and honey; and lentil moussaka are typical choices.

Open 12–3 6–11 **Bar Meals** L served all week 12–2 D served all week 7–9 **Restaurant** L served all week 12–2 D served all week 7–9 ⊕ Free House ◀ Interbrew Flowers IPA, Butcombe Bitter, Archers Best. ♀ 7 **Facilities** Garden Dogs allowed Parking Play Area

CHEW MAGNA   MAP 04 ST56

Pick of the Pubs

The Bear and Swan ♀

South Pde BS40 8SL

☎ 01275 331100 🖹 01275 331204

e-mail: enquiries@bearandswan.co.uk

dir: *A37 from Bristol. Turn right signed Chew Magna onto B3130. Or from A38 turn left on B3130*

The Bear and Swan is a light and airy, oak-beamed gastro-pub with a large open fire, comfy chairs and tables, real ales, and a good selection of fine wines and beers in the bar. A big screen shows requested sports games. The restaurant offers a menu changing menu made from the finest locally sourced produce, along with an à la carte menu with a large range of fish, game, seafood, local meats and vegetarian dishes. A lunchtime menu at the bar highlights filled baguettes, soups and old favourites like locally made sausages, mash and mustard gravy; and gammon, free range eggs and chips. This list changes daily, too, to ensure

that only the freshest produce is used. Fish aficionados will find different surprises everyday – from smoked haddock on wilted spinach with poached egg; and baked salmon en croute on chive butter sauce; to fresh scallops on risotto with pea purée; and pan-fried skate wing on caper salad.

Open 11–12 (Sun 11–7) **Bar Meals** L served all week 12–2 D served Mon-Sat 7–9.30 Av main course £6.50 **Restaurant** L served all week 12–2 D served Mon-Sat 7–9.30 (Sun 12–3) Av 3 course à la carte £25 ⊕ Free House ◀ Butcombe Bitter, Courage Best. ♀ 10 **Facilities** Garden Dogs allowed Parking

CHISELBOROUGH   MAP 04 ST41

The Cat Head Inn ♀

Cat St TA14 6TT ☎ 01935 881231

e-mail: info@thecatheadinn.co.uk

dir: *1m off A303, take slip road to Crewkerne (A356)*

This creeper-clad honey-gold hamstone pub with its award-winning beer garden was converted from an old farmhouse in 1896. Today, the flagstone floors, open fires and contemporary artefacts create a unique atmosphere. Choose from several real ales and local ciders while browsing the menu – the lunchtime range includes smoked chicken and pine nut salad; pork tenderloin with Dijon mash and Calvados sauce; or battered wholetail scampi are supper options.

Open 12–3 6–12 Closed: 25 Dec eve **Bar Meals** L served all week 12–2 D served all week 7–9.30 **Restaurant** L served all week 12–2 D served all week 7–9.30 ⊕ Enterprise Inns ◀ Butcombe, Otter, Speckled Hen, Tribute & London Pride. ♀ 8 **Facilities** Garden Dogs allowed Play Area

CHURCHILL   MAP 04 ST45

The Crown Inn ♀

The Batch BS25 5PP ☎ 01934 852995

dir: *From Bristol take A38 S. Right at Churchill lights, left in 200mtrs, up hill to pub*

Totally unspoilt gem of a stone-built pub situated at the base of the Mendip Hills and close to invigorating local walks. Originally a coaching stop on the old Bristol to Exeter route, it once housed the village grocer's and butcher's shop before real ale became its main commodity. Today, an ever-changing range of local brews are tapped straight from the barrel in the two rustic stone-walled and flagstone-floored bars. Freshly prepared food is served at lunchtime only, the blackboard listing rare beef sandwiches, filled jacket potatoes, cauliflower cheeses, locally-caught trout and popular casseroles. Peaceful front terrace for summer alfresco sipping.

Open 11–11 **Bar Meals** L served Mon-Sat 12-2.30 (Sun 12–3) Av main course £5 ⊕ Free House ◀ Palmers IPA, Draught Bass, P G Steam, Butcombe. ♀ 7 **Facilities** Children's licence Garden Dogs allowed Parking **Notes** ⊕

England

CLAPTON-IN-GORDANO   MAP 04 ST47

Pick of the Pubs

The Black Horse ☙

Clevedon Ln BS20 7RH ☎ 01275 842105
e-mail: theblack.horse@tiscali.co.uk
dir: *M5 junct 19, 3m to village. 2m from Portishead, 10m from Bristol*

Down a little lane behind a stone wall is the pretty, whitewashed Black Horse, built in the 14th century and at one time what is now the small Snug Bar was the village lock up, as the surviving bars on one of the windows testify. The traditional bar features low beams with jugs and pint pots hanging from them, flagstone floors, wooden settles and old guns above the big open fireplace. The kitchen in this listed building is tiny, which limits its output to traditional pub food served lunchtimes only (and not at all on Sundays), but very tasty it is too. The repertoire includes hot filled baguettes and baps, moussaka, cottage pie, beef stew, chilli and lasagne. The large rear garden includes a children's play area, and there's a separate family room. On Monday nights someone usually turns up with a guitar. Outside there's a large beer garden and children's play area.

Open 11–11 **Bar Meals** L served Mon-Sat 12–2 ⊕ Enterprise Inns
◀ Courage Best, Wadworth 6X, Shepherd Neame Spitfire, Butcombe Best. ☙ 7 **Facilities** Garden Dogs allowed Parking Play Area
Notes ⊜

CLUTTON   MAP 04 ST65

Pick of the Pubs

The Hunters Rest ★★★★ INN ☙
See Pick of the Pubs on opposite page

COMBE HAY   MAP 04 ST75

Pick of the Pubs

The Wheatsheaf Inn ☙

BA2 7EG ☎ 01225 833504 📄 01225 833504
e-mail: info@wheatsheafcombehay.com
dir: *From Bath take A369 (Exeter road) to Odd Down, left at park towards Combe Hay. Follow for 2m to thatched cottage & turn left*

This pretty black and white timbered free house nestles on a peaceful hillside close to the route of the former Somerset Coal Canal, just four miles south of Bath off the A367. The 17th-century building is decorated with flowers in summer, and the gorgeous south-facing garden is an ideal spot for summer dining. The rambling, unspoilt bar is stylishly decorated, with massive wooden tables and sporting prints, and boasts an open log fire in cold weather. An integral part of the local community, this picturesque setting has also featured as a BBC TV documentary location. The daily menus feature ploughman's lunches, and an impressive selection of freshly-cooked hot dishes. Terrine of home-smoked partridge with green tea jelly and apple chutney; and crisp belly pork with south coast scallops and pork juices are typical choices. Don't miss the fresh artisan breads, or desserts such as hot raspberry soufflé.

Open 10.30–3 6–11 (Fri-Sat 11–11, Sun 12–6) Closed: 25–26 Dec & 1st 2wks Jan **Bar Meals** L served Tue-Sat 12–2.30 (10 Fri and Sat) Av main course £8.50 **Restaurant** L served all week 12–2 D served all week 6.30–9.30 (Fri & Sat 6.30–10) Av 3 course à la carte £28 ⊕ Free House ◀ Butcombe Bitter, Butcombe Brunel, Cheddar Valley Cider. ☙ 13 **Facilities** Garden Dogs allowed Parking

PICK OF THE PUBS

CLUTTON-SOMERSET

The Hunters Rest

Paul Thomas has been running this popular free house for 20 years, and has established a great reputation for its warm welcome and good home-made food. The views over the Cam Valley to the Mendip Hills and across the Chew Valley to Bristol are breathtaking – well worth a visit on their own account.

The Hunters Rest was originally built around 1750 for the Earl of Warwick as a hunting lodge; when the estate was sold in 1872, the building became a tavern serving the growing number of coal miners working in the area. Mining has finished now and the inn has been transformed into an attractive place to eat and stay, with its five well-appointed bedrooms, including some four-poster suites. A range of real beers and a reasonably priced wine list are offered, with a good choice by the glass. The menu includes filled rolls; oggies (giant filled pastries); grills using meat from local farms; and a variety of vegetarian dishes such as stilton and broccoli oggie, and roasted vegetable lasagne. Dishes among the blackboard specials might include

salmon and smoked haddock fishcakes with dill hollandaise; smoked local trout and king prawn salad with lime vinaigrette; rack of lamb with rosemary and garlic gravy; slow-roast belly pork, crackling, cider gravy and blackpud mash; and crispy duck breast with bramble sauce. There are some real old favourites among the desserts, such as blackcurrant cheesecake and sticky toffee pudding, alongside banoffee meringue roulade and lemon sorbet. In the summer you can sit out in the landscaped grounds and watch the miniature railway take customers on rides around the garden, while in winter you can cosy up to the crackling log fires.

★★★★ INN ♥
MAP 04 ST65
King Ln, Clutton Hill BS39 5QL
☎ 01761 452303
▤ 01761 453308
e-mail: info@huntersrest.co.uk
web: www.huntersrest.co.uk
dir: *On A37 follow signs for Wells through Pensford, at large rdbt left towards Bath, 100mtrs right into country lane, pub 1m up hill*

Open 11.30–3 6–11 (Fri-Sun all day)
Bar Meals L served Mon-Sat 12–2 D served Mon-Sat 6.30–9.45 (Sun 12–9)
Restaurant L served Mon-Sat 12–2 D served Mon-Sat 6.30–9.45 (Sun 12–9)
⊕ Free House ◖ Interbrew Bass, Otter Ale, Sharp's Own, Hidden Quest & Butcombe. ♥ 14
Facilities Garden Dogs allowed Parking Play Area
Rooms 5

CORTON DENHAM   MAP 04 ST62

The Queens Arms ♛

DT9 4LR ☎ 01963 220317
e-mail: relax@thequeensarms.com
dir: *From A30 (Sherborne) take B3145 signed Wincanton. Approx 1.5m turn left at red sign to Corton Denham. 1.5m, turn left down hill, right at bottom into village. Pub on left*

The Queens Arms nestles at the heart of the ancient village of Corton Denham, just north of Sherborne on the Somerset/Dorset border, surrounded by beautiful countryside. Food is served in the bar, adjoining dining room and private dining room of the late 18th-century free house. You can also sit out in the garden at the rear. Drink is taken seriously; choose from a range of world classic bottled beers, locally brewed ales, and a selection of Somerset apple juices and ciders. The imaginative wine and whisky list is also well chosen and reasonably priced. Earthy British dishes using the freshest local and seasonal produce include light bites, platters and sandwiches at lunch, with dishes such as poacher's risotto; and sausage and mash. In the evening, there might be confit of duck leg on bruschetta with orange and marjoram ricotta; and local venison cobbler with curly kale and baby carrots.

Open 11–3 6–11 (Sat-Sun & BHs 11–11) **Bar Meals** L served Mon-Sat 12-3 D served Mon-Sat 6–10 (Sun 12–3.30, 6–9.30) Av main course £10.50 **Restaurant** L served Mon-Sat 12-3 D served Mon-Sat 6–10 (Sun 12–3.30, 6–9.30) Av 3 course à la carte £22 ⊕ Free House ◀ Butcombe, Timothy Taylor Landlord, Bath Spa. ♛ 16 **Facilities** Garden Dogs allowed Parking **Rooms** available

CRANMORE   MAP 04 ST64

Strode Arms ♛

BA4 4QJ ☎ 01749 880450
dir: *S of A361, 3.5m E of Shepton Mallet, 7.5m W of Frome*

Just up the road from the East Somerset Railway, this rambling old coaching inn boasts a splendid front terrace overlooking the village duck pond. Spacious bar areas are neatly laid-out with comfortable country furnishings and warmed by winter log fires. The bar menu features filled baguettes and pub favourites like Wiltshire ham, eggs and chips. Meanwhile, restaurant diners might choose roast guinea fowl; or bubble and squeak with asparagus.

Open 11.30–2.30 6–11 Closed: Sun eve **Bar Meals** L served all week 12–2 D served Mon-Sat 6.30–9 **Restaurant** L served all week 12–2 D served Mon-Sat 6.30–9 ⊕ Wadworth ◀ Henry's IPA, Wadworth 6X, JCB. ♛ 9 **Facilities** Garden Dogs allowed Parking

CREWKERNE   MAP 04 ST40

The Manor Arms Ⓤ ♛

North Perrott TA18 7SG ☎ 01460 72901 🖩 01460 74055
e-mail: bookings@manorarmshotel.co.uk
dir: *From A30 (Yeovil/Honiton) take A3066 towards Bridport. North Perrott 1.5m*

On the Dorset-Somerset border, this 16th-century Grade II listed pub and its neighbouring hamstone cottages overlook the village green. The popular River Parrett trail runs by the door. The inn has been lovingly restored and an inglenook fireplace, flagstone floors and oak beams are among the charming features inside. Bar food includes fillet steak medallions, pan-fried whole plaice, and chicken supreme.

Open 11–11 (Sun 12–10.30) **Bar Meals** L served all week 12–2.30 D served all week 7–9 Av main course £6 **Restaurant** L served all week 12–2.30 D served all week 7–9 ⊕ Free House ◀ Butcombe, Otter, Fuller's London Pride, 5 guest ales. ♛ 8 **Facilities** Garden Parking **Rooms** 8

CROSCOMBE   MAP 04 ST54

The Bull Terrier ★★★ INN

Long St BA5 3QJ ☎ 01749 343658
e-mail: barry.vidler@bullterrierpub.co.uk
dir: *Halfway between Wells & Shepton Mallet on A371*

Formerly known as the 'Rose and Crown', the name of this unspoiled village free house was changed in 1976. First licensed in 1612, this is one of Somerset's oldest pubs. The building itself dates from the late 15th century, though the fireplace and ceiling in the inglenook bar are later additions. One menu is offered throughout, including ginger chicken; bacon, mushroom and tomato pasta special; hot smoked mackerel with horseradish; and vegan tomato crumble.

Open 12–2.30 7–11.30 **Bar Meals** L served Mon-Sat 12–2 D served all week 7–9 (Sun 12–1.45) **Restaurant** L served Mon-Sat 12–2 D served all week 7–9 (Sun 12–1.45) ⊕ Free House ◀ Butcombe, Courage Directors, Marston's Pedigree, Greene King Old Speckled Hen & Ruddles County. **Facilities** Garden Dogs allowed Parking **Rooms** 2

DINNINGTON   MAP 04 ST41

Dinnington Docks

TA17 8SX ☎ 01460 52397 🖩 01460 52397
e-mail: hilary@dinningtondocks.co.uk
dir: *S of A303 between South Petherton & Ilminster*

This welcoming and traditional village pub on the old Fosse Way has been licensed for over 250 years. Rail or maritime enthusiasts will enjoy the large collection of memorabilia, and it's an ideal location for cycling and walking. The pub is well known for the quality of its cask ales, and farmhouse cider is also available. You won't find any pool tables, loud music or fruit machines, but instead good conversation and a varied selection of freshly prepared food available every lunchtime and evening, made using local produce wherever possible.

Open 11.30–3.30 6–12 **Bar Meals** L served all week 12–2.30 D served Mon-Sat 6–9.30 (Sun 7–9.30) **Restaurant** L served all week 12–2.30 D served Mon-Sat 6–9.30 (Sun 7–9.30) ⊕ Free House ◀ Butcombe Bitter, Wadworth 6X, guests. **Facilities** Garden Dogs allowed Parking Play Area

DITCHEAT
MAP 04 ST63

Pick of the Pubs

The Manor House Inn ♟

BA4 6RB ☎ 01749 860276 📄 0870 286 3379

e-mail: giles@themanoratditcheat.co.uk

dir: *From Shepton Mallet take A371 towards Castle Cary, in 3m turn right to Ditcheat*

Tucked away in a charming Mendip village offering easy access to the Bath and West showground and the East Somerset steam railway, this delightful brick-built free house with its flagstone floors was originally known as the White Hart. Here you'll find Butcombe Bitter, John Smith's and regular guest ales, as well as local brandies and up to 19 wines served by the glass. Starters include pan-fried pigeon breast with bacon on mixed leaves; and smoked salmon on risotto with roasted beetroot and dill dressing. Main course dishes range from rack of lamb with herb crust, parsnip purée and red wine sauce; to sea bass fillets on stir-fry vegetables with spring onion and beetroot sauce. Round off with plum tart and lemon zest sorbet; or Bakewell tart with clotted cream.

Open 12–3 7–11 **Bar Meals** L served all week 12–2.30 D served Mon-Sat 6–10 (Sun 7–9) Av main course £12.50 **Restaurant** L served all week 12–2 D served all week 7–9.30 (Sun 12–2.30, 7–9) ⊕ Free House ◀ Butcombe, John Smiths's & guest ales. ♟ 19 **Facilities** Garden Dogs allowed Parking

DUNSTER
MAP 03 SS94

Pick of the Pubs

The Luttrell Arms ★★★ HL ⊛

High St TA24 6SG ☎ 01643 821555 📄 01643 821567

e-mail: info@luttrellarms.fsnet.co.uk

dir: *A39 Bridgewater to Minehead, A396 Dunster. 2m before Minehead*

Built in the 15th-century as a guesthouse for the Abbots of Cleeve, this beguiling hotel has retained all its atmospheric charms. Open fires and oak beams make the bar a welcoming place in winter, while the bedrooms are period pieces complete with leather armchairs and four-poster beds. A rib-sticking wild venison casserole with ale and horseradish sauce is just the thing for a chilly day, while in the more formal restaurant you could tuck into smoked haddock fishcakes, followed by wild pigeon and mushroom parcels with cider jus. Desserts include sticky ginger

parkin with vanilla-steeped pineapple and ginger ice cream in the restaurant, and clotted cream rice pudding in the bar. Locally brewed beers and a good value wine list make staying the night an appealing option, especially since the murmuring of ghostly monks is rumoured to cure even the most stubborn insomnia.

Open 10–11 **Bar Meals** L served all week 12–3 D served all week 7–10 Av main course £10.95 **Restaurant** L served all week 12–3 D served all week 7–10 Av 3 course fixed price £28.50 ⊕ Free House ◀ Exmoor Gold Fox, Cheddar Valley Cider & guest ale. **Facilities** Garden Dogs allowed **Rooms** 28

EAST COKER
MAP 04 ST51

Pick of the Pubs

The Helyar Arms ★★★★ INN ⊛ ♟

Moor Ln BA22 9JR

☎ 01935 862332 📄 01935 864129

e-mail: info@helyar-arms.co.uk

dir: *3m from Yeovil. Take A57 or A30, follow East Coker signs*

Log fires warm the old world bar in this charmingly traditional 15th-century inn, reputedly named after Archdeacon Helyar, a chaplain to Queen Elizabeth I. A Grade II listed building, it dates back in part to 1468 and its separate restaurant occupies an original apple loft. The kitchen makes full use of local produce, especially cheeses, beef and bread. Bar snacks include ploughman's lunches; the Helyar chargrilled pizza; and speciality sandwiches such as bacon, Somerset brie and cranberry ciabatta. A main meal could begin with warm, crusty bread with olive tapenade followed by a starter of sautéed lamb's kidneys with roasted red onion and deep-fried sage leaves. Main courses range from traditional favourites such as shepherd's pie (made with hogget lamb mince and served with glazed carrots) to a spicy Thai red chicken curry with jasmine rice. You could finish with profiteroles or rhubarb crème brûlée.

Open 11–3 6–11 (Sun 12–10.30) **Bar Meals** L served all week 12–2.30 D served all week 6.30–9.30 (Sun 12–2.30, 6.30–9) Av main course £11 **Restaurant** L served all week 12–2.30 D served all week 6.30–9.30 (Sun 6.30–9) Av 3 course à la carte £22 ⊕ Punch Taverns ◀ Butcombe Bitter, Greene King IPA, Flowers Original. ♟ 30 **Facilities** Garden Dogs allowed Parking

EXFORD
MAP 03 SS83

Pick of the Pubs

The Crown Hotel ★★★ HL ⊛⊛ ♟

See Pick of the Pubs on page 498

PICK OF THE PUBS

EXFORD-SOMERSET

The Crown Hotel

The 17th-century Crown Hotel was the first purpose-built coaching inn on Exmoor, providing a change of horses for the Taunton to Barnstaple run. This venerable establishment surrounded by beautiful countryside and moorland is located in a pretty village amid three acres of gardens and woodland, with a fast flowing trout stream running through.

Outdoor pursuits are popular with the patrons here, including walking, hunting, horse-riding and shooting – horses and dogs can be accommodated if required. The cosy country bar remains very much at the heart of village life, populated by a mix of visitors and colourful locals, many of whom enjoy the weekly curry night. Welcoming log fires are lit in the lounge and bar in winter, and there are lovely water and terrace gardens for summer use. Other permanent fixtures are the real ales, fine wines and good food, alL served in a relaxing and homely atmosphere. Lunchtime snacks include a range of sandwiches and baguettes, and baked potatoes brimming with cheese and pickle; tuna and red onion; or chicken and bacon. Quality ingredients are sourced locally where possible and cooked to order. In the smart dining room you might anticipate a meal starting with home-made smoked haddock, chive and coriander fishcake, or confit of duck salad. Main courses include organic meats and a good selection of fish dishes such as poached fillets of plaice; and pan-fried cajun tuna. Vegetarian options are plentiful and delicious: try tomato and balsamic risotto, and gruyère cheese with herb salad. A fitting finish could be home-made vanilla pavlova with Chantilly cream; or a West Country cheese plate with crackers and quince jelly. If you fancy staying over and exploring the delights of this lovely area, accommodation is available in 17 en suite bedrooms.

★★★ HL ◎◎ ♀
MAP 03 SS83
TA24 7PP
☎ 01643 831554
🖹 01643 831665
e-mail:
info@crownhotelexmoor.co.uk
web:
www.crownhotelexmoor.co.uk
dir: *From M5 junct 25 follow Taunton signs. Take A358 then B3224 via Wheddon Cross to Exford*

Open 11–11
Bar Meals L served all week 12–5.50 D served all week 6–9.30 Av main course £9.95
Restaurant D served all week 7–9 Av 3 course à la carte £32.50
⊕ Free House ◄ Exmoor Ale, Quantock Ales. ♀ 12
Facilities Garden Dogs allowed Parking
Rooms 17

FAULKLAND   MAP 04 ST75

Tuckers Grave

Faulkland BA3 5XF ☎ 01373 834230

dir: *Telephone for directions*

Tapped ales and farm cider are served at Somerset's smallest pub, a tiny atmospheric bar with old settles. Lunchtime sandwiches and ploughman's lunches are available, and a large lawn with flower borders makes an attractive outdoor seating area. The grave in the pub's name is the unmarked one of Edward Tucker, who hung himself here in 1747.

Open 11–3 6–11 Closed: 25 Dec ⊕ Free House ◀ Interbrew Bass, Butcombe Bitter. **Facilities** Garden Dogs allowed Parking **Notes** ⊛

FRESHFORD   MAP 04 ST76

The Inn at Freshford ♥

BA2 7WG ☎ 01225 722250 📄 01225 723887

dir: *1m from A36 between Beckington & Limpley Stoke*

With its 15th-century origins, and log fires adding to its warm and friendly atmosphere, this popular inn in the Limpley Valley is an ideal base for walking, especially along the Kennet & Avon Canal. Extensive gardens. The à la carte menu changes weekly to show the range of food available, and a daily specials board and large children's menu complete the variety. Typical home-made dishes are patés, steak and ale pie, lasagne and desserts; a nice selection of fish dishes includes fresh local trout.

Open 11–3 6–11 (Sun 7–11) **Bar Meals** L served all week 12–2 D served all week 6–9 **Restaurant** L served Mon-Sat 12–2 D served Mon-Sat 6–9 (Sun 12–3, 7–9) ⊕ Latona Leisure ◀ Butcombe Bitter, Courage Best & guest ale. ♥ 12 **Facilities** Garden Dogs allowed Parking

FROME   MAP 04 ST74

Pick of the Pubs

The Horse & Groom ♥

East Woodlands BA11 5LY
☎ 01373 462802 📄 01373 462802

e-mail: kathybarrett@btconnect.com

dir: *A361 towards Trowbridge, over B3092 rdbt, take immediate right towards East Woodlands, pub 1m on right*

Located at the end of a single track lane, this attractive 17th-century building is adorned with colourful hanging baskets in summer and surrounded by lawns fronted by severely pollarded lime trees. The bar, furnished with pine pews and settles on a flagstone floor and a large inglenook fireplace, offers shove ha'penny, cribbage, dominoes and a selection of daily newspapers for your diversion. There's also a carpeted lounge, including three dining tables in addition to the conservatory-style garden room with 32 covers. A great choice of drinks includes smoothies and milkshakes, and designated drivers are provided with free soft drinks. The lunch and bar menu is offered at lunchtime along with baguettes, salads and daily specials. In the evening, the bar and baguette menus are complemented by a full carte served in all areas. Typical dishes are smoked salmon roulade followed by peppered venison with Cumberland sauce.

Open 11.30–2.30 6.30–11 (Sun 12–3, 7–10) **Bar Meals** L served Tue-Sun 12–2 D served Tue-Sat 6.30–9 (Sun 12–2.30) Av main course £9 **Restaurant** L served Tue-Sun 12–2 D served Tue-Sat 6.30–9 (Sun 12–2.30) Av 3 course à la carte £25 Av 2 course fixed price £10 ⊕ ◀ Wadworth 6X, Butcombe Bitter, Branscombe Branoc, Timothy Taylor Landlord. ♥ 9 **Facilities** Garden Dogs allowed Parking

HASELBURY PLUCKNETT   MAP 04 ST41

Pick of the Pubs

The White Horse at Haselbury ♥

North St TA18 7RJ ☎ 01460 78873

e-mail: haselbury@btconnect.com

dir: *Just off A30 between Crewkerne & Yeovil on B3066*

Set in the peaceful village of Haselbury Plucknett, the building started life as a rope works and flax store, later becoming a cider house. Its interior feels fresh and warm, but retains the original character of exposed stone and open fires. Patrick and Jan Howard have run the hostelry for over ten years, with the explicit promise to provide the best food, service and value for money possible. This is confirmed by the lunchtime set menu served from Tuesday to Saturday, when leek and potato soup could be followed by baked trout fillets with bacon and almond sauce, and rounded off with spotted dick and custard. However, an excellent selection of fish specials may tempt: fillet of hake on a bed of mixed leaves, perhaps; or grilled fillet of turbot served on a mound of chargrilled Mediterranean vegetables. The eclectic carte also includes beef stroganoff, roasted rack of English lamb, and pan-fried pork medallions.

Open 11.45–2.30 6–11 Closed: Sun eve & Mon **Bar Meals** L served Mon-Sat 12–2 D served all week 6.30–9.30 (Sun 12–3) **Restaurant** L served Mon-Sat 12–2 D served all week 6.30–9.30 (Sun 12–3) ⊕ Free House ◀ Palmers IPA, Otter Ale. ♥ 10 **Facilities** Garden Parking

England

HINTON BLEWETT   MAP 04 ST55

Ring O'Bells 🍷

BS39 5AN ☎ 01761 452239 📄 01761 451245
e-mail: jonjenssen@btinternet.com
dir: *11m S of Bristol on A37 toward Wells, small road signed in Clutton & Temple Cloud*

On the edge of the Mendips, this 200–year-old pub offers good views of the Chew Valley. An all-year-round cosy atmosphere is boosted by a log fire in winter, and a wide choice of real ales. The bar-loving shove ha'penny players attract a good following. Good value dishes include beef in Guinness served in a giant Yorkshire pudding, and chicken breast with stilton and bacon. Baguettes, sandwiches and ploughman's also available.

Open 11–3.30 5–11 (Sat 11–4, 6–11 Sun 12–4, 7–10.30)
Bar Meals L served all week 12–2 D served all week 6.30–10
Restaurant L served all week 12–2 D served all week 7–10 (Sat 12–2.30)
🍺 Free House 🍺 Butcombe, Fuller's London Pride, Badger Tanglefoot, Gem. **Facilities** Garden Dogs allowed Parking Play Area

HINTON ST GEORGE   MAP 04 ST41

Pick of the Pubs

The Lord Poulett Arms 🍷

High St TA17 8SE ☎ 01460 73149
e-mail: steveandmichelle@lordpoulettarms.com
dir: *2m N of Crewkerne, 1.5m S of A303*

Fronting the street in one of Somerset's loveliest and most peaceful villages is this stone-built, 17th-century thatched pub. It has been superbly restored by its owners Michelle Paynton and Steve Hill, to include a pale green bar with bare flagstones and boarded floors, a pleasing mix of old oak and elm tables, and ladderback, spindleback and Windsor chairs. Helping to make the darker green dining room a delightful place to eat are real fires, including one with a huge bressemer beam across the top, more wooden floors, a big old settle, and yet more harmoniously mixed chairs and tables. The versatile lunch menu lists gourmet sandwiches (melted Somerset brie and caramelised red onions), a light snack of Cornish mussels in a red Thai curry broth, or perhaps cumin and apple glazed pork belly. In the evening you might find foie gras torchon, to start, and then venison bangers and mash, or slow-braised beef with winter vegetables and dumplings.

Open 12–3 6.30–11 **Bar Meals** L served all week 12–2 D served all week 7–9 **Restaurant** L served all week 12–2 D served all week 7–9 🍺 Free House 🍺 Hopback, Branscombe, Cotleigh, Archers. 🍷 7 **Facilities** Garden Dogs allowed Parking

HOLCOMBE   MAP 04 ST64

The Holcombe Inn 🍷

Stratton Rd BA3 5EB ☎ 01761 232478 📄 01761 233737
e-mail: info@ringoroses.co.uk
dir: *On A367 to Stratton-on-the-Fosse, take concealed left turn opposite Downside Abbey signed Holcombe, take next right, pub 1.5m on left*

This country inn boasts a large garden with views of nearby Downside Abbey and the Somerset countryside. The lunch menu runs to various sandwiches and wraps, while the evening choice is supplemented by a specials board: start with crispy squid with sweet chilli dip; or asparagus tips with tomato and basil hollandaise sauce, and move on to grilled Scottish salmon with cucumber and prawn cream; pork stroganoff; or spinach and ricotta ravioli.

Open 11.30–11 (Sat 11.30–2.30, 6.30–11 Sun 12.30, 7–10.30) Closed: Sun eve & Mon in winter **Bar Meals** L served Mon-Sat 12–2 D served Mon-Sat 7–9 (Sun 12–1.30, 7–8.30) **Restaurant** L served Mon-Sat 12–2 D served Mon-Sat 7–9 (Sun 12–1.30, 7–8.30) 🍺 Free House 🍺 Otter Ale, Guinness, guest bitter. 🍷 7 **Facilities** Garden Dogs allowed Parking

ILCHESTER   MAP 04 ST52

Ilchester Arms 🍷

The Square BA22 8LN ☎ 01935 840220 📄 01935 841353
e-mail: ilchester@yahoo.co.uk
dir: *From A303 take A37 to Ilchester/Yeovil, left at 2nd Ilchester sign. Hotel 100yds on right*

First licensed in 1686, this elegant Georgian building was owned between 1962 and 1985 by the man who developed Ilchester cheese. Brendan McGee, the head chef, and his wife Lucy are well settled in now, enabling Brendan to create an extensive bistro menu offering pan-fried fillet of red snapper, rich lamb casserole, and vegetable moussaka. Sandwiches, paninis, salads, the house burger, and beef and ale pie are available at the bar.

Open 11–11 Closed: 26 Dec **Bar Meals** L served all week 12–2.30 D served Mon-Sat 7–9.30 Av main course £11.50 **Restaurant** L served all week 12–2.30 D served Mon-Sat 7–9.30 Av 3 course à la carte £21.50 🍺 Free House 🍺 Butcombe, Flowers IPA, London Pride & local breweries' ales. 🍷 12 **Facilities** Children's licence Garden Parking Play Area

ILMINSTER   MAP 04 ST31

New Inn 🍷

Dowlish Wake TA19 0NZ ☎ 01460 52413
dir: *From Ilminster follow Kingstone & Perry's Cider Museum signs, in Dowlish Wake follow pub signs*

Deep in rural Somerset, you'll find this 350–year-old stone-built pub tucked away in the village of Dowlish Wake, close to Perry's thatched cider mill. Inside there are two bars with wood-burning stoves and a restaurant, and outside there is a large secluded beer garden. The menu of home-cooked food features local produce in dishes such as Perry's pork steak, with a rich cider, apple and cream sauce; and Aunt Sally's home-made apple pie.

Open 11.30–3 6–11 **Bar Meals** L served all week 12–2.30 D served all week 6–9 Av main course £7.50 **Restaurant** L served all week 12–2.30 D served all week 6–9 Av 3 course à la carte £15 🍺 Enterprise Inns 🍺 Butcombe Bitter, Poachers Bitter, Otter Ale & Thatcher's Gold. 🍷 10 **Facilities** Children's licence Garden Dogs allowed Parking

KILVE

MAP 03 ST14

The Hood Arms ★★★★ INN ☻

TA5 1EA ☎ 01278 741210 🖹 01278 741477

e-mail: easonhood@aol.com

dir: *From M5 junct 23/24 follow A39 to Kilve. Village between Bridgwater & Minehead*

This traditional, friendly 17th-century coaching inn is set among the Quantock Hills and provides thirsty walkers with traditional ales. A good range of fresh fish includes whole sea bass with apple and almond butter, and always on the menu are the inn's famous beef and ale pie, and stilton-topped steaks. Vegetarians get their own choice of dishes.

Open 11–3 6–11 (Sun 12–2, Winter Sun-Mon 12–2, 6–10)
Bar Meals L served Mon-Sat 12–2.30 D served 6.15–9 (Sun 12–2, Winter Sun-Tue 7–8.30) **Restaurant** L served all week 12–2 D served all week 7–9 (Winter Sun-Tue 7–8.30) ⊕ Free House ◗ Sharp's Doom Bar, Cotleigh Tawney Ale, Tribute, St Austell. ☻ 8 **Facilities** Garden Dogs allowed Parking Play Area **Rooms** 12

KINGSDON

MAP 04 ST52

Kingsdon Inn ☻

TA11 7LG ☎ 01935 840543

e-mail: enquiries@kingsdoninn.co.uk

dir: *A303 onto A372, right onto B3151, right into village, right at post office*

The three charmingly decorated, saggy-beamed rooms in this pretty thatched pub give off a relaxed and friendly feel. Stripped pine tables and cushioned farmhouse chairs are judiciously placed throughout, and there are enough open fires to keep everywhere well warmed. Traditional country cooking includes pheasant, venison and other game in season; pork fillets with apricot and almonds; roast half duck with local scrumpy cider sauce; and seared sea bass with fennel and cream.

Open 12–3 5.30–11 **Bar Meals** L served all week 12–2 D served Mon-Sat 6.30–9.30 (Sun 7–9) **Restaurant** L served all week 12–2 D served Mon-Sat 6.30–9.30 (Sun 7–9) ⊕ Free House ◗ Butcombe Cask, Otter Cask, guest ale. ☻ 10 **Facilities** Children's licence Garden Dogs allowed Parking

LANGLEY MARSH

MAP 03 ST02

The Three Horseshoes

TA4 2UL ☎ 01984 623763 🖹 01984 623763

e-mail: marellahopkins@hotmail.com

dir: *M5 junct 25 take B3227 to Wiveliscombe. Turn right up hill at lights. From square, turn right, follow Langley Marsh signs, pub in 1m*

This handsome 17th-century red sandstone pub has had only four landlords during the last century. It remains a free house, with traditional opening hours, child-free bars and a good choice of ales straight from the barrel. The landlord's wife prepares home-cooked meals, incorporating local ingredients and vegetables from the pub garden. Typical specials include halibut steak baked with tomatoes and wine; and pheasant breast with smoked bacon and cranberries. There's an enclosed garden with outdoor seating.

Open 12–2.30 7–11 (Sun 7–9, off season) Closed: early Jul
Bar Meals L served Tue-Sun 12–1.45 D served Tue-Sun 7–9 (Sun 7–9) Av main course £7.25 **Restaurant** L served all week 12–1.45 D served all week 7–9 (Sun 12–2.30, 7–9) ⊕ Free House ◗ Palmer IPA, Otter Ale, Fuller's London Pride, Adnams Southwold. **Facilities** Garden Parking

---

LANGPORT

MAP 04 ST42

The Old Pound Inn ★★★ INN ☻

Aller TA10 0RA ☎ 01458 250469 🖹 01458 250469

e-mail: oldpoundinn@btconnect.com

dir: *2.5m N of Langport on A372. 8m SE of Bridgwater on A372*

Built as a cider house, the Old Pound Inn dates from 1571 and retains plenty of historic character with oak beams, open fires and a garden that used to be the village pound. It's a friendly pub with a good reputation for its real ale and home-cooked food, but also provides function facilities for 200 with its own bar.

Open 11–2.30 5–11 (Sat-Sun 11–11) **Bar Meals** L served Mon-Sat 12–1.45 D served Mon-Sat 6–9.45 (Sun 12–7.45) Av main course £8 **Restaurant** L served Mon-Sat 12–1.45 D served Mon-Sat 6–8.45 (Sun 12–7.45) Av 3 course à la carte £22 ◗ Tribute, Sharp's, Cotleigh, Branscombe. ☻ 8 **Facilities** Garden Dogs allowed Parking **Rooms** 8

Rose & Crown

Huish Episcopi TA10 9QT ☎ 01458 250494

dir: *M5 junct 25, A358 towards Ilminster. Left onto A378. Village in 14m (1m from Langport). Pub near church in village*

Destined forever to be known as Eli's, after the landlady's grandfather, this traditional inn has no bar, just a flagstone taproom lined with casks of ales and farmhouse ciders, an upright piano and some fairly basic seating. No wonder folk music and storytelling evenings are a regular feature. Home-made food includes sandwiches, soups, jacket potatoes, pork cobbler and cottage pie. Vegetarian meals, such as cauliflower cheese, are always available, along with puddings like apple crumble.

Open 11.30–2.30 5.30–11 (Fri-Sat 11.30–11, Sun 12–10.30)
Bar Meals L served all week 12–2 D served Mon-Sat 6–7.30 Av main course £6.75 ⊕ Free House ◗ Teignworthy Reel Ale, Mystery Tor, Hop Back Summer Lightning, Butcombe Bitter. **Facilities** Garden Dogs allowed Parking Play Area **Notes** ☻

England

LEIGH UPON MENDIP   MAP 04 ST64

The Bell Inn ♀

BA3 5QQ ☎ 01373 812316 ▤ 01373 812434

e-mail: rodcambourne@aol.com

dir: *From Frome take A37 towards Shepton Mallet. Turn right, through Mells, on to Leigh upon Mendip*

The Bell was built in the early 16th century to house workers constructing the village church, and Pilgrims used to stop here en route to Glastonbury. There is a bar with two inglenook fireplaces, a 30-seat restaurant, a skittle alley/function room and a large garden with children's play equipment. Snacks and meals are served (mussels with Thai curry, lamb stew and dumplings). A three-mile walk around the lanes starts and finishes at the pub.

Open 12–3 6–12 (Sun 12–12) **Bar Meals** L served all week 12–2 D served all week 6.30–9.30 (Sun 12–2.30) **Restaurant** L served all week 12–2 D served all week 6.30–9.30 (Sun 12–2.30) Av 3 course à la carte £16 ⊕ Wadworth ◀ Wadworth 6X, Butcombe Bitter, Wadworths JCB, Henrys IPA. ♀ 12 **Facilities** Garden Dogs allowed Parking Play Area

LONG SUTTON   MAP 04 ST42

Pick of the Pubs

The Devonshire Arms ★★★ INN ⊛ ♀

TA10 9LP ☎ 01458 241271 ▤ 01458 241037

e-mail: mail@thedevonshirearms.com

dir: *Exit A303 at Podimore rdbt onto A372. Continue for 4m, left onto B3165.*

A fine-looking, stone-built former hunting lodge on a pretty village green. Step through its imposing portico, decorated with the Devonshire family crest, to discover unexpectedly contemporary styling complementing the large open fire and other original features. The pub is renowned locally for its food, which, whenever possible, is made with the best local produce. For lunch try home-smoked chicken salad with rosemary dressing; chargrilled whole plaice with garlic mayonnaise; or just a ploughman's with cheddar, Somerset brie, honey roast ham and spring onions. For dinner, give thought to grilled sea bream with roasted root vegetables and white wine and tarragon sauce; roasted wood pigeon with caramelised shallots, savoy cabbage and mash; or Quantock duck breast with stir-fried vegetables and balsamic jus. Pear and almond tart with cinnamon ice cream would be a tasty dessert. The bar serves good West Country ales and the cellar provides a refreshingly manageable wine list.

Open 12–3 6–11 Closed: 25 Dec, 1 Jan **Bar Meals** 12–2.30 D served all week 7–9.30 Av main course £9.95 **Restaurant** D served all week 7–9.30 Av 3 course à la carte £26 ⊕ Free House ◀ Teignworthy 'Real Ale', Hopback 'Crop Circle'. ♀ 10 **Facilities** Children's licence Garden Parking Play Area **Rooms** 8

LOVINGTON   MAP 04 ST53

Pick of the Pubs

The Pilgrims ★★★★ INN ♀

See Pick of the Pubs on opposite page

LOWER VOBSTER   MAP 04 ST74

Pick of the Pubs

Vobster Inn ★★★★ INN ⊛ ♀

See Pick of the Pubs on page 504

LUXBOROUGH   MAP 03 SS93

Pick of the Pubs

The Royal Oak Inn ♀

See Pick of the Pubs on page 507

MARTOCK   MAP 04 ST41

The Nag's Head Inn

East St TA12 6NF ☎ 01935 823432

dir: *Telephone for directions*

Expect a warm welcome at this 200-year-old former cider house set in a picturesque village in rural south Somerset. Alfresco eating and drinking is encouraged in the landscaped garden and a huge orchard area, with the home-made food being much sought after locally. Lamb shanks, venison casserole, various Thai and other oriental dishes, and delicious steaks are also available in the bar and restaurant.

Open 12–2.30 6–11 (Fri-Sun all day) **Bar Meals** L served Tue-Sun 12–2 D served Wed-Sat 6–9 (Mon-Tue 6–8) **Restaurant** L served Tue-Sun 12–2 D served Wed-Sat 6–8.30 (Mon-Tue 6–8) ⊕ Free House ◀ Guinness, Worthington, Toby. **Facilities** Garden Dogs allowed Parking

The Pilgrims

As the deeds to the Pilgrims were lost in a fire in 1980, not much about the pub is written down; it's generally accepted that the building is around 300 years old. With disarming honesty owners Sally and Jools Mitchison admit that it will never be pretty from the outside. Step inside, however, and the interior tells another story.

Wicker and leather seating is backed by the rich woods of the bar, where locals' pewter mugs hang in readiness for the next pint of village ale brewed just around the corner. 'Local' is a much used word here, especially when describing the quality food. Many herbs and vegetables are grown in the pub's own garden, and then every effort is made to source nearby produce; suppliers are proudly listed in the pub's literature. Starters and light lunches include smoked eel (from the nearby Somerset Levels) and bacon, and West Country mussels cooked in cider (from Burrow Hill) with leeks and garlic. Local rack of lamb roasted pink or roast pheasant with bacon, pistachios and wild mushrooms are among the main courses. World-class cheeses "all made between three and 30 miles of where you're sitting" include goat's and ewes' milk varieties. Finally desserts are all home made (except the ice cream, which is made in the village); examples are Somerset apple crumble; chocolate mousse; and lemon posset. Wisely, Sally and Jools observe that children prefer small portions of adult food to their own menu, so dishes can be produced in smaller quantities for a lower price, and that goes for less hungry adults too.

★★★★ INN ☗
MAP 04 ST53
BA7 7PT
☎ 01963 240597
e-mail: jools@
thepilgrimsatlovington.co.uk
web:
www.thepilgrimsatlovington.co.uk
dir: *From A303 take A37 to Lyford, right at lights, 1.5m to The Pilgrims on B3153.*

Open 12–3 7–11 Closed: Oct Sun eve & Mon
Bar Meals L served Tue-Sun 12–2 D served Tue-Sat 7–9 Av main course £17
Restaurant L served Tue-Sun 12–2 D served Tue-Sat 7–9 Av 3 course à la carte £27
⊕ Free House ◀ Cottage Brewing Champflower & Erdinger.
☗ 12
Facilities Children's licence Garden Dogs allowed Parking
Rooms 5

PICK OF THE PUBS

LOWER VOBSTER-SOMERSET

Vobster Inn

The original part of the building, which stands in four acres of grounds and mature gardens, dates back to the 17th century – though there was probably an inn on the site even before that. Surrounded by stunning countryside, it is a popular destination for walkers.

Rafael and Peta Davila took up residence in the Vobster Inn in 2005 after more than a year of searching for the right business and home. With warm support from their regulars and neighbours, they have been putting their stamp on it ever since. Both bar and restaurant menus feature seafood and West Country meats, but there's a distinctive Spanish bias, reflecting Rafael's birthplace on the rugged Galician coast. So, along with seared breast of woodpigeon, sweet pear and black pudding, the starter menu also includes a platter of Spanish meats with salad, olives, houmous and crusty bread. Main courses options include beef featherblade with cheddar parsnip purée and buttered Savoy cabbage; gammon steak with fries,

mushroom and free-range egg; chicken and chorizo paella; and mixed bean and Catalan sauce ragout with crusty bread. Fish lovers should check the blackboard for a selection of fresh fish from St Mawes; whole roast sea bass with pesto; and salmon and ginger fishcake are typical. All desserts are home made: expect warm upside-down pineapple cake with vanilla parfait and mango coulis; bread and butter pudding with clotted cream; and coconut and citrus rice pudding with passion fruit jelly. Children are particularly welcome and have their own menu as well, although they are also encouraged to try smaller portions from the main menus.

★★★★ INN ◉ ♥
MAP 04 ST74
BA3 5RJ
☎ 01373 812920
🖷 01373 812920
e-mail: info@vobsterinn.co.uk
dir: *4m W of Frome*

Open 12–3 6.30–11 Closed: Sun eve
Bar Meals L served Mon-Sat 12–2 D served Mon-Thu 7–9 (Fri-Sat 7–9.30, Sun 12–6) Av main course £12.50
Restaurant L served all week 12–2 D served Mon-Sat 7–11 Av 3 course à la carte £23
⊕ Free House ◼ Butcombe Blonde, Ashton, Press Cider. ♥ 8
Facilities Garden Parking
Rooms 3

MILVERTON MAP 03 ST12

Pick of the Pubs

The Globe NEW ☝

Fore St TA4 1JX ☎ 01823 400534

e-mail: info@theglobemilverton.co.uk

dir: *On B3187*

A village free house with a difference. Originally a coaching inn, its now not-so-new owners have refurbished it in a clean-looking, contemporary style that creates both its distinctive character and its warm, friendly atmosphere. As a result, the local community has taken them to their hearts in a big way. Local artists' work adorns the walls of the restaurant and bar. Menus draw heavily on West Country sources, and change frequently to offer attractions such as broccoli and gorgonzola soup; River Fowey mussels; grilled pollack with kale; Cornish rib-eye steak; Mark's mum's faggots (Mark, by the way, is the co-owner); baked parsnip and onion tart with roasted root vegetables; and linguine carbonara with parmesan shavings. The children's menu is thoughtfully compiled. Resist if you can sticky toffee pudding, not with just toffee sauce, but with clotted cream too.

Open 12–3 6–11 (Sat-Sun 6–11.30, Sun 6–10.30) Closed: Mon **Bar Meals** L served Tue-Sun 12–3 D served Tue-Thu 6–11 (Fri-Sat 6–11.30, Sun 6–10.30) Av main course £8.95 **Restaurant** L served Tue-Sun 12–3 D served Tue-Thu 6–11 (Fri-Sat 6–11.30, Sun 6–10.30) Av 3 course à la carte £22.95 ◀ Exmoor Ale, Cotleigh 25 & guest ales. ☝8 **Facilities** Parking

MONKSILVER MAP 03 ST03

Pick of the Pubs

The Notley Arms ☝

See Pick of the Pubs on page 508

MONTACUTE MAP 04 ST41

The Kings Arms Inn ☝

49 Bishopston TA15 6UU ☎ 01935 822513

e-mail: kingsarmsmont@aol.com

dir: *From A303 onto A3088 at rdbt signed Montacute. Hotel in village centre*

Mons Acutus (thus Montacute) is the steep hill at whose foot the hamstone-built Kings Arms has stood since 1632. Have a snack in the fire-warmed bar, or something more substantial chosen from the daily changing restaurant menu, such as fillet of beef in oyster sauce; baked salmon fillet with hollandaise; or baked tomatoes stuffed with olives, spring onions and feta.

Open 7–11 **Bar Meals** L served all week 12 D served all week 9 (Sun carvery) Av main course £11.95 **Restaurant** L served all week 12–2.30 D served all week 7–9 ⊕ Greene King ◀ Ruddles County, Abbot Ale, Old Speckled Hen. ☝10 **Facilities** Garden Dogs allowed Parking

The Phelips Arms ☝

The Borough TA15 6XB ☎ 01935 822557 🖹 01935 822557

e-mail: infophelipsarms@aol.com

dir: *From Cartgate rdbt on A303 follow signs for Montacute*

A 17th-century listed ham stone building overlooking the village square and close to historic Montacute House (NT). The emphasis is on the quality of the food, and everything is prepared on the premises using the best local and West Country produce. The menu features an eclectic selection of dishes cooked in a robust style, and there is a small but delicious pudding menu, and an extensive wine list.

Open 11.30–2.30 6–11 Closed: 25 Dec **Bar Meals** L served all week 12–2 D served Tue-Sat 7–9 Av main course £12 **Restaurant** L served all week 12–2 D served Tue-Sat 6–9 (Sun 12–2.30) Av 3 course à la carte £21 ⊕ Palmers ◀ Palmers IPA & 200 Premium Ale, Copper Ale. ☝35 **Facilities** Garden Dogs allowed Parking

NORTH CURRY MAP 04 ST32

The Bird in Hand ☝

1 Queen Square TA3 6LT ☎ 01823 490248

dir: *5m from M5 junct 25*

A friendly 300–year-old village inn, with large stone inglenook fireplaces, flagstone floors, exposed beams and studwork. Cheerful staff provide a friendly welcome, and the place is atmospheric at night by candlelight. Blackboard menus feature local produce including vegetarian options and steak dishes, and the constantly changing seafood is supplied by a Plymouth fishmonger.

Open 12–3 6–11 (Fri-Sat 6–12) **Bar Meals** L served all week 12–2 D served Sun-Thu 7–9 (Fri-Sat 7–9.30) **Restaurant** L served all week 12–2 D served all week 7–9.30 ⊕ Free House ◀ Badger Tanglefoot, Exmoor Gold, Otter Ale, Cotleigh Barn Owl. ☝8 **Facilities** Dogs allowed Parking

NORTON ST PHILIP MAP 04 ST75

Pick of the Pubs

George Inn ☝

See Pick of the Pubs on page 510

NUNNEY MAP 04 ST74

The George at Nunney ★★ HL ☝

Church St BA11 4LW ☎ 01373 836458 🖹 01373 836565

e-mail: enquiries@georgeatnunneyhotel.wanadoo.co.uk

dir: *0.5m N off A361, Frome/Shepton Mallet*

The garden was used in the Middle Ages as a place of execution, but this rambling old coaching inn is deservedly popular these days. Set in a historic conservation village, it serves a wide choice of food. Big steaks, mixed grill, steak and ale pie, and double chicken breasts with choice of sauces, plus a separate fish menu including brill, sea bass, hake, red mullet and fresh dressed crabs.

Open 12–3 5–11 **Bar Meals** L served all week 12–2 D served all week 7–9 Av main course £8 **Restaurant** L served all week 12–2 D served all week 7–9 Av 3 course à la carte £18 Av 3 course fixed price £12 ⊕ Free House ◀ Highgate Brewery Saddlers Best Bitter, Wadworth 6X, Interbrew Bass and guest ales. ☝8 **Facilities** Garden Parking **Rooms** 10 (9 en suite)

England

OVER STRATTON   MAP 04 ST41

The Royal Oak

TA13 5LQ ☎ 01460 240906
e-mail: info@the-royal-oak.net
dir: *Exit A303 at Hayes End rdbt (South Petherton). 1st left after Esso garage signed Over Stratton*

Blackened beams, flagstones, log fires, pews and settles set the scene in this welcoming old thatched inn built from warm Hamstone, which has the added attraction of a garden, children's play area and barbecue. Expect real ales, including Tanglefoot from the Badger brewery in Blandford Forum, and dishes ranging from beer battered haddock and chips with home-made tartare sauce to supreme of chicken in an apricot, ginger and white wine sauce.

Open 11.30–3 6.30–11 **Bar Meals** L served all week 12–2.30 D served all week 6.30–9.30 **Restaurant** L served all week 12–2.30 D served all week 6.30–9.30 ⊕ Hall & Woodhouse ◀ Badger Best, Tanglefoot, Sussex Best Bitter. **Facilities** Garden Dogs allowed Parking Play Area

---

PITNEY   MAP 04 ST42

The Halfway House ⏲

TA10 9AB ☎ 01458 252513
dir: *On B3153, 2m from Langport & Somerton*

This pub is largely dedicated to the promotion of real ale, and there are always six to ten available in tip-top condition, shown on a blackboard. This delightfully old-fashioned rural pub has three homely rooms boasting open fires, books and games, but no music or electronic games. Home-cooked meals (except Sundays when it is too busy with drinkers) include soups, local sausages, sandwiches and a good selection of curries and casseroles in the evening.

Open 11.30–3 5.30–11 (Sun 12–3, 7–10.30) Closed: 25 Dec
Bar Meals L served Mon-Sat 12–2.30 D served Mon-Sat 7–9.30 Av main course £6.95 ⊕ Free House ◀ Butcombe Bitter, Teignworthy, Otter Ale, Cotleigh Tawny Ale. ⏲ 8 **Facilities** Garden Dogs allowed Parking Play Area

---

PORLOCK   MAP 03 SS84

The Ship Inn

High St TA24 8QD ☎ 01643 862507 📄 01643 863224
e-mail: mail@shipinnporlock.co.uk
dir: *A358 to Williton, then A39 to Porlock. 6m from Minehead.*

Many travellers have been welcomed to this 13th-century inn, including Wordsworth, Coleridge and even Nelson's press gang. Nestling at the foot of Porlock's notorious hill, where Exmoor tumbles into the sea, its thatched roof and traditional interior provide an evocative setting for a meal, drink or overnight stay. Regularly changing menus include ploughman's, light bites and dishes such as supreme of salmon on horseradish mash with parsley and lemon crème. There's a beer garden with children's play area.

Open 11–12 (Sun 12–11) **Bar Meals** L served all week 12–2 D served all week 6.30–9 (Sun 12.30–2.30 7–9) Av main course £8 **Restaurant** L served Sun 12–2 D served all week 7–9 Av 3 course à la carte £17 ⊕ Free House ◀ Tribute, Exmoor Ale, Butcombe, Otter. **Facilities** Garden Dogs allowed Parking Play Area

The Anchor Hotel & Ship Inn

Porlock Weir TA24 8PB ☎ 01643 862753 📄 01643 862843
e-mail: info@theanchorhotelandshipinn.co.uk
web: www.theanchorhotelandshipinn.co.uk

A three-star hotel restaurant and 16th-century inn all in one, right on the harbour front at the point where the road ends. Just offshore is an ancient submarine forest, visible during only the lowest tides. Traditional pub food in Mariners Bar includes smoked mackerel; hot and fruity chicken curry; home-made steak and kidney pie; and four-cheese and roast onion quiche. Among dinner choices in the Harbourside Restaurant are rack of lamb; lobster thermidor; and cannelloni verde.

Open 11–11 **Bar Meals** L served all week 12–3 D served all week 6.30–8.30 **Restaurant** L served all week 12–2.30 D served all week 7–9.30 ⊕ Free House ◀ Exmoor Ale, Exmoor Fox, Cotleigh Barn Owl, Cotleigh 25. **Facilities** Children's licence Garden Dogs allowed Parking

---

PRIDDY   MAP 04 ST55

New Inn

Priddy Green BA5 3BB ☎ 01749 676465
dir: *M4 junct 18, A39 right to Priddy 3m before Wells. M4 junct 19 through Bristol onto A39. From M5 junct 21,A371 to Cheddar, then B3371*

Overlooking the village green high up in the Mendip Hills, this old, former farmhouse is popular with walkers, riders and cavers, and once served beer to the local lead miners. A typical dinner menu features liver and bacon, chargrilled steaks, Brixham plaice, and fillet of pork with braised red cabbage. There's also a skittle alley, and Priddy's 'friendliest folk festival in England' every July.

Open 12–3 7–11 **Bar Meals** L served all week 12–2 D served all week 7–9.30 Av main course £6.50 **Restaurant** L served all week 12–2 D served all week 7–9.30 Av 3 course à la carte £12 ⊕ Free House ◀ Interbrew Bass, Fuller's London Pride, Wadworth 6X, New Inn Priddy. **Facilities** Garden Dogs allowed Parking Play Area

PICK OF THE PUBS

LUXBOROUGH-SOMERSET

The Royal Oak Inn

Set directly on the Coleridge Way walk amid the beauty Exmoor National Park, this 14th-century building has been an inn for as long as anyone can remember. At some point, though, the back bar was an abattoir, as the hooks in the ceiling beams testify, and it has also served as a tailor's shop and post office.

There is no piped music, no fruit machine and mobile phones can't receive a signal here, which many will find a huge blessing. Until 1996, drinkers in the Blazing Stump bar (so called after a stingy former landlord who put only one log on the fire at a time) held their breath as the ceiling sagged four inches when someone walked overhead. Renovation has resolved that problem, while leaving its rustic character intact, although during a downpour you still might need Wellington boots when an unstoppable torrent rushes down the hill, through the front door and out the back, without even stopping to buy a pint of Exmoor Gold. Tastefully traditional dining areas include the Green Room, ideal for intimate candlelit dinners, the

Red Room for family gatherings or parties, and the Old Dining Room, just off the bar. The fine food, ranging from lunchtime snacks to classic country fare, makes full use of excellent local ingredients and has a well-deserved reputation. Selected from a winter menu are starters of chicken liver parfait with a fig and red wine compote; and potted venison and foie gras with a sweet wine jelly and toasted brioche. Main courses include local game casserole cooked in a sloe gin sauce with pearl barley; and roast tail of monkfish with curried mussels and coriander – but be sure to check the daily specials board before deciding. The suntrap courtyard patio makes a delightful setting for a meal or peaceful drink.

MAP 03 SS93
TA23 0SH
☎ 01984 640319
🖷 01984 641561
e-mail: info@
theroyaloakinnluxborough.co.uk
dir: *From A38 (Taunton/Minehead) at Washford take minor road S through Roadwater*

Open 12-2.30 6-11 (Open all day June-mid Sep) Closed: 25 Dec
Bar Meals L served all week 12-2 Av main course £8.25
Restaurant L served all week 12-2 D served all week 7-9 (Cream Tea served 1 Jun-15 Sep, 2-6) Av 3 course à la carte £25.95
⊕ Free House ◀ Tawney, Palmers 200, Exmoor Gold, Palmers IPA. ♟ 8
Facilities Garden Dogs allowed Parking

PICK OF THE PUBS

MONKSILVER-SOMERSET

The Notley Arms

An English country drinking and dining pub in a hamlet on the edge of Exmoor, built in the 1860s and named after a prominent local family. The stream that runs through the village and alongside the pub garden is called the Silver, derived from silva, which is Latin for wooded area.

When monks from Monmouthshire arrived at nearby Cleeve Abbey, the village became known as Silva Monachorum, which over the centuries has mutated to Monksilver. Jane and Russell Deary prepare and cook everything themselves, with a distinct bias towards traditional but imaginative British dishes, using fresh produce from the south west of England. That said, you'll soon spot ostrich steaks, biltong, droewors and bobotie, southern African specialities that reflect the Dearys' Zimbabwean origins. Menus also offer pork and three-mustard stroganoff; Exmoor sirloin steak; Somerset lamb shank braised in red wine and redcurrant jus; 'deerstalker' venison pie; chicken teriyaki with stir-fry vegetables

and egg noodles; and Thai-style butternut and pineapple curry. Depending on fish catches delivered fresh from St Mawes in Cornwall, there may be baked red mullet, chunky cod fillet, sea bass en papillote, and much more. Smaller portions of most dishes are available for children. Puddings include Somerset apple and hazelnut cake with toffee sauce and clotted cream, and raspberry yoghurt meringue with raspberry coulis and toasted almonds. Well-tended flower borders make the garden look very pretty, and there's a selection of outdoor toys to keep children happy. The pub stands on the 36–mile Coleridge Way, which runs from Nether Stowey, the poet's one-time home, to Porlock.

MAP 03 ST03
TA4 4JB
☎ 01984 656217
dir: *Village on B3227 N of Wiveliscombe towards Watchet & Minehead*

Open 12–2.30 6.30–11 (Fri 12–2, 6.30–9)
Bar Meals L served Tue-Sun 12–2 D served all week 7–9 (Mon-Fri in winter 7–9) Av main course £7.50
⊕ Enterprise Inns ◀ Exmoor Ale, Wadworth 6X & Bath Ales. ☻ 10
Facilities Garden Dogs allowed Parking Play Area

RODE
MAP 04 ST85

The Mill at Rode ♥

BA11 6AG ☎ 01373 831100 📄 01373 831144

e-mail: info@themillatrode.co.uk

dir: *6m S of Bath*

A sympathetically modernised, former grist mill with an original waterwheel that the River Frome, which runs through the beautiful gardens, still coaxes into turning. According to the menu, the owners are "making a huge effort" to provide the best local ingredients – judge for yourself with Wiltshire pheasant breast on celeriac mash with gin and juniper sauce; savoury ragout of Bath blue cheese, celery and sweet potato; or Springleaze fillet steak with wholegrain mustard sauce.

Open 12–11 **Bar Meals** L served all week 12–10 D served all week 12–10 **Restaurant** L served all week 12–10 D served all week 12–10 ⊕ Free House ◀ Butcombe Bitter, Erdinger, Guinness, guest ales. ♥ 8 **Facilities** Garden Parking Play Area

---

RUDGE
MAP 04 ST85

The Full Moon at Rudge ★★★★ INN

BA11 2QF ☎ 01373 830936 📄 01373 831366

e-mail: info@thefullmoon.co.uk

dir: *From A36 (Bath to Warminster road) follow Rudge signs*

Strategically placed at the crossing of two old drove roads, this inn enjoys great views of Westbury White Horse. The venerable 16th-century building had been sympathetically updated and retains its small, stone-floored rooms furnished with scrubbed tables. Modern British cooking is the watchword: perhaps lime and coriander crab cakes, followed by lamb chump chop with bubble and squeak and a rosemary jus, or simple steak and kidney pie.

Open 11–11 (Sun 12–10.30) **Bar Meals** L served all week 12–2 D served Mon-Sat 6.30–9.30 (Sun 7–9) **Restaurant** L served all week 12–2 D served Mon-Sat 6.30–9.30 (Sun 7–9) ⊕ Free House ◀ Butcombe Bitter, Wadworth 6X, John Smith's. **Facilities** Garden Dogs allowed Parking **Rooms** 16

SHEPTON BEAUCHAMP
MAP 04 ST41

Duke of York NEW ♥

TA19 0LW ☎ 01460 240314

e-mail: sheptonduke@tiscali.co.uk

In the lovely village of Shepton Beauchamp is this 17th-century free house, run by husband and wife team Paul and Hayley Rowlands, and Purdy, the 'famous' pub dog. The bar stocks some good West Country real ales and ciders, while the restaurant's varied menu and blackboard specials offer chargrilled steaks, delicious fish from Bridport, and a selection of home-made pub classics.

Open 12–2.30 6.30–11 (Sat-Sun, all day) **Bar Meals** L served Tue-Sun 12–2 D served Tue-Sat 7–9 Av main course £8 **Restaurant** L served Tue-Sun 12–2 D served Tue-Sat 7–9 Av 3 course à la carte £16.95 ⊕ Free House ◀ Teignworthy Reel Ale, Otter Bright. ♥ 7 **Facilities** Garden Dogs allowed Parking

---

SHEPTON MALLET
MAP 04 ST64

Pick of the Pubs

The Three Horseshoes
Inn ★★★★ INN ❀ ♥

See Pick of the Pubs on page 512

Pick of the Pubs

The Waggon and Horses ♥

Frome Rd, Doulting Beacon BA4 4LA

☎ 01749 880302 📄 01749 880602

e-mail: portsmouthpnni@hotmail.com

dir: *1.5m N of Shepton Mallet at x-roads with Old Wells-Frome road, 1m off A37*

This rural coaching inn has views over Glastonbury, and is very much at the heart of artistic life in the local community. A pretty, whitewashed building with leaded windows and a large garden, it has a flower-filled paddock and an upstairs skittle alley that doubles as a concert hall and gallery, with regular exhibitions and monthly live music. Food choices are based on traditional country food which is locally sourced and seasonal. The bar offers a varying range of real beers, a good choice of wines by the glass, local Somerset Royal cider brandy, and an interesting selection of cocktails.

Open 11.30–3 6–11 (Fri-Sun all day in summer) **Bar Meals** L served all week 11.30–2.30 D served all week 6–9.30 (Sat-Sun all day in summer) **Restaurant** L served all week 11.30–2.30 D served all week 6–9.30 (Sat-Sun all day in summer) Av fixed price £10 ◀ Wadworth 6X, Greene King IPA, Butcombe. ♥ 12 **Facilities** Children's licence Garden Dogs allowed Parking

---

SHEPTON MONTAGUE
MAP 04 ST63

The Montague Inn ♥

BA9 8JW ☎ 01749 813213 📄 01749 813213

e-mail: themontagueinn@aol.com

dir: *From Wincanton & Castle Cary turn right off A371*

This comfortably refurbished, stone-built village inn nestles in rolling unspoilt Somerset countryside on the edge of sleepy Shepton Montague. Tastefully decorated throughout, with the homely bar featuring old dark pine and an open log fire, and a cosy, yellow-painted dining room. Menu choices include bacon and brie ciabatta, Scottish venison steak, home-made pies, mushroom lasagne, and organic lamb. Local beers and ciders are served directly from the cask. The attractive terrace with rural views is perfect for summer sipping.

Open 12–3 6–11 Closed: Sun eve & Mon **Bar Meals** L served Tue-Sun 12–2 D served Tue-Sat 7–9 **Restaurant** L served Tue-Sun 12–2 D served Tue-Sat 7–9 Av 3 course à la carte £26 ⊕ Free House ◀ Bath Ale, Butcombe Gold, Abbot Ale & guest ale. ♥ 7 **Facilities** Garden Dogs allowed Parking

PICK OF THE PUBS

George Inn

A Grade I listed property, the George is one of the oldest continually licensed inns in England, dating back to the 13th century. The beautiful building is of great historical and architectural interest, particularly the stone slated roof.

Famous visitors include diarist Samuel Pepys, who called in on 12 June 1668 with his wife and servants en route from Salisbury to Bath, and dined well for 10 shillings. Also, the Duke of Monmouth, the illegitimate son of Charles II, who fought his uncle for the throne on his father's death and made the inn his base as he retreated from Bath in June 1685. The infamous Judge Jeffreys held court here, too, and while he was shaving at the window of the Monmouth Room, an attempt was made on his life. As a result of Jeffreys' judgements, 12 men were hanged just across the road from the inn. These days the outlook is more gently bucolic, with views over the local cricket pitch and the 13th-century church. Seats are also available in the cobbled and galleried courtyard, where knights of old once walked. The Norton (or Dungeon) Bar, with its flagstone floor and arched stone ceiling is a favourite with locals, while the intimate main bar features a bar bench (made from a 700-year-old monks' writing table) and an inglenook fireplace. There's a choice of dining rooms, too, in the main restaurant with its oak-beamed ceiling and the smaller Charterhouse Room. Typical dishes are game casserole; fillet of sea bass on roasted vegetables with balsamic dressing; Mediterranean chicken; and steak, mushroom and 6X pie. An hourly bus service from the inn to the centre of Bath makes it an ideal base for visiting the city.

🍷
MAP 04 ST75
High St BA2 7LH
☎ 01373 834224
▤ 01373 834861
e-mail: georgeinnnsp@aol.com
dir: *From Bath take A36 to Warminster, after 6m take A366 on right to Radstock, village 1m*

Open 11–2.30 5.30–11 (Sat-Sun all day summer)
Bar Meals L served all week 12–2 D served all week 7–9.30 (Sun all day from Mar)
Restaurant L served all week 12–2 D served all week 7–9.30 (Sun all day from Mar)
⊕ Wadworth ◧ Wadworth 6X, Henrys IPA, Wadworth Bishops Tipple, J.C.B. 🍷 30
Facilities Garden Dogs allowed Parking

SPARKFORD   MAP 04 ST62

The Sparkford Inn

High St BA22 7JH ☎ 01963 440218 ▤ 01963 440358
e-mail: sparkfordinn@sparkford.fsbusiness.co.uk
dir: *Just off A303, 400yds from rdbt at Sparkford*

A 15th-century former coaching inn with beamed bars and a fascinating display of old prints and photographs. It is set in an attractive garden just off the A303 between Wincanton and Yeovil. The restaurant offers a popular lunchtime carvery, light meals and a full evening menu, featuring steaks from the grill. Dishes include marinated Cajun chicken breast; smoked haddock and bacon au gratin; and bean, celery and coriander chilli.

Open 11–3 5.30–11 (Summer 11–11) **Bar Meals** L served all week 12–2 D served all week 7–9.30 **Restaurant** L served all week 12–2 D served all week 7–9.30 ⊕ Free House ◀ Marstons Pedigree, Banks Bitter & guest ales. **Facilities** Garden Dogs allowed Parking Play Area

STANTON WICK   MAP 04 ST66

Pick of the Pubs

The Carpenters Arms ⏟

BS39 4BX ☎ 01761 490202 ▤ 01761 490763
e-mail: carpenters@buccaneer.co.uk
web: www.the-carpenters-arms.co.uk
dir: *A37 to Chelwood rdbt, then A368. Pub 8m S of Bath*

Formerly a row of miners' cottages, this charming stone-built free house has oodles of cottagey style. It stands just 20 minutes drive from Bath and Bristol in the tranquil hamlet of Stanton Wick, overlooking the Chew Valley. Outside is a landscaped patio for al fresco drinks or meals, while behind the flower-bedecked façade lies a comfortable bar with low beams, a chatty, music-free atmosphere, and real ales. Seasonal and local produce are a priority, so menus and daily specials change regularly. A typical meal might include a warm duck salad with orange and maple-glazed walnuts and mixed leaves, followed by seared fillets of sea bass on lemon-crushed potato with wilted spinach and tomato, chive and prawn butter. At the heartier end of the scale are grilled steaks or honey-roasted ham with double egg and chips, while lighter options include sandwiches.

Open 11–11 Closed: 25–26 Dec **Bar Meals** L served all week 12–9 D served all week 7–10 **Restaurant** L served Mon-Sat 12–2 D served Mon-Sat 7–10 (Sun 12–9) Av 3 course à la carte £24 ⊕ Buccaneer Holdings ◀ Butcombe Bitter, Courage Best, Wadworth 6X. ⏟ 12 **Facilities** Garden Parking **Rooms** available

STAPLE FITZPAINE   MAP 04 ST21

Pick of the Pubs

The Greyhound Inn ★★★★ INN ⏟
See Pick of the Pubs on page 514

STOGUMBER   MAP 03 ST03

The White Horse

High St TA4 3TA ☎ 01984 656277 ▤ 01984 656873
e-mail: info@whitehorsestogumber.co.uk
dir: *From Taunton take A358 to Minehead. After 8m turn left to Stogumber, 2m into village centre. Right at T-junct & right again. Pub opposite church*

Nestling between the Quantock Hills and Exmoor in an area of outstanding beauty, with the West Somerset Steam Railway only a mile away. The dining room of this traditional free house was once the historic village's Market Hall and Reading Room. Home-cooked menus change daily; typical dishes are smoked salmon tartare with cucumber salad, followed by pan-fried pheasant breast with caramelised apple and cider. The courtyard garden is a perfect place to sample one of the local ales.

Open 11–11 (Sun 12–11) **Bar Meals** L served all week 12–2 D served all week 7–9 Av main course £8.50 **Restaurant** L served all week 12–2 D served all week 7–9 Av 3 course à la carte £16.50 ⊕ Free House ◀ Cotleigh Tawny Bitter, Marstons Pedigree, Greene King, Abbot Ale. **Facilities** Garden Dogs allowed Parking **Rooms** available

STOKE ST GREGORY   MAP 04 ST32

Rose & Crown ⏟

Woodhill TA3 6EW ☎ 01823 490296 ▤ 01823 490996
e-mail: info@browningpubs.com
dir: *M5 junct 25, follow A358 towards Langport, bear left at Thornfalcon, then left again, follow signs to Stoke St Gregory*

Set in the Somerset Levels at the heart of the willow industry, this 18th-century building became a pub in 1867. It has been run by the same family for over 27 years, and enjoys a well deserved reputation for good food, local produce and a warm reception. The interior is cluttered and cosy, full of nooks and crannies with a well in the middle of the bar. Expect lots of fish – roasted whole sea bream, perhaps, or grilled skate wing with capers and black butter.

Open 11–3 7–11 **Bar Meals** L served Mon-Sat 12.30–2 D served Mon-Sat 7–9.30 (Sun 12–2, 7–9) **Restaurant** L served Mon-Sat 12.30–2 D served Mon-Sat 7–9.30 (Sun 12–2, 7–9) Av 3 course à la carte £22.50 ⊕ Free House ◀ Exmoor Fox, Stag, Butcombe, Otter Ale. ⏟ 8 **Facilities** Children's licence Garden Parking

PICK OF THE PUBS

SHEPTON MALLET-SOMERSET

The Three Horseshoes Inn

A 17th-century, honey-coloured stone inn, which once had its own smithy, and whose lovely rear garden overlooks the old parish church. It is now a popular dining pub, with a friendly and relaxed atmosphere, and attentive service. Exposed beams, terracotta walls and an inglenook fireplace are features of the long main bar, where hand-pumped real ales are served.

By the way, don't be confused by one of them, Butcombe Bitter, which comes from near Bristol – this pub is in Batcombe, near Shepton Mallet. The menus draw partly on regional sources for inspiration, but expect too dishes from farther afield, such as starters of Loch Fyne oak-smoked salmon, and West Highland haggis on toast with morels and a shot of Scotch. Main courses with more local provenance include slow-braised shoulder of organic Somerset lamb; fillet of West Country beef; and grilled whole Cornish plaice. For a lighter lunch opt for the seasonally governed, brasserie-style menu, which might offer home-made bangers and mash with onion gravy; cassolette of shellfish and white fish; 100 per cent fillet steak beefburger; and fresh pasta tagliolini with autumn mushrooms. Desserts include sticky toffee pudding with butterscotch sauce and vanilla ice cream; classic treacle sponge with lemon zest, ginger and 'real English' custard; and local and continental cheeses with celery biscuits and home-made chutney. The wines are reasonably priced, with a more or less equal split between European and New World. There are three stylishly decorated letting bedrooms, two with en suite facilities and one with a private bathroom.

★★★★ INN ◉ ♟
MAP 04 ST64
Batcombe BA4 6HE
☎ 01749 850359
🖹 01749 850615
dir: *Take A359 from Frome to Bruton. Batcombe signed on right. Pub by church*

Open 12–3 6.30–11 Closed: Mon
Bar Meals L served Tue-Sun 12–2 D served Tue-Sat 7–9 Av main course £8.50
Restaurant L served Tue-Sun 12–2 D served Tue-Sat 7–9 Av 3 course à la carte £25
⊕ Free House ◼ Butcombe Bitter, Bats in the Belfry & Adnams Palmers 200. ♟ 8
Facilities Garden Dogs allowed Parking
Rooms 3

TAUNTON MAP 04 ST22

The Hatch Inn NEW ★★★ INN

Village Rd, Hatch Beauchamp TA3 6SG ☎ 01823 480245
e-mail: gemma@thehatchinn.co.uk
dir: *M5 junct 25, S on A358 for 3m. Left to Hatch Beauchamp, pub in 1m*

This family-run pub prides itself on its friendly atmosphere and the quality of its beers and wines, including regular guest ales. Traditional home-cooked food is served, prepared from regional produce. Options range through lunchtime snacks (baguettes, ploughman's, jacket potatoes), light bites (Greek salad, fishcakes, meatloaf), and main dishes such as rustic pasta; chunky beef chilli; pan-fried salmon fillet with hollandaise sauce; and sausage with herb mash and onion gravy. A children's menu is also available.

Open 12-2.30 5-12 (Sun 12-3, 7-10.30) Closed: Mon lunch Oct-Feb **Bar Meals** L served Mon-Sat 12-2 D served Mon-Sat 6.30-9 (Sun 12.30-2.30) **Restaurant** L served Mon-Sat 12-2 D served Mon-Sat 6.30-9 (Sun 12.30-2.30) Free House Exmoor Ale, Sharp's Doom Bar & Worthington's. **Facilities** Dogs allowed Parking **Rooms** 5

Pick of the Pubs

Queens Arms

Pitminster TA3 7AZ ☎ 01823 421529 01823 451068
e-mail: enquiries@queensarms-taunton.co.uk
dir: *4m from town centre. On entering Corfe, turn right signed Pitminster. 0.75m, pub on left*

Situated in the heart of Pitminster, the Queens Arms even gets a mention in the Domesday Book of 1086, recording that this ancient building was then a mill. Today, the pub combines the traditional welcome of a classic country inn with a touch of continental influence. Oak and slate floors and roaring log fires in winter add to the appeal, while in summer the patio garden is the perfect spot for a cold drink or after-dinner coffee. The chef uses only the finest locally produced ingredients, with fish delivered daily from Brixham. Meat and game are produced in Somerset, and the vegetables are grown locally. Starters include smoked salmon, moules marinière, and mushroom and blue cheese bouchee. Among the main courses are beef and otter pie, fish and chips, traditional Irish stew, liver and bacon, Somerset lamb shank, and home-made fishcakes. Extensive and impresive wine list.

Open 12-3 6-11 Closed: Mon-Tue L Jan-Etr **Bar Meals** L served Tue-Sun 12-2.15 D served Mon-Sat 7-9.15 Av main course £9.95 **Restaurant** L served Tue-Sun 12-2.15 D served Mon-Sat 7-9.15 Enterprise Inns Otter Ale, Otter Bitter & Exmoor Ale. 8 **Facilities** Garden Dogs allowed Parking

TRISCOMBE MAP 04 ST13

Pick of the Pubs

The Blue Ball

TA4 3HE ☎ 01984 618242 01984 618371
e-mail: info@blueballinn.co.uk
web: www.blueballinn.co.uk
dir: *From Taunton take A358 past Bishops Lydeard towards Minehead*

Hidden away down a narrow lane in the Quantock Hills, the pub is actually a converted 18th-century thatched barn. Inside are A-frame wood ceilings, solid beech furniture, log fires and, through the windows, super views south to the Brendon Hills. The chefs produce dishes from fresh ingredients sourced from local suppliers all, of course, chosen with considerable care. For a three-course lunch try smoked salmon, capers and lemon; warm salad of chicken, chorizo and black pudding; and vanilla pannacotta with berry and mango sauce. In the evening, there may be carpaccio of beef, rocket and parmesan; whole roasted sea bass with lemon hollandaise; and sticky toffee pudding with toffee sauce. Also not to be missed are home-made ice creams and sorbets. Meals are also served in the large beer garden and on the patio. West Country real ales are kept, and there's an extensive wine list.

Open 12-4 6-11 Closed: 25-26 Dec eve & 1 Jan eve **Bar Meals** L served all week 12-2.30 D served all week 7-9.30 (Sun 12-6) Av main course £9.95 **Restaurant** L served all week 12-2.30 D served Mon-Sat 7-9.30 (Sun 12-6) Av 3 course à la carte £23 Punch Taverns Cotleigh Tawny, Exmoor Gold & Stag, St Austell, Tribute. 8 **Facilities** Garden Dogs allowed Parking

WASHFORD MAP 03 ST04

The Washford Inn

TA23 0PP ☎ 01984 640256
e-mail: washfordinn@freedomnames.co.uk
dir: *Telephone for directions*

A pleasant family inn located beside Washford Station, a stop on the West Somerset Railway between Minehead and Bishop's Lydeard – the longest privately-owned line in Britain. A service runs all year, using both diesel and nostalgic old steam locos. A good range of beers and a simple menu of proven pub favourites such as omelette and chips, grilled steaks, and all-day breakfast. Chicken nuggets, sausages or pizzas for young trainspotters.

Open 12-11 **Bar Meals** L served all week 12-8.30 D served all week Av main course £7.50 **Restaurant** L served all week 12-2.30 D served all week 5-9 Scottish & Newcastle Adnams Broadside, Theakstons Best Mild, Ringwood. **Facilities** Garden Dogs allowed Parking Play Area

PICK OF THE PUBS

STAPLE FITZPAINE-SOMERSET

The Greyhound Inn

In a dip in the Blackdown Hills that surround the tucked-away village of Staple Fitzpaine, is this creeper-clad, award-winning 16th-century free house. Extended over the years, it has become by default rather than design a series of rambling rooms linked by flagstone floors, old timbers and natural stone walls.

In the locals' bar, with its barrel stools and wood burning stove, real ales and traditional Somerset cider, all on hand pump, are kept in fine condition, while in the restaurant candle-topped tables and open winter fires are clearly designed with a warm welcome in mind. Freshly prepared seasonal food is cooked to order, to be complemented by a fine wine, served by the glass or bottle. The comprehensive menu features a variety of dishes using the best local Somerset ingredients, including local pork, beef, lamb and cheeses, with fish freshly delivered each morning from Brixham in Devon. A typical menu lists starters of home-made tomato and basil soup; chorizo, mushroom and prosciutto salad; and mussels

tossed in garlic, onion, parsley and cream. It continues with main courses of chargrilled sirloin steak with smoked bacon, asparagus and stilton with port wine reduction; salmon and spinach en croûte with spring onion mash and white wine grape butter sauce; and Mexican-style pancakes filled with tomato, red pepper and kidney bean salsa. It ends with desserts such as raspberry pavlova; apple pie with custard or cream; and blackcurrant cheesecake. Pub classics include home-made curries and pies of the day. In the summer you can enjoy the large split-level beer garden that surrounds the building. The four en suite bedrooms are furnished to a high standard and are extremely comfortable.

★★★★ INN ♥
MAP 04 ST21
TA3 5SP
☎ 01823 480227
📄 01823 481117
e-mail: thegreyhound-inn@btconnect.com
dir: *From M5 take A358 E, signed Yeovil, in 1m turn right, signed Staple Fitzpaine, left at T-junct, pub on right at x-rds.*

Open 12–3 5.30–11
Bar Meals L served Mon-Sat 12–2 D served Mon-Fri 6.45–9
Restaurant L served all week 12–2 D served all week 6.30–9
⊕ Free House ◼ Badgers First Gold, King & Barnes Sussex, Hofbrau Export, Otter Ale. ♥ 7
Facilities Garden Dogs allowed Parking
Rooms 4

WATERROW   MAP 03 ST02

Pick of the Pubs

The Rock Inn ★★★★ INN ♛

TA4 2AX ☎ 01984 623293 🖹 01984 623293
e-mail: lnp@rockinn.co.uk
dir: *From Taunton take B3227. Waterrow approx 14m W*

The name derives from the rock face a third of this former smithy was once carved out of. Indeed, part of its still visible behind the bar, next to a cheerfully roaring fire. The inn dates back over 400 years and is set in a lovely green valley beside the River Tone. Award-winning ales and home-made food are served, including fresh fish daily from Brixham, and Aberdeen Angus beef from their own farm two miles away. Start with double-baked jubilee soufflé, followed by local pan-fried pork fillet; free-range chicken and ham pie; Exmoor venison steak; or, for the vegetarians, red onion and goats' cheese tart. Miles of wonderful walking and fishing country make this region much cherished by outdoor types. Stop off for a night or two in one of eight cosy rooms: the promise is that your dog will be made as welcome as you!

Open 12–3 6–11 **Bar Meals** L served all week 12–2.30 D served all week 6.30–9.30 (Sun 7–9) Av main course £9.50 **Restaurant** L served all week 12–2.30 D served all week 6.30–9.30 (Sun 7–9) Av 3 course à la carte £19.50 ⊕ Free House ◖ Cotleigh Tawny, Exmoor Gold, Otter Ale, London Pride. ♛ 11 **Facilities** Children's licence Dogs allowed Parking **Rooms** 8

WELLS   MAP 04 ST54

The City Arms ♛

69 High St BA5 2AG ☎ 01749 673916 🖹 01749 672901
e-mail: query@thecityarmsatwells.co.uk

This pub prides itself on serving well-kept ales and generous fresh local food at a reasonable price. It is one of the historic sights of Wells, built in 1539. By 1591 it had become a jail, hence the small barred windows and cell doors. It has been through a period of refurbishment, adding more seating and relaxed bistro-style dining in the restaurant; the room has a romantic candle-lit atmosphere, and an area with soft chairs and sofas for pre- and post-dinner relaxation.

Open 8–11 (Fri-Sat 8am-12, Sun 9am-11) **Bar Meals** L served all week 9 D served all week 10 (Winter 9) **Restaurant** L served all week 12 D served all week 6–9 ◖ Butcombe, Greene King, Sharps', Morland Old Speckled Hen. ♛ 16 **Facilities** Children's licence Garden Dogs allowed

Pick of the Pubs

The Fountain Inn & Boxer's Restaurant ♛

1 Saint Thomas St BA5 2UU
☎ 01749 672317 🖹 01749 670825
e-mail: eat@fountaininn.co.uk
dir: *City centre, at A371 & B3139 junct. Follow signs for The Harringtons. Inn on junct of Tor St & St Thomas St*

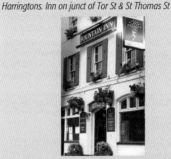

Dating back to the 16th century and built to house builders working on nearby Wells Cathedral, the award-winning Fountain Inn & Boxer's Restaurant has a well-earned reputation for good food. Chef manager Julie Pearce uses the finest local produce to create an impressive selection of quality home-cooked food served in both the bar and the restaurant. Old favourites on the bar specials board may include lasagne bolognaise with dressed side salad; fresh cod in beer batter with chips and home-made tartare sauce; and Butcombe, beef and mushroom pie with new potatoes and fresh vegetables. Among the restaurant mains are fillet steak stuffed with haggis and wrapped in smoked bacon, blackberry and red wine jus, gratin dauphinoise and fresh vegetables; oven-baked wild salmon escalope topped with fresh asparagus, balsamic, bell pepper and red onion dressing, new potatoes and fresh vegetables; and roasted rump of lamb with an orange, redcurrant and red wine jus.

Open 10.30–2.30 6–11 (Sun 12–3, 7–10.30) Closed: 25–26 Dec **Bar Meals** L served Mon-Sat 12–2 D served Mon-Sat 6–10 (Sun 12–2.30, 7–9.30) **Restaurant** L served Mon-Sat 12–2.30 D served Mon-Sat 6–10 (Sun 7–9.30) ◖ Butcombe Bitter, Interbrew Bass, Courage Best. ♛ 23 **Facilities** Parking

The Pheasant Inn ♛

Worth, Wookey BA5 1LQ ☎ 01749 672355
e-mail: pheasant@dsl.pipex.com
dir: *W of Wells on B3139 towards Wedmore*

Popular country pub at the foot of the Mendips, where you can enjoy some impressive views and relax with a pint of real ale beside a welcoming log fire. The menu ranges through light bites, a pasta and pizza section, and dishes such as slow roast lamb shank with minty Somerset sauce, and escalope of pork with cider and sage cream sauce. Friday night is fish night, and there are some great home-made puddings.

Open 11.30–2.30 6–11 (Sat 11.30–11 Sun 12–10.30) **Bar Meals** L served all week 12–2 D served all week 6.30–9.30 (Sun 7–9) **Restaurant** L served all week 12–2 D served all week 6.30–9.30 (Sun 7–9) ⊕ Enterprise Inns ◖ Butcombe, Greene King Old Speckled Hen, Pedigree, Butcombe Blond. ♛ 6 **Facilities** Children's licence Garden Dogs allowed Parking

WEST BAGBOROUGH   MAP 04 ST13

The Rising Sun Inn NEW

TA4 3EF ☎ 01823 432575

e-mail: jon@risingsuninn.info

In 2002 the Sun rose from the ashes of a devastating fire. Rebuilt around the original 16th-century cob walls and magnificent door, this craftsmen-led reincarnation is both bold and smart. For lunch try Exmoor lamb shank with rosemary juices; or Glenarm salmon with linguini. In the evening, perhaps roast loin of Hampshire black pork; or roasted Cornish cod with prosciutto, pease pudding and crayfish dressing. With Exmoor in view, savour a Somerset-brewed real ale.

Open 11–3 6–11 **Bar Meals** L served Mon-Sat 12–2 D served Mon-Sat 6.30–9.30 (Sun 12–3, 7–9) Av main course £14 **Restaurant** L served Mon-Sat 12–2 D served Mon-Sat 6.30–9.30 (Sun 12–3, 7–9) Av 3 course à la carte £22 ◀ Exmoor Ale, Butcombe & Taunton Castle. **Facilities** Dogs allowed

WEST CAMEL   MAP 04 ST52

The Walnut Tree ★★ HL ◉

Fore St BA22 7QW ☎ 01935 851292 📠 01935 851292

e-mail: info@thewalnuttreehotel.com

dir: *Off A303 between Sparkford & Yeovilton Air Base*

Close to the border between Dorset and Somerset, this well-kept inn is in a quiet village. The Leyland Trail passes close by and brings plenty of walkers. The cosily carpeted lounge bar and two restaurants entice the hungry with smoked duck breast with caramelised onions in an apple and brandy sauce; venison fillet on dauphinoise potatoes in a port and redcurrant sauce; and roasted beef fillet with a wild mushroom farci wrapped in bacon.

Open 11–3 6.30–11.30 Closed: 25–26 Dec, 1 Jan **Bar Meals** L served Tue-Sun 12–2 D served Mon-Sat 6–9.30 (Sun 6–8.30) Av main course £12 **Restaurant** L served Tue-Sun 12–2 D served All 7–9.30 Av 3 course à la carte £23 ⊕ Free House ◀ Otter Ale & Bitter. **Facilities** Garden Parking **Rooms** 13

WEST HUNTSPILL   MAP 04 ST34

Pick of the Pubs

Crossways Inn ♀

Withy Rd TA9 3RA ☎ 01278 783756 📠 01278 781899

e-mail: crossways.inn@virgin.net

dir: *On A38 3.5m from M5*

Run by Mike and Anna Ronca since 1973, this 17th-century coaching inn is an integral part of village life. The interior is warmly furnished and free of piped music, although live jazz, blues, Gaelic music and even opera get the green light some evenings. Blackboards display the day's temptations, from snacks to traditional pies, various curries and a selection from the grill. There's a family room, skittle alley and secluded garden.

Open 12–3 5.30–11 (Sun 12–4.30, 7–10.30) Closed: 25 Dec **Bar Meals** L served all week 12–2.30 D served all week 6.30–9 Av main course £7.50 **Restaurant** L served all week 12–2 D served all week 6.30–9 Av 3 course à la carte £14.50 ⊕ Free House ◀ Interbrew Bass, Flowers IPA, Fuller's London Pride, Exmoor Stag. ♀8 **Facilities** Garden Dogs allowed Parking

WHEDDON CROSS   MAP 03 SS93

The Rest and Be Thankful Inn ★★★★

INN

TA24 7DR ☎ 01643 841222 📠 01643 841813

e-mail: stay@restandbethankful.co.uk

dir: *5m S of Dunster*

Years ago, travellers were grateful for a break at this coaching inn, nearly 1,000 feet up in Exmoor's highest village. Old world charm blends with friendly hospitality in the bar and spacious restaurant, where log fires burn in winter and home-cooked food is served. In addition to the restaurant menu there is a weekly specials board, a ligh

England

unch menu and a traditional Sunday carvery. The pub also has a skittle
alley and pool table.

Open 10–2.30 6.30–12 **Bar Meals** L served all week 12–2 D served
all week 7–9 **Restaurant** L served all week 12–2 D served all week
7–9 ⊕ Free House ◖ Exmoor Ale, Proper Job, Tribute, Guinness.
Facilities Garden Parking **Rooms** 8

WOOKEY   MAP 04 ST54

The Burcott Inn

Wells Rd BA5 1NJ ☎ 01749 673874

e-mail: ian@burcottinn.co.uk

dir: *2m from Wells on B3139*

Set on the edge of a charming village, this 300–year-old stone-built
inn features low beamed ceilings, a flagstone floor, log fires and a
copper top bar. The range of real ales changes frequently as does the
blackboard menu, featuring seafood specialities and locally sourced
beef and lamb. Options range through lunchtime snacks, steak and ale
pie, slow roasted lamb rump, and vegetable and cashew nut bake. The
large garden affords views of the Mendip Hills.

Open 11.30–2.30 6–11 Closed: 25–26 Dec, 1 Jan **Bar Meals** L served
all week 12–2.30 D served Tue-Sat 6.30–9.30 **Restaurant** L served all
week 12–2 D served Tue-Sat 6.30–9.30 Av 3 course à la carte £19 ⊕ Free
House ◖ Teignworthy Old Moggie, Cotleigh Barn Owl Bitter, RCH Pitchfork,
Branscombe BVB. **Facilities** Garden Parking **Rooms** available

YARLINGTON   MAP 04 ST62

The Stags Head Inn

Pound Ln BA9 8DG ☎ 01963 440393 ◻ 01963 440393

e-mail: mrandall1960@tiscali.co.uk

dir: *Leave A303 at Wincanton onto A37 signed Castle Carey. In
1m turn left signed Yarlington, take 2nd right into village. Pub
opposite church*

Halfway between Wincanton and Castle Cary lies this completely
unspoilt country inn with flagstones, real fires and no electronic
intrusions. A sample menu includes slow-roasted lamb shank on
creamed mash with redcurrant and rosemary; haddock fillet in
beer batter; or chargrilled rump steak with chips, onion rings and
mushrooms. Burgers and light bites also available.

Open 12–2.30 6–11 (Sat-Sun 12–3) Closed: 25 Dec **Bar Meals** L served
Tue-Sun 12–2 D served Tue-Sat 7–9 ⊕ Free House ◖ Greene King, IPA,
Bass, Guinness. **Facilities** Children's licence Garden Dogs allowed Parking

---

STAFFORDSHIRE

ALREWAS   MAP 10 SK11

The Old Boat ♟

DE13 7DB ☎ 01283 791468 ◻ 01283 792886

dir: *Telephone for directions*

Standing on the Trent and Mersey Canal, the pub was originally used by
canal construction workers and bargemen. The snug at the end of the
bar was once the cellar, where casks of ale were rolled off the barges
and kept cool in up to two feet of water. Typical dishes include roast
Packington pork belly with sage and apple mash; roast lamb with braised
red onions; and grilled turbot with sautéed cabbage and chorizo.

Open 12–2 6–11 (Sun 12–3) **Restaurant** L served all week 12–2 D served
all week 6–9 (Sun 12–3) Av 3 course à la carte £21.95 ◖ Marston's
Pedigree & John Smith's. ♟ 8 **Facilities** Garden Parking

ALSAGERS BANK   MAP 15 SJ74

The Gresley Arms

High St ST7 8BQ ☎ 01782 720297 ◻ 01782 720297

dir: *3m from Newcastle-under-Lyme town centre on B5367*

A 200–year-old pub in a semi-rural location set between two country
parks, making it a popular stopping off point for walkers and cyclists.
It is a friendly local, with a traditional bar, separate lounge and large
family room, serving real ale and real food at a reasonable price. The
menu encompasses basket meals (chicken, scampi, beefburger), steaks
with sauces, light bites, main meals and daily specials, such as braised
lamb shank, and tagliatelle Nicoise.

Open 12–11 **Bar Meals** L served all week 12–9 D served all week 12–9 Av
main course £9.95 **Restaurant** L served all week 12–9 D served all week
12–9 ◖ 6 guest ales. **Facilities** Garden Dogs allowed Parking **Notes** ⊕

ALSTONEFIELD   MAP 16 SK15

Pick of the Pubs

The George ♟

See Pick of the Pubs on page 518

ALTON   MAP 10 SK04

Bulls Head Inn

High St ST10 4AQ ☎ 01538 702307 ◻ 01538 702065

e-mail: janet@thebullshead.freeserve.co.uk

dir: *M6 junct 14, A518 to Uttoxeter. (Follow Alton Towers signs).
Onto B5030 to Rocester, then B5032 to Alton. Pub in village centre*

Traditional beers and home cooking are provided in the heart of
Alton, less than a mile from Alton Towers theme park. Oak beams
and an inglenook fireplace set the scene for the old world bar, the
cosy snug and the country-style restaurant. Menus offer the likes of
sirloin steak, deep fried breaded plaice, lasagne verde, steak, ale and
mushroom pie, and hunters chicken.**Bar Meals** L served all week 12–2
D served all week 6–9.30 (Sat 12–2.30, Sun 12–3) Av main course £8
Restaurant L served all week 12–2 D served all week 6.30–9.30 Av 3
course à la carte £15 ⊕ Free House ◖ Guest ales. **Facilities** Parking

517

The George

Situated right at the heart of Alstonefield, this 18th-century coaching inn has been run by three generations of the same family since the 1960s. The current generation in the form of landlady Emily Hammond has undertaken a sympathetic restoration of the dining room, which revealed many original features including a Georgian fireplace hidden for over a century.

She is currently developing the coach house, also 18th-century, into a farm shop. But the prime raison d'être behind Emily's operation remains the selection of real ales and wines by the glass behind the bar, and an impressive local reputation for excellent home-cooked food – the chef makes all his own jams, pickles and chutneys on the premises. The emphasis is on seasonal, regional and traditional dishes, with plenty of hearty options for the walkers and fishermen who flock to the pub by day: a range of sandwiches (home-cooked Derbyshire ham; free-range egg mayonnaise); Welsh rarebit on bloomer bread with piccalilli; salads such as spring lettuce, asparagus and duck egg; and game and ale pie with seasonal vegetables. By night,

sample the likes of duck and ham hock terrine. Follow with roast loin of venison with baby fondant potatoes and rhubarb ribbons, local steaks or fish fillet on a Devon crab and pea risotto topped with poached egg and hollandaise sauce. For the sweet of tooth, Bakewell pudding, hot chocolate fondant, or sticky toffee pudding are three agreeable options, served with a scoop of home-made ice cream. Alternatively a plate of Hartington stilton with walnut and raisin loaf and a glass of port might suit your mood. Food and drink can be served in the garden, and dogs are welcome.

MAP 16 SK15
DE6 2FX
☎ 01335 310205
e-mail: emily@
thegeorgeatalstonefield.com
web: www.
thegeorgeatalstonefield.com
dir: *7m N of Ashbourne, signed
Milldale/Alstonefield to left*

Open 11.30–3 6–11 (Sat
11.30–11, Sun 12–11)
Bar Meals L served all week
12–2.30 D served Mon-Sat 7–9
(Sun 6.30–8, varies BH) Av main
course £9
Restaurant L served all week
12–2.30 D served Mon-Sat 7–9
(Sun 6.30–8, varies BH) Av 3
course à la carte £20
⊕ Marstons ◀ Marston's Bitter
& Pedigree, Jennings Cumberland
Ale & Sneck Lifter, & guest ale. ⚐ 8
Facilities Children's licence
Garden Dogs allowed Parking

ANSLOW — MAP 10 SK22

The Burnt Gate Inn

opley Rd DE13 9PY ☎ 01283 563664

-mail: info@burntgate.co.uk

ir: *From Burton take B5017 towards Abbots Bromley. At top of enhurst Hill turn right Inn on Hopley Rd, 2m from town centre*

riginally two cottages and a farmhouse, parts of this uniquely named ub are up to 300 years old. A recent refurbishment has given the nterior some contemporary touches (wi-fi access, for example), while etaining the traditional elements of oak-floored bar, open fires and ewspapers. As well as steaks and home-made pies, there is game (in eason), Thai-style chicken and rice, fresh fish, tapas and deli boards nd a gluten-free selection.

pen 12–2.30 6–11 (Sat-Sun 12–11) **Bar Meals** L served Mon-Fri 12–2.15) served all week 12–8.30 **Restaurant** L served Mon-Fri 12–2 D served Mon-Fri 6.30–9 (Sat-Sun all day) Free House Pedigree, guest ales. 17 **Facilities** Parking

BURTON UPON TRENT — MAP 10 SK22

Burton Bridge Inn

4 Bridge St DE14 1SY ☎ 01283 536596

ir: *Telephone for directions*

ith its own brewery at the back, this is one of the oldest pubs in the rea. The unspoilt old-fashioned interior has oak panelling, feature replaces, and a distinct lack of electronic entertainment. A full range f Burton Bridge ales is on tap, and the menu includes straightforward neals like roast pork, jacket potatoes, or beef cobs, as well as raditional filled Yorkshire puddings. Long skittles alley upstairs.

pen 11.30–2.30 5–11 **Bar Meals** L served Mon-Sat 12–1.45 Burton Bridge – Gold Medal Ale, Festival Ale, Golden Delicious & Bridge itter. 15 **Facilities** Garden Dogs allowed **Notes**

AULDON — MAP 16 SK04

ew Tree Inn

T10 3EJ ☎ 01538 308348 01782 212064

ir: *Between A52 & A523. 4.5m from Alton Towers*

he Yew Tree is so well known that people come from all over the orld to see it. The pub dates back 300 years and has plenty of haracter and lots of fascinating artefacts, including Victorian music oxes, pianolas, grandfather clocks, a crank handle telephone, and a ub lantern. A varied snack menu offers locally made, hand-raised pork ies, sandwiches, baps, quiche and sweets.

pen 10–2.30 6–11 (Sun 12–3) Free House Burton Bridge, Grays ild, Bass. **Facilities** Dogs allowed Parking **Notes**

CHEADLE — MAP 10 SK04

The Queens At Freehay

Counslow Rd, Freehay ST10 1RF

☎ 01538 722383 01538 723748

dir: *4m from Alton Towers*

Very much a family-run establishment, the pub dates from the 18th century and has a pretty setting surrounded by mature trees and garden. The interior is refreshingly modern in style, with elegant tables and chairs. The pub has established a good reputation for food, and dishes from the menu are supplemented by chef's specials from the fish or meat boards. Expect traditional fish and chips; lamb or vegetable tagine; and beef and Guinness pie,

Open 12–2.30 6–11 (Sun 6.30–11) Closed: 25–26, 31 Dec-1 Jan **Bar Meals** L served Mon-Sat 12–2 D served Mon-Sat 6–9.30 (Sun 12–2.30, 6.30–9.30) **Restaurant** L served Mon-Sat 12–2 D served Mon-Sat 6–9.30 (Sun 12–2.30, 6.30–9.30) Free House Draught Bass, Draught Worthington Bitter. **Facilities** Garden Parking

ECCLESHALL — MAP 15 SJ82

The George

Castle St ST21 6DF ☎ 01785 850300 01785 851452

e-mail: information@thegeorgeinn.freeserve.co.uk

dir: *6m from M6 junct 14*

A family-run, 16th-century former coaching inn with its own micro-brewery, where the owners' son produces award-winning Slater's ales. Occasional beer festivals are held, and the menu features a wide variety of dishes, including spicy chilli tortillas; fish stew; roast salmon with hoi sin sauce, chive mash and stir-fry veg; and cod in Slater's ale batter. A selection of salads, baked potatoes and sandwiches is also available.

Open 11–11 (Sun 12–10.30) Closed: 25 Dec **Bar Meals** L served Mon-Sat 12–9.30 D served Mon-Sat 6–9.30 (Sun 12–8.30) Av main course £8 **Restaurant** L served all week 12–2.30 D served all week 6–9.45 Av 3 course à la carte £15 Free House Slaters Ales. **Facilities** Dogs allowed Parking

KING'S BROMLEY	MAP 10 SK11

Royal Oak ♀

Manor Rd DE13 7HZ ☎ 01543 472 289

e-mail: shropshall@btinternet.com

dir: *Off A515*

The Royal Oak looks and feels like a quaint village local but award-winning chef and licensee Mathew Shropshall offers cooking of serious intent alongside more familiar pub grub. There are lunchtime wraps, melts and sandwiches, and comfort food such as steak and ale pie or beer battered cod and chips. The serious stuff might include Barbary duck with a Seville orange and mustard sauce; or braised oxtails with sauce bourguignon and parsnip mash.

Open 11.45–3 6–11 **Bar Meals** L served all week 12–2.30 D served all week 6–9 Av main course £9.95 **Restaurant** L served all week 12–2.30 D served all week 6–9 ⊕ Marstons ◀ Pedigree Bitter, Banks Bitter, Sneck Lifter, Cocker Hoop. ♀ 10 **Facilities** Garden Dogs allowed Parking

LEEK	MAP 16 SJ95

Three Horseshoes Inn ★★★ HL ⊛ ♀

Buxton Rd, Blackshaw Moor ST13 8TW

☎ 01538 300296 📄 01538 300320

e-mail: enquiries@threeshoesinn.co.uk

dir: *on A53, 3m N of Leek*

There are great views from the attractive gardens of this sprawling, creeper-covered inn. Inside, the main bar features wood fires in the winter, with a good selection of real ales. Visitors can choose from traditional decor and roast meats in the bar carvery, the relaxed atmosphere of the brasserie (one rosette), and the more formal restaurant. Choices include eggs Benedict with smoked haddock and spinach; and roasted vegetable, rosemary and goats' cheese tarte Tatin.

Open 12–3 6–11 **Bar Meals** L served all week 12–2 D served all week 6.30–9 (Sun 12–3, 6–8.30 & all day in summer) Av main course £8 **Restaurant** L served Wed-Sat D served Sat 6.30–9 (Sun 12.15–1.30) Av 3 course à la carte £25 ⊕ Free House ◀ Theakstons XB Courage Directors, Morland Old Speckled Hen, John Smiths. ♀ 12 **Facilities** Garden Parking Play Area **Rooms** 27 (26 en suite)

NORBURY JUNCTION	MAP 15 SJ72

The Junction Inn ♀

ST20 0PN ☎ 01785 284288 📄 01785 284288

dir: *From M6 take road for Eccleshall, left at Gt Bridgeford towards Woodseaves, left towards Newport, left for Norbury Junct*

Not a railway junction, but a beautiful stretch of waterway where the Shropshire Union Canal meets the disused Newport arm. The inn's large beer garden gives a ringside view of everything happening on the canal, as well as hosting summer BBQs. Food ranges from baguettes to specials such as home-made rabbit stew with fresh crusty bread; traditional belly pork with black pudding; and bangers and mash with onion gravy. Disabled access at both front and rear.

Open 11–11 (Winter 11–3, 6–11) **Bar Meals** L served all week 11–9 D served all week 11–9 Av main course £6 **Restaurant** L served all week 12–9 D served all week 12–9 Av 3 course à la carte £12.95 ⊕ Free House ◀ Banks Mild, Banks Bitter, Junction Ale and guest ales. ♀ 4 **Facilities** Garden Dogs allowed Parking Play Area

STAFFORD	MAP 10 SJ92

Pick of the Pubs

The Holly Bush Inn ♀

See Pick of the Pubs on opposite page

Pick of the Pubs

The Moat House ★★★★ HL ⊛⊛ ♀

Lower Penkridge Rd, Acton Trussell ST17 0RJ

☎ 01785 712217 📄 01785 715344

e-mail: info@moathouse.co.uk

dir: *M6 junct 13 towards Stafford, 1st right to Acton Trussell*

Grade II listed mansion dating back to the 15th century and situated behind its original moat. Quality bedrooms, conference facilities and corporate events are big attractions, and with four honeymoon suites, the Moat House is a popular venue for weddings. Inside are oak beams and an inglenook fireplace, and the bar and food trade brings in both the hungry and the curious who like to savour the charm and atmosphere of the place. Major refurbishments have contributed a stylish lounge area serving brasserie-style food. Among the more popular dishes are rocket and goats cheese soup or tuna spring roll, followed by braised shank of lamb with bubble and squeak and a rosemary jus; seared seabass with fennel, baby spinach and a mussel nage; or plaice fillets with crab mousse, asparagus and saffron broth. If there's room afterwards, try bread and butter pudding, steamed treacle sponge or chocolate fudge brownie.

Open 10–11 Closed: 25–26 Dec, 1–2 Jan **Bar Meals** L served Mon-Sat 12–2.15 D served Sun-Fri 6–9.30 Av main course £12.50 **Restaurant** L served all week 12–2 D served all week 7–9.30 Av 3 course à la carte £34.50 Av 3 course fixed price £29.50 ⊕ Free House ◀ Bank's Bitter, Marston's Pedigree, Murphys. ♀ 13 **Facilities** Children's licence Garden Parking **Rooms** 32

STOURTON	MAP 10 SO88

The Fox Inn ♀

Bridgnorth Rd DY7 5BL

☎ 01384 872614 & 872123 📄 01384 877771

e-mail: fox-inn-stourton@dial.pipex.com

dir: *5m from Stourbridge town centre. On A458 Stourbridge to Bridgnorth road*

Late 18th-century pub set amid beautiful countryside near Kinver village. Walkers from many nearby rambling areas are attracted by its warm atmosphere and historic surroundings, with many original features still in place. There's also a large garden to enjoy, complete with weeping willow, gazebo and an attractive patio area. Stefan Caron has been the landlord here since 1971, which must be something of a record.

Open 11.30–3 5–11 (Sat-Sun 11–11) **Bar Meals** L served Mon-Sat 12.30–2.15 D served Tue-Sat 7–9.30 (Sun lunch 3–5.30) **Restaurant** L served Tue-Sat 12–9.30 D served Tue-Sat 7–9.30 (Sun 12.30–5.15) ⊕ Free House ◀ Bathams Ale, Enville Ale, Murphy's, Boddingtons. ♀ 8 **Facilities** Garden Parking

PICK OF THE PUBS

STAFFORD-STAFFORDSHIRE

The Holly Bush Inn

The Holly Bush is well-known for the quality of its food and welcome, but it boasts two other notable distinctions. It is generally recognised as the second pub in the country to have been licensed. This event took place during Charles II's reign (1660–1685), though the building itself is far older, possibly dating back to 1190.

Secondly, when landlord Geoff Holland's son became a joint licensee at the age of 18 years and 6 days, he was the youngest person ever to be granted a licence. The pub's comfortably old-fashioned interior contains all the vital ingredients: heavy carved beams, open fires, attractive prints and cosy alcoves. The team are more enthusiastic than ever in their attempts to reduce food miles and support local producers, with regular visits made to local farms to source new products – mose recently Jersey milk ice cream and true free-range eggs. Other innovations include a wood fired brick oven which has expanded the pub's menu to include pizzas. Also on the menu are traditional Staffordshire oatcakes -perhaps filled with crispy cooked duck and redcurrant sauce or flaked salmon, herbs and a light cream sauce; and modern adaptations of medieval dishes such as braised venison with chestnuts. Other typical dishes include rabbit casserole with herb dumplings; braised ham hock with horseradish sauce; hand-made pork, leek and stilton sausages with a brace of fried eggs and chipped potatoes; and pan-fried fillet of local pork with apples and cider. A lengthy seafood menu attests to the excellent relationships developed with Torbay's fishermen: try chargrilled skate wings with black butter; monkfish and scallop kebabs with a tomato and basil chutney; and chargrilled red snapper with Jamaican spiced tomato chutney.

MAP 10 SJ92
Salt ST18 0BX
☎ 01889 508234
🖨 01889 508058
e-mail:
geoff@hollybushinn.co.uk
dir: *Telephone for directions*

Open 12–11
Bar Meals L served Mon-Sat
12–9.30 D served Mon-Sat
12–9.30 (Sun 12–9)
⊕ Free House ◀ Adnams,
Pedigree & guest ales. ♟ 12
Facilities Garden Parking

TATENHILL
MAP 10 SK22

Horseshoe Inn ♥

Main St DE13 9SD ☎ 01283 564913 🖹 01283 511314

dir: *From A38 at Branston follow signs for Tatenhill*

Probably five to six hundred years old, this historic pub retains much original character, including evidence of a priest's hiding hole. In winter, log fires warm the bar and family area. In addition to home-made snacks like chilli con carne, and Horseshoe brunch, there are sizzling rumps and sirloins, chicken curry, moussaka, battered cod with chips and mushy peas, and a pasta dish of the week. And specials too – beef bourguignon, or steak and kidney pudding, for instance.

Open 11–11 **Bar Meals** L served all week 12–9.30 D served all week 12–9.30 (Sun 12–9) Av main course £7.50 **Restaurant** L served all week 12–9.30 D served all week 12–9.30 Av 3 course à la carte £14 ⊕ ◀ Marstons Pedigree. ♥ 14 **Facilities** Garden Dogs allowed Parking Play Area

TUTBURY
MAP 10 SK22

Ye Olde Dog & Partridge Inn

High St DE13 9LS ☎ 01283 813030 🖹 01283 813178

e-mail: info@dogandpartridge.net

dir: *On A50 NW of Burton-on-Trent (signed from A50 & A511)*

A beautiful period building resplendent in its timbers and whitewashed walls, with abundant flower displays beneath the windows. The inn has stood in this charming village since the 15th century when Henry IV was on the throne. Five hundred years of offering hospitality has resulted in a well-deserved reputation for good food, served in two smart eating outlets.

Open 11–11 **Bar Meals** L served all week 11.30–11 D served all week ⊕ Free House ◀ Marston's Pedigree, Courage Director's. **Facilities** Garden Parking

WATERHOUSES
MAP 16 SK05

Ye Olde Crown

Leek Rd ST10 3HL ☎ 01538 308204 🖹 01538 308204

e-mail: kerryhinton@hotmail.co.uk

dir: *From Ashbourne take A52 then A523 towards Leek. Village in 8m*

A traditional village local, Ye Olde Crown dates from around 1647 when it was built as a coaching inn. Sitting on the bank of the River Hamps, and on the edge of the Peak District National Park and the Staffordshire moorlands, it's ideal for walkers. Inside are original stonework and interior beams, and open fires are lit in cooler weather.

Open 12–2.30 6–11 (Sat-Sun all day) Closed: Mon lunch **Bar Meals** L served Tue-Sat 12–2.30 D served Mon-Sat 6.30–8.30 (Sun 12–6) Av main course £7.50 **Restaurant** L served Tue-Sat 12–2.30 D served Tue-Sat 6–8.30 (Sun 12–6) ⊕ Marstons ◀ Marstons, Burton Bitter, Guinness, guest ale. **Facilities** Children's licence Parking

WETTON
MAP 16 SK15

Ye Olde Royal Oak

DE6 2AF ☎ 01335 310287

e-mail: brian@rosehose.wanadoo.co.uk

dir: *A515 towards Buxton, left in 4m to Manifold Valley-Alstonfield, follow signs to Wetton*

The stone-built inn dates back over 400 years and features wooden beams recovered from oak ships at Liverpool Docks. It was formerly part of the Chatsworth estate, and the Tissington walking and cycling trail is close by. Cask marque real ales are served along with dishes such as home-made soup; large battered cod; and treacle sponge. Separate vegetarian and children's menus are available. The pub's moorland garden includes a campsite with showers and toilets.

Open 12–2.30 6–11 (Sat-Sun all day Etr-Sep) Closed: Mon-Tue (Winter) **Bar Meals** L served Wed-Mon 12–2 D served Wed-Mon 7–9 (Closed Mon-Tue in Winter) Av main course £7 ⊕ Free House ◀ Greene King Abbot Ale, Sharp's Doom Bar & guest ales. **Facilities** Garden Dogs allowed Parking

WOODSEAVES
MAP 15 SJ72

The Plough Inn ♥

Newport Rd ST20 0NP ☎ 01785 284210

dir: *From Stafford take A5013 towards Eccleshall. Turn left onto B4505. Woodseaves at junct with A519. 5m from Eccleshall on A519 towards Newport*

Built in the mid-18th century for workers constructing the nearby canal, the Plough is a traditional country pub with winter fires and hanging baskets for the summer. There's a good selection of real ales, and the bar menu features favourites like sausages, mash and red wine gravy. The restaurant menu offers more adventurous options like deep-fried goat's cheese with ratatouille and chargrilled potatoes; or pan-fried duck with cranberry and orange sauce.

Open 12–2 6–11 **Bar Meals** L served Wed-Sun 12–2.30 D served Wed-Sat 6–9.30 (Sun 12–4, Summer 6–8) Av main course £8.95 **Restaurant** L served 12–2 D served Wed-Sat 6–9 (Sun 12–8) ⊕ Free House ◀ Spitfire, 6X, Grumpy Chef, Titanic Full Kiln Ale. ♥ 2 **Facilities** Garden Parking

WRINEHILL
MAP 15 SJ74

Pick of the Pubs

The Crown Inn ♥

See Pick of the Pubs on opposite page

PICK OF THE PUBS

WRINEHILL-STAFFORDSHIRE

The Crown Inn

This 19th-century former coaching inn is very much a family affair. Charles and Sue Davenhill have owned it for over 30 years, and in 2001 were joined by their daughter and son-in-law, Anna and Mark Condliffe. Mark is now the joint licensee with Charles, who is reputedly the longest-serving licensee in Staffordshire.

Food is a major part of the pub's success, famed locally not just for the generosity of its portions, but also for consistency in quality and use of seasonal produce. The appealingly organised menu offers a wide range of dishes for varying appetites. The not-so-hungry might prefer a soft floury bap, served open with salad and home-made coleslaw; the choice of fillings range from a four-ounce fillet steak topped with melted Hartington stilton, to flakes of tuna with lemon mayonnaise. The more ravenous will find meat dishes which may encompass sirloin rarebit, the steak topped with wholegrain mustard, cheddar cheese and a dash of Worcestershire sauce; Somerset pork medallions; or piri-piri chicken. Fish comes in the form of breaded plaice, baked monkfish or a seafood basket – a selection of plaice and haddock goujons, wholetail scampi, calamari, scallops and barbecued crab claws, all coated in breadcrumbs and deep fried. With Sue and Anna both vegetarian, the tasty options here are numerous and well above the average pub's token gesture: try the Moroccan tagine with chickpeas, couscous and coriander; or chef's cheesy leek cakes with a Dijon sauce; a vegan dish completes the savoury choices. From the sweet menu try Debbie's home-made traditional toffee pudding 'obviously served with custard'; sensational Jersey cream-based ice creams are made by Snugbury's in Nantwich. At the bar there's always a choice of six traditional cask ales.

♀
MAP 15 SJ74
Den Ln CW3 9BT
☎ 01270 820472
🖹 01270 820547
e-mail:
mark_condliffe@hotmail.com
dir: *Village on A531, 1m S of Betley. 6m S of Crewe; 6m N of Newcastle-under-Lyme*

Open 12–3 6–11 (Sun 6–10.30, closed Mon lunch) Closed: 26 Dec
Bar Meals L served Tue-Sat 12–2 D served Mon-Fri 6.30–9.30 (Sat 6–10, Sun 12–3, 6–9) Av main course £8.50
⊕ Free House ◀ Marstons Pedigree & Bitter, Adnams Bitter, Cumberland Ale, Timothy Taylor Landlord & guest ales. ♀ 9
Facilities Garden Parking

England

WRINEHILL continued

The Hand & Trumpet NEW ⚑

Main Rd CW3 9BJ ☎ 01270 820048 📄 01270 821911
e-mail: hand.and.trumpet@brunningandprice.co.uk
dir: *M6 junct 16 follow signs for Keele, continue onto A531, 7m on right*

The Hand & Trumpet was refurbished and re-opened in February 2006. It has a friendly, comfortable interior with original floors, old furniture, open fires and rugs. A deck to the rear overlooks the sizeable grounds, which include a large pond. Light bites range from home-made fish finger buttie to hand raised hare and ham pie. Main courses include vegetable cobbler; lobby (a Staffordshire mutton stew); and fish pie with green vegetables in lemon butter.

Open 11.30–11 Closed: 25 Dec **Bar Meals** L served Mon-Sat 12–10 D served Mon-Sat 12–10 (Sun 12–9.30) Av main course £9.95 ⊕ Free House ◀ Timothy Taylor Landlord, Deuchars IPA, Thwaites Original & Guest ales. ⚑22 **Facilities** Garden Dogs allowed Parking

SUFFOLK

ALDEBURGH   MAP 13 TM45

The Mill Inn ★★★ INN

Market Cross Place IP15 5BJ ☎ 01728 452563
e-mail: peeldennisp@aol.com
dir: *Follow Aldeburgh signs from A12 on A1094. Pub last building on left before sea*

A genuine fisherman's inn located less than 100 metres from the seafront, and a short walk from the town and bird sanctuaries. Seafood bought fresh from the fishermen on the beach is a speciality here, backed by pub favourites such as sirloin steak, ham and eggs, and lamb shank. Well-kept Adnams Bitter, Broadside, Regatta and Fisherman can all be enjoyed at this favourite haunt of the local lifeboat crew.

Open 11–3 6–11 (11–11 summer) **Bar Meals** L served all week 12–2 D served Tue-Sat 7–9 **Restaurant** L served Tue-Sun 12–2 D served Tue-Sat 7–9 ⊕ Adnams ◀ Adnams Bitter, Broadside, Regatta & Fisherman, OLD. **Facilities** Dogs allowed **Rooms** 4

ALDRINGHAM   MAP 13 TM46

The Parrot and Punchbowl Inn & Restaurant ⚑

Aldringham Ln IP16 4PY ☎ 01728 830221
e-mail: paul@parrotandpunchbowl.fsnet.co.uk
dir: *On B1122 1m from Leiston, 3m from Aldeburgh, on x-rds to Thorpeness*

Originally called The Case is Altered, it became the Parrot in 1604 and as such enjoyed considerable notoriety, particularly during the 17th century, as the haunt of Aldringham's smuggling gangs. Don't ask if there's any contraband rum on offer; just study the menu and try and decide between medallions of pork fillet, whole baked sea bass, deep-fried cod in Adnam's beer batter, or an Aberdeen Angus fillet steak. 'Parrot sandwiches' are generously overfilled.

Open 12–3 5.30–12 **Bar Meals** L served all week 12–2.30 D served all week 6.30–9.30 Av main course £5 **Restaurant** L served all week 12–2.30 D served all week 6.30–9.30 Av 3 course à la carte £20 ⊕ Enterprise Inns ◀ Adnams, guest ale. ⚑10 **Facilities** Garden Parking Play Area

BARNBY   MAP 13 TM49

Pick of the Pubs

The Swan Inn ◉

See Pick of the Pubs on page 526

BILDESTON   MAP 13 TL94

Pick of the Pubs

The Bildeston Crown NEW ★★★ HL

◉◉◉ ⚑

High St IP7 7EB ☎ 01449 740510 📄 01449 741583
e-mail: info@thebildestoncrown.co.uk
dir: *Telephone for directions*

Located in the heart of Suffolk's picturesque countryside, close to the historic towns of Bury St Edmunds and Ipswich. Originally built for a wealthy wool merchant, the Bildeston Crown is a beautiful 15th-century half-timbered former coaching inn with oak-beamed bars and lounge; its original charming character is largely intact and it claims to be one of the most-haunted pubs in Britain. Don't miss the opportunity to try one of the excellent Mauldons ales, but dining here is undoubtedly the irresistible attraction for most people. Head chef Chris Lee's passion for food is exemplified by his signature dish of rabbit gnocchi, Braeburn purée, caper berries and ceps. The mid-week set menu available at both lunch and dinner represents excellent value, while the seven-course tasting menu amply demonstrates Chris's skills. Dishes made with beef from the owner's own Red Poll herd, and a wide range of local game are much lauded too.

Open 11–11 (Sun 11–10.30) **Bar Meals** L served all week 12–3 D served Mon-Sat 7–10 (Sun 7–9.30) Av main course £10 **Restaurant** L served all week 12–3 D served Mon-Sat 7–10 (Sun 7–9.30) Av 3 course à la carte £30 Av 2 course fixed price £19 ⊕ Free House ◄ Mauldons, Meantime London Stout, Adnams. ☻ 18 **Facilities** Garden Dogs allowed Parking **Rooms** 13

BRANDESTON
MAP 13 TM26

The Queens Head ☻

The Street IP13 7AD ☎ 01728 685307

e-mail: thequeensheadinn@btconnect.com

dir: *From A14 take A1120 to Earl Soham, then S to Brandeston*

Originally four cottages, the pub has been serving ale to the villagers of Brandeston since 1811. A large open bar allows drinkers and diners to mix, and good use is made of the huge garden in summer. Local food, Adnams ales and award-winning Adnams wines are served, with dishes like Suffolk cider-poached mackerel with hazelnut and rocket salad and horseradish dressing; and saddle of rabbit wrapped in pancetta with lentil and confit leg broth.

Open 12–3 5–11 (Sun 12–5) Closed: Sun eve **Bar Meals** L served Mon-Sat 12–2 D served all week 6.30–9 (Sun 12–3) **Restaurant** L served Mon-Sat 12–2 D served all week 6.30–9 (Sun 12–3) ⊕ Adnams ◄ Adnams Broadside & Bitter, Explorer & seasonal ales. ☻ 8 **Facilities** Garden Dogs allowed Parking

---

BROCKLEY GREEN
MAP 12 TL74

The Plough Inn ☻

CO10 8DT ☎ 01440 786789 📄 01440 786710

e-mail: info@theploughhundon.co.uk

dir: *Take B1061 from A143, approx 1.5m beyond Kedington*

Originally a small alehouse providing local farmers with liquid refreshments, this friendly inn has been skilfully renovated to create a

rustic interior featuring oak beams and soft red brickwork. Its seafood is a major reason for visiting, but look out for the 'Simply Wild' blackboard during the game season. The garden offers glorious views over the Suffolk countryside.

Open 12–3 6–11 **Bar Meals** L served all week 12–2.30 D served all week 6–9 (Sun 12–7) Av main course £6.50 **Restaurant** L served all week 12–2.30 D served all week 6–9 (Sun 12–7) Av 3 course à la carte £20 ⊕ Free House ◄ Greene King IPA, Woodforde's Wherry Best Bitter, Theakstons XB, Abbot Ale. ☻ 12 **Facilities** Garden Parking **Rooms** available

---

BURY ST EDMUNDS
MAP 13 TL86

The Linden Tree

7 Out Northgate IP33 1JQ ☎ 01284 754600

dir: *Opposite railway station*

Built to serve the railway station, this is a big, friendly Victorian pub, with stripped pine bar, dining area, non-smoking conservatory and charming garden. The family-orientated menu ranges from beef curry, home-made pies, and liver and bacon, to crab thermidor, fresh sea bass, and mushroom and lentil moussaka. Youngsters will go for the burgers, scampi, or pork chipolatas. Freshly filled ciabattas at lunchtime.

Open 11–3 5–11 (Fri-Sat 11–11, Sun 12–4 5.30–10.30) Closed: 25 Dec **Bar Meals** L served Mon-Sat 12–2 D served Mon-Sat 6–9.30 (Sun & BH 12–3 5.30–9) Av main course £7.99 **Restaurant** L served Mon-Sat 12–2 D served Mon-Sat 6–9.30 (Sun 12–3 5.30–9) ⊕ Greene King ◄ Greene King, IPA & Old Speckled Hen & guest. **Facilities** Garden Dogs allowed Play Area

---

The Nutshell

17 The Traverse IP33 1BJ ☎ 01284 764867

dir: *Telephone for directions*

Unique pub measuring 15ft by 7ft, and said to be Britain's smallest. Somehow more than 100 people and a dog managed to fit inside in the 1980s. The bar's ceiling is covered with paper money, and there have been regular sightings of ghosts around the building, including a nun and a monk who apparently weren't praying! No food is available, though the pub jokes about its dining area for parties of two or fewer.

Open 11–11 (Sun 12–10.30) ⊕ Greene King ◄ Greene King IPA, Abbot Ale & guest ales. **Facilities** Dogs allowed **Notes** ⊛

PICK OF THE PUBS

BARNBY-SUFFOLK

The Swan Inn

Two windows upstairs, two down and a central door – the classic front elevation of buildings everywhere.

Behind the distinctive pink-painted façade of this warm and friendly gem in the Suffolk countryside is one of Suffolk's foremost fish restaurants – it is, after all, owned by Donald and Michael Cole, whose family have been fish wholesalers in Lowestoft since grandfather set up the business in 1936. With deep-sea trawling in deep decline by the mid-1980s, Donald thought it prudent to diversify and bought the run-down Swan. It was during the refurbishment that he had a dinghy installed up in the rafters (although he might try and kid you there's just been a particularly high tide!). The property dates from 1690, and in the rustic Fisherman's Cove restaurant you'll find the original low beams and a collection of nautical memorabilia, including trawlers' bells, wheels and a binnacle, all placed on show as 'a tribute to the brave people who bring ashore the fruits of the sea'. The menu, which lists some 80 different seafood dishes, is very much aimed at fish-lovers, with starters including smoked sprats, smoked trout paté and Italian seafood salad, and main dishes such as whole grilled wild sea bass; whole grilled turbot; whole grilled Dover sole; monkfish tails in garlic butter; and crab gratin. The Swan has its own smokehouse, one of just three remaining out of 200 in what was once one of Britain's busiest fishing ports. Anyone preferring meat to fish has a choice of fillet, rump and gammon steaks.

⊚
MAP 13 TM49
Swan Ln NR34 7QF
☎ 01502 476646
🖷 01502 562513
dir: *Just off A146 between Lowestoft & Beccles*

Open 11–3 6–12
Bar Meals L served all week 12–2 D served all week 7–9.30
Restaurant L served all week 12–2 D served all week 7–9.30
⊕ Free House ⬤ Interbrew Bass, Adnams Best, Broadside, Greene King Abbot Ale.
Facilities Garden Parking Play Area

BURY ST EDMUNDS continued

The Old Cannon Brewery ★★★ INN ☉

36 Cannon St IP33 1JR ☎ 01284 768769
e-mail: info@oldcannonbrewery.co.uk
web: www.oldcannonbrewery.co.uk

dir: *From A14 follow signs to Bury St Edmunds town centre, at 1st rdbt take 1st left onto Northgate St, then 1st right onto Cadney Ln, left at end onto Cannon St, pub 100yds on left*

'The Old Can' is the only independent brewpub in the brewing town of Bury St Edmunds. A spacious former beer house built in 1845, it has something of a conversation piece in the bar – two giant stainless steel brewing vessels. The menu might offer Norfolk mussels marinière, followed by Old Cannon ale-braised guinea fowl with mushrooms, chestnuts and pan haggerty. Overnight guests are treated to fresh Suffolk apple juice and a hearty farmhouse breakfast.

Open 12–3 5–11 (Sun 7–10.30) Closed: 25 Dec, 1 Jan & Mon lunch **Bar Meals** L served Tue-Sun 12–2 **Restaurant** L served Tue-Sun 12–2 D served Tue-Sat 6.30–9.15 Av 3 course à la carte £22 ⊕ Free House ◀ Old Cannon Best Bitter, Old Cannon Gunner's Daughter, Old Cannon Blonde Bombshell, Adnams Bitter. ☉ 12 **Facilities** Garden Parking **Rooms** 5

The Three Kings ★★★ INN ☉

Hengrave Rd, Fornham All Saints IP28 6LA
☎ 01284 766979
e-mail: thethreekings@keme.co.uk
dir: *Bury St Edmunds (2m), A14 junct 42 (1m)*

A 17th-century coaching inn with a pretty village setting, the Three Kings features wood panelled bars, a conservatory, restaurant and courtyard. A new Saturday night menu for 2008 offers an elegant à la carte dining experience in additional to traditional bar food of burgers, beer battered fish and chips, and spicy vegetable chilli. There is also a popular Sunday roast carvery, for which booking is advised. Nine comfortable en suite bedrooms are available in converted outbuildings.

Open 12–11 **Bar Meals** L served Mon-Fri 12–2 D served Tue-Sat 5.30–9 (Mon 6–8, Sat 12–2.30, Sun 12–2.30, 6–8) Av main course £7.50 **Restaurant** L served Sun 12–2.30 D served Sat 7–9 ⊕ Greene King ◀ Greene King IPA, Abbot & Ridleys Rumps. ☉ 14 **Facilities** Children's licence Garden Parking **Rooms** 9

CAVENDISH   **MAP 13 TL84**

Bull Inn

High St CO10 8AX ☎ 01787 280245

dir: *A134 (Bury St Edmunds to Long Melford), then right at green, pub 3m on right*

A Victorian pub set in one of Suffolk's most beautiful villages, with an unassuming façade hiding a splendid 15th-century beamed interior. Expect a good atmosphere and decent food, with the daily-changing blackboard menu listing perhaps curries, shank of lamb, fresh fish and shellfish, and a roast on Sundays. Outside there's a pleasant garden.

Open 11–3 6–11 (Sun 12–4) **Bar Meals** L served all week 12–2 D served Tue-Sat 6.30–9 (Sun 12–2.30) Av main course £9 **Restaurant** L served all week 12–2 D served Mon-Sat 6.30–9 (Sun 12–2.30) Av 3 course à la carte £16 ⊕ Adnams ◀ Adnams Bitter & Broadside, Nethergate Suffolk County. **Facilities** Dogs allowed Parking

CHILLESFORD   **MAP 13 TM35**

The Froize Inn ☉

The Street IP12 3PU ☎ 01394 450282
e-mail: dine@froize.co.uk
dir: *On B1084 between Woodbridge (8m) & Orford (3m)*

This former gamekeeper's cottage, built on the site of Chillesford Friary, is a distinctive red-brick building dating to around 1490. Inside is a thoroughly traditional English pub, with a modern dining room which champions a variety of East Anglian growers and suppliers. Starters may include hare brawn with crab apple jelly; or English snails with garlic, parsley and lemon butter. Main courses from the hot buffet could offer free-range Blythburgh pork; or devilled lambs' kidneys. The pub stands on the popular Suffolk Coastal Path.

Open 11.30–2.30 6.30–11 Closed: Mon **Bar Meals** L served Tue-Sun 12–2 D served Thu-Sat 7–8.30 **Restaurant** L served Tue-Sun 12–2 D served Thu-Sat 7–8.30 ⊕ Free House ◀ Adnams. ☉ 14 **Facilities** Garden Parking

COTTON   **MAP 13 TM06**

Pick of the Pubs

The Trowel & Hammer Inn

Mill Rd IP14 4QL ☎ 01449 781234 🖷 01449 781765
e-mail: sallyselvage@tiscali.co.uk

dir: *From A14 follow signs to Haughley, then Bacton, then turn left for Cotton*

A herd of nine carved teak elephants trekking through the main hall way to the outdoor swimming pool gives you a clue that this is no ordinary pub. At first sight the well maintained, wisteria-clad building belies its 16th-century origins; but, once inside, the old oak timbers and traditional fireplace give a better idea of its age. Nevertheless contemporary needs haven't been forgotten, and licensee Sally Burrows has created secluded areas within the main bars to cater for all age groups. In the summer months the garden, with its tropical theme and thatched poolside umbrellas, is a relaxing place for a drink and a bite to eat. The menus are a blend of traditional farmhouse cooking and international cuisine,

CONTINUED

COTTON continued

so expect to find the regular Sunday roast rubbing shoulders with more exotic dishes that include crocodile and kangaroo.

Open 12–11 (Fri-Sat 12-1am) **Bar Meals** L served all week 12–3 D served all week 6–9.30 (Sun all day) Av main course £9.45 **Restaurant** L served all week 12–3 D served Mon-Sat 6–9.30 ⊕ Free House ◣ Adnams Bitter & Broadside, Greene King IPA & Old Speckled Hen. **Facilities** Garden Parking

DENNINGTON   MAP 13 TM26

The Queens Head

The Square IP13 8AB ☎ 01728 638241 📄 01728 638037
e-mail: denningtonqueen1@btinternet.com
dir: From Ipswich take A14 to turn off for Lowestoft (A12). Turn off to Framlingham on the B1116, from Framlingham follow signs to Dennington.

A 500–year-old inn with a resident ghost, a bricked-up tunnel to the neighbouring church, and a coffin hatch. Locally brewed cider is available alongside the real ales. On the extensive main menu, which changes every six months, might be duck with port and raspberry sauce; cottage pie; Irish hotpot with dumplings; and fillet of plaice parcels. Daily specials, sandwiches, griddles and children's meals, vegetarian and gluten-free dishes add to the choice.

Open 9–3 6.30–11 (Summer 6–11 Winter 6.30–10 ex Sat-Sun) Closed: 25–26 Dec **Bar Meals** L served all week 12–2 D served all week 6.30–9 Av main course £8.50 **Restaurant** L served all week 12–2 D served all week 6.30–9 Av 3 course à la carte £16 ⊕ Free House ◣ Adnams, St Peters, Woodfordes & Mauldons. **Facilities** Garden Parking Play Area

DUNWICH   MAP 13 TM47

The Ship Inn

St James St IP17 3DT ☎ 01728 648219 📄 01728 648675
web: www.shipatdunwich.co.uk
dir: N on A12 from Ipswich through Yoxford, right signed Dunwich

The once-thriving medieval port of Dunwich has long since been claimed by the sea, but thankfully this old smugglers' haunt looks invulnerable. As one would expect, fresh fish usually features on the daily-changing menu, including plaice, mackerel, prawns, scampi and fishcakes, as do steak and ale pie; lamb, pea and mint casserole; and jam roly poly. In fine weather you can eat in the garden then slip down to the beach, two minutes away.

Open 11–11 (Sun 12–10.30) **Bar Meals** L served all week 12–3 D served all week 6–9 Av main course £9.50 **Restaurant** L served all week 12–3 D served all week 6–9 Av 3 course à la carte £18 ⊕ Free House ◣ Adnams Earl Soham. **Facilities** Children's licence Garden Dogs allowed Parking

EARL SOHAM   MAP 13 TM26

Victoria

The Street IP13 7RL ☎ 01728 685758
dir: From A14 at Stowmarket take A1120 towards Yoxford

This friendly, down to earth free house is a showcase for Earl Soham beers, which for many years were produced from a micro-brewery behind the pub. In 2001 the brewery moved to the Old Forge building opposite the village green, where production still continues. The Victoria offers traditional pub fare, including ploughman's, jacket potatoes, macaroni cheese, and smoked salmon salad. Heartier meals include a variety of casseroles and curries, followed by home-made desserts.

Open 11.30–3 6–11 (Sun 12–3, 7–10.30) **Bar Meals** L served Mon-Sat 11.30–2 D served all week 7–10 (Sun 12–2) ⊕ Free House ◣ Earl Soham-Victoria Bitter, Albert Ale, & Gannet Mild (all brewed on site). Earl Soham Porter. **Facilities** Garden Dogs allowed Parking

ERWARTON   MAP 13 TM23

The Queens Head

The Street IP9 1LN ☎ 01473 787550
dir: From Ipswich take B1456 to Shotley

This handsome 16th-century Suffolk free house provides an atmospheric stop for a pint of locally-brewed Adnams or Greene King ales. There's a relaxed atmosphere in the bar with its bowed black oak beams, low ceilings and cosy coal fires, and magnificent views over the fields to the Stour estuary. The wide-ranging menu offers traditional hot dishes and snacks, while daily specials include pheasant casserole, spinach and red lentil curry, Guinness-battered cod and chips, and home-made fishcakes. Booking is advised at weekends.

Open 11–3 6.30–11 (Sun 12–3, 7–10.30) Closed: 25 Dec **Bar Meals** L served all week 12–1.45 D served all week 7–9 **Restaurant** L served all week 12–2 D served all week 7–9.30 ⊕ Free House ◣ Adnams Bitter & Broadside, Greene King IPA, Aspall Cider, Guinness. **Facilities** Garden Parking

EYE   MAP 13 TM17

The White Horse Inn ★★★★ INN

Stoke Ash IP23 7ET ☎ 01379 678222 📄 01379 678800
e-mail: mail@whitehorse-suffolk.co.uk
dir: On A140 between Ipswich & Norwich

A 17th-century coaching inn set amid lovely Suffolk countryside. The heavily-timbered interior accommodates an inglenook fireplace, two bars and a restaurant. There are seven spacious motel bedrooms in the grounds, as well as a patio and secluded grassy area. An extensive menu is supplemented by lunchtime snacks, grills and daily specials from the blackboard. Try grilled butterflied breast of chicken; Lincolnshire sausages and mash; lasagne; or salmon and haddock tagliatelle are typical.

Open 8–11 (Sun 8–10.30) **Bar Meals** L served all week 11–9.30 D served all week 11–9.30 **Restaurant** L served all week 11–9.30 D served all week 11–9.30 ⊕ Free House ◣ Adnams, Greene King Abbot, IPA Smooth. **Facilities** Children's licence Garden Parking **Rooms** 11

FRAMLINGHAM

MAP 13 TM26

The Station Hotel ♈

Station Rd IP13 9EE ☎ 01728 723455

e-mail: framstation@btinternet.com

dir: *Bypass Ipswich towards Lowestoft on A12. In approx 6m turn left onto B1116 towards Framlingham*

Built as part of the local railway in the 19th century, The Station Hotel has been a pub since the 1950s, outliving the railway which closed in 1962. During the last decade it has established a fine reputation for its seafood and locally brewed beers. Expect the likes of smoked mackerel terrine with beetroot and horseradish; pan-fried skate wing with samphire and caper butter; or pigeon breasts with warm puy lentil and green bean salad.

Open 12–2.30 5–11 Closed: 25–27 Dec **Bar Meals** L served all week 12–2 D served Sun-Thu 7–9 (Fri-Sat 7–9.30) **Restaurant** L served all week 12–2 D served Sun-Thu 7–9 (Fri-Sat 7–9.30) ⊕ Free House ◀ Earl Soham Victoria, Albert & Mild, Veltins, Nusto. **Facilities** Garden Dogs allowed Parking

FRAMSDEN

MAP 13 TM15

The Dobermann Inn

The Street IP14 6HG ☎ 01473 890461

dir: *S off A1120 (Stowmarket/Yoxford)*

Previously The Greyhound, the pub was renamed by its current proprietor, a prominent breeder and judge of Dobermanns. The thatched roofing, gnarled beams, open fire and assorted furniture reflect its 16th-century origins. Food ranges from sandwiches and salads to main courses featuring game from a local estate in season, and plenty of fish choices. Reliable favourites include steak and mushroom pie, Dover sole, and sirloin steak. Vegetarians can feast on mushroom stroganoff or spicy nut loaf.

Open 12–3 7–11 Closed: 25–26 Dec & Sun & Mon eve
Bar Meals L served Tue-Sun 12–2 D served Tue-Sat 7–10 ⊕ Free House ◀ Adnams Bitter & Broadside, Mauldons Moletrap Bitter, Adnams Old WA. **Facilities** Garden Parking **Notes** ⊛

GREAT BRICETT

MAP 13 TM05

Pick of the Pubs

Red Lion NEW

Green St Green IP7 7DD

☎ 01473 657799 📠 01473 658492

e-mail: janwise@fsmail.net

dir: *4.5m from Needham Market on B1078*

This fine example of a 17th-century village pub was, arguably, just another hostelry until Jan Wise came along and turned it into East Anglia's only vegetarian pub. She has a fixed rule – nothing is served that means killing an animal, so there's no Sunday carvery, no mixed grill, no scampi in a basket. Passionate about meat-free dining, and wanting to 'celebrate the fantastic flavours that only vegetables can provide', Jan uses her 30 years' experience as a vegetarian caterer to provide garlic mushroom tart; Mexican chimichangas (tortillas filled with refried beans, salsa, red onions and cheese); African sweet potato stew; Caribbean pasta; and

porcini risotto fritters. She's back on more familiar territory with her desserts, including chocolate brownies, strawberry knickerbockers and caramel apple sponge pudding. Not only is it advisable to book, but you'll need a healthy appetite.

Open 12–3 6–11 (Summer, Sun all day) Closed: Mon
Bar Meals L served all week 12–2 D served all week 6–9 Av main course £6.90 **Restaurant** L served all week 12–2 D served all week 6–9 Av 3 course à la carte £15 ⊕ Greene King ◀ Greene King IPA, Speckled Hen. **Facilities** Children's licence Garden Dogs allowed Parking Play Area

GREAT GLEMHAM

MAP 13 TM36

The Crown Inn ⊛ ♈

IP17 2DA ☎ 01728 663693

dir: *A12 (Ipswich to Lowestoft), in Stratford-St-Andrew left at Shell garage. Pub 1.5m*

Cosy 17th-century village pub overlooking the Great Glemham Estate and within easy reach of the Suffolk Heritage Coast. You can eat in the extensively renovated bars and large flower-filled garden, where moussaka, carbonnade of beef, Somerset lamb casserole, roasted vegetables with pasta, and spinach and feta cheese tart from the specials menu might be followed by fresh fruit pavlova or traditional sherry trifle.

Open 11.30–2.30 6.30–11 Closed: Mon **Bar Meals** L served Tue-Sun 11.30–2.30 D served Tue-Sun 6.30–10 ⊕ Free House ◀ Adnams Bitter & Broadside. ♈7 **Facilities** Garden Dogs allowed Parking Play Area

HALESWORTH

MAP 13 TM37

Pick of the Pubs

The Queen's Head ♈

The Street, Bramfield IP19 9HT

☎ 01986 784214 📠 01986 784797

e-mail: qhbfield@aol.com

dir: *2m from A12 on the A144 towards Halesworth*

The Queen's Head is a lovely old building in the centre of Bramfield village on the edge of the Suffolk Heritage Coast, just 15 minutes from Southwold. The enclosed garden, ideal for children, is overlooked by the thatched village church which has an unusual separate round bell tower. The pub interior welcomes with scrubbed pine tables, exposed beams, a vaulted ceiling in the bar and enormous fireplaces. In the same capable hands for over ten years, the pub's reputation is built on enthusiastic support for the 'local and organic' movement – reflected by the menu which proudly names the farms and suppliers from which the carefully chosen ingredients are sourced. As well as baguettes and ploughman's displayed on boards, newly-introduced dishes maintain the menu's appeal: a starter of stilton and port ramekin; and main courses like locally-smoked kipper served with champ and poached free-range egg; or Longwood Organic Farm pork, apple and Aspalls Cider pie.

Open 11.45–2.30 6.30–11 (Sun 12–3, 7–10.30) Closed: 26 Dec
Bar Meals L served all week 12–2 D served Mon-Sat 6.30–9.15 (Sun 7–9) Av main course £10.95 ⊕ Adnams ◀ Adnams Bitter & Broadside. ♈8 **Facilities** Garden Dogs allowed Parking

The White Horse Inn ♥

The Street IP7 7NQ
☎ 01449 740981 📠 01449 740981
e-mail: lewis@thewhitehorse.wanadoo.co.uk
dir: *13m from Ipswich & Bury St Edmunds*

This semi-detached Grade II listed building in two storeys is the only pub in Hitcham, and estimated in parts to be around 400 years old. The family run inn has a welcoming atmosphere where you can relax and enjoy home-cooked food washed down by one of the large selection of wines. Please note that from November to the end of March this pub is closed on Mondays and Tuesdays.

Open 12–3 6–11 Closed: Mon & Tue Nov-Mar **Bar Meals** L served all week 12–2 D served all week 6–9 **Restaurant** L served all week 12–2 D served Sun-Thu 6–9 (Fri-Sat 6–9.30) ◀ IPA, Adnams Best Bitter, Rattlesden Best, Stowmarket Porter & Adnams Fisherman. ♥ 8 **Facilities** Garden Dogs allowed Parking

The Compasses

Ipswich Rd IP9 2QR
☎ 01473 328332 📠 01473 327403
e-mail: compasses.holbrook@virgin.net

dir: *From A137 S of Ipswich, take B1080 to Holbrook, pub on left. From Ipswich take B1456 to Shotley. At Freston Water Tower right onto B1080 to Holbrook. Pub 2m right*

Holbrook is bordered by the rivers Orwell and Stour, and this traditional country pub, which dates from the 17th century, is on the Shotley peninsula. A good value menu includes ploughman's, salads and jacket potatoes; pub favourites such as pork tenderloin or chicken with cashew nuts; and a fish selection. Party bookings are a speciality, and look out for Wine of the Week deals. Pensioners' weekday lunches complete this pub's honest offerings.

Open 11.30–2.30 6–11 (Sun 12–3, 6–10.30) Closed: 25–26 Dec, 1 Jan **Bar Meals** L served all week 12–2.15 D served all week 6–9.15 Av main course £9.45 **Restaurant** L served all week 12–2.15 D served all week 6–9.15 Av 3 course à la carte £18 🌐 Punch Taverns ◀ Greene King IPA, Adnams Bitter & guest ales. **Facilities** Garden Parking Play Area

The Lion ♥

CO6 4NX ☎ 01206 263434 📠 01206 263434
e-mail: enquiries@lionhoneytye.co.uk
dir: *On A134 midway between Colchester & Sudbury*

Located in an Area of Outstanding Natural Beauty this traditional country dining pub has low-beamed ceilings and an open log fire inside and a patio with tables and umbrellas for outside eating and drinking. The menu offers a good choice of daily fresh fish (oven baked red snapper supreme with tomato and prawn confit), pub favourites (home-made steak and ale pie), and main dishes such as braised lamb shank with rosemary, garlic and red wine jus.

Open 11–3 5.30–11 (Sun 12–10.30) **Bar Meals** L served all week 12–2 D served all week 6–9.30 (Sun 12–9.30) Av main course £8 **Restaurant** L served all week 12–2 D served all week 6–9.30 (Sun 12–9.30) Av 3 course à la carte £17 🌐 Free House ◀ Greene King IPA, Adnams Bitter, guest ale. ♥ 7 **Facilities** Garden Parking

Beehive ◉ ♥

The Street IP29 5SN
☎ 01284 735260 📠 01284 735523
dir: *From A14 1st turn for Bury St Edmunds, sign for Westley & Ickworth Park*

Small rooms, antique tables and white linen napkins characterise this Victorian flint and stone cottage, which is full of period features. In summer, visitors head for the patio and the picnic benches in the walled beer garden. Expect home-made pork and apple sausages; seared fresh tuna; and warm roast vegetable and tomato tart. Located on the High Street in Horringer, the pub is handy for Bury St Edmunds and the National Trust's Ickworth Park.

Open 11.30–2.30 7–11 Closed: 25–26 Dec Sun eve **Bar Meals** L served all week 12–2 D served Mon-Sat 7–9.45 Av main course £10.95
Restaurant L served all week 12–2 D served all week 7–9.30 Av 3 course à la carte £20 ⊕ Greene King ◄ Greene King IPA & Abbot Ale, guest ales.
♀ 8 **Facilities** Garden Parking

HOXNE   MAP 13 TM17

The Swan ♀

Low St IP21 5AS ☎ 01379 668275
e-mail: info@hoxneswan.co.uk
dir: *Telephone for directions*

This 15th-century Grade II listed lodge, reputedly built for the Bishop of Norwich, has large gardens running down to the River Dove, with a vast willow tree. Inside, the restaurant and front bar boast a 10ft inglenook fireplace, ornate beamed ceilings and old planked floors. Food ranges from lunchtime snacks like golden whitebait or soup of the day, to a weekly changing lunch and dinner menu. Traditional dishes include venison and wild mushroom pie, with innovative options like sweet potato and saffron fricassée.

Open 11.30–3 6–11 (Sun 12–10.30) **Bar Meals** L served all week 12–2.30 D served all week 7–9.30 (Sun 12–4, 7–9) Av main course £10
Restaurant L served all week 12–2.30 D served all week 7–9.30 (Sun 12–4, 7–9) ⊕ Enterprise Inns ◄ Adnams Best Bitter & 4 other real ales. ♀ 10
Facilities Garden Dogs allowed Parking

ICKLINGHAM   MAP 13 TL77

The Plough Inn ♀

The Street IP28 6PL ☎ 01638 711770 📄 01638 583885
e-mail: info@ploughpubinn.co.uk

This old, flint-built village pub is part of the Iveagh Estate. Among the numerous fish dishes are grilled red snapper with rougail sauce; and pan-fried skate wing in rosemary and caper butter. Other main courses include beef fillet pie; cottage pie; pork and herb sausages; lemon basil chicken; and poacher's pot, which contains wild boar, rabbit, pheasant and venison in real ale and red wine.

Open 11–12 **Bar Meals** L served all week 12–8.45 D served all week **Restaurant** L served Mon-Sat 11.30–8.45 D served Mon-Sat (Sun 12–8.45) ⊕ Free House ◄ IPA, Wherry, London Pride, Adnams. ♀ 26
Facilities Garden Parking

The Red Lion ♀

The Street IP28 6PS ☎ 01638 711698
dir: *Follow A1101 from Bury St Edmunds 8m. In Icklingham pub on main street on left*

A sympathetically restored, 16th-century thatched country inn set back from the road behind a grassed area with flower beds and outdoor furniture. The interior, glowing by candlelight in the evening, features exposed beams, a large inglenook fireplace, wooden floors, and antique furniture. The pub backs onto the River Lark, and was formerly the site of a coal yard and a maltings. An interesting menu offers a variety of choices, and all dishes are freshly prepared.

Open 12–3 6.30–11 (Sun 7–10.30) Closed: 25 Dec
Bar Meals L served all week 12–2.30 D served all week 6.30–10 (Sun 7–9) Av main course £9 **Restaurant** L served all week 12–2.30 D served all week 6.30–10 (Sun 7–9) ⊕ Greene King ◄ Greene King Abbot Ale & IPA, Norlands Speckled Hen. ♀ 15 **Facilities** Garden Parking

---

IXWORTH   MAP 13 TL97

Pykkerell Inn ♀

38 High St IP31 2HH ☎ 01359 230398 📄 01359 230398
dir: *On A143 from Bury St Edmunds towards Diss*

This former coaching inn dates from 1530 and still retains most of its original beams, inglenook fireplace and other features. The wood-panelled library is just off the lounge, and the 14th-century barn encloses a patio and barbecue. The extensive menu includes vegetarian options and children's meals, as well as traditional Sunday roast lunch. Menu boards highlight a variety of fresh fish, and may include red snapper, monkfish and Dover sole.

Open 12–3 6–11 **Bar Meals** L served all week 12–2.30 D served all week 7–10 Av main course £9.50 **Restaurant** L served all week 12–2.30 D served all week 6–10 Av 3 course à la carte £15.95 ⊕ Greene King ◄ Greene King IPA & Abbot Ale. **Facilities** Garden Dogs allowed Parking

---

KETTLEBURGH   MAP 13 TM26

The Chequers Inn

IP13 7JT ☎ 01728 723760 & 724369 📄 01728 723760
e-mail: info@thechequers.net
dir: *From Ipswich A12 onto B1116, left onto B1078 then right through Easton*

The Chequers is set in beautiful countryside on the banks of the River Deben. The landlord serves a wide range of cask ales, including two guests. In addition to snack and restaurant meals, the menu in the bar includes local sausages and ham with home-produced free-range eggs. The riverside garden can seat up to a hundred people.

Open 12–2.30 6–11 **Bar Meals** L served all week 12–2 D served all week 7–9.30 (Sun 12–2, 7–9) Av main course £5.50 **Restaurant** L served all week 12–2 D served all week 7–9.30 (Sun 12–2, 7–9) Av 3 course à la carte £16.50 ⊕ Free House ◄ Greene King IPA, Black Dog Mild & 3 guest ales. **Facilities** Garden Dogs allowed Parking Play Area

Lavenham , Suffolk

England

LAKENHEATH   MAP 12 TL78

The Half Moon Restaurant & Bar

4 High St IP27 9JX ☎ 01842 861484 📄 01842 861484

e-mail: info@halfmoonrestaurant.co.uk

web: www.halfmoonrestaurant.co.uk

dir: *6m N of Mildenhall between Newmarket & Thetford on A11. Signed to Lakenheath & RAF Lakenheath (B1112)*

A brick and flint pub with an extensive range of drinks including Belhaven Best Original. A broad menu includes pasta, steaks and other pub favourites.

Open 12–3 6–11.30 (Fri-Sun 12–12) Closed: Mon **Bar Meals** L served all week 12–2.30 D served all week 6–9.30 (Sat 12–9.30, Sun 12–8) Av main course £6 **Restaurant** L served all week 12–2.30 D served all week 6–9.30 (Sat 12–9.30, 12–8.30) Av 3 course à la carte £18 ⊕ Greene King ◀ Greene King IPA, Abbot Ale, guest ale. **Facilities** Garden Parking

---

LAVENHAM   MAP 13 TL94

Pick of the Pubs

Angel Hotel Ⓤ ◉ ♟

See Pick of the Pubs on page 534

LAXFIELD   MAP 13 TM27

The Kings Head ♟

Gorams Mill Ln IP13 8DW ☎ 01986 798395

e-mail: bob-wilson5505@hotmail.co.uk

dir: *On B1117*

Beautifully situated overlooking the river, the garden of this thatched 16th-century alehouse was formerly the village bowling green. Beer is still served straight from the cask in the original tap room, whilst high-backed settles and wooden seats add to the charming atmosphere. Traditional home-cooked dishes complement the à la carte menu and chef's specials and, on warmer evenings, the rose gardens and arbour are perfect for al fresco dining.

Open 12–3 6–11 (Sun 12–3, 7–11, Sat-Sun all day Summer) **Bar Meals** L served all week 12–2 D served all week 7–9 Av main course £8 **Restaurant** L served all week 12–2 D served all week 7–9 Av 3 course à la carte £15 ⊕ Adnams ◀ Adnams Best & Broadside, Adnams seasonal & guest ales. ♟ 8 **Facilities** Garden Dogs allowed Parking Play Area

---

LEVINGTON   MAP 13 TM23

Pick of the Pubs

The Ship Inn ♟

See Pick of the Pubs on page 536

LIDGATE   MAP 12 TL75

Pick of the Pubs

The Star Inn

The Street CB8 9PP ☎ 01638 500275 📄 01638 500275

e-mail: tonyaxon@aol.com

dir: *From Newmarket clocktower in High St follow signs towards Clare on B1063. Lidgate 7m*

This pretty, pink-painted Elizabethan building is made up of two cottages with gardens front and rear; inside, two traditionally furnished bars with heavy oak and pine furniture lead into the dining room. Yet the Star's quintessentially English appearance holds a surprise, for here you'll find a renowned Spanish restaurant offering authentic Mediterranean cuisine. No mere gastro-pub, the Star provides an important meeting place for local residents. It's also popular with Newmarket trainers on race days, and with dealers and agents from all over the world during bloodstock sales. The menu offers appealingly hearty food: starters like Catalan spinach; and Mediterranean fish soup might precede Spanish meatballs; or hake a la vasca. English tastes are also catered for, with dishes such as smoked salmon and avocado; roast lamb with garlic; and fillet steak in pepper sauce. There's an extensive wine list, too.

Open 11–3 6–11 Closed: 25–26 Dec, 1 Jan **Bar Meals** L served Mon-Sat 12–2 D served Mon-Sat 7–10 (Sun 12–2.30, 7–11) Av main course £16.95 **Restaurant** L served Mon-Sat 12–2 D served Mon-Sat 7–10 (Sun 12–2.30) Av 2 course fixed price £12 ⊕ Greene King ◀ Greene King IPA, Ruddles County & Abbot Ale. **Facilities** Garden Parking

PICK OF THE PUBS

LAVENHAM-SUFFOLK

Angel Hotel

The attractive, bustling Angel Hotel stands in the market place of beautiful Lavenham, a historical village whose streets are lined with crooked timber-framed houses. First licensed in 1420, it was originally a 'high hall' house: smoke from a central fire would drift out through roof vents.

Around 1500 ventilation improved when two wings with brick chimneys were added to the building, along with a first-floor solar room. Now the residents' sitting room, it contains a rare pargetted ceiling, in which patterns were applied to the wet plaster. In the cellar is a huge Elizabethan brick arch supporting the chimney above. There is no real division between the bar and restaurant areas, both of which have historic features including exposed timbers, a large inglenook fireplace, and a Tudor shuttered shop window. The Angel does its best to source all its produce from local suppliers; the menu changes daily, with everything prepared on the premises. There are always home-made soups, pies and casseroles, fresh fish, game in season and vegetarian dishes. Typical starters from a dinner menu include chicken, apricot and sun-dried tomato terrine; haddock, crab and chilli fishcakes with spicy tomato sauce; and tomato, butternut squash and sweet potato soup. Main courses might be steak and ale pie; chargrilled tuna with lemon and thyme risotto; lamb, chick pea and butternut squash casserole; or Gressingham duck breast with sweet potato and chestnut rösti. You could finish with a selection of English cheeses, or perhaps steamed syrup sponge pudding with custard. Eight en suite bedrooms enable excellent dinner, bed and breakfast packages to be offered, and the chance to linger.

[U] ⊛ ♀
MAP 13 TL94
Market Place CO10 9QZ
☎ 01787 247388
📄 01787 248344
e-mail:
angel@maypolehotels.com
dir: *7m from Sudbury on A1141 between Sudbury & Bury St Edmunds*

Open 11–11 (Sun 12–10.30)
Bar Meals L served all week
12–2.15 D served all week
6.45–9.15 Av main course £12
Restaurant L served all week
12–2.15 D served all week
6.45–9.15
🍺 Adnams Bitter, Nethergate, Greene King IPA, Broadside & Old Growler. ♀ 10
Facilities Children's licence
Garden Parking
Rooms 8

MELTON

MAP 13 TM25

Wilford Bridge

Wilford Bridge Rd IP12 2PA

☎ 01394 386141 📠 01394 386141

e-mail: wilfordbridge@yahoo.com

dir: *From A12 towards coast, follow signs to Bawdsey & Orford, cross rail lines, next pub on left*

Just down the road from the famous Sutton Hoo treasure ship, Mike and Anne Lomas have been running the free house at Wilford Bridge for the last 17 years. As a former West End chef, Mike specialises in seafood dishes; look out for mussels and sprats in season, as well as king prawns, cod, salmon, trout, sea bass and others as available. At the bar, guest ales supplement the regular choice of beers.

Open 11–11 Closed: 25–26 Dec **Bar Meals** L served all week 11.30–9.30 D served all week 11.30–9.30 Av main course £10 **Restaurant** L served all week 11.30–9.30 D served all week 11.30–9.30 Av 3 course à la carte £19.25 ⊕ Free House ◀ Adnams Best, Broadside, John Smiths's + guest ales. **Facilities** Garden Parking

---

MONKS ELEIGH

MAP 13 TL94

Pick of the Pubs

The Swan Inn ⊚⊚ ♥

The Street IP7 7AU ☎ 01449 741391

e-mail: carol@monkseleigh.com

dir: *On B1115 between Sudbury & Hadleigh*

This thatched free house first welcomed customers In the 14th century. In those days its interior would have been open to the roof; you can still see evidence of the former smokehole. Other historical features include original wattle and daub, which was exposed during renovation work. The main restaurant, with its magnificent open fireplace, may once have been used as the manorial court. Menus change almost daily to make the most of local ingredients, and autumn sees a steady stream of game from local shoots. The cooking combines British, Italian and Asian influences. Starters could include pigeon breast with crispy bacon and walnut salad; or mussels steamed in coconut milk with green chilli, lemongrass, coriander and spring onions. Follow with braised lamb knuckle with a puy lentil sauce on creamy mashed potatoes with buttered broad beans; or Italian-style sweet and sour duck leg on buttered spinach with lemon and rosemary potatoes.

Open 12–3 7–11 Closed: 25–26 Dec, 1–2 Jan & Mon-Tue (ex BH)
Bar Meals L served Wed-Sun 12–2 D served Wed-Sun 7–9.30 Av main course £14 **Restaurant** L served Wed-Sun 12–2 D served Wed-Sun 7–9.30 Av 3 course à la carte £27.50 ⊕ Free House ◀ Greene King IPA, Adnams Bitter & Broadside. ♥ 20 **Facilities** Garden Parking

---

NAYLAND

MAP 13 TL93

Pick of the Pubs

Anchor Inn

26 Court St CO6 4JL ☎ 01206 262313 📠 01206 264166

e-mail: enquiries@anchornayland.co.uk

dir: *From Colchester follow signs to N rail station, under railway bridge, take A134 towards Sudbury, right towards Nayland signed Horkesley Rd. Pass bridge, pub on right*

This 15th-century inn by the River Stour is reputedly the last remaining place from where press gangs recruited their 'volunteers'. What also makes it rather special is that the adjoining non-intensive Heritage Farm, where visitors can see Suffolk Punch horses at work, English longhorn cattle grazing, and conservation projects in progress, provides the kitchen with much of its daily requirement of meat, vegetables and herbs. This farm-kitchen relationship is crucial to the quality of food, all of which, from sausages to sauces, is prepared here from scratch for regularly changing menus shaped by the seasons. Try the platter of home-smoked fish, meat and cheese; grilled escalope of salmon; classic Irish stew; spicy mutton tagine; or home-made linguine. The estate's Pitfield Brewery supplies some of the beers, while wines from Carter's Vineyards three miles away contribute to the world wine list.

Open 11–3 5–11 (Sat 11–11, Sun 11–10.30) **Bar Meals** L served Mon-Sat 12–2.30 D served Mon-Thu 6.30–9 (Fri-Sat 6.30–9.30, Sun 10–3, 4.30–8.30) Av main course £9 **Restaurant** L served Mon-Sat 12–2.30 D served Mon-Thu 6.30–9 (Fri-Sat 6.30–9.30 Sun 10–3, 4.30–8.30) Av 3 course à la carte £20 ⊕ Free House ◀ Adnams, IPA, Mild. **Facilities** Garden Parking

---

ORFORD

MAP 13 TM45

Jolly Sailor Inn

Quay St IP12 2NU ☎ 01394 450243 📠 0870 128 7874

e-mail: jacquie@jollysailor.f9.co.uk

dir: *On B1084 E of Woodbridge, Orford signed from A12 approx 10m*

Until the 16th century, Orford was a bustling coastal port. This ancient, timber-framed smugglers' inn stood on the quayside – but, as Orford Ness grew longer, the harbour silted up and fell out of use. Nevertheless, the pub still serves visiting yachtsmen, and local fishermen supply fresh fish to the kitchen. There's also a daily roast, and other dishes might include seasonal local pheasant in red wine; or fresh pasta with a choice of sauces.

Open 11.30–2.30 7–11 **Bar Meals** L served all week 12–2 D served all week 7.15–8.45 Av main course £6.50 ⊕ Adnams ◀ Adnams Bitter & Broadside. **Facilities** Garden Dogs allowed **Notes** ⊛

PICK OF THE PUBS

The Ship Inn

The timbers of this part-14th-century thatched inn are impregnated with the salt of the sea. It stands within sight of the Orwell estuary and the Suffolk marshes, where old sailing vessels were beached and their hulks broken up for their precious beams. Attractive front and rear patios are adorned with hanging and potted plants.

Walls and flat surfaces inside are full of seafaring pictures, curiosities and keepsakes, and it may seem a bit too ordered and cosy ever to have been the smugglers' haunt it once was. But wait, read the old newspaper cuttings on the wall and you'll be in no doubt that excise men and contraband often ended up here, though ideally not at the same time. In summer, when shellfish comes into season, the kitchen buys huge quantities of lobster, crab, mussels, clams and oysters in addition to haddock, hake, salmon, mackerel and snapper from around the coast. This means a good choice of fish and seafood starters and main courses from the daily changing blackboard menu – perhaps something griddled in herb, lemon and garlic oil, or

accompanied by a light sauce. Local game includes pigeon, pheasant, partridge, rabbit, hare and estate-reared venison, although the kitchen is also noted for its meats, including chargrilled chicken brochettes; fillet of pork or beef; and liver and bacon, served with black pudding and Madeira sauce. Homemade desserts range from crème brûlée to baked chocolate and pecan tart. Alternatively, there is a good selection of British cheeses. Finish your meal with coffee (again, a good selection available) and home-made almond biscuits. Regional ales include Adnams and Greene King, plus a range of Scottish and Irish malts and wines by the glass, including champagne. Everything is served by smiling, attentive staff.

MAP 13 TM23
Church Ln IP10 0LQ
☎ 01473 659573
dir: *Off A14 towards Felixstowe. Nr Levington Marina*

Open 11.30–3 6.30–11 (Sat-Sun 11.30–11) Closed: 25–26 Dec D only, 31 Dec-1 Jan
Bar Meals L served Mon-Sat 12–2 D served all week 6.30–9.30 (Sun 12–3)
Restaurant L served Mon-Sat 12–2 D served Mon-Sat 6.30–9.30 (Sun 12–3, 6.30–9)
⊕ Punch Taverns ◀ Greene King IPA, Adnams Best & Broadside.
♀ 11
Facilities Garden Parking

ORFORD continued

King's Head

Front St IP12 2LW ☎ 01394 450271

e-mail: ian_thornton@talk21.com

dir: From Woodbridge follow signs for Orford Castle on B1084. Through Butley & Chillesford on to Orford

An inn with a smuggling history, The King's Head stands on the old market square, a short walk from the quay. The atmospheric interior includes a beamed bar serving Adnams ales, and a wood-floored restaurant offering plenty of local produce. Typical starters include garlic mushrooms, whitebait, and smoked mackerel, followed perhaps by 'boozy beef' (made with Adnams ale); cod in beer batter; or vegetable stir fry. Bar snacks include sandwiches, burgers and things with chips.

Open 11.30–3 6–11 **Bar Meals** L served all week 12–2 D served all week 6–9 (Sun 12–2.45, 7–9) Av main course £7.25 **Restaurant** L served all week 12–2 D served all week 6–9 (Sun 12–2.30, 7–9) Av 3 course à la carte £14 ⊕ Adnams ◀ Adnams Bitter, Adnams Broadside, Adnams Regatta, Adnams Tally Ho & Adnams Explorer. **Facilities** Garden Dogs allowed Parking

---

POLSTEAD   MAP 13 TL93

Pick of the Pubs

The Cock Inn ♥

The Green CO6 5AL ☎ 01206 263150 ▤ 01206 263150

dir: Colchester/A134 towards Sudbury then right, follow signs to Polstead

There has been a change of hands at this delightful 17th-century pub, which stands in award-winning gardens overlooking the village green. It is a lovely place to sit outside in summer, with a play area for children. Inside is an oak beamed and quarry-tiled bar with log fires in winter, and a restaurant in the Victorian extension. The food – locally sourced where possible – is constantly changing, but Suffolk huffers are a menu fixture – large triangle-shaped rolls with a wide choice of fillings. Also from the bar menu come lasagne and garlic bread, steak and ale pies (both home made), and beer-battered fish and chips. The carte features fillet steak with thick hand cut chips, and fillet of salmon on a bed of creamed spinach and fondant potatoes. Eton mess and crème brûlée might finish a meal. Thursday is senior citizens' day and Friday is fresh fish day. Regular events include quiz nights, poetry evenings and barbecues.

Open 12–3 6–11 (Sat-Sun all day, Apr-Sep, Sun & BH 12–3 6–10.30) **Bar Meals** L served Tue-Sat 12–3 D served Tue-Sat 6.30–9.30 (Sun 12–2.30, 6.30–9 all day in Summer) Av main course £7.99 **Restaurant** L served Tue-Sat 12–3 D served Tue-Sat 6.30–9.30 (Sun 12–2.30, 6.30–9 & all day in Summer) Av 3 course à la carte £20 ⊕ Free House ◀ Greene King IPA, Adnams, Ansels Mild & Guinness. ♥8 **Facilities** Garden Dogs allowed Parking Play Area

---

REDE   MAP 13 TL85

The Plough

IP29 4BE ☎ 01284 789208

dir: On A143 between Bury St Edmunds & Haverhill

A picture-postcard half-thatched 16th-century pub, with an old plough outside. A revamp has given the building a cream exterior and restored the beams to their original colour, promoting a fresher, more open feel inside. Light snacks in the form of carpaccio of wild boar or grilled scallops are backed by an adventurous array of blackboard-listed dishes: grilled sea bass with a cream and bacon sauce; wild woodpigeon with lentils; and traditional country recipes with a Mediterranean twist like lamb, olive and artichoke stew.

Open 11–3 6.30–11 **Bar Meals** L served all week 12–2 D served Mon-Sat 7–9 **Restaurant** L served all week 12–2 D served Mon-Sat 7–9 ◀ Greene King IPA, Abbot Ale, London Pride & Adnams. **Facilities** Garden Parking

---

ST PETER SOUTH ELMHAM   MAP 13 TM38

Pick of the Pubs

Wicked at St Peter's Hall ♥

NR35 1NQ ☎ 01986 782288 ▤ 01986 782505

e-mail: mail@wickedlygoodfoodltd.co.uk

dir: From A143/A144 follow brown signs to St Peter's Brewery

A pub and brewery in a magnificent moated hall that originally dates from 1280. In 1539 it was enlarged using stones salvaged from nearby Flixton Priory, destroyed during the Dissolution. Look for the chapel above the porch, the carvings on the façade, and the tombstone in the entrance, not to mention the stone floors, lofty ceilings, and period furnishings. The brewery, which you can visit, produces seventeen (yes, seventeen) different beers, and is housed in what until 1996 were long-derelict former agricultural buildings. Starters may include home-made game paté with spiced ale chutney; and stilton, grape and spicy olive salad with wholegrain mustard dressing. There are usually six to eight main courses, among them St Peter's steak and ale pie; pork fillet in sage and white wine cream sauce; and plaice fillet with lemon and dill cream sauce. For vegetarians, there's wild mushroom risotto with truffle oil, lemon and thyme.

Open 12–3 6–11 (Sat-Sun & BH all day) **Bar Meals** L served Mon-Sat 12–3 D served Mon-Sat 6.30–9.30 (Sun 11–4) Av main course £10 **Restaurant** L served all week 12–3 D served all week 6.30–9.30 Av 3 course à la carte £28 ⊕ St Peters Brewery ◀ Golden Ale, Organic Ale, Grapefruit ale, Cream Stout. ♥20 **Facilities** Garden Parking

SNAPE
MAP 13 TM35

Pick of the Pubs

The Crown Inn ♀

Bridge Rd IP17 1SL ☎ 01728 688324

e-mail: snapecrown@tiscali.co.uk

dir: *A12 N to Lowestoft, right to Aldeburgh, then right again in Snape at x-rds by church, pub at bottom hill.*

Visitors to Snape Maltings, home of the Aldeburgh Music Festival, will find this 15th-century former smugglers' inn perfect for a pre- or post-concert dinner. Set close to the River Alde, the pub is highly atmospheric, with abundant old beams, brick floors and, around the large inglenook, a very fine double Suffolk settle. Once installed, you'll realise (at least on a cold day) just how wonderful burning logs sound when there is no gaming machine or piped music to drown the crackles. Modern British menus, with daily specials, include starters of rope-grown Shetland mussels with Aspall's cider; and warm leek and rosemary tart. Main courses might be home-reared pork sausages, mash and shallot gravy; rib-eye steak with flat mushroom and tomato; and crisp battered cod and chips. For pudding, iced coconut parfait with red chilli-marinated pineapple may be on the menu. A dozen or so wines are available by the glass.

Open 12–3 6–11 **Bar Meals** L served Mon-Fri 12–2.30 D served Mon-Fri 6–9.30 (Sat-Sun 12–3, Sat 6–10) Av main course £10 **Restaurant** L served Mon-Fri 12–2.30 D served Mon-Fri 6–9.30 (Sat-Sun 12–3, 6–10) ⊕ Adnams ◀ Adnams Best, Broadside, Old Ale, Regatta. ♀ 18 **Facilities** Garden Dogs allowed Parking

The Golden Key ♀

Priory Ln IP17 1SQ ☎ 01728 688510

dir: *Telephone for directions*

Since taking the helm in 2006 landlord Nick Attfield has seen the Golden Key through an extensive refurbishment and redecoration program aimed at returning the 17th-century building to its former glory. Today it retains its identity as a true local but has a fast-growing reputation for food. You could dine on Aldeburgh crab and spring onion fishcakes, followed by local lamb chops with fondant potatoes, braised red cabbage and rosemary jus.

Open 12–3 6–11 **Bar Meals** L served Mon-Sat 12–2 D served Mon-Sat 6–9 (Sun 12–2.30, 7–9) Av main course £10 **Restaurant** L served Mon-Sat 12–2 D served Mon-Sat 6–9 (Sun 12–2.30, 7–9) Av 3 course à la carte £22 ⊕ Adnams ◀ Adnams Bitter, Broadside & Explorer. ♀ 12 **Facilities** Garden Dogs allowed Parking

Plough & Sail ♀

Snape Maltings IP17 1SR

☎ 01728 688413 📠 01728 688930

e-mail: enquiries@snapemaltings.co.uk

dir: *Snape Maltings on B1069 S of Snape. Signed from A12*

An enjoyable and popular part of any visit to Snape Maltings, the Plough and Sail rubs shoulders with the famous concert hall, art gallery and shops. The rambling interior includes a restaurant, and the large terrace provides summer seating. Sweet potato moussaka or wild boar sausages with green pea mash are typical light lunches, whilst evening

diners might expect a slow braised lamb shank, or baked cod with Welsh rarebit and creamed leeks.

Open 11–3 5.30–11 **Bar Meals** L served all week 12–2.30 **Restaurant** L served all week 12–2.30 D served all week 7–9 (Sat-Sun 7–9.30) ⊕ Free House ◀ Adnams Broadside, Adnams Bitter, Explorer, Fishermans. ♀ 10 **Facilities** Garden Dogs allowed Parking

SOUTHWOLD
MAP 13 TM57

Pick of the Pubs

The Crown Hotel ★★ HL ⊕ ♀

The High St IP18 6DP

☎ 01502 722275 📠 01502 727263

e-mail: crown.hotel@adnams.co.uk

dir: *A12 onto A1095 to Southwold. Into town centre, pub on left*

As the flagship operation for Adnams' brewery, the Crown fulfils the roles of pub, wine bar, eatery and small hotel. Originally a posting inn dating from 1750, it offers a wide selection of Adnams' ales, with some 20 wines by the glass. Alternatively you can visit the cellar and kitchen store in the hotel yard for a full selection of wines and bottled beers. The bar area has been expanded, so the whole place buzzes with lively informality as blue-shirted waiting staff attend to customers installed on green leather cushioned settles or at the green-washed oak-panelled bar. It's a popular place, especially in summer when customers are queueing at the door. The seaside location means seafood is well represented, with roasted fillet of hake or seared sea bass. Land-based options may include braised lamb sweetbreads or roast local partridge, Norfolk smoked eel, or confit of rabbit ravioli. Excellent puddings include warm treacle tart with clotted cream.

Open 8–3 6–11 (all day during peak times) **Bar Meals** L served all week 12–2.30 D served all week 6.30–9.30 Av main course £13 ⊕ Adnams ◀ Adnams Ales. ♀ 20 **Facilities** Children's licence Parking **Rooms** 14

The Randolph ⊕ ♀

41 Wangford Rd, Reydon IP18 6PZ

☎ 01502 723603 📠 01502 722194

e-mail: reception@therandolph.co.uk

dir: *A1095 from A12 at Blythburgh 4m, Southwold 1m from Darsham Train Station.*

This grand late-Victorian pile in large gardens was built by Adnams, the ubiquitous local brewers, who named it after Lord Randolph Churchill, Sir Winston's father. Standing just out of town, it successfully combines its functions as pub, restaurant and hotel; more accurately perhaps, this happy state of affairs is all down to owners David and Donna Smith. Their menus are full of interesting twists.

Open 11–11 **Bar Meals** L served all week 12–2 D served all week 6.30–9 **Restaurant** L served all week 12–2 D served all week 6.30–9 ◀ Adnams Bitter, Adnams Broadside. ♀ 6 **Facilities** Garden Parking **Rooms** available

STANTON   MAP 13 TL97

The Rose & Crown

Bury Rd IP31 2BZ ☎ 01359 250236

dir: *On A413 from Bury St Edmunds towards Diss*

Three acres of landscaped grounds surround this 16th-century coaching inn. Curl up on one of the comfy sofas in the split-level bar for a pint of locally brewed Adnam's Broadside, before perusing a menu that offers the likes of seared scallop, chorizo and black pudding salad; glazed pork loin chops; and sea bass with crayfish and saffron risotto. The adjoining Cobbled Barn is a popular spot for weddings and parties.

Bar Meals L served Mon-Sat 12–3 D served all week 6–10 Av main course £9.95 **Restaurant** L served all week 12–3 D served all week 6–10 Av 3 course à la carte £18 ⊕ Punch Taverns ◀ Greene King IPA, Adnams Broadside, Guinness. **Facilities** Garden Parking Play Area

---

STOKE-BY-NAYLAND   MAP 13 TL93

Pick of the Pubs

The Angel Inn Ⓤ ◉ ♥

CO6 4SA ☎ 01206 263245 📄 01206 263373
e-mail: the.angel@tiscali.co.uk

dir: *From A12 take Colchester right turn, then A134, 5m to Nayland. From A12 S take B1068*

Set in a landscape immortalised in the paintings of local artist, John Constable, the Angel is a 16th-century inn with beamed bars, log fires and a long tradition of hospitality. The relaxed, modern feel extends to the air-conditioned conservatory, the patio and sun terrace. Tables for lunch and dinner may be reserved in The Well Room, which has a high ceiling open to the rafters, a gallery leading to the pub's accommodation, rough brick and timber studded walls, and the well itself, fully 52 feet deep. Eating in the bar, by comparison, is on a strictly first-come, first-served basis but the same menu is served throughout. Starters might feature baked goats' cheese with roasted field mushroom, beefsteak tomato and red onion confit for example. Main courses offer a range of meat, seafood and vegetarian options, typically including griddled whole plaice served with salad and French fries. There is an extensive wine list.

Open 11–11 **Bar Meals** L served all week 12–2 D served all week 6.30–9.30 (Sun 12–5, 5.30–9.30) **Restaurant** L served all week 12–2 D served all week 6.30–9.30 (Sun 12–5, 5.30–9.30) ⊕ Free House ◀ Greene King IPA & Abbot Ale, Adnams Best. ♥ 9 **Facilities** Garden Parking **Rooms** 6

Pick of the Pubs

The Crown ◉◉ ♥

CO6 4SE ☎ 01206 262001 📄 01206 264026
e-mail: thecrown@eoinns.co.uk

dir: *Exit A12 signed Stratford St Mary/Dedham. Through Stratford St Mary 0.5m, left, follow signs to Higham. At village green turn left, left again 2m, pub on right*

From this modernised and extended mid-16th century village inn you can see over the Box Valley, one of the most beautiful parts of Suffolk. Wherever possible, local produce is the basis for a monthly changing modern British menu, all freshly prepared by a team of eleven chefs. Typically available might be local wild rabbit, bacon and onion pie; smoked haddock, horseradish mash and poached egg; roast chicken breast, wild mushroom pappardelle, sage and brandy cream; and deep-fried goat's cheese with roasted beetroot, artichoke heart and butternut squash. Consult the blackboard for the day's fresh fish, mostly landed on the East Coast, and never ever frozen. Every dish is given its 'wine match' – Sauvignon Blanc in the case of smoked haddock, for instance. Another sign of the owner's passion for wine is his wine shop, where bottles may be bought to accompany a meal or to take away.

Open 11–11 (Sun 12–10.30) Closed: 25–26 Dec **Bar Meals** L served Mon-Sat 12–2.30 D served Mon-Thu 6–9.30 (Fri-Sat 12–2.30 6–10, Sun 12–9) **Restaurant** L served all week 12–2.30 D served all week 6–9.30 (Fri-Sat 12–12.30 6–10, Sun & BH 12–9) Av 3 course à la carte £23.50 ⊕ Free House ◀ Adnams Best Bitter, Greene King IPA, Guinness, guest ales. ♥ 28 **Facilities** Garden Dogs allowed Parking

STOWMARKET MAP 13 TM05

Pick of the Pubs

The Buxhall Crown ♀

Mill Rd, Buxhall IP14 3DW ☎ 01449 736521

dir: *Telephone for directions*

A 17th-century building that has been transformed from just another rundown village local into one of East Anglia's most welcoming and applauded gastro-pubs, now under new management. Hand-pumped real ales and an extensive wine list complement an interesting and varied menu that changes every few weeks. Fire up your palate with shredded duck and hoi sin sauce pancake rolls; or a simple, warm smoked chicken Caesar salad. Main courses range from the ever-popular haddock in beer batter with home-cut chips to more adventurous fare: try chestnut potato cakes with rarebit topping and port sauce; roasted lambs' hearts with apricot stuffing, mashed potato and red wine gravy; or suet crust game pie with juniper gravy and seasonal vegetables.

Open 12–3 6.30–11 Closed: Sun eve & Mon **Bar Meals** L served Tue–Sun 12–2 D served Tue–Sat 6.30–9.30 **Restaurant** L served Tue–Sun 12–2 D served Tue–Sat 6.30–9.30 ⊕ Greene King ◀ Greene King IPA, Woodforde's Wherry, Tindals Best Bitter, Cox & Holbrook. ♀ 10 **Facilities** Garden Dogs allowed Parking

STRADBROKE MAP 13 TM27

The Ivy House ♀

Wilby Rd IP21 5JN ☎ 01379 384634

e-mail: stensethhome@aol.com

A grade two listed thatched pub just off the main street in Stradbroke. The separate restaurant has been recently refurbished to include beech tables and chairs and white china. There's an extensive wine list plus an impressive, daily changing menu that makes good use of local produce. Typical dishes include crayfish salad with lemon dressing followed by roast Gressingham duck breast with stir-fried vegetables, noodles and plum sauce. Outside is a lawn and pond.

Open 12–2.30 6–11 **Restaurant** L served all week 12–2 D served all week 6.30–9 ⊕ Free House ◀ Adnams, Woodtorde's, Buffy's. ♀ 7 **Facilities** Garden Dogs allowed Parking

SWILLAND MAP 13 TM15

Moon & Mushroom Inn ♀

High Rd IP6 9LR ☎ 01473 785320

e-mail: nikki@ecocleen.fsnet.co.uk

dir: *6m N of Ipswich on Westerfield road*

This 300–year-old free house has a reputation as 'the pub that time passed by', and the owners intend to keep it that way. Winter fires, good company and a choice of six East Anglian ales straight from the barrel all play their part. Steaks and fish and chips with mushy peas are staples, while ever popular are beef in ale with dumplings; pan-fried partridge breast; shoulder of lamb; and a good vegetarian selection.

Open 11.30–2.30 6–11 (Sun 12–3 & 7–10.30) **Bar Meals** L served Tue–Sat 12–2 D served Tue–Sat 6.30–9 (Sun 12–3) Av main course £7.95 **Restaurant** L served Tue–Sun 12–2 D served Tue–Sat 6.30–9 Av 3 course à la carte £18 ⊕ Free House ◀ Nethergate Suffolk County, Woodfords Wherry, Buffy's Hopleaf, Brewers Gold. ♀ 10 **Facilities** Garden Dogs allowed Parking

THORPENESS MAP 13 TM45

The Dolphin Inn ♀

Peace Place IP16 4NA ☎ 01728 454994

e-mail: info@thorpenessdolphin.com

dir: *A12 onto A1094 & follow Thorpeness signs*

In the heart of Thorpeness, this traditional village inn offers good food, and alfresco dining in the summer. Pan-fried pigeon breasts are served as a starter with red pepper dressing; lamb kleftiko is marinated in red wine and served the Cypriot way with onions, herbs, rice and Greek salad; and there's a fish selection too.

Open 11–3 6–11 Restricted hours in winter **Bar Meals** L served all week 12–2 D served all week 6.30–9 Av main course £9 **Restaurant** L served all week 12–2 D served all week 6.30–9 Av 3 course à la carte £18 ◀ Adnams Best, Adnams Broadside. ♀ 8 **Facilities** Garden Dogs allowed Parking

TOSTOCK MAP 13 TL96

Gardeners Arms

IP30 9PA ☎ 01359 270460

e-mail: robert.richards@btconnect.co.uk

dir: *A14 follow signs to Tostock, turn at slip road through Beyton. Left at T-junct over A14 turn left into Tostock. 1st right to end of road, pub on right*

Parts of this charming pub, at the end of the village green, near the horse chestnut tree, date back 600 years. The basic bar menu – salads, grills, ploughman's, sandwiches, toasties, etc – is supplemented by specials boards offering six starters and 12 main courses in the evening. Look out for lamb balti, Thai king prawn green curry, steak and kidney pie, and chicken and stilton roulade. There's a large grassy garden.

Open 11.30–3 6.30–11 (Sun 12–3.30, 7–10.30) **Bar Meals** L served all week 12–2.30 D served Mon–Sat 7–9 **Restaurant** L served all week 12–2.30 D served Mon–Sat 7–9 ⊕ Greene King ◀ Greene King IPA, Greene King Abbot, Greene King seasonal ales. **Facilities** Garden Parking

PICK OF THE PUBS

The Westleton Crown

Nestling in a quiet village close to the RSPB's Minsmere reserve, this atmospheric and hospitable inn is handy for exploring Suffolk's Heritage Coast and the picturesque towns of Southwold and Aldeburgh. Its origins date back to the 12th century when it belonged to nearby Sibton Abbey, before becoming a coaching inn in the 17th century.

Today the Westleton Crown has succeeded in combining the rustic charms of its heritage with the comforts of contemporary living. Inside you will find two crackling log fires, real ales and good wines. The team at the Crown are passionate about their cooking, for which two AA Rosettes have been awarded. Meals are prepared from fresh locally-sourced ingredients, and can be served in the parlour, the dining room or the conservatory. Starters and lighter dishes include warm salt-cured haddock topped with a prawn rarebit; and wild duck and pheasant terrine served with an Adnams beer and mixed fruit chutney. Main courses embrace steamed steak and kidney suet pudding; and poached breast and confit leg of guinea

fowl. At this stage seafood lovers will probably look to the specials list, which may proffer a grilled assiette of sea fish with a bacon and herb salad and buttered charlotte potatoes; a whole grilled East Coast plaice with a prawn, caper and herb butter; and the Crown's own smoked fish platter. Save some space for accomplished desserts like pear and blackberry crumble tart with custard; caramelised banana tarte Tatin with hazelnut ice cream; and steamed spotted dick. After a meal such as this, you may wish to repose in one of the 25 comfortable, individually styled and recently refurbished bedrooms complete with flat screen TV. Outside are large terraced gardens, floodlit in the evening.

★★★ HL ⊛⊛ ♀
MAP 13 TM46
The Street IP17 3AD
☎ 01728 648777
🖹 01728 648239
e-mail: reception@
westletoncrown.co.uk
dir: *Turn off A12 just past Yoxford N'bound, follow signs for Westleton for 2m*

Open 7 -11 (Sun 7.30–10.30)
Closed: 25 Dec
Bar Meals L served all week
12–2.30 D served all week 7–9.30
Av main course £16
Restaurant L served all week
12–2.30 D served all week 7–9.30
Av 3 course à la carte £25
⊕ Free House ◀ Adnams Bitter,
& range of real ales. ♀ 9
Facilities Garden Dogs allowed
Parking
Rooms 25

541

England

WALBERSWICK   MAP 13 TM47

Bell Inn ♟

Ferry Rd IP18 6TN ☎ 01502 723109 📠 01502 722728

e-mail: bellinn@btinternet.com

dir: *From A12 take B1387, follow to beyond village green, bear right down track*

The inn dates back 600 years and is located near the village green, beach and the ancient fishing harbour on the River Blyth. The large garden has beach and sea views, while inside, the building's great age is evident from the low beams, stone-flagged floors, high wooden settles and open fires. Food is all home cooked with local produce featuring strongly, particularly fresh fish. Specialities include starters of locally smoked sprats or Suffolk smokies – flaked smoked haddock in a creamy cheese sauce – both served with granary toast and a salad garnish. Among the main courses are grilled skate wing with caper and almond butter, new potatoes and mixed leaf salad, or Walberswick fish pie. There are non-fishy dishes too, like baked Suffolk ham, lamb burger in toasted ciabatta, hot and spicy chilli, and chargrilled sirloin steak. Snack lunches are also offered, and a further treat is afternoon tea in the bar, with a choice of teas, coffees and pastries.

Open 11–3 6–11 (Sun 12–10.30, Fri-Sat 6–12) **Bar Meals** L served all week 12–2 D served all week 6–9 (Sun 12–2.30, D in Winter 7–9) Av main course £8.50 **Restaurant** D served Fri-Sat 7–9 Av 3 course à la carte £25 ⊕ Adnams ◀ Adnams Best, Broadside, Regatta, Old Ale. ♟ 15 **Facilities** Garden Dogs allowed Parking

WESTLETON   MAP 13 TM46

The Westleton Crown ★★★ HL ◉◉ ♟

See Pick of the Pubs on page 541

SURREY

ABINGER   MAP 06 TQ14

The Volunteer ♟

Water Ln, Sutton RH5 6PR

☎ 01306 730798 📠 01306 731621

dir: *Between Guildford & Dorking, 1m S of A25*

Enjoying a delightful rural setting with views over the River Mole, this popular village pub was originally farm cottages and first licensed about 1870. An ideal watering hole for walkers who want to relax over a pint in the attractive pub garden. Typical fish dishes include lobster thermidor, Mediterranean squid pasta and fillet of sea bass, while Thai coconut chicken, partridge with red wine and junipers and fillet of braised beef on fennel feature among the meat dishes.

Open 11.30 -11 (Sun 12–10.30) **Bar Meals** L served all week 12–2.30 D served all week 6–9.30 (Sat 12–9.30, Sun 12–8) **Restaurant** L served all week 12–2.30 D served all week 6–9.30 (Sat 12–9.30, Sun 12–8) ⊕ Hall & Woodhouse ◀ Badger Tanglefoot, King & Barns Sussex, plus guest ales. ♟ 9 **Facilities** Garden Parking

The Bat and Ball Freehouse

Bat and Ball Lane, Boundstone, Farnham, Surrey GU10 4SA   *Tel: 01252 792108*
www.thebatandball.co.uk   *E-mail: info@thebatandball.co.uk*

The Bat and Ball Freehouse nestles in the bottom of the Bourne valley in Boundstone near Farnham. Over 150 years old, the Pub has a relaxed, rural feel, surrounded by woodland and wildlife, and is the focal point of 5 footpaths which connect to local villages. Customers can eat or drink throughout the Pub, patio area and the large south-facing garden (which backs onto the Bourne stream and has a popular children's play structure). All the food is cooked in-house and this is very much a pub that serves restaurant quality food and not a restaurant that sells beer! The bar area has both a traditional and modern style to it to provide for our differing customer tastes, both young and old, and we have a tempting selection of 6 well-kept Cask Ales.

ALBURY
MAP 06 TQ04

The Drummond Arms Inn ☻

The Street GU5 9AG
☎ 01483 202039 📄 01483 205361
e-mail: info@thedrummondarms.co.uk
dir: *6m from Guildford*

Triple gables at the second-floor level add an interesting architectural twist to this village pub, set in an attractive garden overlooking the River Tillingbourne. The menu offers sandwiches, old favourites (fish and chips; sausage and mash), and regular main courses such as braised lamb shank, or chicken New Yorker (with barbecue sauce and mozzarella cheese); fish dishes feature strongly. There is also a choice of daily specials.

Open 11–11 **Bar Meals** L served all week 12–2.30 D served Mon-Sat 6.30–9.30 (Sun 12–6, Summer 12–9) Av main course £10 **Restaurant** L served all week 12–2.30 D served Mon-Sat 7–9.30 (Sun 12–6, Summer 12–9) Av 3 course à la carte £20 ⊕ Merlin Inns Ltd ◀ Courage Best, Fuller's HSB, Old Speckled Hen & Shere Drop. ☻ 8 **Facilities** Garden Parking

William IV

Little London GU5 9DG ☎ 01483 202685
dir: *Just off A25 between Guildford & Dorking. Near Shere*

A quaint country pub just a stone's throw from Guildford, yet deep in the heart of the Surrey countryside. The area is great for hiking and the pub is popular with walkers, partly due to its attractive garden, which is ideal for post-ramble relaxation. A choice of real ales and a blackboard menu that changes daily are also part of the attraction. Expect steak and kidney pie, pot-roast lamb shank, battered cod and chips, and Sunday roasts.

Open 11–3 5.30–11 (Sun 12–3, 7–10.30) Closed: 25 Dec **Bar Meals** L served all week 12–2 D served Mon-Sat 7–9 Av main course £9 **Restaurant** L served all week 12–2 D served Mon-Sat 7–9 Av 3 course à la carte £17.20 ⊕ Free House ◀ Flowers IPA, Hogs Back, Surrey Hills Brewery. **Facilities** Garden Dogs allowed Parking

BETCHWORTH
MAP 06 TQ25

The Red Lion Ⓤ ☻

Old Reigate Rd RH3 7DS
☎ 01737 843336 📄 01737 845242
e-mail: info@redlion-betchworth.com
dir: *Telephone for directions*

Set in 18 acres with a cricket ground and rolling countryside views, this award-winning, 200–year-old pub offers an extensive menu. Beyond baguettes and ploughman's lunches the choice includes sole and smoked salmon, Barbary duck breast, aubergine and broccoli fritters, deep-fried plaice and chips, Toulouse sausage and mash, and steak and ale pie. The area is ideal for walkers.

Open 12–11.30 (Sun 12–11) **Bar Meals** L served all week 12–3 D served all week 6–10 (Sun 12–9.30) Av main course £9 **Restaurant** L served all week 12–3 D served all week 6–10 (Sun 12–9.30) ⊕ Punch Taverns ◀ Fuller's London Pride, Greene King, IPA, Adnams Broadside. ☻ 6 **Facilities** Garden Parking

BLACKBROOK
MAP 06 TQ14

The Plough at Blackbrook ☻

RH5 4DS ☎ 01306 886603 📄 01306 886603
dir: *A24 to Dorking, then towards Horsham, 0.75m from Deepdene rdbt left to Blackbrook*

Once a coaching inn and a popular haunt of highwaymen, this pub offers outstanding views and a charming cottage garden. The ever-changing menu may include rabbit and bacon pie; roast herb crusted rack of lamb with a red wine jus; and baked spinach and potato dauphinoise. Alternatively, try moussaka, chilli and rice, sirloin steak or deep-fried battered cod and chips. Jacket potatoes, ploughman's and toasted deli bagels round off the appetising menu.

Open 11–3 6–11 (Sun 12–10.30) Closed: 25–26 Dec, 1 Jan **Bar Meals** L served all week 12–2 D served Tue-Sat 7–9 **Restaurant** L served Mon-Sun 12–2 D served Tue-Sat 7–9 (Sun 12–4) Av 3 course à la carte £25 ⊕ Hall & Woodhouse ◀ Badger King & Barnes Sussex, Tanglefoot, Badger Best, Fursty Ferret & Festive Feasant. ☻ 18 **Facilities** Children's licence Garden Dogs allowed Parking Play Area

BLACKHEATH
MAP 06 TQ04

The Villagers Inn

Blackheath Ln GU4 8RB ☎ 01483 893152
e-mail: kbrampton@ringstead.co.uk

More than a hundred years old, this free house stands on the edge of Blackheath, a natural woodland area of several square miles in the heart of Surrey. A menu of traditional pub food includes steak and kidney pie, chicken pie, and fillet steak. A covered patio extends the opportunity for alfresco dining. Real ales are represented by London Pride, Hair of the Dog and Youngers Special.

Open 12–3 6–11 (Fri-Sat 12–11, Sun 12–10.30) **Bar Meals** L served all week 12–2.30 D served all week 6–9 Sun all day Av main course £7 **Restaurant** L served all week 12–2.30 D served all week 6–9 Av 3 course à la carte £16 ◀ T.E.A, London Pride, Youngs Special, Teardrop. **Facilities** Garden Dogs allowed Parking Play Area

England

BRAMLEY   **MAP 06 TQ04**

Jolly Farmer Inn ♥

High St GU5 0HB ☎ 01483 893355 📠 01483 890484

e-mail: enquiries@jollyfarmer.co.uk

dir: *From Guildford take A281 (Horsham road). Bramley 3.5m S of Guildford*

The family that own this friendly 16th-century free house have a passion for cask ales, and you'll always find up to eight real ales and six lagers, as well as an impressive range of Belgian bottled beers. All meals are freshly cooked to order: expect the likes of slow-roast chicken supreme; seafood tagliatelle; and wild boar steak with foie gras on the specials board, alongside old favourites such as burgers and grills.

Open 11–12.30 (Sun 12–12) **Bar Meals** L served all week 12–2.30 D served Mon-Sat 6.30–10 (Sun 7–9.30) Av main course £11 **Restaurant** L served all week 12–2.15 D served Mon-Sat 6.30–10 (Sun 7–9.30) Av 3 course à la carte £22 ⊕ Free House ◀ 8 continually changing cask ales. ♥ 16 **Facilities** Garden Dogs allowed Parking

CHIDDINGFOLD   **MAP 06 SU93**

The Crown Inn ♥

The Green GU8 4TX ☎ 01428 682255 📠 01428 685736

dir: *On A283 between Milford & Petworth*

Historic inn, dating back over 700 years, with lots of charming features, including ancient panelling, open fires, distinctive carvings and huge beams. Reliable food ranges from sausage and mash with onion gravy, chicken tagliatelle, freshly battered fish and chips, and decent sandwiches, warm salads and ploughman's at lunchtime, to Torbay sole, monkfish and tiger prawns pan-fried with ginger and lime cream sauce and served on tagliatelle, and roast duck with sweet plum sauce on the evening menu.

Open 11–11 (Sun 12–10.30) **Bar Meals** L served 12–3 D served Mon-Sat 6.30–9.30 (Sun 12–9) Av main course £9.95 **Restaurant** L served all week 12–3 D served Wed-Sun 6.30–9.30 ⊕ Hall & Woodhouse ◀ London Pride, Moon Dance, Crown Bitter, Summer Lightning. ♥ 9 **Facilities** Garden Dogs allowed

The Swan Inn & Restaurant ★★★★ INN ♥

Petworth Rd GU8 4TY ☎ 01428 682073 📠 01428 683259

e-mail: the-swan-inn@btconnect.com

dir: *10m from Guildford city centre. Between Petworth & Godalming on A283*

This appealing 14th-century village pub successfully manages to balance the traditional and contemporary, with bare floors, wooden furniture and big leather sofas giving a relaxed, stylish feel. The chef makes impressive use of quality produce: look out for lamb shank; Cumberland sausages; tournados of poached or roast salmon; and rib-eye steak with spinach, fries and peppercorn sauce.

Open 11–11 (Sun 12–10.30) **Bar Meals** L served all week 12–2.30 D served all week 6.30–10 **Restaurant** L served Mon-Fri 12–2.30 D served all week 6.30–10 (Sat-Sun 12–3) ⊕ Free House ◀ Hogs Back TEA, Ringwood Best, Fuller's London Pride. ♥ 15 **Facilities** Garden Parking **Rooms** 11

CHURT   **MAP 05 SU83**

Pick of the Pubs

Pride of the Valley ♥

Tilford Rd GU10 2LH

☎ 01428 605799 📠 01428 605875

e-mail: reservations@prideofthevalleyhotel.com

dir: *4m from Farnham on outskirts of Churt Valley*

Named after a local beauty spot, this charming and traditional inn sits in the heart of the Surrey countryside within its own idyllic country garden. Built in 1867, it enjoyed the regular patronage of David Lloyd George and then Britain's first Formula One champion Mike Hawthorn when they lived nearby. At the bar you'll find a mix of local ales and international beers, together with a tasty bar menu: home-cured gravadlax or beer-battered tiger prawns for the smaller appetite; pie of the day, chicken Caesar salad, or organic rump steak with fries for the more hungry. The restaurant menu is refreshingly concise, but steps up a gear or two in complexity: pan-seared chicken livers, pancetta and dressed leaves as a starter could be followed by a grilled fillet of West County ling with kale and moules à la crème. Choose from desserts such as chocolate brownie with hot chocolate sauce.

Open 10.30–11 **Bar Meals** L served all week 12–2.30 D served all week 6.30–9.30 **Restaurant** L served all week 12–2.30 D served all week 6.30–9.30 ⊕ Free House ◀ Doom Bar, Hogs Back brewery ales. ♥ 8 **Facilities** Garden Dogs allowed Parking

CLAYGATE   **MAP 06 TQ16**

Swan Inn & Lodge ♥

2 Hare Ln KT10 9BS ☎ 01372 462582 📠 01372 467089

e-mail: info@theswanlodge.co.uk

dir: *At Esher/Oxshott junct of A3 take A244 towards Esher. Right at 1st lights, pub 300yds on right*

Rebuilt in 1905 overlooking the village green and cricket pitch, yet barely 15 miles from Charing Cross. There's an attractively furnished Continental-style bar and a Thai restaurant offering nearly 75 starters, soups, curries, stir-fries, and seafoods. The Thai menu is available at lunchtime and in the evenings, as are calamari, Cajun chicken burgers, scampi, roast beef and lamb, and paninis. Dishes of the day appear on the specials board.

Open 11–11.30 **Bar Meals** L served all week 12–2.30 D served Mon-Sat 6–10.30 (Sun 12–4) Av main course £5 **Restaurant** L served all week 12–2.30 D served Mon-Sat 6–10.30 (Sun 12–4) Av 3 course à la carte £13.50 ⊕ Wellington Pub Co ◀ London Pride, Adnams, Brakspear. ♥ 8 **Facilities** Children's licence Garden Dogs allowed Parking Play Area

---

COBHAM   MAP 06 TQ16

The Cricketers ♥

Downside KT11 3NX ☎ 01932 862105 🖹 01932 868186
e-mail: info@thecricketersdownside.co.uk

dir: *M25 junct 10, A3 towards London. 1st exit signed Cobham. Straight over 1st rdbt, right at 2nd. In 1m right opposite Waitrose into Downside Bridge Rd*

Traditional, family-run pub, parts of which date back to 1540, with beamed ceilings and log fires. The inn's charming rural setting makes it popular with walkers, and the pretty River Mole is close by. There is a salad and light meals menu, with dishes like fishcakes and Barnsley chops. The main menu offers pan-fried cod fillet with saffron mash, steamed mussels and creamy sorrel sauce, or lamb shank cooked in aromatics and red wine sauce.

Open 11–11 (Sun 12–10.30) **Bar Meals** L served Mon-Sat 12–3 D served Mon-Sat 6.30–10 (Sun 12–8) **Restaurant** L served Sun 12–4 D served Thu-Sat 6.30–10 ⊕ Enterprise Inns ◀ Speckled Hen, London Pride, IPA . ♥ 9 **Facilities** Children's licence Garden Dogs allowed Parking Play Area

---

COLDHARBOUR   MAP 06 TQ14

Pick of the Pubs

The Plough Inn ♥

Coldharbour Ln RH5 6HD
☎ 01306 711793 🖹 01306 710055
e-mail: ploughinn@btinternet.com

dir: *M25 junct 9, A24 to Dorking. A25 towards Guildford. Coldharbour signed from one-way system*

For fifteen years, the husband-and-wife owners of this 17th-century pub have been slowly rebuilding, refurbishing and upgrading it to create a warm, welcoming hostelry with superb food, and ~ since 1996 ~ its own real ales. This labour of love perhaps results from the air here – the pub is 25 minutes walk from the top of Leith Hill, southern England's highest point. A well-worn smugglers' route from the coast to London once passed its door, which probably explains why the resident ghost is a matelot. The surrounding North Downs draw customers in the shape of walkers, horseback riders, cyclists, and Londoners simply anxious to escape the city and relax in convivial surroundings. Food is freshly prepared and home cooked, while three real fires in winter and candlelight in the evenings create a suitable ambience. On the menu fish dishes are always plentiful, and could feature pan-fried baby squid, grilled sardines, and monkfish. Other representative dishes are confit of duck; braised beef with onions in home-brewed porter; and pork fillet with fresh asparagus roulade. Desserts like apple and red fruit crumble with custard are

irresistible; and the collection of fine wines completes a thoroughly agreeable experience.

Open 11.30–11 Closed: 25 Dec **Bar Meals** L served all week 12–2.30 D served all week 6.30–9.30 (Sun 6–9) Av main course £9.50 **Restaurant** L served all week 12–2.30 D served all week 6.30–9.30 (Sun 6.30–9) Av 3 course à la carte £21.50 ⊕ Free House ◀ Crooked Furrow, Leith Hill Tallywhacker, Ringwood Old Thumper, Timothy Taylor Landlord. ♥ 8 **Facilities** Children's licence Garden Dogs allowed Parking

---

COMPTON   MAP 06 SU94

The Withies Inn ♥

Withies Ln GU3 1JA ☎ 01483 421158 🖹 01483 425904

dir: *Telephone for directions*

Set amid unspoiled country on Compton Common, just below the Hog's Back, this low-beamed, 16th-century pub has been carefully modernised to incorporate a small restaurant. There is also a splendid garden where meals are served in the pergola. Snacks are available in the bar, while in the restaurant there is a selection from the chargrill, and dishes such as roast duckling with orange sauce; rack of lamb with rosemary; and scampi meunière with mushrooms.

Open 11–3 6–11 Closed: Sun eve **Bar Meals** L served all week 12–2.30 D served Mon-Sat 7–10.30 Av main course £5.25 **Restaurant** L served all week 12–2.30 D served Mon-Sat 7–10 Av 3 course à la carte £30 ⊕ Free House ◀ TEA, Sussex & Adnams. ♥ 8 **Facilities** Garden Dogs allowed Parking

---

DORKING   MAP 06 TQ14

Pick of the Pubs

The Stephan Langton ♥

Friday St, Abinger Common RH5 6JR ☎ 01306 730775
e-mail: info@stephan-langton.co.uk

dir: *Exit A25 between Dorking & Guildford at Hollow Lane, W of Wootton. 1.5m then left into Friday St. At end of hill right at pond*

In a tranquil valley, this unspoilt brick and timber country pub is named after a 13th-century local boy who later, as Archbishop of Canterbury, helped draw up the Magna Carta, a copy of which is pinned to a wall. Although looking much older, it wasn't built until the 1930s, after its predecessor burnt down. The lunchtime food, like the décor, is unpretentious, but will go down well following a strenuous walk through some of Surrey's most challenging terrain, not least Leith Hill, the highest summit in south-east England. Rabbit pie, pigeon breasts and other game are often on the menu, while classics include Abinger watercress soup; sausage and mash; corned beef hash; and home-made pork pie and piccalilli. In the evening more elaborate cuisine on offer might include breast of Gressingham duck with rösti potato and pickled beetroot. Surrey Hills Ranmore Ale and Hogs Back TEA are the local beers.

Open 11–3 5–11 (Sat-Sun 11–11) **Bar Meals** L served Tue-Sun 12.30–2.30 D served Tue-Sat 7–9 Av main course £12 **Restaurant** L served Tue-Sun 12.30–2.30 D served Tue-Sat 7–9 Av 3 course à la carte £30 ⊕ Free House ◀ Fuller's London Pride, Hogsback Tea, Ranmore Ale. ♥ 14 **Facilities** Children's licence Garden Dogs allowed Parking

England

DUNSFOLD
MAP 06 TQ03

The Sun Inn ♥
The Common GU8 4LE
☎ 01483 200242 🖹 01483 201141
e-mail: suninn@dunsfold.net
dir: *A281 through Shalford & Bramley, take B2130 to Godalming. Dunsfold on left after 2m*

In the summer you can hear the sound of willow on leather coming from the cricket green opposite this 500-year-old family-run inn. Inside you'll find a warm welcome, blazing fires and a broad selection of home-made food. Dishes range from sausages and mash, or steak burgers with a variety of toppings, through to Thai fish cakes with sweet chilli dipping sauce. Regular live music and quiz nights.

Open 11–3 5–12 (Fri-Sat 11–1am, Sun 12–12.30am) **Bar Meals** L served all week 12–2.30 D served Mon-Sat 7–9.15 (Sun 7–8.30)
Restaurant L served all week 12–2.30 D served Mon-Sat 7–9.15 (Sun 7–8.30) ⊕ Punch Taverns ◀ Harveys Sussex, Adnams, guest ales. ♥ 9
Facilities Garden Dogs allowed Parking

EFFINGHAM
MAP 06 TQ15

The Plough ♥
Orestan Ln KT24 5SW ☎ 01372 458121 🖹 01372 458121
dir: *Between Guildford & Leatherhead on A246*

A modern pub with a traditional feel, The Plough provides a peaceful retreat in a rural setting close to Polesden Lacy National Trust property. Home-cooked dishes include the likes of wild boar with mushroom sauce, bangers with spring onion mash and gravy, rib-eye steak, and pan-fried sea bass with saffron broth and green beans. Once owned by Jimmy Hanley and used in the 1960s TV series *Jim's Inn*, it also boasts a popular beer garden.

Open 11.30–3 5.30–11 (Sun 12–3, 7–10.30) Closed: 25–26 Dec & 1 Jan eve **Bar Meals** L served all week 12–2.30 D served all week 7–10 **Restaurant** L served all week 12–2.30 D served all week 7–10 ⊕ Young & Co ◀ Youngs IPA, Special, Winter Warmer, Bombardier. ♥ 12
Facilities Garden Parking

EGHAM
MAP 06 TQ07

The Fox and Hounds ♥
Bishopgate Rd, Englefield Green TW20 0XU
☎ 01784 433098 🖹 01784 438775
e-mail: thefoxandhounds@4cinns.co.uk
dir: *From village green left into Castle Hill Rd, then right into Bishopsgate Rd*

The Surrey border once ran through the centre of this pub, on the edge of Windsor Great Park, convenient for walkers and riders. Features include a large garden, handsome conservatory and weekly jazz nights. Menus offer a range of daily-changing fish specials as well as dishes like orange and sesame chicken fillets on coriander and lime noodles, or roast pork with grain mustard glaze and parmesan crisps.

Open 11–11 (Sun 12–10.30) (Fri-Sat, all day) **Bar Meals** L served all week 12–2.30 D served all week 6.30–9.30 Av main course £7
Restaurant L served all week 12–2.30 D served all week 6.30–10
◀ Hogsback Brewery Traditional English Ale, Brakspears Bitter. ♥ 8
Facilities Garden Dogs allowed Parking

ELSTEAD
MAP 06 SU94

Pick of the Pubs

The Woolpack ♥
See Pick of the Pubs on opposite page

EPSOM
MAP 06 TQ26

White Horse NEW ♥
63 Dorking Rd KT18 7JU ☎ 01372 726622
e-mail: enquiries@whitehorseepsom.com
dir: *On A24 next to Epsom General Hospital*

The town's oldest surviving pub focuses on four areas – real ales, freshly cooked traditional British food, being family friendly and, as host of the Epsom Jazz Club on Tuesday evenings, live entertainment. Typical starters are pork rillette with fruit chutney; and prawn platter; mains include chef's own pie of the week; pan-fried sea bass with rocket and lemon pesto dressing; and chicken and mature cheese wrap. Traditional roasts are available all day Sunday.

Open 11–11 (Tue, Fri & Sat 11–12, Sun 12–10) **Bar Meals** L served Mon-Fri 12–3 (Sun 12–6) Av main course £5 **Restaurant** L served Mon-Sat 12–3 D served Mon-Sat 6–9 (Sun 12–6) ⊕ Punch Taverns ◀ guest ales. ♥ 15 **Facilities** Children's licence Garden Dogs allowed Parking Play Area

PICK OF THE PUBS

ELSTEAD-SURREY

The Woolpack

Sheep were so plentiful round here in the 17th century that the area needed a wool exchange. Once in possession of this simple fact, it shouldn't take much to deduce from its name that this quaint old pub once performed that very function.

Times change, of course, and over the years the building has also been a butcher's shop, a bicycle repairer's and even the local Co-op, before becoming the popular pub it is today. The surrounding hundreds of acres of common land attract ramblers galore, especially at lunchtime, and their arrival in the bar is often heralded by the rustle of protective plastic shopping bags over their muddy boots. In the carpeted bar, weaving shuttles and other remnants of the wool industry make appealing features, as do the open log fires, low beams, high-backed settles, window seats and spindle-backed chairs. A good range of cask-conditioned beers is offered, and large blackboards display frequently changing main meals, sandwiches, ploughman's and burgers. An enthusiastic team of chefs produces menus planned around the best of local produce, taking account of the seasons. Lunchtime brings an extensive menu with a broad appeal, whilst in the evening a range of traditional pub food is served: perhaps crayfish and chardonnay tagliolini; a selection of steaks; smoked mackerel salad; pan-fried sea bass with couscous; and pork and leek sausages with mustard mash. A particularly good vegetarian selection includes cherry tomato and mozzarella risotto; leek and shiitake mushrooms en cro?te; and goats' cheese crostini with salad. An extensive range of fresh, home-made desserts is always on offer. A recent garden makeover now incorporates a children's play area.

MAP 06 SU94
The Green GU8 6HD
☎ 01252 703106
🖷 01252 705914
e-mail: woolpack.elstead@
yahoo.co.uk
dir: *A3 S, take Milford exit, follow signs for Elstead on B3001*

Open 12–3 5.30–11 (Sat 12–11, Sun 12–10.30)
Bar Meals L served Mon-Sat 12–2.30 D served Mon-Sat 7–9.30 (Sun 12–3, 7–9) Av main course £10
Restaurant L served all week 12–2.30 D served Mon-Sat 7–9.30 (Sun 7–9)
⊕ Punch Taverns ◀ Greene King Abbot Ale, Hog Goblin, Youngs, Spitfire & London Pride. ♟ 13
Facilities Garden Dogs allowed Parking Play Area

547

FARNHAM   MAP 05 SU84

The Bat & Ball Freehouse ⚑

15 Bat & Ball Ln, Boundstone GU10 4SA
☎ 01252 792108 📄 01252 794564
e-mail: info@thebatandball.co.uk
web: www.thebatandball.co.uk
dir: *From A31 Farnham bypass follow signs for Birdworld. Left at Bengal Lounge into School Hill. At top over staggered x-rds into Sandrock Hill Road. After 0.25m left into Viler Bourne Lane, signed*

It's well worth the effort of finding this 150–year-old inn, tucked away at the end of a lane in a wooded valley to the south of Farnham. Not surprisingly, cricketing memorabilia features, and there are six hand pumps serving a constantly changing selection of cask conditioned ales. A varied menu includes home-made puff pastry pies, and fresh fish is usually offered from the daily blackboard, maybe whole baked sea bass drizzled with pesto olive oil.

Open 11–11 (Sun 12–10.30) **Bar Meals** L served all week 12–2.15 D served all week 7–9.30 (Sun 12–3, 6–8.30) Av main course £8.95 **Restaurant** L served all week 12–2.15 D served all week 7–9.30 (Sun 12–3, 6–8.30) Av 3 course à la carte £17.95 ⊕ Free House ◀ Youngs Bitter, Hogs Back TEA, Bat & Ball Bitter, Archers Ales. ⚑ 8 **Facilities** Garden Dogs allowed Parking Play Area

See advertisement under ABINGER

FOREST GREEN   MAP 06 TQ14

The Parrot Inn ⚑

RH5 5RZ ☎ 01306 621339 📄 01306 621255
e-mail: drinks@theparrot.co.uk
dir: *B2126 from A29 at Ockley, signed Forest Green*

Set opposite the village green and cricket pitch in a rural hamlet, this attractive 17th-century building is in many ways the archetypal British inn. But besides the expected oak beams and huge fire, it also has its own butchery, charcuterie and farm shop. Owners Charles and Linda Gotto have a farm just a couple of miles away, where they raise shorthorn cattle, saddleback pigs, Suffolk sheep and Black Rock hens. The pub makes its own sausages, preserves and chutneys, and much of the menu uses home-grown or home-made produce. The dishes blend modern, traditional and European influences: perhaps coarse pork, hare and juniper berry terrine with fruit chutney and home-made bread, followed by slow-braised shorthorn beef in Guinness with sauteed potatoes and purple sprouting broccoli. Not to be forgotten is a good range of real ales, which can be enjoyed in the bar or one of the four pub gardens.

Open 11–11 (Fri-Sat 11–12) **Bar Meals** L served Mon-Sat 12–3 D served Mon-Sat 6–10 (Sun 12–6) Av main course £11.75 **Restaurant** L served Mon-Sat 12–3 D served Mon-Sat 6–9.30 (Sun 12–6) Av 3 course à la carte £22.50 ⊕ Free House ◀ Ringwood Best, Youngs PA, Timothy Taylor Landlord, Sharp's Doom Bar. ⚑ 14 **Facilities** Garden Dogs allowed Parking

GUILDFORD   MAP 06 SU94

The Keystone ⚑

3 Portsmouth Rd GU2 4BL ☎ 01483 575089
e-mail: drink@thekeystone.co.uk
dir: *0.5m from Guildford train station. Right out of station. Cross 2nd pedestrian crossing, follow road downhill. Past Savills Estate Agents. Pub 200yds on left*

This town bar has a stylish, well-kept feel, from its outdoor seating areas to the wood floors and leather sofas of its interior. Pub games, a book swap facility, and live music most Saturday nights add to its distinctive character. Expect fairly priced, home-made modern pub food – from tapas or sharing plates to mains such as moules frites; or home-roasted ham with a rum, honey and mustard glaze, a free-range egg and chips.

Open 12–11 (Fri-Sat 12–12, Sun 12–7) Closed: 25–26 Dec, 1 Jan **Bar Meals** L served Mon-Fri 12–3 D served Mon-Thu 6–9 (Sat-Sun 12–5) Av main course £8 ◀ Black Sheep, 6X, Guinness. ⚑ 13 **Facilities** Garden

HASCOMBE · MAP 06 TQ03

The White Horse ♥

The Street GU8 4JA ☎ 01483 208258 🖷 01483 208200

dir: *From Godalming take B2130. Pub on left 0.5m after Hascombe*

Freshly prepared, locally sourced food is always on the menu at this friendly pub owned by John Beckett (a local farmer) and Ossie Gray (River Cafe). Surrounded by picturesque walking country, the 16th-century building is unmissable in summer thanks to its flower-filled garden. A meal might include field mushroom and spinach tart with roasted tomatoes, followed by grilled sea bass with roasted tomatoes and new potatoes; or grilled rib-eye steak with gratin dauphinoise.

Open 12–11 (Fri-Sat 12-12) **Bar Meals** L served Mon-Sat 12–3 D served all week 7–10 (Sun 12–3.30) Av main course £12 **Restaurant** L served all week 12–3 D served Mon-Sat 7–10 Av 3 course à la carte £25 ⊕ Punch Taverns ◀ Harveys, Adnams Broadside, Black Sheep Bitter & Youngs. ♥ 6 **Facilities** Garden Dogs allowed Parking

HASLEMERE · MAP 06 SU93

The Wheatsheaf Inn ★★★ INN ♥

Grayswood Rd, Grayswood GU27 2DE
☎ 01428 644440 🖷 01428 641285
e-mail: thewheatsheaf@aol.com
web: www.thewheatsheafgrayswood.co.uk
dir: *Leave A3 at Milford, A286 to Haslemere. Grayswood approx 7.5m N*

A stunning display of hanging baskets adorns this Edwardian village inn at the start of one of Surrey's loveliest walks. Award-winning chefs provide a high standard of cuisine, showcased in themed evenings that include special dessert or gourmet fish nights, when you might encounter poached plaice and scampi roulade; or grilled sea bass on sautéed leeks with chervil sauce. The magnificent viewpoint at Black Down, beloved of Alfred, Lord Tennyson, is nearby.

Open 11–3 6–11 **Bar Meals** L served Mon-Sat 12–2 D served Mon-Sat 7–10 (Sun 12–2.30 7–9.45) Av main course £9.95 **Restaurant** L served all week 12–2 D served all week 7–10 Av 3 course à la carte £25 ⊕ Free House ◀ Badger 1st Gold, Ringwood Best, Ringwood 49er & Greene King IPA. ♥ 8 **Facilities** Garden Parking **Rooms** 7

HINDHEAD · MAP 06 SU83

Devil's Punchbowl Inn ♥

London Rd GU26 6AG
☎ 01428 606565 🖷 01428 605713
e-mail: hotel@punchbowlhotels.co.uk
web: www.punchbowlhotels.co.uk
dir: *A3 N of Hindhead, opp National Trust car park for Devils Punch Bowl*

The hotel, which dates from the early 1800s, stands 900ft above sea level with wonderful views as far as London on a clear day. The 'punchbowl' is a large natural bowl in the ground across the road. The menu, while not large, has something for everybody, with chilli con carne, steak and Guinness pie, Surrey shepherds pie, sausage and mash, and hand-made burger with chunky chips.

Open 7am-11 **Bar Meals** L served all week 12 D served all week 9.15 (Sun carvery 12–5.30, std menu 5.30–9.15) Av main course £8.95 **Restaurant** L served Sun 12–5.30 D served all week 6–9.15 (Sun carvery only) Av 3 course à la carte £17.95 ⊕ Eldridge Pope ◀ Bass, 6X, Tetleys, Bombardier. ♥ 15 **Facilities** Garden Parking

LEIGH · MAP 06 TQ24

The Plough ♥

Church Rd, LEIGH RH2 8NJ
☎ 01306 611348 🖷 01306 611299
e-mail: sarah@theploughleigh-wanadoo.co.uk
dir: *Telephone for directions*

A welcoming country pub overlooking the village green and situated opposite St Bartholomew's Church. Varied clientele, good atmosphere and quaint low beams which are conveniently padded! A hearty bar menu offers steak sandwiches, burgers, melts, salads, ploughmans' and jacket potatoes, while the restaurant area menu features tomato and artichoke pasta, smoked haddock fillet mornay, or Mexican style tortilla wraps.

Open 11–11 (Sun 12–10.30) **Bar Meals** L served all week all day D served all week all day Av main course £8 **Restaurant** L served all week all day D served all week all day ⊕ Hall & Woodhouse ◀ Badger Best , Tanglefoot, Sussex Bitter. ♥ 15 **Facilities** Garden Dogs allowed Parking

LINGFIELD — MAP 06 TQ34

Pick of the Pubs

Hare and Hounds ♀

Common Rd RH7 6BZ
☎ 01342 832351 📄 01342 832351
e-mail: hare.hounds@tiscali.co.uk
web: www.hareandhoundslingfield.co.uk/index.htm
dir: *From A22 follow signs for Lingfield Racecourse into Common Rd*

An 18th-century country pub close to Lingfield Park racecourse, the Hare and Hounds has a good name for its innovative modern English and European food. The menus provide early clues to the original approach taken by the kitchen – for a start, there's 'Something soup' rather than the more conventional 'Soup of the day'. Start with aubergine caviar blinis with oven-dried plum tomatoes and mushroom salad; or seared scallops with pea purée, orange and vanilla sauce. Then, maybe swordfish loin with truffle mash, pak choi and cannelloni bean relish, or even roast veal chop with spinach and sage gnocchi, Parma ham and garlic jus; or perhaps risotto primavera, available as a large or small portion. The Sunday menu goes beyond traditional roasts with Cumberland sausages, chargrilled gammon steak, and pan-fried fillet of John Dory with clam chowder. Head for the split-level decked garden for a drink in the sun.

Open 11.30–11 Closed: 1 Jan **Bar Meals** L served all week 12–2.30 D served Mon-Sat 7–9.30 (Sun 12–3.30) **Restaurant** L served all week 12–2.30 D served Mon-Sat 7–9.30 (Sun 12–3.30) ⊕ Punch Taverns ◀ Greene King IPA, Flowers Original, Old Speckled Hen, Guinness. ♀ 8 **Facilities** Children's licence Garden Dogs allowed Parking

MICKLEHAM — MAP 06 TQ15

King William IV ♀

Byttom Hill RH5 6EL ☎ 01372 372590
dir: *From M25 junct 9, A24 signed to Dorking, pub just before Mickleham*

Former ale house for Lord Beaverbrook's staff at his nearby Cherkley estate, the building dates from 1790 and has a terraced garden with fine country views. There's a panelled snug and larger back bar with an open fire, cast iron tables and grandfather clock. The chef proprietor serves good food alongside real ales including vegetarian specialities. Expect fisherman's pie, calves' liver and smoked bacon, baked tagliatelle with wild mushroom sauce, and the weekly Sunday roast.

Open 11.30–3 6.30–11 (Sun 12–10.30) Closed: 25 Dec **Bar Meals** L served Mon-Sat 12–2 D served Mon-Sat 7–9.30 (Sun 12–5) Av main course £13 **Restaurant** L served Mon-Sat 12–2 D served Mon-Sat 7–9.30 (Sun 12–5) ⊕ Free House ◀ Hogs Back TEA, Adnams Best, guest ales. ♀ 11 **Facilities** Garden

The Running Horses ♀

Old London Rd RH5 6DU
☎ 01372 372279 📄 01372 363004
e-mail: info@therunninghorses.co.uk
web: www.therunninghorses.co.uk
dir: *1.5m from M25 junct 9. Off A24 between Leatherhead & Dorking*

This pub has a history of sheltering highwaymen; a secret ladder-way leading to the roof once helped them evade capture. Its interior may resonate with history, right down to its bare beams and real fires, but the menus have a modern edge. Bar food ranges from sandwiches to shank of lamb braised in balsamic and burgundy.

Open 11.30–11 (Sun 12–10.30) Closed: 25–26 Dec, 31 Dec-1 Jan eve **Bar Meals** L served Mon-Fri 12–2.30 D served all week 7–9.30 (Sat-Sun 12–3) **Restaurant** L served Mon-Fri 12–2.30 D served Mon-Fri 7–9.30 (Sat-Sun 12–3, 6–9) Av 3 course à la carte £32 ⊕ Punch Taverns ◀ Fuller's London Pride, Young's Bitter, Abbot, Adnams Bitter. ♀ 9 **Facilities** Garden Dogs allowed

NEWDIGATE — MAP 06 TQ14

The Surrey Oaks ♀

Parkgate Rd RH5 5DZ ☎ 01306 631200 📄 01306 631200
e-mail: ken@surreyoaks.co.uk
web: www.surreyoaks.co.uk
dir: *From A24 follow signs to Newdigate, at T-junct turn left, pub 1m on left*

Picturesque oak-beamed pub located one mile outside the village of Newdigate. Parts of the building date back to 1570, and it became an inn around the middle of the 19th century. There are two bars, one with an inglenook fireplace, as well as a restaurant area, patio and beer garden with boules pitch. A typical specials board features Barnsley lamb chop with minted gravy, chicken and ham pie, and grilled plaice with parsley butter.

Open 11.30–2.30 5.30–11 (Sat 11.30–3, 6–11 Sun 12–10.30) **Bar Meals** L served all week 12–2 D served Tue-Sat 7–9 Av main course £8 **Restaurant** L served all week 12–2 D served Tue-Sat 7–9 ◀ Harveys Sussex Best, Surrey Hills Ranmore Ale and rotating guest ales. ♀ 8 **Facilities** Garden Dogs allowed Parking Play Area

OCKLEY
MAP 06 TQ14

Pick of the Pubs

Bryce's at The Old School House ⊛ ♥

RH5 5TH ☎ 01306 627430 🖹 01306 628274

e-mail: bryces.fish@virgin.net

dir: 8m S of Dorking on A29

Formerly a boarding school, this Grade II listed building dates back to 1750 and was bought by Bill Bryce in 1982. He's passionate about fresh fish and offers a huge range, despite the location in rural Surrey. It's more of a restaurant than a pub, although there is a bar with its own interesting bar menu (open sandwiches; white Portland crab risotto, battered cod and chips). The restaurant offers seven starters and seven main courses – all fish – with some non-fish daily specials. Options to start include a soufflé of Arbroath smokie, Avruga caviar and parsley, or tartar of swordfish with lime, ginger and cinnamon. Mains take in fillet of sea bream on a porridge of mussels, chorizo and Parma ham with plum tomatoes and thyme fish cream; and pan-seared king scallops and calves' liver served with cauliflower and red wine and rosemary jus. Private parties are a speciality.

Open 11–3 6–11 Closed: 25–26 Dec & 1 Jan & Sun eve Nov, Jan & 2 Feb **Bar Meals** L served all week 12–2.30 D served Mon-Sat 6.30–9.30 Av main course £11.50 **Restaurant** L served all week 12–2.30 D served Mon-Sat 7–9.30 Av 3 course à la carte £31 Av 3 course fixed price £31 ⊕ Free House ◖ London Pride, W J King Sussex, John Smith's Smooth. ♥ 15 **Facilities** Dogs allowed Parking

The Kings Arms Inn ♥

Stane St RH5 5TS ☎ 01306 711224 🖹 01306 711224

e-mail: enquiries@thekingsarmsockley.co.uk

dir: From M25 junct 9 take A24 through Dorking towards Horsham, A29 to Ockley

The many charms of this heavily-beamed 16th-century inn include welcoming log fires, a priest hole, a friendly ghost, and an award-winning garden. Set in the picturesque village of Ockley and overlooked by the tower of Leith Hill, it's an ideal setting in which to enjoy home-cooked food such as honey-glazed pork belly with roast onions and mashed potato; coq au riesling; or rabbit and winter vegetable casserole.

The Kings Arms Inn

Open 11–2.30 6–11 (Sat 11–3, Sun 12–3, 7–10.30) **Bar Meals** L served all week 12–2 D served Sun-Thu 7–9 (Fri-Sat 7–10) **Restaurant** L served all week 12–2 D served Sun-Thu 7–9 (Fri-Sat 7–10) ⊕ Free House ◖ Flowers IPA, Old Speckled Hen, Castlemaine 4X, & Murphy's. ♥ 15 **Facilities** Garden Parking

PIRBRIGHT
MAP 06 SU95

The Royal Oak ♥

Aldershot Rd GU24 0DQ ☎ 01483 232466

dir: M3 junct 3, A322 towards Guildford, then A324 towards Aldershot

A genuine old world pub specialising in real ales (up to nine at any time), and well known for its glorious prize-winning garden. The Tudor cottage pub has an oak church door, stained glass windows and pew seating, and in winter there are welcoming log fires in the rambling bars. The menu may include smoked salmon and pesto, braised lamb shoulder, steak and ale pie, and penne pasta Alfredo, along with various specials.

Open 11–11 (Sun 11–10.30) **Bar Meals** L served all week 12–6 D served all week 6–10 (Sat-Sun 12–9.30) Av main course £7 ◖ Flowers IPA, Hogsback Traditional English Ale, Bass Ringwood Ale, Abbots Ales. ♥ 18 **Facilities** Garden Dogs allowed Parking

SOUTH GODSTONE
MAP 06 TQ34

Fox & Hounds ♥

Tilburstow Hill Rd RH9 8LY ☎ 01342 893474

Parts of this cosy, traditional inn date back to 1368, though Thomas Hart first opened it as a pub in 1601. There's a large inglenook in the restaurant, and a real fire in the lower bar. Regular visitors to the specials board include pan-fried swordfish with paprika and black olives; beef medallions in brandy and peppercorn sauce; and sizzling asparagus and tiger prawns. Outside is a large garden with pleasant rural views.

Open 12–11 **Bar Meals** L served Mon-Thu 12–3 D served Mon-Thu 6–9 (Fri-Sun 12–9) **Restaurant** L served Mon-Thu 12–3 D served Mon-Thu 6–9 (Fri-Sun 12–9) ⊕ Greene King ◖ All Greene King. ♥ 13 **Facilities** Garden Dogs allowed Parking

The Inn @ West End

The Inn @ West End has been a pub for almost 200 years, but has few original features and is not naturally pretty. However, over the last eight years it has developed into a destination inn as well as a main road local and a thriving business. Somewhat Tardis-like, you will either love it or hate it, but most people love it.

Customers devoted to the place are those who can walk, cycle or get the bus from home. They might also be ladies who lunch, gentlemen who shoot at Bisley ranges, friends who use the inn as a halfway meeting point, or local business people – whoever they are they know they will get a cheery welcome, a good pint, a glass of wine, decent coffee and great food prepared from quality ingredients. Although it is definitely a dining pub, it still has a great crowd of regular drinkers, and with just two real ales on hand pumps they are always in good condition. The wine list is extensive and eclectic with a leaning towards Portugal and Spain, and Bordeaux having an unfair advantage. About 50% of produce is sourced locally, with some home-grown herbs and vegetables. Fresh fish is collected in the inn's own chiller van from the coast, and meat from Hyden Organic Farm. Game features strongly (the proprietor is a keen shot) and the inn has its own game room and plucking machine. Try half a roast pheasant with red wine and juniper sauce, braised red cabbage and dauphinoise potatoes, or a selection of fresh fish with fennel seed beurre blanc, green vegetables and new potatoes. Quizzes and themed events are a regular feature. Older children are only allowed in when dining.

MAP 06 SU96
42 Guildford Rd GU24 9PW
☎ 01276 858652
e-mail: greatfood@the-inn.co.uk
dir: *On A322 towards Guildford. 3m from M3 junct 3, just beyond Gordon Boys rdbt*

Open 12–3 5–11
Bar Meals L served Mon-Sat 12–2.30 D served Mon-Sat 6–9.30 (Sun 12–3 6–9) Av main course £15
Restaurant L served Mon-Sat 12–2.30 D served Mon-Sat 6–9.30 (Sun 12–3 6–9) Av 3 course à la carte £27.75 Av 2 course fixed price £11.95
⊕ Free House ◀ Youngs Bitter, Fuller's London Pride. ♥ 12
Facilities Garden Dogs allowed Parking

552

STAINES
MAP 06 TQ07

The Swan Hotel ♥

The Hythe TW18 3JB ☎ 01784 452494 📠 01784 461593
e-mail: swan.hotel@fullers.co.uk
dir: *Just off A308, S of Staines Bridge. 5m from Heathrow*

This 18th-century inn stands just south of Staines Bridge and was once the haunt of river bargemen who were paid in tokens which could be exchanged at the pub for food and drink. It has a spacious, comfortable bar, and a menu based on traditional home-cooked food. Examples range from sausage and mash; pot-roast lamb shank; and steak and ale pie, to seafood risotto or vegetarian noodle bowl.

Open 12–11 **Bar Meals** L served all week 12–6 D served all week 6–9.30 (Sun 12–8) **Restaurant** L served all week 12–6 D served all week 6–9.30 ⊕ Fullers ◀ Fuller's London Pride, ESB. ♥ 10 **Facilities** Garden Dogs allowed

VIRGINIA WATER
MAP 06 TQ06

The Wheatsheaf Hotel ♥

London Rd GU25 4QF ☎ 01344 842057 📠 01344 842932
e-mail: wheatsheaf.hotel.4306@thespiritgroup.com
dir: *From M25 junct 13, take A30 towards Bracknell*

The Wheatsheaf dates back to the second half of the 18th century and is beautifully situated overlooking Virginia Water on the edge of Windsor Great Park. Chalkboard menus offer a good range of freshly prepared dishes with fresh fish as a speciality. Popular options are beer battered cod and chips, roast queen fish with pesto crust, and braised lamb shank on mustard mash.

Open 11–10 (Sun 12–10) **Bar Meals** L served all week 12–10 D served all week (Sun 12–9.30) Av main course £8 **Restaurant** L served all week 12–10 D served all week ◀ guest ales. ♥ 6 **Facilities** Garden Parking

WARLINGHAM
MAP 06 TQ35

The White Lion ♥

CR6 9EG ☎ 01883 629011

This listed 15th-century inn on Warlingham Green has low ceilings, oak beams and inglenook fireplace, along with an extension that carefully combines the old and the new. Four real ales and five lagers are always available, and there's a varied menu offering sandwiches, light bites and dishes of Thai green chicken; lamb shank with rosemary and stilton; and Roquefort tortelloni among a good vegetarian choice.

Open 12–11 (Sun 12–10.30) **Bar Meals** L served all week 12–9 D served all week 12–9 Av main course £6 ⊕ Bass ◀ Fuller's London Pride, Bass, Youngs, Pedigree. ♥ 18 **Facilities** Garden Parking

WEST CLANDON
MAP 06 TQ05

Onslow Arms ♥

The Street GU4 7TE ☎ 01483 222447 📠 01483 211126
e-mail: onslowarms@massivepub.com
dir: *A3 then A247, approx 7m from Guildford*

An old English pub with a French restaurant attached, the Onslow Arms dates from 1623. For the high flying clientele a helipad is provided, and there's a large patio and even larger car park. The Cromwell Bar has a good choice of real ales, and the beamed interior provides a contrast to the contemporary restaurant. L'Auberge serves traditional French cuisine while the separate rotisserie offers an appetising range of soups, salads, omelettes and baguettes.

Open 11–11 (Sun 12–10.30) **Bar Meals** L served Mon-Sat 12–2.30 D served Mon-Thu 7–9.30 (Fri-Sat 7–10, Sun 12–9) Av main course £8.50 **Restaurant** L served all week 12.30–2.30 D served Mon-Sat 7–10 (Sun 7–9) Av 3 course à la carte £30 ◀ Courage Best & Directors, Bombardier Premium, Hogs Back TEA, Pedigree & 2 rotating guest ales. ♥ 11 **Facilities** Children's licence Garden Dogs allowed Parking

WEST END
MAP 06 SU96

Pick of the Pubs

The Inn @ West End ♥

See Pick of the Pubs on opposite page

England

WEST HORSLEY — MAP 06 TQ05

Pick of the Pubs

The King William IV ♀

83 The Street KT24 6BG

☎ 01483 282318 🖹 01483 282318

e-mail: kingbilly4th@aol.com

dir: *On The Street off A246 (Epsom to Guildford)*

When laws limiting the consumption of gin were passed in the 1830s, the King William IV began a swift trade in ale through its street-level windows. Fortunately, many of the original Georgian features have been preserved, giving this traditional countryside local a warm and welcoming atmosphere, augmented by open fires in winter and a light and airy conservatory restaurant. Today it's popular with walkers, not least for the large garden and terrace to the rear, with colourful tubs and floral baskets. Beers include several lagers, while the generously proportioned wine list proffers a good selection by the glass. The well-priced menu ranges over reliable starters such as deep-fried French brie or crispy garlic mushrooms, and leads on to equally popular mains like seared tuna, or marinated minty lamb rumps. Children can tuck into home-made lasagne and a shot of sugar-free 'safari juice'.

Open 11.30–11 (Fri 11.30–12) **Bar Meals** L served all week 12–3 D served all week 6.30–9.30 **Restaurant** L served all week 12–3 D served all week 6.30–9.30 ⊕ Enterprise Inns ◀ Sheerdrop, Courage Best. ♀ 12 **Facilities** Children's licence Garden Dogs allowed Parking

---

WITLEY — MAP 06 SU93

The White Hart ♀

Petworth Rd GU8 5PH ☎ 01428 683695

e-mail: thewhitehartwitley@yahoo.co.uk

dir: *From A3 follow signs to Milford, then A283 towards Petworth. Pub 2m on left*

A delightfully warm and welcoming pub, built in 1380 as a hunting lodge for Richard II; the white hart became his personal emblem. Licensed since 1700, the three log fires, oak beams, Shepherd Neame ales and hearty portions of good value home-cooked food continue to attract. Soups, sandwiches, salads and pastas make a light lunch; steak and kidney pudding, venison casserole, and sausages and mash are some of the main course options. Families and dogs welcome.

Open 11–3 5.30–11 (Sun 12–5) Closed: Sun eve **Bar Meals** L served all week 12–2.30 D served Mon-Sat 6.30–9.30 Av main course £7.95 **Restaurant** L served all week 12–2.30 D served Tue-Sat 6.30–9.30 ⊕ Shepherd Neame ◀ Shepherd Neame Master Brew, Spitfire, Holsten Export, seasonal ale. ♀ 7 **Facilities** Garden Dogs allowed Parking Play Area

---

SUSSEX, EAST

ALCISTON — MAP 06 TQ50

Pick of the Pubs

Rose Cottage Inn ♀

BN26 6UW ☎ 01323 870377 🖹 01323 871440

e-mail: ian@alciston.freeserve.co.uk

dir: *Off A27 between Eastbourne & Lewes*

A traditional Sussex pub, with roses round the door in a cul-de-sac village below the South Downs. Ramblers will find it a good base for long walks in unspoilt countryside, especially along the old traffic-free coach road to the south. The inn has been in the same family for over 40 years, and is well known for its good, 'fresh daily' home-cooked food. This includes the best local meats, poultry and game, served in rambling dining rooms, in the bar or in the patio garden. The local butcher's sausages are particularly excellent, and the wide-ranging fish selection includes fresh Scottish mussels delivered every Friday (when in season) and cooked French or Italian-style. Blackboard specials include authentic curries using fresh spices; braised pheasant in red wine and juniper sauce; and rolled pancakes with cream cheese, spinach and pinenuts. Lunchtime eating is primarily casual, with booking necessary only on Sundays.

Open 11.30–3 6.30–11 (Sun 12–3, 7–10.30) Closed: 25–26 Dec **Bar Meals** L served all week 12–2 D served Mon-Sat 7–9.30 (Sun 7–9) Av main course £10 **Restaurant** L served all week 12–2 D served Mon-Sat 7–9 ⊕ Free House ◀ Harveys Best, Dark Star. ♀ 9 **Facilities** Garden Dogs allowed Parking

---

ALFRISTON — MAP 06 TQ50

George Inn ♀

High St BN26 5SY ☎ 01323 870319 🖹 01323 871384

e-mail: info@thegeorge-alfriston.com

dir: *Telephone for directions*

Splendid 14th-century, Grade II listed flint and half-timbered inn set in a magical South Downs village. The George boasts heavy oak beams, an ancient inglenook fireplace and a network of smugglers' tunnels leading from its cellars. The team of three chefs create delights such as flat mushrooms sautéed in garlic with smoked bacon and goats' cheese; skate wings in black butter and capers; and monkfish wrapped in Parma ham on a mixed bean cassoulet.

Open 12–11 (Fri-Sat 12–12, Sun 12–10.30) Closed: 25–26 Dec **Bar Meals** L served all week 12–2.30 D served all week 7–10 **Restaurant** L served all week 12–2.30 D served all week 7–10 ⊕ Greene King ◀ Greene King Old Speckled Hen, Abbot Ale, 2 guests. ♀ 12 **Facilities** Garden Dogs allowed

The Sussex Ox ♟

Milton St BN26 5RL ☎ 01323 870840 📠 01323 870715

e-mail: mail@thesussexox.co.uk

dir: *Off A27 between Wilmington & Drusillas. Follow brown signs to pub*

Idyllically situated pub, tucked away down a meandering country lane and set in almost two acres of gardens. In recent years, improvements and adjustments have been made, but the friendly welcome and cosy atmosphere of a country pub have been retained. You can eat in the bar, the Garden Room, or the more formal Dining Room. A typical menu includes shoulder of lamb roasted in honey and mustard, and chargrilled venison steak with red onion and juniper reduction. Bar snacks, sandwiches and ploughman's are also available.

Open 11.30–3 6–11 (Winter Sun 12–5) Closed: 25–31 Dec
Bar Meals L served all week 12–2 D served all week 6–9 (Winter Sun 12–3) ⊕ Free House ⚫ Harveys Best, Dark Star Hophead, Golden Gate, Hop Back Summer Lightning. ♟ 10 **Facilities** Garden Parking

ASHBURNHAM PLACE   MAP 06 TQ61

Ash Tree Inn

Brownbread St TN33 9NX ☎ 01424 892104

dir: *From Eastbourne take A271 at Boreham Bridge towards Battle. Next left, follow pub signs*

The Ash Tree is a friendly old pub with three open fires, plenty of exposed beams and a traditional local atmosphere. Bar food includes ploughman's, salads and sandwiches, while the restaurant serves steaks, local lamb, steak and ale pie, or salmon in a variety of sauces.

Open 12–3 7–11 (Summer 6.30–11, closed Mon eve) **Bar Meals** L served all week 12–2 D served Tue-Sat 7–9 **Restaurant** L served all week 12–2 D served Tue-Sun 7–9 ⊕ Free House ⚫ Harveys Best, Greene King Old Speckled Hen, Brakspear Bitter + guest ales. **Facilities** Garden Dogs allowed Parking

BERWICK   MAP 06 TQ50

Pick of the Pubs

The Cricketers Arms ♟

BN26 6SP ☎ 01323 870469 📠 01323 871411

e-mail: pbthecricketers@aol.com

dir: *Off A27 between Polegate & Lewes (follow signs for Berwick Church)*

A traditional flint and stone cottage pub in beautiful gardens close to many popular walks, including the South Downs Way running along the crest of the chalk scarp to the south. It was formerly two 16th-century farmworkers' cottages, which then became an alehouse for 200 years before Harvey's of Lewes bought it around 50 years ago and turned it into a 'proper' pub. Three beamed, music-free rooms with stone floors and open fires are simply furnished with old pine furniture. Home-made food, using local produce, found on the simple but perfectly adequate bar menu includes starters such as crayfish cocktail, and duck and pistachio terrine, and main courses like sausages with white bean mash and red wine gravy; and warm chicken Waldorf salad. Nearby is

Charleston Farmhouse, the country rendezvous of the London writers, painters and intellectuals known as the Bloomsbury Group, and scene of an annual literary festival.

Open 11–3 6–11 (Sat-Sun all day, Jul-Aug 11–11) Closed: 25 Dec
Bar Meals L served Mon-Fri 12–2.15 D served Mon-Fri 6.30–9 (Sat-Sun all day) ⊕ Harveys of Lewes ⚫ Harveys Best Bitter, Pale & Armada. ♟ 11 **Facilities** Garden Dogs allowed Parking

BLACKBOYS   MAP 06 TQ52

The Blackboys Inn ♟

Lewes Rd TN22 5LG

☎ 01825 890283 📠 01825 890283

e-mail: blackboys-inn@btconnect.com

dir: *From A22 at Uckfield take B2102 towards Cross in Hand. Or from A267 at Esso service station in Cross in Hands take B2102 towards Uckfield. Village in 1.5m at junct of B2102 & B2192*

Set in 12 acres of beautiful countryside, the rambling, black-weatherboarded Blackboys Inn was first recorded as an ale house as long ago as 1349; parts of the building date from even earlier. It has a large garden overlooking a pond and a splendid beamed interior, complete with resident ghost. A meal might include mussels marinière, followed by half a pheasant slow roasted in red wine and brandy.

Open 12 -11 Closed: 1 Jan **Bar Meals** L served all week 12 D served all week 10 **Restaurant** L served Mon-Sat 10 D served Mon-Sat 10 (Sun 3–6 Bar menu only) ⊕ Harveys of Lewes ⚫ Harveys Sussex Best Bitter, Sussex Halow, Sussex XXXX Old Ale & seasonal. ♟ 8 **Facilities** Garden Dogs allowed Parking

BRIGHTON & HOVE   MAP 06 TQ30

The Basketmakers Arms

12 Gloucester Rd BN1 4AD

☎ 01273 689006 📠 01273 682300

e-mail: bluedowd@hotmail.co.uk

dir: *From Brighton station main entrance 1st left (Gloucester Rd). Pub on right at bottom of hill*

This Victorian corner pub in the North Laines conservation area has bags of character. Seven hand pumped beers are offered, plus 90 malt whiskies, and an exceptional selection of vodkas and gins. The food is prepared, where possible, from free-range, locally sourced meat and produce. Dishes include locally caught fish with chips, fish chowder, steak and ale pie, burgers (and veggie burgers), and home-cooked Sunday roasts with a choice of three meats and a vegetarian option.

Open 11–11 (Thu-Sat 11–12, Sun 12–11) **Bar Meals** L served Mon-Sat 12–8.30 D served Mon-Sat 12–8.30 (Sun 12–5) Av main course £6.50 ⊕ Fullers ⚫ Fuller's HSB, Butser Bitter, London Pride, ESB & Discovery & seasonal ales. **Facilities** Dogs allowed

England

BRIGHTON & HOVE continued

The Chimney House ⚑

28 Upper Hamilton Rd BN1 5DF

☎ 01273 556708 🖶 01273 556708

e-mail: info@chimneyhouse.co.uk

The Chimney House has an open-plan kitchen where you can watch chefs prepare such delights as sautéed calves' sweetbread tartlet; or salt cod brandade with home-made aioli. Dishes like roast rack of hill-reared Blackface lamb are sourced from owner Jackie Nairn's family farm in northwest Scotland. Finish up with chocolate brownie mousse, and don't forget the wine list, compiled with the help of Hamish Anderson, award-winning buyer for Tate Britain.

Bar Meals L served Fri-Sat 12–2.30 D served Mon 6–9.30 (Sun 12–3.30. 6.30–9) 🍺 Harvey's Sussex Best Bitter, Staropramen, Guinness. ⚑ 10 **Facilities** Children's licence Dogs allowed

---

Pick of the Pubs

The Greys

105 Southover St BN2 9UA

☎ 01273 680734 & 606475

e-mail: chris@greyspub.com

dir: 0.5m from St Peters Church in Hanover area of Brighton

Renowned for its high quality food, Belgian beers and live country/folk music, The Greys is something of an institution. Chris Beaumont and Gill Perkins are the driving force behind this dynamic little back-street pub in Brighton's Hanover district, though some of the credit must go to new chef Paul Collins, who has managed to sustain the reputation forged by his predecessor. The menu has a bright, flavourful, international feel, with the occasional reference to Paul's South African origins – Bunny Chow, for instance, which comprises a hollowed-out organic bread roll filled with delicately spiced Cape Malan style curry made with local mutton. Other dishes could include starters of Thai prawn and crab cakes with sweet chilli sauce and fresh lime; or hot peppered beef green salad with horseradish and yoghurt dressing, followed by duck breast with a sour cherry glaze; or a home-made Aberdeen Angus burger.

Open 12–11 (Mon-Thu 4–11) **Bar Meals** L served Sun 12–3 D served Tue-Sat 6–9 (Tapas on Fri 6–9) Av main course £11.50 **Restaurant** L served Sun 12–3 D served Tue-Thu, Sat 6–9 Av 3 course à la carte £19 ⊕ Enterprise Inns 🍺 Timothy Taylor Landlord, Harveys. **Facilities** Dogs allowed Parking

---

The Market Inn ★★ INN ⚑

1 Market St BN1 1HH ☎ 01273 329483 🖶 01273 777227

e-mail: marketinn@reallondonpubs.com

dir: In Lanes area, 50mtrs from junct of North St & East St

In the heart of Brighton's historic Lanes, this classic pub is within easy reach of the Royal Pavilion and seafront. The building was used by George IV for romantic liaisons, and now features two en suite bedrooms. Daily blackboard specials supplement the inexpensive pub menu which features salmon and dill fishcakes, jacket potatoes, and home-cooked curry. Seafood, vegetarian or spicy platters are available for sharing over a pint of Harveys or Bombardier ale.

Open 11–11 (Fri-Sat 11–1am Sun 12–10.30) **Bar Meals** L served Mon-Sat 11–9 D served Mon-Sat 11–9 (Sun 12–5) Av main course £6.50 ⊕ Scottish Courage 🍺 Harveys, Wells Bombardier, Youngs Bitter. ⚑ 7 **Facilities** Dogs allowed **Rooms** 2

CHAILEY   MAP 06 TQ31

The Five Bells Restaurant and Bar ⚑

East Grinstead Rd BN8 4DA

☎ 01825 722259 🖶 01825 723368

e-mail: info@fivebellschailey.co.uk

dir: 5m N of Lewes on A275

Handy for Sheffield Park, the Bluebell Railway, Plumpton racecourse and walks around Chailey. With origins in the 15th century and serving ale since the 17th, this country pub cum wine bar cum smart restaurant has many original features, including a large inglenook fireplace. The highly qualified kitchen team create modern European dishes rooted in English tradition from fresh, organic and free-range ingredients. Friday evenings host live jazz, and in summer the large bar terrace and secluded restaurant garden come into their own. New owners for 2008.

Open 12–3 6–11 (Closed Sun Eve) **Bar Meals** L served all week 12–2.30 D served Tue-Sat 6.30–9.30 (Sun 6.30–8.30) **Restaurant** D served Tue-Sun 7–9.30 Av 3 course à la carte £30 Av 2 course fixed price £25 ⊕ Enterprise Inns 🍺 Harvey's Best, Old Speckled Hen, Youngs Special. ⚑ 9 **Facilities** Children's licence Garden Dogs allowed Parking

---

CHIDDINGLY   MAP 06 TQ51

The Six Bells

BN8 6HE ☎ 01825 872227

dir: E of A22 between Hailsham & Uckfield (turn opp Golden Cross PH)

Inglenook fireplaces and plenty of bric-a-brac are to be found at this large characterful free house which is where various veteran car and motorbike enthusiasts meet on club nights. The jury in the famous Onion Pie Murder trial sat and deliberated in the bar before finding the defendant guilty. Live music at weekends. Exceptionally good value bar food includes stilton and walnut pie, lemon peppered haddock, Six Bells Yorkshire pudding with beef or sausage, vegetarian lasagne, cannelloni, lasagne, and shepherd's pie.

Open 11–3 6–11 (Fri-Sun all day) **Bar Meals** L served Mon-Thu 11–2.30 D served Mon-Thu 6–10.30 (Fri-Sun 12–9) Av main course £6.95 ⊕ Free House 🍺 Courage Directors, John Smiths, Harveys Best. **Facilities** Garden Dogs allowed Parking

PICK OF THE PUBS

The Bull

Dating back to 1563, the Bull is one of the oldest buildings in this famously pretty Sussex village. First used as an overnight resting place for travelling monks, the inn has also served as a courthouse and staging post for the London-Brighton coach.

Owner Dominic Worrall took over in 2003, and locals claim the inn has never been so popular. Real ale lovers will be delighted by the four cask conditioned ales, including the local Harvey's Best, while wine drinkers can enjoy 13 regularly changing wines by the glass. The modern British menu also changes frequently (up to four times a week) to make the most of the freshest local supplies, be it game from the Balcombe Estate, South Downs lamb from village farms or fish from the nearby coast. These show up in such dishes as seared venison loin marinated in raspberry vinegar with walnut salad; and smoked mackerel and horseradish rillette with melba toast. Example mains could range from pork tenderloin stuffed with red onion marmalade; or roasted duck breast with courgette spaghetti and Marsala jus; to poached fillet of salmon with tiger prawn gateaux; or stuffed aubergine with feta, pine nut and spinach au gratin. No one should miss the rare opportunity to sample Sussex pond pudding, a local speciality made with an alarming amount of butter, and here served with lemon and lime crème anglaise. Strawberry and mint crème brûlée, and rich chocolate and fudge brownie are equally alluring. Families are made very welcome, and half-sized portions are generally available for children. A huge garden commands stunning views over the South Downs.

MAP 06 TQ31
2 High St BN6 8TA
☎ 01273 843147
🖹 01273 843147
e-mail:
info@thebullditchling.com
dir: *S on M23/A23 5m. N of Brighton, follow signs to Pyecombe/Hassocks then signed to Ditchling 3m*

Open 11–11 (Sun 12–10.30)
Bar Meals L served Mon-Sat 12–2.30 D served Mon-Sat 7–9.30 (Sun 12–6)
🍺 Free House ⬛ Harveys Best, Timothy Taylor Landlord, Hop Back Summer Lightning, Gribble Plucking Pheasant. 🍷 13
Facilities Children's licence Garden Dogs allowed Parking Play Area

England

COWBEECH — MAP 06 TQ61

Pick of the Pubs

The Merrie Harriers ♥

BN27 4JQ ☎ 01323 833108 🖹 01323 833108
e-mail: rmcotton@btopenworld.com

dir: Off A271, between Hailsham & Herstmonceux

A Grade II listed, 17th-century, white clapboard building at the centre of the village with great country views. The beamed bar has a large inglenook fireplace, and there is another open fire in the lounge bar/dining room, which leads into the restaurant. The latter opens on to a pretty terrace with garden tables among the flowering tubs. A good choice of real ales and nine wines by the glass are served, and all the food is prepared on the premises using local suppliers and produce – free range and organic wherever possible. Dishes, prepared from local free-range and organic produce where possible, might include slow roasted lamb shank with parsnip purée, Sussex steak and kidney pie with shortcrust pastry, and pan-fried fillet of sea bass with roast Mediterranean vegetables. Starters like wild mushroom risotto can double as mains.

Open 11.30–3 6–11 **Bar Meals** L served all week 12–2 D served all week 7–9 Av main course £20 **Restaurant** L served all week 12–2 D served all week 7–9 ⊕ Free House ◀ Harveys, Timothy Taylor. ♥ 9 **Facilities** Garden Dogs allowed Parking

DANEHILL — MAP 06 TQ42

Pick of the Pubs

The Coach and Horses ♥

RH17 7JF ☎ 01825 740369 🖹 01825 740369

dir: From East Grinstead, S through Forest Row on A22 to junct with A275 (Lewes road), right on A275, 2m to Danehill, left onto School Lane, 0.5m, pub on left

Here is proof that some classic hostelries still exist in an age when the traditional village local is under increasing threat. The Coach and Horses has provided hospitality since 1847 when it was built as an ale house with stabling and a courtyard between two large country estates. These days the stables form part of the comfortable country-style restaurant. Open fires and neatly tended gardens add colour to a characterful setting: expect half-panelled walls, highly polished wooden floorboards and vaulted beamed ceilings. Food plays a key role in its success. Typical choices range from lunchtime sandwiches to main meals such as home-cured gravadlax of salmon on rocket, pine nut and caper salad, followed by chargrilled rib eye of Scotch beef with buttered baby spinach, curried parsnips, sweet potatoes and red wine jus; or Rye Bay plaice with caper and parsley butter, and a mixed leaf salad.

Open 11.30–3 6–11 **Bar Meals** L served all week 12–2 D served Mon-Sat 7–9 **Restaurant** L served all week 12–2 D served Mon-Sat 7–9 Av 3 course à la carte £23 ⊕ Free House ◀ Harveys Best & Old Ale, Brakspear, Wadsworth IPA, Archers Golden. ♥ 10 **Facilities** Garden Dogs allowed Parking Play Area

DITCHLING — MAP 06 TQ31

Pick of the Pubs

The Bull ♥

See Pick of the Pubs on page 557

EAST CHILTINGTON — MAP 06 TQ31

The Jolly Sportsman ♥

Chapel Ln BN7 3BA ☎ 01273 890400 🖹 01273 890400
e-mail: thejollysportsman@mistral.co.uk

dir: From Lewes take A275, left at Offham onto B2166 towards Plumpton, take Novington Ln, after approx 1m left into Chapel Ln

This characterful and sympathetically upgraded Victorian-style dining inn is the work of respected restaurateur Bruce Wass from Thackerays in Tunbridge Wells. Tucked down a quiet no-through road surrounded by downland, it feels isolated and romantic. Begin your meal with seared scallops, chilli and garlic linguini, followed by roast Sussex pork loin with caramelised garlic and seed mustard sauce, or perhaps poached skate wing with lemon, chive and butter sauce. Lovely garden.

Open 12–2.30 6–11 (Sun 12–4) Closed: 25–26 Dec & Mon (ex BH) **Bar Meals** L served Tue-Sat 12.30–2.15 D served Tue-Thu 7–9 (Fri-Sat 7–10, Sun 12–3) Av main course £12.50 **Restaurant** L served Tue-Sat 12.30–2.15 D served Tue-Thu 7–9.15 (Fri-Sat 7–10, Sun 12–3) Av 3 course à la carte £28 Av 3 course fixed price £15.75 ⊕ Free House ◀ Changing guest ales. ♥ 9 **Facilities** Children's licence Garden Dogs allowed Parking Play Area

EXCEAT — MAP 06 TV59

The Golden Galleon ♥

Exceat Bridge BN25 4AB
☎ 01323 892555 🖹 01323 896238

dir: On A259, 1.5m E of Seaford

Once this was just a shepherd's bothy, but it has grown enough to comfortably accommodate TV crews making an episode of *EastEnders*, a Gary Rhodes commercial, and a Dickens costume drama. The pub overlooks Cuckmere Haven, and the Seven Sisters Country Park. A sample menu includes lemon chicken, fish and chips, Mediterranean vegetable and brie open pie, chicken carbonara linguine, traditional mixed grill, and beef, mushroom and ale pie.

Open 10.30–11 (Sun 11.30–10.30) **Bar Meals** L served all week 12–10 D served all week (Sun 12–9.30) Av main course £6.95 ⊕ Free House ♥ 21 **Facilities** Garden Dogs allowed Parking

PICK OF THE PUBS

The Hatch Inn

Classically picturesque and reputedly dating from 1430, the Hatch Inn was converted from three cottages thought to have housed workers for the local water-driven hammer mill. It may also have been a smugglers' haunt, and is named after the coalmen's gate at the nearby entrance to Ashdown Forest.

The pub is superbly placed for a country walk (dogs are welcome), it features in a number of 'top ten pubs' lists, and has often served as a filming location for television dramas and advertisements. Only minutes away is the restored Poohsticks Bridge, immortalised in A.A. Milne's 'Winnie the Pooh' stories. There are two large beer gardens for al fresco summer dining, one of which enjoys views out over the forest. Cooking by the owner Nicholas Drillsma, combined with the customer service skills of his partner Sandra, have created a recipe for success. Quality ingredients and imaginative techniques produce an exciting menu, which includes a good selection of light bites and traditional dishes like home-cured gravadlax of tuna loin; and oven-roasted Mediterranean vegetables with grilled goats' cheese. Fish dishes are well represented, with smoked haddock and leek risotto, Cajun salmon, pan-fried scallops, oven-roasted halibut, and Shetland mussels all making appearances. Lunchtime reservations are not taken, but evening booking is essential. This is when to look out for a starter of hot duck salad, served pink with fresh mango and field mushrooms; or poached pears with roquefort and balsamic syrup. Main courses might include locally-reared beef fillet with pont-neuf potatoes and béarnaise sauce; or pan-fried fillet of brill with salsa verde. For dessert, try the double crunch rhubarb and apple crumble, or sticky toffee pudding.

MAP 06 TQ43
Coleman's Hatch TN7 4EJ
☎ 01342 822363
🖹 01342 822363
e-mail: nickad@bigfoot.com
dir: *A22, 14m, left at Forest Row rdbt, 3m to Colemans Hatch, right by church. Straight on at next junct, pub on right*

Open 11.30–3 5.30–11 (Sat-Sun all day in summer & BHs) Closed: 25 Dec
Bar Meals L served Mon-Sat 12–2.30 D served Mon-Thu 7–9.15 (Fri-Sat 7–9.30 Sun 12–3, 6.30–8.30)
Restaurant L served Mon-Sat 12–2.30 D served Mon-Sat 7–9.15 (Sun 12–3, 7–8.30)
🍺 Free House 🍺 Harveys, Fuller's London Pride, Larkins & Harvey's Old. 🍷 10
Facilities Garden Dogs allowed Play Area

FLETCHING
MAP 06 TQ42

Pick of the Pubs

The Griffin Inn ♀

TN22 3SS ☎ 01825 722890 📄 01825 722810

e-mail: info@thegriffininn.co.uk

dir: *M23 junct 10 to East Grinstead, then A22, then A275. Village signed on left, 15m from M23*

The Grade II listed Griffin is reputedly the oldest licensed building in Sussex. Since it's been in this unspoilt village overlooking the lovely Ouse Valley for over 400 years, the claim sounds entirely reasonable. The two-acre, west-facing garden offers glorious views, while inside old beams, wainscotting, open fires and pews make up the character of the main bar. Menus change daily, with organic, locally sourced ingredients used wherever possible to create modern British, but Mediterranean-influenced, food. A typical restaurant meal might start with half a dozen rock oysters with shallot vinegar; or borlotti bean soup; followed by saltimbocca of Rye Bay monkfish in Parma ham with soft polenta and roasted pepper jam; or roast guinea fowl with wild mushrooms, mash and Madeira cream.

Open 12–3 6–11 (Sat-Sun all day summer) Closed: 25 Dec
Bar Meals L served all week 12–2.30 D served Mon-Sat 7–9.30 (Sun 7–9) Av main course £13 **Restaurant** L served all week 12.15–2.30 D served Mon-Sat 7.15–9.30 Av 3 course à la carte £28 Av 3 course fixed price £30 ⊕ Free House ◀ Harvey Best, Kings of Horsham, Hepworths. ♀ 15 **Facilities** Garden Parking Play Area

GUN HILL
MAP 06 TQ51

Pick of the Pubs

The Gun Inn ♀

TN21 0JU ☎ 01825 872361 📄 01622 851881

e-mail: enquiries@thegunhouse.co.uk

dir: *5m S of Heathfield, 1m off A267 towards Gun Hill. 4m off A22 between Uckfield & Hailsham.*

A lovely 17th-century building and former courthouse set in delightful East Sussex countryside, with extensive views from a pretty terrace and garden. Wood dominates the interior, with beams, a beautiful wooden floor, and lots of hideaway places for quiet eating and drinking. A separate panelled dining room with a stunning fireplace is ideal for private parties. Three deli board selections can be shared by a gathering of friends – the fish board, for example, includes anchovies, marinated octopus, taramasalata, smoked salmon and trout. From the menu come starters of whole oven-baked camembert served with toast, and a pint or half pint of fresh prawns with tarragon mayonnaise. Main dishes include home-made pies (steak and kidney, shepherd's), and chef's favourite Sussex beef cuts (rib-eye, fillet) with sauce of your choice. The Old Coach House behind the Gun has been transformed into a farmer's market offering a wide selection of fresh local fruits and vegetables, organic foods, fish and meats.

Open 11–11 (Sun 11–10.30) **Bar Meals** L served all week 12–9.30 D served all week 12–9.30 Av main course £8 **Restaurant** L served all week 12–9.30 D served all week 12–9.30 Av 3 course à la carte £19 Av 2 course fixed price £9.95 ⊕ Free House ◀ Harveys, Guinness, Leffe, Youngs. ♀ 13 **Facilities** Children's licence Garden Parking Play Area

HARTFIELD
MAP 06 TQ43

Anchor Inn

Church St TN7 4AG ☎ 01892 770424

dir: *On B2110*

A 14th-century inn at the heart of Winnie the Pooh country, deep within the scenic Ashdown Forest. Inside are stone floors enhanced by a large inglenook fireplace. Sandwiches and salads are among the bar snacks, while for something more substantial you could try whole Dover sole; grilled pork loin on a bed of spaghetti; or medallions of beef fillet. Puddings include crème brûlée; ice cream gateau; and orange marmalade bread and butter pudding.

Open 11–11 **Bar Meals** L served all week 12–2 D served all week 6–10 **Restaurant** L served all week 12–2 D served Tue-Sat 7–9.30 ⊕ Free House ◀ Fuller's London Pride, Harveys Sussex Best Bitter, Interbrew Flowers IPA, Flowers Original Bitter. **Facilities** Garden Dogs allowed Parking

Pick of the Pubs

The Hatch Inn ♀

See Pick of the Pubs on page 559

ICKLESHAM
MAP 07 TQ81

The Queen's Head ♀

Parsonage Ln TN36 4BL

☎ 01424 814552 📄 01424 814766

dir: *Between Hastings & Rye on A259. Pub in village on x-rds near church*

Two centuries elapsed between 1632, when these distinctive tile-hung cottages were built, and their first days as an alehouse in 1831. The traditional atmosphere has been conserved, with high-beamed ceilings, large inglenook fireplaces, church pews and a clutter of old farm implements, and a bar from the old Midland Bank in Eastbourne. Hearty food usually includes home-made pies; steak and kidney pudding; curry of the day; all-day breakfast; jacket potatoes and plenty of other snacks.

Open 11–11 (Sun 12–10.30) **Bar Meals** L served Mon-Fri 12–2.30 D served Mon-Fri 6.15–9.30 (Sat-Sun 12–9.30) Av main course £8.95 **Restaurant** L served all week D served all week ⊕ Free House ◀ Rother Valley Level Best, Greene King Abbot Ale, Whites 1066, Harveys Best. ♀ 10 **Facilities** Garden Parking Play Area

KINGSTON (NEAR LEWES)
MAP 06 TQ30

The Juggs ♀

The Street BN7 3NT

☎ 01273 472523 📄 01273 483274

e-mail: juggs@shepherd-neame.co.uk

dir: *E of Brighton on A27*

Named after the women who walked from Brighton with baskets of fish for sale, this rambling, tile-hung 15th-century cottage, tucked beneath the South Downs, offers an interesting selection of freshly-cooked food. The area is ideal for walkers, and families are very welcome.

Open 11–11 (Sun 12–10.30) **Bar Meals** L served all week 12–2.30 D served Mon-Sat 6–9 (Sun 12–3.30, Sat-Sun snacks 12–9) Av main course £7.50 **Restaurant** L served all week 12–2.30 D served Mon-Sat 6–9 (Sun 12–3.30) Av 3 course à la carte £15.50 ⊕ Shepherd Neame ◄ Shepherd Neame Spitfire, Best & Oranjeboom. ♈ 7 **Facilities** Garden Dogs allowed Parking

---

LEWES   MAP 06 TQ41

The Snowdrop ♈

119 South St BN7 2BU ☎ 01273 471018

dir: Telephone for directions

In 1836 Britain's biggest ever avalanche fell from the cliff above this pub, hence its deceptively gentle name. The owners provide good-value fresh food (all meat is free range, including tempting ranges of doorstep sandwiches (try Sussex cheese and home-made chutney), pizzas, home-made vegetable burger; and wild boar sausages. Vegetarians are well catered for. Beer garden with a waterfall.

Open 11–11 (Sun 12–10.30) **Bar Meals** L served all week 12–9 D served all week 12–9 Av main course £7 **Restaurant** L served all week 12–9 D served all week 12–9 ⊕ Free House ◄ Harveys Best, Adnams Broadside plus guests. **Facilities** Garden Dogs allowed

---

MAYFIELD   MAP 06 TQ52

Pick of the Pubs

The Middle House ♈

See Pick of the Pubs on page 562

OFFHAM   MAP 06 TQ41

The Blacksmiths Arms ★★★★ INN ♈

London Rd BN7 3QD ☎ 01273 472971

e-mail: blacksmithsarms@tiscali.co.uk

web: www.theblacksmithsarms-offham.co.uk

dir: 2m N of Lewes on A275

An attractive, mid-18th-century free house popular with walkers and cyclists on the South Downs Way. Harvey's ales are served in the bar, where log fires burn in the inglenook. Bernard and Sylvia Booker's use of excellent local produce is shown in dishes like Auntie Kate's crispy roast duckling with spiced orange and Cointreau sauce; rack of South Downs lamb with poached pear and apricot sauce; and locally caught seafood.

Open 12–2.30 6.30–10.30 Closed: Mon **Bar Meals** L served Tue-Sat 12–2 D served Tue-Sat 7–9 (Sun 12–2.30) Av main course £6.50 **Restaurant** L served Tue-Sat 12–2 D served Tue-Sat 7–9 (Sun 12–2.30) Av 3 course à la carte £24 Av 2 course fixed price £9.95 ⊕ Free House ◄ Harveys Ales. ♈ 7 **Facilities** Garden Parking **Rooms** 4

RINGMER   MAP 06 TQ41

The Cock ♈

Uckfield Rd BN8 5RX

☎ 01273 812040 🖶 01273 812040

e-mail: matt@cockpub.co.uk

web: www.cockpub.co.uk

dir: On A26 approx 2m N of Lewes (just outside Ringmer)

Expect a friendly welcome at this family-run 16th-century free house. Original oak beams, flagstone floors and a blazing fire set a cosy scene. Harvey's ales and guest beers accompany the extensive menu, where typical choices include pork Dijonnaise; sea bass in white wine, cream and mustard sauce; and traditional favourites like steak and kidney pudding. The west-facing restaurant and garden have splendid views to the South Downs, with wonderful sunsets on clear evenings.

Open 11–3 6–11.30 (Sun 11–11.30) **Bar Meals** L served Mon-Sat 12–2 D served Mon-Sat 6–9.30 (Sun & BH 12–9.30) Av main course £9 **Restaurant** L served Mon-Sat 12–2 D served Mon-Sat 6–9.30 (Sun & BH 12–9.30) Av 3 course à la carte £18 ⊕ Free House ◄ Harveys Sussex Best Bitter, Sussex XXXX Old Ale , Fuller's London Pride, Harvey's Olympia. ♈ 9 **Facilities** Garden Dogs allowed Parking Play Area

PICK OF THE PUBS

MAYFIELD-SUSSEX, EAST

The Middle House

This Grade I listed 16th-century village inn is a superb specimen of Elizabethan architecture, described as 'one of the finest examples of a timber framed building in Sussex'. The timber, wattle and daub structure has survived since 1575, when it was built for Sir Thomas Gresham, Elizabeth I's Keeper of the Privy Purse, and founder of the London Stock Exchange.

A private residence until the 1920s, still incorporating a private chapel, it retains a fireplace by master carver Grinling Gibbons, and a splendid oak-panelled restaurant. Occupying a dominant position in the High Street of this 1000–year-old village, the inn is typical of the many black-and-white properties in this part of the country, with its heavily beamed frontage incorporating ornate timber patterning. A truly family-run business from start to finish, the Middle House is owned by Monica and Bryan Blundell; their son Darren is general manager, and daughter Kirsty manages the restaurant, while son-in-law Mark is the head chef. An impressive selection of imaginative dishes is served, ranging from blackboard choices in the bar to more than 40 options on the more formal restaurant carte. Expect starters here like honey roast scallops served with chestnut purée and crispy bacon, or smoked haddock and vegetable terrine with a lemon vinaigrette. Main courses make good use of local produce in delicious dishes like roast lamb cutlets topped with black olive and rosemary risotto. Another traditional choice would be fanned marinated duck breast with a caramelised plum and ginger sauce. Vegetarians might try beetroot, red onion marmalade and goats' cheese tart with a balsamic glaze.

MAP 06 TQ52
High St TN20 6AB
☎ 01435 872146
🖹 01435 873423
e-mail:
kirsty@middle-house.com
dir: *E of A267, S of Tunbridge Wells*

Open 11–11 (Sun 12–10.30)
Bar Meals L served all week 12–2 D served all week 7–9.30 (Sun 12–2.30, 7–9) Av main course £11.95
Restaurant L served all week 12–2 D served Tue-Sat 7–9 Av 3 course à la carte £27
⊕ Free House ◀ Harveys Best, Greene King Abbot Ale, Black Sheep Best, Theakston Best. ♀ 9
Facilities Garden Parking Play Area

RUSHLAKE GREEN   MAP 06 TQ61

Pick of the Pubs

Horse & Groom ♥

TN21 9QE ☎ 01435 830320 🖹 01435 830310

e-mail: chappellhatpeg@aol.com

dir: *Telephone for directions*

Just across the road from the village green, this whitewashed inn dates from around 1650. The building was first licensed in 1775, and two years later it was listed as the Horse and Groom. Today you'll find a welcoming atmosphere surrounded by old beams, with Shepherd Neame ales dispensed from a row of hand pumps in the bar. Antique shotguns decorate the walls of the Gun Room restaurant, where you can choose an entirely fishy flavour for your meal: monkfish and organic salmon baked in parchment vanilla and vermouth; scallops sautéed with smoked bacon, spring onions, white wine and a butter oyster sauce; wild seabass fillets pan-fried and served with crushed olive, potato and white wine sauce; and mussels steamed in leeks, onions, white wine and pink peppercorns. On warmer days, meals are served in the garden, with fantastic views of the Sussex countryside.

Open 11.30–3 5.30–11 (Sun 11.30–4 winter, all day summer) Rest: (25–26 Dec Eve only) **Bar Meals** L served all week 12–2.15 D served Mon-Sat 7–9.30 (Sun 7–9) Av main course £10 **Restaurant** L served all week 12–2.30 D served Mon-Sat 7–9.30 (Sun7–9) Av 3 course à la carte £22 ⊕ Shepherd Neame ◄ Master Brew, Spitfire, Kent Best, Late Red & Bishop's Finger. ♥ 8 **Facilities** Garden Dogs allowed Parking

---

RYE   MAP 07 TQ92

The Globe Inn ♥

10 Military Rd TN31 7NX ☎ 01797 227918

e-mail: info@theglobe-inn.com

dir: *M20 junct 11 onto A2080*

A small, informal free house just outside the ancient town walls. An absence of gaming machines, jukeboxes and TV screens encourages even husbands and wives to talk to each other over their drinks, or while they enjoy their contemporary British food in the modern, wood-floored bar and restaurant area. Fresh fish comes from a local fisherman, organic meat from a National Trust farm at Winchelsea, and fruit and vegetables from Kent, the Garden of England.

Open 12–3 7–11 Closed: 2wks Jan & Mon, Sun eve & Tue Jan-Mar **Bar Meals** L served Tue-Sat 12–3 (Sun 12–2, closed Tue Jan-March) **Restaurant** L served Tue-Sun 12–2 D served Tue-Sat 7–9.30 (Closed Tue Jan-March) ⊕ Free House ◄ ESB, Harveys & Guinness. ♥ 20 **Facilities** Children's licence Garden Dogs allowed Parking

Pick of the Pubs

Mermaid Inn ★★★ HL ◉ ♥

Mermaid St TN31 7EY

☎ 01797 223065 🖹 01797 225069

e-mail: info@mermaidinn.com

dir: *A259, follow signs to town centre, then into Mermaid Street*

Rye is a Cinque Port, and the now silted-up harbour was once England's premier point of embarkation for France. Smugglers congregated here, including the infamous Hawkhurst Gang, and one or two of them may yet haunt the Mermaid's corridors and secret passages. Even the street is cobbled, as if to prepare the senses for the interior of an inn whose doors first opened in 1156. The public rooms have huge beams, some recycled from ships' timbers, and fireplaces carved from French stone ballast rescued from the harbour. There is also a priest's hole in the lounge bar. Food is served in the bar and restaurant (with its notable linenfold panelling), and in the summer you can relax under sunshades on the patio. Bar food ranges from sandwiches or steak and kidney pudding, to smoked fish chowder and seafood platter.

Open 11–11 **Bar Meals** L served all week 12–2.30 D served Sun-Fri 7–9.30 Av main course £7.50 **Restaurant** L served all week 12–2.15 D served all week 7–9.15 Av 3 course à la carte £35 Av 3 course fixed price £24 ⊕ Free House ◄ Greene King Old Speckled Hen, Courage Best. ♥ 11 **Facilities** Garden Parking **Rooms** 31

The Lamb Inn

A family-run white-painted inn built in 1526, the Lamb did not begin dispensing ale until 1640. It's a popular watering hole for locals and walkers enjoying the tiny hamlet and lovely surrounding East Sussex countryside. Settle down in one of the comfortable cream sofas drawn up to the fire and enjoy a thoughtful selection of real ales and wines by the glass.

Aside from liquid refreshment, the pub is well known for its food, which mixes traditional ingredients with modern techniques. Everything is home made including the bread, and top quality produce is locally sourced as much as possible. Chilley Farm, just two miles away, specialises in raising stock without additives in unhurried fashion, rearing animals such as Gloucester Old Spot pigs, Southdowns and Kent Cross lamb, and Sussex beef which is extra matured on the bone before delivery. Fish from Hastings and Newhaven is a house speciality, offered daily on the specials board. Baps loaded with Chilley Farm smoked bacon, and ploughman's are served at lunchtime, as is a steakburger stuffed with smoked cheddar and served with fries, rocket mayonnaise and tomato relish. Main meals range from home-made pie of the day, to the Lamb's own chicken Kiev – succulent Suffolk farm chicken breast stuffed with smoked cheddar and garlic butter. Alternatively braised shank of lamb on roasted smoked garlic mash, or crispy roasted pork belly with apple dauphinoise potatoes should hit the spot. Non-carnivores will enjoy home-made vegetarian Wellington of chestnuts, mushrooms, peppers, gruyère and butter onions; or winter vegetable casserole with a parmesan and breadcrumb crust. Traditional desserts along the lines of vanilla and blackcurrant cheesecake with cream, or steamed apple sponge pudding with custard.

MAP 06 TQ60
BN27 1RY
☎ 01323 832116
web: www.lambinnwartling.co.uk
dir: *A259 from Polegate to Pevensey rdbt. Take 1st left to Wartling & Herstmonceux Castle. Pub 3m on right.*

Open 11–3 6–11
Bar Meals L served Mon-Sat 11.45–2.15 (Sun 12–2.30) D served all week 6.45–9
Restaurant L served Mon-Sat 11.45–2.15 (Sun 12–2.30) D served all week 6.45–9
Harveys, Red River, Horsham Best, Toff's. 8
Facilities Garden Parking

RYE continued

Pick of the Pubs

The Ypres Castle Inn 🍷

Gun Garden TN31 7HH ☎ 01797 223248

e-mail: info@yprescastleinn.co.uk

dir: *Behind parish church & adjacent to medieval Ypres Tower*

'The Wipers', as locals call it, was once the haunt of smugglers. Built in 1640 in weather-boarded style and added to in Victorian times, it's the only pub in the citadel area of Rye. Another plus is its garden – the roses, shrubs and views to the 13th-century Ypres Tower and River Rother make it an ideal spot for a pint from the range of tapped ales. Colourful art and furnishings help give the interior a warm and friendly atmosphere. The seasonally changing menu is largely sourced locally. A good range of lunchtime snacks includes ploughman's, jacket potatoes, and sandwiches backed by half a dozen daily specials. The evening menu may propose fishy starters like moules marinières or cracked Dungeness crab, a theme which could be continued with grilled Rye Bay plaice or pan-fried fillets of lemon sole. Meaty options are no less appealing: grilled rack of Romney salt-marsh lamb, or the pub's home-made prime beefburger with relish. New landlord for 2008.

Open 11.30–11 (Fri 11–1am) **Bar Meals** L served all week 12–3 D served all week 6–9 Av main course £10 **Restaurant** L served all week 12–3 D served Mon-Sat 6–9 Av 3 course à la carte £18.20 ⊕ Free House ◀ Harveys Best, Adnams Broadside, Wells Bombardier, Timothy Taylor Landlord. 🍷 11 **Facilities** Garden

---

SHORTBRIDGE   MAP 06 TQ42

Pick of the Pubs

The Peacock Inn 🍷

TN22 3XA ☎ 01825 762463 📠 01825 762463

e-mail: enquiries@peacock-inn.co.uk

dir: *Just off A272 (Haywards Heath to Uckfield road) & A26 (Uckfield to Lewes road)*

Mentioned in Samuel Pepys' diary, this traditional inn dates from 1567 and is full of old world charm, both inside and out. Today it is renowned for its food (created by no fewer than three chefs), and also the resident ghost of Mrs Fuller. The large rear patio garden is a delightful spot in summer. Food choices include toasted ciabatta and toasted foccacia with a variety of fillings. For the hungry there are starters such as chicken and duck liver paté, or crayfish tails and smoked salmon, followed by seafood crepe, pan-fried sea bass fillets; steak, Guinness and mushroom pie or fillet steak with garlic and stilton butter. For the non-meat eaters there's Mediterranean vegetable and mozzarella tartlet, or vegetarian tagine. Look out for chefs' specials.

Open 11–3 6–11 Closed: 25–26 Dec **Bar Meals** L served all week 12–2.30 D served all week 6–9.30 (Sun 6–9) **Restaurant** L served all week 12–2.30 D served all week 7–10 (Sun 6–9) Av 3 course à la carte £21 ⊕ Free House ◀ Abbot Ale, Harveys Best Bitter, Fuller's London Pride. 🍷 8 **Facilities** Garden Dogs allowed Parking

---

THREE LEG CROSS   MAP 06 TQ63

The Bull 🍷

Dunster Mill Ln TN5 7HH

☎ 01580 200586 📠 01580 201289

e-mail: enquiries@thebullinn.co.uk

dir: *From M25 exit at Sevenoaks toward Hastings, right at x-rds onto B2087, right onto B2099 through Ticehurst, right for Three Legged Cross*

Based around a 14th-century Wealden hall house and set in a peaceful hamlet close to Bewl Water, the Bull features oak beams, inglenook fireplaces and quarry tiled floors. There's a duck pond in the garden, together with a pétanque pitch and children's play area. Menus are full of pub favourites high in comfort factor: garlic mushrooms, prawn cocktail or deep-fried brie to start; chicken Kiev, bangers and mash, or beef lasagne to follow; and desserts like treacle pudding or apple tart.

Open 12–11 Closed: 25–26 Dec eve **Bar Meals** L served Mon-Fri 12–2.30 D served Mon-Sat 6.30–9 (Sat 12–3, Sun 12–8) **Restaurant** L served Mon-Sat 12–2.30 D served Mon-Sat 6.30–9 (Sun 12–8) ⊕ Free House ◀ Harveys, Spitfire, Speckled Hen, Wealdell Bitter. 🍷 7 **Facilities** Children's licence Garden Dogs allowed Parking Play Area

---

UPPER DICKER   MAP 06 TQ50

The Plough 🍷

Coldharbour Rd BN27 3QJ ☎ 01323 844859

dir: *Off A22, W of Hailsham*

17th-century former farmhouse which has been a pub for over 200 years, and now comprises two bars and two restaurants. Excellent wheelchair facilities, a large beer garden and a children's play area add to the appeal, and the Plough is also a handy stop for walkers. Expect such fish dishes as Sussex smokie or prawn, brie and broccoli bake, while other options include duck breast in spicy plum sauce, veal in lemon cream, or lamb cutlets in redcurrant and rosemary.

Open 11–11 (Sun 12–3, 7–10.30) **Bar Meals** L served all week 12–2.30 D served all week 6–9 (Sat-Sun all day) **Restaurant** L served all week 12–2.30 D served all week 6–9 ⊕ Shepherd Neame ◀ Shepherd Neame Spitfire Premium Ale, Best & Bishop's Finger. 🍷 6 **Facilities** Garden Dogs allowed Parking Play Area

WADHURST   MAP 06 TQ63

The Best Beech Inn ♀

Mayfield Ln TN5 6JH

☎ 01892 782046 📠 01982 782046

e-mail: bestbeech@tesco.net

dir: *7m from Tunbridge Wells. On A246 at traffic lights turn left onto London Rd A26, left at mini rdbt onto A267, left then right onto B2100. At Mark Cross signed Wadhurst, 3m on right*

The unusually-named Best Beech Inn is going from strength to strength. The inn dates back to 1680, and has been sympathetically refurbished in recent years to preserve the essentially Victorian character of its heyday. The result is a place bursting with personality, characterised by comfy chairs, exposed brickwork and open fireplaces. Ideally situated near the Kent and Sussex border, in an area of outstanding natural beauty, the inn includes a fine à la carte restaurant offering excellent European cuisine with a French influence. For those who prefer a more informal atmosphere, there is the bar bistro with a comprehensive menu available from the blackboard. Dinner could begin with pork rillette and apricot chutney, move on to bouillabaisse with saffron new potatoes, and finish with tarte au chocolate, marmalade syrup and vanilla ice cream.

Open 11–11 **Bar Meals** L served all week 12–2.30 D served all week 6–9.30 Av main course £10 **Restaurant** L served all week 12–2.30 D served all week 6–9 Av 3 course à la carte £20 ⊕ Free House 🍺 Harveys, Level Best, Youngs, London Pride. ♀7 **Facilities** Garden Dogs allowed Parking

---

WARBLETON   MAP 06 TQ61

The War-Bill-in-Tun Inn

Church Hill TN21 9BD

☎ 01435 830636 📠 01435 830636

e-mail: whitton@thewarbillintun.wanadoo.co.uk

dir: *From Hailsham take A267 towards Heathfield. Turn right for village (15m from Hailsham)*

A 400–year-old smugglers' haunt, visited by The Beatles when they came to see their manager, Brian Epstein, who lived half a mile away. Locals still recall meeting Lennon and McCartney, as well as the resident ghost. Family run, the owners aim to offer good food and friendly service. Representative dishes include Gressingham duck, grilled trout with an almond and wine sauce, and light lunch dishes like jacket potatoes and scampi.

Open 12–3 7–11 **Bar Meals** L served all week 12–1.45 D served all week 7–9.30 **Restaurant** L served all week 12–1.45 D served all week 7–9.30 ⊕ Free House 🍺 Harveys Best, Bishop's Finger, Tanglefoot & Spitfire Smooth. **Facilities** Garden Dogs allowed Parking

---

WARTLING   MAP 06 TQ60

The Lamb Inn ♀

See Pick of the Pubs on page 564

WILMINGTON   MAP 06 TQ50

The Giants Rest ♀

The Street BN26 5SQ

☎ 01323 870207 📠 01323 870207

e-mail: abecjane@aol.com

dir: *2m outside Polegate on A27 towards Brighton*

With the famous chalk figure of the Long Man of Wilmington standing guard opposite, this family-owned, Victorian free house is admirably committed to home-prepared, seasonal food. Sit at a pine table, play a game or puzzle, and order roast chicken and leek pie; beef in Guinness with rosemary dumplings; hake with coriander, spring onion and chilli fishcakes; or haloumi warm salad. There are daily specials too. Harveys real ales from Lewes are among those offered.

Open 11.30–3 6–11 (Sat 11.30–11, Sun 12–10.30) **Bar Meals** L served Mon-Sat 12–2 D served Mon-Sat 7–9 (Sun 12–9) Av main course £9 **Restaurant** L served Mon-Sat 12–2 D served Mon-Sat 7–9 (Sun 12–9) ⊕ Free House 🍺 Harveys Best, Timothy Taylor Landlord, Summer Lightning, Harveys Old. ♀7 **Facilities** Garden Dogs allowed Parking

---

WINCHELSEA   MAP 07 TQ91

The New Inn ♀

German St TN36 4EN ☎ 01797 226252

dir: *Telephone for details*

Elegant Winchelsea has seen much change over the centuries, not least the sea's retreat that ended its days as a thriving seaport. The 18th-century New Inn has witnessed change of a far more beneficial nature and is known today for its comfort, hospitality and excellent cuisine. Chalkboard specials include lobster tails with chips and salad, Rye Bay lemon sole, and chicken Klev. The lovely walled garden is a delight on a sunny day.

Open 11.30–12 **Bar Meals** L served all week 12–3 D served all week 6.30–9.30 (Sun 12–9) **Restaurant** L served all week 12–2.30 D served all week 6.30–9.30 (Sun 12–9) ⊕ Greene King 🍺 Morlands Original, Abbots Ale, Greene King IPA, Old Speckled Hen. ♀10 **Facilities** Garden Dogs allowed Parking

---

WITHYHAM   MAP 06 TQ43

The Dorset Arms ♀

See Pick of the Pubs on opposite page

PICK OF THE PUBS

WITHYHAM-SUSSEX, EAST

The Dorset Arms

Back in the 15th century this white, weather-boarded building was an open-halled farmhouse with earthen floors. It has been an inn since the 18th century, and the name derives from the arms of the local Sackville family of Buckhurst Park, who were once the Dukes of Dorset.

Set on the borders of Kent and Sussex, the inn is ideally situated for explorations of nearby Ashdown Forest, home to everybody's favourite bear, Winnie the Pooh. It has many interesting features, including the massive wall and ceiling beams in the restaurant, the oak-floored bar, the huge open fireplace, and an old ice house buried in the hillside at the back. The prize-winning beers come from Harveys of Lewes, and a good number of wines from the extensive wine list are available by the glass. Bar snacks and daily specials are among the food choices, and the à la carte menu lists starters such as home-made chicken liver pate and toast; crispy coated camembert with port and redcurrant jelly; and deep-fried tempura battered

king prawns with chilli dip. Main courses can include pan-fried loin of venison in Cumberland sauce; large tiger prawns sautéed in garlic, white wine and cream; half roast duckling with cherry and Amaretto sauce; and sliced boneless breast of chicken with bacon, leeks, cream and cider. Where possible the owners source all their ingredients locally. Blackboard specials might feature cheese-topped ratatouille bake; salmon fishcakes; or griddled whole plaice. The pub is a popular venue for the fishing and cricket teams, and holds regular quiz nights and music evenings.

MAP 06 TQ43
TN7 4BD
☎ 01892 770278
🖷 01892 770195
e-mail: pete@dorset-arms.co.uk
dir: 4m W of Tunbridge Wells on B2110 between Groombridge & Hartfield

Open 11–3 6–11 (Sun 12–3, 7–10.30)
Bar Meals L served all week 12–2 D served Tue-Sat 7–9 Av main course £8
Restaurant L served all week 12–2 D served Tue-Sat 7–9 Av 3 course à la carte £20
🍺 Harveys of Lewes ◀ Harveys Sussex Best & seasonal ales. 🍷 8
Facilities Garden Dogs allowed Parking

SUSSEX, WEST

AMBERLEY
MAP 06 TQ01

Black Horse

High St BN18 9NL ☎ 01798 831552

e-mail: theblackhorse@btconnect.com

A traditional 17th-century tavern with a lively atmosphere, in a beautiful South Downs village. Look out for the display of sheep bells donated by the last shepherd to have a flock on the local hills. Food is served in the large restaurant and bar, including extensive vegetarian choice and children's menu. Lovely gardens, good local walks, and nice views of the South Downs. Dogs are welcome in the bar.

Open 11–11 (Sun 12–10.30) **Bar Meals** L served all week 12–3 D served all week 6–9 Av main course £9.45 **Restaurant** L served all week 12–3 6–9 ⊕ Punch Taverns ◄ Bombardier, Greene King IPA. **Facilities** Garden Dogs allowed

The Bridge Inn ☻

Houghton Bridge BN18 9LR ☎ 01798 831619

e-mail: bridgeamberley@aol.com

dir: 5m N of Arundel on B2139. Next to Amberley main line station

This traditional country pub stands in the stunning Arun Valley on the half-way point of the South Downs Way. The building is Grade II listed and dates from 1650. Personally owned and managed by Dave and Natasha Challis, the inn offers an extensive menu ranging from hearty steak and kidney pudding to Mediterranean daily specials made by Greek chef George Koulouris. Picturesque Amberley, Arundel Castle and Bignor Roman Villa are all close by.

Open 12–11 (Sun 12–10.30) **Bar Meals** L served Mon-Fri 12–2.30 D served Mon-Sat 6–9 (Sat 12–4 & Sun 12–8) Av main course £8.95 **Restaurant** L served Mon-Sat 12–2.30 D served Mon-Sat 6–9 (Sun 12–8) Av 3 course à la carte £20 ⊕ Free House ◄ Harveys Sussex, Youngs, Fuller's London Pride, Hopback Summer Lightning & Skinner's Betty Stogs. ☻8 **Facilities** Garden Dogs allowed Parking

ASHURST
MAP 06 TQ11

Pick of the Pubs

The Fountain Inn ☻

BN44 3AP ☎ 01403 710219

e-mail: fountainashurst@aol.com

dir: On B2135 N of Steyning

This 16th-century free house is located just north of Steyning in a picturesque setting in the historic village of Ashurst. The interior features flagstone floors, low beams and a fantastic inglenook fireplace. There are two large garden areas in a delightfully tranquil setting by the large duck pond with seating for 200 people. The inn offers an extensive selection of home-made dishes to delight your taste buds, including its renowned burgers and steak and ale pies, and the regular range of well-kept real ales is supplemented by a weekly guest ale from local breweries. At lunchtime there are ploughman's, salads, freshly cut sandwiches, and Sussex smokie – smoked haddock and prawns in a cheese sauce. In the evening there is a good choice from the chargrill, notably steaks, and dishes like chicken breast with a sunblush tomato and pesto dressing. A fishy option might be sea bass, or a choice from the specials board.

Open 11.30 -11 (Sun 12–10.30) **Bar Meals** L served Mon-Sat 11.30–2 D served Mon-Sat 6–9.30 (Sun 12–3) **Restaurant** L served Mon-Sat 11.30–2 D served Mon-Sat 6–9.30 (Sun 12–3) ⊕ Free House ◄ Harveys Sussex, Fuller's London, Adnams Broadside and seasonal and guest ales. ☻10 **Facilities** Garden Dogs allowed Parking

BARNHAM
MAP 06 SU90

The Murrell Arms ☻

Yapton Rd PO22 0AS ☎ 01243 553320

dir: From Brighton follow A27 through Arundel for 2m, left at The Oaks, follow road to end. Turn right at The Olive Branch

An attractive white-painted inn distinguished by lavish window boxes and hanging baskets that add a wonderful splash of colour in summer. Built in 1750 as a farmhouse, it became a pub shortly after the railway station opened over 100 years later. With the briefest of menus at the lowest of prices, there's no more affordable place to sit down for a ploughman's or two king-size bangers, new potatoes and baked beans, washed down with a reliable pint of Fullers.

Open 11–2.30 6–11 (Sat 11–11, Sun 12–10.30) **Bar Meals** L served all week 12–2 D served Fri-Wed 6–9 ⊕ Fullers ◄ Fuller's London Pride, ESB & Butser Best – Horndean Special Brew. ☻28 **Facilities** Garden Dogs allowed Parking Play Area **Notes** ⊛

BURPHAM
MAP 06 TQ00

Pick of the Pubs

George & Dragon ◉

See Pick of the Pubs on opposite page

BURY
MAP 06 TQ01

The Squire & Horse ☻

Bury Common RH20 1NS ☎ 01798 831343 📄 01798 831343

dir: On A29, 4m S of Pulborough, 4m N of Arundel

The original 16th-century building was extended a few years ago, with old wooden beams and country fireplaces throughout. All the food is freshly cooked to order. The fish specials change daily and main courses are served with a selection of vegetables. These could include barbequed barracuda fillet on a bed of prawn risotto, or calves' liver with bacon and red wine glaze. Thai food is a speciality, and the pub is renowned for its desserts.

Open 11.30–3 6–11 (Sun 12–3 6–10.30) (May-Sep Sat 11.30–11, Sun 12–10.30) **Bar Meals** L served all week 12–2 D served all week 12–10.30) **Bar Meals** L served all week 12–2 D served all week **Restaurant** (May-Sep Sat 11.30–11, Sun 12–10.30) L served all week 12–2 D served all week 6–9 ◄ Greene King IPA, Harveys Sussex, guest ales. ☻8 **Facilities** Garden Parking

George & Dragon

An old smuggling inn down what is essentially a two and a half mile cul-de-sac in peaceful Burf'm (although next-door Wepham is Wep'm!). The Arun cuts through the chalk downs here, with mighty Arundel Castle guarding the gap. The riverside and other local walks are lovely, but be ready to remove muddy footwear in the pub porch.

Inside this lovely old inn are beamed ceilings and modern prints on the walls, and worn stone flags on the floor. The original old rooms have been opened out into one huge space that catches the afternoon and evening light. One alcove is hidden away up a few steps, with a couple of tables tucked away for an intimate drink or meal, and there's another nook with more tables. A small bar is accessed around a corner. It's very much a dining pub, attracting visitors from far and wide. The à la carte menu and specials board offer a good choice of dishes between them: for starters you could try prawn and crab cake on seasonal leaves; deep-fried whitebait with lemon and dill mayonnaise; or smoked chicken and duck terrine with orange chutney and melba toast; main courses might include walnut-crusted cod loin with parsnip pur?e and new minted potatoes; roasted duck breast with redcurrant and black cherry sauce and dauphinoise potatoes; pan-seared scallops with a lobster risotto and white wine sauce; slow-cooked lamb shank in a red wine and rosemary sauce, and favourites like battered fillet of haddock with fries. There are tables outside, ideal for whiling away an afternoon or evening in summer, listening to the cricket being played on the green a few steps away. New owners now in situ.

MAP 06 TQ00
BN18 9RR
☎ 01903 883131
e-mail:
sara.cheney@btinternet.com
dir: *Off A27 1m E of Arundel, signed Burpham, 2.5m pub on left*

Open 11–2.30 6–12
Bar Meals L served Mon-Fri 12–2 (Sat-Sun 12–3) D served Mon-Sat 7–9
Restaurant L served all week 12–2 D served Mon-Sat 7–9 Av 3 course à la carte £30
⊕ Free House ◀ Harvey Best, Brewery-on-Sea Spinnaker Bitter, Fuller's London Pride, King Brewery Red River. Arundel Ales & guests.
Facilities Dogs allowed Parking

PICK OF THE PUBS

CHARLTON-SUSSEX, WEST

The Fox Goes Free

A favoured hunting lodge of William III, this 16th-century pub also hosted the first Women's Institute meeting in 1915. The lovely old brick and flint building nestles in unspoilt countryside, and with its two huge fireplaces, old pews and brick floors, it exudes charm and character.

The Weald and Downland open-air museum is close by, where fifty historic buildings have been niched into the South Downs in a unique collection. The pub is also only a few furlongs away from Goodwood Racecourse, and attracts many a punter in the racing season – especially during the July festival known as 'Glorious Goodwood'. A little further on Goodwood House, home to the Dukes of Richmond for over 300 years, hosts the annual 'Festival of Speed'; and the historic Goodwood Motor Racing Circuit is a mecca for vintage car enthusiasts during the 'Revival' meeting. Lest this all sounds rather fancy, the Fox Goes Free is nonetheless a friendly and welcoming drinkers' pub – a good selection of real ales includes one named after the pub – and

eating here is not prohibitive either. There are five places where your meal can be served: the main bar with open fire, the main restaurant, the Snug, the Bakery and the Stable. Carefully prepared ingredients mingle on a menu of home-made food that may include starters of smoked and poached salmon, or baked goat's cheese crotin; mains can vary from lasagne, chips and salad through to rib-eye steak with rocket salad, red onion marmalade and a peppercorn sauce; vanilla rice pudding is a dessert to sample. Solid timber benches and tables to the front and an equally well furnished lawned garden to the rear are also attractive settings in which to sup a quiet pint while picking your winners.

MAP 06 SU81
PO18 0HU
☎ 01243 811461
e-mail:
thefoxgoesfree.always@virgin.net
dir: *A286, 6m from Chichester towards Midhurst. 1m from Goodwood racecourse*

Open 11–11 (Sun 12–10.30)
Bar Meals L served all week
12–2.30 D served all week
6.30–10 (Sat-Sun 12–10) Av main course £9.50
Restaurant L served Mon-Fri
12–2.30 D served Mon-Fri 6.30–10
(Sat-Sun all day) Av 3 course à la carte £25
⊕ Free House ◀ Ballards Best
& The Fox Goes Free, Harvey's
Sussex. ♥ 7
Facilities Garden Dogs allowed
Parking
Rooms available

CHARLTON   MAP 06 SU81

Pick of the Pubs

The Fox Goes Free ⚲
See Pick of the Pubs on opposite page

CHICHESTER   MAP 05 SU80

Crown and Anchor ⚲
Dell Quay Rd PO20 7EE ☎ 01243 781712
e-mail: crown&anchor@thespiritgroup.com
dir: *Take A286 from Chichester towards West Wittering, turn right for Dell Quay*

Nestling at the foot of the Sussex Downs with panoramic views of Chichester harbour, this unique hostelry dates in parts to the early 18th century when it also served as a custom house for the old port. It has a superb terrace overlooking the quay for al fresco dining. Menu choices include fish (battered to order) and chips, grilled steaks, and steak and ale pie.

Open 11–11 (Sun 12–10.30) **Bar Meals** L served all week 12–3 D served all week 6–9 (Sun 12–9) Av main course £10 **Restaurant** L served all week 12–3 D served all week 6–9 (Sun 12–9) Av 3 course à la carte £40 Av 3 course fixed price £10 ⊕ Punch Taverns ◀ Bombardier, Theakstons, Guinness. ⚲ 17 **Facilities** Children's licence Garden Dogs allowed Parking

Pick of the Pubs

Royal Oak Inn ★★★★★ INN ◉ ⚲
Pook Ln, East Lavant PO18 0AX
☎ 01243 527434 📄 01243 775062
e-mail: info@royaloakeastlavant.co.uk
dir: *A286 from Chichester signed Midhurst, 2m then right at mini-rdbt, pub is over bridge on left*

Set just two miles north of the Georgian streets of Chichester, this coaching inn is tucked away in a pretty Downland village within easy reach of the rolling hills of Sussex. The Royal Oak was a pub for many years, but has been exceptionally well converted to offer not only an elegant restaurant, but also stylish, sleekly furnished accommodation complete with state of the art entertainment systems. The brick-lined restaurant and bar achieve a crisp, rustic chic: details include fresh flowers, candles, and wine attractively displayed in alcoves set into the walls. A lengthy wine list will be the delight of any connoisseur. New owners for 2008.

Royal Oak Inn

Open 10 -11 Closed: 25 Dec **Bar Meals** L served all week 12–2 D served all week 6–9.30 **Restaurant** L served all week 12–2 D served all week 6–9.30 Av 3 course à la carte £28 ◀ Ballards, HSB, Sussex, Arundel. ⚲ 20 **Facilities** Garden Parking **Rooms** 8

CHILGROVE   MAP 05 SU81

Pick of the Pubs

The Fish House Ⓤ ◉◉ ⚲
High St PO18 9HX ☎ 01243 519444
e-mail: info@thefishhouse.co.uk
dir: *On B2141 between Chichester & Petersfield*

Built in 1756, this long wisteria-covered hostelry is tucked right into the South Downs, a few miles outside Chichester. New owner David Barnard has completely renovated and refurbished it for the summer of 2008, and now offers a completely transformed venue for eating, drinking and longer stays too. The bar area is elegant and welcoming, with its open fire and comfy sofas, and here an oyster and Guinness counter serves modern versions of classic dishes. The restaurant is a sophisticated spot to sample some fine dining, based on the freshest seafood, while the bedrooms are luxurious enough to warrant return visits.

Open 8am-11 **Bar Meals** L served all week 12–5 D served all week 6–10 Av main course £12 **Restaurant** L served all week 12–2.30 D served all week 6–10 Av 3 course à la carte £30 Av 3 course fixed price £19.50 ⊕ Free House ◀ Ballard's. ⚲ 15 **Facilities** Garden Dogs allowed Parking **Rooms** 17

COMPTON   MAP 05 SU71

Coach & Horses
The Square PO18 9HA ☎ 02392 631228
dir: *On B2146 S of Petersfield, to Emsworth, in centre of Compton*

The 16th-century pub is set quite remotely in the prettiest of downland villages, a popular spot for walkers and cyclists. The front bar features two open fires and a bar billiards table, while the restaurant is in the oldest part of the pub, with many exposed beams. Up to five guest beers from independent breweries are usually available, and there is an extensive menu of home-cooked dishes, all made to order.

Open 12–3 6–11 **Bar Meals** L served all week 12–2 D served all week 6–9 Av main course £9.75 **Restaurant** L served Tue-Sun 12–2 D served Tue-Sat 6–9 Av 3 course à la carte £25.75 ⊕ Free House ◀ Fuller's ESB, Ballard's Best, Dark Star Golden Gate, Oakleaf Brewery Nuptu'ale. **Facilities** Dogs allowed

England

DUNCTON
MAP 06 SU91

The Cricketers ♀

GU28 0LB ☎ 01798 342473 📄 01799 344753

e-mail: info@thecricketersinn.com

Attractive white-painted pub situated in spectacular walking country at the western end of the South Downs. Rumoured to be haunted, the inn has changed little over the years. There is a delightful and very popular garden with extensive deck seating and weekend barbecues. The menus sometimes change four times a day, offering good hearty meals like beer-battered haddock or rib-eye steak, both with hand-cut chips. An ideal stop-off point for coach parties visiting Goodwood.

Open 11–11 **Bar Meals** L served Mon-Sat 12–2.30 D served Mon -Sat 6–9.30 (Sun all day) **Restaurant** L served Mon-Sat 12–2.30 D served Mon-Sat 6–9.30 (Sun all day) ⊕ Free House ◖ Betty Stogs, Horsham Best, Arundel Gold & wkly guest ale. ♀ 10 **Facilities** Garden Dogs allowed Parking Play Area

EAST ASHLING
MAP 05 SU80

Horse and Groom ★★★★ INN ♀

East Ashling PO18 9AX ☎ 01243 575339 📄 01243 575560

e-mail: info@thehorseandgroomchichester.co.uk

web: www.thehorseandgroomchichester.com

dir: 3m from Chichester on B1278 between Chichester & Rowland's Castle. 2m off A27 at Fishbourne

A substantially renovated 17th-century inn located at the foot of the South Downs. This is good walking country, and top tourist attractions lie within easy reach. The flagstoned and beamed bar is cosy, with a working range at one end and an open fire at the other. The underground cellar keeps ales at a constant temperature, and there are bar snack, blackboard and full à la carte menus.

Open 12–3 6–11 (Sun 12–6) Closed: Sun eve **Bar Meals** L served Mon-Sat 12–2.15 D served Mon-Sat 6.30–9.15 (Sun 12–2.30) **Restaurant** L served Mon-Sat 12–2.15 D served Mon-Sat 6.30–9.15 (Sun 12–2.30) ⊕ Free House ◖ Youngs, Harveys, Summer Lightning, Hop Head. ♀ 6 **Facilities** Garden Dogs allowed Parking **Rooms** 11

EAST DEAN
MAP 06 SU91

Pick of the Pubs

The Star & Garter ♀

PO18 0JG ☎ 01243 811318 📄 01243 811826

e-mail: thestarandgarter@hotmail.com

dir: On A286 between Chichester & Midhurst. Exit A286 at Singleton. Village in 2m

East Dean is one of the county's prettiest villages, and the Star and Garter has been a pub there since 1740. There are bar snacks, of course, and the beer from the cellar comes from Ballards and other guest breweries. Seafood is the speciality, and the Shellfish Bar serves crab and lobster from Selsey as well as most other kinds of crustacea. Fish does not monopolise the menu, though. It is also possible to have the likes of grilled Buche Ruffec goats' cheese with baby beetroot; chicken breast wrapped in Parma ham with a white wine and tarragon sauce; and herb-crusted rack of lamb with rosemary jus from the daily-changing menu.

Open 11–3 6–11 (Fri 11.30–3, 5.30–11 Sat 11–11 Sun 12–10.30) **Bar Meals** L served Mon-Sat 12–2.30 D served Mon-Sat 6.30–10.30 (Sun 12–9.30) **Restaurant** L served Mon-Fri 12–2.30 D served Mon-Fri 6.30–10.30 (Sat 12–10, Sun 12–9.30) ⊕ Free House ◖ Ballards Best, Leffe, Guinness, Arundel Castle & Gold. ♀ 10 **Facilities** Garden Parking

ELSTED
MAP 05 SU81

Pick of the Pubs

The Three Horseshoes

GU29 0JY ☎ 01730 825746

dir: A272 from Midhurst to Petersfield, after 2m left to Harting & Elsted, after 3m pub on left

Tucked below the steep scarp slope of the South Downs is the peaceful village of Elsted, and this 16th-century former drovers' ale house. It's one of those quintessential English country pubs that Sussex specialises in, full of rustic charm, with unspoilt cottagey bars, worn tiled floors, low beams, latch doors, a vast inglenook, and a motley mix of furniture. On fine days the extensive rear garden, with roaming chickens and stunning southerly views, is hugely popular. Tip-top real ales, including Cheriton Pots from across the Hampshire border, are drawn from the cask, and a daily-changing blackboard menu offers good old country cooking. Main courses are likely to include steak, kidney and Murphy's pie; pheasant breast in cider with shallot and prune sauce; and in summer, crab and lobster. Excellent ploughman's are served with unusual cheeses. Puddings include treacle tart and raspberry and hazelnut meringue.

Open 11–2.30 6–11 (Sun 12–3, 7–10.30) **Bar Meals** L served all week 12–2 D served Mon-Sat 7–9 (Sun 7–8.30) **Restaurant** L served all week 12–2 D served Mon-Sat 7–9 (Sun 7–8.30) Av 3 course à la carte £22.50 ⊕ Free House ◖ Flowerpots Ale, Ballard's Best, Fuller's London Pride, Timothy Taylor Landlord. **Facilities** Garden Dogs allowed Parking

PICK OF THE PUBS

HALNAKER-SUSSEX, WEST

The Anglesey Arms at Halnaker

This charmingly old-fashioned Georgian inn stands in two acres of landscaped grounds on the Goodwood estate. The famous Boxgrove archaeological site is only a mile away – home to the 500,000–year-old remains of the Boxgrove Man. There's a traditional atmosphere in the wood-floored bar with its winter fires and real ales.

Ethical produce is taken seriously, and the kitchen team makes skilful use of meat from fully traceable and organically raised animals, as well as locally-caught fish from sustainable stocks – a stipulation that even applies to the cod. The Anglesey has built a special reputation over the years for its steaks cut from British beef hung for at least 21 days. The Goodwood Estate's Home Farm supplies additional meats, while vegetables are sourced from Wayside Organics. Eggs are also organic, and free-range poultry has the 'label rouge' classification. The area is noted for shooting, so game birds and venison are seasonally available. The extensive wine list contains unusual wines from small vineyards. A recent addition is a sparkling Ridgeview

Bloomsbury, received with rave reviews and made with grapes grown behind the pub. Order a bottle after a successful flutter at Goodwood, settle back and enjoy the simply decorated restaurant, which is candle-lit in the evening. A recently appointed head chef has added his flair to the menu, and a Mediterranean touch can be found in dishes of charcuterie, marinated olives and artichokes with warm ciabatta. A representative choice could be a starter of home-made Selsey crab paté with brown toast; and noisettes of organic lamb with hand-made black pudding and leeks. Desserts are now all home made along traditional lines: sticky toffee and bread and butter puddings, apple and berry crumble.

MAP 06 SU90
PO18 0NQ
☎ 01243 773474
🖷 01243 530034
e-mail: angleseyarms@aol.com
dir: *4m E from centre of Chichester on A285 (Petworth road)*

Open 11–3 5.30–12 (Sat-Sun all day)
Bar Meals L served Mon-Sat 12–2.30 D served all week 6.30–9.30 (Sun 12–4)
Restaurant L served Mon-Sat 12–2 D served all week 6.30–9.30 (Sun 12–4) Av 3 course à la carte £22.50
⊕ Punch Taverns ◀ Young's Bitter, Adnams Bitter, Hop Back Summer Lightning & Staropramen, Black Sheep Bitter.
♟ 10
Facilities Garden Dogs allowed Parking

Pick of the Pubs

The King's Arms ♥

Midhurst Rd GU27 3HA

☎ 01428 652005 📠 01428 658970

dir: *On A286 between Haslemere & Midhurst, 1m S of Fernhurst*

A Grade II-listed, 17th-century free house and restaurant set amidst rolling Sussex farmland, which can be seen at its best from the garden. The pub and its outbuildings are built from Sussex stone and decorated with hanging baskets, flowering tubs, vines and creepers. The L-shaped interior is very cosy, with beams, lowish ceilings, and a large inglenook fireplace, with the bar one side and restaurant and small dining room the other. Everything is home made and freshly prepared on the premises, from salad dressings to sorbets. Fish is an important commodity, and Michael regularly visits the south coast to buy direct from the boats, bringing back what later appears on the menu as, for instance, goujons of plaice with tartare sauce; monkfish loin in Parma ham with courgette ribbons, prawn and saffron sauce; or perhaps seared scallops with bacon and pea risotto. Alternatives to fish usually include Barbary duck breast with Savoy cabbage, baby roast potatoes and orange and port sauce; rack of English lamb with redcurrant and rosemary mash with lightly minted gravy; and fillet steak with dauphinoise potatoes, wild mushrooms and rich red wine jus. In addition to the monthly changing menu, there are daily changing specials such as steak, kidney and mushroom pudding. No food is served in the bar in the evenings. The large garden has some lovely trees, including a mature willow and pretty white lilacs, and views over surrounding fields. A wisteria-clad barn is used for the pub's annual three-day beer festival at the end of August.

Open 11.30–3 5.30–11 Closed: 25 Dec **Bar Meals** L served all week 12–2.30 D served Mon-Sat 7–9.30 Av main course £12.50 **Restaurant** L served all week 12–2.30 D served Mon-Sat 7–9.30 Av 3 course à la carte £24 ⊕ Free House ◀ W J King Brewery Horsham Best Bitter, Ringwood Brewery 49er, Hogsback TEA, Caledonian IPA. ♥ 10 **Facilities** Garden Dogs allowed Parking

The Red Lion ♥

The Green GU27 3HY

☎ 01428 643112 📠 01428 643939

dir: *Just off A286 midway between Haslemere & Midhurst*

Built in the 16th-century, this pretty village inn is popular with walkers. Traditional features include beams and open fires, as well as well-kept gardens back and front. The varied menu of freshly cooked dishes is supplemented by blackboard specials. Typical are slow-cooked lamb shank; deep-fried Selsey cod in beer batter; and profiteroles. Seasonal guest ales accompany the likes of Fuller's ESB and London Pride.

Open 11–11.30 Closed: Mon-Wed 3–5 **Bar Meals** L served all week 12–2.30 D served all week 6–9.30 **Restaurant** L served all week 12–2.30 D served all week 6–9.30 ⊕ Fullers ◀ Fuller's ESB, Chiswick, London Pride, and seasonal guest. ♥ 8 **Facilities** Garden Dogs allowed Parking

Pick of the Pubs

The Foresters Arms NEW ♥

The Street GU28 0QA ☎ 01798 867202

e-mail: info@forestersgraffham.co.uk

Clare and Robert Pearce bought this 16th-century country freehouse in 2007. In the bar you'll find old beams and a large smoke-blackened fireplace while, in the restaurant, a move back to basics results in a short, daily-changing menu using produce sourced from within a 50-mile radius. Thus, panfried skate wing; salt beef; and mushroom and leek fritta are among Robert's repertoire. Sixteen wines by the glass on a personally chosen list from selected vintners.

Open 12–3 6–11 (Sun 12–4 Summer all day) Closed: Mon **Bar Meals** L served Tue-Sat 12–2.30 D served Tue-Sat 6.30–9.30 (Sun 12–3) **Restaurant** L served Tue-Sat 12–2.30 D served Tue-Sat 6.30–9.30 (Sun 12–3) ⊕ Free House ♥ 16 **Facilities** Garden Dogs allowed Parking

Pick of the Pubs

The Anglesey Arms at Halnaker ♥

See Pick of the Pubs on page 573

Pick of the Pubs

Unicorn Inn ♥

GU29 0DL ☎ 01730 813486 📠 01730 814896

e-mail: unicorninnheyshott@hotmail.co.uk

dir: *Telephone for directions*

This cosy village pub dates from 1750, although it was not granted its first licence until 1839. Set within the South Downs Area of Outstanding Natural Beauty (there's a good view of the Downs from the beautiful, south-facing rear gardens), the Unicorn is popular not just with locals, but with walkers and cyclists detouring from the South Downs Way. The bar, with beams and large log fire, is part of the original building, and very atmospheric it is too. The subtly lit, cream-painted restaurant, with matching table linen, is also in perfect historical tune. Locally sourced food is important, although some of the meats come from Smithfield, while fish arrives daily from Selsey a few miles away, and Portsmouth.

Open 11.30–3 6.30–11 (Sun 12–4, Winter 7–11) Closed: Mon **Bar Meals** L served Tue-Sat 12–2.30 D served Tue-Sat 7–9 (Sun 12–3) Av main course £10 **Restaurant** L served Tue-Sat 12–2 D served Tue-Sat 7–9 (Sun 12–2.30) ⬤ Timothy Taylor Landlord, Horsham Best Bitter, Unicorn Best Bitter. ⚲ 10 **Facilities** Garden Dogs allowed Parking

HORSHAM   MAP 06 TQ13

The Black Jug ⚲

31 North St RH12 1RJ
☎ 01403 253526 📠 01403 217821
e-mail: black.jug@brunningandprice.co.uk
dir: Telephone for directions

This busy town centre pub is close to the railway station and popular with Horsham's professional classes. Here you'll find a congenial atmosphere with friendly staff, an open fire, large conservatory and courtyard garden. Meals are freshly prepared using local ingredients wherever possible; light bites include chilli beef with cheese topping and crusty bread, whilst larger appetites might go for roasted vegetable Wellington; or pan-fried mackerel with horseradish mash.

Open 12–11 (Fri-Sat 12–12, Sun 12–10.30) **Bar Meals** L served Mon-Sat 12–10 D served Mon-Sat 12–10 (Sun 12–9.30) **Restaurant** L served Mon-Sat 12–10 D served Mon-Sat 12–10 (Sun 12–9.30) ⬤ Weltons, Adnams Broadside, Greene King IPA & guest ales. ⚲ 25 **Facilities** Garden Dogs allowed

KINGSFOLD   MAP 06 TQ13

The Dog and Duck

Dorking Rd RH12 3SA ☎ 01306 627295
e-mail: info@thedoganduck.fsnet.co.uk
dir: On A24, 3m N of Horsham

A 16th-century, family-run country pub with a very large garden, children's play equipment and a summer ice cream bar. The pub has been steadily building a reputation for wholesome home-made food, such as liver and bacon, breaded plaice with prawns, chicken curry, chilli con carne and lasagne. It hosts many events, including quizzes, arts evenings, a big beer festival and fundraising activities for St George's Hospital.

Open 12–3 6–11 (Sat-Sun 12–10 BHs 12–11) **Bar Meals** L served Mon-Sat 12–2.30 D served Mon-Sat 6–9 (Sun 12–3, 6–8) Av main course £9.50 **Restaurant** L served Mon-Sat 12–2.30 D served Mon-Sat 6–9 (Sun 12–3, 6–8) Av 3 course à la carte £18 ⊕ Hall & Woodhouse ⬤ King & Barnes Sussex, Badger Best, seasonal variations, guest ales. **Facilities** Garden Dogs allowed Parking Play Area

KIRDFORD   MAP 06 TQ02

The Half Moon Inn

RH14 0LT ☎ 01403 820223 📠 01403 820224
e-mail: halfmooninn.kirdford@virgin.net
dir: Off A272 between Billingshurst & Petworth. At Wisborough Green follow Kirdford signs

This red-tiled 16th-century village inn is covered in climbing rose bushes, and sits directly opposite the church in this unspoilt Sussex village near the River Arun. Although drinkers are welcome, the Half Moon is mainly a dining pub. The interior, with its low beams and log fires, has been fully redecorated. Lunch choices from the bistro menu might include medallions of lobster, followed by pan-fried venison with black pudding mash; pan-fried medallions of pork; or fillet of salmon on a bed of buttered pasta. Lunchtime snacks might be battered haddock with chips, Caesar salad, or vegetarian pasta. At dinner, the menu is broadly similar, although the atmosphere changes, with candlelight, tablecloths and polished glassware. Well-tended gardens are an added draw in the summer, while for the more energetic, a pamphlet featuring local country walks is available.

Open 11–3 6–11 Closed: Sun eve **Bar Meals** L served Mon-Sun 12–2.30 D served Mon-Sat 6–9.30 Av main course £10 **Restaurant** L served all week 12–2.30 D served Mon-Sat 6–9.30 ⬤ Fuller's London Pride. **Facilities** Garden Parking Play Area

LAMBS GREEN   MAP 06 TQ23

The Lamb Inn ⚲

RH12 4RG
☎ 01293 871336 & 871933 📠 01293 871933
e-mail: ben@benbokoringram.wanadoo.co.uk
dir: 6m from Horsham between Rusper & Faygate. 5m from Crawley

Recently purchased by the former tenants, the Lamb remains unchanged, with an emphasis on sourcing real ales from independent breweries and using as much local produce as they can get their hands on. Everything on the menu from starters to puddings is home made. Baguettes, omelettes, a fresh fish board and 28–day matured steaks feature, along with specials such as wild rabbit casserole; and chicken breast in a creamy stilton and Madeira sauce.

Open 11–3 5.30–11 (Sat 11.30–11, Sun 12–10.30) Closed: 25–26 Dec **Bar Meals** L served Mon-Sat 12–2 D served Mon-Sat 7–9.30 (Sun 12–9) ⬤ Horsham Best Bitter, Kings Old Ale, Dark Star Original, Hepworth Prospect & Hogs Back Tea. ⚲ 12 **Facilities** Dogs allowed Parking

LICKFOLD — MAP 06 SU92

Pick of the Pubs

The Lickfold Inn ⊛ ♥

GU28 9EY ☎ 01798 861285

e-mail: thelickfoldinn@aol.com

dir: *From A3 take A283, through Chiddingfold, 2m on right signed 'Lurgashall Winery', pub in 1m*

The hamlet of Lickfold may not have a shop or post office, but a bus occasionally turns up, and it does have this delightful free house, dating back to 1460. Furthermore, it's thriving, in the capable hands of Camilla Hanton and Mark Evans who took over the running early in 2008. Period features include an ancient timber frame containing attractive herringbone-patterned bricks, and a huge central chimney. Inside are two restaurant areas with oak beamed ceilings, and a cosy bar dominated by a large inglenook fireplace with a spit, Georgian settles, more beams and moulded panelling. Look for the recurring garlic motif, which picks up on the village's Anglo-Saxon name, 'leac fauld', meaning an enclosure where garlic grows. The pub is heavily food oriented, offering seasonal dishes cooked to order, complemented by a choice of well-kept real ales and a comprehensive selection of wines. The large courtyard and rambling terraced gardens are suitable for outdoor eating.

Open 11–3.30 6–11.30 (BH Mon 12–2.30) Closed: 25–26 Dec **Bar Meals** L served Tue-Sun 12–2.30 D served Tue-Sat 7–9.30 Av main course £10.75 **Restaurant** L served Tue-Sun 12–2.30 D served Tue-Sat 7–9.30 Av 3 course à la carte £26 ⊕ Free House ◀ Harveys Best Bitter, Youngs, 49er, Hogsback TEA. ♥ 12 **Facilities** Children's licence Garden Dogs allowed Parking

LODSWORTH — MAP 06 SU92

Pick of the Pubs

The Halfway Bridge Inn ♥

See Pick of the Pubs on opposite page

Pick of the Pubs

The Hollist Arms ♥

The Street GU28 9BZ ☎ 01798 861310

e-mail: george@thehollistarms.co.uk

dir: *0.5m between Midhurst & Petworth, 1m N of A272, adjacent to Country Park.*

The Hollist Arms, a pub since 1823, is full of traditional charm and character. The 15th-century building overlooks a lawn where a grand old tree stands ringed by a bench. Step through the pretty entrance porch and you'll find roaring open fires, leather sofas and a blissful absence of fruit machines. You'll probably need to book to enjoy dishes such as tiger prawns and leek gratin with fresh bread; home-made steak, Guinness and mushroom pie; or hoi sin duck in soy sauce with ginger, mushrooms and spring onions. Bar snacks range from toasties or sausages and mash. Wash it down with real ales such as Timothy Taylor's Landlord; Horsham Best or the locally-brewed Langham's Halfway to Heaven. The Hollist

Arms is conveniently situated for Goodwood, Cowdray Park and Petworth House, and has its own business providing picnic hampers for any event.

The Hollist Arms

Open 11–3 6–12 **Bar Meals** L served Mon-Sat 12–2 D served all week 7–9 (Sun 12–2.30) **Restaurant** L served Mon-Sat 12–2 D served Mon-Sat 7–9 (Sun 12–3, 6.30–8.30) ⊕ Free House ◀ Youngs, Timothy Taylor Landlord, Horsham Best. ♥ 7 **Facilities** Children's licence Garden Dogs allowed Parking

LURGASHALL — MAP 06 SU92

The Noah's Ark ♥

The Green GU28 9ET ☎ 01428 707346 🗎 01428 707742

e-mail: amy@noahsarkinn.co.uk

dir: *B2131 from Haslemere towards Petworth/Lurgashall*

Thanks to its owners – young and full of enthusiasm – the pub has undergone a sympathetic refurbishment, which maintains both modern standards and the charming character of the 16th-century village pub. Foodwise the focus is on fresh local produce sourced from butchers, greengrocers and other suppliers in West Sussex, and the menus are going down very well with the clientele. The place gets particularly busy in summer when there are cricket matches right outside the pub.

Open 11–3.30 6–11 (Fri-Sat 11–11.30 Sun 12–4, all day in Summer) **Bar Meals** L served Mon-Sat 12–2.30 D served Mon-Sat 7–9.30 Av main course £8 **Restaurant** L served all week 12–2.30 D served all week 7–9.30 Av 3 course à la carte £22 ⊕ Greene King ◀ Greene King IPA , Abbot & guest ale. ♥ 8 **Facilities** Children's licence Garden Dogs allowed Parking Play Area

MAPLEHURST — MAP 06 TQ12

The White Horse

Park Ln RH13 6LL ☎ 01403 891208

dir: *5m SE of Horsham, between A281& A272*

In the tiny Sussex hamlet of Maplehurst, this traditional pub offers a break from modern life: no music, no fruit machines, no cigarette machines, just hearty, home-cooked pub food and an enticing range of ales. Sip Harvey's Best, Welton's Pride & Joy, or Dark Star Espresso Stout in the bar or whilst admiring the rolling countryside from the quiet, south-facing garden. Village-brewed cider is a speciality.

Open 12–2.30 6–11 (Sun 12–3, 7–10.30) **Bar Meals** L served Mon-Sat 12–2 D served Mon-Sat 6–9 (Sun 12–2.30, 7–9) ⊕ Free House ◀ Harvey's Best, Welton's Pride & Joy, Dark Star Espresso Stout, King's Red River. **Facilities** Children's licence Garden Dogs allowed Parking Play Area **Notes** ⊛

PICK OF THE PUBS

LODSWORTH-SUSSEX, WEST

The Halfway Bridge Inn

This charming 17th-century brick-and-flint coaching inn stands in lovely countryside midway between Midhurst and Petworth, making it ideal for antique hunters drawn to Petworth's fabled shops, as well as the polo crowd heading for nearby Cowdray Park.

Locally it is popular, not least because owners Paul and Sue Carter have made the inn an attractive destination for diners. Winter cosiness is guaranteed: the inn boasts two open fires, while in summer the sheltered patio and lawn come into their own. An intimate and casual atmosphere pervades the numerous dining rooms where the food emphasis is on local produce, along with fresh meats, fish and vegetables from the London markets. Daily specials are chalked up on the blackboards. The lunchtime bar menu consists of sandwiches – roast beef and horseradish, fresh crab, smoked Applewood cheddar – or a choice of appetizers from the main menu. These include crispy fried whitebait with caper mayonnaise; rabbit and pancetta terrine with

lambs leaf and cranberry chutney; and twice-cooked belly of pork served with creamed Savoy, sage and bacon lardons. Typical of the vegetarian main courses is chestnut and wild mushroom risotto with apple compote and a parmesan crisp. Otherwise you may find a trio of partridge, pheasant and pigeon breasts with parsnip, sweet potato and swede purées; calve's liver served with lyonnaise potatoes and chargrilled bacon; and a pan-baked tranche of halibut with chive creamed potatoes and buttered baby carrots. A good range of half a dozen puddings includes the likes of warm treacle tart served with home-made honeycombe ice cream; dark and white chocolate mousse with broken chocolate; and orange and cardamom brûlée with a brandy snap.

MAP 06 SU92
Halfway Bridge GU28 9BP
☎ 01798 861281
e-mail: enquiries@
halfwaybridge.co.uk
dir: *Between Petworth & Midhurst, next to Cowdray Estate & Golf Club on A272*

Open 11–11 (Sun 12–10.30)
Closed: 25 Dec
Bar Meals L served Mon-Sat
12–2.30 D served Mon-Sat
6.30–9.15 (Sun 12–2.30,
6.30–8.30)
Restaurant L served Mon-Sat
12–2.30 D served Mon-Sat
6.30–9.15 (Sun 12–2.30,
6.30–8.30) Av 3 course à la
carte £25
⊕ Free House ◀ Skinners
Betty Stogs, Ballards Best Bitter,
Ringwood Best Bitter. ♥ 14
Facilities Garden Dogs allowed
Parking

England

MIDHURST — MAP 06 SU82

The Angel Hotel ♈

North St GU29 9DN ☎ 01730 812421 📠 01730 815928

dir: *Telephone for directions*

An imposing and well-proportioned, late-Georgian façade hides the true Tudor origins of this former coaching inn. Its frontage overlooks the town's main street, while at the rear attractive gardens give way to meadowland and the ruins of Cowdray Castle. Bright yellow paintwork on local cottages means they are Cowdray Estate-owned. Gabriel's is the main restaurant, or try The Halo Bar where dishes range from snacks and pasta to sizzlers and steaks, with additional specials.

Open 11–11 **Bar Meals** L served all week 12–2.30 D served all week 6–9.30 Av main course £8 ⊕ Free House ◀ Fuller's HSB & Best. ♈ 6 **Facilities** Children's licence Garden Dogs allowed Parking **Rooms** available

NUTHURST — MAP 06 TQ12

Pick of the Pubs

Black Horse Inn ♈

Nuthurst St RH13 6LH ☎ 01403 891272

e-mail: clive.henwood@btinternet.com

web: www.theblackhorseinn.com

dir: *4m S of Horsham, off A281 & A24*

Built of clay tiles and mellow brick, this one-time smugglers' hideout is still appropriately secluded in a quiet backwater. It is a lovely old building, half masked by impressive window boxes in summer, forming part of what was originally a row of workers' cottages on the Sedgwick Park estate. The building was first recorded as an inn in 1817, and plenty of its history remains. Inside you'll find stone-flagged floors, an inglenook fireplace

and an exposed wattle and daub wall. The place is spotlessly maintained with a warm and cosy atmosphere that's perfect for dining or just enjoying a drink. The pub has a reputation for good beers, including Harvey's, London Pride, Timothy Taylor Landlord and numerous guest beers. On sunny days, visitors can sit out on the terraces at the front and rear, or take their drinks across the stone bridge over a stream into the delightful back garden.

Open 12–3 6–11 (Sat-Sun, BH all day) **Bar Meals** L served all week 12–2.30 D served all week 6–9.30 Sat-Sun & BH all day) **Restaurant** L served all week 12–2.30 D served all week 6–9.30 (Sat-Sun & BH all day) ⊕ Free House ◀ Harveys Sussex, W J King, Timothy Taylor Landlord, London Pride and guest ales. ♈ 7 **Facilities** Children's licence Garden Dogs allowed Parking

OVING — MAP 06 SU90

The Gribble Inn ♈

PO20 2BP ☎ 01243 786893 📠 01243 788841

e-mail: dave@thegribble.co.uk

dir: *From A27 take A259. After 1m left at rdbt, 1st right to Oving, 1st left in village*

Named after local schoolmistress Rose Gribble, the inn retains all of its 16th-century charm. Large open fireplaces, wood burners and low beams set the tone. There's no background music at this peaceful hideaway, which is the ideal spot to enjoy any of the half dozen real ales from the on-site micro-brewery. Liver and bacon; spinach lasagne with red peppers; and special fish dishes are all prepared and cooked on the premises.

Open 11–3 5.30–11 (Sat 11–11, Sun 12–10.30) **Bar Meals** L served all week 12–2.30 D served all week 6–9.30 Av main course £8.95 **Restaurant** L served all week 12–2.30 D served all week 6–9.30 ⊕ Hall & Woodhouse ◀ Gribble Ale, Reg's Tipple, Fursty Ferret, Badger First Gold & Pigs Ear. ♈ 10 **Facilities** Garden Dogs allowed Parking

PARTRIDGE GREEN — MAP 06 TQ11

Pick of the Pubs

The Green Man Inn and Restaurant

Church Rd RH13 8JT ☎ 01403 710250 📠 01403 713212

dir: *Between A24 & A281, just S of A272. Pub on B2135*

A stylish and attractive gastropub with a pretty garden, and decorated in a clean-looking, unfussy way that accentuates the late-Victorian interior. Seasonal menus with daily specials use only fresh, mostly locally sourced, ingredients. Examples of the range are pan-roasted breast of Barbary duckling with sweet potato purée; pan-fried calf's liver with streaky bacon and bubble and squeak; supreme of salmon with red pepper and courgette linguine; and cheese and sage croquettes with creamed caraway Savoy cabbage. From the specials board come monkfish fillet with Chinese spices; smoked haddock with Welsh rarebit; and Chateaubriand with béarnaise sauce. Tapas, bar snacks, light meals and sandwiches are also available at lunchtime. A short list of puddings could well feature crème brûlée, and pears and blackberries poached in red wine. Seating in the restaurant is supplemented by al fresco dining on the terrace.

Open 11.30–3.30 6.30–12 **Bar Meals** L served Tue-Sun 12–2.15 D served Tue-Sat (Sun 12–2.30) Av main course £12 **Restaurant** L served Tue-Sun 12–2.15 D served Tue-Sat 7–9.30 (Sun 12–2.30) Av 3 course à la carte £25 ◀ Harveys Sussex Best, Guinness. **Facilities** Children's licence Garden Dogs allowed Parking

---

PETWORTH   MAP 06 SU92

The Black Horse

Byworth GU28 0HL ☎ 01798 342424 🖨 01798 342868
e-mail: blackhorsebyworth@btconnect.com
dir: *A285 from Petworth, 2m, turn right signed Byworth, pub 50yds on right*

Flagstone floors, scrubbed wooden tables and open fires set the scene at this 16th-century free house, once part of the old tanneries. The former kitchen has been transformed into a snug dining area complete with original Aga, whilst the large sloping garden offers views to the South Downs. Expect a range of home-made fresh pizza, light bites and daily specials; main meals include hand-made Thai fishcakes; and lamb shoulder in mint gravy.

Open 11.30–11 (Sun 12–10.30) **Bar Meals** L served all week 12–9 D served all week 12–9 Av main course £8.95 **Restaurant** L served all week 12–9 D served all week 12–9 (Fri-Sat 12–9.30) Av 3 course à la carte £17.50 ◀ Arundel Gold, Youngs Bitter, Hogs Back Brew, London Pride. **Facilities** Garden Dogs allowed Parking

Pick of the Pubs

The Grove Inn NEW

Grove Ln GU28 0HY ☎ 01798 343659
e-mail: steveandvaleria@tiscali.co.uk
dir: *On outskirts of town, 0.5m from Petworth Park*

A 17th-century free house on the outskirts of historic Petworth, home to numerous antique shops. It offers a bar with oak-beamed ceilings and large fireplace, conservatory restaurant, garden with views to the South Downs, and a patio area with pergola. The seasonal menu is completely rewritten every six to eight weeks, with some daily changes for good measure. Typical starters include smoked salmon, chive and cream cheese roulade; home-made parsnip soup; and duck liver and mushroom terrine. Among the main courses are natural smoked haddock topped with Welsh rarebit; well-matured chargrilled fillet steak with truffle mash and cracked black peppercorn sauce; and wild mushroom risotto with parmesan and truffle oil. And to follow there could be banana pancake with honey rum toffee sauce and vanilla ice cream; or lemon posset. Three whites, three reds and a rosé are available by the glass.

Open 12–3 6–11.30 Closed: 2nd & 3rd wk Jan, Sun eve & Mon **Bar Meals** L served Tue-Sat 12–2 D served Tue-Sat 6–9 (Sun 12–3) Av main course £13 **Restaurant** L served Tue-Sat 12–2 D served Tue-Sat 6–9 (Sun 12–3) Av 3 course à la carte £25 ⊕ Free House ◀ Youngs, Betty Stogs, Arundel Gold. **Facilities** Garden Parking

---

POYNINGS   MAP 06 TQ21

Pick of the Pubs

Royal Oak Inn ♥

The Street BN45 7AQ
☎ 01273 857389 🖨 01273 857202
e-mail: ropoynings@aol.com
web: www.royaloakpoynings.biz
dir: *N on A23 just outside Brighton, take A281 (signed for Henfield & Poynings), then follow signs into Poynings*

Tucked away in a fold of the South Downs below the Devil's Dyke, the Royal Oak has eye-catching window blinds and cream-painted exterior and roaring winter fires within. Solid oak floors and old beams hung with hop bines blend effortlessly with contemporary décor and comfy sofas. In the bar, Sussex-bred Harveys real ales rub shoulders with offerings from Greene King and Morland, and a decent wine list includes a red and a white from a Sussex vineyard. The menu combines local and seasonal produce with sometimes ambitious international twists. Starters and light meals include sandwiches and ciabattas, or more elaborate preparations such as goat's cheese stuffed with basil and sun-blush tomatoes on a warm chick pea and capsicum salad. For the main course you may find pan-fried milk-fed calves' liver with pancetta and black pudding, roasted leek and mustard mash and a red wine jus. Puddings are ordered at the bar – chocolate and Amaretto terrine perhaps.

Open 11–11 (Sun 12–10.30) **Bar Meals** L served all week 12–9.30 D served all week 12–9.30 ⊕ Free House ◀ Harveys Sussex, Abbot Ale, Greene King Morland Old Speckled Hen, Fuller's London Pride. ♥ 12 **Facilities** Garden Dogs allowed Parking Play Area

PICK OF THE PUBS

The Countryman Inn

The inn is set in open countryside close to the small village of Shipley, surrounded by 3,500 acres of farmland owned by the Knepp Castle Estate. The estate is being turned back into a more natural state, with fallow deer, free roaming Tamworth pigs, Exmoor ponies and longhorn cattle.

Wild birds have returned to the area, encouraged by the new growth of wild grasses and plant life, which provide a welcoming habitat. In fine weather, the inn's garden is a great place to do a spot of bird watching. Inside you'll find warming log fires in cold weather, and cask conditioned ales in the cosy bar, together with a great choice of wines from around the world. Local produce is used wherever possible, and free-range meat and vegetables from local farms make their appearance on the menu alongside home-grown herbs, fresh fish from Shoreham and Newhaven, and local game in season. Menus are frequently changing, but lunch classics include Aunt Bettie's mutton cobbler; fish pie; and steak and kidney pudding. From the dinner

menu come roasted saddleback pork with crackling, potato rösti and apple and parsnip purée; and pan-fried fillet of wild sea bass on beetroot and pear salsa with chunky chips. Shipley's historic eight-sided smock mill is worth a visit (fictional home of the BBC's Jonathan Creek), and is just a mile's walk along a woodland bridle path from The Countryman. The mill is so called because of its likeness to the farm labourer's traditional cotton smock. Shipley church, one of the oldest Norman churches in Sussex, is also of interest, built by the Knights Templar in the 12th century.

MAP 06 TQ12
Countryman Ln RH13 8PZ
☎ 01403 741383
🖹 01403 741115
e-mail: countrymaninn@btopenworld.com
web:
www.countrymanshipley.co.uk
dir: *From A272 at Coolham into Smithers Hill Lane. 1m to junct with Countryman Lane*

Open 11–3 6.30–11
Bar Meals L served all week 12–3 D served all week 7–9.30
Restaurant L served all week 12–2.30 D served all week 7–9.30
Av 3 course à la carte £25
🍺 Harverys, Kings & London Pride. 🍷 20
Facilities Garden Parking

England

ROWHOOK
MAP 06 TQ13

Neals Restaurant at The Chequers Inn
◎ ♥

RH12 3PY ☎ 01403 790480 📄 01403 790480
e-mail: thechequers1@aol.com
dir: *Off A29 NW of Horsham*

A hamlet on the Sussex, Surrey border provides the setting for this 15th-century inn of great character, with original beams, flagstones and open fires. Having been tenants for over six years, Tim and Katy Neal have now bought the pub. Master Chef Tim offers a good choice of food from beer battered haddock in the bar to restaurant mains like roast loin of South Downs venison with bubble and squeak and chestnut jus.

Open 11.30–3.30 6–11.30 Closed: 25 Dec **Bar Meals** L served Mon-Sat 12–2 D served Mon-Sat 7–9.30 (Sun 12–2.30) Av main course £12.50 **Restaurant** L served Mon-Sat 12–2 D served Mon-Sat 7–9.30 (Sun 12–2.30) Av 3 course à la carte £25.50 ⊕ Punch Taverns ◀ Harvey's Sussex Ale, Young's, Fuller's London Pride, plus guest ale each week. ♥ 7 **Facilities** Garden Dogs allowed Parking

RUDGWICK
MAP 06 TQ03

The Fox Inn ♥

Guildford Rd, Bucks Green RH12 3JP
☎ 01403 822386 📄 01403 823950
e-mail: seafood@foxinn.co.uk
dir: *on A281 midway between Horsham & Guildford*

'Famous for Fish!' is the claim of this attractive 16th-century inn, a message borne out by the extensive menu. Food offered includes all-day breakfast and afternoon tea, while the bar menu focuses on seafood, from fish and chips to the huge fruits de mer platter. Dishes include Foxy's famous fish pie; roasted cod loin with chorizo; and hand-made Cumberland sausage on stilton mash. A horse is apparently walked through the pub each Christmas day!

Open 11–11 **Bar Meals** L served all week 12–10 D served all week 12–10 **Restaurant** L served all week 12–10 D served all week 12–10 Av 3 course à la carte £25.28 ⊕ Hall & Woodhouse ◀ King & Barnes Sussex, Badger Tanglefoot, Fursty Ferret. ♥ 8 **Facilities** Garden Dogs allowed Parking Play Area

SHIPLEY
MAP 06 TQ12

Pick of the Pubs

The Countryman Inn ♥

See Pick of the Pubs on opposite page

George & Dragon

Dragons Green RH13 7JE ☎ 01403 741320
dir: *Signed from A272 between Coolham & A24*

A 17th-century, tile-hung cottage that provides welcome peace and quiet, especially on balmy summer evenings when the peaceful garden is a welcome retreat. Its interior is all head-banging beams and character inglenook fireplaces where a pint of Badger or Tanglefoot will not come amiss. The food is home made using fresh vegetables and 'real' chips and offers dishes such as roasts of lamb and crispy coated chicken breast with sweet-and-sour sauce. Shipley is famous for its smock mill.

Open 12–3 6–11 (Sun-Sun, BHs & summer all day) **Bar Meals** L served all week 12–2 D served Mon-Sat 6.30–9 (Sun 12–2.30) Av main course £8.50 **Restaurant** L served all week 12–2 6.30–9 ⊕ Hall & Woodhouse ◀ Badger Best, Sussex Best, Firsty Ferret, guest ale. **Facilities** Garden Dogs allowed Parking

SINGLETON
MAP 05 SU81

The Partridge Inn

PO18 0EY ☎ 01243 811251 📄 0870 804 4566
dir: *Telephone for directions*

Once known as the Fox and Hounds, the building probably dates from the 16th century, when it would have been part of a huge hunting park owned by the Fitzalan family, Earls of Arundel. Today, it is popular with walkers enjoying the rolling Sussex countryside and visitors to Goodwood for motor and horse-racing. A menu of typical pub fare includes liver and bacon, steak and ale pie, Goodwood gammon, salmon fishcakes, fish and chips, and home-made puddings.

Open 11.30–3 6–11 (Sat-Sun 11–11) **Bar Meals** L served all week 12–2 D served all week 6.30–9 Sat-Sun 12–9 Av main course £9.50 **Restaurant** L served all week 12–2 D served all week 6.30–9 ⊕ Enterprise Inns ◀ London Pride, Ringwood Best Bitter, Hopworths Sussex. **Facilities** Garden Dogs allowed Parking

SLINDON
MAP 06 SU90

The Spur ♥

BN18 0NE ☎ 01243 814216 📄 01243 814707
dir: *Off A27 on A29 outside village of Slindon*

Nestling on top of the South Downs, just outside the village of Slindon, sits this 17th-century pub. Inside are an open plan bar and restaurant, warmed by log fires that create a friendly atmosphere. If you book in advance you can use the skittle alley, or enjoy a game of pool or other pub games.

Open 11.30–3 6–11 (Sun, 12–3, 7–10.30) **Bar Meals** L served all week 12–2 D served Wed-Sat –9.30 (Sun-Tue 7–9) **Restaurant** L served all week 12–2 D served Wed-Sat 7–9.30 (Sun-Tue 7–9) Av 3 course à la carte £25 ⊕ Free House ◀ Abbot, Greene King IPA, Courage Directors. ♥ 7 **Facilities** Garden Dogs allowed Parking

England

SOUTH HARTING
MAP 05 SU71

The Ship Inn

GU31 5PZ ☎ 01730 825302

dir: *From Petersfield take B2146 towards Chichester (5m)*

17th-century inn made from a ship's timbers, hence the name. Home-made pies are a feature, and other popular dishes include fish pie, mussel chowder, calves' liver, rack of lamb, ham and asparagus mornay, and Hungarian goulash. A range of vegetarian dishes and bar snacks is also available.

Open 11–11 **Bar Meals** 12–2.30 D served Mon-Sat 7–9 **Restaurant** L served all week 12–2.30 D served Mon-Thu 7–9 (Fri-Sat 7–9.30) ⊕ Free House ◀ Palmer IPA, Darkstar Brewery Hophead, Ballards Wassail & Palmers Copper Ale. **Facilities** Garden Dogs allowed Parking

STEDHAM
MAP 05 SU82

Hamilton Arms/Nava Thai Restaurant ♥

Hamilton Arms School Ln GU29 0NZ
☎ 01730 812555 ▤ 01730 817459
e-mail: hamiltonarms@hotmail.com
web: www.thehamiltonarms.co.uk
dir: *Off A272 between Midhurst & Petersfield*

Set in a picturesque village, this pub's colourful parasols overflow from its patio onto the common opposite. A popular destination in any weather, it is renowned for its authentic Thai cuisine, offered from a huge menu of soups, curries, salads and speciality meat, seafood and vegetarian dishes, also available to takeaway. Oriental beers, too, are available alongside local real ales. The pub is the base for a charitable trust to help prevent child prostitution in Thailand.

Open 11–3 6–11 (Sun 12–4, 7–11, Fri-Sat 11–12) Closed: Mon (ex BH) **Bar Meals** L served Tue-Sun 12–2.30 D served Tue-Sat 6–10.30 (Sun 7–9.30) **Restaurant** L served Tue-Sun 12–2.30 D served Tue-Sat 6–10.30 (Sun 7–9.30) Av 3 course à la carte £20 Av 4 course fixed price £22.50 ⊕ Free House ◀ Ballard's Best, Fuller's London Pride, Everards Tiger Best, Fuller's HSB. ☎8 **Facilities** Garden Dogs allowed Parking Play Area

TROTTON
MAP 05 SU82

The Keepers Arms ♥

GU31 5ER ☎ 01730 813724
e-mail: enquiries@keepersarms.co.uk
dir: *5m from Petersfield on A272, pub on right just after narrow bridge*

Set amid spectacular countryside, this charming 17th-century free house backs onto Terwick Common, an area of outstanding natural beauty. A log fire provides a warm welcome in the lovely, low-ceilinged bar, and the beamed dining room, themed around a Scottish hunting lodge, is also a treat with its warm colours and tartan fabrics. By day, it offers fabulous views over the South Downs. Food is taken seriously here, with real efforts made to source local and seasonal produce. Menus change frequently, and dishes range from simple pub favourites from the blackboards, such as steak and chips or sausage and mash, to the likes of seared salmon with herb risotto and red wine sauce; or fillet of beef with dauphinoise potatoes, baby spinach and wild mushrooms from the carte. Finish with sticky toffee pudding with toffee sauce and vanilla ice cream, or a selection of British and European cheeses with biscuits.

Open 12–3 6–11 (Sun 11.30–5, 7–10.30) **Bar Meals** L served Mon-Sat 12–2 D served Mon-Sat 7–9.30 (Sun 12–2.30, 7–9) Av main course £12 **Restaurant** L served Mon-Sat 12–2 D served Mon-Sat 7–9.30 (Sun 12–2.30, 7–9) Av 3 course à la carte £25 ⊕ Free House ◀ Dark Star Hophead, Ringwood Best, Ballards Best, Ringwood 49'er & Triple fff Moondance. ☎8 **Facilities** Children's licence Garden Dogs allowed Parking

WALDERTON
MAP 05 SU71

The Barley Mow ♥

PO18 9ED ☎ 023 9263 1321 ▤ 023 9263 1403
e-mail: mowbarley@aol.co.uk
dir: *B2146 from Chichester towards Petersfield. Turn right signed Walderton, pub 100yds on left*

A pretty, ivy-clad 18th-century pub in the rolling Sussex Downs, famous locally for its skittle alley, and used by the local Home Guard as its HQ in World War II. A value-for-money menu offers succulent chargrilled steaks; home-made meat pies and burgers; trout, tuna and jumbo cod; and vegetarian hot bake. Less filling options include ploughman's and sandwiches. The secluded, stream-bordered garden is a real sun-trap – perfect for a pint of Ringwood Old Thumper.

Open 11–3 6–11.30 (Sun 12–10.30) **Bar Meals** L served Mon-Sat 12–2 D served Mon-Sat 6–9.30 (Sun 12–9.30) **Restaurant** L served Mon-Sat 12–2.15 D served Mon-Sat 6–9.30 (Sun 12–2.30, 6–9.30) ⊕ Free House ◀ Ringwood Old Thumper & Fortyniner, Fuller's London Pride, & Harveys Best. ☎8 **Facilities** Garden Dogs allowed Parking

WARNHAM   MAP 06 TQ13

The Greets Inn 🍷

47 Friday St RH12 3QY ☎ 01403 265047 📠 01403 265047

dir: *Off A24 N of Horsham*

A fine Sussex hall house dating from about 1350 and built for Elias Greet, a local merchant. A magnificent inglenook fireplace and low beams will be discovered in the flagstone-floored bar. There is a rambling series of dining areas where diners can sample the wares of the kitchen team. Look out for some good pasta and fish dishes.

Open 11–2.30 6–11 (Sun 12–2, 7–10.30) **Bar Meals** L served all week 12–2 D served all week 7–9.30 **Restaurant** L served all week 12–2 D served all week 7–9.30 🍺 Interbrew, Greene King IPA, Fuller's London Pride, Abbot Ale. 🍷 5 **Facilities** Garden Dogs allowed Parking

WARNINGLID   MAP 06 TQ22

The Half Moon 🍷

The Street RH17 5TR ☎ 01444 461227

e-mail: Info@thehalfmoonwarninglid.co.uk

dir: *1m from Warninglid/Cuckfield junct of A23 & 6m from Haywards Heath*

This 19th-century pub continues to flourish and grow in the hands of its dedicated owners, yet all improvements preserve the natural character of the building. The food-led business is growing all the time, thanks to inspired specials such as smoked tomato and courgette gnocchi with chard and goat's cheese; and roast belly pork with Thai noodle, shitake and bok choi broth. Puddings could include rhubarb pannacotta; and passionfruit mousse with pomegranate syrup.

Open 11.30–2.30 5.30–11 (Sun 12–10.30) **Bar Meals** L served all week 12–2 D served Mon-Sat 6–9.30 Av main course £9.50 🍺 Free House 🍺 Harveys Sussex, Black Sheep, Spitfire, Wadworth 6X. 🍷 8 **Facilities** Garden Dogs allowed Parking

WINEHAM   MAP 06 TQ22

The Royal Oak

BN5 9AY ☎ 01444 881252 📠 01444 881530

e-mail: theroyaloakwineham@sky.com

dir: *Wineham Lane – between A272 (Cowfold-Bolney) & B2116 (Hurst-Henfield)*

After dispensing ale straight from the barrels for more than two centuries, this delightful 14th-century half-timbered cottage still retains its traditional, unspoilt character. It is a true rural alehouse – so expect rustic furnishings, and food like venison sausage toad-in-the-hole; cauliflower cheese; steak and ale pie; and home-made soups. Snacks

of potted and smoked mackerel, and ploughman's on a wooden board are served weekdays, with roasts on Sundays. Outside, the extensive gardens are ideal for summer drinking.

Open 11–2.30 5.30–11 (Sun 12–3, 7–10.30) **Bar Meals** L served Mon-Fri 11–2.30 D served Mon-Sat 5.30–11 (Sat 11–4, Sun 11–5) 🍺 Punch Taverns 🍺 Harveys Sussex Best Bitter. **Facilities** Garden Dogs allowed Parking

WISBOROUGH GREEN   MAP 06 TQ02

Cricketers Arms 🍷

Loxwood Rd RH14 0DG ☎ 01403 700369

e-mail: craig@cricketersarms.com

dir: *On A272 between Billingshurst & Petworth. In centre of Wisborough Green turn at junct next to village green, pub 100yds on right*

A traditional village pub dating from the 16th century with oak beams, wooden floors and open fires. Fans of extreme sports should be aware that the Cricketers is the home of the British Lawn Mower Racing Association. A full bar menu ranges from snacks to three course meals and Sunday roasts, with a large selection of specials. Typical dishes include steak pie, sea bass in a prawn and oyster sauce, game dishes in season, and 'mega' salads.

Open 12–11 **Bar Meals** L served all week 12–2 D served Mon-Wed, Fri-Sat 6.30–9.30 (Thu & Sun 6.30–9) **Restaurant** L served all week 12–2 D served Mon-Wed, Fri-Sat 6.30–9.30 (Thu & Sun 6.30–9) 🍺 Enterprise Inns 🍺 Harveys Sussex, Fuller's London Pride, Swift One. 🍷 34 **Facilities** Garden Dogs allowed Parking

TYNE & WEAR

NEWCASTLE UPON TYNE   MAP 21 NZ26

Shiremoor House Farm 🍷

Middle Engine Ln, New York NE29 8DZ

☎ 0191 257 6302 📠 0191 257 8602

dir: *Telephone for directions*

A swift pint of Jarrow River Catcher in New York? Since that's the name of the village, it's eminently feasible at this popular North Tyneside pub, brilliantly converted from an old farm. Particularly appealing is the glazed former granary where a wide range of traditional pub food is served, including steak, ale and mushroom casserole; fillet of salmon with prawn and dill sauce; and sizzling strips of chicken with sweet chilli sauce.

Open 11–11 **Bar Meals** L served all week 12–10 D served all week 12–10 Av main course £8.45 🍺 Free House 🍺 Timothy Taylor Landlord, Mordue Workie Ticket, Theakston BB, John Smiths. 🍷 12 **Facilities** Children's licence Garden Parking

England

TYNEMOUTH
MAP 21 NZ36

Copperfields ★★★ HL

Grand Hotel, Hotspur St NE30 4ER

☎ 0191 293 6666 📠 0191 293 6665

e-mail: info@grandhotel-uk.com

dir: *On NE coast, 10m from Newcastle upon Tyne*

The bar is at the rear of the imposing Grand Hotel, where Stan Laurel and Oliver Hardy always stayed when they played Newcastle's Theatre Royal. Worth a visit for the great views up and down the coast, as well as an extensive bar menu that includes home-made ham, leek and cheddar clanger (a steamed pudding); smokie fish pie; sticky chilli belly pork; Mexican beefburger; and riccia pasta ribbons. A blackboard lists daily specials.

Open 12–12 (Thu-Sat 12–1am) **Bar Meals** L served all week 12–3 D served Sun-Fri 3–9.45 (Sat 3–8) Av main course £6 **Restaurant** L served all week 12–3 D served Mon-Sat 6.30–9.45 Av 3 course à la carte £30 Av 3 course fixed price £22 ◀ Bass '9', Black Sheep, Durham Brewery ales. **Facilities** Children's licence Parking **Rooms** 44

WHITLEY BAY
MAP 21 NZ37

The Waterford Arms

Collywell Bay Rd, Seaton Sluice NE26 4QZ

☎ 0191 237 0450 📠 0191 237 7760

dir: *From A1 N of Newcastle take A19 at Seaton Burn then follow signs for A190 to Seaton Sluice*

The building dates back to 1899 and is located close to the small local fishing harbour, overlooking the North Sea. Splendid beaches and sand dunes are within easy reach, and the pub is very popular with walkers. Seafood dishes are the speciality, including a jumbo cod, seared swordfish, lemon sole, halibut, and crab-stuffed plaice.

Open 12–11 (Sun 12–10.30) **Bar Meals** L served all week 12–4 D served all week (Sun 12–4) Av main course £5.95 **Restaurant** L served all week 12–9 D served all week (Sun 12–4) Av 3 course à la carte £7.25 ⊕ Pubmaster ◀ Tetleys, John Smiths, Scotch. **Facilities** Parking

WARWICKSHIRE

ALDERMINSTER
MAP 10 SP24

Pick of the Pubs

The Bell ♥

CV37 8NY ☎ 01789 450414 📠 01789 450998

e-mail: info@thebellald.co.uk

dir: *On A3400 3.5m S of Stratford-upon-Avon*

An 18th-century coaching inn, whose interior blends modern touches with traditional charms. The spacious conservatory restaurant overlooks a delightful old courtyard with views of the Stour Valley beyond. A good selection of starters and 'little dishes' could include avocado and crayfish tails with tomato vinaigrette on mixed leaves; pan-fried duck livers with Grand Marnier, spiced apple and toasted brioche; and a platter of mixed hors d'oeuvre. Follow with pork fillet filled with apricots and lemongrass, wrapped in Parma ham and served with Madeira jus and vegetables; or fillet of beef mignon with green beans, cherry tomatoes and a Jack Daniels and gorgonzola sauce. If you prefer a snack, there is also a selection of baguettes and light bites including hot cheese and bacon bruschetta; smoked salmon and cream cheese baguette with mixed leaves; and bacon, lettuce and tomato baguette. Those fond of fresh fish should keep an eye on the blackboard menu. New owners for Summer 2008.

Open 11.30–2.30 6.30–11 **Bar Meals** L served all week 12–2 D served all week 7–9.30 **Restaurant** L served all week 12–2 D served all week 7–9.30 ⊕ Free House ◀ Greene King IPA, Abbot Ale, Hook Norton. ♥ 11 **Facilities** Garden Dogs allowed Parking

ALVESTON
MAP 10 SP25

Pick of the Pubs

The Baraset Barn

1 Pimlico Ln CV37 7RF

☎ 01789 295510 📠 01789 292961

e-mail: barasetbarn@lovelypubs.co.uk

Surrounded by Warwickshire countryside, the Baraset Barn has a dramatic interior styled from granite, pewter and oak. The original flagstones remind customers of its 200–year history, but the glass-fronted kitchen introduces an up-to-the-minute visual appeal. From the bar, stone steps lead to the main dining area with high oak beams and brick walls, and the open mezzanine level makes for a perfect vantage point. The menu brings together eclectic flavours from fresh products sourced when possible from the Vale of Evesham: pressed game terrine with quince jelly and caramelised apple; or Lyonnaise salad with belly pork and free range poached duck egg are likely starters. The excellent fish choices features the Baraset bouillabaisse for two, served with croutons, rouille and parmesan. Carnivores will relish classic coq au vin; or spit-roast Gressingham duck, while vegetarians could tuck into wild mushroom and blushed tomato 'arichini' with sautéed spinach and porcini beurre blanc.

Open 11–12 Closed: 25 Dec & 1 Jan Sun eve & Mon (Jan-Feb) **Bar Meals** L served Mon-Sat 12–2 Av main course £15 **Restaurant** L served Mon-Sat 12–2.30 D served Mon-Sat 6.30–9.30 (Sun 12–4) ◀ Leffe, Moretti, UBU. **Facilities** Garden Dogs allowed Parking

England

ARDENS GRAFTON   MAP 10 SP15

Pick of the Pubs

The Golden Cross ♀

B50 4LG ☎ 01789 772420 🖹 01789 773697

e-mail: steve@thegoldencross.net

dir: *Telephone for directions*

The Golden Cross offers a mellow, rug-strewn bar with a flagstone floor, massive beams and roaring fires, and a spacious dining room with restful décor and beautifully laid tables. On warmer days the patio is every bit as inviting. Well kept cask ales and good food at sensible prices are served, with dishes such as pheasant, chestnut and apricot terrine, followed by pan-fried fillet of brill with colcannon, purple sprouting broccoli and citrus butter.

Open 12–3 5–11 (Sat-Sun all day) **Bar Meals** L served Mon-Fri 12–2.30 D served Mon-Fri 5.30–9.30 (Sat 12–9.30, Sun 12–8) **Restaurant** L served Mon-Fri 12–2.30 D served Mon-Fri 5.30–9.30 (Sat 12–9.30, Sun 12–8) Av 3 course à la carte £20 Av 3 course fixed price £15 ⊕ Charles Wells ◀ Tetley Cask, Hook Norton, UBU Purity Brewing & guest ales. ♀ 8 **Facilities** Garden Parking

ASTON CANTLOW   MAP 10 SP16

Pick of the Pubs

King's Head ♀

21 Bearley Rd B95 6HY

☎ 01789 488242 🖹 01789 488137

dir: *Telephone for directions*

It is reputed that William Shakespeare's parents held their wedding reception at the King's Head after they were married next door in the village church in 1557. These days, the colourful hanging baskets and wisteria-clad exterior of this lovingly restored Tudor hostelry invite further exploration; inside, you'll discover a comfortable village bar with wooden settles, a massive inglenook fireplace and an old-fashioned snug. There's also a quarry-tiled main room with attractive window seats and oak tables. A single menu serves all areas: a lunchtime sandwich could be filled with smoked mackerel paté or roast beef and aubergine tapenade. Other dishes might include ham hock and honey glazed parsnip terrine with balsamic shallot jus; followed by saddle of rabbit with braised cabbage and juniper sauce, or venison casserole with calvados sauce and salsify purée. From the specials board, grilled halibut on truffle oil fettuccine; and roast monkfish fillet on artichokes, spinach and sun blushed cherry tomatoes. In summer, food is also served in the large and pretty garden.

Open 11–3 5.30–11 (Winter Sun 5.30–8.30) **Bar Meals** L served all week 12–2.30 D served all week 6.30–9.30 (Sun 12–3) **Restaurant** L served all week 12–2.30 D served all week 6.30–9.30 (Sun 12–3) Av 3 course à la carte £25 Av 3 course fixed price £15 ◀ Greene King Abbot Ale, Purity Gold & Mitchell and Butler Brew XI. ♀ 8 **Facilities** Garden Dogs allowed Parking

BROOM   MAP 10 SP05

Broom Tavern ♀

High St B50 4HL ☎ 01789 773656 🖹 01789 773656

e-mail: webmaster@broomtavern.co.uk

dir: *N of B439 W of Stratford-upon-Avon*

Once a haunt of William Shakespeare, this 16th-century brick and timber inn is smartly furnished, with a large beer garden where barbecues are held in summer. Very much at the heart of village life, it is home to the Broom Tavern Golf Society, and fun days, charity events and outings are a feature. The menu offers a large selection of vegetarian dishes and seafood specials.

Open 12–3 6–11 (Fri-Sat 12–11, Sun 12–3) **Bar Meals** L served all week 12–2 D served Mon-Thu 6–9 (Fri-Sat 6–9.30) **Restaurant** L served all week 12–2 D served Mon-Thu 6.30–9 (Fri-Sat 6–9.30, Sun 5.30–8) ⊕ Punch Taverns ◀ Greene King IPA, Black Sheep & Timothy Taylors Landlord, Wells Bombardier. ♀ 20 **Facilities** Garden Dogs allowed Parking

EDGEHILL   MAP 11 SP34

The Castle Inn ♀

OX15 6DJ ☎ 01295 670255 🖹 01295 670521

e-mail: thecastle-edgehill@beeb.net

dir: *M40 then A422. 6m until Upton House, then turn next right 1.5m*

A fascinating property, the inn was built as a copy of Warwick Castle in 1742 to commemorate the centenary of the Battle of Edgehill, and stands on the summit of Edgehill, 700 feet above sea level. It opened on the anniversary of Cromwell's death in 1750, was first licensed in 1822, and acquired by Hook Norton a hundred years later. Bar snacks, sandwiches, hot platters and steaks are served.

Open 12–3 6–11 (Summer Sat-Sun all day) **Bar Meals** L served all week 12–2 D served all week 6.30–9 **Restaurant** L served all week 12–2 D served all week 6.30–9 (Summer extended hrs) ⊕ Hook Norton ◀ Hook Norton Best, Old Hooky & Generation, Hooky Dark, guest ales. **Facilities** Children's licence Garden Parking

ETTINGTON MAP 10 SP24

The Houndshill ♀

Banbury Rd CV37 7NS

☎ 01789 740267 📠 01789 740075

dir: *On A422 SE of Stratford-upon-Avon*

Family-run inn situated at the heart of England, making it a perfect base for exploring popular tourist attractions such as Oxford, Blenheim, Stratford and the Cotswolds. The pleasant tree-lined garden is especially popular with families. Typical dishes range from poached fillet of salmon, and faggots, mash and minted peas, to supreme of chicken and ham and mushroom tagliatelle. Alternatively, try cold ham off the bone or home-made steak and kidney pie.

Open 12–3 6–11 (Sun 12–3, 7–10.30) Closed: 25–28 Dec **Bar Meals** L served all week 12–2 D served all week 7–9.30 Av main course £8.50 **Restaurant** L served all week 12–2 D served all week 9.30 Av 3 course à la carte £16.50 ⊞ Free House ⛃ Hook Norton Best, Spitfire. ♀ 7 **Facilities** Garden Dogs allowed Parking Play Area

FARNBOROUGH MAP 11 SP44

Pick of the Pubs

The Inn at Farnborough ⊛ ♀

OX17 1DZ ☎ 01295 690615

e-mail: enquiries@innatfarnborough.co.uk

dir: *M40 junct 11 towards Banbury. Right at 3rd rdbt onto A423 signed Southam. 4m & onto A423. Left onto single track road signed Farnborough. Approx 1m turn right into village, pub on right*

This Grade II listed free house enjoys a picturesque setting in a National Trust village. Formerly known as the Butcher's Arms, it once served as the butcher's house on the Farnborough Estate. Parts of the building, including an original inglenook fireplace, date back 400 years. A good range of real ales and 14 wines by the glass are served alongside dishes based on high-quality Heart of England produce. Typical examples from the fixed price menu are smoked salmon croquette with lemon and saffron aioli; half a roasted corn-fed poussin with winter greens and peppercorn sauce; and a dessert of apple crumble. Daily specials might include roasted Gressingham duck breast with winter greens, braised red cabbage and black cherry jus. Families are welcome, with smaller portions available for children, and there is a funky private dining room with claret walls and a zebra print ceiling.

Open 12–3 6–11 (Sat-Sun 6–12) Closed: 25 Dec **Bar Meals** L served Mon-Fri 12–3 D served Mon-Fri 6–11 (Sat-Sun all day) **Restaurant** L served Mon-Fri 12–3 D served Mon-Fri 6–11 (Sat-Sun all day) Av 3 course à la carte £25 Av 2 course fixed price £10.95 ⊞ Free House ⛃ Old Speckled Hen, Greene King IPA, Guinness & Hook Norton. ♀ 16 **Facilities** Children's licence Garden Dogs allowed Parking

GREAT WOLFORD MAP 10 SP23

Pick of the Pubs

The Fox & Hounds Inn ★★★★ INN

CV36 5NQ ☎ 01608 674220 📠 01608 674160

e-mail: enquiries@thefoxandhoundsinn.com

dir: *Off A44 NE of Moreton-in-Marsh*

An unspoilt village hostelry nestling in glorious countryside on the edge of the Cotswolds. Good food, good beer and exceptional whiskies are all on offer, along with an inviting ambience enhanced by old settles, Tudor inglenook fireplaces and solid ceiling beams adorned with jugs or festooned with hops. The bar entrance is a double-hinged 'coffin door' which once allowed coffins to be brought in and laid out prior to the funeral service. Allegedly, a secret tunnel, along which bodies were sometimes carried, linked the cellar with the nearby church, and obviously, there have been many ghostly sightings. The famously controversial pub sign features Tony Blair and a number of foxes and foxhounds. As well as a range of traditional ales, the bar offers a staggering selection of almost 200 fine whiskies. On the menu, look for home-made salmon fishcakes, oven-roasted guinea fowl, grilled Dover sole, and rib-eye steak.

Open 12–2.30 6–11 Closed: 1st 2wks Jan & Mon **Bar Meals** L served Tue-Sat 12–2 D served Tue-Sat 6.30–9 **Restaurant** L served Tue-Sun 12–2 D served Tue-Fri 7–9 (Sat-Sun 7–9.30) ⊞ Free House ⛃ Hook Norton Best, guest ales. **Facilities** Garden Dogs allowed Parking **Rooms** 3

HATTON MAP 10 SP26

The Case is Altered

Case Ln, Five Ways CV35 7JD ☎ 01926 484206

This traditional free house proudly carries the standard for the old style of pub. It serves no food and does not accept children or dogs. That aside, it's a thoroughly welcoming spot for adults who appreciate the pleasures of a quiet pint. Hook Norton beers have a strong presence, and there is always a local and national guest ale to sup while enjoying lively conversation or just appreciating the atmosphere.

Open 12–2.30 6–11 (Sun 12–2, 7–10.30) ⛃ Greene King IPA, Sharp's Doom Bar, guest ales. **Facilities** Parking **Notes** ⊛

The Howard Arms

The Howard Arms stands on the picturesque village green at Ilmington in a crook of the Cotswold Hills. Built of Cotswold stone, the inn dates back 400 years and features polished flagstones and a welcoming blaze in the inglenook fireplace.

The interior, with its collection of friendly old furniture, is light and airy, and there's an attractive garden with lawns, fruit trees and a York stone terrace. A good choice of cask ales is served alongside organic soft drinks, ciders and an eclectic list of Old and New World wines, including more than 20 available by the glass. The imaginative menu changes two or three times a week and is based on locally sourced ingredients. The freshly prepared dishes offer plenty of variety, with starters such as butter-fried chicken cake with rocket and watercress salad, and tomato and red onion salsa; or oak smoked organic salmon on a warm potato cake with sour cream and chives. Main courses range from pan-fried sea bass with coriander houmous, roasted artichoke and red onion dressing, to marinated lamb rump with aubergine purée and tomato jus. A vegetarian alternative might be potato, blue cheese and spring onion cake with wilted spinach, poached egg and mustard hollandaise sauce. The inn is known for its desserts, so don't miss out on the likes of warm chocolate brownie with chocolate sauce and vanilla ice cream; or pear and apple flapjack crumble with custard, cream or ice cream. If you are planning to walk off your meal, you can take a leisurely stroll around the village or head for the nearby hills.

MAP 10 SP24
Lower Green CV36 4LT
☎ 01608 682226
🖹 01608 682226
e-mail: info@howardarms.com
dir: *Off A429 or A3400, 7m from Stratford-upon-Avon*

Open 11–11 (Sun 12–10.30)
Bar Meals L served Mon-Fri 12–2.30 D served Sat-Sun 12–10
Restaurant L served Mon-Fri 12–2.30 D served Mon-Thu 6.30–9.30 (Fri-Sat 6.30–10)
🌐 Free House ◀ Everards Tiger Best, Hook Norton Gold, Prurity Brewing 'Ubu', Bard's Brewery Nobel Fool. ♀ 20
Facilities Garden Parking

ILMINGTON   MAP 10 SP24

Pick of the Pubs

The Howard Arms ▼

See Pick of the Pubs on page 587

LAPWORTH   MAP 10 SP17

Pick of the Pubs

The Boot Inn ▼

Old Warwick Rd B94 6JU
☎ 01564 782464 📠 01564 784989
e-mail: the bootinn@lovelypubs.co.uk
dir: *Telephone for directions*

Beside the Grand Union Canal in the unspoilt village of Lapworth, this lively and convivial 16th-century former coaching inn is well worth seeking out. Apart from its smartly refurbished interior, the attractive garden is a great place to relax on warm days, while a canopy and patio heaters make it a comfortable place to sit even on cooler evenings. But the main draw is the modern brasserie-style food, with wide-ranging menus that deliver home-produced dishes. A selection from the menu might include prawn, smoked haddock and spring onion fishcake, served with lemon gremolata and herb aioli; haddock in tempura batter with pea purée, sauce gribiche and frites; and fillet steak with smoked roast garlic, spinach and mascarpone mash.

Open 11–12 Closed: 25 Dec **Bar Meals** L served all week 12–2.30 D served all week 7–10 Av main course £9 **Restaurant** L served all week 12–2.30 D served all week 7–10 Av 3 course à la carte £19 Av 4 course fixed price £27.50 🍺 Greene King Old Speckled Hen, Wadworth 6X, John Smiths's, Brew XI. ▼8 **Facilities** Garden Dogs allowed Parking

LONG ITCHINGTON   MAP 11 SP46

Pick of the Pubs

The Duck on the Pond ▼

The Green CV47 9QJ
☎ 01926 815876 📠 01926 815766
e-mail: duckonthepond@aol.com
dir: *On A423 in middle of Long Itchington, 1m N of Southam*

Children will be delighted to discover that the name of this attractive village inn does indeed indicate the presence of a pond replete with drakes and mallards. Adults, meanwhile, will be comforted to learn that the inn's appearance, which is reminiscent of a French bistro, is entirely substantiated by the food. Winter fires light an entirely intriguing interior, crammed with French artwork, road signs and bottles, not to mention an unusual willow baton ceiling. The passion is evident in an appealing and well thought out menu that mixes traditional dishes with more innovative selections. Start with an impressive tower of prawns and filo pastry; or fresh Scottish mussels steamed with chorizo, garlic and tomato sauce. Follow on with breast of chicken stuffed with spinach and brie; roast pork with nettle stuffing on apple

mash with cider cream; or grilled salmon with braised fennel and a caramelised lime, mango and pineapple salsa. Specials might include seared king scallops with sautéd black pudding, or Thai-marinated red snapper stir fry.

Open 12–3 5–11 (Sat 12–11, Sun 12–10.30) Closed: Mon (ex BH) **Bar Meals** L served Tue-Sun 12–2 D served Tue-Sun 6.30–10 (Sat-Sun 12–10) Av main course £12 **Restaurant** L served Tue-Sun 12–2.30 D served Tue-Sun 6.30–10 (Sat 12–10, Sun 12–9) Av 3 course à la carte £20 ⊕ Charles Wells 🍺 Wells Bombardier, Young's Winter Warmer & Guinness. ▼10 **Facilities** Garden Parking

MONKS KIRBY   MAP 11 SP48

The Bell Inn

Bell Ln CV23 0QY ☎ 01788 832352 📠 01788 832352
e-mail: belindagb@aol.com
dir: *Off The Fosseway junct with B4455*

The Spanish owners of this quaint, timbered inn, once a Benedictine priory gatehouse and then a brewhouse cottage, describe it as "a corner of Spain in the heart of England". Mediterranean and traditional cuisine play an important role on the menu. Red snapper gallega, saddle of lamb, fillet Catalan, chicken piri piri, and Mexican hot pot are popular favourites. Extensive range of starters and speciality dishes.

Open 12–2.30 7–11 Closed: 26 Dec, 1 Jan **Bar Meals** L served Tue-Sun 12–2.30 D served all week 7–10.30 **Restaurant** L served Tue-Sun 12–2.30 D served all week 7–10.30 ⊕ Free House 🍺 Boddingtons, IPA & Ruddles. **Facilities** Garden Parking

NAPTON ON THE HILL   MAP 11 SP46

The Bridge at Napton

Southam Rd CV47 8NQ ☎ 01926 812466
e-mail: info@thebridgeatnapton.co.uk
dir: *At Bridge 111 on Oxford Canal on A425, 2m from Southam & 1m from Napton-on-the-Hill*

This is an ideal place to moor the narrow boat, though travellers by car or bike are equally welcome. Built as a stabling inn at bridge 111 on the Oxford canal, the pub has a restaurant, three bars and a large garden, plus its own turning point for barges. There are some excellent ales, and food choices range from Aberdeen Angus beefburger with chips to the likes of honey-roasted belly pork with caramelised onions.

Open 12–3 6–11 (Apr-Nov Sat-Sun 12–11) Closed: Sun eve & Mon (Nov-Apr) **Bar Meals** L served all week 12–2 (Winter Tue-Sun) Av main course £6.50 **Restaurant** L served all week 12–2 D served all week 6–9 (Winter lunch Tue-Sun, dinner Tue-Sat) Av 3 course à la carte £18.50 ⊕ Punch Taverns 🍺 3 guest ales. **Facilities** Garden Dogs allowed Parking Play Area

England

PRESTON BAGOT
MAP 10 SP16

The Crabmill ⚈

B95 5EE ☎ 01926 843342 📠 01926 843989
e-mail: thecrabmill@lovelypubs.co.uk

dir: *M42 junct 8, A3400 towards Stratford-upon-Avon. Take A4189 Henley-in-Arden lights. Left, pub 1.5m on left*

The name is a reminder that crab apple cider was once made at this 15th-century hostelry, which is set in beautiful rural surroundings. Restored to create an upmarket venue, the pub has a light, open feel. Even the menu seems fresh and stylish, with dishes ranging from a lunchtime croque monsieur or panini, to evening dishes such as Moroccan chicken with spiced potatoes and cucumber yogurt relish, and crab, crayfish and saffron risotto.

Open 11–11 (Sun 12–6) Closed: 25 Dec **Bar Meals** L served all week 12–2.30 D served Mon-Sat 6.30–9.30 (Sun 12.30–3.30) Av main course £12 **Restaurant** L served all week 12–2.30 D served Mon-Sat 6.30–9.30 (Sun 12.30–3.30) Av 3 course à la carte £23 ◀ Wadworth 6X, Tetleys, Greene King Abbot Ale. ⚈8 **Facilities** Garden Dogs allowed Parking

PRIORS MARSTON
MAP 11 SP45

Pick of the Pubs

The Hollybush Inn ⚈

Hollybush Ln CV47 7RW
☎ 01327 260934 📠 01327 262507

dir: *From Southam A425, off bypass and take 1st right, 6m to Priors Marston. Turn left after War memorial, next left, 150yds left again*

Many pubs are central to their communities, but this one goes a step further – it provides lunches for the local school and is committed to supporting the village sports club. Set in the beautiful village of Priors Marston in the heart of Warwickshire, the Hollybush was a farmhouse that started selling beer in 1927 and became fully licensed twenty years later. Recent extensions have added the 40–seat restaurant and a games room. With its large fireplace burning brightly, it's a warm hub of village social activity with a very relaxed atmosphere; people can eat and/or drink wherever they choose. The bar menu ranges from baguettes to steak, Guinness and mushroom pie; and a dish of charcuterie is served with olives, spicy cornichons and bread. A three-course dinner could comprise pan-fried pigeon breast with beetroot salad; medallions of pork fillet; and blackberry and apple crumble – with custard of course!

Open 12–2 5.30–11 (Fri 5.30–12, Sat-Sun 12–3, Sat 6–12, Sun 7–10.30) **Bar Meals** L served all week 12–2 D served all week 6.30–9.30 (Wed 6.30–9, Sun 12.2.30, 7–9) Av main course £7.50 **Restaurant** L served all week 12–2 D served all week 6.30–9.30 (No à la carte Wed eve or Sun) Av 3 course à la carte £20 Av 3 course fixed price £14.95 ◀ Hook Norton, London Pride, Guinness & guest ale. ⚈8 **Facilities** Garden Dogs allowed Parking

RATLEY
MAP 11 SP34

The Rose and Crown

OX15 6DS ☎ 01295 678148
e-mail: k.marples@btinternet.com

dir: *Follow Edgehill signs, 7m N of Banbury (13m SE of Stratford-upon-Avon) on A422.*

Following the Battle of Edgehill in 1642, a Roundhead was discovered in the chimney of this 11th (or 12th)-century pub and beheaded in the hearth. His ghost reputedly haunts the building. Enjoy the peaceful village location and the traditional pub food, perhaps including beef and ale pie, scampi and chips, chicken curry and the Sunday roast, plus vegetarian options.

Open 12–3 6–11 (Fri-Sat 12–3, 6.30–12, Sun 12–4, 7–11) **Bar Meals** L served all week 12–2 D served all week 7–9 Av main course £8.95 **Restaurant** L served Tue-Sun 12–2.30 D served Tue-Sat 7–9 ⊕ Free House ◀ Wells Bombardier & Eagle IPA, Greene King Old Speckled Hen & guest ale. **Facilities** Garden Dogs allowed Parking

RED HILL
MAP 10 SP15

The Stag at Redhill NEW ⚈

Alcester Rd B49 6NQ
☎ 01789 764634 📠 01789 764431
e-mail: info@thestagatredhill.co.uk

dir: *On A46 between Stratford-upon-Avon and Alcester*

A family run business, The Stag is a 16th-century coaching inn, which has also been a court house and prison (you can still see a cell door in the court room restaurant). Food is freshly prepared and service begins with breakfast from 7.30am. Seating is provided for 150 people, and there is a large patio eating area outside, popular in fine weather. A helipad facility allows customers to fly in for a meal at their convenience.

Open 7.30am-11 **Bar Meals** L served all week 12–5 D served all week 5–8 Av main course £11 **Restaurant** L served all week 12–5 D served all week 5–9 Av 3 course à la carte £20 ⊕ Greene King ◀ Greene King IPA, Abbot Ale, Old Speckled Hen, Ruddles & Morland Original. ⚈7 **Facilities** Garden Parking

England

Pick of the Pubs

Golden Lion Hotel ★★★ HL ♀

Easenhall CV23 0JA

☎ 01788 832265 🖹 01788 832878

e-mail: reception@goldenlionhotel.org

web: www.goldenlionhotel.org

dir: *From Rugby take A426, follow signs for Nuneaton. Through Newbold, follow brown sign, turn left, pub in 1m*

A charming 16th-century free house with low oak-beamed ceilings and narrow doorways. James and Claudia are the third generation of the Austin family at the Golden Lion, where you'll find traditional ales, roaring winter fires and an extensive wine list. Choose between home-cooked bar food such as red Thai chicken curry, or breast of chicken wrapped in bacon with tomato sauce, and melted cheese on spaghetti. For gourmet dining in the candlelit restaurant, start perhaps with tian of avocado and Marie Rose prawns, or a continental mixed meat platter with olives and crusty bread. Continue with oven-roasted loin of monkfish wrapped in Parma ham; whole grilled lemon sole; or lambs' liver, bacon, black pudding, mash, red wine and onion gravy. The pub is set amidst idyllic countryside in one of Warwickshire's best-kept villages, and its 21 en suite bedrooms, some with four-poster beds, offer outstanding accommodation.

Open 11–11 **Bar Meals** L served all week 12–3 D served all week 6–9.30 (Sun carvery 12–2.30, bar menu 4–8.45) Av main course £9.85 **Restaurant** L served Mon-Sun 12–2 D served Mon-Sun 6–9.30 (Sun carvery 12–2.30, bar menu 4–8.45) Av 3 course à la carte £19 ⊕ Free House ♀ 7 **Facilities** Garden Parking **Rooms** 21

The Cherington Arms ♀

Cherington CV36 5HS ☎ 01608 686233

e-mail: thecheringtonarms@hooknorton.tablesir.com

dir: *12m from Stratford -upon-Avon. 14m from Leamington & Warwick. 10m from Woodstock. 4m from Shipston on Stour.*

An attractive 17th-century inn with exposed beams and Cotswold stone walls, stripped wood furniture and roaring log inglenook fire. The ever-changing chalkboard menus might announce crab fishcakes with mango and chilli salsa; home-made beef and Hooky (ie Hook Norton beer, as sold in the bar) pie; breast of chicken stuffed with sun-dried tomato and cream pesto; and risotto of chargrilled artichoke, asparagus and green beans. Outside are large riverside gardens with a mill race.

Open 12–3 6.30–11.30 (Sat-Sun all day summer) **Bar Meals** L served Mon-Sat 12–2 D served Tue-Sun 7–9 (Sun 12–3) Av main course £9.75 **Restaurant** L served Mon-Fri 12–2 D served Sun-Thu 7–9 (Fri-Sat 7–9.30, Sat 12–2.30, Sun 12–3) ⊕ Hook Norton ◀ Hook Norton Best Bitter, Generation & Old Hooky, guest ales. ♀ 11 **Facilities** Garden Dogs allowed Parking

Pick of the Pubs

The Red Lion ★★★★ INN ♀

See Pick of the Pubs on opposite page

White Bear Hotel ♀

High St CV36 4AJ

☎ 01608 661558 🖹 01608 662612

e-mail: info@whitebearhotel.co.uk

dir: *From M40 junct 15, follow signs to Stratford-upon-Avon, then take A3400 to Shipston-on-Stour*

Open fires and wooden settles give the bars of this Georgian hotel a comfortable, timeless appeal. You'll find a range of real ales and keg beers, with up to eight wines available by the glass. The refurbished restaurant with its crisp white tablecloths makes dining a delicious experience: starters like pan-fried kidneys with black pudding precede main course options that include rack of lamb; and haddock with spinach and Welsh rarebit.

Open 11–12 (Sun 11–11) **Bar Meals** L served all week 12–2 D served Mon-Sat 6.30–9.30 Av main course £10 **Restaurant** L served all week 12–2 D served Mon-Sat 6.30–9.30 Av 3 course à la carte £18 ⊕ Punch Taverns ◀ Adnams Old Hooky, Bass & guest ales. ♀ 8 **Facilities** Children's licence Garden Parking

The Red Lion

Originally built as a coaching inn in 1748, this grade II listed stone free house is located in an area of outstanding natural beauty.

Though it is ideally situated for such major attractions as Stratford upon Avon, Warwick, Oxford and the Cotswold Wildlife Park, tales of witches in the village and a nearby prehistoric stone circle mean there is as much to interest the historian as the tourist. The inside retains an old world atmosphere with oak beams, log fires, gleaming wood and comfy leather chairs. The bar is full of atmosphere, and visitors can eat there or in the restaurant area, choosing food from one long menu and specials from the blackboard. All tastes are catered for, from interesting sandwiches (hand-carved ham and wholegrain mustard on granary bread; buffalo mozzarella and beef tomato on ciabatta) to a lightly battered cod fillet, served on a sheet of 'The Red Lion Times'. Look out otherwise for such adventurous starters as home-made ham hock, leek and Parma ham terrine with grape chutney; or celeriac remoulade on a salad of roasted beetroot, apples and walnuts. Mains might include herb-crusted rack of lamb; steak and Hook Norton pie, or grilled sea bass with wilted garlic spinach and ratatouille. Round off with a warm pear and almond flan and mascarpone cheese, or an iced lime and ginger parfait. Those who choose to dine in the well-kept garden may be lucky enough to be joined by Cocoa, the pub's glamorous chocolate Labrador. Five elegant en suite bedrooms all feature such modern luxuries as Egyptian cotton bed linen and flat screen televisions.

★★★★ INN ♥
MAP 10 SP24
Main St, Long Compton CV37 5JS
☎ 01608 684221
🖷 01608 684968
e-mail:
info@redlion-longcompton.co.uk
web:
www.redlion-longcompton.co.uk
dir: *On A3400 between Shipston on Stour & Chipping Norton*

Open 11–2.30 6–11 (Fri-Sun 11–11)
Bar Meals L served all week 12–2.30
D served all week 6–9.30 (Fri-Sun 12–9.30) Av main course £9.95
⊕ Free House ◀ Hook Norton Best, Adnams, Timothy Taylor. ♥ 7
Facilities Garden Dogs allowed Parking Play Area
Rooms 5

PICK OF THE PUBS

STRATFORD-UPON-AVON-WARWICKSHIRE

The Fox & Goose Inn

A busy, privately owned inn, formerly two cottages and a blacksmith's forge. It is located in Armscote, a beautiful village eight miles south of Stratford-upon-Avon, set in lovely countryside and within easy reach of Warwick and several Cotswold villages.

The inn was given the total refurb treatment a few years ago, and the result is stylish and utterly distinctive. It includes a smart dining room and a cosy bar. The bar, with its real ales, has lots of squishy velvet cushions, an open fire, flagstone floors and piles of reading matter to enjoy while supping a pint of Butcombe or Black Sheep. If you prefer wine (or even champagne) there is a selection by the glass or bottle, and for further refreshments there is a new country-style menu: look out for home-cooked pie and vegan choices. The dining room offers a menu created from fresh produce and much imagination. Out in the garden there's a large grassy area, a decked space and 20 seats for dining under the vines and enjoying

some lovely country views. Nearby attractions include Warwick Castle and Museum, Hill Close Gardens, St Edwards Church, Queens Own Hussars Museum, and Stow Toy Museum.

Ｕ ♀
MAP 10 SP25
CV37 8DD
☎ 01608 682293
▤ 01608 682293
e-mail: mail@foxandgoose.co.uk
dir: *1m off A3400, between Shipston-on-Stour & Stratford-upon-Avon*

Open 12–3 6–11
Bar Meals L served all week 12–2.30 D served all week 7–9.30 Av main course £11.95
Restaurant L served all week 12–2.30 D served all week 7–9.30 Av 3 course à la carte £23.50
⊕ Free House ◀ Butcombe, Black Sheep & Bombardier. ♀ 8
Facilities Garden Parking

SHREWLEY   MAP 10 SP26

Pick of the Pubs

The Durham Ox Restaurant and Country Pub ♀

Shrewley Common CV35 7AY

☎ 01926 842283 📄 0121 705 9315

e-mail: reservations@durham-ox.com

dir: *M40 junct 15 onto A46 towards Coventry. 1st exit signed Warwick, turn left onto A4177. After Hatton Country World pub signed 1.5m*

An award-winning pub/restaurant in a peaceful village just four miles from Warwick and Leamington. Warm and inviting, its old beams, roaring fire and traditional hospitality combine with a city chic that give it a competitive edge. Success is in no small measure due to the restaurant, where Master Chef Simon Diprose prepares impressive, seasonally changing classic and contemporary dishes. A meal might consist of deep-fried Boursin with ratatouille and basil sorbet; roast fillet of five-spice salmon with sweet corn, pak choi and coriander dressing; and hot chocolate and Snickers fondant with vanilla ice cream. For more examples of his style, consider roast vegetables with North African spices, couscous and yoghurt dressing; and fresh plaice fillet in crispy Cajun coating with buttered peas and chunky chips. Children are offered penne pasta, and home-made fishcakes from their own menu. Extensive gardens incorporate a safe children's play area.

Open 12–11 **Bar Meals** L served all week 12–3 D served all week 6–10 (Sun 12–9) Av main course £13.50 **Restaurant** L served all week 12–3 D served all week 6–10 (Sun 12–9) Av 3 course à la carte £24 ⊕ Greene King ◖ IPA, Old Speckled Hen, Guinness & Abbot Ale. ♀ 21 **Facilities** Garden Parking Play Area

---

STRATFORD-UPON-AVON   MAP 10 SP25

The Dirty Duck

Waterside CV37 6BA ☎ 01789 297312 📄 01789 293441

dir: *Telephone for directions*

Frequented by members of the Royal Shakespeare Company from the nearby theatre, this traditional, partly Elizabethan inn has a splendid raised terrace overlooking the River Avon. In addition to the interesting range of real ales, a comprehensive choice of food is offered. Light bites, pastas, salads and mains at lunchtime, plus pub classics and 'make it special' dishes at night, from rustic sharing bread with herbs, garlic and olives to roast rack of lamb.

Open 11–12 (Sun 12–10.30) **Bar Meals** L served all week 12–5 D served Mon-Sat 5–10 Av main course £6 **Restaurant** D served Mon-Sat 5–10 Av 3 course à la carte £15 ⊕ Whitbread ◖ Flowers Original, Morland Old Speckled Hen. **Facilities** Garden Dogs allowed

Pick of the Pubs

The Fox & Goose Inn Ⓤ ♀

See Pick of the Pubs on opposite page

The One Elm ♀

1 Guild St CV37 6QZ ☎ 01789 404919

dir: *In town centre*

Standing on its own in the heart of town, the One Elm has two dining rooms: downstairs is intimate, even with the buzzy bar close by, while upstairs feels grander. The menu features chargrilled côte de boeuf for two, Aberdeen Angus rump steak, and tuna, as well as other main courses. The deli board offers all-day nuts and seeds, cheeses, charcuterie and antipasti. The secluded terrace induces in some a feeling of being abroad.

Open 11.30–11 Closed: 25 Dec **Bar Meals** L served all week 12–2.30 D served all week 6.30–10 (Sun all day) Av main course £10.50 **Restaurant** L served all week 12–2.30 D served all week 6.30–10 (Sun all day) ◖ London Pride, Old Speckled Hen, Timothy Taylor Landlord. ♀ 9 **Facilities** Garden Dogs allowed Parking

---

STRETTON ON FOSSE   MAP 10 SP23

The Plough Inn

GL56 9QX ☎ 01608 661053

e-mail: ploughinn053@aol.com

dir: *From Moreton In Marsh, 4m on A429 N. From Stratford Upon Avon, 10m on A429 S*

Family-run, 17th-century village pub, built from Cotswold stone, its traditional charms include bare beams and a real fire. Starters of home-made soup with crusty bread or a goats' cheese crouton with smoked bacon on salad could be followed by beer-battered cod with chips and salad. There's a spit roast over a log fire on Sundays (September-May), and in addition the French chef prepares traditional dishes from his homeland for the specials board.

Open 11.30–2.30 6–11 (Sun all day) **Bar Meals** L served Mon-Sat 12–2 D served Mon-Sat 6–9 (Sun 12–8) Av main course £9.95 **Restaurant** L served Mon-Sat 12–2 D served Mon-Sat 6–9 (Sun 12–8) ⊕ Free House ◖ Butcombe, Timothy Taylor Landlord, Bath Spa. **Facilities** Garden Parking Play Area

---

TEMPLE GRAFTON   MAP 10 SP15

The Blue Boar Inn ♀

B49 6NR ☎ 01789 750010 📄 01789 750635

e-mail: blueboar@rutlandpubco.net

dir: *From A46 (from Stratford to Alcester) turn left to Temple Grafton. Pub at 1st x-rds*

The oldest part of the inn dates from the early 1600s, and the restaurant features a 35-foot glass-covered well, home to a family of

CONTINUED

TEMPLE GRAFTON continued

koi carp, from which water was formerly drawn for brewing. There are four open fires in the bar and restaurant areas, and a patio garden with views of the Cotswold Hills. A menu of traditional dishes is served, with variety provided by daily specials prepared from local produce, game in particular.

Open 11–12 **Bar Meals** L served all week 12–3 D served all week 6–10 (Sat 12–10, Sun 12–9) Av main course £9.95 **Restaurant** L served all week 12–3 D served all week 6–10 ◀ Morland Old Speckled Hen, Best, Deuchars IPA, guest ale. ♀ 18 **Facilities** Children's licence Garden Parking

WARWICK   MAP 10 SP26

The Rose & Crown ♀

30 Market Place CV34 4SH
☎ 01926 411117 📄 01926 492117
e-mail: roseandcrown@peachpubs.com
dir: 5mins from A46 & M40

Stylish gastropub located in the centre of Warwick with large leather sofas in the bar, a good choice of real ales and wines by the glass. Breakfast, lunch and dinner are served in the vibrant red restaurant. The deli board is a popular feature, with nuts and seeds, cheese, charcuterie, antipasti, fish and bread. Mains take in free range coq au vin, Porterhouse steak, roast hake, and sausage of the week.

Open 8–11 Closed: 25 Dec **Bar Meals** L served Mon-Sat 12–10 D served Mon-Sat 6.30–10 (Sun 12–9.30) Av main course £12 **Restaurant** L served Mon-Sat 12–2.30 D served Mon-Sat 6.30–10 (Sun 12–3, 6.30–9.30) ◀ Speckled Hen, Black Sheep & London Pride. ♀ 8 **Facilities** Dogs allowed

WELFORD-ON-AVON   MAP 10 SP15

The Bell Inn ♀

Binton Rd CV37 8EB
☎ 01789 750353 📄 01789 750893
e-mail: info@thebellwelford.co.uk

Set deep in the heart of the Warwickshire countryside, this 17th-century inn has all the classic touches – open fires, flagstone floors, exposed beams and oak furniture – that make country pubs so charming. On a literary note, rumour has it that William Shakespeare contracted fatal pneumonia after stumbling home from a drink at the Bell in the pouring rain. In addition to the extensive list of wines and real ales, food is taken seriously here and the local suppliers of quality ingredients are credited on the menu. Typical dishes are cod on leek risotto with wholegrain mustard sauce and crispy onions; four-cheese pancake cannelloni; and chicken wrapped in Parma ham on roasted potatoes and parsnips with wilted spinach and a plum and orange sauce. Home-made desserts include ginger crème brûlée with a spicy pepper biscuit.

Open 11.30–3 6.30–11 (Sat 11.30–11, Sun 12–11) **Bar Meals** L served Mon-Sat 11.30–2.30 D served Mon-Thu 6.45–9.30 (Fri-Sat 6.45–10, Sun 12–9.30) **Restaurant** L served Mon-Sat 11.30–2.30 D served Mon-Thu 6.45–9.30 (Fri-Sat 6.45–10, Sun 12–9.30) ⊞ Enterprise Inns ◀ Hook Norton (various), Flowers Original, Hobsons Best, Wadsworth 6X. ♀ 16 **Facilities** Garden Parking

The Four Alls ♀

Binton Bridges CV37 8PW
☎ 01789 750228 📄 01789 750262
e-mail: andrew@thefouralls.co.uk
dir: B439 from Stratford-upon-Avon then left

This centuries-old inn was completely refurbished in spicy Mediterranean tones after the dramatic floods of 2007. Its charming location features a riverside garden and patio, whilst inside is a warm and cosy atmosphere in which to sample the varied menus. The bar and tapas menu features rustic breads, a choice of meat, fish or veggie boards, as well as burgers and filled baguettes. Restaurant options include braised lamb; poached salmon; and wild mushroom stroganoff.

Open 11–3 6–11 (Sat-Sun all day & BHs, Mon-Sun all day in summer) **Bar Meals** L served Mon-Sat 12–2.30 D served Mon-Sat 7–10 (Sun 12–3, 7–9.30) Av main course £12.95 **Restaurant** L served all week 12–2.30 D served Mon-Sat 7–10 (Sun 7–9.30) Av 3 course à la carte £22 ⊞ Enterprise Inns ◀ Old Hooky, Purity Gold, Deuchars IPA. ♀ 12 **Facilities** Children's licence Garden Parking Play Area

WITHYBROOK   MAP 11 SP48

The Pheasant ♀

Main St CV7 9LT ☎ 01455 220480 📄 01455 221296
e-mail: thepheasant01@hotmail.com
dir: 7m from Coventry

This well-presented 17th-century free house stands beside the brook where withies were once cut for fencing. An inglenook fireplace, farm implements and horse-racing photographs characterise the interior. Under the same ownership since 1981, the pub has a tried and tested menu of over 100 dishes backed by blackboard specials such as beef sirloin in red wine and mushroom sauce. Regular choices include chicken kiev; and venison pie. Outside tables overlook the Withy Brook.

Open 11–3 6–1am (Sun 12–11) Closed: 25–26 Dec **Bar Meals** L served Mon-Sat 12–2 D served Mon-Sat 6.15–10 (Sun 12–9) Av main course £11.95 ⊞ Free House ◀ Courage Directors, Theakstons Best, John Smiths Smooth. ♀ 9 **Facilities** Garden Dogs allowed Parking

WOOTTON WAWEN   MAP 10 SP16

The Bulls Head ♀

See Pick of the Pubs on opposite page

The Bulls Head

Since changing hands in 2006, the Bull's Head has developed into a serious dining destination. Originally two separate 16th-century cottages, the extensively refurbished Bulls Head is set in the ancient village of Wootton Wawen, and is ideally placed for touring and exploring the lovely landscapes of Warwickshire and the Cotswolds.

Low beams, leather sofas, open fires and old church pews set the scene in the bar and snug areas, and the same tone and style are maintained in the magnificent 'great hall' restaurant, with its vaulted ceiling and exposed beams. Outside, you'll find a lawned garden and paved patio surrounded by mature trees. Owners Andrew and Wendy Parry describe their cooking style quite simply as "food we love to eat and food we love to cook." Local suppliers are personally visited in order to ensure the very best of the county's produce finds its way to the kitchen. Start with herb-baked whole camembert with tomato and sweet chilli chutney; home-cured Sambuca and lemongrass salmon with citrus potato salad; or a tower of prawns and filo pastry with rocket mayonnaise. Mains might take in pan-fried duck breast with leeks and bacon; Lighthorne shoulder of lamb stuffed with apricot, prune, pistachio and mint, or pea and lemon risotto served on roasted butternut squash with truffle oil. Keep an eye out for the daily specials, which could include smoked halibut; grilled mahi mahi with niçoise salad and a poached egg; and pork fillet stuffed with black pudding. What's more, service is taken seriously here, promising to be attentive without being overbearing.

MAP 10 SP16
Stratford Rd B95 6BD
☎ 01564 792511
dir: *On B3400, 4m N of Stratford-upon-Avon, 1m S of Henley-in-Arden*

Open 12–3 5–11 (Sun 12–10.30)
Bar Meals L served all week 12–9 D served all week 2–9 Av main course £12
Restaurant L served all week 12–2.30 D served all week 6–9.30 (Sat-Sun all day) Av 3 course à la carte £19
◀ Marston's Pedigree, Banks Bitter, Banks Original plus guest ales. ☻ 10
Facilities Garden Parking

595

WEST MIDLANDS

BARSTON
MAP 10 SP27

Pick of the Pubs

The Malt Shovel at Barston ● ♀

Barston Ln B92 0JP
☎ 01675 443223 📠 01675 443223
web: www.themaltshovelatbarston.com
dir: *Telephone for directions*

Heralded as a country pub and restaurant with a difference, the Malt Shovel certainly does not disappoint. It has been converted from an early 20th-century mill and stylishly decorated with modern soft furnishings and interesting art and artifacts. There is also a pretty garden for summer use. The bar is cosy and relaxed with log fires in winter, and the restaurant is housed in a converted barn next door. Fresh local produce is cooked to order, with some imaginative dishes making the best of seasonal ingredients. Seafood is a particular strength, and dishes include seared scallops on braised honey and vanilla potato fondant; and roasted fillet of wild marlin with red pepper risotto, rocket and white truffle oil. An alternative might be slow braised Royal Balmoral venison with sweet red cabbage, followed by an intriguing dessert: warm stack of kirsch blinis with plum and apricot chutney and caramelita ice cream.

Open 12–3.30 5.30–11 (Sun & BHs 12–7) **Bar Meals** L served Mon-Sat 12–2.30 D served Mon Sat 6.30–9.45 (Sun 12–3.30) **Restaurant** L served Mon-Sat 12–2.30 D served Mon-Sat 7–9.45 (Sun 12–3.30) ⊕ Free House ◀ Tribute, Brew XI, Timothy Taylor Landlord. ♀ 8 **Facilities** Children's licence Garden Parking

BIRMINGHAM
MAP 10 SP08

The Peacock ♀

Icknield St, Forhill, nr King's Norton B38 0EH
☎ 01564 823232 📠 01564 829593
dir: *Telephone for directions*

Despite its out of the way location, at Forhill just outside Birmingham, the Peacock keeps very busy serving traditional ales and a varied menu, (booking essential). Chalkboards display the daily specials, among which you might find braised partridge on a bed of pheasant sausage and mash, whole sea bass with crab, grilled shark steak with light curry butter, pan-fried sirloin steak with mild mushroom and pepper sauce, or lamb fillet with apricot and walnut

stuffing. Several friendly ghosts are in residence, and one of their tricks is to disconnect the taps from the barrels. Large gardens with two patios.

Open 11–11 (Sun 12–10.30) **Bar Meals** L served all week 11 D served all week 10 Av main course £7.95 **Restaurant** L served all week 12–10 D served all week 6–10 ◀ Hobsons Best Bitter, Theakstons Old Peculier, Enville Ale. ♀ 20 **Facilities** Garden Parking

CHADWICK END
MAP 10 SP27

Pick of the Pubs

The Orange Tree ♀

Warwick Rd B93 0BN
☎ 01564 785364 📠 01564 782988
e-mail: theorangetree@lovelypubs.co.uk
dir: *3m from Knowle towards Warwick*

A pub/restaurant in beautiful and peaceful countryside, yet only minutes from the National Exhibition Centre, Solihull and Warwick. Visitors will find a relaxed Italian influence, reflected in the furnishings and the food, not least the deli counter from which breads, cheeses and olive oils are served. Start with a plate of antipasti, perhaps, or chilli-crusted squid with pineapple and red onion salsa. A small section of the menu is devoted to dishes featuring salad leaves, of which chicory with gorgonzola and pear is an example. There are several pastas, including orechiette with tomatoes, garlic broad beans and gnat's cheese; fired pizzas; and a range of stove-cooked, grilled or spit-roasted meats and fish. Comfortable seating and ambient music in the bar makes it great for just mingling and relaxing, while the sunny lounge area, all sumptuous leather sofas and rustic décor, opens up though oversized French doors to the patio.

Open 11–11 Closed: 25 Dec **Bar Meals** L served Mon-Sat 12–2.30 D served Mon-Sat 6–9.30 (Sun 12–4.30) Av main course £12.95 **Restaurant** L served all week 12–2.30 D served Mon-Sat 6.30–9.30 Av 3 course à la carte £25 Av 2 course fixed price £12.50 ◀ IPA, Tetleys, Old Hooky. ♀ 8 **Facilities** Garden Dogs allowed Parking Play Area

England

HAMPTON IN ARDEN MAP 10 SP28

Pick of the Pubs

The White Lion

10 High St B92 0AA ☎ 01675 442833 🖹 01675 443168
e-mail: info@thewhitelioninn.com
dir: *Opposite church*

A listed 400-year-old timber-framed village pub, originally a farmhouse although licensed since at least 1836. The lounge bar has the more comfortable furniture and open fires, and provides an appealing range of traditional bar food. In the attractively designed and furnished restaurant you'll find modern English cuisine based on local, seasonal produce, including fresh fish on daily specials boards. For dinner, try a starter of spicy lamb koftas with Greek salad, followed by pan-fried duck breast with braised red cabbage, orange and blackberry and port jus; chargilled chicken supreme and confit chicken leg with red wine, bacon and mushroom sauce; or salmon and prawn fishcakes with fine green beans and hollandaise sauce. Plenty of choice for children, and roasts on Sundays.

Open 12–11 **Bar Meals** L served Mon-Sat 12–2.30 D served Mon-Fri 6.30–8.30 (Sun 12–3) Av main course £9 **Restaurant** L served all week 12–2.30 D served all week 6.30–10 ⊕ Punch Taverns ◀ Brew XI, Black Sheep, Adnams, Old Hooky. **Facilities** Garden Parking

OLDBURY MAP 10 SO98

Waggon & Horses

17a Church St B69 3AD ☎ 0121 552 5467
e-mail: andrew.gale@unicombox.co.uk
dir: *Telephone for directions*

A listed back-bar, high copper-panelled ceiling and original tilework are among the character features to be found at this real ale pub in the remnants of the old town centre. Traditional pub food includes faggots and mash, pork and leek sausages, lasagne, chilli, and fish and chips. Beers from Brains of Cardiff and guests.

Open 12–11 (Fri-Sat 12–12, Sun 12–10.30) **Bar Meals** L served Mon-Sat 12–3 D served Mon-Sat 5.30–8 ◀ Enville White, Brains IPA, Oakham JHB, 3 guest ales. **Facilities** Parking

SEDGLEY MAP 10 SO99

Beacon Hotel & Sarah Hughes Brewery ♥

129 Bilston St DY3 1JE
☎ 01902 883380 🖹 01902 884020
dir: *Telephone for directions*

Little has changed in 150 years at this traditional brewery tap, which still retains its Victorian atmosphere. The rare snob-screened island bar serves a taproom, snug, large smoke-room and veranda. Proprietor John Hughes reopened the adjoining Sarah Hughes Brewery in 1987, 66 years after his grandmother became the licensee. Flagship beers are Sarah Hughes Dark Ruby, Surprise and Pale Amber, with guest bitters also available.

Open 12–2.30 5.30–11 (Sat 12–3 6–11, Sun 12–3 7–10.30) ◀ Sarah Hughes Dark Ruby, Surprise & Pale Amber, plus guest & seasonal ales. ♥ 8 **Facilities** Children's licence Garden Dogs allowed Parking Play Area **Notes** ⊛

SOLIHULL MAP 10 SP17

The Boat Inn ♥

222 Hampton Ln, Catherine-de-Barnes B91 2TJ
☎ 0121 705 0474 🖹 0121 704 0600
e-mail: steven-hickson@hotmail.com
dir: *Telephone for directions*

Village pub with a small, enclosed garden located right next to the canal in Solihull. Real ales are taken seriously and there are two frequently changing guest ales in addition to the regulars. There is also a choice of 14 wines available by the glass. Fresh fish is a daily option, and other favourite fare includes chicken cropper, Wexford steak, and beef and ale pie.

Open 11–11 (Sun 12–10.30) **Bar Meals** L served all week 12–10 D served all week 12–10 Av main course £7.95 ◀ Bombardier, Greene King IPA, 2 guest ales. ♥ 14 **Facilities** Children's licence Garden Parking

WEST BROMWICH MAP 10 SP09

The Vine

Roebuck St B70 6RD ☎ 0121 553 2866 🖹 0121 500 0700
e-mail: bharat@thevine.co.uk
dir: *0.5m from junct 1 of M5. 2m from town centre*

Well-known, family-run business renowned for its good curries and cheap drinks. Since 1978 the typically Victorian alehouse has provided the setting for Suresh "Suki" Patel's eclectic menu. Choose from a comprehensive range of Indian dishes (chicken tikka masala, goat curry, lamb saag), a barbecue menu and Thursday spit roast, offered alongside traditional pub meals like sausage and chips, chicken and ham pie, and toasted sandwiches. The Vine boasts the Midlands' only indoor barbeque.

Open 11.30–2.30 5–11 (Fri-Sun all day) **Bar Meals** L served Mon-Sat 12–2 D served Mon-Sat 5–10.30 (Sun 1–10.30) **Restaurant** L served Mon-Fri 12–2 D served Mon-Fri 5–10.30 (Sat-Sun 1–10.30) Av 3 course à la carte £10 ⊕ Free House ◀ Banks, Brew XI, John Smiths. **Facilities** Garden

WIGHT, ISLE OF

ARRETON — MAP 05 SZ58

The White Lion

PO30 3AA ☎ 01983 528479
e-mail: chrisandkatelou@hotmail.co.uk
dir: *B3056 (Newport to Sandown road)*

Sited in an outstandingly beautiful conservation area, this 300–year-old former coaching inn offers a genuinely hospitable welcome. Oak beams, polished brass and open fires set the cosy tone inside, while a safe outside seating area enjoys views of the Arreton scenery. Well-priced pub grub is served all day, ranging from traditional snacks to specials such as nasi goreng – Indonesian spicy rice with chicken and prawns. Favourite puddings of spotted dick and jam roly poly sell out quickly.

Open 11–11 (Sun 12–10.30) **Bar Meals** L served all week 12–9 D served all week 12–9 Av main course £8 ⊕ Enterprise Inns ◼ Badger Best, Fuller's London Pride, Timothy Taylor Landlord, John Smiths Smooth & Flowers Best. **Facilities** Garden Dogs allowed Parking Play Area

BEMBRIDGE — MAP 05 SZ68

The Crab & Lobster Inn ♟

32 Foreland Field Rd PO35 5TR
☎ 01983 872244 ▤ 01983 873495
e-mail: allancrab@aol.com
dir: *Telephone for directions*

Refurbished, award-winning 19th-century pub just yards from the popular 65–mile coastal path, and including a raised deck and patio area offering superb sea views. Originally a fisherman's cottage built of island stone. Locally caught seafood is one of the pub's great attractions, with lemon sole, sea bass and fresh tuna among the dishes.

Open 11–3 6–11 (Summer 11–11) **Bar Meals** L served all week 12–2.30 D served all week 6–9.30 Av main course £8.95 **Restaurant** L served all week 12–2.30 D served all week 7–9.30 Av 3 course à la carte £25 ⊕ Enterprise Inns ◼ Interbrew Flowers Original, Goddards Fuggle-Dee-Dum, Greene King IPA, John Smiths. ♟ 10 **Facilities** Children's licence Garden Dogs allowed Parking

The Pilot Boat Inn

Station Rd PO35 5NN ☎ 01983 872077 & 874101
e-mail: michelle@pilotboatinn.com
dir: *On corner of harbour at bottom of Kings Rd*

Just a stone's throw from Bembridge harbour, this strikingly designed free house enjoys a strong local following, whilst being handy for yachtsmen and holidaymakers. Owners Nick and Michelle Jude offer an attractive menu of traditional favourites, including cod in beer batter with chips and peas; and bangers and mash with red wine and onion gravy. There's also a children's menu, together with specials like vegetable balti with rice; and chunky lamb stew and mash.

Open 11–11 **Bar Meals** L served all week 12–2.30 D served all week 6–9 (Wed 6–8.30) Av main course £7.95 **Restaurant** L served all week 12–2.30 D served all week 6–9 ⊕ Free House ◼ London Pride, Guinness & IPA. **Facilities** Dogs allowed Parking

BONCHURCH — MAP 05 SZ57

The Bonchurch Inn

Bonchurch Shute PO38 1NU
☎ 01983 852611 ▤ 01983 856657
e-mail: gillian@bonchurch-inn.co.uk
dir: *Off A3055 in Bonchurch*

Charles Dickens wrote part of *David Copperfield* while staying in this village. The pub itself is a splendidly preserved former coaching inn and stables, tucked away in a secluded continental-style courtyard. The menu focuses on Italian specialities (pastas include spaghetti, lasagne and tagliatelle); fish dishes such as crevettes, scampi and breaded plaice; and a small range of meats: chicken (Kiev, chilli, or provençale), sausages and steaks. Pizzas with your choice of toppings can also be taken away.

Open 12–3.30 6.30–11 Closed: 25 Dec **Bar Meals** L served all week 11–2.15 D served Mon-Sat 6.30–9 (Sun 6.30–8.30) **Restaurant** D served all week 6.30–8.45 Av 3 course à la carte £17 ⊕ Free House ◼ Courage Directors & Best. **Facilities** Garden Dogs allowed Parking

COWES — MAP 05 SZ49

The Folly ♟

Folly Ln PO32 6NB ☎ 01983 297171
dir: *Telephone for directions*

Reached by land and water, and very popular with the boating fraternity, the Folly is one of the island's more unusual pubs. Timber from an old sea-going French barge was used in the construction, and wood from the hull can be found in the bar. The menus are wide ranging with something for everyone. House specialities include Venison Wellington, prime British beef ribs and slow cooked lamb.

Open 9–11 **Bar Meals** L served all week 12–9.30 D served all week 12–9.30 (Sun 12–9) Av main course £8 ⊕ Greene King ◼ Greene King IPA, Old Speckled Hen & Goddards Best Bitter. ♟ 10 **Facilities** Garden Dogs allowed Parking

FRESHWATER
MAP 05 SZ38

Pick of the Pubs

The Red Lion ♀
Church Place PO40 9BP

☎ 01983 754925 🖹 01983 754483

dir: *In Freshwater follow signs for parish church*

An unashamedly English pub where 'tradition and care' is the motto of owners Michael and Lorna Mence. The origins go back to the 11th century, although today's climber-clad building is clearly more recent. A garden at the rear is well furnished with hardwood chairs and tables, and a canvas dome comes into its own for candle-lit alfresco dinners. The bar is comfortable with settles and chairs around scrubbed pine tables, the log fire burns throughout the winter, and pop music is definitely not played. Lorna is the talented head chef who prepares a mix of favourites for lunch and dinner seven days a week. Apart from their daily-changing blackboard, which includes a lot of English Channel seafood, there are light lunches of tortilla wraps, baguettes, ploughman's, bangers and mash, scampi, or ham, egg and chips. In the evening options range from asparagus in smoked salmon, to tagine of lamb with apricots.

Open 11.30–3 5.30–11 (Sun 12–3, Sun 7–10.30) **Bar Meals** L served all week 12–2 D served Mon-Sat 6.30–9 (Sun 7–9) Av main course £13 ⊞ Enterprise Inns ◀ Interbrew Flowers Original, Spitfire, Goddards, Wadworth 6X. ♀ 16 **Facilities** Garden Dogs allowed Parking

NITON
MAP 05 SZ57

Buddle Inn ♀
St Catherines Rd PO38 2NE ☎ 01983 730243

e-mail: buddleinn@aol.com

dir: *Take A3055 from Ventnor. In Niton take 1st left signed 'to the lighthouse'*

A spit away from the English Channel one way and the Coastal Path the other, this 16th-century, former cliff-top farmhouse can claim to be one of the island's oldest hostelries. Popular with hikers and ramblers (and their muddy boots and dogs), the interior has the full traditional complement – stone flags, oak beams and large open fire. Simple but well prepared food is served, including local crab (summer only), and grilled fresh sardines.

Open 11–12 **Bar Meals** L served all week 12–2.45 D served all week 6–9 ⊞ Enterprise Inns ◀ Wight Spirit, Buddle Best, London Pride, Greene King. ♀ 9 **Facilities** Garden Dogs allowed Parking

NORTHWOOD
MAP 05 SZ49

Travellers Joy
85 Pallance Rd PO31 8LS ☎ 01983 298024

e-mail: tjoy@globalnet.co.uk

Ruth and Derek Smith run this 300–year-old alehouse, just a little way inland from Cowes. Don't expect dishes described on the menu as 'drizzled' or 'pan-roasted' here because the food is, well, uncomplicated – grilled gammon steak, scampi, breaded plaice, double sausage with egg, chips and beans, honey-roast ham, home-made steak and kidney pie, burgers and children's meals. Outside is a pétanque terrain, pets' corner and play area.

Open 11–3 5–12 (Sun 7–12) **Bar Meals** L served all week 12–2 D served Mon-Sat 6–9 (Sun 7–9) ⊞ Free House ◀ Goddards Special Bitter, Courage Directors, Ventnor Golden Bitter, Deuchars IPA. **Facilities** Garden Dogs allowed Parking Play Area

ROOKLEY
MAP 05 SZ58

The Chequers
Niton Rd PO38 3NZ

☎ 01983 840314 🖹 01983 840820

e-mail: richard@chequersinn-iow.co.uk

dir: *Telephone for directions*

Horses in the neighbouring riding school keep a watchful eye on comings and goings at this 250–year-old family-friendly free house. In the centre of the island, surrounded by farms, the pub has a reputation for good food at reasonable prices. Fish, naturally, features well, with sea bass, mussels, plaice, salmon and cod usually available. Other favourites are mixed grill, pork medallions, T-bone steak, and chicken supreme with BBQ sauce and cheese.

Open 11–11 **Bar Meals** L served all week 12–10 D served all week 12–10 (Sun 12–9.30) Av main course £7.95 **Restaurant** L served all week 12–10 D served all week (Sun 12–9.30) ⊞ Free House ◀ John Smiths, Courage Directors, Best, Wadworth 6X. **Facilities** Children's licence Garden Dogs allowed Parking Play Area

SEAVIEW
MAP 05 SZ69

Pick of the Pubs

The Seaview Hotel & Restaurant
★★★ HL ◉◉

See Pick of the Pubs on page 600

The Seaview Hotel & Restaurar

In a sailing-mad village (the derivation of whose name can surely present no challenge) this smart, sea-facing hotel is crammed with nautical associations. There are ships' wheels, oars, model ships, old pictures, and lots of polished wood and brass, particularly in the two bars.

The two areas at the front are ideal in summer when you can look out at the passing holidaymakers and the yachts, while the Pump Bar at the back is more like a traditional English pub. The Modern British menu includes fish straight from the sea; pork and beef from the island's lush grazing land; venison from a farm in nearby Carisbrooke; and tomatoes, garlic and herbs from the hotel's own garden. There's a choice of places to eat including the spacious AA award winning restaurant with its own conservatory, or the smaller, more traditional Victorian dining room. If the menu offers it, weigh up roasted Island lobster, potato and carrot fettuccine with saffron sauce as a starter; Godshill free-range duck, braised red cabbage, creamed potato, golden sultanas and jasmine tea sauce; or lightly salted cod, pumpkin mash, Jerusalem artichoke, buttered spinach and curry oil as a main course; and pineapple parfait, black pepper ice cream, and sweet red pepper and chilli syrup as a dessert. But if that's not what you'd go for, there's still plenty of choice.

★★★ HL ◉◉
MAP 05 SZ69
High St PO34 5EX
☎ 01983 612711
🖷 01983 613729
e-mail:
reception@seaviewhotel.co.uk
dir: *B3330 (Ryde to Seaview road), left via Puckpool along seafront road, hotel on left*

Open 11–2.30 6–11
Bar Meals L served all week
12–2 D served all week 7–9.30
Restaurant L served all week 12–
1.30 D served all week 7.30–9.30
(Fixed menu Sun lunch only) Av
3 course à la carte £28.50 Av 3
course fixed price £28.50
⊕ Free House ◀ Goddards,
Greene King Abbot Ale, Ventnor
Bitter & Adnams Ale.
Rooms 24 & 3 suites

SHALFLEET   MAP 05 SZ48

Pick of the Pubs

The New Inn ☻

Mill Ln PO30 4NS ☎ 01983 531314 ▤ 01983 531314
e-mail: info@thenew-inn.co.uk
dir: 6m from Newport to Yarmouth on A3054

This is one of Wight's best-known dining pubs and, owing to its location on the National Trust-owned Newtown River estuary, an absolute mecca for yachties. Its name reflects how it rose phoenix-like from the charred remains of an older inn, which burnt down in 1743, and its original inglenook fireplaces, flagstone floors and low-beamed ceilings give it bags of character. The waterside location helps to explain its reputation for excellent fish and seafood dishes, such as grilled fillets of sole with lime, ginger and rocket; whole cracked-crab salad; prawn platter with garlic mayo; and seafood royale, a mammoth plate of fresh fish and crustaceans for two people. Other favourites include hot cooked baguettes; prime steaks with chips, onion rings and mushrooms; gammon, egg and chips; lamb steak with Moroccan-style bean salad; and home-made lasagne. With over 60 worldwide wines, the New Inn offers one of the island's most extensive selections.

Open 12–11 (Sun 12–10.30) **Bar Meals** L served all week 12–2.30 D served all week 6–9.30 **Restaurant** L served all week 12–2.30 D served all week 6–9.30 ⊕ Enterprise Inns ◀ Interbrew Bass, Goddards Special Bitter, Greene King IPA, Marston's Pedigree. ☻ 6 **Facilities** Garden Dogs allowed Parking

---

SHANKLIN   MAP 05 SZ58

Fisherman's Cottage

Shanklin Chine PO37 6BN
☎ 01983 863882 ▤ 01983 866145
e-mail: jill@shanklinchine.co.uk
dir: Telephone for details

At the foot of a deep ravine known as Shanklin Chine, the cottage was built about 1817 by William Colenutt, who also excavated the path through the Chine. Always on offer are stilton and vegetable crumble, lasagne, gammon and egg, salads, jacket potatoes, ploughman's and sandwiches, as well as a children's selection. Wider choice at dinner includes fisherman's pie, salmon mornay, Thai green curried chicken, and various specials. Sit outside and you're virtually on the beach.

Open 11–3 7–11 (Mar-Oct all wk) Closed: Nov-Feb **Bar Meals** L served all week 11–2 D served all week 7–9 ⊕ Free House ◀ Courage Directors & John Smiths Smooth. **Facilities** Garden Dogs allowed **Notes** ⊛

SHORWELL   MAP 05 SZ48

Pick of the Pubs

The Crown Inn

Walkers Ln PO30 3JZ
☎ 01983 740293 ▤ 01983 740293
e-mail: info@crownshorwell.com
web: www.crownshorwell.com
dir: Turn left at top of Carrisbrooke High Street, Shorwell approx 6m

Set in a pretty village in picturesque West Wight, with thatched cottages, a small shop, three manor houses, and the church opposite. In summer arum lilies decorate the garden stream, and a Wendy house, slide and swings keep youngsters amused. The building dates in parts from the 17th century, and different floor levels attest to many alterations. Log fires, antique furniture, and a friendly female ghost who disapproves of card playing complete the picture of this traditional family-run pub. Beers on tap include an island brew, and food consists of home-made favourites based on locally sourced lamb and beef, game in winter and fish in summer. The award-winning specials board usually features ten dishes, which may include steak and kidney pie, cottage pie, crown of pheasant, or lamb tagine. If fish is favoured, you may find a seafood platter, fish pie, crab and prawn gratin, or sea bass with red onion and sweet pepper salsa.

Open 10.30–3 6–11 (Sun 6–10:30 summer holidays all day) **Bar Meals** L served all week 12–2.30 D served all week 6–9 (Sat-Sun & summer 6–9.30) **Restaurant** L served all week 12–2.30 D served all week 6–9 ⊕ Enterprise Inns ◀ Interbrew, Flowers Original, Badger Tanglefoot, Wadworth 6X. **Facilities** Garden Dogs allowed Parking Play Area

England

VENTNOR

MAP 05 SZ57

The Spyglass Inn 🍷

The Esplanade PO38 1JX
☎ 01983 855338 🖹 01983 855220
e-mail: info@thespyglass.com
dir: *Telephone for directions*

For centuries this area was a haunt of smugglers, and echoes of these activities can be seen in the huge collection of nautical memorabilia on the walls of this famous 19th-century inn. It has a superb position, right at the end of Ventnor Esplanade. Much of the food here is, naturally, fishy, with home-made fish chowder, Ventnor crab and lobster, but other dishes might include several varieties of pie; local sausages; or ham and leek bake.

Open 10.30–11 **Bar Meals** L served all week 12–9.30 D served all week 12–9.30 Av main course £7.50 ⊕ Free House ◖ Badger Best & Tanglefoot, Ventnor Golden, Goddards Fuggle-Dee-Dom, Yates Undercliff Experience. 🍷 8 **Facilities** Garden Dogs allowed Parking

YARMOUTH

MAP 05 SZ38

Bugle Coaching Inn ★★★ INN 🍷

The Square PO41 0NS ☎ 01983 760272 🖹 01983 760883
e-mail: buglecoachinginn@btconnect.com

The 17th-century inn stands in Yarmouth's market square, close to the sea and the yachting harbour. Food is served in the bar, the heated and stone-flagged courtyard garden, and the more recently added Brasserie at the Inn. The oak-panelled bar, with its beams and log fires, opens into an attractive conservatory area. Sandwiches, ploughman's, hot and cold dishes are served in the bar, while the brasserie specialises in locally landed fish and island produce.

Open 11–11 (Sun 12–10.30) **Bar Meals** L served all week 12–3 D served Mon-Sat 6–9.30 (Sun 6–9) Av main course £8.95 ◖ Greene King IPA, London Pride, 6X, Ringwood 49. 🍷 6 **Facilities** Garden Dogs allowed Parking **Rooms** 7

WILTSHIRE

ALDERBURY

MAP 05 SU12

The Green Dragon 🍷

Old Rd SP5 3AR ☎ 01722 710263
dir: *1m off A36 (Southampton/Salisbury rd)*

There are fine views of Salisbury Cathedral from this 15th-century pub, which is probably named after the heroic deeds of Sir Maurice Berkeley, the Mayor of Alderbury, who slew a green dragon in the 15th century. Dickens wrote *Martin Chuzzlewit* here, and called the pub the Blue Dragon. An interesting and daily changing menu features home-made meat and vegetarian dishes using locally sourced produce.

Open 11.30–3 6–11 (Sun 12–3, 7–11) **Bar Meals** L served all week 12–2.30 D served Mon-Sat 6.30–9.30 Av main course £6.50
Restaurant L served 12–2.30 D served all week 7–9 Av 3 course à la carte £16 ⊕ Hall & Woodhouse ◖ Badger First Gold & Tanglefoot, Ferret. 🍷 14 **Facilities** Garden Dogs allowed Parking

ALVEDISTON

MAP 04 ST92

Pick of the Pubs

The Crown

See Pick of the Pubs on opposite page

AXFORD

MAP 05 SU27

Red Lion Inn 🍷

SN8 2HA ☎ 01672 520271
e-mail: info@redlionaxford.com
dir: *M4 junct 15, A246 Marlborough centre. Follow Ramsbury signs. Inn 3m*

A pretty, 17th-century brick and flint pub with fine views over the Kennet Valley. In the bar there's a large inglenook, and a pleasing mix of sofas and more solid seating, while the restaurant is attractively laid out with white linen-covered tables and upholstered ladderback chairs. In addition to bar snacks, the menus offer plenty of choice, including chargrilled prime Aberdeen Angus steak; baked Barbary duck breast; grilled Brixham brill; and bean and mixed pulse casserole.

Open 12–2.30 6.30–11 Closed: Sun eve **Bar Meals** L served all week 12–2 D served all week 7–9 (Sat 7–9.30) Av main course £10
Restaurant L served all week 12–2 D served Mon-Fri 7–9 (Sat 7–9.30) Av 3 course à la carte £25 ⊕ Free House ◖ Ashford Ale, Ramsbury Gold & guest ales. 🍷 16 **Facilities** Garden Parking

PICK OF THE PUBS

ALVEDISTON-WILTSHIRE

The Crown

Tucked away in the Ebble Valley between Salisbury and Shaftesbury, the Crown is a well-known landmark with its pink-washed walls, thatched roof, clinging creepers and colourful window boxes.

Its old world setting is characterised by head-cracking low beams, two inglenook fireplaces that burn invitingly on cooler days, and comfortable furnishings. The inn serves entirely home-made food, with particular emphasis on fresh local produce whenever possible. The cosy bar sets the scene for anything from a simple sandwich to fresh fish and rib-eye steaks. Listed weekly on the specials board, expect to find a wide range of starters from a hearty leek and potato soup, through deep-fried camembert with redcurrant jelly; field mushrooms stuffed with garlic, parsley, bacon, breadcrumbs and cashew nuts; and filo-wrapped king prawns with a sweet chilli dip; to Chinese spring rolls with a hoisin dip. Main choices are just

as appetizing, with pub favourites like chilli con carne with garlic bread; scampi, chips and salad; beef lasagna; and steak and kidney pie with a rich shortcrust pastry; and imaginative dishes like roast rump of lamb with a minted pea veloute; smoked haddock and spinach gratin topped with breadcrumbs and cheese; pan-fried duck breast with a plum sauce; and fresh whole lemon sole with herb butter. The pub makes a handy stopover for splendid local walks and visits to Salisbury Cathedral and Stonehenge. Outside there's a beer garden where food is also served.

MAP 04 ST92
SP5 5JY
☎ 01722 780335
📠 01722 780836
dir: *2.5m off A30 approx halfway between Salisbury & Shaftesbury*

Open 12–3 6.30–11 (Sun 7–10.30)
Bar Meals L served all week 12–2.30 D served all week 6.30–9 Av main course £9.75
Restaurant L served all week 12–2 D served all week 6.30–9.30 Av 3 course à la carte £18
⊕ Free House ◀ Ringwood Best, Timothy Taylor Landlord, Youngs Special Bitter.
Facilities Garden Dogs allowed Parking Play Area

BARFORD ST MARTIN   MAP 05 SU03

Barford Inn ♟

SP3 4AB ☎ 01722 742242 📄 01722 743606
e-mail: thebarfordinn@btconnect.com
dir: *On A30 5m W of Salisbury*

Customer satisfaction and service are the keynotes in this 16th-century former coaching inn five miles outside Salisbury. A welcoming lounge, lower bar area and intimate snug have greeted visitors for generations – during World War II the Wiltshire Yeomanry dedicated a tank to the pub, known then as The Green Dragon. The varied menu includes freshly cut ciabattas, chargrilled medallions of beef, seafood linguini, or vegetarian stuffed Creole-style aubergine, and there's a range of exotic coffees to finish.

Open 11–3 6–11 Closed: 25 Dec **Bar Meals** L served Mon, Wed-Thu 12–2.30 D served Mon-Sat 7–9.30 **Restaurant** L served all week 12–2.30 D served Mon-Sat 7–9.30 ⊞ Hall & Woodhouse ◀ Badger Dorset Best & Fursty Ferret, Festive. ♟ 6 **Facilities** Garden Parking **Rooms** available

BOX   MAP 04 ST86

The Northey ♟

Bath Rd SN13 8AE ☎ 01225 742333
e-mail: office@ohhcompany.co.uk
dir: *4m from Bath on A4 towards Chippenham. Between M4 juncts 17 & 18*

Following a magnificent transformation, this former station hotel is now a favourite in the area for eating, drinking and listening to the soothing tones of Sinatra and Fitzgerald. Designed throughout by owner Sally Warburton, the interior makes good use of wood and flagstone flooring, high-back oak chairs, leather loungers and handcrafted tables around the bar, where sandwiches, ciabattas and Italian platters hold sway. The main menu ranges from home-made shepherd's pie to roast Orkney salmon.

Open 10.30–3 6.30–12 **Bar Meals** L served all week 11–2 D served all week 6.30–9.30 **Restaurant** L served all week 11–2 D served all week 6.30–9.30 ⊞ Wadworth ◀ Wadworth 6X, IPA, Malt 'n' Hops & Old Father Timer. ♟ 10 **Facilities** Garden Dogs allowed Parking

The Quarrymans Arms ♟

Box Hill SN13 8HN ☎ 01225 743569 📄 01225 742610
e-mail: john@quarrymans-arms.co.uk
dir: *Telephone for accurate directions*

Built above Brunel's famous Box railway tunnel, this 300-year-old pub is packed with stone-mining memorabilia (take a tour of the old mine workings). Great views through the restaurant window of the valley, abundantly laced with marked paths and trails. In addition to the regular menu – fillet of pecials board. Some good hand-pumped West Country beers, good wines and over sixty malt whiskies.

Open 11–3.30 6–11 (Fri-Sun all day) **Bar Meals** L served all week 11–3 D served all week 6.30–10.30 **Restaurant** L served all week 11–3 D served all week 6.30–10.30 ⊞ Free House ◀ Butcombe Bitter, Wadworth 6X, Moles Best & local guest ales. ♟ 10 **Facilities** Garden Dogs allowed Parking

BRADFORD-ON-AVON   MAP 04 ST86

The Dandy Lion ♟

35 Market St BA15 1LL
☎ 01225 863433 📄 01225 869169
e-mail: dandylion35@aol.com
dir: *Telephone for directions*

The owners have refurbished this 17th-century town centre pub. But the spirit of the original Dandy Lion lives on through its well-kept ales and continental lagers, together with a mix of traditional English and rustic European food. The café-bar menu offers tasty grazing boards, hot-filled flatbreads, and thick-cut sandwiches alongside old comforts. Dinner in the air-conditioned restaurant could start with rich Tuscan paté, and continue with poached chicken supreme. Home-made desserts include New York baked cheesecake.

Open 10.30–11 **Bar Meals** L served all week 12–8.30 D served all week 12–8.30 (Sun 12–3) Av main course £8.95 **Restaurant** L served Sun 12–2.30 D served all week 6–9.30 (Sun 12–8.30) Av 3 course à la carte £23 ⊞ Wadworth ◀ Butcombe, Wadworth 6X, Henrys IPA, Wadworth Seasonal. ♟ 11

Pick of the Pubs

The Kings Arms ♟

Monkton Farleigh BA15 2QH
☎ 01225 858705 📄 01225 858999
e-mail: enquiries@kingsarms-bath.co.uk
dir: *Off A363 (Bath to Bradford-on-Avon road), follow brown tourist signs to pub*

Dating back to the 11th century, this historic Bath stone building is situated in an attractive village just outside Bradford-on-Avon. Conversion into an alehouse took place in the 17th century, but original features remain, including the mullioned windows, flagged floors and a vast inglenook – said to be the largest in Wiltshire – in the medieval-style Chancel restaurant, which is hung with tapestries and pewter plates. The Bar and Garden menu offers light lunches such as Bath sausages, spring onion and smoked bacon mash; steak frites; three-egg omelette (with various fillings) and chips; and wild mushroom, spinach and asparagus lasagne. From the à la carte menu come main dishes such as duck breast with balsamic glaze, mascarpone and almond dauphinoise; game casserole with herb dumplings; brochette of sirloin steak and tiger prawns (known as the 'Trawler and Tractor'), while specials may include roast poussin with smoked bacon, parsley mash and cheddar cheese sauce; pork schnitzel with sesame-fried potatoes and dolcelatte cheese sauce; and chicken piri piri sizzle with white and wild rice.

Open 12 -11 (Sun 12–10.30) **Bar Meals** L served all week fr 12 D served all week 12–10.30 Av main course £10 🍺 Wadworth 6X, Butcombe Bitter, Wychwood Hobgoblin, Shepherd Neame Spitfire. ♀8 **Facilities** Garden Dogs allowed Parking

Pick of the Pubs

The Tollgate Inn ★★★★ INN ◉◉ ♀

See Pick of the Pubs on page 606

BRINKWORTH   MAP 04 SU08

Pick of the Pubs

The Three Crowns ♀

SN15 5AF ☎ 01666 510366

dir: *From Swindon take A3102 to Wootton Bassett, then B4042, 5m to Brinkworth*

The Three Crowns stands on the village green facing the church in the longest village in England. Run by the same licensees for over 20 years, it is one of the area's most popular eating venues. The building extends into a large, bright conservatory and garden room, then out onto a heated patio and garden with extensive views of the Dauntsey Vale. In winter an open log fire warms the bars, which are decorated with farming memorabilia donated by customers. Settle there for a pint of Archers Best or Bath Gem, and perhaps a game of draughts, cribbage or chess. When it's time to eat, the imaginative menu will offer traditionally-inspired steaks alongside more adventurous options: crocodile or wild boar, for example, or kangaroo, venison and ostrich meat in a dish called 'A Taste of the Wild'. There are plenty of fish options too, and classic sweets like raspberry meringue.

Open 11–3 6–11 Closed: 25–26 Dec **Bar Meals** L served Mon-Sat 12–2 D served all week 6–9.30 (Sun 12–3, 6–9) **Restaurant** L served all week 12–2 D served all week 6–9.30 ⊕ Enterprise Inns 🍺 Wadworth 6X, Archers Best, Castle Eden, Bath Gem. ♀20 **Facilities** Garden Dogs allowed Parking Play Area

---

BROAD CHALKE   MAP 05 SU02

The Queens Head Inn ♀

1 North St SP5 5EN

☎ 01722 780344 & 0870 7706634

📠 0870 7706635 & 01722 781322

dir: *Take A354 from Salisbury towards Blandford Forum, at Coombe Bissett turn right towards Bishopstone, pub in 4m*

Attractive 15th-century-inn with friendly atmosphere and low-beamed bars, once the village bakehouse. On sunny days, enjoy the flower-bordered courtyard, whilst in colder weather the low beams and wood burner in the bar provide a cosy refuge. Menus include light snacks such as sandwiches, ploughman's lunches and home-made soups, as well as more substantial main courses: perhaps grilled trout with almonds, sirloin steak with a choice of vegetables, or wild game casserole.

Open 11–3 6–11 (Sun 12–3, 7–11) **Bar Meals** L served all week 12–2 D served all week 7–9 **Restaurant** L served all week 12–2 D served all week 7–9 ⊕ Free House 🍺 Greene King IPA & Old Speckled Hen, Wadworth 6X, Ruddles County & Morlands Best. ♀7 **Facilities** Garden Parking

---

BURCOMBE   MAP 05 SU03

The Ship Inn ♀

Burcombe Ln SP2 0EJ

☎ 01722 743182 📠 01722 743182

e-mail: theshipburcombe@mail.com

dir: *In Burcombe, off A30, 1m from Wilton & 5m W of Salisbury*

A 17th-century village pub with low ceilings, oak beams and a large open fire. In summer the riverside garden is a great place to enjoy a leisurely meal in the company of the resident ducks. Seasonal menu examples include home-made fishcakes; braised lamb shank with pumpkin and gruyere mash; grilled lemon sole; braised beef, carrot and mushroom pie; and butternut squash, chickpea, spinach and mushroom casserole. Daily changing specials, sandwiches and light bites are also available.

Open 11–3 6–11 (Sun 6.30–10.30) **Bar Meals** L served all week 12–2.30 D served Mon-Sat 6.30–9 (Sun 7–9) Av main course £12 **Restaurant** L served all week 12–2.30 D served Mon-Sat 6.30–9 (Sun 7–9) Av 3 course à la carte £23 🍺 Flowers IPA, Wadworth 6X, Courage Best, Guinness. ♀10 **Facilities** Children's licence Garden Dogs allowed Parking

---

BURTON   MAP 04 ST87

The Old House at Home ♀

SN14 7LT ☎ 01454 218227

e-mail: office@ohhcompany.co.uk

dir: *On B4039 NW of Chippenham*

A stone, ivy-clad pub with beautiful landscaped gardens and a waterfall, and inside, low beams and an open fire. Overseen by the same landlord for some twenty years, the crew here are serious about food. The kitchen offers a good fish choice, vegetarian and pasta dishes, and traditional pub meals. Favourites include lamb cutlets with champ; salmon and crab cakes; Woodland duck breast with stuffing; butterfly red mullet; and king scallops in Cointreau.

Open 11.30–2.30 7–12 (Fri-Sat 11.30–3, Sun 7.30–10) Closed: 25 & 26 Dec **Bar Meals** L served all week 12–2 D served Mon-Sat 7–10 (Sun 7–9.30) ⊕ Free House 🍺 Wadworth 6X, Butcombe Gold. ♀40 **Facilities** Garden Dogs allowed Parking

PICK OF THE PUBS

BRADFORD-ON-AVON-WILTSHIRE

The Tollgate Inn

Built in the 16th century, the Tollgate used to be a cider house known as the White Hart – and a den of iniquity it was, by all accounts. As with many old buildings, it has a chequered history, having been part weaving mill, part Baptist chapel, and even the village school.

When the nearby Kennet and Avon Canal was cut, some of the building was knocked down to make way for an approach road. The bar serves a rotating selection of guest ales, mostly from small West Country micro-breweries. You can eat in a small adjoining room with wood-burning stove and country-style decoration. The restaurant proper is up wooden stairs in what was originally the chapel for the weavers working below. Regular customers are attracted by modern British cooking with Mediterranean influences, locally sourced and supplied whenever possible. For example, hand-reared beef comes from the lush pastures of nearby Broughton Gifford and Corsham; the pub produces its own lamb; village shoots provide game; vegetables are grown in the surrounding fertile soils; and a specialist in town supplies cheeses. Lunchtime light bites (Tuesday to Saturday only) include omelette Arnold Bennett; Valley Smokehouse kipper topped with free-range poached egg; and traditional fish pie. Fresh seafood from Brixham market appears in a panaché of Cornish fish in a white wine and tarragon cream sauce; and pan-fried skate wing with a brown butter sauce. Other possibilities could be roasted breast of mallard on Savoy cabbage and Wiltshire bacon; and pan-fried pork tenderloin with apple purée and glazed Somerset brie. The well-established garden and terrace (out of bounds to children under 12) is a tranquil and delightful place to eat when the weather permits.

★★★★ INN ◉◉ ♥
MAP 04 ST86
Holt BA14 6PX
☎ 01225 782326
🖷 01225 782805
e-mail: alison@tollgateholt.co.uk
dir: M4 junct 18, A46 towards Bath, then A363 to Bradford-on-Avon, then B3107 towards Melksham, pub on right

Open 11–2.30 5.30–11
Bar Meals L served Tue-Sun 12–2 D served Tue-Sat 7–9.30
Restaurant L served Tue-Sun 12–2 D served Tue-Sat 7–9.30
⊕ Free House ◀ Exmoor Gold, Glastonbury Ales Mystery Tor, York Ales, Sharp's Doom Bar. ♥ 9
Facilities Garden Dogs allowed Parking
Rooms 4

CASTLE COMBE   MAP 04 ST87

Pick of the Pubs

Castle Inn ♀

SN14 7HN ☎ 01249 783030 🖹 01249 782315
e-mail: enquiries@castle-inn.info
dir: From M4 junct 17 straight over rdbt towards Cirencester/
Chippenham. At next rdbt take 2nd exit onto A350, 2.5m. 2nd
exit onto A350, 1m. 4th exit off rdbt onto A420. Right into
Castle Combe

All the properties in drop-dead gorgeous Castle Combe are
listed. The inn takes its name from a Norman castle, now almost
vanished thanks to stone-filching villagers. The inn has faced
the market place since the 13th century, but recent careful and
considerate restoration has conserved its ancient charm, not least
in the beamed bar with its large stone fireplaces. The bar menu
follows the well-trodden path of baguettes and ploughman's;
sausage, mash and onion gravy; fresh cod in beer batter; and
chicken, bacon and avocado salad. In Oliver's Restaurant main
courses include chargrilled rib-eye steak with pepper and shallot
sauce; roast breast of duck with rösti potato and plum sauce;
Cajun salmon with mash and roasted cherry tomatoes; and
pavé of tomato and mozzarella risotto on buttered spinach. A
conservatory leads out to a pleasant courtyard.

Open 9.30–11 Closed: 25 Dec **Bar Meals** L served all week
11.30–3 D served Mon-Sat 6–9.30 (Sun 6–9) Av main course £8.10
Restaurant D served Mon-Sat 6–9.30 (Sun 6–9) Av 3 course à la carte
£27.55 ⊕ Free House ◀ Guinness, Tunnel Vision, Figgy Pudding,
Spitfire & Butcombe. ♀7 **Facilities** Garden

CHRISTIAN MALFORD   MAP 04 ST97

The Rising Sun

Station Rd SN15 4BL ☎ 01249 721571
dir: M4 junct 17, B4122 towards Sutton Benger, left onto B4069,
1m to Christian Malford. Pub last building on left

Built in 1832, the pub is set in the picturesque village of Christian
Malford, and used to have a blacksmith's attached to it. Bi-monthly
themed evenings, quiz nights and sports' club events are regular
features, and the pub is one of the hosts of the Malford Challenge,
every May, when the men of the village compete with their
counterparts in Foxham in 10 events over a day. Seafood figures
strongly on the menu.

Open 12–2.30 6.30–11 **Bar Meals** L served Thu-Sun 12–2 D served
Mon-Sun 6.30–9.30 Av main course £6 **Restaurant** L served Thu-Sun
12–2 D served Mon-Sun 6.30–9.30 Av 3 course à la carte £22 ⊕ Free House
◀ Sussex, Rucking Mole. **Facilities** Garden Dogs allowed Parking

COLLINGBOURNE DUCIS   MAP 05 SU25

The Shears Inn & Country Hotel ♀

The Cadley Rd SN8 3ED
☎ 01264 850304 🖹 01264 850301
e-mail: info@the-shears-inn.co.uk
dir: On A338 NW of Andover & Ludgershall

As the name attests, this thatched 16th-century building was formerly
a shearing shed for market-bound sheep. Now a thriving country inn,
the daily chalkboard menus round up all the usual suspects as well
as more unusual dishes such as poached chicken, spinach and Parma
ham roulade; roasted goose breast and sweet cherry gravy; or oxtail
in red wine.

Open 11–11 **Bar Meals** L served all week 12–2.30 D served all week
6.30–10 Av main course £14 **Restaurant** L served Mon-Sat 12–3 D served
Mon-Sat 6–9.30 (Sun 12–9.30) ⊕ Brakspear ◀ Brakspear Bitter, Hobgoblin
& guest ales. ♀12 **Facilities** Children's licence Garden Dogs allowed
Parking

CORSHAM   MAP 04 ST87

Pick of the Pubs

The Flemish Weaver ♀

63 High St SN13 0EZ ☎ 01249 701929
e-mail: nibags@blueyonder.co.uk
dir: Next to town hall on Corsham High St

Historic Corsham Court is just a stone's throw away, as is a row
of Flemish weavers' cottages in original condition. Previously
called the Packhorse, the pub was closed for several months
before being taken over by the current team. Work to restore the
interiors followed, when original beams and fittings were carefully
preserved. 'A breath of fresh air' is the ethos of the place, reflected
in its well-kept real ales and the traceability of its food – a full list
of suppliers is displayed in the bar, together with dates of local
farmers' markets. Menus change daily, so specials are eschewed.
At lunchtime choose from baguettes, salads, or larger plates such
as diced venison in red wine, or free-range gammon steak and
pineapple. For dinner choose from the likes of organic rump steak
with stilton sauce, or five fish crumble with leeks; leave space for
puddings which are all home made.

Open 10.30–3 5.30–11 (Sun 12–3 only) **Bar Meals** L served all
week 12–2.30 D served Mon-Sat 7–9.30 Av main course £10.50
Restaurant L served all week 12–2.30 D served Mon-Sat 7–9.30 Av 3
course à la carte £17.50 ⊕ Unique Pub Co ◀ Bath Spa, Doom Bar,
Speckled Hen, Bath Gem. ♀10 **Facilities** Garden Dogs allowed
Parking

CORTON   MAP 04 ST94

Pick of the Pubs

The Dove Inn ★★★ INN ☼

BA12 0SZ ☎ 01985 850109 📄 01985 851041

e-mail: info@thedove.co.uk

dir: *A36 (Salisbury towards Warminster), in 14m turn left signed Corton & Boyton. Cross rail line, right at T-junct. Corton approx 1.5m, turn right into village.*

A thriving traditional pub tucked away in a lovely Wiltshire village near the River Wylye. A striking central fireplace is a feature of the refurbished bar, and the spacious garden is the venue for barbecues, and the perfect spot for a drink on long summer days. Award-winning menu is based firmly on West Country produce, with many ingredients coming from within just a few miles. Popular lunchtime bar snacks give way to a full evening carte, featuring starters like pan-fried pigeon breast with a redcurrant jus, or garlic king prawns with a sweet chilli dip, followed by oven-baked sea bass stuffed with fresh herbs; beef and ale pie served with mashed potato or fries; spicy chicken curry with basmatic rice; and pan-fried venison steak with a juniper berry and red wine sauce. Five en suite bedrooms arranged around a courtyard make The Dove an ideal touring base. Bath, Salisbury and Stonehenge are all close by.

Open 12–2.30 6–11 (Sun 7–10.30) **Bar Meals** L served all week 12–2 D served all week 7–9 (Sat 12–3, 7–9.30 Sun 12–3, 7–9) Av main course £9 **Restaurant** L served all week 12–2 D served all week 7–9 (Sun 12–3, 7–10.30) Av 3 course à la carte £18 ⊕ Free House ◀ Spitfire, Youngs, Butcombe & Hop Back GFB. ☼ 10 **Facilities** Children's licence Garden Dogs allowed Parking **Rooms** 5

DEVIZES   MAP 04 SU06

The Bear Hotel ★★★ HL ☼

The Market Place SN10 1HS

☎ 0845 456 5334 📄 01380 722450

e-mail: info@thebearhotel.net

dir: *In town centre, follow Market Place signs*

Right in the centre of Devizes, home of Wadworth's Brewery, this old coaching inn dates from at least 1559 and lists Judge Jeffreys, George III, and Harold Macmillan amongst its notable former guests. You'll find old beams, log fires, fresh flowers, three bars and two restaurants. The menu offers pot-roasted partridge perhaps, and broccoli and mushroom strudel. Music fans, check out the weekly jazz sessions in the cellar.

Open 9.30–11 Closed: 25–26 Dec **Bar Meals** L served all week 11.30–2.30 D served Mon-Sat 7–9.30 (Sun 7–9) **Restaurant** L served Sun 12.15–1.45 D served Mon-Sat 7–9.30 ⊕ Wadworth ◀ Wadworth 6X, Wadworth IPA, Wadworth JCB, Old Timer. ☼ 18 **Facilities** Garden Dogs allowed Parking **Rooms** 25

The Raven Inn ☼

Poulshot Rd SN10 1RW

☎ 01380 828271 📄 01380 828271

dir: *A361 from Devizes towards Trowbridge, left at Poulshot sign*

A characterful half-timbered 18th-century pub in an attractive village – an easy walk to the Kennet and Avon Canal and the towpath by the famous Caen Hill flight of locks. The extensive menu of home-cooked food includes light bites such as avocado, prawn and apple salad; and deep-fried tiger prawns in filo pastry. There are usually a trio of vegetarian options, perhaps four fish dishes, main courses of steak and kidney pie or pork stroganoff, and traditional desserts like banana split.

Open 11–2.30 6.30–11 (Sun 12–3, 7–10.30) Closed: Mon **Bar Meals** L served Tue-Sun 12–2 D served Tue-Sat 7–9.30 (Sun 7–9) **Restaurant** L served Tue-Sun 12–2 D served Tue-Sun 7–9.30 ⊕ Wadworth ◀ Wadworth 6X, Wadworth IPA, Summersault, Wadworth Old Timer. ☼ 8 **Facilities** Garden Parking

---

DONHEAD ST ANDREW   MAP 04 ST92

Pick of the Pubs

The Forester Inn ☼

Lower St SP7 9EE ☎ 01747 828038

e-mail: possums1@btinternet.com

dir: *4.5m from Shaftesbury off A30 towards Salisbury.*

A traditional 16th-century inn close to the Dorset and Wiltshire border, the Forester has warm stone walls, a thatched roof, original beams and an inglenook fireplace. In recent years the inn has been extended to include a restaurant and a restaurant/meeting room, which has double doors opening on to the lower patio area. The garden and large patio area are pleasant for eating and drinking outside, where there is hardwood garden furniture as well as traditional pub-style bench seating. The restaurant has a reputation for its freshly cooked food and interesting choice of dishes including many seafood dishes as there are deliveries from Cornwall five times a week. Starters such as Gran Reserva Parma ham with fresh figs, gorgonzola and honey dressing, or crab tian with lamb's lettuce, tarragon and ginger dressing; mains take in poussin, poached and chargrilled with black-eye bean cassoulet, and broucette of lambs' kidney with black pudding, mashed swede and a sherry and shallot vinegar. The wine list has been painstakingly compiled by the landlord and reflects his passion for the subject.

Open 12–3 6.30–11 Closed: Sun eve **Bar Meals** L served all week 12–2 D served all week 6.30–9 Av main course £11.50 **Restaurant** L served all week 12–2 D served all week 7–9 Av 3 course à la carte £22.50 ⊕ Free House ◀ 6X, Ringwood, Butcombe. ☼ 17 **Facilities** Garden Dogs allowed Parking

PICK OF THE PUBS

EAST KNOYLE-WILTSHIRE

The Fox and Hounds

A traditional, late 15th-century thatched and beamed free house, built originally as three cottages. East Knoyle itself is situated on a greensand ridge and is surrounded by excellent walking country with views to the west of the delightful Blackmore Vale.

As well as once being home to the family of Jane Seymour, Henry VIII's second wife, it was the village where Sir Christopher Wren grew up, his father being the local vicar. A stone alongside the main road records that Wren was an 'Architect, Mathematician, Patriot'. The pub's interior is quaint and cosy, with wooden flooring, natural stone walls, flagstones and sofas within toasting distance of a winter fire. The conservatory has a New England feel – calm, light and comfortable. Snacks and main meals include ploughman's, ciabatta melts and pizzas (from the clay oven) and good old favourites like steamed steak and kidney pudding, bangers and mash, lasagne and smoked haddock, cod and salmon fishcakes. The specials menu, which points out that all meat, chicken and game is sourced from local farms and suppliers, is extensive. Starters include mussels in red Thai curry sauce; braised capsicums, chorizo and smoked paprika on garlic toast; and pork rillette, onion marmalade and pickles on toasted brioche. For a main dish there may be a 21–day old fillet or sirloin steak with a choice of sauces; venison medallions with port and cranberry sauce; beer-battered catch of the day with tartare sauce and chunky chips; Asian-style duck on noodles with hoi sin; or caramelised onion and leek tart with watercress and walnut salad. Pavlova with passion fruit coulis and cream, or warm chocolate fudge cake number among the desserts.

MAP 04 ST83
The Green SP3 6BN
☎ 01747 830573
🖷 01747 830865
e-mail: pub@foxandhounds-eastknoyle.co.uk
web: www.foxandhounds-eastknoyle.co.uk
dir: *1.5m off A303 at the A350 turn off, follow brown signs*

Open 12–2.30 6–11
Bar Meals L served all week 12–2.30 D served all week 6.30–9.30
Restaurant L served all week 12–2.30 D served all week 6.30–9.30 Av 3 course à la carte £20
⊕ Free House ◁ Hidden, Wessex, Dorset Brewing Co, Youngs Bitter. 🍷 10
Facilities Garden Dogs allowed Parking

England

EAST KNOYLE — MAP 04 ST83

Pick of the Pubs

The Fox and Hounds ♟

See Pick of the Pubs on page 609

EBBESBOURNE WAKE — MAP 04 ST92

Pick of the Pubs

The Horseshoe

Handley St SP5 5JF ☎ 01722 780474

dir: *Telephone for directions*

A gem of a 17th-century village inn that was possibly – and nobody's sure about this – a former farm building. Nothing very much has changed for at least 50 years, not counting the very necessary grafting on of a conservatory to accommodate more diners. The village is not that easy to find, but a good navigator and perseverance pay dividends. Beyond the climbing roses are two rooms filled with simple furniture, old farming implements and country bygones, linked to a central servery dispensing cask-conditioned ales straight from their barrels. Good value bar food is freshly prepared from local produce, with steak and kidney and pheasant and cranberry pies; fresh fish bake; lamb shank with rosemary and redcurrant sauce; honey roasted duckling; lambs' liver and bacon casserole; and pork and leek sausages in leek and onion gravy. All meals are accompanied by plenty of vegetables. Children are welcome, dogs are allowed, and there's a pretty, flower-filled garden.

Open 12–3 6.30–11 Closed: 26 Dec Sun eve & Mon lunch **Bar Meals** L served Tue-Sun 12–2 D served Tue-Sat 7–9.30 **Restaurant** D served Tue-Sat 7–9.30 ⊕ Free House ◀ Ringwood Best Bitter, Keystone & other bitters. **Facilities** Children's licence Garden Parking Play Area

FONTHILL GIFFORD — MAP 04 ST93

Pick of the Pubs

The Beckford Arms

See Pick of the Pubs on opposite page

GREAT BEDWYN — MAP 05 SU26

Pick of the Pubs

The Three Tuns ♟

High St SN8 3NU ☎ 01672 870280 📠 01672 870890
e-mail: jan.carr2@btinternet.com

dir: *Off A4 between Marlborough & Hungerford*

You'll find this popular country inn in the centre of the village, close to the Ridgeway Path and the Kennet and Avon Canal. A roaring winter fire in the inglenook and lovely beer garden in summer attract a healthy year-round trade. Food is served at candlelit tables in the open plan bar area and there is a choice of lunch dishes, traditional bar food and a full evening carte menu. Local meat and game, augmented by twice-weekly deliveries of fresh Devon fish, feature in such dishes as slow-roasted lamb shank with cinnamon and red wine sauce; chicken, chorizo, belly pork and mixed sausage cassoulet; Spanish-style rabbit with peppers, tomatoes, white wine, onions and garlic; and tagliatelle with clams, slightly spicy tomato sauce and basil sauce. Chargrills are available every day except Sunday. Out back is a pleasant raised garden.

Open 11.30–3 6–11.30 **Bar Meals** L served all week 12–2 D served all week 7–9 (Sun 12–2.30) Av main course £10 **Restaurant** L served all week 12–2 D served Mon-Sat 7–9 (Sun 2–2.30) Av 3 course à la carte £20 ⊕ Punch Taverns ◀ Wadworth 6X, Fuller's London Pride, Flowers IPA & Theakstons Black Sheep. ♟9 **Facilities** Garden Parking

GREAT CHEVERELL — MAP 04 ST95

Pick of the Pubs

The Bell Inn ♟

High St SN10 5TH ☎ 01380 813277
e-mail: gillc@clara.co.uk

dir: *N side of Salisbury plain. A360 from Salisbury through West Lavington, 1st left after black & yellow striped bridge to Great Cheverell*

A family friendly former coaching inn located on the northern edge of Salisbury Plain, run by mother and daughter team Gill and Sara Currie. The Curries were helped to find the premises in 2005 by the Channel 4 programme *Relocation, Relocation*. It's an 18th-century building, Grade II listed, with an L-shaped bar and an oak beamed restaurant. A further 40 people can be seated in the 200–foot garden, where popular barbecues are held in the summer months. There is also a function room available for receptions, private parties and meetings, which can accommodate up to 120 people. The menu is flexible enough to provide anything from a casual lunch to a special occasion dinner, with dishes based on local produce. Choose from grilled steaks, sizzling stir-fries, and the likes of cod bourguignon, medallions of chicken with prunes and Calvados, and liver and bacon with a twist.

Open 12–3 6–11 (Fri-Sat 6pm-1am) Closed: 26 Dec, 1 Jan **Bar Meals** L served all week 12–2 D served all week 7–9 Av main course £8.50 **Restaurant** L served all week 12–2 D served all week 7–9 Av 3 course à la carte £16 Av 2 course fixed price £6.75 ⊕ Free House ◀ 6X, IPA, guest ale. ♟9 **Facilities** Garden Dogs allowed Parking

PICK OF THE PUBS

FONTHILL GIFFORD-WILTSHIRE

The Beckford Arms

Substantial 18th-century stone-built inn peacefully situated opposite the Fonthill Estate and providing a good base from which to explore the unspoilt Nadder Valley. New owners have maintained this rural retreat since arriving here recently.

Beyond the basic locals' bar, you will find a rambling main bar, adjoining dining area and an airy garden room all decorated in a tastefully rustic style, complete with scrubbed plank tables topped with huge candles, and warm terracotta-painted walls. Expect a roaring log fire in winter, a relaxed, laid-back atmosphere, and interesting modern pub menus. From petit pain baguettes, hearty soups, salads, Asian-style fishcakes with sweet chilli dip, or a Thai curry at lunchtime, the choice of well presented dishes extends, perhaps, to rack of lamb with tomatoes, wine and Italian herbs, sautéed medallions of Wiltshire pork with caramelised apple, Calvados and cider, and salmon with Vermouth glaze in the evening. Generous bowls of fresh vegetables, colourful plates and friendly service all add to the dining experience here. Sun-trap patio and a delightful garden – perfect for summer sipping.

MAP 04 ST93
SP3 6PX
☎ 01747 870385
🖷 01747 870385
e-mail:
enquiries@the-beckford.co.uk
dir: *2m from A303 (Fonthill Bishop turning) halfway between Hindon & Tisbury at x-rds by Beckford Estate*

Open 12–11 (Sun 12–10.30)
Bar Meals L served all week 12–2.15 D served Mon-Sat 7–9
Restaurant L served all week 12–2.15 (Sun 12–6) D served Mon-Sat 7–9
⊕ Free House ◾ Timothy Taylor Landlord, Abbot, Hopback Summer Lightning.
Facilities Garden Dogs allowed Parking

GREAT HINTON

MAP 04 ST95

Pick of the Pubs

The Linnet ♥

BA14 6BU ☎ 01380 870354 📠 01380 870354

dir: *Just off A361 (Devizes to Trowbridge road)*

In the 19th century this building was a woollen mill. It was converted into a village local circa 1914, and has been in the safe hands of chef/landlord Jonathan Furby for the past five years. Don't miss the chance to eat here. Everything is prepared on the premises – bread, ice cream, pasta and sausages – with fresh, locally produced ingredients to the fore. There is a light lunch menu, and more substantial dinner choice. You might try honey-roasted duck breast on watercress and orange couscous with a soy dressing, followed by steamed sea bass and prawn dumplings with Thai broth, or the award-winning baked tenderloin of pork, filled with prunes and spinach, wrapped in smoked bacon and served with a wild mushroom sauce. Finish with rhubarb and vanilla cheesecake; or stem ginger pudding with toffee sauce. In summer there are seats in the large patio area in front of the pub.

Open 11–2.30 6–11 (Sun 12–3, 7–10.30) Closed: 25–26 Dec, 1 Jan Mon **Bar Meals** L served Tue-Sun 12–2 D served Tue-Sun 6.30–9.30 **Restaurant** L served Tue-Sat 12–2 D served Tue-Sat 6.30–9.30 (Sun 12–3, 7–10.30) Av 3 course à la carte £22 Av 3 course fixed price £14.25 ⊕ Wadworth ◀ Wadworth 6X & Henrys IPA. ♥ 11 **Facilities** Garden Parking

GRITTLETON

MAP 04 ST88

The Neeld Arms

The Street SN14 6AP
☎ 01249 782470 📠 01249 782168
e-mail: neeldarms@zeronet.co.uk

dir: *Telephone for directions*

This 17th-century Cotswold stone pub stands at the centre of a pretty village in lush Wiltshire countryside. Quality real ales and freshly prepared food are an equal draw to diners who will eagerly tuck in to lamb shanks, home-made steak and kidney pie or sausage and mash. Children are welcome and the small garden is especially popular for al fresco eating in fine weather.

Open 12–3 5.30–11 **Bar Meals** L served all week 12–2 D served all week 7–9.30 Av main course £5 **Restaurant** L served all week 12–2 D served all week 7–9.30 Av 3 course à la carte £19 ⊕ Free House ◀ Wadworth 6X, Buckleys Best, Brakspear Bitter & IPA. **Facilities** Garden Dogs allowed Parking **Rooms** available

HANNINGTON

MAP 05 SU19

The Jolly Tar ♥

Queens Rd SN6 7RP ☎ 01793 762245 📠 01793 765159
e-mail: info@jollytar.co.uk

dir: *M4 junct 15, A419 towards Cirencester. At Bunsdon/ Highworth sign follow B4109. Towards Highworth, left at Freke Arms, follow Hannington & Jolly Tar pub signs.*

Although it's a fair old trek to the sea, there is a connection – the marriage of a lady from a local land-owning family to a 19th-century battleship captain. Inside are old timbers, a log fire and locally brewed

Arkells ales. On the menu, chicken, olive and prosciutto ribbon pasta; home-made lamb burger; Gloucester Old Spot sausages; and Jolly Fantastic fish pie. Specials may include tuna, prawn and red pepper chowder; and shepherds pie.

Open 12–2.30 6–11 **Bar Meals** L served Tue-Sun 12–2.30 D served Tue-Sat 6.30–9 (Sun 7–9.30) **Restaurant** L served Tue-Sun 12–2.30 D served Tue-Sat 6.30–9 (Sun 7–8.30) ◀ Arkells 3B, Noel Ale & Kingsdown. ♥ 11 **Facilities** Children's licence Garden Dogs allowed Parking Play Area

HEYTESBURY

MAP 04 ST94

Pick of the Pubs

The Angel Coaching Inn ♥

See Pick of the Pubs on opposite page

HINDON

MAP 04 ST93

Pick of the Pubs

Angel Inn

High St SP3 6DJ ☎ 01747 820696
e-mail: info@theangelathindon.com

dir: *1.5m from A303, on B3089 towards Salisbury*

An elegant gastro pub where rustic charm meets urbane sophistication in a Georgian coaching inn with a brasserie menu. The interior is characterised by wooden floors, beams, large stone fireplaces and comfortable leather seating. Lunch provides an extensive choice, with rolled shoulder of lamb stuffed with chicken and tarragon mousse, served with Madeira sauce; cold poached salmon with smoked trout mousse; open sandwich filled with prawn salad and smoked salmon; and Wiltshire ham, eggs and chips offering something for everyone. The main menu extends to confit of duck leg and slices of breast; grilled whole sole with lemon and caper butter; noisettes of lamb on pureed fennel with a lime and Pernod sauce; and seared calves' liver with smoked bacon on creamed potato. Outside is an attractive paved courtyard with garden furniture, where food is also served in fine weather.

Open 11–11 **Bar Meals** L served Mon-Sat 12–3 D served Mon-Sat 6–9.30 (Sun 12–9) **Restaurant** L served all week 12–3 D served all week 6–9.30 ⊕ Free House ◀ Wadworth 6X, Sharp's, Ringwood. **Facilities** Garden Dogs allowed Parking

PICK OF THE PUBS

HEYTESBURY-WILTSHIRE

The Angel Coaching Inn

This 16th-century inn is surrounded by stunning countryside so if you have the time, take one of the walks which start and end there. The Angel itself has been transformed by a complete refurbishment into a striking blend of original features and contemporary comfort.

The beamed bar has scrubbed pine tables, warmly decorated walls and an attractive fireplace with a wood-burning stove. In summer, the secluded courtyard garden is very popular. Although very much a dining pub, it has not forsaken the traditional charm and character of its coaching inn past. You can eat in the restaurant, the bar, or, during the summer months, alfresco in the secluded courtyard garden which leads off the restaurant. Steaks are a speciality and are hung for 35 days in the pub's ageing rooms for the best possible quality and taste. Lunch might take in a starter of home-cured gravadlax with a lemon and caper dressing and wild rocket, followed by roast haunch of venison with peppercorn sauce, sautéed Savoy cabbage and mashed potato.

If you fancy something simpler, plump for an aged steak, mushroom and Guinness pie; eggs Benedict; or sandwiches. The dinner menu is divided into starters (grilled goats' cheese, roasted vegetables and pesto; chicken liver parfait with fig chutney); 'simple classics' (perhaps classic fish pie with cod, haddock, salmon and prawns); and main courses such as wild mushroom gnocchi with blue cheese and rocket; or seared calves' liver with Lyonaise potatoes and bacon.

♥
MAP 04 ST94
High St BA12 0ED
☎ 01985 840330
🖷 01985 840931
e-mail:
admin@theangelheytesbury.co.uk
dir: *From A303 take A36 toward Bath, 8m Heytesbury on left*

Open 12–12
Bar Meals L served all week
12–2.30 D served all week 7–9.30
(Sun 12–3)
Restaurant L served all week
12–2.30 D served all week 7–9.30
(Sun 12–2.30)
⊕ Greene King ◀ Moorlands,
Greene King IPA, 6X. ♥ 10
Facilities Garden Dogs allowed
Parking

England

HINDON continued

Pick of the Pubs

The Lamb at Hindon ★★★★ INN ⬤

High St SP3 6DP ☎ 01747 820573 📠 01747 820605

e-mail: info@lambathindon.co.uk

dir: *From A303 follow signs to Hindon. At Fonthill Bishop right onto B3089 to Hindon. Pub on left*

Set in the heart of this charming Wiltshire village just 20 minutes from Salisbury, The Lamb began trading as a public house as long ago as the 12th century. By 1870 it supplied 300 horses for coaches going to and from London and the West Country. Today, the building retains plenty of its original character, with inglenook fireplaces, flagstone floors and heavy wooden beams. It also has 14 individually furnished bedrooms. In addition to a good selection of real ales there are extensive wine and whisky lists. The modern menu makes use of the best ingredients: you could start with a parfait of foie gras with Glenmorangie 10 year old malt whisky, red onion marmalade and olive oil crostini; then move on to red Thai chicken curry, or perhaps Macsween haggis with swede and potato gratin, buttered savory cabbage and thyme jus.

Open all day, incl breakfast **Bar Meals** L served all week 12–2.30 D served Mon-Sat 6.30–9.30 (Sun 7–9) **Restaurant** L served all week 12–2.30 D served Mon-Sat 6.30–9.30 (Sun 7–9) Av 3 course à la carte £22 ◀ Youngs Bitter, Youngs Special & 2 guest ales. **Facilities** Garden Dogs allowed Parking **Rooms** 14

HORTON   MAP 05 SU06

The Bridge Inn ⬤

Horton Rd SN10 2JS ☎ 01380 860273 📠 01380 860273

dir: *A361 from Devizes, right at 3rd rdbt*

The buildings that now constitute the Bridge Inn were originally a family-run farm, built around 1800, and then a flour mill and bakery. It makes a perfect place for a pint, while narrowboats cruise past on the Kennet and Avon Canal. Menus start with filled rolls and end with appetising hot dishes such as pan-fried Barbary duck breast; or stincotta – a hefty shank of pork marinated in Italian wine and herbs and slow roasted.

Open 11.30–3 6.30–11 (Sun 12–3, 6.30–10.30) **Bar Meals** L served all week 12–2.15 D served Mon-Sat 6.45–9.15 (Sun 6.45–9) **Restaurant** L served all week 12–2.15 D served Mon-Sat 6.45–9.15 (Sun 6.45–9) ⊕ Wadworth ◀ Wadworth Henry's original IPA, 6X, Old Father Timer. ⬤8 **Facilities** Garden Dogs allowed Parking

---

KILMINGTON   MAP 04 ST73

The Red Lion Inn ⬤

BA12 6RP ☎ 01985 844263

dir: *B3092 off A303 N towards Frome. Pub 2.5m from A303 on right on B3092 just after turning to Stourhead Gardens*

There's a good local pub atmosphere at this 14th-century former coaching inn, which once provided spare horses to assist coaches in the climb up nearby White Sheet Hill. Inside, you'll find flagstone floors, beams, antique settles and blazing log fires, and outside a large garden and a smoking shelter in the car park. Good value meals are served, such as home-made chicken casserole; and steak and kidney pie, plus snacks at lunchtime.

Open 11.30–2.30 6.30–11 (Sun 12–3, 7–10.30) **Bar Meals** L served all week 12–1.50 (ex 25–26 Dec & 1 Jan) Av main course £6.10 ⊕ Free House ◀ Butcombe Bitter, Jester, guest ale. ⬤7 **Facilities** Garden Dogs allowed Parking **Notes** ⊛

LACOCK   MAP 04 ST96

The George Inn ⬤

4 West St SN15 2LH ☎ 01249 730263 📠 01249 730186

dir: *M4 junct 17 take A350, S*

Steeped in history and much used as a film and television location, this beautiful National Trust village includes an atmospheric inn. The George dates from 1361 and boasts a medieval fireplace, a low-beamed ceiling, mullioned windows, flagstone floors and an old tread wheel by which a dog would drive the spit. Wide selection of steaks and tasty pies, and fish options include specials in summer; finish with the home-made bread and butter pud.

Open 10–2.30 5–11 (Sat-Sun all day) **Bar Meals** L served all week 12–2 D served all week 6–9.30 **Restaurant** L served all week 12–2 D served all week 6–9.30 (Eve hrs vary in winter) ⊕ Wadworth ◀ Wadworth 6X, Henrys IPA, J.C.B & Henrys Smooth. ⬤13 **Facilities** Garden Dogs allowed Parking Play Area

---

Red Lion Inn ⬤

1 High St SN15 2LQ ☎ 01249 730456 📠 01249 730766

e-mail: redlionlacock@wadworth.co.uk

dir: *Just off A350 between Chippenham & Melksham*

This historic 18th-century inn has kept its original features intact, from the large open fireplace to the flagstone floors and Georgian interior. Wadworth ales and a varied wine list accompany the home-cooked meals and daily specials. Fresh lunchtime sandwiches are accompanied by a portion of chips, whilst more substantial evening dishes include home-made spinach and mushroom lasagne; caramelised red onion and balsamic tart; or venison steak in red wine sauce.

Open 11.30–11 **Bar Meals** L served all week 12–2.30 D served all week 6–9 Av main course £8.50 **Restaurant** L served all week 12–2.30 D served all week 6–9 ⊕ Wadworth ◀ Wadworth Henry's IPA & 6X, Seasonal & mild. ⬤14 **Facilities** Garden Dogs allowed Parking

---

The Rising Sun ⬤

32 Bowden Hill SN15 2PP ☎ 01249 730363

The pub is located close to the National Trust village of Lacock, on a steep hill, providing spectacular views over Wiltshire from the large garden. Live music and quiz nights are a regular feature, and games and reading material are provided in the bar. Thai curries and stir-fries are popular options, alongside traditional liver, bacon and onions; steaks; and beef, ale and Stilton pie.

Open 12–3 6–11 (Sun all day, Summer Fri-Sun all day) **Bar Meals** L served all week 12–2 D served all week 6–9 Sun 12–3 **Restaurant** L served all week 12–2 D served all week 6–9 (Sun 12–2.30) ◀ Moles Best, Molecatcher, Tap Bitter, Rucking Mole. ⬤10 **Facilities** Garden Dogs allowed Parking Play Area

PICK OF THE PUBS

LOWER CHICKSGROVE-WILTSHIRE

Compasses Inn

This immensely characterful 14th-century thatched inn stands in a tiny hamlet on the old drovers' track from Poole to Birmingham – a route that can still be traced today. The rolling countryside that unfolds around it is part of a designated Area of Outstanding Natural Beauty.

Inside the latched door, there's a long, low-beamed bar with high-backed stools, stone walls, worn flagstone floors and a large inglenook fireplace in which a wood-burning stove blazes in colder months. The adjacent dining room is perfect for private parties. Dishes are written up on a regularly changing blackboard menu and everything is freshly made from seasonally available produce. Two chefs, Toby Hughes and Ian Chalmers, oversee operations. Typical starters could include duck, pheasant and pigeon terrine with a port and onion chutney; goats' cheese and roasted red pepper soufflé; and mussels in a bacon, white wine and onion cream sauce. Follow with the likes of goose breast on roasted baby vegetables with a grape compote; chicken breast filled with goats' cheese, wrapped in bacon and served with a red onion confit; or slow-roasted shoulder of lamb with a red wine and mint jus. An impressive selection of fish and seafood dishes might include lemon sole fillets stuffed with salmon mousse; poached smoked haddock with black pudding and tomato concasse; and West Country lobster thermidor. The garden has a large grassed area with some lovely views and seats for 40 people. Four bedrooms are available, providing an ideal base for an exploration of the area.

★★★★ INN ☺ ♀
MAP 04 ST92
SP3 6NB
☎ 01722 714318
e-mail: thecompasses@aol.com
dir: *On A30 (1.5m W of Fovant) take 3rd right to Lower Chicksgrove. In 1.5m turn left into Lagpond Lane, pub 1m on left*

Open 12–3 6–11 (Sun 7–10.30)
Closed: 25–26 Dec
Bar Meals L served all week 12–2 D served all week 6.30–9
Restaurant L served all week 12–2 D served all week 6.30–9 Av 3 course à la carte £23
⊕ Free House ◀ Keystone Large One & Bedrock, Hidden Quest. ♀ 24
Facilities Garden Dogs allowed Parking
Rooms 4

615

LIMPLEY STOKE — MAP 04 ST76

The Hop Pole Inn ♀

Woods Hill, Lower Limpley Stoke BA2 7FS

☎ 01225 723134 📠 01225 723199

e-mail: latonahop@aol.com

dir: *Telephone for directions*

Set in the beautiful Limpley Stoke valley, the Hop Pole dates from 1580 and takes its name from the hop plant that still grows outside the pub. Eagle-eyed film fans may recognise it as the hostelry in the 1992 film *Remains of the Day*. A hearty menu includes Thai vegetable curry; home-made pies; fresh local trout; and steaks. Giant filled baps and other light bites are available too.

Open 11–2.30 6–11 Closed: 25 Dec **Bar Meals** L served all week 12–2 D served Mon-Sat 6.30–9 (Sun 7–9) Av main course £8.95 **Restaurant** L served all week 12–2.15 D served Mon-Sat 6.30–9.15 (Sun 7–9) Av 3 course à la carte £18 ⊕ Free House ◖ Courage Best, Butcombe Bitter, Marstons Pedigree, guest ales. ♀8 **Facilities** Garden Dogs allowed Parking

LITTLE CHEVERELL — MAP 04 ST95

The Owl

Low Rd SN10 4JS ☎ 01380 812263 📠 01380 812263

dir: *A344 from Stonehenge, then A360, after 10m left onto B3098, right after 0.5m. Pub signed*

Sit in the pretty garden after dark and you'll discover that this pub is aptly named. As well as the hoot of owls, woodpeckers can be heard in summer. A brook runs at the bottom of the garden and there are views of Salisbury Plain. The pub itself is a cosy hideaway with oak beams and a fire in winter. Typical dishes include lasagne; Thai chicken curry; sizzling beef Szechwan; and stilton and mushroom pork.

Open all day **Bar Meals** L served all week 12–9 D served all week 12–9 **Restaurant** L served all week 12–9 D served all week 12–9 ⊕ Enterprise Inns ◖ Wadworth 6X, Hook Norton Best, Cotleigh Tawney Owl, Courage Directors. **Facilities** Children's licence Garden Dogs allowed Parking Play Area

LOWER CHICKSGROVE — MAP 04 ST92

Pick of the Pubs

Compasses Inn ★★★★ INN ◉ ♀

See Pick of the Pubs on page 615

LUDWELL — MAP 04 ST92

The Grove Arms ♀

SP7 9ND ☎ 01747 828328 📠 01747 828960

e-mail: info@grovearms.com

dir: *On A30 (Shaftesbury to Salisbury road), 3m from Shaftesbury*

This friendly 17th-century village inn was once owned by the aristocratic Grove family. The smartly turned out restaurant features the family coat of arms in pride of place, alongside a menu that makes good use of British produce. If you've ever dreamed of running a pub, look out for the sample days, designed to give you a taste of the realities of life behind the bar.

Open 12–12 **Bar Meals** L served all week 12–2.15 D served all week 6.15–9 Av main course £10 **Restaurant** L served all week 12–2.15 D served all week 6.15–9 ⊕ Hall & Woodhouse ◖ Badger Gold, Festive Feasant & Hopping Hare. **Facilities** Dogs allowed Parking

MALMESBURY — MAP 04 ST98

Pick of the Pubs

Horse & Groom ♀

See Pick of the Pubs on opposite page

The Smoking Dog ♀

62 The High St SN16 9AT ☎ 01666 825823

e-mail: smokindog@sabrain.com

dir: *5m N of M4 junct 17*

A winged wheel on the outside front wall greets visitors to this refined 17th-century stone-built pub, right in the heart of Malmesbury. Inside log fires and wooden floors make for a warm and cosy atmosphere. Freshly cooked food and live music have broad appeal, while the wide choice of refreshments includes continually changing guest ales and scrumpy ciders. A renowned beer and sausage festival over Whitsun weekend is the time to sample over 30 brews and 15 banger varieties.

Open 12–11 (Fri-Sat 12–12, Sun 12–10.30) **Bar Meals** L served Mon-Sat 12–2.30 D served Sat-Thu 6.30–9.30 (Sun 12–3, 6.30–9) Av main course £10 **Restaurant** L served Mon-Sat 12–3 D served Mon-Sat 6.30–9.30 (Sun 12–3, 6.30–9) Av 3 course à la carte £20 ◖ Archers Best, Buckleys Best, Reverend James plus 3 guest bitters. ♀7 **Facilities** Garden Dogs allowed

Pick of the Pubs

The Vine Tree ♀

Foxley Rd, Norton SN16 0JP

☎ 01666 837654 📠 01666 838003

e-mail: tiggi@thevinetree.co.uk

dir: *M4 junct 17, A429 towards Malmesbury. Turn left for village*

The Vine Tree used to be a mill, and workers apparently passed beverages out through front windows to passing carriages – an early drive-through it would seem. These days, it is well worth seeking out for its interesting modern pub food and memorable outdoor summer dining. In today's central bar a large open fireplace burns wood all winter, and there's a wealth of old beams, flagstone and oak floors. Ramblers and cyclists exploring Wiltshire's charms are frequent visitors, and the inn is situated on the official county cycle route. Cooking is modern British in style, with menus changing daily in response to local produce availability. Everything on the menus is produced in-house, including bread. Dishes include light bites and vegetarian options, local game and well-sourced fish and meats. There's also a terrific stock of wines. In addition to the suntrap terrace, there's a two-acre garden with two boules pitches.

Open 12–3 6–12 (Sun 12–12) **Bar Meals** L served all week 12–2 D served all week 6–9.30 (Fri 6–10, Sat 12–2.30, 6–10 Sun 12–3.30, 7–9.30) **Restaurant** L served all week 12–2 D served all week 6–9.30 (Fri 6–10, Sat 12–2.30, 6–10 Sun 12–3.30, 7–9.30) ⊕ Free House ◖ Tinners, Bath Ales, Badger & Butcombe. ♀30 **Facilities** Garden Dogs allowed Parking Play Area

PICK OF THE PUBS

MALMESBURY-WILTSHIRE

Horse & Groom

The golden Cotswold stone exterior of this 16th-century coaching inn gives way to stone flags and roaring fires inside – the epitome of the rural pub. Substantially refurbished in recent years, it has a pristine but atmospheric interior that retains its original country charm.

Wiltshire's only outdoor bar is to be found within the lovely walled garden, while children can make use of a separate play area. In the cosy, dog-friendly bar, weekly-changing guest ales include Cotswold Way and London Pride. Though the drinks side of things is an integral part of the inn, don't expect any old pub grub to appear from the kitchens. The kitchen has earned a number of accolades for its unpretentious but skilled and imaginative cooking. Head chef Justin Brown is passionate about local produce and most of what's on the menu comes from within 40 miles of the pub. In the bar, alongside an appetising range of nibbles you could tuck into a warm braised duck leg baguette, or an array of hearty main courses ranging from fresh battered pollock with hand cut

chips and crushed peas, to braised Moroccan lamb stew with mashed potatoes and glazed carrots. In the restaurant, you could start with risotto of Cornish crab, or pan-roasted scallops with gnocchi, black pudding and a pea dressing, followed by open ravioli of pan-fried wild mushrooms with spinach and fine beans and a wild mushroom sauce; or honey-roasted Gressingham duck breast with wilted spinach, truffle crushed potatoes and a red wine jus. A range of 'classics' includes Wiltshire ham, egg and chips; and local sausages with mash, buttered greens and shallot sauce. Vanilla cheesecake with warm berry compote; apple and pear bread and butter pudding with an orange Anglaise; and glazed lemon tart with mascarpone cream leave the sweet-toothed spoiled for choice.

MAP 04 ST98
The Street, Charlton SN16 9DL
☎ 01666 823904
e-mail:
info@horseandgroominn.com
web:
www.horseandgroominn.com
dir: *M4 junct 17 follow signs to Cirencester on A429. Through Corston & Malmesbury. Straight on at Priory rdbt, at next rdbt take 3rd exit to Cricklade, then to Charlton*

Open 12–11
Bar Meals L served Mon-Sat 12–2.30 D served Mon-Sat 6.30–9.30 (Sun 7–9) Av main course £8.95
Restaurant L served all week 12–2.30 D served all week 6.30–9.30 Av 3 course à la carte £24 Av 3 course fixed price £14.95
🍺 guest ales, Moorland Original, Old Speckled Hen. ♟ 8
Facilities Garden Dogs allowed Parking Play Area
Rooms available

England

MARDEN

MAP 05 SU05

The Millstream ♥

SN10 3RH ☎ 01380 848308 📄 01380 848337

e-mail: mail@the-millstream.net

dir: Signed from A342

The Millstream sits in lovely countryside in the Vale of Pewsey, within sight of both Salisbury Plain and the Marlborough Downs. It was tastefully refurbished a few years ago without losing its traditional feel: wooden floors, beamed ceilings, log fires and pretty muted colours create a cosy, welcoming interior. Books, games and comfy sofas add their own homely touch. A good choice of hand-pulled beers and an impressive wine list are an ideal accompaniment for the contemporary menu, where locally sourced seasonal produce, plus fish from Cornwall, hold sway. Look out for braised lamb shank, and spatchcock poussin, with all the trimmings.

Open 11.30–12 Closed: 25 Dec & Mon (ex BHs) **Bar Meals** L served all week 12–3 D served all week 6.30–9.30 (Sun 12–4, longer hrs Fri-Sat) Av main course £10.95 **Restaurant** L served Tue-Sun 12–3 D served Tue-Sun (Sun 12–4) Av 3 course à la carte £25 Av 2 course fixed price £11.50 ⊕ Wadworth ◀ 6X, Henry's IPA, JCB, Bishops Tipple. ♥ 16 **Facilities** Children's licence Garden Dogs allowed Parking Play Area

MINETY

MAP 05 SU09

Pick of the Pubs

Vale of the White Horse Inn ♥

SN16 9QY ☎ 01666 860175 📄 01666 860175

e-mail: info@vwhi.net

dir: On B4040 (3m W of Cricklade, 6m & E of Malmesbury)

This handsome and beautifully restored inn overlooks its own lake and in summer, sitting out on the large raised terrace surrounded by rose beds, it's hard to think of a better spot. The lower ground floor originally provided stabling for horses, and nowadays the village bar still serves the local community well. Here you'll find a good selection of real ales and a range of sandwiches and simple bar meals. Upstairs, lunch and dinner are served in the stone-walled restaurant with its polished tables and bentwood chairs. The menus offer something for most tastes, with starters including stilton, onion and sweet pepper quiche; and home-cured Bresaola beef salad. Main course options range from beer-battered cod and chips to roast chicken breast wrapped in smoked bacon and stuffed with brie, with daily specials featuring the likes of aubergine risotto, or baked salmon fillet with a black olive crust.

Open 11–11.30 **Bar Meals** L served all week 12–9.30 D served all week 12–9.30 (Sun 12–9) Av main course £9.50 **Restaurant** L served all week 12–9.30 D served all week 12–9.30 (Fri-Sat 12–10, Sun 12–9) Av 3 course à la carte £20 ⊕ Free House ◀ Wadworth 6X, Three Castle Vale Ale & Adnams Broadside. ♥ 12 **Facilities** Children's licence Garden Parking

NEWTON TONY

MAP 05 SU24

Pick of the Pubs

The Malet Arms

SP4 0HF ☎ 01980 629279 📄 01980 629459

e-mail: maletarms@hotmail.com

dir: 8m N of Salisbury on A338, 2m from A303

A 17th-century inn on the River Bourne in a quiet village. It was originally built as a dwelling house, much later becoming The Three Horseshoes, named after a nearby smithy. An earlier Malet Arms, owned by lord of the manor Sir Henry Malet, closed in the 1890s and its name was transferred. It's not just the village that's quiet: the pub is too, as fruit machines and piped music are banned. All food on the ever-changing blackboard menus is home cooked. Game is plentiful in season, often courtesy of the landlord who shoots pheasant and deer. Other choices might include roasted duck legs and Toulouse sausages on puy lentils braised in white wine; and chargrilled pork chop with scrumpy-soused shallots and grain mustard. The landlady makes all the puddings, often sourced from obscure old English recipes. There's a good range of real ales and ciders.

Open 11–3 6–11 (Sun 12–3, 7–10.30) Closed: 25–26 Dec, 1 Jan **Bar Meals** L served all week 12–2.30 D served all week 6.30–10 (Sun 7–9.30) ⊕ Free House ◀ Ramsbury, Stonehenge, Tripple fff, Palmers & Archers. **Facilities** Garden Dogs allowed Parking Play Area

NUNTON

MAP 05 SU12

The Radnor Arms ♥

SP5 4HS ☎ 01722 329722

dir: From Salisbury ring road take A338 to Ringwood. Nunton signed on right

A popular pub in the centre of the village dating from around 1750. In 1855 it was owned by the local multi-talented brewer/baker/grocer, and bought by Lord Radnor in 1919. Bar snacks are supplemented by an extensive fish choice and daily specials, which might include braised lamb shank, wild mushroom risotto, tuna with noodles, turbot with spinach or Scotch rib-eye fillet, all freshly prepared. Fine summer garden with rural views. Hosts an annual local pumpkin competition.

Open 11–3 6–11 (Sun 12–3, 7–10.30) **Bar Meals** L served all week 12–2.30 D served Mon-Sat 7–9.30 **Restaurant** L served all week 12–2.30 D served all week 7–9.30 ⊕ Hall & Woodhouse ◀ Badger Tanglefoot, Best & Golden Champion. **Facilities** Garden Dogs allowed Parking Play Area

---

OAKSEY
MAP 04 ST99

The Wheatsheaf Inn ⊛⊛ ♥

Wheatsheaf Ln SN16 9TB ☎ 01666 577348

e-mail: info@thecompletechef.co.uk

dir: Off A419, 6m S of Cirencester

A village inn built in the 14th century from mellow Cotswold stone, the Wheatsheaf has one rather bizarre feature: an 18th-century 'royal' coffin lid displayed above the open fireplace. All the food is made on the premises from fresh local produce, and Sharp's Doom Bar, Hook Norton, and Wychwood Hobgoblin are some of the real ales kept in good condition behind the bar.

Open 11.30–2.30 6–11 (Sun 12–10.30) **Bar Meals** L served Tue-Sun 12–2 D served Tue-Sun 6.30–9.30 Av main course £7 **Restaurant** L served Tue-Sun 12–2 D served Tue-Sun 6.30–9.30 ◀ Sharp's Doom Bar, London Pride, Hook Norton, Wychwood Hobgoblin. ♥ 9 **Facilities** Children's licence Garden Dogs allowed Parking

---

PEWSEY
MAP 05 SU16

The Seven Stars ♥

Bottlesford SN9 6LU

☎ 01672 851325 📠 01672 851583

e-mail: sevenstarsinn@hotmail.com

dir: Off A345

Set in a splendid seven acre garden, the front door of this creeper-clad 16th-century free house opens straight onto the low-beamed, oak-panelled bar, now tastefully refurbished. Meals are served both here and in the restaurant; at lunchtime, expect filled baguettes, ploughman's, and hot dishes like home-made Mexican chilli with rice. In the evening, typical choices may include calves' liver with bacon and red wine sauce; and pan-fried monkfish with tiger prawns and leek sauce. Under new management for 2008.

Open 11.30–3 6–11 **Bar Meals** L served all week 12–2.30 D served all week 6–9.30 Av main course £8 **Restaurant** L served all week 12–2.30 D served all week 6–9.30 Av 3 course à la carte £22 ⊕ Free House ◀ Wadworth 6X, Badger Dorset Best, London Pride & guest ales. ♥ 9 **Facilities** Garden Dogs allowed Parking

---

PITTON
MAP 05 SU23

Pick of the Pubs

The Silver Plough ♥

White Hill SP5 1DU ☎ 01722 712266 📠 01722 712262

e-mail: thesilverplough@hotmail.co.uk

dir: From Salisbury take A30 towards Andover, Pitton signed (approx 3m)

Surrounded by rolling countryside and with a peaceful garden, this popular pub is at the heart of a village full of thatched houses. Converted from a farmstead around 60 years ago, inside you will find beams strung with antique glass rolling pins – said to bring good luck – along with bootwarmers, Toby jugs and various other artefacts. It also features a skittle alley adjacent to the snug bar and there are darts and board games available. It is within easy reach of many lovely downland and woodland walks. Hughen and Joyce Riley offer a range of dishes at both lunchtime and evening, including children's meals. House specialities include half a roast shoulder of lamb with mint and garlic gravy, and red bream fillet with caramelised onions, prosciutto and pesto sauce.

Open 11–5 6–11 (Sun 12–3, 6–10.30) **Bar Meals** L served all week 12–2.15 D served Mon-Fri 6–9 (Sat 6–9.30, Sun 6–8.30) **Restaurant** L served all week 12–2.15 D served Mon-Fri 6–9 (Sat 6–9.30, Sun 6–8.30) ⊕ Hall & Woodhouse ◀ Badger Tanglefoot, Badger Gold, King Barnes Sussex, guest ale. ♥ 9 **Facilities** Garden Dogs allowed Parking

---

RAMSBURY
MAP 05 SU27

Pick of the Pubs

The Bell NEW ♥

The Square SN8 2PE ☎ 01672 520230

e-mail: jeremy@thebellramsbury.com

dir: Telephone for directions

The Bell, originally a 16th-century coaching inn, stands on ancient crossroads in the centre of the village, probably the site of a hostelry since medieval times. Head chef Paul Kinsey's passion for cooking stems from a training background in France and Hampshire, and two years working for celebrity chef, Antony Worrall-Thompson. Wherever possible, Paul sources food from within Wiltshire or neighbouring Berkshire, for a menu that includes classics such as 28–day rib-eye steak with béarnaise sauce; sausages made with Ramsbury Gold Bell bitter; and River Kennet crayfish. A typical meal might be balsamic glazed chicken livers with goat's cheese risotto; salmon baked in puff pastry with spinach and watercress sauce; or roast Gressingham duck breast with braised beetroot, parsnip purée and Madeira sauce; and finally, caramelised apple tart with vanilla ice cream, accompanied by a glass of Muscat dessert wine. The main wine list has spawned a totally Iberian spin-off.

Open 12–3 5.30–11 (Sun 12–5) Closed: Sun eve (ex BHs) **Bar Meals** L served Mon-Sat 12–2 D served Mon-Sat 7–9 Av main course £8.95 **Restaurant** L served Mon-Sat 12–2 D served Mon-Sat 7–9 (Sun 12–3) Av 3 course à la carte £27.50 ⊕ Free House ◀ Ramsbury Gold & Bell Bitter. ♥ 8 **Facilities** Garden Dogs allowed Parking

England

ROWDE   MAP 04 ST96

Pick of the Pubs

The George & Dragon ◉ ♥

High St SN10 2PN ☎ 01380 723053
e-mail: thegandd@tiscali.co.uk

dir: *1m from Devizes, take A342 towards Chippenham*

Winter log fires warm the panelled bars and dining room of this free house, not far from the Caen Hill lock flight on the Kennet and Avon Canal. The building dates from the 15th century, and has a Tudor rose carved on one of the restaurant beams. The pub specialises in seafood from Cornwall, so take your pick from the latest catch – whatever is available is chalked up on the blackboard. From the menu, you could try tomato and basil soup, or carpaccio of beef with light mustard dressing as a starter. Main course dishes might include oven-roasted chicken breast with dauphinoise potatoes, or an 8oz fillet steak with herb and blue cheese crust. Some starters are also available as a main course: try king prawn tagliatelle with pesto, rocket and chilli sauce, or double-baked cheese soufflé. Puddings include favourites like treacle tart with clotted cream, and chocolate bread and butter pudding.

Open 12–3 7–11 (Sat-Sun 12–4, Sat 6.30–11) Closed: Sun eve **Bar Meals** L served Mon-Fri 12–3 D served Mon-Fri 7–10 (Sat-Sun 12–4, Sat 6.30–11) Av main course £15 **Restaurant** L served Mon-Fri 12–3 D served Mon-Fri 7–10 (Sat-Sun 12–4, Sat 6.30–11) ⊕ Free House ◀ Butcombe Bitter, Milk Street Brewery Ales, Bath Ales Gem, ESB. ♥ 11 **Facilities** Garden Dogs allowed Parking

SALISBURY   MAP 05 SU12

Pick of the Pubs

The Haunch of Venison ♥

1–5 Minster St SP1 1TB ☎ 01722 411313
e-mail: info@haunchofvenisonsalisbury.co.uk

dir: *In city centre. Opposite Poultry Cross Monument, adjacent to market place*

Probably the oldest hostelry in Salisbury, the earliest records for this heavily beamed and reputedly haunted inn date from 1320, when it housed craftsmen working on the cathedral spire. Charming details include what is believed to be the country's only surviving complete pewter bar top, as well as original gravity-fed spirit taps. With such a past, ghosts are inevitable. The one-handed Demented Whist Player is a favourite; his missing hand, severed in

a card game as punishment for cheating, was found mummified in the 19th century, and it remains to this day, despite attempts on the part of thieves to remove it. The eclectic restaurant features modern and classic dishes with 'an upbeat slant'. Try venison toad in the hole, bubble and squeak, or haddock chowder, and keep an eye out for local game and fish on the specials board. A thoughtfully coded menu offers plenty of scope for vegetarians and dairy-free diners.

Open 11–11 (Sun 12–10.30) Closed: 25 Dec eve **Bar Meals** L served all week 12–2 D served all week 6–9.30 **Restaurant** L served all week 12–2.30 D served Mon-Sat 6–10 (Sun 6–9.30) Av 3 course fixed price £9.90 ⊕ Enterprise Inns ◀ Courage Best, Summer Lightning, Directors & Greene King IPA. ♥ 12

SEEND   MAP 04 ST96

Bell Inn

Bell Hill SN12 6SA ☎ 01380 828338
e-mail: bellseend@aol.com

According to local tradition, Oliver Cromwell and his troops enjoyed breakfast at this inn, quite possibly on 18 September 1645 when he was advancing from Trowbridge to attack Devizes Castle. The extensive menu runs to poached salmon with a prawn and cream sauce; spicy bean burgers; and barbecue pork ribs, while the specials board highlights liver and bacon casserole; chicken balti; and Highland sausages in whisky. The two-floor restaurant has lovely valley views.

Open 11.15–3 6–12 **Bar Meals** L served all week 11.45–2.15 D served all week 6.15–9.30 (Sun 12–2.15) Av main course £7.50 **Restaurant** L served all week 11.45–2.15 D served all week 6.15–9.30 (Sun 12–2.15) Av fixed price £7.50 ⊕ Wadworth ◀ Wadworth 6X, Henry's IPA & Henrys Smooth. **Facilities** Garden Dogs allowed Parking Play Area

SEMINGTON   MAP 04 ST86

The Lamb on the Strand ♥

99 The Strand BA14 6LL

☎ 01380 870263 & 870815 ▤ 01380 871203

dir: *1.5m E on A361 from junct with A350*

An 18th-century farmhouse that later became a beer and cider house. Today's popular dining pub typically offers starters of grilled goat's cheese with spiced beetroot; and grilled fig, chorizo and parmesan salad. Almost sure to be found on the generous list of main courses are sausages, mash and onion gravy; fillet of cod with herb crust, leeks and new potatoes; medallions of venison, parsnip purée, vegetables and Madeira jus; and cheesy pudding, salad and sauté potatoes.

Open 11.30–3 6.30–11 Closed: 25–26 Dec & 1 Jan, & Sun eve **Bar Meals** L served all week 12–2 D served Mon-Sat 6.30–9 Av main course £9.50 ⊕ Free House ◀ Butcombe Bitter, Ringwood Bitter, Shepherd Neame Spitfire, Guinness. ♥ 12 **Facilities** Garden Dogs allowed Parking

SHERSTON — MAP 04 ST88

Carpenters Arms

SN16 0LS ☎ 01666 840665

dir: *On B4040 W of Malmesbury*

A 17th-century traditional village inn offering a warm welcome to families, dogs and walkers in wellies. The inn has four interconnecting rooms, with low, beamed ceilings, a wood-burner and a cosy old-world atmosphere. The sunny conservatory restaurant overlooks a beautiful garden. The menu offers a choice of starters like home-made soup, then a selection of meat dishes, curries, fish dishes, vegetarian options and blackboard specials. BBQs and hog roasts in summer.

Open 12–3 5–12 (Sat-Sun all day) **Bar Meals** L served Tue-Sun 12–4 D served Tue-Sun 6.30–9.30 Av main course £7 **Restaurant** L served Tue-Sun 12–3 D served Tue-Sun 6.30–9.30 ⊕ Enterprise Inns ◀ Whitbread Best, Bath Gem, Wickwar Bob & guest ale. **Facilities** Garden Dogs allowed Parking Play Area

STOFORD — MAP 05 SU03

The Swan Inn ★★★ INN ☗

Warminster Rd SP2 0PR ☎ 01722 790236

e-mail: info@theswanatstoford.co.uk

dir: *From Salisbury take A36 towards Warminster. Stoford on right 4m from Wilton*

A landmark former coaching inn overlooking the River Wylye, meadows and farmland. Family-owned since 1993, it offers good value, mostly locally sourced meals, such as mozzarella and beef tomato salad, followed perhaps by home-made beef chilli, or grilled whole rainbow trout, then tangy lemon meringue pie. Other facilities include a skittle alley and two gardens, one at the rear of the property, the other on the river bank. Guest rooms are comfortable and homely.

Open 11–3 6–11 **Bar Meals** L served all week 12–2 D served all week 6.30–9.15 (Sun 7–9) Av main course £9 **Restaurant** L served all week 12–2.15 D served all week 6.30–9.15 (Sun 7–9) Av 3 course à la carte £18 ⊕ Free House ◀ Ringwood Best, Fuller's London Pride, Odyssey Best Bitter, Old Speckled Hen. ☗ 7 **Facilities** Garden Parking **Rooms** 9

STOURTON — MAP 04 ST73

Pick of the Pubs

Spread Eagle Inn ★★★★ INN ☗

BA12 6QE ☎ 01747 840587 📠 01747 840954

e-mail: enquiries@spreadeagleinn.com

dir: *N of A303 off B3092*

Built at the beginning of the 19th century, this charming inn stands in the heart of the 2,650-acre Stourhead Estate, one of the country's most-visited National Trust properties. Before or after a walk through the magnificent gardens and landscapes there is plenty on offer here, including locally produced beers and traditional food. Expect perhaps Wiltshire pasty with onion gravy and chips; lamb casserole and roasted root vegetables; and Old Spot sausages with bubble and squeak mash and sweet mustard sauce. The restaurant menu shifts things up a gear with breast of Gressingham duck with parsnip purée and apple sauce; escalope

---

of cod with lentils and bacon; and chump of Cotswold lamb with spiced apricots and rosemary. Finish with treacle tart with clotted cream; hot sticky toffee pudding; or chocolate roulade. The interior is smartly traditional.

Open 9–11 (Sun 9–10.30) **Bar Meals** L served all week 12–3 D served all week 7–9 Av main course £9 **Restaurant** L served all week 12–3 D served all week 7–9 Av 3 course à la carte £25 ⊕ Free House ◀ Kilmington, Butcombe & Wadworth 6X. ☗ 8 **Facilities** Garden Parking **Rooms** 5

SWINDON — MAP 05 SU18

The Sun Inn ☗

Lydiard Millicent SN5 3LU ☎ 01793 770425

e-mail: thesuninnlm@yahoo.co.uk

dir: *3m W of Swindon, 1.5m from M4 junct 16*

This 18th-century free house is set in a conservation area, near Lydiard House and Park. The walls display an eclectic mix of artwork from local artists. There's an emphasis on real ale, and traditional food with a bistro touch is served. It would be a mistake to miss the smoked haddock and king prawns fish pot, while monkfish wrapped in bacon with as green bean and mussel sauce is also an appetising option.

Open 11.30–3 5.30–11 (Mar-Sep Sun all day) **Bar Meals** L served all week 12–2.30 D served all week 6.30–9.30 (Sun 6.30–9) Av main course £8.95 **Restaurant** L served all week 12–2.30 D served all week 6.30–9.30 (Sun 6.30 -9) Av 3 course à la carte £17.95 ⊕ Free House ◀ Sharp's Doom Bar, West Berkshire, Wadsworth 6X, Wye Valley Brewery. ☗ 8 **Facilities** Garden Dogs allowed Parking

TOLLARD ROYAL — MAP 04 ST91

King John Inn

SP5 5PS ☎ 01725 516207

dir: *On B3081 (7m E of Shaftesbury)*

Named after one of King John's hunting lodges, this Victorian building was opened in 1859. A friendly and relaxing place, it is today perhaps better known as Madonna's local after she and husband Guy Ritchie moved in close by. Also nearby is a 13th-century church, and the area is excellent rambling country. A typical menu offers old English favourites like bangers and apple mash; bacon, liver and kidney casserole; Dorset lamb cutlets; and Wiltshire gammon with peaches.

Open 11–3 6–12 (Sun 12–10.30) **Bar Meals** L served all week 12–2 D served all week 7–9 (Sun summer all day) **Restaurant** L served all week 12–2 D served all week 7–9 (Sun 12–2.30) ⊕ Free House ◀ Courage Best, John Smith's, Wadworth 6X, Ringwood. **Facilities** Garden Dogs allowed Parking

UPTON LOVELL   MAP 04 ST94

Prince Leopold Inn ▼

BA12 0JP ☎ 01985 850460 📠 01985 850737

e-mail: Princeleopold@Lineone.net

web: www.princeleopoldinn.co.uk

dir: *From Warminster take A36 after 4.5m turn left into Upper Lovell*

Built in 1887 as the local shop, post office and store to service the then prosperous woollen industry, the inn's name was chosen to honour Prince Leopold who lived nearby. Possibly unique in England, the Mediterranean-style restaurant has an eye-level fireplace with a charcoal barbecue grill. Seafood features strongly on a wide ranging menu, offering brill fillet on champ mash with hollandaise sauce and thyme scented onions alongside Thai green chicken curry.

Open 12–3 7–11 **Bar Meals** L served all week 12–2.30 D served all week 7–10 **Restaurant** L served all week 12–2.30 D served all week 7–10 ⊕ Free House ◀ Ringwood Best, John Smith's & San Miguel. ▼ 8 **Facilities** Garden Parking **Rooms** available

WARMINSTER   MAP 04 ST84

Pick of the Pubs

The Angel Inn ▼

Upton Scudamore BA12 0AG

☎ 01985 213225 📠 01985 218182

e-mail: mail@theangelinn.co.uk

dir: *From Warminster take A350 towards Trowbridge*

The Angel is a restored 16th-century coaching inn located in a small village close to Warminster. Access to the pub is via a walled garden and terrace, where meals and drinks can be taken in fine weather. Inside, the open fires and natural wood flooring create a relaxed atmosphere. Meals open with a selection of home-made breads and flavoured olive oil. Chef's specials from the chalk board feature fresh sea fish from Brixham, which might include gilthead bream, barramundi or sea bass. Dishes from the menu might include steamed River Fowey mussels cooked in white wine, garlic and herbs, and roast rump of lamb with slow roast potato, confit tomatoes and sweet onion jus. For a vegetarian alternative, perhaps fresh linguine with baby bell peppers, cashew nuts, baby spinach and goats' cheese, finished with pesto dressing. Desserts range from iced white chocolate parfait with mango sorbet to sticky toffee pudding with butterscotch sauce.

Open 11–3 6–11 Closed: 25–26 Dec, 1 Jan **Bar Meals** L served all week 12–2 D served all week 7–9.30 **Restaurant** L served all week 12–2 D served all week 7–9.30 Av 3 course à la carte £25 ⊕ Free House ◀ Wadworth 6X, Butcombe, John Smith's Smooth, guest ales. ▼ 8 **Facilities** Garden Parking

The Bath Arms ▼

Clay St, Crockerton BA12 8AJ

☎ 01985 212262 📠 01985 218670

e-mail: batharms@aol.com

dir: *From Warminster on A36 take A350 towards Shaftesbury then left to Crockerton, follow signs for Shearwater*

Standing close to the Shearwater Lake on the Longleat Estate, this well-known free house attracts locals, walkers and tourists. In recent years the garden has been landscaped to provide a pleasant spot for outdoor dining. The new Garden Suite, with views across the lawn, provides additional seating on busy weekends. Expect steak and horseradish baguettes; shepherd's pie with crushed peas; or Bath Arms fish cake with Cornish crab and broad beans.

Open 11–3 6–11 (Sat-Sun all day in Summer) **Bar Meals** L served all week 12–2.30 D served all week 6–9.30 **Restaurant** L served all week 12–2.30 D served all week 6–9.30 ⊕ Free House ◀ Crockerton Classic, Naughty Ferrit & guest ales. ▼ 10 **Facilities** Garden Dogs allowed Parking Play Area

The George Inn ★★★★ INN ▼

BA12 7DG ☎ 01985 840396 📠 01985 841333

dir: *Telephone for directions*

A 17th-century coaching inn at the heart of the pretty village of Longbridge Deverill. Customers can enjoy a pint of real ale by the fire in the oak-beamed Longbridge bar, or sit outside in the two-acre garden on the banks of the River Wylye. Food is served in a choice of two restaurants, and there is a Sunday carvery in the Wylye Suite.

Function facilities are available, plus accommodation in 11 en suite bedrooms.

Open 11–11 (Fri 11–12pm, Sun 12 -10.30) Closed: 25–Dec from 3
Bar Meals L served all week 12–2.30 D served Mon-Sat 6–9.30 (Sun 6–9)
Restaurant L served all week 12–2.30 D served Mon-Sat 6–9.30 (Sun 6–9)
⊞ Free House ◀ John Smiths's, Wadworth 6X, Hobdens Doverills Advocat.
♀ 11 **Facilities** Garden Parking Play Area **Rooms** 11

WEST LAVINGTON   MAP 04 SU05

Pick of the Pubs

The Bridge Inn ♀

26 Church St SN10 4LD
☎ 01380 813213 ▤ 01380 813213
e-mail: portier@btopenworld.com
web: www.the-bridge-inn.co.uk
dir: *Approx 7m S of Devizes on A360 towards Salisbury. On the edge of village, past the church.*

The Bridge is a small but perfectly formed pub and restaurant in a village setting on the edge of Salisbury Plain. Inside is a beamed bar and log fire with displays of local paintings for sale. Outside, the large garden features a boule pitch. Light lunch options of baguettes and salads can be augmented by choosing a starter as a snack if you wish. Pub favourites are offered on the specials board – fresh haddock in beer batter; salmon, cod and dill fishcakes; and Wiltshire ham with free-range eggs and pomme frites. The distinctly French flavour of the main menu includes entrées of burgundy snails or warm smoked duck salad, and main courses of coq au vin or seared Badminton estate pheasant. Desserts include an irresistible sample of six miniatures from the carte. Regular fund-raising events include a 'rook supper' in May, harvest festival, and a charity beer festival over August bank holiday weekend.

Open 12–3 6.30–11 Closed: 2wks Feb Sun eve & Mon
Bar Meals L served Tue-Sat 12–2 D served Tue-Sat 6.30–9
Restaurant L served Tue-Sun 12–2 D served Tue-Sat 6.30–9
⊞ Enterprise Inns ◀ Brakspear Organic Oxford Gold, Hobgoblin, Wadworth Henry's IPA, Greene King IPA. ♀ 12 **Facilities** Garden Parking

---

WHADDON   MAP 05 SU12

The Three Crowns ♀

Southampton Rd SP5 3HB
☎ 01722 710211 ▤ 01722 711537
e-mail: pubstuff@thethreecrowns.com
dir: *4m from Salisbury on A27*

Standing on the old Salisbury-Southampton road, this mid-18th-century pub is left in peace as traffic hurtles along the by-pass. According to legend, Edward III and his two royal prisoners, David of Scotland and John of France, visited an earlier hostelry in 1356 – thus the name. Warm and welcoming, with inglenook fireplaces, leather sofa and a miscellany of chairs. Blackboards offer a good choice, including steaks, red snapper, wild mushroom stroganoff, sandwiches, and Sunday roasts.

Open 12–2.30 5–11 (Sun all day) **Bar Meals** L served all week 12–2
D served all week 6–9 (Sun 12–8) **Restaurant** L served all week 12–2
D served all week 6–9 (Sun 12–8) ⊞ Greene King ◀ Greene King IPA,
Abbot Ale & guest ale. ♀ 8 **Facilities** Garden Dogs allowed Parking
Rooms available **Notes** ⊛

WHITLEY   MAP 04 ST86

Pick of the Pubs

The Pear Tree Inn ★★★★★ RR ◉◉ ♀

See Pick of the Pubs on page 624

WINTERBOURNE BASSETT   MAP 05 SU07

The White Horse Inn ♀

SN4 9QB ☎ 01793 731257 ▤ 01793 739030
e-mail: ckstone@btinternet.com
web: www.whitehorsewinterbournebassett.co.uk
dir: *5m S of Swindon on A4361 (Devizes road)*

Lying just two miles north of the mysterious Avebury stone circle, the White Horse is an ideal base for walks on the historic Ridgeway path. Food is served in the bar and conservatory restaurant, as well as in the safe, lawned garden. Budget lunches and snacks are supported by a full menu and daily specials: look out for baked cod topped with tomato, herbs and mozzarella; mushroom stroganoff; and beef, ale and mushroom pie.

Open 11–3 6–11 **Bar Meals** L served all week 12–2 D served Mon-Sat
6–9.30 (Sun 7–10) **Restaurant** L served all week 12–2 D served Mon-Sat
6–9.30 (Sun 7–10) ⊞ Wadworth ◀ Wadworth 6X, IPA, Hophouse Brews.
♀ 11 **Facilities** Garden Parking

The Pear Tree Inn

The agricultural antiques that adorn this pub's interior are a testament to its past life as a farmstead. It has a lived-in, comfortable feel, with flagstone floors, two log fires, three or four real ales always on tap, and a wine list displaying over 40 choices.

So drinkers are still very much welcome – the bar is open all day – while the cosy restaurant attracts diners with its fresh and innovative menu. Outside a large boules piste, an extensive patio area and a cottage garden are agreeable surroundings for al fresco relaxation in summer. The surrounding acres of wooded farmland make it feel as though you are in the heart of a country estate. You can work up a thirst or an appetite by visiting Lacock Abbey which is just up the road, or Avebury and Silbury Hill which are close by; alternatively Stonehenge is a lovely drive across Salisbury Plain. The menu delivers a modern take on hearty, traditional British food, all prepared by an experienced team of chefs with ingredients from locally based suppliers. Organic meats from the local Neston Park Farm shop are reared on the estate, and delicious free-range chickens are very popular. Fruit and vegetables of the highest quality come from local Bromham growers, or further afield when necessary – try the lemon tart made with lemons from the Amalfi coast. There is also a healthy children's menu. The success of this operation lies in the staff's ability to balance a laid back country pub ambience with the fine dining ethos from the kitchen. To this end food is served throughout the pub, giving customers the option to choose a dining style to suit their mood and dress.

★★★★★ RR ◉◉ ♀
MAP 04 ST86
Top Ln SN12 8QX
☎ 01225 709131
🖷 01225 702276
e-mail:
enquries@thepeartreeinn.com
dir: *A365 from Melksham towards Bath, at Shaw right onto B3353 into Whitley, 1st left in lane, pub at end*

Open 11–3 6–11 Closed: 25–26 Dec, 1 Jan
Bar Meals L served all week 12–2.30 D served all week 6.30–9.30
Restaurant L served all week 12–2.30 D served all week 6.30–9.30
⊕ Free House ◀ Wadworth 6X, Bath Ales Gem, Stonehenge Ales, Pigswill. ♀ 12
Facilities Garden Dogs allowed Parking
Rooms 8

WOODFALLS
MAP 05 SU12

The Woodfalls Inn ♀

The Ridge SP5 2LN ☎ 01725 513222 ▤ 01725 513220
e-mail: enquiries@woodfallsinn.co.uk
dir: *B3080 to Woodfalls*

Located on an old coaching route on the northern edge of the New Forest, the Woodfalls Inn has provided hospitality to travellers since the early Victorian era. A more recent extension accommodates a purpose built function suite, in addition to the bar areas, conservatory, lounge and restaurant. Home-made dishes include chicken curry, beef or vegetable lasagne, and steak and ale pie. There is also a comprehensive selection of grills.

Open 11–11 **Bar Meals** L served all week 12–2.15 D served all week 6.30–9.30 Av main course £6.95 **Restaurant** L served all week 12–2.15 D served all week 6.30–9 Av 3 course à la carte £20 ⊕ Free House ◀ Courage Directors & Best, Hopback's GFB, John Smiths, Ringwood 49er. ♀ 9 **Facilities** Garden Dogs allowed Parking

WOOTTON RIVERS
MAP 05 SU16

Pick of the Pubs

Royal Oak ♀

SN8 4NQ ☎ 01672 810322 ▤ 01672 811168
e-mail: royaloak35@hotmail.com
dir: *3m S from Marlborough*

Just 100 yards from the Kennet and Avon Canal, this 16th-century thatched and timbered inn presents a picture of rural idyll. It's also very handy for exploring the 2600 ancient oaks of Savernake Forest, as well as visiting Stonehenge, Avebury, Bath and Marlborough. The interior is as charming as the setting, comprising low-beamed ceilings, exposed brickwork and toasty open fires. Menus tend to be flexible, with an array of starters, main courses and fish dishes. Typical examples include starters of fresh pan-fried scallops with bacon and mushrooms; or home-made chicken liver and brandy paté with berry compote, followed by green Thai chicken curry; Gloucester Old Spot pork with mustard mash; or rich beef and Burgundy casserole with a parsley dumpling. The Royal Oak has 20 years experience in hosting weddings, and holds a licence for civil ceremonies. Discos, parties, film screenings and meetings can also be accommodated.

Open 10.30–3.30 6–11 (Sun 6–10.30) **Bar Meals** L served Mon-Sat 12–2.30 D served Mon-Sat 6.30–9.30 (Sun 12–3, 6.30–9) **Restaurant** L served Mon-Sat 12–2.30 D served Mon-Sat 6.30–9.30 (Sun 12–3, 6.30–9) ⊕ Free House ◀ Wadworth 6X, guest ales inc local Ramsbury Bitter. ♀ 7 **Facilities** Garden Dogs allowed Parking **Rooms** available

WYLYE
MAP 04 SU03

The Bell Inn ♀

High St, Wylye BA12 0QP
☎ 01985 248338 ▤ 01985 248491
e-mail: thebellatwyle@hotmail.co.uk
dir: *From Salisbury take A36 N'bound to Warminster, then Wylye & A303 Honiton signed off A36. Follow signs for Wylye*

There's a wealth of old oak beams, log fires and an inglenook fireplace at this 14th-century coaching inn, situated in the pretty Wylye valley.

Owned by the Hidden Brewery (located just two miles away in Dinton), and so Hidden beers are available, but thankfully, not too well hidden. Lunch and dinner menus feature mainly local ingredients.

Open 11.30–2.30 6–11 (Sun 12–3, 6–10.30) **Bar Meals** L served all week 12–2.30 D served all week 6.30–9.30 (Mon, Thu & Sun 6.30–9) Av main course £9 **Restaurant** L served all week 12–2 D served all week 6–9.30 (Mon, Thu & Sun 12–2.30, 6.30–9) ⊕ Free House ◀ Hidden Pint, Hidden Quest, Hidden Oldsarum, Hidden Fantasy. ♀ 10 **Facilities** Garden Dogs allowed Parking

WORCESTERSHIRE

ABBERLEY
MAP 10 SO76

The Manor Arms at Abberley
★★★ INN ♀

WR6 6BN ☎ 01299 896507 ▤ 01299 896723
e-mail: themanorarms@btconnect.com
dir: *Signed from A443, Abberley B4202 towards Crofts Toft*

Set just across the lane from the Norman church of St Michael, the interior of this 300-year-old inn is enhanced by original oak beams and a log-burning fire. For food, expect a wide choice of grills and roasts, plus alternatives such as poached haddock with a poached egg and chive and butter sauce, or cheese and lentil terrine on a smooth tomato coulis. Good choice of real ales.

Open 12–3 6–11 Closed: Mon lunchtime winter **Bar Meals** L served all week 12–2.30 D served all week 6–9 (Sat-Sun 12–3.30, Sun 6–8) Av main course £9 **Restaurant** D served all week 6–9 ⊕ Enterprise Inns ◀ Timothy Taylor, Hookey Bitter, Hereford HPA, Flowers IPA. ♀ 11 **Facilities** Garden Dogs allowed Parking **Rooms** 10 (8 en suite)

BECKFORD
MAP 10 SO93

The Beckford ★★★★ INN NEW ♀

Cheltenham Rd GL20 7AN
☎ 01386 881532 ▤ 01386 882021
e-mail: norman@thebeckford.com
dir: *On A46 Evesham to Cheltenham road*

Parts of this traditional, family run coaching inn date back to the 18th century. But time has not stood still, and owners Sue and Norman Hughes have carried out extensive refurbishment. There's a pleasant bar area with a real fire, and an attractive formal dining room. Menu choices include red snapper with stir-fried vegetables; beef, Guinness and mushroom pie; and pork fillet with apple and Calvados sauce.

Open 10.30–11.30 Closed: 25 Dec eve & 26 Dec eve **Bar Meals** L served Mon-Sat 12–2.30 D served Mon-Sat 6.30–9.50 (Sun 12–8, May-Sep food all day) Av main course £10.95 **Restaurant** L served Mon-Sat 12–2.30 D served Mon-Sat 6.30–9.40 (Sun 12–8, Sat in summer 12–9.40) Av 3 course à la carte £24 ⊕ Free House ◀ London Pride, Greene King Abbot, Marstons Pedigree. ♀ 8 **Facilities** Children's licence Garden Dogs allowed Parking **Rooms** 10

BEWDLEY

MAP 10 SO77

Little Pack Horse ♥

31 High St DY12 2DH ☎ 01299 403762 📄 01299 403762
e-mail: enquires@littlepackhorse.co.uk

dir: *From Kidderminster follow ring road & signs for Safari Park.
Then follow signs for Bewdley over bridge, turn left, then right,
right at top of Lay Lane. Pub in 20mtrs*

The interior of this historic timber-framed inn is warmed by cosy log
fires and lit by candles at night. There are low beams, an elm bar, and
a small outside patio for alfresco summer dining. Fresh fish and an
extensive wine list are the house specialities. Expect trout with lemon
butter; swordfish with caper and herb crust; lobster thermidore; and an
impressive range of vegetarian and vegan dishes: aubergine, leek and
parsnip crumble, perhaps.

Open 12–3 6–11 (Thu-Sat 6–12) **Bar Meals** L served Mon-Fri 12–2.15
D served Mon-Fri 6–9.30 (Sat 12–9.30, Sun 12–8) **Restaurant** L served
Mon-Fri 12–3 D served Mon-Fri 6–9.30 (Sat 12–9.30, Sun 12–8) Av 3 course
à la carte £20 ⊕ Punch Taverns ◀ Theakstons Best Wye Valley HPA,
Dorothy Goodbodies Golden Ale, Black Sheep Bitter, Shepherd Neame
Spitfire. ♥ 21 **Facilities** Garden Dogs allowed

The Mug House Inn & Angry Chef
Restaurant ★ ★ ★ ★ INN ♥

12 Severnside North DY12 2EE
☎ 01299 402543 📄 01299 402543
e-mail: drew@mughousebewdley.co.uk

dir: *A456 from Kidderminster to Bewdley. Pub in town on river*

Nestled beside the River Severn in picturesque Bewdley, the inn's
riverside seating area is popular on warmer days. The unusual name
dates back to the 17th century, when 'mug house' was a popular term
for an alehouse. Nowadays, visitors will find an extensive lunchtime bar
menu, with à la carte options in the restaurant. Typical choices include
rack of lamb with ratatouille and mash; butternut squash crumble;
roast pollock and grilled lobster in garlic butter.

Open 12 -11 **Bar Meals** L served Mon-Sat 12–2.30 (Sun 12–5)
Restaurant L served Mon-Sat 12–2.30 D served Mon-Sat 6.30–9 (Sun lunch
12–5) ⊕ Punch Taverns ◀ Timothy Taylor Landlord, Wye Valley, Hereford
Pale Ale plus 2 guest ales. ♥ 10 **Facilities** Children's licence Garden Dogs
allowed **Rooms** 7

BRANSFORD

MAP 10 SO75

The Bear & Ragged Staff ♥

Station Rd WR6 5JH ☎ 01886 833399 📄 01886 833106
e-mail: mail@bear.uk.com

dir: *3m from Worcester or Malvern, clearly signed from A4103
or A449*

Built in 1861 as an estate rent office, this lovely old pub's reputation
is founded on good food. Wide choices are available: in the bar, beef
pasanda curry and beer-battered, deep-fried haddock, for example
and, in the restaurant, shallow-fried calf's liver in sage and black
pepper butter; trio of English lamb; grilled Cornish Dover sole; and red
onion and baked savoury cheesecake. Sunday roast could be loin of
Woodland pork, or prime Herefordshire beef.

Open 11.30–2.30 6–11 (Sat 6.30–11, Sun 7–10.30) Closed: 25 Dec eve, 1
Jan eve **Bar Meals** L served all week 12–2 D served Mon-Fri 6.30–9 (Sun
7–8.30) Av main course £10 **Restaurant** L served all week 12–2 D served
Mon-Sat 7–9 (Sun 7–8.30) Av 3 course à la carte £28 ♦ Free House ◀ St
Georges Best & Shepherd Neame Spitfire. ♥ 10 **Facilities** Garden Parking

BRETFORTON

MAP 10 SP04

Pick of the Pubs

The Fleece Inn ♥

See Pick of the Pubs on opposite page

CLENT

MAP 10 SO97

The Bell & Cross ♥

Holy Cross DY9 9QL ☎ 01562 730319 📄 01562 731733
dir: *Telephone for directions*

Several rooms make up this award-winning pub at the foot of the Clent
Hills, and there's a covered patio for pleasant al fresco dining. The
building dates from the early 19th century, and today Roger Narbett
serves modern British food in a traditional setting. Light bar lunches
include toasted paninis, pasta and daily specials, whilst the main menu
might feature seared salmon; Thai red pumpkin curry; or calves' liver
with onions and black pudding.

Open 12–3 6–11 Closed: 25 Dec **Bar Meals** L served Mon-Sat
12–2 D served Mon-Sat 6.30–9.15 (Sun 12–7) Av main course £6.95
Restaurant L served Mon-Sat 12–2 D served Mon-Sat 6.30–9.15 (Sun
12–7) ⊕ Enterprise Inns ◀ Pedigree, Mild, Bitter & guest ales. ♥ 14
Facilities Children's licence Garden Dogs allowed Parking

PICK OF THE PUBS

BRETFORTON-WORCESTERSHIRE

The Fleece Inn

The Fleece, or The Ark as it is known locally, has been part of Cotswold history for the six centuries since it was built as a longhouse. Amazingly, its last private owner, Lola Taplin, who died in front of the fire in the snug in 1977, was a direct descendant of the man who built it.

Before departing for premises celestial she bequeathed it to the National Trust, its first licensed property. In February 2004 it caught fire and a massive restoration programme followed, but it looks as good as ever. The pub is well known for its British Asparagus Festival Day, held in May every year. Fresh asparagus naturally features on the menu when seasonal, in starters like oven-baked camembert with asparagus and crusty baguette; other openers might be crown of mackerel mousse with baby spinach and walnut dressing. Main courses include grilled meats and fish; traditional faggots with mash, mushy peas and gravy; Mexican beef chilli and rice; Whitby scampi with chips; and baked field mushrooms

with spinach and cream cheese topping. To follow there's bread and butter pudding, apple crumble, and chocolate brandy cake with raspberry purée, and all home made too. A separate children's menu might feature tomato, pasta and cheesy bake with salad; and silly sausage, chips and beans. Various fillings in lunchtime sandwiches could include warm chicken, rocket and parmesan, or mature cheddar and pickle.

MAP 10 SP04
The Cross WR11 7JE
☎ 01386 831173
e-mail: nigel@thefleeceinn.co.uk
dir: *From Evesham follow signs for B4035 towards Chipping Campden. Through Badsey into Bretforton. Right at village hall, past church, pub in open parking area.*

Open 11–11 (Sun 12–10.30
Winter Mon-Fri 11–3, 6–11)
Bar Meals L served all week 12–2.30 D served Mon-Sat 6.30–9
Av main course £6.50
⊕ Free House ◀ Hook Norton Best Bitter, Pigs Ear, Goff's White Knight, Slaters Supreme & Purity Ubu. ♀ 12
Facilities Children's licence Garden Play Area

England

CLOWS TOP

MAP 10 SO77

The Colliers Arms ♀

Tenbury Rd DY14 9HA ☎ 01299 832242

e-mail: colliersarms@aol.com

dir: On A456 pub 4m from Bewdley & 7m from Kidderminster

This popular pub-restaurant is family owned and run. A new outdoor patio and drinkers' garden offers superb views. All the food is home cooked, and varies from light lunches such as beef and Guinness pie with mustard mash, to a full carte. Here you could start with a warming bowl of kale and bacon soup, follow with cider-marinated rack of pork with roasted apples and parsnips; and finish with steamed jam sponge with crème anglaise.

Open 11–3 6–11 (Sat all day, Sun 11–6) Closed: Sun eve Winter **Bar Meals** L served Mon-Sat 12–2 D served Mon-Sat 6.30–9 (Sun 11–3) Av main course £11 **Restaurant** L served Mon-Sat 12–2 D served all week 6.30–9 (Sun 11–3) Av 3 course à la carte £19.50 ⊕ Free House ◀ Hobsons Best, Town Crier, Guinness, guest ale. ♀ 14 **Facilities** Garden Dogs allowed Parking

DROITWICH

MAP 10 SO86

Pick of the Pubs

The Chequers ♀

Cutnall Green WR9 0PJ

☎ 01299 851292 📄 01299 851744

dir: Telephone for directions

A display of football memorabilia on the bar wall reveals that this is the home of Roger Narbett, chef to the England football team. The Chequers, which he runs with his wife Joanne remains a charming and traditional village pub, with an open fire, panelled bar and richly coloured furnishings. Next to the bar is the Garden Room with warmly painted walls, a plush sofa and hanging tankards. Lunchtime offers sandwiches, toasted paninis, pastas, light hot dishes and desserts. The carte menu includes starters of potted farmhouse duck confit; and oak-smoked salmon with quail eggs, and lemon and chive crème fraîche. Typical main courses are thyme-roasted chicken breast with colcannon cake, black pudding and wild mushrooms; corned beef hash with free-range eggs and capers; and beer-battered fish and chips. Finish, perhaps, with red berries with lemon curd, yoghurt and brandy snap.

Open 12–3 6–11 Closed: 25 Dec & 1 Jan **Bar Meals** L served Mon-Sat 12–2 D served Mon-Sat 6.30–9.15 (Sun 12–2.30, 7–9) **Restaurant** L served Mon-Sat 12–2 D served Mon-Sat 6.30–9.15 (Sun 12–2.30, 7–9) ⊕ Enterprise Inns ◀ Timothy Taylors, Enville Ale, Banks Bitter, Banks Mild. ♀ 11 **Facilities** Children's licence Garden Dogs allowed Parking

The Old Cock Inn ♀

Friar St WR9 8EQ ☎ 01905 774233

dir: M5 junct 5, A449 in Droitwich town centre opposite theatre

Three stained-glass windows, rescued from a church destroyed during the Civil War, are a feature of this charming pub, first licensed during the reign of Queen Anne. The stone carving above the front entrance is believed to portray Judge Jeffreys, who presided over local magistrates' court. A varied menu, including snacks and more

substantial dishes – beer battered fish and chips, vegetarian risotto, and local sausages and mash – is supplemented by the daily specials.

Open 11.30–3 5.30–11.30 **Bar Meals** L served Mon-Sat 11.30–2.30 D served all week 5.30–9.30 (Sun 12–3) Av main course £7.50 **Restaurant** L served Mon-Sat 11.30–2.30 D served all week 5.30–9.30 (Sun 12–3) Av 3 course à la carte £20 ⊕ Marstons ◀ 3 guest ales. ♀ 8 **Facilities** Children's licence Garden Dogs allowed

FLADBURY

MAP 10 SO94

Chequers Inn

Chequers Ln WR10 2PZ ☎ 01386 860276 📄 01386 861286

e-mail: fretwelljohn.fretwell4@btinternet.com

dir: Off A4538 between Evesham and Pershore

The Chequers is a 14th-century inn with plenty of beams and an open fire, tucked away in a pretty village in the shadow of the glorious Bredon Hills. Local produce from the Vale of Evesham provides the basis for home-cooked dishes offered from the monthly-changing menu, plus a choice of daily specials. There is also a traditional Sunday carvery. The pretty walled garden enjoys outstanding views, and the nearby River Avon is ideal for walking.

Open 11–3 5.30–11 **Bar Meals** L served all week 12–2 D served Tue-Sat 6–10 **Restaurant** L served all week 12–2 D served Mon-Sat 6–9 ⊕ Free House ◀ Hook Norton Best, Fuller's London Pride, Black Sheep, plus guests. **Facilities** Garden Parking

FLYFORD FLAVELL

MAP 10 SO95

The Boot Inn ★ ★ ★ ★ INN ♀

Radford Rd WR7 4BS ☎ 01386 462658 📄 01386 462547

e-mail: enquiries@thebootinn.com

web: www.thebootinn.com

dir: From Worcester take A422 towards Stratford. Turn right to village

Parts of this family-run coaching inn date back to the 13th century, as heavy beams and slanting doorways attest. The bar area has been completely refurbished to make it larger and more comfortable, with pool table and TV in a separate room. Good food ranging from bar snacks to specials from the blackboard is served by friendly staff. Outside are gardens front and back, with a heated patio and sheltered smoking area. Five charming bedrooms in the converted coach house complete the picture.

Open 12–12 **Bar Meals** L served Mon-Sat 12–2 D served Mon-Sat 6.30–9.45 (Sun 12–3, 7–9) **Restaurant** L served Mon-Sat 12–2 D served Mon-Fri 6.30–9.45 (Sat 6–10, Sun 12–3, 7–9) ⊕ Punch Taverns ◀ Old Speckled Hen, Greene King IPA, London Pride, Adnams & John Smith's. ♀ 8 **Facilities** Garden Dogs allowed Parking **Rooms** 5

PICK OF THE PUBS

KEMPSEY-WORCESTERSHIRE

Walter de Cantelupe Inn

With its whitewashed walls bedecked with flowers, this authentic and charming little inn is a magnet for passing motorists and knowing locals alike. Outside, a walled and paved garden has been fragrantly planted with clematis, roses and honeysuckle, and its south-facing position is a sun-trap on hot days. A gas heater has extended its use into the cooler months.

The inn is named after the mid-13th-century Bishop of Worcester, Walter de Cantelupe, who was strongly against his parishioners' habit of brewing and selling of ales as a way to raise church funds. The pub was formed out of a row of cottages three centuries later, and its naming is presumably ironic! The food is written up each day on a blackboard, with choices to please both traditionalists and those seeking hearty, modern cooking. You could begin with celery and almond soup served with crusty granary bread; or perhaps deep-fried whitebait with a home-made tartar sauce. Main courses have a similar scope; there might be beef and local ale pie; plate-sized gammon steak with a fried free range egg; thick grilled

pork chop with a cider, onion and cream sauce; seared tuna steak with chilli and lime butter; and a glazed chicory and butternut squash pancake. You could finish with hot marmalade bread and butter pudding; or local farmhouse ice creams. Look out for food-themed events such as the Balti Bonanza or the Outdoor Paella Fiesta. Other events include malt whiskey tastings and cookery demonstrations by Martin Lloyd-Morris who trained as a chef in France and worked at the London Hilton before bringing his talents to the Walter de Cantalupe. The pub's en suite accommodation is popular with visitors to historic Worcester, the Malvern Hills and Severn Vale.

★★★ INN
MAP 10 SO84
Main Rd WR5 3NA
☎ 01905 820572
dir: *4m S of Worcester city centre on A38. Pub in village centre*

Open 12–2 6–11 (Sun 12–3, 7–10.30 summer 11.30–2.30)
Closed: 25–26 Dec, 1 Jan
Bar Meals L served Tue-Sat 12–2 D served Tue-Thu 6.30–9 Sun 12–2.30, Fri-Sat 6.30–10 Av main course £8
Restaurant L served Tue-Sun 12–2 D served Tue-Thu 7–9 Fri-Sat 7–10 Av 3 course à la carte £17
⊕ Free House ◀ Timothy Taylor Landlord, Cannon Royal, Kings Shilling, Hobsons Best Bitter.
Facilities Garden Dogs allowed Parking
Rooms 3

KEMPSEY   **MAP 10 SO84**

Pick of the Pubs

Walter de Cantelupe Inn ★★★ INN

See Pick of the Pubs on page 629

KINGTON   **MAP 10 SO95**

Pick of the Pubs

The Red Hart ♥

See Pick of the Pubs on opposite page

KNIGHTWICK   **MAP 10 SO75**

Pick of the Pubs

The Talbot ♥

WR6 5PH ☎ 01886 821235 🖹 01886 821060

e-mail: admin@the-talbot.co.uk

dir: *A44 (Leominster road) through Worcester, 8m W turn right onto B4197 (at River Teme bridge)*

Over the 25 years that the Clift family have owned The Talbot, a late 14th-century coaching inn, they have developed their own style and are firmly rooted in the traditions and produce of the Teme Valley. Nearly everything is made in house, including bread, preserves, black pudding, paté, raised pies and so on. The inn has a large kitchen garden run on organic principles, which produces a wide range of salads, herbs and, of course, vegetables. Other items – sausages, hams, bacon and cheeses, are sourced from local suppliers. The Talbot is also the home of The Teme Valley Brewery, started in 1997, using hops grown in the parish. The cask conditioned ales, all on hand pump in the bar, are called This, That, T'Other and Wot. Wot is a seasonal brew, so there is Spring Wot, Wassail Wot, Wotever Next etc. Hobson's best bitter is also served.

Open 11–11 (Sun 12–10.30) Closed: 25 Dec pm **Bar Meals** L served all week 12–2 D served Mon-Sat 6.30–9.30 (Sun 7–9) Av main course £13 **Restaurant** L served all week 12–2 D served Mon-Sat 6.30–9.30 (Sun 7–9) Av 3 course à la carte £30 Av 3 course fixed price £30 ⊕ Free House ◀ Teme Valley This, That , T'Other & Wot, Hobsons Best Bitter Choice. ♥ 9 **Facilities** Garden Dogs allowed Parking **Rooms** available

MALVERN   **MAP 10 SO74**

The Anchor Inn ♥

Drake St, Welland WR13 6LN ☎ 01684 592317

e-mail: theanchor13@hotmail.com

dir: *M50 follow signs to Upton upon Severn. Turn left onto A4104 through town 2.5m. Pub on right*

The Anchor is an attractive pub with views of the Malvern Hills from its patio. There's a garden where children can play, and a welcoming fire in the dining room. Light bites and main meals are marked up on the chalkboard, with dishes such as pork loin stuffed with apple in stilton sauce, steak and kidney pie, and shank of lamb simmered in mint and rosemary gravy. Themed menus and quiz nights feature regularly.

Open 12–3 6.45–11 Closed: Sun eve **Bar Meals** L served all week 12–2.50 D served Mon-Sat Av main course £10.99 **Restaurant** L served all week 12–2 D served all week 7–9 ⊕ Free House ◀ Black Sheep, Woods, Hook Norton, Greene King. ♥ 20 **Facilities** Garden Dogs allowed Parking

The Red Lion

4 St Ann's Rd WR14 4RG ☎ 01684 564787

e-mail: johnholmes25@btintenet.com

dir: *In town centre*

An authentic Thai restaurant complete with chefs and waitresses from the Land of Smiles has been added to this thriving pub. The existing pub menu continues to be available, offering a wide choice of snacks, starters and main courses, all freshly cooked to order. Seafood is a particular speciality: try pan-fried king prawns, or a hearty paella. One of the main walking routes in the Malvern Hills runs right by, so expect plenty of ramblers.

Open 12–3 5.30–11 (Sat-Sun 12–11) **Bar Meals** L served Mon-Fri 12–2.45 D served Mon-Fri 6–9.30 (Sat-Sun all day) **Restaurant** L served Mon-Fri 12–2.45 D served Mon-Fri 6–9.30 (All day Sat-Sun) ⊕ Marstons ◀ Marstons Bitter, 4 guest ales. **Facilities** Children's licence Garden

PICK OF THE PUBS

The Red Hart

From a derelict shell in 2001, this beautiful, easy-going country pub and restaurant has been completely restored by a team of local craftsmen. The interior has been stripped to reveal its original looks, while some stunning contemporary touches have been added.

The aim is to make everyone's dining experience, whether in bar or restaurant, utterly memorable. The main bar has been furnished in wine bar style, while the secondary bar area boasts deep leather sofas surrounding a log burner. The restaurant is also smart and full of atmosphere. You could go for local game casserole with suet dumplings; beer-battered fish and chips with minted mushy peas; or rustic bean casserole with red onions, peppers and tomato. From the short lunch menu come specials like bangers and mash; black pudding and bacon salad; and smoked salmon and prawn risotto, while the evening might yield pan-seared scallops followed by crispy belly of pork, or pan-fried duck breast. Puddings could range from the sticky toffee classic to spiced winter fruit bread and butter pudding. Heated log burners are dotted strategically around the outside decking.

🍷
MAP 10 SO95
Stratford Rd WR7 4DD
☎ 01386 792559
📠 01386 793748
e-mail: enquiries@redhart.co.uk
dir: *On A422, Stratford Rd, Nr Flyford Flavell 4m from Worcester, junct 6 of M5, 6m from Redruth.*

Open 12–3 5–11 (Fri-Sat 12–12, Sun 12–11)
Bar Meals L served all week 12–2.30 D served all week 6–10 (Sat-Sun 12–10)
Restaurant L served all week 12–2.30 D served all week 6–10 (Sun 12–10) Av 3 course à la carte £25
⊕ Marstons 🍺 Banks, Marstons Pedigree. 🍷 10
Facilities Children's licence Garden Dogs allowed Parking

MARTLEY   **MAP 10 SO76**

Admiral Rodney Inn ★★★★ INN

Berrow Green WR6 6PL

☎ 01886 821375 📄 01886 822048

e-mail: rodney@admiral.fslife.co.uk

dir: *M5 junct 7, A44 signed Leominster. Approx 7m at Knightwick right onto B4197. Inn 2m on left at Berrow Green*

An early 17th-century farmhouse-cum-alehouse standing in the heart of the countryside on the Worcester Way footpath. The stylishly traditional interior includes a split-level restaurant housed in an old barn. Fish – freshly delivered from Cornwall – features strongly. In the bar, expect home-made pies, fish and chips, and perhaps Malaysian lamb curry.

Open 12–3 5–11 (Mon 5–11, Sat-Sun all day) **Bar Meals** L served Tue-Sat 12–2 D served Sun-Fri 6.30–9 (Sun 12–4, Sat 6.30–9.30) **Restaurant** L served Sun 12–2.30 D served Sun-Fri 7–9 (Sat 7–9.30) ⊕ Free House ◀ Wye Valley Bitter, local guest ales eg. Black Pear, Malvern Hills Brewery, Muzzle Loader & Cannon Royal. **Facilities** Children's licence Garden Dogs allowed Parking

The Crown Inn NEW

Berrow Green Rd WR6 6PA ☎ 01886 888840

dir: *7m W of Worcester on B4204*

A Victorian village pub with a large extension formed from redundant outbuildings, which now houses the dining area. In one bar is an open fire, Sky TV, pool table and jukebox, while the other has dining tables and french windows to the garden. The pub is on the Worcester Way, so many lunchers tend to be walkers. Locally sourced, freshly cooked food includes seafood bake; 10oz Kobe beefburger; chicken supreme in parma ham; and penne pasta.

Open 12–11 **Bar Meals** L served Mon-Sat 12–2 D served all week 6–9 (Sun 12–3) Av main course £10 **Restaurant** L served Mon-Sat 12–2 D served all week 6–9 (Sun 12–3) Av 3 course à la carte £19 Av 2 course fixed price £7.95 ⊕ Marstons ◀ Banks Bitter, Marston's Burton, Jennings Cocker Hoop. **Facilities** Children's licence Garden Dogs allowed Parking Play Area

OMBERSLEY   **MAP 10 SO86**

Pick of the Pubs

Crown & Sandys Arms ♀

Main Rd WR9 0EW

☎ 01905 620252 📄 01905 620769

e-mail: enquiries@crownandsandys.co.uk

dir: *3m from Droitwich, off A449*

A classy establishment run by Richard Everton who also owns the village deli and wine shop, so you can expect an ample range of wines by the glass and a good selection of real ales. The décor is bang up-to-date, yet the original beams and fireplaces seem to blend effortlessly with the trendy furnishings. Regular 'wine dinners' and themed evenings complement the modern menus, which burst with the latest flavours. Freshly-made sandwiches, paninis and baguettes are supplemented on weekdays by home-made pizzas prepared to order, with different topping requests usually accommodated. Choose from dishes such as beef carpaccio marinated with wasabi and herbs, sushi ginger, noodle and scallion salad; and pan-fried breast of chicken wrapped in Parma ham, porcini mushroom and blue cheese risotto. If seafood is your preference, exotic options (barramundi, mahi-mahi) may vie with the likes of red mullet, gurnard and mackerel in daily changing specials.

Open 11–3 5–11 **Bar Meals** L served Mon-Sat 12–2.30 D served Mon-Sat 6–10 (Sun 12–9) Av main course £14 **Restaurant** L served Mon-Sat 12–2.30 D served Mon-Sat 6–10 (Sun 12–9) Av 3 course à la carte £25 ⊕ Free House ◀ Sadlers Ale, Marstons, Woods Shropshire Lad, Burtons Bitter. ♀ 16 **Facilities** Garden Parking

POWICK   **MAP 10 SO85**

The Halfway House Inn

Bastonford WR2 4SL

☎ 01905 831098 📄 01905 831704

dir: *From A15 junct 7 take A4440 then A449*

Situated on the A449 between Worcester and Malvern, this delightful pub is just a few minutes' drive from the picturesque spa town of Malvern, a popular centre for exploring the Malvern Hills. The menu choice ranges from Herefordshire fillet steak or roasted Gressingham duck breast to baked fillet of Scottish salmon and spinach, ricotta and beef tomato lasagne.

Open 12–3 6–11 Closed: Mon lunch (ex BHs) **Bar Meals** L served all week 12–2 D served all week 6–9 **Restaurant** L served all week 12–2 D served all week 6–9 ⊕ Free House ◀ Abbot Ale, St Georges Bitter, Fuller's London Pride, Timothy Taylor. **Facilities** Garden Parking Play Area

PICK OF THE PUBS

TENBURY WELLS-WORCESTERSHIRE

The Fountain Hotel

A fine example of the black and white timbered inns that are common in these parts, the Fountain comes complete with all the hoped-for welcoming country atmosphere. In 1855 this former farmhouse began selling beer and cider to Welsh drovers herding their sheep to English markets; at that time it was known as the Hippodrome, after the horse-racing that used to take place on the common outside.

The hotel has been providing rest and sustenance for travellers ever since, as its motto suggests: 'Weary and thin they stagger in; happy and stout they waddle out'. The Fountain's oldest resident is its mischievous but friendly ghost, a landlord who died in 1958 while saving his dogs from a fire. Now run by Russell Allen, a well-travelled big-game fisherman, and his chef wife Michaela, the inn has been winning plaudits for its quality food and real ales. The theme in the restaurant is nautical, and its carefully prepared fish dishes are a real strength: they may include line-caught wild salmon from the river Tay, or local rainbow trout; among more exotic species you may find roast blue-fin tuna; barracuda cooked in home-made

organic herb butter; red snapper sushi; and porbeagle shark. To complete the theme, book a table near the 1,000–gallon aquarium for a grandstand view of many unusual fish. Non-aquatic starters could include melon and sorbet, or garlic bruschetta. For a main course, try Berrington chicken in leek and stilton sauce; or oven-roasted duck with honey, ginger and soy sauce. Outside is a large secluded garden which includes the plot where organic herbs and vegetables are grown for the kitchen, a children's play area with a trampoline, and a heated patio. The hotel is open all day, and also serves food throughout the day.

🍷
MAP 10 SO56
Oldwood, St Michaels WR15 8TB
☎ 01584 810701
🖷 01584 819030
e-mail:
enquiries@fountain-hotel.co.uk
dir: *1m from Tenbury Wells on A4112 (Leominster road)*

Open 9–11
Bar Meals L served all week 12–9 D served all week 12–9
Restaurant L served all week 12–10 D served all week 12–10
⊕ Free House ◀ Fountain Ale, Old Speckled Hen, Greene King IPA, Wye Valley Bitter. 🍷 20
Facilities Children's licence Garden Parking Play Area
Rooms available

633

England

STONEHALL   MAP 10 SO84

The Fruiterer's Arms

Stonehall Common WR5 3QG
☎ 01905 820462 ▤ 01905 820501
e-mail: thefruiterersarms@btopenworld.com
dir: *2m from M5 junct 7. Stonehall Common 1.5m from St Peters Garden Centre Norton*

Pub on Stonehall Common, once frequented by the area's fruit pickers. Four guest ales are rotated weekly, and there's a main menu, specials menu and Sunday menu offered in the bar, restaurant, garden pavilion and garden. Favourite dishes include Swiss chicken with Alpine cheese, fillet of lamb with Madeira and rosemary, and the fresh fish of the day. The garden is large and has a purpose-built play area for children.

Open 12–3 6–11 (Sat-Sun all day Summer) **Bar Meals** L served all week 12–2 D served all week 6–9.15 Av main course £6.50 **Restaurant** L served all week 12–2.30 D served all week 6–9.15 (Sun all day) Av 3 course à la carte £28 ◀ Bombardier, St Austell Tribute, guest ales. **Facilities** Children's licence Garden Parking Play Area

TENBURY WELLS   MAP 10 SO56

Pick of the Pubs

The Fountain Hotel ♥

See Pick of the Pubs on page 633

Pick of the Pubs

The Peacock Inn

WR15 8LL ☎ 01584 810506 ▤ 01584 811236
e-mail: thepeacockinn001@aol.com
dir: *Exit M5 junct 3, follow A456 for 40m then A443 to Tenbury Wells, 0.75m on right*

A 14th-century coaching inn overlooking the River Teme, with a sympathetic extension and pleasant patio eating area. The relaxing bars and oak-panelled restaurant are enhanced by oak beams, dried hops and open log fires, while upstairs the ghost of Mrs Brown, a former landlady, does its best to enliven the place. Local market produce features on the menus, specialities being fresh fish and game. Starters might include millefeuilles of black pudding and apple with wholegrain mustard dressing. For a main course try green Thai curry of chicken and tiger prawns served with jasmine rice, or a more traditional option like home-made steak pie with herb dumplings. Desserts include classics like sticky toffee pudding, alongside innovative options like pineapple mousse served with passion fruits.

Open 11.30–3.30 5.30–12 **Bar Meals** L served all week 12–2 D served all week 6.30–9 Av main course £10.50 **Restaurant** L served all week 12–2 D served all week 6.30–9 Av 3 course à la carte £17.50 ⊕ Free House ◀ Hobsons Best Bitter, Spitfire, Tetley Cask. **Facilities** Children's licence Garden Dogs allowed Parking

UPTON SNODSBURY   MAP 10 SO95

Bants ★★★★ INN

Worcester Rd WR7 4NN ☎ 01905 381282 ▤ 01905 381173
e-mail: info@bants.co.uk
dir: *Exit M5 junct 6 and follow signs for Evesham. At 2nd rdbt turn left onto A422 towards Stratford. Bants 2m on left*

A few years ago Sue and Steve Bant changed the pub's name (from the Coventry Arms) to celebrate twenty years of ownership. It's a 16th-century free house serving traditional ales, with real fires in winter warming an eclectic mix of ancient beams and modern furnishings. Food served in three lounge bars and the dedicated conservatory restaurant has a high comfort factor: you may find faggots with garlic mash, or corned beef hash on bubble and squeak with fried egg.

Open 12–3 5.30–11.30 (Opening times can vary) **Bar Meals** L served all week 12–2 D served all week 6–9.30 Av main course £6.95 **Restaurant** L served all week 12–2 D served all week 6–9.30 Av 3 course à la carte £25 ◀ Guinness, London Pride, Cats Whiskas & Pettermans. **Facilities** Garden Parking **Rooms** 7

YORKSHIRE, EAST RIDING OF

BEVERLEY   MAP 17 TA03

White Horse Inn

22 Hengate HU17 8BN ☎ 01482 861973 ▤ 01482 861973
e-mail: anna@nellies.co.uk
dir: *A1079 from York to Beverley*

Gas lighting, open fires, old cartoons and high-backed settles add to the charm of this classic 16th-century local. John Wesley preached in the back yard in the mid-18th century, and the pub's atmospheric little rooms arranged around the central bar are probably much as they were back then. Traditional bar food might include pasta dishes, fresh jumbo haddock, bangers and mash, and steak and ale pie. Toasted and plain sandwiches and daily specials also feature.

Open 11–11 (Sun 12–10.30) **Bar Meals** L served Mon-Sat 11–2.45 ⊞ Samuel Smith ◀ Samuel Smith Old Brewery Bitter & Sovereign Bitter. **Facilities** Garden Parking Play Area **Notes** ⊛

DRIFFIELD   MAP 17 TA05

Best Western The Bell ★★★ HL

46 Market Place YO25 6AN
☎ 01377 256661 ▤ 01377 253228
e-mail: bell@bestwestern.co.uk
dir: *Enter town from A164, turn right at lights. Car park 50yds on left behind black railings*

A delightful 18th-century coaching inn furnished with antiques, with an oak-panelled bar serving a good range of cask beers and 300 whiskies. Food ranges through broiled salmon fillet cooked with red peppers, lemon, garlic and capers; roasted whole pork fillet coated with honey and Dijon mustard; and oven roasted breast of English duckling with spicy plum sauce. Fresh coffee is served in the mornings 9.30–11.30 with scones, jam and cream.

Open 10–11 (Sun 11–10.30) Closed: 25 Dec, 1 Jan **Bar Meals** L served Mon-Sat 12–1.30 D served Mon-Sat 5–8.30 (Sun 6.30–8.30) Av main course £6.50 **Restaurant** L served Mon-Sat 12–1.30 D served all week 6.30–8.30 ⊕ Free House ◀ World Top, Falling Stones, Mars Magic, Hambleton Stallion & Stud. **Facilities** Parking **Rooms** 16

Castle Howard, North Yorkshire

England

FLAMBOROUGH   MAP 17 TA27

The Seabirds Inn ☻

Tower St YO15 1PD ☎ 01262 850242 ▤ 01262 851874

dir: *On B1255 E of Bridlington, 6m from train station*

Head westwards from famous Flamborough Head and you'll swiftly arrive at this 200-year-old village pub. Good eating is the emphasis here, with a daily changing specials board that includes seasonal fresh fish: typical examples are sea bass served whole with garlic butter prawns; halibut supreme in a prawn and champagne sauce; and home-made luxury fish pie with monkfish, scallops and salmon. Meat options include steaks, loin of pork, and chicken breast stuffed with apricot stilton.

Open 12–3 6.30–11 (Sun 7–10.30) Closed: Mon Winter
Bar Meals L served all week 12–2 D served Mon-Fri 6.30–9 (Sat 6.30–9.30, Sun 7–9) **Restaurant** L served all week 12–2 D served Mon-Fri 6.30–9 (Sat 6.30–9.30, Sun 7–9) ⊕ Free House ◀ John Smith's, Interbrew Boddingtons Bitter, Tetleys Creamflow. ☻ 9 **Facilities** Garden Dogs allowed Parking

HOLME UPON SPALDING MOOR   MAP 17 SE83

Ye Olde Red Lion Hotel ☻

Old Rd YO43 4AD ☎ 01430 860220 ▤ 01430 861471

dir: *Off A1079 (York to Hull road). At Market Weighton take A614. Right at painted rdbt in village centre,100yds, right then 1st left*

A historic 17th-century coaching inn that once provided hospitality for weary travellers who were helped across the marshes by monks. It's still a great refuge, with a friendly atmosphere, oak beams and a cosy fire. The inspiring menu could include oven-baked duck breast with star anise sauce, corn fed chicken coq-au-vin or pan-seared sea bass with wilted greens and vierge sauce.

Open 11.30–2.30 5.30–11 (Sun 12–11) **Bar Meals** L served Mon-Sat 12–2 D served Mon-Sat 5.30–9 (Sun 12–9) Av main course £8.45
Restaurant L served Mon-Sat 12–2 D served Mon-Sat 5.30–9 (Sun 12–9) ⊕ Free House ◀ John Smiths, Black Sheep, Guinness. ☻ 9
Facilities Garden Parking

HUGGATE   MAP 19 SE85

The Wolds Inn ★★★ INN ☻

YO42 1YH ☎ 01377 288217

e-mail: huggate@woldsinn.freeserve.co.uk

dir: *S off A166 between York & Driffield*

Probably the highest inn on the Yorkshire Wolds, 16th century in origin, with tiled roofs and white-painted chimneys, and a wood-panelled interior with open fires and gleaming brassware. Its elevation explains why the Wolds Topper, 'the mixed grill to remember', is so named; other main courses include steaks with a variety of sauces, rack of lamb, loin of pork, roast duckling, and Scottish salmon fillet, while vegetarians may consult their own blackboard.

Open 12–2 6.30–11 (Sun 6.30–10.30, May-Sep Sun 6–10.30) Closed: Mon (ex BHs) **Bar Meals** L served Tue-Thu, Sat & Sun 12–2 D served Tue-Sun 6.30–9 (May-Sep 6–9) Av main course £8 **Restaurant** L served Tue-Thu, Sat-Sun 12–2 D served Tue-Sat 6.30–9 (May-Sep Sun 6–9) Av 3 course à la carte £19 ⊕ Free House ◀ Tetley Bitter & Timothy Taylor Landlord. ☻ 10
Facilities Garden Parking **Rooms** 3

KILHAM   MAP 17 TA06

The Old Star Inn ☻

Church St YO25 4RG ☎ 01262 420619

dir: *Between Driffield & Bridlington on A164. (6m from Driffield; 9m from Bridlington)*

Situated in the historic village of Kilham, with easy access to Bridlington, Scarborough and the Yorkshire Wolds, this quaint pub offers home-cooked food, real ale and a warm welcome. Food is sourced from local suppliers, with particular attention to reducing the travelling time of ingredients. Special diets are catered for, and children have half price portions for half price. John Smiths is the resident beer, the three other pumps operating a rotation of guest ales.

Open 12–2.30 5–11 (Mon 6–11, Fri 4–11, Sat 5.30–11, Sun all day) **Bar Meals** L served Wed-Sun 12–2.30 D served Tue-Sun 5–9.30 (Mon 6–8, Winter L & D Fri-Sun) **Restaurant** L served Sun 12–5 D served Tue-Sun 6–9.30 ⊕ Free House ◀ John Smiths Cask, Deuchars, Theakstons, Black Sheep. ☻ 7 **Facilities** Garden Dogs allowed Parking

PICK OF THE PUBS

SOUTH DALTON-YORKSHIRE, EAST RIDING OF

The Pipe & Glass Inn

Dating from the 15th century, this much-praised inn stands on the site of the original gatehouse to Dalton Hall. It was here that visitors to the 'great house' were offered hospitality and lodgings during their stay. The old gatehouse was eventually replaced by the present building, part of which is 17th century.

James and Kate Mackenzie took over in 2006, and undertook a full refurbishment, making sure they kept a country pub feel in the bar, while transforming the restaurant into a warm, more contemporary area. A large conservatory looking out over the garden houses a magnificent long table seating twenty-four; there is also plenty of room for dining outside. Chef-proprietor James is committed to sourcing as much local and seasonal produce as possible for his regularly changing menus. From a sample come starters of cold pressed terrine of locally shot hare, salt beef hash with fried egg, devilled sauce, ox tongue and capers; and potted Hornsea crab with spiced butter, crab sticks, sorrel and blood orange. Mains include Harpham-raised lamb with mutton and kidney Turbigo and champ potato; baked leek tart with Lincolnshire Poacher rarebit and scallion and chive salad; and grilled Filey Bay sea bass with wilted samphire, crab and lovage beignet. In the unlikely event that you'd like something not on the menu, James and his chefs will do their best to make it for you. Puddings are equally alluring, with rhubarb trifle and rum-soaked parkin crumbs; and lemon posset with mulled autumn fruits and East Yorkshire sugar cakes. The wine list is sourced entirely from small producers, a wide selection of regularly changing hand-pulled guest ales, and Old Rosie cider.

◉ ♛
MAP 17 SE94
West End HU17 7PN
☎ 01430 810246
e-mail:
email@pipeandglass.co.uk
dir: *Just off B1248 Beverley to Malton road. 7m from Beverley*

Open 12–3 6.30–11 (Sun 12–10.30) Closed: 2wks Jan & Mon
Bar Meals L served Tue-Sat 12–2 D served Tue-Sat 6.30–9.30 (Sun 12–4) Av main course £12.95
Restaurant L served Tue-Sat 12–2 D served Tue-Sat 6.30–9.30 (Sun 12–4) Av 3 course à la carte £28
⊕ Free House ◖ Wold Top, Copper Dragon, Black Sheep, Cropton. ♛ 10
Facilities Garden Parking

KINGSTON UPON HULL **MAP 17 TA02**

The Minerva Hotel ₽

Nelson St, Victoria Pier HU1 1XE

☎ 01482 326909 📄 01482 617434

dir: *M62 onto A63, then Castle St, right at fruit market sign into Queens St. At top of Queens St on right of pier*

The Minerva boasts old-fashioned rooms and cosy snugs at its riverside location with its ferry port, marina, and fishing fleet. It has a reputation for hospitality and delicious home-cooked food, and a good range of guest ales. Part of the Tattershall Castle Group.

Open 11–11 (Sun 12–10.30) **Bar Meals** L served all week 12–9.45 D served all week Sun 12–8.45 Av main course £5.95 **Restaurant** L served all week 12–9.45 D served all week Sun 12–8.45 ◀ Tetley Bitter, usually 4 guest beers. ₽ 7 **Facilities** Children's licence

---

LOW CATTON **MAP 17 SE75**

The Gold Cup Inn ₽

YO41 1EA ☎ 01759 371354 📄 01759 373833

dir: *1m S of A166 or 1m N of A1079, E of York*

Solid tables and pews – reputedly made from a single oak tree – feature in the restaurant of this 300-year-old, family-run free house. There's a large beer garden, and the adjoining paddock drops down to the River Derwent. On the menu expect to find braised beef in red wine gravy on mashed potato; grilled gammon with port and mushroom sauce; baked cod loins with herb crust; and deep-fried brie with cranberry and orange dip.

Open 12–2.30 6–11.30 (Sat-Sun all day) Closed: Mon lunch **Bar Meals** L served Tue-Sun 12–2 D served Mon-Fri 6–9 (Sat-Sun 12–9) Av main course £8.50 **Restaurant** D served Mon-Sat 6.30–9.30 (Sun 12–5.30) Av 3 course à la carte £19 Av 2 course fixed price £12 ⊕ Free House ◀ John Smiths, Black Sheep. ₽ 15 **Facilities** Garden Dogs allowed Parking Play Area

---

LUND **MAP 17 SE94**

The Wellington Inn ₽

19 The Green YO25 9TE ☎ 01377 217294 📄 01377 217192

dir: *On B1248 NE of Beverley*

Nicely situated opposite the picture-postcard village green, the Wellington Inn is popular with locals and visitors alike, whether for a pint of real ale, a glass of house wine, or a plate of decent food. You can choose to eat from the bar menu or à la carte, and there's an extensive wine list. Expect king scallops with bacon and garlic risotto; or perhaps beef, mushroom and red onion suet pudding.

Open 12–3 6.30–11 **Bar Meals** L served Tue-Sun 12–2 D served Tue-Sat 6.30–9.30 Av main course £12.95 **Restaurant** D served Tue-Sat 7–9.30 Av 3 course à la carte £26 ⊕ Free House ◀ Timothy Taylor Landlord, Black Sheep Best, John Smiths, regular guest. ₽ 8 **Facilities** Garden Parking

---

SOUTH CAVE **MAP 17 SE93**

The Fox and Coney Inn ₽

52 Market Place HU15 2AT

☎ 01430 424336 📄 01430 421552

e-mail: foxandconey@mail.com

dir: *4m E of M62 on A63. 4m N of Brough mainline railway*

Right in the heart of South Cave, this family run pub dates from 1739 and is probably the oldest building in the village. The inn, which is handy for walkers on the nearby Wolds Way, was known simply as The Fox until William Goodlad added the Coney (rabbit) in 1788. Jacket potatoes, salads and baguettes supplement varied hot dishes like steak in ale pie, chicken curry, seafood platter and mushroom stroganoff.

Open 11.30 -11 **Bar Meals** L served Mon-Sat 12–2.30 D served Mon-Sat 5–9 (Sun 12–8) Av main course £7.50 **Restaurant** L served Mon-Sat 12–2.30 D served Mon-Sat 5–9 (Sun 12–8) Av 3 course à la carte £19 ⊕ Enterprise Inns ◀ Timothy Taylor Landlord, John Smiths & Theakston Cool Cask, Deuchars IPA, guest ales. ₽ 10 **Facilities** Garden Parking

---

SOUTH DALTON **MAP 17 SE94**

Pick of the Pubs

The Pipe & Glass Inn ⊛ ₽

See Pick of the Pubs on page 637

SUTTON UPON DERWENT **MAP 17 SE74**

St Vincent Arms ₽

Main St YO41 4BN ☎ 01904 608349

e-mail: enquiries@stvincentarms.co.uk

dir: *From A64 follow signs for A1079. Turn right, follow signs for Elvington on B1228. Through Elvington to Sutton upon Derwent*

The name comes from John Jervis, created the first Earl of St Vincent in the 18th century, and mentor to Admiral Lord Nelson. This is a warm family-run pub with an old-fashioned welcoming atmosphere, minus music or gaming machines but plus great food and beer. Food options include sandwiches, ciabatta, salads and full meals such as curried crab mayonnaise followed by chicken and ginger stir fry.

Open 11.30–3 6–11 **Bar Meals** L served all week 12–2 D served all week 7–9.30 **Restaurant** L served all week 12–2 D served all week 7–9.30 ◀ Timothy Taylor Landlord, Fuller's ESB, Yorkshire Terrier, Wells Bombardier. ₽ 8 **Facilities** Garden Parking

YORKSHIRE, NORTH

AKEBAR

MAP 19 SE19

The Friar's Head ♥

Akebar Park DL8 5LY

☎ 01677 450201 & 450591 📠 01677 450046

e-mail: info@akebarpark.com

web: www.akebarpark.com/pub.html

dir: From A1 at Leeming Bar onto A684, 7m towards Leyburn. Entrance at Akebar Park

The Friar's Head is a traditional stone-built Yorkshire Dales hostelry with a terrace overlooking lower Wensleydale. The wow factor comes from the large south-facing conservatory dining room, called The Cloister, with its stone flags, lush planting and fruiting vines. At night, by candlelight, the effect is quite magical. The blackboard menu offers daily changing fish, meat and vegetarian dishes, and from the carte comes stuffed breast of local pheasant, steaks, and Thai-style beef stir fry.

Open 10–2.30 6–11.30 (Sun 7–10.30) **Bar Meals** L served all week 12–2 D served Mon-Sat 6–9.30 (Sun 7–9.30) Av main course £10 **Restaurant** L served all week 12–2 D served Mon-Fri 6–9.30 (Sat 6–10, Sun 7–9.30) Av 3 course à la carte £24 ⊕ Free House ◖ John Smiths's & Theakston Best Bitter, Black Sheep Best. ♥ 14 **Facilities** Garden Parking

See advert on this page

APPLETON-LE-MOORS

MAP 19 SE78

The Moors Inn

YO62 6TF ☎ 01751 417435

e-mail: enquiries@moorsinn.co.uk

dir: On A170 between Pickering & Kirbymoorside

Whether you're interested in walking or sightseeing by car, this family-run inn is a good choice for its location and good home-cooked food. Set in a small moors village with lovely scenery in every direction, in summer you can sit in the large garden and enjoy the splendid views. Dishes include pheasant casserole and fish pie, and in addition to hand-pumped Black Bull and Black Sheep, there is a selection of 50 malt whiskies.

Open 7–11 (Sun 12–2 7–11) Closed: Mon **Bar Meals** L served Sun 12–2 D served Tue-Sun 7–9 Av main course £10 **Restaurant** L served Sun 12–2 D served Tue-Sun 7–9 ⊕ Free House ◖ Black Sheep, Black Bull. **Facilities** Garden Dogs allowed Parking **Notes** ◉

England

APPLETREEWICK

MAP 19 SE06

The Craven Arms ♀

BD23 6DA ☎ 01756 720270

e-mail: thecravenarms@ukonline.co.uk

dir: *From Skipton take A59 towards Harrogate, B6160 N. Village signed on right. Pub just outside village.*

Originally a farm built for Sir William Craven (a Lord Mayor of London) in the mid-16th century, and later used as a weaving shed and courthouse, this historic building retains its original beams, flagstone floors and magnificent fireplace. The village stocks are still outside, with spectacular views of the River Wharfe and Simon's Seat. Food options range through sandwiches, home-made kids' food, jacket potatoes and dishes such as ratatouille bake and steak and mushroom pie.

Open 11.30–3 6.30–11 **Bar Meals** L served all week 12–2 D served Mon-Sat 6.30–9 (Sun 6.30–8.30) **Restaurant** L served all week 12–2 D served Mon-Sat 6.30–8.45 (Sun 6.30–8.30) ⊕ Free House ◀ Tetley, Folly Ale, Timothy Taylor Landlord & Golden Best. ♀8 **Facilities** Garden Dogs allowed Parking

ASENBY

MAP 19 SE37

Pick of the Pubs

Crab & Lobster ◉◉ ♀

Dishforth Rd YO7 3QL

☎ 01845 577286 🖺 01845 577109

e-mail: reservations@crabandlobster.co.uk

web: www.crabandlobster.co.uk

dir: *From A1(M) take A168 towards Thirsk, follow signs for Asenby*

Amid seven acres of garden, lake and streams stands this unique 17th-century thatched pub and adjacent small hotel. It is an Aladdin's cave of antiques and artefacts from around the world. Equally famous for its innovative cuisine and special gourmet extravaganzas, the menus show influences from France and Italy, with some oriental dishes too. The famous fish club sandwich (lunch only); and starters like chunky fish soup; mussels with Yorkshire ale, cabbage and bacon; or perhaps Thai green fish curry or fish pie, scallops and capers. Meat eaters are not ignored, with main dishes like pan-fried Dutch calves' liver alongside an array of fish dishes including roast local cod chunk with slow-roasted belly pork, honey and capers and duck fat roastie. Alfresco eating and summer barbecues are on offer. There are good real ales and an extensive wine list, plus a pavilion open all day for food, drinks and coffees.

Open 11.30–11 **Bar Meals** L served all week 12–2.30 D served all week 7–9.30 (Sat 6.30–9.30) **Restaurant** L served all week 12–2 D served all week 7–9.30 (Sat 6.30–9.30) ◀ John Smiths, Scots 1816, Golden Pippin, Guinness. ♀16 **Facilities** Garden Dogs allowed Parking

ASKRIGG

MAP 18 SD99

Kings Arms ♀

Market Place DL8 3HQ ☎ 01969 650817 🖺 01969 650856

e-mail: kingsarms@askrigg.fsnet.co.uk

dir: *N off A684 between Hawes & Leyburn*

At the heart of the Yorkshire Dales, Askrigg's pub was known as The Drovers in the TV series *All Creatures Great and Small*. Built in 1762 as racing stables and converted to a pub in 1860, today it boasts a good range of real ales and an extensive menu and wine list. Favourites are roasted rack of Dales lamb with a mustard and herb crust, beer-battered haddock fillet with chips, chicken breast with linguini, seared sea bass on fresh pasta with a shellfish nage, or grilled gammon steak with eggs or pineapple rings. Look out for the spectacular inglenook fireplace in the main bar.

Open 11–3 6–11 (Sat 11–11, Sun 12–10.30) **Bar Meals** L served all week 12–2 D served all week 6.30–9 Av main course £12 **Restaurant** L served 12–2 D served all week 7–9 Av 3 course à la carte £20.25 ⊕ Free House ◀ John Smiths, Black Sheep, Theakstons Best Bitter, Theakstons Old Peculier. ♀6 **Facilities** Garden Dogs allowed

AUSTWICK

MAP 18 SD76

The Game Cock Inn

The Green LA2 8BB ☎ 015242 51226

e-mail: richardlord495@hotmail.com

dir: *Telephone for directions*

Richard and Trish Lord offer a warm welcome to this award-winning pub, set in the limestone village of Austwick. There's a large garden and children's play area, with winter log fires in the cosy bar. Expect real ale, a range of malt whiskies, and an imaginative menu. Typical dishes include giant ham shank with mash and pickled red cabbage, whilst one of the regular French evenings might feature fresh Toulouse sausage on provençal couscous.

Open 11.30–3 6–1am (Sun all day) **Bar Meals** L served all week 11.30–2 D served all week 6–9 (Sun 12–9) Av main course £6 **Restaurant** L served all week 11.30–2 D served all week 6–9 (Sun 12–9) Av 3 course à la carte £10 ◀ Thwaites Best Bitter & Smooth, Warfsteiner. **Facilities** Garden Parking Play Area

AYSGARTH

MAP 19 SE08

Pick of the Pubs

The George & Dragon Inn ★★ HL ♀

See Pick of the Pubs on opposite page

PICK OF THE PUBS

The George & Dragon Inn

The George & Dragon Inn is a 17th-century Grade II listed building in a superb location in the Yorkshire Dales National Park, near the beautiful Aysgarth Falls. This is Herriot country, of All Creatures Great and Small fame, and where Robin Hood Prince of Thieves was filmed.

The area is perfect for walking, touring and visiting local attractions, including Forbidden Corner, the cheese factory and the Wensleydale Railway. The owners are proud to continue a centuries-long tradition of Yorkshire hospitality at the inn, with visitors returning again and again to stay in the seven comfortable en suite bedrooms. In winter you can keep cosy by the fireside and in summer there is a flower-filled patio with tables and chairs where meals and drinks can be taken outside. A good choice of well-kept real ales is available and 16 wines are served by the glass. The inn has a great reputation for its food. Only the best, freshest produce is used, local wherever possible. The regular menu is supplemented by

daily specials, including a good fresh fish element in dishes such as home-made Thai fishcakes with saffron rouille, and monkfish wrapped in Parma ham with a mango and pumpkin seed salsa. Alternative options are smooth chicken liver parfait with red onion marmalade, and local fillet of beef with Lyonnaise potatoes, sunblush tomatoes and Madeira wine sauce. Desserts range from traditional apple crumble with ice cream to the more exotic vanilla cheesecake with fruits of the forest and mulled wine.

★★ HL ♀
MAP 19 SE08
DL8 3AD
☎ 01969 663358
🖷 01969 663773
e-mail: info@
georgeanddragonaysgarth.co.uk
dir: *On A684 midway between Leyburn & Hawes. Pub in village centre*

Open 11–11 Closed: 2wks Jan
Bar Meals L served all week
12–2 D served all week 6–9
(Afternoon snacks 2–5 spring/
summer) Av main course £12
Restaurant L served all week
12–2 D served all week 6–9 (Sun
12–3) Av 3 course fixed price £25
⊕ Free House ◼ Black
Sheep Best, John Smith's Cask,
Smooth, Theakstons Bitter. ♀ 16
Facilities Garden Dogs allowed
Parking
Rooms 7

PICK OF THE PUBS

The Three Hares Country Inn & Restaura

Race-goers, foodies and locals alike flock to this 18th-century country pub, which is renowned for the quality of its food. A light and smartly turned-out brick-walled dining room provides an elegant setting for the culinary delights in store.

Local, seasonal produce, a menu that wisely balances tradition with simplicity, and assured cooking techniques combine to create an award-winning kitchen output. For lunch, tuck into chicken liver parfait; goats' cheese ravioli, or ham and pea risotto with crispy leeks, to be followed by confit duck leg with parmesan mash and red wine jus; baked Whitby fish pie topped with cheese; or pan-fried salmon with dressed spinach. The dinner menu might well open with the likes of smoked mackerel fillets, toasted brioche, concasse, capers and shallot rings. Follow with open lasagne of wild mushrooms, white wine, cream and herbs; oven-baked pork loin, crispy black pudding and caramelised Bramley apples; pan-fried sea bass fillet

with saffron potatoes, or duck breast with buttered cabbage and bacon. Desserts such as apple and pear tarte Tatin with cinnamon ice cream, or chocolate brownie and griottine cherries maintain the momentum, and the selection of Yorkshire cheeses is excellent. Race-goers should look out for the racing brunch, which includes such trencherman fare as Yorkshire ploughman's; a 'Full Monty' breakfast; fillet steak sandwich with home-made chips; and roast ham sandwiches. In combination with a pint of Black Sheep bitter, it's just the thing to toast a win or console oneself after a loss. A heated terrace completes the package.

MAP 16 SE54
Main St YO23 3PH
☎ 01937 832128
🖷 01937 834626
e-mail:
info@thethreehares.co.uk
dir: *Off A64 between A659 Tadcaster & A1237 York junct*

Open 12-12.30 Closed: Mon Jan-Feb
Bar Meals L served Tue-Sun 12–3
Restaurant L served Tue-Sun 12–3 D served Tue-Sat 7–9 (Sun 12–3) Av 3 course à la carte £21.50
⊕ Free House ◀ Timothy Taylor Landlord, Black Sheep, Farmers Blond, guest ales each week. ⦿ 10
Facilities Garden Parking

England

BILBROUGH   MAP 16 SE54

Pick of the Pubs

The Three Hares Country Inn & Restaurant ♚

See Pick of the Pubs on opposite page

BOROUGHBRIDGE   MAP 19 SE36

Pick of the Pubs

The Black Bull Inn ♚

See Pick of the Pubs on page 646

BREARTON   MAP 19 SE36

Pick of the Pubs

Malt Shovel Inn ♚

See Pick of the Pubs on page 649

BROUGHTON   MAP 18 SD95

The Bull ♚

BD23 3AE ☎ 01756 792065
e-mail: janeneil@thebullatbroughton.co.uk
web: www.thebullatbroughton.co.uk
dir: *On A59 3m from Skipton on A59*

Like the village itself, the pub is part of the 3,000–acre Broughton Hall estate, owned by the Tempest family for 900 years. The locally brewed Bull Bitter and guest ales are backed by a dozen wines served by the glass. Chef-cum-manager Neil Butterworth's compact, thoughtful menu features sausages, fishcakes, sauces and ice creams all made on the premises. Children will be delighted with their own selection of scrambled eggs; chicken fillets; and mini shepherd's pie, rounded off with hot chocolate and marshmallows.

Open 12–3 5.30–11 (Sat 12–11, Sun & BHs 12–8) **Bar Meals** L served Mon-Sat 12–2 D served Mon-Sat 6–9 (Sun 12–6) **Restaurant** L served Mon-Sat 12–2 D served Mon-Sat 6–9 (Sun & BHs 12–6) Av 3 course à la carte £19 Av 2 course fixed price £9.95 ⊕ Free House ◀ John Smith's Smooth, Bull Bitter (Local), guest ales, Copper Dragon. ♚ 12 **Facilities** Garden Dogs allowed Parking

BURNSALL   MAP 19 SE06

Pick of the Pubs

The Red Lion ★★ HL ❀ ♚

See Pick of the Pubs on page 650

BYLAND ABBEY   MAP 19 SE57

Pick of the Pubs

Abbey Inn ♚

See Pick of the Pubs on page 651

CARTHORPE   MAP 19 SE38

Pick of the Pubs

The Fox & Hounds

DL8 2LG ☎ 01845 567433 🖹 01845 567155
dir: *Off A1, signed on both N'bound & S'bound carriageways*

The Fox and Hounds has been standing in the sleepy village of Carthorpe for over 200 years. The restaurant was once the village smithy, and the old anvil and other tools of the trade are still on display, giving a nice sense of history to the place. The pub has an excellent reputation for its food, which might include starters of honey roast ham hock terrine with home-made piccalilli; caramelised onion and goats' cheese tart; or Loch Fyne smoked salmon. Typical main courses include half roasted Gressingham duckling; or chicken breast with Yorkshire blue cheese and leeks. Vegetarians won't go hungry – there's a dedicated menu of five dishes, each available as a starter or main course. Leave room for desserts such as meringue with lemon curd ice cream served with seasonal fruit. All wines are available by the glass.

Open 12–3 7–11 Closed: 25–26 Dec eve & 1st wk Jan & Mon **Bar Meals** L served Tue-Sun 12–2 D served Tue-Sun 7–9.30 Av main course £12.95 **Restaurant** L served Tue-Sun 12–2 D served Tue-Sun 7–9.30 Av 3 course à la carte £24 Av 3 course fixed price £15.95 ⊕ Free House ◀ Black Sheep Best, Worthington's Bitter. **Facilities** Parking

New Inn Hotel
'Jewel of the Dales'
Clapham LA2 8HH
Yorkshire Dales National Park

This family run inn is set amidst a geological wonderland of limestone, cavern and fell country.

Being a true 18th Century village coaching inn, experience the warmth and friendliness that we give to the New Inn. Now a 19 bedroomed inn with four poster

and kingsize beds, 2 bars with open fires, cask beers, quality wines and malt whiskies, restaurant and residents lounge.

A wonderful blend of old and new to retain the ambience of a true Dales village inn.

Nestling below Ingleborough mountain, the beautiful Dales village straddles either side of Clapham Beck, one half linked to the other by three bridges – the church is at the top, the New Inn at the bottom.

Walk from our doorstep or tour the Dales or Lakes, Windermere being only a forty minute drive away.

**Contact us for details of
our special offers.**

Tel: 01524 251203
Email: info@newinn-clapham.co.uk
Website: www.newinn-clapham.co.uk

Pets welcome.

CHAPEL LE DALE — MAP 18 SD77

The Old Hill Inn

LA6 3A4 ☎ 015242 41256

dir: *From Ingleton take B6255 4m, on the right*

Built in 1615 as a farm, and later serving as a stopping place for drovers, this characterful inn specializes in delicious home-cooked food. The Old Hill is owned and run by a family of chefs: look out for Colin Martin's award-winning sugar sculptures on display. Sample dishes include beef casserole; pan-fried sea bass; and sautéed duck breast, while vegetarians can tuck into mushroom stuffed with ratatouille, chickpeas and Wensleydale cheese.

Open (telephone for details) Closed: 24–25 Dec & Mon (ex BHs) **Bar Meals** L served Tue-Sun 12–2.30 D served Tue-Sun 6.30–8.45 **Restaurant** L served Tue-Sun D served Tue-Sun ⊕ Free House ◀ Black Sheep Best & Ale, Timothy Taylor Landlord, Theakstons Best & Dent Aviator. **Facilities** Garden Parking

CLAPHAM — MAP 18 SD76

New Inn ♀

LA2 8HH ☎ 01524 251203 📠 01524 251496

e-mail: info@newinn-clapham.co.uk

dir: *On A65 in Yorkshire Dale National Park*

There's a warm and friendly welcome at this 18th-century free house, nestling beneath the famous summit of Ingleborough. Outdoor enthusiasts Keith and Barbara Mannion have run the former coaching inn since 1987, and walkers and visitors to the Yorkshire Dales certainly appreciate the honest, wholesome food served in their dining room. Typical dishes include ricotta and spinach tortellini; poached salmon on mustard mash; and venison steak with redcurrant sauce.

Open 11–11 **Bar Meals** L served all week 12–2 D served all week 6.30–8.30 (Sun 6.30–8) Av main course £8.95 **Restaurant** L served all week 12–2 D served all week 6.30–8.30 (Sun 6.30–8) Av 3 course à la carte £22 Av 5 course fixed price £24 ⊕ Free House ◀ Black Sheep Best, Tetley Bitter, Copper Dragon Pippin, Thwaites Best & Thwaites Bomber. ♀ 18 **Facilities** Children's licence Garden Dogs allowed Parking **Rooms** available

See advert on opposite page

COLTON — MAP 16 SE54

Ye Old Sun Inn ♀

Main St LS24 8EP ☎ 01904 744261 📠 01904 744261

e-mail: kelly.mccarthy@btconnect.com

dir: *3–4m from York, off A64*

An 18th-century, whitewashed local, formerly a coaching inn, in the heart of the village. Tables and chairs on the lawns await warm days, and customers who want to look at the rolling countryside. Menu choices include monkfish skewer marinated in Thai spices; rabbit pie with shortcrust pastry; a wide choice of grills; Cumberland sausage; and vegetarian rösti. Among the home-made desserts appears the British classic, jam roly poly. Cookery demonstrations are held throughout the year.

Open 12–2.30 6–11 Closed: 1–26 Jan & Mon **Bar Meals** L served Tue-Sat 12–2 D served Tue-Sun 6.30–9.30 (Sun 12–4) **Restaurant** L served Tue-Sat 12–2 D served Tue-Sun 6–9.30 (Sun 12–4) Av 3 course à la carte £24 ⊕ Enterprise Inns ◀ John Smith, Timothy Taylors, Black Sheep, guest ale. ♀ 18 **Facilities** Garden Parking

CRAY — MAP 18 SD97

Pick of the Pubs

The White Lion Inn ♀

See Pick of the Pubs on page 652

CRAYKE — MAP 19 SE57

Pick of the Pubs

The Durham Ox ★★★★ RR 🅰 ♀

See Pick of the Pubs on page 654

The Black Bull Inn

Built in 1258, The Black Bull was one of the main watering holes for coaches travelling what is now the A1. Back then it had stables and a blacksmith's shop attached. These days, it retains plenty of original features, including old beams, low ceilings and roaring open fires, not to mention the supposed ghost of a monk.

Plenty of traditional pub fare is the order of the day here, with extensive menus covering all the options. Starters such as chicken liver paté with Cumberland sauce; king prawn tails and queen scallops; and Scottish smoked salmon are sure to whet the appetite. The main courses that follow might include rump of English lamb with rosemary and olive mashed potato; duck breast with orange and Grand Marnier jus; pork tenderloin with pink peppercorn sauce; chicken breast wrapped in Parma ham with pan-fried wild mushroom; and a selection of very substantial steak dishes. Several fish options are also available, including the likes of salmon, halibut, sea bass, tuna and Dover sole. Some of the wicked desserts for the sweet-toothed are

banoffee meringue roulade with toffee sauce; dark chocolate truffle torte; apple pie with custard; and mixed ice creams encased in brandy snap with fruit purées. Sizeable bar snacks range from pork and chive sausage with onion gravy, and deep-fried prawns, to Thai beef strips with egg noodles and stir-fry vegetables. Among the mouth-watering array of sandwiches are hot roast pork and applesauce; and cold smoked salmon with dill mayonnaise. Yorkshire beers are well represented in the bar, and there is a splendid selection of 17 malts to choose from.

🍷
MAP 19 SE36
6 St James Square YO51 9AR
☎ 01423 322413
🖥 01423 323915
dir: *From A1(M) junct 48 take B6265 E for 1m*

Open 11–11 (Sun 12–10.30)
Bar Meals L served all week
12 2 D served all week 6–9 (Fri-Sat 6–9.30, Sun 12–2.30, 6–9)
Restaurant L served all week
12–2 D served all week 6–9 (Fri-Sat 6–9.30, Sun 12–2.30, 6–9)
⊕ Free House ◀ Black Sheep, John Smiths, Timothy Taylor Landlord, Cottage Brewing. 🍷 10
Facilities Dogs allowed Parking

CROPTON MAP 19 SE78

The New Inn ♀

YO18 8HH ☎ 01751 417330 📄 01751 417582
e-mail: info@croptonbrewery.co.uk
dir: *Telephone for directions*

Home of the award-winning Cropton micro-brewery, this family-run free house on the edge of the North York Moors National Park is popular with locals and visitors alike. Meals are served in the restored village bar and in the elegant Victorian restaurant: choices could include Whitby cod with mushy peas and home-made chips; three cheese and roasted vegetable frittata; an extensive range from the grill; plus lunchtime sandwiches and ciabatta rolls.

Open 11–11 **Bar Meals** L served all week 12–2 D served all week 6–9 Av main course £9 **Restaurant** L served all week 12–2 D served all week 6–9 Av 3 course à la carte £16 ⊕ Free House ◀ Cropton Two Pints, Monkmans Slaughter, Yorkshire Moors Bitter, Honey Gold Bitter & Theakstons Best Bitter. ♀ 7 **Facilities** Garden Dogs allowed Parking Play Area **Rooms** available

---

EAST WITTON MAP 19 SE18

Pick of the Pubs

The Blue Lion ♀

DL8 4SN ☎ 01969 624273 📄 01969 624189
e-mail: enquiries@thebluelion.co.uk
dir: *From Ripon take A6108 towards Leyburn, approx 20mins*

A coaching inn built towards the end of the 18th century, the Blue Lion has been sought out by travellers from far and wide since cattle drovers rested here on their journey through glorious Wensleydale. The pub's stone facade can hardly have changed since it first opened, while inside an extensive but sympathetic refurbishment has created rural chic interiors with stacks of atmosphere and charm. The bar with its open fire and flagstone floor is a beer drinker's haven, where the best of North Yorkshire's breweries present a pleasant dilemma for the real ale lover. A blackboard displays imaginative but unpretentious bar meals. Diners in the candlelit restaurant can expect award-winning culinary treats which incorporate a variety of Yorkshire ingredients. A fulfilling repast may comprise a terrine of ham hock, parsley and foie gras with yellow split pea purée; a roast fillet of Hartlepool halibut with leeks, sage and cannelloni beans; and apple Tatin with vanilla ice cream.

Open 11–11 **Bar Meals** L served all week 12–2.15 D served all week 7–9.30 Av main course £17.25 **Restaurant** L served Sun 12–2.15 D served all week 7–9.30 Av 3 course à la carte £29 ⊕ Free House ◀ Black Sheep Bitter, Theakston Best Bitter, Black Sheep Riggwelter, Worthingtons. ♀ 12 **Facilities** Garden Dogs allowed Parking

---

EGTON MAP 19 NZ80

Pick of the Pubs

The Wheatsheaf Inn

YO21 1TZ ☎ 01947 895271 📄 01947 895391
dir: *Off A169 NW of Grosmont*

This unassuming old pub sits back from the wide main road, so be careful not to miss it. The main bar is cosy and traditional, with low beams, dark green walls and comfy settles. There's a locals' bar too, but it only holds about twelve, so get there early. The pub is very popular with fishermen, as the River Esk runs along at the foot of the hill, and is a big draw for fly-fishers in particular. The menu offers white nut and artichoke heart roast with mushroom stroganoff, and chicken and smoked bacon puff pastry pie among others.

Open 11.30–3 5.30–11.30 **Bar Meals** L served Tue-Sun 12–2 D served Tue-Sat 6–9 **Restaurant** L served Tue-Sun 12–2 D served Tue-Sat 6–9 ⊕ Free House ◀ Black Sheep Bitter, Black Sheep Special, John Smith, Adnams. **Facilities** Garden Dogs allowed Parking

---

EGTON BRIDGE MAP 19 NZ80

Horseshoe Hotel ♀

YO21 1XE ☎ 01947 895245
dir: *From Whitby take A171 towards Middlesborough. Village signed in 5m.*

An 18th-century country inn by the River Esk, handy for visiting the North Yorkshire Moors Railway. Inside are oak settles and tables, local artists' paintings and, depending on the weather, an open fire. Lunchtime bar food consists of sandwiches in granary bread and hot baguettes. The main menu includes starters like crab cakes with a sweet chilli dip, and mains like lasagne, scampi, or pie of the day. There is also a specials board.

Open 11.30–3 6.30–11 (Sat, Sun & BH's all day in Summer) Closed: 25 Dec **Bar Meals** L served all week 12–2 D served all week 7–9 **Restaurant** L served all week 12–2 D served all week 7–9 ⊕ Free House ◀ Copper Dragon & John Smiths, Durham, Black Sheep & Archers. ♀ 7 **Facilities** Garden Dogs allowed Parking

England

FADMOOR   MAP 19 SE68

Pick of the Pubs

The Plough Inn ♥

See Pick of the Pubs on page 655

FELIXKIRK   MAP 19 SE48

Pick of the Pubs

The Carpenters Arms

YO7 2DP ☎ 01845 537369 📠 01845 537889

dir: *2m from Thirsk on A170*

This 18th-century inn stands in the pretty hamlet of Felixkirk, a mere skip away from the market town of Thirsk, where much-loved writer and vet James Herriott once practised. The inn has been in the capable hands of mother and daughter team Linda and Karen Bumby since 2000, and very welcoming they've made it too. The Bistro bar is a cosy spot, with soft seating and big cushions, oil lamps, coloured checked tablecloths, carpenters' tools, old-fashioned toy balloons and various other knick-knacks on display. Tuck into home-made fisherman's pie; Indonesian chicken curry; or venison and beef casserole with suet dumplings. In the slightly more formal restaurant, with its white linen cloths and napkins, crystal glasses and locally made furniture, the menu also moves up a notch. Try duck breast with port wine sauce and parsnip crisps; or bacon-wrapped pork fillet stuffed with black pudding and apple, with wholegrain mustard sauce.

Open 11.30–3 6.30–11 Closed: 1wk Jan or Feb, 25 Dec, Sun eve **Bar Meals** L served Tue-Sun 12–2 D served Tue-Sat 6.30–9 **Restaurant** L served Tue-Sun 12–2 D served Tue-Sat 6.30–9 ⊕ Free House **Facilities** Parking

GIGGLESWICK   MAP 18 SD86

Black Horse Hotel

32 Church St BD24 0BE ☎ 01729 822506

e-mail: blackhorse-giggle@tiscali.co.uk

dir: *Telephone for directions*

Set in the 17th-century main street, this traditional free house stands next to the church and behind the market cross. Down in the warm and friendly bar you'll find a range of hand-pulled ales. The menu of freshly-prepared pub favourites ranges from hot sandwiches or giant filled Yorkshire puddings to main course dishes like steak and ale pie; broccoli and sweetcorn vol-au-vent; and crispy battered haddock.

Open 12–2.30 5.30–11 (Sun 5.30–10.30) Closed: Mon 12–2.30 **Bar Meals** L served Tue-Sun 12–1.45 D served all week 7–8.45 **Restaurant** L served Tue-Sun 12–1.45 D served all week 7–8.45 ⊕ Free House ◀ Carlsberg-Tetley Bitter, Timothy Taylor Landlord, John Smiths, Timothy Taylor Golden Best. **Facilities** Garden Parking **Rooms** available

GOATHLAND   MAP 19 NZ80

Birch Hall Inn

Beckhole YO22 5LE ☎ 01947 896245

e-mail: glenys@birchhallinn.fsnet.co.uk

dir: *9m from Whitby on A169*

This delightful little free house, tucked away in a remote valley close to the North York Moors steam railway, has been in the same ownership for 25 years. With just two tiny rooms separated by a sweet shop, it offers an open fire in the main bar, well-kept local ales and a large garden with tempting views of the local walks. The simple menu features locally-baked pies, butties, home-made scones and buttered beer cake.

Open 11–3 7.30–11 (Summer & Sun 11–11) Closed: Mon eve & Tue Winter **Bar Meals** L served all week 11–3 D served all week 7.30–11 ⊕ Free House ◀ Black Sheep Best, Theakstons Black Bull, Cropton Yorkshire Moors Bitter, Daleside Brewery Legover. **Facilities** Garden Dogs allowed **Notes** ☺

GREAT AYTON   MAP 19 NZ51

The Royal Oak ★★★ INN ♥

123 High St TS9 6BW ☎ 01642 722361 📠 01642 724047

e-mail: info@royaloak-hotel.co.uk

dir: *Telephone for directions*

Real fires and a relaxed atmosphere are part of the attraction at this traditional corner pub, run by the Monaghan family since 1978. Expect traditional pub food.

Open 11–11 (Sun 12–10.30) Closed: 25 Dec **Bar Meals** L served all week 12–2 D served all week 6.30–9.30 **Restaurant** L served all week 12–2 D served all week 6.30–9.30 ⊕ Scottish & Newcastle ◀ Theakstons, John Smiths Smooth, Directors. ♥ 10 **Facilities** Children's licence Garden **Rooms** 4

PICK OF THE PUBS

Malt Shovel Inn

A 16th-century beamed free house, the Malt Shovel is one of the oldest buildings in an ancient village. Open fires in winter, flagstoned floors and pianos in the bar and conservatory give the place both atmosphere and character.

The rural setting has some good examples of ancient strip farming, and although the pub is surrounded by rolling farmland, it's just fifteen minutes from Harrogate and within easy reach of both Knaresborough and Ripon. The Bleiker family took it over in 2006, having previously run the Old Deanery in Ripon and established the hugely successful Bleiker's Smokehouse. Swiss-born Jurg's fine cooking specialises in fresh fish, classic sauces and well-sourced local produce. He and his wife Jane draw on their wealth of experience in food, hospitality and entertainment to create an ambience that combines elegance and theatricality – his son and daughter-in-law are international opera soloists, so the occasional impromptu performance in the bar is not unknown. However it's their commitment to great food, fine wine (nearly twenty are served by the glass), impeccable service and the warmest of welcomes that bring customers back again and again. A light lunch of Bleiker's oak roast salmon or moules frites may suffice for some; others may plump for the traditional pub lunch of fresh North Sea haddock in a Timothy Taylor Landlord beer batter, or a rib-eye steak sandwich with chips. There are also lunchtime and evening cartes, when sophisticated cooking techniques become apparent: seared foie gras with poached pear; queenie scallops 'Newburg'; WienerschnitzeL served with gratin dauphinoise or chips; and acorn-fed Black Leg pig cheeks with an apple and black pudding mash. Children can choose between mini fish and chips and sausage and mash.

MAP 19 SE36
HG3 3BX
☎ 01423 862929
e-mail: bleikers@
themaltshovelbrearton.co.uk
dir: *From A61 (Ripon/ Harrogate) onto B6165 towards Knaresborough. Left & follow Brearton signs. In 1m right into village*

Open 12–3 6–11 (Sun 12–7)
Closed: Mon & Tue
Bar Meals L served Wed-Sat
12–2 D served Wed-Sat 6–9 (Sun 12–7) Av main course £10.95
Restaurant L served Wed-Sat
12–2 D served Wed-Sat 6–9 (Sun 12–7) Av 3 course à la carte £25
⊕ Free House ◀ Daleside Blond, Timothy Taylor Landlord, Black Sheep Best. ☘ 18
Facilities Garden Parking

649

PICK OF THE PUBS

The Red Lion

A 16th-century ferryman's inn with large gardens and terraces, overlooking the River Wharfe as it gently curves its way under a magnificent old five-arch bridge. The Grayshon family have sympathetically upgraded The Lion, retaining of course its beamed ceilings and creaky sloping floors – in short, its historic character.

The cellars are inhabited by a mischievous ghost who amuses himself (or is it herself?) by turning off the beer taps and icemaker. The original 'one-up, one-down' structure, now the oak-panelled and floored main bar, is the focal point of the hotel. The Grayshons like to namecheck Jim, the head chef, not just because he's their son-in-law, but also because he is the reason for their AA Rosette. His extensive brasserie menu features game in season from the nearby estates, beef from another son-in-law, Robert, and lamb from the Daggett family (both of whom farm just across the river). On the bar menu at lunchtime and in the evening are gravadlax of salmon with dill mustard mayo; smoked chicken and avocado salad; fish and chips with mushy peas; and goat's cheese tart. The main restaurant menu offers starters of saffron, prawn and sweet corn risotto; asparagus and parma ham; and chick pea fritters with cucumber and mint yoghurt. Among a good choice of main courses are pan-fried fillet of venison, wild mushrooms, ch,teau potato and cranberry chutney; woodpigeon with rösti potato, wild mushroom and smoked bacon sauce; pot roasted Wharfedale lamb confit with redcurrant and garlic, parsnip mash and roasted shallots; and roast corn-fed chicken breast, grilled tomatoes, mushrooms and grilled smoked bacon. If you're staying in one of the 25 bedrooms, note the horse-trough – it was easier to build the stone steps around it than move it.

★★ HL ◉ ♀
MAP 19 SE06
By the Bridge BD23 6BU
☎ 01756 720204
▤ 01756 720292
e-mail: redlion@daelnet.co.uk
dir: *From Skipton take A59 E, take B6160 towards Bolton Abbey, Burnsall 7m*

Open 8–11.30
Bar Meals L served Mon-Sat 12–2.30 D served Mon-Sat 6–9.30 (Sun all day) Av main course £12
Restaurant L served all week 12–2.30 D served all week 7–9.30 Av 3 course à la carte £31.95
⊕ Free House ◪ Theakston Black Bull, Greene King Old Speckled Hen, Timothy Taylor Landlord, John Smith's. ♀ 14
Facilities Garden Dogs allowed Parking Play Area
Rooms 25

PICK OF THE PUBS

BYLAND ABBEY-YORKSHIRE, NORTH

Abbey Inn

Byland Abbey, a Cistercian monastery built almost 1,000 years ago, was probably Europe's largest ecclesiastical building at the time. Thanks to Henry VIII it is now a ruin, albeit a beautiful one, set in the shadow of the Hambleton Hills.

Over the road is the ivy-clad Abbey Inn, built in 1845 as a farmhouse by Fr John Molyneux and a team of monks, using some of the old abbey stones. In 2005 the whole site was taken over by English Heritage, and many Abbey Inn patrons are comforted in the knowledge that some of its profits are invested in preserving the historic ruins for future generations. A recent refurbishment has been sympathetic, and a new colour scheme fictires, fittings and some furniture are part of the new look. Unusual objets d'art lurking in corners may take some noticing, as a pint of the inn's own real ale slips down. Two dining rooms at the front overlook the haunting profile of the abbey itself; a third is known, commemoratively, as the Piggery. The award-winning

gastro-pub uses only fresh seasonal Yorkshire produce, and is booked up to four weeks ahead for its renowned Sunday lunch. A daily changing menu might offer starters and light bites of pressed Yorkshire gammon with pease pudding and toasted sourdough, or confit of mallard with broad bean and crispy bacon casserole; main dishes should include the chef's signature dish – roast cod and boulangère potatoes wrapped in Parma ham with tomato chutney; Bolton Abbey braised lamb shank shepherds pie with parsnip purée; and free range pork au feu with home-made black pudding and a Calvados and apple jus. Children are offered the same healthy food but in half-size portions, while early-bird diners benefit from a discounted menu.

♥
MAP 19 SE57
YO61 4BD
☎ 01347 868204
📠 01347 868678
e-mail: abbeyinn@
english-heritage.org.uk
web: www.bylandabbeyinn.com
dir: *From A19 Thirsk/York follow signs to Byland Abbey/Coxwold*

Open 12–2.30 6–9 (6–8.30 in winter) Closed: 25–26 Dec, 24 & 31 Dec eve, 1 Jan, Sun eve & Mon-Tue
Bar Meals L served Wed-Sun 12–2.30 D served Wed-Sat 6–8.30 Av main course £12.95
Restaurant L served Wed-Sun 12–2 D served Wed-Sat 6.30–9 (Sun 12–3) Av 3 course à la carte £28 Av fixed price £16.50
⊕ Free House ● Black Sheep Best, Timothy Taylor. ♥ 8
Facilities Garden Parking

PICK OF THE PUBS

The White Lion Inn

Nestling beneath Buckden Pike, The White Lion is Wharfedale's highest inn. It also boasts some spectacular scenery, since it's set right at the heart of the Yorkshire Dales. Indeed, the celebrated fell-walker Wainwright once described this former drovers' hostelry as a 'tiny oasis', a claim that's just as accurate today.

All the qualities of a traditional Yorkshire inn have been maintained here, from warm hospitality to oak beams, log fire and flagstone floors. The age-old game of bull'ook is still played here alongside the more contemporary Giant Jenga. A good choice of hand-pulled real ales is offered and 20–plus malt whiskies. You can eat and drink in the bar or dining room, though the sight of the cascading Cray Gill, which runs past the inn, is sure to lure children out to the garden. Before or after a meal, you can also make your way across the stepping-stones in the gill to the open fells and many locally recognised walks, long and short. In the bar, wholesome food is cooked to order and served in generous portions. Lunchtime options include filled baguettes,

ploughman's, and plate-sized Yorkshire puddings with a choice of fillings like Cumberland sausage or three-bean chilli. Also available, lunchtime and evenings, is a variety of substantial dishes such as pork fillet in a honey and mustard cream sauce; whole steamed Kilnsey trout, or steak and mushroom casserole cooked with root vegetables and beer gravy. A children's menu is also on offer. Ten en suite bedrooms are available if you want to linger, with well-behaved dogs welcome in ground floor rooms.

♀
MAP 18 SD97
Cray BD23 5JB
☎ 01756 760262
e-mail:
admin@whitelioncray.com
dir: *Take B6265 from Skipton towards Grassington, then B6160 towards Aysgarth. Cray 10m from Aysgarth*

Open 11–11 Closed: 25 Dec
Bar Meals L served all week
12–2 D served all week 5.45–8.30
Av main course £10
⊕ Free House ◀ Timothy Taylor
Golden Best, Copper Dragon
Golden Pippin, Copper Dragon
1816, Wensleydale brewery
Semerwater. ♀ 9
Facilities Garden Dogs allowed
Parking
Rooms available

GREEN HAMMERTON   MAP 19 SE45

The Bay Horse Inn

York Rd YO26 8BN ☎ 01423 330338 ▤ 01423 331279
e-mail: info@bayhorseinn.uk.com

A 200–year-old coaching inn located in a small village near the A1 and close to both York and Harrogate. Food is served in the bar and restaurant, and there is further seating outside, sheltered by the boundary hedge. Dishes might include bangers and mash, fish and chips, chicken and stilton, and a home-made pie of the day. Various steaks and grills are also a key feature of the menu.

Open 12–3 6–12 (Summer 12–12) **Bar Meals** L served Mon-Sun 12–2 D served Mon-Sat 6–9 (Fri-Sat 12–2.30, Sun 12–3) **Restaurant** L served Mon-Sun 12–2 D served Mon-Sat 6–9 (Fri-Sat 12–2.30, Sun 12–3) ⊕ New Century Inns ◀ Worthington, Timothy Taylor, Black Sheep & guest. **Facilities** Garden Dogs allowed Parking

GRINTON   MAP 19 SE09

Pick of the Pubs

The Bridge Inn ♟

See Pick of the Pubs on page 656

HAROME   MAP 19 SE68

Pick of the Pubs

The Star Inn ◉◉ ♟

YO62 5JE ☎ 01439 770397 ▤ 01439 771833

dir: *From Helmsley take A170 towards Kirkbymoorside 0.5m. Turn right for Harome*

This award-winning gastro-pub is housed in a fine example of a 14th-century cruck-framed longhouse, with the former monks' dormitory converted into a distinctive coffee loft. A byre houses the dining room, while the bar is full of Mousey Thompson hand-carved oak furniture. Additional developments are afoot: the kitchen will become a new dining area, the reception a cocktail bar, a private 'chef's table' will be placed in the new kitchen, and a terrace and English kitchen garden will also have dining space. Accomplished cooking continues to draw customers looking to savour starters such as grilled black pudding with pan-fried foie gras; main courses of roast rack of Leckenby's-reared Ryedale lamb and hotpot potatoes; and desserts like brioche bread and butter pudding with hot spiced syrup and black treacle ice cream. The strong vegetarian menu may offer omelette of Lowna Dairy goats' cheese with wilted Pickering watercress and scallion salad.

Open 11.30–3 6.30–11 Closed: 2wks spring & Mon am **Bar Meals** L served Tue-Sat 11.30–2 D served Tue-Sat 6.30–9.15 (Sun 12–6) Av main course £18 **Restaurant** L served Tue-Sat 11.30–2 D served Tue-Sat 6.30–9.15 (Sun 12–6) Av 3 course à la carte £40 ⊕ Free House ◀ Black Sheep Special, Copper Dragon, Hambleton Ales, John Smith's & Theakston Best. ♟10 **Facilities** Garden Parking

HARROGATE   MAP 19 SE35

Pick of the Pubs

The Boars Head Hotel ★★★ HL ◉◉ ♟

See Pick of the Pubs on page 658

HAWES   MAP 18 SD88

The Moorcock Inn ♟

Garsdale Head LA10 5PU
☎ 01969 667488 ▤ 01969 667488
e-mail: admin@moorcockinn.com

dir: *On A684 5m from Hawes, 15m from Sedbergh at junct for Kirkby Stephen (10m). Garsdale Station 1m*

A heart-warming 18th-century hostelry, where owners Caz and Simon welcome weary walkers with or without muddy boots and dogs. Candles glow in the windows, while inside fairy lights pick out a cosy blend of original stonework and bright colours, furnished with comfy sofas and traditional wooden chairs. Savour the pub's local ales around the wood-burning stove, or enjoy the spectacular views from the garden. Traditional fare ranges from hot ciabattas, lasagne or chilli, through to hotpots, steaks and local game.

Open 11–11 **Bar Meals** L served all week 12–3 D served all week 6.30–9 (Soups & sandwiches all day) Av main course £7.95 **Restaurant** L served all week 12–3 D served all week 6.30–9 Av 3 course à la carte £17 ⊕ Free House ◀ Black Sheep, Copper Dragon, Boddingtons Cask & guest ales. ♟7 **Facilities** Garden Dogs allowed Parking

HETTON   MAP 18 SD95

Pick of the Pubs

The Angel ♟

BD23 6LT ☎ 01756 730263 ▤ 01756 730363
e-mail: info@angelhetton.co.uk

dir: *From A59 take B6265 towards Grassington. Turn left at Rylstone Pond as signed then left at T junct*

Now renowned for its modern British cooking, this ivy-clad Dales inn dates back to the 15th century. Starting life as a drovers' inn in the early 1800s, the Angel has evolved through a number of guises, and some local residents remember it as a traditional farmhouse pub in the 1950s. Today, the interior is all oak beams and winter log fires; in summer you can eat or drink on the flagged forecourt and enjoy the views of Cracoe Fell. Dennis and Juliet Watkins have fulfilled their vision of 'good food and great value'. Locally sourced meats, seasonal game and fresh Fleetwood fish are the foundation of the Angel's varied menus. The informal brasserie blackboard might offer slow-cooked suckling pig or vegetarian cassoulet, whilst à la carte diners might enjoy braised Bolton Abbey mutton; pan-seared silver hake; or roasted courgette, cauliflower and broccoli crumble.

Open 12–3 6–11 Closed: 25 Dec & 1wk Jan **Bar Meals** L served all week 12–2.15 D served Sun-Fri 6–9 (Sat 6–10) **Restaurant** L served Sun 12–2 D served Mon-Sat 6–9 ⊕ Free House ◀ Blacksheep Bitter, Timothy Taylor Landlord. ♟24 **Facilities** Garden Parking **Rooms** available

The Durham Ox

Situated in the historic village of Crayke, with breathtaking views over the vale of York on three sides, and a charming view up the hill to the medieval church. Crayke is less than 20 minutes from York city centre in the heart of Herriot Country, well placed for visits to Castle Howard, the walled gardens at Scampston, Byland Abbey and other historic sites.

Notes on the inn's menu tell us the eponymous ox was born around 1796 and grew to enormous proportions – five feet six inches tall, 11 feet from nose to tail, the same around its girth, and weighing 171 stone. Little wonder the animal created such a sensation that over 2,000 prints of it were sold, one of which hangs in the bottom bar. Another claim to fame for this delightful country pub is that the hill outside is reputedly the one up which the Grand Old Duke of York marched his men. Today the Durham Ox prides itself on serving good pub food properly, and uses the best ingredients sourced locally when possible. The cosy oak-panelled bar with roaring fires and award-winning restaurant are equally acceptable venues for indulging in the justifiably revered menus. From the à la carte, simple and tasty snacks include poached eggs and cured bacon on toast; chargrilled Ox burger with cheese, bacon, chips and onion rings; and a variety of open sandwiches. For a three-course meal, you could start with warm Golden Cross goat's cheese and beetroot salad; follow with roast Mount Grace lamb rump with minted crushed new potatoes and spinach; and finish with Yorkshire rhubarb and apple pie with vanilla egg custard and clotted cream ice cream. The specials board is the place to find fresh fish dishes such as grilled langoustines and pan-roasted monkfish. The Ox was AA Pub of the Year for England 2007-8.

★★★★ RR 🅰 ♀
MAP 19 SE57
Westway YO61 4TE
☎ 01347 821506
🖹 01347 823326
e-mail:
enquiries@thedurhamox.com
dir: *Off A19 from York to Thirsk, then to Easingwold. From market place to Crayke, turn left up hill, pub on right*

Open 12–3 6–11 (Sat-Sun 12–11)
Closed: 25 Dec
Bar Meals L served all week
12–3 D served Mon-Fri 6–9.30
(Sat 6–10, Sun 12–3, 6–8.30)
Restaurant L served all week
12–2.30 D served Mon-Fri 6–9.30
(Sat 6–10, Sun 12–3, 6–8.30)
⊕ Free House ◀ John Smiths, Theakstons, Black Bull, Theakstons Old Peculier. ♀ 9
Facilities Garden Dogs allowed Parking
Rooms 6

PICK OF THE PUBS

FADMOOR-YORKSHIRE, NORTH

The Plough Inn

Ramblers sampling the delights of the North Yorkshire Moors National Park will be pleased to find this stylishly well-appointed country pub and restaurant in the pretty village of Fadmoor. The setting overlooking the village green could not be more idyllic, and the inn boasts dramatic views over the Vale of Pickering and the Wolds.

Inside it is cosy, snug and welcoming with log fires, beams and brasses in the bar – the ideal place to enjoy a pint of Black Sheep Best while plotting further hikes. Alternatively the wine list makes good reading, with an honest selection of house wines all at the same good value price, ranging up to some choice bottles from vineyards around the world. The food is an undoubted attraction, with meals available in the bar or in the attractively furnished rustic-style restaurant. A two-course special menu is available for lunch and early evenings (except Saturday evening and Sunday lunch). From the main carte starter options include pan-fried award-winning black pudding with caramelised sliced buttered onions; and deep-fried duck and mango spring rolls

with sweet chilli and ginger sauce. These could be followed by griddled fillet of beef medallions; or braised shank of lamb with a Bramley apple mash. Desserts home made on the premises offer half a dozen choices along the lines of smooth chocolate orange terrine with a black cherry and brandy compote; and caramelised lemon and lime tart with strawberry and raspberry sorbet. A dedicated menu for vegetarians has a thoughtful range of options, including Thai green vegetable curry with flavoured basmati rice; brie and mango puff pastry tartlet with roasted sweet cherry tomatoes; and fresh penne pasta in a rustic tomato, garlic and butter sauce. The Sunday lunch menu brims with good things, including the traditional choice of roast meats.

MAP 19 SE68
Main St YO62 7HY
☎ 01751 431515
🖹 01751 432492
dir: *1m N of Kirkbymoorside on A170 (Thirsk to Scarborough road)*

Open 12–2.30 6.30–11 Closed: 25–26 Dec, 1 Jan
Bar Meals L served Mon-Sun 12–1.45 D served Mon-Sat 6.30–8.45 (Sun 7–8.30) Av main course £9.50
Restaurant D served Mon-Sat 6.30–8.45 (Sun 7–8.30) Av 3 course à la carte £22 Av 2 course fixed price £12.95
⊕ Free House ◀ Black Sheep Best, John Smith's, Tetley Cask + guest ales. ♀ 8
Facilities Garden Parking

The Bridge Inn

Situated on the banks of the River Swale in the heart of the Yorkshire Dales National Park, the Bridge Inn stands opposite St Andrew's church in the picturesque village of Grinton. Dating from the 13th century, this former coaching inn with its beamed ceilings and open fires has now been tastefully restored.

Most visitors head for the Dales in search of country pursuits, and a range of activities can be found on the pub's doorstep. Walking, horse riding and mountain biking are all close at hand, and fishermen can buy their day tickets from the hotel. The Bridge Inn is fast becoming known for its great food and ales. Customers are invited to sample Jennings award-winning cask ales, or maybe try something a little different from a micro-brewery. There is also a fine extensive cellar of handpicked wines. Menus are based on seasonal local produce under the experienced eye of resident chef John Scott, and flavoured with herbs plucked from the pub's own garden. Hot or cold baguettes are served in the bar with a handful of chips, and baked jacket potatoes are also on offer. In the fine à la carte restaurant, starters include courgette and tomato bake; smoked mackerel paté; and black pudding with chorizo, red chard and three pepper dressing. Typical main course choices range from lamb shank in red wine and rosemary; to spiced parsnip pie with herby pastry; and salmon steak in white wine on lemon mash. If you've room to spare, the dessert menu includes a daily choice of old-fashioned traditional puddings.

MAP 19 SE09
DL11 6HH
☎ 01748 884224
e-mail:
atkinbridge@btinternet.com
web: www.bridgeinngrinton.co.uk
dir: *Exit A1 at Scotch Corner & towards Richmond. At Richmond take A6108 towards Reeth, 10m*

Open 12–11
Bar Meals L served Mon-Sat 12–3 D served all week 12–9 (Sun 3–9) Av main course £9.95
Restaurant L served Mon-Sat 12–5 D served all week 5–9 (Sun 12–3)
⊕ Jennings ◀ Cumberland Ale, Cocker Hoop, Deuchars IPA, Adnams. ♟ 7
Facilities Garden Dogs allowed Parking
Rooms available

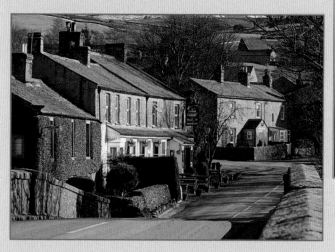

HOVINGHAM
MAP 19 SE67

The Malt Shovel

Main St YO62 4LF ☎ 01653 628264 🖹 01653 628264

dir: *18m NE of York, 5m from Castle Howard*

Tucked away amid the Howardian Hills, in the Duchess of Kent's home village, the stone-built 18th-century Malt Shovel offers a friendly and traditional atmosphere with good-value food prepared from quality local ingredients. Popular options include pork and leeks, beef stroganoff, sirloin steak garni, chicken stilton, and supreme of salmon. Fresh vegetables, hand-crafted chips and daily specials board featuring speciality game dishes complete the picture.

Open 11.30–2.30 6–11 (Fri-Sat 5–11, Sun all day) **Bar Meals** L served all week 12–2 D served all week 6–9 Sun 6–8 Av main course £6 **Restaurant** L served all week 12–2 D served all week 6–9 (Sun 6–8) Av 3 course à la carte £20 ⊕ Punch Taverns ◀ Tetley's, Greene King IPA. **Facilities** Garden Parking

---

Pick of the Pubs

The Worsley Arms Hotel ★★★ HL ♥

Main St YO62 4LA ☎ 01653 628234 🖹 01653 628130

e-mail: worsleyarms@aol.com

dir: *On B1257 between Malton & Helmsley*

In 1841 Sir William Worsley thought he would turn the village of Worsley into a spa to rival Bath, and built a spa house and a hotel. However, he reckoned without the delicate nature of his guests who disliked the muddy track between the two. Inevitably the spa failed, but the hotel survived and, together with the separate pub, forms part of the Worsley family's historic Hovingham Hall estate, birthplace of the Duchess of Kent, and currently home to her nephew. You can eat in the restaurant or the Cricketer's Bar (the local team has played on the village green for over 150 years). Hambleton Stallion beer from nearby Thirsk is on tap, and food choices include speciality ciabatta sandwiches, and dishes such as trio of local sausages with creamy leek mash and sweet shallot gravy, and pan-fried sea bass with Whitby crab risotto and bloody Mary dressing.

Open 12–2.30 7–11 **Bar Meals** L served all week 12–2 D served all week 7–10 **Restaurant** L served Sun 12–2 D served all week 7–10 Av 3 course à la carte £27.50 ⊕ Free House ◀ John Smith's, Hambleton Stallion. ♥ 20 **Facilities** Garden Dogs allowed Parking **Rooms** 20

HUBBERHOLME
MAP 18 SD97

The George Inn

BD23 5JE ☎ 01756 760223

dir: *From Skipton take B6265 to Threshfield. Continue on B6160 to Buckden. Follow signs for Hubbleholme.*

To check if the bar is open, look for a lighted candle in the window. Another old tradition is the annual land-letting auction on the first Monday night of the year, when local farmers bid for 16 acres of land owned by the church. Stunningly located beside the River Wharfe, this pub has flagstone floors, an open fire and an inviting summer terrace. Lunches include baguettes or gammon and eggs; evening choices include pork escalope topped with Wensleydale cheese.

Open 12–3 6–11 Closed: 1st 2wks Dec & Mon **Bar Meals** L served all week 12–2 D served all week 6–8.30 Av main course £9 ⊕ Free House ◀ Black Sheep Best, Black Sheep Special, Skipton Brewery. **Facilities** Garden Parking

---

KILBURN
MAP 19 SE57

The Forresters Arms

YO61 4AH

☎ 01347 868386 & 868550 🖹 01347 868386

e-mail: fiona@forrestersarms.com

dir: *6m from Thirsk*

Sturdy stone former coaching inn still catering for travellers passing close by the famous White Horse of Kilburn on the North York Moors. The cosy lower bar has some of the earliest oak furniture by Robert Thompson, with his distinctive mouse symbol on every piece. Evidence of the inn's former stables can be seen in the upper bar. Steak and ale pie, pheasant casserole, home-made lasagne and lamb chops are popular dishes.

Open 11–11 **Bar Meals** L served all week 12–2.30 D served all week 6.30–9 **Restaurant** L served all week 12–2.30 D served all week 6.30–9 ⊕ Free House ◀ John Smiths, Tetley's, Hambleton. **Facilities** Dogs allowed Parking

---

KIRBY HILL
MAP 19 NZ10

The Shoulder of Mutton Inn

DL11 7JH ☎ 01748 822772 🖹 01325 718936

e-mail: info@shoulderofmutton.net

dir: *4m N of Richmond, 6m from A1 A66 junct at Scotch Corner*

A traditional 18th-century inn with panoramic views over Holmedale and beyond. Open log fires burn in the bar area and dining room, where stone walls and original beams provide just the right kind of backdrop for renowned daily-changing home-cooked dishes such as scallops with black pudding, and seafood sausage with lobster and crayfish sauce.

Open 6–11 12–3 **Bar Meals** L served Sat-Sun 12–2 D served Wed-Sun 7–9 **Restaurant** L served Sun 12–2 D served Wed-Sun 7–9 ⊕ Free House ◀ Daleside, Black Sheep, Copper Dragon, Deuchars. **Facilities** Garden Parking **Rooms** available

PICK OF THE PUBS

The Boars Head Hotel

A lovely old coaching inn at the heart of the Ripley Castle Estate has been transformed by Sir Thomas and Lady Ingilby into an impressive hotel with luxurious furnishings. Originally known as the Star Inn, this was once the breakfast stop for the crowded charabancs that linked Leeds with Edinburgh.

Sir William Ingilby closed all three of Ripley's inns when he inherited the estate soon after the First World War, and Ripley remained dry until the Star was re-opened as the Boar's Head Hotel in 1990. The current name recalls an incident during the 14th century when a former Thomas Ingilby earned his knighthood by killing a wild boar that had attacked King Edward III. Coming back to the present day, stable partitions in the bar and bistro bring intimacy to the relaxed, candlelit atmosphere. Food options begin with classic sandwiches (BLT; poached salmon with lemon and dill crème fraîche), which can be served with a jacket potato instead of bread, and starters like tower of Mediterranean vegetables glazed with goat's cheese, or fish

terrine with citrus dressing. More substantial dishes include pork and leek sausage with sun-blushed tomato mash; pot roasted breast of chicken with ginger scented cabbage; and wild mushroom stroganoff with fresh pasta. In the restaurant, main course prices are inclusive of a starter, dessert and coffee, so the price of your meal depends on your choice of main course – the rest is thrown in. Mains range from seared duck breast with bean cassoulet and herb dumpling, to classic beef Wellington, to which you might add king prawn tempura to start, and the hot soufflé of the day for dessert.

★★★ HL ⌘⌘ ☂
MAP 19 SE35
Ripley Castle Estate HG3 3AY
☎ 01423 771888
🖹 01423 771509
e-mail: reservations@
boarsheadripley.co.uk
dir: *On A61 (Harrogate/Ripon road). Hotel in village centre*

Open 11–11 (Winter 12–3, 5–10.30)
Bar Meals L served all week 12–2.30 D served Sun-Wed 6.30–9 (Winter lunch 12–2, Thu-Sat 6.30–9.30) Av main course £9.50
Restaurant L served all week 12–2 D served all week 7–9 Av 2 course fixed price £16
⊕ Free House ◧ Theakston Best & Old Peculier, Daleside Crackshot, Hambleton White Boar, Black Sheep Best. ☂ 10
Facilities Garden Parking
Rooms 25

KIRKBYMOORSIDE   MAP 19 SE68

Pick of the Pubs

George & Dragon Hotel ♈

17 Market Place YO62 6AA

☎ 01751 433334 📠 0870 7060004

dir: *Just off A170 between Scarborough & Thirsk. In town centre*

This 17th-century former coaching inn has seen dramatic changes over the years: the restaurant used to be the brewhouse and the garden room is the former rectory. Despite all this, centuries on, the inn is still providing a haven of hospitality in the heart of Kirkbymoorside. In the beamed interior visitors can sit by the log fire and sample hand-pulled real ales, wines by the glass and a choice of 30 malt whiskies. A good variety of food is served, from snacks and blackboard specials in the bar to candlelit dinners in the Knights' Restaurant (themed around George and the dragon). There's also a bistro, which opens partially onto the bar lounge.

Bar Meals L served all week 12–2 D served Mon-Sat 6.30–9 (Sun 7–9) **Restaurant** L served all week 12–2 D served Mon-Sat 6.30–9 (Sun 7–9) ⊕ Free House ◀ Black Sheep Best, Tetley, Copper Dragon, guest ale. ♈ 10 **Facilities** Garden Dogs allowed Parking **Rooms** available

KIRK DEIGHTON   MAP 16 SE35

The Bay Horse Inn ♈

Main St LS22 4DZ ☎ 01937 580058 📠 01937 582443

e-mail: karl.mainey@btconnect.com

dir: *1m N of Wetherby on the Knaresborough road*

Originally two pubs side by side (the other being the Greyhound), knocked through over 50 years ago. Today's thriving gastro-pub with locals' bar sources locally-grown and organic food to support Yorkshire farmers and fishermen. Many of the bar lunch dishes come in two sizes, such as smoked salmon Benedict, or queenie scallop gratin glazed with parmesan. In the evening choose between the likes of Swaledale George Fells lamb saddle, or lemon sole.

Open 12–2.15 6–9.30 **Bar Meals** L served Tue-Sun 12–2.30 Av main course £8.50 **Restaurant** L served Tue-Sun 12–2.15 D served Mon-Sat 6–9.30 Av 3 course à la carte £25 ⊕ Free House ◀ Copper Dragon, Timothy Taylors Landlord, Black Sheep Bitter, John Smiths Cask & Deuchars IPA. ♈ 12 **Facilities** Dogs allowed Parking

KIRKHAM   MAP 19 SE76

Pick of the Pubs

Stone Trough Inn ⊛ ♈

Kirkham Abbey YO60 7JS

☎ 01653 618713 📠 01653 618819

e-mail: info@stonetroughinn.co.uk

dir: *1.5m off A64, between York & Malton*

This free house has a great reputation for its friendliness, fine food and real ales. It stands high above Kirkham Priory and the River Derwent, and was sympathetically converted into licensed

premises in the early 1980s from Stone Trough Cottage. The cottage took its name from the base of a cross erected by a 12th-century French knight to commemorate a son killed in a riding accident. The cross has long since disappeared, but its hollowed-out base now stands at the entrance to the car park. A real fire, bare beams and wooden settles make for a pleasingly traditional interior. Food-wise there's a menu of serious intent that includes roast breast of guinea fowl with confit leg and a chanterelle sauce; whole grilled lemon sole with a shrimp beurre noisette dressing; and fillet of turbot with a basil and ginger sauce.

Open 12–2.30 6–11 (Sat 12–11, Sun 11.45–10.30) Closed: 25 Dec & 2–5 Jan **Bar Meals** L served Tue-Sun 12–2 D served Tue-Sun 6.30–8.30 Av main course £9.50 **Restaurant** L served Sun 12–2.15 D served Tue-Sat 6.45–9.30 Av 3 course à la carte £25 ⊕ Free House ◀ Tetley Cask, Timothy Taylor Landlord, Black Sheep Best, Malton Brewery Golden Chance. ♈ 14 **Facilities** Garden Parking

KNARESBOROUGH   MAP 19 SE35

Pick of the Pubs

The General Tarleton Inn ★★★★★

RR ⊛⊛ ♈

See Pick of the Pubs on page 660

LANGTHWAITE   MAP 19 NZ00

The Red Lion Inn ♈

DL11 6RE ☎ 01748 884218 📠 01748 884133

e-mail: rlionlangthwaite@aol.com

dir: *Through Reeth into Arkengarthdale, 18m from A1*

The unusually photogenic Red Lion Inn has appeared in several feature films as well as starring in the long running BBC serial *All Creatures Great and Small*. Owned by the same family for 43 years, it's also very much a traditional pub, hosting the local darts and quoits teams, and providing Black Sheep bitter and bar snacks for the hundreds of visitors attracted to this unspoiled stretch of the Yorkshire Dales.

Open 11–3 7–11 **Bar Meals** L served all week 11–3 D served all week 7–10) ⊕ Free House ◀ Black Sheep Riggwelter, Worthington Cream Flow, Tetleys & Guinness. ♈ 8 **Facilities** Garden Parking

PICK OF THE PUBS

The General Tarleton Inn

Sir Banastre Tarleton distinguished himself during the American War of Independence, and the inn was probably opened by a member of his platoon in his honour. What started as an 18th-century coaching inn is now known for its contemporary comforts, unstuffy atmosphere, and top-class dining.

The low-beamed bar area is warm and welcoming, with log fires and cosy corners, the perfect setting in which to enjoy the range of real ales. The covered courtyard is a light, modern setting, while the garden offers a further option for summertime refreshment. The kitchen takes great care to source the best of local, seasonal produce from Yorkshire's larder, establishing supplies from local farmers and producers who share the same passion for good food. The restaurant offers a brasserie-style menu supported by an extensive wine list. There are open sandwiches at lunchtime, with Lishmans rare breed bacon and Nidderdale smoked salmon on English muffins or walnut bread. Smaller dishes or starters with

Yorkshire roots include crisp slowly braised belly pork with prunes, rolled in bacon and served with red onion chutney and scrumpy reduction; and classic fish soup with rouille, gruyère and croutons. Main courses take in confit of Dales lamb with hot pot potatoes, garlic and thyme jus; and chargrilled haunch of venison with a Yorkshire buffalo blue cheese polenta, shallots and salsa verde. Fish and chips is a popular option prepared, with sustainable fishing in mind, from ling and pollock. Yorkshire treacle tart comes with clotted cream for dessert; or try trio of rhubarb (brûlée, crumble and compote) with strawberry ice cream.

★★★★★ RR ◉◉ ♀
MAP 19 SE35
Boroughbridge Rd, Ferrensby
HG5 0PZ
☎ 01423 340284
🖷 01423 340288
e-mail: gti@generaltarleton.co.uk
dir: *A1(M) junct 48 at Boroughbridge, take A6055 to Knaresborough. Inn 4m on right*

Open 12–3 6–11
Bar Meals L served all week 12–2.15 D served Mon-Sat 6–9.30 (Sun 6–8.30) Av main course £14
Restaurant L served Sun 12–2 D served Mon-Sat 6–9.30 Av 3 course à la carte £28.30
⊕ Free House ◼ Black Sheep Best, Timothy Taylor Landlord.
♀ 10
Facilities Garden Parking
Rooms 14

LASTINGHAM   MAP 19 SE79

Blacksmiths Arms ♥

YO62 6TL ☎ 01751 417247 📠 01751 417247

e-mail: pete.hils@blacksmithslastingham.co.uk

dir: *7m from Pickering & 4m from Kirbymoorside. A170 (Pickering to Kirbymoorside road), follow Lastingham & Appleton-le-Moors signs*

This 17th-century, stone-built free house retains its original low-beamed ceilings and open range fireplace; outside there's a cottage garden and decked seating area. Home-cooked dishes include toasted filled paninis; Whitby wholetail scampi; tender chunks of beef in a giant Yorkshire pudding; gammon steak; and vegetable balti. Snacks, sandwiches and daily specials are also available.

Open 12–2.30 6–11 (May-Nov all day) Closed: Tue lunch Nov-May **Bar Meals** L served Mon-Sat 12–2 D served all week 7–9 (Sun 12–5) Av main course £8.50 **Restaurant** L served Mon-Sat 12–2 D served all week 7–9 (Sun 12–5) ⊕ Free House ◀ Theakstons Best Bitter, 2 rotating guest ales e.g. Pheonix, Roosters. ♟ 10 **Facilities** Garden

---

LEYBURN   MAP 19 SE19

The Old Horn Inn

Spennithorne DL8 5PR ☎ 01969 622370

e-mail: desmond@furlong1706.fsbusiness.co.uk

dir: *From Leyburn on A684 approx 1.5 m E. Turn right signed Spennithorne. From Bedale & A1 on A684 approx 9m W. Turn left signed Spennithorne*

Low beams and open log fires characterise this traditional 17th-century free house. The former farmhouse, which has been a pub for at least 100 years, is named after the horn that summoned the farmer's workers to lunch. Today's customers enjoy good food in the dining room. Expect local hog and hop sausages with mash and red onion marmalade; baked salmon with prawns and basil sauce; or roasted vegetable lasagne with garlic ciabatta bread.

Open 12–3 6–11 (Sat & BHs all day during Jul-Aug) **Bar Meals** L served Tue-Sun 12–2 D served Tue-Sun 6.30–9 (12–3 summer) Av main course £9 **Restaurant** L served Tue-Sun 12–2 D served Tue-Sun 7–9 (12–3 summer) ◀ Black Sheep Bitter & Special, John Smiths's Cask, Coors Worthington's Cream Flow. **Facilities** Garden Dogs allowed **Notes** ⊛

Pick of the Pubs

Sandpiper Inn ♥

Market Place DL8 5AT

☎ 01969 622206 📠 01969 625367

e-mail: hsandpiper@aol.com

dir: *From A1 take A684 to Leyburn*

Although it has been a pub for only 30 years, the building that houses the Sandpiper Inn in is the oldest in Leyburn, dating back to around 1640. It has a beautiful summer garden, and inside, a bar, snug and dining room where an exciting and varied mix of traditional and more unusual dishes is served. Lunch brings sandwiches (prawn and rocket, avocado and bacon); and omelette Arnold Bennett. An evening meal could take in black pudding with caramelised apple and foie gras; and Moroccan spiced chicken with couscous; or roasted vegetable risotto with parmesan curls. Sunday lunch ranges from roasted rib-eye of Dales beef with onion gravy and Yorkshire pudding, to Masham sausage with mash and onion gravy.

Open 11.30–3 6.30–11 (Sun 12–3, 6.30–10.30) Closed: Mon & occas Tue **Bar Meals** L served Tue-Sun 12–2.30 D served Tue-Thu 6.30–9.00 (Fri-Sat 6.30–9.30, Sun 7–9) Av main course £9 **Restaurant** L served Tue-Sat 12–2.30 D served Tue-Thu 6.30–9 (Fri-Sat 6.30–9.30, Sun 12–2, 7–9) ⊕ Free House ◀ Black Sheep Best, Black Sheep Special, Daleside, Copperdragon. ♟ 8 **Facilities** Garden Dogs allowed

---

LITTON   MAP 18 SD97

Queens Arms NEW ♥

BD23 5QJ ☎ 01756 770208

e-mail: wdmgoldie@yahoo.co.uk

dir: *N of Skipton*

Surrounded by the beauty of the Yorkshire Dales, this is an ideal refreshment stop for everyone from walkers to potholers. The inn dates from the 16th century and is full of original features including flagstones and beams. An open fire provides a warm winter welcome. The pub serves its own cask-conditioned ales, which are brewed on the premises, as well as fine wines and home-cooked food made with ingredients from local farms.

Open 12–3 6–11.30 (Sun 6–10.30) Closed: Mon **Bar Meals** L served Tue-Sun 12–2.30 D served Tue-Sat 6–9 (Sun 7–9) Av main course £10 **Restaurant** L served Tue-Sun 12–2.30 D served Tue-Sat 6–9 (Sun 7–9) Av 3 course à la carte £20 ⊕ Free House ◀ Litton Ale, Tetley Cask & guest ales. ♟ 12 **Facilities** Children's licence Garden Dogs allowed Parking

England

LONG PRESTON — MAP 18 SD85

Maypole Inn ⚲

Maypole Green BD23 4PH
☎ 01729 840219 ▤ 01729 840727
e-mail: landlord@maypole.co.uk
dir: On A65 between Settle & Skipton

This inn has been welcoming visitors since 1695, when Ambrose Wigglesworth welcomed his first customers. Hand-drawn ales and traditional home cooking underpin the operation. Located at the edge of the Yorkshire Dales National Park, it's a good base for walking and cycling. Relax in the beamed dining room or cosy bar over a pint and a simple snack, sandwich, steak or salad; or try a 'special' like beef in ale pie, braised shoulder of lamb, or pork in Pernod.

Open 11–3 6–11 (Sat 11–11 Sun 12–10.30) **Bar Meals** L served all week 12 D served all week 6.30–9 (Sun 12–11) Av main course £8
Restaurant L served all week 12–2 D served all week 6.30–9 (Sun 12–9, Sat 12–9.30) ⊕ Enterprise Inns ◀ Timothy Taylor Landlord, Moorhouses Premier, Jennings, Cumberland. ⚲ 10 **Facilities** Garden Dogs allowed Parking **Rooms** available

---

LOW ROW — MAP 18 SD99

The Punch Bowl Inn ★★★★ INN NEW ⚲

DL11 6PF ☎ 01748 886233 ▤ 01748 886945
e-mail: info@pbinn.co.uk
dir: From Scotch Corner, take A6108 to Richmond then B6270 to Low Row

An ideal location for walking, the Punch Bowl stands on Alfred Wainwright's 'Coast to Coast' walk and close to the Pennine Way. Dating from the 17th century, the inn reopened in 2006 and has been refurbished using local wood and stone. The latest addition is 11 en-suite bedrooms. Food could include spiced crab samosa with sweet chilli sauce followed by loin of local lamb with home-made black pudding, ratatouille and a bordelaise sauce.

Open 11–12 Closed: 25 Dec **Bar Meals** 12–2 6.30–9 Av main course £10.50 **Restaurant** L served all week 12–2 D served all week 6.30–9 Av 3 course à la carte £21 ⊕ Free House ◀ Theakstons Best Bitter, Black Sheep Best Bitter, John Smiths Cask & Smooth. ⚲ 14 **Facilities** Parking

---

MARTON — MAP 19 SE78

Pick of the Pubs

The Appletree ☺ ⚲

YO62 6RD ☎ 01751 431457 ▤ 01751 430190
e-mail: info.appletreeinn@virgin.net
dir: From Kirkbymoorside on A170 turn right after 1m. 2m to Marton

Warm, rich colours, a huge fire in the cosy lounge and hundreds of evening candles make this a cosy and inviting place to enjoy a quiet drink or a relaxing dinner. Formerly a working farm, the Appletree became a pub when the farmer's wife began serving beer from her living room in earthenware jugs. Today, local farmers are still regulars at the bar, and their produce is a mainstay of the kitchen. Quality ingredients are hugely important to owners

'TJ' and Melanie Drew, who grow salad leaves, herbs and fruit in their orchard garden. Menus change daily: start, perhaps, with sweet potato pancake or steamed Scottish mussels, before moving on to Wintringham Shoot pheasant; salmon poached in mulled wine; or chestnut, spinach and ricotta roulade. Leave room for appetising desserts like marbled chocolate pyramid; and Amaretto meringue mess. Please note that the Appletree is closed on Monday and Tuesday.

Open 12–2.30 6–11 (Sun 12–3, 7–10.30) Closed: 2wks Jan & Mon-Tue **Bar Meals** L served Wed-Sun (booking essential) 12–2 **Restaurant** L served Wed-Sun (booking essential) 12–2 D served Wed-Sat (booking essential) 6–9.30 (Sun 7–9) Av 3 course à la carte £25 ⊕ Free House ◀ John Smiths Cask, Malton, York, Wychwood. ⚲ 14 **Facilities** Garden Parking

---

MASHAM — MAP 19 SE28

The Black Sheep Brewery

HG4 4EN ☎ 01765 689227 & 680100 ▤ 01765 689746
e-mail: sue.dempsey@blacksheep.co.uk
web: www.blacksheep.co.uk
dir: Off A6108, 9m from Ripon & 7m from Bedale.

Paul Theakston, of Masham's famous brewing family, founded the Black Sheep Brewery in the early nineties according to traditional brewing principles. The complex boasts a visitor centre where you can enjoy a 'shepherded' tour of the brewhouse, before popping into the cosy bistro and 'baa…r' to sample the ales. The beers also find their way into a range of hearty dishes, including steak and Riggwelter casserole served with jacket potato.

Open (Please phone for details) **Bar Meals** L served all week **Restaurant** L served all week 12–2.30 D served Thu-Sat 6.30–9 Av 3 course à la carte £22 ⊕ ◀ Black Sheep Best Bitter, Emmerdale, Riggwelter & Black Sheep Ale. **Facilities** Garden Parking

See advert on opposite page

Kings Head Hotel ★★ HL ⚲

Market Place HG4 4EF
☎ 01765 689295 ▤ 01765 689070
dir: B6267 towards Masham, 7m from A1

Overlooking Masham's large market square with its cross and maypole, this tastefully renovated Georgian inn boasts open fires in the public rooms and a pleasant terrace for summer dining. Unwind over a pint of Theakston's in the bar, or sample a range of traditional and contemporary dishes in the wood panelled restaurant. Options might include minted lamb shoulder with creamy mash; chicken with thyme dumplings and Savoy cabbage; and smoked salmon penne pasta.

Open 10.30am-1am **Bar Meals** L served all week 12–2.45 D served all week 6–9.45 Av main course £10.95 **Restaurant** L served all week 12–2.45 D served all week 6–9.45 Av 3 course à la carte £19.95 ◀ Theakstons Best Bitter, Black Bull & Old Peculier, Theakstons XB, Black Sheep. ♟ 14 **Facilities** Garden **Rooms** 27

MIDDLEHAM MAP 19 SE18

Black Swan Hotel ♟

Market Place DL8 4NP
☎ 01969 622221 📄 01969 622221
e-mail: blackswanmiddleham@breathe.com
dir: *Telephone for directions*

Dating back to the 17th-century and backing onto Middleham Castle, home of Richard III, this historic pub is at the heart of Yorkshire's racing country. Horses can be seen passing outside every morning on their way to the gallops. The emphasis here is on good food, with an appealing choice including Black Swan grill, chicken curry, bangers and mash, lasagne, and Kilnsey trout roasted with parsley and thyme dressing. There's also a good vegetarian choice.

Open 10–3.30 6–12 (Sun 12–11.30) **Bar Meals** L served all week 12–2 D served all week 6.30–9 **Restaurant** L served all week 12–2 D served all week 6.30–9 ⊕ Free House ◀ John Smiths, Theakstons Best Bitter, Black Bull, Old Peculier & guest ales. ♟ 7 **Facilities** Garden Dogs allowed

---

MIDDLESMOOR MAP 19 SE07

Crown Hotel ♟

HG3 5ST ☎ 01423 755204
dir: *Telephone for directions*

The original building dates back to the 17th century; today it offers the chance to enjoy a good pint of local beer by a cosy, roaring log fire, or in a sunny pub garden. Stands on a breezy 900ft hilltop with good views towards Gouthwaite Reservoir. Ideal for those potholing or following the popular Nidderdale Way.

Open 12–3 7–11 (closed Mon & Thu lunch) **Bar Meals** L served Fri-Sun 12–2 D served Tue-Wed 7–8.30 (closed BHs) **Restaurant** L served Fri-Sun 12–2 D served Tue-Wed 7–8.30 ⊕ Free House ◀ Black Sheep Best, Worthingtons Smooth, Guinness. ♟ 20 **Facilities** Garden Dogs allowed Parking

---

MIDDLETON MAP 19 SE78
(NEAR PICKERING)

The Middleton Arms ♟

Church Ln YO18 8PB ☎ 01751 475444
e-mail: themiddletonarms@aol.com
dir: *1m W of Pickering on A170*

Formerly known as The New Inn, the pub dates from the 17th century and retains much of its traditional charm. Menus draw on the best local produce and food is prepared to order by chef proprietor Andy Green. Seasonal fish and meat dishes are featured on the daily specials board, while regulars might include roasted Nidderdale chicken breast with creamy risotto, or pan-fried fillet of sea bass with watercress, orange and pine nut salad.

Open 6–11 Closed: Mon **Bar Meals** D served Tue-Sat 6–9 (Sun 12–2, 6–10.30) Av main course £12.25 **Restaurant** L served Sun 12–2 D served Tue-Sat 6–9 ⊕ Free House ◀ Timothy Taylor Landlord, Tetleys Smooth, Nick Stafford Hambleton Ales, Black Sheep. ♟ 7 **Facilities** Parking

Good Pub Guide Brewery of the Year 2006 & 2007

Enjoy a 'Shepherded' tour, a delicious meal in the Bistro & Baa....r, or browse the Black Sheep Shop.

Tel: 01765 680100 / 680101
www.blacksheepbrewery.co.uk

MOULTON MAP 19 NZ20

Black Bull Inn

DL10 6QJ ☎ 01325 377289 📄 01325 377422
e-mail: blackbullinn1@btconnect.com
dir: *1m S of Scotch Corner off A1, 5m from Richmond Town.*

A pub that continues to impress for its consistency and value. A fixed-price Sunday lunch is now available, and dining in the 1932 Brighton Belle Pullman carriage is always an attraction. The pub specialises in fresh seafood, but various meat dishes are also served. Choose a cold starter of Gigas oysters from Cork, or a hot one such as moules marinières. Grilled Dover sole and lobster thermidor compete with herb-roasted rack of lamb and pan-fried beef fillet as main courses.

Open 12–2.30 6.30–9.30 (Fri-Sat 6.30–10) Closed: Sun eve **Bar Meals** L served Mon-Sat 12–2 (Sun 12–4) **Restaurant** L served Mon-Fri 12–2.30 D served Mon-Thu 6.45–9.30 (Fri-Sat 6.45–10) Av 3 course fixed price £19.95 ⊕ Free House ◀ Theakstons Best, John Smiths Smooth. **Facilities** Garden Parking

England

MUKER

MAP 18 SD99

The Farmers Arms ♥

DL11 6QG ☎ 01748 886297 🖹 01748 886375

dir: *From Richmond take A6108 towards Leyburn, turn right onto B6270*

The last remaining pub in the village of Muker, at the head of beautiful Swaledale, the Farmers Arms is understandably popular with walkers. A welcoming coal fire burns in the stone-flagged bar in cooler weather, while in summer the south facing patio is a relaxing place to sit. Award-winning cask marque ales are served along with good home-cooked food (the steak pie is a particular favourite). Dogs on leads are welcome in the bar.

Open 11–11 (Sun 11.30–11) **Bar Meals** L served all week 12–2.30 D served all week 6–8.45 Av main course £7.50 ⊕ Free House ◀ Theakston Best & Old Peculier, John Smith's, Black Sheep, guest ales. ♥ 10 **Facilities** Garden Dogs allowed Parking

NORTH RIGTON

MAP 19 SE24

Pick of the Pubs

The Square and Compass ♥

LS17 0DJ ☎ 01423 734228

e-mail: l13hud@aol.com

dir: *Just off A658, in village centre*

The Square and Compass was originally part of the Harewood estate and probably got its name by being used, many years ago, as a Mason's lodge. Today this pub, set in the beautiful Yorkshire village of North Rigton, is the ideal setting for celebrating special occasions, corporate dinners or simply enjoying a meal or drink with friends. You can relax and soak up the atmosphere while enjoying a light bar meal in the oak beamed bar and lounge, or go for a gourmet meal with fine wines in the tastefully restored restaurant. Both lunchtime and evening à la carte menus use only the freshest of local ingredients: starters could include a large Yorkshire pudding with onion gravy; and smooth paté of chicken liver, brandy, garlic and orange. Mains dishes of rib-eye steak with garnish; chicken breast with smoked Wensleydale cheese wrapped in dry cured bacon; crispy haddock in beer batter; and chef's luxury fish pie provide a good variety.

Open 12–3 5–11 **Bar Meals** L served all week 12–2.30 D served all week 6–9.30 (Sun 12–6) Av main course £9.50 **Restaurant** L served Sun 12–6 D served Fri-Sat 6–9.30 Av 3 course à la carte £22.50 ◀ Black Sheep, Timothy Taylor Landlord, Hoegaarden. ♥ 46 **Facilities** Garden Parking

NUNNINGTON

MAP 19 SE67

The Royal Oak Inn ♥

Church St YO62 5US ☎ 01439 748271 🖹 01439 748271

dir: *Village centre, close to Nunnington Hall*

A solid stone pub in this sleepy rural backwater in the Howardian Hills, a short drive from the North Yorkshire Moors. The immaculate open-plan bar is furnished with scrubbed pine and decorated with farming memorabilia, just the place for a pint of Theakstons and a bite to eat. New landlord for 2008.

Open 12–2.30 6.30–11 Closed: Mon **Bar Meals** L served Tue-Sun 12–2 D served Tue-Sun 6.30–9 **Restaurant** L served Tue-Sun 12–2 D served Tue-Sun 6.30–9 ⊕ Free House ◀ Black Sheep, Wold Top, John Smith's. ♥ 11 **Facilities** Parking

OLDSTEAD

MAP 19 SE57

Pick of the Pubs

The Black Swan NEW ⓤ ◉ ♥

Main St YO61 4BL ☎ 01347 868387

e-mail: enquiries@blackswanoldstead.co.uk

dir: *From Coxwold village turn towards Byland Abbey. After 2m, turn left for Oldstead, 1m on left*

The Black Swan, which dates from the 16th century, is owned and run by the Banks family, who have lived and farmed in the village for generations. The bar is full of character with a log fire, flagstone floor, window seats, antique furniture and oak fittings by Robert 'Mousey' Thompson. Choice at the bar includes real ales, good wines by the glass, malt whiskies and old port. Both lunch and evening menus offer home-made fare including traditional and more sophisticated dishes. Options from the specials board include braised home-made faggots with parsley mash; and hot smoked eel with minted mushy peas, crispy pancetta and game chips. Ingredients are fresh, and the beef, pork and lamb comes from local farms. Printed details of walks from the pub are available at the bar, and you are welcome to leave your vehicle in the car park while you enjoy your walk.

Open 12–3 6–11 (Sat-Sun 12–11) **Bar Meals** L served Mon-Sat 12–2 D served all week 6–9 (Sun 12–2.30) Av main course £10 **Restaurant** L served Mon-Sat 12–2 D served all week 6–9 (Sun 12–2.30) Av 3 course à la carte £22 ◀ Black Sheep, Copper Dragon & John Smiths. ♥ 11 **Facilities** Children's licence Garden Parking

OSMOTHERLEY
MAP 19 SE49

Pick of the Pubs

The Golden Lion

6 West End DL6 3AA ☎ 01609 883526

The Golden Lion is a cosy sandstone building of some 250 years standing. The atmosphere is warm and welcoming, with open fires and wooden flooring on one side of the downstairs area. Furnishings are simple with a wooden bar, bench seating and tables, whitewashed walls, mirrors and fresh flowers. The extensive menu ranges through basic pub grub to more refined dishes. The starters are divided between fish, soups, vegetarian, pastas and risottos, meat and salads, and might include smoked salmon; buffalo mozzarella with tomato and basil; spicy pork ribs; and avocado and king prawn salad. Mains are along the lines of grilled seabass with new potatoes and peas; coq au vin; calve's liver with fried onions and mash; home-made beef burger with Mexican salsa; and spicy chilladas with fresh tomato sauce. Also interesting specials like pork stroganoff and rice, or lamb and feta lasagne. Sherry trifle, and bread and butter pudding with cream, are popular desserts.

Open 12–3 6–11 Sat–Sun all day Closed: 25 Dec **Bar Meals** L served all week 12–2.30 D served all week 6–9.15 Food all day when busy Av main course £9.95 **Restaurant** L served all week 12–2.30 D served all week 6–9.15 Av 3 course à la carte £18 ◀ Timothy Taylors Landlord, Hambleton Bitter, Jennings Bitter, Caledonian IPA. **Facilities** Garden Dogs allowed

Queen Catherine ★★★ INN

7 West End DL6 3AG ☎ 01609 883209

e-mail: queencatherine@yahoo.co.uk

Named after Henry VIII's wife, Catherine of Aragon, who left her horse and carriage here while sheltering from her husband with nearby monks. There's no sense of menace around this friendly hotel nowadays, believed to be the only one in Britain bearing its name, and visitors can enjoy a well-cooked meal: monkfish tails, crab-stuffed chicken breast, lamb shank with minted gravy, Icelandic cod, and Whitby breaded scampi are all on the menu.

Open 12–11 **Bar Meals** L served Mon–Sat 12–2 D served Mon–Sat 6–9 (Sun 12–9) **Restaurant** L served all week 12–2 D served all week 6–9 ⊕ Free House ◀ Hambleton Ales-Stud, Stallion, Bitter, Goldfield. **Facilities** Dogs allowed **Rooms** 5

PADSIDE
MAP 19 SE15

The Stone House Inn NEW ♟

Thruscross HG3 4AH

☎ 01943 880325 📄 01943 880347

e-mail: info@stonehouseinn.co.uk

Throughout its 300–year history, the Stone House Inn has been a place of refreshment for travellers as well as a community hub. Run by John McEwan since 2007, it features open fires, exposed beams and stone flagged floors. Locally sourced ingredients are the starting point for varied, home made dishes; expect specials such as Ramsgill oxtail casserole with root vegetables; black pudding salad; and wild mushroom and feta lasagne. Lunchtime sandwiches are also available.

Open 12–12 Closed: Mon (Jan–Etr) **Bar Meals** L served all week 12–5 D served all week 12–9 **Restaurant** L served all week 12–5 D served all week 5–9 Av 3 course à la carte £20 ⊕ Free House ◀ Black Sheep Bitter, Deuchars IPA, Old Bear Honeypot, Riggwelter & Daleside. ♟ 7 **Facilities** Children's licence Garden Dogs allowed Parking

PATELEY BRIDGE
MAP 19 SE16

Pick of the Pubs

The Sportsmans Arms Hotel ♟
See Pick of the Pubs on page 666

PICKERING
MAP 19 SE78

Pick of the Pubs

Fox & Hounds Country Inn ★★ HL
◉ ♟

Sinnington YO62 6SQ

☎ 01751 431577 📄 01751 432791

e-mail: foxhoundsinn@easynet.co.uk

dir: *3m W of town, off A170*

This handsome 18th-century coaching inn lies in Sinnington, just off the main road. The village has a large green with its own maypole, and there is a packhorse bridge nearby over the River Seven. The inn's cosy interior offers oak-beamed ceilings, old wood panelling and open fires. Modern British dishes are served in the restaurant and lounge bar, and a small dining room is available for private parties, seating up to 12 people. A selection of freshly cooked dishes prepared from meat and produce supplied by local farmers might include pot roast chicken breast with Yorkshire ale; shoulder of lamb casserole; and beer battered fresh haddock and chips. Traditional Sunday lunches are popular, with plenty to choose from, though local roast beef and Yorkshire puddings are a given. The inn has ten well equipped en suite bedrooms and a newly refurbished residents' lounge, where guests can relax by the fire before dinner.

Open 12–2 6–11 (Sun 6–10.30) **Bar Meals** L served all week 12–2 D served Mon–Sat 6.30–9 (Sun 6.30–8.30) Av main course £12.95 **Restaurant** L served all week 12–2 D served Mon–Sat 6.30–9 (Sun 6.30–8.30) ⊕ Free House ◀ Theakston Best, Black Sheep Special, Worthingtons Creamflow. ♟ 7 **Facilities** Garden Dogs allowed Parking **Rooms** 10

The Sportsmans Arms Hotel

Wath-in-Nidderdale is a conservation village, and one of the most picturesque and unspoilt settlements in the Yorkshire Dales National Park. Ray and Jane Carter have been running this unpretentious hotel for nearly 30 years, although son Jamie and daughter Sarah have leading roles too these days.

Dating from the 17th century, the sandstone-built Sportsmans Arms stands on the 53–mile, circular Nidderdale Way, hard by the dam over the River Nidd (some fishing rights belong to the hotel) that creates Gouthwaite Reservoir. Approach via an old pack-horse bridge, enter the hallway and find open log fires, comfortable chairs, a warm and welcoming bar and a charming restaurant. As much of the food as possible is locally sourced, but Ray has no qualms about occasionally buying foreign produce if he thinks it better. Always good, though, are the Nidderdale lamb, pork, beef, trout and game (season permitting) that can always be found on the menu. Fish arriving daily from Whitby and Redcar on the East

Coast, typically appears on the plate as turbot with spinach and mousseline; seared tuna with rocket salsa and Greek salad; or maybe lightly-cooked halibut with beurre blanc glazed with fresh parmesan. Best end of Nidderdale lamb is perfectly accompanied by creamy garlic mash, natural jus and tomato concassée; and chestnuts, cranberries and pancetta go well with saddle of venison. The wine list offers a wide selection of styles and prices. The annual Lobster Festival at the end of May is hugely popular.

♀
MAP 19 SE16
Wath-in-Nidderdale HG3 5PP
☎ 01423 711306
🖨 01423 712524
dir: *A59/B6451, hotel 2m N of Pateley Bridge*

Open 12–2 7–11 (Sun 7–10.30)
Closed: 25 Dec
Bar Meals L served all week
12–2 D served all week 7–9 Av main course £11.50
Restaurant L served all week
12–2 D served all week 7–9.30 Av 3 course à la carte £28
⊞ Free House ◖ Black Sheep, Worthingtons, Folly Ale. ♀ 12
Facilities Garden Parking

PICKERING continued

Horseshoe Inn ♀

Main St, Levisham YO18 7NL ☎ 01751 460240
e-mail: info@horseshoelevisham.co.uk
dir: *A169, 5m from Pickering. 4m, pass Fox & Rabbit Inn on right. In 0.5m left to Lockton. Follow steep winding road to village*

A 16th-century inn standing at the head of the tranquil moorland village of Levisham in the North York Moors National Park, with the steam railway running through. The Horseshoe reopened in February 2008 under the ownership of the Wood family. Chef/proprietor Toby prepares a simple menu which is served in the bar warmed by a lovely log fire. Expect dishes such as ham hock terrine, mini roast brisket with Yorkshire pudding, and chocolate mousse.

Open 10–3 6–11 (summer all day) Closed: Sun eve winter
Bar Meals L served all week 12–2 D served all week 6–8.30 Av main course £10.95 **Restaurant** L served all week 12–2 D served all week 6.30–9 ⊕ Free House ◀ Theakstons Best Bitter, John Smiths, Old Peculier. ♀9
Facilities Garden Dogs allowed Parking

Pick of the Pubs

The White Swan Inn ★★★ HL ⊛ ♀

Market Place YO18 7AA
☎ 01751 472288 📄 01751 475554
e-mail: welcome@white-swan.co.uk
dir: *From N: A19 or A1 to Thirsk, A170 to Pickering, left at lights, 1st right onto Market Place. Pub on left. From S: A1 or A1(M) to A64 to Malton rdbt, A169 to Pickering*

Standing just off the market place in this thriving Yorkshire town, the White Swan has been owned by the Buchanan family for two decades. Originally built in 1532 as a four-room cottage, the building was soon converted to a coaching inn on the York to Whitby route. Nowadays the inn blends traditional simplicity with understated luxury and style; the owners and staff pay careful attention to every detail. There are comfy, relaxing sofas, whilst the restaurant has stone flagged floors and a roaring winter fire. A set price lunch menu offers a choice of two or three courses: expect grilled sardines, followed by salmon, leek and potato hash, with glazed lemon tart and raspberries for dessert. The dinner menu might range from pan-fried venison with bubble and squeak, glazed shallots and redcurrant jelly, to posh Whitby fish and chips with mushy peas and tartare sauce.

Open 10 -11 (Occasionally closed Winter 3–6) **Bar Meals** L served all week 12–2 Av main course £16.71 **Restaurant** L served all week 12–2 D served all week 6.45–9 Av 3 course à la carte £29.74 Av 3 course fixed price £15 ⊕ Free House ◀ Black Sheep Best & Special, Yorkshire Moors Cropton Brewery, Timothy Taylor Landord. ♀15
Facilities Dogs allowed Parking **Rooms** 21

PICKHILL
MAP 19 SE38

Pick of the Pubs

Nags Head Country Inn ★★ HL ⊛ ♀

YO7 4JG ☎ 01845 567391 📄 01845 567212
e-mail: enquiries@nagsheadpickhill.co.uk
dir: *1m E of A1(4m N of A1/A61 junct)*

This region of Yorkshire is known as 'Herriot country', after the books by the famous country vet. A direct descendant of the coaching inn tradition, the Nag's Head is a 200–year-old free house, set in the village of Pickhill. It's perfectly situated for exploring the local fells, playing a round of golf, fishing or having a flutter at nearby Thirsk, Ripon and Catterick races. Once you've worked up an appetite head inside, where beamed ceilings, stone-flagged floors and winter fires make for a most welcoming atmosphere. A lengthy, thoughtful menu is equally appealing. Starters like queenie scallops glazed with gruyere cheese precede main course options that include locally smoked Whitby haddock on a Welsh rarebit muffin; casserole of local game topped with suet pastry, or duo of pork loin and belly on root vegetable mash. On sunny days, meals can be taken in the secluded walled garden.

Open 11–11 Closed: 25 Dec **Bar Meals** L served Mon-Sat 12–2 D served Mon-Sat 6–9.30 (Sun 12–2.30, 6–9) Av main course £12 **Restaurant** L served all week 12–2 D served Mon-Sat 7–9.30 (Sun 7–9) Av 3 course à la carte £25 ⊕ Free House ◀ Hambleton Bitter & Goldfield, Black Sheep Best & Special, Old Peculier, Theakstons Best Bitter. ♀8 **Facilities** Garden Dogs allowed Parking **Rooms** 16

PICTON
MAP 19 NZ40

The Station Pub

TS15 0AE ☎ 01642 700067
dir: *1.5m from A19*

A family-run and family-friendly village pub, offering real food at reasonable prices. Just about everything is home made, with one menu serving both bar and dining room. While the children enjoy the outdoor play area, Mum and Dad can relax in front of the open fire and scan the extensive specials board. If fish is the order of the day, you may find oven-roasted cod with Wensleydale cheese, lime and ginger crumb; or sea bass fillets with stirfry.

Open 6–12 (Sat-Sun 12–3, 6–12) **Bar Meals** L served Sat 12–2 D served all week 6.30–9 (Sun 12–4) **Restaurant** L served Sat-Sun 12–2 D served all week 6.30–9 ⊕ Free House ◀ John Smiths Cask, John Smiths Smooth, Guinness. **Facilities** Garden Parking Play Area

Muker, Swaledale in the Yorkshire Dales National Park , North Yorkshire

REETH | MAP 19 SE09

Pick of the Pubs

Charles Bathurst Inn ★★★★ INN ♀

See Pick of the Pubs on page 671

ROBIN HOOD'S BAY | MAP 19 NZ90

Laurel Inn

New Rd YO22 4SE ☎ 01947 880400

dir: *Telephone for directions*

Picturesque Robin Hood's Bay is the setting for this small, traditional pub which retains lots of character features, including beams and an open fire. The bar is decorated with old photographs, and an international collection of lager bottles. This coastal fishing village was once the haunt of smugglers who used a network of underground tunnels and secret passages to bring the booty ashore. Straightforward simple menu offers wholesome sandwiches and soups.

Open 12–11 (Sun 12–10.30 Mon-Fri Nov-Feb 2–11) ⊕ Free House ◀ Old Peculier, Theakstons Best & Deuchars IPA. **Facilities** Dogs allowed **Notes** ⊕

ROSEDALE ABBEY | MAP 19 SE79

Pick of the Pubs

The Milburn Arms Hotel ♀

YO18 8RA ☎ 01751 417312 📠 01751 417541

e-mail: info@millburnarms.co.uk

dir: *A170 W from Pickering 3m, right at sign to Rosedale then 7m N*

In the heart of the Yorkshire Moors lies the picturesque village of Rosedale Abbey. Opposite the village green you will find this charming country house hotel dating back to 1776, and a perfect rural retreat. The family-run hotel offers a welcoming bar and log fires in the public rooms. Rosedale, once a centre for ironstone mining, is great for walking and you can quite literally begin a local hike at the front door of the hotel. Also close by are some of Yorkshire's best-loved attractions, including Castle Howard, Rievaulx Abbey and the region's famous steam railway. The Priory Restaurant is known for its quality cuisine: lobster and crab bisque, or a slice of pink melon and Parma ham sharpen the appetite for chicken breast with apricot and pork; pan-fried calves' liver with red wine shallot; or poached fillet of plaice filled with fresh prawns.

Open 11.30–3 6–11 Closed: 25 Dec **Bar Meals** L served all week 12–2.15 D served all week 6–9 (Sun 12–3) Av main course £15 **Restaurant** L served Sun 12–2.30 D served all week 6–9.15 Av 3 course à la carte £22.50 Av fixed price £10 ⊕ Free House ◀ Black Sheep Best, Tetely Bitter, John Smith's, Theakstons. ♀8 **Facilities** Garden Dogs allowed Parking

---

SAWDON | MAP 17 SE98

The Anvil Inn ♀

Main St YO13 9DY ☎ 01723 859896

e-mail: theanvilinnsawdon@btinternet.com

web: www.theanvilinnsawdon.co.uk

dir: *1.5m N of Brompton-by-Sawdon, on A170 8m E of Pickering & 6m W of Scarborough*

Set in a walkers' and birdwatchers' paradise on the edge of Dalby Forest, this was a working forge for over 200 years until 1985; many artefacts remain, and the bar features the original furnace under a high pitched roof. At least two Yorkshire brews and 10 wines are always available. Local produce, nicely cooked and well priced, appears in chef's specials such as paté of Yorkshire blue and leek, skate wing in clarified butter, and toffeed banana crêpes.

Open 12–2.30 6.30–11 (Summer 6–11) Closed: 26 Dec & 1 Jan & Mon **Bar Meals** L served Tue-Sat 12–2 (Sun 12–3) **Restaurant** L served Tue-Sat 12–2 D served Tue-Sat 6.30–9 (Sun 12–3) Av 3 course à la carte £32 ⊕ Free House ◀ Black Sheep Best, Daleside Blonde, Hobgoblin Ale, Fuller's London Pride. ♀9 **Facilities** Children's licence Garden Dogs allowed Parking

---

SAWLEY | MAP 19 SE26

The Sawley Arms ♀

HG4 3EQ ☎ 01765 620642

e-mail: junehawes1@aol.co.uk

dir: *A1, Knaresborough-Ripley, or A1, Ripon B6265–Pateley Bridge. 1m from Fountains Abbey*

This delightful 200–year-old pub stands just a mile from Fountains Abbey. Run by the same owners for nearly 40 years, it was a frequent haunt of the late author and vet James Herriot. Surrounded by its own stunning gardens, the pub is big on old world charm. The menu is

CONTINUED

England

SAWLEY continued

suitably traditional, with dishes ranging from pies and casseroles to fresh plaice mornay with sautéed leeks, creamed potatoes and a rich cheese glaze.

Open 11.30–3 6.30–10.30 Closed: 25 Dec (Sun eve winter)
Bar Meals L served all week 12–2.30 D served Tue-Sat 6.30–9 (Sun 6–8 in summer) **Restaurant** L served all week 12–2.30 D served Tue-Sat 6.30–9 (Sun 6–8 in summer) Av 3 course à la carte £16.50 ⊕ Free House ◀ Theakston Best, John Smiths. ♥ 8 **Facilities** Garden Parking

SCAWTON   MAP 19 SE58

Pick of the Pubs

The Hare Inn ♥

YO7 2HG ☎ 01845 597524
dir: *Telephone for directions*

Mentioned in the Domesday Book, and once frequented by the abbots and monks of Rievaulx Abbey. In the 17th century ale was brewed here for local iron workers. Inside, as you might expect, are low-beamed ceilings and flagstone floors, a wood-burning stove providing a warm welcome in the bar, and an old-fashioned kitchen range in the dining area. Diners may find baked Whitby haddock with a minted pea crust, Aberdeen Angus sirloin steak and caramelized red onion sandwich, crab and king scallop thermidor with a crunchy parmesan topping, tagliatelle in crab and salmon cream sauce, and poached lemon sole with crisp pancetta and pimientos.

Open 12–3 6.30–11 (Sun 12–3.30, 6.30–11, summer varies)
Bar Meals L served Tue-Sat 12–2.30 D served Tue-Sat 6.30–8.45 (Sat-Sun 12– 3) **Restaurant** L served Tue-Sun 12–2.30 D served Tue-Sat 6.30–8.45 ⊕ Free House ◀ Black Sheep, John Smiths, guest ales. ♥ 14 **Facilities** Garden Parking

SETTLE   MAP 18 SD86

Golden Lion ♥

Duke St BD24 9DU ☎ 01729 822203 ▤ 01729 824103
e-mail: info@goldenlion.yorks.net
dir: *Telephone for directions*

This traditional Dales coaching inn has been the silent witness to incalculable comings and goings in Settle's market place since around 1640. Its cosy bars, open fire, commodious restaurant and comfy bedrooms often meet the needs of travellers on the spectacular Settle-Carlisle railway line. There is a good choice of beers and a strong emphasis on food prepared from fresh ingredients, with specials such as moules marinière, Moroccan lamb curry and vegetable stirfry.

Open 11–11 **Bar Meals** L served all week 12–2.30 D served all week 6–10 Av main course £7.50 **Restaurant** L served all week 12–2.30 D served all week 6–10 Av 3 course à la carte £18 ⊕ Thwaites ◀ Thwaites Bitter, Bomber, Thoroughbred, Smooth & guest ales. ♥ 9 **Facilities** Children's licence Parking

SKIPTON   MAP 18 SD95

Devonshire Arms ♥

Grassington Rd, Cracoe BD23 6LA
☎ 01756 730237 ▤ 01756 730142
dir: *Telephone for directions*

A convivial 17th-century inn convenient for the Three Peaks, and original setting for the Rhylstone Ladies WI calendar. There are excellent views of Rhylstone Fell. A wide range of cask ales plus extensive wine list will wash down a menu that includes steak and mushroom pie cooked in Jennings Snecklifter ale, lamb Jennings, chicken Diane, and haddock and chips.

Open 12–3 6–12 (Sat 12–1am, Sun 12–12) **Bar Meals** L served all week 12–2 D served all week 6.30–9 (Fri-Sat 6.30–9, Sun 12–4) **Restaurant** L served all week 12–2 D served all week 6.30–8.30 Fri-Sat 6.30–9, Sun 12–4 ◀ Jennings, Jennings Cumberland, Snecklifter, Tetley's. ♥ 7 **Facilities** Garden Parking

SNAINTON   MAP 17 SE98

Coachman Inn ♥

Pickering Rd West YO13 9PL
☎ 01723 859231 ▤ 01723 850008
e-mail: james@coachmaninn.co.uk
dir: *5m from Pickering, off A170 on B1258*

The Coachman is an imposing Grade II listed Georgian coaching inn, run by James and Rita Osborne. Main courses include asparagus, spinach and wild mushroom puff pastry tartlet with poached egg and hollandaise; slow-roast belly of pork with cider, celeriac, apples and crackling; wild salmon with casserole of summer vegetables; and roast fillet of Scarborough halibut with mushrooms, and pea and bacon risotto. Outside is a large lawned area with flowers, trees and seating.

Open 12–2 6–11 **Bar Meals** L served Wed-Sun 12–2 D served 7–9 (Sun 6.30-8.30) **Restaurant** L served pre booking only 12–2 D served Tue-Sat 7–9 Av 3 course à la carte £25 ⊕ Free House ◀ John Smiths, Wold Top, Guinness. ♥ 7 **Facilities** Children's licence Garden Parking

STARBOTTON   MAP 18 SD97

Fox & Hounds Inn ♥

BD23 5HY ☎ 01756 760269 & 760367
dir: *Telephone for directions*

Situated in a picturesque limestone village in Upper Wharfedale, this ancient pub was originally built as a private house, but has been a pub for more than 160 years. Make for the cosy bar, with its solid furnishings and flagstones, and enjoy a pint of Black Sheep or one of the guest ales. The menu offers steak and ale pie, lamb shank, pork medallions in brandy and mustard sauce, and a selection of steaks.

Open 11.30–3 6–11 (BH open lunch only) Closed: 1–22 Jan
Bar Meals L served Tue-Sat 12–2.30 D served Tue-Sat 6–9 (Sun 12–8.15) ⊕ Free House ◀ Black Sheep, Timothy Taylor Landlord, Boddingtons White Horse & guest ales. ♥ 8 **Facilities** Garden Parking **Rooms** available

PICK OF THE PUBS

Charles Bathurst Inn

Strategically located about halfway along the St Bee's Head to Robin Hood's Bay coast-to-coast walk, this 18th-century inn is predictably popular with ramblers. Set in remote and beautiful Arkengarthdale, the CB (as regulars call it) was a bunkhouse for lead miners employed by the man himself, an 18th-century lord of the manor and son of Oliver Cromwell's physician.

Customers entering the bar and restaurant, once a barn and stable, are greeted by cosy fires and antique pine furniture. The owners pride themselves on knowing the provenance of all their food, which is purchased locally and prepared and cooked on the premises. The menu, written up daily on an imposing mirror hanging at the end of the bar, reflects the frequently changing availability of fresh, seasonal food, and features lamb and beef from Swale Hall, game (in season) from the surrounding moors, and fish from Hartlepool (delivered six times weekly). Starters might include asparagus and Wensleydale cheese tartlet with sour cherry confit; and home-made black pudding with tomato fondue and seared queen scallops. For a hearty lunch try Swaledale shank of lamb, mixed beans and juniper jus; or the lighter aubergine, tomato and feta gratin. An evening meal of line-caught wild sea bass with smoked salmon mousseline and roasted root vegetables could prove a winner, followed perhaps by pear frangipane with lemon, honey and crème fraîche ice cream. Wines are supplied by award-winning Playford Ros of Thirsk. While in the area visit the CB's sister establishment, the 17th-century Punch Bowl Inn, in neighbouring Swaledale.

★★★★ INN ☕
MAP 19 SE09
Arkengarthdale DL11 6EN
☎ 01748 884567
🖹 01748 884599
e-mail: info@cbinn.co.uk
dir: *B6270 to Reeth. At Buck Hotel turn N to Langthwaite, pass church on right, inn 0.5m on right*

Open 11–12 Closed: 25 Dec
Bar Meals L served all week 12–2 D served all week 6.30–9 Av main course £11
Restaurant L served all week 12–2 D served all week 6.30–9 Av 3 course à la carte £21.50
🍺 Free House ◀ Theakstons, John Smiths Bitter, John Smiths Smooth, Black Sheep Best & Riggwelter. ☕ 10
Facilities Garden Parking Play Area
Rooms 19

SUTTON-ON-THE-FOREST   MAP 19 SE56

Pick of the Pubs

The Blackwell Ox Inn ★★★★ INN
@ ♀

Huby Rd YO61 1DT ☎ 01347 810328 📄 01347 812738

e-mail: enquiries@blackwelloxinn.co.uk

dir: *7m from centre of York off A1237. Take B1363, at t-junct turn left and pub on the right*

Originally a private residence, built in the early 1820s, the Blackwell Ox takes its name from a shorthorn Teeswater ox that was slaughtered in 1779. Today, it's a friendly village pub, with open winter fires in the cosy bar and lounge, hand-pulled cask ales and summer dining in the garden. Seven individually designed en suite bedrooms make this an inviting base for touring the Yorkshire countryside or visiting the nearby city of York. Head chef Steven Holding draws inspiration from the robust flavours of French and Spanish regional cookery, and sources his ingredients from local producers named on the menus. Dinner might begin with pan-seared scallops with confit pork, onion purée and roasting juices, followed by roast stuffed loin of rabbit with tagliatelle and herby girolle mushrooms. A good choice of desserts ranges from crème brûlée to spotted dick; alternatively try the Yorkshire cheeses with biscuits and chutney.

Open 12–2 5–11 **Bar Meals** L served Mon-Sat 12–2 D served Mon-Sat 6–9.30 (Sun 12–2.30, 6.30–9) **Restaurant** L served Sun 12–2.30 D served Mon-Sat 6–9.30 (Sun 6.30–9) ⊕ Free House ◀ Black Sheep, John Smiths Cask, John Smiths Smooth, Guinness. ♀ 9 **Facilities** Garden Parking **Rooms** 7

THORNTON LE DALE   MAP 19 SE88

The New Inn

Maltongate YO18 7LF ☎ 01751 474226

e-mail: enquire@the-new-inn.com

dir: *A69N from York to Scarborough, follow signs to Malton/ Pickering, after 5m right at Pickering rdbt, take A170 for 2m, pub on right*

This Georgian coaching inn stands at the heart of a picturesque village complete with stocks and a market cross. The old world charm of the surroundings is echoed inside the bar and restaurant, whose large windows illuminate real log fires and exposed beams. Well-behaved dogs sit patiently while their owners ponder the array of guest ales, bitters, lagers and wines. Freshly cooked food ranges from ploughman's to prime fillet steaks and roast of the day.

Open 11–3 5–11 (Sun & Summer all day) **Bar Meals** L served all week 12–2 D served Mon-Sat 6–8.30 Av main course £8.50 **Restaurant** L served all week 12–2 D served Mon-Sat 6–8.30 ⊕ Scottish & Newcastle ◀ Theakston Best, Bombardier, Black Sheep & guest ales. **Facilities** Garden Dogs allowed Parking

THORNTON WATLASS   MAP 19 SE28

Pick of the Pubs

The Buck Inn ★★★ INN ♀

See Pick of the Pubs on opposite page

TOPCLIFFE   MAP 19 SE37

The Angel Inn Ⓤ ♀

YO7 3RW ☎ 01845 577237 📄 01845 578000

e-mail: mail@angelinn.co.uk

dir: *Located on the A168(M) trunk rd 3m from the A1*

A refurbishment has given this old country inn a more contemporary feel, but with more than a nod to tradition. The restaurant has a good local reputation for creative dishes such as fillet of red mullet with warm potato, celeriac and beetroot salad; pheasant pot au feu with stuffed cabbage and spätzle; and, for two, seafood casserole under puff pastry. Most of the 15 bedrooms are in a new wing.

Open 11–11 **Bar Meals** L served all week 12–9 D served all week 12–9 Av main course £8.95 **Restaurant** L served all week D served all week ◀ John Smith, Black Sheep, Timothy Taylors. ♀ 8 **Facilities** Children's licence Garden Dogs allowed Parking **Rooms** 15

WASS   MAP 19 SE57

Pick of the Pubs

Wombwell Arms ♀

YO61 4BE ☎ 01347 868280

e-mail: wykes@wombwellarms.wanadoo.co.uk

dir: *From A1 take A168 to A19 junct. Take York exit, then left after 2.5m, left at Coxwold to Ampleforth. Wass 2m*

The building was constructed around 1620 as a granary, probably using stone from nearby Ryland Abbey, and it became an ale house in about 1645. A series of stylishly decorated rooms provide the setting for bistro-style cooking. Local suppliers have been established for all the produce used: at least three vegetarian dishes are offered daily along with a good choice of fresh fish, including Whitby cod. Popular options are steak, Guinness and mushroom pie, country rabbit, and game casserole. Great location for those walking the North Yorks National Park.

Open 11–3 6.15–11 Closed: Sun pm in low season **Bar Meals** L served all week 12–2.30 D served all week Sun 12–3 Av main course £12 **Restaurant** L served all week 12–2.30 D served all week 6.30–8.30 (Sun 12–3) Av 3 course à la carte £20 ⊕ Free House ◀ Black Sheep Best, Timothy Taylor Landlord, Tetley Extra Smooth. ♀ 7 **Facilities** Children's licence Garden Parking

PICK OF THE PUBS

THORNTON WATLASS-YORKSHIRE, NORTH

The Buck Inn

The picturesque village of Thornton Watlass is where Wensleydale, gateway to the Yorkshire Dales National Park, begins. It's also where much of the television programme Heartbeat is filmed – a little quieter than the better known Goathland.

After more than 20 years caring for the Buck, Michael and Margaret Fox have no trouble maintaining its welcoming and relaxed atmosphere. The pub overlooks the triangular village green, incorporating a cricket pitch whose boundary is actually the pub wall. There are three separate dining areas – the bar for informality, the restaurant for dining by candlelight, and on busy days the large function room is opened. The menu ranges from traditional, freshly prepared pub fare to exciting modern cuisine backed by daily changing blackboard specials. Typical bar favourites are omelettes, with most combinations possible; the prawn and potted shrimp platter – the shrimps from the Solway Firth prepared in a lightly spiced melting butter glaze; and a Greek salad with feta cheese, fresh basil, black olives, cherry tomatoes and mixed leaves served with freshly baked bread. From the à la carte menu you'll probably find a starter salad of crispy shredded duck and bacon; or scallops with smoked bacon. Main courses are hearty and wholesome: the game casserole, for example, comprises venison, hare, game sausage and herb dumplings served with parsnip mash; and monkfish stuffed with tapenade is wrapped in Parma ham and served with spinach and sautéed potatoes. Beer drinkers have a choice of five real ales pulled from hand pumps, including Masham-brewed Black Sheep, while whisky drinkers have a selection of some forty different malts to try, ideal when relaxing by the real coal fire. Live music most Sundays.

★★★ INN ?
MAP 19 SE28
HG4 4AH
☎ 01677 422461
📠 01677 422447
e-mail:
innwatlass1@btconnect.com
dir: *From A1 at Leeming Bar take A684 to Bedale, then B6268 towards Masham. Village 2m on right, hotel by cricket green*

Open 11–11 Closed: 25 Dec eve
Bar Meals L served Mon-Sat 12–2 D (Sun 12–3) served all week 6.30–9.30 Av main course £9
Restaurant L served Mon-Sat 12–2 D (Sun 12–3) served all week 6.30–9.30 Av 3 course à la carte £24 Av 3 course fixed price £16.50
⊕ Free House ◖ Theakston Best, Black Sheep Best, John Smith's & guest ales. ? 7
Facilities Garden Dogs allowed Parking Play Area
Rooms 5

WEAVERTHORPE — MAP 17 SE97

Pick of the Pubs

The Star Country Inn

See Pick of the Pubs on opposite page

WEST BURTON — MAP 19 SE08

Fox & Hounds

DL8 4JY ☎ 01969 663111 📠 01969 663279
e-mail: foxandhounds.westburton@virgin.net
web: www.fhinn.co.uk
dir: *A468 between Hawes & Leyburn, 0.5m E of Aysgarth*

Overlooking the village green in the unspoilt village of West Burton, this inn offers log fires and home cooking. Hand-pulled ales on offer at the bar include Black Sheep and Copper Dragon. Traditional pub food includes steak and kidney pie, curry, and lasagne will fortify you for country walks or visits to nearby waterfalls, castles or cheese-tasting at the Wensleydale Creamery.

Open 11–12 **Bar Meals** L served all week 12–2 D served all week 6–8.30 Av main course £6.95 **Restaurant** L served all week 12–2 D served all week 6–8.30 Av 3 course à la carte £15 ⊕ Free House ◀ Black Sheep, John Smiths, Tetleys, Copper Dragon. **Facilities** Dogs allowed Parking

---

WESTOW — MAP 19 SE76

The Blacksmiths Inn

Main St YO60 7NE ☎ 01653 618365
dir: *From A64, Westow signed from top of Whitwell Hill. Turn right and onto T-junct. Pub on right on Main St*

A 19th-century free house in the old village blacksmith's, where nothing much has changed and the old oven, anvil and bellows are still in place. Tuesday night is pie night, when the new owners serve a selection of home-made pies, washed down with Jennings' Bitter or Cumberland. Reports please.

Open 12–2 5.30–11 (Sat-Sun all day) Closed: Sun eve **Bar Meals** L served Wed-Sat 12–2 D served Wed-Sat 6–9 (Tue 8.30–9, Sun 12–4) **Restaurant** L served Wed-Sat 12–2 D served Wed-Sat 5.30–9 (Sun 12–4) ⊕ Free House ◀ Jennings Bitter, Jennings Cumberland & Guinness. **Facilities** Garden Parking

---

WEST TANFIELD — MAP 19 SE27

Pick of the Pubs

The Bruce Arms 🍷

See Pick of the Pubs on page 676

WEST WITTON — MAP 19 SE08

Pick of the Pubs

The Wensleydale Heifer Inn ★★ HL ◉ 🍷

See Pick of the Pubs on page 678

WHASHTON — MAP 19 NZ10

Hack & Spade

DL11 7JL ☎ 01748 823721
dir: *A66 Penrith for 5m. Left exit towards Ravensworth, follow for 2m. Left at x-rds for Whashton*

This unusually titled free house stands opposite the former quarry from which its name is derived. Nowadays, however, the quarry has been filled in to form part of the village green. Starters such as four cheese focaccia bites precede main course dishes like lamb shank in red wine and rosemary gravy; vegetarian Glamorgan sausage with tomatoes, and bubble and squeak; and salmon with breadcrumbs, lemon and parsley. Finish with organic country fruit crumble.

Open 11–11 (Sun 12–3) **Bar Meals** L served Tue-Sun 12–2.30 D served Tue-Sat 7–9 Av main course £9.95 **Restaurant** L served Tue-Sun 12–2.30 D served Tue-Sat 7–9 ⊕ Free House ◀ John Smiths Smooth, Theakstons Original. **Facilities** Parking

PICK OF THE PUBS

The Star Country Inn

This brightly-shining Star has expanded over the years to incorporate adjoining cottages to house an extended dining room and provide guest accommodation.

Situated in the heart of the Yorkshire Wolds, it makes a handy base for exploring the area and visiting such attractions as Nunnington Hall, Sledmere House, and Castle Howard, which was used extensively in the classic television series Brideshead Revisited. The area is also popular with bird watchers and cyclists. The rustic facilities of bar and dining room, with large winter fires and a welcoming, convivial atmosphere, complement food cooked to traditional family recipes using fresh local produce. Theakstons is the major real ale on tap in the bar, alongside handles for popular lagers such as Fosters and Kronenbourg. Bar meals may include chicken breast wrapped in bacon with mozzarella, and king prawn balti

served with rice, poppadoms, and home-made mango chutney. The specials board tempts with the likes of pan-fried pigeon breast and slow-roasted lamb shank. Fresh fish from Whitby is a major strength, with langoustines, brill with a crab sauce, and roasted cod among the options. To finish, home-made desserts such as apple and blackberry crumble, spiced roast rhubarb served with creamy rice pudding, and rich chocolate tart ensure that there's something for the sweet tooth in everyone.

MAP 17 SE97
YO17 8EY
☎ 01944 738273
📄 01944 738273
e-mail:
starinn.malton@btconnect.com
dir: *From Malton take A64 towards Scarborough. 12m, at Sherborn right at lights. Weaverthorpe 4m, inn opposite junct*

Open 12–11 (Fri-Sat 12–12)
Bar Meals L served all week
12–9 D served all week Av main course £8
Restaurant L served all week
12–9 D served all week
⊕ Free House ◙ Theakstons, Bitter, John Smiths, Wold Top.
Facilities Garden Parking

The Bruce Arms

The Bruce Arms is a stone-built ivy-clad house dating from 1820, with its bistro-style interior enjoying traditional exposed beams, log fires and candles on the tables. Situated in the heart of the pretty village of West Tanfield, just five miles north west of Ripon, the pub is rapidly earning a reputation for providing great food in relaxed surroundings.

It's handy for racing at both Ripon and Thirsk, as well as visiting famous sights such as Fountains Abbey and Staley Royal Water Garden. The pub is run by husband and wife team Russell and Rosie Caines, who between them have a keen eye for quality food and first-class customer service. A good wine list and real ales such as Black Sheep Best guarantee that customers find what they want to drink. Russell's menu is best described as modern British; he uses only the finest ingredients, all of which are sourced locally when possible. A brunch choice served until 3pm starts with dry-cured bacon with fried eggs on champ potato; it also features a ploughman's with a pork pie along with cheeses, fruit and pickle. The carte takes the form of a fixed-price two- or three-course selection, with five options at each course. You could start with a warm salad of curried monkfish tail with Granny Smith apple salad and purée; or spiced belly of pork with pickled plums and braised onion. Main courses embrace pan-fried fillet of smoked haddock with braised celery, shrimps and brown butter; and maple-glazed supreme of guinea fowl with poached pears and ham hock. The dessert list is equally accomplished: why not try vanilla soaked savarin sponge, tangerines and vanilla ice cream; or iced amaretto mousse with blackberry compote. For those looking to enjoy a short break, the pub offers two letting bedrooms.

♟
MAP 19 SE27
Main St HG4 5JJ
☎ 01677 470325
📠 01677 470925
e-mail: info@bruce-arms.co.uk
web: www.bruce-arms.co.uk
dir: *On A6108 Ripon/Masham Rd, close to A1*

Open 12–11 Closed: Mon
Bar Meals L served Tue-Sun 12–9.30 D served Tue-Sat 12–9.30 Av main course £6.95
Restaurant L served Tue-Sun 12–2 D served Tue-Sun 6.30–9.30 Av 3 course fixed price £20.95
⊕ Free House 🍺 Black Sheep Best, Black Sheep Ale & Worthington Smooth. ♟ 10
Facilities Garden Dogs allowed Parking

WHITBY

MAP 19 NZ81

The Magpie Café ♀

14 Pier Rd YO21 3PU

☎ 01947 602058 📄 01947 601801

e-mail: ian@magpiecafe.co.uk

dir: *Telephone for directions*

More a licensed restaurant than a pub, the award-winning Magpie has been the home of North Yorkshire's best-ever fish and chips since the late 1930s when it moved to its present site in Pier Road. The dining rooms command excellent views of the harbour, the Abbey and St Mary's Church. Given its proximity to the Fish Market, fresh fish dishes abound – up to 10 daily. Ranges of salads and over 20 home-made puddings continue the choice.

Open 11.30–9 (Sun Nov-Mar 11.30–6.30) Closed: 5 Jan-6 Feb
Restaurant L served all week 11.30–9 D served all week Av 3 course à la carte £20 ⊕ Free House ◄ Crompton, Scoresby Bitter, Tetley Bitter. ♀ 11

WIGGLESWORTH

MAP 18 SD85

The Plough Inn ♀

BD23 4RJ ☎ 01729 840243 📄 01729 840638

e-mail: sue@ploughinn.info

dir: *From A65 between Skipton & Long Preston take B6478 to Wigglesworth*

Dating back to 1720, the bar of this traditional country free house features oak beams and an open fire. There are fine views of the surrounding hills from the conservatory restaurant, where the pub's precarious position on the Yorkshire/Lancashire border is reflected in a culinary 'War of the Roses'. Yorkshire pudding with beef casserole challenges Lancashire hotpot and pickled red cabbage – the latest score is published beside the daily blackboard specials!

Open 11–3 6–11 Closed: 8–24 Jan & Mon Nov-Mar **Bar Meals** L served all week 12–2 D served all week 6.30–9 Av main course £9
Restaurant L served all week 12–2 D served all week 7–9 Av 3 course à la carte £21.50 ⊕ Free House ◄ Tetley Bitter, Black Sheep Best. ♀ 6
Facilities Garden Parking **Rooms** available

YORK

MAP 16 SE65

Blue Bell ♀

53 Fossgate YO1 9TF ☎ 01904 654904

e-mail: robsonhardie@aol.com

dir: *Located in York City Centre*

It's easy to do, but don't walk past the narrow frontage of York's smallest pub, which has been serving customers in the ancient heart of the city for 200 years. In 1903 it was given a typical Edwardian makeover, since when hardly anything has changed, and this includes the varnished wall and ceiling panelling, the two cast-iron tiled fireplaces, and the old settles. The layout is original too, with the taproom at the front and the snug down a long corridor at the rear, both with servery hatches. Quite fittingly, the whole interior is now Grade II-listed. The only slight drawback is that the pub's size leaves no room for a kitchen, so although sandwiches are available, don't go expecting anything more complicated. No fewer than six real ales are usually on tap, including rotating guests.

Open 11–11 **Bar Meals** L served all week 11–6.30 ⊕ Punch Taverns ◄ Deuchars IPA, Timothy Taylors Landlord, Adnams Bitter, Abbot Greene King. ♀ 10 **Facilities** Dogs allowed **Notes** ⊛

Lysander Arms ♀

Manor Ln, Shipton Rd YO30 5TZ

☎ 01904 640845 📄 01904 624422

The Lysander Arms is a recently constructed pub built on the site of an old RAF airfield. The contemporary feel of the pub's interior includes a long, fully air-conditioned bar with modern furnishings, brick-built fireplace and large-screen TV. The lunch menu features a choice of ciabatta, melted bloomer and poppy bagel sandwiches; specialities such as blackened Cajun chicken with chargrilled peppers; and in the evening, beef from the char grill, accompanied by thick chips.

Open 11–11 (Sat 11–12.30, Sun 12–10.30) **Bar Meals** L served Tue-Sat 12–2 D served Tue-Sat 5.30–9 (Sun 12–3) **Restaurant** L served Tue-Sat 12–2 D served Tue-Sat 5.30–9 (Sun 12–3) ◄ John Smiths Cask, Deuchars IPA, John Smiths Smooth, Bombardier. ♀ 18 **Facilities** Garden Dogs allowed Parking Play Area

England

PICK OF THE PUBS

The Wensleydale Heifer Inn

Despite its inland location in the heart of Wensleydale, fish features strongly at the Wensleydale Heifer and is the winner of the AA Seafish Pub of the Year for England 2007. The inn, now under the new ownership and management of award-winning chef David Moss, has its own restaurant and fish bar, both with a uniquely chic look.

The restaurant provides a lovely setting for a 'special occasion' meal, with chocolate brown leather chairs, linen clothed tables and original Doug Hyde pictures. Alternatively, the fish bar and snug are less formal in style with sea grass flooring, rattan chairs and wooden tables, perfect for a light meal in relaxing surroundings. For sitting comfortably with a coffee, pint, or a glass of the finest malt, there's the Whisky Club Lounge, where an open fire burns in cooler weather. The 17th-century former coaching inn has a whitewashed stone exterior with a sculptured garden and an attractive area of decking for sitting outside. Overnight accommodation is provided in nine en suite bedrooms, some with four-posters. The menu has something to appeal to all tastes, from traditional fish and chips to warm salad of maple roasted lobster. Ingredients include locally produced farmed meats and hand-made after dinner chocolates. At lunchtime, the house speciality is hot fish ciabatta with Marie Rose sauce and frites, or for something more substantial choose from the two or three-course fixed-price lunch. From the carte you might try cured fish platter, famous fish pie with fennel and capers, or roast organic pork chop with black pudding mash, apple sauce and cider braised Savoy cabbage.

★★ HL ❀ ♟
MAP 19 SE08
DL8 4LS
☎ 01969 622322
🖷 01969 624183
e-mail:
info@wensleydaleheifer.co.uk
dir: *A684, at west end of village.*

Open 11–11
Bar Meals L served all week
12–2 D served all week 6–9 Av
main course £6.95
Restaurant L served all week
12 2 D served all week 6.30–9
⊕ Free House ◀ Burst ale, John
Smiths, Black Sheep Best. ♟ 7
Facilities Garden Parking
Rooms 9

YORKSHIRE, SOUTH

BRADFIELD

MAP 16 SK29

The Strines Inn

Bradfield Dale S6 6JE ☎ 0114 2851247

dir: *Off A57 between Sheffield toward Manchester*

Nestled amid breathtaking moorland scenery overlooking Strines Reservoir, this popular Peak District free house feels a world away from nearby Sheffield but is in fact within its border. Most of the present building is 16th century, and the traditional charm is enhanced by winter open fires. Traditional home-made fare ranges from sandwiches, salads and daily fresh fish to substantial Yorkshire puddings with a choice of fillings, plus grilled steaks, or pie of the day.

Open 10.30–3 5.30–11 (Mar-Sep Sat-Sun all day) Closed: 25 Dec **Bar Meals** L served all week 12–2.30 D served all week 5.30–9 (Sat-Sun & Mar-Sep all day) Av main course £7.90 ⊕ Free House ◄ Marston's Pedigree, Kelham Island, Mansfield Cask, Bradfield Bitter & Old Speckled Hen. **Facilities** Garden Dogs allowed Parking Play Area

CADEBY

MAP 16 SE50

Pick of the Pubs

Cadeby Inn ♟

Main St DN5 7SW ☎ 01709 864009

e-mail: info@cadeby-inn.co.uk

Before being converted into a picturesque whitewashed pub, with a stone-walled traditional bar and a more contemporary restaurant, this was a farmhouse. Sandstone walls enclose the large front garden, while a patio and smaller garden lie at the rear. Robert and Susan Craggs took over in late 2007; he was previously executive chef at Harvey Nicks in Manchester, so clearly knows what he is doing. Depending on the month, his modern European menu might bring Mrs Bell's blue cheese and caramelised onion tart, rocket and aged balsamic as a starter, followed by main courses such as Old Spot belly pork with cider-braised red cabbage and wholegrain mustard mash; line-caught sea bass with saffron mash, vine tomato and Niçoise olives; Northumbrian Blackface lamb navarin with white bean purée; and Middle Eastern-style feta and spinach pastries with tomato and chickpeas. Lemon meringue pie with lime syrup will follow any of those.

Open 11–11 (Fri-Sat 11–12, Sun 11–10.30) **Bar Meals** L served all week 12–5 D served all week 6.30–9 **Restaurant** L served all week 12–5 D served all week 6–9 Av 3 course à la carte £24.50 ◄ John Smiths Cask, Black Sheep Best Bitter, Guinness. ♟ 6 **Facilities** Children's licence Garden Dogs allowed Parking

DONCASTER

MAP 16 SE50

Waterfront Inn ♟

Canal Ln, West Stockwith DN10 4ET ☎ 01427 891223

dir: *From Gainsborough take either A159 N, then minor road to village. Or A631 towards Bawtry/Rotherham, then right onto A161, then minor road*

Built in the 1830s overlooking the Trent Canal basin and the canal towpath, the pub is now popular with walkers and visitors to the nearby marina. Real ales and good value food are the order of the day,

including pasta with home-made ratatouille, broccoli and cheese bake, deep fried scampi, half honey-roasted chicken, and lasagne.

Open 11.30–11 **Bar Meals** L served Mon-Sat 12–2 D served all week 6.30–8.30 (Sun 12–3) **Restaurant** L served Mon-Sat 12–2 D served all week 6.30–8.30 (Sun 12–3) ⊕ Enterprise Inns ◄ John Smiths Cask, Timothy Taylors, Greene King Old Speckled Hen, Deuchars IPA. ♟ 9 **Facilities** Garden Dogs allowed Parking Play Area

PENISTONE

MAP 16 SE20

Pick of the Pubs

Cubley Hall ♟

Mortimer Rd, Cubley S36 9DF

☎ 01226 766086 🖷 01226 767335

e-mail: info@cubleyhall.co.uk

dir: *M1 junct 37, A628 towards Manchester, or M1 junct 35a, A616. Hall just south of Penistone*

Over the centuries, Cubley Hall has seen service as everything from a gentleman's residence to a children's home. Despite those years of youthful battering, many original features such as mosaic floors, ornate plasterwork, oak panelling and stained glass survived, ready for the conversion in 1983 to a free house. Another seven years passed before the massive hewn-stone barn was converted into Cubley Hall's renowned restaurant, with its imaginative cuisine and all day Sunday carvery. There's also a simple bar menu, featuring such popular choices as chicken and ricotta pasta; bangers with cheddar and chive mash; vegetarian pizza with mountain goats' cheese; jumbo cod, chips and mushy peas; and fresh seasonal salads. Children have their own menu, and the best of local produce often finds its way into the blackboard specials.

Open 11–11 **Bar Meals** L served all week 12–9.30 D served all week 12–9.30 **Restaurant** L served Sun 12–9.30 D served Sat-Sun ⊕ Free House ◄ Tetley Bitter, Burton Ale, Greene King Abbot Ale, Young's Special. ♟ 7 **Facilities** Garden Parking Play Area **Rooms** available

PENISTONE continued

The Fountain Inn Hotel ♥

Wellthorne Ln, Ingbirchworth S36 7GJ
☎ 01226 763125 📄 01226 761336
e-mail: enquiries@fountain-Ingbirchworth.co.uk
dir: *M1 junct 37, A628 to Manchester then A629 to Huddersfield*

Parts of this former coaching inn date from the 17th century; it is attractively located by Ingbirchworth Reservoir in the foothills of the southern Pennines. The interior is cosy and stylish, the locals' bar has real log fires and traditional games, and the food focus is on quality with value for money: expect the likes of prawn cocktail, roast sirloin of local beef, and apple and blackberry crumble with custard. Garden with large decking and seating area.

Open 11.45–11 **Bar Meals** L served Mon-Sat 12–9.30 D served Mon-Sat 12–9.30 (Sun 12–8) **Restaurant** L served Mon-Sat 12–9.30 D served Mon-Sat 12–9.30 (Sun 12–8) ⊕ Enterprise Inns ◀ Tetleys Cask, Theakstons Best, Black Sheep, John Smith Smooth. ♥ 8 **Facilities** Children's licence Garden Parking Play Area

---

SHEFFIELD MAP 16 SK38

Pick of the Pubs

The Fat Cat

23 Alma St S3 8SA ☎ 0114 249 4801 📄 0114 249 4803
e-mail: info@thefatcat.co.uk
dir: *Telephone for directions*

This reputedly haunted back-street pub was built in 1832, and is Grade II-listed. Beer-wise, it's hard to imagine anywhere better: there is a constantly changing list of guest beers from across the country, especially from micro-breweries. Traditional scrumpy and unusual bottled beers are also sold, while the Kelham Island Brewery, owned by the pub, accounts for at least four of the ten traditional draught real ales sold. The smart interior is very much that of a traditional, welcoming city pub; outside there's an attractive walled garden complete with Victorian-style lanterns, bench seating and shrubbery. Real fires in winter complete the cosy feel. Home-cooked food is offered at lunch and in the evening from a simple weekly menu that might feature steak pie with potatoes, peas and gravy; ploughman's lunch; and sausage and bacon casserole with rice. Look out for special events such as a beer and food evening.

Open 12–12 Closed: 25 Dec **Bar Meals** L served all week 12–2.30 D served Mon-Sat 6–7.30 Av main course £3.50 ⊕ Free House ◀ Timothy Taylor Landlord, Kelham Island Bitter, Pale Rider, Pride of Sheffield. **Facilities** Garden Dogs allowed Parking

---

Lions Lair

31 Burgess St S1 2HF ☎ 0114 263 4264 📄 0114 263 4265
e-mail: info@lionslair.co.uk
dir: *On Burges Street next to John Lewis, between City Hall & Peace Gardens*

A modern café bar offering a friendly welcome from your hosts. It makes an intimate retreat, situated at the heart of the city with a small terrace outside. The menu is limited but there is a popular Sunday social where you're invited to come and chill out every Sunday and enjoy lunch, served from 1–5pm along with cheap cocktails.

Open 12–12 **Bar Meals** L served all week 12–3 D served all week 5–7 (Sun 12–5) Av main course £4.95 ⊕ Punch Taverns ◀ Black Sheep, Tetley. **Facilities** Garden

---

TOTLEY MAP 16 SK37

Pick of the Pubs

The Cricket Inn ♥

Penny Ln, Totley Bents S17 3AZ ☎ 0114 236 5256
dir: *Follow A621 from Sheffield 8m. Turn right onto Hillfoot Rd, 1st left onto Penny Ln*

Run by a new partnership between Simon Webster and Jim Harrison of the Thornbridge Brewery, and restaurateurs Richard and Victoria Smith, the Cricket Inn opened for business in 2007. The building was originally a farmhouse, which started selling beer to navvies building the Totley Tunnel on the nearby Sheffield to Manchester railway. Today, it's a forward-looking venture that links an innovative brewery with great pub food. Beers like Jaipur IPA, Ashford, and Lord Marples are the foil for a comprehensive menu of pub classics. Fill the odd corner with tasty snacks like crispy pork crackling with apple cinnamon sauce; or dive into wooden platters of seafood; roast and cured meats; and a vegetarian selection. Main course offerings include Sheffield-style hash and dumplings; and pot-roasted lamb shank with sweet and sour red cabbage. There are pies, grills and Sunday roasts, too, as well as sandwiches and a decent children's menu.

Open 11–11 **Bar Meals** L served Mon-Fri 12–2.30 D served Mon-Fri 5–9.30 (Sat 12–9.30, Sun 12–8) Av main course £12 ◀ Black Sheep, Stonies. ♥ 8 **Facilities** Children's licence Garden Dogs allowed Parking

YORKSHIRE, WEST

ADDINGHAM
MAP 19 SE04

Pick of the Pubs

The Fleece ♀
154 Main St LS29 0LY ☎ 01943 830491

dir: *Between Ilkley & Skipton*

This 17th-century coaching inn is popular with walkers, situated as it is at the intersection of several well-tramped footpaths. The stone-flagged interior boasts an enormous fireplace, wooden settles and a friendly bunch of locals. A pint of Black Sheep might be all you want, but if you feel peckish, be sure to consult the daily chalkboard. Much of the produce is local and organic, with beef and lamb coming from a nearby farm, allotment holders bringing surplus vegetables, and seasonal game delivered straight to the door. Simple flavoursome dishes are the speciality here. Favourites include meat and potato pie, and whole roast chicken, while fish is also a big draw. Try the likes of naturally smoked haddock and leek gratin; line-caught sea bass with celeriac fondant; or hand-dived king scallops with mint and pea purée.

Open 12–11 (Sun 12–10.30) **Bar Meals** L served Mon-Sat 12–2.15 D served Mon-Sat 6–9.15 (Sun & BH 12–8) ⊕ Punch Taverns ◀ Black Sheep, Copper Dragon, Timothy Taylor Landlord, Tetleys. ♀ 15 **Facilities** Dogs allowed Parking

---

BRADFORD
MAP 19 SE13

New Beehive Inn
171 Westgate BD1 3AA ☎ 01274 721784 📠 01274 735092
e-mail: newbeehiveinn@talk21.com
web: www.newbeehiveinn.co.uk

dir: *A606 into Bradford, A6161 200yds B6144, left after lights, pub on left.*

Classic Edwardian inn, dating from 1901 and retaining its period atmosphere with separate bars and gas lighting. Outside, with a complete change of mood, you can relax in the Mediterranean-style courtyard. The pub offers a good range of unusual real ales and a selection of over 100 malt whiskies, served alongside some simple bar snacks.

Open 12–11 (Sun 12–10.30) **Bar Meals** L served Mon-Sat 12–2 Av main course £5 ⊕ Free House ◀ Timothy Taylor Landlord, Kelham Island Bitter, Hop Back Summer Lightning, Abbeydale Moonshine. **Facilities** Garden Parking **Rooms** available

---

CLIFTON
MAP 16 SE12

The Black Horse Inn ◉ ♀
HD6 4HJ ☎ 01484 713862 📠 01484 400582
e-mail: mail@blackhorseclifton.co.uk
web: www.blackhorseclifton.co.uk
dir: *1m from Brighouse town centre. 0.5m from M62 junct 25*

The white-painted, 15th-century building was originally a farmhouse, which helps to explain why a six-inch layer of chicken droppings was found here during conversion in the 1970s. At the pub's heart is a well-kept bar serving traditional Yorkshire ales and a wide-ranging wine selection. Three separate dining areas provide a seasonal menu of locally sourced food, such as slow-braised lamb shank; pan-fried breast of chicken; beer-battered Whitby haddock; and leek and pea tartlet.

Open 11–12 **Bar Meals** L served Mon-Sat 12–2.30 D served Mon-Sat 5.30–9.30 (Sun 12–8.30) **Restaurant** L served Mon-Sat 12–2.30 D served Mon-Sat 5.30–9.30 (Sun 12–8.30) ⊕ Enterprise Inns ◀ Black Sheep, Timothy Taylor Landlord, Old Speckled Hen. ♀ 18 **Facilities** Garden Dogs allowed Parking

See advert on page 682

HALIFAX
MAP 19 SE02

The Rock Inn Hotel
Holywell Green HX4 9BS ☎ 01422 379721 📠 01422 379110
e-mail: reservations@rockinnhotel.com
dir: *From M62 junct 24 follow Blackley signs, left at x-rds, approx 0.5m on left*

Substantial modern extensions have transformed this attractive 17th-century wayside inn into a thriving hotel and conference venue in the scenic valley of Holywell Green. All-day dining in the brasserie-style conservatory is truly cosmopolitan; kick off with freshly prepared parsnip and apple soup or crispy duck and seaweed, followed by liver and bacon, Thai-style steamed halibut, or vegetables jalfrezi.

Open 12 -11 **Bar Meals** L served all week 12–2.30 D served all week 5–9 Av main course £6 **Restaurant** L served all week 12–2.30 D served all week 5–9 Av 3 course fixed price £14.95 ⊕ Free House ◀ Black Sheep, Taylor Landlord, John Smiths. **Facilities** Garden Dogs allowed Parking

HALIFAX continued

Pick of the Pubs

Shibden Mill Inn ★★★★ INN ◉ ♥

See Pick of the Pubs on page 684

HAWORTH
MAP 19 SE03

The Old White Lion Hotel ★★ HL ♥

Main St BD22 8DU ☎ 01535 642313 📠 01535 646222

e-mail: enquiries@oldwhitelionhotel.com

dir: *A629 onto B6142, hotel 0.5m past Haworth Station*

This traditional 300–year-old coaching inn is set in the famous Brontë village of Haworth. In the charming bar the ceiling beams are held up by what look for all the world like pit props. From the carte in the candlelit restaurant choose between smoked haddock rarebit; fillet of sea bass with roast feta and olives; or asparagus and wild mushroom crêpe.

Open 11–11 **Bar Meals** L served Mon-Fri 11.30–2.30 D served Mon-Fri 5.30–9.30 (Sat-Sun 12–9.30) **Restaurant** L served Sun 12–2.30 D served all week 7–9.30 ⊕ Free House ⬛ Theakstons Best (Green Label), Tetley Bitter, John Smith's, Websters. **Facilities** Parking **Rooms** 14

HORBURY
MAP 16 SE21

The Quarry Inn

70 Quarry Hill WF4 5NF ☎ 01924 272523

dir: *On A642 approx 2.5m from Wakefield*

In the hollow of a disused quarry, this creeper-clad pub is built with stone actually quarried here, as are the bar fronts. Just beyond the main road outside are the River Calder and the Calder and Hebble Navigation. A good range of simple but appetising dishes in the bar and restaurant includes cottage pie, steaks, gammon, fish and chips, liver and onions, and Yorkshire puddings with various fillings.

Open 12–11 **Bar Meals** L served all week 12–2 Av main course £3.99 **Restaurant** L served all week 12–2 Av 3 course fixed price £5 ⊕ Marstons ⬛ Marston's Pedigree, Mansfield Smooth. **Facilities** Parking **Notes** ⊗

KIRKBURTON
MAP 16 SE11

The Woodman Inn ★★★★ INN ♥

Thunderbridge HD8 0PX

☎ 01484 605778 📠 01484 604110

e-mail: thewoodman@connectfree.co.uk

dir: *Approx 5m S of Huddersfield, just off A629*

Lovely old stone-built inn set in the wooded hamlet of Thunderbridge. One menu is offered throughout, but customers can eat in the bar downstairs or the more sophisticated ambience of the restaurant upstairs. Dishes include daily fresh fish (grilled brill with chilli), and the likes of wild boar and apple sausages. Wine is selected by the owners, whose family has been in the licensed trade since 1817. Accommodation is provided in adjacent converted weavers' cottages.

Open 12–11 (Fri-Sat 12.30–11) **Bar Meals** L served all week 12–6.30 D served all week 6.30–9 (Sun 12–8) Av main course £12 **Restaurant** L served all week 12–2 D served all week 6.30–9 (Sun 12–8) ⊕ Free House ⬛ Taylors Best Bitter, Tetleys Bitter. ♥ 13 **Facilities** Parking **Rooms** 12

LEDSHAM
MAP 16 SE42

The Chequers Inn

Claypit Ln LS25 5LP ☎ 01977 683135 📠 01977 680791

e-mail: cjwrath@btconnect.com

dir: *Between A1 & A656 above Castleford. 1m from A1M, junct 42.*

A quaint, creeper-clad inn located in an old estate village, with low beams, wooden settles, and a history traceable back to 1540. Ever since the lady of the manor was offended by her over-indulgent farm workers over 160 years ago, the pub has been closed on Sundays. But otherwise, you can tuck into leek and stilton bread and butter pudding with roasted capsicums; traditional cassoulet; or baked halibut with mussel and dill cream.

Open 11–11 Closed: Sun **Bar Meals** L served Mon-Sat 12–9.15 D served Mon-Sat 12–9.15 **Restaurant** D served Mon-Sat 7–9.15 ⊕ Free House ⬛ Theakston, John Smiths, Timothy Taylor Landlord, Brown Cow. **Facilities** Garden Dogs allowed Parking

---

LEEDS
MAP 19 SE23

Whitelocks ♥

Turks Head Yard, Briggate LS1 6HB

☎ 0113 245 3950 📠 0113 242 3368

e-mail: charliehudson@whitelocks.co.uk

dir: *Next to Marks & Spencer in Briggate*

First licensed in 1715 as the Turks Head, this is the oldest pub in Leeds. Recent restoration has highlighted its classic long bar with polychrome tiles, stained-glass windows, advertising mirrors and a mid-Victorian-style Top Bar known as Ma'Gamps. Food beef, rack of lamb, lots of fish – there's a daily sis sourced entirely from the city's Kirkgate market, to reappear as traditional British Yorkshire puddings with gravy; steak and stilton or vegetable pie; breaded scampi; and ham, egg and chips.

Open 11–11 (Sun 12–10.30) **Bar Meals** L served all week 12–7 D served all week (Sun 12–6) Av main course £6.95 **Restaurant** L served Mon-Sat 12–9 D served Mon-Sat (Sun 12–6) ⬛ Theakston Best, Old Peculier, John Smiths, Deuchars. ♥ 16 **Facilities** Children's licence Garden Dogs allowed

---

LINTHWAITE
MAP 16 SE11

The Sair Inn

Hoyle Ing HD7 5SG ☎ 01484 842370

dir: *From Huddesfield take A62 (Oldham road) for 3.5m. Left just before lights at bus stop (in centre of road) into Hoyle Ing & follow sign*

You won't be able to eat here, but this old hilltop ale house has enough character in its four small rooms to make up for that. Three are heated by hot (landlord Ron Crabtree's word) Yorkshire ranges in winter. Ron has brewed his own beers for 25 years and much sought after they are by real ale aficionados. In summer the outside drinking area catches the afternoon sun and commands views across the Colne Valley.

Open 5.30–11 (Sat 12–11 Sun 12–10.30) ⊕ Free House ⬛ Linfit Special Bitter, Linfit Bitter, Linfit Gold Medal, Autumn Gold. **Facilities** Dogs allowed **Notes** ⊗

Shibden Mill Inn

A 17th-century free house tucked into a fold of the Shibden Valley, overlooking Red Beck. The first mention by name of an ancient manorial water corn mill on this site is found in Wakefield's court rolls dating it to the second year of Edward II's reign, 1308. (Curiously the rolls also tell us that Shibden used to be spelled Schepedene, and that Chippendale derives from Schepedendale.)

It appears that the mill was used for corn right up to the 19th century. In 1845 a change of ownership brought a change of use – machinery for spinning worsted was installed. However a disastrous fire in 1859 closed the business, and the mill was sold in 1890 to a Halifax brewer. The original mill pond was filled in, possibly to prevent water leaking into the local mine shafts; today this area is the inn's car park. The interior has been sympathetically renovated while retaining much of the character of these long-gone times, particularly in the log fire-warmed, oak-beamed bar and candlelit restaurant. Real ales include two guests, and the wine list cheers the hearts of all oenophiles. The menus offer plenty of options, including an excellent value early bird served Monday to Friday at lunchtime and between 6 and 7pm: warm terrine of smoked haddock, roast rump of English lamb, and dark chocolate and cherry cheesecake could be a typical selection. The bar menu has antipasti; starters such as steak tartare with warm toast; fish in the form of grilled tuna steak niçoise or seared supreme of salmon; and traditional mains such as steak and kidney pudding and home-made cottage pie. Vegetarian options are equally attractive, and can be served as starters or main courses; one possibility is poached egg with asparagus, hollandaise and sautéed spinach. Children tuck into haddock goujons or crispy chicken strips with potato wedges and peas.

★★★★ INN ⊕ ☻
MAP 19 SE02
Shibden Mill Fold HX3 7UL
☎ 01422 365840
🖹 01422 362971
e-mail:
shibdenmillinn@zoom.co.uk
web: www.shibdenmillinn.com
dir: *From A58, turn onto Kell Ln. After 0.5M turn left onto Blake Hill*

Open 12–11 Closed: 25–26 Dec eve & 1 Jan eve
Bar Meals L served Mon-Sat 12–2 D served Mon-Sat 6–9.30 (Sun 12–7.30) Av main course £9.95
Restaurant L served Mon-Sat 12–2 D served Mon-Sat 6–9.30 (Sun 12–7.30) Av 2 course fixed price £10.95
⊕ Free House ◄▌ John Smiths, Theakston XB, Shibden Mill & 2 guest ales. ☻ 14
Facilities Garden Dogs allowed Parking
Rooms 11

LINTON
MAP 16 SE34

The Windmill Inn ♀

Main St LS22 4HT ☎ 01937 582209 📄 01937 587518

dir: *From A1 exit at Tadcaster/Otley junction, follow Otley signs. In Collingham follow Linton signs*

A coaching inn since the 18th century, the building actually dates back to the 14th century, and originally housed the owner of the long-disappeared windmill. Stone walls, antique settles, log fires, oak beams and lots of brass set the scene in which to enjoy good bar food prepared by enthusiastic licensees. Expect the likes of chicken breast on mustard mash with onion jus, sea bass on pepper mash with tomato and basil sauce, baked salmon on Italian risotto, or king prawns in lime and chilli butter. While you're there, ask to take a look at the local history scrapbook.

Open 11.30–3 5–11 (Sat-Sun all day) **Bar Meals** L served Mon-Sat 12–2 D served Mon-Sat 5.30–9 (Sun 12–6) Av main course £8.50 **Restaurant** L served Mon-Sat 12–2 D served Mon-Sat 5.30–9 (Sun 12–6) Av 3 course à la carte £19 ⊕ Scottish Courage ◀ John Smith & Theakston Best, Daleside, Greene King Ruddles County. ♀ 12 **Facilities** Garden Dogs allowed Parking

MARSDEN
MAP 16 SE01

The Olive Branch ★★★★ RR ◉ ♀

Manchester Rd HD7 6LU ☎ 01484 844487

e-mail: mail@olivebranch.uk.com

dir: *On A62 between Marsden & Slaithwaite, 6m from Huddersfield*

This old moorland inn by a former packhorse route offers daily-changing, seasonally dependent brasserie-style menus. Choice is wide, with starters such as spiced parsnip soup; baked Whitby crab; and smoked duck and chicken salad; and mains that include Round Green Farm venison loin; pan-fried organic salmon fillet; and fresh tagliatelle with wild mushroom sauce. Locally brewed real ales are always available. Four designer bedrooms include one with ducks – plastic, one assumes – in the bath.

Open 12–2 6.30–9.30 Closed: 1st 2wks Jan **Restaurant** L served Wed-Fri 12–2 D served Wed-Fri 6.30–9.30 (Sun 1–8.30) Av 3 course à la carte £33 ⊕ Free House ◀ Dogcross Bitter, Greenfield Red Ale, Boddingtons. ♀ 16 **Facilities** Garden Parking **Rooms** 3

MYTHOLMROYD
MAP 19 SE02

Shoulder of Mutton ♀

New Rd HX7 5DZ ☎ 01422 883165

dir: *A646 Halifax to Todmorden, in Mytholmroyd on B6138, opposite rail station*

Award-winning Pennines' pub situated by a trout stream in the village where Poet Laureate Ted Hughes was born. Popular with walkers, cyclists, families and visitors to the area, the pub's reputation for real ales and hearty fare using locally sourced ingredients remains intact after 30 years of ownership. The menu ranges from snacks and sandwiches to vegetarian quiche; filled giant Yorkshire pudding; Cumberland sausages; and beef in ale.

Open 11.30–3 7–11 (Sat 11.30–11, Sun 12–10.30) **Bar Meals** L served Mon, Wed-Sat 11.30–2 D served Mon, Wed-Sat 7–8.15 (Sun 12–10.30) Av main course £4.50 **Restaurant** L served Wed-Mon 11.30–2 D served Wed-Mon 7–8.15 ⊕ Enterprise Inns ◀ Black Sheep, Copper Dragon, Greene King IPA, Taylor Landlord. ♀ 10 **Facilities** Garden Dogs allowed Parking Play Area **Notes** ◉

NEWALL
MAP 19 SE14

The Spite Inn ♀

LS21 2EY ☎ 01943 463063

dir: *Telephone for directions*

'There's nowt but malice and spite at these pubs', said a local who one day did the unthinkable – drank in both village hostelries, renowned for their feuding landlords. The Traveller's Rest, which became The Malice, is long closed, but the Roebuck has survived as The Spite. Salmon mornay, haddock, scampi, steak and ale pie, ostrich fillet and speciality sausages are likely to be on offer.

Open 12–3 6–11 (Thu-Sat 12–11, Sun 12–10.30) **Bar Meals** L served all week 12–2 D served Tue-Thu 6–8.30, (Fri-Sat 6–9 6–9 Sun 12–5) Av main course £7.50 **Restaurant** L served all week 11.30–2 D served Tue-Thu 6–8.30, (Sat 6–9 Sun 12–5) ⊕ Unique Pub Co ◀ John Smiths Smooth, Tetleys, Copper Dragon, plus guest ales. ♀ 10 **Facilities** Garden Dogs allowed Parking

PICK OF THE PUBS

The Three Acres Inn

Neil Truelove and Brian Orme have owned this country inn for over 30 years, building a reputation for good quality food, tasteful accommodation and a welcoming atmosphere. In a sense, perhaps, nothing changes for it was once a favourite with drovers bringing their sheep to market from their Pennine pastures.

The inn's spacious interior is lavishly traditional in style – all rich reds, greens and yellows, exposed beams and large fireplaces. On summer evenings, sit out on the decked area to enjoy a pint of Timothy Taylor Landlord, or one of several wines available by the glass. Food, served in both bar and restaurant, successfully fuses traditional English and international influences, including plenty of fresh fish prepared as you watch: flash-grilled Loch Fyne queenies; gratin of monkfish, scallops and langoustines; or fresh Irish oysters. To continue in a fishy vein, you could choose fresh Whitby haddock in crisp Timothy Taylor batter, with proper chips and mushy peas; or fresh pan-fried Dover sole with caper butter. Meat lovers will not

be disappointed with Hinchliffe Farm's beef, matured on the bone for three or four weeks, and prime Texel lamb is renowned for its quality. These appear in dishes such as chargrilled rib-eye steaks, and confit of lamb shoulder in winter vegetable broth, with rosemary dumplings and hot-pot potatoes. The three-course Sunday lunch menu offers half a dozen choices at each stage. You could start with fresh rope-grown Hebridean mussels marinière, follow with Wigton Cumberland sausage served in a Yorkshire pudding, and finish with dark chocolate Amaretto mousse with candied orange and white chocolate sauce.

MAP 16 SE21
HD8 8LR
☎ 01484 602606
▤ 01484 608411
e-mail: 3acres@globalnet.co.uk
dir: *From Huddersfield take A629 then B6116, turn left for village*

Open 12–3 7–11 Closed: 25–26 Dec, 1–2 Jan
Bar Meals L served all week 12–2 D served all week 7–9.45
Restaurant L served Sun-Fri 12–7 D served all week 7–9.45 Av 3 course à la carte £32.50
⊕ Free House ◀ Timothy Taylor Landlord, Black Sheep, Tetley Smooth, Tetley Bitter. ▼ 16
Facilities Garden Parking

RIPPONDEN
MAP 16 SE01

Old Bridge Inn ⚦

Priest Ln HX6 4DF ☎ 01422 822595

dir: *5m from Halifax in village centre by church*

An award-winning pub prettily situated on the banks of the River Ryburn in a lovely Pennine conservation village. It boasts a fine cruck frame, wattle and daub, and remnants of an old bread oven. Fixed-price buffet lunches served Monday to Friday, popular since 1963, include rare roast beef and Virginia ham, home-made scotch eggs and quiches. The blackboard menu for evenings and weekends may offer warm salad of pigeon breast, followed by spicy sausage cassoulet. Traditional puddings like treacle tart are all home made.

Open 12–3 5.30–11 **Bar Meals** L served all week 12–2 D served Mon-Fri 6.30–9.30 ⊕ Free House ◀ Timothy Taylor Landlord, Golden Best & Best Bitter, Black Sheep Best. ⚦ 12 **Facilities** Garden Parking

SHELLEY
MAP 16 SE21

Pick of the Pubs

The Three Acres Inn ⚦

See Pick of the Pubs on opposite page

SOWERBY
MAP 16 SE02

Pick of the Pubs

The Travellers Rest ⚦

Steep Ln HX6 1PE ☎ 01422 832124 🖷 01422 831365

The stone built Travellers Rest was built in 1730 and fully renovated in 2002 by Caroline Lumley. It sits high on a steep hillside with glorious views, a dining terrace, duck pond, huge car park and helipad. The cosy stone-flagged bar boasts fresh flowers and an open fire, while in the restaurant, beams, animal print sofas, more warmth from a wood-burning stove, and exposed stonework continue the emphasis on comfort and relaxation. Dishes cooked to order from local produce are rooted in Yorkshire tradition yet refined with French flair, yielding an immaculate and happy mix of classic and contemporary cooking. Bar meals start with sandwiches, and continue with steak and ale pie with pastry crust, or sausage and mash with onion gravy. In the restaurant you'll find starters like potted crayfish, or creamy garlic and herb mushrooms on toasted brioche; and main courses such as caramelized pork fillet with baked apple mash. Resist the jam sponge with custard if you can.

Open 5–late (Sat 12–3, 5.30–late, Sun 12–late) Closed: Mon-Tue **Bar Meals** L served Sat 12–2.30 D served Wed-Fri 5–9.30 (Sat 5–10, Sun 12–3.30, 5.30–8.30) Av main course £10 **Restaurant** L served Sat 12–2.30 D served Wed-Fri 5–9.30 (Sat 5–10, Sun 12–3.30, 5.30–8.30) Av 3 course à la carte £24 ◀ Timothy Taylor Landlord, Timothy Taylor & Best Bitter. ⚦ 8 **Facilities** Garden Dogs allowed Parking

SOWERBY BRIDGE
MAP 16 SE02

Pick of the Pubs

The Millbank ⚦

HX6 3DY ☎ 01422 825588

e-mail: eat@themillbank.com

dir: *A58 from Sowerby Bridge to Ripponden, right at Triangle*

A contemporary dining pub that retains the function and traditional feel of the village free house it's always been. It stands in the Pennine conservation village of Mill Bank, home since 1971 to writer and poet Glyn Hughes; you can read one of his sonnets, 'The Rock Rose', in the churchyard, engraved on a slate slab in the wall. Back in the pub, head for the cosy stone-flagged tap room for a real ale, or the main wooden-floored drinking area for more of a wine bar feel and stunning views of the gardens and valley. The dining room chairs are recycled mill and chapel seats, complete with prayer-book racks. The main menu has modern bistro touches: you could start with crab fritters with chilli sauce and raita, then move on to roast suckling pig from Garstang with grilled black pudding, potato rösti, oriental sauce and bok choi.

Open 12–3 5.30–11 (Sun 12–10.30) Closed: 1st 2wks Oct & 1st wk Jan & Mon **Bar Meals** L served Tue-Sat 12–2.30 D served Tue-Thu 6–9.30 (Fri-Sat 6–10, Sun 12–4.30, 6–8) **Restaurant** L served Tue-Sat 12–2.30 D served Tue-Thu 6–9.30 (Fri-Sat 6–10, Sun 12–4.30, 6–8) ⊕ Free House ◀ Timothy Taylor Landlord, Tetley Bitter, & Erdinger. ⚦ 20 **Facilities** Garden

THORNTON
MAP 19 SE03

Pick of the Pubs

Ring O'Bells Country Pub & Restaurant ⚦

See Pick of the Pubs on page 688

PICK OF THE PUBS

Ring O'Bells Country Pub & Restauran

On a clear day, views from the Ring O'Bells stretch up to 30 miles across rugged Pennine moorland. It stands just minutes away from the village of Thornton, where the Brontë sisters were born and their father was curate. The pub was converted from a Wesleyan chapel, and the restaurant was formerly two mill workers' cottages.

It has been successfully run by Ann and Clive Preston for the past 17 years, and their cuisine, service and professionalism have been recognised with accolades from visitors far and wide. The wood-panelled and welcoming bar and dining area serves Black Sheep cask-conditioned ales and a fine selection of malt whiskies, speciality liqueurs and wines by the glass. The fully air-conditioned Brontë restaurant has a new contemporary look; a conservatory running its whole length rewards diners with stunning valley views. Meat, fish, game and vegetables sourced from local farmers and suppliers are carefully prepared and served by a team of award-winning chefs. The à la carte menu and daily specials board offer traditional British dishes

with European influences. Starters such as lamb and spinach meatballs on a tsatziki sauce; sun-blushed tomato risotto cake; and deep-fried goats' cheese with spinach are typical. Main courses may include pan-fried duck breast with roasted potatoes and porcini mushrooms in creamy paprika and redcurrant sauce; and grilled snapper fillet served on dill and Dijon mustard sauce with a crab potato cake. More traditional dishes comprise locally-made sausages, chef's steak and kidney or meat and potato pies; imaginative vegetarian options are on the blackboard, and all dietary requirements can be catered for. A range of desserts is made to order, from chef's creative crème brûlée to traditional warm lattice apple pie served with vanilla ice cream and toffee sauce.

MAP 19 SE03
212 Hilltop Rd BD13 3QL
☎ 01274 832296
🖷 01274 831707
e-mail:
enquiries@theringobells.com
dir: *From M62 take A58 for 5m, right onto A644. 4.5m follow Denholme signs, onto Well Head Rd into Hilltop Rd.*

Open 11.30–3.30 5.30–11 (Sat-Sun 6.15–11) Closed: 25 Dec
Bar Meals L served all week 12–2 D served Mon-Fri 5.30–9.30 (Sat-Sun 6.15–8.45) Av main course £9.95
Restaurant L served all week 12–2 D served Mon-Sat 7–9.30 (Sun 6.15–8.45) Av 3 course à la carte £19.95 Av 2 course fixed price £9.95
⊕ Free House ◖ John Smiths & Courage Directors, Black Sheep ales. ♟ 12
Facilities Parking

WAKEFIELD   MAP 16 SE32

Pick of the Pubs

Kaye Arms Inn & Brasserie 🍷

29 Wakefield Rd, Grange Moor WF4 4BG
☎ 01924 848385 📄 01924 848977
e-mail: kayearms@hotmail.co.uk
dir: *On A642 between Huddersfield & Wakefield*

This family-run dining pub stands alone on the Huddersfield to Wakefield road. Its bar menu offers the likes of cold rare roast beef with celeriac remoulade; braised veal and mushroom pasta; and honey-baked ham sandwiches. Over in the brasserie, try crab tart or chicken liver parfait; then confit of duck leg with French-style peas and dauphinoise potatoes; smoked haddock and poached egg with beetroot and spinach; or mature cheddar cheese soufflé with roquefort salad. Specials might take in braised shin beef or grilled fillet of John Dory with Greek salad. Raspberry soufflé is the house speciality, though bread and butter pudding with whisky and honey cream; and almond tart with vanilla crème anglaise are equally appealing. An extensive wine list comprehensively roams the world. The popular National Coal Mining Museum is close by.

Open 11.30–3 7–11 Closed: 25 Dec–2 Jan & Mon **Bar Meals** L served Tue-Sun 12–2 **Restaurant** L served Tue-Sun 12–2 D served Tue-Fri & Sun 7.15–9.30 (Sat 6.30–10) ⊕ Free House ◀ John Smiths, Theakstons Best, Guinness. 🍷 15 **Facilities** Parking

WIDDOP   MAP 18 SD93

Pack Horse Inn 🍷

HX7 7AT ☎ 01422 842803 📄 01422 842803
dir: *Off A646 & A6033*

The Pack Horse is a converted Laithe farmhouse dating from the 1600s, complete with welcoming open fires. A beautiful location just 300 yards from the Pennine Way makes it popular with walkers, but equally attractive are the home-cooked meals, good range of real ales and fabulous choice of 130 single malt whiskies. Please note that from October to Easter the pub is only open in the evening.

Open 12–3 7–11 Closed: Mon **Bar Meals** L served Tue-Sun (summer only) 12–2 D served Tue-Sun 7–10 Av main course £7.95 ⊕ Free House ◀ Thwaites, Theakston XB, Morland Old Speckled Hen, Black Sheep Bitter. 🍷 8 **Facilities** Dogs allowed Parking

CHANNEL ISLANDS
GUERNSEY

CASTEL   MAP 24

Pick of the Pubs

Fleur du Jardin 🍷

Kings Mills GY5 7JT ☎ 01481 257996 📄 01481 256834
e-mail: info@fleurdujardin.com
dir: *2.5m from town centre*

This friendly hotel, bar and restaurant stands in a picturesque village, home to some of Guernsey's finest farmhouses. Dating from the 15th century, it has been restyled with an eye for contemporary design, but historical features such as granite walls, solid wood beams and real fireplaces remain intact. Those taller than the average Tudor might have to stoop in the bar, but that needn't prevent enjoyment of a pint of Guernsey Special. Imaginative use of local produce is what sets the award-winning restaurant apart; it is not unusual to see a local fisherman delivering his catch to the kitchen. You could start with a Mediterranean vegetable tower with tangy tomato coulis and herbed crème fraîche; or an antipasti plate to share. Move on to oak-smoked chicken supreme with gratin potatoes, sweet potato purée and braised endive; or penne pasta with Italian sausage, fresh peas and mascarpone.

Open 12–12.45 **Bar Meals** L served all week 12–2 D served all week 6–9 Av main course £10 **Restaurant** L served all week 12–2 D served all week 6–9 Av 3 course à la carte £20 ◀ Sunbeam, Guernsey Special, London Pride & guest ales. 🍷 12 **Facilities** Children's licence Garden Dogs allowed Parking

Hotel Hougue du Pommier ★★★ HL 🍷

Hougue du Pommier Rd GY5 7FQ
☎ 01481 256531 📄 01481 256260
e-mail: hotel@houguedupommier.guernsey.net
dir: *Telephone for directions*

Old Guernsey farmhouse with the only feu du bois (literally 'cooking on the fire') in the Channel Islands. Fish, steaks, chicken and vegetarian dishes are offered along with a selection of bar meals. Play 'get the hook on the nose of the large black bull', again, the only one left in Guernsey. The 10-acre gardens have a swimming pool, barbecue and medieval area, where banquets are held the first Saturday of the month.

Open 10.30–11.45 **Bar Meals** L served all week 12–2.15 D served all week 6.30–9 **Restaurant** L served Sun 12–2.30 D served all week 6.30–9 Av 3 course à la carte £25 Av 5 course fixed price £21.95 ◀ John Smith's, Extra Smooth, Guernsey Best Bitter. 🍷 8 **Facilities** Children's licence Garden Dogs allowed Parking **Rooms** 43

England

JERSEY

GOREY   MAP 24

Castle Green Gastropub ♥

La Route de la Cote JE3 6DR

☎ 01534 840218 📠 01534 840229

e-mail: enquiries@jerseypottery.com

dir: *Opposite main entrance of Gorey Castle*

A superbly located pub overlooking Gorey harbour and, in turn, overlooked by dramatic Mont Orgueil Castle. The views from the wooden sun terrace are breathtaking. An imaginative menu offers pan-Pacific-style dishes like Moroccan spiced lamb shoulder; Thai chicken burger; sushi and sashimi plate with pickled ginger and wasabi; along with fresh fillets of the day's catch , and summer seafood platter.

Open 11–11 Closed: Sun eve & Mon **Bar Meals** L served all week 12–2.30 D served all week 6–8.30 **Restaurant** L served all week 12–2.30 D served all week 6–9 Av 3 course à la carte £20 ◀ Directors, John Smith Extra Smooth, Theakstons. ☏ 8 **Facilities** Children's licence

ST AUBIN   MAP 24

Old Court House Inn ♥

St Aubin's Harbour JE3 8AB

☎ 01534 746433 📠 01534 745103

e-mail: info@oldcourthousejersey.com

dir: *From Jersey Airport, right at exit, left at lights, 0.5m to St Aubin*

The original courthouse at the rear of the property dates from 1450 and was first restored in 1611. Beneath the front part are enormous cellars where privateers stored their plunder. Three bars offer food, and there are two restaurants, the Granite and the Mizzen, with terrific views over the harbour, plus an attractive courtyard. There's lots of locally caught fish on the menus, of course, and the wine list incorporates a worthy Director's Bin.

Open 11–11.30 **Bar Meals** L served Mon-Sun 12.30–2.15 D served Mon-Sat 7.30–9.30 **Restaurant** L served all week 12.30–2.30 D served all week 7.30–10 Av 3 course à la carte £25 Av 3 course fixed price £25 ∰ Free House ◀ Directors, Theakstons, John Smith, Jersey Brewery. ☏ 8 **Facilities** Garden

ST MARTIN   MAP 24

Royal Hotel ♥

La Grande Route de Faldouet JE3 6UG

☎ 01534 856289 📠 01534 857298

e-mail: johnbarker@jerseymail.co.uk

dir: *2m from Five Oaks rdbt towards St Martyn. Pub on right next to St Martin's Church*

A friendly atmosphere, value for money, and great food and drink are the hallmarks of this friendly local in the heart of St Martin. Roaring log fires welcome winter visitors, and there's a sunny beer garden to relax in during the summer months. Among the traditional home-made favourites are steak and ale pie, fresh grilled trout, monkfish and prawn Thai curry, and vegetarian lasagne. Ploughman's lunches, filled jacket potatoes, grills and children's choices are also on offer.

Open 9.30 -11.30 (Sun 11–11.30) **Bar Meals** L served Mon-Sat 12–2.15 D served Mon-Sat 6–8.30 (Sun 12–2.30) **Restaurant** L served Mon-Sat 12–2.15 D served Mon-Sat 6–8.30 (Sun 12–2.30) ◀ John Smiths Smooth, Theakstons cool, Guinness, Ringwood Real Ale. ☏ 9 **Facilities** Garden Parking Play Area

ISLE OF MAN

PEEL   MAP 24 SC28

The Creek Inn ♥

Station Place IM5 1AT ☎ 01624 842216 📠 01624 843359

e-mail: jeanmcaleer@manx.net

dir: *On quayside opposite House of Mannanan Museum*

Ideal for walkers, wildlife lovers and yachting enthusiasts, this family-run free house overlooks the harbour at Peel. Expect live music on Friday and Saturday nights, and a good selection of beers including locally brewed Okells ales. Fish and seafood dominate the menu, with the following available on any given day: Manx kippers, crab, lobster, seafood lasagne, salmon and broccoli bake, and king prawn thermidore.

Open 10–12 (Fri-Sat 10–1am) **Bar Meals** L served all week 10–9.30 D served all week 10–9.30 **Restaurant** L served all week 10–9.30 D served all week 10–9.30 ∰ Free House ◀ Okells Bitter, Okells Seasonal, Bushy's Bitter, 4 guest ales. ☏ 9 **Facilities** Children's licence Garden Parking

PORT ERIN   MAP 24 SC26

Falcon's Nest Hotel ★★ HL

The Promenade, Station Rd IM9 6AF

☎ 01624 834077 📠 01624 835370

e-mail: falconsnest@enterprise.net

A popular hotel overlooking a beautiful, sheltered harbour and beach. In 1865 Gladstone, then prime minister, was responsible while staying here with his son for what he called "an amusing incident" involving a teapot. The lounge and saloon bars serve local beers, over 150 whiskies, snacks and meals, although there is also a restaurant with carvery option. Fish include local crab, prawns, sea bass, lobster and local scallops known as queenies.

Open 10.30–12 **Bar Meals** L served all week 12–2 D served all week 6–9 Av main course £9 **Restaurant** L served all week 12–2 D served all week 6–9 Av 3 course à la carte £18 Av fixed price £15 ∰ Free House ◀ Manx guest ale, Guinness & John Smith. **Facilities** Children's licence Dogs allowed Parking **Rooms** 35

Scotland

CITY OF ABERDEEN

ABERDEEN
MAP 23 NJ90

Old Blackfriars ♀

52 Castle St AB11 5BB ☎ 01224 581922 📄 01224 582153

dir: *From train station down Deeside to Union St. Turn right. Pub at end on right*

Stunning stained glass and a warm, welcoming atmosphere are features of this traditional city centre pub, situated in Aberdeen's historic Castlegate. It is built on the site of property owned by Blackfriars Dominican monks, hence the name. The menu runs from sandwiches and filled potatoes through to hearty dishes such as bangers and mash; chicken tikka masala; and beef au poivre. Finish with sticky toffee pudding or pancakes in maple syrup.

Open 11–12 (Fri-Sat 10–1, Sun 12.30–11) Closed: 25 Dec, 1 Jan **Bar Meals** L served Mon-Thu 12–8.45 D served Mon-Thu (Sun 12.30–8.45, Fri-Sat 12–7.45) 🍺 Belhaven 🍺 Abbot Ale, Deuchars IPA, Caledonian 80/-, Inveralmond. ♀ 12 **Facilities** Children's licence

ABERDEENSHIRE

BALMEDIE
MAP 23 NJ91

The Cock & Bull Bar & Restaurant ♀

Ellon Rd, Blairton AB23 8XY

☎ 01358 743249 📄 01358 742466

e-mail: info@thecockandbull.co.uk

dir: *11m N of city centre, located on left hand side of main A90 between Balmedie junct & Foveran*

What was once a coaching inn has been developed into a cosy gastro-pub. The bar area, warmed by a cast-iron range, has big sofas and a gallimaufry of hanging junk, from a ship's lifebelt to a trombone. The menu ranges from bar dishes of fish and chips, and cheese and bacon burger to restaurant fare like loin of monkfish wrapped in Parma ham with tarragon and chilli couscous and roasted red pepper reduction.

Open 10.30–12 (Sun 12–9) Closed: 25–26 Dec, 1–2 Jan **Bar Meals** L served Mon-Sat 12–5.30 D served Mon-Thu 5.30–9 (Sun 12–7) Av main course £10 **Restaurant** L served Mon-Sat 12–5.30 D served Mon-Sat 5.30–9 (Sun 12–7) Av 3 course à la carte £24 🍺 Free House 🍺 Directors Ale, Guinness & guest ale. ♀ 7 **Facilities** Children's licence Garden Parking Play Area

MARYCULTER
MAP 23 NO89

Old Mill Inn

South Deeside Rd AB12 5FX

☎ 01224 733212 📄 01224 732884

e-mail: Info@oldmillinn.co.uk

dir: *5m W of Aberdeen on B9077*

This delightful family-run country inn stands on the edge of the River Dee, just over five miles from Aberdeen city centre. A former mill house, the 18th-century granite building has been tastefully modernised to include a restaurant where the finest Scottish ingredients feature on the menu: venison stovies, peppered carpaccio of beef, cullen skink, and chicken and venison terrine are typical.

Open 11–11 **Bar Meals** L served all week 12–2 D served all week 5.30–9 **Restaurant** L served all week 12–2 D served all week 5.30–9.30 🍺 Free House 🍺 Interbrew Bass, Caledonian Deuchars IPA, Timothy Taylor, Landlord. **Facilities** Garden Parking **Rooms** available

NETHERLEY
MAP 23 NO89

Pick of the Pubs

The Lairhillock Inn ♀

AB39 3QS ☎ 01569 730001 📄 01569 731175

e-mail: info@lairhillock.co.uk

dir: *From Aberdeen take A90. Right at Durris turn*

Set in beautiful rural Deeside yet only 15 minutes drive from Aberdeen, this award-winning 200–year-old former coaching inn offers real ales in the bar and real fires in the lounge to keep out the winter chill. Dishes are robust and use a bounty of fresh, quality, local produce. Starters from the pub menu range from traditional cullen skink to king prawns in a lime, chilli, sweet pepper and coconut sauce, while main courses could include Aberdeen Angus steak and chips or chicken supreme stuffed with haggis and skirlie. For a more formal dining option head for the atmospheric Crynoch restaurant where the menu might feature grilled wood pigeon salad followed by a duo of beef medallion and roast venison fillet with peppercorn sauce and port jus topped with crispy celeriac. Finish with sticky toffee pudding or a platter of four desserts.

Open 11–11 (Fri-Sat 11–12) Closed: 25–26 Dec, 1–2 Jan **Bar Meals** L served all week 12–2 D served Mon-Thu 6–9.30 (Fri-Sat 6–10, Sun 5.30–9) Av main course £9.25 **Restaurant** L served Sun 12–1.45 D served Tue-Sat 7–9.30 🍺 Free House 🍺 Timothy Taylor Landlord, Courage Directors, Cairngorm, Tradewinds. ♀ 7 **Facilities** Garden Dogs allowed Parking

PICK OF THE PUBS

Crinan Hotel

The Crinan Hotel dates back some 200 years and has been run by owners Nick and Frances Ryan for over 36 years, making it a very long-standing place of welcome at the heart of community life in this tiny fishing village. From its location at the northern end of the Crinan Canal, it enjoys fabulous views across the sound of Jura to the islands of Mull and Scarba.

You can eat in the ground floor Panther Arms and Mainbrace Bar or in the Westward restaurant with its views over Loch Crinan to Jura, Scarba and the mountains of Mull. Whatever you choose, you can be sure of the freshest seafood – landed daily just 50 metres from the hotel! Typical choices from the Mainbrace menu include Loch Fyne princess clams with organic salad leaves, beurre blanc and French fries; and authentic Hungarian goulash with fresh bread. In the Westward restaurant you could enjoy crab ravioli with roast courgettes and shellfish cream, followed by pan-seared Scottish salmon with crushed potatoes, green beans and caper lemon butter; or perhaps roast loin of Duntrune venison with gratin potatoes, savoy cabbage, leeks and redcurrant jus lie. Finish, perhaps, with clafoutis of Scottish berries; or a selection of fine cheeses with hand crafted oat cakes and quince jelly. The hotel has 20 artistically decorated bedrooms, some with private balconies and all with breathtaking views of Loch Crinan or the Isles of Scarba, Jura and the whirlpool of the Corryvreckan. Boat trips can be arranged to the islands, and there is a classic boats regatta in the summer.

MAP 20 NR79
PA31 8SR
☎ 01546 830261
🖷 01546 830292
e-mail: reservations@ crinanhotel.com
dir: *From M8, at end of bridge take A82, at Tarbert left onto A83. At Inverary follow Campbeltown signs to Lochgilphead, follow signs for A816 to Oban. 2m, left to Crinan on B841*

Open 11–11 (Sun 11–12 May-Oct Mon-Sat 11–12) Closed: Xmas
Bar Meals L served all week 12–2.30 D served all week 6–8.30 Av main course £10.50
Restaurant D served all week 7–8.30 Av 5 course fixed price £45
⊕ Free House ◼ Belhaven, Interbrew Worthington Bitter, Tennents Velvet, Guinness.
Facilities Children's licence Garden Dogs allowed Parking
Rooms available

OLDMELDRUM   MAP 23 NJ82

The Redgarth ☙

Kirk Brae AB51 0DJ ☎ 01651 872353 📠 01651 873763
e-mail: redgarth1@aol.com
dir: On A947

A family-run inn, The Redgarth was built as a house in 1928 and has an attractive garden offering magnificent views of Bennachie and the surrounding countryside. Cask-conditioned ales and fine wines are served along with dishes prepared on the premises using fresh local produce. A typical selection might be honey and ginger prawns on a bed of salad leaves; roast Aberdeen Angus beef in a rich gravy with Yorkshire pudding; and raspberry white chocolate cheesecake.

Open 11–3 5–11 (Fri-Sat 5–11.45) Closed: 25–26 Dec, 1–3 Jan
Bar Meals L served all week 12–2 D served all week 5–9 (Fri-Sat 9.30)
Restaurant L served all week 12–2 D served all week 5–9 (Fri-Sat 5–9.30)
⊕ Free House ◀ Inveralmond Thrappledouser, Caledonian Deuchars IPA, Taylor Landlord, Isle of Skye Red Cullin. ☙ 6 **Facilities** Children's licence Garden Parking **Rooms** available

ARGYLL & BUTE

ARDUAINE   MAP 20 NM71

Pick of the Pubs

Loch Melfort Hotel ★★★ HL ◉◉

PA34 4XG ☎ 01852 200233 📠 01852 200214
e-mail: reception@lochmelfort.co.uk
dir: On A816, 20m south of Oban

One of the finest locations on the west coast of Scotland awaits visitors to this award-winning hotel and restaurant – the perfect place for a relaxing holiday or short break at any time of the year. The hotel stands in 26 acres of grounds next to the National Trust's Arduaine Gardens, and its loch-side location gives spectacular views across Asknish Bay and the Sound of Jura. To the rear, the hotel is framed by woodlands and the magnificent mountains of Argyll. The restaurant offers superb dining with fresh local produce including meats, cheeses and locally caught fish and seafood. Meanwhile, the Skerry Bar/Bistro is very popular with both guests and locals for light lunches, teas and suppers. Here, the menu ranges from, baguettes and toasties to dishes like warm Cajun chicken salad; tomato and basil pasta with mushrooms, spinach and crème fraîche; and venison sausages with champ mash and onion gravy.

Open 10.30–10.30 (Fri-Sat 10.30–11) Closed: early Jan & Feb
Bar Meals L served all week 12–2.30 D served all week 6–9
Restaurant D served all week 7–9 Av 3 course à la carte £26 ⊕ Free House ◀ 80/-, Theakstons, Guinness, Miller. **Facilities** Garden Dogs allowed Parking **Rooms** 25

CLACHAN-SEIL   MAP 20 NM71

Pick of the Pubs

Tigh an Truish Inn

PA34 4QZ ☎ 01852 300242
dir: 14m S of Oban take A816. 12m, onto B844 towards Atlantic Bridge

Following the Battle of Culloden in 1746, kilts were outlawed on pain of death. In defiance of this edict the islanders wore their kilts at home; but, on excursions to the mainland, they would stop at the Tigh an Truish – the 'house of trousers' – and change into the hated trews. Now popular with tourists and members of the yachting fraternity, the Tigh an Truish is handy for good walks and lovely gardens. It offers an appetising menu based on the best local produce, with a range of starters like sweet pickled herring with brown bread and salad; and home-made paté with toast. Main course dishes include home-made vegetable lasagne with garlic bread; smoked haddock mornay with cheese crumble topping; home-made steak and ale pie; and locally caught prawns with garlic mayonnaise and salad. Watch out for the summer daily specials of locally caught seafood.

Open 11–3 5–11 (May-Sept all day) Closed: 25 Dec & 1 Jan
Bar Meals L served all week 12–2 D served all week 6–8.30 Av main course £7.50 **Restaurant** L served all week 12–2 D served all week 6–8.30 ⊕ Free House ◀ Local guest ales changing regularly.
Facilities Garden Dogs allowed Parking

CRINAN   MAP 20 NR79

Pick of the Pubs

Crinan Hotel

See Pick of the Pubs on page 695

The Crinan Canal at Cairnbaan, Argyll & Bute

PICK OF THE PUBS

Cairnbaan Hotel

Once upon a time, this late 18th-century coaching inn was frequented by fishermen on the Crinan Canal in flat-bottomed boats called puffers, but today's waterborne clientele is almost entirely sailing the waterway for pleasure.

The hotel offers high standards of hospitality and smart accommodation in en suite bedrooms, so there is no excuse for speeding away after a meal or drink. It's owned by ex-QE2 catering officer Darren Dobson, ashore now for some 20 years, and wife Christine, a former teacher, who plans the menus and does all the baking. Enjoy a meal in the serene restaurant, where the carte specialises in the use of fresh local produce, notably seafood and game. On the menu, look out for starters of moules marinière using secretly sourced large local mussels; deep-fried haggis balls with whisky gravy and neeps; and smoked lamb with gooseberry and mint jelly and fresh pear. Mains might include seared scallops with sauce vièrge, creamed

potatoes and prosciutto crisp; Thai-spiced butternut squash risotto with vegetable crisps and red onion and coriander sambal; and confit of duck with redcurrant glaze, potatoes and vegetables. From the dessert menu come Mississippi mud pie; or fruit crumble with cream and custard. For a lunchtime snack, opt for ciabatta rolls with fillings such as smoked chicken with sun-blushed tomatoes and mayonnaise; or sausage, red onion and leaves. From nearby Oban there are sailings to Mull, Tiree, and Colonsay among other islands, and Inveraray Castle is well worth a visit, as is Dunadd Fort where the ancient kings of Scotland were crowned.

★★★ HL ◉ ♥
MAP 20 NR88
Cairnbaan PA31 8SJ
☎ 01546 603668
🖹 01546 606045
e-mail: info@cairnbaan.com
dir: *2m N, take A816 from Lochgilphead, hotel off B841*

Open 11–11
Bar Meals L served all week 12–2.30 D served all week 6–9.30
Restaurant D served all week 6–9.30 Av 3 course à la carte £24
⊕ Free House ◀ Local Ales. ♥ 8
Facilities Garden Parking
Rooms 12

DUNOON   MAP 20 NS17

Coylet Inn

Loch Eck PA23 8SG ☎ 01369 840426
e-mail: reservations@coylet-locheck.co.uk
web: www.coylet-locheck.co.uk
dir: *9m N of Dunoon on A815*

Overlooking the shores of Loch Eck, this beautifully refurbished 17th-century coaching inn is a blissful hideaway with no television or games machines to disturb the peace. The inn is famous for its ghost, the Blue Boy; a film was even made of the story, starring Emma Thompson. Unwind by one of three log fires or plunder the impressive menus, where choices range from venison burger and chips to grilled sole with mussel cream.

Open 11–12 Closed: 25 Dec **Bar Meals** L served all week 12–2 D served all week 6–8.45 **Restaurant** L served all week 12–2 D served all week 6–8.45 ⊕ Free House ◖ Caledonian Deuchars IPA, Highlander. **Facilities** Garden Parking **Rooms** 4

KILFINAN   MAP 20 NR97

Kilfinan Hotel Bar

PA21 2EP ☎ 01700 821201 🖷 01700 821205
e-mail: kilfinanhotel@btconnect.com
dir: *8m N of Tighnabruaich on B8000*

The hotel, on the eastern shore of Loch Fyne set amid spectacular Highland scenery, has been welcoming travellers since the 1760s. The bars are cosy with log fires in winter, and offer a fine selection of malts. There are two intimate dining rooms, with the Lamont room for larger parties. Menus change daily and offer the best of local produce: Loch Fyne oysters, of course, and langoustine grilled in garlic butter; cullen skink soup; and moules marinière, plus game, Aberdeen Angus beef and a variety of Scottish sweets and cheeses.

Bar Meals L served all week 12.30–2.30 D served all week 6.30–10 Av main course £6.95 **Restaurant** 12.30–2.30 D served all week 6.30–10.30 Av 3 course à la carte £25 ⊕ Free House ◖ McEwens 70/-, McEwens 80/-, Fosters & Kronenbourg. **Facilities** Garden Parking

LOCHGILPHEAD   MAP 20 NR88

Pick of the Pubs

Cairnbaan Hotel ★★★ HL ◉ ♈

See Pick of the Pubs on opposite page

PORT APPIN   MAP 20 NM94

Pick of the Pubs

The Pierhouse Hotel & Seafood Restaurant ★★★ SHL

See Pick of the Pubs on page 700

STRACHUR   MAP 20 NN00

Pick of the Pubs

Creggans Inn ★★★ HL ◉ ♈

PA27 8BX ☎ 01369 860279 🖷 01369 860637
e-mail: info@creggans-inn.co.uk
web: www.creggans-inn.co.uk
dir: *A82 from Glasgow, at Tarbet take A83 to Cairndow, then A815 down coast to Strachur*

From the hills above this informal family-friendly free house on the edge of Loch Fyne, you can gaze across the Mull of Kintyre to the Western Isles beyond. It has been a coaching inn since Mary Queen of Scots' day. Owned and run by the Robertson family for the last seven years, it maintains a good selection of real ales, wines by the glass and malt whiskies. There's a formal terraced garden and patio for alfresco summer drinking, and regional produce plays a key role in the seasonal menus: the famed Loch Fyne oysters of course, but also mussels, scallops and langoustines from the same waters. Robust main courses may feature venison sausages, steak and ale pie, and pan-fried rump of beef, the venison, beef and lamb coming from the surrounding hills. Choose from the selection of home-made puddings and Scottish cheeses to finish.

Open 11–11 **Bar Meals** L served all week 12–2.30 D served all week 6–8.30 Av main course £10 **Restaurant** D served all week 7–8.30 Av 4 course fixed price £30 ⊕ Free House ◖ Coniston Bluebird Bitter, Fyne Ales Highlander, Atlas Latitude, Deuchars IPA. ♈ 7 **Facilities** Garden Dogs allowed Parking **Rooms** 14

Scotland

PICK OF THE PUBS

The Pierhouse Hotel & Seafood Restauran

It is hard to imagine a more spectacular or romantic setting than this. The Pierhouse sits on the edge of Loch Linnhe with views of the island of Lismore and the Morvern Hills. You arrive by a narrow road from Appin or by sea, where you can tie up to one of the hotel's ten moorings near the pier.

Originally the home of the Pier Master at Port Appin, who oversaw the steam packets plying up and down the loch, The Pierhouse is now a renowned small hotel with an excellent seafood restaurant. There is a popular bar with a pool room and a terrace with views of one of Scotland's last remaining small working piers. Lunch and dinner are served in both the bar and restaurant, from fresh locally sourced produce and seafood from Lismore, Loch Etive, Loch Linnhe, Mull and Inverawe – the latter not surprisingly since The Pierhouse is a past winner of an AA Seafish Pub of the Year Award. Favourite dishes are lobster served in a half shell fresh from The Pierhouse creel; a sumptuous seafood platter; plump scallops from Mull; and a mountain of langoustine served

with fresh bread and seafood dips. Meaty alternatives include local venison cooked pink and served with potato and leek croquette and blackcurrant port butter; and locally farmed beef sirloin with all the trimmings. Vegetarian options might include pappardelle with fresh mushrooms, herbs, white wine, garlic and cream topped with gruyere cheese. Twelve individually designed bedrooms include two with four-poster beds and superb loch views and three triple family rooms. All are en suite, with either bath or shower, and are equipped with wi-fi hotspot internet access, flatscreen televisions, direct dial telephones, hairdryers and tea and coffee making facilities. Other treats include a traditional Finnish sauna for guests and an excellent range of massage treatments.

★★★ SHL
MAP 20 NM94
PA38 4DE
☎ 01631 730302
📄 01631 730400
e-mail: marketingandpr@
pierhousehotel.co.uk
dir: *A828 from Ballachulish to Oban. In Appin right at Port Appin & Lismore ferry sign. After 2.5m left after post office, hotel at end of road by pier*

Open 8–11.30 Closed: 25 Dec
Bar Meals L served all week
12.30–2.30 D served all week
6.30–9.30 Av main course £19.45
Restaurant L served all week
12.30–2.30 D served all week
6.30–9.30 Av 3 course à la carte
£31.85 Av 3 course fixed price £30
⊕ Free House ◼ Calders 80/-,
Belhaven Best & Guinness.
Facilities Children's licence
Garden Dogs allowed Parking
Rooms 12

TAYVALLICH MAP 20 NR78

Pick of the Pubs

Tayvallich Inn

PA31 8PL ☎ 01546 870282 📠 01546 870333

e-mail: rfhanderson@aol.com

dir: *From Lochgilphead take A816 then B841/B8025*

This 'house in the pass', as it translates, was converted from an old bus garage in 1976 and stands by a natural harbour at the head of Loch Sween with stunning views over the anchorage, especially from the picnic tables that front the inn in summer. The cosy bar with its yachting theme and the more formal dining-room feature original works by local artists and large picture windows from which to gaze out over the village and Tayvallich Bay. Those interested in the works of 19th-century engineer Thomas Telford will find plenty of bridges and piers in the area. Expect a lot of seafood, including Loch Etive mussels steamed in white wine, garlic and cream; seared scallops on pea purée and black pudding; and the Tayvallich Seafood Platter. Other options could include prime Scottish rib-eye with onion rings and tomatoes; and beer-battered haddock and chips.

Open 11-2.30 5.30-12 (Fri-Sat 5-1am, Sun 5-12) Closed: 25 Dec **Bar Meals** L served all week 12-2 D served all week 6-9 Av main course £12 **Restaurant** L served all week 12-2 D served all week 6-9 Free House Tennents, Guinness, Loch Fynk Ales. **Facilities** Garden Dogs allowed Parking

CLACKMANNANSHIRE

DOLLAR MAP 21 NS99

Castle Campbell Hotel ★★★ SHL

11 Bridge St FK14 7DE ☎ 01259 742519 📠 01259 743742

e-mail: bookings@castle-campbell.co.uk

dir: *A91 (Stirling to St Andrews road). In centre of Dollar by bridge overlooking Dollar Barn and Clock tower*

Find a real taste of Scotland at this 19th-century coaching inn, handy for the romantic castle and Dollar Glen's spectacular gorges. Recognised as a Whisky Ambassador, the hotel has over 50 malts; local ale is always on tap and the wine list runs to several pages. Prime Scottish produce features on both bar and restaurant menus, with options ranging from lunchtime sandwiches to Arbroath haddock fillet in crisp beer batter, or lamb with minted mash.

Open 12-11.30 (Fri 12-1am, Sun 12-11) **Bar Meals** L served Mon-Sat 12-2 D served Mon-Sat 5.30-8.45 (Sun 12-3, 5-8.45) **Restaurant** L served Mon-Sat 12-2 D served Mon-Sat 5.30-8.45 (Sun 12-3, 5-8.45) Av 3 course à la carte £20 Free House Harviestoun Bitter & Twisted, Deuchars IPA (guest), McEwans 70'. 7 **Facilities** Children's licence Dogs allowed Parking **Rooms** 9

DUMFRIES & GALLOWAY

ISLE OF WHITHORN MAP 20 NX43

Pick of the Pubs

The Steam Packet Inn

Harbour Row DG8 8LL

☎ 01988 500334 📠 01988 500627

e-mail: steampacketinn@btconnect.com

dir: *From Newton Stewart take A714, then A746 to Whithorn, then Isle of Whithorn*

This lively quayside pub stands in a picturesque village at the tip of the Machars peninsula. Sit by the picture windows and watch the fishermen at work, then look to the menu for a chance to sample the fruits of their labours. Extensive seafood choices – perhaps local lobster thermidor or a kettle of fish with vermouth crème fraîche – are supported by the likes of steak and baby onion suet pudding or Thai pork ciabatta.

Open 11-11 Closed: 25 Dec Winter Tue-Thu 2.30-6 **Bar Meals** L served all week 12-2 D served all week 6.30-9 Av main course £8 **Restaurant** L served Sun 12-2 D served Mon-Sat 6.30-9 Av 3 course à la carte £25 Av 3 course fixed price £25 Free House Theakston XB, Caledonian Deuchars IPA, Black Sheep Best Bitter, Houston Killellan. 9 **Facilities** Children's licence Garden Dogs allowed Parking

KIRKCUDBRIGHT MAP 20 NX65

Selkirk Arms Hotel ★★★ HL

Old High St DG6 4JG ☎ 01557 330402 📠 01557 331639

e-mail: reception@selkirkarmshotel.co.uk

dir: *M74 & M6 to A75, halfway between Dumfries & Stranraer on A75*

A privately owned hotel in the centre of 'Artists' Town', as Kirkcudbright is known. Many first-time visitors head, sometimes inadvertently,

CONTINUED

KIRKCUDBRIGHT continued

straight into the lively public bar for a taste of local life. The Bistro menu offers a terrifically good choice, including haggis and tattie scone tower with Drambuie cream sauce; oven-roast partridge with bubble and squeak; and Galloway scampi with chips and peas. The menu in Artistas Restaurant is similar, but the surroundings are more intimate.

Open 11–12 **Bar Meals** L served all week 12–2 D served all week 6–9.30 Av main course £10 **Restaurant** L served all week 12–2 D served all week 7–9.30 Av 3 course à la carte £25 Av 2 course fixed price £19 ⊕ Free House ◀ Youngers Tartan, John Smiths Bitter, Criffel, Timothy Taylor Landlord. ♀8 **Facilities** Children's licence Garden Dogs allowed Parking **Rooms** 16

MOFFAT   MAP 21 NT00

Black Bull Hotel ♀

Churchgate DG10 9EG ☎ 01683 220206 📄 01683 220483
e-mail: hotel@blackbullmoffat.co.uk
dir: *Telephone for directions*

This historic pub was the headquarters of Graham of Claverhouse during the 17th-century Scottish rebellion, and was frequented by Robert Burns around 1790. The Railway Bar, in former stables across the courtyard, houses a collection of railway memorabilia and traditional pub games. Food is served in the lounge, Burns Room or restaurant. Dishes include Black Bull sizzlers (steak, chicken fillets, gammon) served on a cast iron platter; the daily roast, and deep-fried breaded haddock fillet.

Open 11–11 (Thu-Sat 11–12) **Bar Meals** L served all week 11.30–9.15 D served all week 11.30–9.15 **Restaurant** L served all week 11.30–3 D served all week 6–9.15 ⊕ Free House ◀ McEwans, Theakston. ♀10 **Facilities** Garden Parking **Rooms** available

NEW ABBEY   MAP 21 NX96

Criffel Inn

2 The Square DG2 8BX
☎ 01387 850305 & 850244 📄 01387 850305
e-mail: criffelinn@btconnect.com
dir: *A74/A74(M) exit at Gretna, A75 to Dumfries, A710 to New Abbey*

A former 18th-century coaching inn set on the Solway Coast in the historic conservation village of New Abbey close to the ruins of the 13th-century Sweetheart Abbey. The Graham family ensures a warm welcome and excellent home-cooked food using local produce. Dishes include chicken wrapped in smoked Ayrshire bacon served with Loch Arthur mature creamy cheese sauce; fish dishes feature sea trout and sea bass among several others. Lawned beer garden overlooking corn-mill and square; ideal for touring Dumfries and Galloway.

Open 12–2.30 5–11 (Sat 12–12 Sun 12–11) **Bar Meals** L served Mon-Sat 12–2 D served Mon-Sat 5.30–8 (Sun 12–8) Av main course £7 **Restaurant** L served Mon-Sat 12–2 D served Mon-Sat 5–8 (Sun 12–8) ⊕ Free House ◀ Belhaven Best, McEwans 60–. **Facilities** Garden Dogs allowed Parking

NEW GALLOWAY   MAP 20 NX67

Cross Keys Hotel ♀

High St DG7 3RN ☎ 01644 420494 📄 01644 701071
e-mail: enquiries@thecrosskeys-newgalloway.co.uk
dir: *At N end of Loch Ken, 10m from Castle Douglas on A712*

An 18th-century coaching inn with a beamed period bar, where food is served in restored, stone-walled cells (part of the hotel was once the police station). The à la carte restaurant offers hearty food with a Scottish accent, chicken stuffed with haggis and served with whisky sauce being a prime example. Real ales are a speciality, and there's a good choice of malts in the whisky bar.

Open 12–2.30 6–11.30 (Apr-Oct 12–12 all wk) **Bar Meals** L served Tue-Sun 12–2 D served Tue-Sat 6–9 (Sun 5.30–7.30, Nov-Mar no food Mon-Tue) **Restaurant** L served Tue-Sun 12–2 D served Tue-Sat 6–9 (Sun 5.30–7.30, Nov-Mar Wed-Sat) Av 3 course à la carte £16.10 ◀ Houston & guest real ales. ♀9 **Facilities** Garden Dogs allowed

NEWTON STEWART   MAP 20 NX46

Pick of the Pubs

Creebridge House Hotel

Minnigaff DG8 6NP ☎ 01671 402121 📄 01671 403258
e-mail: info@creebridge.co.uk
dir: *From A75 into Newton Stewart, turn right over river bridge, hotel 200yds on left*

A listed building dating from 1760, this family-run hotel is set in three acres of idyllic gardens and woodland at the foot of Kirroughtree forest. It was formerly the Earl of Galloway's shooting lodge and part of his estate. The refurbished Bridge's bar and brasserie offers malt whiskies, real ales and an interesting menu, perfect for an informal lunch. For a candlelit dinner the alternative dining venue is the Creebridge Garden Restaurant. The emphasis is on fresh Scottish produce, and both menus feature Kirkcudbrightshire beef, hung for 14 days, and an award-winning house speciality: best loin of lamb with creamed kale and roulade of braised shin. Fish dishes range from the brasserie's local sea bass set on chive mash with dill butter sauce, to the restaurant's seared Solway salmon with lemon risotto and chive velouté.

Open 12–2.30 6–11 (Sun all day) **Bar Meals** L served all week 12–2 D served all week 6–9 **Restaurant** L served all week 12–2 D served all week 6–9 (a la carte available Apr-Oct) Av 3 course à la carte £25 ⊕ Free House ◀ Fuller's London Pride, Tennents, Deuchars & Guinness. **Facilities** Children's licence Garden Dogs allowed Parking **Rooms** available

PORTPATRICK MAP 20 NW95

Crown Hotel ♀

9 North Crescent DG9 8SX ☎ 01776 810261
e-mail: info@crownportpatrick.com
web: www.crownportpatrick.com
dir: *Take A77 from ferry port at Stranraer*

Just a few yards from the water's edge in one of the region's most picturesque villages, the Crown has striking views across the Irish Sea. The rambling old bar has seafaring displays and a warming winter fire. Naturally seafood is a speciality: starters range from crab and scallop fish soup, to fresh local crab claws in dill sauce; main courses continue the briny celebration with a hot seafood platter, or whole fresh pan-fried sea bass.

Open 12–12 (Thu-Sat 12–1am) **Bar Meals** L served all week 12–6 D served all week 6–9 Av main course £7.95 **Restaurant** D served all week 6–9 Av 4 course fixed price £22.95 ⊕ Free House ◄ John Smith's, McEwans 80/-, McEwans 70/-, Guinness. ♀ 8 **Facilities** Children's licence Garden Parking

CITY OF DUNDEE

BROUGHTY FERRY MAP 21 NO43

The Royal Arch Bar ♀

285 Brook St DD5 2DS ☎ 01382 779741 📠 01382 739174
dir: *3m from Dundee. 0.5 min from Broughton Ferry rail station*

In Victorian times, the jute industry made Broughty Ferry the 'richest square mile in Europe'. Named after the Masonic Arch, demolished to make way for the Tay road bridge, the pub dates from 1856. In the 1930s the landlady, Mrs Cardwell, sold her own label whisky, bottles of which are still displayed. An extensive selection of bar meals ranges from light snacks to three-course meals, served in the bar, lounge or pavement cafe.

Open 11–12 (Sun 12.30–12) Closed: 1 Jan **Bar Meals** L served Mon-Thu 11.30–2.30 (Sun 12.30–2.30) D served Sun-Thu 5–8 (Fri-Sat 11.30–7.30) **Restaurant** L served Mon-Thu 11.30–2.30 (Sun 12.30–2.30) D served Sun-Thu 5–8 (Fri-Sat 11.30–7.30) ⊕ Free House ◄ McEwans 80/-, Belhaven Best, Guinness, Clark Caledonian. ♀ 12 **Facilities** Children's licence Garden Dogs allowed

DUNDEE MAP 21 NO43

Speedwell Bar NEW ♀

165–167 Perth Rd DD2 1AS ☎ 01382 667783
e-mail: jonathan_stewart@fsmail.net
dir: *From city centre along Perth Rd, pass university, last bar on right*

Popularly known as Mennies, this surviving Edwardian pub is listed for an interior that has no need of imported nicknacks to give it period character. The same family owned it for 90 years, until the present landlord's father bought it in 1995. The bar offers 157 whiskies. A kitchen would be good, but since the pub is listed this is impossible, so signs encourage customers to bring in pies from next door.

Open 11–12 (Sun 12.30–12) ⊕ Free House ◄ McEwans, Belhaven Best. ♀ 10 **Facilities** Dogs allowed **Notes** ⊛

EAST AYRSHIRE

DALRYMPLE MAP 20 NS31

The Kirkton Inn

1 Main St KA6 6DF ☎ 01292 560241 📠 01292 560835
e-mail: kirkton@cqm.co.uk
dir: *6m SE from centre of Ayr just off A77*

This inn's motto is, 'There are no strangers here, only friends who have never met', and the welcoming atmosphere makes it easy to feel at home. It's a stoutly traditional setting, with open fires and polished brasses, set in the village of Dalrymple. A meal might include haggis with a dram of Drambuie, cream and redcurrants, followed by the chef's home-made steak pie.

Open 11–12 **Bar Meals** L served all week 12–4 D served all week 12–9 Av main course £9 **Restaurant** L served all week 12–4 D served all week 12–9 Av 3 course à la carte £18 ⊕ Free House ◄ Belhaven Best, Tennents. **Facilities** Children's licence Garden Dogs allowed Parking

GATEHEAD
MAP 20 NS33

The Cochrane Inn ♥

45 Main Rd KA2 0AP ☎ 01563 570122

dir: From Glasgow A77 to Kilmarnock, then A759 to Gatehead

The emphasis is on contemporary British food at this village centre pub, just a short drive from the Ayrshire coast. There's a friendly, bustling atmosphere inside. Good choice of starters may include soused herring and grilled goat's cheese, while main courses might feature stuffed pancake, pan-fried trio of seafood with tiger prawns, or smoked haddock risotto.

Open 12–2 6–11 (Fri-Sat 6–12.30, Sun all day) **Bar Meals** L served all week 12–2 D served all week 6–9 (Sat-Sun 5.30–9) Av main course £10 **Restaurant** L served all week 12–2 D served all week 6–9 (Sat-Sun 5.30–9) Av 3 course à la carte £17 ⊕ Free House ◀ John Smith's. ♥ 20 **Facilities** Garden Parking

SORN
MAP 20 NS52

The Sorn Inn ★★★★ RR ◉◉ ♥

35 Main St KA5 6HU ☎ 01290 551305 📄 01290 553470

e-mail: craig@sorninn.com

The Sorn is an 18th-century coaching inn on the Kilmarnock to Edinburgh route, now comprising a public bar, chop house and restaurant with four comfortable letting rooms. The chop house serves steaks, burgers, baguettes and simple dishes such as cod and chips, while the restaurant offers the likes of pheasant supreme with fondant potato, creamed Savoy cabbage and smoked bacon cream. The inn is on the River Ayr, which has good salmon and trout fishing.

Open 12–2.30 6–11 (Fri-Sat 6–12, Sun 12.30–10) Closed: 2wks Jan & Mon **Bar Meals** L served Tue-Sat 12–2.30 D served Tue-Sat 6–9 (Sun 12.30–7) Av main course £12 **Restaurant** L served Tue-Sat 12–2.30 D served Tue-Sat 6–9 (Sun 12.30–6.30) Av 3 course à la carte £20 ⊕ Free House ◀ John Smiths, McEwans 60/-. ♥ 13 **Facilities** Children's licence Parking **Rooms** 4

EAST LINTON
MAP 21 NT57

The Drovers Inn

5 Bridge St EH40 3AG ☎ 01620 860298 📄 01620 860205

dir: Off A1, 5m past Haddington, follow road under rail bridge, then left

Herdsmen used to stop here as they drove their livestock to market. Those old drovers are long gone but the bar, with wooden floors, beamed ceilings and half-panelled walls, retains an old-world charm. Upstairs, though, is more sumptuous with rich colours, low-beamed ceilings and antique furniture. The menus change every six weeks or so, but may include the likes of grilled halibut and black tiger prawns with chervil and garlic butter. The bistro downstairs next to the bar offers a more informal dining choice.

Open 11.30–11 **Bar Meals** L served all week 12.30–2.30 D served all week 6–9.30 Av main course £10 **Restaurant** L served all week 12–2.30 D served all week 6–9.30 (Sun all day) Av 3 course à la carte £22.50 ⊕ Free House ◀ Adnams Broadside, Deuchars IPA, Old Speckled Hen, Burton Real Ale. **Facilities** Garden Dogs allowed

CITY OF EDINBURGH

EDINBURGH
MAP 21 NT27

Bennets Bar ♥

8 Leven St EH3 9LG ☎ 0131 229 5143

dir: Next to Kings Theatre. Please phone for more detailed directions

Bennets is a friendly pub, popular with performers from the adjacent Kings Theatre, serving real ales, over 120 malt whiskies and a decent selection of wines. It's a listed property dating from 1839 with hand-painted tiles and murals on the walls, original stained glass windows and brass beer taps. Reasonably priced home-made food ranges from toasties, burgers and salads to stovies, steak pie, and macaroni cheese. There's also a daily roast and traditional puddings.

Open 11–1am (Sun 12–12) Closed: 25 Dec **Bar Meals** L served Mon-Sat 12–2 D served Mon-Sat 5–8.30 (Sun 12–5) Av main course £5.85 **Restaurant** L served all week 12–2 D served Mon-Sat 5–8.30 ◉ Scottish & Newcastle ◀ Caledonian Deuchars IPA, Miller, Guinness, Caledonian 80/-. ♥ 14

The Bow Bar ♥

80 The West Bow EH1 2HH ☎ 0131 226 7667

dir: Telephone for directions

Located in the heart of Edinburgh's old town, the Bow Bar reflects the history and traditions of the area. Tables from decommissioned railway carriages and a gantry from an old church used for the huge selection of whiskies create interest in the bar, where 150 malts are on tap, and eight cask ales are dispensed from antique equipment. Bar snacks only are served, and there are no gaming machines or music to distract from conversation.

Open 12–11.30 (Sun 12.30–11) Closed: 25–26 Dec, 1–2 Jan ⊕ Free House ◀ Deuchars IPA, Belhaven 80/-, Taylors Landlord, Harviestown Bitter & Twisted. ♥ 6 **Facilities** Dogs allowed

Pick of the Pubs

Doric Tavern ♥

15–16 Market St EH1 1DE

☎ 0131 225 1084 📄 0131 220 0894

e-mail: info@mowco.co.uk

dir: Centre of Edinburgh opposite Waverly Station & Edinburgh Dungeons

The property dates from 1710, when it was built as a private residence. It became a pub in the mid-1800s and later the Nor Loch was drained to make way for the railway; Waverley Station was conveniently built nearby, just a short walk from Princes Street and Edinburgh Castle. Public rooms include the regular bar, a wine bar and bistro, and in these pleasantly informal surroundings a wide choice of fresh, locally sourced food is available, prepared by the chefs on site. Typical bar options are cullen skink; mince and tatties; or steak sandwich, while the bistro offers carpaccio of prime Border beef with quenelle of horseradish mousse, baby capers and lemon; and Hebridean chicken breast stuffed with haggis and Stornoway black pudding, with bubble and squeak and pink peppercorn sauce. A vegetarian alternative is vegetable and lentil pie topped with a creamy potato and parsnip mash.

Open 12–1am Closed: 25–26 Dec, 1 Jan **Bar Meals** L served all week 12–11 **Restaurant** L served all week 12–5 D served all week 5–11.30 ⊕ Free House ⬛ Deuchars IPA, Tennents, McEwans 80/-, Guinness. ♀13

The Shore Bar & Restaurant ♀

3 Shore, Leith EH6 6QW
☎ 0131 553 5080 📠 0131 553 5080
e-mail: enquiries@the.shore.ukf.net

Part of this historic pub was a 17th-century lighthouse and, befitting its location beside the Port of Leith, it has a fine reputation for fish and seafood. The carte changes at every sitting during the day to ensure the freshest produce is on offer. A typical meal could be pan-fried pigeon breasts and pancetta followed by sautéed monkfish tail with a fennel and orange sauce. The bustling bar hosts regular live Latin-jazz and folk sessions.

Open 11–12 (Sun 11–11) Closed: 25–26 Dec, 1–2 Jan **Bar Meals** L served all week 12–2.30 (Sat-Sun 12–3) D served all week 6.30–10 Av main course £15 **Restaurant** L served all week 12–2.30 (Sat-Sun 12–3) D served all week 6.30–10 Av 3 course à la carte £26 Av 3 course fixed price £15.50 ⊕ Free House ⬛ Belhaven 80/-, Deuchars IPA, Guinness. ♀14 **Facilities** Dogs allowed

---

RATHO　　　　　　　　　　**MAP 21 NT17**

Pick of the Pubs

The Bridge Inn

27 Baird Rd EH28 8RA
☎ 0131 333 1320 📠 0131 333 3480
e-mail: info@bridgeinn.com
dir: *From Newbridge B7030 junction, follow signs for Ratho*

In 1822 the Union Canal reached to the door of this former farmhouse, which seized the opportunity of increased traffic to become an inn. Unfortunately, a century or so later the barge traffic declined and the rot set in. In 1971 the inn was transformed once again, becoming the lively multi-function establishment that still thrives today. The informal Pop Inn Lounge serves snacks and bar meals all day – to be eaten while gazing out over the canal. In the award-winning waterways-themed restaurant you can enjoy the likes of pan-fried chicken breast stuffed with haggis, and served with Drambuie, cream and mushroom sauce; poached smoked haddock and salmon with creamy prawn sauce; casserole of Highland venison, cooked with a whisky and port sauce; and pappardelle pasta with spring onion sauce. The Edinburgh Canal Centre arranges three-hour cruise dinners from here.

Open 12–11 (Sat 11–12, Sun 12.30–11) Closed: 26 Dec, 1–2 Jan **Bar Meals** L served all week 12–9 D served all week 12–9 (Sun 12.30–9) Av main course £8 **Restaurant** L served all week 12–2.30 D served all week 6.30–9 (Sun 12.30–9) Av 3 course à la carte £20 ⊕ Free House ⬛ Belhaven, Deuchars IPA, Tennents. **Facilities** Children's licence Garden Parking

---

ANSTRUTHER　　　　　　**MAP 21 NO50**

The Dreel Tavern ♀

16 High St West KY10 3DL
☎ 01333 310727 📠 01333 310577
e-mail: dreeltavern@aol.com
dir: *From Anstruther centre take A917 towards Pittenweem*

Complete with a local legend concerning an amorous encounter between James V and a local gypsy woman, the 16th-century Dreel Tavern has plenty of atmosphere. Its oak beams, open fire and stone walls retain much of the distant past, while home-cooked food and cask-conditioned ales are served to hungry visitors of the present. Peaceful gardens overlook Dreel Burn. Under new management.

Open 11–12 (Sun 12.30–12) **Bar Meals** L served Mon-Sat 12–2.30 (Sun 12.30–2.30) D served all week 5.30–9 **Restaurant** L served all week 12–2.30 D served all week 5.30–9 ⊕ Free House ⬛ Tetley's Bitter, Harviestoun Bitter & Twisted, Greene King IPA, London Pride. ♀20 **Facilities** Children's licence Garden Dogs allowed Parking

---

BURNTISLAND　　　　　**MAP 21 NT28**

Burntisland Sands Hotel

Lochies Rd KY3 9JX ☎ 01592 872230 📠 01592 872230
e-mail: clarkelinton@hotmail.com
dir: *Towards Kirkcaldy, Burntisland on A921. Hotel on right before Kinghorn*

This small, family-run hotel, just 50 yards from an award-winning sandy beach, was once a highly regarded girls' boarding school. Reasonably priced breakfasts, snacks, lunches and evening meals are always available, with a good selection of specials. Try breaded haddock and tartare sauce; gammon steak Hawaii; or crispy shredded beef. Desserts include hot naughty fudge cake, and banana boat. There is also an excellent choice of hot and cold filled rolls, and a children's menu.

Open 12–12 **Bar Meals** L served all week 12–2.30 D served all week 6–8.30 (Sat-Sun 12–8.30) Av main course £5.95 **Restaurant** L served all week 12–2.30 D served all week 5–8.30 (Sat-Sun all day) Av 3 course à la carte £15 ⊕ Free House ⬛ Scottish Courage ales, Guinness & guest ales. **Facilities** Children's licence Garden Parking Play Area

---

CRAIL　　　　　　　　　**MAP 21 NO60**

The Golf Hotel

4 High St KY10 3TD ☎ 01333 450206 📠 01333 450795
e-mail: enquiries@thegolfhotelcrail.com
dir: *On corner of High Street*

Reputedly one of the oldest licensed inns in Scotland, the present day Golf Hotel occupies an 18th-century Grade I-listed building, but the first inn on the site opened its doors 400 years earlier. In 1786, the Crail Golfing Society was established here, although the pub's present name appeared only in the mid-1800s. The pub is known for home-cooked meals such as smoked haddock and poached salmon fishcakes; and high teas with home-made scones.

Open 11–12 **Bar Meals** L served all week 12–7 D served all week 7–9 Av main course £7 **Restaurant** L served all week 12–7 D served all week 7–9 ⊕ Free House ⬛ McEwans 60/-, 80/-, 70/-, Belhaven Best & Real ale. **Facilities** Garden Dogs allowed Parking **Rooms** available

ELIE
MAP 21 NO40

The Ship Inn ▿
The Toft KY9 1DT ☎ 01333 330246 ▤ 01333 330864
e-mail: info@ship-elie.com
dir: *Follow A915 & A917 to Elie. From High Street follow signs to Watersport Centre & The Toft*

Run by the enthusiastic Philip family for over two decades, this lively free house stands right on the waterfront at Elie Bay. The Ship has been a pub since 1838, and there's still plenty going on. The cricket team plays regular fixtures on the beach, live music is performed, and a programme of summer Sunday barbecues is eagerly anticipated. Local bakers, butchers and fishmongers and their produce feature in the pub's colourful and concise menu.

Open 11–11 Closed: 25 Dec **Bar Meals** L served all week 12–2 D served all week 6–9 **Restaurant** L served all week 12–2 D served all week 6–9 ⊕ Free House ◀ Caledonian Deuchars IPA, Belhaven Best, Tetleys Xtra Cold, Caledonian 80I. ▿ 7 **Facilities** Garden Dogs allowed Play Area

KINCARDINE
MAP 21 NS98

The Unicorn ▿
15 Excise St FK10 4LN ☎ 01259 739129
e-mail: info@theunicorn.co.uk
dir: *Exit M9 at Kincardine Bridge, across bridge & bear left. 1st left, then sharp left at rdbt*

This 17th-century pub-restaurant in the heart of the historic port of Kincardine used to be a coaching inn. And it was where, in 1842, Sir James Dewar, inventor of the vacuum flask, was born. Leather sofas and modern d?cor blend in well with the older parts of the building. There is a comfortable lounge bar, a grillroom, and a more formal dining room upstairs. In decent weather, have a drink by the old well in the walled garden.

Open 12–2 5.30–12 Closed: 1st wk Jan & 3rd wk Jul Sun-Mon **Bar Meals** L served Tue-Sat 12–2 D served Tue-Sat 5.30–9 **Restaurant** D served Fri-Sat 7–9 ◀ Extra Cold Guinness, Belhaven Best, Bitter & Twisted, Schiallion. ▿ 8 **Facilities** Parking

LOWER LARGO
MAP 21 NO40

The Crusoe Hotel
2 Main St KY8 6BT ☎ 01333 320759 ▤ 01333 320865
e-mail: relax@crusoehotel.co.uk
dir: *A92 to Kirkcaldy East, A915 to Lundin Links, then right to Lower Largo*

This historic inn is located on the sea wall in Lower Largo, the birthplace of Alexander Selkirk, the real-life castaway immortalised by Daniel Defoe in his novel, *Robinson Crusoe*. In the past the area was also the heart of the once-thriving herring fishing industry. Today it is a charming bay ideal for a golfing break. A typical menu may include 'freshly shot' haggis, Pittenweem haddock and a variety of steaks.

Open 11–12 (Fri 11-1am, Sun 12–12) **Bar Meals** L served all week 12–9 Av main course £6 **Restaurant** D served all week 6.45–9 ⊕ Free House ◀ Belhaven 80/-, Best, Deuchars. **Facilities** Dogs allowed Parking Play Area **Rooms** available

ST ANDREWS
MAP 21 NO51

The Inn at Lathones ★★★★ INN ⊛⊛ ▿
Largoward KY9 1JE ☎ 01334 840494 ▤ 01334 840694
e-mail: lathones@theinn.co.uk
dir: *5m from St Andrews on A915*

This is St Andrews' oldest inn, and parts of the building date back over 400 years. Up to fifteen Scottish real ales are served in pewter tankards in the bar lounge, with its big leather sofas and log burning fires. The finest fresh, local produce features on the daily changing menus: typical dishes include oven-roasted salmon with pesto crust, shallots and cherry tomatoes; and roast Perthshire black-faced lamb with lemon and mint stuffing.

Open 7–12.30 Closed: 1st 2wks Jan **Bar Meals** L served all week 12–2.30 D served all week 6–9.30 **Restaurant** L served all week 12–2.30 D served all week 6–9.30 Av 3 course à la carte £45 Av 3 course fixed price £17.50 ◀ Boddingtons, Miller, Scottish Ales. ▿ 11 **Facilities** Garden Dogs allowed Parking **Rooms** 13

CITY OF GLASGOW

GLASGOW
MAP 20 NS56

Rab Ha's
83 Hutchieson St G1 1SH
☎ 0141 572 0400 ▤ 0141 572 0402
e-mail: management@rabhas.com
dir: *Telephone for directions*

In the heart of Glasgow's revitalised Merchant City, Rab Ha's takes its name from Robert Hall, a local 19th-century character known as 'The Glasgow Glutton'. This hotel, restaurant and bar blend Victorian character with contemporary Scottish décor. Pre-theatre and set menus show extensive use of carefully sourced Scottish produce in starters like poached egg on grilled Stornoway black pudding, and pan-seared Oban scallops, followed by roast saddle of Rannoch Moor venison.

Open 12–12 (Sun 12.30–12) **Bar Meals** L served all week 12 D served all week 8 Av main course £8 **Restaurant** L served all week 12–2.30 D served all week 5–10 Av 3 course à la carte £25 Av 3 course fixed price £13.95 ⊕ Free House ◀ Tennents, Belhaven Best, Guinness. **Facilities** Children's licence Dogs allowed

Pick of the Pubs

Ubiquitous Chip ⊛⊛ ▿
12 Ashton Ln G12 8SJ
☎ 0141 334 5007 ▤ 0141 337 6417
e-mail: mail@ubiquitouschip.co.uk
dir: *In West End of Glasgow, off Byres Rd. Beside Hillhead subway station*

The Ubiquitous Chip opened in 1971 with the intention of bringing Scotland's endangered cuisine out of the home and into the restaurant – in this case a glass-covered mews with cobbled floor, water fountains and enough greenery to fill an arboretum. Traditional draught beers, over a hundred malt whiskies and excellent wines are served from three bars; the new roof terrace is a quiet space in which to enjoy them. The original upper level bar with its coal fire and the sound of no music is a regular haunt for Glasgow's media types. The Wee bar, reputed to be the smallest in Scotland, is intimate and cosy – attracting tourists as well as regulars. Finally the Corner bar boasts an imported tin ceiling and a granite bar top reclaimed from a mortuary. The food continues to showcase the best of Scotland's produce in dishes of Ayrshire ham, Seil Island crab, Ritchie's of Rothesay black pudding, and nine hole beef stovies.

Open 11–12 (Sun 12.30–12) Closed: 25 Dec, 1 Jan
Bar Meals L served Mon-Sat 12–5.30 D served all week 5.30–11 (Sun 12.30–4) Av main course £5.50 **Restaurant** L served Mon-Sat 12–2.30 D served Mon-Sat 5.30–11 (Sun 12.30–3, 6.30–11) Av 3 course à la carte £34.85 ⊕ Free House ◀ Deuchars IPA, The Chip 71 Ale. ♥ 21

HIGHLAND

ACHILTIBUIE   MAP 22 NC00

Summer Isles Hotel & Bar ◉◉
IV26 2YG ☎ 01854 622282 ▤ 01854 622251
e-mail: info@summerisleshotel.co.uk
dir: *Take A835 N from Ullapool for 10m, Achiltibuie signed on left, 15m to village. Hotel 1m on left*

Located in a stunningly beautiful and unspoilt landscape, it would be hard to discover a more individual and relaxing place in which to drink and unwind. The emphasis here is on locally caught and home-produced quality food, with a wide choice of malts and real ale. Seafood platter, seared local scallops, fresh lobster and dressed crab are popular favourites, as well as vegetarian dishes, steaks, casseroles and freshly made sandwiches.

Open 11–11 Closed: Mon-Wed (Nov-Feb) **Bar Meals** L served all week 12–2.30 D served all week 5.30–8.30 **Restaurant** L served all week 12.30–2 D served all week at 8 ⊕ Free House ◀ Red Cuillin, Misty Isle, Hebridean Gold, Young Pretender & IPA Deuchars. **Facilities** Garden Dogs allowed Parking

ALTNAHARRA   MAP 23 NC53

Altnaharra Hotel
IV27 4UE ☎ 01549 411222 ▤ 01549 411222
e-mail: office@altnaharra.co.uk
dir: *A9 to Bonar Bridge, A836 to Lairg & Tongue*

Originally a drover's inn understood to date back to the late 17th century, the Altnaharra is located in the beautiful Flow Country of Scotland, with endless views over timeless moorland. Interesting items of fishing memorabilia decorate the walls, including some fine historical prints and fishing records. The imaginative menu features the best of Scottish produce and options might include scallops in a brandy and cream sauce, Aberdeen Angus roast rib of beef, whole baked sea bass, Kyle of Tongue oysters, and Scottish rack of lamb.

Open 11–12.45 **Bar Meals** L served all week 12–10 D served all week 12–10 Av main course £7 **Restaurant** D served all week 7–10 Av 3 course à la carte £32.50 Av 5 course fixed price £45 ⊕ Scottish & Newcastle ◀ No real ale. **Facilities** Garden Dogs allowed Parking Play Area

AVIEMORE   MAP 23 NH81

The Old Bridge Inn ♥
Dalfaber Rd PH22 1PU ☎ 01479 811137 ▤ 01479 810270
e-mail: nigel@oldbridgeinn.co.uk
dir: *Exit A9 to Aviemore, 1st left to Ski Rd, then 1st left again 200mtrs*

Cosy and friendly Highland pub overlooking the River Spey. Dine in the relaxing bars, the comfortable restaurant, or in the attractive riverside garden. A tasty chargrill menu includes lamb chops in redcurrant jelly, Aberdeen Angus sirloin or rib-eye steaks, and butterflied breast of chicken marinated in yoghurt, lime and coriander. Seafood specials include monkfish pan fried in chilli butter, mussels poached in white wine, and seafood crumble. Large selection of malt whiskies.

Open 11–11 (Sun 12.30–11) **Bar Meals** L served Mon-Sat 12–2 D served all week 6–9 (Sun 12.30–2) **Restaurant** L served Mon-Sat 12–2 D served all week 6–9 (Sun 12.30–2) ⊕ Free House ◀ Caledonian 80/-, Cairngorm Highland IPA. ♥ 18 **Facilities** Children's licence Garden Parking Play Area

BADACHRO   MAP 22 NG77

The Badachro Inn ♥
IV21 2AA ☎ 01445 741255 ▤ 01445 741319
e-mail: Lesley@badachroinn.com
dir: *Off A832 onto B8056, right onto Badachro after 3.25m, towards quay.*

A commanding position on the cusp of Badachro Bay, one of Scotland's finest anchorages, makes this atmospheric local in the north Highlands very popular in summer with yachting folk. Log fires burn cheerily in the bar in winter as the sea laps against the windows in high tides. Seals and otters can also be seen from the pub. Local seafood is, unsurprisingly, a speciality, and includes hot-smoked salmon, marinated herring, and Gairloch prawns.

Open 12–12 Closed: 25 Dec **Bar Meals** L served all week 12–3 D served all week 6–9 (Sun 12.30–3) **Restaurant** L served all week 12–3 D served all week 6–9 (Sun 12.30–3) ⊕ Free House ◀ Red Cullen, Anceallach, Blaven, 80/-. ♥ 11 **Facilities** Children's licence Garden Dogs allowed Parking

Scotland

707

CAWDOR   MAP 23 NH85

Pick of the Pubs

Cawdor Tavern ♥

The Lane IV12 5XP ☎ 01667 404777 📋 01667 404777
e-mail: enquiries@cawdertavern.info
dir: *From A96 (Inverness-Aberdeen) take B9006 & follow Cawdor Castle signs. Tavern in village centre.*

Standing close to the famous castle in a beautiful conservation village, the tavern was formerly a joinery workshop for the Cawdor Estate. Oak panelling from the castle, gifted by the late laird, is used to great effect in the bar. Roaring log fires keep the place cosy and warm on long winter evenings, while the garden patio comes into its own in summer. A single menu is offered for both restaurant and bar, where refreshments include a choice of real ales and 100 malt whiskies. The pub's reputation for seafood draws diners from some distance for dishes like fresh Mallaig haddock, and sea bass fillet on creamed potatoes. Other favourites include steak and Orkney beer pie; chicken Culloden (breast of local chicken filled with home-made haggis, served with a Drambuie and mushroom cream sauce); and desserts like caramelised pear and honey crème brûlée.

Open 11–3 5–11 (May-Oct 11–11) Closed: 25 Dec, 1 Jan
Bar Meals L served Mon-Sat 12 2 D served all week 5.30–9 (Sun 12.30–3) **Restaurant** L served Mon-Sat (prior arrangement) 12–2 D served Mon-Sat 6.30–9 (Sun 12.30–3, 5.30–9) ⊕ Free House
⬛ Red McGregor, 3 Sisters, Orkney Dark Island, Raven Ale. ♥ 8
Facilities Children's licence Garden Dogs allowed Parking

CONTIN   MAP 23 NH45

Achilty Hotel ★★★ SHL ◉ ♥

IV14 9EG ☎ 01997 421355 📋 01997 421923
e-mail: info@achiltyhotel.co.uk
web: www.achiltyhotel.co.uk
dir: *On A835, at N outskirts of Contin*

The original stone walls and log fire keep this former drovers' inn warm when the Highlands weather closes in. On the edge of the village near a fast-flowing mountain river, the cosy Achilty Hotel serves good Scottish food made from fresh local produce. The bar/restaurant menu offers an extensive choice with a seafood slant: bouillabaisse (Scottish style), scampi provençal, seafood thermidor, halibut and monkfish, plus chicken with haggis in a creamy whisky and onion sauce, duck breasts, mushroom stroganoff, and a large selection of steaks and home-made desserts.

Achilty Hotel

Open 11–2 5–10 (Sun 12.30–2.30, 5–9. Apr-Oct 11–11) Closed: 25 Dec & 2nd wk Jan, Mon & Tue lunch **Bar Meals** L served Wed-Sat 12–2 D served Wed-Sun 5–9 (Sun 12.30–2.30, Etr-Sep 12–2, 5–8.30) Av main course £24 **Restaurant** L served Mon-Sat 12–2 D served Mon-Sat 5–9 (Sun 12.30–2.30, fixed price menu only) Av 3 course à la carte £24 Av 3 course fixed price £10.95 ⊕ Free House ⬛ Calders Cream, Calders 70/-. ♥ 8
Facilities Children's licence Garden Parking **Rooms** 12

FORT WILLIAM   MAP 22 NN17

Moorings Hotel ★★★ HL ◉

Banavie PH33 7LY ☎ 01397 772797 📋 01397 772441
e-mail: reservations@moorings-fortwilliam.co.uk
dir: *From A82 in Fort William follow signs for Mallaig, then left onto A830 for 1m. Cross canal bridge then 1st right signed Banavie*

This modern hotel lies alongside Neptune's Staircase, on the coast-to-coast Caledonian Canal. The canal is a historic monument, its eight locks able to raise even sea-going craft a total of 64 feet. Most hotel bedrooms and the Upper Deck lounge bar have good views of Ben Nevis (1344m) and Aonach Mor (1219m). A range of eating options includes Mariners cellar bar, and the Caledonian split-level lounge bar overlooking the canal, plus the fine dining Jacobean Restaurant.

Open 12–11.45 (Thu-Sat 12–1am) **Bar Meals** L served all week 12–9.30 D served all week 12–9.30 Av main course £7 **Restaurant** D served all week 7–9.30 Av 3 course à la carte £25 ⊕ Free House ⬛ Calders 70/-, Tetley Bitter, Guinness. **Facilities** Children's licence Garden Dogs allowed Parking **Rooms** 27

GAIRLOCH   MAP 22 NG87

Pick of the Pubs

The Old Inn ★★★ INN ♥

See Pick of the Pubs on opposite page

PICK OF THE PUBS

GAIRLOCH-HIGHLAND

The Old Inn

On a good day, you might be able to spy the Outer Hebrides from this attractive inn, though the setting is pretty fabulous whatever the weather. The pub sits at the foot of the Flowerdale Valley, looking out across Gairloch Harbour to the isles of Rona, Raasay and Skye.

Among the many activities in the area are walking, fishing, golf, birdwatching and boat trips from the adjacent harbour to see whales, porpoises and, if you are lucky, bottlenose dolphins. The inn provides a comfortable base for exploring these activities, or simply resting and lolling about on the golden beaches. The 14 bedrooms are named after famous pipers, and the atmosphere is friendly and hospitable. In the two bars you'll find the inn's own beer, the Blind Piper of Gairloch, which was created by the landlord and enthusiastic locals, alongside a good range of real ales. An extensive range of Highland malt whiskies is also available. Seafood will be the main draw in an area where Gairloch lobster, Loch Ewe scallops, Minch langoustines, mussels, brown crab and fresh fish are regularly landed. Tuck into the traditional Cullen Skink, a soup of smoked haddock, potato and cream, or steamed langoustine tails with aioli and salsa, before launching into cod and monkfish bakes; pan-seared scallops with smoked bacon mash and tamarind sauce, or grilled seafood platter with shoestring fries. Those less inclined towards the fruits of the sea might like pheasant and venison game casserole; or vegetable stuffed cannelloni topped with sherry cream. A large grassy area by the pretty stream with picnic tables is an attractive place to eat and enjoy the views. Dogs are more than welcome, with bowls, baskets and rugs to help them feel at home.

★★★ INN ♥
MAP 22 NG87
IV21 2BD
☎ 01445 712006
🖷 01445 712044
e-mail: info@theoldinn.net
dir: *Just off A832, near harbour at south end of village*

Open 11–12 (Winter eve & wknds only)
Bar Meals L served all week 12–2.30 D served all week 5–9.30
Restaurant L served all week 12–5 D served all week 5–9.30 Av 3 course à la carte £25
🌐 Free House 🍺 Adnams Bitter, Isle of Skye Red Cullin, Blind Piper, An Teallach. ♥ 8
Facilities Children's licence Garden Dogs allowed Parking Play Area
Rooms 14

PICK OF THE PUBS

Kylesku Hotel

Legendary fell-walker Alfred Wainwright didn't write only about the Lake District, as this quote shows: "Anyone with an eye for impressive beauty will not regard time spent at Kylesku as wasted. I could spend a day here, just looking."

On the shores of two sea-lochs, Glendhu and Glencoul, it certainly is a delightful place. This former coaching inn, dating from 1680, stands by the former ferry slipway between the two expanses of water, which gives the restaurant and bar splendid views over to the mountains beyond. The chef uses fresh local produce wherever possible, and with local fishing boats landing daily in Kylesku, seafood, such as langoustine, spineys, lobster, crab, scallops, haddock and mussels, are usually available. Salmon is hot-and cold-smoked on the premises,†beef and lamb all comes from the Scottish Highlands and the venison (in season) is wild. Alternative bar meals to all that fish and shellfish could be grilled breast of chicken with bacon; grilled rib-eye steak; or mixed mushroom tagliatelle, while a typical restaurant meal might be buttered asparagus with poached egg and parmesan shavings; fillet of Scottish lamb with red onion pickle and redcurrant and rosemary sauce; and a platter of Isle of Mull cheddar with celery and spicy fruit chutney. Also available is a wide selection of wines, real ales from the Black Isle Brewery, Skye Cuillin bottled beers, and malt whiskies. The Kylesku Hotel is now at the centre of Scotland's first designated Global Geopark, a 2,000–square kilometre area of lochs, mountains and coastal scenery with an abundance of wildlife and a wide range of outdoor activities.

MAP 22 NC23
IV27 4HW
☎ 01971 502231
🖹 01971 502313
e-mail: info@kyleskuhotel.co.uk
web: www.kyleskuhotel.co.uk
dir: *35m N of Ullapool on A835, then A837 & A894 into Kylesku. Hotel at end of road at Old Ferry Pier*

Open 11–11 Closed: Nov-Feb
Bar Meals L served all week 12–2.30 D served all week 6–9 Av main course £10
Restaurant D served Tue-Sun 7–8.30 Av 2 course fixed price £24.50
⊕ Free House ◀ Tennents Ember 80/-, Selection of Black Isle Brewery and Skye Cuillin bottled ales.
Facilities Children's licence Garden

GARVE   MAP 23 NH36

Inchbae Lodge Guesthouse

IV23 2PH ☎ 01997 455269 📄 01997 455207

e-mail: contact@inchbae.co.uk

dir: *30m from Inverness, 26m from Ullapool, A835 from Tore rdbt*

You can watch stags feeding in the garden of this 19th-century hunting lodge, and residents can fish for free in the river Blackwater, which flows just outside. Inside you'll find a bistro and a conservatory dining room with panoramic views, and a large residents' lounge warmed by a log fire on cooler days. The menu includes hearty traditional choices such as venison casserole or liver and onions, and an extensive list of curries.

Open all day **Bar Meals** L served all week 9–8.30 D served all week 9–8.30 Av main course £6.25 **Restaurant** L served all week 9–8.30 D served all week 9–8.30 ⊕ Free House 🍺 Guinness, Isle of Skye Red Cullin & An Teallach Brewhouse Special. **Facilities** Garden Parking

---

GLENELG   MAP 22 NG81

Glenelg Inn

IV40 8JR ☎ 01599 522273 📄 01599 522283

e-mail: christophermain7@glenelg-inn.com

dir: *From Shiel Bridge (A87) take unclassified road to Glenelg*

The inn is a conversion of 200–year-old stables set in a large garden stretching down to the sea, with stunning views across the Sound of Sleat. Musicians are frequent visitors to the bar, where at times a ceilidh atmosphere prevails. Menus offer traditional Scottish fare based on local produce, including plenty of fresh fish and seafood, hill-bred lamb, venison and seasonal vegetables. In the bar are seafood casserole and pies, while the dinner menu offers West Coast turbot with fennel and new potatoes.

Open 12–11 (Bar closed lunch in winter) **Bar Meals** L served all week 12.30–2 D served all week 6–9.30 **Restaurant** L served 12.30–2 D served 7.30–9 ⊕ Free House **Facilities** Garden Dogs allowed Parking

---

INVERIE   MAP 22 NG70

The Old Forge

PH41 4PL ☎ 01687 462267 📄 01687 462267

e-mail: info@theoldforge.co.uk

dir: *From Fort William take A830 (Road to the Isles) towards Mallaig. Take ferry from Mallaig to Inverie*

Accessible only by boat, The Old Forge stands literally between heaven and hell (Loch Nevis is Gaelic for heaven and Loch Hourn is Gaelic for hell). The most remote pub in mainland Britain is, however, a mecca for musicians and is popular for its impromptu ceilidhs. It is also the ideal place to sample local fish and seafood – especially the renowned prawn platters. There are nine boat moorings and a daily ferry from Mallaig.

Open 10.30–1am (Sun 12–11.45) (5–1am Tue & Thu Dec-Mar) **Bar Meals** L served all week 12–3 D served all week 6.30–9.30 **Restaurant** L served all week 12–3 D served all week 6.30–9.30 ⊕ Free House 🍺 80 Shilling, Guinness, Black Cuillin & Red Cuillin. **Facilities** Children's licence Garden Dogs allowed Parking Play Area

---

KYLESKU   MAP 22 NC23

Pick of the Pubs

Kylesku Hotel

See Pick of the Pubs on opposite page

LYBSTER   MAP 23 ND23

Portland Arms Ⓤ

KW3 6BS ☎ 01593 721721 📄 01593 721722

e-mail: manager.portlandarms@ohiml.com

dir: *Exit A9 signed Latheron, take A99 to Wick. Then 12m to Lybster*

This 19th-century coaching inn has evolved into a comfortable modern hotel. The bar and dining areas feature the best of fresh Scottish produce in settings that range from farmhouse to formal. The extensive menus cater for all tastes, with everything from a simple cheese ploughman's to chargrilled haunch of venison with haggis and black pudding. There's a children's menu too, and the home-made puddings include a tempting oat-baked fruit crumble.

Open 7.30–11 Closed: 31 Dec-3 Jan **Bar Meals** L served all week 12–3 D served all week 5–9 (Sat-Sun 12–9) Av main course £8.50 **Restaurant** L served all week 12–3 D served all week 5–9 (Sat-Sun 12–9) Av 3 course à la carte £20 ⊕ Free House 🍺 McEwans 70/-, Tennents Lager, Guinness. **Facilities** Children's licence Dogs allowed Parking **Rooms** 22

NORTH BALLACHULISH   MAP 22 NN06

Loch Leven Hotel

Old Ferry Rd PH33 6SA ☎ 01855 821236 📄 01855 821550

e-mail: reception@lochlevenhotel.co.uk

web: www.lochlevenhotel.co.uk

dir: *Off A82, N of Ballachulish Bridge*

With its relaxed atmosphere, beautiful loch-side setting, and dramatic views, this privately owned hotel lies in the heart of Lochaber,

Continued

NORTH BALLACHULISH continued

The Outdoor Capital of the UK'. It began life over 300 years ago accommodating travellers from the adjacent Ballachulish ferry. Food is available in the restaurant and the bar, both of which offer spectacular views over the fast-flowing narrows to the mountains. Home-cooked meals are built around local produce, especially fresh seafood, game and other traditional Scottish dishes.

Open 11–12 (Sun 12.30–11.45) Closed: afternoons in winter
Bar Meals L served all week 12–3 D served all week 6–9 Av main course £9.50 **Restaurant** L served all week 12–3 D served all week 6–9 (Sun 12.30–3) Av 3 course à la carte £20 ⊕ Free House ◀ John Smith's Extra Smooth. **Facilities** Garden Dogs allowed Parking Play Area

See advert below

Loch Leven Hotel

Old Ferry Road, North Ballachulish, Inverness shire PH33 6SA
Tel: 01855 821236   Fax: 01855 821550

Loch Leven Hotel, a small, informal, family run hotel with excellent food and it's own idyllic surroundings of loch and mountains make it the perfect place to relax and unwind and a perfect base to see the rest of this beautiful region, near to Glencoe and Fort William.

Enjoy the spectacular scenery and the tranquillity from the Lochview Restaurant, garden and new decking or toast yourself by the log fire in the Public Bar. Inexpensive menu, freshly prepared.

Children and pets always welcome.

Email: reception@lochlevenhotel.co.uk
Website: www.lochlevenhotel.co.uk

PLOCKTON   MAP 22 NG83

Pick of the Pubs

The Plockton Hotel ★★★ SHL ♟
See Pick of the Pubs on opposite page

Pick of the Pubs

Plockton Inn & Seafood Restaurant
See Pick of the Pubs on page 714

SHIELDAIG   MAP 22 NG85

Pick of the Pubs

Shieldaig Bar & Coastal Kitchen ★ SHL ◉◉ ♟
See Pick of the Pubs on page 715

TORRIDON   MAP 22 NG95

Pick of the Pubs

AA PUB OF THE YEAR FOR SCOTLAND 2008-9

The Torridon Inn ♟
See Pick of the Pubs on page 716

ULLAPOOL   MAP 22 NH19

Pick of the Pubs

The Ceilidh Place ♟
14 West Argyle St IV26 2TY
☎ 01854 612103 ▤ 01854 613773
e-mail: stay@theceilidhplace.com
dir: *On entering Ullapool, along Shore Street, pass pier, take 1st right. Hotel straight ahead at top of hill*

Organic growth has seen this old boatshed café metamorphose over 37 years into an all-day bar, coffee shop, restaurant, bookshop and art gallery. The late founder Robert Urquhart had aspirations for a place for serious writing – life histories, postcards; a place for eating, meeting, talking and singing. This all came to pass and it is now known mostly for live traditional Scottish music, although some jazz slips in. The heart of The Ceilidh Place is the café/bar, with its big open fire and solid wooden furniture. It's a place to stay all day, and some do. Simple delights conjured up by the menu include mince and tatties, kedgeree, homity pie, and bone-warming cullen skink. Among the main dishes are braised venison chop; pan-roasted whole Loch Broom prawns; and seafood platter. A specials board offering seasonally available fish, meat, vegetables and fruits complements the printed menu.

Open 11–11 Closed: 2wks mid-Jan **Bar Meals** L served all week 12–6 D served all week 6.30–9 **Restaurant** D served all week 6.30–9.30 Av 3 course à la carte £24 ⊕ Free House ◀ Belhaven Best, Guinness, Scottish ales. ♟ 8 **Facilities** Children's licence Garden Dogs allowed Parking

PICK OF THE PUBS

PLOCKTON-HIGHLAND

The Plockton Hotel

Constructed in 1827 as a private house, the stone-built Plockton Hotel stands in an incomparable location just fifty metres from the gently lapping waters of Loch Carron; this sheltered sea loch is warmed by the Gulf Stream and fringed with palm trees.

It is the only waterfront hostelry in this lovely National Trust village, surrounded by a bowl of hills, which makes it an ideal base for visiting the nearby Isle of Skye. The view across the bay from the hotel to the castle and the Applecross Hills is simply breathtaking. Plockton itself was the location for both The Wicker Man in the 1970s and the fishing village of Lochdubh in the 1990s Hamish Macbeth TV series. The hotel was converted from a ship's chandlery in 1913, and has now been run by the Pearson family and their staff for nearly 20 years; the adjoining house was added to the hotel in 2000. Menus are based on the very best of Highland produce, with seafood a major strength: locally caught langoustines, shellfish from Skye, fresh fish landed at Gairloch and Kinlochbervie, and smoked fish from Aultbea. Products from the smokehouse feature in one of the hotel's specialities – cream of smoked fish soup. Other starters may include Talisker whisky paté; a small haggis with a tot of whisky; and fresh Plockton prawns. Top quality Highland beef supplied by the hotel's butcher in Dingwall appears in flamed peppered whisky steaks from the charcoal grill. Other main course choices may include casserole of Highland venison, Argyle chicken, and wild boar burger served with salad and fries. For fish lovers a large whole trout, a local fresh salmon fillet, roasted monkfish, and traditional fish and chips are among the options. A fine range of malts is available to round off that perfect Highland day.

★★★ SHL ⬧
MAP 22 NG83
Harbour St IV52 8TN
☎ 01599 544274
📠 01599 544475
e-mail: info@plocktonhotel.co.uk
web: www.plocktonhotel.co.uk
dir: *On A87 to Kyle of Lochalsh take turn at Balmacara. Plockton 7m N*

Open 11–11.45 (Sun 12.30–11)
Bar Meals L served Mon-Sat 12–2.15 D served all week 6–9 (Sun 12.30–2.15)
Restaurant L served all week 12–2.15 D served all week 6–9 Av 3 course à la carte £35
⊕ Free House ◨ Caledonian Deuchars IPA, Hebridean Gold – Isle of Skye Brewery, Harvieston Blonde ale, Tennents Emper. ⬧ 6
Facilities Children's licence Garden
Rooms 15

PICK OF THE PUBS

Plockton Inn & Seafood Restaurant

Mary Gollan and her brother Kenny, the proprietors of this attractive stone-built free house, were born and bred in Plockton. Their great grandfather built this property as a manse, just 100 metres from the harbour in the fishing village where BBC Scotland's Hamish Macbeth series was filmed in the mid-1990s.

Mary, Kenny and his partner, Susan Trowbridge, bought the inn in 1997 and have since elevated it to award-winning status, Mary and Susan doing the cooking, Kenny running the bar. The atmosphere is relaxed and friendly, with winter fires in both bars, and a selection of more than 50 malt whiskies. Taking pride of place on the regular and daily changing specials menus in the dining room and the lounge bar are fresh West Coast fish and shellfish, and West Highland beef, lamb and game. Starters include fish-based soup of the day; hot Plockton prawns with garlic butter; and roasted red pepper paté. Haggis and clapshot is a particular speciality (including a vegetarian version), served with neeps, tatties and home-made pickled beetroot. Seafood main dishes take in creel-caught langoustines from the waters of Loch Carron, served cold with Marie Rose sauce; and hake fillet with pesto crust. Other dishes include braised lamb shank; venison in ale; chicken Caesar salad; and aubergine parmigiana. Among some truly mouth-watering desserts is lemon and ginger crunch pie, as well as a selection of Scottish cheeses served with Orkney oatcakes. Comfortable en suite bedrooms are provided in both the main building and an annexe over the road. The National Centre of Excellence in Traditional Music is based in Plockton, which is why the inn's public bar resonates with fantastic live sounds twice a week.

MAP 22 NG83
Innes St IV52 8TW
☎ 01599 544222
🖷 01599 544487
e-mail: info@plocktoninn.co.uk
dir: *On A87 to Kyle of Lochalsh take turn at Balmacara. Plockton 7m N*

Open 11–1am (Sun 12.30–11)
Bar Meals L served all week 12–2.30 D served all week 6–9.30 (Winter 6–8.30)
Restaurant L served all week D served all week 6–9.30 (Winter 6–8.30) Av 3 course à la carte £18
⊕ Free House ◀ Greene King Abbot Ale & Old Speckled Hen, Fuller's London Pride, Isle Of Skye Blaven, Caledonian 80/-.
Facilities Children's licence Garden Dogs allowed Parking Play Area
Rooms available

PICK OF THE PUBS

Shieldaig Bar & Coastal Kitchen

You can enjoy stunning views across Loch Torridon to the sea beyond from this popular loch-front bar. Set in a charming fishing village, it comes alive on summer Friday nights with the sound of local musicians, among them owner Chris Field, playing guitar, banjo or pipes.

In fact, all over Wester Ross you are likely to find music like this being played somewhere. A new first floor eating area – called the Coastal Kitchen – makes the most of the views. Throughout the day a full range of alcoholic and non-alcoholic beverages is served to suit the hour, and there's always a ready supply of newspapers and magazines to read. The pub has a fine reputation for its bar snacks – sandwiches, home-made soups, burgers and bangers and mash – and for its daily-changing specials, such as Shieldaig crab cakes with tarragon mayonnaise; moules marinière; whole loch Torridon langoustines with a lemongrass, chilli and coriander dipping sauce; and the speciality Shieldaig bar seafood stew. All the seafood is caught locally, some from local prawn-fishing grounds which have won a sustainable fishery award. Alternatives are local venison sausages with mash and a red wine and onion gravy; or a shallot and goats' cheese tart with salad and new potatoes. Food is now served all day in summer, when you can also dine in the lochside courtyard, warmed, if necessary, by patio heaters. A good range of real ales is on tap from the Isle of Skye Brewery and Black Isle Ales, plus malt whiskies and a choice of wines by the glass. It's the sort of place you'll want to linger, so take note that the Fields also own the Tigh an Eilean Hotel next door.

★ SHL ☺☺ ♀
MAP 22 NG85
IV54 8XN
☎ 01520 755251
📠 01520 755321
e-mail:
tighaneilean@kerne.co.uk
dir: *Off A896, in centre of village.*

Open 11–11 (Sun 11–10.30)
Bar Meals L served all week 12–9 D served all week 12–9 (Winter 12–2.30, 6–9) Av main course £8.25
Restaurant L served all week 12–9 D served all week 12–9 (Winter 12–2.30, 6–9) Av 3 course à la carte £25
⊕ Free House ◀ Isle of Skye Brewery Ales. ♀ 8
Facilities Children's licence Garden Dogs allowed Parking
Rooms 11

TORRIDON-HIGHLAND

The Torridon Inn

Modern convenience meets cosy surroundings at The Torridon Inn, which stands on the shores of Loch Torridon. The inn was created by converting the stable block, buttery and farm buildings of nearby Ben Damph House in 1996; the latter is now known as The Torridon Hotel.

Whether you use it as a base to enjoy some of the many activities on offer, or simply want to unwind with a warm fire and relaxing drink after a hard day's walking, you can be sure of a memorable visit. The cosy bar offers a Highland welcome from both staff and locals. Choose from a range of 60 malt whiskies, or enjoy the local real ale and recount the adventures of the day. Entertainment ranges from indoor games to regular traditional live music sessions. The inn has its own restaurant where you can sample high quality, locally sourced food at any time. Hearty soups, sandwiches and bar meals are available during the day, and in the evening there's a choice of succulent starters, delicious main courses and legendary desserts. Local produce

is the foundation of menus that feature venison, salmon, haggis and home-made specials. Dinner might begin with beef carpaccio with rocket and parmesan shavings; Gairloch black pudding with mushy peas and crisp wild boar bacon; or smoked haddock and mackerel fishcakes. Typical main course choices include roast Scottish cod with parsley crust, creamy mash, mangetout and lemon butter sauce; breaded striploin of pork with Parma ham and applewood smoked cheddar; and linguine tossed with pesto, asparagus and rocket. Tea and coffee is served throughout the day.

MAP 22 NG95
IV22 2EY
☎ 01445 791242
🖷 01445 712253
e-mail: Inn@thetorridon.com
dir: *From Inverness take A9 N, then follow signs to Ullapool. Take A835 then A832. In Kinlochewe take A896 to Annat . Pub 200yds on right after village*

Open 11–11 Closed: Nov-Feb
Bar Meals L served all week
12–2 D served all week 6–8.45 Av main course £13.50
Restaurant L served all week
12–2 D served all week 6–8.45 Av 3 course à la carte £23.50
◀ Isle of Skye Red Cullen, Cairngorm Brewery Stag, Torridon Ale, Blaven & Tradewinds. ☻ 8
Facilities Children's licence Garden Dogs allowed Parking Play Area

MIDLOTHIAN

PENICUIK MAP 21 NT25

The Howgate Restaurant

Howgate EH26 8PY ☎ 01968 670000 01968 670000
e-mail: peter@howgate.com
dir: *10m N of Peebles. 3m E of Penicuik on A6094 between Leadburn junct & Howgate village*

Once a racehorse stables and a dairy, this long, low building makes a warm and welcoming bar and restaurant. There is an impressive wine list from all the corners of the world, a regularly changing menu, and a 'dishes of the moment' selection. Options might include fresh steamed mussels in tomato and coriander sauce; and braised lamb shank with chive mash and honey roasted root vegetables. Alternatively try a vegetarian risotto.

Open 12-2 6-11 Closed: 25-26 Dec, 1 Jan **Bar Meals** L served all week 12-2 D served all week 6-9.30 Av main course £9.95 **Restaurant** L served all week 12-2 D served all week 6-9.30 Av 3 course à la carte £22 Free House Belhaven Best, Hoegaarden & Wheat Biere. 12 **Facilities** Children's licence Garden Parking

MORAY

FOCHABERS MAP 23 NJ35

Gordon Arms Hotel

80 High St IV32 7DH ☎ 01343 820508 01343 820300
e-mail: info@gordonarms.co.uk
dir: *A96 approx halfway between Aberdeen & Inverness, 9m from Elgin*

This 200-year-old former coaching inn, close to the River Spey and within easy reach of Speyside's whisky distilleries, is understandably popular with salmon fishers, golfers and walkers. Its public rooms have been carefully refurbished, and the hotel makes an ideal base from which to explore this scenic corner of Scotland. The cuisine makes full use of local produce: venison, lamb and game from the uplands, fish and seafood from the Moray coast, beef from Aberdeenshire and salmon from the Spey – barely a stone's throw from the kitchen!

Open 11-3 5-11 (Sun 12-3, 6-10.30) **Bar Meals** L served all week 12-2 D served all week 5-6.45 **Restaurant** L served all week 12-2 D served all week 7-9 Free House Caledonian Deuchars IPA, John Smiths Smooth, Marstons Pedigree. **Facilities** Children's licence Dogs allowed Parking

NORTH LANARKSHIRE

CUMBERNAULD MAP 21 NS77

Castlecary House Hotel ★★★ HL

Castlecary Rd G68 0HD ☎ 01324 840233 01324 841608
e-mail: enquiries@castlecaryhotel.com
web: www.castlecaryhotel.com
dir: *Off A80 onto B816 between Glasgow & Stirling . 7m from Falkirk, 9m from Stirling*

Run by the same family for over 30 years, this friendly hotel is located close to the historic Antonine Wall and Forth and Clyde Canal. Meals in the lounge bars plough a traditional furrow with options such as home-made lasagna; oven-roasted Scottish salmon fillet with a cherry tomato and spring onion hollandaise; and a range flame-grilled burgers. More formal restaurant fare is available in Camerons Restaurant.

Open 11-11.30 (limited times during festive period) **Bar Meals** L served all week 12-9 D served all week 12-9 **Restaurant** D served Mon-Sat 6-9.45 (Sun high tea 12.30-6.45) Av 3 course à la carte £20 Free House Arran Blonde, Harviestoun Brooker's Bitter & Twisted, Inveralmond Ossian's Ale, Housten Peter's Well. 8 **Facilities** Children's licence Garden Dogs allowed Parking **Rooms** 55

PERTH & KINROSS

GLENDEVON MAP 21 NN90

Pick of the Pubs

The Tormaukin Country Inn and Restaurant ★★★★ INN

FK14 7JY ☎ 01259 781252 01259 781526
e-mail: info@anlochon.co.uk
dir: *N from Edinburgh, exit M90 junct 6 onto A977 to Kincardine, follow signs to Stirling. Exit at Yelts of Muckhard onto A823/Crieff*

The name Tormaukin is Gaelic for 'hill of the mountain hare', which reflects this inn's serene, romantic location in the midst of the Ochil Hills. The attractive whitewashed building was built in 1720 as a drovers' inn, at a time when Glendevon was frequented by cattlemen making their way from the Tryst of Crieff to the market place at Falkirk. It has been sympathetically refurbished throughout, but still bristles with real Scottish character and charm. Original features like stone walls, exposed beams and blazing winter fires in the cosy public rooms ensure a warm and

CONTINUED

Scotland

GLENDEVON continued

welcoming atmosphere. Typical lunch choices are smoked haddock chowder; and braised Highland beef with root vegetables. An evening meal could include gravadlax and a potato scone, then wild boar with celeriac mash, black pudding and Calvados compote. Live music is a regular feature at the inn, and golfing breaks are available.

Open 12–11 **Bar Meals** L served Mon-Fri 12–3 D served Mon-Fri 5.30–9 (Sat-Sun all day) **Restaurant** L served Mon-Fri 12–3 D served Mon-Fri 5.30–9 (Sat-Sun all day) ⊕ Free House ◀ Bitter & Twisted. ♀ 8 **Facilities** Garden Dogs allowed Parking **Rooms** 12

GLENFARG   MAP 21 NO11

The Famous Bein Inn

PH2 9PY ☎ 01577 830216 🖹 01577 830211
e-mail: enquiries@beininn.com
web: www.beininn.com
dir: Telephone for details

Many famous musicians have performed in this inn's lively Bistro Bar, and the memorabilia collection in the Basement Bar rivals anything to be seen in a Hard Rock Café. It has been welcoming guests since 1861, with its warm atmosphere enhanced by a log fire and wood burning stove. A typical dinner choice could be traditional prawn cocktail followed by a T-bone steak from the grill with all the trimmings, finishing with sticky toffee pudding.

Open 11–2.30 5–11 (Sat-Sun all day) **Bar Meals** L served all week 12–2 D served all week 5–9 **Restaurant** L served Sat-Sun 12–2 D served all week 5–9 (Sat-Sun all day) ⊕ Free House ◀ Independence, Ossian, Guinness, Boddingtons & Tennents. **Facilities** Children's licence Dogs allowed Parking

GUILDTOWN   MAP 21 NO13

Anglers Inn NEW ♀

Main Rd PH2 6BS ☎ 01821 640329
e-mail: enquiries@theanglersinn.co.uk
dir: 6m N of Perth on A93

Shona and Jeremy Wares bought the Anglers in 2007 and gave it a complete refurbishment before reopening it as a contemporary gastro-pub. Comfortable leather chairs and a log fire maintain a homely atmosphere, ideal for enjoying the Inveralmond Brewery ales dispensed at the bar. Jeremy's award-winning pedigree as a chef ensures that a meal here will not disappoint: expect the likes of venison fillet carpaccio, cuts of Angus beef, and sticky toffee pudding with butterscotch sauce.

Open 10-11 (Fri-Sat 10-12.30) Closed: 1–15 Jan **Bar Meals** L served Mon-Sat 12–2 **Restaurant** L served all week 12–2 D served Mon-Sat 6–9 (Sun 6–8) Av 3 course à la carte £20 Av 2 course fixed price £14.95 ⊕ Free House ♀ 13 **Facilities** Children's licence Garden Dogs allowed Parking

KILLIECRANKIE   MAP 23 NN96

Pick of the Pubs

Killiecrankie House Hotel ◉◉ ♀

PH16 5LG ☎ 01796 473220 🖹 01796 472451
e-mail: enquiries@killiecrankiehotel.co.uk
dir: Take B8079 N from Pitlochry. Hotel in 3m after NT Visitor Centre

Built in 1840 as a dower house, and established as a hotel in 1940, Killiecrankie House is set in four sprawling acres of wooded grounds at the northern end of the historic Killiecrankie Pass. It stands near the site of the Battle of Killiecrankie and overlooks the intriguingly named Soldier's Leap. It holds such a special place in Scottish history that it has a National Trust Visitor Centre dedicated to its history and current wildlife. The menu offers the best local produce, including seasonal vegetables, fruits and herbs from the garden. The conservatory makes an ideal spot for informal eating, while dinner is served in the elegant dining room. Options range from open sandwiches at lunchtime – coronation chicken; smoked salmon and prawn – and bar meals such as deep-fried haddock with chips, or game pie. Pan-fried fillet of Highland venison with Madeira and apricot sauce is typical of the restaurant menu.

Open 12–2.30 6–11 Closed: Jan & Feb **Bar Meals** L served all week 12.30–2 D served all week 6.30–9 Av main course £10.50 **Restaurant** D served all week 6.15–8.30 Av 4 course fixed price £38 ⊕ Free House ◀ Tennents Velvet Ale, Red McGregor, Deuchars IPA, Brooker's Bitter & Twisted. ♀ 8 **Facilities** Children's licence Garden Dogs allowed Parking

Moulin Hotel

French-speakers might instinctively pronounce Moulin as they do in France. After all, it looks like their word for mill, but Moulin is actually derived from the Gaelic 'maohlinn', meaning either smooth rocks or calm water – a tad confusing, but presumably the locals know.

This old inn faces Moulin's square, a rewarding three-quarters of a mile from the busy tourist centre of Pitlochry. Awarded the accolade of AA Scottish Pub of the Year 2006, its popularity is partly due to the fact that it opened its own microbrewery in 1995 to celebrate the building's tercentenary. Since the area is known as the Vale of Atholl, don't be too surprised to find that the name of one of the house beers is the same. A major refurbishment of the building in the 1990s opened up old fireplaces and beautiful stone walls that had been hidden for many years, and lots of cosy niches were created using timbers from the old Coach House (now the brewery). The courtyard garden is lovely in summer, while blazing log fires warm the Moulin's innards

in winter. Menus partly reflect the inn's Highlands location, and although more familiar dishes are available such as seafood pancake, lamb shank, and trio of salmon, you also have the opportunity to try something more ethnic, such as deep-fried haggis; venison Braveheart; Scotsman's bunnet, which is a meat and vegetable stew-filled batter pudding; or a plate of sauté potatoes, smoked bacon and fried egg, otherwise known as vrackie grostel. You might then round off your meal with ice cream with Highland toffee sauce, or bread and butter pudding. A specials board broadens the choice further. Around 20 wines by the glass and more than 30 malt whiskies are available.

★★★ SHL ♥
MAP 23 NN95
11–13 Kirkmichael
Rd, Moulin PH16 5EH
☎ 01796 472196 🖹 01796 474098
e-mail:
enquiries@moulinhotel.co.uk
dir: *From A924 at Pitlochry take A923. Moulin 0.75m*

Open 12–11 (Fri-Sat 12–11.45)
Bar Meals L served all week 12–9.30 D served all week 12
Restaurant D served all week 6–9
⊕ Free House ◀ Moulin Braveheart, Old Remedial, Ale of Atholl & Moulin Light. ♥ 20
Facilities Garden Parking
Rooms 15

KINNESSWOOD   MAP 21 NO10

Pick of the Pubs

Lomond Country Inn ⚑

KY13 9HN ☎ 01592 840253 📠 01592 840693

e-mail: info@lomondcountryinn.co.uk

dir: *M90 junct 5, follow signs for Glenrothes then Scotlandwell, Kinnesswood next village*

A small, privately owned hotel on the slopes of the Lomond Hills that has been entertaining guests for more than 100 years. It is the only hostelry in the area with uninterrupted views over Loch Leven to the island on which Mary Queen of Scots was imprisoned. The cosy public areas offer log fires, a friendly atmosphere, real ales and a fine collection of single malts. If you want to make the most of the loch views, choose the charming restaurant, a relaxing room freshly decorated in country house style. Specials may include supreme of guinea fowl on creamed mash with Calvados sauce, roast sirloin of beef, or strips of chicken with a leek and stilton sauce, plus a selection of grills.

Open 11–11 (Fri-Sat 11–12.45, Sun 12.30–11) Closed: 25 Dec **Bar Meals** L served all week 12.30–2 D served all week 6–9 Av main course £7 **Restaurant** L served all week 12–2.30 D served all week 6–9.30 (Sun all day) Av 3 course à la carte £25 ⊕ Free House ◖ Deuchers IPA, Calders Cream, Tetleys, Orkney Dark Island. ⚑ 6 **Facilities** Garden Dogs allowed Parking Play Area

PITLOCHRY   MAP 23 NN95

Pick of the Pubs

Moulin Hotel ★★★ SHL ⚑

See Pick of the Pubs on page 719

RENFREWSHIRE

HOUSTON   MAP 20 NS46

Fox & Hounds ⚑

South St PA6 7EN

☎ 01505 612448 & 612991 📠 01505 614133

e-mail: jonathan@foxandhoundshouston.co.uk

dir: *A737, W from Glasgow. Take Johnstone Bridge off Weir exit, follow signs for Houston. Pub in village centre*

Beer lovers flock to this 18th-century village inn, home to the award-winning Houston Brewing Company. Alongside an impressive list of international bottled beers are two equally appealing bar and restaurant menus. Try smoked trout, rocket and potato salad in the bar; followed by Irish stew with creamy mash. Alternately, in the restaurant sample crayfish and tomato bisque, and a main course of chicken breast stuffed with tomato and basil.

Fox & Hounds

Open 11–12 (Fri-Sat 11–1am, Sun 12.30–12) **Bar Meals** L served all week 12–10 D served all week 12–10 Av main course £9 **Restaurant** L served all week 12–10 D served all week 12–10 Av 3 course à la carte £22 ⊕ Free House ◖ St Peters Well, Killelan, Warlock Stout, Texas & Jock Frost. ⚑ 10 **Facilities** Children's licence Garden Dogs allowed Parking

SCOTTISH BORDERS

ALLANTON   MAP 21 NT85

Allanton Inn

TD11 3JZ ☎ 01890 818260

e-mail: info@allantoninn.co.uk

dir: *From A1 at Berwick take A6105 for Chirnside (5m). At Chirnside Inn take Coldstream Rd for 1m to Allanton*

Highly acclaimed for its food, this award-winning establishment is housed in an 18th-century coaching inn. Outside is a large lawned area with fruit trees overlooking open countryside. Inside are two restaurants and a cosy bar serving real ales and a range of malt whiskies. Daily changing menus may offer braised beef and Guinness casserole with a puff pastry crust at lunch, and monkfish tail sautéed onto a risotto of asparagus, mussels and rocket for dinner.

Open 12–2 6–10.30 Closed: Mon **Bar Meals** L served Wed-Sun 12–1 D served all week 6–8.30 **Restaurant** L served Fri-Sun 12–1 D served all week 6–8.30 ⊕ Free House ◖ Ossian, Bitter and Twisted, Tradewinds. **Facilities** Children's licence Garden Dogs allowed Parking

ETTRICK   MAP 21 NT21

Tushielaw Inn

TD7 5HT ☎ 01750 62205 📠 01750 62205

e-mail: robin@tushielaw-inn.co.uk

dir: *At junction of B709 & B711(W of Hawick)*

An 18th-century former toll house and drover's halt on the banks of Ettrick water, making a good base for trout fishing and those tackling the Southern Upland Way. An extensive menu is always available with daily changing specials. Fresh produce is used according to season, with local lamb and Aberdeen Angus beef regular specialities, and gluten-free and vegetarian meals. Home-made steak and stout pie and sticky toffee pudding rate among other dishes.

Open 12–2.30 6.30–11 **Bar Meals** L served all week 12–2 D served all week 7–9 **Restaurant** L served all week 12–2 D served all week 7–9 ⊕ Free House **Facilities** Children's licence Dogs allowed Parking

Scotland

GALASHIELS MAP 21 NT43

Kingsknowes Hotel ★★★ SHL

1 Selkirk Rd TD1 3HY ☎ 01896 758375 🖹 01896 750377
e-mail: enquiries@kingsknowes.co.uk
dir: *Off A7 at Galashiels/Selkirk rdbt*

In over three acres of grounds on the banks of the Tweed, a splendid baronial mansion built in 1869 for a textile magnate. There are lovely views of the Eildon Hills and Abbotsford House, Sir Walter Scott's ancestral home. Meals are served in two restaurants and the Courtyard Bar, where fresh local or regional produce is used as much as possible. The impressive glass conservatory is the ideal place to enjoy a drink.

Open 12–12 **Bar Meals** L served all week 11.45–2 D served all week 5.45–9.30 Av main course £8.50 **Restaurant** L served all week 11.45–2 D served all week 5.45–9.30 ⊕ Free House ◀ McEwans 80/-, John Smith's. **Facilities** Garden Dogs allowed Parking Play Area **Rooms** 12

INNERLEITHEN MAP 21 NT33

Corner House

1 Chapel St EH44 6HN ☎ 01896 831181 🖹 01896 831182
e-mail: cornerhouse@hotmail.com
dir: *From Galashiels take A72 W. Innerleithen in 12m*

This family-run hotel occupies a characterful street-corner building in the heart of Innerleithen and is a great place to relax after a day spent walking or biking at Glentress or Innerleithen. With well-equipped rooms and a generous menu in the restaurant, it may tempt you to stay longer than you first intended.

Open 11–12 **Bar Meals** L served all week 12–8.45 D served all week 12–8.45 Av main course £6 **Restaurant** L served all week 12–8.45 D served all week 12–8.45 ⊕ Belhaven ◀ Belhaven Best, Guinness. **Facilities** Children's licence Garden Dogs allowed Parking

---

LAUDER MAP 21 NT54

Pick of the Pubs

The Black Bull ★★★★ INN 💡

See Pick of the Pubs on page 722

LEITHOLM MAP 21 NT74

The Plough Hotel 💡

Main St TD12 4JN ☎ 01890 840252 🖹 01890 840252
e-mail: theplough@leitholm.wanadoo.co.uk
dir: *5m N of Coldstream on A697. Take B6461, Leitholm in 1m*

The only pub remaining in this small border village (there were originally two), the Plough dates from the 17th century and was once a coaching inn. A programme of major refurbishment and expansion is highlighting the building's historic features. Locally bred Aberdeen Angus beef is a speciality of the menu, along with fresh fish from Eyemouth. Frequent barbecues in the summer make the most of the long south facing beer garden, complete with decking.

The Plough Hotel

Open 12–12 (Fri-Sat 12–1am) **Bar Meals** L served Tue-Sun 12–2 D served Tue-Sun 6–9 Av main course £7.95 **Restaurant** L served Tue-Sun 12–2 D served Tue-Sun 6–9 ⊕ Free House ◀ Tennents, Guinness, & real ale. 💡 8 **Facilities** Children's licence Garden Parking

---

MELROSE MAP 21 NT53

Pick of the Pubs

Burts Hotel ★★★ HL ◉◉ 💡

Market Square TD6 9PL
☎ 01896 822285 🖹 01896 822870
e-mail: enquiries@burtshotel.co.uk
web: www.burtshotel.co.uk
dir: *A6091, 2m from A68 3m S of Earlston*

Built in 1722 as a townhouse for a local dignitary, this civilised hotel overlooks the picturesque market square in the historic town of Melrose. For some time it was a temperance hotel, but with today's selection of several real ales, 80 single malt whiskies and a good range of wines by the glass, there's no danger of running dry. Graham and Anne Henderson have been running the award-winning business for over 35 years, more recently supported by their son Nicholas and wife Trish. Their personal attention ensures the highest standards of comfort, service and cuisine. The food offers a true taste of the Borders, with a starter of Teviot Smokery smoked salmon, and a main course of braised shank of Border lamb, with garlic mash and red onion jus. The menu also includes a grills section – steaks and chops – with a choice of classic sauces.

Open 11–2.30 5–11 **Bar Meals** L served all week 12–2 D served all week 6–9.30 Av main course £11 **Restaurant** L served all week 12–2 D served all week 7–9 Av 3 course fixed price £33 ⊕ Free House ◀ Caledonian 80/-, Deuchars IPA, Timothy Taylor Landlord, Fuller's London Pride. 💡 8 **Facilities** Children's licence Garden Dogs allowed Parking **Rooms** 20

PICK OF THE PUBS

LAUDER-SCOTTISH BORDERS

The Black Bull

Dazzlingly white in the sun, a three-storey coaching inn dating from 1750. The large dining room was once a chapel, and the church spire remains in the roof!

Proprietor Maureen Rennie bought the hotel in a decrepit state but has transformed it into a cosy, characterful hotel with lots of interesting pictures and artefacts. She has gone on to win a host of prestigious awards, including AA Pub of the Year for Scotland a few years ago. Maureen uses only the best quality local beef, lamb, fish and seasonal game, all, of course, prepared to order. Lunch could begin with that hearty fish and potato soup, cullen skink; a platter of Belhaven smoked salmon with lemon and granary bread; or Italian-style meatballs with tomato sauce, spaghetti and fresh parmesan. Scottish fare is prominent among the mains too, with Wedderlie (a farm) Aberdeen Angus beef, Guinness and mushroom pie; grilled Stichill

(a nearby village) cream cheese croutons with mixed leaves and balsamic vinaigrette; and wholetail Scottish scampi. Bar suppers echo lunch, although again don't expect everything to be Scottish. Perhaps terrine of pheasant, duck and pistachios with tomato chutney to start; grilled fillet of salmon with sun-blushed tomato and olive crust; or lamb and spinach curry with cucumber raita, poppadom and steamed basmati rice. A selection of specials might include breast of duck with puy lentils and teriyaki vegetables; or corn-fed chicken breast with herbed mascarpone, pea and pancetta risotto. For hotel guests who have had a successful day on the Leader Water, a tributary of the Tweed, the kitchen will happily prepare your catch for dinner.

★★★★ INN ♀
MAP 21 NT54
Market Place TD2 6SR
☎ 01578 722208
🖷 01578 722419
e-mail:
enquiries@blackbull-lauder.com
dir: *In centre of Lauder on A68*

Open 12–2.30 5–9 (Winter 12–2, 5.30–9) Closed: Feb
Bar Meals L served all week 12–2.30 D served all week 5–9 Av main course £8.50
Restaurant L served all week 12–2.30 D served all week 5–9 Av 3 course à la carte £22
⊕ Free House ◼ Broughton Ales, Guinness, Worthington & Caffreys. ♀ 16
Facilities Children's licence Dogs allowed Parking
Rooms 8

ST BOSWELLS   MAP 21 NT53

Buccleuch Arms Hotel ★★★ SHL ♟

The Green TD6 0EW ☎ 01835 822243 🖹 01835 823965
e-mail: info@buccleucharms.com

dir: *On A68, 10m N of Jedburgh. Hotel on village green*

'Relax, unwind, enjoy' is the exhortation of this smart and friendly country house hotel. Built in the 16th century, it boasts a spacious garden and children's play area. Local produce is used unstintingly in lunches of steak and ale pie, club sandwiches or home-made beef lasagne, and dinner dishes of coconut sweet potato curry; chargrilled lamb cutlets, or grilled fillet of sea bream from the extensive menus. The nineteen en suite bedrooms are well appointed and luxurious.

Open 7.30am–11 Closed: 25 Dec **Bar Meals** L served Mon-Sat 12–9 D served Mon-Sat 6–9 (Sun 12–8.30) **Restaurant** D served Mon-Sat 6–9 (Sun 12–8.30) ⊕ Free House ◀ John Smiths, Guinness, Broughton, guest ales. ♟ 8 **Facilities** Children's licence Garden Dogs allowed Parking Play Area **Rooms** 19

SWINTON   MAP 21 NT84

Pick of the Pubs

The Wheatsheaf at Swinton

★★★★ RR ◉◉ ♟

Main St TD11 3JJ ☎ 01890 860257 🖹 01890 860688
e-mail: reception@wheatsheaf-swinton.co.uk

dir: *From Edinburgh A697 onto B6461. From East Lothian A1 onto B6461*

In the past few years, the award-winning Wheatsheaf has built up an impressive reputation as a dining destination. Run by husband and wife team Chris and Jan Winson, this popular venue is tucked away in the picturesque village of Swinton. The Wheatsheaf's secret is to use carefully sourced local ingredients, used in imaginative combinations, and there are various menus to choose from including gluten-free and vegetarian. The lunch menu offers the likes of roast pigeon breast on black pudding and Cumberland sauce; and casseroled shin of beef with herb and potato mash. The dinner menu offers a similar choice of starters, perhaps including smoked haddock, salmon and dill fishcakes, and moves on to walnut crusted halibut with asparagus and lemon; and braised lamb shank on a spring onion potato mash. Vegetarians will find wild mushroom and spinach risotto, and desserts maintain the high standards: perhaps glazed lemon tart with passion fruit sorbet.

Open 11–3 6–11 Closed: 25–27 & 31 Dec-1 Jan **Bar Meals** L served all week 12–2 D served Mon-Sat 6–9 (Sun 6–8.30) Av main course £15 **Restaurant** L served all week 12–2 D served Mon-Sat 6–9 (Sun 6–8.30) Av 3 course à la carte £29 ⊕ Free House ◀ Deuchars IPA, Broughton Greenmantle Ale, Belhaven Best. ♟ 12 **Facilities** Children's licence Parking **Rooms** 10

TIBBIE SHIELS INN   MAP 21 NT22

Pick of the Pubs

Tibbie Shiels Inn

St Mary's Loch TD7 5LH
☎ 01750 42231 🖹 01750 42302

dir: *From Moffat take A708. Inn 14m on right*

On the isthmus between St Mary's Loch and the Loch of the Lowes, this waterside Inn is named after the woman who first opened it in 1826 and expanded the inn from a small cottage to a hostelry capable of sleeping around 35 people, many of them on the floor! Famous visitors during her time included Walter Scott, Thomas Carlyle and Robert L. Stevenson. Tibbie Shiels herself is rumoured to keep watch over the bar, where the selection of over 50 malt whiskeys will sustain you for ghost watching! Meals can be enjoyed either in the bar or the non-smoking dining room; the inn also offers packed lunches for your walking, windsurfing or fishing expedition (residents fish free of charge). The menu offers a wide range of vegetarian options as well as local fish and game: highlights include Yarrow trout and Tibbie's mixed grill.

Open 11–11 (Sun 12.30–11) **Bar Meals** L served all week 12.30–8 D served all week 12.30–8 Av main course £6.50 **Restaurant** L served all week 12.30–8 D served all week 12.30–8 Av 3 course à la carte £11.25 ⊕ Free House ◀ Broughton Greenmantle Ale, Belhaven 80/-. **Facilities** Children's licence Garden Parking

---

WEST LINTON   MAP 21 NT15

The Gordon Arms

Dolphinton Rd EH46 7DR
☎ 01968 660208 🖹 01968 661852
e-mail: info@thegordon.co.uk

Set in the pretty village of West Linton but within easy reach of the M74, this 17th-century inn has a real log fire in the cosy lounge bar, and a lovely sun-trap beer garden. The pub's aim is to support the Scottish microbrewery industry as much as possible, so expect a changing selection of excellent ales. A meal might include Jamaican jerked chicken, followed by grilled sea bass with an orange sauce.

Open 10–12 (Winter 10–11, Fri-Sat 10–1am) **Bar Meals** L served all week 12–3 D served all week 6–9 (Sat-Sun 12–9) **Restaurant** L served all week 12–3 D served all week 6–9 (Sat-Sun 12–9) Av 3 course fixed price £25 ⊕ Scottish & Newcastle ◀ Tennents, John Smiths, Guinness, real ales. **Facilities** Children's licence Garden Dogs allowed Parking

Scotland

SOUTH AYRSHIRE

SYMINGTON — MAP 20 NS33

Wheatsheaf Inn

Main St KA1 5QB ☎ 01563 830307 📠 01563 830307

dir: *Telephone for directions*

This 17th-century inn lies in a lovely village setting close to the Royal Troon Golf Course, and there has been a hostelry here since the 1500s. Log fires burn in every room and the work of local artists adorns the walls. Seafood dominates the menu – maybe pan-fried scallops in lemon and chives – and alternatives include honey roasted lamb shank; haggis, tatties and neeps in Drambuie and onion cream, and the renowned steak pie.

Open 11–11 (Fri-Sat 11–12) Closed: 25 Dec, 1 Jan **Bar Meals** L served all week 12–4 D served all week 4–9 Av main course £8 **Restaurant** L served all week 12–4 D served all week 4–9 Av 3 course à la carte £15 ⊕ Belhaven ◀ Belhaven Best, St Andrews Ale & Tennents. **Facilities** Garden Parking

STIRLING

ARDEONAIG — MAP 20 NN63

The Ardeonaig Hotel ♀

South Lock Tay Side FK21 8SU

☎ 01567 820400 📠 01567 820282

e-mail: info@ardeonaighotel.co.uk

dir: *On South Rd Loch Tay, 6m from Killin, 8m from Kenmore*

A romantic rural retreat on the south shore of Loch Tay with views of the Ben Lawers mountains, this hotel has undergone total refurbishment and development to provide a new kitchen, five thatched garden lodges, a fine dining wine cellar, a new dining room and the landscaping of 13 acres of grounds. The Ardeonaig has a solid reputation for food ranging from oat-crusted East Coast herring with salad leaves, to braised shoulder of Ardeonaig lamb.

Open 12–11 (Fri-Sat 12–12) **Bar Meals** L served all week 11–10 D served all week 11–10 **Restaurant** L served all week 12–3 D served all week 6.30–10 Av 3 course à la carte £30.35 Av 3 course fixed price £26.50 ⊕ Free House ◀ Arran Blonde, Tusker, Castle Larger, Windhoek Larger. ♀ 8 **Facilities** Garden Dogs allowed Parking **Rooms** available

CALLANDER — MAP 20 NN60

The Lade Inn ♀

Kilmahog FK17 8HD ☎ 01877 330152

e-mail: info@theladeinn.com

dir: *From Stirling take A84 to Callander. Left at Kilmahog Woollen Mills onto A821 towards Aberfoyle. Pub immediately on left.*

Built in 1935 as a tearoom serving the Trossachs National Park area, the Lade Inn was licensed in the 1960s, taking its name from the river that feeds the local woollen mills. It's a family-friendly traditional pub/restaurant, committed to providing value for money while supporting regional food producers and caring for the environment. The real ales certainly don't travel far – the Trossachs Craft Brewery is on site; its shop offers over 100 bottled Scottish varieties.

Open 12–11 (Sat 12–1am, Sun 12.30–10.30) **Bar Meals** L served Mon-Sat 12–9 D served Mon-Sat 12–9 (Sun 12.30–9) Av main course £9 **Restaurant** L served Mon-Sat 12–9 D served Mon-Sat 12–9 (Sun 12.30–9) Av 3 course à la carte £17 ⊕ Free House ◀ Waylade, LadeBack, LadeOut. ♀ 9 **Facilities** Children's licence Garden Dogs allowed Parking Play Area

DRYMEN — MAP 20 NS48

The Clachan Inn

2 Main St G63 0BG ☎ 01360 660824

dir: *Telephone for directions*

Quaint, white-painted cottage, believed to be the oldest licensed pub in Scotland, situated in a small village on the West Highland Way, and once owned by Rob Roy's sister. Locate the appealing lounge bar for freshly-made food, the varied menu listing filled baked potatoes, salads, fresh haddock in crispy breadcrumbs, spicy Malaysian lamb casserole, vegetable lasagne, a variety of steaks, and good daily specials.

Open 11–12 (Sun 12.30–12) Closed: 25 Dec & 1 Jan **Bar Meals** L served all week 12–4 D served all week 6–10 (Sun 12.30–4, 5–10) **Restaurant** L served all week 12–4 D served all week 6–10 (Sun 12.30–4, 5–10) ⊕ Free House ◀ Caledonian Deuchars IPA, Belhaven Best, Tennents Lager & Guinness. **Facilities** Dogs allowed Parking **Rooms** available

KIPPEN — MAP 20 NS69

Cross Keys Hotel

Main St FK8 3DN ☎ 01786 870293

e-mail: info@kippencrosskeys.co.uk

dir: *10m W of Stirling, 20m from Loch Lomond off A811*

Freshly refurbished by new owners Debby and Brian, this cosy inn now serves food and drink all day. Nearby Burnside Wood is managed by a local community woodland group, and is perfect for walking and nature trails. The pub's interior, warmed by three log fires, is equally perfect for resting your feet afterwards. Regular events include a weekly Tuesday folk night.

Open 12–11 (Fri-Sat 12–1am) Closed: 25 Dec, 1–2 Jan & Mon **Bar Meals** L served Tue-Sun 12–11 D served Tue-Sun 12–11 Av main course £9 **Restaurant** L served all week 12–11 D served all week 12–11 ⊕ Free House ◀ Belhaven Best, Harviestoun Bitter, Twisted & Guinness. **Facilities** Children's licence Garden Dogs allowed Parking

Pick of the Pubs

The Inn at Kippen 🍷

Fore Rd FK8 3DT ☎ 01786 871010 🖹 01786 871011

e-mail: info@theinnatkippen.co.uk

dir: From Stirling take A811 to Loch Lomond. Take 1st left at Kippen station rdbt, then 1st right onto Fore Road. Inn on left

Previously the Crown, the Inn at Kippen was taken over in 2003 by James Fletcher who set about creating a chic yet cosy gastro-pub. The pretty little beer garden comes into its own during the summer when it hosts small festivals celebrating beer, wine or whisky, while a cider fair and hog roast takes place in August or September. The stylish interior is a relaxing place for a drink and a taste of home-cooked bar food, and a fine dining restaurant serves fresh local produce in a comfortable and informal atmosphere. The beef and lamb come from Kippen itself, and the best of Scotland's ingredients appear in starters such as warm partridge, orange and crispy pancetta salad; or little venison bridies with home-made ketchup. International influences can be found in dishes such as lamb and spinach curry; and cannelloni with butternut squash and goat's cheese.

Open 11–1am (Mon-Thu 11–11) Closed: 25 Dec & 1–2 Jan **Bar Meals** L served all week 12–2.30 D served all week 6–9 (Nov-Feb Sun 5–7) **Restaurant** L served all week 12–2.30 D served all week 6–9 (Nov-Feb Sun 5–7.30) ⊕ Free House ◀ Thrappledouser, Ossian, Baltika & John Smiths. 🍷7 **Facilities** Children's licence Garden Dogs allowed Parking

WEST LOTHIAN

LINLITHGOW   **MAP 21 NS97**

Pick of the Pubs

Champany Inn – The Chop and Ale House ◉◉

Champany EH49 7LU

☎ 01506 834532 🖹 01506 834302

e-mail: reception@champany.com

dir: 2m N.E of Linlithgow on corner of A904 & A803

A collection of buildings dating from the 17th century houses the Chop and Ale House and its superior sister, the main restaurant. The whole place is full of traditional charm and atmosphere, not to mention wine bottles, with one of the two extensive cellars visible from the bar. If you want to sample the best Scottish beef, this place, described as the Rolls Royce of steak restaurants, is

not to be missed. Starters take in peppered mackerel with sweet horseradish, or dressed salmon fillets, while mains offer several choices of Aberdeen Angus steaks, and an extensive range of Champany burgers made from the same meat as the steaks and cooked medium rare. Alternatives are home-made sausages (including a vegetarian option), speciality fish and chips, and chargrilled chicken. A popular dessert is hot home-made waffles with maple syrup and whipped cream.

Open 12–2 6.30–10 (Fri-Sun all day) Closed: 25–26 Dec, 1 Jan **Bar Meals** L served Mon-Thu 12–2 D served Mon-Thu 6.30–10 (Fri-Sun all day) Av main course £16.95 **Restaurant** L served Mon-Fri 12.30–2 D served Mon-Sat 7–10 ⊕ Free House ◀ Belhaven. **Facilities** Garden Parking

SCOTTISH ISLANDS

COLL, ISLE OF

ARINAGOUR   **MAP 22 NM25**

Pick of the Pubs

Coll Hotel

PA78 6SZ ☎ 01879 230334 🖹 01879 230317

e-mail: info@collhotel.com

dir: Ferry from Oban. Located at head of Arinagour Bay, 1m from Pier (collections by arrangement)

The Coll Hotel is the only inn on the Isle of Coll, and commands stunning views over the sea to Jura and Mull. The island only has 170 inhabitants, so is perfect for a holiday away from it all. The hotel is a popular rendezvous for locals, and food is served in the Gannet Restaurant, bar or garden. Fresh produce is landed and delivered from around the island every day and features on the specials board. Try local seafood open sandwiches; or Coll crab and local prawn spaghetti with chilli and parmesan at lunch, and for dinner perhaps Argyll venison casserole with port, juniper and clove gravy; or roasted locally caught monkfish tail with crispy Parma ham, tomato and basil sauce, and rice. The hotel has a private helipad in the garden, and guests are welcome to land and enjoy a meal or an overnight stay.

Open 11–12 (Winter 11–2, 5–10) **Bar Meals** L served all week 12–2 D served all week 6–9.30 (Winter 6–8.30) Av main course £10 **Restaurant** L served all week 12–2 D served all week 6–9.30 (Winter 6–8.30) Av 3 course à la carte £18 ⊕ Free House ◀ Loch Fyne Ale, Pipers Gold, Guinness, Staropramen. **Facilities** Garden Parking Play Area **Rooms** available

Scotland

SKYE, ISLE OF

ARDVASAR   MAP 22 NG60

Ardvasar Hotel ★★ HL ♀

IV45 8RS ☎ 01471 844223 📄 01471 844495
e-mail: richard@ardvasar-hotel.demon.co.uk
web: www.ardvasarhotel.com
dir: *From ferry terminal, 50yds & turn left*

An early 1800s white-painted cottage-style inn, the second oldest on Skye, renowned for its genuinely friendly hospitality and informal service. Sea views over the Sound of Sleat reach the Knoydart Mountains beyond. Malt whiskies are plentiful, but beer drinkers will not be disappointed. Food is served in the informal lounge bar throughout the day and evening, with a sumptuous four-course dinner in the dining room during high season. Local produce figures prominently, particularly freshly-landed seafood, venison, and Aberdeen Angus beef.

Open 12–12 **Bar Meals** L served all week 12–2.30 D served all week 5.30–9 Av main course £11.50 **Restaurant** D served all week 7–9 Av 3 course à la carte £23 ⊕ Free House ◀ 80/-, Deuchars, IPA, Isle of Skye Red Cuillin. ♀ 6 **Facilities** Children's licence Garden Dogs allowed Parking **Rooms** 10

CARBOST   MAP 22 NG33

The Old Inn

IV47 8SR ☎ 01478 640205 📄 01478 640325
e-mail: reservations@oldinn.f9.co.uk

Two-hundred-year-old free house on the edge of Loch Harport with wonderful views of the Cuillin Hills from the waterside patio. Not surprisingly, the inn is popular with walkers and climbers (inn and bunkhouse accommodation is available). Open fires welcome winter visitors, and live music is a regular feature. The menu includes daily home-cooked specials, with numerous fresh fish dishes, including local prawns and oysters and mackerel from the loch.

Open 11–1am **Bar Meals** L served all week 12–3 D served all week 6–9 **Restaurant** L served all week 12–3 D served all week 6–9 ⊕ Free House ◀ Red Cuillin, Black Cuillin, Hebridean ale & Cuillin Skye Ale. **Facilities** Children's licence Garden Dogs allowed Parking

ISLE ORNSAY   MAP 22 NG71

Pick of the Pubs

Hotel Eilean Iarmain ★★ SHL ◉◉

IV43 8QR ☎ 01471 833332 📄 01471 833275
e-mail: hotel@eileaniarmain.co.uk
dir: *A851, A852 right to Isle Ornsay harbour front*

An award-winning Hebridean hotel with its own pier, overlooking the Isle of Ornsay harbour and Sleat Sound. The old-fashioned character of the hotel remains intact, and décor is mainly cotton and linen chintzes with traditional furniture. More a small private hotel than a pub, the bar and restaurant ensure that the standards of food and drinks served here – personally chosen by the owner Sir Iain Noble – are exacting. The head chef declares: "We never accept second best, it shines through in the standard of food served in our restaurant." Here you can try dishes like Eilean Iarmain estate venison casserole, pan-seared sirloin steak, or grilled fillet of cod with hollandaise sauce. If you call in at lunchtime, a more humble range of baked potatoes, sandwiches and toasties is also available. Half portions are served for children, or the chef can usually find chicken wings, fish fingers, sausages and baked beans.

Open 11–1am (Sun 12.30–1am) **Bar Meals** L served all week 12–2.30 D served all week 6–9.30 Av main course £8.50 **Restaurant** L served all week 12–2 D served all week 6.30–9 Av 5 course fixed price £31 ⊕ Free House ◀ McEwans 80/-, Guinness & Isle of Skye real ale. **Facilities** Children's licence Garden Dogs allowed Parking **Rooms** 16

Scotland

STEIN   MAP 22 NG25

Stein Inn ☝

Macleod's Ter IV55 8GA ☎ 01470 592362

e-mail: angus.teresa@steininn.co.uk

dir: *Take A87 from Portree. In 5m take A850 for 15m. Right onto B886, 3m to T-junct. Turn left.*

The oldest inn on the island, set in a lovely hamlet right next to the sea, the Stein Inn provides a warm welcome, fine food, and an impressive selection of drinks: fine wines, real ales and no fewer than a hundred malt whiskies. Highland game and local seafood feature strongly on daily-changing menus that range from lunchtime toasties and jacket potatoes to moules marinière, venison pie, and salmon in a vermouth and tarragon sauce.

Open 11–12 (Sun 12.30–11, Winter 12–11) **Bar Meals** L served Mon-Sat 12–4 D served all week 6–9 (Sun lunch 12.30–4)
Restaurant D served all week 6–9 ⊕ Free House ◀ Red Cuillin, Trade Winds, Reeling Deck, Deuchars IPA. ☝ 8 **Facilities** Children's licence Garden Dogs allowed Parking

LOCHBOISDALE   MAP 22 NF71

The Polochar Inn

Polochar HS8 5TT ☎ 01878 700215 🖹 01878 700768

e-mail: polocharinn@btconnect.co.uk

dir: *W from Lochboisdale, take B888. Hotel at end of road*

Overlooking the sea towards the islands of Eriskay and Barra, this superbly situated 18th-century inn enjoys beautiful sunsets. The bar menu offers fresh seafood dishes and steaks with various sauces, while restaurant fare includes venison, fresh scallops or steak pie.

Open 11–11 (Thu-Sat 11–1, Sun 12.30–11) **Bar Meals** L served all week 12.30–2.30 D served all week 6–9 Av main course £8 **Restaurant** L served all week 12–2.30 D served all week 6–9 Av 3 course à la carte £17 ⊕ Free House ◀ Syke Ales. **Facilities** Garden Parking

Scotland

Wales

Wales

ANGLESEY, ISLE OF

BEAUMARIS MAP 14 SH67

Pick of the Pubs

Ye Olde Bulls Head Inn ★★★★★

INN ◉◉ ☕

Castle St LL58 8AP ☎ 01248 810329 ▤ 01248 811294
e-mail: info@bullsheadinn.co.uk
web: www.bullsheadinn.co.uk
dir: *From Britannia Road Bridge follow A545. Inn in town centre*

Situated a stone's throw from the gates of imposing Beaumaris castle, The Bull (as it is commonly known) is inextricably linked to Anglesey's history. Built in 1472 as a coaching house, it has welcomed such distinguished guests as Samuel Johnson and Charles Dickens. Inside there's a traditional bar leading on to the popular brasserie which offers modern European cuisine – perhaps shredded duck salad with plum sauce, followed by pork saltimbocca with celeriac purée and Marsala sauce. Or it's up the stairs to the smartly modern, first-floor Loft restaurant which offers a more formal menu. Try a terrine of wild rabbit, foie gras and Parma ham, followed by fillet of Anglesey black beef with spinach, red wine, shallots, ceps, fine beans, pancetta, fondant potatoes and Madeira jus. Delectable desserts like caramelised hazelnut and sweet apple semifreddo with Bramley apple fritters and hazelnut tuile will be hard to resist.

Open 11–11 (Sun-12–10.30) Closed: 25 Dec **Bar Meals** L served all week 12–2 D served all week 7–9 (Sun 12–3) Av main course £9.35 **Restaurant** D served Mon-Sat 7–9 (Sun on BH wknds 12–1.30) Av 3 course fixed price £37.50 ⊕ Free House ◀ Bass, Hancocks, guest ales. ☕ 16 **Facilities** Parking **Rooms** 13

RED WHARF BAY MAP 14 SH58

Pick of the Pubs

The Ship Inn ☕

LL75 8RJ ☎ 01248 852568 ▤ 01248 851013
dir: *Telephone for directions*

Wading birds in their hundreds flock to feed on the extensive sands of Red Wharf Bay, making the Ship's waterside beer garden a birdwatcher's paradise on warm days. Before the age of steam, sailing ships landed cargoes here from all over the world; now the boats bring fresh Conwy Bay fish and seafood to the kitchens of this traditional free house. A single menu is served to diners in the bars and restaurant. Lunchtime sandwiches are a cut above the usual: choose from the likes of Perl Wen cheese and bacon, or seared strips of Welsh beef fillet with horseradish crème fraîche. Starters such as ham hock and leek terrine on toasted crumpet with poached free range egg is almost a meal in itself. Main courses may include rabbit and root vegetable casserole, or grilled fillets of lemon sole. If not quite replete, round off with banana custard and strawberry jam tart.

Open 11–11 **Bar Meals** L served Mon-Sat 12–2.30 D served Mon-Sat 6–9 (Sun 12–9) **Restaurant** D served Fri-Sat 7–9.30 ⊕ Free House ◀ Brains SA, Adnams, guest ales. ☕ 16 **Facilities** Garden Parking Play Area

BRIDGEND

KENFIG MAP 09 SS88

Prince of Wales Inn ☕

CF33 4PR ☎ 01656 740356
e-mail: prince-of-wales@bt.connect.com
dir: *M4 junct 37 into North Cornelly. Left at x-rds, follow signs for Kenfig & Porthcaw. Pub 600yds on right*

A 16th-century property, this stone-built inn has been many things in its time: a school, town hall and courtroom among others. The town hall, incorporated into the inn, has recently been restored and one of the landlord's family will happily show it to you. Local fare on the menu includes award-winning sausages, Welsh minted lamb chops and Welsh braised faggots. Also worth attention are the daily specials on the blackboard and traditional Sunday lunches.

Open 11–11 **Bar Meals** L served Tue-Sun 12–3 D served Tue-Sun 6–9 Av main course £6.50 **Restaurant** L served Tue-Sun 12–3 D served Tue-Sun 6–9 ⊕ Free House ◀ Bass Triangle, Worthington Best, guest ales. ☕ 15 **Facilities** Garden Dogs allowed Parking

CARDIFF

CREIGIAU   MAP 09 ST08

Pick of the Pubs

Caesars Arms ☕

Cardiff Rd CF15 9NN
☎ 029 2089 0486 📠 029 2089 2176
e-mail: caesarsarms@btconnect.com
dir: *1m from M4 junct 34*

Cardiff is nearby, but the Caesars Arms is reached through a network of winding country lanes that make city life seem a world away. The heated patio and terrace, both boasting views over the surrounding countryside, attract a well-heeled clientele. The menu is based around a ravishing range of fresh meat, game, fish and seafood displayed in shaven-ice display cabinets. Start with fresh Pembrokeshire dressed crab; tiger prawns in garlic; or scallops with leek and bacon. You could follow with fresh fish such as hake or lemon sole; venison from the Brecon Beacons; award-winning Welsh Black beef slowly reared and dry-aged for four weeks; or a real showstopper – sea bass baked in rock salt and filleted at your table. The pub has its own 'smokery', and the garden provides organically-grown herbs, salad and vegetables – plus honey from its bee hives.

Open 12–2.30 6–10.30 (Sun 12–4) Closed: 25 Dec
Bar Meals L served Mon-Sat 12–2.30 D served Mon-Sat 6–10.30
(Sun 12–4) **Restaurant** L served Mon-Sat 12–2.30 D served
Mon-Sat 6–10.30 (Sun 12–4) ⊕ Free House ◀ Felinfoel. ☕ 8
Facilities Garden Dogs allowed Parking

Gwaelod-y-Garth Inn NEW ☕

Main Rd, Gwaelod-y-Garth CF15 9HH
☎ 029 2081 0408 & 07855 313247
dir: *From M4 junct 32, N on A470, left at next exit, at rdbt turn right 0.5m. Right into village*

Meaning 'foot of the garth (mountain)', this welcoming pub was originally part of the Marquess of Bute's estate. Every window of the pub offers exceptional views, and it's a much favoured watering hole for ramblers, cyclists and hang-gliders as well as some colourful locals. Real ales change every week, while the pub's food has won awards with starters such as mussels in a tomato and garlic sauce; and main courses like rack of lamb with a herb crust, or duck breast with a kumquat and blackcurrant sauce.

Open 11–11 (Sun 12–11) **Bar Meals** L served Mon-Sat 12–2 D served Mon-Sat 6.30–9 (Sun 12–3.30) **Restaurant** L served Mon-Sat 12–2 D served Mon-Sat 6.30–9.30 (Sun 12–3.30) ⊕ Free House ◀ HPA (Wye Valley), Otley OI, RCH Pitchfork, Vale of Glamorgan. ☕ 7 **Facilities** Garden Dogs allowed Parking

CARMARTHENSHIRE

ABERGORLECH   MAP 08 SN53

The Black Lion

SA32 7SN ☎ 01558 685271
e-mail: michelle.r@btinternet.com
dir: *A40 E from Carmarthen, then B4310 signed Brechfa & Abergorlech*

A 17th-century coaching inn in the Brechfa Forest, with a beer garden overlooking the Cothi River, and an old packhorse bridge. Flagstone floors, settles and a grandfather clock grace the antique-furnished bar, while the modern dining room is welcoming in pink and white. Try home-made chicken and leek pie, home-made curry of the day, or a fresh salmon steak. Miles of forest and riverside walks are easily reached from the pub.

Open 12–3.30 7–11 (Sat 12–11, Sun 12–10) **Bar Meals** L served Tue-Sun 12–2 D served Tue-Sun 7–9 (Sun 7–8.30) Av main course £6.50 **Restaurant** L served Sun 12–2 D served Sat 7–9 Av 3 course à la carte £12 ⊕ Free House ◀ Brains SA, Buckley's Best, Spitfire, Young's Bitter. **Facilities** Garden Dogs allowed Parking

LLANDDAROG   MAP 08 SN51

White Hart Thatched Inn & Brewery

SA32 8NT ☎ 01267 275395
dir: *6m E of Carmarthen towards Swansea, just off A48 on B4310, signed Llanddarog*

The White Hart's thick stone walls, heavy beams and thatched roof have stood in this rural Welsh village since 1371. Now, the Coles family invites you to sit by a cosy log fire with a pint from the on-site microbrewery, or eat out on the summer patio. Expect snacks and sandwiches, as well as specials such as duck breast in red wine and plum sauce; and sizzling marlin with garlic, wine and mushrooms.

Open 11.30–3 6.30–11 (Sun 12–3, 7–10.30) **Bar Meals** L served all week 11.30–2 D served all week 6.30–10 (Sun 12–2, 7–9.30) Av main course £6 **Restaurant** L served all week 11.30–2 D served all week 6.30–10 (Sun 12–2, 7–9.30) Av 3 course à la carte £20 ⊕ Free House ◀ Roasted Barley Stout, Llanddarog Ale, Bramling Cross. **Facilities** Garden Parking Play Area

Wales

LLANDEILO
MAP 08 SN62

The Angel Hotel ☻

Rhosmaen St SA19 6EN ☎ 01558 822765 📠 01558 824346

e-mail: capelbach@hotmail.com

dir: *In centre of town next to post office.*

This popular pub in the centre of Llandeilo has something for everyone. Real ales are available in the bar area, which hosts regular live music nights. Upstairs, the Yr Eglwys function room ceiling is decorated with soaring frescoes inspired by Michelangelo's Sistine Chapel, and at the rear is an intimate bistro, where dishes might include butternut squash ravioli, followed by rack of salt marsh lamb with a blueberry and port jus and a nut crust.

Open 11–3.30 6.30–12 Closed: Sun **Bar Meals** L served Mon-Sat 11.30–2.30 D served Mon-Sat 7–9 Av main course £6 **Restaurant** L served Mon-Sat 11.30–2.30 D served Mon-Sat 7–9.30 Av 3 course à la carte £20 ⊕ Free House ◀ Evan Evans Ales, Tetleys, Butty Bach. ☻ 12 **Facilities** Garden

The Castle Hotel

113 Rhosmaen St SA19 6EN

☎ 01558 823446 📠 01558 822290

dir: *Telephone for directions*

A 19th-century Edwardian-style hotel within easy reach of Dinefwr Castle and wonderful walks through classic parkland. A charming, tiled and partly green-painted back bar attracts plenty of locals, while the front bar and side area offer smart furnishings and the chance to relax in comfort over a drink. A good range of Tomas Watkins ales is available, and quality bar and restaurant food is prepared with the finest of fresh local ingredients. Under new management.

Open 12–11 (Sun 12–10.30) **Bar Meals** L served Wed-Sun 12–2.30 D served Wed-Sun 6.30–9 Av main course £6.95 **Restaurant** L served all week 12–2.30 D served Mon-Sat 6.30–9 ◀ Tomas Watkins, Hancoats Bitter, Archers Golden, London Pride. **Facilities** Garden Parking

NANTGAREDIG
MAP 08 SN42

Pick of the Pubs

Y Polyn ◉◉ ☻

SA32 7LH ☎ 01267 290000

e-mail: ypolyn@hotmail.com

dir: *From A48 follow signs to National Botanic Garden of Wales. Then follow brown signs to Y Polyn*

A 250–year-old inn set in a lovely spot in the verdant Towy Valley. Long ago it was a tollhouse – its name means 'pole', probably after the original barrier across the road. It is handily placed by a fork in the roads, with Aberglasney in one direction and the National Botanic Garden of Wales in the other. Though drinkers are undoubtedly welcome to prop up the bar, or in reality sit by the fire in the squashy armchairs, the inn continues to make its name primarily as a food destination. Lunch could begin with pear, roquefort and toasted pecan salad, and continue with Carmarthenshire free range chicken coq au vin. The dinner fixed-price menu follows similar lines: Y Polyn fish soup is served with the full set of accompaniments – rouille, croûtons and gruyère; a main course of roast rump of saltmarsh lamb comes with onion, garlic and thyme purée.

Open 12–2 7–11 Closed: Mon **Bar Meals** L served Tue-Sun D served Tue-Sat Av main course £13.50 **Restaurant** L served Tue-Sun 12–2 D served Tue-Sat 7–9 Av 3 course à la carte £27.50 Av 3 course fixed price £27.50 ⊕ Free House ◀ Deuchars IPA, Ffos-y-ffin ales. ☻ 7 **Facilities** Garden Parking

CEREDIGION

ABERAERON
MAP 08 SN46

Pick of the Pubs

Harbourmaster Hotel ★★★★★ INN
◉ ☻

Pen Cei SA46 0BA ☎ 01545 570755

e-mail: info@harbour-master.com

dir: *From A487, once in town follow signs for tourist information centre. The pub is next door on the harbourside.*

A renovated Grade-II listed harbourmaster's residence, the hotel has been a landmark on the Aberaeron quayside since 1811. A recent extension into the adjoining grain warehouse has greatly increased the bar capacity, and the bar, restaurant and hotel all have fabulous views of the harbour – there is no better place to enjoy a pint of real ale or a glass of wine. The light interior decor is complemented by original features like the Welsh slate masonry and listed spiral staircase. The food is modern in style but substantial in character, with plenty of opportunities to sample fresh local produce in the restaurant. The bar menu, in Welsh and English, offers Harbourmaster fishcakes with lime mayonnaise; Welsh Black beef burger with chips and Snowdonia cheddar; and treacle tart with cinnamon ice cream. The Harbourmaster is proudly bilingual, and a mixture of Welsh and English is spoken in the bar.

Open 10–11 (Mon 3–11) Closed: 25 Dec **Bar Meals** L served Tue-Sun 12–2.30 D served all week 6–9 **Restaurant** L served Tue-Sun 12–2 D served all week 6.30–9 Av 3 course à la carte £25 ⊕ Free House ◀ Tomas Watkins Cwrw Braf, Evan Evans Best Bitter. ☻ 12 **Facilities** Parking **Rooms** 13

LLWYNDAFYDD

MAP 08 SN35

The Crown Inn & Restaurant

SA44 6BU ☎ 01545 560396 📄 01545 560857

dir: *Off A487 NE of Cardigan*

A traditional Welsh longhouse dating from 1799, with original beams, open fireplaces, and a pretty restaurant. A varied menu offers a good selection of dishes, including sautéed ballottine of chicken supreme; roast monkfish wrapped in Parma ham; and warm spiced couscous. Blackboard specials and bar meals are available lunchtimes and evenings. Outside is a delightful, award-winning garden. An easy walk down the lane leads to a cove with caves and National Trust.

Open 12–3 6–11 (Fri-Sat all day Etr-Sep) Closed: Sun eve winter
Bar Meals L served all week 12–2 D served all week 6–9 Av main course £8 **Restaurant** D served all week 6.30–9 Av 3 course à la carte £30 ⊕ Free House ◀ Interbrew Flowers Original & Flowers IPA , Greene King Old Speckled Hen, Honey ales Envill Ale, Fuller's London Pride.
Facilities Children's licence Garden Dogs allowed Parking Play Area

CONWY

Pick of the Pubs

Ty Gwyn Inn ★★★ INN

LL24 0SG ☎ 01690 710383 & 710787 📄 01690 710383
e-mail: mratcl1050@aol.com
dir: *At junct of A5 & A470, 100yds S of Waterloo Bridge*

Set in the heart of the Snowdonia National Park, this atmospheric inn overlooks the Conwy River, and enjoys some beautiful views of the mountains. It began life in 1636 as a coaching inn on the London to Holyhead road, and in 1815 Thomas Telford built the impressive cast iron Waterloo Bridge opposite. The interior features the expected exposed beams, so minding your head is recommended. Food is home-cooked and full of imagination,

CONTINUED

Wales

BETWS-Y-COED continued

with typical starters including home-made wood pigeon pie; crispy confit of oriental duck with spicy Thai salad, sweet chilli, sesame and soya; and local smoked king prawns with fresh crab and wild garlic. Main courses could include roast rack of venison with wild mushroom risotto; fresh fillet of wild turbot with creamed cabbage and smoked salmon; or local roast goose with red onion and mature cheddar pudding. The twelve bedrooms include some with four-poster beds, and a honeymoon suite.

Open 12–3 6–11 Closed: 1wk Jan **Bar Meals** L served all week 12–2 D served all week 6.30–9 **Restaurant** L served all week 12–2 D served all week 6.30–9 ⊕ Free House ◀ Adnams Broadside, Reverend James Old Speckled Hen, Bombardier & IPA, Orms Best. **Facilities** Parking **Rooms** 10

See advert on page 733

White Horse Inn ★★★ INN

Capel Garmon LL26 0RW
☎ 01690 710271 📧 01690 710721
e-mail: r.alton@btconnect.com
dir: *Telephone for directions*

Picturesque Capel Garmon perches high above Betws-y-Coed, with spectacular views of the Snowdon Range, a good 20 kilometres away. To make a detour to find this cosy 400–year-old inn is to be rewarded by a menu featuring fresh local produce.

Open 6–11 (Sat-Sun 12–2.30) Closed: 25 Dec **Bar Meals** L served Sat-Sun 12–2.30 D served all week 4.30–8 (Fri-Sat 6.30–9.30, Sun 6.30–9) Av main course £8.85 **Restaurant** L served Sat-Sun 12–2.30 D served all week 9–9 Av 3 course à la carte £19 ⊕ Free House ◀ Tetley Imperial, Tetley Smoothflow, Hob Goblin. **Facilities** Dogs allowed Parking **Rooms** 5

BETWS-YN-RHOS   MAP 14 SH97

The Wheatsheaf Inn

LL22 8AW ☎ 01492 680218 📧 01492 680666
e-mail: perry@jonnyp.fsnet.co.uk
dir: *A55 to Abergele, take A548 to Llanrwst from High Street. 2m turn right B5381, 1m to Betws-yn-Rhos*

This 13th-century alehouse was licensed as a coaching inn in 1640. Splendid oak beams, old stone pillars and an original hayloft ladder combine to make this an ideal spot to enjoy a pint of John Smiths or one of the Wheatsheaf's special malt whiskies. A single menu serves the lounge bar and restaurant with dishes that may include grilled halibut with prawns and royal game pie and Madeira sauce.

Open 12–3 6–11 **Bar Meals** L served all week 12–2 D served all week 6–9 (Sun 12–3) Av main course £10 **Restaurant** L served all week 12–2 D served all week 6–9.30 (Sun 12–3) Av 3 course à la carte £17 ⊕ Enterprise Inns ◀ John Smiths, Brains, Hobgoblin, Conwy Castle. **Facilities** Garden Parking Play Area

---

CAPEL CURIG   MAP 14 SH75

Cobdens Hotel ★★ SHL

LL24 0EE ☎ 01690 720243 📧 01690 720354
e-mail: info@cobdens.co.uk
dir: *Telephone for directions*

Situated in a beautiful mountain village in the heart of Snowdonia, this 250-year-old inn offers wholesome, locally sourced food and real ales. Start with local rabbit and pancetta terrine. Mains include roasted Welsh lamb with garlic and thyme mash; Welsh beef steaks; and pasta with roasted courgette, blue cheese and chestnut. Snacks and sandwiches also available.

Open 11–11 Closed: 6–26 Jan **Bar Meals** L served all week 12–2.30 D served all week 6–9 Av main course £10 **Restaurant** L served all week 12–2 D served all week 6–9 Av 3 course à la carte £22 ⊕ Free House ◀ Conwy Castle ale, Cobdens Ale & guest ale. **Facilities** Children's licence Garden Dogs allowed Parking **Rooms** 17

COLWYN BAY   MAP 14 SH87

Pick of the Pubs

Pen-y-Bryn ♥

Pen-y-Bryn Rd LL29 6DD
☎ 01492 533360 & 535808 📧 01492 536127
e-mail: pen.y.bryn@brunningandprice.co.uk
dir: *Kings Rd to top of hill, right Pen-y-Bryn Rd, pub on left*

From the front, this 1970s building looks rather more like a medical centre than a pub. The interior, though, is very attractive with oak floors, open fires, bookcases, rugs and old furniture. To the rear there is a stunning garden and terrace with panoramic views over the sea and looming headland known as the Great Orme. The modern British menu opens with a good selection of starters, including sticky chilli chicken with Thai salad; mushroom tart with tarragon crust; and light dishes like Welsh rarebit, or Menai mussels in a wine and cream sauce. Among the main courses are Guinness braised blade of beef; crispy lamb and feta salad; and grilled herring fillet in oatmeal crust with crab and lemon butter. To finish try warm treacle tart with custard; or cinnamon choux pastry fritters with apricot sauce and ice cream.

Open 11.30–11 (Sun 12–11, 25 Dec 12–2) **Bar Meals** L served Mon-Sat 12–9.30 D served Mon-Sat 12–9.30 (Sun 12–9) **Restaurant** L served Mon-Sat 12–9.30 D served Mon-Sat 12–9.30 (Sun 12–9) ◀ Timothy Taylor Landlord, Thwaites Original, Brag D.Y.R Bryn, Ormes Best & Weetwoods Eastgate. ♥ 14 **Facilities** Garden Parking

Llynau Mymbyr lake near Capel Curig with a view to Mount Snowdon, Conwy

PICK OF THE PUBS

CONWY-CONWY

The Groes Inn

Built as a small two-storey house in the 15th century, and first recorded as an inn in 1573. The location is stunning, with a panorama over the River Conwy and the surrounding hills from the front, and slopes rising towards Snowdonia at the rear. Rambling rooms, beamed ceilings and historic settles – this inn has them all.

For centuries it has maintained a tradition of welcoming travellers; drovers would rest here while drying their wet clothes in front of a blazing fire. Today it makes a great base for exploring the mountains, coastline, castles and gardens of North Wales. Owners Dawn and Justin Humphreys have decorated the interior with stone cats, military hats, saucy Victorian postcards, historic cooking utensils and old advertisements. You can eat in the bar or more stylishly in the award-winning restaurant. Dishes using fresh local produce reflect traditional tastes with some European influences. You can choose a small meal that doubles as a starter in the bar, from choices like butternut squash and sage ravioli; grilled kippers and crispy bacon with brown bread and butter; and fresh linguini with smoked chicken and carbonara sauce. Or perhaps plump for the favourites such as haddock, prawn and mushroom mornay; thick juicy Anglesey gammon and eggs; poached salmon with hollandaise sauce; and chicken curry. From the restaurant set menu come starters like deep-fried devilled whitebait with garlic mayonnaise; and salad of smoked chicken fillets with crispy bacon and avocado pear. Move on to chilli bean casserole; seafood platter; pot-roast widgeon stuffed with herbs, bacon and chestnuts; or steak and mushroom pie. For dessert try bara brith (Welsh fruit bread), white chocolate and vanilla bean panacotta; toffee and banana pie; or orange and rosemary jelly with roasted apricots and orange and Cointreau ice cream.

★★★ HL ◉ ♀
MAP 14 SH77
LL32 8TN
☎ 01492 650545
▤ 01492 650855
e-mail: reception@groesinn.com
dir: *Off A55 to Conwy, left at mini rdbt by Conwy Castle onto B5106, 2.5m inn on right.*

Open 12–3 6.30–11
Bar Meals L served Mon-Sat 12–2.15 D served Mon-Sat 6.30–9 (Sun 12–9)
Restaurant L served all week 12–2.15 D served all week 6.30–9
⊕ Free House ◀ Tetley, Burton Ale, Ormes Best, Welsh Black.
♀ 10
Facilities Garden Parking
Rooms 14

CONWY   MAP 14 SH77

Pick of the Pubs

The Groes Inn ★★★ HL 🏵 ♀

See Pick of the Pubs on opposite page

LLANDUDNO JUNCTION   MAP 14 SH77

The Queens Head ♀

Glanwydden LL31 9JP ☎ 01492 546570 📠 01492 546487

e-mail: enquiries@queensheadglanwydden.co.uk

dir: *From A55 take A470 towards Llandudno. At 3rd rdbt right towards Penrhyn Bay, then 2nd right into Glanwydden, pub on left*

Set amidst dramatic scenery with a bounty of beaches and castles nearby, this pub majors on traditional comfort and charm. The bar, fire-warmed when it's cold, is the perfect pre-prandial rendezvous. The menu is in tune with the inn's surroundings: try game from the local shoot; seared Anglesey scallops with pea purée and pancetta; Conwy mussels marinière; or a home-made Welsh steak, mushroom and ale pie. Spicier options include Thai-style fishcakes or Jamaican chicken curry.

Open 11–3 6–11 (Sun 11–10.30) **Bar Meals** L served Mon-Sat 12–2 D served Mon-Sat 6–9 (Sun 12–9) **Restaurant** L served Mon-Sat 12–2 D served Mon-Sat 6–9 (Sun 12–9) ⊕ Free House 🍺 Carlsberg-Tetley, Weetwood Ales, Great Orme Brewery. ♀ 7 **Facilities** Garden Parking **Rooms** available

---

LLANNEFYDD   MAP 14 SH97

The Hawk & Buckle Inn

LL16 5ED ☎ 01745 540249 📠 01745 540316

e-mail: hawkandbuckle@btinternet.com

web: www.hawkandbuckleinn.com

dir: *Telephone for directions*

A 17th-century coaching inn 200mtrs up in the hills, with wonderful views to the sea beyond. Traditional dishes using local produce – shoulder of Welsh lamb, chicken breast stuffed with Welsh cheese or duck breast with port and redcurrant sauce, sit comfortably alongside international flavours – lamb pasanda, beef and Guinness casserole or chicken tikka masala, for example.

Open 12–2 6–11 Closed: 25–26 Dec **Bar Meals** L served Wed & Sun 12–2 D served Tue-Sat 6–9 (Sun 7–10.30) Av main course £8.50 **Restaurant** L served Sun D served Sat-Sun 6–9 Av 3 course à la carte £16 ⊕ Free House 🍺 Brains Bitter, Interbrew Boddingtons Bitter, Bass Bitter. **Facilities** Parking

---

ST GEORGE   MAP 14 SH97

Pick of the Pubs

The Kinmel Arms ★★★★★ RR 🏵 ♀

LL22 9BP ☎ 01745 832207 📠 01745 822044

e-mail: info@thekinmelarms.co.uk

dir: *From Bodelwyddan towards Abergele take slip road at St George. Take 1st left & Kinmel Arms on left at top of hill*

Nestling in the foothills of the stunning Elwy valley, this rural free house offers ready access to the coast, mountains and cwms of beautiful North Wales. Despite its neo-Elizabethan style, the Kinmel Arms dates from the last decade of the Victorian era. It was built to replace the Dinorben Arms, which was demolished to make way for a new village hall in 1899. The building has been stylishly renovated by owners Lynn and Tim Watson, who have decorated the rooms with their own mountain photography. Good fresh food is offered from an à la carte menu at dinner, with a brasserie-style choice at lunchtime. Fish features strongly with dishes such as Menai mussels served with a cream and white wine sauce; and roast halibut fillet with braised fennel and red chicory in a lemon and thyme, balsamic peppers and rocket salad.

Open 12–3 6.30–11 (Sun 12–5, BH Sun-Mon all day) Closed: 25 Dec, 1–2 Jan **Bar Meals** L served Tue-Sun 12–2 D served Tue-Sat 7–9.30 (Fri-Sat 6.30–9.30, Sun 12–3) Av main course £15 **Restaurant** L served Tue-Sun 12–2 D served Tue-Sat 7–9.30 (Fri-Sat 6.30–9.30, Sun 12–3) Av 3 course à la carte £25 ⊕ Free House 🍺 4 real ales (change weekly). ♀ 16 **Facilities** Garden Parking **Rooms** 4

DENBIGHSHIRE

LLANGOLLEN   MAP 15 SJ24

The Corn Mill NEW ♀

Dee Ln LL20 8PN ☎ 01978 869555 📠 01978 869930

The first two things to strike you as you walk through the door are the great jumble of old beams, and the waterwheel turning slowly behind the bar. The decks outside are built directly over the millrace and the rapids, and on the opposite bank of the river, steam trains huff and puff in the restored railway station. Mains include cold honey-roast ham; Cumberland sausage; lamb and vegetable suet pudding; and macaroni cheese.

Open 12–11 (Sun 12–10.30) **Bar Meals** L served Mon-Sat 12–9.30 D served Mon-Sat 12–9.30 (Sun 12–9) Av main course £10 **Restaurant** L served Mon-Sat 12–9.30 D served Mon-Sat 12-9.30 (Sun 12–9) ⊕ Free House 🍺 Boddingtons, Plassey ales. ♀ 12 **Notes** 🏵

Wales

PICK OF THE PUBS

White Horse Inn

A whitewashed, 400–year-old inn in the lovely vale of Clwyd. Part of the building was originally the village shop and, together with the pub, used to be a much favoured resting place for sheep drovers making their way over the Clwydian Range to markets in England.

Today's visitors tend to arrive without woolly companions and are able to relax in more civilised style with a newspaper or magazine in front of a log fire. The bar serves regularly changing guest real ales, as well as a wide variety of malts and some unusual spirits. Meals are served at any time, the speciality of the house being farm-cured ham and fresh farm eggs, while sandwiches and dishes such as Hungarian goulash, and fish, chips and mushy peas tend to be bar menu fixtures. The main menu includes starters of baked sardines with herbed crust; Chinese-style spicy chicken salad with lime; and field mushrooms with thyme and garlic. Typical main courses are duck cakes with spring onions, figs, hot salsa and elderberry jus;

Moroccan lamb tagine; fresh fish of the day from Llandudno Smokery; and local rump steak cooked to order. For dessert, rice pudding with caramelised figs; and sticky toffee pudding. The reasonably priced wine list is interesting, and there's also a more expensive Cellar Selection which peaks at £64.50 for a Chassagne-Montrachet white Burgundy. Outside is an attractive decked patio and garden with views of distant Snowdonia. For the sightseer, Ruthin Castle and the ruins of Denbigh Castle are not too far away. Pony trekking is a popular pastime from nearby Cilcain.

MAP 15 SJ15
Hendrerwydd LL16 4LL
☎ 01824 790218
e-mail: vintr74@hotmail.com
dir: *A494 (Ruthin to Mold road). 10m, turn left opposite The Griffin pub to Llandyrnog. Through Gellifar to Hendrerwydd*

Open 12–2.30 6–11 Closed: Sun eve & Mon
Bar Meals L served all week 12–2.30 D served all week 6–9.15
Restaurant L served all week 12–2.30 D served Tue-Sat 6–9.15 (Sun 6–8.30)
⊕ Free House
◀ Regular changing guest ales.
♀ 7
Facilities Garden Dogs allowed Parking

PRESTATYN
MAP 15 SJ08

Nant Hall Restaurant & Bar ♥

Nant Hall Rd LL19 9LD ☎ 01745 886766 🖹 01745 886998
e-mail: mail@nanthall.com

dir: *E towards Chester, 1m on left opposite large car garage*

Nant Hall, a Grade II listed Victorian country house in seven acres of grounds, operates as a gastro-pub with a great variety of food, beers and wines. Dawsons Bar Cuisine menu offers local and regional dishes alongside recipes from around the world: Conwy award-winning pork and leek sausages with mash and onion gravy, vegetarian fajitas, lamb koftas with couscous, and sweet and sour king prawns. The large outdoor eating area is great in summer.

Open 11–12 (Oct-Mar Mon 11–3, Tue-Thu 11–11 Sun 11–6)
Bar Meals L served Mon-Sat 12 D served Mon-Sat 6–9.30 (Sun 12–6)
Av main course £11 ⊕ Free House ◀ Bass Smooth, Boddintons. ♥14
Facilities Garden Parking

RHEWL
MAP 15 SJ16

The Drovers Arms, Rhewl

Denbigh Rd LL15 2UD ☎ 01824 703163 🖹 01824 703163
e-mail: Allen_Given@hotmail.com
dir: *1.3m from Ruthin on the A525*

A small village pub whose name recalls a past written up and illustrated on storyboards displayed inside. Main courses are divided on the menu into poultry, traditional meat, fish, grills and vegetarian; examples from each section are chicken tarragon; Welsh lamb's liver and onions; Vale of Clwyd sirloin steak; home-made fish pie; and fresh mushroom stroganoff. Desserts include treacle sponge pudding.

Open 12–3 5–11 (Times vary Summer & Winter) **Bar Meals** L served all week 12–2 D served all week 5–8 (Fri-Sat 6–9, Sun 12–2.30)
Restaurant L served all week 12–2 D served Mon-Sun 5–8 (Fri-Sat 6–9, Sun 12–2.30) ⊕ Free House ◀ London Pride, Youngs, Tetley Smooth.
Facilities Children's licence Garden Parking Play Area

RUTHIN
MAP 15 SJ15

Ye Olde Anchor Inn

Rhos St LL15 1DY ☎ 01824 702813 🖹 01824 703050
e-mail: info@anchorinn.co.uk
dir: *At junction of A525 and A494*

In the centre of town, this impressive-looking old inn has 16 windows at the front alone – all with award-winning window boxes. An extensive bar snack menu is available lunchtimes and evenings, while the main menu offers two types of lasagne, baked beef or Mediterranean vegetable; honey-spiced Welsh lamb shank; trinity of grilled fish; carpetbag fillet steak; and chestnut, mushroom and asparagus linguine, all eminently worth following with one of the freshly prepared desserts.

Open 12–11 **Bar Meals** L served Mon-Sat 12–7 D served all week 12–9.30 (Sun 12–3) **Restaurant** L served all week 12–9.30 D served all week Av 3 course à la carte £18 ⊕ Free House ◀ Timothy Taylor, Worthington, guest ales. **Facilities** Dogs allowed Parking

---

White Horse Inn ♥

See Pick of the Pubs on opposite page

ST ASAPH
MAP 15 SJ07

The Plough Inn ♥

The Roe LL17 0LU ☎ 01745 585080 🖹 01745 585363
dir: *Exit A55 at Rhyl/St Asaph signs, left at rdbt, pub 200yds on left*

An 18th-century former coaching inn, the Plough has been transformed. The ground floor retains the traditional pub concept, cosy with open fires and rustic furniture, while upstairs there are two very different restaurants: an up-market bistro and an Italian-themed art deco restaurant, divided by a wine shop. All the kitchens are open so you can see the food being prepared. Desserts are a great strength throughout.

Open 12–11 Fri-Sat 12–1 **Bar Meals** L served all week 12–9.30 D served all week Av main course £8.50 **Restaurant** L served all week 12–3 D served all week 6–10 ⊕ Free House ◀ Greene King Old Speckled Hen, Shepherd Neame Spitfire, Plassey brewery. ♥9 **Facilities** Garden Parking

---

BABELL
MAP 15 SJ17

Black Lion Inn

CH8 8PZ ☎ 01352 720239
e-mail: theblacklioninn@btinternet.com
dir: *From Holywell take B5121 towards A541 & take 2nd right to Babell*

Ancient inns spawn ghost stories, but the 13th-century Black Lion boasts more than its fair share. Ask about them when you visit, but don't be put off savouring a local real ale on the outside decking while the children enjoy the play area. Alternatively tuck into good home-cooked dishes like black pudding layered with crisp back bacon; and pork escalope with fresh asparagus sauce. Irish music keeps the spirits awake on the last Wednesday of the month.

Open 6–11 (Sat-Sun all day) **Bar Meals** L served Sat-Sun D served Thu-Fri 6–9 (Sat 12–9.30, Sun 12–9) Av main course £11.95 **Restaurant** L served Sat-Sun D served Thu-Fri 6.30–9 (Sat 12–9.30, Sun 12–9) Av 3 course à la carte £22 ⊕ Free House ◀ Thwaites Lancaster Bomber, Thwaites Smooth Bitter, Purple Moose Brewery – Traeth Mawr, Thirstquencher Spitting Feathers. **Facilities** Garden Parking Play Area

CILCAIN
MAP 15 SJ16

White Horse Inn
CH7 5NN ☎ 01352 740142 📠 01352 740142
e-mail: christine.jeory@btopenworld.com
dir: *From Mold take A541 towards Denbigh. After approx 6m turn left*

A 400–year-old pub, which is the last survivor of five originally to be found in this lovely hillside village – no doubt because it was the centre of the local gold-mining industry in the 19th century. Today the White Horse is popular with walkers, cyclists, and horse-riders. The dishes are home made by the landlord's wife using the best quality local ingredients, including filled omelettes, grilled ham and eggs, breaded fillet of trout, cig oen Cymraeg (Welsh lamb pie), and various curries.

Open 12–3 6.30–11 (Sat-Sun 12–11) **Bar Meals** L served all week 12–2 D served all week 7–9 Av main course £7 ⊕ Free House ◀ Marston's Pedigree, Bank's Bitter, Timothy Taylor Landlord, Draught Bass. **Facilities** Garden Dogs allowed Parking

NORTHOP
MAP 15 SJ26

Stables Bar Restaurant ⬤
CH7 6AB ☎ 01352 840577 📠 01352 840382
e-mail: info@soughtonhall.co.uk
dir: *From A55, take A119 through Northop*

This destination pub is housed in the magnificent setting of the 17th-century Soughton Hall stables. Fortunately, it has kept many original features intact, including the cobbled floors, stalls and roof timbers. The tables are named after famous racecourses and their winners. Menus continue the racing theme. Try pan-seared scallops with bacon polenta, followed by grilled sea bass and shellfish chowder. 'Final Furlong' sweets make for a spectacular finish.

Open 11–11.30 **Bar Meals** L served all week 12–3 D served all week 7–9.30 (Sun 4–9.30) **Restaurant** L served all week 12–3 D served all week 7–10 (Sun 1–3, 7–10) ⊕ Free House ◀ Shepherd Neame Spitfire, Shepherd Neame Bishops Finger, Coach House Honeypot, Dick Turpin. ⬤ 6 **Facilities** Garden Parking

MOLD
MAP 15 SJ26

Pick of the Pubs

Glasfryn ⬤
Raikes Ln, Sychdyn CH7 6LR
☎ 01352 750500 📠 01352 751923
e-mail: glasfryn@brunningandprice.co.uk
dir: *From Mold follow signs to Theatr Clwyd, 1m from town centre*

Built as a judge's residence in around 1900, later a farm and then divided into bedsits, this building was rescued by the present owners in 1999 and transformed into a wonderful pub. It attracts a variety of visitors from farmers and business people to holidaymakers along the north Wales coast. Outside, the newly landscaped garden is maturing well, while inside is a bright open space with lots of polished wooden tables and chairs. Puddings and cheeses are not to be missed. The comprehensive daily menu runs from sandwiches and snacks through to meals such as beetroot gravad lax followed by crab and prawn noodles with lime and chilli; or perhaps Welsh lamb sausage with braised tomato beans followed by beer battered haddock with chips.

Open 11.30–11 (Sun 12–10.30) Closed: 25–26 Dec **Bar Meals** L served Mon-Sat 12–9.30 D served Mon-Sat 12–9.30 (Sun 12–9) **Restaurant** L served Mon-Sat 12–9.30 D served Mon-Sat 12–9.30 (Sun 12–9) ◀ Timothy Taylor, Thwaites, Deuchars IPA, Wadworth 6X. ⬤ 20 **Facilities** Children's licence Garden Dogs allowed Parking

GWYNEDD

ABERDYFI
MAP 14 SN69

Pick of the Pubs

Penhelig Arms Hotel & Restaurant ⬤
Terrace Rd LL35 0LT ☎ 01654 767215 📠 01654 767690
e-mail: info@penheligarms.com
dir: *On A493 W of Machynlleth*

The Penhelig Arms has been in business since the late 18th century. It enjoys glorious views over the tidal Dyfi estuary, and is idyllically placed for breezy sea strolls or hill walks. Cader Idris and a variety of majestic mountains and historic castles are within easy reach. Locals and visitors alike experience a warm welcome in the wood-panelled Fisherman's bar, where traditional ales are to be found; many customers relax on the sea wall opposite during fine weather. Nibbles include toasted flatbread with houmous and bowls of mixed olives. Starters range from fillets of sweet cured herrings to sardines grilled with spring onions. Fish dishes are indeed plentiful, continuing with main courses such as whole black sea bream roasted with Mediterranean vegetables; and pan-fried swordfish, with rocket, red onion and tomato salad. Offal lovers will relish a plate of pan-fried Welsh lambs' liver and bacon, with sautéed potatoes and broccoli.

Open 11.30–3.30 5.30–11 (Sun 12–3.30, 6–11) Closed: 25–26 Dec **Bar Meals** L served all week 12–2.30 D served all week 6–9.30 **Restaurant** L served all week 12–2.30 D served all week 7–9.30 ⊕ Free House ◀ Speckled Hen, Greene King Abbot Ale, Adnams Broadside, Brains Reverend James & SA. ⬤ 12 **Facilities** Children's licence Garden Dogs allowed Parking

740

BLAENAU FFESTINIOG   MAP 14 SH74

The Miners Arms

Llechwedd Slate Caverns LL41 3NB
☎ 01766 830306 📄 01766 831260
e-mail: quarrytours@aol.com
dir: *From Llandudno take A470 south. Through Betwys-y-Coed, 16m to Blaenau Ffestiniog*

Slate floors, open fires and staff in Victorian costume emphasise the heritage theme of this welcoming pub nestling in the centre of a Welsh village. On the site of Llechwedd Slate Caverns, one of the country's leading tourist attractions, it caters for all comers and tastes: expect steak and ale casserole, pork pie and salad, various ploughman's lunches, and hot apple pie, as well as afternoon tea with scones and cream.

Open 11–5.30 Closed: Oct-Etr **Bar Meals** L served all week 11–5 ⊕ Free House **Facilities** Garden Dogs allowed Parking Play Area

---

LLANBEDR   MAP 14 SH52

Victoria Inn ★★★★ INN ♈

LL45 2LD ☎ 01341 241213 📄 01341 241644
e-mail: junevicinn@aol.com
dir: *Telephone for directions*

Heavily beamed and wonderfully atmospheric, the Victoria is perfect for the pub connoisseur seeking authentic features such as flagged floors, an unusual circular wooden settle, an ancient stove and a grandfather clock. Good food in the bars and restaurant includes honey roast ham, sausage in onion gravy, Japanese torpedo prawns served with a lemon mayonnaise dip, and Welsh dragon tart. Relax with a leisurely drink in the pub's well-kept garden.

Open 12–11 (Fri-Sat 12–12, Sun 12–10.30) **Bar Meals** L served all week 12–9 D served all week 6–9 (Sun 12–8) Av main course £7.95 **Restaurant** L served all week 12–3 D served all week 6–9 Av 3 course à la carte £18 ◀ Robinson's Best Bitter, Hartleys XB. ♈ 10 **Facilities** Garden Dogs allowed Parking Play Area **Rooms** 5

MALLWYD   MAP 14 SH81

Pick of the Pubs

Brigands Inn ★★★★ INN ♈

SY20 9HJ ☎ 01650 511999 📄 01650 531208
dir: *On A487 between Dolgellau and Machynlleth*

At the heart of the Cambrian Mountains, on the upper banks of the gin-clear River Dovey, lies the Brigands Inn, a renowned 15th-century coaching establishment. The pub's impressive setting makes it a popular base for exploring this scenic, spectacular corner of Wales. Fly fishing is a much-loved activity here, as is walking, and one well-worn route offers the chance to stroll up Camlan Mountain to inspect the site of King Arthur's last battle. Alternatively, or afterwards, opt for a glass of wine in the pub's sunny garden with its fine country views. The chef sources the finest local produce to create a fusion of contemporary and classic Welsh cuisine. The menus reflect the changing seasons with a good selection of fish, meat and game. A typical example is grilled fillet of sea bass with sun-dried tomato and pesto; grilled sirloin steak with tomato, mushrooms and onions; and loin of venison on caramelised red onions with a port and juniper sauce.

Open 8am-11 **Bar Meals** L served all week 12–3 D served all week 6–9 **Restaurant** L served all week 12–2.30 D served all week 6–9 ◀ Worthington Cream, Worthington Cask, Archers guest ale. **Facilities** Children's licence Garden Dogs allowed Parking Play Area **Rooms** 11

NANTGWYNANT   MAP 14 SH65

Pen-Y-Gwryd Hotel

LL55 4NT ☎ 01286 870211
dir: *A5 to Capel Curig, left on A4086 to T-junct*

This slate-roofed climbers' pub and rescue post in the heart of Snowdonia has long been the home of British mountaineering. The 1953 Everest team used it as their training base, and etched their signatures on the ceiling. The appetising and inexpensive menus make good use of Welsh lamb and local pork; other options include home-made paté with pickles, salad and crusty bread; or ham and cannellini bean spaghetti with home-made olive and herb flatbread.

Open 11–11 Closed: Nov-1 Jan & mid wk (Jan-Feb) **Bar Meals** L served all week 12–2 **Restaurant** D served all week 7.30–8 ⊕ Free House ◀ Interbrew Bass & Boddingtons Bitter. **Facilities** Garden Dogs allowed Parking Play Area

Wales

TUDWEILIOG
MAP 14 SH23

Lion Hotel ♥
LL53 8ND ☎ 01758 770244 📠 0871 256 5207
dir: *A499 from Caernarfon, B4417 Tudweiliog*

The beach is only a mile away from this friendly inn, run by the Lee family for over 30 years. The large garden and children's play area makes the pub especially popular with the cyclists, walkers and families who flock to the Lleyn Peninsula. The bar features an extensive list of over 80 malt whiskies. A typical menu might consist of Tuscan bean soup, Welsh lamb bake, and rice pudding.

Open 11.30–11 (Sun 12–2 Winter 12–2, 7–11) **Bar Meals** L served all week 12–2 D served all week 6–9 ⊕ Free House ◀ Purple Moose Brewery Ale. ♥ 6 **Facilities** Garden Parking Play Area

WAUNFAWR
MAP 14 SH55

Snowdonia Parc Brewpub & Campsite
LL55 4AQ ☎ 01286 650409 & 650218
e-mail: info@snowdonia-park.co.uk
dir: *Telephone for directions*

This pub stands 400 feet above sea level at Waunfawr Station on the Welsh Highland Railway. There are steam trains on site (the building was originally the stationmaster's house), plus a micro-brewery and campsite. The foot of Mount Snowdon is four miles away. Expect home-cooked food based on locally produced and traditionally reared beef, lamb, chicken and pork. In addition to its own brews, the bar serves guest ales and popular lagers, cider and Guinness. Children and dogs welcome.

Open 11–11 **Bar Meals** L served all week 11–8.30 D served all week 11–8.30 **Restaurant** L served all week 11–8.30 D served all week 11–8.30 ⊕ Free House ◀ Marston's Bitter & Pedigree, Welsh Highand Bitter (ownbrew), Mansfield Dark Mild. **Facilities** Garden Dogs allowed Parking Play Area

MONMOUTHSHIRE

ABERGAVENNY
MAP 09 SO21

Pick of the Pubs

Clytha Arms ♥
Clytha NP7 9BW ☎ 01873 840209 📠 01873 840209
e-mail: theclythaarms@tiscali.co.uk
dir: *From A449/A40 junction (E of Abergavenny) follow signs for 'Old Road Abergavenny/Clytha'*

After 15 years at the Clytha Arms, Andrew and Beverley Canning are opening up the kitchen and investing in a wood-burning Aga to make their own bread and cut down on carbon emissions. Formerly a dower house, this family-run free house now functions as both an informal pub and an outstanding restaurant. Wild boar, mutton and poultry come from nearby Madgetts Organic Farm, whilst Andrew and Beverley are growing more herbs and vegetables in their large garden. Expect mixed Clytha grill with bubble and squeak; goat's cheese with asparagus soufflé; and lemon sole goujons with fennel coleslaw and salad. Felinfoel and Rhymney ales are joined by an ever-changing selection of guest beers, and there's also a good choice of wines by the glass. The inn is surrounded by two acres of lawns and gardens – perfect for an al fresco supper in the sun.

Open 12–3 6–12 (Fri-Sat 12–12, Sun 12–10.30) Closed: 25 Dec & Mon lunch **Bar Meals** L served Tue-Sun 12.30–2.15 D served Mon-Sat 7–9.30 Av main course £10 **Restaurant** L served Tue-Sun 12.30–2.15 D served Mon-Sun 7–9.30 Av 3 course à la carte £31 Av 3 course fixed price £23 ⊕ Free House ◀ Felinfoel Double Dragon, Hook Norton, Rhymer Bitter & 3 guest ales (300+ per year). ♥ 10 **Facilities** Garden Dogs allowed Parking Play Area

CHEPSTOW   MAP 04 ST59

Castle View Hotel ★★ HL ⚐

16 Bridge St NP16 5EZ ☎ 01291 620349 🗎 01291 627397
e-mail: castleviewhotel@btconnect.com
dir: *Opposite Chepstow Castle*

This hotel was built as a private house some 300 years ago, and has solid walls up to five feet thick in places. It stands opposite the castle, alongside the River Wye, and has a lovely secluded walled garden. Food choices include cold options such as sandwiches, ploughman's and baguettes, plus omelettes and full meals – perhaps duck and orange paté with chilli dressing followed by lamb cutlets with parsnip purée.

Bar Meals L served all week 12–2.30 D served all week 6.30–9.30 (Sun 12–3, 7–9) Av main course £9 **Restaurant** D served all week 6.30–9.30 ⊕ Free House 🍺 Wye Valley Real Ale, Double Dragon, Felinfuel Best Bitter. **Facilities** Garden Dogs allowed Parking **Rooms** 13

LLANGYBI   MAP 09 ST39

Pick of the Pubs

The White Hart Village Inn NEW

NP15 1NP ☎ 01633 450258
e-mail: info@whitehartvillageinn.com
dir: *M4 junct 25 onto B4596 Caerleon road, through town centre on High St, straight over rdbt onto Usk Rd continue to Llangybi*

This sensitively restored inn, located in the beautiful Usk Vale, was built in the 12th century. In the early 1500s it became the property of Henry VIII as part of Jane Seymour's wedding dowry, and a century later Oliver Cromwell is reputed to have used it as his headquarters in Gwent. Inside, fireplaces from the 12th- and 16th-century survive, alongside ancient beams, plasterwork and a priest's hole. For years, students of English literature where puzzled by a couple of lines from T S Eliot's poem Usk: 'Do not hope to find the White Hart behind the white well …' Only recently has it been established that Eliot was referring not to any animal but to this very pub, which stands not far from the (once white) village well. A good choice of food includes Welsh rib-eye steak; slow-roasted Welsh lamb shank; hand-made faggots; and fisherman's pie.

Open 11.30–3 5.30–11 (Sun 11.30–6) Closed: Mon **Bar Meals** L served Tue-Sat 12–2 D served Tue-Sat 6–9.30 (Sun 12–3) Av main course £9.50 **Restaurant** L served Tue-Sat 12–2 D served Tue-Sat 6–9.30 (Sun 12–3) 🍺 Timothy Taylor Landlord, Rhymney Brewery Bevan's Bitter, Hobby Horse, Wye Valley Butty Bach & Old Speckled Hen. **Facilities** Garden Parking

LLANTRISANT   MAP 09 ST39

Pick of the Pubs

The Greyhound Inn ⚐

NP15 1LE ☎ 01291 672505 & 673447 🗎 01291 673255
e-mail: enquiry@greyhound-inn.com
dir: *From M4 take A449 towards Monmouth, 1st junct to Usk, left onto Usk Sq. Take 2nd left signed Llantrisant, 2.5m to inn*

During the 17th century this traditional Welsh longhouse oversaw a 400-acre farm estate; then in 1845 the milk parlour was converted into an inn. Over the decades land was sold off, and by 1980 the whole complex was in a sorry state, as pictures hanging in the Cocktail and Llangibby lounges bear witness. Today, after a quarter of a century in the same family's hands, the Greyhound has two acres of award-winning gardens, a four-acre paddock, and an array of restored outbuildings. Owner Nick Davies heads the kitchen team, serving customers in the relaxed lounges or more formal candle-lit dining room. The regular menu is complemented by a daily specials blackboard offering unusual and seasonal dishes. Otherwise choose from well-prepared standards such as deep-fried breaded brie wedges or whitebait; home-made chicken curry, or chilli con carne; and fish in the form of grilled local trout or battered plaice.

Open 11–11 (Sun 12–4, 7–11) Closed: 25 & 31 Dec, 1 Jan **Bar Meals** L served all week 12–2.15 D served Mon-Sat 6–10 **Restaurant** L served all week 12–2.15 D served Mon-Sat 6–10.30 ⊕ Free House 🍺 Interbrew Flowers Original & Bass, Greene King Abbot Ale & guest ale. ⚐ 10 **Facilities** Garden Parking

Wales

LLANVAIR DISCOED   MAP 09 ST49

Pick of the Pubs

The Woodland Restaurant & Bar ♥

NP16 6LX ☎ 01633 400313 📄 01633 400313

e-mail: lausnik@aol.co.uk

dir: *5m from Caldicot & Magor*

This old inn has been extended to accommodate a growing number of diners, but remains at heart a friendly, family-run village local serving a good range of beers. The pub is located close to the Roman fortress town of Caerwent and Wentworth's forest and reservoir. Its nickname, 'the war office' recalls the fact that Irish navvies building the reservoir used to hold bare-knuckle fights here. A varied menu of freshly prepared dishes caters for all tastes from ciabatta bread with various toppings to seared fillets of sea bream, crayfish risotto and buttered samphire; and devilled Cornish mackerel with tomato, onion and basil salad. Meat is sourced from a local butcher who slaughters all his own meat, and the fish is mostly from Cornwall. Various guest ales back up a regular supply of Felinfoel Double Dragon and Tomas Watkins OSB.

Open 11–3 6–11 (Sun 12–3) Closed: Sun eve & Mon
Bar Meals L served Tue-Sat 12–2 D served Tue-Sat 6–10 (Sun 12–3) Av main course £7.95 **Restaurant** L served Tue-Sat 12–2 D served Tue-Sat 6–9.30 (Sun 12–3, fixed price menu only) Av 3 course à la carte £22 Av 2 course fixed price £9.95 ⊕ Free House ◀ Brains, Felinfoel Double Dragon, Tomas Watkins OSB, guest ales. ♥ 8 **Facilities** Dogs allowed Parking

MAMHILAD   MAP 09 SO30

Pick of the Pubs

Horseshoe Inn NEW ♥

NP4 8QZ ☎ 01873 880542

e-mail: horseshoe@artizanleisure.com

dir: *A4042 Pontypool to Abergavenny road, at Mamhilad estate rdbt take 1st exit onto Old Abergavenny Rd. 2m over canal bridge on right*

One of the Artizan Collection, a small group of historic country inns dedicated to the Slow Food movement set up to counteract fast food and the disappearance of local food traditions. The kitchen is headed by Wales Culinary Olympic team member Kurt Flemming, whose weekly-changing menus support the movement's philosophy of working with local suppliers. Typical dishes are grilled whole sea bass with confit of lemon and dill dressing, and minted new potatoes; steak and stilton baguette with chips; goat's cheese, pepper and leek

strudel and tomato and basil sauce; Thai chicken curry with fragrant rice; steak and stout pie with mushrooms; and roasted rump of lamb with minted mash and braised leeks.

Open 12–3 5.30–11 (Fri-Sun all day) **Bar Meals** L served all week 12–2.30 D served Mon-Sat 6.30–9.30 Av main course £9 **Restaurant** L served all week 12.30–2.30 D served Mon-Sat 6.30–9.30 Av 3 course à la carte £33 ⊕ Free House ◀ Abbot Ale, London Pride, Rymney Bitter, Guest ales. ♥ 10 **Facilities** Children's licence Garden Dogs allowed Parking

PENALLT   MAP 04 SO51

The Boat Inn

Lone Ln NP25 4AJ ☎ 01600 712615 📄 01600 719120

dir: *From Monmouth take A466. In Redbrook, pub car park signed. Access by foot across rail bridge over River Wye*

Dating back over 360 years, this riverside pub has served as a hostelry for quarry, mill, paper and tin mine workers, and even had a landlord operating a ferry across the Wye at shift times. The unspoilt slate floor is testament to the age of the place. The excellent selection of real ales and local ciders complements the menu well, with choices ranging from various ploughman's to lamb steffados or the charmingly-named pan haggerty. Ideal for walkers taking the Offa's Dyke or Wye Valley walks.

Open 11–11 (Sun 12–10.30) **Bar Meals** L served all week 12–2.30 D served all week 6–9 (Sun 12–3 winter, Sat-Sun 12–9 summer) Av main course £5 ⊕ Free House ◀ Freeminer Bitter, Wadworth 6X, Abbot Ale & Old Speckled Hen, Wye Valley Butty Bach. **Facilities** Garden Dogs allowed Parking

RAGLAN   MAP 09 SO40

Pick of the Pubs

The Beaufort Arms Coaching Inn & Restaurant ★★★ HL ♥

High St NP15 2DY ☎ 01291 690412 📄 01291 690935

e-mail: enquiries@beaufortraglan.co.uk

dir: *0.5m from junct of A40 and A449 Abergavenny/ Monmouth*

This atmospheric inn, nestling between the Wye Valley and the Usk, dates from the 15th century. It was used by Parliamentarian soldiers during the Siege of Raglan Castle in 1646, and was later an important staging post on the London to Fishguard road. The beautifully refurbished interior still resonates with history: the large stone fireplace in the lounge allegedly came from the castle, and locals believe a stash of vintage champagne lies hidden in tunnels beneath the inn. Expect excellent ales, continental lagers and food served in the bar, lounge and restaurant. The daytime menu offers paninis, sandwiches, prime Welsh steak, beer battered catch of the day, wild mushroom risotto, and seared leg of chicken with chorizo mousse and braised lentils. There are light meals in the evening too, doubling as starters (chicken Caesar salad, salmon and smoked haddock fishcakes), and mains like slow roasted herb crusted loin of pork.

Open 7–11 (Sat 8–11, Sun 8–10.30) **Bar Meals** L served all week 12–5 D served Mon-Thu 6–9 (Fri-Sat 6–9.30, Sun 6–8.30, Summer all day) Av main course £8.95 **Restaurant** L served all week 12–3 D served Mon-Thu 6–9 (Fri-Sat 6–9.30, Sun 6–8.30) Av 3 course à la carte £23 ⊕ Free House ◀ London Pride, Reverend James, Warsteiner & Old Speckled Hen. ♀ 12 **Facilities** Garden Parking **Rooms** 15

SHIRENEWTON MAP 09 ST49

The Carpenters Arms

Usk Rd NP16 6BU ☎ 01291 641231 🖹 01291 641231

dir: M48 junct 2, A48 to Chepstow then A4661, B4235. Village 3m on left

A 400-year-old hostelry, formerly a smithy and carpenter's shop, with flagstone floors, open fires and antiques. It's set in a pleasant wooded location in the valley of the Mounton Brook which lies between the bigger valleys of the Wye and Usk. Straightforward bar food is typified by chicken in leek and stilton sauce, steak and mushroom pie, smoked haddock and potato pie, guinea fowl in orange sauce, and lamb rogan josh. New owners.

Open 11–11 **Bar Meals** L served all week 12–2 D served all week 7–9.30 Av main course £6.95 **Restaurant** L served all week 12–9.30 D served all week 12–9.30 Av 3 course à la carte £12 ⊕ Punch Taverns ◀ Fuller's London Pride, Wadworth 6X, Marston's Pedigree, Theakston Old Peculier. **Facilities** Children's licence Dogs allowed Parking

---

SKENFRITH MAP 09 SO42

The Bell at Skenfrith ★ ★ ★ ★ ★ RR

⊛ ⊛ ♀

NP7 8UH ☎ 01600 750235 🖹 01600 750525
e-mail: enquiries@skenfrith.co.uk
dir: M4 junct 24 onto A449. Exit onto A40, through tunnel & lights. At rdbt take 1st exit, right at lights onto Hereford Rd. Left onto B4521 towards Abergavenny, 3m on left

From its setting by the historic arched bridge over the River Morrow, this 17th-century coaching inn has views of Skenfrith Castle. An oak bar, flagstone floors, comfortable sofas and old settles provide plenty of character, and there are eight well-equipped bedrooms, some with four-poster beds. The pub flies the flag for superb food and drink. Guest real ales, hand-pumped local cider and wines by the glass are a treat in themselves. Locally sourced and mainly organic ingredients are used in dishes offered from a daily menu. One day's selection might include roast local woodcock with pancetta and mushroom dumplings, sautéed spinach and winter vegetable broth, followed by pan-roasted fillet of sea bass with green olive and herb crushed new potatoes, baby leeks, fine ratatouille and basil pesto. Hot chocolate fondant with vanilla ice cream and crème anglaise would be a fitting finale, or a selection of Neal's Yard cheeses.

Open 11–11 Closed: Last wk Jan & 1st wk Feb **Bar Meals** L served all week 12–2.30 D served Mon-Sat 7–9.30 (Sun 7–9) **Restaurant** L served all week 12–2.30 D served Mon-Sat 7–9.30 (Sun 7–9) ⊕ Free House ◀ Golden Valley, Timothy Taylor Landlord, St Austell Tribute. ♀ 13 **Facilities** Garden Dogs allowed Parking **Rooms** 11

TINTERN PARVA
MAP 04 SO50

Fountain Inn
Trellech Grange NP16 6QW
☎ 01291 689303 🖹 01291 689303
e-mail: thefountaininn@msn.com
dir: *From M48 junct 2 follow Chepstow then Tintern signs. In Tintern turn by George Hotel for Raglan. Bear right, inn at top of hill*

A fire nearly destroyed this fine old inn, but the thick 17th-century walls survived the flames, and its character remains unspoilt. It enjoys views of the Wye Valley from the garden, and is close to Tintern Abbey. Home-cooked food includes grilled sardines with balsamic vinegar and cherry tomatoes; leek and Caerphilly sausages with onion gravy; and beef and Guinness pie. Also a good selection of steaks, omelettes, and seafood choices.

Open 12–3 6.30–11 **Bar Meals** L served all week 12–2.30 D served all week 7–9.15 **Restaurant** L served all week 12–2.30 D served all week 7–9.15 ⊕ Free House ◀ Hook Norton, Spinning Dog, Ring of Bells, Interbrew Bass. **Facilities** Garden Dogs allowed Parking

TREDUNNOCK
MAP 09 ST39

Pick of the Pubs

The Newbridge ♥
NP15 1LY ☎ 01633 451000 🖹 01633 451001
e-mail: newbridge@evanspubs.co.uk
dir: *M4 junct 24/26 from Usk take road towards Llangybi. 0.5m, turn left for Tredunnock. Pub in 800yds*

The Newbridge occupies an idyllic riverside location: to be there in the early morning and watch the mist over the river is magical. The decor is warm and welcoming, with comfortable sofas and subtle lighting. Head Chef Iain Sampson has worked in some of the country's finest kitchens and the quality and consistency of his modern British with Mediterranean-influenced food is well reflected in exciting seasonal menus, based extensively on local produce. Expect a typical meal of Welsh oak-smoked haddock risotto with parmesan wafer and herb oil; mustard-crusted rack of local Penperlleni lamb with fondant potatoes and carved vegetables; and banana Tatin with caramel ice cream. Dinner could be watercress, spinach and goats' cheese tart with beetroot coulis; Gloucestershire Old Spot pork loin with potato cake, baby vegetables and buttered tarragon jus; and home-made ice cream. The day's catch, purchased from the quayside in Cornwall, is displayed on the specials board. New landlord for 2008.

Open 12–2.30 6.30–9.30 (Sun 12–3, 6.30–8.30) **Bar Meals** L served all week 12–2.30 D served all week 6–9.30 (Sun 12–3, 6.30–8.30) **Restaurant** L served all week 12–2.30 D served all week 6–9.30 (Sun 12–3, 6.30–8.30) ⊕ Free House ◀ Hancock's HB, Brains Rev James, Brains Smooth & guest ale. ♥ 12 **Facilities** Garden Parking

TRELLECH
MAP 04 SO50

Pick of the Pubs

The Lion Inn
NP25 4PA ☎ 01600 860322 🖹 01600 860060
e-mail: debs@globalnet.co.uk
dir: *From A40 S of Monmouth take B4293, follow signs for Trellech. From M8 junct 2, straight across rdbt, 2nd left at 2nd rdbt, B4293 to Trellech*

Once an Elizabethan stone pig cot, this multi-award-winning pub has also been a coaching inn and a brewhouse. Much effort has been made to preserve that authentic sense of history. There are beams and open fires in both bar and restaurant, and all the accoutrements of the traditional English pub have been maintained: hearty wholesome grub, traditional beers, ciders and games, and no plastic flowers, jukebox, or gaming machines. But homage to tradition is not total, since authentic Hungarian dishes are also served, like Kecskemét stuffed chicken, in which chicken breast is stuffed with apricots, cherries and cheese, then wrapped in bacon. Keep an eye out too for the Back to the Earth board, which touts such hedgerow-foraged foodstuffs as nettle soup; wild mushroom stroganoff; or pan-fried puffball and bacon. Unusual spirits are a house speciality, especially for absinthe and Hungarian plum brandy.

Open 12–3 6–11 (Mon 7–11, Thu-Sat 6–12, Sat all day summer) Closed: Sun eve **Bar Meals** L served Mon-Fri 12–2 D served Mon-Sat 6–9.30 (Sat-Sun 12–2.30) Av main course £9 **Restaurant** L served Mon-Fri 12–2 D served Mon-Sat 6–9.30 (Sat-Sun 12–2.30) Av 3 course à la carte £23 ⊕ Free House ◀ Bath Ales, Wye Valley Butty Bach, Sharp's Cornish Coaster, Rhymney Best. **Facilities** Garden Dogs allowed Parking

USK
MAP 09 SO30

The Nags Head Inn ♥
Twyn Square NP15 1BH ☎ 01291 672820 🖹 01291 672720
dir: *On A472*

This 15th-century coaching inn overlooks the square just a short stroll from the River Usk, and boasts magnificent hanging flower baskets. The traditional bar is furnished with polished tables and chairs, and decorated with collections of horse brasses, farming tools and lanterns hanging from exposed oak beams. Game in season figures strongly among the speciality dishes, including whole stuffed partridge (one of the hardest birds to shoot), pheasant in port, and wild boar steak with apricot and brandy sauce. There is a good choice for vegetarians, too, such as Glamorgan sausage filled with cheese and leek and served with a chilli relish.

Open 10–2.30 5.30–11 Closed: 25 Dec **Bar Meals** L served Mon-Sat 10–2 D served Mon-Sat 5.30–9.30 (Sun 12–2, 6–9.30) **Restaurant** L served all week 11.30–2 D served all week 5.30–10.30 ⊕ Free House ◀ Brains Bitter, Dark, Buckleys Best, Reverend James & Bread of Heaven. ♥ 8 **Facilities** Garden Dogs allowed Parking

Raglan Arms ◉ ♥

Llandenny NP15 1DL ☎ 01291 690800 📠 01291 690155
e-mail: raglanarms@aol.com
dir: Monmouth A449 to Raglan, left in village

Giles Cunliffe and Charlott Fagergard have put their own stamp on the Raglan Arms since taking over three years ago, offering well-cooked modern British food from local ingredients. Whilst the choice of dishes is fairly small, menus are changed daily and a good selection of Welsh and English cheeses supports a well-chosen range of starters, mains and puddings. At lunchtime, expect open sandwiches, too: slow-roast pork with apples, perhaps, or smoked salmon with rocket and horseradish.

Open 12–3 6.30–9.30 Closed: Sun eve & Mon **Bar Meals** L served Tue-Sun 12–3 D served Tue-Sat 6.30–9.30 **Restaurant** L served Tue-Sun 12–3 D served Tue-Sat 6.30–9.30 ◀ Wye Valley Bitter, Butty Bach & Guinness. ♥ 12 **Facilities** Garden Parking

PEMBROKESHIRE

ABERCYCH   MAP 08 SN24

Nags Head Inn NEW

SA37 0HJ ☎ 01239 841200
dir: On B4332 Carmarthen to Newcastle Emlyn

Crossing into Pembrokeshire from the Teifi Falls at Cenarth, the Nag's Head is the first building you see over the county boundary. The famous old inn, with its beamed bars and riverside gardens, is located at the entrance to an enchanted valley immortalised in Welsh folklore. Old Emrys Ale is brewed on the premises and good food options include coracle caught Teifi sewin; hungry farmer's mixed grill; and home-made faggots with chips and mushy peas.

Open 11.30–3 6–11.30 Closed: Mon **Bar Meals** L served Tue-Sun 12–2 D served Tue-Sun 6–9 Av main course £7.50 **Restaurant** L served Sun 12–2 D served Tue-Sun 6–9 ⊕ Free House ◀ Old Emrys. **Facilities** Children's licence Garden Dogs allowed Parking Play Area

AMROTH   MAP 08 SN10

The New Inn

SA67 8NW ☎ 01834 812368
dir: A48 to Carmarthen, A40 to St Clears, A477 to Llanteg then left

A 400–year-old inn, originally a farmhouse, belonging to Amroth Castle Estate. It has old world charm with beamed ceilings, a Flemish chimney, a flagstone floor and an inglenook fireplace. It is close to the beach, and local lobster and crab are a feature, along with a popular choice of home-made dishes including steak and kidney pie, soup and curry. Enjoy food or drink outside on the large lawn complete with picnic benches.

Open 11–11 Closed: Nov-Mar **Bar Meals** L served all week 12–9 D served all week **Restaurant** L served all week 12–9 D served all

week ⊕ Free House ◀ Brains, Tetley Bitter, Speckled Hen & guest ales. **Facilities** Garden Dogs allowed Parking **Notes** ⊛

CAREW   MAP 08 SN00

Carew Inn

SA70 8SL ☎ 01646 651267
e-mail: mandy@carewinn.co.uk
dir: From A477 take A4075. Inn 400yds opp castle & Celtic cross

A traditional stone-built country inn situated opposite the Carew Celtic cross and Norman castle. Enjoy the one-mile circular walk around the castle and millpond. A good range of bar meals includes Welsh black steak and kidney pie; chilli con carne; Thai red chicken curry; and seafood pancakes. Fruit crumble and old favourite jam roly poly feature among the puddings. Live music every Thursday night under the marquee.

Open 11–11 Closed: 25 Dec **Bar Meals** L served all week 11.30–2 D served all week 5.30–9 Av main course £8.50 **Restaurant** L served all week 11.30–2 D served all week 5.30–9 Av 3 course à la carte £15 ⊕ Free House ◀ Worthington Best, SA Brains Reverend James & guest ales. **Facilities** Garden Dogs allowed Parking Play Area

CILGERRAN   MAP 08 SN14

Pendre Inn

Pendre SA43 2SL ☎ 01239 614223
dir: Off A478 south of Cardigan

Dating back to the 14th century, this is a pub full of memorabilia and featuring exposed interior walls, old beams, slate flooring and an inglenook fireplace. An ancient ash tree grows through the pavement in front of the white stone, thick-walled building. Typical menu includes lamb steaks with red wine and cherries, rump and sirloin steaks, pork loin with honey and mustard glaze, and salmon with hollandaise.

Open 12 -11 **Bar Meals** L served Wed-Sun 12–2 D served Wed-Sun 6–8.30 Av main course £6 **Restaurant** L served Wed-Sun 12–2 D served Wed-Sun 6–8 Av 3 course à la carte £12 ⊕ Free House ◀ Tomas Watkins, OSB, Murphys, Worthington. **Facilities** Garden Parking

Wales

Wales

HAVERFORDWEST MAP 08 SM91

Pick of the Pubs

The Georges Restaurant/Cafe Bar ☕

24 Market St SA61 1NH

☎ 01437 766683 📠 01437 760345

e-mail: llewis6140@aol.com

dir: *In town centre*

Formerly George's Brewery, this remarkable 18th-century building incorporates many original features in its restored vaulted cellar and eating areas. Its delightful walled garden, with spectacular views over the ruins of 12th-century Haverfordwest Castle, has outdoor heating for chillier days and evenings. Genuine local character is a feature of the all-day café bar and cellar bistro, where freshly-prepared food and sheer enthusiasm sets it apart from the norm. An extensive range of home-made dishes is served all day in the Celtic-themed restaurant. Given the proximity of the sea, there are plenty of fish dishes including crab cakes, black bream, poached turbot and scallops. Locally-sourced meat appears in choices such as Welsh venison steak with a rich port and berry sauce; Welsh lamb-steak with red wine, mushroom and fresh mint sauce; and Pembrokeshire sausage pie with mashed potatoes and rich onion gravy topped with toasted cheese. For those whose tastebuds are tickled by the exotic, George's Creole rump steak is marinated in Cajun spices with a hot chilli and ginger sauce. Among over a dozen vegetarian options are spinach and cream cheese cannelloni with traditional tomato sauce, topped with béchamel and Welsh cheddar; and garlic mushrooms in flaky pastry with a creamy sauce.

Open 10–5.30 (Sat 10.30–11) Closed: 25 Dec, 1 Jan **Bar Meals** L served Mon-Sat 12–5.30 D served Fri-Sat 6–9.45 Av main course £7 **Restaurant** L served Mon-Sat 12–2.30 D served Fri-Sat 6–9.30 Av 3 course à la carte £20 ⊕ Free House ◀ Marston's Pedigree, Wye Valley Bitter, Adnams Broadside, Brains Bitter. ☕ 10 **Facilities** Garden

LAMPHEY MAP 08 SN00

The Dial Inn ☕

Ridegway Rd SA71 5NU ☎ 01646 672426 📠 01646 672426

dir: *Just off A4139 (Tenby to Pembroke road)*

The Dial started life around 1830 as the Dower House for nearby Lamphey Court, and was converted into a pub in 1966. It immediately established itself as a popular village local, and in recent years the owners have extended the dining areas. Food is a real strength, and Pembrokeshire farm products are used whenever possible. You can choose from traditional bar food, the imaginative restaurant menu, or the daily blackboard.

Open 11–3 6–12 **Bar Meals** L served all week 12–3 D served all week 6.30–9.30 **Restaurant** L served all week 12–3 D served all week 6.30–9.30 ⊕ Free House ◀ Coors ale, Runmey Bitter. ☕ 8 **Facilities** Children's licence Garden Parking

LETTERSTON MAP 08 SM92

The Harp Inn ☕

31 Haverfordwest Rd SA62 5UA

☎ 01348 840061 📠 01348 840812

dir: *On A40*

This 15th-century free house was once a working farm, as well as home to a weekly market. After remaining largely unchanged for 500 years, the inn is now firmly grounded in the 21st century with new disabled facilities and a 130–seater restaurant. Two comprehensive menus and a chalkboard offer dishes ranging from grilled sea bass to tenderloin pork in red plum sauce; and Welsh steaks garni to stir-fried vegetables in black bean sauce.

Open 11–3 6–11 (Sun 12–3, 6–10.30) **Bar Meals** L served all week 12–2.30 D served all week 6–9.30 **Restaurant** L served all week 12–2.30 D served all week 6.30–9.30 ⊕ Free House ◀ Tetleys, Greene King, Abbot Ale. ☕ 8 **Facilities** Garden Parking Play Area

LITTLE HAVEN MAP 08 SM81

Pick of the Pubs

The Swan Inn NEW ☕

Point Rd SA62 3UL ☎ 01437 781880 📠 04137 781880

e-mail: enquiries@theswanlittlehaven.co.uk

dir: *From Haverfordwest take B4341 (Broad Haven road). In Broad Haven follow seafront and signs for Little Haven, 0.75m*

This 300–year-old inn has been impeccably renovated but retains its beams, real fires and exposed stone walls. It stands so near the beach that the fisherman who built it could almost have stepped straight into his boat. Cooking is very accomplished, but informal in style. Dishes could include corn-fed chicken and foie gras terrine or dressed Saint Brides crab followed by Welsh rib-eye with béarnaise sauce, red onion confit and chips.

Open 11–3 5–11 (Sat-Sun all day) Closed: Mon (Jan) **Bar Meals** L served Tue-Sun 12.30–2 D served Tue-Sat 7–9 Av main course £9 **Restaurant** L served Tue-Sat 12.30–2 D served Tue-Sat 7–9 (Sun 12.30–2.30) Av 3 course à la carte £28 ◀ Worthington Best Bitter, Brains Reverend James, Timothy Taylor Landlord, Hook Norton Old Hooky. ☕ 8 **Facilities** Children's licence Garden

NEWPORT   MAP 08 SN03

Salutation Inn

Felindre Farchog, Crymych SA41 3UY
☎ 01239 820564 🖹 01239 820355
e-mail: JohnDenley@aol.com
dir: *On A487 between Cardigan and Fishguard*

Set right on the banks of the River Nevern, this 16th-century coaching inn stands in a quiet village in the heart of the Pembrokeshire Coast National Park. Travellers will find a comfortable bar, a lounge and a restaurant. The varied menu might include potted asparagus and smoked Cerwyn cheese, or rustic game paté to start, with perhaps prime fillet of Welsh Black beef on rösti and roasted shallots to follow.

Open 12–12 **Bar Meals** L served all week 12.30–2.30 D served all week 6.30–9.30 Av main course £8.50 **Restaurant** L served all week 12.30–2.30 D served all week 6.30–9.30 ⊕ Free House ◀ Local guest ales, Felinfoel, Brains. **Facilities** Garden Dogs allowed Parking **Rooms** available

---

PEMBROKE DOCK   MAP 08 SM90

Ferry Inn

Pembroke Ferry SA72 6UD ☎ 01646 682947
e-mail: ferryinn@aol.com
dir: *A477, off A48, right at garage, signs for Cleddau Bridge, left at rdbt*

There are fine views across the Cleddau estuary from the terrace of this 16th-century free house. Once the haunt of smugglers, the riverside inn has a nautical-themed bar with a 'great disaster' corner highlighting pictures of local catastrophes! The pub is also said to be haunted. Fresh fish features strongly on the menu: favourites include locally caught trout; salmon fillet with dill butter; and brill with cherry tomatoes and crème frâiche.

Open 12–2.45 7–11 Closed: 25–26 Dec **Bar Meals** L served Mon-Sat 12–2 D served Mon-Sat 7–9.30 (Sun 12–1.30, 7–9) **Restaurant** L served Mon-Sat 12–2 D served Mon-Sat 7–9.30 (Sun 12–1.30, 7–9) ⊕ Free House ◀ Worthington, Bass, Felinfoel Double Dragon, guest ale. **Facilities** Garden Parking

---

PORTHGAIN   MAP 08 SM83

The Sloop Inn ♟

SA62 5BN ☎ 01348 831449 🖹 01348 831388
e-mail: matthew@sloop-inn.freeserve.co.uk
dir: *Take A487 NE from St Davids for 6m. Left at Croesgooch for 2m to Porthgain*

A mere 100 metres from the harbour side at Porthgain, this is the ideal place for watching village activity on the village green including fishermen landing the fish you may well eat for dinner. The Sloop Inn has been in the same hands for 20 years, and the landlord catches most of his own crab, lobster and scallops.

Open 9.30–11 Closed: 25 Dec **Bar Meals** L served all week 12–2.30 D served all week 6–9.30 Av main course £8.50 **Restaurant** L served all week 12–2.30 D served all week 6–9.30 ⊕ Free House ◀ Reverend James, Brains Draught & Felinfoel. ♟ 4 **Facilities** Children's licence Garden Parking

---

ROSEBUSH   MAP 08 SN02

Tafarn Sinc

Preseli SA66 7QT ☎ 01437 532214

High in the Preseli Hills, the looming presence of this large red corrugated-iron free house stands testament to its rapid construction in 1876. Now deserted by the railway it was built to serve, Tafarn Sinc boasts woodburning stoves, a sawdusted floor, and a charming garden. This idiosyncratic establishment is popular with walkers, who can stoke up on traditional favourites like faggots with onion gravy, and Preseli lamb burgers.

Open 12–12 Closed: Mon (ex BHs & Summer) **Bar Meals** L served all week 12–2 D served Tue-Sat 6–9 ◀ Worthington, Tafarn Sinc, guest ale. **Facilities** Garden Dogs allowed Parking

PICK OF THE PUBS

The Stackpole Inn

A now-famous phrase sums up this 17th-century inn – location, location, location. It stands in beautiful gardens within the Pembrokeshire Coast National Park, just 15 minutes walk from the coastal path, Stackpole Quay and Barafundle Bay – described by the Sunday Times as 'a desert island dream beach in Wales'.

In the mellow stone wall outside is a rare King George V post box, a hangover from when one of the two original stone cottages was a post office. It's a freehouse, so there's always a guest beer from elsewhere in the UK to accompany three Welsh ales. The bar surface is made from slate, while the wood for the ceiling beams came from ash trees grown on the estate. Warmth is provided by a wood-burning stove set within the stone fireplace. Local produce from the surrounding countryside and fish from the nearby coast play a major part in the home-cooked menu. From its snack section might come battered cod, chips and peas, a home-made cheeseburger, Thai green curry, or a filled baguette. On the lunch and dinner menu starters include home-cured gravadlax, poached pear salad, and baked camembert. Among the main courses are marinated chicken breast in coriander, lime and honey; Moroccan-style lamb cutlets; and home-made Thai-style fishcakes; and a daily vegetarian dish. Finish with a dessert such as rich chocolate, blackberry and Tia Maria torte, or fresh raspberry brûlée. Specials, which are always available, will include a selection of fresh fish dishes. Bed and breakfast accommodation consists of four high-quality twin/double bed en suite rooms in a separate building in the grounds.

MAP 08 SR99
SA71 5DF
☎ 01646 672324 🖷 01646 672716
e-mail: info@stackpoleinn.co.uk
dir: *From Pembroke take B4319 & follow signs for Stackpole, approx 4m.*

Open 12–2.30 6–11 (Summer 12–3, 5.30–11)
Bar Meals L served all week 12–2 D served all week 6.30–9 (Summer Sat-Sun 12–3, 5.30–9)
Restaurant L served all week 12–2 D served all week 6.30–9 (Summer Sat-Sun 12–3, 5.30–9)
⊕ Free House ◖ Brains Reverend James, Felinfoel, Double Dragon, Best Bitter & Variable guest ale. ☗ 12
Facilities Children's licence Garden Dogs allowed Parking
Rooms available

ST DOGMAELS
MAP 08 SN14

Webley Waterfront Inn & Hotel ⟨wine glass⟩

Poppit Sands SA43 3LN ☎ 01239 612085
e-mail: webleyhotel@btconnect.com
web: www.webleyhotel.com
dir: *A484 from Carmarthen to Cardigan, then to St Dogmaels, right in village centre to Poppit Sands on B4546*

From its spectacular location at the start of the Pembrokeshire Coast National Park, the inn offers outstanding views across the River Teifi and Poppit Sands to Cardigan Bay. Being where it is naturally means fresh seafood, with specialities such as line-caught sea bass, dressed crab and lobster, and Teifi sewin (sea trout), while fresh lamb and beef comes from local farms, and organic ice cream from Mary's Farmhouse in nearby Crymych.

Open 9–11 (Easter to Oct all day) **Bar Meals** L served all week 12–3 D served all week 6–9 Av main course £7.95 **Restaurant** L served all week 12–2.30 D served all week 6–8.30 ⊕ Free House ⟨tankard⟩ Brains Buckleys Bitter, Worthington, Rev James, DSB. ⟨wine glass⟩ 8 **Facilities** Children's licence Garden Dogs allowed Parking

SOLVA
MAP 08 SM82

The Cambrian Inn ⟨wine glass⟩

Main St SA62 6UU ☎ 01437 721210 ▤ 01437 720661
e-mail: thecambrianinn@btconnect.com
dir: *13m from Haverfordwest on A487 towards St David's*

Something of an institution in this pretty fishing village is a Grade II listed 17th-century inn that attracts local and returning visitors alike. A sample bar menu offers Welsh black beef curry, vegetable pancakes topped with melted cheese or Welsh sirloin steak, while the carte dinner menu offers lots of fresh fish dishes. Sandwiches, jackets, salads and ploughman's also available.

Open 10 -11 (Sun 10–10.30) **Bar Meals** L served all week 8–6 D served all week 6–10 **Restaurant** L served all week 8–6 D served all week 6–10 Av 3 course à la carte £25 ⊕ Free House ⟨tankard⟩ Tomas Watkins OSB & Cwrw Braf/Haf, Butty Bach, guest ales. ⟨wine glass⟩ 15 **Facilities** Garden Parking

STACKPOLE
MAP 08 SR99

Pick of the Pubs

The Stackpole Inn ⟨wine glass⟩
See Pick of the Pubs on opposite page

WOLF'S CASTLE
MAP 08 SM92

The Wolfe Inn ⟨wine glass⟩

SA62 5LS ☎ 01437 741662 ▤ 01437 741676
dir: *On A40 between Haverfordwest & Fishguard, (7m from both towns)*

The Wolfe is an oak-beamed, stone-built property in a lovely village setting. The bar-brasserie and restaurant comprise four interconnecting but distinctly different rooms: the Victorian Parlour, Hunters' Lodge, the Brasserie and a conservatory. The inn uses mainly local produce in its 'robust, real food'. Example dishes are fillet of beef Bordelaise, lamb all'aglio e menta, chicken piccante, salmon fillet with cream and Pernod sauce, and mussels in garlic, white wine and cream. Award-winning local cheeses and scrumptious home-made desserts follow.

Open 12–2 6–11 **Bar Meals** L served all week 12–2 D served all week 7–9 Av main course £12 **Restaurant** L served all week 12–2 D served all week 7–9 Av 3 course à la carte £25 Av 3 course fixed price £15 ⊕ Free House ⟨tankard⟩ Interbrew Worthington Bitter, guest ale. ⟨wine glass⟩ 11 **Facilities** Garden Parking

POWYS

BERRIEW
MAP 15 SJ10

The Lion Hotel

SY21 8PQ ☎ 01686 640452 ▤ 01686 640604
e-mail: patrick@okeeffe.demon.co.uk
dir: *5m from Welshpool on A483, right to Berriew. Centre of village next to church.*

Behind the black and white timbered grid of this 17th-century coaching inn lie bars and dining areas where yet more old timbers testify to its age. Menus include loin of venison with pan-fried wild mushrooms and redcurrant jus; slow-roasted Welsh lamb shoulder with red wine mint gravy; leek and mozzarella-filled crîpe with spiced tomato sauce; and a fish board with sea bream, halibut, red snapper and salmon based dishes.

Open 12–3 5–11 (Sat 12–11, Sun 6–10.30) **Bar Meals** L served all week 12–2 D served all week 7–8.45 **Restaurant** L served all week 12–2 D served all week 6–8.45 ⟨tankard⟩ Banks Bitter/Mild, Pedigree, Old Empire. **Facilities** Children's licence Parking

Wales

BRECON   MAP 09 SO02

Pick of the Pubs

The Felin Fach Griffin ★★★★ INN

🌑🌑 🍷

Felin Fach LD3 0UB ☎ 01874 620111 📠 01874 620120
e-mail: enquiries@eatdrinksleep.ltd.uk
dir: *4.5m N of Brecon on the A470 (Brecon to Hay-on-Wye road)*

This much-feted country inn exemplifies owner Charles Inkin's passion for 'the simple things in life done well'. The ethos is applied to food, wines, beers and bedrooms. In the bar are deep leather sofas surrounding a newspaper-strewn table and open fire. Food is served in rambling bare-floored rooms where original features, including an Aga, are teamed with tasteful modern touches. Set on the edge of the Brecon Beacons, the Griffin draws much of its ingredients from the surrounding area, while the garden keeps up a steady flow of organic produce. The freshest seafood could feature as a rich Mediterranean fish soup or wild sea bass with chervil root purée, cep marmalade and red wine butter. Other choices might include gnocchi with wild mushrooms, pumpkin and parmesan, or local Welsh venison with roasted parsnip, parsnip pureé and dauphinoise potato. Finish with superb Welsh cheeses, or vanilla crème brûlée with warm rum grog.

Open 11.30–11 Closed: 24–25 Dec & occasional Mon lunch **Bar Meals** L served Tue-Sat 12.30–2.30 D served Mon-Sat 6.30–9.30 (Sun 12–2.30, 6.30–9) Av main course £12 **Restaurant** L served Tue-Sat 12.30–2.30 D served Mon-Sat 6.30–9.30 (Sun 12–2.30, 6.30–9) Av 3 course à la carte £34 ⊕ Free House ◀ Breckonshire Breweries, Tomas Watkin OSB & Evan Evans. ☂ 10 **Facilities** Garden Dogs allowed Parking **Rooms** 7

The Old Ford Inn NEW ★★★ INN

Llanhamlach LD3 7YB ☎ 01874 665391 📠 01874 665391
e-mail: lynxcymru@aol.com
dir: *2.5m from Brecon town centre on Abergavenny road*

The Old Ford is a 900–year-old inn set in the foothills of the Brecon Beacons, affording outstanding views over the mountains, the River Usk and the canal. The business is family run and offers cosy beamed bars and a restaurant serving home-cooked food using local produce. Chef's specials include Old Ford cow pie, with beef, vegetables and ale under a puffed pastry lid; and braised Welsh lamb shank with mint and rosemary sauce and creamy mash.

Open 12–3 6–12 (Etr-Sep all day) Closed: 3–6 months winter **Bar Meals** L served Tue-Sat 12 D served Tue-Sat 6 (Sun, all day) Av main course £7.95 **Restaurant** L served Tue-Sat 12–3 D served Tue-Sat 6–9 (Sun, all day) ⊕ Free House ◀ Worthington, Guinness. **Facilities** Children's licence Garden Parking **Rooms** 5

Pick of the Pubs

The Usk Inn ★★★★ INN 🌑 🍷

Talybont-on-Usk LD3 7JE
☎ 01874 676251 📠 01874 676392
e-mail: stay@uskinn.co.uk
dir: *6m E of Brecon, just off A40 towards Abergavenny & Crickhowell*

The inn was established in the 1840s, just as the Brecon to Merthyr Railway arrived. In 1878 the locomotive Hercules failed to stop at the former station opposite and crashed into the street, seriously disrupting conversations and beer consumption in the bar. The owner Andrew Felix is making sure you can still partake of interesting food like fried haggis and chilli dressing. This haggis, by the way, is prefixed by the all-important word Celtic. Alternatively, opt for risotto of smoked garlic and porcini mushrooms, then half a honey-roast duck with apricot and tarragon, or a fish special, and home-made treacle tart to finish. The Brecon to Monmouth Canal runs through the village, in some places at rooftop level.

Open 8am-11 Closed: 25–26 Dec **Bar Meals** L served all week 12–3 D served all week 6.30–9 **Restaurant** L served all week 12–3 D served all week 6.30–9 ⊕ Free House ◀ Hancocks HB, Brains, Guinness, Worthington. ☂ 11 **Facilities** Garden Parking **Rooms** 11

Pick of the Pubs

The White Swan Inn 🌑 🍷

Llanfrynach LD3 7BZ
☎ 01874 665276 📠 01874 665362
dir: *3m E of Brecon off A40, take B4558, follow Llanfrynach signs*

The long white-painted frontage of the White Swan overlooks St Brynach's churchyard in the heart of the Brecon Beacons National Park. With its exposed oak beams, stone walls and inglenook fireplace, this is an unpretentious gastro-pub with character and atmosphere. The theme is good quality food using locally sourced produce – Welsh beef, lamb, pork and venison, together with a variety of fish, are all served with fresh seasonal vegetables. Typical main courses could be tenderloin of local pork stuffed with stilton mousse and wrapped in Parma ham; rump of Welsh lamb with a black pudding crust; chargrilled sirloin of Welsh beef with traditional punchnep; and pan-fried supreme of pollack served with ribbons of fresh pasta. The White Swan is especially popular with walkers and cyclists, there's trout fishing on the nearby River Usk, and the Monmouthshire and Brecon Canal runs close by. Brains SA and Brecon County are served at the bar.

Open 12–2 6.30–11 Closed: 25–26 Dec, 1 Jan & Mon (ex BHs summer & Dec) **Bar Meals** L served Tue-Sat 12–2 D served Tue-Sat 7–9.30 (Sun 12–2.30, 7–9) Av main course £9.95 **Restaurant** L served Tue-Sat 12–2 D served Tue-Sat 7–9.30 (Sun 12–2.30, 7–9) Av 3 course à la carte £25 ⊕ Free House 🍺 HB, Brains SA, Brains Smooth, Guinness. ▼ 8 **Facilities** Garden Parking

---

COEDWAY   MAP 15 SJ31

The Old Hand and Diamond Inn

SY5 9AR ☎ 01743 884379 🖷 01743 884379
e-mail: moz123@aol.com
web: www.oldhandanddiamond.co.uk

dir: *9m from Shrewsbury*

Close to the River Severn and the Welsh border, this 17th-century inn retains many original features. Open winter fires crackle in the beamed interior, whilst outside you'll find a children's play area and a beer garden with plenty of seating on the patio. Local produce underpins the extensive restaurant menu, offering dishes like braised venison; corn-fed chicken; and a selection of fresh fish, as well as light bites and the popular lunchtime carvery.

Open 11–11 **Bar Meals** L served Mon-Thu 12–2 D served Mon-Thu 6–9.30 (Fri-Sun 12–9.30) **Restaurant** L served Mon-Thu 12–2 D served Mon-Thu 6–9.30 (Fri-Sun 12–9.30) ⊕ Free House 🍺 Bass, Worthington, Shropshire Lad & guest ales. **Facilities** Garden Dogs allowed Parking Play Area

---

CRICKHOWELL   MAP 09 SO21

Pick of the Pubs

The Bear Hotel ★★★ HL ◉ ▼

See Pick of the Pubs on page 754

Pick of the Pubs

Nantyffin Cider Mill ◉ ▼

Brecon Rd NP8 1SG ☎ 01873 810775 🖷 01873 810986
e-mail: info@cidermill.co.uk

dir: *At junct of A40 & A479, 1.5m west of Crickhowell*

Originally a drovers' inn, located at the foot of the Black Mountains between Crickhowell and Brecon, the Nantyffin dates from the 16th century. It became well known for the cider it produced in the 19th century and the original cider press, fully working until the 1960s, has been incorporated into the Mill Room Restaurant. These days the Nantyffin is renowned for its successful pairing of traditional pub values with acclaimed French bistro-style food. The bars are full of character and offer a range of ales, draught and bottled Welsh ciders, and a comprehensive wine list. Menus are based on locally sourced produce such as beef, pork, lamb and poultry from a farm only six miles away. Under new stewardship for 2008.

Open 12–3 6–11 Closed: Mon (Oct-Mar ex BH) **Bar Meals** L served Tue-Sun 12–2.30 D served Tue-Sun 6.30–9.30 **Restaurant** L served Tue-Sun 12–2.30 D served Tue-Sun 6.30–9.30 Av 3 course à la carte £20 ⊕ Free House 🍺 Reverend James, Rhymney Best Bitter. ▼ 12 **Facilities** Garden Dogs allowed Parking

Wales

PICK OF THE PUBS

The Bear Hotel

A quaint and comfortable 15th-century coaching inn, The Bear has been restored and maintained to a high standard and continues to provide rest and refreshment in the centuries' old tradition. Some of the bedrooms may still have four-posters, but these days they also have en suite facilities and even Jacuzzis.

The hotel is located in Crickhowell, a delightful little market town set amid the hills of the Brecon Beacons National Park. There are two dining rooms, the first with oak beams, stone walls and a flagstone floor; while the other is smaller, with candles, flowers and lace tablecloths. Cooking is modern British but the trend is towards the wholesome dishes of the past. Slow cooking is a long established practice here, and wherever possible locally produced ingredients are used. Welsh lamb is always a favourite, offered alongside Usk and Wye salmon, and local game is also used to advantage. From time to time a selection of popular dishes from other countries is introduced. Hand-pulled ales are served in the bar, locally brewed where possible,

and seasonal guest ales feature. The bar bistro goes from strength to strength, offering comfort foods and more country-style items, such as slow roast lamb shank; Welsh Champion sausages; braised belly pork with lentils; baked salmon fillet; Welsh lamb shank; smoked haddock fishcakes; Welsh black beef steaks and home-made faggots. Vegetarian meals are always listed, and a daily specials board adds to the choice. The Bear also has a charming small garden where you can sit with a drink or have a meal, and listen to the birds.

★★★ HL ◎◎♥
MAP 09 SO21
Brecon Rd NP8 1BW
☎ 01873 810408
🖷 01873 811696
e-mail: bearhotel@aol.com
dir: *On A40 between Abergavenny & Brecon (6m)*

Open 11–3 6–11 (Sun 12–3, 7–10.30)
Bar Meals L served all week 12–2 D served Mon-Sat 6–10 (Sun 12–2, 7–9.30)
Restaurant L served Tue-Sat 12–2 D served Tue-Sat 7–9.30
Av 3 course à la carte £30
⊕ Free House ◀ Interbrew Bass, Ruddles Best, Evans & Jones (Premium Welsh), Brains Reverend James. ♥ 12
Facilities Children's licence Garden Dogs allowed Parking
Rooms 35

DYLIFE   MAP 14 SN89

Star Inn ★★ INN

SY19 7BW ☎ 01650 521345 🖺 01650 521345

dir: *Between Llanidloes & Machynlleth on mountain road*

Situated at 1300 feet in some of Wales' most breathtaking countryside, the inn is in an area favoured by Dylan Thomas and Wynford Vaughn Thomas; red kites swoop overhead, and the magnificent Clywedog reservoir is close by. A varied choice of wholesome pub fare includes cottage pie, big banger and chips, chicken in mushroom cream sauce, and gammon with egg or pineapple. Between November and March the inn is not open for weekday lunch.

Open 12–2.30 7–10 Closed: Winter Mon–Fri lunch **Bar Meals** L served all week 12–2.30 D served all week 7–10 **Restaurant** L served all week 12–2 D served Mon–Sat 7–10 (Sun 7–9) ⊕ Free House ⬛ Tetley Smooth, Abbots. **Facilities** Children's licence Dogs allowed Parking **Rooms** 2

GLADESTRY   MAP 09 SO25

The Royal Oak Inn ♀

HR5 3NR ☎ 01544 370669 & 370342

dir: *4m W of Kington, 10m from Hay-on-Wye on B4594*

The huge inglenook fireplace, heavily beamed ceilings and a flagstone floor set a scene befitting a 300–year-old inn that once welcomed drovers travelling between Kington and Painscastle. The Offa's Dyke footpath is nearby, and Hay-on-Wye is a 12–mile trek away. Meals include home-made soup; steak and stout pie; three bean chilli; and Greek salad pizza.

Open 12–3 7–11 **Bar Meals** L served Tue–Sat 12–2 D served Tue–Sat 7–9 Av main course £8 **Restaurant** L served Tue–Sun 12–2 D served Tue–Sat 7–9 Av 3 course à la carte £16 ⊕ Free House ⬛ Hancocks HB, Brains Reverend James, Butty Bach, S A. ♀ 8 **Facilities** Garden Dogs allowed Parking

HAY-ON-WYE   MAP 09 SO24

Kilverts Hotel ♀

The Bullring HR3 5AG ☎ 01497 821042 🖺 01497 821580

e-mail: info@kilverts.co.uk

dir: *From A50 take A49, then left onto B4348 into Hay-on-Wye. Pub in town centre near Butter Market*

A timber-framed, olde worlde style bar, offering a range of local beers. The gardens have lawns and flower beds with a pond and fountain, as well as a pavement terrace at the front. Pizza and pasta menus are supplemented by daily specials offering fresh fish and local lamb dishes, as well as the carte. There's a new landlady for 2008.

Open 8 -11.30 (Fri–Sat 8–12.30) **Bar Meals** L served all week 12–2.30 D served all week 6–9.30 (Sat–Sun all day May–Sep) Av main course £8.95 **Restaurant** D served all week 6.30–9.30 Av 3 course à la carte £25 ⊕ Free House ⬛ Wye Valley Butty Bach, Brains Cream Flow & Hancock's HB, The Reverend James. ♀ 7 **Facilities** Garden Dogs allowed Parking **Rooms** available

Pick of the Pubs

The Old Black Lion ★★★★ INN ⚫ ♀

See Pick of the Pubs on page 756

LLANDRINDOD WELLS   MAP 09 SO06

The Gold Bell Country Inn

Llanyre LD1 6DX ☎ 01597 823959 🖺 01597 823959

dir: *1.5m NW of Llandrindod Wells on A4081*

New owners have just completed a complete refit of this former drovers' inn set in the hills above Llandrindod Wells. Two bars and a restaurant serve a range of beers and seasonally changing menus. Bar food embraces jacket potatoes, baguettes, and the likes of Welsh lamb shank on creamed mash; or turkey, ham and mushroom pie. Head for the conservatory restaurant for fillet of beef wrapped in smoked bacon, or line-caught rainbow trout on a potato cake.

Open 7am-1.30am **Bar Meals** L served all week 12–2 D served Mon–Sat 6–9 (Sun ex Winter) **Restaurant** L served all week 12–2 D served Mon–Sat 6–9 (Sun ex Winter) ⊕ Free House ⬛ Brain's, Hancock's, guest ales. **Facilities** Garden Parking Play Area

LLANFYLLIN   MAP 15 SJ11

Cain Valley Hotel ★★ HL

High St SY22 5AQ ☎ 01691 648366 🖺 01691 648307

e-mail: info@cainvalleyhotel.co.uk

dir: *From Shrewsbury & Oswestry follow signs for Lake Vyrnwy & onto A490 to Llanfyllin. Hotel on right*

Family-run coaching inn dating from the 17th century, with a stunning Jacobean staircase, oak-panelled lounge bar and a heavily beamed restaurant with exposed hand-made bricks. A full bar menu is available at lunchtime and in the evening. Local lamb steak with red wine and rosemary sauce, vegetable risotto, prime steak braised in real ale, and salmon fillet in a dill butter and lemon sauce may be on the menu.

Open 11.30–12 (Sun 12–11) Closed: 25 Dec **Bar Meals** L served all week 12–2 D served all week 7–9 **Restaurant** L served all week 12–2 D served all week 7–9 ⊕ Free House ⬛ Worthingtons, Ansells Mild, Guinness & Tetleys. **Facilities** Dogs allowed Parking **Rooms** 13

Wales

PICK OF THE PUBS

The Old Black Lion

Expect a warm welcome and a tranquil atmosphere at this charming old inn, close to the centre of Hay-on-Wye. Parts of this historic building date back to the 1300s, but structurally most of it is 17th century. It stands on Lion Street, near the site of the Lion Gate, one of the original entrances to the walled town of Hay-on-Wye.

With the Brecon Beacons to the west and the Black Mountains to the south, Hay is the world's largest second-hand book centre, with bookshops at every turn. It also hosts a renowned annual literary festival and marks the crossing point of the Offa's Dyke Path and the Wye Valley Walk. Oliver Cromwell is reputed to have stayed at the inn during the siege of Hay Castle, although he would not have found a teddy bear in his room as guests do today. The oak-timbered bar is furnished with scrubbed pine tables and comfy armchairs – an ideal setting in which to enjoy beers from Rhymney and Wye Valley Breweries (including Wye Valley's Old Black Lion) beside the log-burning stove. The inn has a long-standing reputation for its

food, and the pretty dining room overlooking the garden terrace provides a perfect environment for the enjoyment of meals. Lunchtime snacks include filled baguettes with chips and salad; and sausages and mash with onion and seed mustard gravy. Other menus include 'bar favourites' (calves' liver with bacon, onion and Madeira gravy with creamed potatoes; baked loin of cod on braised leeks and fennel with a light cheese sauce and new potatoes); and an à la carte offering the likes of confit of duck on spicy noodles with a plum sauce followed by fillet of fallow venison with a quenelle of parsnip and spring onion purée with a pink peppercorn sauce.

★★★★ INN ◉ ♞
MAP 09 SO24
HR3 5AD
☎ 01497 820841
🖹 01497 822960
e-mail: info@oldblacklion.co.uk
dir: *In town centre*

Open 11–11 Closed: 24–26 Dec
Bar Meals L served all week
12–2.30 D served all week
6.30–9.30
Restaurant D served all week
6.30–9
⊕ Free House ◀ Old Black Lion
Ale, Wye Valley, Rev James. ♞ 7
Facilities Garden Parking
Rooms 10

LLANGATTOCK
MAP 09 SO21

The Vine Tree Inn ♀
The Legar NP8 1HG ☎ 01873 810514

dir: *Take A40 W from Abergavenny then A4077 from Crickhowell*

A pretty pink pub on the River Usk, at the edge of the National Park and within walking distance of Crickhowell. The large garden overlooks the river, bridge and Table Mountain. It is predominantly a dining pub serving a comprehensive menu, with traditional roast lunches on Sundays. Tuesdays now feature the weekly Mexican evening, when authentic Latin dishes cooked to order include nachos, spicy bean soup, a choice of fajitas and enchiladas, and chilli con carne.

Open 12–3 6–11 (Sun 12–3, 6.30–9) **Bar Meals** L served all week 12–3 D served all week 6–10 (Sun 12–3, 6.30–9) **Restaurant** L served all week 12–3 D served all week 6–10 Av 3 course à la carte £15 ⊞ Free House ◗ Fuller's London Pride, Coors Worthington's, Golden Valley. ♀ 8 **Facilities** Garden Parking

LLANGYNIDR
MAP 09 SO11

The Coach & Horses
Cwmcrawnon Rd NP8 1LS ☎ 01874 730245

dir: *A40 from Brecon to Abergavenny, 12m from Brecon. Through village of Bwlch, after bend turn right*

Real ales from local breweries are a feature of this free house, which stands just two minutes' walk from the nearby canal moorings. Local ingredients including Welsh black beef are the basis for the seasonal menus: look out for local lamb on crushed new potatoes with sautéed bacon and white pudding; salmon, prawn and coriander fishcakes with Thai chilli jam; and pasta with spinach, chargrilled vegetables and parmesan shavings.

Open 12–11.30 **Bar Meals** L served all week 12–2.30 D served all week 7–9 (Sun 12–2.30) **Restaurant** L served all week 12.30–2 D served all week 7–9 Av 3 course à la carte £22.50 ⊞ Free House **Facilities** Children's licence Garden Parking

LLOWES
MAP 09 SO14

The Radnor Arms ♀
HR3 5JA ☎ 01497 847460 ▤ 01497 847460
e-mail: brian@radnorsarms.freeserve.co.uk

dir: *A438 between Glasbury & Clyro*

This Grade II, 400-year-old former drovers' inn provides outstanding views from the garden, looking over the Wye Valley to the Black Mountains, to the west of the Brecon Beacons. Local Felinfoel bitter is amongst the beers served beside blazing winter fires in the cosy bar. The extensive blackboard menus offer French and English cuisine, with good vegetarian options and a selection of fish dishes, including sardines and monkfish. Long wine list.

Open 11–2.30 6.30–11 (Sun 12–3) **Bar Meals** L served Tue-Sun 12–2.30 D served Tue-Sun 6.30–9 (Sat 6.30–10, Sun 12–3) **Restaurant** L served Tue-Sun 12–2.30 D served Tue-Sun 6.30–9 Av 3 course à la carte £18 ⊞ Free House ◗ Felinfoel, Worthington, Bitburger. ♀ 9 **Facilities** Garden Dogs allowed Parking

MACHYNLLETH
MAP 14 SH70

Pick of the Pubs

Wynnstay Hotel
SY20 8AE ☎ 01654 702941 ▤ 01654 703884
e-mail: info@wynnstay-hotel.com

dir: *Junct A487 & A489 & 5m from A470*

In the middle of Machynlleth, once the capital of Wales, the Wynnstay is an attractive old coaching inn dating from 1780. Famous visitors have included David Lloyd-George, who addressed the town from the hotel's balcony. Today some people drop in to the lively bars for tea, coffee and cakes, while others come for a pint of beer and something more substantial to eat. Head chef Gareth Johns flies the flag for Wales at home and abroad, and here he and his team have created a menu based firmly on good Welsh produce, with influences from France and Italy. Lunch is a mix of lighter snacks (parsnip and apple soup; Conwy mussels with garlic and parsley) and more substantial fare (Welsh lambs' liver and bacon; pollack with chips and mushy peas). At dinner the daily-changing carte may offer a celebration of Welsh beef in the form of grilled Y Wig sirloin steak.

Open 12–2.30 6–11 (Sun 6–10.30) **Bar Meals** L served all week 12–2 D served all week 6.30–9 **Restaurant** L served all week 12–2 D served all week 6.30–9 Av 5 course fixed price £27.50 ⊞ Free House ◗ Greene King IPA, Reverend James, Old Speckled Hen & Guinness. **Facilities** Children's licence Dogs allowed Parking **Rooms** available

MONTGOMERY
MAP 15 SO29

Pick of the Pubs

Dragon Hotel ★★ HL ⊛
SY15 6PA ☎ 01686 668359 ▤ 0870 011 8227
e-mail: reception@dragonhotel.com

dir: *A483 towards Welshpool, right onto B4386 then B4385. Behind town hall*

A striking black and white, timber-framed coaching inn with an enclosed patio created from the former coach entrance. The bar, lounge and most bedrooms contain beams and masonry allegedly removed from the ruins of Montgomery Castle after Oliver Cromwell destroyed it in 1649. Today the hotel prides itself on the quality of its kitchen, where fresh local produce is prepared to a high standard. In addition to daily blackboard specials and soups, the bar menu includes starters such as breaded Welsh brie with spiced cranberry sauce, and home-made game paté, followed by main courses ranging from red Thai prawn curry and rice to tortellini formaggio in tomato and black olive sauce. The restaurant menu may include local fillet of beef with rösti potato, celeriac purée and rich port sauce; and vegetarian kebabs coated in sesame with fried polenta and peanut sauce. Follow with pear and apple crumble with custard.

Open 11–11 **Bar Meals** L served all week 12–2 D served all week 7–9 Av main course £8 **Restaurant** L served bookings only 12–2 D served bookings only 7–9 Av 3 course à la carte £25 Av 3 course fixed price £22.50 ⊞ Free House ◗ Wood Special, Interbrew Bass & guest. **Facilities** Children's licence Garden Parking **Rooms** 20

NEW RADNOR
MAP 09 SO26

Pick of the Pubs

Red Lion Inn

Llanfihangel-nant-Melan LD8 2TN
☎ 01544 350220 ▤ 01544 350220
e-mail: theredlioninn@yahoo.co.uk
dir: *A483 to Crossgates then right onto A44, 6m to pub. (3m W of New Radnor on A44)*

Old habits die hard here: this ancient drover's inn still provides water, though nowadays it's for hosing down the bike. Next door is one of four churches named after St Michael that encircle the burial place of the last Welsh dragon. According to legend, should anything happen to them the dragon will rise again. The inn has a lounge and a locals' bar, two small restaurants and a sun-trap garden. A broad menu draws extensively on local produce, including herbs from the garden. Mussels, usually served as a starter in white wine, garlic and cream, come from the River Conwy up north. Main courses might include game terrine with Cognac and grape preserve; Welsh Black beef fillet with béarnaise sauce; organic salmon fish cakes; and leek, wild mushroom and chestnut gâteau. Round off with Welsh cheeses and home-made walnut bread.

Open 12–2.30 6–11 (Summer all day) **Bar Meals** L served Wed-Mon 12–2 D served Wed-Mon 6–9 Av main course £7 **Restaurant** L served Wed-Mon 12–2 D served Wed-Mon 6–9 Av 3 course à la carte £17.50 ⊕ Free House ◾ Parish (Woods), Springer (Spinning Dog Brewery). **Facilities** Garden Dogs allowed Parking

OLD RADNOR
MAP 09 SO25

Pick of the Pubs

The Harp

LD8 2RH ☎ 01544 350655
e-mail: info@harpinnradnor.co.uk
dir: *Old Radnor signed off A44 (Kington – New Radnor)*

There are spectacular views over the Radnor countryside from this seemingly untouched village inn, just yards from Old Radnor's fine parish church of St Stephen. The building is a Welsh longhouse made from local stone and slate, and dating back to the 15th century. Open the simple wooden door and you'll step in to a cosy lounge and bars with oak beams, open log fires, semi-circular wooden settles, flagstone floors, and lots of guide books to browse through. Pictures of local history adorn the walls. A changing menu is served in the two dining rooms, and two bar areas, and dining here is a casual, relaxing experience. Look out for steaks with a selection of sauces, and home-made pies, and there are real ales to help wash it all down.

Open 6–11 (Sat-Sun 12–3) Closed: Mon **Bar Meals** L served Sat-Sun 12–2 D served Tue-Sun 6.30–9 Av main course £11 **Restaurant** L served Sat-Sun 12–2 D served Tue-Sun 7–9 Av 3 course à la carte £20 ⊕ Free House ◾ Timothy Taylor, Guinness, Three Tuns, Hopback. **Facilities** Garden Parking

TALGARTH
MAP 09 SO13

Castle Inn

Pengenffordd LD3 0EP ☎ 01874 711353 ▤ 01874 711353
e-mail: castleinnwales@aol.com
dir: *4m S of Talgarth on the A479*

Located in the heart of the Black Mountains, in the Brecon Beacons National Park, the Castle takes its name from nearby Castell Dinas, the highest Iron Age fort in England and Wales. Substantial pub food includes gammon steak, sausage and mash, fisherman's pie, and chick pea tagine, with apple and blackberry crumble, and chocarocka pie with cream or ice cream to follow. The pub also offers bunkhouse accommodation and a camping field.

Open 12–11 Closed Mon (Nov-Etr) **Bar Meals** L served Sat-Sun 12–3 D served Tue-Fri 6–9 (Sat-Sun 6–9.30) Av main course £7 **Restaurant** L served Sat-Sun 12–3 D served Tue-Fri 6–9 (Sat-Sun 6–9.30) Av 3 course à la carte £13.50 ⊕ Free House ◾ Butty Bach, Rumney Bitter & guest ales. **Facilities** Garden Parking

TALYBONT-ON-USK
MAP 09 SO12

Star Inn

LD3 7YX ☎ 01874 676635
dir: *Telephone for directions*

With its pretty riverside garden, this traditional 250–year-old inn stands in a picturesque village within the Brecon Beacons National Park. The pub, unmodernised and with welcoming fireplace, is known for its constantly changing range of well-kept real ales, and hosts quiz nights on Monday and live bands on Wednesday. Hearty bar food with dishes such as chicken in leek and stilton sauce, Hungarian pork goulash, traditional roasts, salmon fish cakes, and vegetarian chilli.

Open 11–3 6.30–11 (Sat all day) **Bar Meals** L served all week 12–2.15 D served all week 6.30–9 Av main course £6.50 ⊕ Free House ◾ Felinfoel Double Dragon, Theakston Old Peculier, Hancock's HB, Bullmastiff Best. **Facilities** Garden Dogs allowed

TRECASTLE
MAP 09 SN82

Pick of the Pubs

The Castle Coaching Inn

See Pick of the Pubs on opposite page

The Castle Coaching Inn

A Georgian coaching inn on the old London to Carmarthen coaching route, now the main A40 trunk road. Family-owned and run, the hotel has been carefully restored in recent years, and has lovely old fireplaces and a remarkable bow-fronted bar window. The inn also offers a peaceful terrace and garden.

Food is served in the bar or more formally in the restaurant, and landlord John Porter continues to maintain high standards. Bar lunches consist of freshly-cut sandwiches (roast beef, turkey, stilton or tuna), ploughman's with tuna, duck and port pate perhaps, and hot filled baguettes (steak with melted stilton, bacon with mushrooms and melted mature cheddar). Specialities include mature Welsh 12oz sirloin steak served with mushrooms and onion rings; home-made lasagne with parmesan cheese; and supreme of chicken with a Marsala and mascarpone sauce. Other options range from battered haddock fillet to chilli con carne. Complete your meal with a dessert of strawberry crush cake, hot jaffa puddle

pudding (an irresistible chocolate sponge with a Jaffa orange centre, topped with a milk chocolate sauce), and Dutch chunky apple flan. Alternatively, sample the selection of Welsh farmhouse cheeses. From the bar you can wash it all down with Red Dragon or Timothy Taylor Landlord real ales, or try one of nine malts. A separate children's list runs through the usual favourites – turkey dinosaurs, fish stars, or jumbo sausage, all served with chips and baked beans.

MAP 09 SN82
LD3 8UH
☎ 01874 636354
🖹 01874 636457
e-mail: guest@
castle-coaching-inn.co.uk
dir: *On A40 W of Brecon*

Open 12–3 6–11
Bar Meals L served Mon-Sun
12–2 D served Mon-Sat 6.30–9
(Sun 7–9) Av main course £10
Restaurant L served Mon-Sun
12–2 D served Mon-Sat 6.30–9
(Sun 7–9) Av 3 course à la carte
£16
⊕ Free House ◀ Fuller's London
Pride, Breconshire Brewery Red
Dragon, Timothy Taylor Landlord.
Facilities Children's licence
Garden Parking

UPPER CWMTWRCH
MAP 09 SN71

Lowther's Gourmet Restaurant and Bar

SA9 2XH ☎ 01639 830938

dir: *2m from Ystalyfera rdbt at Upper Cwmtwrch. Establishment by river*

A traditional family-owned pub and restaurant, which occupies a scenic riverside location at the foot of the Black Mountains. Relax by the cosy wood-burner on a cold winter's day or, in summer, make use of the colourful garden and patio for alfresco dining. The pub brews its own beers and offers wholesome fare made from Welsh produce wherever possible. Traditional roasts, sizzling bass in garlic, and Welsh black beef feature on the extensive menu.

Open 12–4 6–11 (Sun 12–3, 6–10.30) Closed: 26 Dec **Bar Meals** 11.30–2.30 6–10 **Restaurant** L served all week 12–3 D served all week 6–9 Av 3 course à la carte £25 ⊕ Free House **Facilities** Garden Parking Play Area

SWANSEA

REYNOLDSTON
MAP 08 SS48

King Arthur Hotel ♥

Higher Green SA3 1AD ☎ 01792 390775 ▤ 01792 391075

e-mail: info@kingarthurhotel.co.uk

dir: *Just N of A4118 SW of Swansea*

A traditional country inn, with real log fires, in a village lying at the heart of the beautiful Gower Peninsula. Eat in the restaurant, main bar or family room, choosing main menu or specials board dishes including seasonal game, Welsh Black beef, locally caught fish and vegetarian options. Try whole trout with cockle and laverbread sauce; crisp garlicky chicken Kiev; or tuna and bean salad.

Open 10–11 Closed: 25 Dec **Bar Meals** L served all week 12–6 D served Sun-Thu 6–9 (Fri-Sat 6–9.30) **Restaurant** L served all week 12–2.30 D served Sun-Thu 6–9 (Fri-Sat 6–9.30) ⊕ Free House ◀ Felinfoel Double Dragon, Worthington Bitter & Bass & Tomas Watkins OSB, King Arthur Ale. ♥ 9 **Facilities** Garden Parking **Rooms** available

VALE OF GLAMORGAN

COWBRIDGE
MAP 09 SS97

Victoria Inn

Sigingstone CF71 7LP ☎ 01446 773943 ▤ 01446 776446

dir: *Off B4270 in Sigingstone*

A quiet, attractively furnished old village inn with a fine reputation for good quality home-prepared food. The beamed interior, decorated with old photographs, prints and antiques, has a good feel about it. The daily menu is extensive, with some 40 different dishes on offer, plus specials and vegetarian boards, and the likes of red snapper, sea bass, salmon and more. Tomos Watkin Bitter is brewed in Swansea.

Open 11.45–3 6–11 **Bar Meals** L served all week 11.45–2 D served all week 6.30–9.30 (Sun 11.45–2.30, 7–9) **Restaurant** L served Sun-Sat D served Mon-Sat 6.30–9.30 (Sun 11.45–2.30, 7–9) ⊕ Free House ◀ Tomas Watkins Best Bitter, Hancocks HB, Worthington Creamflow. **Facilities** Garden Parking

EAST ABERTHAW
MAP 09 ST06

Pick of the Pubs

Blue Anchor Inn

See Pick of the Pubs on opposite page

MONKNASH
MAP 09 SS97

The Plough & Harrow

CF71 7QQ ☎ 01656 890209

e-mail: info@theploughmonknash.com

dir: *M4 junct 35 take dual carriageway to Bridgend. At rdbt follow St Brides sign, then brown tourist signs. Pub 3m NW of Llantwit Major*

In a peaceful country setting on the edge of a small village with views across the fields to the Bristol Channel, this low, slate-roofed, 14th-century building was originally built as the chapter house of a monastery, although it has been a pub for 500 of its 600–year existence. Expect an atmospheric interior, open fires, up to eight guest ales on tap, and home-cooked food using fresh local ingredients. Great area for walkers.

Open 12–11 (Sun 12–10.30) **Bar Meals** L served all week 12–2.30 D served Mon-Sat 6–9 **Restaurant** L served All 12–2.30 D served Mon-Sat 6–9 Av 3 course à la carte £18 ⊕ Free House ◀ Archers Goldon, Shepherd Neame Spitfire, Hereford Pale ale, Sharp's IPA. **Facilities** Garden Parking

PICK OF THE PUBS

EAST ABERTHAW-VALE OF GLAMORGAN

Blue Anchor Inn

Dating from around 1380, the Blue Anchor has been trading as a pub virtually non-stop for over 600 years. The only break came in 2004 when a serious fire destroyed the top half of this medieval building, forcing its closure for restoration.

It's a stone-built inn, heavily thatched, and legend has it that an underground passage leads down to the shore; it would have been used by wreckers and smugglers who roamed this wild Bristol Channel coastline. The interior comprises a warren of small rooms separated by thick walls, with low, beamed ceilings and a number of open fires including a large inglenook. The inn was part of the Fonmon estate until 1941 when it was acquired by the grandfather of the present owners, Jeremy and Andrew Coleman. A good selection of regional real ales plus guest beers from around the country are always on tap. An enticing range of food is offered by both the bar menu and the upstairs restaurant carte. Down in the bar expect starters such as duck and sour cherry spring roll, or Glamorgan cheese sausage; follow these with a main course of braised pork belly with celeriac purée; or calves' liver and onions with dauphinoise potatoes. In the restaurant may be found home-cured gravadlax with sweet pickled beetroot and candied lemons to start, followed by roast Merthyr Mawr pheasant on a sauté of wild mushrooms, spinach and baby onions. Fresh fish dishes may include whole lemon sole with a mussel and clam chowder; pan-fried fillet of red bream with pickled courgettes and sautéed potatoes; seared fillet of salmon on a lemon and crab risotto; and grilled fillet of wild sea bass on aromatic Chinese greens. Desserts follow classic lines, with chocolate orange and honeycomb parfait, or sticky toffee pudding with rum sauce.

MAP 09 ST06
CF62 3DD
☎ 01446 750329
🖹 01446 750077
dir: *From Barry take A4226, then B4265 towards Llantwit Major. Follow signs, turn left for East Aberthaw. (3m W of Cardiff Airport)*

Open 11–11
Bar Meals L served Mon-Sat 12–2 D served Mon-Fri 6–8 Av main course £8.50
Restaurant L served Sun 12–2.30 D served Mon-Sat 7–9.30 Av 3 course à la carte £20 Av 3 course fixed price £13.95
⊕ Free House ◀ Theakston Old Peculier, Wadworth 6X, Wye Valley Hereford Pale Ale, Brains Better.
Facilities Garden Parking

ST HILARY
MAP 09 ST07

Pick of the Pubs

The Bush Inn ♥
CF71 7DP ☎ 01446 772745
dir: *S of A48, E of Cowbridge*

This thatched village pub in the Vale of Glamorgan has overlooked the old church for more than 400 years. Bare stone walls, flagstones, oak beams, and a huge fireplace with a stone spiral staircase leading to the first floor are features of the cosy interior. It has a resident ghost, a highwayman who was cornered in a nearby cave and hanged on Stalling Down half a mile away. The pretty restaurant has French windows leading out to the garden. Depending on which you choose, bar or restaurant menus offer choices of light bites, sandwiches and salads, chargrilled steaks, a fresh fish special of the day, and vegetarian options. Other likely options are main courses of pan-fried rib-eye of Welsh beef; trio of mutton and mint sausages; deep-fried plaice in beer batter; and wild mushroom risotto cake. A selection of desserts appears on the blackboard menu.

Open 11.30–11 (Sun 12–10.30) **Bar Meals** L served Mon-Sat 12–2.30 D served Mon-Sat 6.45–9.30 (Sun 12.15–3.30) **Restaurant** L served Mon-Sat 12–2.30 D served Mon-Sat 6.45–9.30 (Sun 12.15–3.30) Av 3 course à la carte £25 ⊕ Punch Taverns ◀ Hancock's HB, Greene King Abbot Ale, Interbrew Worthington Bitter & Bass, guest ale. ♥ 10 **Facilities** Children's licence Garden Dogs allowed Parking

---

WREXHAM

ERBISTOCK
MAP 15 SJ34

The Boat Inn
LL13 0DL ☎ 01978 780666 🖻 01978 780607
e-mail: info@theboatinn.co.uk
dir: *A483 Whitchurch/Llangollen exit, towards Whitchurch on A539. After 2m turn right at signs for Erbistock & The Boat Inn. Follow to inn*

A 16th-century pub in a great spot on the Dee, where you can still see the landing stage for the one-time ferry and windlass that wound it across the river. Lunch includes pasta, home-made pie of the day, and beer-battered cod and chips. In the evening, pan-fried fillet of salmon with puy lentils, fresh asparagus and mustard, cream and chive sauce; and chargrilled veal chop with parsnip purée and red wine, orange and garlic sauce.

Open 12–11 (Sun 12–10.30) **Bar Meals** L served all week 12–9 (Sun Winter 12–5) **Restaurant** L served all week 12–2.30 D served all week 6.30–9 (Sun Winter Sun 12–5) ⊕ Free House ◀ Tetleys, Export, Addlestones, Guinness & guest ales. **Facilities** Children's licence Garden Dogs allowed Parking

---

GRESFORD
MAP 15 SJ35

Pant-yr-Ochain ♥
Old Wrexham Rd LL12 8TY
☎ 01978 853525 🖻 01978 853505
e-mail: pant.yr.ochain@brunningandprice.co.uk
dir: *From Chester take exit for Nantwich. Holt off A483. Take 2nd left, also signed Nantwich Holt. Turn left at 'The Flash' sign. Pub 500yds on right*

A sweeping drive leads to this 16th-century manor house overlooking a small lake and a sculpted, tree-dotted landscape. Its interior delivers on the promise of its picture-perfect exterior, with an inglenook fireplace and a wealth of nooks and crannies. Food ranges from sandwiches to main meals such as five spice roasted belly pork, followed by fillet of haddock with pea and bacon risotto and mustard butter.

Open 12–11 (Sun 12–10.30) Closed: 25–26 Dec **Bar Meals** L served Mon-Sat 12–9.30 D served Mon-Sat 12–9.30 (Sun 12–9) Av main course £11 **Restaurant** L served Mon-Sat 12–9.30 D served Mon-Sat 12–9.30 (Sun 12–9) Av 3 course à la carte £22 ◀ Timothy Taylor Landlord, Interbrew Flowers Original, Thwaites Original, Weetwood Eastgate. ♥ 22 **Facilities** Children's licence Garden Parking

LLANARMON DYFFRYN CEIRIOG

MAP 15 SJ13

The Hand at Llanarmon ★★★ INN 🏮🏮 ♥

LL20 7LD ☎ 01691 600666 📠 01691 600262
e-mail: reception@thehandhotel.co.uk
web: www.thehandhotel.co.uk
dir: *Turn off A5 at Chirk, follow B4500 for 11m. Through Ceiriog Valley to Llanarmon D C. Pub straight ahead*

Old world charm and modern comforts blend easily at this 16th-century free house, located at the head of the beautiful Ceiriog Valley – David Lloyd George once described the area as 'a little bit of heaven on earth'. Seasonal home-cooked dishes are prepared to a high standard. The menu featuring Welsh Black beef and local trout is backed by bar meals such as Helen's hand-made steak and ale pie, and half a honey-roast chicken with chips and gravy.

Open 11–11 (Fri-Sat 11–12.30) **Bar Meals** L served all week 12–2.20 D served all week 6.30–8.45 (Sun 12.30–2.45) Av main course £11 **Restaurant** L served Mon-Sat 12–2.20 D served all week 6.30–8.45 (Sun 12.30–2.45, fixed price menu Sun) Av 3 course à la carte £21 Av 3 course fixed price £17 ⊕ Free House ◀ Coors, Worthington Cream Flow, Guinness, guest ale. ♥ 7 **Facilities** Garden Dogs allowed Parking **Rooms** 13

Pick of the Pubs

The West Arms Hotel ★★★ HL 🏮🏮 ♥

LL20 7LD ☎ 01691 600665 📠 01691 600622
e-mail: gowestarms@aol.com
dir: *Leave A483 at Chirk, follow signs for Ceiriog Valley B4500, 11m from Chirk*

Take slate-flagged floors, ancient timberwork, inglenooks and open fires. Add some period furniture and warm hospitality, and the precious traditions of this 17th-century drovers' inn are kept well and truly alive. Long ago the drovers would come down from the Welsh hills by way of three tracks that converged here. After resting for the night they continued their slow, arduous journeys to markets in Chirk, Oswestry, Wrexham and as far away as London. Award-winning chef Grant Williams has travelled too, working in kitchens around the world, appearing on several TV cookery programmes, and even cooking for Prince Charles. Grant's seafood dishes are sheer indulgence: grilled fillets of Dover sole with thyme-roasted asparagus; truffled scallops with Anglesey lobster; grilled rosettes of sole and wild River Dee smoked salmon. Or you can simply relax outside with a pint, view the Berwyn mountains, and lose track of time as the Ceiriog River burbles away in the valley.

The West Arms Hotel

Open 8–11 **Bar Meals** L served all week 12–2 D served all week 7–9 Av main course £11.95 **Restaurant** L served Sun 12–2 D served all week 7–9 Av 3 course fixed price £32.90 ⊕ Free House ◀ Interbrew Flowers IPA, Tetleys Smooth, Dave's Hoppy ale. ♥ 11 **Facilities** Garden Dogs allowed Parking **Rooms** 15

MARFORD

MAP 15 SJ35

Trevor Arms Hotel ♥

LL12 8TA ☎ 01244 570436 📠 01244 570273
e-mail: info@trevorarmsmarford.fsnet.co.uk
web: www.trevorarmshotel.com
dir: *Off A483 onto B5102 then right onto B5445 into Marford*

The early 19th-century coaching inn takes its name from Lord Trevor of Trevallin, who was killed in a duel; public executions, both by beheading and hanging, took place in the village. Grisly history notwithstanding, today's Trevor Arms is a charming hostelry, offering a selection of real ales and a varied menu. Bar specials may include deep-fried breaded plaice; minted lamb steak with home-made chips; or braised steak cooked in a rich mushroom and red wine gravy.

Open 11–11.30 (Fri-Sat 11–12) **Bar Meals** L served Mon-Sat 11–10 D served Mon-Sat 6–10 (Sun 12–8.30) Av main course £7.75 **Restaurant** L served Mon-Sat 11–10 D served Mon-Sat 11–10 (Sun 12–8.30) Av 3 course à la carte £15 Av 3 course fixed price £10.95 ⊕ Scottish Courage ◀ Greenalls, Bombardier & John Smiths, Morland Old Speckled Hen & 2 guest ales. ♥ 12 **Facilities** Garden Parking Play Area

Wales

How to Find a
Pub in the Atlas Section

Pubs are located in the gazetteer under the name of the nearest town or village. If a pub is in a small village or rural area, it may appear under a town within fives miles of its actual location. The black dots and town names shown in the atlas refer to the gazetteer location in the guide. Please use the directions in the pub entry to find the pub on foot or by car. If directions are not given, or are not clear, please telephone the pub for details.

Key to County Map

The county map shown here will help you identify the counties within each country. You can look up each county in the guide using the county names at the top of each page. Towns featured in the guide use the atlas pages and index following this map.

England

1 Bedfordshire
2 Berkshire
3 Bristol
4 Buckinghamshire
5 Cambridgeshire
6 Greater Manchester
7 Herefordshire
8 Hertfordshire
9 Leicestershire
10 Northamptonshire
11 Nottinghamshire
12 Rutland
13 Staffordshire
14 Warwickshire
15 West Midlands
16 Worcestershire

Scotland

17 City of Glasgow
18 Clackmannanshire
19 East Ayrshire
20 East Dunbartonshire
21 East Renfrewshire
22 Perth & Kinross
23 Renfrewshire
24 South Lanarkshire
25 West Dunbartonshire

Wales

26 Blaenau Gwent
27 Bridgend
28 Caerphilly
29 Denbighshire
30 Flintshire
31 Merthyr Tydfil
32 Monmouthshire
33 Neath Port Talbot
34 Newport
35 Rhondda Cynon Taff
36 Torfaen
37 Vale of Glamorgan
38 Wrexham

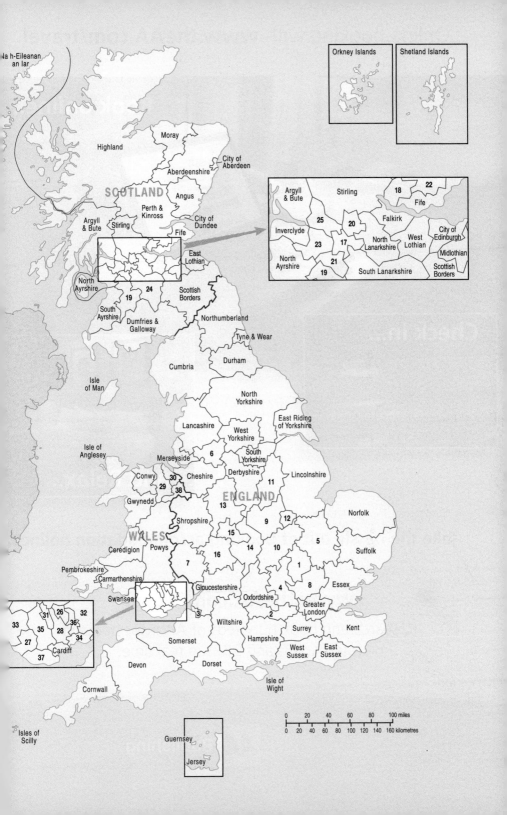

KEY TO ATLAS

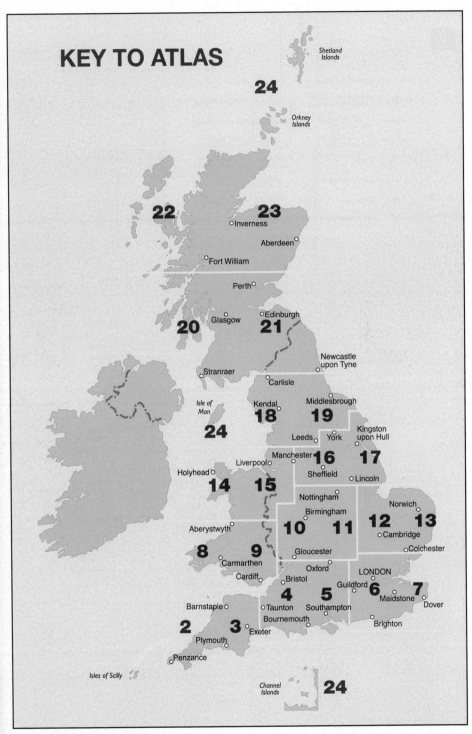

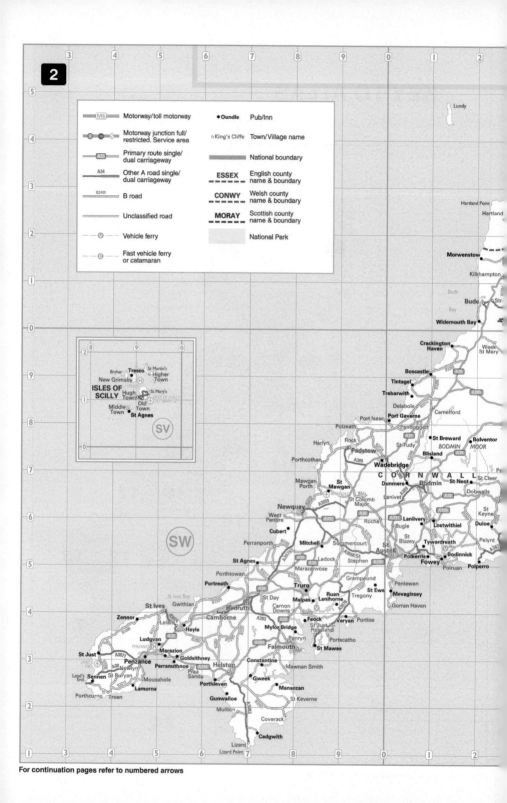

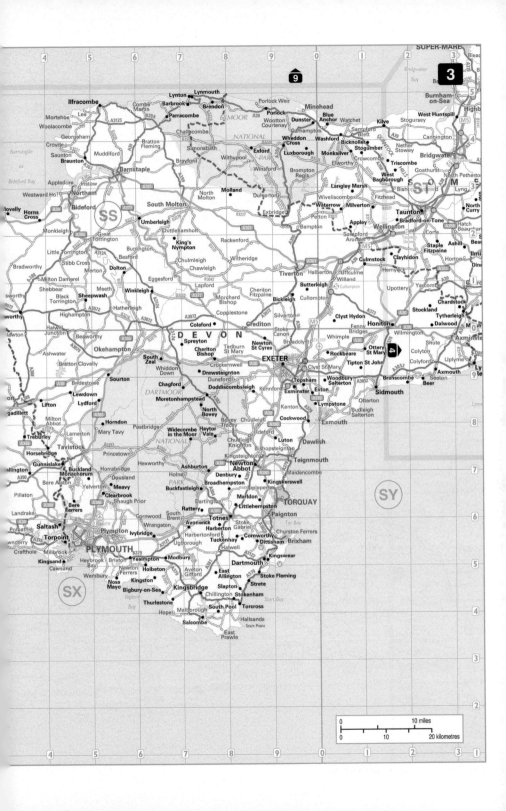

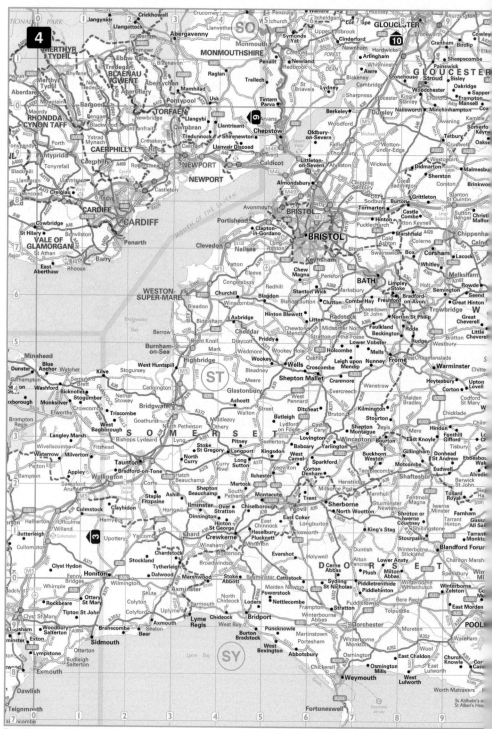

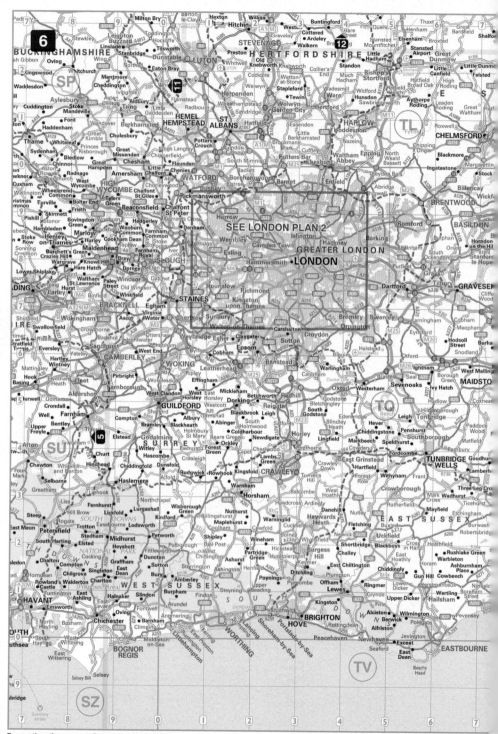

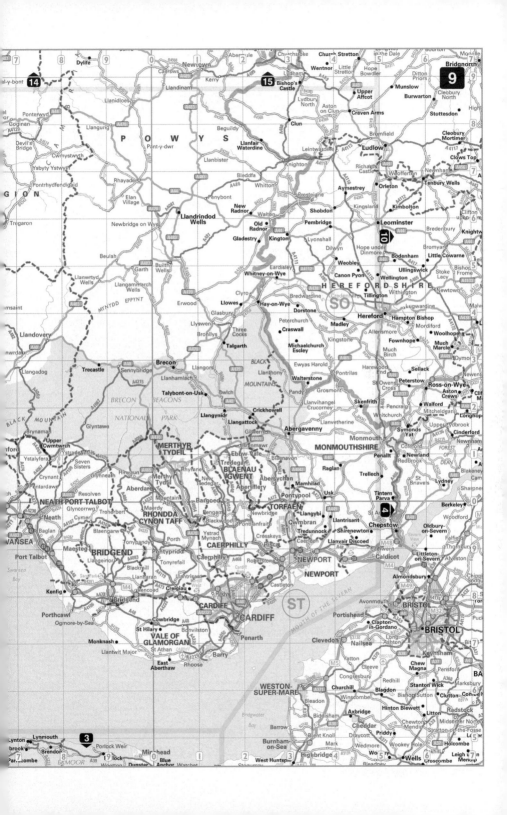

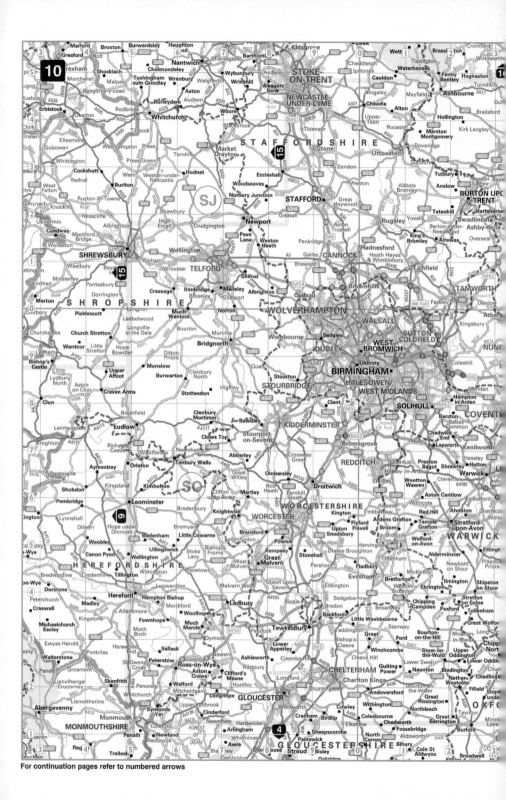

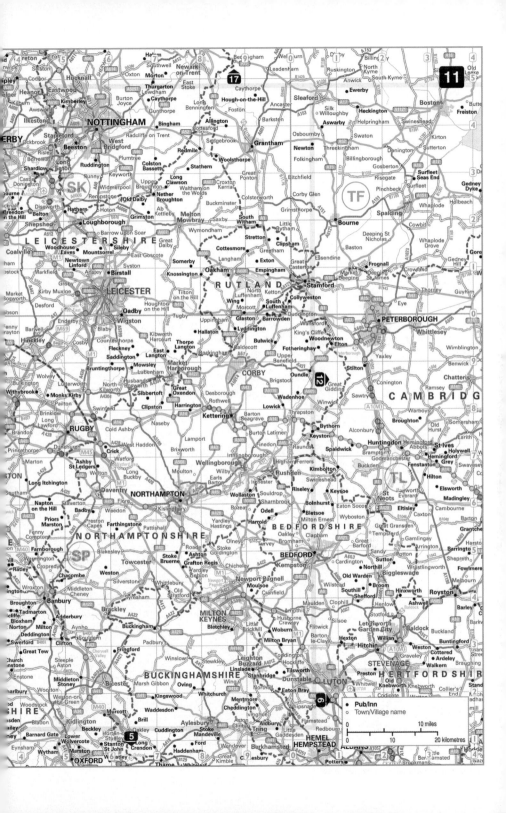

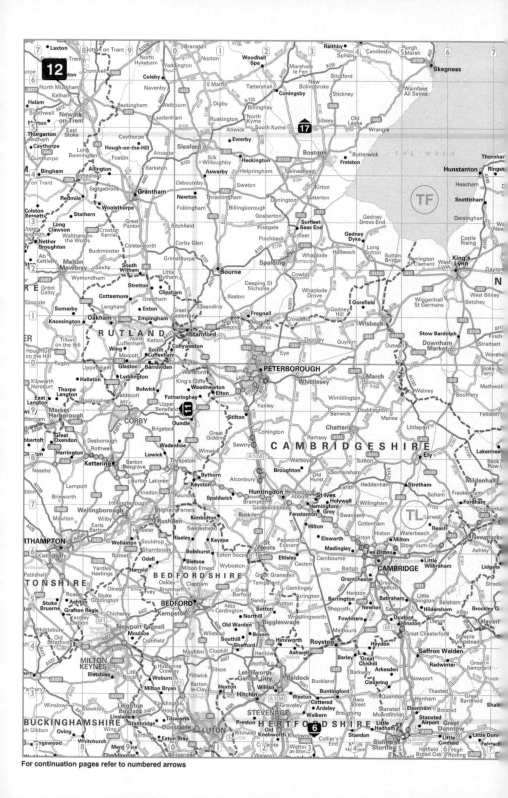

Pub/Inn
○ Town/Village name

0   10 miles
0   10   20 kilometres

ISLE OF
ANGLESEY

Cemaes
Amlwch
Llanerchymedd
Holyhead
Llanfachraeth
Benllech
Red Wharf Bay
Trearddur Bay
Pentraeth
Llangoed
Llandudno
Rhôs-on-Sea
Holy Island
Llangefni
Deganwy
Colwyn Bay
Aberg
Rhosneigr
Menai Bridge
Bangor
Penmaenmawr
Llandudno Junction
Conwy
Llanddulas
St George
Beaumaris
Llanfairfechan
Llansanffraid Glan Conwy
Aberffraw
Llanfair P.G.
Betws-yn-Rhos
Llannefy
Y Felinheli
Llanllechid
Tal-y-Cafn
Newborough
Bethesda
Tal-y-Bont
Llanfair Talhaiarn
Caernarfon
Llanrug
Trefriw
Llangernyw
Llansanna
Bethnewydd
Llanberis
CONWY
Waunfawr
Llanrwst
Bylchau
Llandwrog
Llanwnda
Capel Curig
Llanddeiniolen
Penygroes
Rhyd-Ddu
Betws-y-Coed
Coernarfon Bay
Clynnog-fawr
Dolwyddelan
Penmachno
Pentrefoelas
Nantgwynant
SNOWDONIA
Beddgelert
Cerrigydrudion
SH
Blaenau Ffestiniog
Y Ma
Llanaelhaearn
Prenteg
Ffestiniog
Morfa Nefyn
Nefyn
Tremadog
Maentwrog
Bodfuan
Llanystumdwy
Porthmadog
Penrhyndeudraeth
NATIONAL
Tudweiliog
Criccieth
Borth-y-Gest
Talsarnau
Bala
LLEYN
PENINSULA
Trawsfynydd
Sarn
Pwllheli
Harlech
GWYNEDD
Y Rhiw
Llanbedrog
Llanuwchllyn
PARK
Aberdaron
Abersoch
Llanbedr
Ganllwyd
Bardsey Island
Dyffryn Ardudwy
Tal-y-bont
Llanv
MOUNTAINS
Barmouth
Doigellau
Dinas-Mawddwy
Fairbourne
Mallwyd
Llangad
Coris
Llwyngwril
Cemmaes Road
Llanbrynmair
Bryncrug
Pennal
Tywyn
Machynlleth
Carno
SN
Aberdyfi
Dylife
Borth
Tal-y-bont
Llandre
CARDIGAN BAY
Llanidloes
9
Aberystwyth
Capel Bangor
Ponterwyd

For continuation pages refer to numbered arrows

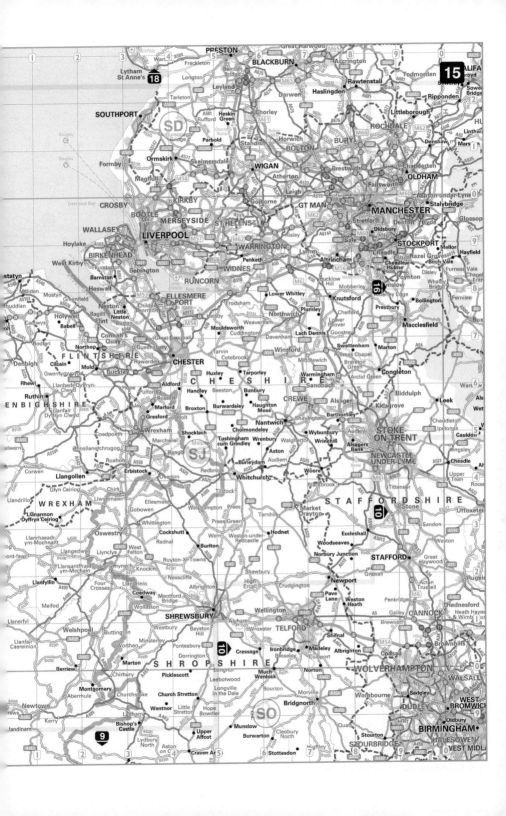

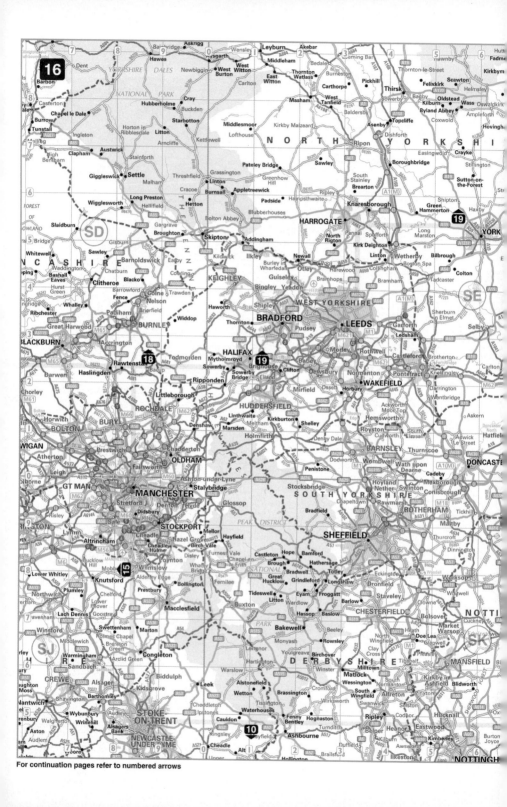

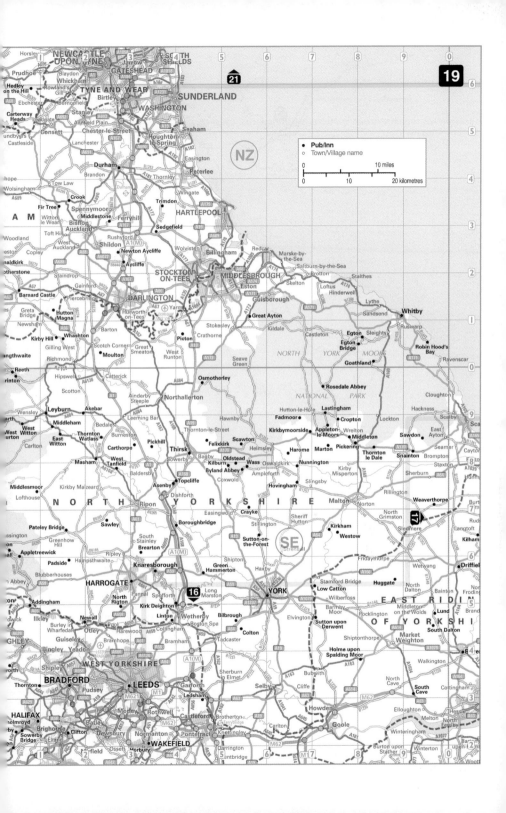

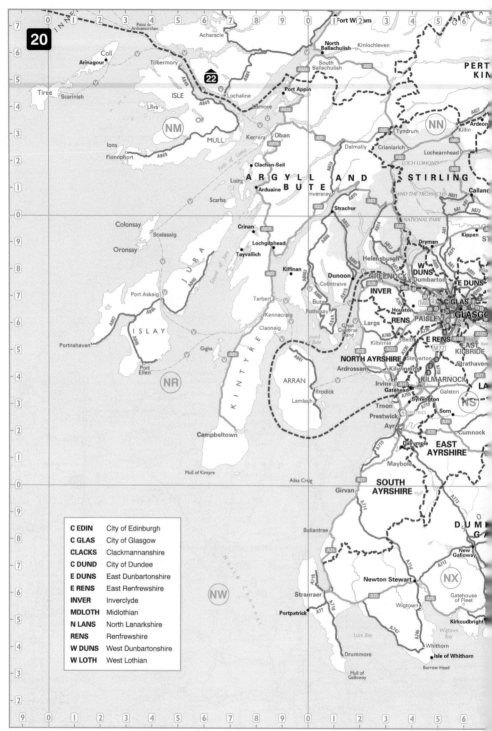

INNER

| | 0 | 1 | 2 | 3 | 4 | 5 | 6 | 7 | 8 | 9 | 0 | 1 | 2 | 3 | 4 | 5 |

7
6
5
4
3
2
1
0

Point or Ardnamurchan

Acharacle

Fort W 2 am

North Ballachulish

Kinlochleven

Coll

Arinagour

Tobermory

South Ballachulish

A82

PERT

KIN

Tiree

Scarinish

ISLE

A849

Lochaline

Port Appin

Ardeon

A827

22

Ulva

OF

Lismore

A828

NN

Killin

Iona

MULL

Kerrera

Oban

Tyndrum

Fionnphort

A849

A816

Dalmally

Crianlarich

Lochearnhead

A84

Clachan-Seil

LOCH LOMOND

A R G Y L L   A N D

S T I R L I N G

NM

Luing

B U T E

Arduaine

Inveraray

A815

A83

AND THE TROSSACHS

A821

Callanc

Scarba

A83

Strachur

A81

A873

Colonsay

Crinan

A816

NATIONAL PARK

Scalasaig

Lochgilphead

Drymen

Kippen

S

Oronsay

Tayvallich

Helensburgh

W

Kilfinan

A83

Dunoon

Colintraive

GREENOCK

DUNS

Kils

Port Askaig

Tarbert

Bute

INVER

Dumbarton

E DUNS

J U R A

Kennacraig

Rothesay

Largs

Houston

C GLAS

GLASGO

Portnahaven

A846

Claonaig

Great Cumbrae Island

RENS

PAISLEY

Port Ellen

Gigha

A83

Sound of Bute

Kilbirnie

Beith

E RENS

NR

NORTH AYRSHIRE

Stevarton

EAST KILBRIDE

K I N T Y R E

A841

ARRAN

Ardrossan

Kilwinning

Strathaven

Brodick

Irvine

Gatehead

KILMARNOCK

LA

Lamlash

A759

Galston

NS

Troon

Symington

Campbeltown

Prestwick

Sorn

A76

Mull of Kintyre

Ayr

Cumnock

Ailsa Craig

Dalrymple

EAST AYRSHIRE

Maybole

SOUTH

NW

AYRSHIRE

Girvan

Ballantrae

DUM

G

New Galloway

A714

NX

Newton Stewart

Stranraer

Gatehouse of Fleet

Portpatrick

A716

Wigtown

Kirkcudbright

Luce Bay

Wigtown Bay

Whithorn

Drummore

Isle of Whithorn

Mull of Galloway

Burrow Head

C EDIN	City of Edinburgh
C GLAS	City of Glasgow
CLACKS	Clackmannanshire
C DUND	City of Dundee
E DUNS	East Dunbartonshire
E RENS	East Renfrewshire
INVER	Inverclyde
MDLOTH	Midlothian
N LANS	North Lanarkshire
RENS	Renfrewshire
W DUNS	West Dunbartonshire
W LOTH	West Lothian

| 9 | 0 | 1 | 2 | 3 | 4 | 5 | 6 | 7 | 8 | 9 | 0 | 1 | 2 | 3 | 4 | 5 | 6 |

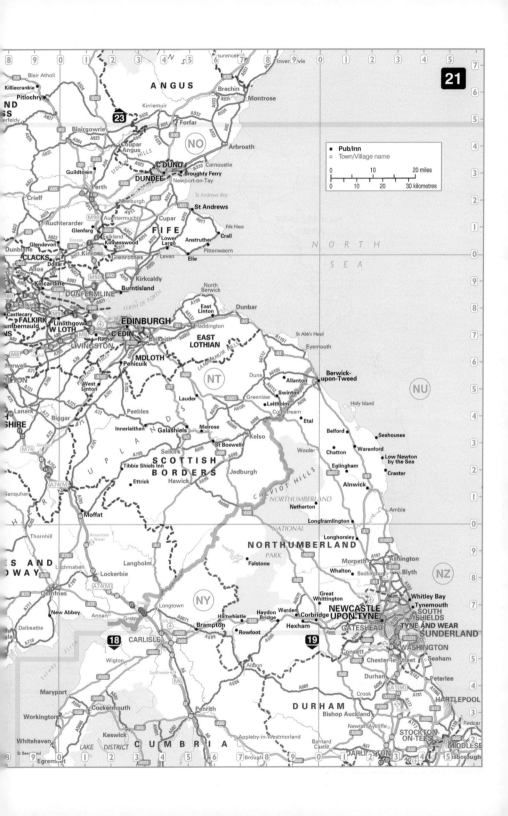

Cape Wrath

Rudha Rhobhanais
(Butt of Lewis)
Port Nis
(Port of Ness)

Cellar
Head

NA

Hands Island

Scourie

LEWIS

NB

A858

A859

A857

Great
Bernera

Carlabhagh
(Carloway)

Kylesku

A894

Tiumpan
Head

Steornabhagh
(Stornoway)

A859

A857

Inchnadan

Lochinver

A837

NA H–EILEANAN
AN IAR

ISLE

OF

Scarp

Achiltibuie

A835

Taransay

Tairbeart
(Tarbert)

Scalpay

Gruinard
Bay

Ullapool

A832

HARRIS

A859

Pabbay

Gairloch

Badachro

A832

Boreray

Berneray

A859

Kinlochewe

A855

A832

NORTH UIST

Loch nam Madadh
(Lochmaddy)

Uig

Torridon

Achnasheen

A867

A865

Ronay

Stein

NG

A890

Shieldaig

Benbecula

A855

NF

Wiay

Dunvegan

ISLE

Portree

Inner Sound

A896

SOUTH
UIST

A863

OF

Raasay

Plockton

A890

Cannich

A865

Carbost

Drynoch

Scalpay

Kyle of
Lochalsh

A87

Loch Baghasdail
(Lochboisdale)

SKYE

A87

Glenelg

A87

A87

Isleornsay

A887

Eriskay

Soay

BARRA

A888

Canna

Ardvasar

Inverie

Invergarry

Bàgh a Chaisteil
(Castlebay)

Rùm

Mallaig

Sandray

NORTH

Eigg

A830

Mingulay

Spean
Bridge

A82

Muck

A861

A861

Fort William

Point of
Ardnamurchan

NM

North
Ballachulish

Kinlochleven

Acharacle

NL

Coll

A884

South
Ballachulish

A82

Arinagour

Tobermory

Port Appin

A828

Tiree

Scarinish

A846

Lochaline

Lismore

ISLE

20

A849

Ulva

Kerrera

Oban

A85

OF

Dalmally

Iona

A849

MULL

Fionnphort

For continuation pages refer to numbered arrows

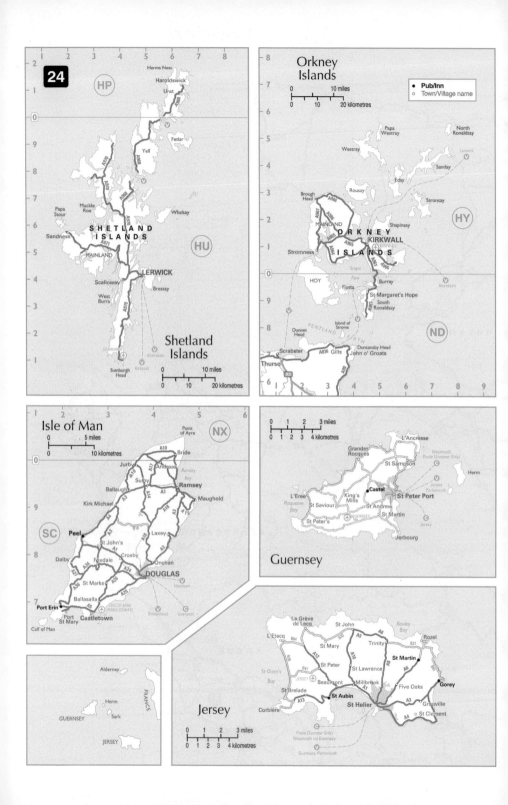

24

HP

Herma Ness
Haroldswick
Unst
A968

V

Fetlar

Yell

A970

A968

Whalsay

Muckle Roe
Papa Stour

SHETLAND ISLANDS

Sandness

MAINLAND

A971

V

LERWICK

Scalloway

Bressay

West Burra

A970

Sumburgh Head
Aberdeen
Kirkwall

Shetland Islands

HU

0   10 miles
0   10   20 kilometres

Orkney Islands

0   10 miles
0   10   20 kilometres

● Pub/Inn
○ Town/Village name

Papa Westray

North Ronaldsay

Westray

Lerwick
V

Sanday

Eday

Brough Head

Rousay

Stronsay

HY

MAINLAND

A967

A986

ORKNEY

Shapinsay

Stromness

A964
A965

KIRKWALL
KIRKWALL
V

ISLANDS

A960
A961

HOY

Scapa
Flow

Burray

Aberdeen
V

Flotta

St Margaret's Hope
A961

South Ronaldsay

Island of Stroma

ND

Dunnet Head

PENTLAND   FIRTH

Scrabster

A836 Gills

Duncansby Head
John o' Groats

Thurso

A9
A99

ND

Isle of Man

0   5 miles
0   10 kilometres

NX

Point of Ayre

A10

Bride

Jurby

A17

Andreas

A10

Ramsey Bay

Sulby

A14

Ballaugh

A3

Ramsey

Kirk Michael

A4

Maughold

A2

A18

A3

75

A15

Peel

B10

Laxey

SC

St John's

A1

Crosby

A2

A18

A5

Dalby

Foxdale

A3

A24

Onchan

DOUGLAS

St Marks

A25

Heysham

Ballasalla

ISLE OF MAN (RONALDSWAY)
V

Birkenhead
C

Liverpool

Port Erin

A5

Port St Mary

Castletown

Calf of Man

0   1   2   3 miles
0 1 2 3 4 kilometres

Grandes Rocques

L'Ancresse

Weymouth
Poole (Summer Only)
C

St Sampson

Herm

L'Eree

King's Mills

Castel

St Peter Port

Raquaine Bay

St Saviour

St Andrew

Jersey
Portsmouth
V

St Peter's

St Martin

GUERNSEY

Jersey
V

Jerbourg

Guernsey

Alderney

Herm

FRANCE

GUERNSEY

Sark

JERSEY

Jersey

0   1   2   3 miles
0 1 2 3 4 kilometres

La Grève de Lecq

St John

Bouley Bay

L'Etacq

B64

St Mary

A8

Trinity

Rozel

B31

A12

St Peter

A10

St Lawrence

A8

St Martin

St Ouen's Bay

B41

JERSEY

Beaumont

Millbrook

Five Oaks

Gorey

St Brelade

A1

Gorey

Corbière

A13

St Aubin

St Helier

A3

Grouville

A4

St Clement

Poole (Summer Only)
Weymouth via Guernsey
C

Guernsey, Portsmouth
V

Central London

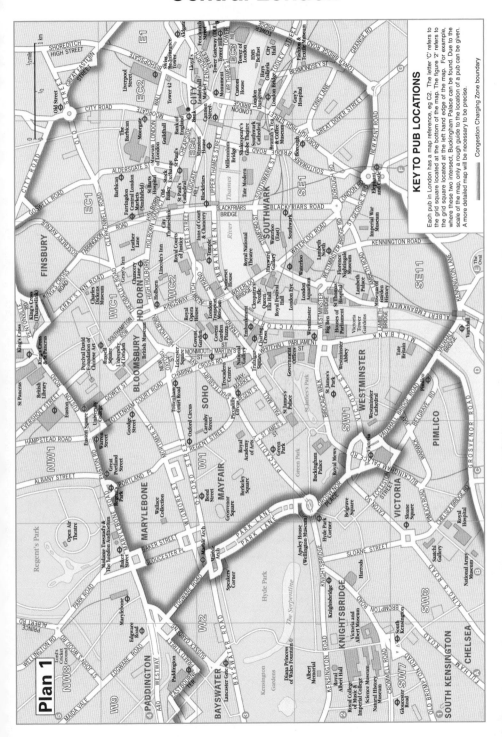

Index

Highlighted entries are Pick of the Pubs

A

ABBERLEY
The Manor Arms at Abberley 625
ABBOTSBURY
Ilchester Arms 180
ABERAERON
Harbourmaster Hotel 732
ABERCYCH
Nags Head Inn 747
ABERDEEN
Old Blackfriars 694
ABERDYFI
Penhelig Arms Hotel & Restaurant 740
ABERGAVENNY
Clytha Arms 742
ABERGORLECH
The Black Lion 731
ABINGDON
The Merry Miller 435
ABINGER
The Volunteer 542
ACHILTIBUIE
Summer Isles Hotel & Bar 707
ADDERBURY
Red Lion 435
ADDINGHAM
The Fleece 681
AKEBAR
The Friar's Head 639
ALBURY
The Drummond Arms Inn 543
William IV 543
ALCISTON
Rose Cottage Inn 554
ALDBURY
The Greyhound Inn 295
The Valiant Trooper 295
ALDEBURGH
The Mill Inn 524
ALDERBURY
The Green Dragon 602
ALDERMASTON
Hinds Head 21
ALDERMINSTER
The Bell 584
ALDFORD
The Grosvenor Arms 67
ALDRINGHAM
The Parrot and Punchbowl Inn &
   Restaurant 524
ALDWORTH
The Bell Inn 21
ALFRISTON
George Inn 554
The Sussex Ox 555
ALLANTON
Allanton Inn 720
ALLENHEADS
The Allenheads Inn 416
ALLINGTON
The Welby Arms 346

ALMONDSBURY
The Bowl 211
ALNWICK
Masons Arms 416
ALREWAS
The Old Boat 517
ALSAGERS BANK
The Gresley Arms 517
ALSTONEFIELD
The George 517
ALTNAHARRA
Altnaharra Hotel 707
ALTON
Bulls Head Inn 517
ALTRINCHAM
The Victoria 249
ALVEDISTON
The Crown 602
ALVESTON
The Baraset Barn 584
AMBERLEY
Black Horse 568
The Bridge Inn 568
AMBLESIDE
Drunken Duck Inn 101
Wateredge Inn 101
AMERSHAM
Hit or Miss Inn 38
AMROTH
The New Inn 747
ANDOVER
Wyke Down Country Pub &
   Restaurant 253
ANDOVERSFORD
The Kilkeney Inn 211
The Royal Oak Inn 211
ANSLOW
The Burnt Gate Inn 519
ANSTRUTHER
The Dreel Tavern 705
APPLEBY-IN-WESTMORLAND
The Royal Oak 101
Tufton Arms Hotel 101
APPLETON-LE-MOORS
The Moors Inn 639
APPLETREEWICK
The Craven Arms 640
APPLEY
The Globe Inn 489
ARDELEY
The Jolly Waggoner 295
ARDENS GRAFTON
The Golden Cross 585
ARDEONAIG
The Ardeonaig Hotel 724
ARDINGTON
The Boar's Head 435
ARDUAINE
Loch Melfort Hotel 696
ARDVASAR
Ardvasar Hotel 726

ARINAGOUR
Coll Hotel 725
ARKESDEN
Axe & Compasses 198
ARLINGHAM
The Old Passage Inn 213
ARMATHWAITE
The Dukes Head Inn 103
ARRETON
The White Lion 598
ASCOT
The Thatched Tavern 22
ASENBY
Crab & Lobster 640
ASHBOURNE
Barley Mow Inn 132
Dog & Partridge Country Inn 132
ASHBURNHAM PLACE
Ash Tree Inn 555
ASHBURTON
The Rising Sun 146
ASHBY ST LEDGERS
The Olde Coach House Inn 406
ASHCOTT
The Ashcott Inn 489
Ring O'Bells 490
ASHILL
Square & Compass 490
ASHLEWORTH
Boat Inn 213
The Queens Arms 213
ASHMORE GREEN
The Sun in the Wood 22
ASHTON
The Old Crown 406
ASHURST
The Fountain Inn 568
ASHWELL
The Three Tuns 296
ASKRIGG
Kings Arms 640
ASTON
The Bhurtpore Inn 67
ASTON CANTLOW
King's Head 585
ASTON CREWS
The Penny Farthing Inn 284
ASWARBY
The Tally Ho Inn 347
AUSTWICK
The Game Cock Inn 640
AVIEMORE
The Old Bridge Inn 707
AVONWICK
The Avon Inn 146
The Turtley Corn Mill 146
AWRE
The Red Hart Inn at Awre 213
AXBRIDGE
Lamb Inn 490

AXFORD
Red Lion Inn 602
AXFORD
The Crown at Axford 253
AXMOUTH
The Harbour Inn 146
The Ship Inn 146
AYCLIFFE
The County 195
AYMESTREY
The Riverside Inn 284
AYSGARTH
The George & Dragon Inn 640
AYTHORPE RODING
Axe & Compasses 198

B

BABCARY
Red Lion 490
BABELL
Black Lion Inn 739
BABRAHAM
The George Inn at Babraham 57
BADACHRO
The Badachro Inn 707
BADBY
The Windmill Inn 408
BAKEWELL
The Bull's Head 132
The Monsal Head Hotel 132
BALMEDIE
The Cock & Bull Bar & Restaurant 694
BAMFORD
Yorkshire Bridge Inn 134
BAMPTON
The Romany 435
BAMPTON
Mardale Inn 103
BANBURY
The George Inn 435
The Wykham Arms 435
Ye Olde Reindeer Inn 437
BARBON
The Barbon Inn 103
BARBROOK
The Beggars Roost 147
BARFORD ST MARTIN
Barford Inn 604
BARLEY
The Fox & Hounds 296
BARLOW
The Tickled Trout 134
BARNARD CASTLE
The Morritt Arms Hotel 195
BARNARD GATE
The Boot Inn 437
BARNBY
The Swan Inn 524
BARNHAM
The Murrell Arms 568
BARNOLDBY LE BECK
The Ship Inn 347
BARNSLEY
The Village Pub 215
BARNSTON
Fox and Hounds 384
BARRINGTON
The Royal Oak 57

BARROWDEN
Exeter Arms 471
BARSTON
The Malt Shovel at Barston 596
BARTHOMLEY
The White Lion Inn 67
BASHALL EAVES
The Red Pump Inn 325
BASINGSTOKE
Hoddington Arms 253
BASLOW
Rowley's 134
BASSENTHWAITE
The Pheasant 103
BATH
The Hop Pole 490
King William 491
The Old Green Tree 491
Pack Horse Inn 491
The Raven 491
The Star Inn 491
BAUGHURST
The Wellington Arms 254
BAWBURGH
Kings Head 384
BEACONSFIELD
The Royal Standard of England 38
BEAUMARIS
Ye Olde Bulls Head Inn 730
BEAUWORTH
The Milburys 254
BECKFORD
The Beckford 625
BECKINGTON
Woolpack Inn 492
BECKLEY
The Abingdon Arms 437
BEDFORD
Knife & Cleaver Inn 16
The Three Tuns 16
BEER
Anchor Inn 147
BEESTON
Victoria Hotel 430
BEETHAM
The Wheatsheaf at Beetham 103
BELCHFORD
The Blue Bell Inn 347
BELFORD
Blue Bell Hotel 416
BELTON
The Queen's Head 338
BEMBRIDGE
The Crab & Lobster Inn 598
The Pilot Boat Inn 598
BENTLEY
The Bull Inn 254
BENTWORTH
The Star Inn 254
The Sun Inn 254
BERE FERRERS
Olde Plough Inn 147
BERKELEY
The Malt House 215
BERRIEW
The Lion Hotel 751
BERWICK
The Cricketers Arms 555

BERWICK-UPON-TWEED
The Rob Roy 416
BETCHWORTH
The Red Lion 543
BETWS-Y-COED
Ty Gwyn Inn 733
White Horse Inn 734
BETWS-YN-RHOS
The Wheatsheaf Inn 734
BEVERLEY
White Horse Inn 634
BEWDLEY
Little Pack Horse 626
The Mug House Inn & Angry Chef
Restaurant 626
BIBURY
Catherine Wheel 215
BICKLEIGH
Fisherman's Cot 147
BICKNOLLER
The Bicknoller Inn 492
BIDDENDEN
The Three Chimneys 305
BIGBURY-ON-SEA
Pilchard Inn 147
BILBROUGH
The Three Hares Country Inn &
Restaurant 643
BILDESTON
The Bildeston Crown 524
BILSBORROW
Owd Nell's Tavern 326
BINGHAM
The Chesterfield 430
BINHAM
Chequers Inn 384
BIRCHOVER
The Druid Inn 134
The Red Lion 134
BIRCH VALE
The Waltzing Weasel Inn 134
BIRDLIP
The Golden Heart 215
BIRMINGHAM
The Peacock 596
BIRSTALL
The Mulberry Tree 338
BISHOP'S CASTLE
Boars Head 477
The Three Tuns Inn 478
BISLEY
The Bear Inn 215
BLACK BOURTON
The Vines 437
BLACKBOYS
The Blackboys Inn 555
BLACKBROOK
The Plough at Blackbrook 543
BLACKBURN
Clog and Billycock 329
The Millstone at Mellor 325
BLACKHEATH
The Villagers Inn 543
BLACKMORE
The Leather Bottle 198
BLACKO
Moorcock Inn 329

Index

BLAENAU FFESTINIOG
The Miners Arms | 741
BLAGDON
The New Inn | 492
BLAKENEY
The Kings Arms | 384
White Horse Hotel | 387
BLANCHLAND
The Lord Crewe Arms | 419
BLANDFORD FORUM
The Anvil Inn | 180
Best Western Crown Hotel | 180
BLEDINGTON
The Kings Head Inn | 217
BLEDLOW
The Lions of Bledlow | 40
BLENCOGO
The New Inn | 103
BLETCHLEY
The Crooked Billet | 40
BLETSOE
The Falcon | 16
BLICKLING
The Buckinghamshire Arms | 387
BLIDWORTH
Fox & Hounds | 430
BLISLAND
The Blisland Inn | 80
BLOXHAM
The Elephant & Castle | 437
BLUE ANCHOR
The Smugglers | 492
BODENHAM
England's Gate Inn | 284
Railway Inn | 284
BODICK
Old Ferry Inn | 80
BODSHAM GREEN
Froggies At The Timber Batts | 305
BOLDRE
The Hobler Inn | 256
The Red Lion | 256
BOLLINGTON
The Church House Inn | 67
BOLNHURST
The Plough at Bolnhurst | 16
BOLTER END
The Peacock | 40
BOLVENTOR
Jamaica Inn | 82
BONCHURCH
The Bonchurch Inn | 598
BOOT
The Boot Inn | 105
Brook House Inn | 105
BOROUGHBRIDGE
The Black Bull Inn | 643
BORROWDALE
The Langstrath Country Inn | 105
BOSCASTLE
The Wellington Hotel | 82
BOSSINGHAM
The Hop Pocket | 305
BOURNE
The Wishing Well Inn | 347
BOURTON
The White Lion Inn | 180

BOURTON-ON-THE-HILL
Horse and Groom | 217
BOUTH
The White Hart Inn | 105
BOVINGDON GREEN
The Royal Oak | 40
BOWLAND BRIDGE
Hare & Hounds Country Inn | 105
BOX
The Northey | 604
The Quarrymans Arms | 604
BOXFORD
The Bell at Boxford | 22
BRABOURNE
The Five Bells | 305
BRADFIELD
The Strines Inn | 679
BRADFORD
New Beehive Inn | 681
BRADFORD-ON-AVON
The Dandy Lion | 604
The Kings Arms | 604
The Tollgate Inn | 605
BRADFORD-ON-TONE
White Horse Inn | 493
BRADWELL
The Old Bowling Green Inn | 137
BRAINTREE
The Green Dragon at Young's End | 200
BRAITHWAITE
Coledale Inn | 105
The Royal Oak | 105
BRAMDEAN
The Fox Inn | 256
The Bell Inn | 256
BRAMLEY
Jolly Farmer Inn | 544
BRAMPTON
Blacksmiths Arms | 106
BRANCASTER STAITHE
The White Horse | 387
BRANDESTON
The Queens Head | 525
BRANSCOMBE
The Masons Arms | 147
BRANSFORD
The Bear & Ragged Staff | 626
BRASSINGTON
Ye Olde Gate Inne | 137
BRAUNTON
The Williams Arms | 148
BRAY
Hinds Head Hotel | 22
BREARTON
Malt Shovel Inn | 643
BRECON
The Felin Fach Griffin | 752
The Old Ford Inn | 752
The Usk Inn | 752
The White Swan Inn | 752
BREEDON ON THE HILL
The Three Horseshoes | 340
BRENDON
Rockford Inn | 148
BRETFORTON
The Fleece Inn | 626

BRIDGNORTH
Halfway House Inn | 478
Pheasant Inn | 478
BRIDPORT
The George Hotel | 180
Shave Cross Inn | 180
The West Bay | 182
BRIGG
The Jolly Miller | 348
BRIGHTON & HOVE
The Basketmakers Arms | 555
The Chimney House | 556
The Greys | 556
The Market Inn | 556
BRIGHTWELL BALDWIN
The Lord Nelson Inn | 439
BRILL
The Pheasant Inn | 40
The Red Lion | 40
BRINKWORTH
The Three Crowns | 605
BRISTOL
Cornubia | 38
Highbury Vaults | 38
Robin Hood's Retreat | 38
BROAD CHALKE
The Queens Head Inn | 605
BROADHEMPSTON
The Monks Retreat Inn | 148
BROADWELL
Chilli Pepper | 439
BROCKLEY GREEN
The Plough Inn | 525
BROOKLAND
The Royal Oak | 307
Woolpack Inn | 307
BROOM
The Cock | 16
BROOM
Broom Tavern | 585
BROUGH
Travellers Rest | 137
BROUGHTON
Saye and Sele Arms | 439
BROUGHTON
The Crown | 57
BROUGHTON
The Bull | 643
BROUGHTON-IN-FURNESS
Blacksmiths Arms | 106
BROUGHTY FERRY
The Royal Arch Bar | 703
BROXTON
The Copper Mine | 67
BRUNTINGTHORPE
Joiners Arms | 340
BUCKFASTLEIGH
Dartbridge Inn | 148
BUCKHORN WESTON
Stapleton Arms | 182
BUCKINGHAM
The Old Thatched Inn | 42
The Wheatsheaf | 42
BUCKLAND MONACHORUM
Drake Manor Inn | 148
BUCKLERS HARD
The Master Builders House Hotel | 257

Index

C

BULWICK
The Queen's Head ... 408
BUNBURY
The Dysart Arms ... 69
BUNTINGFORD
The Sword Inn Hand ... 296
BURCHETT'S GREEN
The Crown ... 24
BURCOMBE
The Ship Inn ... 605
BURCOT
The Chequers ... 439
BURFORD
The Inn for All Seasons ... 441
The Lamb Inn ... 441
BURHAM
The Golden Eagle ... 307
BURLEY
The Burley Inn ... 257
BURLEYDAM
The Combermere Arms ... 69
BURLTON
The Burlton Inn ... 478
BURNHAM MARKET
The Hoste Arms ... 387
BURNHAM-ON-CROUCH
Ye Olde White Harte Hotel ... 200
BURNHAM THORPE
The Lord Nelson ... 389
BURNSALL
The Red Lion ... 643
BURNTISLAND
Burntisland Sands Hotel ... 705
BURPHAM
George & Dragon ... 568
BURROW
The Highwayman ... 329
BURTON
The Old House at Home ... 605
BURTON BRADSTOCK
The Anchor Inn ... 182
BURTON UPON TRENT
Burton Bridge Inn ... 519
BURWARDSLEY
The Pheasant Inn ... 69
BURWARTON
The Boyne Arms ... 479
BURY
The Squire & Horse ... 568
BURY ST EDMUNDS
The Linden Tree ... 525
The Nutshell ... 525
The Old Cannon Brewery ... 527
The Three Kings ... 527
BUTLEIGH
The Rose & Portcullis ... 493
BUTTERLEIGH
The Butterleigh Inn ... 150
BUTTERMERE
Bridge Hotel ... 106
BYLAND ABBEY
Abbey Inn ... 643
BYTHORN
The White Hart ... 59

CADEBY
Cadeby Inn ... 679
CADGWITH
Cadgwith Cove Inn ... 82
CADNAM
Sir John Barleycorn ... 257
CALDBECK
Oddfellows Arms ... 110
CALLANDER
The Lade Inn ... 724
CALLINGTON
The Coachmakers Arms ... 82
Manor House Inn ... 82
CAMBRIDGE
The Anchor ... 59
Cambridge Blue ... 59
Free Press ... 59
CANON PYON
The Nags Head Inn ... 286
CANTERBURY
The Chapter Arms ... 307
The Dove Inn ... 307
The Granville ... 309
The Old Coach House ... 309
The Red Lion ... 309
The White Horse Inn ... 309
CAPEL CURIG
Cobdens Hotel ... 734
CARBOST
The Old Inn ... 726
CAREW
Carew Inn ... 747
CARNFORTH
Old Station Inn ... 331
CARSHALTON
Greyhound Hotel ... 248
CARTERWAY HEADS
The Manor House Inn ... 419
CARTHORPE
The Fox & Hounds ... 643
CARTMEL
The Cavendish Arms ... 110
CASTEL
Fleur du Jardin ... 689
Hotel Hougue du Pommier ... 689
CASTLE COMBE
Castle Inn ... 607
CASTLE HEDINGHAM
The Bell Inn ... 200
CASTLETON
The Castle ... 137
The Peaks Inn ... 137
Ye Olde Nag's Head ... 138
The Coach and Horses Inn ... 140
CATFORTH
The Running Pump ... 331
CATTISTOCK
Fox & Hounds Inn ... 182
CAULDON
Yew Tree Inn ... 519
CAUNTON
Caunton Beck ... 431
CAVENDISH
Bull Inn ... 527
CAWDOR
Cawdor Tavern ... 708

CAYTHORPE
Black Horse Inn ... 431
CERNE ABBAS
The Royal Oak ... 184
CHACOMBE
George and Dragon ... 408
CHADDLEWORTH
The Ibex ... 24
CHADLINGTON
The Tite Inn ... 441
CHADWICK END
The Orange Tree ... 596
CHAGFORD
Ring O'Bells ... 150
The Sandy Park Inn ... 150
Three Crowns Hotel ... 150
CHAILEY
The Five Bells Restaurant and Bar ... 556
CHALFONT ST GILES
The Ivy House ... 42
The White Hart ... 42
CHALFONT ST PETER
The Greyhound Inn ... 42
CHALGROVE
The Red Lion Inn ... 441
CHALTON
The Red Lion ... 257
CHAPEL LE DALE
The Old Hill Inn ... 645
CHAPPEL
The Swan Inn ... 200
CHARDSTOCK
The George Inn ... 150
CHARING
The Bowl Inn ... 310
CHARLBURY
The Bull Inn ... 441
CHARLTON
The Fox Goes Free ... 571
CHARTER ALLEY
The White Hart Inn ... 258
CHATTON
The Percy Arms Hotel ... 419
CHAWTON
The Greyfriar ... 258
CHEADLE
The Queens At Freehay ... 519
CHEADLE HULME
The Church Inn ... 249
CHECKENDON
The Highwayman ... 441
CHEDDINGTON
The Old Swan ... 44
CHEDWORTH
Hare & Hounds ... 217
Seven Tuns ... 217
CHELMSFORD
The Alma ... 201
CHENIES
The Red Lion ... 44
CHEPSTOW
Castle View Hotel ... 743
CHERITON
The Flower Pots Inn ... 258
CHERITON BISHOP
The Old Thatch Inn ... 151

CHESHAM
The Black Horse Inn — 44
The Swan — 44
CHESTER
Albion Inn — 69
Old Harkers Arms — 69
CHEW MAGNA
The Bear and Swan — 493
CHICHESTER
Crown and Anchor — 571
Royal Oak Inn — 571
CHIDDINGFOLD
The Crown Inn — 544
The Swan Inn & Restaurant — 544
CHIDDINGLY
The Six Bells — 556
CHIDDINGSTONE
Castle Inn — 310
CHIDEOCK
The Anchor Inn — 184
CHIEVELEY
The Crab at Chieveley — 24
CHILGROVE
The Fish House — 571
CHILHAM
The White Horse — 310
CHILLENDEN
Griffins Head — 310
CHILLESFORD
The Froize Inn — 527
CHILWORTH
Chilworth Arms — 258
CHINNOR
The Sir Charles Napier — 442
CHIPPING
Dog & Partridge — 331
CHIPPING CAMPDEN
The Bakers Arms — 218
Eight Bells — 218
The Kings — 218
Noel Arms Hotel — 218
The Volunteer Inn — 221
CHIPPING NORTON
The Chequers — 442
CHISELBOROUGH
The Cat Head Inn — 493
CHISLEHAMPTON
Coach & Horses Inn — 442
CHOLESBURY
The Full Moon — 44
CHOLMONDELEY
The Cholmondeley Arms — 69
CHRISTCHURCH
Fishermans Haunt — 184
The Ship In Distress — 184
CHRISTIAN MALFORD
The Rising Sun — 607
CHRISTMAS COMMON
The Fox and Hounds — 445
CHURCH ENSTONE
The Crown Inn — 445
CHURCHILL
The Crown Inn — 493
CHURCH KNOWLE
The New Inn — 184
CHURCH STRETTON
The Royal Oak — 479

CHURT
Pride of the Valley — 544
CILCAIN
White Horse Inn — 740
CILGERRAN
Pendre Inn — 747
CINDERFORD
The New Inn — 221
CIRENCESTER
The Crown of Crucis — 221
CLACHAN-SEIL
Tigh an Truish Inn — 696
CLAPHAM
New Inn — 645
CLAPTON-IN-GORDANO
The Black Horse — 494
CLAVERING
The Cricketers — 201
CLAYGATE
Swan Inn & Lodge — 544
CLAYHIDON
The Merry Harriers — 151
CLEARBROOK
The Skylark Inn — 151
CLENT
The Bell & Cross — 626
CLEOBURY MORTIMER
The Crown Inn — 479
CLEY NEXT THE SEA
The George Hotel — 389
CLIFFORD'S MESNE
The Yew Tree — 221
CLIFTON
Duke of Cumberland's Head — 445
CLIFTON
The Black Horse Inn — 681
CLIPSHAM
The Olive Branch — 473
CLIPSTON
The Bulls Head — 408
CLITHEROE
The Assheton Arms — 331
The Shireburn Arms — 331
CLOVELLY
Red Lion Hotel — 151
CLOWS TOP
The Colliers Arms — 628
CLUN
The Sun Inn — 479
CLUTTON
The Hunters Rest — 494
CLYST HYDON
The Five Bells Inn — 152
COATES
The Tunnel House Inn — 221
COBHAM
The Cricketers — 545
COCKERMOUTH
The Trout Hotel — 110
COCKSHUTT
The Leaking Tap — 479
COCKWOOD
The Anchor Inn — 152
COEDWAY
The Old Hand and Diamond Inn — 753
COLCHESTER
The Rose & Crown Hotel — 201

COLDHARBOUR
The Plough Inn — 545
COLEBY
The Bell Inn — 348
COLEFORD
The New Inn — 152
COLESBOURNE
The Colesbourne Inn — 221
COLLINGBOURNE DUCIS
The Shears Inn & Country Hotel — 607
COLLYWESTON
The Collyweston Slater — 408
COLN ST ALDWYNS
The New Inn At Coln — 223
COLSTON BASSETT
The Martins Arms Inn — 431
COLTISHALL
Kings Head — 389
COLTON
Ye Old Sun Inn — 645
COLWYN BAY
Pen-y-Bryn — 734
COMBE HAY
The Wheatsheaf Inn — 494
COMPTON
Coach & Horses — 571
COMPTON
The Withies Inn — 545
CONGLETON
The Plough At Eaton — 73
CONINGSBY
The Lea Gate Inn — 348
CONISTON
The Black Bull Inn & Hotel — 110
Sun Hotel & 16th Century Inn — 110
CONSTANTINE
Trengilly Wartha Inn — 83
CONTIN
Achilty Hotel — 708
CONWY
The Groes Inn — 737
COOKHAM DEAN
Chequers Brasserie — 24
CORBRIDGE
The Angel of Corbridge — 419
CORFE CASTLE
The Greyhound Inn — 184
CORFE MULLEN
The Coventry Arms — 186
CORNWORTHY
Hunters Lodge Inn — 153
CORSHAM
The Flemish Weaver — 607
CORTON
The Dove Inn — 608
CORTON DENHAM
The Queens Arms — 496
COTHERSTONE
The Fox and Hounds — 195
COTTERED
The Bull at Cottered — 296
COTTESMORE
The Sun Inn — 473
COTTON
The Trowel & Hammer Inn — 527
COWBEECH
The Merrie Harriers — 558

COWBRIDGE
Victoria Inn — 760
COWES
The Folly — 598
COWLEY
The Green Dragon Inn — 223
CRACKINGTON HAVEN
Coombe Barton Inn — 83
CRAIL
The Golf Hotel — 705
CRANHAM
The Black Horse Inn — 223
CRANMORE
Strode Arms — 496
CRASTER
Cottage Inn — 420
Jolly Fisherman Inn — 420
CRASWALL
The Bulls Head — 286
CRAVEN ARMS
The Sun Inn — 481
CRAWLEY
The Fox and Hounds — 258
CRAY
The White Lion Inn — 645
CRAYKE
The Durham Ox — 645
CRAY'S POND
The White Lion — 445
CRAZIES HILL
The Horns — 25
CREIGIAU
Caesars Arms — 731
Gwaelod-y-Garth Inn — 731
CRESSAGE
The Riverside Inn — 481
CREWKERNE
The Manor Arms — 496
CRICK
The Red Lion Inn — 408
CRICKHOWELL
The Bear Hotel — 753
Nantyffin Cider Mill — 753
CRINAN
Crinan Hotel — 696
CRONDALL
The Hampshire Arms — 259
CROOK
The Sun Inn — 112
CROPTON
The New Inn — 647
CROSCOMBE
The Bull Terrier — 496
CROSTHWAITE
The Punch Bowl Inn — 112
CUBERT
The Smugglers' Den Inn — 83
CUDDINGTON
The Crown — 44
CULMSTOCK
Culm Valley Inn — 153
CUMBERNAULD
Castlecary House Hotel — 717
CUMNOR
Bear & Ragged Staff — 446
The Vine Inn — 446

CURRIDGE
The Bunk Inn — 25
CUXHAM
The Half Moon — 446

D

DALRYMPLE
The Kirkton Inn — 703
DALWOOD
The Tuckers Arms — 153
DAMERHAM
The Compasses Inn — 259
DANEHILL
The Coach and Horses — 558
DARTFORD
The Rising Sun Inn — 310
DARTMOUTH
Royal Castle Hotel — 154
DEAL
The King's Head — 310
DEDDINGTON
Deddington Arms — 446
The Unicorn — 449
The White Hart — 450
DEDHAM
Marlborough Head Hotel — 201
The Sun Inn — 201
DENBURY
The Union Inn — 154
DENHAM
The Falcon Inn — 47
The Swan Inn — 47
DENNINGTON
The Queens Head — 528
DENSHAW
The Rams Head Inn — 249
DERBY
The Alexandra Hotel — 138
DEREHAM
Yaxham Mill — 389
DEVIZES
The Bear Hotel — 608
The Raven Inn — 608
DIDMARTON
The Kings Arms — 223
DIDSBURY
The Metropolitan — 249
DINNINGTON
Dinnington Docks — 496
DITCHEAT
The Manor House Inn — 497
DITCHLING
The Bull — 558
DITTISHAM
The Ferry Boat — 154
DODDISCOMBSLEIGH
The Nobody Inn — 154
DOE LEA
Hardwick Inn — 138
DOLLAR
Castle Campbell Hotel — 701
DOLTON
Rams Head Inn — 154
The Union Inn — 156
DONCASTER
Waterfront Inn — 679

DONHEAD ST ANDREW
The Forester Inn — 608
DONINGTON ON BAIN
The Black Horse Inn — 348
DORCHESTER (ON THAMES)
Fleur De Lys — 449
The George — 449
DORKING
The Stephan Langton — 545
DORNEY
The Palmer Arms — 47
DORSTONE
The Pandy Inn — 286
DOVER
The Clyffe Hotel — 313
DOWNTON
The Royal Oak — 259
DREWSTEIGNTON
The Drewe Arms — 156
DRIFFIELD
Best Western The Bell — 634
DROITWICH
The Chequers — 628
The Old Cock Inn — 628
DRYMEN8
The Clachan Inn — 724
DULOE
Ye Olde Plough House Inn — 83
DUMMER
The Queen Inn — 259
DUNCTON
The Cricketers — 572
DUNDEE
Speedwell Bar — 703
DUNMERE
The Borough Arms — 83
DUNOON
Coylet Inn — 699
DUNSFOLD
The Sun Inn — 546
DUNSTER
The Luttrell Arms — 497
DUNWICH
The Ship Inn — 528
DURHAM
Victoria Inn — 196
DUXFORD
The John Barleycorn — 59
DYLIFE
Star Inn — 755

E

EARLS COLNE
The Carved Angel — 203
EARL SOHAM
Victoria — 528
EAST ABERTHAW
Blue Anchor Inn — 760
EAST ALLINGTON
Fortescue Arms — 156
EAST ASHLING
Horse and Groom — 572
EAST CHALDON
The Sailors Return — 186
EAST CHILTINGTON
The Jolly Sportsman — 558

Index

EAST COKER
The Helyar Arms 497
EAST DEAN
The Star & Garter 572
EAST END
The East End Arms 260
EAST GARSTON
The Queen's Arms Country Inn 27
EAST HENDRED
The Wheatsheaf 450
EAST KNOYLE
The Fox and Hounds 610
EAST LANGTON
The Bell Inn 340
EAST LINTON
The Drovers Inn 704
EAST MEON
Ye Olde George Inn 260
EAST MORDEN
The Cock & Bottle 186
EASTON
The Chestnut Horse 260
The Cricketers Inn 260
EAST RUSTON
The Butchers Arms 389
EAST TYTHERLEY
The Star Inn Tytherley 261
EAST WITTON
The Blue Lion 647
EATON
The Red Lion 390
EATON BRAY
The White Horse 18
EBBESBOURNE WAKE
The Horseshoe 610
EBRINGTON
The Ebrington Arms 227
ECCLESHALL
The George 519
EDGEHILL
The Castle Inn 585
EDINBURGH
Bennets Bar 704
The Bow Bar 704
Doric Tavern 704
The Shore Bar & Restaurant 705
EFFINGHAM
The Plough 546
EGHAM
The Fox and Hounds 546
EGLINGHAM
Tankerville Arms 420
EGTON
The Wheatsheaf Inn 647
EGTON BRIDGE
Horseshoe Hotel 647
ELIE
The Ship Inn 706
ELKESLEY
Robin Hood Inn 431
ELSENHAM
The Crown 203
ELSTEAD
The Woolpack 546
ELSTED
The Three Horseshoes 572

ELSWORTH
The George & Dragon 60
ELTERWATER
The Britannia Inn 112
ELTISLEY
The Leeds Arms 60
ELTON
The Black Horse 60
The Crown Inn 60
ELY
The Anchor Inn 60
EMPINGHAM
The White Horse Inn 473
EMSWORTH
The Sussex Brewery 261
ENNERDALE BRIDGE
The Shepherd's Arms Hotel 112
EPSOM
White Horse 546
ERBISTOCK
The Boat Inn 762
ERPINGHAM
The Saracen's Head 390
ERWARTON
The Queens Head 528
ESKDALE GREEN
Bower House Inn 112
King George IV Inn 112
ETAL
Black Bull 420
ETTINGTON
The Houndshill 586
ETTRICK
Tushielaw Inn 720
EVERSHOT
The Acorn Inn 187
EVERSLEY
The Golden Pot 261
EWERBY
The Finch Hatton Arms 348
EXCEAT
The Golden Galleon 558
EXETER
Red Lion Inn 156
The Twisted Oak 156
EXFORD
The Crown Hotel 497
EXMINSTER
Swans Nest 156
EXTON
The Puffing Billy 157
EXTON
Fox & Hounds 473
EYAM
Miners Arms 138
EYE
The White Horse Inn 528

F

FADMOOR
The Plough Inn 648
FAKENHAM
The Wensum Lodge Hotel 390
The White Horse Inn 390
FALSTONE
The Blackcock Inn 420
The Pheasant Inn 420

FARINGDON
The Lamb at Buckland 450
The Trout at Tadpole Bridge 450
FARNBOROUGH
The Inn at Farnborough 586
FARNHAM
The Museum Inn 187
FARNHAM
The Bat & Ball Freehouse 548
FARNHAM COMMON
The Foresters 47
FARNHAM ROYAL
The King of Prussia 47
FARTHINGSTONE
The Kings Arms 410
FAULKLAND
Tuckers Grave 499
FAVERSHAM
Shipwrights Arms 313
FEERING
The Sun Inn 203
FELIXKIRK
The Carpenters Arms 648
FELSTED
The Swan at Felsted 203
FENCE
Fence Gate Inn 332
Ye Old Sparrow Hawk Inn 332
FEN DITTON
Ancient Shepherds 60
FENNY BENTLEY
Bentley Brook Inn 138
FENSTANTON
King William IV 62
FEOCK
The Punch Bowl & Ladle 83
FERNHURST
The King's Arms 574
The Red Lion 574
FIFIELD
Merrymouth Inn 451
FILKINS
The Five Alls 451
FINGRINGHOE
The Whalebone 203
FIR TREE
Duke of York Inn 196
FLADBURY
Chequers Inn 628
FLAMBOROUGH
The Seabirds Inn 636
FLAUNDEN
The Bricklayers Arms 296
FLECKNEY
The Old Crown 341
FLETCHING
The Griffin Inn 560
FLYFORD FLAVELL
The Boot Inn 628
FOCHABERS
Gordon Arms Hotel 717
FOLKESTONE
The Lighthouse Inn 313
FONTHILL GIFFORD
The Beckford Arms 610
FORD
The Dinton Hermit 49

FORD
The Plough Inn · 227
FORDCOMBE
Chafford Arms · 313
FORDHAM
White Pheasant · 62
FORDINGBRIDGE
The Augustus John · 261
FOREST GREEN
The Parrot Inn · 548
FORTON
The Bay Horse Inn · 332
FORT WILLIAM
Moorings Hotel · 708
FOSSEBRIDGE
The Inn at Fossebridge · 227
FOTHERINGHAY
The Falcon Inn · 410
FOWEY
The Ship Inn · 85
FOWLMERE
The Chequers · 62
FOWNHOPE
The Green Man Inn · 286
FRAMLINGHAM
The Station Hotel · 529
FRAMPTON MANSELL
The Crown Inn · 227
The White Horse · 227
FRAMSDEN
The Dobermann Inn · 529
FREISTON
Kings Head · 348
FRESHFORD
The Inn at Freshford · 499
FRESHWATER
The Red Lion · 599
FRIETH
The Prince Albert · 49
The Yew Tree · 49
FRINGFORD
The Butchers Arms · 451
FRITHAM
The Royal Oak · 262
FROGGATT
The Chequers Inn · 140
FROGNALL
The Goat · 349
FROME
The Horse & Groom · 499
FYFIELD
The White Hart · 451

G

GAIRLOCH
The Old Inn · 708
GALASHIELS
Kingsknowes Hotel · 721
GARRIGILL
The George & Dragon Inn · 112
GARVE
Inchbae Lodge Guesthouse · 711
GATEHEAD
The Cochrane Inn · 704
GEDNEY DYKE
The Chequers · 349

GIGGLESWICK
Black Horse Hotel · 648
GILLINGHAM
The Kings Arms Inn · 187
GLADESTRY
The Royal Oak Inn · 755
GLASGOW
Rab Ha's · 706
Ubiquitous Chip · 706
GLASTON
The Old Pheasant · 473
GLENDEVON
The Tormaukin Country Inn and
   Restaurant · 717
GLENELG
Glenelg Inn · 711
GLENFARG
The Famous Bein Inn · 718
GLOUCESTER
Queens Head · 229
GOATHLAND
Birch Hall Inn · 648
GOLDSITHNEY
The Trevelyan Arms · 85
GOODNESTONE
The Fitzwalter Arms · 313
GOOSNARGH
The Bushell's Arms · 332
GOREFIELD
Woodmans Cottage · 62
GOREY
Castle Green Gastropub · 690
GORING
Miller of Mansfield · 451
GOSFIELD
The Green Man · 203
GOSFORTH
The Globe Hotel · 116
GOSPORT
The Seahorse · 262
GOUDHURST
Green Cross Inn · 314
The Star & Eagle · 314
GRAFFHAM
The Foresters Arms · 574
GRAFTON REGIS
The White Hart · 410
GRANTCHESTER
The Rupert Brooke · 63
GRANTHAM
The Beehive Inn · 349
GRASMERE
The Travellers Rest Inn · 116
GRAVESEND
The Cock Inn · 314
GREAT AYTON
The Royal Oak · 648
GREAT BARRINGTON
The Fox · 229
GREAT BEDWYN
The Three Tuns · 610
GREAT BRAXTED
Du Cane Arms · 205
GREAT BRICETT
Red Lion · 525
GREAT CHEVERELL
The Bell Inn · 610

GREAT CHISHILL
The Pheasant · 63
GREAT GLEMHAM
The Crown Inn · 529
GREAT HAMPDEN
The Hampden Arms · 49
GREAT HINTON
The Linnet · 612
GREAT HUCKLOW
The Queen Anne Inn · 140
GREAT LANGDALE
The New Dungeon Ghyll Hotel · 116
GREAT MISSENDEN
The Nags Head · 49
The Polecat Inn · 50
The Rising Sun · 50
GREAT OXENDON
The George Inn · 410
GREAT RISSINGTON
The Lamb Inn · 229
GREAT RYBURGH
The Boar Inn · 390
GREAT SALKELD
The Highland Drove Inn and Kyloes
   Restaurant · 116
GREAT TEW
The Falkland Arms · 453
GREAT WHITTINGTON
Queens Head Inn · 422
GREAT WOLFORD
The Fox & Hounds Inn · 586
GREAT YELDHAM
The White Hart · 205
GREEN HAMMERTON
The Bay Horse Inn · 653
GREET
The Harvest Home · 229
GRESFORD5
Pant-yr-Ochain · 762
GRIMSTON
The Black Horse · 341
GRINDLEFORD
The Maynard · 140
GRINTON
The Bridge Inn · 653
GRITTLETON
The Neeld Arms · 612
GUILDFORD
The Keystone · 548
GUILDTOWN
Anglers Inn · 718
GUITING POWER
The Hollow Bottom · 229
GUN HILL
The Gun Inn · 560
GUNNISLAKE
The Rising Sun Inn · 85
GUNWALLOE
The Halzephron Inn · 85
GUSSAGE ALL SAINTS
The Drovers Inn · 188
GWEEK
The Gweek Inn · 86

H

HADDENHAM
The Green Dragon · 50

Index

HAILEY
Bird in Hand 453
HALAM
The Waggon and Horses 432
HALESWORTH
The Queen's Head 529
HALIFAX
The Rock Inn Hotel 681
Shibden Mill Inn 683
HALLATON
The Bewicke Arms 341
HALNAKER
The Anglesey Arms at Halnaker 574
HALTWHISTLE
Milecastle Inn 422
HAMBLEDEN
The Stag & Huntsman Inn 50
HAMBLEDON
The Vine at Hambledon 262
HAMBLE-LE-RICE
The Bugle 262
HAMPTON BISHOP
The Bunch of Carrots 287
HAMPTON IN ARDEN
The White Lion 597
HANDLEY
The Calveley Arms 73
HANNINGTON
The Jolly Tar 612
HANNINGTON
The Vine at Hannington 262
HAPPISBURGH
The Hill House 392
HARBERTON
The Church House Inn 157
HARBY
Bottle & Glass 432
HARE HATCH
The Queen Victoria 27
HAROME
The Star Inn 653
HARRIETSHAM
The Pepper Box Inn 314
HARRINGTON
The Tollemache Arms 411
HARROGATE
The Boars Head Hotel 653
HARROLD
The Muntjac 18
HARTFIELD
Anchor Inn 560
The Hatch Inn 560
HARTLEY WINTNEY
The Phoenix Inn 262
HARTSHORNE
The Mill Wheel 141
HASCOMBE
The White Horse 549
HASELBURY PLUCKNETT
The White Horse at Haselbury 499
HASLEMERE
The Wheatsheaf Inn 549
HASLINGDEN
Farmers Glory 333
HASSOP
Eyre Arms 141

HATHERN
The Anchor Inn 341
HATHERSAGE
Millstone Inn 141
The Plough Inn 141
HATTON
The Case is Altered 586
HAUGHTON MOSS
The Nags Head 73
HAVANT
The Royal Oak 262
HAVERFORDWEST
The Georges Restaurant/Cafe Bar 748
HAWES
The Moorcock Inn 653
HAWKHURST
The Great House 315
The Queens Inn 315
HAWKSHEAD
Kings Arms 116
Queens Head Hotel 116
The Sun Inn 118
The Kings Head 121
The Swinside Inn 121
HAWORTH
The Old White Lion Hotel 683
HAYDON BRIDGE
The General Havelock Inn 422
HAYFIELD
The Royal Hotel 141
HAYLE
The Watermill 86
HAY-ON-WYE
Kilverts Hotel 755
The Old Black Lion 755
HAYTOR VALE
The Rock Inn 157
HECKINGTON
The Nags Head 349
HEDGERLEY
The White Horse 52
HEDLEY ON THE HILL
The Feathers Inn 422
HEMEL HEMPSTEAD
Alford Arms 296
HEMINGFORD GREY
The Cock Pub and Restaurant 63
HENLEY-ON-THAMES
The Cherry Tree Inn 453
The Five Horseshoes 454
Three Tuns Foodhouse 454
WhiteHartNettlebed 457
HENNY STREET
The Henny Swan 205
HEREFORD
The Crown & Anchor 287
HERMITAGE
The White Horse of Hermitage 27
HESKET NEWMARKET
The Old Crown 118
HESKIN GREEN
Farmers Arms 333
HEST BANK
Hest Bank Hotel 333
HETTON
The Angel 653

HEVER
The Wheatsheaf 315
HEVERSHAM
Blue Bell Hotel 118
HEVINGHAM
Marsham Arms Freehouse 392
HEXHAM
Battlesteads Hotel & Restaurant 424
Dipton Mill Inn 424
Miners Arms Inn 424
Rat Inn 424
HEXTON
The Raven 296
HEYDON
Earle Arms 392
HEYSHOTT
Unicorn Inn 574
HEYTESBURY
The Angel Coaching Inn 612
HILDERSHAM
The Pear Tree 63
HILTON
The Prince of Wales 63
HINDHEAD
Devil's Punchbowl Inn 549
HINDON
Angel Inn 612
The Lamb at Hindon 614
HINTON
The Bull Inn 230
HINTON BLEWETT
Ring O'Bells 500
HINTON ST GEORGE
The Lord Poulett Arms 500
HINXTON
The Red Lion 64
HINXWORTH
Three Horseshoes 299
HITCHAM
The White Horse Inn 530
HITCHIN
The Greyhound 299
HODNET
The Bear at Hodnet 481
HODSOLL STREET
The Green Man 315
HOGNASTON
The Red Lion Inn 143
HOLBETON
The Mildmay Colours Inn 158
HOLBROOK
The Compasses 530
HOLCOMBE
The Holcombe Inn 500
HOLKHAM
Victoria at Holkham 392
HOLLINGTON
The Red Lion Inn 143
HOLME UPON SPALDING MOOR
Ye Olde Red Lion Hotel 636
HOLSWORTHY
The Bickford Arms 158
HOLYWELL
The Old Ferryboat Inn 64
HONEY TYE
The Lion 530

HONITON
The Otter Inn — 158
HOOK
Crooked Billet — 265
HOOK NORTON
The Gate Hangs High — 457
Sun Inn — 457
HOPE
Cheshire Cheese Inn — 143
HORBURY
The Quarry Inn — 683
HORNDON
The Elephant's Nest Inn — 158
HORNDON ON THE HILL
Bell Inn & Hill House — 205
HORNS CROSS
The Hoops Inn & Country Hotel — 156
HORRINGER
Beehive — 530
HORSEBRIDGE
The Royal Inn — 159
HORSEBRIDGE
John O'Gaunt Inn — 265
HORSEY
Nelson Head — 393
HORSHAM
The Black Jug — 575
HORSTEAD
Recruiting Sergeant — 393
HORTON
The Bridge Inn — 614
HOUGH-ON-THE-HILL
The Brownlow Arms — 349
HOUSTON
Fox & Hounds — 720
HOVINGHAM
The Malt Shovel — 657
The Worsley Arms Hotel — 657
HOXNE
The Swan — 531
HUBBERHOLME
The George Inn — 657
HUGGATE
The Wolds Inn — 636
HUNGERFORD
The Crown & Garter — 27
The Swan Inn — 29
HUNSDON
The Fox and Hounds — 299
HUNSTANTON
The King William I — 393
HUNTINGDON
The Three Horseshoes — 64
HURST
The Green Man — 29
HUTTON MAGNA
The Oak Tree Inn — 196
HUXLEY
Stuart's Table at the Farmer's Arms — 73

I

IBSLEY
Old Beams Inn — 265
ICKLESHAM
The Queen's Head — 560
ICKLINGHAM
The Plough Inn — 531

The Red Lion — 531
IDEN GREEN
The Peacock — 315
IGHTHAM
The Harrow Inn — 316
ILCHESTER
Ilchester Arms — 500
ILFRACOMBE
The George & Dragon — 159
ILMINGTON
The Howard Arms — 588
ILMINSTER
New Inn — 500
INGATESTONE
The Red Lion — 205
INNERLEITHEN
Corner House — 721
INVERIE
The Old Forge — 711
IRONBRIDGE
The Malthouse — 481
ISLE OF WHITHORN
The Steam Packet Inn — 701
ISLE ORNSAY
Hotel Eilean Iarmain — 726
ITCHEN ABBAS
The Trout — 265
ITTERINGHAM
Walpole Arms — 393
IVYBRIDGE
The Anchor Inn — 159
IVY HATCH
The Plough at Ivy Hatch — 316
IXWORTH
Pykkerell Inn — 531

K

KELMSCOTT
The Plough Inn — 457
KEMPSEY
Walter de Cantelupe Inn — 630
KENDAL
Gateway Inn — 118
KENFIG
Prince of Wales Inn — 730
KESWICK
The Farmers — 118
The Horse & Farrier Inn — 118
The Whoop Hall — 122
KETTERING
The Overstone Arms — 411
KETTLEBURGH
The Chequers Inn — 531
KEYSOE
The Chequers — 18
KEYSTON
Pheasant Inn — 64
KILBURN
The Forresters Arms — 657
KILFINAN
Kilfinan Hotel Bar — 699
KILHAM
The Old Star Inn — 636
KILLIECRANKIE
Killiecrankie House Hotel — 718
KILMINGTON
The Red Lion Inn — 614

KILVE
The Hood Arms — 501
KIMBERLEY
The Nelson & Railway Inn — 432
KIMBOLTON
Stockton Cross Inn — 288
KIMBOLTON
The New Sun Inn — 64
KINCARDINE
The Unicorn — 706
KINGSAND
The Halfway House Inn — 86
KINGSBRIDGE
The Crabshell Inn — 159
KING'S BROMLEY
Royal Oak — 520
KINGSDON
Kingsdon Inn — 501
KINGSFOLD
The Dog and Duck — 575
KINGSKERSWELL
Barn Owl Inn — 159
Bickley Mill Inn — 160
KING'S LYNN
The Stuart House Hotel, Bar &
Restaurant — 393
KING'S NYMPTON
The Grove Inn — 160
KING'S STAG
The Greenman — 188
KINGSTON
The Dolphin Inn — 160
KINGSTON (NEAR LEWES)
The Juggs — 560
KINGSTON UPON HULL
The Minerva Hotel — 638
KINGSWEAR
The Ship — 160
KINGSWOOD
Crooked Billet — 52
KINGTON
The Stagg Inn and Restaurant — 288
KINGTON
The Red Hart — 630
KINNESSWOOD
Lomond Country Inn — 720
KINTBURY
The Dundas Arms — 29
KIPPEN
Cross Keys Hotel — 724
The Inn at Kippen — 725
KIRBY HILL
The Shoulder of Mutton Inn — 657
KIRDFORD
The Half Moon Inn — 575
KIRKBURTON
The Woodman Inn — 683
KIRKBY LONSDALE
The Pheasant Inn — 121
The Sun Inn — 121
KIRKBYMOORSIDE
George & Dragon Hotel — 659
KIRKBY STEPHEN
The Bay Horse — 122
KIRKCUDBRIGHT
Selkirk Arms Hotel — 701

Index

KIRK DEIGHTON
The Bay Horse Inn — 659
KIRKHAM
Stone Trough Inn — 659
KNARESBOROUGH
The General Tarleton Inn — 659
KNIGHTWICK
The Talbot — 630
KNOSSINGTON
The Fox & Hounds — 342
KNOWL HILL
Bird In Hand Country Inn — 31
KNUTSFORD
The Dog Inn — 74
KYLESKU
Kylesku Hotel — 711

L

LACH DENNIS
The Duke of Portland — 74
LACOCK
The George Inn — 614
Red Lion Inn — 614
The Rising Sun — 614
LAKENHEATH
The Half Moon Restaurant & Bar — 533
LAMBERHURST
The Swan at the Vineyard — 316
LAMBS GREEN
The Lamb Inn — 575
LAMORNA
Lamorna Wink — 86
LAMPHEY
The Dial Inn — 748
LANCASTER
The Stork Inn — 333
The Sun Hotel and Bar — 333
The Waterwitch — 334
Ye Olde John O'Gaunt — 334
LANGHAM
The Shepherd and Dog — 207
LANGLEY MARSH
The Three Horseshoes — 501
LANGPORT
The Old Pound Inn — 501
Rose & Crown — 501
LANGTHWAITE
The Red Lion Inn — 659
LANLIVERY
The Crown Inn — 86
LAPWORTH
The Boot Inn — 588
LARLING
Angel Inn — 395
LASTINGHAM
Blacksmiths Arms — 661
LAUDER
The Black Bull — 721
LAVENHAM
Angel Hotel — 533
LAXFIELD
The Kings Head — 533
LAXTON
The Dovecote Inn — 432
LECHLADE ON THAMES
The Trout Inn — 230

LECKHAMPSTEAD
The Stag — 31
LEDBURY
The Farmers Arms — 288
The Feathers Hotel — 286
The Talbot — 289
The Trumpet Inn — 289
LEDSHAM
The Chequers Inn — 683
LEEDS
Whitelocks — 683
LEEK
Three Horseshoes Inn — 520
LEIGH
The Plough — 549
LEIGH
The Greyhound Charcott — 316
LEIGH UPON MENDIP
The Bell Inn — 502
LEITHOLM
The Plough Hotel — 721
LEOMINSTER
The Grape Vaults — 289
The Royal Oak Hotel — 289
LETTERSTON
The Harp Inn — 748
LEVINGTON
The Ship Inn — 533
LEWDOWN
The Harris Arms — 161
LEWES
The Snowdrop — 561
LEWKNOR
The Leathern Bottel — 457
LEYBURN
The Old Horn Inn — 661
Sandpiper Inn — 661
LICKFOLD
The Lickfold Inn — 576
LIDGATE
The Star Inn — 533
LIFTON
The Arundell Arms — 161
LIMPLEY STOKE
The Hop Pole Inn — 616
LINCOLN
Pyewipe Inn — 350
The Victoria — 350
Wig & Mitre — 350
LINGFIELD
Hare and Hounds — 550
LINLITHGOW
Champany Inn – The Chop and Ale House — 725
LINSLADE
The Globe Inn — 18
LINTHWAITE
The Sair Inn — 683
LINTON
The Bull Inn — 317
LINTON
The Windmill Inn — 685
LINWOOD
The High Corner Inn — 265
LITTLEBOROUGH
The White House — 249

LITTLEBOURNE
King William IV — 317
LITTLE BRAXTED
The Green Man — 207
LITTLE CANFIELD
The Lion & Lamb — 207
LITTLE CHALFONT
The Sugar Loaf Inn — 52
LITTLE CHEVERELL
The Owl — 616
LITTLE COWARNE
The Three Horseshoes Inn — 289
LITTLE DUNMOW
Flitch of Bacon — 207
LITTLE FRANSHAM
The Canary and Linnet — 395
LITTLE HADHAM
The Nags Head — 301
LITTLE HAVEN
The Swan Inn — 748
LITTLEHEMPSTON
Tally Ho Inn — 161
LITTLE LANGDALE
Three Shires Inn — 122
LITTLE NESTON
The Old Harp — 74
LITTLETON
The Running Horse — 266
LITTLETON–ON–SEVERN
White Hart — 230
LITTLE WALSINGHAM
The Black Lion Hotel — 395
LITTLE WASHBOURNE
The Hobnails Inn — 230
LITTLE WILBRAHAM
Hole in the Wall — 64
LITTON
Red Lion Inn — 143
LITTON
Queens Arms — 661
LIVERPOOL
Everyman Bistro — 384
LLANARMON DYFFRYN CEIRIOG
The Hand at Llanarmon — 763
The West Arms Hotel — 763
LLANBEDR
Victoria Inn — 741
LLANDDAROG
White Hart Thatched Inn & Brewery — 731
LLANDEILO
The Angel Hotel — 732
The Castle Hotel — 732
LLANDRINDOD WELLS
The Gold Bell Country Inn — 755
LLANDUDNO JUNCTION
The Queens Head — 737
LLANFAIR WATERDINE
The Waterdine — 481
LLANFYLLIN
Cain Valley Hotel — 755
LLANGATTOCK
The Vine Tree Inn — 757
LLANGOLLEN
The Corn Mill — 737
LLANGYBI
The White Hart Village Inn — 743

Index

LLANGYNIDR
The Coach & Horses 757
LLANNEFYDD
The Hawk & Buckle Inn 737
LLANTRISANT
The Greyhound Inn 743
LLANVAIR DISCOED
The Woodland Restaurant & Bar 744
LLOWES
The Radnor Arms 757
LLWYNDAFYDD
The Crown Inn & Restaurant 733
LOCHBOISDALE
The Polochar Inn 727
LOCHGILPHEAD
Cairnbaan Hotel 699
LODERS
Loders Arms 188
LODSWORTH
The Halfway Bridge Inn 576
The Hollist Arms 576
LONDON E1
Town of Ramsgate 354
LONDON E9
The Empress of India 354
LONDON E14
The Grapes 354
The Gun 354
LONDON EC1
The Bleeding Heart Tavern 355
The Eagle 355
The Jerusalem Tavern 355
The Peasant 355
The Well 356
Ye Olde Mitre 356
The White Swan 357
LONDON EC2
Old Dr Butler's Head 356
LONDON EC4
The Black Friar 356
The Old Bank of England 356
LONDON N1
The Barnsbury 357
The Compton Arms 357
The Crown 357
The Drapers Arms 357
The Duke of Cambridge 358
The House 358
The Northgate 358
LONDON N6
The Flask 358
LONDON N19
The Landseer 358
LONDON NW1
The Chapel 359
The Engineer 359
The Globe 359
The Lansdowne 359
The Queens 360
The Lord Palmerston 361
The Vine 361
LONDON NW3
The Holly Bush 360
Spaniards Inn 360
Ye Olde White Bear 360
LONDON NW5
Dartmouth Arms 360

The Junction Tavern 360
LONDON NW6
The Salusbury Pub and Dining Room 361
LONDON NW8
The Salt House 361
LONDON NW10
The Greyhound 362
William IV Bar & Restaurant 362
LONDON SE1
The Anchor 362
The Anchor & Hope 362
The Bridge House Bar & Dining Rooms 362
The Fire Station 363
The Garrison 363
The George Inn 363
The Market Porter 363
The Old Thameside 363
LONDON SE5
The Sun and Doves 363
LONDON SE10
The Cutty Sark Tavern 365
Greenwich Union Pub 365
North Pole Bar & Restaurant 365
LONDON SE16
The Mayflower 365
LONDON SE21
The Crown & Greyhound 365
LONDON SE22
Franklins 367
LONDON SE23
The Dartmouth Arms 367
LONDON SW1
The Albert 367
The Buckingham Arms 367
The Clarence 367
The Grenadier 368
Nags Head 368
The Orange Brewery 368
The Wilton Arms 368
The Builders Arms 369
The Coopers of Flood Street 369
The Cross Keys 369
The Phene Arms 369
The Pig's Ear 369
LONDON SW3
The Admiral Codrington 368
LONDON SW4
The Belle Vue 370
The Coach & Horses 370
The Royal Oak 370
The Windmill on the Common 370
LONDON SW6
The Atlas 370
The Imperial 371
The Salisbury Tavern 371
The White Horse 371
LONDON SW7
The Anglesea Arms 371
Swag and Tails 371
LONDON SW8
The Masons Arms 371
LONDON SW10
The Chelsea Ram 373
The Hollywood Arms 373
Lots Road Pub and Dining Room 373
The Sporting Page 373

LONDON SW11
The Castle 374
The Fox & Hounds 374
LONDON SW13
The Bull's Head 374
The Idle Hour 374
LONDON SW15
The Spencer Arms 376
LONDON SW18
The Alma Tavern 376
The Cat's Back 376
The Earl Spencer 376
The Freemasons 377
The Old Sergeant 377
The Ship Inn 377
LONDON SW19
The Brewery Tap 377
LONDON W1
The Argyll Arms 377
French House 377
Red Lion 378
The Swan 379
LONDON W2
The Cow 378
The Prince Bonaparte 378
The Westbourne 378
LONDON W4
The Devonshire House 378
The Pilot 378
LONDON W5
The Red Lion 379
The Wheatsheaf 379
LONDON W6
Anglesea Arms 379
The Dartmouth Castle 380
The Stonemasons Arms 380
The Windsor Castle 381
LONDON W8
The Churchill Arms 380
Mall Tavern 380
The Scarsdale 380
LONDON W9
The Waterway 381
LONDON W10
The Fat Badger 381
Golborne Grove 381
The North Pole 381
LONDON W11
Portobello Gold 382
LONDON W14
The Cumberland Arms 382
The Havelock Tavern 382
LONDON WC1
The Bountiful Cow 382
The Lamb 383
LONDON WC2
The Lamb and Flag 383
The Seven Stars 383
LONG CLAWSON
The Crown & Plough 342
LONG CRENDON
The Angel Inn 52
LONGFRAMLINGTON
The Anglers Arms 424
LONGHOPE
The Glasshouse Inn 230

Index

LONGHORSLEY
Linden Tree 428
LONG ITCHINGTON
The Duck on the Pond 588
LONGPARISH
The Plough Inn 266
LONG PRESTON
Maypole Inn 662
LONGSHAW
Fox House 143
LONG SUTTON
The Devonshire Arms 502
LOSTWITHIEL
The Royal Oak 88
LOUGHBOROUGH
The Swan in the Rushes 342
LOUTH
Masons Arms 350
LOVINGTON
The Pilgrims 502
LOW CATTON
The Gold Cup Inn 638
LOWER ANSTY
The Fox Inn 188
LOWER APPERLEY
The Farmers Arms 231
LOWER CHICKSGROVE
Compasses Inn 616
LOWER LARGO
The Crusoe Hotel 706
LOWER ODDINGTON
The Fox 231
LOWER SHIPLAKE
The Baskerville Arms 459
LOWER VOBSTER
Vobster Inn 502
LOWER WHITLEY
Chetwode Arms 74
LOWER WIELD
The Yew Tree 266
LOWER WOLVERCOTE
The Trout Inn 459
LOWESWATER
Kirkstile Inn 122
LOWICK
The Snooty Fox 412
LOW NEWTON BY THE SEA
The Ship Inn 428
LOW ROW
The Punch Bowl Inn 662
LUDGVAN
White Hart 88
LUDLOW
The Church Inn 482
The Clive Bar & Restaurant with Rooms 482
The Roebuck Inn 482
Unicorn Inn 482
LUDWELL
The Grove Arms 616
LUND
The Wellington Inn 638
LURGASHALL
The Noah's Ark 576
LUTON (NEAR CHUDLEIGH)
The Elizabethan Inn 161
LUXBOROUGH
The Royal Oak Inn 502

LYBSTER
Portland Arms 711
LYDDINGTON
Old White Hart 475
LYDFORD
Dartmoor Inn 161
LYDNEY
The George Inn 231
LYME REGIS
Pilot Boat Inn 188
LYMINGTON
The Kings Arms 266
Mayflower Inn 268
LYMPSTONE
The Globe Inn 163
LYNDHURST
New Forest Inn 268
The Oak Inn 268
The Trusty Servant 268
LYNMOUTH
Rising Sun Hotel 163
LYNTON
The Bridge Inn 163

M

MACCLESFIELD
The Windmill Inn 76
MACHYNLLETH
Wynnstay Hotel 757
MADELEY
All Nations Inn 483
The New Inn 483
MADINGLEY
The Three Horseshoes 65
MADLEY
The Comet Inn 289
MAIDENHEAD
The Belgian Arms 31
The White Hart 31
MAIDSTONE
The Black Horse Inn 317
MALLWYD
Brigands Inn 741
MALMESBURY
Horse & Groom 616
The Smoking Dog 616
The Vine Tree 616
MALPAS
The Heron Inn 88
MALVERN
The Anchor Inn 630
The Red Lion 630
MAMHILAD
Horseshoe Inn 744
MANACCAN
The New Inn 88
MANCHESTER
Dukes 92 251
Marble Arch 251
The Queen's Arms 251
MANNINGTREE
The Mistley Thorn 207
MAPLEDURWELL
The Gamekeepers 269
MAPLEHURST
The White Horse 576

MARAZION
Godolphin Arms 88
MARDEN
The Millstream 618
MARFORD
Trevor Arms Hotel 763
MARKBEECH
The Kentish Horse 317
MARLDON
The Church House Inn 163
MARLOW
The Kings Head 52
MARSDEN
The Olive Branch 685
MARSHAM
The Plough Inn 395
MARSH BENHAM
The Red House 33
MARSHFIELD
The Catherine Wheel 232
The Lord Nelson Inn 232
MARSHWOOD
The Bottle Inn 189
MARSTON
Victoria Arms 459
MARSTON MONTGOMERY
The Crown Inn 144
MARTLEY
Admiral Rodney Inn 632
The Crown Inn 632
MARTOCK
The Nag's Head Inn 502
MARTON
The Sun Inn 483
MARTON
The Davenport Arms 76
MARTON
The Appletree 662
MARYCULTER
Old Mill Inn 694
MASHAM
The Black Sheep Brewery 662
Kings Head Hotel 662
MATLOCK
The Red Lion 144
MAYFIELD
The Middle House 561
MEAVY
The Royal Oak Inn 164
MELBOURNE
The Melbourne Arms 144
MELLOR
The Moorfield Arms 251
The Oddfellows Arms 251
MELMERBY
The Shepherds Inn 122
MELROSE
Burts Hotel 721
MELTON
Wilford Bridge 535
MENTMORE
Il Maschio @ The Stag 52
MEVAGISSEY
The Rising Sun Inn 89
The Ship Inn 89
MEYSEY HAMPTON
The Masons Arms 232

MICHAELCHURCH ESCLEY
The Bridge Inn — 290
MICHELDEVER
Half Moon & Spread Eagle — 269
MICKLEHAM
King William IV — 550
The Running Horses — 550
MIDDLEHAM
Black Swan Hotel — 663
MIDDLESMOOR
Crown Hotel — 663
MIDDLESTONE
Ship Inn — 196
MIDDLETON (NEAR PICKERING)
The Middleton Arms — 663
MIDDLETON-IN-TEESDALE
The Teesdale Hotel — 196
MIDDLETON STONEY
Best Western Jersey Arms Hotel — 459
MIDHURST
The Angel Hotel — 578
MILLTOWN
The Nettle Inn — 144
MILTON
The Black Boy Inn — 459
MILTON
Waggon & Horses — 65
MILTON ABBAS
The Hambro Arms — 189
MILTON BRYAN
The Red Lion — 20
MILVERTON
The Globe — 505
MINCHINHAMPTON
The Old Lodge — 232
The Weighbridge Inn — 232
MINETY
Vale of the White Horse Inn — 618
MITCHELL
The Plume of Feathers — 89
MODBURY
California Country Inn — 164
MOFFAT
Black Bull Hotel — 702
MOLD
Glasfryn — 740
MOLLAND
The London Inn — 164
MONKNASH
The Plough & Harrow — 760
MONKS ELEIGH
The Swan Inn — 535
MONKSILVER
The Notley Arms — 505
MONKS KIRBY
The Bell Inn — 588
MONTACUTE
The Kings Arms Inn — 505
The Phelips Arms — 505
MONTGOMERY
Dragon Hotel — 757
MONXTON
The Black Swan — 269
MORETONHAMPSTEAD
The White Hart Hotel — 164
MORTIMER WEST END
The Red Lion — 270

MORTON
The Full Moon Inn — 432
MORWENSTOW
The Bush Inn — 89
MOTCOMBE
The Coppleridge Inn — 189
MOULDSWORTH
The Goshawk — 76
MOULSOE
The Carrington Arms — 55
MOULTON
Black Bull Inn — 663
MOUNTSORREL
The Swan Inn — 342
MOWSLEY
The Staff of Life — 342
MUCH MARCLE
The Slip Tavern — 290
MUCH WENLOCK
The Feathers Inn — 483
The George & Dragon — 483
Longville Arms — 483
The Talbot Inn — 484
Wenlock Edge Inn — 484
MUKER
The Farmers Arms — 664
MUNDFORD
Crown Hotel — 397
MUNGRISDALE
The Mill Inn — 122
MUNSLOW
The Crown Country Inn — 484
MURCOTT
The Nut Tree Inn — 459
MYLOR BRIDGE
The Pandora Inn — 91
MYTHOLMROYD
Shoulder of Mutton — 685

N

NAILSWORTH
The Britannia — 232
Egypt Mill — 235
Tipputs Inn — 235
NANTGAREDIG
Y Polyn — 732
NANTGWYNANT
Pen-Y-Gwryd Hotel — 741
NANTWICH
The Thatch Inn — 76
NAPTON ON THE HILL
The Bridge at Napton — 588
NAUNTON
The Black Horse — 235
NAYLAND
Anchor Inn — 535
NEAR SAWREY
Tower Bank Arms — 122
NETHER BROUGHTON
The Red House — 342
NETHERLEY
The Lairhillock Inn — 694
NETHERTON
The Star Inn — 428
NETHER WASDALE
The Screes Inn — 125

NETHER WESTCOTE
The Westcote Inn — 235
NETTLECOMBE
Marquis of Lorne — 189
NEW ABBEY
Criffel Inn — 702
NEWALL
The Spite Inn — 685
NEW ALRESFORD
The Globe on the Lake — 270
NEWBURY
The Yew Tree Inn — 33
NEWCASTLE UPON TYNE
Shiremoor House Farm — 583
NEWDIGATE
The Surrey Oaks — 550
NEW GALLOWAY
Cross Keys Hotel — 702
NEWLAND
The Ostrich Inn — 235
NEWNHAM
The George Inn — 317
NEWPORT
Salutation Inn — 749
NEW RADNOR
Red Lion Inn — 758
NEWTON
The Red Lion — 350
NEWTON
The Queen's Head — 65
NEWTON ABBOT
The Wild Goose Inn — 164
NEWTON AYCLIFFE
Blacksmiths Arms — 196
NEWTON-ON-THE-MOOR
The Cook and Barker Inn — 428
NEWTON ST CYRES
The Beer Engine — 166
NEWTON STEWART
Creebridge House Hotel — 702
NEWTON TONY
The Malet Arms — 618
NEWTOWN LINFORD
The Bradgate — 344
NITON
Buddle Inn — 599
NORBURY JUNCTION
The Junction Inn — 520
NORTHAMPTON
The Fox & Hounds — 412
NORTH BALLACHULISH
Loch Leven Hotel — 711
NORTH BOVEY
The Ring of Bells Inn — 166
NORTH CERNEY
Bathurst Arms — 237
NORTH CURRY
The Bird in Hand — 505
NORTH FAMBRIDGE
The Ferry Boat Inn — 208
NORTHILL
The Crown — 20
NORTHLEACH
The Puesdown Inn — 237
NORTHOP
Stables Bar Restaurant — 740

NORTH RIGTON
The Square and Compass 664
NORTH WALTHAM
The Fox 270
NORTHWOOD
Travellers Joy 599
NORTH WOOTTON
The Three Elms 189
NORTON
The Hundred House Hotel 484
NORTON ST PHILIP
George Inn 505
NORWICH Adam & Eve 397
The Mad Moose Arms 397
Ribs of Beef 397
NOSS MAYO
The Ship Inn 166
NOTTINGHAM
Cock & Hoop 432
Fellows Morton & Clayton 434
Ye Olde Trip to Jerusalem 434
NUNNEY
The George at Nunney 505
NUNNINGTON
The Royal Oak Inn 664
NUNTON
The Radnor Arms 618
NUTHURST
Black Horse Inn 578
OADBY
Cow and Plough 344
OAKHAM
Barnsdale Lodge Hotel 475
The Blue Ball 475
The Grainstore Brewery 475
The Old Plough 475

O

OAKRIDGE
The Butcher's Arms 237
OAKSEY
The Wheatsheaf Inn 619
OCKLEY
Bryce's at The Old School House 551
The Kings Arms Inn 551
ODELL
The Bell 20
OFFHAM
The Blacksmiths Arms 561
OLD BASING
The Millstone 270
OLDBURY
Waggon & Horses 597
OLDBURY-ON-SEVERN
The Anchor Inn 237
OLD DALBY
The Crown Inn 344
OLDHAM
The Roebuck Inn 251
The White Hart Inn 252
OLD KNEBWORTH
The Lytton Arms 301
OLDMELDRUM
The Redgarth 696
OLD RADNOR
The Harp 758
OLDSTEAD
The Black Swan 664

OLD WARDEN
Hare and Hounds 20
OMBERSLEY
Crown & Sandys Arms 632
ORFORD
Jolly Sailor Inn 535
King's Head 537
ORLETON
The Boot Inn 290
ORMSKIRK
Eureka 334
OSMINGTON MILLS
The Smugglers Inn 190
OSMOTHERLEY
The Golden Lion 665
Queen Catherine 665
OTTERY ST MARY
The Talaton Inn 166
OUNDLE
The Montagu Arms 412
OUTGATE
Outgate Inn 125
OVER STRATTON
The Royal Oak 506
OVING
The Gribble Inn 578
OVING
The Black Boy 55
OVINGTON
The Bush 272
OWSLEBURY
The Ship Inn 272
OXFORD
The Anchor 461
Turf Tavern 461

P

PADSIDE
The Stone House Inn 665
PAINSWICK
The Falcon Inn 239
PALEY STREET
The Royal Oak 33
PARBOLD
The Eagle & Child 334
PARRACOMBE
The Fox & Goose 166
PARTNEY
Red Lion Inn 351
PARTRIDGE GREEN
The Green Man Inn and Restaurant 578
PATELEY BRIDGE
The Sportsmans Arms Hotel 665
PATTISWICK
The Compasses at Pattiswick 208
PAVE LANE
The Fox 484
PAXFORD
The Churchill Arms 239
PEEL
The Creek Inn 691
PELDON
The Peldon Rose 208
PEMBRIDGE
New Inn 290
PEMBROKE DOCK
Ferry Inn 749
The Sloop Inn 749

PENALLT
The Boat Inn 744
PENICUIK
The Howgate Restaurant 717
PENISTONE
Cubley Hall 679
The Fountain Inn Hotel 680
PENKETH
The Ferry Tavern 76
PENSHURST
The Bottle House Inn 318
The Leicester Arms 318
The Spotted Dog 318
PENZANCE
Dolphin Tavern 91
The Turks Head Inn 91
PERRANUTHNOE
The Victoria Inn 91
PETERBOROUGH
The Brewery Tap 65
Charters Bar & East Restaurant 65
PETERSFIELD
The Good Intent 272
The Trooper Inn 272
The White Horse Inn 274
PETERSTOW
The Red Lion Inn 290
PETWORTH
The Black Horse 579
The Grove Inn 579
PEWSEY
The Seven Stars 619
PICKERING
Fox & Hounds Country Inn 665
Horseshoe Inn 667
The White Swan Inn 667
PICKHILL
Nags Head Country Inn 667
PICKLESCOTT
Bottle & Glass Inn 484
PICTON
The Station Pub 667
PIDDLEHINTON
The Thimble Inn 190
PIDDLETRENTHIDE
The Piddle Inn 190
The Poachers Inn 190
PILLEY
The Fleur de Lys 274
PIRBRIGHT
The Royal Oak 551
PISHILL
The Crown Inn 461
PITLOCHRY
Moulin Hotel 720
PITNEY
The Halfway House 506
PITTON
The Silver Plough 619
PLOCKTON
The Plockton Hotel 712
Plockton Inn & Seafood Restaurant 712
PLUCKLEY
The Dering Arms 318
The Mundy Bois 318
PLUMLEY
The Golden Pheasant Hotel 76
The Smoker 78

PLUSH
The Brace of Pheasants 190
POLKERRIS
The Rashleigh Inn 91
POLPERRO
Old Mill House Inn 92
POLSTEAD
The Cock Inn 537
POOLE
The Guildhall Tavern Ltd 191
PORLOCK
The Ship Inn 506
The Anchor Hotel & Ship Inn 506
PORT APPIN
The Pierhouse Hotel & Seafood Restaurant 699
PORT ERIN
Falcon's Nest Hotel 691
PORT GAVERNE
Port Gaverne Hotel 92
PORTHLEVEN
The Ship Inn 92
PORTPATRICK
Crown Hotel 703
PORTREATH
Basset Arms 92
PORTSMOUTH & SOUTHSEA
The Wine Vaults 274
POTTERS CROUCH
The Hollybush 301
POULTON
The Falcon Inn 239
POWERSTOCK
Three Horseshoes Inn 191
POWICK
The Halfway House Inn 632
POYNINGS
Royal Oak Inn 579
PRESTATYN
Nant Hall Restaurant & Bar 739
PRESTBURY
The Legh Arms & Black Boy Restaurant 78
PRESTON
Cartford Country Inn & Hotel 336
PRESTON BAGOT
The Crabmill 589
PRIDDY
New Inn 506
PRIORS MARSTON
The Hollybush Inn 589
PUNCKNOWLE
The Crown Inn 191

R

RADNAGE
The Three Horseshoes Inn 55
RADWINTER
The Plough Inn 208
RAGLAN
The Beaufort Arms Coaching Inn & Restaurant 744
RAITHBY
Red Lion Inn 351
RAMSBURY
The Bell 619
RAMSDEN
The Royal Oak 461

RATHO
The Bridge Inn 705
RATLEY
The Rose and Crown 589
RATTERY
Church House Inn 166
RAVENSTONEDALE
The Black Swan 125
The Fat Lamb Country Inn 125
King's Head 125
RAWTENSTALL
The Boars Head 336
REACH
Dyke's End 66
READING
The Crown 34
The Flowing Spring 34
The Shoulder of Mutton 34
REDE
The Plough 537
RED HILL
The Stag at Redhill 589
REDMILE
Peacock Inn 345
RED WHARF BAY
The Ship Inn 730
REEPHAM
The Old Brewery House Hotel 397
REETH
Charles Bathurst Inn 669
REYNOLDSTON
King Arthur Hotel 760
RHEWL
The Drovers Arms, Rhewl 739
RIBCHESTER
The White Bull 336
RICKMANSWORTH
The Rose and Crown 301
RINGMER
The Cock 561
RINGSTEAD
The Gin Trap Inn 397
RIPLEY
The Moss Cottage Hotel 144
RIPPONDEN
Old Bridge Inn 687
ROBIN HOOD'S BAY
Laurel Inn 669
ROCKBEARE
Jack in the Green Inn 168
ROCKBOURNE
The Rose & Thistle 274
ROCKFORD
The Alice Lisle 275
RODE
The Mill at Rode 509
ROKE
Home Sweet Home 461
ROMALDKIRK
Rose & Crown 198
ROMSEY
The Dukes Head 275
The Three Tuns 275
ROOKLEY
The Chequers 599
ROSEBUSH
Tafarn Sinc 749

ROSEDALE ABBEY
The Milburn Arms Hotel 669
ROSS-ON-WYE
The Moody Cow 292
ROWDE
The George & Dragon 620
ROWFOOT
The Wallace Arms 428
ROWHOOK
Neals Restaurant at The Chequers Inn 581
ROWLAND'S CASTLE
The Castle Inn 275
The Fountain Inn 275
ROWSLEY
The Grouse & Claret 144
ROYSTON
The Cabinet Free House and Restaurant 301
RUAN LANIHORNE
The Kings Head 93
RUDDINGTON
Three Crowns 434
RUDGE
The Full Moon at Rudge 509
RUDGWICK
The Fox Inn 581
RUGBY
Golden Lion Hotel 590
RUSHLAKE GREEN
Horse & Groom 563
RUTHIN
Ye Olde Anchor Inn 739
White Horse Inn 739
RYE
The Globe Inn 563
Mermaid Inn 563
The Ypres Castle Inn 565

S

SADDINGTON
The Queens Head 345
SAFFRON WALDEN
The Cricketers' Arms 206
ST AGNES
Driftwood Spars 93
ST AGNES (ISLES OF SCILLY)
Turks Head 93
ST ALBANS
Rose & Crown 301
ST ANDREWS
The Inn at Lathones 706
ST ASAPH
The Plough Inn 739
ST AUBIN
Old Court House Inn 690
Royal Hotel 690
ST BOSWELLS
Buccleuch Arms Hotel 723
ST BREWARD
The Old Inn & Restaurant 93
ST DOGMAELS
Webley Waterfront Inn & Hotel 751
ST EWE
The Crown Inn 94
ST GEORGE
The Kinmel Arms 737
ST HILARY
The Bush Inn 762

Index

ST JUST (NEAR LAND'S END)
Star Inn 94
ST MARGARET'S AT CLIFFE
The Coastguard 321
ST MARY BOURNE
The Bourne Valley Inn 276
ST MAWES
The Rising Sun 94
The Victory Inn 94
ST MAWGAN
The Falcon Inn 95
ST NEOT
The London Inn 95
ST PETER SOUTH ELMHAM
Wicked at St Peter's Hall 537
SALCOMBE
The Victoria Inn 168
SALISBURY
The Haunch of Venison 620
SALTASH
The Crooked Inn 95
The Weary Friar Inn 95
SALTHOUSE
The Dun Cow 397
SANDWICH
George & Dragon Inn 321
SAPPERTON
The Bell at Sapperton 239
SAWDON
The Anvil Inn 669
SAWLEY
The Spread Eagle 336
SAWLEY
The Sawley Arms 669
SCAWTON
The Hare Inn 670
SEAHOUSES
The Olde Ship Hotel 428
SEAVIEW
The Seaview Hotel & Restaurant 599
SEDBERGH
The Dalesman Country Inn 125
SEDGEFIELD
Dun Cow Inn 198
SEDGLEY
Reaçon Hotel & Sarah Hughes Brewery 597
SEEND
Bell Inn 620
SELBORNE
The Selborne Arms 276
SELLACK
The Lough Pool Inn at Sellack 292
SELLING
The Rose and Crown 321
SEMINGTON
The Lamb on the Strand 620
SENNEN
The Old Success Inn 96
SETTLE
Golden Lion 670
SEVENOAKS
The White Hart Inn 321
SHALFLEET
The New Inn 601
SHALFORD
The George Inn 210
SHANKLIN
Fisherman's Cottage 601

SHARDLOW
The Old Crown 145
SHEEPSCOMBE
The Butchers Arms 240
SHEEPWASH
Half Moon Inn 168
SHEFFIELD
The Fat Cat 680
Lions Lair 680
SHEFFORD
The Black Horse 20
SHELLEY
The Three Acres Inn 687
SHENINGTON
The Bell 461
SHEPTON BEAUCHAMP
Duke of York 509
SHEPTON MALLET
The Three Horseshoes Inn 509
The Waggon and Horses 509
SHEPTON MONTAGUE
The Montague Inn 509
SHERBORNE
The Digby Tap 191
Half Moon Inn 191
Queen's Head 192
Skippers Inn 192
White Hart 192
SHERSTON
Carpenters Arms 621
SHIELDAIG
Shieldaig Bar & Coastal Kitchen 712
SHIFNAL
Odfellows Wine Bar 487
SHIPLEY
The Countryman Inn 581
George & Dragon 581
SHIPSTON ON STOUR
The Cherington Arms 590
The Red Lion 590
White Bear Hotel 590
SHIPTON-UNDER-WYCHWOOD
The Shaven Crown Hotel 461
SHIRENEWTON
The Carpenters Arms 745
SHOBDON
The Bateman Arms 292
SHOCKLACH
Bull Inn Country Bistro 78
SHORTBRIDGE
The Peacock Inn 565
SHORWELL
The Crown Inn 601
SHREWLEY
The Durham Ox Restaurant and Country Pub 593
SHREWSBURY
The Armoury 487
The Mytton & Mermaid Hotel 487
The Plume of Feathers 487
SHROTON OR IWERNE COURTNEY
The Cricketers 192
SIBBERTOFT
The Red Lion 412
SIDMOUTH
Dukes 168
SILCHESTER
Calleva Arms 276

SILEBY
The White Swan 345
SINGLETON
The Partridge Inn 581
SKEGNESS
Best Western Vine Hotel 351
SKENFRITH
The Bell at Skenfrith 745
SKIPTON
Devonshire Arms 670
SKIRMETT
The Frog 55
SLAIDBURN
Hark to Bounty Inn 336
SLAPTON
The Tower Inn 168
SLINDON
The Spur 581
SMARDEN
The Bell 321
The Chequers Inn 322
SNAINTON
Coachman Inn 670
SNAPE
The Crown Inn 538
The Golden Key 538
Plough & Sail 538
SNETTISHAM
The Rose & Crown 395
SOLIHULL
The Boat Inn 597
SOLVA
The Cambrian Inn 751
SOMERBY
Stilton Cheese Inn 345
SOMERFORD KEYNES
The Bakers Arms 240
SORN
The Sorn Inn 704
SOURTON
The Highwayman Inn 171
SOUTHAMPTON
The White Star Tavern & Dining Rooms 276
SOUTH CAVE
The Fox and Coney Inn 638
SOUTH DALTON
The Pipe & Glass Inn 638
SOUTH GODSTONE
Fox & Hounds 551
SOUTH HARTING
The Ship Inn 582
SOUTHILL
The White Horse 20
SOUTH LUFFENHAM
The Coach House Inn 477
SOUTH MORETON
The Crown Inn 463
SOUTH POOL
The Millbrook Inn 171
SOUTHPORT
The Berkeley Arms 384
SOUTHROP
The Swan at Southrop 240
SOUTHSEA; SOUTH STOKE
The Perch and Pike 463
SOUTH WINGFIELD
The White Hart 145

SOUTH WITHAM
Blue Cow Inn & Brewery 351
SOUTHWOLD
The Crown Hotel 536
The Randolph 538
SOUTH ZEAL
Oxenham Arms 171
SOWERBY
The Travellers Rest 687
SOWERBY BRIDGE
The Millbank 687
SPALDWICK
The George Inn 66
SPARKFORD
The Sparkford Inn 511
SPARSHOLT
The Plough Inn 278
SPELDHURST
George & Dragon 322
SPREYTON
The Tom Cobley Tavern 171
STACKPOLE
The Stackpole Inn 751
STADHAMPTON
The Crazy Bear 463
STAFFORD
The Holly Bush Inn 520
The Moat House 520
STAINES
The Swan Hotel 553
STALYBRIDGE
The Royal Oak 252
Stalybridge Station Buffet Bar 252
STAMFORD
The Bull & Swan Inn 351
The George of Stamford 352
STANBRIDGE
The Five Bells 21
STANDON
The Kick & Dicky 303
STANFORD DINGLEY
The Bull Country Inn 34
The Old Boot Inn 36
STANTON
The Rose & Crown 539
STANTON ST JOHN
Star Inn 463
The Talkhouse 463
STANTON WICK
The Carpenters Arms 511
STAPLE FITZPAINE
The Greyhound Inn 511
STAPLEFORD
Papillon Woodhall Arms 303
STARBOTTON
Fox & Hounds Inn 670
STATHERN
Red Lion Inn 346
STEDHAM
Hamilton Arms/Nava Thai Restaurant 582
STEEP
Harrow Inn 278
STEIN
Stein Inn 727
STILTON
The Bell Inn Hotel 66
STOCK
The Hoop 210

STOCKBRIDGE
Mayfly 278
The Peat Spade 278
STOCKLAND
The Kings Arms Inn 171
STOCKPORT
The Arden Arms 252
The Nursery Inn 252
STOFORD
The Swan Inn 621
STOGUMBER
The White Horse 511
STOKE ABBOTT
The New Inn 193
STOKE BRUERNE
The Boat Inn 414
STOKE-BY-NAYLAND
The Angel Inn 539
The Crown 539
STOKE FLEMING
The Green Dragon Inn 171
STOKE HOLY CROSS
The Wildebeest Arms 399
STOKE MANDEVILLE
The Wool Pack 55
STOKENHAM
The Tradesman's Arms 173
STOKE ROW
Crooked Billet 464
STOKE ST GREGORY
Rose & Crown 511
STONEHALL
The Fruiterer's Arms 634
STONEHOUSE
The George Inn 240
STOTTESDON
Fighting Cocks 488
STOURPAINE
The White Horse Inn 193
STOURTON
Spread Eagle Inn 621
STOURTON
The Fox Inn 520
STOW BARDOLPH
The Hare Arms 399
STOWMARKET
The Buxhall Crown 540
STOW-ON-THE-WOLD
The Eagle and Child 242
The Unicorn 242
STRACHUR
Creggans Inn 695
STRADBROKE
The Ivy House 540
STRATFIELD TURGIS
The Wellington Arms 278
STRATFORD-UPON-AVON
The Dirty Duck 593
The Fox & Goose Inn 593
The One Elm 593
STRATTON
Saxon Arms 193
STRETE
Kings Arms 173
STRETHAM
The Lazy Otter 66
STRETTON
The Jackson Stops Inn 477

Ram Jam Inn 477
STRETTON ON FOSSE
The Plough Inn 593
STROUD
Bear of Rodborough Hotel 242
The Ram Inn 242
Rose & Crown Inn 242
The Woolpack Inn 242
STUDLAND
The Bankes Arms Hotel 193
SURFLEET SEAS END
The Ship Inn 352
SUTTON
John O'Gaunt Inn 21
SUTTON-ON-THE-FOREST
The Blackwell Ox Inn 672
SUTTON UPON DERWENT
St Vincent Arms 638
SWALCLIFFE
Stag's Head 464
SWALLOWFIELD
The George & Dragon 36
SWANTON MORLEY
Darbys Freehouse 399
SWERFORD
The Mason's Arms 464
SWETTENHAM
The Swettenham Arms 78
SWILLAND
Moon & Mushroom Inn 540
SWINDON
The Sun Inn 621
SWINTON
The Wheatsheaf at Swinton 723
SYDENHAM
The Crown Inn 464
SYDLING ST NICHOLAS
The Greyyuurpain Inn 193
SYMINGTON
Wheatsheaf Inn 724
SYMONDS YAT (EAST)
The Saracens Head Inn 292

T

TADMARTON
The Lampet Arms 464
TALGARTH
Castle Inn 758
TALYBONT-ON-USK
Star Inn 758
TANGLEY
The Fox Inn 278
TARPORLEY
Alvanley Arms Inn 79
The Boot Inn 79
TARRANT MONKTON
The Langton Arms 194
TATENHILL
Horseshoe Inn 522
TAUNTON
The Hatch Inn 513
Queens Arms 513
TAYVALLICH
Tayvallich Inn 701
TEMPLE GRAFTON
The Blue Boar Inn 593
TENBURY WELLS
The Fountain Hotel 634

Index

The Peacock Inn 634
TENTERDEN
White Lion Inn 324
TETBURY
Gumstool Inn 245
The Priory Inn 245
The Trouble House 245
TETSWORTH
The Old Red Lion 467
TEWIN
The Plume of Feathers 303
TEWKESBURY
The Fleet Inn 246
THAME
The Swan Hotel 467
THATCHAM
The Bladebone Inn 36
THEALE
Thatchers Arms 36
THOMPSON
Chequers Inn 401
THORNHAM
Lifeboat Inn 401
The Orange Tree 401
THORNTON
Ring O'Bells Country Pub & Restaurant 687
THORNTON LE DALE
The New Inn 672
THORNTON WATLASS
The Buck Inn 672
THORPE LANGTON
The Bakers Arms 346
THORPE MARKET
Green Farm Restaurant & Hotel 403
THORPENESS
The Dolphin Inn 540
THREE LEG CROSS
The Bull 565
THURGARTON
The Red Lion 434
THURLESTONE
The Village Inn 173
TIBBIE SHIELS INN
Tibbie Shiels Inn 723
TICHBORNE
The Tichborne Arms 280
TIDESWELL
The George Hotel 145
Three Stags' Heads 145
TILLINGTON
The Bell 292
TILSWORTH
The Anchor Inn 21
TINTAGEL
The Port William 96
TINTERN PARVA
Fountain Inn 746
TIPTON ST JOHN
The Golden Lion Inn 173
TIRRIL
Queen's Head Inn 129
TITCHWELL
Titchwell Manor Hotel 403
TODENHAM
The Farriers Arms 246
TOLLARD ROYAL
King John Inn 621

TOOT BALDON
The Mole Inn 467
TOPCLIFFE
The Angel Inn 672
TOPSHAM
Bridge Inn 175
The Lighter Inn 175
TORCROSS
Start Bay Inn 175
TORMARTON
Best Western Compass Inn 246
TORPOINT
Edgcumbe Arms 96
TORRIDON
The Torridon Inn 712
TOSTOCK
Gardeners Arms 540
TOTLEY
The Cricket Inn 680
TOTNES
The Durant Arms 175
Royal Seven Stars Hotel 175
Rumour 175
Steam Packet Inn 177
The White Hart Bar 177
TREBARWITH
The Mill House Inn 96
TREBURLEY
The Springer Spaniel 99
TRECASTLE
The Castle Coaching Inn 758
TREDUNNOCK
The Newbridge 746
TREGADILLETT
Eliot Arms (Square & Compass) 99
TRELLECH
The Lion Inn 746
TRENT
Rose & Crown Inn 194
TRESCO (ISLES OF SCILLY)
The New Inn 99
TRIMDON
The Bird in Hand 198
TRISCOMBE
The Blue Ball 513
TROTTON
The Keepers Arms 582
TROUTBECK
Queens Head 129
TRURO
Old Ale House 99
The Wig & Pen Inn 99
TUCKENHAY
The Maltsters Arms 177
TUDWEILIOG
Lion Hotel 742
TUNBRIDGE WELLS (ROYAL)
The Beacon 324
The Crown Inn 324
The Hare on Langton Green 324
TUNSTALL
The Lunesdale Arms 129
TURVILLE
The Bull & Butcher 56
TUSHINGHAM CUM GRINDLEY
Blue Bell Inn 79

TUTBURY
Ye Olde Dog & Partridge Inn 522
TUXFORD
The Mussel & Crab 434
TWICKENHAM
The White Swan 248
TYLERS GREEN
The Old Queens Head 56
TYNEMOUTH
Copperfields 584
TYTHERLEIGH
Tytherleigh Arms Hotel 177
TYWARDREATH
The Royal Inn 99

U

ULLAPOOL
The Ceilidh Place 712
ULLINGSWICK
Three Crowns Inn 292
ULVERSTON
The Devonshire Arms 129
Farmers Arms 129
UMBERLEIGH
The Rising Sun Inn 177
UPPER AFFCOT
The Travellers Rest Inn 488
UPPER CWMTWRCH
Lowther's Gourmet Restaurant and Bar 760
UPPER DICKER
The Plough 565
UPPER FROYLE
The Hen & Chicken Inn 280
UPPER ODDINGTON
The Horse and Groom Inn 246
UPTON LOVELL
Prince Leopold Inn 622
UPTON SNODSBURY
Bants 634
USK
The Nags Head Inn 746
Raglan Arms 747

V

VENTNOR
The Spyglass Inn 602
VERYAN
The New Inn 100
VIRGINIA WATER
The Wheatsheaf Hotel 553

W

WADEBRIDGE
The Quarryman Inn 100
Swan 100
WADENHOE
The King's Head 414
WADHURST
The Best Beech Inn 566
WAKEFIELD
Kaye Arms Inn & Brasserie 689
WALBERSWICK
Bell Inn 542
WALDERTON
The Barley Mow 582
WALFORD
The Mill Race 294

WALKERN
The White Lion 303
WALTERSTONE
Carpenters Arms 294
WALTHAM ST LAWRENCE
The Bell 36
WANTAGE
The Hare 467
WARBLETON
The War-Bill-in-Tun Inn 566
WARDEN
The Boatside Inn 428
WARENFORD
The White Swan 430
WARGRAVE
St George and Dragon 36
WARHAM ALL SAINTS
Three Horseshoes 403
WARLINGHAM
The White Lion 553
WARMINGHAM
The Bear's Paw 79
WARMINSTER
The Angel Inn 622
The Bath Arms 622
The George Inn 622
WARNHAM
The Greets Inn 583
WARNINGLID
The Half Moon 583
WARSASH
The Jolly Farmer Country Inn 280
WARTLING
The Lamb Inn 566
WARWICK
The Rose & Crown 594
WASDALE HEAD
Wasdale Head Inn 129
WASHFORD
The Washford Inn 513
WASS
Wombwell Arms 672
WATERHOUSES
Ye Olde Crown 522
WATERMILLOCK
Brackenrigg Inn 131
WATERROW
The Rock Inn 515
WAUNFAWR
Snowdonia Parc Brewpub & Campsite 742
WEAVERTHORPE
The Star Country Inn 674
WELFORD-ON-AVON
The Bell Inn 594
The Four Alls 594
WELL
The Chequers Inn 282
WELLINGTON
The Wellington 294
WELLS
The City Arms 515
The Fountain Inn & Boxer's Restaurant 515
The Pheasant Inn 515
WELLS-NEXT-THE-SEA
Carpenter's Arms 403
The Crown 406

WENTNOR
The Crown Inn 488
WEOBLEY
The Salutation Inn 294
WESSINGTON
The Three Horseshoes 145
WEST BAGBOROUGH
The Rising Sun Inn 516
WEST BECKHAM
The Wheatsheaf 406
WEST BEXINGTON
The Manor Hotel 194
WEST BROMWICH
The Vine 597
WEST BURTON
Fox & Hounds 674
WEST CAMEL
The Walnut Tree 516
WEST CLANDON
Onslow Arms 553
WEST END
The Inn @ West End 553
WESTERHAM
The Fox & Hounds 324
WEST HORSLEY
The King William IV 554
WEST HUNTSPILL
Crossways Inn 516
WEST LAVINGTON
The Bridge Inn 623
WESTLETON
The Westleton Crown 542
WEST LINTON
The Gordon Arms 723
WEST LULWORTH
The Castle Inn 194
WEST MALLING
The Farmhouse 325
WESTON
The Crown 414
WESTON
The Rising Sun 303
WESTON HEATH
The Countess's Arms 488
WESTOW
The Blacksmiths Inn 674
WEST TANFIELD
The Bruce Arms 674
WEST WITTON
The Wensleydale Heifer Inn 674
WEST WYCOMBE
The George and Dragon Hotel 56
WETTON
Ye Olde Royal Oak 522
WEYMOUTH
The Old Ship Inn 195
WHADDON
The Three Crowns 623
WHALLEY
Freemasons Arms 336
The Three Fishes 336
WHALTON
Beresford Arms 430
WHASHTON
Hack & Spade 674
WHEATLEY
Bat & Ball Inn 467

WHEDDON CROSS
The Rest and Be Thankful Inn 516
WHEELEREND COMMON
The Chequers 56
WHERWELL
The White Lion 282
WHITBY
The Magpie Café 677
WHITCHURCH
Watership Down Inn 282
WHITCHURCH
Willeymoor Lock Tavern 489
WHITEHAVEN
The Waterfront 131
WHITELEAF
Red Lion 57
WHITEWELL
The Inn At Whitewell 336
WHITLEY
The Pear Tree Inn 623
WHITLEY BAY
The Waterford Arms 584
WHITNEY-ON-WYE
Rhydspence Inn 294
WHITSBURY
The Cartwheel Inn 282
WHITSTABLE
The Sportsman 325
WHITWAY
Carnarvon Arms 282
WICKHAM
Greens Restaurant & Pub 282
WICKHAM BISHOPS
The Mitre 211
WIDDOP
Pack Horse Inn 689
WIDECOMBE IN THE MOOR
The Old Inn 178
WIDEMOUTH BAY
Bay View Inn 100
WIGAN
Bird I'th Hand 253
WIGGLESWORTH
The Plough Inn 677
WILLIAN
The Fox 305
WILMINGTON
The Giants Rest 566
WINCHCOMBE
The White Hart Inn and Restaurant 248
WINCHELSEA
The New Inn 566
WINCHESTER
The Westgate Inn 284
The Wykeham Arms 284
WINDERMERE
The Angel Inn 131
Eagle & Child Inn 131
WINEHAM
The Royal Oak 583
WING
Kings Arms 477
WINKFIELD
Rose & Crown 37
WINKLEIGH
The Duke of York 178
The Kings Arms 178

WINTERBORNE ZELSTON
Botany Bay Inne 195
WINTERBOURNE
The Winterbourne Arms 37
WINTERBOURNE BASSETT
The White Horse Inn 623
WINTERTON-ON-SEA
Fishermans Return 406
WISBOROUGH GREEN
Cricketers Arms 583
WITHINGTON
The Mill Inn 248
WITHYBROOK
The Pheasant 594
WITHYHAM
The Dorset Arms 566
WITLEY
The White Hart 554
WITNEY
The Bell Inn 471
The Three Horseshoes 471
WIVETON
Wiveton Bell 406
WOBURN
The Birch at Woburn 21
WOLF'S CASTLE
The Wolfe Inn 751
WOLLASTON
The Wollaston Inn 414
WOOBURN COMMON
Chequers Inn 57
WOODBASTWICK
The Fur & Feather Inn 406
WOODBURY SALTERTON
The Digger's Rest 178

WOODCHESTER
The Old Fleece 248
WOODFALLS
The Woodfalls Inn 625
WOODHALL SPA
Village Limits Country Pub, Restaurant &
Motel 352
WOODHAM MORTIMER
Hurdle Makers Arms 211
WOODHOUSE EAVES
The Wheatsheaf Inn 346
WOODNEWTON
The White Swan 414
WOODSEAVES
The Plough Inn 522
WOOKEY
The Burcott Inn 517
WOOLHOPE
The Crown Inn 295
WOOLSTHORPE
The Chequers Inn 352
WOOLSTONE
The White Horse 471
WOORE
Swan at Woore 489
WOOTTON RIVERS
Royal Oak 625
WOOTTON WAWEN
The Bulls Head 594
WORKINGTON
The Old Ginn House 131
WORLD'S END
The Langley Hall Inn 37
WRENBURY
The Dusty Miller 80

WRINEHILL
The Crown Inn 522
The Hand & Trumpet 524
WYBUNBURY
The Swan 80
WYE
The New Flying Horse 325
WYLYE
The Bell Inn 625
WYTHAM
White Hart 471

Y

YANWATH
The Yanwath Gate Inn 132
YARLINGTON
The Stags Head Inn 517
YARMOUTH
Bugle Coaching Inn 602
YATTENDON
The Royal Oak Hotel 37
YEALAND CONYERS
The New Inn 338
YEALMPTON
Rose & Crown 178
YORK
Blue Bell 677
Lysander Arms 677

Z

ZENNOR
The Gurnards Head 101
The Tinners Arms 101

The Automobile Association would like to thank the following photographers, companies and picture libraries for their assistance in the preparation of this book.

Abbreviations for the picture credits are as follows: (t) top; (b) bottom; (l) left; (r) right; (AA) AA World Travel Library.

Front Cover t The Durham Ox Restaurant and Country Pub, Shrewley; front cover bl The Wellington Arms, Baughurst; Front cover br Red Lion, Shipton on Stour; Back Cover l 2nd Image Photography, Rose & Crown, Romaldkirk; Back Cover c Hare and Hounds Country Inn, Grange-Over-Sands; Back Cover r Cock & Hoop, Nottingham;

1 Kings Arms, Bradford-On-Avon; 2 Rose & Crown, Snettisham; 3t Sarah Montgomery, The Bull & Butcher, Turville; 3bl Puffing Billy, Exton; 3br Crown Inn, Shorwell; 4t Sarah Montgomery, The Five Horseshoes, Henley-On-Thames; 4c Falcon Inn, Denham; 5t Sarah Montgomery, The Bull & Butcher, Turville; 5c Titchwell Manor Hotel, Titchwell; 6 Sarah Montgomery, The Five Horseshoes, Henley-On-Thames; 7t Sarah Montgomery, The Bull & Butcher, Turville; 7b Bell at Sapperson, Sapperton; 8tl Sarah Montgomery, The Five Horseshoes, Henley-on-Thames; 8tr Sarah Montgomery, The Five Horseshoes, Henley-on-Thames; 8b Queens Arms, Corton Denham; 9tc Torridon Inn, Torridon; 9tr Sarah Montgomery, The Bull & Butcher, Turville; 9b The Bush Inn, St Hilary; 10t Sarah Montgomery, The Five Horseshoes, Henley-on-Thames; 10bl Bell at Skenfrith; 10br Foresters, Farnham Common;11t Sarah Montgomery, The Bull & Butcher, Turville; 11b Crooked Billet, Stoke Row; 12tl Sarah Montgomery, The Five Horseshoes, Henley-on-Thames; 12tr AA/C Sawyer; 12bl AA/C Sawyer; AA/C Sawyer; 13t Sarah Montgomery, The Bull & Butcher, Turville; 13bl AA/C Sawyer; 13br Sarah Montgomery, The Bull & Butcher, Turville;

Argyll&Bute AA/S Anderson; Berkshire AA/D Forss; Cheshire AA/T Mackie; Conwy AA/S Watkins; Cornwall AA/A Besley; Cumbria AA/A Mockford & N Bonetti; Dorset AA/R Newton; Gloucestershire AA/S Day; Hampshire AA/M Moody; Hertfordshire AA/C Jones; Lancashire AA/J Beazley; Norfolk AA/S&O Mathews; Northumberland AA/J Beazley; Oxford AA; Powys AA/C&A Molyneux; Rutland AA/R Newton; Suffolk AA/W Voysey; North Yorkshire AA/P Bennett; North Yorkshire AA/T Mackie;

Every effort has been made to trace the copyright holders, and we apologise in advance for any accidental errors. We would be happy to apply the corrections in the following edition of this publication.

Please send this form to:
  Editor, The Pub Guide,
  Lifestyle Guides,
  The Automobile Association,
  Fanum House,
  Basingstoke RG21 4EA

Readers' Report form

or fax: 01256 491647
or e-mail: lifestyleguides@theAA.com

Please use this form to tell us about any pub or inn you have visited, whether it is in the guide or not currently listed. We are interested in the quality of food, the selection of beers and the overall ambience of the establishment.

Feedback from readers helps us to keep our guide accurate and up to date. However, if you have a complaint to make during a visit, we do recommend that you discuss the matter with the pub management there and then, so that they have a chance to put things right before your visit is spoilt.

Please note that the AA does not undertake to arbitrate between you and the pub management, or to obtain compensation or engage in protracted correspondence.

Date: ....

Your name (block capitals) ....

Your address (block capitals) ....

....

....

.... Post Code....................

e-mail address: ....

Name of pub: ....

Location ....

Comments ....

....

....

....

(please attach a separate sheet if necessary)

Please tick here if you DO NOT wish to receive details of AA offers or products ☐

PTO

Readers' Report Form

	YES	NO
Have you bought this guide before?	☐	☐

Do you regularly use any other pub, accommodation or food guides?
If yes, which ones?

....

....

What do you find most useful about The AA Pub Guide?

....

....

....

....

Do you read the editorial features in the guide?..

Do you use the location atlas? ....

Have you tried any of the walks included in this guide?................................

Is there any other information you would like to see added to this guide?

....

....

....

....

....

What are your main reasons for visiting pubs (tick all that apply)

food ☐	business ☐	accommodation ☐
beer ☐	celebrations ☐	entertainment ☐
atmosphere ☐	leisure ☐	other ....

How often do you visit a pub for a meal?

more than once a week	☐
one a week	☐
once a fortnight	☐
once a month	☐
once in six months	☐